MACRO-ECONOMICS

CONTENTS

PART III

PART IV

THIRD EDITION

MACRO-ECONOMICS

RUDIGER DORNBUSCH
STANLEY FISCHER

Department of Economics
Massachusetts Institute of Technology

McGRAW-HILL BOOK COMPANY

New York St. Louis San Francisco Auckland Bogotá
Hamburg Johannesburg London Madrid Mexico
Montreal New Delhi Panama Paris
São Paulo Singapore Sydney Tokyo Toronto

TO RHODA

This book was set in Caledonia by Progressive Typographers, Inc.
The editors were Patricia A. Mitchell and Scott Amerman;
the designer was Joan E. O'Connor;
the production supervisor was Phil Galea.
New drawings were done by J & R Services, Inc.
R. R. Donnelley & Sons Company was printer and binder.

MACROECONOMICS

1 2 3 4 5 6 7 8 9 0 DOCDOC 8 9 8 7 6 5 4 3

ISBN 0-07-017770-8

Library of Congress Cataloging in Publication Data

Dornbusch, Rudiger.
Macroeconomics.

Includes bibliographical references and index.
1. Macroeconomics. I. Fischer, Stanley. II. Title.
HB172.5.D67 1984 339 83-19553
ISBN 0-07-017770-8

PREFACE

This third edition presents a complete rewriting of our book. We have remained faithful to our basic approach—presenting the relevant theory and at the same time showing both its empirical relevance and policy applications. We have, of course, stayed with our general eclectic outlook on macroeconomics. But in the details of presentation and development, and in the weight given to various topics, much has changed to meet the changing emphasis of macroeconomic issues and theory over the last few years. More than before, the book focusses on *current* policy issues, ranging from budget deficits and the public debt to the tradeoff between inflation and unemployment. On the theory side we give more room to the discussion of the challenge rational expectations poses for traditional macroeconomics, and to a mainstream synthesis of the ideas of the 1970s as they apply to the policy issues of the 1980s.

Although few paragraphs remain unchanged from the two earlier editions, the book remains recognizably the same in that it develops, and teaches students to use, a broad-based, critical, and useful macroeconomics. Our overriding objective is still to explain how modern macroeconomics is used in understanding important economic issues, and to help the reader analyze macroeconomic problems for herself or himself. The book provides full coverage of basic macroeconomics, such as national income accounting, aggregate demand, and the *IS-LM* analysis. It goes beyond the standard coverage in presenting also the theory of aggregate supply, the interesting and vitally important topics of inflation and unemployment, and a detailed treatment of open-economy macroeconomics. No important topic has been omitted because it is too difficult, but we have taken great pains to make nothing more difficult than it need be.

THIS EDITION

There are major innovations in the organization of chapters and in the material covered. Most visibly, boxes with topical material, either conceptual or applied, have been added to broaden the coverage and develop some points without detracting from the flow of the main topic. The content of the boxes ranges from post-Keynesian economics to the use of econometric models, to descriptions of the chief financial instruments in the assets markets. We have also added legends to the diagrams to make them a more self-contained tool for review and summary.

We have gone beyond revision and updating to recast our treatment altogether in three areas. We have split the treatment of the *IS-LM* model into two chapters. In this way we develop this central material more slowly, and with applications that immediately demonstrate the usefulness of the apparatus. Fiscal policy and crowding-out receive special attention in the new Chapter 5.

Most important, the treatment of aggregate demand and supply has been completely recast to simplify the analysis and make it more accessible than before. We thus make it possible to draw on the inflation-unemployment analysis throughout the remainder of the book. This is a major change and advantage because it opens up the really interesting issues in stabilization policy for treatment in this course. We have achieved that simplification by no longer attempting to trace out the dynamics of a formal model, but rather using short-run and long-run Phillips curves as the basic tools.

Our third major rewriting effort has been in the policy chapters dealing with the inflation-unemployment tradeoff, the budget, and the development of macroeconomic policy and ideas. That block of chapters has been entirely recast to focus on the policy concerns of the 1980s, and also to understand the issues in the broader context of alternative approaches—Keynesian economics, monetarism, rational expectations, and supply-side economics. The discussion of actual policy issues and the U.S. experience makes it possible to sort out and incorporate the valid and valuable contributions of the rational expectations school and the more limited validity of supply-side economics. The discussion serves to show how mainstream macroeconomics has evolved substantially over the last 10 years—and how it has been enriched by the challenges. We include this material because one of the most useful things a student can get from a course in macroeconomics is the ability to sort out the competing claims for alternative approaches made in the media.

Beyond these three specific areas, we have completely updated the material and references. We have also used the opportunity of this revision to follow up on the suggestions received from many readers and users.

A word on the organization of the book: Some users have suggested that we move directly from the *IS-LM* model to the aggregate supply chapters. We see some advantages in doing that, particularly because the student gets quickly to the central issues of inflation and unemployment. But we prefer to pause for consolidation and extension, after the basic aggregate demand *IS-LM* model has been introduced. That is why Chapter 5 on fiscal policy is followed by chapters on consumption, investment, money demand, and money supply that deepen understanding of the *IS-LM* framework, and by Chapter 10 on policymaking. By the end of those ten chapters the student should have a thorough understanding of the aggregate demand side of the economy — including the financial markets — and will be ready to move on to aggregate supply. However, those instructors who prefer to move ahead directly to aggregate supply can easily go from Chapter 5 to Chapter 11, and later come back to fill in the details presented in Chapters 6 through 10.

An *Instructor's Manual,* prepared for this edition by Patricia Pando of Houston Baptist College, is available to accompany this edition. Professor Pando has updated, expanded, and improved the *Instructor's Manual* that accompanied the second edition. Returning to a practice we initiated with the first edition of *Macroeconomics,* we shall each year be preparing an *Update* to this book, which will be made available to instructors by McGraw-Hill.

ACKNOWLEDGMENTS

In writing this book in its various editions we have had much help from friends, present and former students, and colleagues who advised us on how to improve the book. We wish to thank especially Andrew Abel, Richard Anderson, Yves Balcer, Robert Bishop, Olivier Blanchard, Cary Brown, Eliana Cardoso, Jacques Cremer, Allen Drazen, Robert Feldman, Jeffrey Frankel, Jacob Frenkel, Ronald Jones, Paul Joskow, Edi Karni, Tim Kehoe, Robert Pindyck, Donald Richter, Michael Rothschild, Paul Samuelson, Steven Sheffrin, Robert Solow, Richard Startz, Larry Summers, Peter Temin, Michael Schmid, Charles Steindel, Hal Varian, and Michael Veall.

Many readers and users of our book have given us the benefit of their teaching experience and particular suggestions. We would like to thank especially Joseph Aubareda, Alan Auerbach, Francis Bator, Thomas Bonsor, Carl Christ, Giacomo Costa, Kevin Davis, Clifford B. Donn, Gerald Egerer, Robert Eisner, George Feiwel, Rendigs Fels, Benjamin Friedman, Joanna Froyden, Charles C. Gillete, Micha Gisser, Robert J. Gordon, Joseph Guerin, John Haltiwanger, Raundi Halvorson, Dennis J. Hanseman, Brian Horrigan, Mike Jacobson, James Johannes, Yoshiaki Kaoru, S. W. Kardasz, John Kareken, M. P. Kidd, David Laidler, Kathleen Langley, Michael Lopez, Barry A. Love, David McClain, Erwin Miller, Richard Miller, Douglas W. Mitchell,

Masanori Morita, John Naylor, Norman Obst, Edward Offenbacher, Patricia Pando, Thomas Russell, Walter Salant, Robert Schenk, Masaki Shinbo, Richard Startz, Kirker Stevens, Houston Stokes, Earl Thompson, Hal Varian, David H. Vrooman, and Randy Williams.

We owe a special debt to reviewers of various editions who prepared very detailed comments and suggestions. We would like to mention especially Lloyd Atkinson, Alan Deardorff, Don Heckerman, Thomas Mayer, William Poole, Steven Shapiro, Michael Babcock, Arnold Collery, William Hosek, Timothy Kersten, Charles Knapp, Charles Lieberman, Andrew Policano, James Duga, Michael Edgmand, Hajime Miyazaki, Aris Protopapadakis, Stephen Van der Ploeg, Ben Bernanke, Shirley Browning, and Roland Artle.

Over the years we have enjoyed and benefitted from the most competent and dedicated research assistance. We would like to thank particularly Carl Shapiro and David Modest who helped us with the first two editions and Michael Gavin and Patricia Mosser who did the work for the present edition. Carol McIntire and Liz Walb were unendingly cheerful and efficient in coping with many drafts of what turned out not to be a small revision, just as Barbara Ventresco, Nancy Johnson, and Carolyn Dedutis had been in previous years. Their willingness to work long hours is deeply appreciated.

TO THE STUDENT

Macroeconomics is not cut and dried. There are disputes over basic issues, for instance over whether the government should try actively to fight unemployment. That makes macroeconomics unsatisfying if you are looking for clear-cut definite answers to all the economy's problems. But it should also make it more interesting because you have to think hard and critically about the material being presented.

Despite the disagreements, there is a substantial basic core of macroeconomics that we present in this book, and that will continue to be useful in understanding the behavior of the economy. We have not hesitated to say where we think theories are incomplete, or where the evidence on a question is not yet decisive. But we have not hesitated, either, to describe the many areas in which macroeconomic theory does a good job of explaining the real world.

Because we have not shied away from important topics even if they are difficult, parts of the book require careful reading. There is no mathematics except simple algebra. Some of the analysis, however, involves sustained reasoning. Careful reading should therefore pay off in enhanced understanding. Chapter 1 gives you suggestions on how to learn from this book. The single most important suggestion is that you learn actively. Some of the chapters (such as Chapter 10) are suitable for bedtime reading, but most are not. Use pencil and paper to be sure you are following the argument. See if you can find reasons to disagree with arguments we make. Work the problem sets! Be sure you understand the points contained in the summaries to each chapter. Follow the economic news in the press, and see how that relates to what you are learning. Try to follow the logic of the budget or any economic packages the administration may present. Occasionally, the chairpersons of the Federal Reserve Board or the Council of Economic Advisers testify before the Congress. Read what they have to say, and see if it makes sense to you.

A *Study Guide*, prepared and updated by Richard Startz of the University of Pennsylvania, is available to accompany this edition. The *Study Guide* contains a wide range of questions, starting from the very easy and progressing in each chapter to material that will challenge the more advanced student. It is a great help in studying, particularly since active learning is so important.

Rudiger Dornbusch
Stanley Fischer

PART ONE

1

INTRODUCTION

Macroeconomics is concerned with the behavior of the economy as a whole — with booms and recessions, the economy's total output of goods and services and the growth of output, the rates of inflation and unemployment, the balance of payments, and exchange rates. To study the overall performance of the economy, macroeconomics focuses on the economic policies and policy variables that affect that performance — on monetary and fiscal policies, the money stock and interest rates, the public debt, and the federal government budget. In brief, macroeconomics deals with the major economic issues and problems of the day.

Macroeconomics is interesting because it deals with important issues. But it is fascinating and challenging too, because it reduces complicated details of the economy to manageable essentials. *Those essentials lie in the interactions among the goods, labor, and assets markets of the economy.*

In dealing with the essentials, we have to disregard details of the behavior of individual economic units, such as households and firms, or the determination of prices in particular markets, or the effects of monopoly on individual markets. These are the subject matter of microeconomics. In macroeconomics we deal with the market for goods as a whole, treating all the markets for different goods — such as the markets for agricultural products and for medical services — as a single market. Similarly, we deal with the labor market as a whole, abstracting from differences between the markets for, say, migrant labor and doctors. We deal with the assets markets as a whole, abstracting from the differences between the markets for AT&T bonds and Rembrandt paintings. The cost of the abstraction is that omitted details sometimes matter. The benefit of the abstraction is increased understanding of the vital interactions among the goods, labor, and assets markets.

Despite the contrast between macroeconomics and microeconomics, there is no basic conflict between them. After all, the economy in the aggregate is nothing but the sum of its submarkets. The difference between microeconomics and macroeconomics is therefore primarily one of emphasis and exposition. In studying price determination in a single industry, it is convenient for microeconomists to assume that prices in other industries are given. In macroeconomics, where we study the price level, it is for the most part sensible to ignore changes in relative prices of goods among different industries. In microeconomics, it is convenient to assume the total income of all consumers is given and to ask how consumers divide their spending out of that income among different goods. In macroeconomics, by contrast, the aggregate level of income or spending is among the key variables to be studied.

The great macroeconomists, including Keynes, and modern American leaders in the field, such as Milton Friedman of the University of Chicago, Franco Modigliani of MIT, and James Tobin of Yale, have all had a keen interest in the applications of macrotheory to problems of policy making. Indeed, developments in macrotheory are closely related to the economic problems of the day. Keynesian economics developed during the great depression of the 1930s and showed the way out of such depressions. Monetarism developed during the 1960s, promising a way of solving the inflation problem. *Supply-side economics* became the fad of the early 1980s, promising an easy way out of the economic mess of the time, by cutting taxes. But supply-side economics overpromised, and there was no easy way out.

Because macroeconomics is closely related to the economic problems of the day, it does not yield its greatest rewards to those whose primary interest is theoretical. The need for compromise between the comprehensiveness of the theory and its manageability inevitably makes macrotheory a little untidy at the edges. And the emphasis in macroeconomics is on the manageability of the theory and on its applications. To demonstrate that emphasis, this book uses the theories we present to illuminate recent economic events from the 1960s to the 1980s. We also refer continually to real world events to elucidate the meaning and the relevance of the theoretical material.

Schools of Thought

There have for long been two intellectual traditions in macroeconomics. One school of thought believes that markets work best if left to themselves; another believes that government intervention can significantly improve the operation of the economy. In the 1960s the debate on these questions involved *monetarists*, led by Milton Friedman, on one side and *Keynesians*, including Franco Modigliani and James Tobin, on the other side. In the 1970s the debate on much the same issues brought to the fore a new group—the *new classical macroeconomists*—including among the leaders Robert Lucas of the University of Chicago and Thomas Sargent of the University of Minnesota.

The new classical macroeconomics shares many policy views with Friedman. It sees the world as one where individuals act rationally in their self-interest in markets that adjust rapidly to changing conditions. The government, it is claimed, is likely only to make things worse by intervening. That model is a challenge to traditional macroeconomics, which sees a role for useful government action in an economy which is viewed as adjusting sluggishly, with rigidities, poor information, and social customs impeding the rapid clearing of markets.

Macroeconomics is often presented as the battleground between implacably opposed schools of thought. There is no denying that there are conflicts of opinion and even theory between different camps. But it is also the case that there are significant areas of agreement and that the different groups, through discussion and research, continually evolve new areas of consensus and a sharper idea of where precisely the differences lie. In this book we do not emphasize the debate, preferring to discuss substantive matters while indicating alternative views of an issue whenever relevant.

We shall now in Section 1-1 present an overview of the key concepts with which macroeconomics deals. Section 1-2 examines relationships among the key macroeconomic variables, while Section 1-3 discusses stabilization policy. Section1-4 presents a diagrammatic introduction to aggregate demand and supply and their interaction; it gives a very general perspective on the fundamentals of macroeconomics and the organization of this book. Then, in Section 1-5, we outline the approach of the book to the study of macroeconomics and macropolicy making, and present a preview of the order in which topics are taken up. Section 1-6 contains brief remarks on how to use the book.

1-1 KEY CONCEPTS

Gross National Product

Gross national product (*GNP*) is the value of all goods and services produced in the economy in a given time period (quarter or year). GNP is the basic measure of economic activity.

Figure 1-1 shows two measures of GNP—*nominal*, or *current dollar*, GNP and *real*, or *constant dollar*, GNP.[1] Nominal GNP measures the value of

[1] Notice that the scale for GNP in Fig. 1-1 is not linear. For example, the distance from 600 to 650 is bigger than the distance from 1,450 to 1,500. The scale is logarithmic, which means that equal ratios are represented by equal distances. For instance, the distance from 600 to 1,200 is the same as the distance from 750 to 1,500 since GNP doubles in both cases. On a logarithmic scale, a variable growing at a constant rate (e.g., 4 percent per annum) is represented by a straight line.

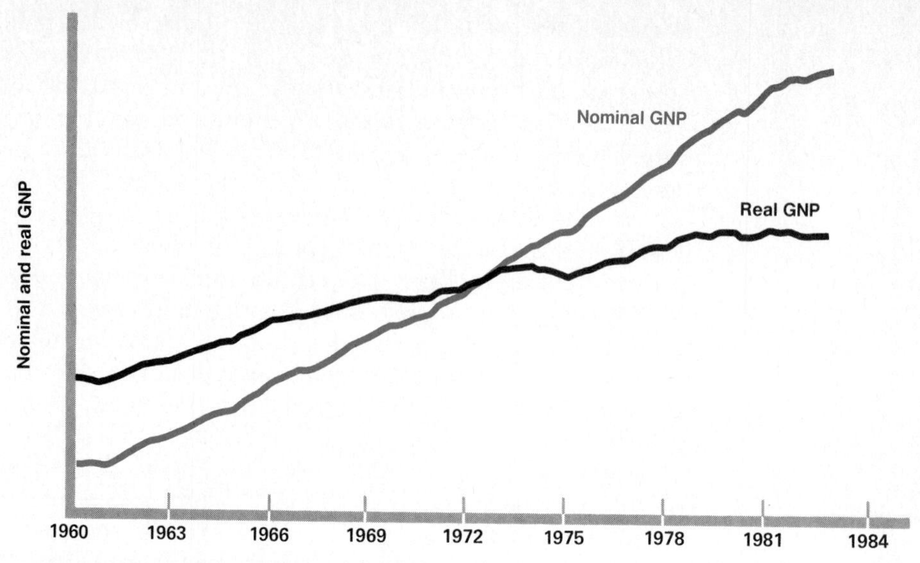

FIGURE 1-1 REAL AND NOMINAL GNP, 1960–1983. (*Source:* Data Resources, Inc.) Nominal GNP measures the output of final goods and services produced in the economy in a given period, using the prices of that period. Real GNP measures the value of the output using the prices of a *given* year, in this case 1972. Nominal GNP has risen more rapidly than real GNP because prices have been rising.

output at the prices prevailing in the period the output is produced, while real GNP measures the output produced in any one period at the prices of some base year. At present, 1972 serves as the base year for real output measurement. GNP statistics become available quarterly.

Figure 1-1 shows that nominal GNP was equal to $3059 billion in 1982 and $1186 billion in 1972. Thus nominal GNP grew at an average rate of 9.9 percent during that period. If we divide total GNP by population, we obtain per capita nominal GNP, which was $13,187 in 1982. Accordingly, the average value of output produced in the United States economy in 1982 was $13,187 per member of the population. The chart shows that real GNP was $1477 billion in 1982 and $1186 billion in 1972,[2] implying an average annual growth rate of real GNP of only 2.2 percent over the period.

Inflation and Nominal GNP

Figure 1-1 shows that nominal GNP has risen much more rapidly than real GNP. The difference between the growth rates of real and nominal GNP occurs because the prices of goods have been rising, or there has been

[2] Why are real and nominal GNP the same in 1972? Because we use 1972 prices to calculate real GNP.

inflation. The inflation rate is the percentage rate of increase of the level of prices during a given period.

Real GNP grew at an average rate of 2.2 percent over the 10 years from 1972–1982, while nominal GNP grew at an average annual rate of 9.9 percent per year. Because real GNP is calculated holding the prices of goods constant, the difference is entirely due to inflation, or rising prices. Over the 10-year period, prices were on average rising at 7.7 percent per year. In other words, the average rate of inflation over that period was 7.7 percent per year.

With 1972 as the base year for the prices at which output is valued, we observe in Figure 1-1 two implications of the distinction between nominal and real GNP. First, in 1972 the two are equal, because in the base year, current and constant dollars are the same dollars. Second, with inflation, nominal GNP rises faster than real GNP, and therefore, after 1972, nominal GNP exceeds real GNP. The converse is, of course, true before 1972.

Growth and Real GNP

We turn next to the reasons for the growth of real GNP. The *growth rate* of the economy is the rate at which real GNP is increasing. Anytime we refer to growth or the growth rate without any other qualifying word, we mean the growth rate of GNP. On average, most economies grow by a few percent per year over long periods. For instance, U.S. real GNP grew at an average rate of 3.1 percent per year from 1962 to 1982. But this growth has certainly not been smooth, as Figure 1-1 confirms.

What causes GNP to grow? The first reason real GNP changes is that the available amount of resources in the economy changes. The resources are conveniently split into capital and labor. The labor force, consisting of people either working or looking for work, grows over time and thus provides one source of increased production. The capital stock, including buildings and machines, likewise has been rising over time, thereby making increased output possible. Increases in the availability of factors of production—the labor and capital used in the production of goods and services—thus account for part of the increase in real GNP.

The second reason for real GNP to change is that the efficiency with which factors of production work may change.[3] Over time, the same factors of production can produce more output. These increases in the efficiency of production result from changes in knowledge, including learning by doing, as people learn through experience to perform familiar tasks better.

Employment and Unemployment

The third source of change in real GNP is a change in the employment of the given resources available for production. Not all the capital and labor available to the economy are actually used at all times.

The *unemployment rate* is the fraction of the labor force that cannot find

[3] These efficiency improvements are often called productivity increases.

jobs. For example, in 1982, a reduction in the employment of labor, or a rise in unemployment, shows up in Figure 1-1 as a fall in real GNP. Indeed, in that year unemployment rose to nearly 11 percent, the highest unemployment rate in the post-World War II period. More than one person out of every ten who wanted to work could not find a job. Such unemployment levels had not been experienced since the great depression of the 1930s.

Inflation, Growth, and Unemployment: The Record

Macroeconomic performance is judged by the three broad measures we have introduced: the *inflation* rate, the *growth* rate of output, and the rate of *unemployment.* News of these three variables makes the headlines, because they affect our daily lives.

When the inflation rate is high, the prices of goods people buy are rising. Partly for this reason, inflation is unpopular, even if people's incomes rise along with the prices. Inflation is also unpopular because it is often associated with other disturbances to the economy—such as the oil price increases of the 1970s—that would make people worse off even if there were no inflation. Inflation is frequently a major political issue, as it was, for instance, in the 1980 presidential election between Presidents Carter and Reagan, when the high rate of inflation contributed to President Reagan's victory.

When the growth rate is high, the production of goods and services is rising, making possible an increased standard of living. Along with the high growth rate typically goes lower unemployment, and more jobs. High growth is a target and hope of most societies.

High unemployment rates are a major social problem. Jobs are difficult to find. The unemployed suffer a loss in their standard of living, personal distress, and sometimes a lifetime deterioration in their career opportunities. When unemployment reaches 11 percent—and even well short of that—it becomes the number one social and political issue.

Table 1-1 confirms that the recent years have not been happy ones economically. Inflation has risen in every 10-year period shown in the table, from 1.3 percent per year to 8.7 percent per year. In 1982 inflation did show a rapid decline, but that decline was associated with a large increase in unemployment.

TABLE 1-1 MACROECONOMIC PERFORMANCE

Period	Inflation % p.a.	Growth % p.a.	Unemployment rate, % of the labor force
1952–1962	1.3	2.9	5.1
1962–1972	3.3	4.0	4.7
1972–1982	8.7	2.2	7.0
1981–1982	6.1	−1.9	9.7

Source: Economic Report of the President and estimates. *Note:* Unemployment rate is average of rates for years shown. Inflation rate is for CPI, year over year.

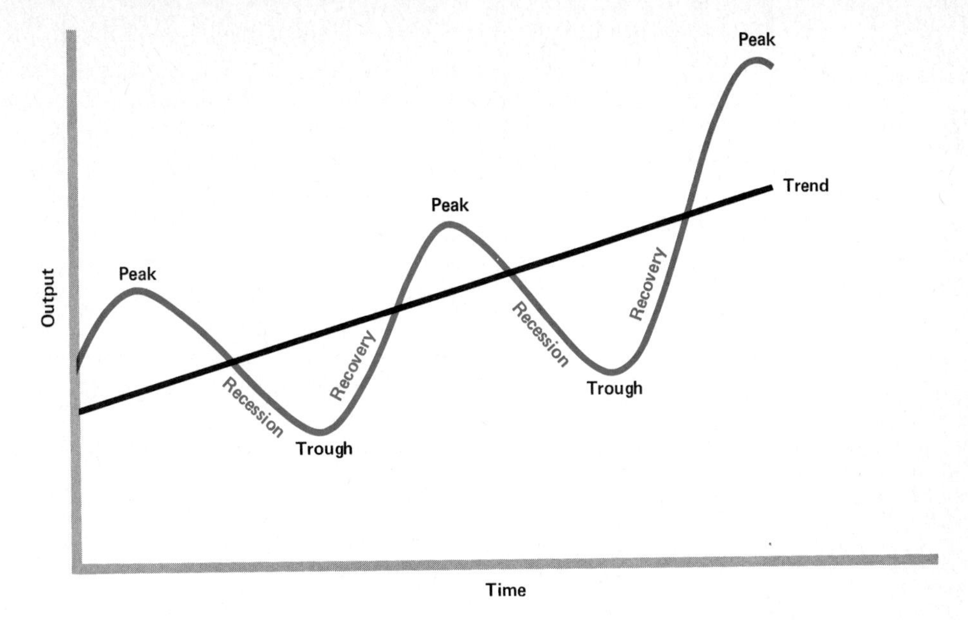

FIGURE 1-2 THE BUSINESS CYCLE. Output or GNP does not grow smoothly at its trend rate. Rather, it fluctuates irregularly around trend, showing business cycle patterns from trough, through recovery, to peak, and then from peak, through recession, back to the trough. Business cycle output movements are not regular in timing or in size.

The growth performance over the last 30 years has been very uneven: high growth in the 1963–1972 period, less in the 1950s, and much less in the most recent decade. And, of course, recent unemployment has been the worst of the post-World War II period.

As we develop macroeconomics in this book, we are looking for answers to the questions that recent macroeconomic performance raises: Why has the inflation rate increased? Why has growth slowed? Why is unemployment so high? And, of course, is there anything that can be done to improve the situation?

The Business Cycle and the Output Gap

Inflation, growth, and unemployment are related through the *business cycle.* The business cycle is the more or less regular pattern of expansion (recovery) and contraction (recession) in economic activity around the path of trend growth. At a cyclical *peak,* economic activity is high relative to trend, and at a cyclical *trough,* the low point in economic activity is reached. Inflation, growth, and unemployment all have clear cyclical patterns as we will show below. For the moment we concentrate on measuring the behavior of output or real GNP relative to trend over the business cycle.

Figure 1-2 shows as the straight line the trend path of real GNP. Over time real GNP will grow for two reasons, as we already noted. First, more resources become available: the size of the population increases; firms acquire machinery or build plants; land is improved for cultivation. This increased availability of resources allows the economy to produce more goods and services every year. Second, given resources are used with increased efficiency. New technology, learning by doing, acquisition of skills, new kinds of products (computers, fertilizers as examples) may dramatically increase the amount of goods that can be produced.

But output does not grow smoothly. Rather, it fluctuates around trend, in the business cycle. During an *expansion* (or *recovery*) the *employment* of factors of production increases, and that is a source of increased production. Output can rise above trend because people work overtime, and machinery is used for several shifts. Conversely, during a *recession* unemployment develops and less output is produced than can in fact be produced with the existing resources and technology. The wavy line in Figure 1-1 shows these cyclical departures of output from trend. Deviations of output from trend are referred to as the *output gap*. The output gap measures the gap between actual output and the output the economy could produce at full employment given the existing resources. Full-employment output is also called *potential output*.

$$\text{Output gap} \equiv \text{potential output} - \text{actual output} \qquad (1)$$

The output gap allows us to measure how large the cyclical deviations of output from potential output or trend output (we use these terms interchangeably) are. Figure 1-3 shows actual and potential output for the United States. The shaded lines represent recessions, with the letters *P* and *T* denoting cyclical peaks and troughs.[4]

The figure shows that the output gap grows during a recession, such as in 1982. More resources become unemployed, and actual output falls below potential. Conversely, during an expansion, most strikingly in the long expansion of the 1960s, the gap declines and ultimately even becomes negative. A negative gap means that there is overemployment, overtime of workers, and more than the usual rate of utilization of machinery. It is worth nothing that the gap is sometimes very sizable. For example, in 1982 it amounted to as much as 10 percent.

Establishing the level of potential output is a difficult problem. In the 1960s it was believed that full employment corresponds to a measured rate of unemployment of 4 to 4.5 percent of the labor force. Changes in the composition of the labor force toward younger workers and female workers who change jobs more frequently have raised the estimate of the full employment rate of unemployment to a range above 5.5 percent in the early 1980s. This is a bench mark for calculating what potential output or full employment output is, but it is only a bench mark, not a rigid, undebatable rule. Even so, the GNP gap provides an important indicator of how the economy is performing and which direction policies should try to move the level of activity.

[4] Dating of the business cycle is done by the National Bureau of Economic Research (NBER). The NBER is a private, nonprofit research organization based in Cambridge, Massachusetts.

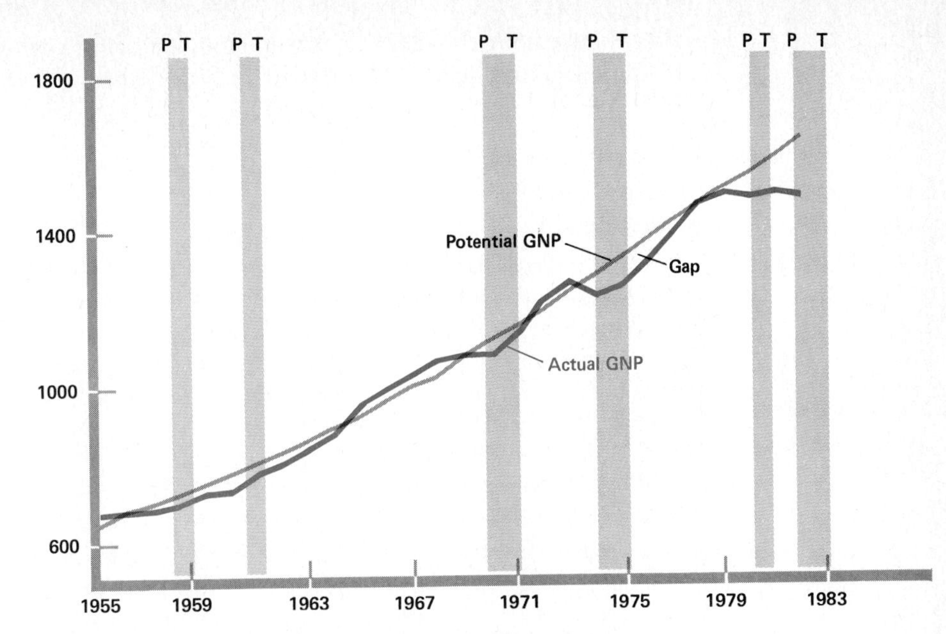

FIGURE 1-3 ACTUAL AND POTENTIAL OUTPUT, 1960–1982. Potential output is the full employment level of output. It grows like trend output in Figure 1-2. Actual GNP fluctuates around potential, falling below during recession, and rising back toward the potential level during recoveries. Shaded areas represent recessions.

Much of recent history can be read from the GNP gap. In the Kennedy-Johnson years (1961–1968) the output gap declined under the impact of expansionary government policies. The policies were successful in reducing the gap, but did so at the cost of building up inflationary pressures. The Nixon administration (1969–1973) inherited this inflation problem and decided to fight it by tight policies that led to a recession and thus a growing gap. In 1972–1973, highly expansionary monetary policies of the Federal Reserve System led to recovery and even overemployment shown by a negative gap, actual output exceeding potential. In 1973–1974, tight policies together with the huge increases in oil prices threw the economy into a deep recession. Recovery from that recession in the 1976–1979 period was too fast and led to sharp increases in inflation. With the aid of another rapid rise in oil prices in 1979, inflation by 1980 had come to exceed 10 percent, and once more tight policies drove the economy into a recession in 1980–1981 and again in 1981–1982. The recessions, as can be seen from the gap, were very severe and in that way made a deep cut in the inflation rate.

1-2 RELATIONSHIPS AMONG MACROECONOMIC VARIABLES

The preliminary look at the data presented above, and our discussion of the business cycle, suggests—correctly—that we should expect to find simple relationships among the major macroeconomic variables, growth, unemployment, and inflation. There are indeed such relationships, as we now document.

Growth and Unemployment

We have already noted that changes in the employment of factors of production provide one of the sources of growth in real GNP. We would then expect high GNP growth to be accompanied by declining unemployment. That is indeed the case, as we observe from Figure 1-4. On the vertical axis, Figure 1-4 shows the growth rate of output in a particular year and on the horizontal axis the change in the unemployment rate in that year. For example, in both 1965 and 1966, the growth rate of output was 6 percent and the reduction in the unemployment rate was 0.7 percentage points. Thus we plot the points labeled 65-66 in the upper left-hand region. That region corresponds to a period of expansion and falling unemployment rates.

By contrast, in the lower right-hand region, such as the points labeled 1980 and 1982, are periods of recession—low growth and rising unemployment rates. Note that even when there is some growth, such as in 1981, unemployment rates may be rising. It takes growth rates above about 3 percent to cause unemployment rates to come down.

Okun's Law

A relationship between real growth and changes in the unemployment rate is known as *Okun's law*, named after its discoverer, the late Arthur Okun of the Brookings Institution, former chairperson of the Council of Economic Advisers (CEA). Okun's law says that for every 2½ percentage points of growth in real GNP above the trend rate that is sustained for a year, the unemployment rate declines by 1 percentage point. This 2½-to-1 relationship, the status of which is somewhat exaggerated by calling it a law rather than an empirical regularity, provides a rule of thumb for assessing the implications of real growth for unemployment.[5] While the rule is only approximate and will not work very precisely from year to year, it still gives a sensible translation from growth to unemployment.

The relation is a useful guide to policy because it allows us to ask how a particular growth target will affect the unemployment rate over time. Suppose we were in a deep recession with 9 percent unemployment. How many years would it take us to return to, say, 6 percent unemployment? The answer depends, of course, on how fast the economy grows in the recovery. Assume the growth rate of potential output is 3 percent per year. One possible path to return to 6 percent unemployment is for output to grow at 5½ percent per year for 3 years. On this path, each year we are growing 2½ percent above trend, and thus each year we take 1 percentage point off the unemployment rate. An alternative recovery strategy is front-loaded: growth is high at the beginning and then slows down. Such a path might be one of growth rates in

[5] For more details on Okun's law, see Chap. 13.

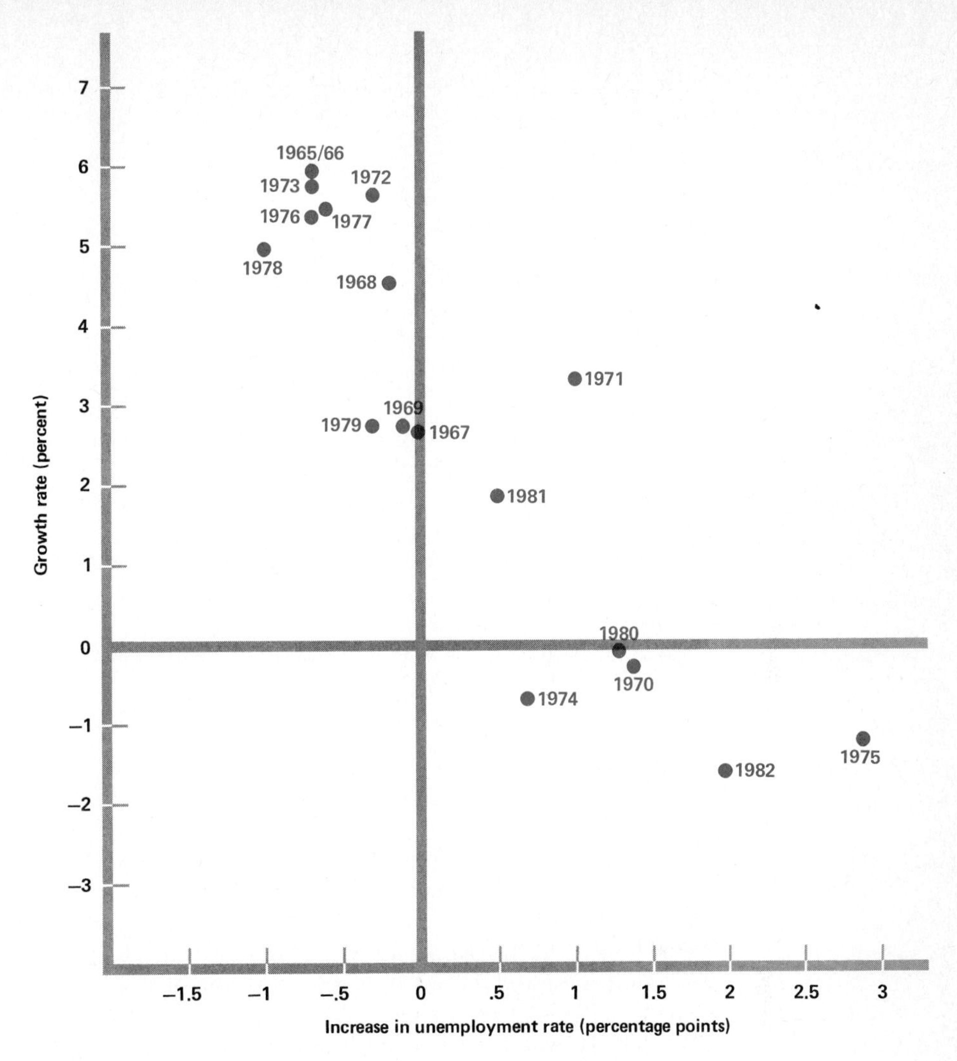

FIGURE 1-4 GROWTH AND THE CHANGE IN THE UNEMPLOYMENT RATE: 1965–1982. High rates of growth cause the unemployment rate to fall, and low or negative rates of growth are accompanied by increases in the unemployment rate. The relationship shown by the scatter of the points in this figure is summarized by *Okun's law,* linking the growth rate to the change in the unemployment rate.

successive years equal to 6½, 5½, and 4½ percent, also allowing a return to 6 percent unemployment in 3 years.

Inflation and the Cycle

Inflation is the rate of increase of prices. Expansionary aggregate demand policies tend to produce inflation, unless they occur when the economy is at

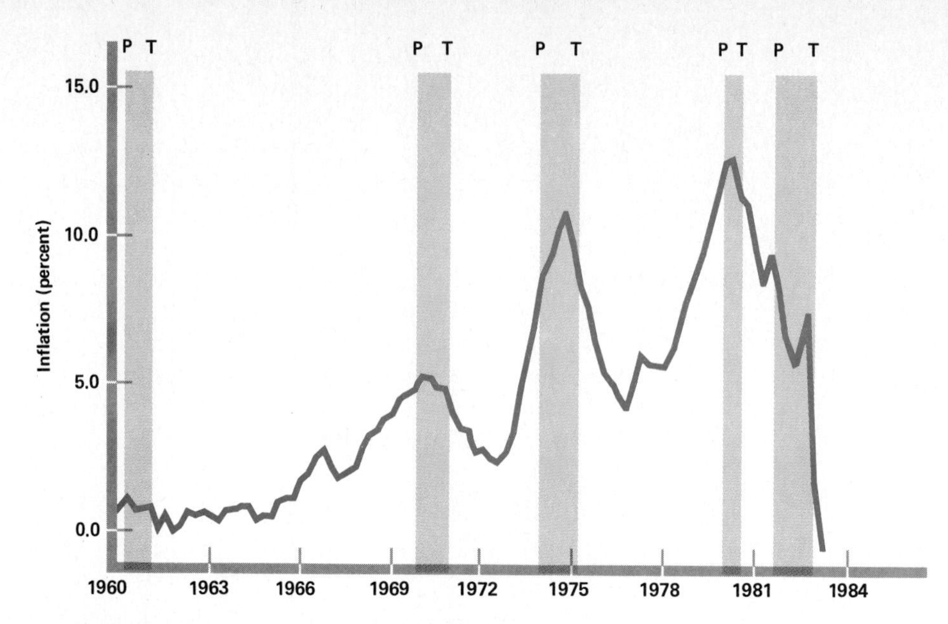

FIGURE 1-5 THE RATE OF INFLATION OF CONSUMER PRICES. The inflation rate falls during and after recessions, and then—over the period shown—tends to rise later in the recovery. (*Source:* Citibank Database.)

high levels of unemployment. Protracted periods of low aggregate demand tend to reduce the inflation rate. Figure 1-5 shows one measure of inflation for the United States economy for the period since 1960. The inflation measure in the figure is the rate of change of the *consumer price index*, the cost of a given basket of goods, representing the purchases of a typical urban consumer.[6]

The rate of inflation shown in Figure 1-5 fluctuates considerably. Just as we could tell much about the recent history of the economy from looking at Figure 1-3's picture of the course of actual and potential GNP, we can likewise see much of recent economic history in Figure 1-5. In particular, there is the period of steady inflation from 1960 through 1964 when the inflation rate hovered around the 2 percent level. Then there is a slow climb in the inflation rate from 1965 to 1970, followed by a slowing down till mid-1972. And finally there are the inflationary bursts from 1972 through 1974 and 1978 to 1981 as the inflation rate rose to 12 percent and above. In 1982–1983 inflation was again down, under the impact of a deep recession.

Figure 1-5 shows the *rate of increase* of prices. We can also look at the *level* of prices. All the inflation of the 1960s and 1970s adds up to a large increase in the price level. In the period from 1960 to 1983 the price level

[6] By contrast, the measure of inflation obtained in Figure 1-1 by comparing nominal and real GNP is the rate of change of the GNP *deflator*. The consumer price index (CPI) rate of inflation is the most frequently used, and the GNP deflator is next most popular. Chapter 2 presents more details on the different price indexes.

more than tripled. A product that cost $1 in 1960 cost $3.40 by 1983. Much of that increase in prices took place since the early 1970s.

Inflation, like unemployment, is a major macroeconomic problem. However, the costs of inflation are much less obvious than those of unemployment. In the case of unemployment, it is clear that potential output is going to waste, and therefore it is clear why the reduction of unemployment is desirable. In the case of inflation, there is no obvious loss of output. As we noted above, consumers in part dislike inflation because it is often associated with disturbances, such as the oil price shocks, that reduce their real incomes. It is also argued that inflation upsets familiar price relationships and reduces the efficiency of the price system. Whatever the reasons, policy makers have been willing to increase unemployment in an effort to reduce inflation—that is, to trade off some unemployment for less inflation.

Inflation-Unemployment Tradeoffs

The *Phillips curve* describes a relationship between inflation and unemployment: the higher the rate of unemployment, the lower the rate of inflation. The Phillips curve is an empirical relationship that relates the behavior of wage and price inflation to the rate of unemployment. It was made famous in the 1950s in Great Britain and has since become a cornerstone of macroeconomic discussion. Figure 1-6 presents a typical downward-sloping Phillips

FIGURE 1-6 A PHILLIPS CURVE. The Phillips curve suggests a tradeoff between inflation and unemployment: less unemployment can always be obtained by incurring more inflation—or inflation can be reduced by allowing more unemployment. Recent events, particularly the combination of high inflation *and* high unemployment in years such as 1975 and 1981, have led to skepticism about the Phillips curve. It nonetheless remains useful, as we shall show later.

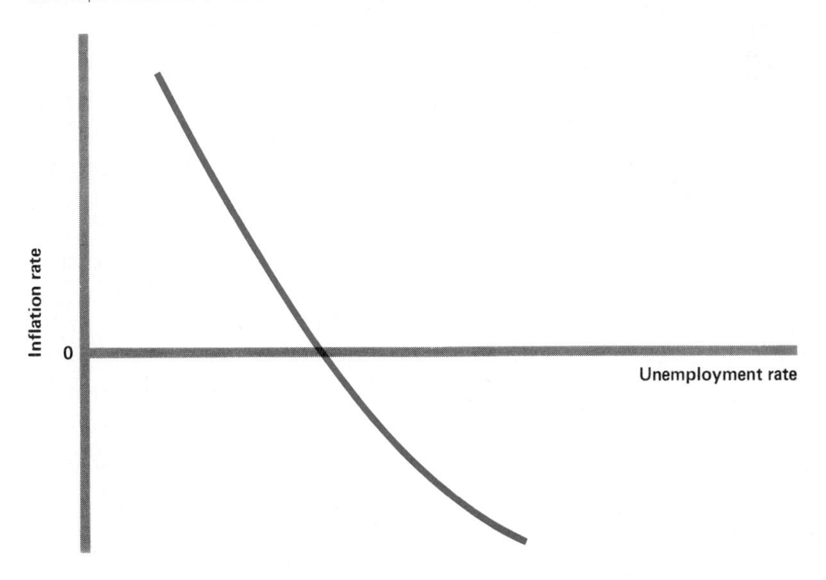

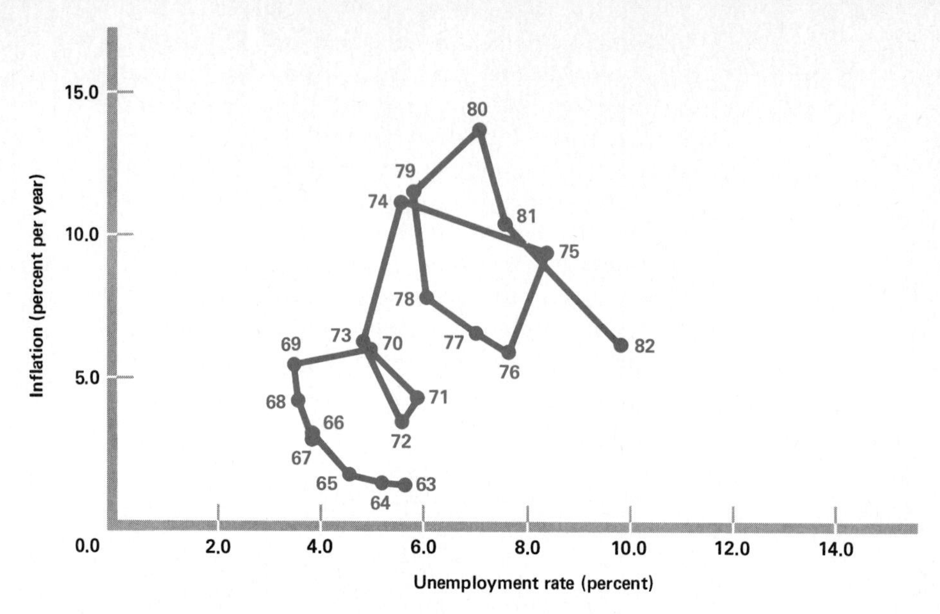

FIGURE 1-7 INFLATION AND UNEMPLOYMENT: 1963–1982. The actual history of inflation and unemployment in the United States since 1963 shows no simple Phillips curve relationship. There are periods, for instance, 1963–1969, 1976–1979, and 1980–1982, which fit the general shape of the Phillips curve, but in-between there are periods where inflation and unemployment both increase or sometimes, (e.g., 1975–1976) decrease.

curve showing that high rates of unemployment are accompanied by low rates of inflation and vice versa. The curve suggests that less unemployment can always be attained by incurring more inflation and that the inflation rate can always be reduced by incurring the costs of more unemployment. In other words, the curve suggests there is a tradeoff between inflation and unemployment.

Economic events of the past decade, particularly the combination of high inflation and high unemployment in 1974 or 1981, have led to considerable skepticism about the unemployment-inflation relation shown in Figure 1-6. Figure 1-7 presents the inflation and unemployment rate combinations for the years 1963 to 1982. Clearly, there is no simple relationship of the form shown in Figure 1-6.

Nonetheless, there remains a tradeoff between inflation and unemployment which is more sophisticated than a glance at Figure 1-6 would suggest, and which will enable us to make sense of Figure 1-7. In the short run, of, say, 2 years, there is a relation between inflation and unemployment of the type shown in Figure 1-6. The *short-run Phillips curve,* however, does not remain stable. It shifts as expectations of inflation change. In the long run, there is no tradeoff worth speaking about between inflation and unemployment. In the long run, the unemployment rate is basically independent of the long-run inflation rate.

The short- and long-run tradeoffs between inflation and unemployment are obviously a major concern of policy making and are the basic determinants of the potential success of stabilization policies.

1-3 MACROECONOMIC POLICY

Policy makers have at their command two broad classes of policies with which to affect the economy. *Monetary policy* is controlled by the Federal Reserve System (the Fed). The instruments of monetary policy are changes in the stock of money, changes in the interest rate — the discount rate — at which the Fed lends money to banks, and some controls over the banking system. *Fiscal policy* is under the control of the Congress, and usually is initiated by the executive branch of the government. The instruments of fiscal policy are tax rates and government spending.

One of the central facts of policy is that the effects of monetary and fiscal policy on the economy are not fully predictable, neither in their *timing* nor in the *extent* to which they affect demand or supply. These two uncertainties are at the heart of the problem of stabilization policy. *Stabilization policies* are monetary and fiscal policies designed to moderate the fluctuations of the economy — in particular, fluctuations in the rates of growth, inflation, and unemployment.

Figure 1-7, which showed the recent fluctuations of the rates of inflation and unemployment, suggests strongly that stabilization policy has not been fully successful in keeping them within narrow bounds. The failures of stabilization policy are due mostly to uncertainty about the way it works.

However, questions of political economy are also involved in the way stabilization policy has been operated. The speed at which to proceed in trying to eliminate unemployment, at the risk of increasing inflation, is a matter of judgment about both the economy and the costs of mistakes. Those who regard the costs of unemployment as high, relative to the costs of inflation, will run greater risks of inflation to reduce unemployment than will those who regard the costs of inflation as primary and unemployment as a relatively minor misfortune.

Political economy affects stabilization policy in more ways than through the costs which policy makers of different political persuasions attach to inflation and unemployment, and the risks they are willing to undertake in trying to improve the economic situation. There is also the so-called *political business cycle*, which is based on the observation that election results are affected by economic conditions. When the economic situation is improving and the unemployment rate is falling, incumbent presidents tend to be reelected. There is thus the incentive to policy makers running for reelection, or who wish to affect the election results, to use stabilization policy to produce booming economic conditions before elections.

Stabilization policy is also known as *countercyclical policy*, that is, policy to moderate the trade cycle or business cycle. Figure 1-3 shows that cycles in the past 20 years have been far from regular. The behavior, and even the existence, of the trade cycle is substantially affected by the conduct of stabilization policy. Successful stabilization policy smooths out the cycle, while unsuccessful stabilization policy may worsen the fluctuations of the economy. Indeed, one of the tenets of monetarism is that the major fluctuations of the economy are a result of government actions rather than the inherent instability of the economy's private sector.

Monetarists and Activists

We noted above that there is some controversy over the existence of a tradeoff between inflation and unemployment. That controversy arose around 1967–1968 in the context of the debate in macroeconomics between monetarists and nonmonetarists, or fiscalists. We have already identified some of the major participants in the debate as Milton Friedman on the monetarist side and Franco Modigliani and James Tobin on the nonmonetarist side. But macroeconomists cannot be neatly classified into one camp or the other. Instead, there is a spectrum of views. There are monetarists who make Friedman look like a Keynesian, and Keynesians who make Modigliani look like a monetarist. Not only that; there is no compelling unity in the views that are identified with monetarism, and the balanced economist is likely to accept some monetarist arguments and reject others. Nor is the debate one in which there is no progress. For example, both theory and empirical evidence have been brought to bear on the issue of the inflation-unemployment tradeoff, and it is no longer central to the monetarist/fiscalist debate.

Another major point of contention is the relation between *money* and *inflation*. *Monetarists* tend to argue that the quantity of money is the prime determinant of the level of prices and economic activity, and that excessive monetary growth is responsible for inflation and unstable monetary growth for economic fluctuations. Since they contend that variability in the growth rate of money accounts for variability of real growth, they are naturally led to argue for a monetary policy of low and constant growth in the money supply—a monetary growth rule. *Activists*, by contrast, point out that there is no close relationship between monetary growth and inflation in the short run and that monetary growth is only one of the factors affecting aggregate demand. Activists maintain that policy makers are—or at least can be—sufficiently careful and skillful to be able to use monetary and fiscal policy to control the economy effectively.

The skill and care of the policy makers are important because monetarists raise the issue of whether aggregate demand policies might not worsen the performance of the economy. Monetarists point to episodes, such as the overexpansionary policies followed by the Fed in 1972, to argue that policy makers cannot and do not exercise sufficient caution to justify using activist policy. Here the activists are optimists, suggesting that we can learn from our past mistakes.

A further issue that divides the two camps concerns the proper role of government in the economy. This is not really an issue that can be analyzed using macroeconomic theory, but it is difficult to follow some of the debate without being aware that the issue exists. Monetarists and the new classical macroeconomists tend to be conservatives who favor small government and abhor budget deficits and a large public debt. They favor tax cuts during recessions and cuts in public spending during booms, with the net effect of winding up with a smaller share of government in the economy. Activists, by contrast, tend to favor an active role for government and are therefore quite willing to use increased government spending and transfers as tools of stabilization policy. Differences between monetarists and activists must, therefore, be seen in a much broader perspective than their particular disagreements about the exact role of money in the short run.

1-4 AGGREGATE DEMAND AND SUPPLY

We have sketched the major issues and variables we shall be discussing and using in the book.

The key overall concepts in analyzing output, inflation and growth, and the role of policy are *aggregate demand* and *aggregate supply.* In this section we provide a brief preview of those concepts and of their interaction, with the aims of showing where we are heading and of keeping the material of Chapters 3 through 10 in perspective.

The level of output and the price level are determined by the interaction of aggregate demand and aggregate supply. Under some conditions, employment depends only on total spending, or aggregate demand. At other times, supply limitations are an important part of the policy problem and have to receive major attention. From the 1930s to the later 1960s, macroeconomics was very much demand-oriented.

But in recent years the emphasis has shifted, and aggregate supply and *supply-side economics* have gained in importance. This shift of emphasis and interest was no doubt fostered by the slow growth and high inflation experienced by the industrialized countries in the 1970s.

What are the relationships among aggregate demand and aggregate supply, output or employment, and prices? Aggregate demand is the relationship between spending on goods and services and the level of prices. If output limitations are not present, increased spending or an increase in aggregate demand will raise output and employment with little effect on prices. In such conditions, for example, during the great depression of the thirties, it would certainly be appropriate to use expansionary aggregate demand policies to increase output.

But if the economy is close to full employment, increased aggregate demand will be reflected primarily in higher prices or inflation. The aggregate supply side of the economy has then to be introduced. The aggregate supply curve specifies the relationship between the amount of output firms produce and the price level. The supply side not only enters the picture in telling us how successful demand expansions will be in raising output and employment, but also has a role of its own. Supply disturbances, or *supply shocks,* can reduce output and raise prices, as was the case when increases in the price of oil reduced the productive capacity of the economy. Conversely, policies that increase productivity, and thus the level of aggregate supply at a given price level, can help reduce inflationary pressures.

Graphical Analysis

Figure 1-8 shows aggregate demand and supply curves. The vertical axis *P* is the price level, and the horizontal axis *Y* is the level of real output or income. Although the curves look like the ordinary supply and demand curves of microeconomics, a full understanding of them will not be reached until Chapter 12.

Aggregate demand is the total demand for goods and services in the economy. It depends on the aggregate price level, as shown in Figure 1-8. It can be shifted through monetary and fiscal policy. The aggregate supply curve shows the price level associated with each level of output. It can, to some extent, be shifted by fiscal policy.

Aggregate supply and demand interact to determine the price level and output level. In Figure 1-8, P_0 is the equilibrium price level and Y_0 the equilibrium level of output. If the *AD* curve in the figure shifts up to the right, then the extent to which output and prices, respectively, are changed depends on the steepness of the aggregate supply curve.[7] If the *AS* curve is very

[7] Experiment with graphs like Fig. 1-8 to be sure you understand this fact.

FIGURE 1-8 AGGREGATE DEMAND AND SUPPLY. The basic tools for analyzing output, inflation, and growth are the aggregate supply and demand curves. Shifts in either aggregate supply or demand will cause the level of output to change—thus affecting growth—and will also change the price level—thus affecting inflation. Through Okun's law, changes in output are linked to changes in the unemployment rate. For the first 10 chapters, we concentrate on aggregate demand. Then in the later chapters we introduce the aggregate supply curve, thereby completing the analysis.

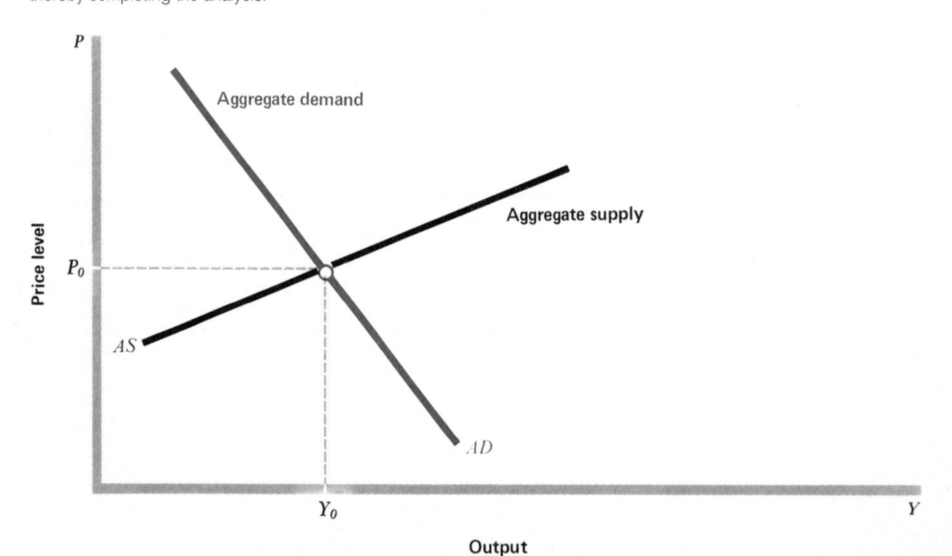

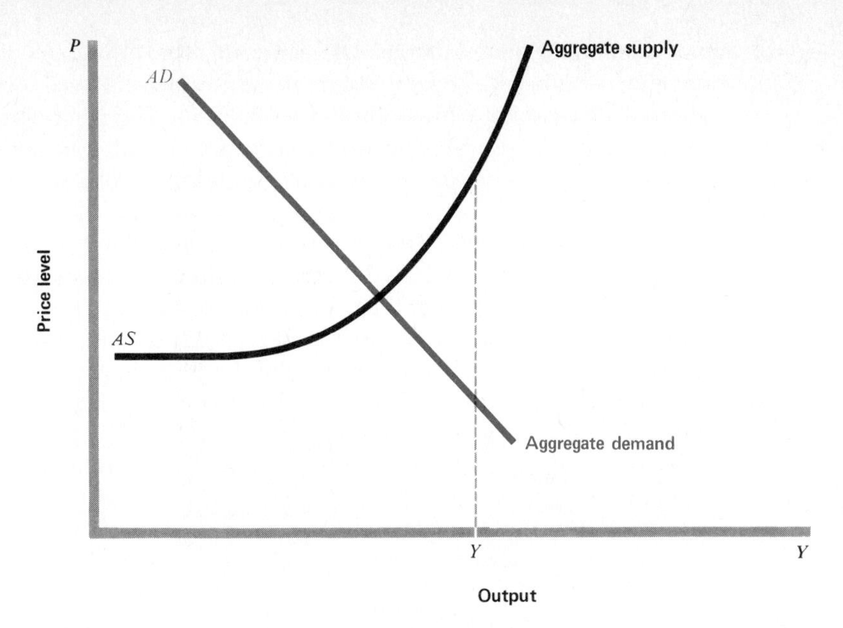

FIGURE 1-9 AGGREGATE DEMAND AND NONLINEAR AGGREGATE SUPPLY. A key fact about the aggregate supply curve is that it is not linear. At low levels of output, prices do not change much on the aggregate supply schedule, implying that more output will be supplied without much increase in prices. But as the economy gets close to full employment or potential output, further increases in output will be accompanied by increased prices.

steep, then a given increase in aggregate demand mainly causes prices to rise and has very little effect on the level of output. If the *AS* curve is flat, a given change in aggregate demand will be translated mainly into an increase in output and very little into an increase in the price level.

One of the crucial points about macroeconomic adjustment is that the aggregate supply curve is not a straight line. Figure 1-9 shows that at low levels of output, below potential output $\bar{Y}$, the aggregate supply curve is quite flat. When output is below potential, there is very little tendency for prices of goods and factors (wages) to fall. Conversely, for output above potential, the aggregate supply curve is steep and prices tend to rise continuously. The effects of changes in aggregate demand on output and prices therefore depend on the level of output relative to potential.

All these observations are by way of a very important warning. In Chapters 3 through 10 we focus on aggregate demand as the determinant of the level of output. We shall assume that prices are given and constant, and that output is determined by the level of demand—that there are no supply limitations. We are thus talking about the very flat part of the aggregate supply curve, at levels of output below potential.

The suggestion that output rises to meet the level of demand without a rise in prices leads to a very activist conception of policy. Under these circumstances, without any obvious tradeoffs, policy makers would favor very expansionary policies to raise demand and thereby cause the economy to move to a high level of employment and output. There are circumstances where such a policy view is altogether correct. The early 1960s are a case in point. Figure 1-3 shows that in those years output was substantially below potential. There were unused resources, and the problem was a deficiency of demand. By contrast, in the late 1960s and the early 1970s the economy was operating at full employment. There was no significant GNP gap. An attempt to expand output or real GNP further would run into supply limitations and force up prices rather than the production of goods. In these circumstances, a model that assumes that output is demand-determined and that increased demand raises output and *not* prices is simply inappropriate.

Should we think that the model with fixed prices and demand-determined output is very restricted and perhaps artificial? The answer is no. There are two reasons for this. First, the circumstances under which the model is appropriate—those of high unemployment—are neither unknown nor unimportant. Unemployment and downward price rigidity are continuing features of the United States economy. Second, even when we come to study the interactions of aggregate supply and demand in Chapter 11 and later, we need to know how given policy actions *shift* the aggregate demand curve at a given level of prices. Thus all the material of Chapters 3 through 10 on aggregate demand plays a vital part in the understanding of the effects of monetary and fiscal policy on the price level as well as output in circumstances where the aggregate supply curve is upward-sloping.

What, then, is the warning of this section? It is simply that the very activist spirit of macroeconomic policy under conditions of unemployment must not cause us to overlook the existence of supply limitations and price adjustment when the economy is near full employment.

1-5 OUTLINE AND PREVIEW OF THE TEXT

We have sketched the major issues we shall discuss in the book. We can now outline our approach to macroeconomics and the order in which the material will be presented. The key overall concepts, as already noted, are aggregate demand and aggregate supply. Aggregate demand is influenced by monetary policy, primarily via interest rates and expectations, and by fiscal policy. Aggregate supply is affected by fiscal policy and also by disturbances such as changes in the supply of oil.

Figure 1-10 presents a schematic view of the approach of the book to macroeconomics. Being schematic, the diagram is not comprehensive, but it does show the most important relationships we shall examine.

The coverage by chapters starts in Chapter 2 with national income accounting, emphasizing data and relationships that are used repeatedly later in the book. Chapters 3 to 5 are concerned with aggregate demand and Chapters 11–13 with aggregate supply and the interactions between aggregate supply and demand. Chapters 6 through 10 present material which clarifies and deepens understanding of aggregate demand and of the ways in

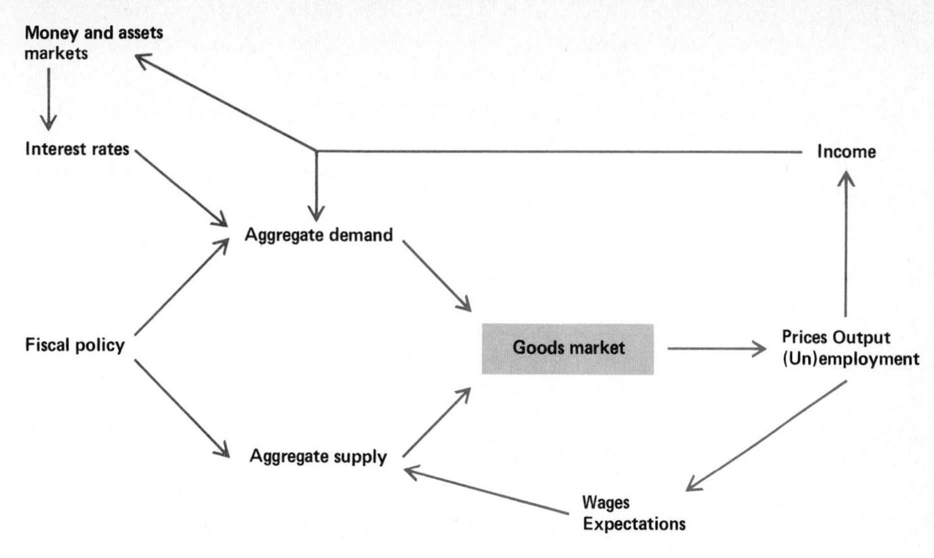

FIGURE 1-10 BASIC APROACH TO MACROECONOMICS. Aggregate demand and aggregate supply are the key elements in determining prices and output. Aggregate supply is affected by fiscal policy and by wage behavior and expectations. Aggregate demand is affected by fiscal policy and by monetary policy. There are also feedbacks through the money market—a high level of income increases the demand for money, which raises interest rates and reduces aggregate demand. This figure is a road map for the rest of the book. It will be helpful to return to it later, to see where the material being covered in later chapters fits in to the overall approach to the economy outlined here.

which monetary and fiscal policies affect the economy. Chapters 14 through 17 perform a similar service for aggregate supply and the interactions of aggregate supply and demand. Chapters 18 and 19 examine the effects of international trade in goods and assets on the economy.

1-6 PREREQUISITES AND RECIPES

A few words on how to use this book are helpful in concluding this introductory chapter. First, we note that there is no mathematical prerequisite beyond high school algebra. We do use equations whenever they appear helpful, but they are not an indispensable part of the exposition. Nevertheless, they can and should be mastered by any serious student of macroeconomics.

The technically harder chapters or sections are marked by an asterisk (*). They can be skipped or dipped into. Either we present them as supplementary material, or we provide sufficient nontechnical coverage to help the reader get on without them later in the book. The reason we do present more advanced material or treatment is to afford a complete and up-to-date coverage of the main ideas and techniques in macroeconomics. Even though you may not be able to grasp every point of a section marked by an asterisk on first reading—and should not even try to—these sections should certainly be read to get the main message and an intuitive appreciation of the issues that are raised.

The main problem you will encounter comes from the interaction of several markets and many variables. As Figure 1-10 already suggests, the direct and feedback effects in the economy constitute a quite formidable system. How can you be certain to progress efficiently and with some ease? The most important thing is to ask questions. Ask yourself, as you follow the argument: Why is it that this or that variable should affect, say, aggregate demand? What would happen if it did not? What is the critical link?

There is no substitute whatsoever for an active form of learning. Reading sticks at best for 7 weeks. Are there simple rules for active study? The best way to study is to use pencil and paper and work the argument by drawing diagrams, experimenting with flowcharts, writing out the logic of an argument, working out the problems at the end of each chapter, and underlining key ideas. The *Study Guide*, by Richard Startz of the University of Pennsylvania, contains both much useful material and problems that will help in your studies. Another valuable exercise is to take issue with an argument or position, or to spell out the defense for a particular view on policy questions. Beyond that, if you get stuck, read on for half a page. If you are still stuck, go back five pages.

You should also learn to use the Index. Several concepts are discussed at different levels in different chapters. If you come across an unfamiliar term or concept, check the Index to see whether and where it was defined and discussed earlier in the book.

As a final word, this chapter is designed for reference purposes. You should return to it whenever you want to check where a particular problem fits or where a particular subject matter is relevant. The best way to see the forest is from Chapter 1.

KEY TERMS

Monetarists
Keynesians
New classical macroeconomists
GNP, nominal and real
Inflation
Growth
Unemployment
Business cycle
Trend or potential output
Peak
Trough
Recovery or expansion
Recession
Output gap
Okun's law
Phillips curve
Monetary policy
Fiscal policy
Stabilization policies
Activists
Aggregate demand and supply

2

NATIONAL INCOME ACCOUNTING

Macroeconomics is ultimately concerned with the determination of the economy's total output, the price level, the level of employment, interest rates, and other variables discussed in Chapter 1. A necessary step in understanding how these variables are determined is *national income accounting.*

The national income accounts give us regular estimates of GNP, the basic measure of the performance of the economy in producing goods and services. The first part of the chapter discusses the measurement and meaning of GNP, nominal and real. But the national income accounts are useful also because they provide us with a conceptual framework for describing the relationships among three key macroeconomic variables: output, income, and spending. Those relationships are described in the second part of the chapter. They are summarized in the circular flow diagram, Figure 2-1.

Figure 2-1 illustrates the interactions of firms and households in the economy. Output is produced by firms. The value of the output produced is the gross national product. GNP includes the value of goods produced, such as automobiles and eggs, along with the value of services, such as haircuts and medical services.

Firms produce the output by employing factors of production — land,

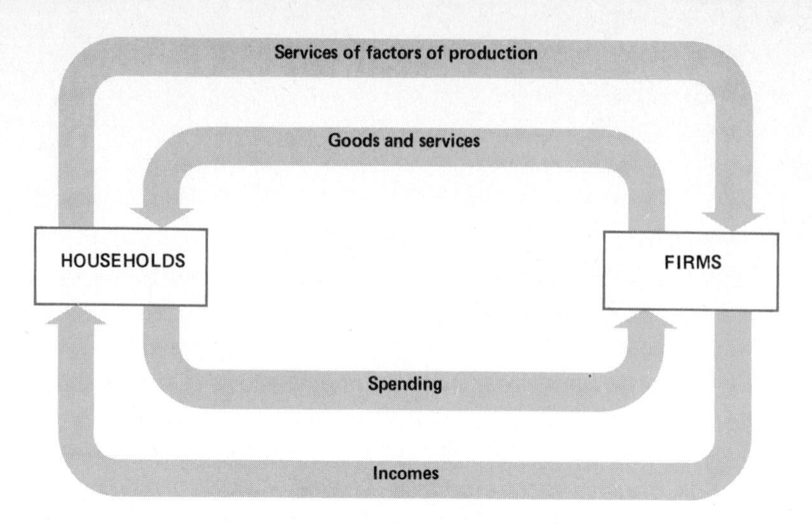

FIGURE 2-1 THE CIRCULAR FLOW OF INCOME AND SPENDING. Production is carried out by firms, whose total output is equal to GNP. The output is produced using the services of factors of production, mostly labor, owned by households and paid for by the firms. The payments for the use of factors of production generate the households' income. Household spending out of those incomes, in turn, generates the demand for the goods produced by the firms. Spending on goods is, in the simple case shown here where there is no government and no foreign trade, equal to GNP, and also equal to the income of households. The diagram shows the key relation: output is equal to income is equal to spending.

labor, and capital — and paying for their use. The payments made by the firms are the *incomes* earned in the economy. The flow of income is shown in the lower bottom loop of the circular flow diagram. Thus the value of output is equal to the value of incomes received in the economy.

The goods produced by the firms are sold to households (and to other firms). Total *spending* on goods is thus also equal to the value of output. The flow of spending is also shown in Figure 2-1.

Looking at the relationships summarized in Figure 2-1, we see that *GNP is equal to total income earned in the economy, and is also equal to total spending.* That is the main lesson of this chapter, and the single most important point to remember about national income accounting. But there is considerable complexity in the actual national income accounts in relating GNP to incomes and to spending. Those complexities arise in large part from the role of the government and from the presence of foreign trade, and we shall have to explain some of them.

We start in Section 2-1 by examining GNP and its measurement. Section 2-2 returns to the distinction between real and nominal GNP, a distinction which is necessary because of inflation. Section 2-3 compares alternative measures of inflation. Then we move in Sections 2-4 to 2-6 to the relationships among output, income, and spending summarized in the circular flow diagram.

TABLE 2-1 CALCULATING GNP IN A SIMPLE ECONOMY, 1984

	Output	Price per unit	Value of output	GNP
Bananas	20	$0.30	$ 6.00	
Oranges	60	$0.25	$15.00	
				$21.00

Section 2-7 paves the way for the economic analysis of the determination of the level of output that begins in Chapter 3, by systematically setting out the national income relationships studied in this chapter.

2-1 GROSS NATIONAL PRODUCT AND NET NATIONAL PRODUCT

GNP is the value of all final goods and services produced by domestically owned factors of production within a given period. It includes the value of such goods produced as houses and bourbon, and the value of services, such as brokers' services and economists' lectures. The output of each of these is valued at its market price, and the values are added together to give GNP.

Table 2-1 shows the calculation of GNP in a simple economy that produces only bananas and oranges. Twenty bananas and sixty oranges are produced. The bananas are valued at $0.30 each and the oranges at $0.25 each. GNP is equal to $21, the total value of output.

GNP in the United States in 1982 was $3,073 billion. Dividing by population, equal to 232 million in 1982, we obtain GNP per person or per capita, which was $13,246. We can also calculate output per person employed. In 1982 there were on average 99.5 million people employed. Thus GNP per person employed or output per person employed was $30,884.

GNP has increased rapidly in the last 20 years, as Figure 1-1 shows. GNP has grown on average at a rate of 8.8 percent per year since 1962. In that year GNP was only $565 billion, one sixth of its value in 1982. Recall that much of the increase is a result of inflation.

A number of subtleties in the calculation of GNP should be kept in mind.

FINAL GOODS AND VALUE ADDED

GNP is the value of *final* goods and services produced. The insistence on final goods and services is simply to make sure that we do not double-count. For example, we would not want to include the full price of an automobile in GNP and then also include the value of the tires that were sold to the automobile producer as part of the GNP. The components of the car, sold to the manufacturers, are called *intermediate* goods, and their value is not included in GNP. Similarly, the wheat that goes into bread is an intermediate good, and we do not count the value of the wheat sold the miller and the value of the flour sold the baker, as well as the value of the bread, as part of GNP.

In practice, double counting is avoided by working with *value added*. At each stage of the manufacture of a good, only the value added to the good at that stage of manufacture is counted as part of GNP. The value of the wheat produced by the farmer is counted as part of GNP. Then the value of the flour sold by the miller minus the cost of the wheat is the miller's value added. If we follow this process along, we will see that the sum of value added at each stage of processing will be equal to the final value of the bread sold.[1]

CURRENT OUTPUT

GNP consists of the value of output *currently produced*. It thus excludes transactions in existing commodities such as old masters or existing houses. We count the construction of new houses as part of GNP, but we do not add trade in existing houses. We do, however, count the value of realtor's fees in the sale of existing houses as part of GNP. The realtor provides a current service in bringing buyer and seller together, and that is appropriately part of current output.

MARKET PRICES

GNP values goods at *market prices*. The market price of many goods includes indirect taxes such as the sales tax and excise taxes, and thus the market price of goods is not the same as the price the seller of the good receives. The price net of indirect taxes is the *factor cost*, which is the amount received by the factors of production that manufactured the good. GNP is valued at market prices and not at factor cost. This point becomes important when we relate GNP to the incomes received by the factors of production.

Valuation at market prices is a principle that is not uniformly applied, because there are some components of GNP that are difficult to value. There is no very good way of valuing the services of housepersons, or a self-administered haircut, or, for that matter, the services of the police force or the government bureaucracy. Some of these activities are simply omitted from currently measured GNP, as, for instance, housepersons' services. Government services are valued at cost, so that the wages of government employees are taken to represent their contribution to GNP. There is no unifying principle in the treatment of these awkward cases, but rather a host of conventions is used.

GNP and Gross Domestic Product

There is a distinction between GNP and *gross domestic product*, or *GDP*. GDP is the value of final goods produced within the country. What is the difference between GNP and GDP? Part of GNP is earned abroad. For instance, the income of an American citizen working in Japan is part of U.S. GNP. But it is

[1] How about the flour that is directly purchased by households for baking in the home? It is counted as a contribution toward GNP since it represents a final sale.

not part of U.S. GDP because it is not earned in the United States. On the other side, the profits earned by the British owners of the Howard Johnson's chain are part of British GNP and not U.S. GNP. But they are part of U.S. GDP because they are earned in the United States.

When GNP exceeds GDP, residents of a given country are earning more abroad than foreigners are earning in that country. In the United States in recent years, GNP has exceeded GDP by about 2 percent of GNP, meaning that U.S. corporations and residents who own factories or work abroad earn more in foreign countries than foreign firms and individuals earn in the United States.

Net National Product

Net national product (*NNP*), as distinct from GNP, deducts from GNP the *depreciation* of the existing capital stock over the course of the period. The production of GNP causes wear and tear on the existing capital stock; for example, machines wear out as they are used. If resources were not used to maintain or replace the existing capital, GNP could not be kept at the current level. Accordingly, we use NNP as a better measure of the rate of economic activity that could be maintained over long periods, given the existing capital stock and labor force.

Depreciation is a measure of the part of GNP that has to be set aside to maintain the productive capacity of the economy, and we deduct that from GNP to obtain NNP. In 1982 depreciation was $359 billion, or about 11.7 percent of GNP. The figure is typically in the 10 to 12 percent range.

We usually work with the GNP rather than the NNP data because depreciation estimates may be quite inaccurate, and also are not quickly available, whereas the GNP estimate for each calendar quarter is available in preliminary form less than a month after the end of the quarter.[2] Indeed, a preliminary "flash" estimate of GNP for a given quarter is also made public before the end of the quarter.

2-2 REAL AND NOMINAL GNP

Nominal GNP measures the value of output in a given period in the prices of that period, or, as it is sometimes put, in *current dollars.* Thus 1984 nominal GNP measures the value of the goods produced in 1984 at the market prices that prevailed in 1984, and 1976 GNP measures the value of goods produced in 1976, at the market prices that prevailed in 1976. Nominal GNP changes from year to year for two reasons. The first is that the physical output of goods changes. The second is that market prices change. As an extreme and unrealistic example, one could imagine the economy producing exactly the same output in 2 years, between which all prices have doubled. Nominal GNP in

[2] National income account data are regularly reported in the *Survey of Current Business.* Historical data are available in *Business Statistics*, a biennial edition, and the *Economic Report of the President.*

TABLE 2-2 REAL AND NOMINAL GNP, AN ILLUSTRATION

1972 nominal GNP		1984 nominal GNP		1984 real GNP*	
15 bananas at $0.10	$1.50	20 bananas at $0.30	$ 6.00	20 bananas at $0.10	$ 2.00
50 oranges at $0.15	$7.50	60 oranges at $0.25	$15.00	60 oranges at $0.15	$ 9.00
	$9.00		$21.00		$11.00

*Measured in 1972 prices.

the second year would be double nominal GNP in the first year, even though the physical output of the economy has not changed at all.

Real GNP measures changes in *physical* output in the economy between different time periods by valuing all goods produced in the two periods *at the same prices*, or in *constant dollars*. Real GNP is now measured in the national income accounts in the prices of 1972. That means that, in calculating real GNP, today's physical output is multiplied by the prices that prevailed in 1972 to obtain a measure of what today's output would have been worth had it been sold at the prices of 1972.

We return to the simple example of Table 2-1 to illustrate the calculation of real GNP. The hypothetical outputs and prices of bananas and oranges in 1972 and 1984 are shown in the first two columns of Table 2-2. Nominal GNP in 1972 was $9, and nominal GNP in 1984 was $21, or an increase in nominal GNP of 133 percent. However, much of the increase in nominal GNP is purely a result of the increase in prices between the 2 years and does not reflect an increase in physical output. When we calculate real GNP in 1984 by valuing 1984 output in the prices of 1972, we find real GNP equal to $11, which is an increase of 22 percent rather than 133 percent. The 22 percent increase is a better measure of the increase in physical output of the economy than the 133 percent increase.

We see from the table that the output of bananas rose by 33 percent, while the output of oranges increased by 20 percent from 1972 to 1984. We should thus expect our measure of the increase in real output to be somewhere between 20 and 33 percent, as it is.[3]

Figure 2-2 shows the behavior of real and nominal GNP over the period since 1960. The data are for annual GNP for each year shown. Note particularly that while nominal GNP increased every year, real GNP actually fell in

[3] The increase in real GNP that is calculated depends on the prices that are used in the calculation. If you have a calculator, you might want to compare the increase in real GNP between 1972 and 1984 if the prices of 1984 are used to make the comparison. (Using 1984 prices, real GNP rises 23.5 percent from 1972 to 1984, compared with 22.2 percent using 1972 prices.) The ambiguities that arise in comparisons using different prices to calculate real GNP are an inevitable result of the attempt to use a single number to capture the increase in output of both bananas and oranges when those two components did not increase in the same proportion. However, the ambiguity is not a major concern when there is inflation at any substantial rate, and that is precisely when we most want to use real (rather than nominal) GNP to study the performance of the economy.

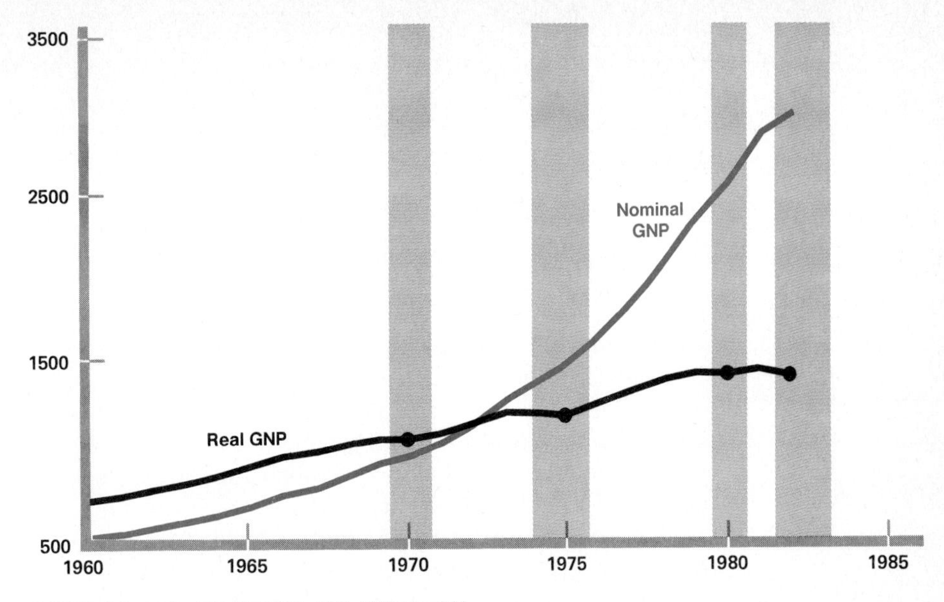

FIGURE 2-2 REAL AND NOMINAL GNP, 1960 TO 1982.

some years. Those years, darkly shaded, are years of recession. The recession years stand out as years of low or negative real GNP growth.

It would clearly be a mistake to regard the increases in *nominal* GNP as indicating that the performance of the economy in producing goods and services was improving from, say, 1981 to 1982. So we look at real and not nominal GNP as the basic measure for comparing output in different years.

Problems of GNP Measurement

GNP data are, in practice, used not only as a measure of how much is being produced, but also as a measure of the welfare of the residents of a country. Economists and politicians talk as if an increase in real GNP means that people are better off. But GNP data are far from perfect measures of either economic output or welfare.

Some of the problems of GNP measurement are described in the Box 2-1, which discusses the underground economy and revisions in GNP data. Here we cover first inadequacies in the measurement of some outputs and then the use of GNP as a measure of economic welfare.

BADLY MEASURED OUTPUTS

Most of the difficulties of measuring GNP arise because some outputs do not go through the market. We already noted that government production is valued at cost. That is because much of government output is not sold in the market, nor is anything comparable available that would make it possible to estimate the value of government output. How would we measure the value of output of safety from attack that defense expenditures are supposed to produce?

But there is also a conceptual problem with much of government output. We include in GNP the value of wages paid for the police and the defense forces. Suppose there was an improvement in public safety and police were taken out of the police force and put to work making candy—at their previous wage. GNP would not change. But the economy's output of useful goods and services certainly would seem to rise.

The problem in this case is that we generally do not deduct negative outputs, or *bads*, from GNP. We do not attempt to value the decline in public safety that requires increased police forces. Nor do we deduct from GNP the value of pollution produced by factories and cars. These are bads, but they do not show up in the GNP accounts. If we were somehow able to value the amount of public safety provided by society, then a shift of labor out of the police force resulting from an increase in public safety would indeed show up as an increase in GNP. Similarly, the improvement in the quality of the environment in the 1970s would show up as having raised output over that decade.

Other nonmarket activities, including do-it-yourself work and volunteer activities, are also excluded from GNP. The most important category here is the value of work done in the home by housepersons. Measured GNP would increase if someone stopped cleaning the house by himself and instead hired a cleaning service to do the same thing. But the output of the economy has not really risen.

Thus real GNP suffers from weaknesses even as a measure of goods and services produced in the economy.

REAL GNP AS A MEASURE OF WELL-BEING

The second use of GNP is as a *measure of economic welfare* (MEW) or well-being of the residents of a country. When GNP rises, it is assumed that people are better off. Of course, it is necessary first to divide real GNP by the number of people to use GNP in this sense: it is per capita (per person) GNP that is used as a welfare measure.

The difficulties of measuring nonmarket outputs already suggest that real GNP per capita is an imperfect measure of economic well-being. In addition, real GNP has to be adjusted to include the value of leisure. If the value of output falls because people have decided they would like to work less, that is not necessarily a sign that they are worse off. Much economic progress over the last century is reflected in a falling workweek. One hundred years ago the average workweek was well above 60 hours—and in manufacturing it was higher still. Now it is under 40 hours. Real GNP should be adjusted to include the value of the increased leisure people have as a result of the declining workweek, if GNP is to be used as a measure of economic welfare.

MEASURE OF ECONOMIC WELFARE

Yale's William Nordhaus and James Tobin in 1972 put together estimates of real GNP, adjusting as best they could for nonmarket outputs and nonmarket bads and for the increased amount of leisure people now have.[4] The value of MEW is larger than that of GNP. But on balance, MEW has grown more slowly than real GNP. Production of bads (pollution) has grown (at least through the seventies), and the increase in leisure time has grown more slowly than the output of goods and services.

MEW is not published regularly, and thus we continue to use real GNP as the chief measure of the economy's output and—although we know its shortcomings—as a measure of how the economy is performing in providing material well-being. The justification for doing so, in addition to the lack of choice, is that, in the short run, changes in real GNP are probably in the same direction as changes in MEW.

[4] William Nordhaus and James Tobin, "Is Growth Obsolete?" in National Bureau of Economic Research, *Fiftieth Anniversary Colloquium* (New York: Columbia University Press, 1972).

BOX 2-1

GNP MEASUREMENT: THE ILLEGAL ECONOMY AND DATA REVISIONS

Two particular (unrelated) problems of GNP measurement are the possibility that large parts of economic activity that are illegal entirely escape measurement, and that the data are frequently and quite substantially revised. We take up the two problems in turn.

THE ILLEGAL ECONOMY

Many illegal economic transactions that go through the market escape not only the law but also measurement. Anyone who pays cash for a handyman's services may be participating in a transaction that is not recorded in the GNP data, for the recipient of the cash is unlikely to declare that income. Similarly, the economic activity generated by the friendly local bookmaker probably does not get recorded in the GNP accounts. Nor does much of the illegal traffic in drugs.

What problems does the illegal or underground economy pose for GNP measurement? The main problem is that the relative importance of illegal activities may have been changing. If, say, illegal activities always produced output equal to 3 percent of measured GNP, then measured GNP would show accurately the *rate* at which total GNP *changes* from year to year. But if illegal activities become more important over time, then measured real GNP will understate the rate of growth of real GNP. And it is precisely the claim that illegal activities have been becoming more important that has led to research on the problem. The claim is made that the low growth rate of real GNP in the seventies is a reflection of the fact that less of actual economic activity was being measured by the government.

The basis for this claim is mainly the behavior of currency holdings in the economy relative to demand deposits. Currency holdings have increased relative to deposit holdings. Since currency is used for illegal transactions, it is argued that this increase shows an increasing share

TABLE 1 GNP DATA REVISIONS, 1980

	NOMINAL GNP, $ BILLION			REAL GNP, 1972 $ BILLION		
	Prerevision	Postrevision	Percentage change	Prerevision	Postrevision	Percentage change
1970	982.4	992.7	1.0	1075.3	1085.6	1.0
1979	2368.5	2413.9	1.9	1431.1	1483.1	3.6

	GROWTH RATE OF REAL GNP, % PER YEAR		
	Prerevision	Postrevision	Difference
1979/78	2.3%	3.2%	0.9%

Sources: Prerevision data are from Economic Report of the President, 1980, *Tables B-1 and B-2. Postrevision data are from "The National Income and Product Accounts of the United States: An Introduction to the Revised Estimates for 1929–80,"* Survey of Current Business, *December 1980, p. 17.*

of illegal transactions in total transactions.* On this basis it has been argued that real GNP in the United States may be understated by as much as 25 percent. Estimates based in part on the number of workers who hold down two jobs (the second with undeclared income) in Italy claim 15 percent of GNP is unrecorded there.

Other estimates for the United States and other countries are far smaller, some being as low as 2 to 3 percent.† Of course, by the nature of the problem, data are hard to come by. Thus we cannot really know. But the evidence in favor of large corrections is quite weak.

Why might there have been an increase in illegal activity? The causes are rising tax rates, which make it more tempting not to declare income, and the growing importance of trade in illegal drugs.

GNP DATA REVISIONS

Preliminary GNP data are published even before the end of the quarter for which they are calculated. The first estimate after the end of the quarter appears about 3 weeks later. For example, the data for the fourth quarter of 1983 will be announced about January 18, 1984. These data are then revised a month later and once more a month after that. Thus four estimates of GNP for a given quarter appear either in that quarter or within the next 3 months. Then in July each year there is a major revision of all GNP data, possibly going back many years.

It is thus clear that GNP data are not, when they first appear, firm estimates. The reason is that many of the data are not measured directly, but rather are based on surveys and guesses. Considering that GNP is supposed to measure the value of *all* production of goods and services in the economy, it is not surprising that not all the data are available within a few weeks after the period of production. The data are revised as new figures come in, and as the Bureau of

* The many estimates of illegal activity for the United States and abroad are reviewed in Adrian Smith, "A Review of the Informal Economy in the European Community," *Economic Papers #3,* July 1981, The Directorate General for Economic and Financial Affairs, Commission of the European Communities, Brussels.

† For a vigorous dissent to the large estimates for the United States, see Edward F. Denison, "Is U.S. Growth Understated because of the Underground Economy? Employment Ratios Suggest Not," *The Review of Income and Wealth,* 1982.

Economic Analysis of the Commerce Department improves its data collection methods and estimates.

The data revisions may be quite large. Table 1 shows the revisions to GNP that were made in 1980. Note in particular the size of the change made in real GNP in 1979. The revised real growth rate for 1979 over 1978, of 3.2 percent, is substantially higher than the prerevision growth rate. A 2.3 percent growth rate is distinctly low, whereas 3.2 percent is respectable. (Note that the levels of GNP for the years 1971–1978 were also raised in the revision, e.g. for 1978 the increase was 2.7 percent.)

The reasons for the revisions are described in the December 1980 *Survey of Current Business*. With such substantial revisions possible, the preliminary data have always to be greeted with caution.

2-3 PRICE INDEXES

The calculation of real GNP gives us a useful measure of inflation known as the *GNP deflator*. Returning to the hypothetical example of Table 2-2, we can get a measure of inflation between 1972 and 1984 by comparing the value of 1984 GNP in 1984 prices and 1972 prices. The ratio of nominal to real GNP in 1984 is 1.91 (=21 ÷ 11). In other words, output is 91 percent higher in 1984 when it is valued using the higher prices of 1984 than valued in the lower prices of 1972. We ascribe the 91 percent increase to price changes, or inflation, over the period 1972–1984.

The GNP deflator is the ratio of nominal GNP in a given year to real GNP, and it is a measure of inflation from the period from which the base prices for calculating real GNP are taken, to the current period. Since the GNP deflator is based on a calculation involving all the goods produced in the economy, it is a very widely based price index that is frequently used to measure inflation.

THE CONSUMER PRICE INDEX

The *consumer price index (CPI)* measures the cost of buying a fixed bundle of goods, representative of the purchases of urban consumers. The GNP deflator differs in four main ways from the CPI. First, the deflator measures the prices of a much wider group of goods than the CPI. These prices are measured by field-workers who go into shops and make phone calls to discuss the prices of the goods. Second, the CPI measures the cost of a given basket of goods, which is the same from year to year. The basket of goods included in the GNP deflator, however, differs from year to year, depending on what is produced in the economy in each year. The goods valued in the deflator in a given year are the goods that are produced in the economy in that year. When corn crops are high, corn receives a relatively large weight in the computation of the GNP deflator. By contrast, the CPI measures the cost of a fixed bundle of goods that does not vary over time.[5] Third, the CPI directly includes prices of imports,

[5] Price indexes are, however, occasionally revised to change weights to reflect current expenditure patterns.

whereas the deflator includes only prices of goods *produced* in the United States. Fourth, until 1983 there was a significant interest cost component in the CPI, representing housing costs. Changes in interest rates through this channel had an important effect on the CPI.[6] The two main indexes used to compute inflation, the GNP deflator and the CPI, accordingly differ in behavior from time to time. For example, at times when the price of imported oil rises rapidly, the CPI is likely to rise faster than the deflator.

THE PRODUCER PRICE INDEX

The *producer price index* (*PPI*) is the third price index that is widely used.[7] Like the CPI, this is a measure of the cost of a given basket of goods. It differs from the CPI partly in its coverage, which includes, for example, raw materials and semifinished goods. It differs, too, in that it is designed to measure prices at an early stage of the distribution system. Whereas the CPI measures prices where urban households actually do their spending—that is, at the retail level—the PPI is constructed from prices at the level of the first significant commercial transaction.

This difference makes the PPI a relatively flexible price index and one that signals changes in the general price level, or the CPI, some time before they actually materialize. For this reason the PPI, and more particularly, some of its subindexes, such as the index of "sensitive materials," serves as one of the business cycle indicators that are closely watched by policy makers.

Table 2-3 shows the CPI, the PPI, and the GNP deflator for the past 32 years. Both the CPI and PPI use 1967 as their base. This means that the weights in the standard basket that is priced are those of 1967.[8] The GNP deflator expresses prices in the current year relative to 1972 prices, using quantities of the current year as weights. Note from the table that all three indexes have been increasing throughout the period. This is a reflection of the fact that the average price of goods has been rising, whatever basket we look at. Note, too, that the cumulative increase (price 1982/price 1950) differs across indexes. This difference occurs because the indexes represent the prices of different commodity baskets.

Although the indexes do not change at the same rate over the entire period, all of them show substantial—and reasonably close—annual rates of inflation. There is no sense in which one of the indexes is "correct" while the others are not. The indexes measure changing prices of different baskets of

[6] Through the seventies and until 1982 the CPI undoubtedly badly miscalculated housing costs and gave too much weight to interest rate changes. The index was revised in 1983 to improve its measurement of housing costs.

[7] It was called the wholesale price index until 1978.

[8] The mechanics of price indexes are briefly described in the appendix to this chapter. Detailed discussion of the various price indexes can be found in the Bureau of Labor Statistics, *Handbook of Methods*, and in the Commerce Department biennial edition of *Business Statistics*.

TABLE 2-3 IMPORTANT PRICE INDEXES

	CPI, 1967 = 100	PPI, 1967 = 100	GNP deflator, 1972 = 100
1950	72.1	81.8	53.6
1960	88.7	94.9	68.7
1967	100.0	100.0	79.1
1972	125.3	119.1	100.0
1980	246.8	268.8	178.6
1982	289.1	299.3	207.2
Increase:			
Price 1982/price 1950	4.009	3.659	3.866
Average annual inflation rate	4.4%	4.1%	4.3%

Source: *Economic Report of the President*, 1983, and *Economic Indicators*, April 1983.

goods. We tend to focus on the deflator or the CPI, the deflator because it measures the prices of a very broad range of goods, and the CPI because the concept it tries to measure—the cost of buying a given basket of goods for the consumer—is a useful one.

We now return to the relationships summarized in the circular flow diagram Figure 2-1, among GNP or output, income, and spending.

2-4 GNP AND INCOME

In this section we show that *income is equal to the value of output* because the receipts from the sale of output must accrue to someone as income. The purchaser of bread is indirectly paying the farmer, the miller, the baker, and the supermarket operator for the labor and capital used in production and is also contributing to their profits.

GNP AND NATIONAL INCOME

Our statement above equating the value of output and income is correct with two qualifications:

1 The first correction arises from depreciation. As already noted, part of GNP has to be set aside to maintain the productive capacity of the economy. Depreciation should not be counted as part of income, since it is a cost of production. As a rule, depreciation amounts to about 11 percent of GNP. Depreciation is usually referred to in the national income accounts as the *capital consumption allowance*. After subtracting depreciation from GNP, we have NNP.

2 The second adjustment arises from indirect taxes, in particular, sales

TABLE 2-4 GNP AND NATIONAL INCOME, 1982 (*In billions of dollars*)

Gross national product		$3059.3
Less:		
Capital consumption allowance	$356.4	
Equals:		
Net national product		$2702.9
Less:		
Indirect taxes	$258.8	
Other (net)	$ 7.5	
Equals:		
National Income		$2436.6

Note: Numbers may not sum to totals because of rounding.
Source: Survey of Current Business, April, 1983.

taxes, that introduce a discrepancy between market price and prices received by producers. GNP is valued at market price, but the income accruing to producers does not include the sales taxes that are part of market price, and thus falls short of GNP. Indirect taxes, along with some other items of the same nature, account for about 10 percent of GNP.

With these two deductions we can derive national income from GNP, as shown in Table 2-4, which gives the dollar figures for 1982.[9] *National income* gives the value of output at *factor cost* rather than market prices, which is GNP. It tells us what the factors of production actually receive as income before direct taxes and transfers.

Factor Shares in National Income

We next ask how national income is split (*factor shares*) among different types of incomes, as shown in Table 2-5.

The most striking fact of Table 2-5 is the very large share of wages and salaries—compensation of employees—in national income. This accounts for 76 percent of national income. Proprietors' income is income from unincorporated businesses. Rental income of persons includes the *imputed* income of owner-occupied housing[10] and income from ownership of patents, royalties, and so on. The net interest category consists of interest payments by

[9] The term "Other (net)" in Table 2-4 includes a statistical discrepancy. In addition, it subtracts from NNP business transfer payments but adds subsidies to, less current surpluses of, government enterprises. The adjustment for government enterprises is required because, in the case of subsidies, market price understates the factor cost. In the case of deficits, similarly, the value of output measured at market prices falls short of the factor cost.

[10] GNP includes an estimate of the services homeowners receive by living in their homes. This is estimated by calculating the rent on an equivalent house. Thus the homeowner is treated as if she pays herself rent for living in her home.

TABLE 2-5 NATIONAL INCOME AND ITS DISTRIBUTION, 1982 (*In billions of dollars*)

National income	$2436.6	100%
Compensation of employees	$1856.5	76.2
Proprietors' income	120.3	4.9
Rental income of persons	34.1	1.4
Corporate profits	160.8	6.6
Net interest	264.9	10.9

Note: Numbers may not sum to totals because of rounding.
Source: Survey of Current Business, April 1983.

domestic businesses and the rest of the world to individuals and firms who have lent to them.

The division of national income into various classes is not too important for our macroeconomic purposes. It reflects, in part, such questions as whether corporations are financed by debt or equity, whether a business is or is not incorporated, and whether the housing stock is owned by persons or corporations—which, in turn, are owned by persons.[11]

National Income and Personal Income

A considerably more important question from the macroeconomic viewpoint is how much the personal sector—households and unincorporated business—actually receives as income, inclusive of transfers. This quantity is measured by *personal income. Transfers* are those payments that do *not* arise out of current productive activity. Thus, pensions, welfare payments, and unemployment benefits are examples of transfer payments. The level of personal income is important because it is a prime determinant of household consumption and saving behavior.

To go from national income to personal income, we have to remove those parts of national income that are earned by the corporate sector and add net transfer payments to the personal sector. Table 2-6 shows the steps needed to make the transition from national income to personal income.

Two items are deducted from national income:

1 Corporate profits (pretax), which clearly are not directly part of personal income.[12]

[11] You might want to work out how Table 2-5 would be modified for each of the possibilities described in this sentence. Problem 9 asks for the answers.

[12] Corporate profits in the national income accounts are adjusted by correcting firms' estimates of (*a*) depreciation (the capital consumption adjustment) and (*b*) the costs of inventories used up in production (the inventory valuation adjustment). The second adjustment occurs because computed profits are affected by the value firms place on the goods they use up in production. In inflationary times, typical ways of valuing inventories *understate* the cost of goods sold and thus *overstate* profits. The inventory valuation adjustment is an attempt to correct that error. The corporate profits deducted from national income in Table 2-6 include the two adjustments mentioned in this footnote.

TABLE 2-6 NATIONAL INCOME AND PERSONAL INCOME, IN 1982 (*In billions of dollars*)

National income		$2,450.4
Less:		
Corporate profits	$164.8	
Social insurance contributions	253.0	
Plus:		
Government and business transfers to persons	374.5	
Interest adjustment	105.1	
Dividends	66.4	
Equals:		
Personal income		$2,578.6

Source: Data Resources, Inc.

2 Contributions for social insurance. These are contributions, by both corporations and the personal sector, which are essentially taxes paid to the government sector and thus not part of personal income.

We then add back three items:

1 *Transfer payments* to persons, consisting mostly of government transfers such as Social Security benefits, state unemployment insurance benefits, and veterans' benefits, along with business transfers such as business contributions to charity.
2 Interest Adjustment: National income only measures payments for productive services. Other payments, not classified as factor payments, still represent income receipts for households or businesses even though they do not apear in national income. Some of the interest income received by households counts as transfer payments in the national income accounts, but has now to be taken into account in calculating the income of households. We therefore add in Table 2-6 an item "interest adjustment."[13]
3 Dividends (distributed after-tax corporate profits).

After making these adjustments, we have a measure of the income received by persons and unincorporated businesses. Personal income is a useful measure particularly because it is available monthly, as opposed to most national income measures which are published only quarterly. The monthly personal income data are used as a guide to the behavior of GNP by those who follow economic events closely.

[13] This interest adjustment is equivalent to adding to national income the item "personal interest income" and subtracting "net interest." These two items can be found in the national accounts tables. The difference between "net interest" (which is net interest paid by businesses to domestic households, plus net interest from abroad) and "personal interest income" (the interest payments received by households) is equal to net interest paid by the government to households and businesses, plus the interest paid by households to businesses.

Although we have derived personal income in Table 2-6 by starting with national income and making adjustments, it is also possible to build up to an estimate of personal income by looking at its components in a way similar to that shown in Table 2-5. In particular, personal income consists of labor income, plus proprietors' income, plus persons' rental, dividend, and interest income, plus transfer payments, minus personal contributions for social insurance.

Disposable Personal Income and Its Allocation

Not all personal income is available for spending by households. The amount available for spending, *disposable personal income*, deducts from personal income the personal tax and certain nontax payments made by the household sector. The nontax payments include such items as license fees and traffic tickets.

Disposable personal income is the amount households have available to spend or save. Table 2-7 shows how households allocate their disposable income. By far the largest outlay is for personal consumption. Most of the remainder is saved. Small amounts of personal disposable income are used to make interest payments and to make transfers to foreigners.

The United States personal saving rate is among the world's lowest. We shall see later why this worries some economists.

This section has shown the relation between GNP and the income that accrues to the household sector. The main steps we have followed arise from taxes, transfers between sectors, depreciation, and profits.

These intermediate steps remind us that there is an important difference

TABLE 2-7 PERSONAL INCOME, DISPOSABLE PERSONAL INCOME, AND ITS DISPOSITION IN 1982

	$ billions		Percent of disposable personal income	
Personal income	$2,578.6			
Less:				
Personal tax and nontax payments	$ 402.1			
Equals:				
Disposable personal income		$2,176.5		100%
Personal outlays:		$2,056.3		94.5%
Personal consumption expenditures	$1,991.9		91.5%	
Interest paid by consumers	$ 58.1		2.7%	
Transfers to foreigners	$ 6.3		0.3%	
Personal savings		$ 125.4		5.8%

Note: Third and fourth columns show the breakdown of disposable personal income as a percentage of disposable personal income. Numbers may not sum to totals because of rounding.
Source: Data Resources, Inc.

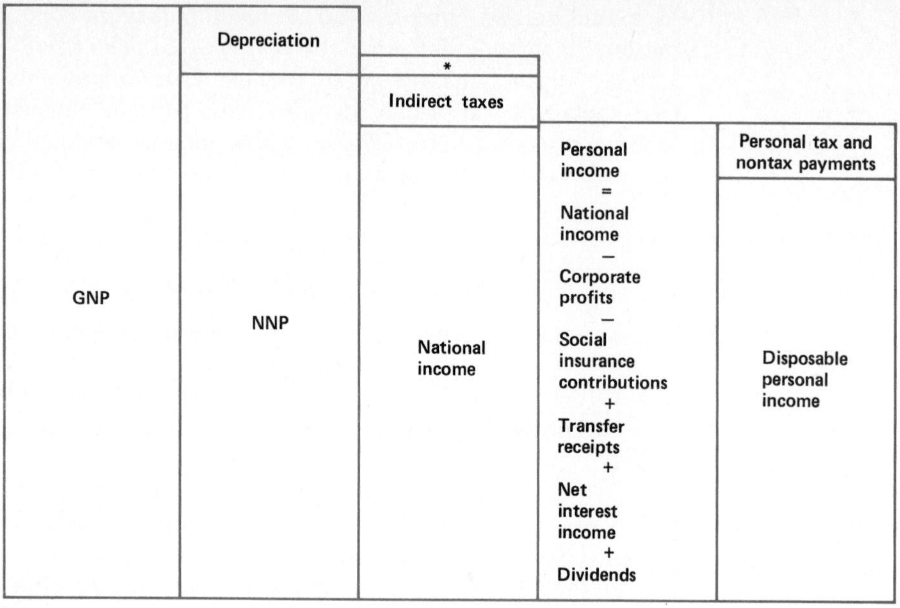

	Depreciation	*	Indirect taxes	Personal tax and nontax payments
GNP	NNP	National income	Personal income = National income − Corporate profits − Social insurance contributions + Transfer receipts + Net interest income + Dividends	Disposable personal income

*Statistical discrepancy plus subsidies less current surplus of government enterprises.

FIGURE 2-3 THE RELATION BETWEEN GNP AND DISPOSABLE PERSONAL INCOME.

between GNP as the value of output at market prices and the spendable receipts of the household sector. We could have a positive disposable personal income even if GNP were zero, provided there was someone to make the necessary transfer payments. Likewise, GNP could be large and disposable income small if the government sector took in a lot of taxes. The larger taxes are relative to government transfers, the smaller is disposable income relative to GNP.

Summary

We summarize here in a few identities (and in the accompanying Figure 2-3) the relationships reviewed in each table:

$$\text{GNP} - \text{capital consumption allowance} \equiv \text{NNP} \qquad \text{(Table2-4)} \qquad (1)$$

$$\text{NNP} - \text{indirect taxes} \equiv \text{national income} \qquad \text{(Table 2-4)} \qquad (2)$$

$$\text{National income} \equiv \text{wages and salaries} + \text{proprietors' income} + \text{rental income of persons} + \text{corporate profits} + \text{net interest} \qquad \text{(Table 2-5)} \quad (3)$$

$$\text{National income} - \text{corporate profits} - \text{social insurance contributions} + \text{transfer receipts} + \text{interest adjustment} + \text{dividends} \equiv \text{personal income} \qquad \text{(Table 2-6)} \quad (4)$$

Personal income − personal tax and nontax payments
$\equiv$ disposable personal income (Table 2-7) (5)

Disposable personal income $\equiv$ personal outlays
+ personal savings (Table 2-7) (6)

2-5 OUTLAYS AND COMPONENTS OF DEMAND

In the previous section, we started with GNP and asked how much of the value of goods and services produced actually gets into the hands of households. In this section we present a different perspective on GNP by asking who buys the output, rather than who receives the income. More technically, we look at the demand for output and speak of the *components* of the aggregate demand for goods and services.

Total demand for domestic output is made up of four components: (1) consumption spending by households; (2) investment spending by businesses or households; (3) government (federal, state, and local) purchases of goods and services; and (4) foreign demand. We shall now look more closely at each of these components.

CONSUMPTION

Table 2-8 presents a breakdown of the demand for goods and services in 1982 by components of demand. The table shows that the chief component of demand is *consumption* spending by the personal sector. This includes anything from food to golf lessons, but involves also, as we shall see in discussing investment, consumer spending on durable goods such as automobiles—spending which might be regarded as investment rather than consumption.

GOVERNMENT

Next in importance we have *government purchases* of goods and services. Here we have such items as national defense expenditures, road paving by state and local governments, and salaries of government employees.

TABLE 2-8 GNP AND COMPONENTS OF DEMAND, 1982 (*In billions of dollars*)

Personal consumption expenditures	$1,991.9	64.8%
Gross private domestic investment	414.5	13.5
Government purchases of goods and services	649.2	21.1
Net exports of goods and services	17.4	0.6
Gross national product	3,073.0	100.0

Note: Numbers do not sum to totals because of rounding.
Source: Data Resources, Inc.

We draw attention to the use of certain words in connection with government spending. We refer to government spending on goods and services as *purchases* of goods and services, and we speak of *transfers plus purchases* as *government expenditure.* The federal government budget, of the order of $650 billion, refers to federal government expenditure. Less than half that sum is for federal government purchases of goods and services.

INVESTMENT

Gross private domestic investment requires some definitions. First, throughout this book, *investment* means additions to the physical stock of capital. As we use the term, investment does *not* include buying a bond or purchasing stock in General Motors. Practically, investment includes housing construction, building of machinery, business construction, and additions to a firm's inventories of goods.

The classification of spending as consumption or investment remains to a significant extent a matter of convention. From the economic point of view, there is little difference between a household building up an inventory of peanut butter and a grocery store doing the same. Nevertheless, in the national income accounts, the individual's purchase is treated as a personal consumption expenditure, whereas the store's purchase is treated as investment in the form of inventory investment. Although these borderline cases clearly exist, we can apply a simple rule of thumb: that investment is associated with the business sector's adding to the physical stock of capital, including inventories.[14]

Similar issues arise in the treatment of household sector expenditures. For instance, how should we treat purchases of automobiles by households? Since automobiles usually last for several years, it would seem sensible to classify household purchases of automobiles as investments. We would then treat the *use* of automobiles as providing consumption services. (We could think of imputing a rental income to owner-occupied automobiles.) However, the convention is to treat all household expenditures as consumption spending. This is not quite so bad as it might seem, since the accounts do separate households' purchases of *durable goods* like cars and refrigerators from their other purchases. When consumer spending decisions are studied in detail, expenditures on consumer durables are usually treated separately.[15]

In passing, we note that in Table 2-8, investment is defined as "gross" and

[14] The GNP accounts record as investment *business sector* additions to the stock of capital. Some government spending, for instance for roads or schools, also adds to the capital stock. Estimates of the capital stock owned by government are available in the *Survey of Current Business,* October 1982, pp. 33–36; this source also provides references to estimates of government investment.

[15] The convention that is adopted with respect to the household sector's purchases of houses also deserves comment. The accounts treat the building of a house as investment by the business sector. When the house is sold to a private individual, the transaction is treated as the transfer of an asset, and not then an act of investment. Even if a house is custom-built by the owner, the accounts treat the builder who is employed by the owner as undertaking the act of investment in building the house. The investment is thus attributed to the business sector.

"domestic." It is gross in the sense that depreciation is not deducted. Net investment is gross investment minus depreciation. Thus NNP is equal to net investment plus the other categories of spending in Table 2-8.

The term *domestic* means that this is investment spending by domestic residents but is not necessarily spending on goods produced within this country. It may well be an expenditure that falls on foreign goods. Similarly, consumption and government spending may also be partly for imported goods. On the other hand, some of domestic output is sold to foreigners.

NET EXPORTS

The item "Net exports" appears in Table 2-8 to show the effects of domestic spending on foreign goods and foreign spending on domestic goods on the aggregate demand for domestic output. The total demand for the goods we produce includes exports, the demand from foreigners for our goods. It excludes imports, the part of our domestic spending that is not for our own goods. Accordingly, the difference between exports and imports, called *net exports*, is a component of the total demand for our goods.

The point can be illustrated with an example. Assume that instead of having spent $1,992 billion, the personal sector had spent $20 billion more. What would GNP have been? If we assume that government and investment spending had been the same as in Table 2-8, we might be tempted to say that GNP would have been $20 billion higher. That is correct if all the additional spending had fallen on our goods. The other extreme, however, is the case where all the additional spending falls on imports. In that event, consumption would be up $20 billion *and* net exports would be down $20 billion, with *no* net effect on GNP.

2-6 SOME IMPORTANT IDENTITIES

In this section we formalize the discussion of the preceding sections by writing down a set of relationships which we use extensively in Chapter 3. We introduce here some notation and conventions that we follow throughout the book.

For analytical work in the following chapters, we simplify our analysis by omitting the distinction between GNP and national income. For the most part we disregard depreciation and thus the difference between GNP and NNP, as well as the difference between gross and net investment. We refer simply to investment spending. We also disregard indirect taxes and business transfer payments. With these conventions in mind *we refer to national income and GNP interchangeably as income or output.* These simplifications have no serious consequence and are made only for expositional convenience. Finally, and only for a brief while, we omit both the government and foreign sector. Thus the assumptions we are making conform to those of the circular flow diagram, Figure 2-1.

A Simple Economy

We denote the value of output in our simple economy, which has neither a government nor foreign trade, by Y. Consumption is denoted by C and investment spending by I. The first key identity we want to establish is that between output produced and output sold. Output produced is Y, which can be written in terms of the components of demand as the sum of consumption and investment spending. (Remember, we have assumed away the government and foreign sectors.) Accordingly, we can write the identity of output sold and output produced[16]:

$$Y \equiv C + I \tag{7}$$

Now the question is whether Equation (7) is really an identity. Is it inevitably true that all output produced is either consumed or invested? After all, do not firms sometimes make goods that they are unable to sell? The answer to each of the questions is yes. Firms do sometimes make output that they cannot sell, and that accumulates on their shelves. *However, we count the accumulation of inventories as part of investment* (as if the firms sold the goods to themselves to add to their inventories), and therefore, all output is either consumed or invested. Note that we are talking here about *actual* investment, which includes investment in inventories that firms might be very unhappy to make. Because of the way investment is defined, output produced is identically equal to output sold.

Identity (7) formalizes the basis of Table 2-8 (we are still assuming away the government and external sectors). The next step is to draw up a corresponding identity for Table 2-7 and identity (6), which examined the disposition of personal income. For that purpose, it is convenient to ignore the existence of corporations and consolidate or add together the entire private sector. Using this convention, we know that private sector income is Y, since the private sector receives as income the value of goods and services produced. Why? Because who else would get it? There is no government or external sector yet. Now the private sector receives, as disposable personal income, the whole of income Y. How will that income be allocated? Part will be spent on consumption, and part will be saved. Thus we can write

$$Y \equiv S + C \tag{8}$$

where S denotes private sector saving. Identity (8) tells us that the whole of income is allocated to either consumption or saving.

Next, identities (7) and (8) can be combined to read:

$$C + I \equiv Y \equiv C + S \tag{9}$$

[16] Throughout the book we distinguish identities from equations. Identities are statements that are *always* true because they are directly implied by definitions of variables or accounting relationships. They do not reflect any economic behavior but are extremely useful in organizing our thinking. Identities, or definitions, are shown with the sign $\equiv$, and equations with the usual equality sign $=$.

The left-hand side of Equation (9) shows the components of demand, and the right-hand side shows the allocation of income. The identity emphasizes that output produced is equal to output sold. The value of output produced is equal to income received, and income received, in turn, is spent on goods or saved.

The identity in Equation (9) can be slightly reformulated to look at the relation between saving and investment. Subtracting consumption from each part of Equation (9), we have

$$I \equiv Y - C \equiv S \tag{10}$$

Identity (10) is an important result. It shows first that in this simple economy, saving is identically equal to income less consumption. This result is not new, since we have already seen it in Equation (8). The new part concerns the identity of the left and right sides: *investment is identically equal to saving.*

One can think of what lies behind this relationship in a variety of ways. In a very simple economy, the only way the individual can save is by undertaking an act of physical investment—by storing grain or building an irrigation channel. In a slightly more sophisticated economy, one could think of investors financing their investing by borrowing from individuals who save.

However, it is important to recognize that Equation (10) expresses the identity between investment and saving, and that some of the investment might well be undesired inventory investment, occurring as a result of mistakes by producers who expected to sell more than they actually did. The identity is really only a reflection of our definitions—output less consumption is investment, output is income, and income less consumption is saving. Even so, we shall find that identity (10) plays a key role in Chapter 3.

Reintroducing the Government and Foreign Trade

We can now reintroduce the government sector and the external sector. First, for the government we denote purchases of goods and services by G and all taxes by TA. Transfers to the private sector (including interest) are denoted by TR. Net exports (exports minus imports) are denoted by NX.

We return to the identity between output produced and sold, taking account now of the additional components of demand G and NX. Accordingly, we restate the content of Table 2-8 by writing

$$Y \equiv C + I + G + NX \tag{11}$$

Once more we emphasize that in Equation (11) we use actual investment in the identity and thus do not rule out the possibility that firms might not at all be content with the investment. Still, as an accounting identity, Equation (11) will hold.

Next we turn to the derivation of the very important relation between output and disposable income. Now we have to recognize that part of income is spent on taxes, and that the private sector receives net transfers TR in addition to national income. Disposable income is thus equal to income plus transfers less taxes:

$$YD \equiv Y + TR - TA \tag{12}$$

We have written YD to denote disposable income. Disposable income, in turn, is allocated to consumption and saving, so that we can write

$$YD \equiv C + S \tag{13}$$

Combining identities (12) and (13) allows us to write consumption as the difference between income, plus transfers minus taxes, and saving:

$$C + S \equiv YD \equiv Y + TR - TA \tag{14}$$

or

$$C \equiv YD - S \equiv Y + TR - TA - S \tag{14a}$$

Identity (14*a*) states that consumption is disposable income less saving, or alternatively, that consumption is equal to income plus transfers less taxes and saving. Now we use the right-hand side of Equation (14*a*) to substitute for C in identity (11). With some rearrangement we obtain

$$S - I \equiv (G + TR - TA) + NX \tag{15}$$

Saving, Investment, the Government Budget, and Trade

Identity (15) cannot be overemphasized. Its importance arises from the fact that the first set of terms on the right-hand side $(G + TR - TA)$ is the *government budget deficit.* $(G + TR)$ is equal to government[17] purchases of goods and services (G) plus government transfer payments (TR), which is total government spending. TA is the amount of taxes received by the government. The difference $(G + TR - TA)$ is the excess of government spending over its receipts, or its budget deficit. The second term on the right-hand side is the excess of exports over imports, or the *trade surplus.*

Thus identity (15) states that the excess of savings over investment $(S - I)$ of the private sector is equal to the government budget deficit plus the trade surplus. The identity suggests—correctly—that there are important relations among the accounts of the private sector, $S - I$, the government budget, $G + TR - TA$, and the external sector. For instance, if, for the private sector, savings is equal to investment, then the government's budget deficit (surplus) is reflected in an equal external deficit (surplus).

Table 2-9 shows the significance of the Equation (15). To fix ideas,

[17] *Government* throughout this chapter means the federal government plus state and local governments. A breakdown between these entities can be found in the *Economic Report of the President.* There one would see, for example, that state and local governments run surpluses in their budgets and are net recipients of interest payments.

TABLE 2-9 THE BUDGET DEFICIT, TRADE, SAVING, AND INVESTMENT

S	*I*	*BD* (budget deficit)	*NX* (trade surplus)
300	300	0	0
300	200	100	0
300	250	0	50
300	150	100	50

suppose that private sector saving S is equal to \$300 (billion). In the first two rows we assume that exports are equal to imports, so that the trade surplus is zero. In row 1, we assume the government budget is balanced. Investment accordingly has to equal \$300 billion. In the next row we assume the government budget deficit is \$100 billion. *Given the level of saving* of \$300 billion and a zero trade balance, it has to be true that investment is now lower by \$100 billion. Rows 3 and 4 show how these relationships are affected when there is a trade surplus.

To interpret these relationships, realize that any sector that spends more than it receives in income has to borrow to pay for the excess spending. The private sector has three ways of disposing of its saving. It can make loans to the government, which thereby pays for the excess of its spending over the income it receives from taxes. Or it can lend to foreigners, who are buying more from us than we are buying from them. They therefore are earning less from us than they need to pay for the goods they buy from us, and we have to lend to cover the difference. Or it can lend to business firms which use the funds for investment.

In Table 2-9 we take saving as fixed at \$300 billion. When the budget and trade are balanced, the private sector has to lend the \$300 billion to firms, which invest that amount. But suppose the government runs a budget deficit of \$100 billion. Then the private sector has to lend \$100 billion to government to cover its excess of spending over revenue. Only \$200 billion is left to lend to firms for investment. Similarly, if we export more than we import, foreigners need to borrow from us to pay for the excess of what they buy from us over what they sell to us. In rows 3 and 4 we are using \$50 billion of our saving to lend to foreigners. Then only \$250 billion is left to lend either to firms or to the government.

2-7 SUMMARY

1 As the circular flow diagram shows, output is equal to income and spending.
2 Nominal GNP is the value of the output of final goods and services produced by domestically owned factors of production, measured at market prices.
3 Gross domestic product is the value of output produced within the

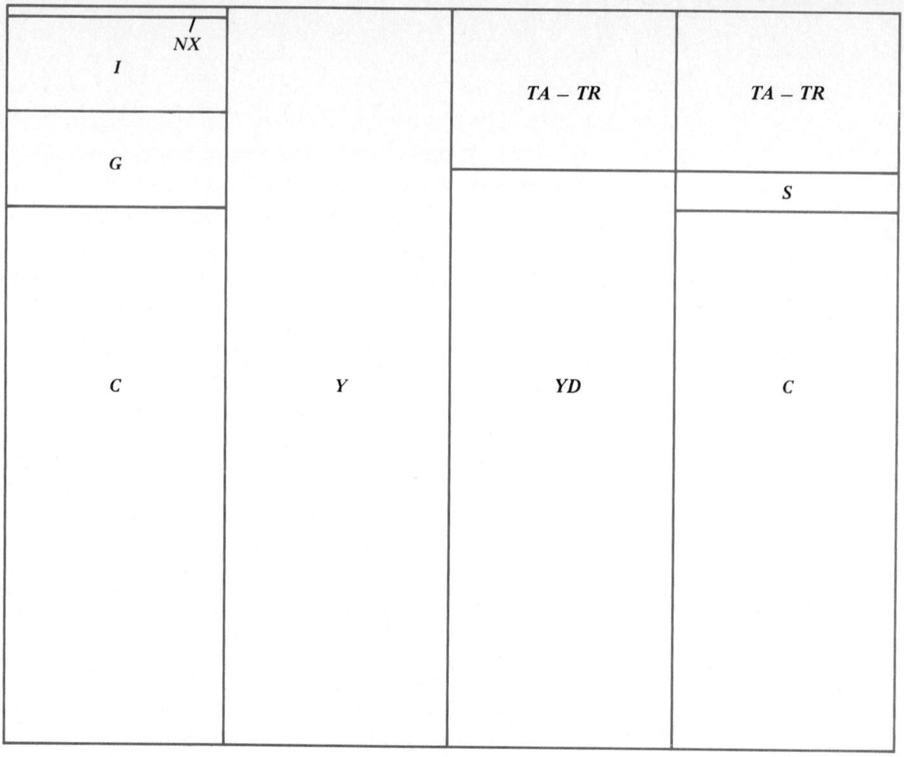

FIGURE 2-4 THE BASIC MACROECONOMIC IDENTITY.

$$C + G + I + NX \equiv Y \equiv YD + (TA - TR) \equiv C + S + (TA - TR) \quad (16)$$

The left-hand side is the demand for output by components which is identically equal to output supplied. Output supplied is equal to income. Disposable income is equal to income plus transfers less taxes. Disposable income is allocated to saving and consumption.

country. It differs from GNP because some of our GNP is produced abroad and because some of our domestic production is produced by foreign-owned factors of production.

4 Real GNP is the value of the economy's output measured in the prices of some base year. Real GNP comparisons, based on the same set of prices for valuing output, provide a better measure of the change in the economy's physical output than nominal GNP comparisons, which also reflect inflation.

5 The GNP deflator is the ratio of nominal to real GNP. It reflects the general rise in prices from the base date by which real GNP is valued. Other frequently used price indexes are the consumer and producer price indexes.

6 National income is equal to GNP minus depreciation and indirect taxes.

7 National income is equal to the incomes received in the economy, valued at factor cost.
8 Spending on GNP is conveniently divided into consumption, investment, government purchases of goods and services, and net exports. The division between consumption and investment in the national income accounts is somewhat arbitrary at the edges.
9 The excess of the private sector's saving over investment is equal to the sum of the budget deficit and the foreign trade surplus.
10 For the remainder of the book we use a simplified model for expositional convenience. We assume away depreciation, indirect taxes, business transfer payments, and the difference between households and corporations. For this simplified model, Figure 2-4 and Equation (16) review the *basic macroeconomic identity:*

$$C + G + I + NX \equiv Y \equiv YD + (TA - TR) \equiv C + S + (TA - TR) \quad (16)$$

The left-hand side is the demand for output by components which is identically equal to output supplied. Output supplied is equal to income. Disposable income is equal to income plus transfers less taxes. Disposable income is allocated to saving and consumption.

KEY TERMS

Final goods
Value added
Market prices
Factor cost
Gross domestic product (GDP)
Net national product (NNP)
Depreciation
Measure of economic welfare (MEW)
The illegal economy
GNP deflator
Consumer price index (CPI)
Producer price index (PPI)
National income
Factor shares
Personal income
Transfers
Disposable personal income
Consumption
Government purchases
Government expenditure
Investment
Net exports
Consumer durables
Government budget deficit

PROBLEMS

1 Show from national income accounting that:
(*a*) An increase in taxes (while transfers remain constant) must imply a change in the trade balance, government purchases, or the saving-investment balance.
(*b*) An increase in disposable personal income must imply an increase in consumption or an increase in saving.
(*c*) An increase in both consumption and saving must imply an increase in disposable income.
[For both (*b*) and (*c*) assume there are no interest payments by households or transfer payments to foreigners.]

2 The following is information from the national income accounts for a hypothetical country:

GNP	2,400
Gross investment	400
Net investment	150
Consumption	1,500
Government purchases of goods and services	480
National income	1,925
Wages and salaries	1,460
Proprietors' income + rental income of persons	160
Dividends	50
Government budget surplus	15
Social insurance contributions	190
Net interest income	60
Government and business transfers to persons	260
Personal tax and nontax payments	300

What is:
(*a*) NNP?
(*b*) Net exports?
(*c*) Indirect taxes?
(*d*) Corporate profits?
(*e*) Taxes—transfers?
(*f*) Personal income?
(*g*) Disposable personal income?
(*h*) Personal saving?

3 What would happen to GNP if the government hired unemployed workers, who had been receiving amount $\$TR$ in unemployment benefits, as government employees to do nothing, and now paid them $\$TR$? Explain.

4 What is the difference in the national income accounts between:
(*a*) A firm's buying an auto for an executive and the firm's paying the executive additional income to buy himself a car?
(*b*) Your hiring your spouse (who takes care of the house) rather than just having him or her do the work without pay?
(*c*) Your deciding to buy an American car rather than a German car?

5 Explain the following terms:
(*a*) Value added (*c*) Inventory investment
(*b*) Factor cost (*d*) GNP deflator

6 (*a*) In 1981 U.S. GNP was $2,954 billion. GDP was $2,905. Why is there a difference?
(*b*) In 1981 U.S. GNP was $2,954 billion. NNP was $2,625. What accounts for the difference? How typical is the difference for 1981 as a fraction of GNP?

7 This question deals with price index numbers. Consider a simple economy where only three items are in the CPI: food, housing, and entertainment (fun). Assume in the base period, say, 1967, the household consumed the following quantities at the then prevailing prices:

	Quantities	Prices per unit, $	Expenditure, $
Food	5	14	70
Housing	3	10	30
Fun	4	5	20
Total			120

(*a*) Define the consumer price index.

(*b*) Assume that the basket of goods that defines the CPI is as given in the table. Calculate the CPI for 1984 if the prices prevailing in 1984 are: food, $30 per unit; housing, $20 per unit; and fun, $6 per unit.

*(*c*) Show that the change in the CPI relative to the base year is a weighted average of the individual price changes, where the weights are given by the base year expenditure shares of the various goods.

8 Here are some 1981 GNP data, in billions:

GNP = $2,954 Indirect taxes = $250

NNP = $2,625 Other (net) = $5

(*a*) What are (*i*) depreciation and (*ii*) national income?

(*b*) Why are indirect taxes deducted from NNP to get national income?

9 After Table 2-5 we asked you to answer certain questions. Here they are:

(*a*) How would a shift by corporations from equity to debt finance affect the distribution of national income in Table 2-5?

(*b*) How would the incorporation of a business affect the table?

(*c*) What difference would it make if some existing houses were owned by corporations instead of individuals?

10 Assume that GNP is $1,200, personal disposable income is $1,000, and the government budget deficit is $70. Consumption is $850, and the trade surplus is $20.

(*a*) How large is saving S?

(*b*) What is the size of investment I?

(*c*) How large is government spending?

APPENDIX: PRICE INDEX FORMULAE

Both the PPI and CPI are price indexes which compare the current and base year cost of a basket of goods of *fixed* composition. If we denote the base year quantities of the various goods by q_0^i and their base year prices by p_0^i, the cost of the basket in the base year is $\Sigma p_0^i q_0^i$, where the summation (Σ) is over all the goods in the basket. The cost of a basket of the *same* quantities but at today's prices is $\Sigma p_t^i q_0^i$, where p_t^i is today's price. The CPI or PPI is the ratio of today's cost to the base year cost, or

$$\text{Consumer or producer price index} = \frac{\Sigma p_t^i q_0^i}{\Sigma p_0^i q_0^i} \times 100$$

This is a so-called *Laspeyres*, or *base-weighted*, price index.

The GNP deflator by contrast uses the weights of the *current* period to calculate the price index. Let q_t^i be the quantities of the different goods produced in the current year.

$$\text{GNP deflator} = \frac{\text{GNP measured in current prices}}{\text{GNP measured in base year prices}}$$

$$= \frac{\Sigma p_t^i q_t^i}{\Sigma p_0^i q_t^i} \times 100$$

This is known as a ***Paasche,*** or ***current-weighted,*** price index.

Comparing the two formulas we see that they differ only in that q_0^i, or the base year quantities, appears in both numerator and denominator of the CPI and PPI formula, whereas q_t^i appears in the formula for the deflator.

Problem: Calculate both Laspeyres and Paasche price indexes for the information in Table 2-2.

3

AGGREGATE DEMAND AND EQUILIBRIUM INCOME AND OUTPUT

In Chapter 2 we studied the measurement of national income and output (GNP). With these fundamental concepts, we are now able to begin our study of the factors that determine the level of national income and product. Ultimately, we want to know why real GNP sometimes falls (and the rate of unemployment rises), as it did in 1974–1975 and 1982, and why at other times income rises very rapidly (and unemployment falls), as it did in 1976–1978.

We also want to know what determines the rate of inflation. Why was it so high in 1974 and 1980? Why did it rise from 1976 to 1979? We want to know whether public policies, such as changes in government spending and tax rates, or changes in the growth rate of the money supply, or changes in interest rates, can affect the level of income and the rates of inflation and unemployment. And if they can, we want to know how.

The study of those questions occupies the rest of the book. But we shall proceed slowly. We begin in this chapter with a simplified model of the economy that isolates the crucial concept of *aggregate demand,* while still omitting both some factors that affect aggregate demand and considerations of aggregate supply. In later chapters we gradually introduce those other factors. By the time we have completed Chapter 13, we shall be able to understand the behavior of the key macroeconomic variables—the rates of unemployment and inflation and the level of GNP.

Our discussion is based on the macroeconomic identities in Equation (16) of Chapter 2 and in Figure 2-4. First, GNP is equal to total spending on goods and services, consisting of consumption C, investment I, government purchases of goods and services G, and net exports NX. Second, GNP is also equal to income received in the economy.[1] Income, in turn, increased by transfers TR and reduced by taxes TA, is allocated to consumption C and saving S.

Thus:
$$C + I + G + NX \equiv Y \equiv C + (TA - TR) + S$$

In this chapter we go beyond that *accounting identity* to begin our study of the factors that determine the level of national product or output. In particular, we focus on the interactions between the level of output and aggregate demand. The main point of the chapter is to show that *there is a single level of equilibrium output at which the aggregate (total) demand for goods and services is equal to the level of output.*

To begin with, we simplify our task by discussing a hypothetical world without a government ($G \equiv TA \equiv TR \equiv 0$) and without foreign trade ($NX \equiv 0$). In such a world, the accounting identity simplifies to

$$C + I \equiv Y \equiv C + S \tag{1}$$

where Y denotes the *real* value of output and income. Throughout this chapter a change in a macroeconomic aggregate is a change in its *real* value. For instance, when we speak of a change in consumption spending, we mean a change in real consumption spending.

The key concept of *equilibrium output* is introduced immediately, in Section 3-1. To keep the analysis as simple as possible, we assume to begin with that the demand for goods is *autonomous*—that is, independent of the level of income.[2] In fact, though, increases in income increase the demand for consumption goods. Accordingly, in Section 3-2 we extend the basic analysis by introducing the *consumption function*, which relates the demand for consumption goods to the level of income. In Sections 3-2 and 3-3 we derive explicit formulas for the equilibrium level of income.

The government sector is reintroduced in Section 3-4, which includes the first discussion of fiscal policy. The government budget is examined in Section 3-5. We do not include foreign trade in this chapter, even though exports account for about 12 percent of GNP. Instead, issues of the open economy are left for an integrated treatment in Chapters 18 and 19. For the impatient reader, problem 14 at the end of the chapter provides an introduction to the role of trade.

[1] Because output is equal to income received in the economy, economists tend to use the terms *income* and *output* interchangeably when discussing the level of economic activity.

[2] The terms *autonomous* and *induced* are traditionally used to indicate spending that is independent of the level of income and dependent on the level of income, respectively. More generally, autonomous spending is spending that is independent of the other variables explained in a given theory.

3-1 EQUILIBRIUM OUTPUT

In this chapter and the next we assume a world where all prices are given and constant.[3] In terms of Figure 1-8, we are dealing with a situation in which the aggregate supply curve is horizontal.

If firms could supply any amount of output at the prevailing level of prices, what would determine the level of output actually produced? *Demand* must enter the picture. We would expect firms to produce at a level just sufficient to meet demand.

To develop this point, we define the concepts of *aggregate demand* and *equilibrium output.*

Aggregate Demand

Aggregate demand is the total amount of goods demanded in the economy. In general, the quantity of goods demanded, or aggregate demand, depends on the level of income in the economy and perhaps—as we shall see later—on interest rates. But for now we shall assume that the amount of goods demanded is constant, independent of the level of income.

Aggregate demand is shown in Figure 3-1 by the horizontal line AD. In the diagram, aggregate demand is equal to 300 (billion dollars). This means that the total amount of goods demanded in the economy is $300 billion, independent of the level of income.

But if the quantity of goods demanded is constant, independent of the level of income, what determines the actual level of income? We have to turn to the concept of equilibrium output.

Equilibrium Output

Output is at its *equilibrium* level when the quantity of output produced is equal to the quantity demanded. An equilibrium situation is one which no forces are causing to change. We now explain why output is at its equilibrium level when it is equal to aggregate demand.

In Figure 3-1 we show the level of output on the horizontal axis. The 45° line serves as a reference line in that it translates any horizontal distance into an equal vertical distance. For any given level of output Y on the horizontal axis, the 45° line gives the level of aggregate demand that is equal to that level of output. For instance, at point E, both output and aggregate demand are equal to 300.

Point E is the point of equilibrium output, at which the quantity of output produced is equal to the quantity demanded. To understand why this should be the equilibrium level of output, suppose that firms were producing some

[3] The assumption that prices are constant is made to simplify the exposition of Chaps. 3 and 4. In later chapters, we use the theories developed in Chaps. 3 and 4 to study the factors that determine the price level and cause it to change over time.

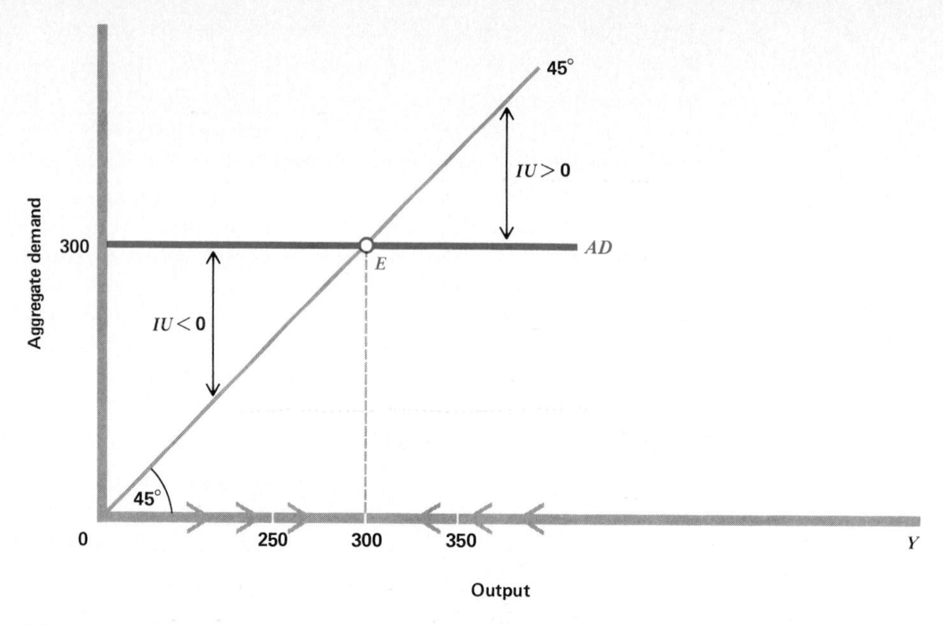

FIGURE 3-1 EQUILIBRIUM WITH CONSTANT AGGREGATE DEMAND. Aggregate demand is shown by the *AD* line, and is equal to 300. Output is at its equilibrium level when it is equal to aggregate demand, equal to 300. Thus the equilibrium is shown at point *E*. At any other output level, inventories are changing in a way that causes firms to change their production in a direction that moves output toward the equilibrium level.

other amount, say, 350 units. Then output would exceed demand. Firms would be unable to sell all they produce, and would find their warehouses filling with inventories of unsold goods. They would then cut their output. This is shown by the horizontal arrow pointing left at the output level of 350 on the horizontal axis.

Similarly, if output were less than 300, say, at 250, firms would either run out of goods or be running down their inventories. They would therefore increase output, as shown by the horizontal arrow pointing to the right from the output level of 250.

Thus at point *E*, the equilibrium level of output, firms are selling as much as they produce, people are buying the amount they want to purchase, and there is no tendency for the level of output to change. At any other level of output, the pressure from increasing or declining inventories causes firms to change the level of output.

Equilibrium Output and the National Income Identity

We have defined equilibrium output as that level of output at which aggregate demand for goods is equal to output. To clarify that definition, we have to dispose of an unsettling issue that arises from the accounting identity in Equation (1), derived from our study of national income accounting. The identity in Equation (1) states that demand, $C + I$, is *identically* equal to supply Y, *whatever* the level of output. That seems to mean that demand equals supply at *any* level of output, so that any level of output could be the equilibrium level.

The issue is resolved by recalling that aggregate demand is the amount of goods people *want to buy,* whereas in the national income accounts investment and consumption are the amounts of the goods *actually* bought for investment or consumption, whether or not people wanted to or planned to buy them. In particular, the investment measured in Equation (1) includes *involuntary,* or *unintended* (or *undesired*), inventory changes, which occur when firms find themselves selling more or less goods than they had planned to sell. Similarly, if households cannot buy all the goods they want, the consumption measured in Equation (1) will be different from planned consumption.

We have to make a distinction between the actual aggregate demand that is measured in an accounting context and the relevant economic concept of planned (desired, intended) aggregate demand.

Actual aggregate demand $(C + I)$ is, by the accounting identity in Equation (1), equal to the level of output (Y). The output level is determined by firms. In deciding how much to produce, firms calculate how much investment, including inventory investment, they want to undertake. They also produce to meet the demand for consumption they forecast will be forthcoming from households. *Planned aggregate demand* consists of the amount of consumption that households plan to carry out plus the amount of investment planned by firms.[4]

If firms miscalculate households' consumption demands, planned aggregate demand does not equal actual aggregate demand. Suppose first that firms overestimate consumption demand. In terms of Figure 3-1, suppose that firms decide to produce 350 units of output, expecting to be able to sell that amount. However, aggregate demand is only 300. The firms thus sell 300 units of output. But they are left with 50, which they have to add to their inventories. It is as if they buy those extra 50 units of output themselves. In the national income accounts, additions to inventories count as investment. Of course, this is not *planned* or *desired* investment, but it does count as part of investment. Looking at the national income accounts for such an economy, we would see output equal to 350 and consumption plus investment equal to 350. But the equality of output and $(C + I)$ does not mean that 350 is the equilibrium level of output, because 50 units of investment were undesired additions to inventories.

[4] From now on we shall assume that actual consumption is equal to planned consumption, so that all differences between actual and planned aggregate demand are reflected in unintended inventory changes. In practical terms, this means we are not considering situations where firms put "Sold Out" signs in their windows and customers cannot buy what they want.

TABLE 3-1 EQUILIBRIUM, OUTPUT, AND INVOLUNTARY INVENTORY CHANGE

Output	Aggregate demand	Involuntary inventory changes
200	300	−100
250	300	−50
300	300	0
350	300	+50
400	300	+100

When aggregate demand, the amount people *want* to buy, is not equal to output, there is unplanned inventory investment. We summarize this in Equation (2):

$$IU = Y - AD \tag{2}$$

where IU is unplanned additions to inventory.

In terms of Figure 3-1, unplanned inventory investment is shown by the vertical arrows. When output exceeds 300, there is unplanned inventory investment. When output is less than 300, there are unplanned reductions in inventories.

An alternative way of seeing the link between the national income accounting relations and the economic concepts is in (2*a*). Here we state that actual output is equal to planned spending or aggregate demand plus involuntary inventory adjustment.

$$\text{Output} = \text{Planned spending} + \text{Involuntary inventory adjustment} \tag{2a}$$

The *equilibrium* level of income is the level of income (or output) at which planned spending is equal to actual output, so that there is no involuntary inventory accumulation or decumulation.

Table 3-1 presents another way of looking at the equilibrium that is shown in both Figure 3-1 and Equation (2*a*). When income is below 300, aggregate demand exceeds output and inventories are being (involuntarily) reduced. When income exceeds 300, output exceeds aggregate demand and inventories are being (involuntarily) accumulated. Only at the output level of 300, when aggregate demand is equal to output, is there no involuntary accumulation or decumulation of inventories: output is then at the equilibrium level.

Equilibrium Output and Demand

We can now define equilibrium output more formally, using Equation (2). Output is at its equilibrium level when it is equal to aggregate demand, or when unplanned inventory accumulation is zero. That is, output is at its equilibrium level when

$$Y = AD \tag{3}$$

There are three essential notions from this section:

1. Aggregate demand determines the equilibrium level of output.
2. At equilibrium, unintended changes in inventories are zero, and households consume the amount they want to consume.
3. An adjustment process for output based on unintended inventory changes will actually move output to its equilibrium level.[5]

Note, too, that the definition of equilibrium implies that actual spending on consumption and investment equals planned spending. In equilibrium, aggregate demand, which is planned spending, equals output. Since output identically equals income, we see also that *in equilibrium, planned spending equals income.*

3-2 THE CONSUMPTION FUNCTION AND AGGREGATE DEMAND

The preceding section studied the equilibrium level of output (and income) on the assumption that aggregate demand was simply a constant. In this section we extend the discussion to a more realistic specification of aggregate demand and begin to examine the economic variables that determine it.

In the simplified model we are working with, which excludes both the government and foreign trade, aggregate demand consists of the demands for consumption and investment. The demand for consumption goods is not in practice autonomous as we have so far assumed, but rather increases with income—families with higher income consume more than families with lower income, and countries where income is higher typically have higher levels of total consumption. The relationship between consumption and income is described by the *consumption function.*

The Consumption Function

We assume that consumption demand increases along with the level of income[6]:

$$C = \overline{C} + cY \tag{4}$$

where $\overline{C} > 0$ and $0 < c < 1$

[5] You may have noticed that the adjustment process we describe raises the possibility that output will temporarily exceed its new equilibrium level during the adjustment to an increase in aggregate demand. This is the *inventory cycle.* Suppose firms desire to keep on hand inventories which are proportional to the level of demand. When demand unexpectedly rises, inventories are depleted. In subsequent periods, the firms have to produce not only to meet the new higher level of aggregate demand, but also to restore their depleted inventories and to raise them to a higher level. While they are rebuilding their inventories and also producing to meet the higher level of demand, their total production will exceed the new level of aggregate demand.

[6] Equation (4) is special because consumption is assumed to be a *linear* function of income. That means that in terms of Fig. 3-2, we can show the consumption function as a straight line. You might want to experiment with nonlinear consumption functions. Note also that because income is equal to output, we use the same symbol, Y, for both income and output.

This consumption function is shown in Figure 3-2*a*. The *intercept* is $\overline{C}$, and the *slope* is c. The consumption function shows that consumption increases as income increases.

The consumption function [Equation (4)] implies that at low levels of income, consumption exceeds income, while at high levels of income, consumption falls short of income. This feature can be seen in Figure 3-2*a*, which includes a 45° line along which income is equal to consumption. At low levels of income, the consumption function lies about the 45° line, and consumption therefore exceeds income. As we shall see, that means that at low levels of income, the individual or household is dissaving. At high levels of income, the household saves, since consumption is less than income.

These relationships between income and consumption arise from the positive intercept $\overline{C}$ in Equation (5) and the fact that the coefficient c is less than unity. The coefficient c is sufficiently important to have a special name. The coefficient c is called the *marginal propensity to consume.* The marginal propensity to consume is the increase in consumption per unit increase in income. In our case, the marginal propensity to consume is less than 1, which implies that out of a dollar increase in income, only a fraction c is spent on consumption. For example, if c is 0.8, then when income rises by $1, consumption increases by $0.80.

Consumption and Saving

What happens to the rest, the fraction $(1 - c)$ that is not spent on consumption? If it is not spent, it must be saved. Income is either spent or saved; there are no other uses to which income can be put.

More formally, we look at Equation (1), which says that income that is not spent on consumption is saved, or

$$S \equiv Y - C \tag{5}$$

What Equation (5) tells us is that by definition, *saving is equal to income minus consumption.* This means that we cannot postulate, in addition to the consumption function, an independent saving function and still expect consumption and saving to add up to income.

The consumption function in Equation (4), together with Equation (5), which we call the *budget constraint*, implies a saving function. The saving function is the function that relates the level of saving to the level of income. Substituting the consumption function in Equation (5) into the budget constraint in Equation (6) yields the saving function

$$\begin{aligned} S &\equiv Y - C \\ &= Y - (\overline{C} + cY) \\ &= -\overline{C} + (1 - c)Y \end{aligned} \tag{6}$$

From Equation (6), saving is an increasing function of the level of income because the *marginal propensity to save, $s = 1 - c$,* is positive. For instance,

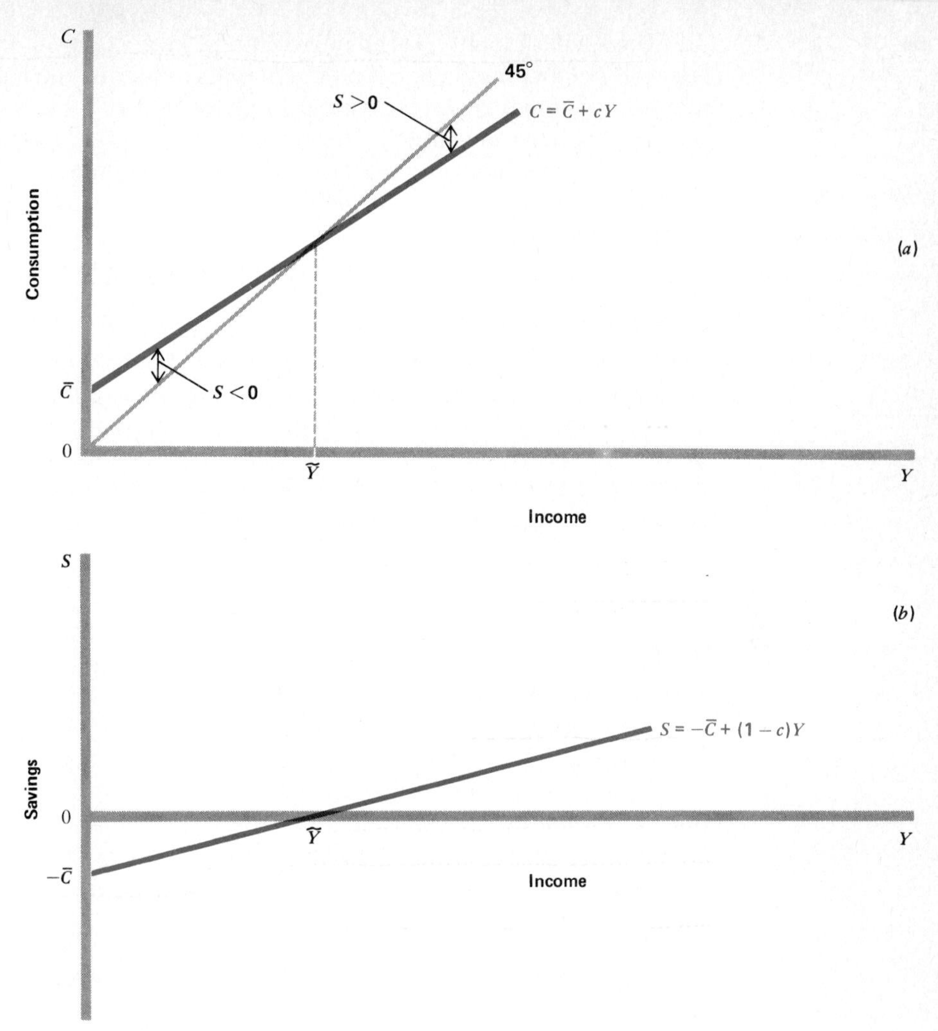

FIGURE 3-2 THE CONSUMPTION AND SAVING FUNCTIONS. (*a*) The consumption function shows consumption increasing with income. Its intercept is $\bar{C}$, and its slope, the marginal propensity to consume, is c. At low levels of income, consumption is above the level of income, implying that people spend more than they earn. At higher levels of income, consumption is below the level of income, implying that people save part of their income. (*b*) The saving function in Figure 3-2*b* is consistent with the consumption function above it: at low income levels, saving is negative, and it is positive at higher income levels. At income level $\tilde{Y}$, saving is exactly zero.

suppose the marginal propensity to consume, c, is 0.8, meaning that 80 cents out of each extra dollar of income is consumed. Then the marginal propensity to save, s, is 0.2, meaning that the remaining 20 cents of each extra dollar of income is saved.

The saving function is the mirror image of the consumption function. At low levels of income, saving is negative, thus reflecting the fact that consumption exceeds income. An individual can have negative saving by using up his assets—his bank account or the stocks he owns—to pay for purchases in excess of his income. Conversely, at sufficiently high levels of income, saving becomes positive and thus reflects the fact that not all income is spent on consumption.

The interrelationship between the consumption and saving functions examined in Equation (6) can also be seen graphically in Figure 3-2, where the vertical distance between the consumption function and the 45° line at each level of income measures saving. Figure 3-2*b* shows the saving function that is derived from the consumption function in Figure 3-2*a* by plotting the vertical distance between income and consumption spending at each level of income. Of course, Figure 3-2*b* is merely a representation of Equation (6). Note that the slope of the saving function in Figure 3-2*b* is the marginal propensity to save, $s = 1 - c$, as defined above.

Planned Investment and Aggregate Demand

We have now specified one component of aggregate demand, consumption demand. We must also consider the determinants of investment spending, or an *investment function*. We cut short the discussion for the present by simply assuming that planned investment spending is at a constant level $\bar{I}$.[7]

Aggregate demand is the sum of consumption and investment demands:

$$\begin{aligned} AD &= C + I \\ &= \bar{C} + cY + \bar{I} \\ &= \bar{A} + cY \end{aligned} \tag{7}$$

The aggregate demand function (7) is shown in Figure 3-3. Part of aggregate demand, $\bar{A}(=(\bar{C} + \bar{I}))$ is independent of the level of income, or autonomous. But aggregate demand also depends on the level of income. It increases with the level of income, because consumption demand increases with income.

Equilibrium Income and Output

The next step is to use the aggregate demand function AD in Figure 3-3 and Equation (7) to determine the equilibrium level of output and input. We plot the AD schedule again in Figure 3-4.

Recall the basic point of this chapter: the equilibrium level of income is such that aggregate demand equals output (which in turn equals income). The 45° line in Figure 3-4 shows points at which output and aggregate demand are equal. The aggregate demand schedule in Figure 3-4 cuts the 45° line at E, and it is accordingly at E that aggregate demand is equal to output (equals

[7] In Chaps. 4, 5, and 7, investment spending will become a function of the rate of interest and will gain an important place in the transmission of monetary policy.

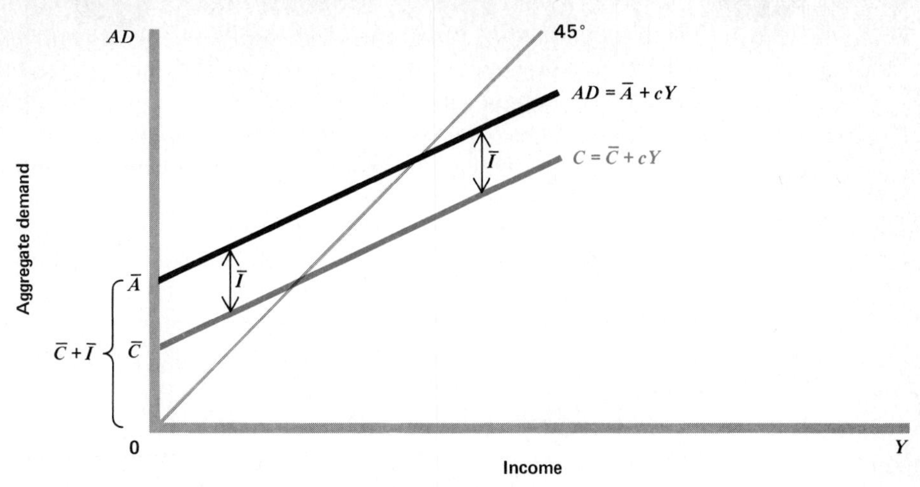

FIGURE 3-3 AGGREGATE DEMAND. Aggregate demand is the sum of the demands for consumption and investment goods. The consumption function is upward-sloping. Investment demand $\bar{I}$ is assumed constant and is added to consumption demand to obtain the level of aggregate demand at each level of income. The line AD shows how aggregate demand increases with income. Its slope is c, the marginal propensity to consume.

FIGURE 3-4 DETERMINATION OF EQUILIBRIUM INCOME AND OUTPUT. Output is at its equilibrium level when aggregate demand is equal to output. This occurs at point E, corresponding to the output (and income) level Y_0. At any higher level of output, aggregate demand is below the level of output, firms are unable to sell all they produce, and there is undesired accumulation of inventories. Firms therefore reduce output, as shown by the arrows. Similarly, at any level of output below Y_0, aggregate demand exceeds output, firms run short of goods to sell, and they therefore increase output. Only at the equilibrium output level Y_0 are firms producing the amount that is demanded, and there is no tendency for the level of output to change.

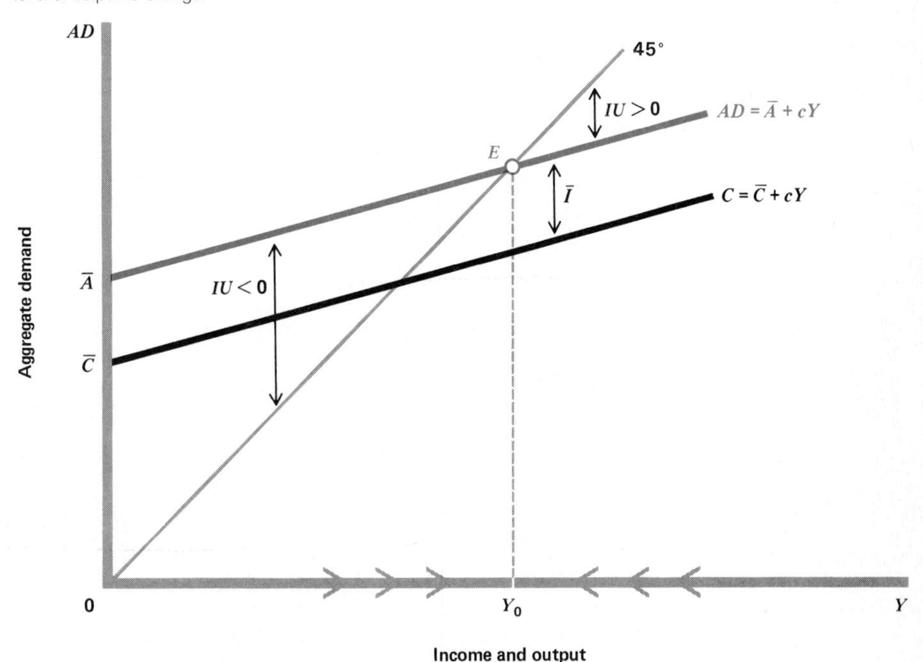

income). Only at E, and at the corresponding equilibrium level of income and output, Y_0, does aggregate demand exactly equal output.[8] At that level of output and income, planned spending precisely matches production.

The arrows in Figure 3-4 indicate once again how we reach equilibrium. If firms expand production whenever they face unintended decreases in their inventory holdings, then they increase output at any level below Y_0, because below Y_0, aggregate demand exceeds output and inventories are declining. Conversely, for output levels above Y_0, firms find inventories piling up and therefore cut production. This process will lead us to the output level Y_0, where current production exactly matches planned aggregate spending. At output level Y_0, unintended inventory changes are equal to zero. Again, the arrows in Figure 3-4 represent the dynamic process by which the economy moves to the equilibrium level of output Y_0.[9]

THE FORMULA FOR EQUILIBRIUM OUTPUT

The determination of equilibrium output in Figure 3-4 can also be described using Equation (7) and the equilibrium condition in the goods market:

$$Y = AD \tag{8}$$

This is the condition that output is equal to aggregate demand.

The level of aggregate demand AD is specified in Equation (7). Substituting for AD in Equation (8), we have the equilibrium condition as

$$Y = \bar{A} + cY \tag{9}$$

Since we have Y on both sides of the equilibrium condition in Equation (9), we can collect the terms and solve for the equilibrium level of income and output, denoted by Y_0:

$$Y - cY = \bar{A}$$

or

$$Y(1 - c) = \bar{A}$$

Thus the equilibrium level of income, at which aggregate demand equals output, is

$$Y_0 = \frac{1}{1 - c}\bar{A} \tag{10}$$

Figure 3-4 sheds light on the meaning of Equation (10). The position of the aggregate demand schedule is characterized by its slope c and intercept $\bar{A}$. The intercept $\bar{A}$ is the level of autonomous spending, that is, spending that is

[8] We frequently use the subscript $_0$ to denote the equilibrium level of a variable.

[9] Do you see that there is once more the possibility of an inventory cycle? Refer to footnote 5.

independent of the level of income. The other determinant of the equilibrium level of income is the marginal propensity to consume, c, which is the slope of the aggregate demand schedule.

Given the intercept, a steeper aggregate demand function—as would be implied by a higher marginal propensity to consume—implies a higher level of equilibrium income. Similarly, for a given marginal propensity to consume, a higher level of autonomous spending—in terms of Figure 3-4 a larger intercept—implies a higher equilibrium level of income. These results, suggested by Figure 3-4, are easily verified from Equation (10), which gives the formula for the equilibrium level of income.

Thus, the equilibrium level of output is higher, the larger the marginal propensity to consume, c, and the larger the level of autonomous spending, $\bar{A}$.

Saving and Investment

There is an alternative, useful formulation of the equilibrium condition that aggregate demand is equal to output. *In equilibrium, planned investment equals saving.* This condition applies only to an economy in which there is no government and no foreign trade.

To understand this relationship, return to Figure 3-4. The vertical distance between the aggregate demand and consumption schedules in that figure is equal to planned investment spending $\bar{I}$. Recall in addition (from Figure 3-2) that the vertical distance between the consumption schedule and the 45° line measures saving at each level of income.

We thus have two vertical distances: between the AD and C schedules in Figure 3-4 and between the 45° line and the C schedule in Figure 3-2*a*. The equilibrium level of income is one where AD crosses the 45° line, at E. Accordingly, at the equilibrium level of income—and only at that level—the two vertical distances are equal. Thus at the equilibrium level of income, saving equals (planned) investment. By contrast, above the equilibrium level of income Y_0, saving (the distance between the 45° line and the consumption schedule) exceeds investment, while below Y_0, investment exceeds saving.

Now, is the equality between saving and investment at equilibrium an essential characteristic of the equilibrium level of income, or is it a mere curiosity? It is an essential characteristic of equilibrium. We can see that by starting with the basic equilibrium condition, Equation (8), which states that in equilibrium, $Y = AD$. If we subtract consumption from both Y and AD, we realize that $Y - C$ is saving and $AD - C$ is planned investment. In symbols,

$$\begin{aligned} Y &= AD \\ Y - C &= AD - C \\ S &= \bar{I} \end{aligned} \tag{11}$$

Thus, the condition $S = \bar{I}$ is merely another way of stating the basic equilibrium condition.[10]

[10] In problem 3 at the end of this chapter, we ask you to derive Eq. (10) for Y_0 by starting from $S = \bar{I}$ and substituting for S from Eq. (6).

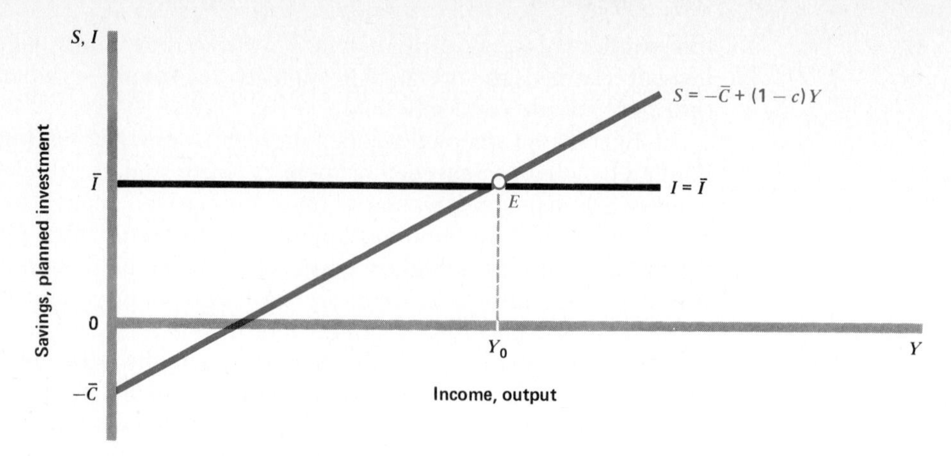

FIGURE 3-5 SAVING AND INVESTMENT. An alternative definition of the equilibrium level of output is that it occurs where saving is equal to (planned) investment. This is shown at point E, with corresponding output level Y_0. At higher levels of output, consumers want to save more than $\bar{I}$. They do not buy all of output, inventories accumulate, and actual investment is made equal to saving because firms undertake undesired inventory investment. They therefore cut output, and the economy moves to output level Y_0.

There is also a diagrammatic derivation of the equilibrium level of income that corresponds to the statement of the equilibrium condition in Equation (11) as the balance between saving and investment. In Figure 3-5, we show the saving function that was derived in Figure 3-2. We have drawn, too, planned investment spending, indicated by the horizontal line with intercept $\bar{I}$. Equilibrium income is shown at the level Y_0.

3-3 THE MULTIPLIER

In this section we develop an answer to the following question: By how much does a \$1 increase in autonomous spending raise the equilibrium level of income?[11] There appears to be a simple answer. Since, in equilibrium, income equals aggregate demand, it would seem that a \$1 increase in (autonomous) demand or spending should raise equilibrium income by \$1. That answer is wrong. Let us now see why.

Suppose first that output increased by \$1 to match the increased level of autonomous spending. This increase in output and income would in turn give rise to further *induced spending* as consumption rises because the level of income has risen. How much of the initial \$1 increase in income would be spent on consumption? Out of an additional dollar of income, a fraction c is

[11] Recall that autonomous spending $\bar{A}$ is spending that is independent of the level of income. Note also that the answer to this question is contained in Eq. (10). Can you deduce the answer directly from Eq. (10)? This section provides an explanation of that answer.

consumed. Assume then that production increases further to meet this induced expenditure, that is, that output and so income increase by $1 + c$. That will still leave us with an excess demand, because the very fact of an expansion in production and income by $1 + c$ will give rise to further induced spending. This story could clearly take a long time to tell. We seem to have arrived at an impasse where an expansion in output to meet excess demand leads to a further expansion in demand without an obvious end to the process.

It helps to lay out the various steps in this chain more carefully. We do this in Table 3-2. We start off in the first round with an increase in autonomous spending $\Delta\bar{A}$. Next we allow an expansion in production to meet exactly that increase in demand. Production accordingly expands by $\Delta\bar{A}$. This increase in production gives rise to an equal increase in income and, therefore, via the consumption function, $C = \bar{C} + cY$, gives rise in the second round to induced expenditures of size $c\,(\Delta\bar{A})$. Assume again that production expands to meet the increase in spending. The production adjustment this time is $c\,(\Delta\bar{A})$, and so is the increase in income. This gives rise to a third round of induced spending equal to the marginal propensity to consume times the increase in income $c\,(c\,\Delta\bar{A}) = c^2\,\Delta\bar{A}$. Careful inspection of the last term shows that induced expenditures in the third round are smaller than those in the second round. Since the marginal propensity to consume, c, is less than 1, the term c^2 is less than c. This can be seen also in the lower part of the table, where we assume $c = 0.6$ and show the steps corresponding to those in the upper part of the table.

If we write out the successive rounds of increased spending, starting with the initial increase in autonomous demand, we obtain

$$\begin{aligned}\Delta AD &= \Delta\bar{A} + c\,\Delta\bar{A} + c^2\,\Delta\bar{A} + c^3\,\Delta\bar{A} + \ldots \\ &= \Delta\bar{A}\,(1 + c + c^2 + c^3 + \ldots)\end{aligned} \tag{12}$$

For a value of $c < 1$, the successive terms in the series become progressively smaller. In fact, we are dealing with a geometric series, the sum of which is calculated as

$$\Delta AD = \frac{1}{1-c}\,\Delta\bar{A} = \Delta Y_0 \tag{13}$$

From Equation (13) therefore, the cumulative change in aggregate spending is equal to a multiple of the increase in autonomous spending. This could also have been deduced from Equation (10).[12] The multiple $1/(1-c)$ is called the *multiplier*. The multiplier is the amount by which equilibrium output changes when autonomous aggregate demand increases by one unit. Because the multiplier exceeds unity, we know that a $1 change in autono-

[12] If you are familiar with the calculus, you will realize that the multiplier is nothing other than the derivative of the equilibrium level of income, Y_0, in Eq. (10) with respect to autonomous spending. Use the calculus on Eqs. (10) and (26) to check the statements of the text.

TABLE 3-2 THE MULTIPLIER

Round	Increase in demand this round	Increase in production this round	Total increase in income
1	$\Delta\bar{A}$	$\Delta\bar{A}$	$\Delta\bar{A}$
2	$c\,\Delta\bar{A}$	$c\,\Delta\bar{A}$	$(1 + c)\,\Delta\bar{A}$
3	$c^2\,\Delta\bar{A}$	$c^2\,\Delta\bar{A}$	$(1 + c + c^2)\,\Delta\bar{A}$
4	$c^3\,\Delta\bar{A}$	$c^3\,\Delta\bar{A}$	$(1 + c + c^2 + c^3)\,\Delta\bar{A}$
.	.	.	.
.	.	.	.
.	.	.	.
.	.	.	$\frac{1}{1-c}\,\Delta\bar{A}$
1	1.0	1.0	1.0
2	0.6	0.6	1.6
3	0.36	0.36	1.96
4	0.216	0.216	2.176
5	0.1296	0.1296	2.3056
.	.	.	.
.	.	.	.
.	.	.	.
.	.	.	2.5

mous spending increases equilibrium income and output by more than $1.[13] The concept of the multiplier is sufficiently important to create a new notation. Defining the multiplier as α, we have

$$\alpha \equiv \frac{1}{1-c} \tag{14}$$

Inspection of the multiplier in Equation (14) shows that the larger the marginal propensity to consume, the larger the multiplier. With a marginal propensity to consume of 0.6 as in Table 3-2, the multiplier is 2.5; for a marginal propensity to consume of 0.8, the multiplier is 5. The reason is simply that a high marginal propensity to consume implies that a large fraction of an additional dollar income will be consumed. Accordingly, expenditures induced by an increase in autonomous spending are high, and therefore, so is

[13] *Two warnings:* (1) The multiplier is necessarily greater than 1 in this very simplified model of the determination of income, but as we shall see in the discussion of "crowding out" in Chap. 4, there may be circumstances in which it is less than 1. (2) The term *multiplier* is used more generally in economics to mean the effect on some endogenous variable (a variable whose level is explained by the theory being studied) of a unit change in an exogenous variable (a variable whose level is not determined within the theory being examined). For instance, one can talk of the multiplier of a change in the income tax rate on the level of unemployment. However, the classic use of the term is as we are using it here—the effects of a change in autonomous spending on equilibrium output.

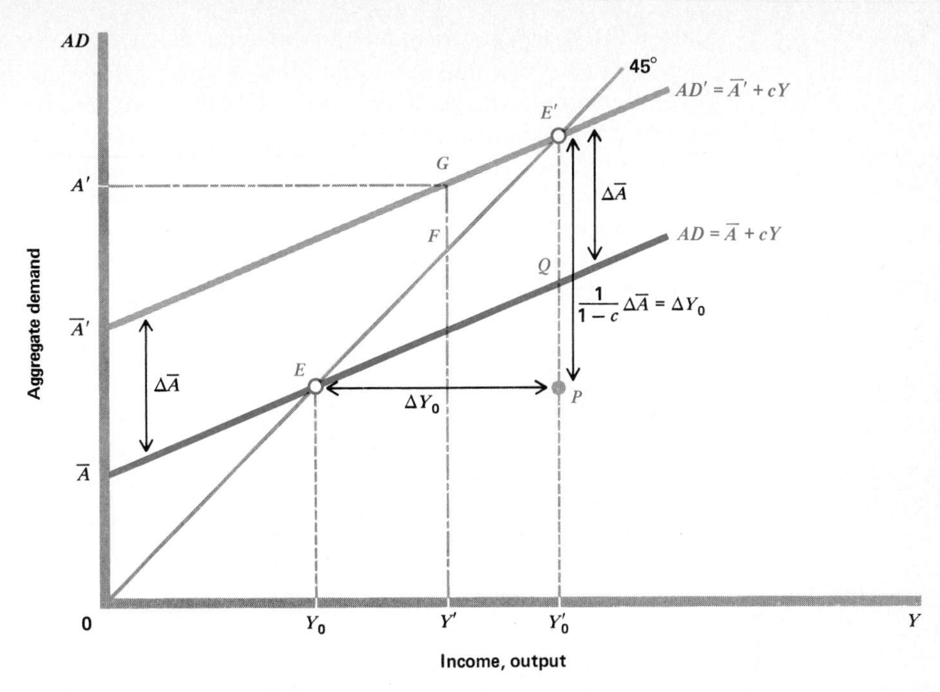

FIGURE 3-6 GRAPHICAL DERIVATION OF THE MULTIPLIER. When there is an increase in autonomous aggregate demand, the aggregate demand schedule shifts up to AD'. The equilibrium moves from E to E'. The increase in equilibrium output ($Y'_0 - Y_0$), equal to distance PE, equal to PE', exceeds the increase in autonomous demand, $E'Q$. From the diagram we see that is a result of the AD curve having a positive slope rather than being horizontal. In other words, the multiplier exceeds 1 because consumption demand increases with output—any increase in output produces further increases in demand.

the expansion in output and income that is needed to restore balance between income and demand (or spending).

Before proceeding further, we note that the relationship between the marginal propensity to consume, c, and the marginal propensity to save, s, allows us to write Equation (14) in a somewhat different form. Remembering from the budget constraint that saving plus consumption adds up to income, we realize that the fraction of an additional dollar of income consumed plus the fraction saved must add up to a dollar, or $1 \equiv s + c$. We can use the relation $s \equiv 1 - c$ and substitute in Equation (14) to obtain an equivalent formula for the multiplier in terms of the marginal propensity to save: $\alpha \equiv 1/s$.

THE MULTIPLIER IN PICTURES

Figure 3-6 provides a graphic interpretation of the effects of an increase in autonomous spending on the equilibrium level of income. The initial equilibrium is at point E with an income level Y_0. Consider next an increase in autonomous spending from $\bar{A}$ to $\bar{A}'$. This is represented by a parallel upward shift of the aggregate demand schedule where the shift is exactly equal to the increase in autonomous spending. The upward shift means that now, at each level of income, aggregate demand is higher by an amount $\Delta\bar{A} \equiv \bar{A}' - \bar{A}$.

At the initial level of income, Y_0, aggregate demand now exceeds income or output. Consequently, unintended inventory decumulation is taking place at a rate equal to the increase in autonomous spending, equal to the vertical distance $\Delta\bar{A}$. Firms will respond to that excess demand by expanding production, say, to income level Y'. This expansion in production gives rise to induced expenditure, increasing aggregate demand to the level A'. At the same time, it reduces the gap between aggregate demand and output to the vertical distance *FG*. Additional spending is induced because the marginal propensity to consume is less than 1.

Thus, a marginal propensity to consume that is positive but less than unity implies that a sufficient expansion in output will restore the balance between aggregate demand and output. In Figure 3-6 the new equilibrium is indicated by point E', and the corresponding level of income is Y_0'. The change in income required is therefore $\Delta Y_0 = Y_0' - Y_0$.

The magnitude of the income change required to restore equilibrium depends on two factors. The larger the increase in autonomous spending, represented in Figure 3-6 by the parallel shift in the aggregate demand schedule, the larger the income change. Furthermore, the larger the marginal propensity to consume—that is, the steeper the aggregate demand schedule—the larger the income change.

As a further check on our results, we verify from Figure 3-6 that the change in equilibrium income exceeds the change in autonomous spending. For that purpose, we use the 45° line to compare the change in income $\Delta Y_0 (= EP = PE')$ with the change in autonomous spending that is equal to the vertical distance between the new and old aggregate demand schedule (QE'). It is clear from Figure 3-6 that the change in income PE' exceeds the change in autonomous spending QE'.

ANOTHER DERIVATION

Finally, there is yet another way of deriving the multiplier. Remember that in equilibrium, aggregate demand equals income or output. From one equilibrium to another, it must therefore be true that the change in income ΔY_0 is equal to the change in aggregate demand ΔAD:

$$\Delta Y_0 = \Delta AD \tag{15}$$

Next we split up the change in aggregate demand into the change in autonomous spending $\Delta\bar{A}$ and the change in expenditure induced by the consequent change in income—that is, $c\,\Delta Y_0$.

$$\Delta AD = \Delta\bar{A} + c\,\Delta Y_0 \tag{16}$$

Combining Equations (15) and (16), we obtain the change in income as

$$\Delta Y_0 = \Delta \bar{A} + c\,\Delta Y_0 \tag{17}$$

or, collecting terms:

$$\Delta Y_0 = \frac{1}{1-c}\,\Delta \bar{A} = \alpha\,\Delta \bar{A} \tag{18}$$

cf. eq. 13

SUMMARY

There are three points to remember from this discussion:

1. An increase in autonomous spending raises the equilibrium level of income.
2. The increase in income is a multiple of the increase in autonomous spending.
3. The larger the marginal propensity to consume, the larger the multiplier, arising from the relation between consumption and income.

As a check on your understanding of the material of this section, you should develop the same analysis, and the same answers, in terms of Figure 3-5.

3-4 THE GOVERNMENT SECTOR

So far, we have ignored the role of the government sector in the determination of equilibrium income. The government affects the level of equilibrium income in two separate ways. First, government purchases of goods and services, G, is a component of aggregate demand. Second, taxes and transfers affect the relation between output and income, Y, and the *disposable income* —income that is available for consumption or saving—that accrues to the private sector, YD. In this section, we are concerned with the way in which government purchases, taxes, and transfers affect the equilibrium level of income.

We start again from the basic national income accounting identities. The introduction of the government restores government purchases (G) on the expenditure side of Equation (1) of this chapter, and taxes (TA) less transfers (TR) on the allocation of income side. We can, accordingly, rewrite the identity in Equation (1) as

$$C + I + G \equiv S + (TA - TR) + C \tag{1a}$$

The definition of aggregate demand has to be augmented to include government purchases of goods and services—the purchases of military equipment and services of bureaucrats, for instance. Thus we have

$$AD \equiv C + \bar{I} + G \tag{7a}$$

Consumption will no longer depend on income, but rather on *disposable* income YD. Disposable income YD is the net income available for spending by households after paying taxes to, and receiving transfers from, the government. It thus consists of income less taxes plus transfers, $Y + TR - TA$. The consumption function is now

$$C = \bar{C} + cYD = \bar{C} + c(Y + TR - TA) \tag{4a}$$

A final step is a specification of *fiscal policy*. Fiscal policy is the policy of the government with regard to the level of government purchases, the level of transfers, and the tax structure. We assume that the government purchases a constant amount $\bar{G}$, that it makes a constant amount of transfers $\overline{TR}$, and that it collects a fraction t of income in the form of taxes. For example, if t equals 0.2, there is an income tax equal to 20 percent of income.

$$G = \bar{G} \qquad TR = \overline{TR} \qquad TR = tY \tag{19}$$

With this specification of fiscal policy, we can rewrite the consumption function, after substitution from Equation (19) for TR and TA in Equation (4a), as

$$\begin{aligned} C &= \bar{C} + c(Y + \overline{TR} - tY) \\ &= (\bar{C} + c\overline{TR}) + c(1 - t)Y \end{aligned} \tag{20}$$

Note from Equation (20) that the presence of transfers raises autonomous consumption spending by the marginal propensity to consume out of disposable income c times the amount of transfers.[14] The presence of income taxes, by contrast, lowers consumption spending at each level of income. That reduction arises because households' consumption is related to *disposable* income rather than income itself, and income taxes reduce disposable income relative to the level of income.

While the marginal propensity to consume out of disposable income remains c, now the marginal propensity to consume out of income is $c(1 - t)$, where $1 - t$ is the fraction of income left after taxes. If the marginal propensity to consume, c, is 0.8 and the tax rate is 0.25, then the marginal propensity to consume out of income, $c(1 - t)$, is 0.6 ($= 0.8 \times (1 - .25)$).

Combining (7a), (19), and (20), we have now

[14] We are assuming no taxes are paid on transfers from the government. As a matter of fact, taxes are paid on some transfers, such as interest payments on the government debt, and not paid on other transfers, such as welfare and unemployment benefits.

$$AD = (\overline{C} + c\overline{TR} + \overline{I} + \overline{G}) + c(1 - t)Y$$
$$= \overline{A} + c(1 - t)Y \tag{21}$$

The effects of the introduction of government on the aggregate demand schedule are shown in Figure 3-7. The new aggregate demand schedule, denoted AD' in the figure, starts out higher than the original schedule AD, but has a flatter slope. The intercept is larger because it now includes both government spending $\overline{G}$ and the part of consumption resulting from transfer payments by the government, $c\overline{TR}$. The slope is flatter because households now have to pay part of every dollar of income in taxes, and are left with only $(1 - t)$ of that dollar. Thus, as (21) shows, the marginal propensity to consume out of income is now $c(1 - t)$ instead of c.

Equilibrium Income

We are now set to study income determination when the government is included. We return to the equilibrium condition for the goods market, $Y = AD$, and using (21), write the equilibrium condition as

$$Y = \overline{A} + c(1 - t)Y$$

We can solve this equation for Y_0, the equilibrium level of income, by collecting terms in Y:

FIGURE 3-7 GOVERNMENT AND AGGREGATE DEMAND. Government affects aggregate demand through its own purchases, assumed here to be fixed at the autonomous level $\overline{G}$, through transfers $\overline{TR}$, and through taxes. Taxes are assumed to be a constant proportion, t, of income. Under these assumptions, the introduction of government shifts the intercept of the aggregate demand curve up and flattens the curve.

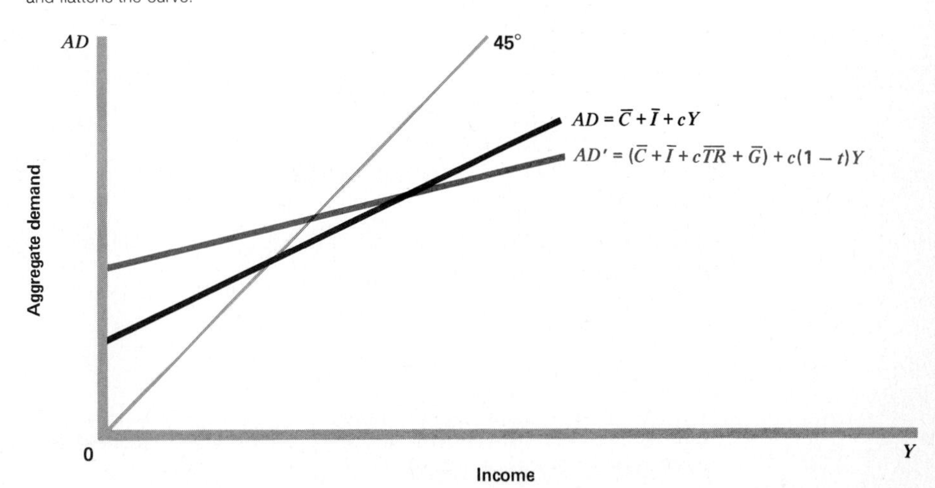

?

$$Y[1 - c(1 - t)] = \overline{A}$$

$$Y_0 = \frac{1}{1 - c(1 - t)} \overline{A} \tag{22}$$

In comparing Equation (22) with Equation (10), we see that the government sector makes a substantial difference. It raises autonomous spending by the amount of government purchases, $\overline{G}$, and by the amount of induced spending out of net transfers, $c\overline{TR}$.

INCOME TAXES AND THE MULTIPLIER

At the same time *income taxes lower the multiplier*. As can be seen from Equation (22), if the marginal propensity to consume is 0.8 and taxes are zero, the multiplier is 5; with the same marginal propensity to consume and a tax rate of 0.25, the multiplier is cut in half to $1/[1 - 0.8(0.75)] = 2.5$. Income taxes reduce the multiplier because they reduce the induced increase of consumption out of changes in income. This can be seen in Figure 3-7, where the inclusion of taxes flattens the aggregate demand curve—recall from Figure 3-6 that the multiplier is larger, the steeper the aggregate demand schedule.

Effects of a Change in Government Purchases

We now consider the effects of changes in fiscal policy on the equilibrium level of income. We distinguish three possible changes in fiscal variables: changes in government purchases, changes in transfers, and income tax changes. The simplest illustration is that of a change in government purchases. This case is shown in Figure 3-8, where the initial level of income is Y_0.

An increase in government purchases is a change in autonomous spending and therefore shifts the aggregate demand schedule upward by an amount equal to the increase in government purchases. At the initial level of output and income, the demand for goods exceeds output, and accordingly, firms expand production until the new equilibrium at point E' is reached. By how much does income expand? We remember that the change in equilibrium income will equal the change in aggregate demand, or

$$\Delta Y_0 = \Delta \overline{G} + c(1 - t)\, \Delta Y_0$$

where the remaining terms ($\overline{C}$, $\overline{TR}$, and $\overline{I}$) are constant by assumption. Thus, the change in equilibrium income is

$$\Delta Y_0 = \frac{1}{1 - c(1 - t)} \Delta \overline{G} = \overline{\alpha}\, \Delta \overline{G} \tag{23}$$

where we have introduced the notation $\overline{\alpha}$ to denote the multiplier in the presence of income taxes:

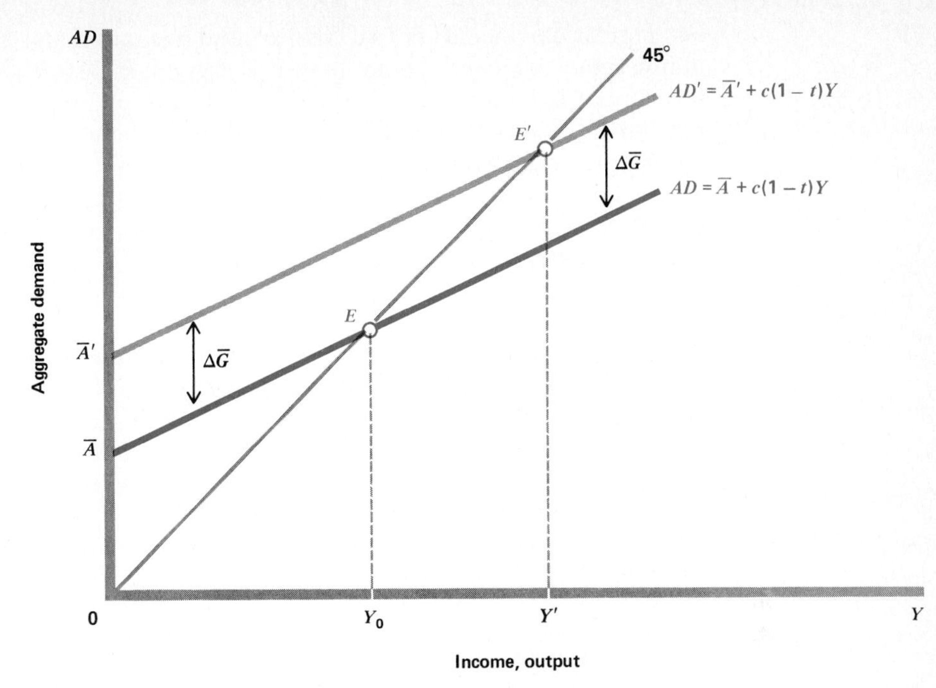

FIGURE 3-8 THE EFFECTS OF AN INCREASE IN GOVERNMENT PURCHASES. An increase in government spending shifts the aggregate demand schedule up from AD to AD'. Output rises from Y_0 to Y'. The multiplier is smaller now than it was in Figure 3-6.

$$\bar{\alpha} \equiv \frac{1}{1 - c(1 - t)} \tag{24}$$

From Equation (23) it is apparent that a \$1 increase in government purchases will lead to an increase in income in excess of a dollar. Thus, as we have already seen, with a marginal propensity to consume of $c = 0.8$ and an income tax rate of $t = 0.25$, we would have a multiplier of 2.5: a \$1 increase in government spending raises equilibrium income by \$2.50.

INCOME TAXES AS AUTOMATIC STABILIZERS

We have just seen that a proportional income tax reduces the multiplier. This means that if any component of autonomous demand changes, output will change by less if there is a proportional income tax than in the absence of such taxes. We say that a proportional income tax is an *automatic stabilizer*. An automatic stabilizer is any mechanism in the economy that reduces the amount by which output changes in response to a change in autonomous demand.

We shall see later that one explanation of the business cycle, the more or less regular movements of real GNP around trend, is that it is caused by shifts in investment demand. Sometimes, it is argued, investors are optimistic and investment is high—and so, therefore, is output. But sometimes they are pessimistic, and both investment and output are low.

Swings in investment demand will have a smaller effect on output when automatic stabilizers are in place. This means that in the presence of automatic stabilizers we should expect output to fluctuate less than it would without them. The income tax, which is an automatic stabilizer, is one reason that the business cycle has been less pronounced since 1945 than it was in earlier years.

The proportional income tax is not the only automatic stabilizer. Unemployment benefits enable the unemployed to continue consuming even if they do not have a job. This means that demand falls less when someone becomes unemployed than it would if there were no benefits. This too makes the multiplier smaller and output more stable. Unemployment benefits and a proportional income tax are two automatic stabilizers that keep the multiplier small, and therefore protect the economy from responding strongly to every small movement in autonomous demand.

Effects of Increased Transfer Payments

An increase in transfer payments increases autonomous demand, as can be seen from Equation (21), where autonomous demand includes a term $c\overline{TR}$. A \$1 increase in transfers therefore increases autonomous demand by an amount c. For instance, if the marginal propensity to consume, c, is 0.8, a \$1 increase in transfers increases autonomous demand by \$0.80. The increase is less than the full \$1 increase in transfers because part of the transfer—\$0.20 in this case—is saved.

Given that a \$1 increase in transfers increases autonomous demand by the amount c, it is clear that the multiplier for an increase in transfers is c times the multiplier for an increase in government spending. For instance, with c equal to 0.8, and a tax rate of 0.25, the government spending multiplier is 2.5. The multiplier for transfers is 0.8 times 2.5, or 2.0.

The Effects of an Income Tax Change

The final fiscal policy question is the effects of a reduction in the income tax rate. This is illustrated in Figure 3-9 by an increase in the slope of the aggregate demand function, because that slope is equal to the marginal propensity to spend out of income, $c(1 - t)$. At the initial level of income, the aggregate demand for goods now exceeds output because the tax reduction causes increased consumption. The new higher equilibrium level of income is Y'.

To calculate the change in equilibrium income, we equate the change in income to the change in aggregate demand. The change in aggregate demand has two components. The first is the change in spending at the initial level of

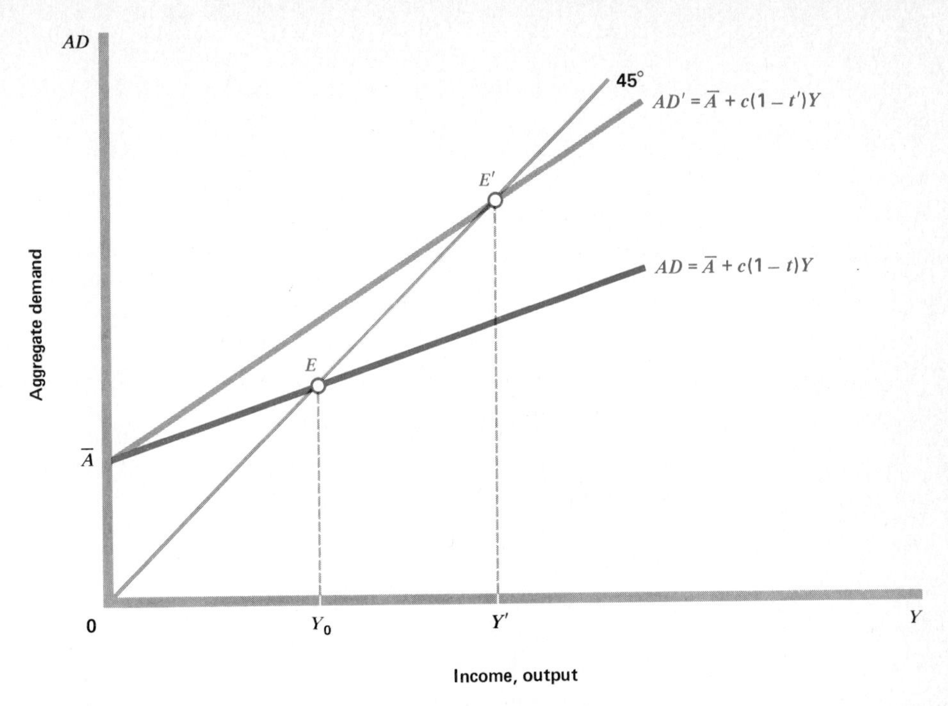

FIGURE 3-9 THE EFFECTS OF A DECREASE IN THE TAX RATE. A reduction in the income tax rate leaves the consumer with a larger proportion of every dollar of income earned. Accordingly, a larger proportion of every extra dollar of income is consumed. The aggregate demand curve swings upward, from AD to AD'. It becomes steeper, because the income tax cut, in effect, acts like an increase in the propensity to consume. The equilibrium level of income rises from Y_0 to Y'.

income that arises from the tax cut. This part is equal to the marginal propensity to consume out of disposable income times the change in disposable income due to the tax cut, $cY_0 \, \Delta t$, where the term $Y_0 \, \Delta t$ is the initial level of income times the change in the tax rate. The second component of the change in aggregate demand is the induced spending due to higher income. This is now evaluated at the new tax rate t' and has the value $c(1 - t') \, \Delta Y_0$. We can therefore write[15]

$$\Delta Y_0 = -cY_0 \, \Delta t + c(1 - t') \, \Delta Y_0 \tag{25}$$

or

$$\Delta Y_0 = -\frac{1}{1 - c(1 - t')} cY_0 \, \Delta t \tag{26}$$

[15] You should check Eq. (26) by using Eq. (22) to write out Y_0 corresponding to a tax rate of t, and Y_0' corresponding to t'. Then subtract Y_0 from Y_0' to obtain ΔY_0 as given in Eq. (26).

EXAMPLE

An exercise clarifies the effects of an income tax cut. Initially the level of income is $Y_0 = 100$, the marginal propensity to consume is $c = 0.8$, and the tax rate $t = 0.2$. Assume now a tax cut that reduces the income tax rate to only 10 percent, or $t' = 0.1$.

At the initial level of income, disposable income rises by $cY_0\ \Delta t = 100(t - t') = \$10$. Out of the increase in disposable income of \$10, a fraction $c = 0.8$ is spent on consumption, so that aggregate demand, at the initial level of income, increases by \$8. This corresponds to the first term on the right-hand side of the Equation (25). The increase in aggregate demand causes an expansion in output and income. Per dollar increase in income, disposable income rises by a fraction $(1 - t')$ of the increase in income. Furthermore, of the increase in disposable income, only a fraction, c, is spent. Accordingly, induced consumption spending is equal to $c(1 - t')\ \Delta Y_0$, which is the second term in Equation (25).

How much does the income tax cut achieve in terms of output expansion? Substituting our numbers in Equation (26), we have

$$\Delta Y_0 = \frac{1}{1 - 0.8(1 - 0.1)}(0.8)(100)(0.2 - 0.1) = (3.57)(8)$$
$$= 28.56 \qquad (26a)$$

In our example, a cut in the tax rate, such that taxes fall by \$10 at the initial level of income, raises equilibrium income by \$28.56.

Note, however, that although taxes are initially cut by \$10, the government's total taxes received fall by less that \$10. Why? The reason is that the government receives 10 percent of the induced increase in income, or \$2.856, as taxes. Thus the final reduction in tax receipts by the government is not the initial \$10, but rather \$7.144.[16]

ACTIVE FISCAL POLICY

Changes in government spending and taxes affect the level of income. This raises immediately the possibility that fiscal policy can be used to stabilize the economy. When the economy is in a recession, perhaps taxes should be cut or spending increased to get output to rise. And when the economy is booming, perhaps taxes should be increased or government spending cut to get back down to full employment.

Fiscal policy is in practice actively used to try to stabilize the economy, as we shall see in the next section when we examine the behavior of the budget. But it is also true that there is some dispute over whether such fiscal policy actions really work. The disputes center on two issues: first, whether they

[16] We leave it to you to calculate the multiplier relating the change in equilibrium income to the total change in taxes received by the government.

work fast enough to help; and second, and more complicated, whether government policy actions don't merely result in private individuals taking offsetting actions. For instance, when government spending rises, private spending might fall.

We cannot at this stage evaluate the arguments against the active use of fiscal policy. But starting in Chapter 5, we continue the discussion.

Summary

1 Government purchases and transfer payments act like increases in autonomous spending in their effects on equilibrium income.
2 Income taxes reduce disposable income relative to the level of income, and their effects on equilibrium income and output are thus the same as those resulting from a reduction in the propensity to consume.[17]

3-5 THE BUDGET

The budget—and especially the budget deficit—has become the major preoccupation of economic policy in the first half of the 1980s. Government budget deficits that sound astronomical are in prospect for the period through 1987, and the fear is strong that the economy cannot prosper with such a threat hanging over it.

In this section we deal with the government budget, with its effects on output, and with the effects of output on the budget. We start by defining the *budget surplus*, denoted by *BS*. The budget surplus is the excess of the government's revenues, consisting of taxes, over its total expenditures, consisting of purchases of goods and services, and transfer payments.

$$BS \equiv TA - G - TR \tag{27}$$

A negative budget surplus, an excess of expenditure over taxes, is a *budget deficit*, denoted *BD*:

$$BD \equiv -BS = G + TR - TA$$

Of course, at the present time, government deficits are the norm, and surpluses are nowhere in prospect. But it was not always so. For most of its

[17] It might be helpful to note that all the results we have derived can be obtained in a straightforward manner by taking the change in aggregate demand at the initial level of income times the multiplier. (Check this proposition for each of the fiscal policy changes we have considered.) You should consider, too, the effect on equilibrium income of an increase in government purchases combined with an equal reduction in transfer payments, $\Delta G = -\Delta TR$. (See problem 9 at the end of this chapter.)

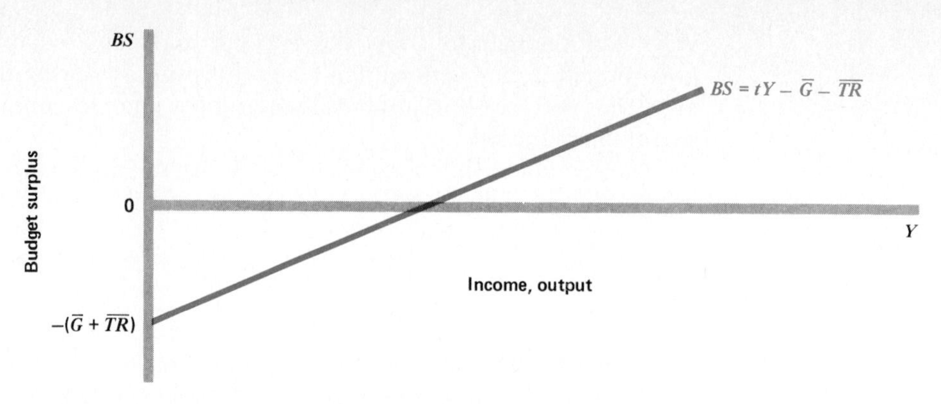

FIGURE 3-10 THE BUDGET SURPLUS. The budget surplus, or deficit, depends in part on the level of income. Given the tax rate, t, and $\overline{G}$ and $\overline{TR}$, the budget surplus will be high if income is high—because then the government takes in a lot of taxes. But if the level of income is low, there will be a budget deficit because tax receipts by the government are small.

history the federal government has run surpluses. It is only in the last 20 years that deficits have become standard.

In the accompanying box, we describe the concepts of government budget surplus and deficit that appear in the national income accounts. For that purpose, the federal government and state and local governments are added together. Thus the government sector in the national income accounts, and in the theory we are developing here, is not just the federal government. It is all government.

However, the budget deficit on which the media and politicians focus is the federal budget deficit. Later in this section we look at the behavior of the federal budget. For now we study the behavior of the budget surplus in relation to income, in the simple theory of this chapter.

Substituting in Equation (27) the assumption of a proportional income tax that yields a tax revenue $TA = tY$ gives us

$$BS = tY - G - TR \tag{27a}$$

In Figure 3-10 we plot the budget surplus as a function of the level of income for given $G = \overline{G}$, $TR = \overline{TR}$, and income tax rate t. At low levels of income, the budget is in deficit (the surplus is negative) because payments $\overline{G} + \overline{TR}$ exceed income tax collection. For high levels of income, by contrast, the budget shows a surplus, since income tax collection outweighs expenditures in the form of government purchases and transfers.

Figure 3-10 demonstrates a significant point about budget surpluses and deficits. The point is that the budget deficit depends not only on the govern-

BOX 3-1

GOVERNMENT IN THE NATIONAL INCOME ACCOUNTS

We distinguish three aspects of fiscal policy in the text. G is government purchases of goods and services, TR is government transfers, and TA is taxes or government receipts. We now give the data for these variables in 1981, when GNP was $2,954 billion. We also show the breakdown of the variables between federal and state and local governments.

GOVERNMENT PURCHASES OF GOODS AND SERVICES

		$ billions	Percent of GNP
Federal government		229.2	7.8
Defense	154.0		
Nondefense	75.2		
State and local		366.5	12.4
Compensation of employees	206.5		
Building	43.0		
Other	116.9		
Total		595.7	20.2

The surprise here is that state and local government purchases of goods and services are substantially larger than those of the federal government.

TRANSFER PAYMENTS

	$ billions	Percent of GNP
Federal government:		
Transfers	286.6	9.7
Net interest payments	73.2	2.5
State and Local:		
Transfers	43.3	1.5
Net interest	−19.3	−0.7
Total	383.9	13.0

Federal government transfer payments are substantially larger than federal government purchases of goods and services. These transfer payments include social security and welfare payments.

The federal government also had to make large interest payments on the national debt. State and local government makes only small transfer payments and actually on balance *receives* interest. We see why on the following page.

GOVERNMENT RECEIPTS

		$ billions	Percent of GNP
Federal government		627.0	21.2
Income taxes	298.6		
Contributions for social insurance	204.5		
Other	123.9		
State and local		418.1	14.2
Sales taxes	90.4		
Property taxes	75.1		
Income taxes	47.9		
Other	204.6		

SURPLUS OR DEFICIT (−) IN GNP ACCOUNTS

	$ billions	Percent of GNP
Federal government	−62.2	−2.1
State and local	35.3	1.2
Net, government sector*	−26.9	−0.9

* Total not equal to sum of components because of rounding.

In 1981, the government sector had a deficit in the national income accounts of $26.9 billion. While the federal government had a deficit, state and local governments on balance were in surplus.

State and local governments have for many years run surpluses. With their surpluses they buy assets, including federal government bonds. That is why they have positive interest earnings.

To summarize, G in 1981 was about 20 percent of GNP, TR was about 13 percent of GNP, and TA was 32.3 percent of GNP (calculated from $TA = G + TR + BS$).

Source: Data Resources, Inc.

ment's policy choices, reflected in the tax rate t, in purchases $\overline{G}$, and in transfers $\overline{TR}$, but also on anything else that shifts the level of income. For instance, suppose there is an increase in investment demand that increases the level of output. Then the budget deficit will fall, or the surplus will increase because tax revenues have risen. But the government has done nothing that changed the deficit.

We should accordingly not be surprised to see budget deficits in recessions. Those are periods when the government's tax receipts are low. And in practice, transfer payments, through unemployment benefits, also increase in recessions, even though in our model we are taking $\overline{TR}$ as autonomous.

The Effects of Government Purchases and Tax Changes on the Budget Surplus

Next we show how changes in fiscal policy affect the budget. In particular, we want to find out whether an increase in government purchases must reduce the budget surplus. At first sight, this appears obvious, because increased government purchases, from Equation (27), are reflected in a reduced surplus, or increased deficit. At further thought, however, the increased government purchases will give rise to an increase (multiplied) in income and, therefore, to increased income tax collection. This raises the interesting possibility that tax collection might increase by more than government purchases.[18]

A brief calculation shows that the first guess is right—increased government purchases reduce the budget surplus. From Equation (23) the change in income due to increased government purchases is equal to $\Delta Y_0 = \overline{\alpha}\, \Delta\overline{G}$. A fraction of that increase in income is collected in the form of taxes, so that tax revenue increases by $t\overline{\alpha}\, \Delta\overline{G}$. The change in the budget surplus, using Equation (24) to substitute for $\overline{\alpha}$, is therefore:

$$\begin{aligned}\Delta BS &= \Delta TA - \Delta\overline{G} \\ &= t\overline{\alpha}\, \Delta\overline{G} - \Delta\overline{G} \\ &= \left[\frac{t}{1 - c(1-t)} - 1\right] \Delta\overline{G} \\ &= -\frac{(1-c)(1-t)}{1 - c(1-t)}\, \Delta\overline{G} \end{aligned} \tag{28}$$

which is unambiguously negative.

We have, therefore, shown that an increase in government purchases will reduce the budget surplus, although by considerably less than the increase in purchases. For instance, for $c = 0.8$ and $t = 0.25$, a \$1 increase in government purchases will create a \$0.375 reduction in the surplus.[19]

In the same way, we can consider the effects of an increase in the tax rate on the budget surplus. We know that the increase in the tax rate will reduce the level of income. It might thus appear that an increase in the tax rate, keeping the level of government spending constant, could reduce the budget

[18] In 1981 the theory that tax cuts would increase government revenue, advanced most strongly by Arthur Laffer of the University of Southern California, was very popular. However, the argument depended on a different mechanism than that discussed here. Laffer did not depend on aggregate demand effects of tax cuts, but rather on the possibility that a tax cut would lead people to work more. This was a strand in supply-side economics, which we examine more closely in Chap. 16.

[19] In this case, $\overline{\alpha} = 1/[1 - 0.8(0.75)] = 2.5$. So $\Delta BS = -2.5(0.2)(0.75) = -0.375$.

TABLE 3-3 EFFECTS OF COMBINED TAX CUT AND GOVERNMENT SPENDING DECREASE

Parameters: Initial tax rate, $t = 0.2$
New tax rate, $t' = 0.1$
Initial level of income, $Y_0 = \$100$
Marginal propensity to consume, $c = 0.8$
Change in government spending, $\Delta\overline{G} = -10$

$$\text{Multiplier: } \overline{\alpha} = \frac{1}{1 - c(1 - t')} = \frac{1}{1 - .72} = 3.57$$

Effects of tax cut: [See Equation (26)]
Change in income $= -\overline{\alpha}\, cY_0\, \Delta t = -(3.57)(0.8)(100)(-0.1) = 28.56$

Effects of cut in government spending: [See Equation (23)]
Change in income $= \overline{\alpha}\, \Delta\overline{G} = -35.70$

Total effect on income: $\Delta Y_0 = -35.70 + 28.56$
$= -7.14$

Therefore: $Y_0' = 100 - 7.14 = 92.86$

Effect on tax receipts: Initial taxes = 20
Taxes in new situation = .1 × 92.86 = 9.29

Therefore: Change in taxes, $\Delta TA = -10.71$

Effects on budget surplus: $\Delta BS = \Delta TA - \Delta\overline{G}$
$= -10.71 + 10.00$
$= -.71$

surplus. In fact, an increase in the tax rate increases the budget surplus, despite the reduction in income that it causes.[20]

A SIMULTANEOUS CHANGE IN TAXES AND PURCHASES

Finally, we can investigate the budgetary effects of simultaneous changes in taxes and government purchases. We do this by working out an example, in Table 3-3. We assume a fiscal policy change that reduces the tax rate and government purchases. The reduction is such that at the initial equilibrium level of income, of 100, the cut in taxes is exactly equal to the cut in government purchases.

What effect would we expect such a fiscal policy to have? A first reaction would be that since taxes are being cut the same amount as spending, there will be no effect. But the table shows that is not right. The combined effect of the two actions is actually to lower income.

Why? The reason is that part of the cut in taxes is saved, so that not all the tax cut goes to increase aggregate demand. But the entire cut in government spending reduces aggregate demand. Therefore this fiscal policy actually reduces aggregate demand, and therefore income.

[20] The effects of an increase in the tax rate on the budget surplus are examined in detail in problem 7 at the end of this chapter.

Notice also from the table that the budget deficit in the end increases slightly — as a result of the fall in income — even though at the initial level of income the cuts in taxes and spending are equal.

BALANCED BUDGET MULTIPLIER

In the previous example, the combined tax cut and reduction of government purchases raised the budget deficit. What would happen to the level of income if government purchases and taxes changed by exactly the same amount, so that the budget surplus remained unchanged between the initial and final level of income? The answer to this question is contained in the famous *balanced budget multiplier* result. The result is that the balanced budget multiplier is exactly 1. That is, an increase in government purchases, accompanied by an equal increase in taxes, increases the level of income by exactly the amount of the increase in purchases.[21] This interesting result is derived in the Appendix at the end of this chapter.

The major points of the preceding discussion are that a balanced budget cut in government purchases lowers equilibrium income and that a dollar increase in government purchases has a stronger impact on equilibrium income than a dollar cut in taxes. A dollar cut in taxes leads only to a fraction of a dollar's increase in consumption spending, the rest being saved, while government purchases are reflected dollar for dollar in a change in aggregate demand.[22]

THE FULL-EMPLOYMENT BUDGET SURPLUS

A final topic to be treated here is the concept of the full-employment budget surplus.[23] Recall that increases in taxes add to the surplus and that increases in government expenditures reduce the surplus. Increases in taxes have been shown to reduce the level of income, and increases in government purchases and transfers to increase the level of income. It thus seems that the budget surplus is a convenient, simple measure of the overall effects of fiscal policy on the economy. For instance, when the budget is deficit, we would say that fiscal policy is expansionary, tending to increase GNP.

However, the budget surplus by itself suffers from a serious defect as a measure of the direction of fiscal policy. The defect is that the surplus can change passively because of changes in autonomous private spending, as we have seen. Thus, if the economy moves into a recession, tax revenue automatically declines and the budget moves into a deficit (or reduced surplus). Conversely, an increase in economic activity causes the budget to move into a

[21] Note that the balanced budget multiplier may well be less than 1 in the more sophisticated models of Chap. 4, in which investment spending depends on the interest rate.

[22] Rather than go through the analysis of changes in transfer payments, we leave it to you to work through an example of the effects on the budget of a change in transfer payments in problem 10 at the end of the chapter.

[23] The concept of the full-employment surplus was first used by E. Cary Brown, "Fiscal Policy in the Thirties: A Reappraisal," *American Economic Review*, December 1956.

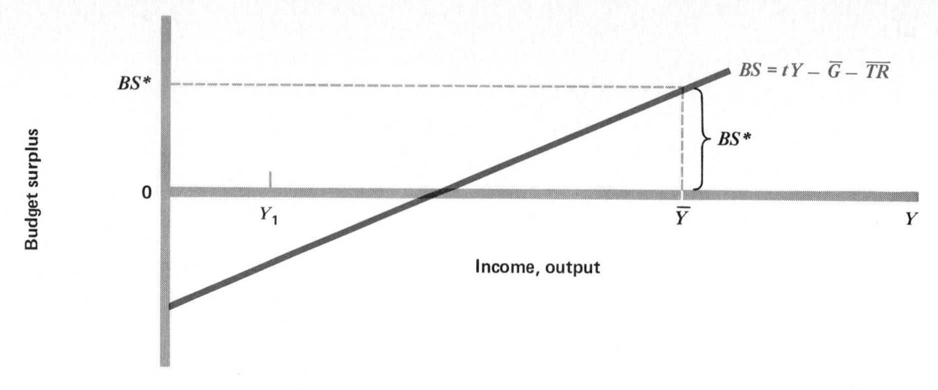

FIGURE 3-11 THE ACTUAL AND FULL-EMPLOYMENT BUDGET SURPLUSES. $\overline{Y}$ is the full-employment level of output. The full-employment budget surplus BS^* is the budget surplus that would exist if the economy were at full employment. If output is below the full-employment level, at a level such as Y_1, the budget surplus would be smaller than BS^*. Indeed, at income level Y_1 the actual budget is in deficit even though there is a full-employment surplus.

surplus (or reduced deficit). These changes in the budget take place automatically for a given tax structure. This implies that we cannot simply look at the budget deficit as a measure of whether government fiscal policy is expansionary or deflationary. A given fiscal policy may imply a deficit if private spending is low and a surplus if private spending is high. Accordingly, an increase in the budget deficit does not necessarily mean that the government has changed its policy in an attempt to increase the level of income.

Since we frequently want to measure the way in which fiscal policy is being actively, rather than passively, used to affect the level of income, we require some measure of policy that is independent of the particular position of the business cycle—boom or recession—in which we may find ourselves. Such a measure is provided by the *full-employment budget surplus,* which we denote by BS^*. The full-employment (high-employment) budget surplus measures the budget, not at the actual level of income, but rather at the full-employment level of income or at potential output. Thus, a given fiscal policy summarized by $\overline{G}$, $\overline{TR}$, and t is assessed by the level of the surplus, or deficit, that is generated at full employment. Using $\overline{Y}$ to denote the full-employment level of income, we can write

$$BS^* = t\overline{Y} - \overline{G} - \overline{TR} \tag{29}$$

In Figure 3-11 we show the budget surplus schedule from Figure 3-10 but add the full-employment level of income $\overline{Y}$. The full-employment budget surplus is indicated by the corresponding point on the budget surplus schedule. To see the difference between the actual and the full-employment budget, we subtract the actual budget in Equation (27*a*) from Equation (29) to obtain

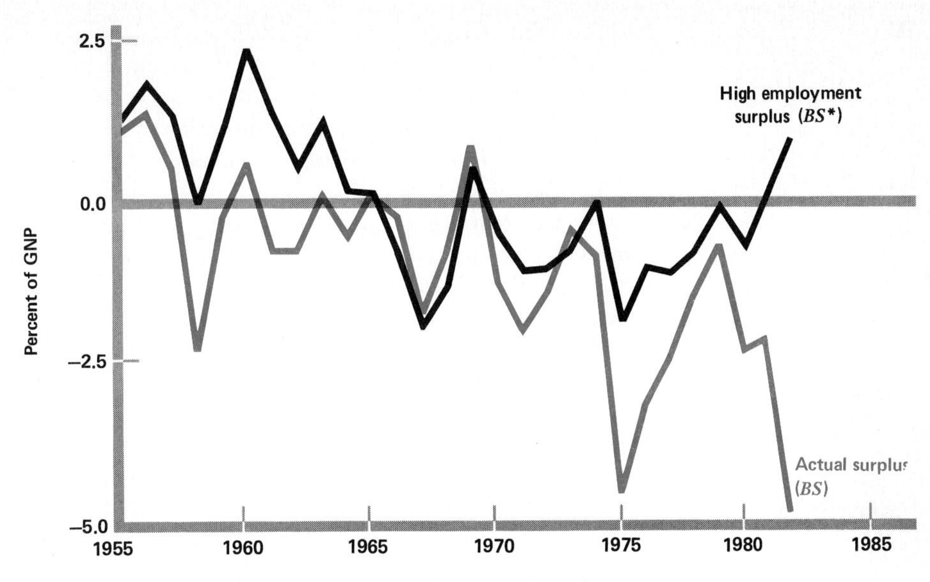

FIGURE 3-12 THE ACTUAL AND FULL-EMPLOYMENT BUDGET SURPLUS AS A FRACTION OF GNP. (*Source: Survey of Current Business*, April and August 1982 and March 1983.)

$$BS^* - BS = t(\overline{Y} - Y) \tag{30}$$

It is apparent that the only difference arises from income tax collection.[24] Specifically, if output is below full employment, the full-employment surplus exceeds the actual surplus. Conversely, if actual output exceeds full-employment (or potential) output, the full-employment surplus is less than the actual surplus.

BUDGET TRENDS

Figure 3-12 shows the actual and full-employment budget surpluses (as a percent of GNP) since 1950. Three facts stand out.

1 The actual budget fluctuates more than the full-employment budget. That is because the actual budget changes as the level of output fluctuates during the business cycle—and the effects of those fluctuations are excluded from the full-employment budget. The recessions of 1974–1975 and 1980–1982 stand out particularly as periods when the actual deficit is far greater than the full-employment deficit. Equivalently, in those years the actual budget surplus is far below the full-employment

[24] In practice, transfer payments, such as welfare and unemployment benefits, are also affected by the state of the economy, so that *TR* also depends on the level of income. But the major cause of differences between the actual surplus and the full-employment surplus is taxes.

surplus. The figure shows in 1975 a good example of the difference between the two budget concepts. Note how much the actual surplus drops in 1975. Mostly that is because there was a deep recession. But note also that the full-employment surplus drops. That was a conscious policy decision, to cut taxes in the face of the recession. That cut in taxes in early 1975 is also reflected in the fall in the actual surplus.

2. Over most of this period, the actual surplus has been below the full-employment surplus. This is because over most of the period output has been below its full-employment level.
3. Over the period since 1950, both budgets have been moving increasingly into deficit. By 1982 it looks as if the full-employment deficit is larger than at any time except in the early 1950s, during the Korean war.

In the early 1980s, the public was very worried about deficits. For many economists, the behavior of the budget deficit during the 1980–1982 recession was not in itself especially worrisome. The actual budget is usually in deficit in recessions. But the shift toward deficit of the full-employment budget was regarded as an entirely different matter. At this stage of our analysis, we are not yet ready to discuss why large persistent deficits might be a problem. That must wait until Chapter 15.

BOX 3-2

CYCLICAL AND POLICY INFLUENCES ON THE BUDGET: THE EARLY 1980s

The actual budget deficit can change because output, and with it tax collection and government transfers, changes. This is the cyclical response of the budget. The budget deficit changes also as a result of discretionary changes in government spending and taxes. In the early 1980s both types of change produced large and controversial increases in the budget deficit. The accompanying figure shows the actual and full employment deficits (the shaded part is the full employment deficit) as well as the unemployment rate.

Cyclical effects on the budget are visible in 1982 when rising unemployment sharply increased the deficit. By contrast, in late 1980 to 1981 the unemployment rate was roughly constant, but the deficit nonetheless increased. In that period changes in the deficit reflected changes in fiscal policy.

How much of the rising deficit was due to policy? An estimate produced by the Council of Economic Advisers is that for every extra point of unemployment, the budget deficit increases by $25 billion. Thus when the civilian unemployment rate increased from 7.6 percent in 1981 to 9.7 percent in 1982, the budget deficit worsened as a result by more than $50 billion. But the actual deficit increased from $62 billion to $147 billion. About $35 billion of the increase in the deficit was thus due to policy changes. These policy changes were mainly the Reagan tax cuts put into effect in 1982.

The discretionary fiscal policy changes—cuts in personal income tax rates, more favorable corporate tax treatment, and increased defense spending—are likely to make the budget deficits become exceedingly large. Table 1 shows a forecast for the actual and full-employment deficits given the policy outlook of early 1983:

TABLE 1 ACTUAL AND FULL-EMPLOYMENT DEFICITS (*% of GNP*)

	1982	1983	1984	1985
Actual deficit	4.8	5.7	4.9	4.1
Full-employment deficit	1.7	2.3	2.2	2.1

Source: Review of the U.S. Economy, Data Resources, Inc., January 1983.

In later chapters we discuss why deficits of this size are so controversial.

FIGURE 1 BUDGET DEFICITS AND UNEMPLOYMENT. (*Source: Survey of Current Business, March 1983 Economic Report of the President.*) The figure shows quarterly data (seasonally adjusted at annual rates) for the actual and the full-employment budget deficit. The full-employment budget deficit is shown by the shaded parts of the bars. Note that during a period where unemployment is constant, as it was from the fourth quarter of 1980 to the third quarter of 1981, the actual and full-employment budgets move together, reflecting only discretionary fiscal policy. By contrast, in 1982 the cyclical component of the actual budget, shown by the unshaded portion of the bars, moves along with the unemployment rate.

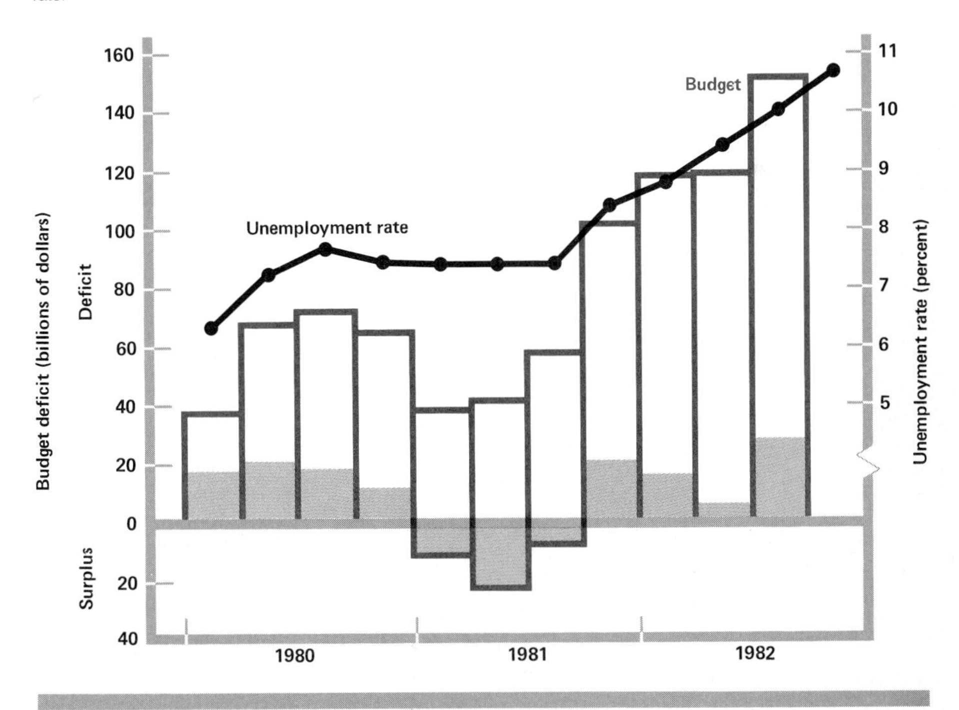

Two final words of warning. First, there is no certainty as to the true full-employment level of output. Various assumptions are possible about the level of unemployment that corresponds to full employment. The usual assumptions now are that full employment means an unemployment rate of 5.5 to even as high as 7 percent. But estimates of the full-employment deficit or surplus will differ depending on the assumptions made about the economy at full employment.[25]

Second, the high-employment surplus is a better measure of the direction of active fiscal policy than the actual budget surplus. But it is not a perfect measure of the thrust of fiscal policy. The reason is that balanced budget increases in government purchases, for example, are themselves expansionary, so that an increase in government purchases matched by a tax increase that keeps the surplus constant leads to an increase in the level of income. Because fiscal policy involves the setting of a number of variables—the tax rate, transfers, and government purchases—it is difficult to describe the thrust of fiscal policy perfectly in a single number.[26] But the high-employment surplus is nevertheless a useful guide to the direction of fiscal policy.

3-6 SUMMARY

1 Output is at its equilibrium level when the aggregate demand for goods is equal to the level of output.
2 Aggregate demand consists of planned spending by households on consumption, firms on investment goods, and government on its purchases of goods and services.
3 When output is at its equilibrium level, there are no unintended changes in inventories and all economic units are making precisely the purchases they had planned to. An adjustment process for the level of output based on the accumulation or decumulation of inventories leads the economy to the equilibrium output level.
4 The level of aggregate demand is itself affected by the level of output (equal to the level of income), because consumption demand depends on the level of income.
5 The consumption function relates consumption spending to income. Consumption rises with income. Income that is not consumed is saved, so that the saving function can be derived from the consumption function.
6 The multiplier is the amount by which a $1 change in autonomous spending changes the equilibrium level of output. The greater the propensity to consume, the higher the multiplier.

[25] For a critique of the concept of the full-employment budget, see William Fellner, "The High Employment Budget and Potential Output," *Survey of Current Business,* November 1982.

[26] A very helpful discussion of the full-employment surplus and other measures—such as the weighted full-employment surplus—that attempt to adjust for the imperfections of the full-employment surplus measure is contained in Alan S. Blinder and Robert M. Solow, "Analytical Foundations of Fiscal Policy," in Alan S. Blinder et al., *The Economics of Public Finance* (Washington, D.C.: The Brookings Institution, 1974).

7 Government purchases and government transfer payments act like increases in autonomous spending in their effects on the equilibrium level of income. A proportional income tax has the same effects on the equilibrium level of income as a reduction in the propensity to consume. A proportional income tax thus reduces the multiplier.
8 The budget surplus is the excess of government receipts over its expenditure. When the government is spending more than it receives, the budget is in deficit. The size of the budget surplus (deficit) is affected by the government's fiscal policy variables—government purchases, transfer payments, and tax rates.
9 The actual budget surplus is also affected by changes in tax collection and transfers resulting from movements in the level of income that occur as a result of changes in private autonomous spending. The full-employment (high-employment) budget surplus is used as a measure of the *active* use of fiscal policy. The full-employment surplus measures the budget surplus that would exist if output were at its potential (full-employment) level.

KEY TERMS

Aggregate demand
Equilibrium output
Unintended (undesired) inventory accumulation
Planned aggregate demand
Consumption function
Marginal propensity to consume
Marginal propensity to save
Multiplier
Automatic stabilizer
Budget surplus
Budget deficit
Balanced budget multiplier
Full-employment (high-employment) surplus

PROBLEMS

1 Here we investigate a particular example of the model studied in Sections 3-2 and 3-3 with no government. Suppose the consumption function is given by $C = 100 + 0.8Y$, while investment is given by $\bar{I} = 50$.
(*a*) What is the equilibrium level of income in this case?
(*b*) What is the level of saving in equilibrium?
(*c*) If, for some reason, output was at the level of 800, what would the level of involuntary inventory accumulation be?
(*d*) If $\bar{I}$ were to rise to 100 (we discuss what determines $\bar{I}$ in later chapters), what would the effect be on equilibrium income?
(*e*) What is the multiplier α here?
(*f*) Draw a diagram indicating the equilibria in both 1(*a*) and 1(*d*).
2 Suppose consumption behavior were to change in problem 1 so that $C = 100 + 0.9Y$, while $\bar{I}$ remained at 50.
(*a*) Would you expect the equilibrium level of income to be higher or lower than in 1(*a*)? Calculate the new Y' to verify this.
(*b*) Now suppose investment increases to $\bar{I} = 100$ just as in 1(*d*). What is the new equilibrium income?

(*c*) Does this change in investment spending have more or less of an effect on Y than in problem 1? Why?
(*d*) Draw a diagram indicating the change in equilibrium income in this case.

3 We showed in the text that the equilibrium condition $Y = AD$ is equivalent to the $S = \bar{I}$, or saving = investment, condition. Starting from $S = \bar{I}$ and the saving function, derive the equilibrium level of income, as in Equation (10).

4 This problem relates to the so-called *paradox of thrift*. Suppose that $I = \bar{I}$ and that $C = \bar{C} + cY$.
(*a*) What is the savings function, that is, the function that shows how saving is related to income?
(*b*) Suppose individuals want to save more at every level of income. Show, using a figure like Figure 3-5, how the saving function is shifted.
(*c*) What effect does the increased desire to save have on the new equilibrium level of saving? Explain the paradox.

5 Now let us look at a model which is an example of the one presented in Sections 3-4 and 3-5; that is, it includes government purchases, taxes, and transfers. It has the same features as the one in problems 1 and 2, except that it also has a government. Thus, suppose consumption is given by $C = 100 + 0.8YD$ and $\bar{I} = 50$, while fiscal policy is summarized by $\bar{G} = 200$, $\overline{TR} = 62.5$, and $t = 0.25$.
(*a*) What is the equilibrium level of income in this more complete model?
(*b*) What is the new multiplier $\bar{\alpha}$? Why is this less than the multiplier in problem 1(*e*)?

6 Using the same model as in problem 5, determine the following:
(*a*) What is the value of the budget surplus BS when $\bar{I} = 50$?
(*b*) What is BS when $\bar{I}$ increases to 100?
(*c*) What accounts for the change in BS from 6(*a*) to 6(*b*)?
(*d*) Assuming that the full-employment level of income $\bar{Y}$ is 1,200, what is the full-employment budget surplus BS^* when $\bar{I} = 50$? 100? (Be careful.)
(*e*) What is BS^* if $\bar{I} = 50$ and $\bar{G} = 250$, with $\bar{Y}$ still equal to 1,200?
(*f*) Explain why we use BS^* rather than simply BS to measure the direction of fiscal policy.

7 Suppose we expand our model to take account of the fact that transfer payments TR do depend on the level of income Y. When income is high, transfer payments such as unemployment benefits will fall. Conversely, when income is low, unemployment is high and so are unemployment benefits. We can incorporate this into our model by writing transfers as $TR = \overline{TR} - bY$, $b > 0$. Remember that equilibrium income is derived as the solution to $Y_0 = C + \bar{I} + \bar{G} = \bar{C} + cYD + \bar{I} + \bar{G}$, where $YD = Y + TR - TA$ is disposable income.
(*a*) Derive the expression for Y_0 in this case, just as Equation (22) was derived in the text.
(*b*) What is the new multiplier now?
(*c*) Why is the new multiplier less than the standard one, $\bar{\alpha}$?
(*d*) How does the change in the multiplier relate to the concept of automatic stabilizers?

8 Now we look at the role taxes play in determining equilibrium income. Suppose we have an economy of the type in Sections 3-4 and 3-5, described by the following functions:

$$C = 50 + 0.8YD$$
$$\bar{I} = 70$$
$$\bar{G} = 200$$
$$\overline{TR} = 100$$
$$t = 0.20$$

(*a*) Calculate the equilibrium level of income and the multiplier in this model.

(*b*) Calculate also the budget surplus BS.
(*c*) Suppose that t increases to 0.25. What is the new equilibrium income? The new multiplier?
(*d*) Calculate the change in the budget surplus. Would you expect the change in the surplus to be more or less if $c = 0.9$ rather than 0.8?
(*e*) Can you explain why the multiplier is 1 when $t = 1$?

9 Suppose the economy is operating at equilibrium with $Y_0 = 1{,}000$. If the government undertakes a fiscal change so that the tax rate t increases by 0.05 and government spending increases by 50, will the budget surplus go up or down? Why?

10 Suppose Congress decides to reduce transfer payments (such as welfare), but to increase government purchases of goods and services by an equal amount. That is, it undertakes a change in fiscal policy such that $\Delta\overline{G} = -\overline{TR}$.
(*a*) Would you expect equilibrium income to rise or fall as a result of this change? Why? Check out your answer with the following example: Suppose initially $c = 0.8$, $t = 0.25$, and $Y_0 = 600$. Now let $\Delta\overline{G} = 10$ and $\Delta\overline{TR} = -10$.
(*b*) Find the change in equilibrium income ΔY_0.
(*c*) What is the change in the budget surplus ΔBS? Why has BS changed?

*11 We have seen in problem 10 that an increase in G accompanied by an equal decrease in TR does not leave the budget unchanged. What would the effect on equilibrium income be if TR and G change to leave the budget surplus BS fixed? [*Hint:* Notice that $BS = TA - TR - G$. We want $\Delta BS = \Delta TA - \Delta TR - \Delta G = 0$(*) so that $\Delta TR = \Delta TA - \Delta G$. Since t is constant, $\Delta TA = t\,\Delta Y_0$(**). We also know that $Y_0 = \overline{\alpha}(\overline{C} + \overline{I} + \overline{G} + c\overline{R})$ and $\Delta Y_0 = \overline{\alpha}(\Delta\overline{G} + c\,\Delta\overline{TR})$.

[Substituting (*) and (**) into this last equation, derive an expression for ΔY in terms of ΔG. Simplify that expression, using the fact that $\overline{\alpha} = \{1/[1 - c(1 - t)]\}$, to obtain the balanced budget result in the case of changes in transfers and government spending.]

*12 In the preceding problem and in the appendix we derived the balanced budget multiplier result. It states that if $\Delta G = \Delta TA$ from the initial to final equilibrium, then $\Delta Y = \Delta G$. Let us look at an example of this balanced budget multiplier in action.
Consider the economy described by the following functions:

$$C = 85 + 0.75YD$$
$$\overline{I} = 50$$
$$\overline{G} = 150$$
$$\overline{TR} = 100$$
$$t = 0.20$$

(*a*) Derive the multiplier $\overline{\alpha}$ and the level of autonomous spending $\overline{A}$.
(*b*) From 12(*a*) calculate the equilibrium level of income and the budget surplus.
(*c*) Now suppose G rises to 250 while t increases to 0.28. Repeat step 12(*a*) for the new fiscal policy.
(*d*) What are ΔTA, ΔG, ΔY, and ΔBS?
(*e*) In view of this result and that of problem 10, what do you think the effect on income would be if we had a balanced budget change where $\Delta TR = \Delta TA$?

*13 Suppose the aggregate demand function is as in the figure on the following page. Notice that at Y_0 the slope of the aggregate demand curve is *greater* than 1. (This would happen if $c > 1$.) Complete this picture as is done in Figure 3-1 to include the arrows indicating adjustment when $Y \neq Y_0$ and show what IU is for $Y < Y_0$ and $Y > Y_0$. What is happening in this example, and how does it differ fundamentally from Figure 3-1?

*14 This problem anticipates our discussion of the open economy in Chapter 18. It is hard, and only the ambitious student should try it. You are asked to derive some of the results that will

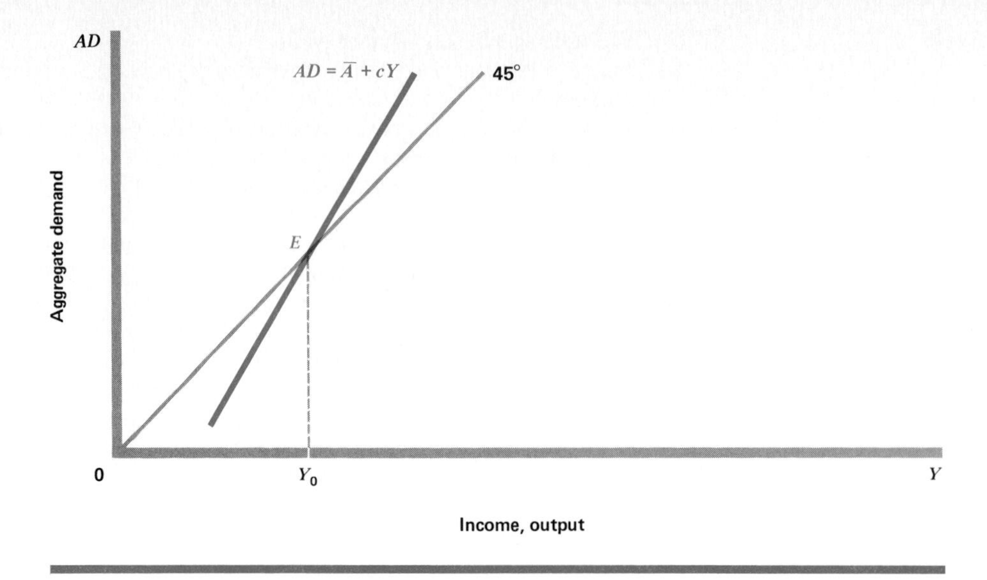

be shown there. We start with the assumption that foreign demand for our goods is given and equal to $\overline{X}$. Our demand for foreign goods or imports, denoted Q, is a linear function of income.

$$\text{Exports} = \overline{X} \qquad \text{Imports} = Q = \overline{Q} + mY$$

where m is the ***marginal propensity to import.***

(*a*) The trade balance, or net exports, NX, is defined as the excess of exports over imports. Write an algebraic expression for the trade balance and show in a diagram net exports as a function of the level of income. (Put Y on the horizontal axis.)

(*b*) Show the effect of a change in income on the trade balance, using your diagram. Show also the effect of a change in exports on the trade balance, given income.

(*c*) The equilibrium condition in the goods market is that aggregate demand for ***our*** goods is equal to supply. Aggregate demand for our goods includes exports but excludes imports. Thus we have

$$Y = C + \bar{I} + NX$$

where we have added net exports (exports less imports) to investment and consumption. Using the expression for net exports developed in 14 (*a*) and the consumption function $C = \overline{C} + cY$, derive the equilibrium level of income, Y_0.

(*d*) Using your expression for the equilibrium level of income in 14(*c*), what is the effect of a change in exports, $\overline{X}$, on equilibrium income? Interpret your result and discuss the multiplier in an open economy.

(*e*) Using your results in 14(*a*) and (*d*), show the effect of an increase in exports on the trade balance.

APPENDIX: THE BALANCED BUDGET MULTIPLIER

This appendix considers the balanced budget multiplier result mentioned earlier. The balanced budget multiplier refers to the effects of an increase in government purchases accompanied by an increase in taxes such that, in the new equilibrium, the budget surplus is exactly the same as in the original equilibrium. The result is that the multiplier of such a policy change, the balanced budget multiplier, is 1.

A multiplier of unity implies that output expands by precisely the amount of the increased government purchases with no induced consumption spending. It is apparent that what must be at work is the effect of higher taxes that exactly offset the effect of the income expansion, and that thus maintain disposable income, and hence consumption, constant. With no induced consumption spending, output expands simply to match the increased government purchases.

We can derive this result formally by noting that the change in aggregate demand ΔAD is equal to the change in government purchases plus the change in consumption spending. The latter is equal to the marginal propensity to consume out of disposable income, c, times the change in disposable income, ΔYD; that is, $\Delta YD = \Delta Y_0 - \Delta TA$, where ΔY_0 is the change in output. Thus:

$$\Delta AD = \Delta\overline{G} + c(\Delta Y_0 - \Delta TA) \tag{A1}$$

Since from one equilibrium to another the change in aggregate demand has to equal the change in output, we have

$$\Delta Y_0 = \Delta\overline{G} + c(\Delta Y_0 - \Delta TA)$$

or

$$\Delta Y_0 = \frac{1}{1-c}(\Delta\overline{G} - c\,\Delta TA) \tag{A2}$$

Next we note that by assumption the change in government purchases between the new equilibrium and the old one is exactly matched by a change in tax collection so that $\Delta\overline{G} = \Delta TA$. It follows from this last equality, after substitution in Equation (A2), that with this particular restriction on fiscal policy we have

$$\Delta Y_0 = \frac{1}{1-c}(\Delta\overline{G} - c\,\Delta\overline{G}) = \Delta\overline{G} = \Delta TA \tag{A3}$$

so that the multiplier is precisely unity.

Another way of deriving the balanced budget multiplier result is by considering the successive rounds of spending changes caused by the government policy changes. Suppose each of government purchases and taxes increased by \$1. Let $c(1-t)$, the induced increase in aggregate demand caused by a \$1 increase in income in the presence of taxes, be denoted by $\overline{c}$.

Table A3-1 shows the spending induced by the two policy changes. The first column shows the changes in spending resulting from the change in government purchases and its later repercussions. The second column similarly gives the spending effects in successive rounds of the tax increase. The third column sums the two effects for each spending round, while the final column adds all the changes in spending induced so far. Since $\overline{c}$ is less than 1, $(\overline{c})^n$ becomes very small as the number of spending rounds, n, increases, and the final change in

TABLE A3-1 THE BALANCED BUDGET MULTIPLIER

	CHANGE IN SPENDING RESULTING FROM			
Spending round	$\Delta\bar{G} = 1$	$\Delta TA = 1$	Net this round	Total
1	1	$-\bar{c}$	$1 - \bar{c}$	$1 - \bar{c}$
2	$\bar{c}$	$-\bar{c}^2$	$\bar{c} - \bar{c}^2$	$1 - \bar{c}^2$
3	$\bar{c}^2$	$-\bar{c}^3$	$\bar{c}^2 - \bar{c}^3$	$1 - \bar{c}^3$
4	$\bar{c}^3$	$-\bar{c}^4$	$\bar{c}^3 - \bar{c}^4$	$1 - \bar{c}^4$
⋮				
n	$\bar{c}^{n-1}$	$-\bar{c}^n$	$\bar{c}^{n-1} - \bar{c}^n$	$1 - \bar{c}^n$

aggregate spending caused by the balanced budget increase in governmental spending is just equal to $1.

Finally, the balanced budget multiplier can also be thought of from a somewhat different perspective. Consider the goods market equilibrium condition in terms of saving, taxes, investment, transfers, and government purchases:

$$S + TA - TR = \bar{I} + G \tag{A4}$$

Now, using the definition of the budget surplus, $BS \equiv TA - TR - G$,

$$BS = \bar{I} - S \tag{A5}$$

If there is no change in the budget deficit, nor a change in investment, the equilibrium change in saving is zero. For saving not to change, disposable income must remain unchanged. This says that $\Delta YD = \Delta Y - \Delta T = 0$, and hence shows once more that the change in income equals the change in taxes. This in turn equals the change in government purchases.

Hence, the balanced budget multiplier, or more precisely, the multiplier associated with an unchanging budget surplus or deficit, is equal to unity. This perspective on the income determination process is very useful because it emphasizes the fact that a change in the surplus or deficit of one sector is matched by a corresponding change in the deficit or surplus of the remaining sectors. If the government surplus is constrained by fiscal policy to be unchanged, so too must be the private sector's surplus, $S - \bar{I}$.

4

MONEY, INTEREST, AND INCOME

The stock of money, interest rates, and the Federal Reserve seemingly had no place in the model of income determination developed in Chapter 3. Clearly, though, we know that money has an important role to play in the determination of income and employment. Interest rates are frequently mentioned as an important determinant of aggregate spending, and the Federal Reserve and monetary policy receive at least as much public attention as fiscal policy. For instance, the blame for the deep 1980–1982 recession and its extraordinarily high interest rates is often placed on the Federal Reserve's tight money policy. This chapter introduces money and monetary policy, and builds an explicit framework of analysis in which the interaction of goods and assets markets can be studied.

This new framework leads to an understanding of the determination of interest rates and of their role in the business cycle. Figure 4-1 shows the interest rate on Treasury bills. The interest rate on Treasury bills represents the payment, per dollar per year, that someone receives who lends to the U.S. government. Thus an interest rate of 10 percent means that someone who lends $100 to the government for 1 year will receive 10 percent, or $10, in interest. Figure 4-1 immediately suggests some questions: What factors cause the interest rate to increase, as occurred for example in 1980–1981, and what factors cause rates to decline as they did

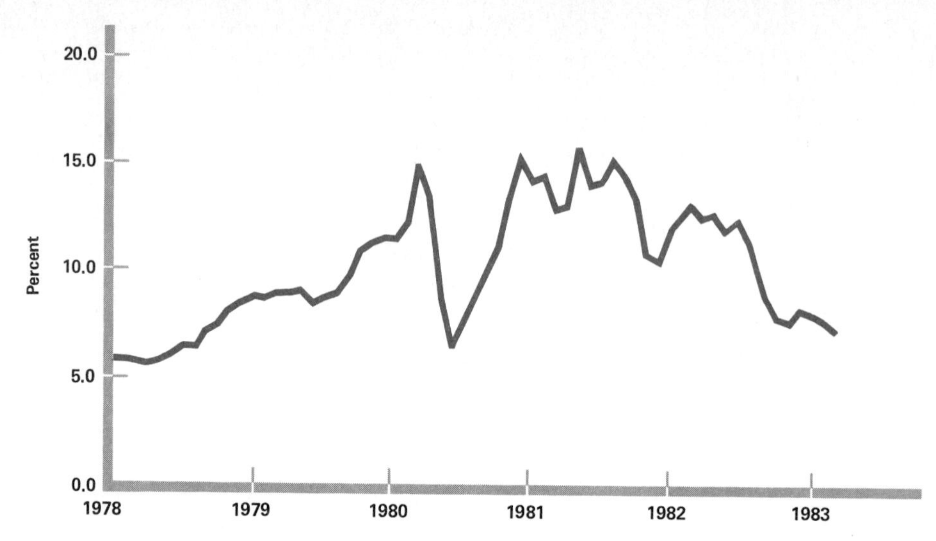

FIGURE 4-1 THE INTEREST RATE ON TREASURY BILLS (Percent per year). (*Source:* Citibank Economic Database.)

in 1982? Furthermore, when interest rates increase, what are the effects on output and employment?

The model we introduce in this chapter, *the IS-LM model,* is the core of modern macroeconomics. It maintains the spirit and, indeed, many details of the previous chapter. The model is broadened, though, by introducing the interest rate as an additional determinant of aggregate demand. In Chapter 3, autonomous spending and fiscal policy were the chief determinants of aggregate spending. Now we add the interest rate and argue that a reduction in the rate of interest raises aggregate demand. This seems a minor extension, which can readily be handled in the context of Chapter 3. This is not entirely correct, because we have to ask what determines the rate of interest. That question extends our model to include the markets for financial assets and forces us to study the interaction of goods and assets markets. Interest rates and income are jointly determined by equilibrium in goods and assets markets.

What is the payoff for that complication? The introduction of assets markets and interest rates serves three important purposes:

1 The extension shows how monetary policy works.
2 The analysis qualifies the conclusions of Chapter 3. Consider Figure 4-2, which lays out the logical structure of the model. So far we looked at the submodel of autonomous spending and fiscal policy as determinants of aggregate demand and equilibrium income. Now the inclusion of assets markets—money demand and supply, as we shall see—introduces an additional channel. An expansionary fiscal policy, for example, would in the first place raise spending and income. That increase in income, though, would affect the assets markets by raising money demand and thereby raising interest rates. The higher interest rates in turn reduce

aggregate spending and thus, as we shall show, dampen the expansionary impact of fiscal policy. Indeed, under certain conditions, the increase in interest rates may be sufficiently important to offset fully the expansionary effects of fiscal policy. Clearly, such an extreme possibility is an important qualification to our study of fiscal policy in Chapter 3.

3 Even if the interest rate changes just mentioned only dampen (rather than offset fully) the expansionary effects of fiscal policy, they nevertheless have an important side effect. The *composition* of aggregate demand between investment and consumption spending will depend on the rate of interest. Higher interest rates dampen aggregate demand mainly by reducing investment. Thus, an expansionary fiscal policy would tend to raise consumption through the multiplier, but it would tend to reduce investment through the induced increase in interest rates. The side effects of fiscal expansion on interest rates and investment continue to be a sensitive and important issue in policy making. An influential view is that fiscal expansion should not be used as a tool for demand management because the increase in government spending takes place at the expense of private investment. Government spending crowds out, or displaces, private investment because it tends to raise interest rates.

These three reasons justify the more complicated model we study in this chapter. There is the further advantage that the extended model helps us to understand the functioning of financial markets.

OUTLINE OF THE CHAPTER

We use Figure 4-2 once more to lay out the structure of this chapter. We start in Section 4-1 with a discussion of the link between interest rates and

FIGURE 4-2 THE STRUCTURE OF THE *IS-LM* MODEL. The *IS-LM* model emphasizes the interaction between goods and assets markets. The model of Chapter 3 looks at income determination by arguing that income affects spending, which in turn determines output and income. Now we add the effects of interest rates on spending and thus income, and the dependence of assets markets on income. Higher income raises money demand and thus link interest rates. Higher interest rates lower spending and thus income. Spending, interest rates, and income are determined jointly by equilibrium in goods *and* assets markets.

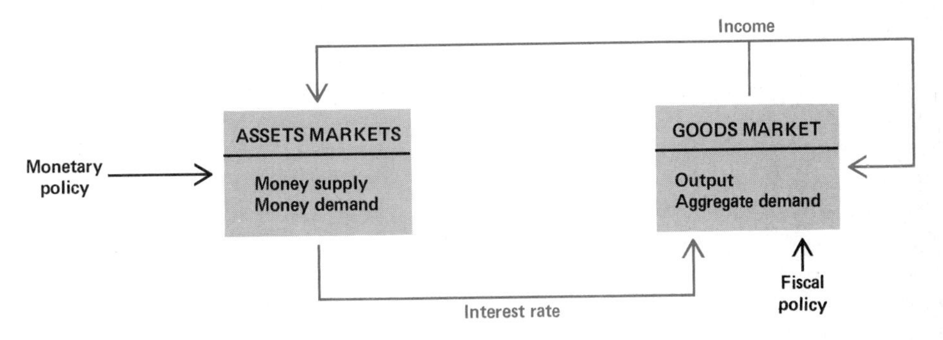

aggregate demand. Here we use the model of Chapter 3 directly, augmented to include an interest rate as a determinant of aggregate demand. We derive a key relationship—the *IS* curve—that shows combinations of interest rates and levels of income for which the goods markets clear. In Section 4-2, we turn to assets markets and, in particular, to the money market. We show that the demand for money depends on interest rates and income and that there is a combination of interest rates and income levels—the *LM* curve—for which the money market clears.[1] In Section 4-3, we combine the two schedules to study the joint determination of interest rates and income. Section 4-4 lays out the adjustment process toward equilibrium. Monetary policy is discussed in Sections 4-5 and 4-6. Fiscal policy and the important issue of the monetary-fiscal policy mix are reserved for Chapter 5. That material is in a separate chapter only to avoid making this chapter too long.

4-1 THE GOODS MARKET AND THE *IS* CURVE

In this section we derive a *goods market equilibrium schedule*. The goods market equilibrium schedule, or *IS* schedule, shows combinations of interest rates and levels of output such that planned spending equals income. The goods market equilibrium schedule is an extension of income determination with a 45° line diagram. What is new here is that investment is no longer fully exogenous but is also determined by the interest rate. To appreciate the extension of Chapter 3 we briefly review what we found there.

In Chapter 3 we derived an expression for equilibrium income:

$$Y_0 = \frac{\overline{A}}{1 - \overline{c}} \qquad \overline{c} = c(1 - t) \tag{1}$$

Equilibrium income in this simple Keynesian model has two determinants: autonomous spending, $\overline{A}$, and the propensity to consume out of income, $\overline{c}$. Autonomous spending includes government spending, investment spending, and autonomous consumption spending. The propensity to consume out of income, as seen from (1), depends on the propensity to consume out of disposable income, c, and on the fraction of a dollar of income retained after taxes, $1 - t$. The higher the level of autonomous spending and the higher the propensity to consume, the higher the equilibrium level of income.

INVESTMENT AND THE INTEREST RATE

So far, investment spending $\overline{I}$ has been treated as *entirely* exogenous—some number like $250 billion determined altogether outside the model of income determination. Now, as we make our macromodel more complete by intro-

[1] The terms *IS* and *LM* are shorthand representations, respectively, of investment equals saving (goods market equilibrium) and money demand (L) equals money supply (M), or money market equilibrium. The classic article that introduced this model is J. R. Hicks, "Mr. Keynes and the Classics: A Suggested Interpretation," *Econometrica*, 1937, pp. 147–159.

ducing interest rates as part of the model, investment spending, too, becomes endogenous. The desired or planned rate of investment is lower the higher the interest rate.

A simple argument shows why. Investment is spending on additions to the capital stock (machinery, structures, inventories). Such investment is undertaken with the aim of making profits in the future by operating machines and factories. Suppose firms borrow to buy the capital (machines and factories) that they use. Then the higher the interest rate, the more firms have to pay out in interest each year from the earnings they receive from their investment. Thus, the higher the interest rate, the less the profits to the firm after paying interest, and the less it will want to invest. Conversely, a low rate of interest makes investment spending profitable and is, therefore, reflected in a high level of planned investment.

THE INVESTMENT DEMAND SCHEDULE

We specify an investment spending function of the form[2]

$$I = \bar{I} - bi \qquad b > 0 \tag{2}$$

where i is the rate of interest and b measures the interest response of investment. $\bar{I}$ now denotes autonomous investment spending, that is, investment spending that is independent of both income and the rate of interest.[3] Equation (2) states that the lower the interest rate, the higher is planned investment, with the coefficient b measuring the responsiveness of investment spending to the interest rate.

Figure 4-3 shows the investment schedule of Equation (2). The schedule shows for each level of the rate of interest the rate at which firms plan to spend on investment. The schedule is negatively sloped to reflect the assumption that a reduction in the rate of interest increases the profitability of additions to the capital stock and therefore leads to a larger rate of planned investment spending.

The position of the investment schedule is determined by the slope — the term b in Equation (2) — and by the level of autonomous investment spending $\bar{I}$. If investment is highly responsive to the interest rate, a small decline in interest rates will lead to a large increase in investment, so that the schedule is almost flat. Conversely, if investment responds little to interest rates, the schedule is more nearly vertical. Changes in autonomous investment spend-

[2] Here and in other places in the book, we specify linear (straight-line) versions of behavioral functions. We use the linear specifications to simplify both the algebra and the diagrams. The linearity assumption does not lead to any great difficulties so long as we confine ourselves to talking about small changes in the economy. You should often draw nonlinear versions of our diagrams to be sure you can work with them.

[3] In Chap. 3, investment spending was defined as autonomous with respect to income. Now that the interest rate appears in the model, we have to extend the definition of autonomous to mean independent of *both* the interest rate and income. To conserve notation, we continue to use $\bar{I}$ to denote autonomous investment, but recognize that the definition is broadened.

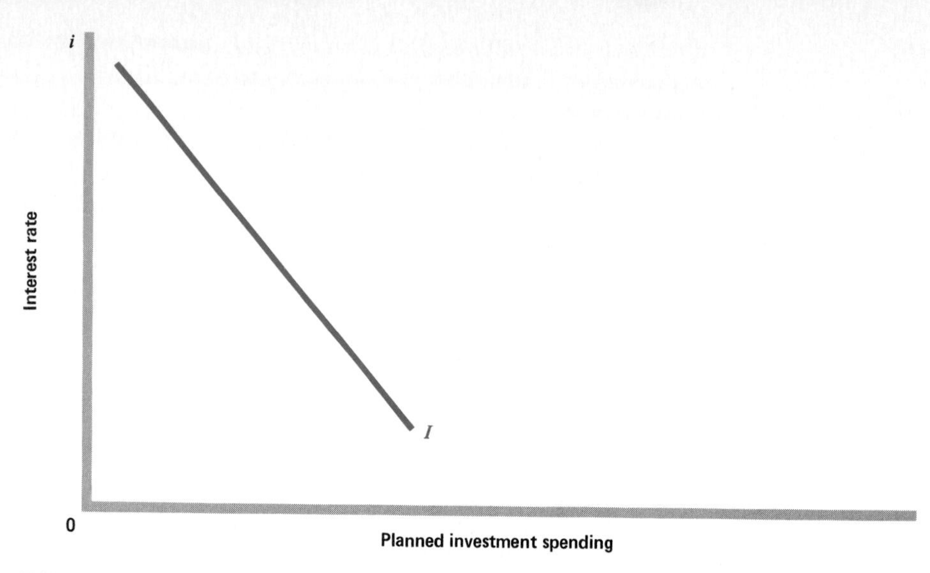

FIGURE 4-3 THE INVESTMENT SCHEDULE. The investment schedule shows the planned level of investment spending at each rate of interest. Because higher interest rates reduce the profitability of additions to the capital stock, higher interest rates imply lower planned rates of investment spending. Changes in autonomous investment shift the investment schedule.

ing $\bar{I}$ shift the investment schedule. An increase in $\bar{I}$ means that at each level of the interest rate firms plan to invest at a higher rate. This would be shown by a rightward shift of the investment schedule.

The Interest Rate and Aggregate Demand: The *IS* Curve

We now modify the aggregate demand function of Chapter 3 to reflect the new planned investment spending schedule. Aggregate demand still consists of the demand for consumption, investment, and government spending on goods and services. Only now investment spending depends on the interest rate. We have

$$\begin{aligned} AD &\equiv C + I + G \\ &= \bar{C} + c\overline{TR} + c(1-t)Y + \bar{I} - bi + \bar{G} \\ &= \bar{A} + \bar{c}Y - bi \end{aligned} \tag{3}$$

where

$$\bar{A} \equiv \bar{C} + c\overline{TR} + \bar{I} + \bar{G} \tag{4}$$

From Equation (3) we observe that an increase in the interest rate reduces aggregate demand at a given level of income because an interest rate increase reduces investment spending. Note that the term $\bar{A}$, which is the part of aggregate demand unaffected by either the level of income or the interest rate, does include part of investment spending, namely, $\bar{I}$. As noted earlier, $\bar{I}$ is the *autonomous* component of investment spending, which is independent of the interest rate (and income).

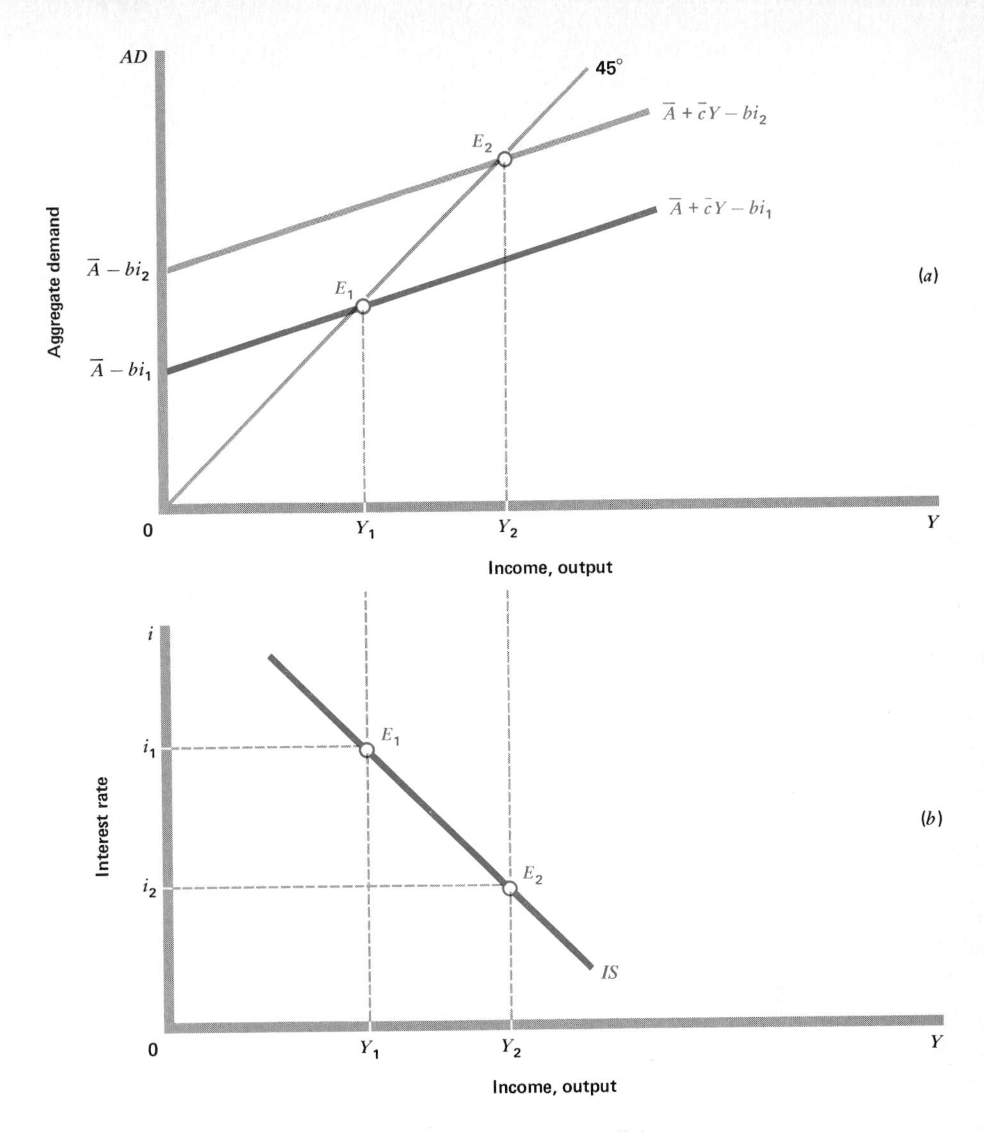

FIGURE 4-4 DERIVATION OF THE *IS* CURVE. At an interest rate i_1, equilibrium in the goods market obtains at point E_1 in the upper panel with an income level Y_1. In the lower panel this is recorded as point E_1. A fall in the interest rate to i_2 raises aggregate demand, shifting the level of spending upward at each income level. The new equilibrium income level is Y_2. In the lower panel, point E_2 records the new equilibrium in the goods market corresponding to an interest rate i_2.

At any given level of the interest rate, we can still proceed as in Chapter 3 to determine the equilibrium level of income and output. As the interest rate changes, however, the equilibrium level of income changes. The relationship we now derive between the interest rate and the equilibrium level of income in the goods market is the *IS* curve.

Figure 4-4 is used to derive the *IS* curve. For a given level of the interest rate, say, i_1, the last term of Equation (3) is a constant (bi_1), and we can in

Figure 4-4*a* draw the aggregate demand function of Chapter 3, this time with an intercept $\overline{A} - bi_1$. The equilibrium level of income obtained in the usual manner is Y_1 at point E_1. Since that equilibrium level of income was derived for a given level of the interest rate i_1, we can plot that pair (i_1, Y_1) in the bottom panel as point E_1. We now have one point, E_1, on the *IS* curve.

Consider next a lower interest rate, i_2. At a lower interest rate, aggregate demand would be higher at each level of income because investment spending is higher. In terms of Figure 4-4*a*, that implies an upward shift of the aggregate demand schedule. The entire aggregate demand schedule shifts upward by $-b\,\Delta i$, where Δi, the assumed change in the interest rate, is negative. The curve shifts upward because the intercept $\overline{A} - bi$ has been increased. Given the increase in aggregate demand, we note that the equilibrium level of income rises to point E_2, with an associated income level Y_2. At point E_2, in the bottom panel, we record the fact that an interest rate i_2 implies an equilibrium level of income, Y_2,—equilibrium in the sense that the goods market is in equilibrium (or that the goods market *clears*). Point E_2 is another point on the *IS* curve.

We can apply the same procedure to all conceivable levels of the interest rate and thereby generate all the points which make up the *IS* curve. They have in common the property that they are combinations of interest rates and income (output) such that the goods market clears. We therefore refer to the *IS* curve as the *goods market equilibrium schedule.*

Figure 4-4 shows that the *IS* curve is negatively sloped, reflecting the increase in aggregate demand associated with a reduction in the interest rate. We can also derive the *IS* curve by using the goods market equilibrium condition, income equals planned spending, or:

$$\begin{aligned} Y &= AD \\ &= \overline{A} + \overline{c}Y - bi \end{aligned} \tag{5}$$

which can be simplified to

$$Y = \overline{\alpha}(\overline{A} - bi) \qquad \overline{\alpha} = \frac{1}{1 - \overline{c}} \tag{6}$$

where $\overline{\alpha}$ is the multiplier of Chapter 3. Equation (6) should now be compared with (1) at the beginning of this chapter. From Equation (6), we note that a higher interest rate implies a lower level of equilibrium income for a given $\overline{A}$, as Figure 4-4 shows.

The construction of the *IS* curve is quite straightforward and may even be deceptively simple. We can gain further understanding of the economics of the *IS* curve by asking and answering the following questions:

- What determines the slope of the *IS* curve?
- What determines the position of the *IS* curve, given its slope, and what causes the curve to shift?

- What happens when the interest rate and income are at levels such that we are not on the *IS* curve?

The Slope of the *IS* Curve

We have already noted that the *IS* curve is negatively sloped because a higher level of the interest rate reduces investment spending, therefore reducing aggregate demand and thus the equilibrium level of income. The steepness of the curve depends on how sensitive investment spending is to changes in the interest rate, and also on the multiplier $\bar{\alpha}$ in Equation (6).

Suppose that investment spending is very sensitive to the interest rate, so that b in Equation (6) is large. Then, in terms of Figure 4-4, a given change in the interest rate produces a large change in aggregate demand, and thus shifts the aggregate demand curve in Figure 4-4*a* up by a large distance. A large shift in the aggregate demand schedule produces a correspondingly large change in the equilibrium level of income. If a given change in the interest rate produces a large change in income, the *IS* curve is very flat. This is the case if investment is very sensitive to the interest rate, that is, if b is large. Correspondingly, with b small and investment spending not very sensitive to the interest rate, the *IS* curve is relatively steep.

THE ROLE OF THE MULTIPLIER

Consider next the effects of the multiplier $\bar{\alpha}$ on the steepness of the *IS* curve. Figure 4-5 shows aggregate demand curves corresponding to different multipliers. The coefficient $\bar{c}$ on the darker aggregate demand curves is smaller than the corresponding coefficient $\bar{c}'$ on the lighter aggregate demand curves. The multiplier is accordingly larger on the lighter aggregate demand curves. The initial levels of income, Y_1 and Y_1', correspond to the interest rate i_1 on the lower of each of the darker and lighter aggregate demand curves, respectively.

A given reduction in the interest rate, to i_2, raises the intercept of the aggregate demand curves by the same vertical distance, as shown in the top panel. However, the implied change in income is very different. For the lighter curve, income rises to Y_2', while it rises only to Y_2 on the darker line. The change in equilibrium income corresponding to a given change in the interest rate is accordingly larger as the aggregate demand curve is steeper; that is, the larger the multiplier, the greater the rise in income. That should not be surprising since effectively the change in the interest rate and induced change in investment act in the same way on the aggregate demand curves as a change in autonomous spending $\bar{A}$. As we see from the lower figure, the smaller the multiplier, the steeper the *IS* curve. Equivalently, the larger the multiplier, the larger the change in income produced by a given change in the interest rate.

We have thus seen that the smaller the sensitivity of investment spending to the interest rate and the smaller the multiplier, the steeper the *IS* curve.

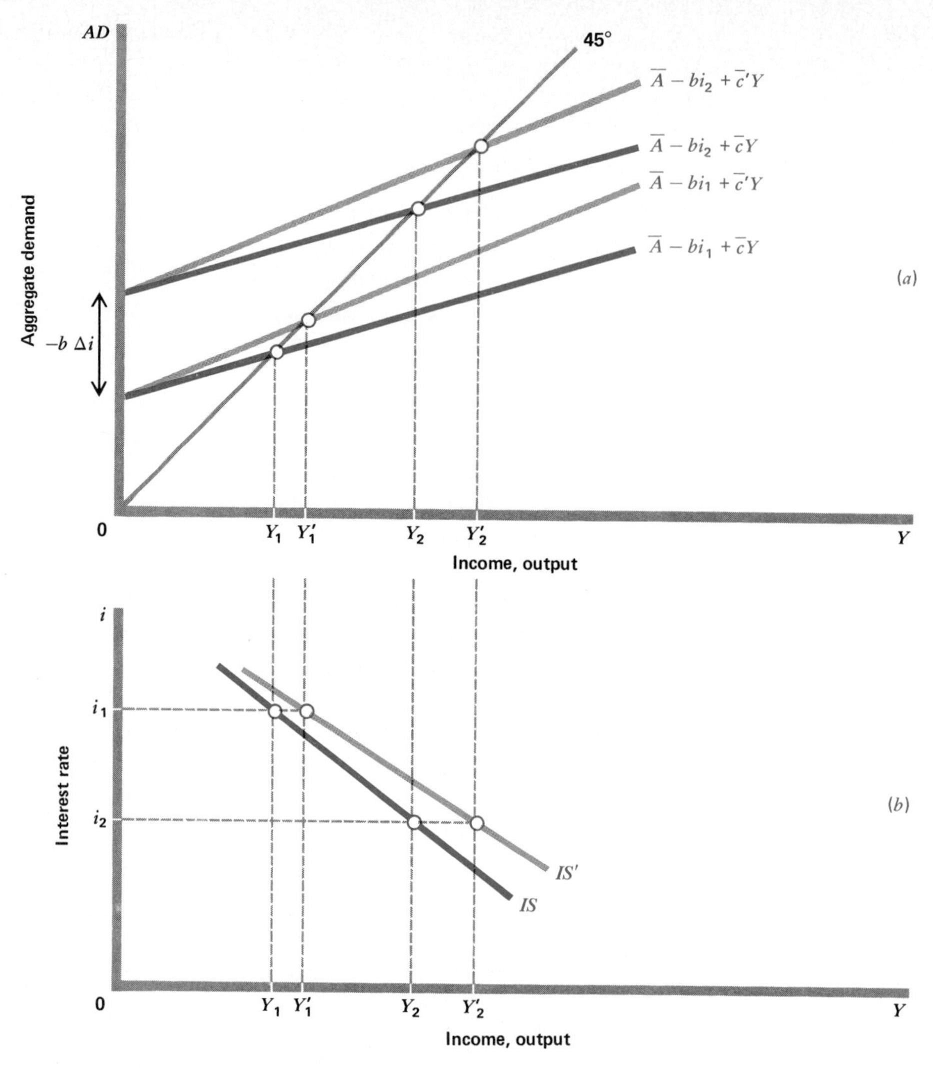

FIGURE 4-5 EFFECTS OF THE MULTIPLIER ON THE STEEPNESS OF THE *IS* CURVE. The diagram shows that corresponding to a higher marginal propensity to spend, and hence a steeper aggregate demand schedule, there is a flatter *IS* schedule.

This conclusion can be confirmed by using Equation (6). We can turn Equation (6) around to express the interest rate as a function of the level of income:

$$i = \frac{\bar{A}}{b} - \frac{Y}{\bar{\alpha} b} \tag{6a}$$

Thus, for a given change in Y, the associated change in i will be larger in size as b is smaller and $\bar{\alpha}$ is smaller.

Given that the slope of the *IS* curve depends on the multiplier, fiscal policy can affect that slope. The multiplier $\bar{\alpha}$ is affected by the tax rate: an increase in the tax rate reduces the multiplier. Accordingly, the higher the tax rate, the steeper the *IS* curve.[4]

The Position of the *IS* Curve

Figure 4-6 shows two different *IS* curves, the lighter one of which lies to the right and above the darker *IS* curve. What might cause the *IS* curve to be at *IS′* rather than at *IS*? The answer is an increase in the level of autonomous spending.

In Figure 4-6*a* we show an initial aggregate demand curve drawn for a level of autonomous spending $\bar{A}$ and for an interest rate i_1. Corresponding to the initial aggregate demand curve is the point E_1 on the *IS* curve in Figure 4-6*b*. Now, at the same interest rate, let the level of autonomous spending increase to $\bar{A}'$. The increase in autonomous spending increases the equilibrium level of income at the interest rate i_1. The point E_2 in Figure 4-6*b* is thus a point on the new goods market equilibrium schedule *IS′*. Since E_1 was an arbitrary point on the initial *IS* curve, we can perform the exercise for all levels of the interest rate and thereby generate our new curve *IS′*. We see that an increase in autonomous spending shifts the curve out to the right.

↑$\bar{A}$ can shift IS curve

By how much does the curve shift? The change in income, as a result of the change in autonomous spending, can be seen from the top panel to be just the multiplier times the change in autonomous spending. That means that the *IS* curve is shifted horizontally by a distance equal to the multiplier times the change in autonomous spending. This can be seen from the fact that the distance between E_1 and E_2, in the lower panel, is the distance between Y_1 and Y_2 in the upper panel.

Now the level of autonomous spending is, from equation (4):

$$\bar{A} \equiv \bar{C} + c\overline{TR} + \bar{I} + \bar{G}$$

Accordingly, an increase in government purchases or transfer payments will shift the *IS* curve out to the right, the extent of the shift depending on the size of the multiplier. A reduction in transfer payments or in government purchases shifts the *IS* curve to the left.

Positions off the *IS* Curve

We gain understanding of the meaning of the *IS* curve by considering points off the curve. Figure 4-7 reproduces Figure 4-4, along with two additional points—the *dis*equilibrium points E_3 and E_4. Consider first the question of what is true for points off the schedule, points such as E_3 and E_4. In Figure 4-7*b* at point E_3 we have the same interest rate i_2 as at point E_2, but the level of income is lower than at E_2. Since the interest rate i_2 at E_3 is the same as at E_2, we must have the same aggregate demand function corresponding to the two

[4] In problem 3 we ask you to relate this fact to the discussion of automatic stabilizers in Chap. 3.

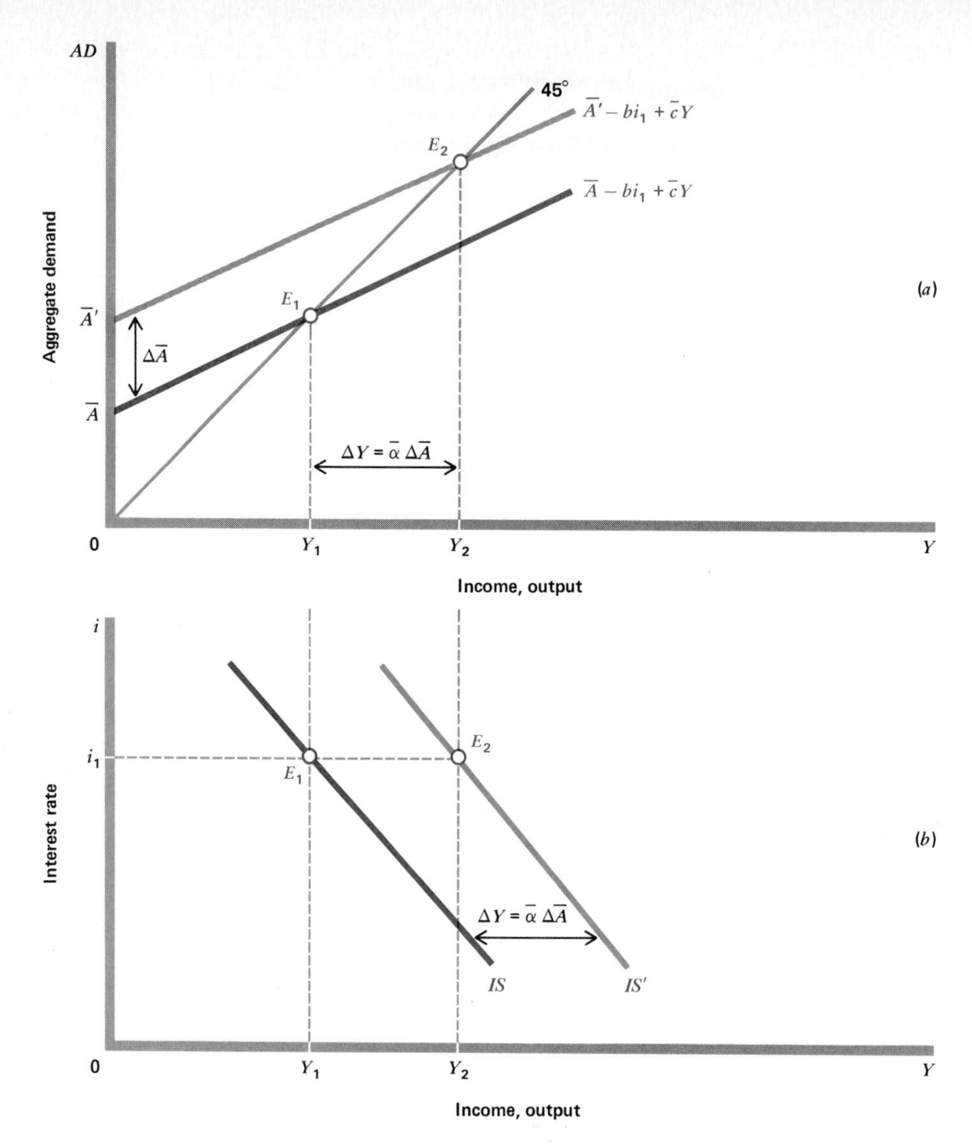

FIGURE 4-6 A SHIFT IN THE *IS* CURVE CAUSED BY A CHANGE IN AUTONOMOUS SPENDING. An increase in aggregate demand due to higher autonomous spending shifts the aggregate demand curve in Figure 4-6(*a*) up, raising the equilibrium level of output at interest rate i_1. The *IS* schedule shifts. At each level of the interest rate, equilibrium income is now higher. The horizontal shift of the *IS* schedule is equal to the multiplier times the increase in autonomous spending.

points. Accordingly, looking now at Figure 4-7*a*, we find both points are on the same aggregate demand schedule. At E_3 on that schedule, aggregate demand exceeds the level of output. Point E_3 is therefore a point of *excess demand for goods:* the interest rate is too low or output is too low for the goods market to be in equilibrium. Demand for goods exceeds output.

Next, consider point E_4 in Figure 4-7*b*. Here we have the same rate of interest i_1 as at E_1, but the level of income is higher. Given the interest rate i_1, the corresponding point in Figure 4-7*a* is at E_4, where we have an *excess supply of goods* since output is larger than aggregate demand—that is, aggregate demand, given the interest rate i_1 and the income level Y_2.

FIGURE 4-7 EXCESS SUPPLY (*ESG*) AND DEMAND (*EDG*) IN THE GOODS MARKET. Points above and to the right of the *IS* schedule correspond to an excess supply of goods, and points below and to the left to an excess demand for goods. At a point such as E_4, interest rates are higher than at E_2 on the *IS* curve. At the higher interest rates, investment spending is too low, and thus output exceeds planned spending and there is an excess supply of goods.

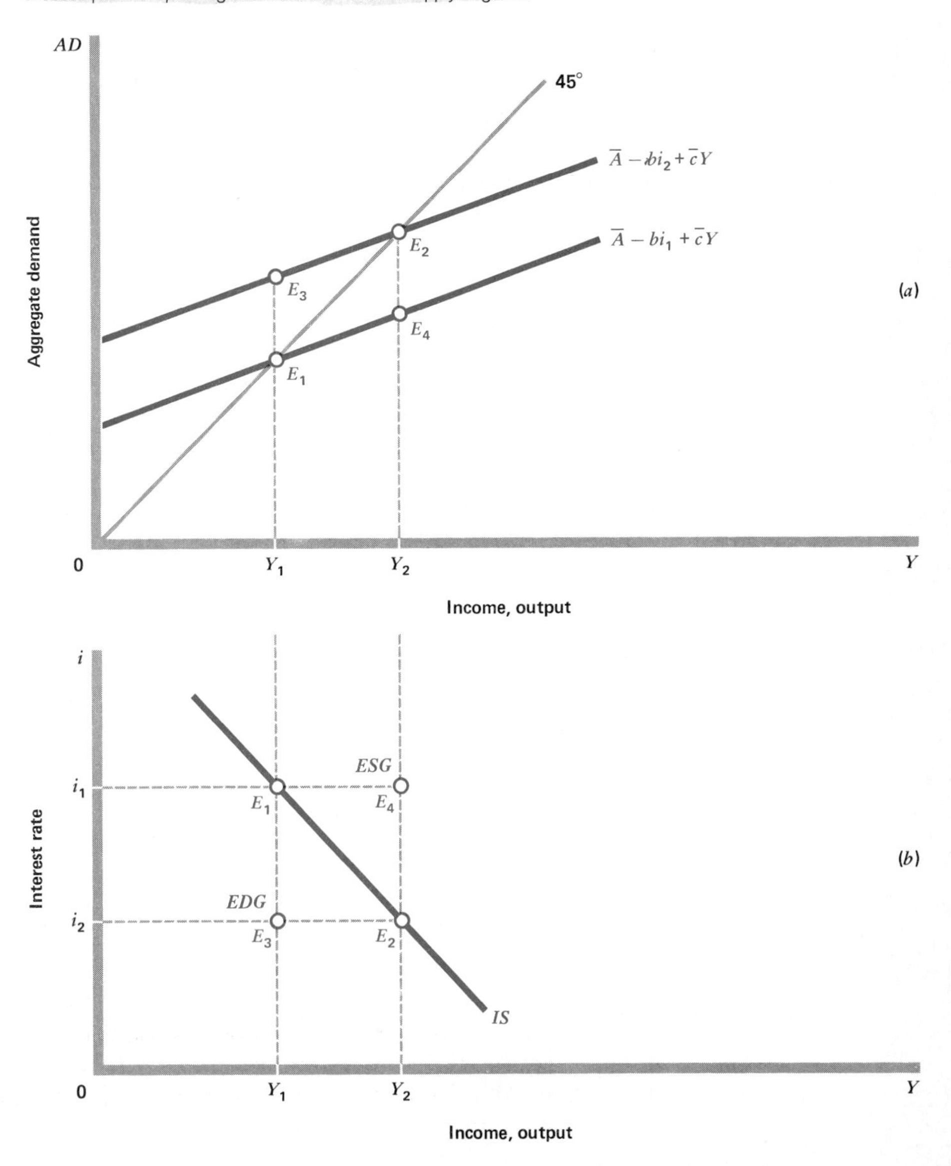

The preceding discussion can be generalized by saying that points above and to the right of the *IS* curve—points like E_4—are points of excess supply of goods. This is indicated by *ESG* (excess supply of goods) in Figure 4-7*b*. Points below and to the left of the *IS* curve are points of excess demand for goods (*EDG*). At a point like E_3, the interest rate is too low and aggregate demand is therefore too high, relative to output. *EDG* shows the region of excess demand in Figure 4-7.

SUMMARY

The major points about the *IS* curve are:

1 The *IS* curve is the schedule of combinations of the interest rate and level of income such that the goods market is in equilibrium.
2 The *IS* curve is negatively sloped because an increase in the interest rate reduces planned investment spending and therefore reduces aggregate demand, thus reducing the equilibrium level of income.
3 The smaller the multiplier and the less sensitive investment spending is to changes in the interest rate, the steeper the curve.
4 The *IS* curve is shifted by changes in autonomous spending. An increase in autonomous spending, including an increase in government purchases, shifts the *IS* curve out to the right.
5 At points to the right of the curve, there is excess supply in the goods market, and at points to the left of the curve, there is excess demand for goods.

We turn now to examine behavior in the assets markets.

4-2 THE ASSETS MARKETS AND THE *LM* CURVE

In the preceding section, we discussed aggregate demand and the goods market. In the present section, we turn to the assets markets. The assets markets are the markets in which money, bonds, stocks, houses, and other forms of wealth are traded. Up to this point in the book, we have ignored the role of those markets in affecting the level of income, and it is now time to remedy the omission.

There is a large variety of assets, and a tremendous volume of trading occurs every day in the assets markets. But we shall simplify matters by grouping all available financial assets into two groups, *money* and *interest-bearing assets.*[5] By analogy with our treatment of the goods market, we

[5] We assume in this section that certain assets, such as the capital that firms use in production, are not traded. That too is a simplification. A more complete treatment of the assets markets would allow for the trading of capital and would introduce a relative price for the capital operated by firms. This treatment is usually reserved for advanced graduate courses. For such a treatment of the assets markets, see James Tobin, "A General Equilibrium Approach to Monetary Theory," *Journal of Money, Credit and Banking,* February 1969, pp. 15–29, and by the same author, "Money, Capital, and Other Stores of Value," *American Economic Review,* May 1961, pp. 26–37.

proceed in the assets markets as if there are only two assets, money and all others. It will be useful to think of the other assets as marketable claims to future income such as *bonds*.

A bond is a promise to pay to its holder certain agreed-upon amounts of money at specified dates in the future. For example, a borrower sells a bond in exchange for a given amount of money today, say, $100, and promises to pay a fixed amount, say, $6, each year to the person who owns the bond, and to repay the full $100 (the principal) after some fixed period of time, such as 3 years, or perhaps longer. In this example, the interest rate is 6 percent, for that is the percentage of the amount borrowed that the borrower pays each year.

BOX 4-1

ASSETS AND ASSET RETURNS

There are four kinds of assets in the economy: money, bonds, equities or stocks, and real assets.

MONEY

The money stock consists of assets that can be immediately used for making payments. Money includes currency (notes and coins) and also deposits on which checks can be written. At the end of 1982, the currency stock was $133 billion, or $570 per person. The stock of deposits on which checks can be written was $345 billion, or about $1,470 per person. Thus the money stock (more detail follows in Chapter 8) was $478 billion, which implies that the amount of money held in the economy was over $2,000 per person.

Until the mid-1970s (and from the 1930s) no interest was paid on checkable deposits. During that period people held checkable deposits purely for the convenience. Now interest is paid on checkable deposits, which people hold both because they pay interest and because they are a convenient way of making payments.

BONDS

A bond is a promise by a borrower to pay the lender a certain amount (the principal) at a specified date (the maturity date of the bond) and in the meantime to pay a given amount of interest per year. Thus we might have a bond, issued by the U.S. Treasury, that pays $10,000 on June 1, 1985, and until that time pays 8 percent interest per year, or $800 each year. Bonds are issued by many types of borrower—the government, municipalities, corporations. The interest rates on bonds issued by different borrowers reflect the differing risk of default. Default occurs when a borrower is unable to meet the commitment to pay interest or principal. Corporations sometimes default, and during the great depression of the 1930s, so did some cities. In the late 1970s there was fear that New York City would default, and in the early 1980s there was the same fear that many foreign governments would do so.

By the end of 1980, individuals in the United States held a total of $2.0 trillion in the form of bonds. Over half that amount was in the form of debt of banks—time and saving deposits. Nearly $300 billion consisted of government bonds held by individuals. Individuals held relatively small amounts of corporate bonds—under $100 billion.

EQUITIES OR STOCKS

Equities or stocks are claims to a share of the profits in an enterprise. For example, a share in Texas Instruments entitles the owner to a share of the profits of that corporation. The shareholder or stockholder receives the return on equity in two forms. Most firms pay regular *dividends*, which means that stockholders receive a certain amount of dollars for each share they own. Firms may also decide not to distribute profits to the stockholders, but rather retain them and reinvest these profits by adding to their stock of machines and structures. When this occurs, the shares become more valuable since they now represent claims on the profits from a larger capital stock. Therefore, the price of the stock in the market will rise, and stockholders make *capital gains*. A capital gain is an increase, per period of time, in the price of an asset. Of course, when the outlook for a corporation turns sour, stock prices can fall and stockholders make capital losses.

Thus the return on stocks or the yield to a holder of a stock is equal to the dividend (as a percent of price) plus the capital gain.

Suppose we look at 1983 and 1984 and consider the yield on a stock in an imaginary company, BioMiracles, Inc. In 1983 the stock trades for $15. In 1984 the stock pays a dividend of $0.75 and the stock price increases to $16.50. What is the yield on the stock? The yield per year is equal to 15.0 percent, which is the dividend as a percent of initial price [5 percent = $(0.75/15) \times 100$] plus 10.0 percent, which is the $1.50 capital gain as a percent of initial price.

At the end of 1980 the value of equity held by individuals in the United States was $1.2 trillion.

REAL ASSETS

Real assets, or tangible assets, are the machines, land, and structures owned by corporations, and the consumer durables (washing machines, stereos, etc.) and houses owned by households. These assets carry a return that differs from one asset to another. Owner-occupied houses provide a return to owners who enjoy living in them and not paying monthly rent; the machines a firm owns contribute to producing output and thus making profits. The assets are called *real* to distinguish them from *financial* assets (money, stocks, bonds). The total value of tangible assets at the end of 1980 was $8.8 trillion, or nearly $39,000 per person.

The value of equities and bonds held by individuals cannot be added to tangible wealth to get the total wealth of individuals. The reason is that the equities and bonds they hold are claims on part of the tangible wealth, that part held by corporations. The equity share gives an individual a part ownership in the factory and machinery. In 1980, the *net* value of assets held by individuals was $8.6 trillion, over $3.7 trillion of that in tangible form (houses, cars, land, etc.).

In macroeconomics, to make things manageable, we lump assets into two categories. On one side we have money, with the specific characteristic that it is the only asset that serves as a means of payment. On the other side we have all other assets. Because money offers the convenience of being a means of payment, it carries a lower return than other assets, but that differential depends on the relative supplies of assets. As we see in this chapter, when the Fed reduces the money stock and increases the supply of other assets (we say "bonds"), the yield on other assets increases.

The Appendix to Chapter 7 develops the relationship between interest rates and asset prices or present values. The Appendix can be read independently of Chapter 7, and the interested student can study that material now.

The Wealth Constraint

At any given time, an individual has to decide how to allocate her financial wealth between alternative assets. The more bonds held, the more interest received on total financial wealth. The more money held, the less likely the individual is not to have money available when she wants to make a purchase. The person who has $1,000 in financial wealth has to decide whether to hold, say, $900 in bonds and $100 in money, or rather, $500 in each type of asset, or even $1,000 in money and none in bonds. Decisions on the form in which to hold assets are *portfolio decisions.*

The example makes it clear that the portfolio decision on how much money to hold and the decision on how many bonds to hold are really the same decision. Given the level of financial wealth, the individual who has decided how many bonds to hold has implicitly also decided how much money to hold. There is thus a *wealth budget constraint* which states that the sum of the individual's demand for money and demand for bonds has to add up to that person's total financial wealth.

REAL AND NOMINAL MONEY DEMAND

At this stage we have to reinforce the crucial distinction between *real* and *nominal* variables. The nominal demand for money is the individual's demand for a given number of dollars, and similarly, the nominal demand for bonds is the demand for a given number of dollars' worth of bonds. The real demand for money is the demand for money expressed in terms of the number of units of goods that money will buy: it is equal to the nominal demand for money divided by the price level. If the nominal demand for money is $100 and the price level is $2 per good—meaning that the representative basket of goods costs $2—then the real demand for money is 50 goods. If the price level later doubles to $4 per good and the demand for nominal money likewise doubles to $200, the real demand for money is unchanged at 50 goods.

Real money balances—real balances for short—are the quantity of nominal money divided by the price level, and the real demand for money is called the *demand for real balances.* Similarly, real bond holdings are the nominal quantity of bonds divided by the price level.

The wealth budget constraint in the assets markets states that the demand for real balances, which we denote L, plus the demand for real bond holdings, which we denote DB, must add up to the real financial wealth of the individual. Real financial wealth is, of course, simply nominal wealth WN divided by the price level P:

$$L + DB \equiv \frac{WN}{P} \tag{7}$$

Note, again, that the wealth budget constraint implies, given an individual's real wealth, that a decision to hold more real balances is also a decision to hold less real wealth in the form of bonds. This implication turns out to be both important and convenient. It will allow us to discuss assets markets entirely in terms of the money market. Why? Because, given real wealth, when the money market is in equilibrium, the bond market will turn out also to be in equilibrium. We now show why that should be.

The total amount of real financial wealth in the economy consists of real money balances and real bonds in existence. Thus, total real financial wealth is equal to

$$\frac{WN}{P} \equiv \frac{M}{P} + SB \tag{8}$$

where M is the stock of nominal money balances and SB is the real value of the supply of bonds. Total real financial wealth consists of real balances and real bonds. The distinction between Equations (7) and (8) is that Equation (7) is a constraint on the amount of assets individuals wish to hold, whereas Equation (8) is merely an accounting relationship which tells us how much financial wealth there is in the economy. There is no implication in the accounting relationship in Equation (8) that individuals are necessarily happy to hold the amounts of money and bonds that actually exist in the economy.

Now we substitute Equation (7) into Equation (8) and rearrange terms to obtain

$$\left(L - \frac{M}{P}\right) + (DB - SB) \equiv 0 \tag{9}$$

Let us see what Equation (9) implies. Suppose that the demand for real balances L is equal to the existing stock of real balances M/P. Then the first term in parentheses in Equation (9) is equal to zero, and therfore the second term in parentheses must also be zero. Thus, if the demand for real money balances is equal to the real money supply, the demand for real bonds DB must be equal to the supply of real bonds SB.

Stating the same proposition in terms of "markets," we can say the following: The *wealth budget constraint* implies that when the money market is in equilibrium ($L = M/P$), the bond market, too, is in equilibrium ($DB = SB$). Similarly, when there is excess demand in the money market, so that $L > M/P$, there is an excess supply of bonds; $DB < SB$. We can therefore fully discuss the assets markets by concentrating our attention on the money market.

The Demand for Money

We now turn to the money market and initially concentrate on the demand for real balances.[6] The demand for money is a demand for *real* balances because the public holds money for what it will buy. The higher the price level, the more nominal balances a person has to hold to be able to purchase a given

[6] The demand for money is studied in depth in Chap. 8; here we only briefly present the arguments underlying the demand for money.

quantity of goods. If the price level doubles, then an individual has to hold twice as many nominal balances in order to be able to buy the same amount of goods.

The demand for real balances depends on the level of real income and the interest rate. It depends on the level of real income because individuals hold money to finance their expenditures, which, in turn, depend on income. The demand for money depends also on the cost of holding money. The cost of holding money is the interest that is foregone by holding money rather than other assets. The higher the interest rate, the more costly it is to hold money, rather than other assets, and accordingly, the less cash will be held at each level of income.[7] Individuals can economize on their holdings of cash, when the interest rate rises, by being more careful in managing their money, by making transfers from money to bonds whenever their money holdings reach any appreciable magnitude. If the interest rate is 1 percent, then there is very little benefit from holding bonds rather than money. However, when the interest rate is 10 percent, one would probably go to some effort not to hold more money than needed to finance day-to-day transactions.

On these simple grounds, then, the demand for real balances increases with the level of real income and decreases with the interest rate. The demand for real balances is accordingly written[8]

$$L = kY - hi \qquad k > 0 \qquad h > 0 \tag{10}$$

The parameters k and h reflect the sensitivity of the demand for real balances to the level of income and the interest rate, respectively. A \$5 increase in real income raises money demand by $5k$ real dollars. An increase in the interest rate by 1 percentage point reduces real money demand by h real dollars.

The demand function for real balances, Equation (10), implies that for a given level of income, the quantity demanded is a decreasing function of the rate of interest. Such a demand curve is shown in Figure 4-8 for a level of income Y_1. The higher the level of income, the larger the demand for real balances, and therefore the further to the right the demand curve. The demand curve for a higher level of real income Y_2 is also shown in Figure 4-8.

The Supply of Money, Money Market Equilibrium, and the *LM* Curve

Now we study equilibrium in the money market. For that purpose we have to say how the supply of money is determined. The nominal quantity of money M

[7] As we discuss in Chap. 9, changes in financial regulations in the early 1980s led to the payment of interest on some forms of money holdings. In Chap. 8 we discuss the effects of such changes on the demand for money and on the *LM* curve. But there do remain sizable parts of money holding—including currency—on which no interest is paid, so that overall, money earns less interest than other assets and the analysis of this chapter is still applicable.

[8] Once again, we use a linear equation to describe a relationship. You should experiment with an alternative form, for example, $L = kY + h'/i$, where k and h' are positive. How would the equivalent of Figure 4-8 look for this demand function?

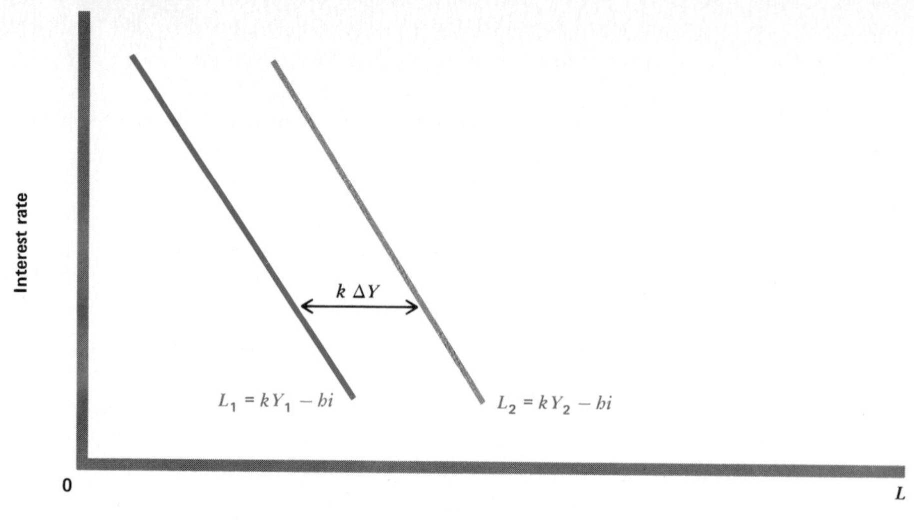

FIGURE 4-8 THE DEMAND FOR REAL BALANCES AS A FUNCTION OF THE INTEREST RATE AND REAL INCOME. The demand for real balances is drawn as a function of the rate of interest. The higher the rate of interest, the lower the quantity of real balances demanded, given the level of income. An increase in income raises the demand for money. This is shown by a rightward shift of the money demand schedule.

is controlled by the Federal Reserve System, and we take it as given at the level $\overline{M}$. We assume the price level is constant at the level $\overline{P}$, so that the real money supply is at the level $\overline{M}/\overline{P}$.[9]

In Figure 4-9, we show combinations of interest rate and income levels such that the demand for real balances exactly matches the available supply. Starting with the level of income Y_1, we have the corresponding demand curve for real balances L_1, in Figure 4-9*b*. It is drawn, as in Figure 4-8, as a decreasing function of the interest rate. The existing supply of real balances $\overline{M}/\overline{P}$ is shown by the vertical line, since it is given and therefore is independent of the interest rate. The interest rate i_1 has the property that it clears the money market. At that interest rate, the demand for real balances equals the supply. Therefore, point E_1 is an equilibrium point in the money market. That point is recorded in Figure 4-9*a* as a point on the *money market equilibrium schedule*, or the *LM curve*.

Consider next the effect of an increase in income to Y_2. In Figure 4-9*b* the higher level of income causes the demand for real balances to be higher at each level of the interest rate, and so the demand curve for real balances shifts

[9] Since for the present we are holding constant the money supply and price level, we refer to them as exogenous and denote that fact by a bar.

up and to the right, to L_2. We require an increase in the interest rate to i_2 to maintain equilibrium in the money market at that higher level of income. Accordingly, our new equilibrium point is E_2. In Figure 4-9*a* we record point E_2 as a point of equilibrium in the money market. Performing the same exercise for all income levels, we generate a series of points that can be linked up to give us the *LM* schedule.

The *LM* schedule, or money market equilibrium schedule, shows all combinations of interest rates and levels of income such that the demand for real balances is equal to the supply. Along the *LM* schedule, the money market is in equilibrium.

The *LM* curve is positively sloped. An increase in the interest rate reduces the demand for real balances. To maintain the demand for real balances equal to the fixed supply, the level of income has, therefore, to rise. Accordingly, money market equilibrium implies that an increase in the interest rate is accompanied by an increase in the level of income.

The *LM* curve can be obtained directly by combining the demand curve for real balances, Equation (10), and the fixed supply of real balances. For the money market to be in equilibrium, we require that demand equals supply, or that

$$\frac{\overline{M}}{\overline{P}} = kY - hi \tag{11}$$

FIGURE 4-9 DERIVATION OF THE *LM* CURVE. The right-hand panel shows the money market. The supply of real balances is the vertical line $\overline{M}/\overline{P}$. The nominal money supply $\overline{M}$ is fixed by the Fed, and the price level $\overline{P}$ is assumed given. Demand for money curves L_1 and L_2 corresponds to different levels of income. When the income level is Y_1, L_1 applies, and the equilibrium interest rate is i_1. This gives point E_1 on the *LM* schedule in Figure 4-9(*a*). At income level Y_2, greater than Y_1, the equilibrium interest rate is i_2, yielding point E_2 on the *LM* curve.

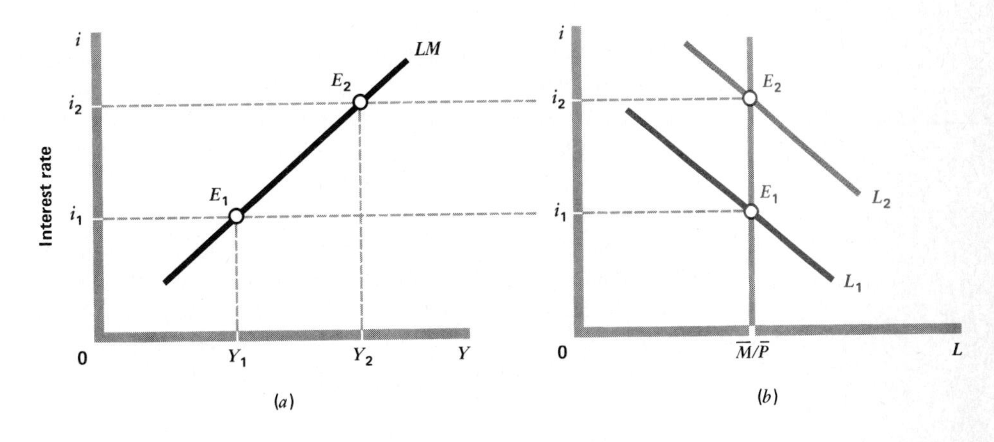

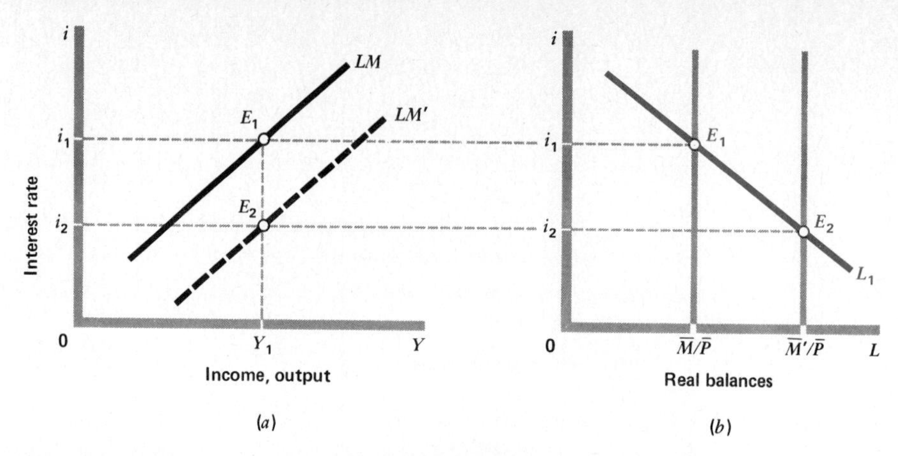

FIGURE 4-10 AN INCREASE IN THE SUPPLY OF MONEY FROM $\overline{M}$ TO $\overline{M}'$ SHIFTS THE *LM* CURVE TO THE RIGHT. An increase in the stock of real balances shifts the supply schedule in the right panel from $\overline{M}/\overline{P}$ to $\overline{M}'/\overline{P}$. At the initial income level Y_1, the equilibrium interest rate in the money market falls to i_2. In the left panel we show point E_2 as one point on the new *LM* schedule, corresponding to the higher money stock. Thus an increase in the real money stock shifts the *LM* schedule down and to the right.

Solving for the interest rate, we have

$$i = \frac{1}{h}\left(kY - \frac{\overline{M}}{\overline{P}}\right) \tag{11a}$$

The relationship (11*a*) is the *LM* curve.

Next we ask the same questions about the properties of the *LM* schedule that we asked about the *IS* curve.

The Slope of the *LM* Curve

The larger the responsiveness of the demand for money to income, as measured by k, and the lower the responsiveness of the demand for money to the interest rate h, the steeper the *LM* curve will be. This point can be established by experimenting with Figure 4-9. It can also be confirmed by examining Equation (11*a*), where a given change in income ΔY has a larger effect on the interest rate i, the larger is k and the smaller is h. If the demand for money is relatively insensitive to the interest rate, so that h is close to zero, the *LM* curve is nearly vertical. If the demand for money is very sensitive to the interest rate, so that h is large, then the *LM* curve is close to horizontal. In that case, a small change in the interest rate is accompanied by a large change in the level of income to maintain money market equilibrium.

The Position of the *LM* Curve

The real money supply is held constant along the *LM* curve. It follows that a change in the real money supply will shift the *LM* curve. In Figure 4-10, we show the effect of an increase in the real money supply. In Figure 4-10*b*, we draw the demand for real money balances for a level of income Y_1. With the initial real money supply $\overline{M}/\overline{P}$, the equilibrium is at point E_1, with an interest rate i_1. The corresponding point on the *LM* schedule is E_1.

Consider the effect of an increase in the real money supply to $\overline{M}'/\overline{P}$, which is represented by a rightward shift of the money supply schedule. At the initial level of income and, hence, on the demand schedule L_1, we now have an excess supply of real balances. To restore money market equilibrium at the income level Y_1, the interest rate has to decline to i_2. The new equilibrium is, therefore, at point E_2. This implies that in Figure 4-10*a*, the *LM* schedule shifts to the right and down to *LM*′. At each level of income the equilibrium interest rate has to be lower to induce people to hold the larger real quantity of money. Alternatively, at each level of the interest rate the level of income has to be higher so as to raise the transactions demand for money and thereby absorb the higher real money supply. These points can be noted, too, from inspection of the money market equilibrium condition in Equation (11).

FIGURE 4-11 EXCESS DEMAND (*EDM*) AND SUPPLY (*ESM*) OF MONEY. Points above and to the left of the *LM* schedule correspond to an excess supply of real balances; points below and to the right to an excess demand for real balances. Starting at point E_1 in the left panel, an increase in income takes us to E_4. At E_4 in the right panel, there is an excess demand for money—and thus at E_4 in the left panel there is an excess demand for money. By a similar argument, we can start at E_2 and move to E_3, at which the level of income is lower. This creates an excess supply of money.

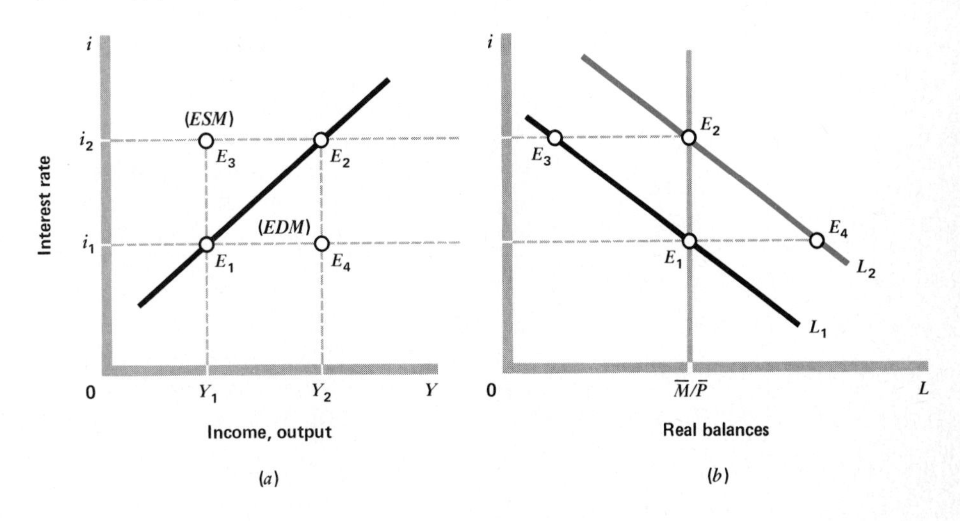

Positions off the *LM* Curve

Next we consider points off the *LM* schedule, to characterize them as points of excess demand or supply of money. For that purpose, we look at Figure 4-11, which reproduces Figure 4-9 but adds the disequilibrium points E_3 and E_4. Look first at point E_1, where the money market is in equilibrium. Next assume an increase in the level of income to Y_2. This will raise the demand for real balances and shift the demand curve to L_2. At the initial interest rate, the demand for real balances would be indicated by point E_4 in Figure 4-11*b*, and we would have an excess demand for money—an excess of demand over supply—equal to the distance E_1E_4. Accordingly, point E_4 in Figure 4-11*a* is a point of excess demand for money: the interest rate is too low and/or the level of income too high for the money market to clear. Consider, next, point E_3 in Figure 4-11*b*. Here we have the initial level of income Y_1, but an interest rate that is too high to yield money market equilibrium. Accordingly, we have an excess supply of money equal to the distance E_3E_2. Point E_3 in Figure 4-11*a* therefore corresponds to an excess supply of money.

More generally, any point to the right and below the *LM* schedule is a point of excess demand for money, and any point to the left and above the *LM* curve is a point of excess supply. This is shown by the *EDM* and *ESM* notations in Figure 4-11*a*.

SUMMARY

The following are the major points about the *LM* curve.

1 The *LM* curve is the schedule of combinations of the interest rate and level of income such that the money market is in equilibrium.
2 When the money market is in equilibrium, so is the bond market in equilibrium. The *LM* curve is, therefore, also the schedule of combinations of the level of income and the interest rate such that the bond market is in equilibrium.
3 The *LM* curve is positively sloped. Given the fixed money supply, an increase in the level of income, which increases the quantity of money demanded, has to be accompanied by an increase in the interest rate. This reduces the quantity of money demanded and thereby maintains money market equilibrium.
4 The *LM* curve is shifted by changes in the money supply. An increase in the money supply shifts the *LM* curve out to the right.
5 At points to the right of the *LM* curve, there is an excess demand for money, and at points to its left, there is an excess supply of money.

We are now ready to discuss the joint equilibrium of the goods and assets markets.

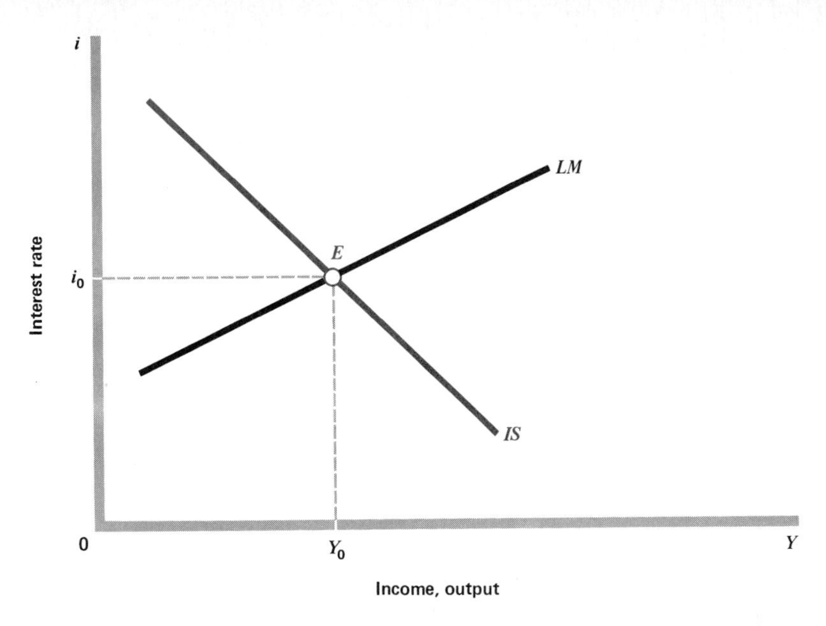

FIGURE 4-12 GOODS AND ASSETS MARKET EQUILIBRIUM. Goods and assets markets clear at point *E*. Interest rates and income are such that the public holds the existing stock of money and planned spending equals output.

4-3 EQUILIBRIUM IN THE GOODS AND ASSETS MARKETS

We have so far studied the conditions that have to be satisfied for the goods and money markets, respectively, to be in equilibrium. These conditions are summarized by the *IS* and *LM* schedules. The task now is to determine how these markets are brought into *simultaneous* equilibrium. For simultaneous equilibrium, interest rates and income have to be such that *both* the goods market *and* the money market are in equilibrium. That condition is satisfied at point *E* in Figure 4-12. The equilibrium interest rate is therefore i_0, and the equilibrium level of income is Y_0, given the exogenous variables, in particular, the real money supply and fiscal policy.[10] At point *E*, both the goods market and the assets markets are in equilibrium.

Figure 4-12 summarizes our analysis: the interest rate and the level of output are determined by the interaction of the assets (*LM*) and goods (*IS*) markets.

It is worth stepping back now to review our assumptions and the meaning of the equilibrium at *E*. The major assumption that we are making is that the price level is constant and that firms are willing to supply whatever amount of output is demanded at that price level. Thus, we assume the level of output Y_0 in Figure 4-12 will be willingly supplied by firms at the price level $\overline{P}$. We

[10] Recall that exogenous variables are those whose values are not determined within the system being studied.

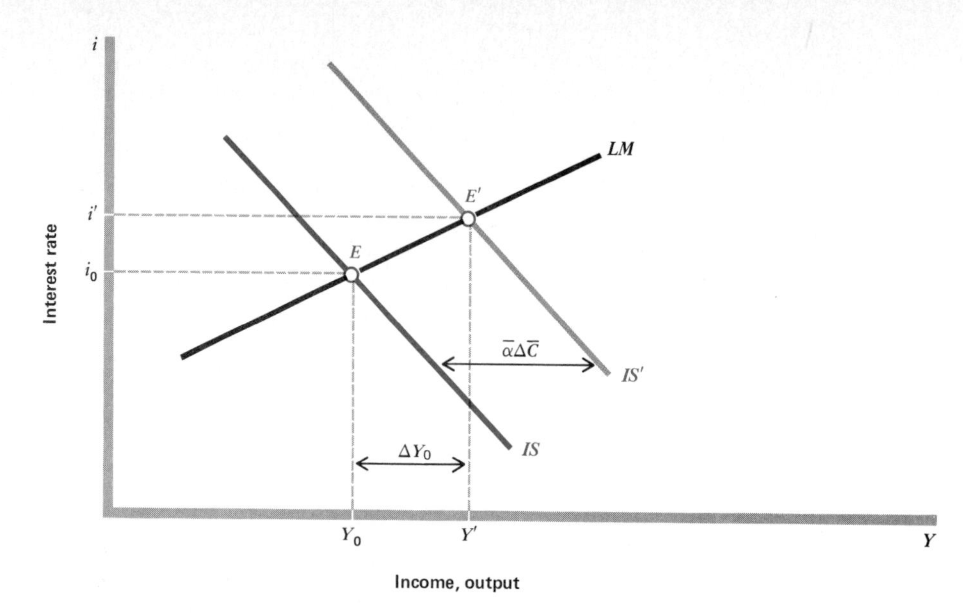

FIGURE 4-13 EFFECTS OF AN INCREASE IN AUTONOMOUS SPENDING ON INCOME AND THE INTEREST RATE. An increase in autonomous spending shifts the *IS* schedule out and to the right. Income increases, and the equilibrium income level rises. The increase in income is less than is given by the simple multiplier $\bar{\alpha}$. This is because interest rates increase and dampen investment spending.

repeat again that this assumption is one that is temporarily needed for the development of the analysis; it will be dropped in Chapter 11 when we begin to study the determinants of the price level.

At the point *E*, in Figure 4-12, the economy is in equilibrium, given the price level, because both the goods and money markets are in equilibrium. The demand for goods is equal to the level of ouput on the *IS* curve. And on the *LM* curve, the demand for money is equal to the supply of money. That also means the supply of bonds is equal to the demand for bonds, as our discussion of the wealth budget constraint showed. Accordingly, at point *E*, firms are producing the amount of output they plan to (there is no unintended inventory accumulation or decumulation), and individuals have the portfolio compositions they desire.

Changes in the Equilibrium Levels of Income and the Interest Rate

The equilibrium levels of income and the interest rate will change when either the *IS* or the *LM* curve shifts. Figure 4-13, for example, shows the effects of an increase in the rate of autonomous consumption $\bar{C}$ on the equilibrium levels of income and the interest rate. Such an increase raises autonomous spending $\bar{A}$, and therefore shifts the *IS* curve to the right. That results in a rise in the level of income and an increase in the interest rate at point *E'*.

We recall that an increase in autonomous spending, equal to $\Delta\overline{C}$, shifts the *IS* curve to the right by the amount $\overline{\alpha}\ \Delta\overline{C}$, as we show in Figure 4-13. In Chapter 3, where we dealt only with the goods market, we would have argued that $\overline{\alpha}\ \Delta\overline{C}$ would be the change in the level of income resulting from the change of $\Delta\overline{C}$ in autonomous spending. But it can be seen in Figure 4-13 that the change in income here is only ΔY_0, which is clearly less than the shift in the *IS* curve $\overline{\alpha}\ \Delta\overline{C}$.

What explains the fact that the increase in income is smaller than the increase in autonomous spending $\Delta\overline{C}$ times the simple multiplier $\overline{\alpha}$? Diagrammatically, it is clear that it is the slope of the *LM* curve. If the *LM* curve were horizontal, there would be no difference between the extent of the horizontal shift of the *IS* curve and the change in income. If the *LM* curve were horizontal, then the interest rate would not change when the *IS* curve shifts.

What is the economics of what is happening? The increase in autonomous spending does tend to increase the level of income. But an increase in income increases the demand for money. With the supply of money fixed, the interest rate has to rise to ensure that the demand for money stays equal to the fixed supply. When the interest rate rises, investment spending is reduced because investment is negatively related to the interest rate. Accordingly, the equilibrium change in income is less than the horizontal shift of the *IS* curve, $\overline{\alpha}\ \Delta\overline{C}$.

We have now provided an example of the use of the *IS-LM* apparatus. That apparatus is most useful for studying the effects of monetary and fiscal policy on income and the interest rate, and we so use it in Sections 4-5 and 4-6 and Chapter 5. Before we do, however, we discuss how the economy moves from one equilibrium, such as *E*, to another, such as *E′*.

4-4 ADJUSTMENT TOWARD EQUILIBRIUM

Suppose the economy were initially at a point like *E* in Figure 4-13, and that one of the curves then shifted, so that the new equilibrium was at a point like *E′*. How would that new equilibrium actually be reached? The adjustment will involve changes in both the interest rate and the level of income. To study how they move over time, we make two assumptions:

1 Output increases whenever there is an excess demand for goods and contracts whenever there is an excess supply of goods. This assumption reflects the adjustment of firms to undesired decumulation and accumulation of inventories.
2 The interest rate rises whenever there is an excess demand for money and falls whenever there is an excess supply of money. This adjustment occurs because an excess demand for money implies an excess supply of other assets (bonds). In attempting to acquire more money, people sell off bonds and thereby cause their prices to fall or their yields (interest rate) to rise.

A detailed discussion of the relationship between the price of a bond and its yield is presented in the Appendix to Chapter 7. Here we give only a brief

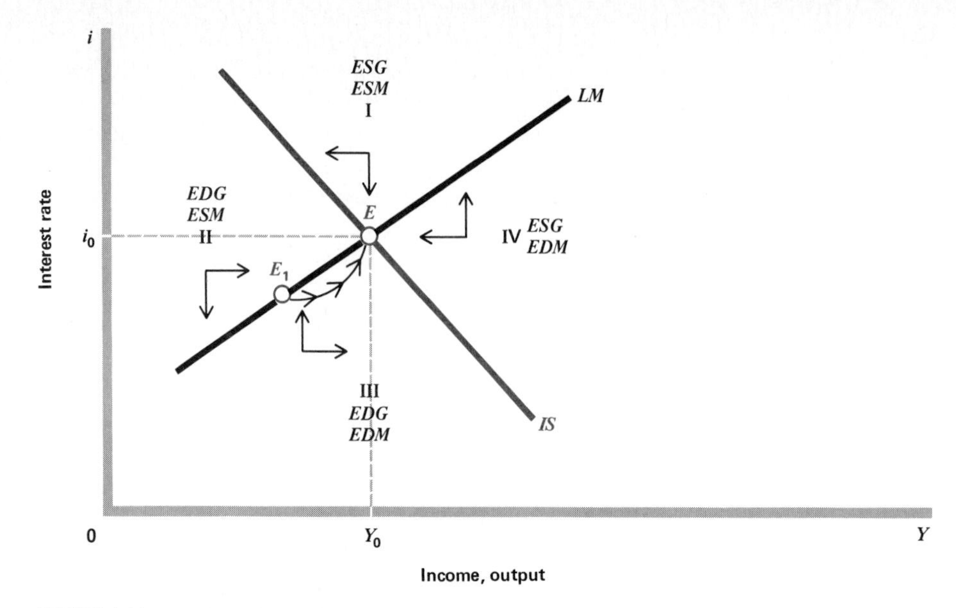

FIGURE 4-14 DISEQUILIBRIUM AND DYNAMICS IN THE GOODS AND MONEY MARKETS. Income and interest rates adjust to the disequilibrium in goods markets and assets markets. Specifically, interest rates fall when there is an excess supply of money and rise when there is an excess demand. Income rises when aggregate demand for goods exceeds output and falls when aggregate demand is less than output. The system converges over time to the equilibrium at *E*.

explanation. For simplicity, consider a bond which promises to pay the holder of the bond \$5 per year forever. The \$5 is known as the bond *coupon*, and a bond which promises to pay a given amount to the holder of the bond forever is known as a *perpetuity*. If the yield available on other assets is 5 percent, the perpetuity will sell for \$100 because at that price it too yields 5 percent (=\$5/\$100). Now suppose that the yield on other assets rises to 10 percent. Then the price of the perpetuity will drop to \$50, because only at that price does the perpetuity yield 10 percent; that is, the \$5 per year interest on a bond costing \$50 gives its owners a 10 percent yield on their \$50. This example makes it clear that the price of a bond and its yield are inversely related, given the coupon.

In point 2 above we assumed that an excess demand for money causes asset holders to attempt to sell off their bonds, thereby causing their prices to fall and their yields to rise. Conversely, when there is an excess supply of money, people attempt to use their money to buy up other assets, raising their prices and lowering their yields.

In Figure 4-14 we apply the analysis to study the adjustment of the economy. Four regions are represented, and they are characterized in Table 4-1. We know from Figure 4-11 that there is an excess supply of money above the *LM* curve, and hence we show *ESM* in regions I and II in Table 4-1. Similarly, we know from Figure 4-7 that there is an excess demand for goods

TABLE 4-1 DISEQUILIBRIUM AND ADJUSTMENT

	GOODS MARKET		MONEY MARKET	
Region	Disequilibrium	Adjustment: Output	Disequilibrium	Adjustment: Interest rate
I	*ESG*	Falls	*ESM*	Falls
II	*EDG*	Rises	*ESM*	Falls
III	*EDG*	Rises	*EDM*	Rises
IV	*ESG*	Falls	*EDM*	Rises

below the *IS* curve. Hence, we show *EDG* for regions II and III in Table 4-1. You should be able to explain the remaining entries of Table 4-1.

The adjustment directions specified in assumptions 1 and 2 above are represented by arrows. Thus, for example, in region IV we have an excess demand for money that causes interest rates to rise as other assets are sold off for money and their prices decline. The rising interest rates are represented by the upward-pointing arrow. There is, too, an excess supply of goods in region IV, and, accordingly, involuntary inventory accumulation to which firms respond by reducing output. Declining output is indicated by the leftward-pointing arrow. The adjustments shown by the arrows will lead ultimately, perhaps in a cyclical manner, to the equilibrium point *E*. For example, starting at E_1 we show the economy moving to *E*, with income and the interest rate increasing along the *adjustment path* indicated.

RAPID ASSET MARKET ADJUSTMENT

For many purposes it is useful to restrict the dynamics by the reasonable assumption that the money market adjusts very quickly and the goods market adjusts relatively slowly. Since the money market can adjust merely through the buying and selling of bonds, the interest rate adjusts rapidly and the money market effectively is always in equilibrium. Such an assumption implies that we are always on the *LM* curve: any departure from the equilibrium in the money market is almost instantaneously eliminated by an appropriate change in the interest rate. In disequilibrium, we therefore move along the *LM* curve, as is shown in Figure 4-15.

The goods market adjusts relatively slowly because firms have to change their production schedules, which takes time. For points below the *IS* curve, we move up along the *LM* schedule with rising income and interest rates, and for points above the *IS* schedule, we move down along the *LM* schedule with falling output and interest rates until point *E* is reached. The adjustment process is *stable* in that the economy does move to the equilibrium position at *E*.

The adjustment process shown in Figure 4-15 is very similar to that of Chapter 3. To the right of the *IS* curve, there is an excess supply of goods, and firms are therefore accumulating inventories. They cut production in re-

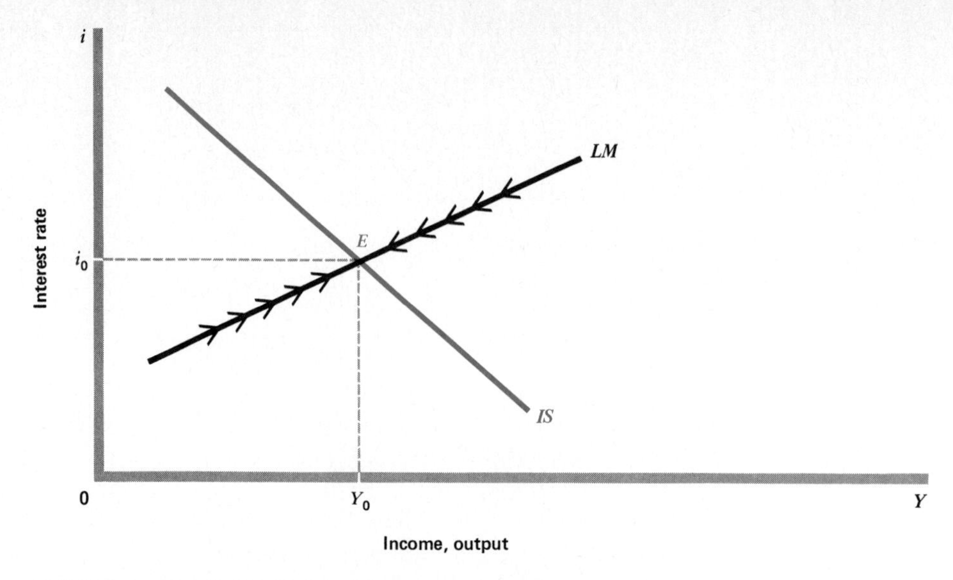

FIGURE 4-15 ADJUSTMENT TO EQUILIBRIUM WHEN THE MONEY MARKET ADJUSTS QUICKLY. If the money market adjusts very rapidly, then the economy is always in monetary equilibrium. In the diagram this corresponds to always being on the *LM* schedule. When there is excess demand for goods, output and interest rates are rising, and when there is excess supply of goods, output and interest rates are falling.

sponse to their inventory buildup, and the economy moves down the *LM* curve. The difference between the adjustment process here and in Chapter 3 is the following: here, as the economy moves toward the equilibrium level of income, with a falling interest rate, desired investment spending is actually rising.[11]

Now that we have established that the economy does adjust toward its equilibrium position, we turn to examine the effects of monetary and fiscal policy on the equilibrium interest rate and level of income.

4-5 MONETARY POLICY

In this section we are concerned with the effect of an increase in the real quantity of money on the interest rate and level of income. We break up that inquiry into two separate questions. First, what is the ultimate effect of the increase in the money supply when the new equilibrium is reached? Second, how is that new equilibrium reached, or what is the transmission mechanism?

Through monetary policy the Federal Reserve affects the quantity of money and thereby the interest rate and income. The chief instrument,

[11] In a more detailed analysis, one would want to allow for the possibility that desired investment would be cut back in response to excess inventories. This again raises the possibility of the inventory cycle, referred to in Chap. 3.

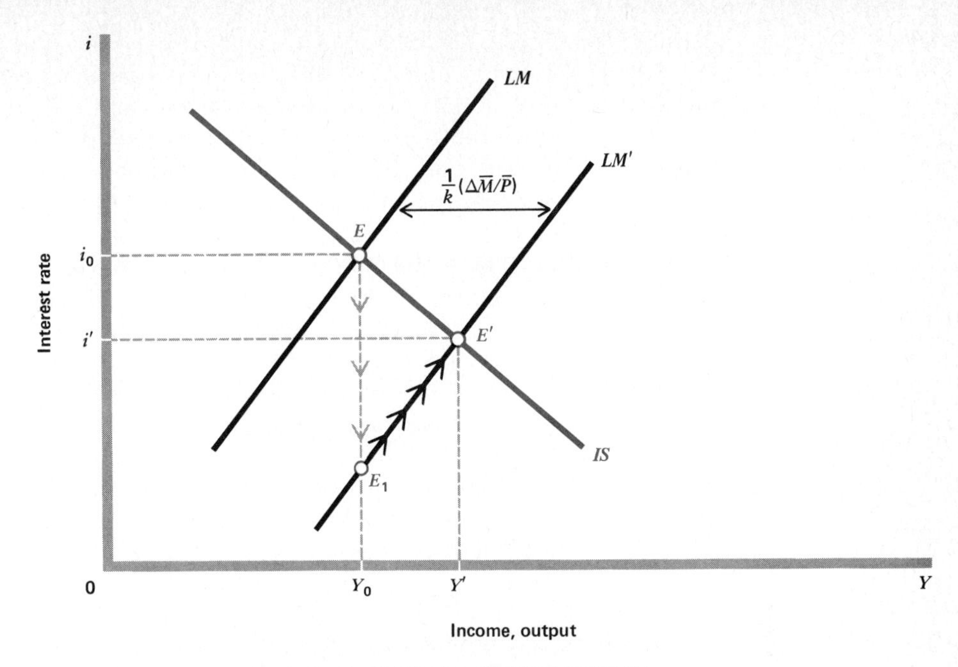

FIGURE 4-16 THE ADJUSTMENT PATH OF THE ECONOMY FOLLOWING AN INCREASE IN THE MONEY STOCK. An increase in the real money stock shifts the *LM* schedule down and to the right. Interest rates immediately decline from *E* to E_1 and then, through their effect on investment, cause spending and income to rise until a new equilibrium is reached at *E'*. Once all adjustments have taken place, a rise in the real money stock raises equilibrium income and lowers equilibrium interest rates.

studied in more detail in Chapter 9, is *open market operations.* In an open market operation the Federal Reserve purchases bonds in exchange for money, thus increasing the stock of money, or it sells bonds in exchange for money paid by the purchasers of the bonds, thus reducing the money stock.

We take here the case of an open market purchase of bonds. The purchase is made by the Federal Reserve System, which pays for its purchases with money that it can create. One can usefully think of the Fed printing money with which to buy bonds, even though that is not strictly accurate, as we shall see in Chapter 9. The purpose of an open market operation is to change the available *relative* supplies of money and bonds and thereby change the interest rate or yield at which the public is willing to hold this modified composition of assets. When the Fed buys bonds, it reduces the supply of bonds available in the market and thereby tends to increase their price, or lower their yield. Only at a lower interest rate will the public be prepared to hold a larger fraction of their given wealth in the form of money, and a lower fraction in the form of bonds.

In Figure 4-16 we show graphically how the open market purchase works. The initial equilibrium at point *E* is on the initial *LM* schedule that corresponds to a real money supply, $\overline{M}/\overline{P}$. Consider next an open market operation that increases the nominal quantity of money, and given the price level, the real quantity of money. We showed before that, as a consequence, the *LM* schedule will shift to *LM'*. Therefore, our new equilibrium will be at point *E'* with a lower interest rate and a higher level of income. The equilibrium level of income rises because the open market purchase reduces the interest rate and thereby increases investment spending.

By experimenting with Figure 4-16, you will be able to show that the steeper the *LM* schedule, the larger the change in income. If money demand is very sensitive to the interest rate, then a given change in the money stock can be absorbed in the assets markets with only a small change in the interest rate. The effects of an open market purchase on investment spending would then be small. By contrast, if the demand for money is not very sensitive to the interest rate, a given change in the money supply will cause a large change in the interest rate and have a big effect on investment demand.[12] Similarly, if the demand for money is very sensitive to income, a given increase in the money stock can be absorbed with a relatively small change in income.

Consider next the adjustment process to the monetary expansion. At the initial equilibrium point *E*, the increase in the money supply creates an excess supply of money to which the public adjusts by attempting to reduce its money holdings by buying other assets. In the process, asset prices increase and yields decline. By our assumption that the assets markets adjust rapidly, we move immediately to point E_1, where the money market clears, and where the public is willing to hold the larger real quantity of money because the interest rate has declined sufficiently. At point E_1, however, there is an excess demand for goods. The decline in the interest rate, given the initial income level Y_0, has raised aggregate demand and is causing inventories to run down. In response, output expands and we start moving up the *LM'* schedule. Why does the interest rate rise in the adjustment process? Because the increase in output raises the demand for money and that increase has to be checked by higher interest rates.

Thus the increase in the money stock first causes interest rates to fall as the public adjusts its portfolio and then—through lower interest rates—increases aggregate demand.

The Transmission Mechanism

Two steps in the *transmission mechanism*—the process by which changes in monetary policy affect aggregate demand—are essential. The first is that an increase in real balances generates a *portfolio disequilibrium*—at the prevailing interest rate and level of income, people are holding more money than they want. This causes portfolio holders to attempt to reduce their money holdings by buying other assets, thereby changing asset prices and yields. In other words, the change in the money supply changes interest rates. The

[12] In problem 3, we ask you to provide a similar explanation of the role of the slope of the *IS* curve—which is determined by the multiplier and the interest sensitivity of investment demand—in determining the effect of monetary policy on income.

TABLE 4-2 THE TRANSMISSION MECHANISM

(1)	(2)	(3)	(4)
Change in real money supply	Portfolio adjustments lead to a change in asset prices and interest rates	Spending adjusts to the change in interest rates	Output adjusts to the change in aggregate demand

second stage of the transmission process occurs when the change in interest rates affects aggregate demand.

These two stages of the transmission process are essential in that they appear in almost every analysis of the effects of changes in the money supply on the economy. The details of the analysis will often differ — some analyses will have more than two assets and more than one interest rate; some will include an influence of interest rates on other categories of demand, in particular consumption and spending by local government.[13]

Table 4-2 provides a summary of the stages in the transmission mechanism. The process starts with a change in the real money stock, which, in the first place, leads to portfolio disequilibrium and changes in interest rates. From here the disturbance spills from assets markets to goods markets, as spending adjusts to the change in interest rates. The change in spending or aggregate demand in turn leads to income adjustments.

There are two critical links between the change in real balances and the ultimate effect on income. First, the change in real balances, by bringing about portfolio disequilibrium, must lead to a change in interest rates. Second, that change in interest rates must change aggregate demand. Through those two linkages, changes in the real money stock affect the level of output in the economy. But that immediately implies the following: if portfolio imbalances do not lead to significant changes in interest rates — for whatever reason — or if spending does not respond to changes in interest rates, the link between money and output does not exist.[14] We now study these linkages in more detail.

[13] Some analyses also include a mechanism by which changes in real balances have a direct effect on aggregate demand through the real balance effect. The argument is that wealth affects consumption demand (as we shall see in Chap. 6) and that an increase in real balances increases wealth and therefore consumption demand. This effect would not apply in the case of an open market purchase, which merely exchanges one asset for another (bonds for money) without changing wealth. The real balance effect is not very important empirically because the relevant real balances are only a small part of wealth.

[14] We refer to the responsiveness of aggregate demand — rather than investment demand — to the interest rate because consumption demand may also respond to the interest rate. Higher interest rates may lead to more saving and less consumption at a given level of income. Empirically, it has been difficult to isolate such an interest rate effect on consumption.

The Liquidity Trap

In discussing the effects of monetary policy on the economy, two extreme cases have received much attention. The first is the *liquidity trap*, a situation in which the public is prepared, at a given interest rate, to hold whatever amount of money is supplied. This implies that the *LM* curve is horizontal and that changes in the quantity of money do not shift it. In that case, monetary policy carried out through open market operations[15] has no effect on either the interest rate or level of income. In the liquidity trap, monetary policy is powerless to affect the interest rate.

There is a liquidity trap at a zero interest rate. At a zero interest rate, the public would not want to hold any bonds, since money, which also pays zero interest, has the advantage over bonds of being usable in transactions. Accordingly, if the interest rate ever, for some reason, was zero, increases in the quantity of money could not induce anyone to shift into bonds and thereby reduce the interest rate on bonds even below zero. An increase in the money supply in that case would have no effect on the interest rate and income, and the economy would be in a liquidity trap.

The belief that there was a liquidity trap at low positive (rather than zero) interest rates was quite prevalent during the forties and fifties. It was a notion associated with the Keynesian followers and developers of the theories of the great English economist John Maynard Keynes—although Keynes himself did state that he was not aware of there ever having been such a situation.[16] The importance of the liquidity trap stems from its presenting a circumstance under which monetary policy has no effect on the interest rate and thus on the level of real income. Belief in the trap, or at least the strong sensitivity of the demand for money to the interest rate, was the basis of the Keynesian belief that monetary policy has no effects on the economy. There is no strong evidence that there ever was a liquidity trap, and there certainly is not one now.

The Classical Case

The polar opposite of the horizontal *LM* curve—which implies that monetary policy cannot affect the level of income—is the vertical *LM* curve. The *LM* curve is vertical when the demand for money is entirely unresponsive to the interest rate. Under those circumstances, any shift in the *LM* curve has a maximal effect on the level of income. Check this by moving a vertical *LM* curve to the right and comparing the resultant change in income with the change produced by a similar horizontal shift of a nonvertical *LM* curve.

[15] We say "through open market operations" because an increase in the quantity of money carried out simply by giving the money away increases individuals' wealth and, through the real balance effect, has some effect on aggregate demand. An open market purchase, however, increases the quantity of money and reduces the quantity of bonds by the same amount, leaving wealth unchanged.

[16] J. M. Keynes, *The General Theory of Employment, Interest and Money* (New York: Macmillan, 1936), p. 207.

The vertical *LM* curve is called the *classical case*. It implies that the demand for money depends only on the level of income and not at all on the interest rate. The classical case is associated with the classical *quantity theory of money*, which argues that the level of nominal income is determined solely by the quantity of money. We return to this view in Chapter 5. As we shall see, a vertical *LM* curve implies not only that monetary policy has a maximal effect on the level of income, but also that fiscal policy has no effect on income. The vertical *LM* curve, implying the comparative effectiveness of monetary policy over fiscal policy, is sometimes associated with the view that "only money matters" for the determination of ouput. Since the *LM* curve is vertical only when the demand for money does not depend on the interest rate, the interest sensitivity of the demand for money turns out to be an important issue in determining the effectiveness of alternative policies.

These two extreme cases, the liquidity trap and the classical case, suggest that the slope of the *LM* curve is a key determinant of the effectiveness of monetary policy in affecting output. The slope of the *LM* curve in turn depends on the interest sensitivity of money demand. The more sensitive to the interest rate is the quantity of money demanded, the flatter the *LM* curve.

4-6 AN APPLICATION OF MONETARY POLICY: TIGHT MONEY IN 1966

From 1963 to 1966 the U.S. economy expanded rapidly under the impact of monetary and fiscal stimulus. The GNP gap in 1963 had been as large as 3.3 percent, but the sustained expansion in output and employment had moved the economy to its potential output level by early 1966. The Fed then became concerned that expansion might get out of hand, with the economy overshooting the full-employment mark and moving into highly inflationary conditions. A tight monetary policy, later known as the *credit crunch*, was initiated in 1966. In terms of the *IS-LM* diagram in Figure 4-18, the *LM* schedule was shifted to the left.

Figure 4-17 shows half-yearly data for real investment spending (excluding inventories) and for the interest rate on Treasury bills. Note that the interest rate rises from an average of 4 percent in the second half of 1965 to more than 5 percent in the second half of 1966. In response to the increase in interest rates, investment spending declines.

We study the dynamics of adjustment using Figure 4-18. The shift of the *LM* schedule to *LM'* first raises interest rates, from point *E* to point *E'*. At *E'* the higher interest rates reduce investment spending and hence lead to a fall in aggregate demand and output as the economy moves to point *E''*. As output declines, interest rates decline somewhat. In this instance they decline quite substantially, because once the sharp slowdown in activity became apparent, the Fed reversed its policy, allowing the money stock to rise again, and thus leading the economy back toward point *E*.

Table 4-3 shows the response of real GNP growth to the tightness of

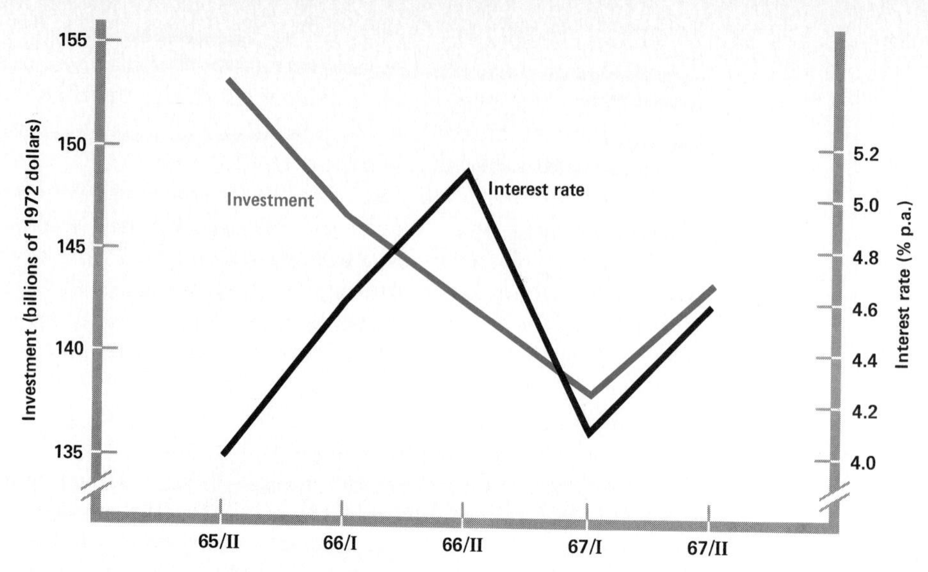

FIGURE 4-17 TIGHT MONEY RAISES INTEREST RATES AND REDUCES INVESTMENT. (*Source: Business Statistics.*)

FIGURE 4-18 In 1966 the Fed tightens monetary policy to avoid an overheating of the economy. The LM schedule shifts to LM'. In the short run, interest rates rise sharply to E', and as a consequence, aggregate demand is reduced. Over time the decline in spending leads to a fall in both output and interest rates at point E''.

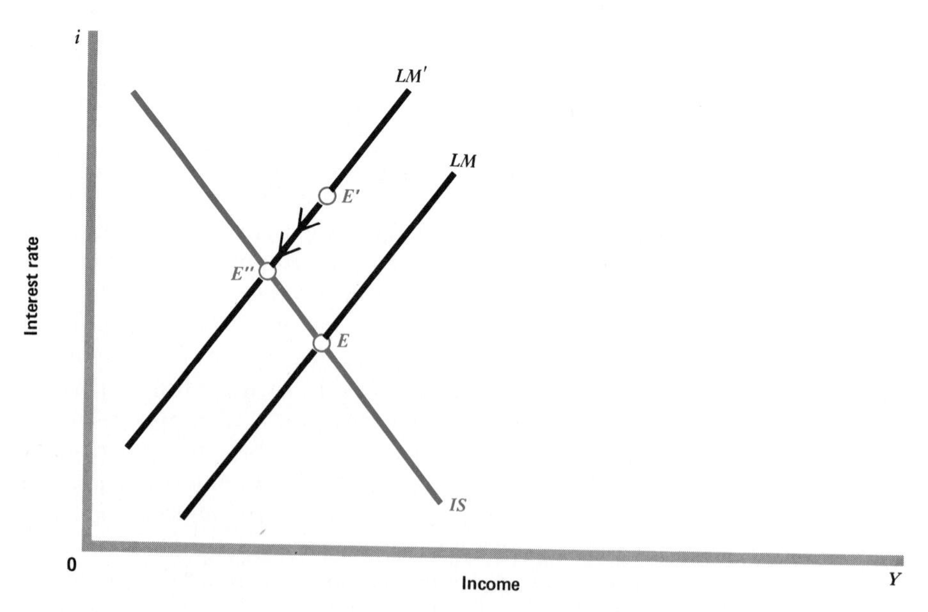

TABLE 4-3 REAL GNP GROWTH IN 1965–1967 *(Percentage change from previous half year at annual rates)*

1965/II	1966/I	1966/II	1967/I	1967/II
7.2	6.9	3.1	1.8	4.2

Source: OECD Economic Outlook, December 1982.

money. In the preceding years real GNP had been growing rapidly, as shown still in the second half of 1965 and the first half of 1966. But once interest rates increased, real growth declined sharply, falling to a low of 1.8 percent in the first half of 1967, before expansion took over again.

It is worth looking for a moment at the timing of interest rate changes and changes in investment. Figure 4-17 shows that there are *lags* in the adjustment of investment spending to changes in interest rates. For example, interest rates peak in the second half of 1966 and are actually way down in the first half of 1967. But investment continues to decline despite the low interest rates.

In later chapters we study these lags further. For the moment we note that lags imply that monetary policy cannot work very quickly—say, within the same quarter—on aggregate demand. Tight money, if sustained for some time, will of course reduce investment, but it may take half a year before these effects become visible. The reason is that much of the investment spending that takes place in a given quarter is based on plans and even financing that were prepared some time ago. For instance, someone starting to build a house this quarter certainly drew up the plans before and probably arranged for the financing a while back. Thus high interest rates today primarily affect plans for investment drawn up now but that will take place over the months to come.

4-7 SUMMARY

1 The *IS-LM* model presented in this chapter is the basic model of aggregate demand that incorporates the assets markets as well as the goods market. It lays particular stress on the channels through which monetary and fiscal policy affect the economy.
2 The *IS* curve shows combinations of the interest rate and level of income such that the goods market is in equilibrium. Increases in the interest rate reduce aggregate demand by reducing the demand for investment goods. Thus at higher interest rates, the level of income at which the goods market is in equilibrium is lower: the *IS* curve slopes downward.
3 The demand for money is a demand for *real* balances. The demand for real balances increases with income and decreases with the interest rate, the cost of holding money rather than other assets. With an exogenously fixed supply of real balances, the *LM* curve, representing money market equilibrium, is upward-sloping. Because of the wealth constraint, equilibrium

of the money market implies equilibrium of the remaining assets markets —summarized here under the catchall "bond market."

4 The interest rate and level of output are jointly determined by simultaneous equilibrium of the goods and money markets. This occurs at the intersection point of the *IS* and *LM* curves.
5 Assuming that output is increased when there is an excess demand for goods, and that the interest rate rises when there is an excess demand for money, the economy does move toward the new equilibrium when one of the curves shifts. Typically we think of the assets markets as clearing rapidly, so that in response to a disturbance, the economy tends to move along the *LM* curve to the new equilibrium.
6 Monetary policy affects the economy in the first instance by affecting the interest rate, and then by affecting aggregate demand. An increase in the money supply reduces the interest rate, increases investment demand and aggregate demand, and thus increases equilibrium output.
7 There are two extreme cases in the operation of monetary policy. In the classical case the demand for real balances is independent of the rate of interest. In this case monetary policy is highly effective. The other extreme is the liquidity trap, where the public is willing to hold *any* amount of real balances at the going interest rate. In that case changes in the supply of real balances have no impact on interest rates and therefore do not affect aggregate demand and output.
8 *A final warning:* We are assuming here that any level of output that is demanded can be produced by firms at the constant price level. Price level behavior, including inflation, is discussed in substantially more detail in Chapters 11 to 13. Those chapters build on the analysis of the *IS-LM* model.

KEY TERMS

IS Curve
LM Curve
Bond
Money
Portfolio decisions
Real balances (real money balances)
Wealth budget constraint
Open market operation
Transmission mechanism
Liquidity trap
Classical case

PROBLEMS

1 The following equations describe an economy. (Think of C, I, G, etc., as being measured in billions and i as percent; a 5 percent interest rate implies $i = 5$.)

$$C = 0.8(1 - t)Y \quad (1)$$
$$t = 0.25 \quad (2)$$
$$I = 400 - 20i \quad (3)$$
$$\overline{G} = 500 \quad (4)$$
$$L = 0.25Y - 30i \quad (5)$$
$$\frac{\overline{M}}{\overline{P}} = 350 \quad (6)$$

(*a*) What is the equation that describes the *IS* curve?
(*b*) What is the general definition of the *IS* curve?
(*c*) What is the equation that describes the *LM* curve?
(*d*) What is the general definition of the *LM* curve?
(*e*) What are the equilibrium levels of income and the interest rate?
(*f*) Describe in words the conditions that are satisfied at the intersection of the *IS* and *LM* curves, and why this is an equilibrium.

2 Continue with the same equations.
(*a*) What is the value of $\overline{\alpha}$, which corresponds to the simple multiplier (with taxes) of Chapter 3?
(*b*) By how much does an increase in government spending of $\Delta\overline{G}$ increase the level of income in this model, which includes the assets markets?
(*c*) By how much does a change in government spending of $\Delta\overline{G}$ affect the equilibrium interest rate?
(*d*) Explain the difference between your answers to 2(*a*) and (*b*).

3 (*a*) Explain in words how and why the multiplier $\overline{\alpha}$ and the interest sensitivity of aggregate demand affect the slope of the *IS* curve.
(*b*) Explain why the slope of the *IS* curve is a factor in determining the working of monetary policy.

4 Explain in words how and why the income and interest sensitivities of the demand for real balances affect the slope of the *LM* curve.

5 (*a*) Why does a horizontal *LM* curve imply that fiscal policy has the same effects on the economy as we derived in Chapter 3?
(*b*) What is happening in this case in terms of Figure 4-2?
(*c*) Under what circumstances might the *LM* curve be horizontal?

6 We mentioned in the text the possibility that the interest rate might affect consumption spending. An increase in the interest rate could, in principle, lead to increases in saving and therefore a reduction in consumption, given the level of income. Suppose that consumption were in fact reduced by an increase in the interest rate. How would the *IS* curve be affected?

7 Suppose that the money supply, instead of being constant, increased (slightly) with the interest rate.
(*a*) How would this change affect the construction of the *LM* curve?
(*b*) Could you see any reason why the Fed might follow a policy of increasing the money supply along with the interest rate?

8 (*a*) How does an increase in the tax rate affect the *IS* curve?
(*b*) How does it affect the equilibrium level of income?
(*c*) How does it affect the equilibrium interest rate?

9 Draw a graph of how i and Y respond over time (that is, use time as the horizontal axis) to an increase in the money supply. You may assume that the money market adjusts much more rapidly than the goods market.

10 (*a*) Show that a given change in the money stock has a larger effect on output the less interest sensitive the demand for money.

(*b*) How does the response of the interest rate to a change in the money stock depend on the interest sensitivity of money demand?

5

FISCAL POLICY, CROWDING OUT, AND THE POLICY MIX

Whenever governments run budget deficits, borrowing to pay for the excess of their spending over the tax revenue they receive, the talk turns to *crowding out*. Crowding out occurs when expansionary fiscal policy causes interest rates to rise, thereby reducing private spending, particularly investment.

When we introduced fiscal policy in Chapter 3, we had not yet included the assets markets in the analysis. Thus we could not discuss the effects of changes in fiscal policy on interest rates. In this chapter we focus on how fiscal policy works when the interdependence of goods and assets markets is taken into account in the *IS-LM* model introduced in Chapter 4.

Our aim is to see how explicit consideration of the role of interest rates affects the conclusions we reached in Chapter 3 about fiscal policy. Is it still the case that an increase in government spending raises output and employment? Do tax cuts still increase output? Or is it possible that the effects of fiscal policy on interest rates are so important that our previous conclusions about the effects of fiscal policy on the economy are reversed?

Figure 5-1 shows how fiscal policy fits into the *IS-LM* model. Fiscal policy affects aggregate demand directly. For instance, an increase in government spending increases aggregate demand, tending to raise output. But the higher output level raises the interest rate in the assets markets, and

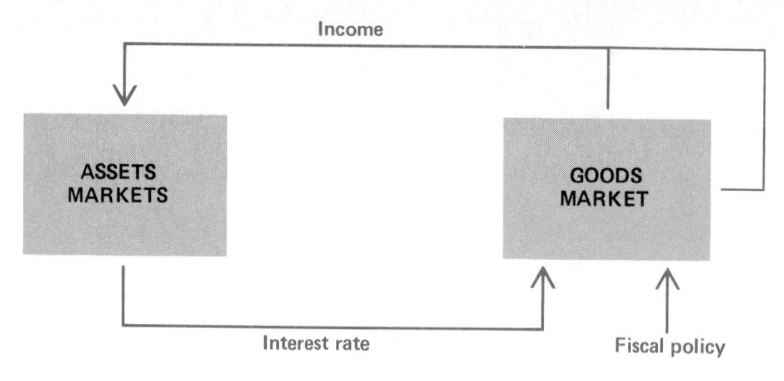

FIGURE 5-1 FISCAL POLICY IN THE *IS-LM* MODEL. Fiscal policy affects aggregate demand and thus has an impact on output and income. But changes in income affect the demand for money and thereby equilibrium interest rates in assets markets. These interest rate changes feed back to the goods market and dampen the impact of fiscal policy.

thereby dampens the effects of the fiscal policy on output. The higher interest rates reduce the level of investment spending, or crowd out investment. Thus a fiscal policy that increases output may actually reduce the rate of investment.

Once we have discussed crowding out, we turn to the issue of the *monetary-fiscal policy mix*. The policy mix is the combination of monetary and fiscal policies. For instance, monetary policy may be easy, with rapid monetary growth, and fiscal policy tight or restrictive, with taxes being increased. We ask what alternative mixes imply for the economy. The question of the appropriate mix is frequently at the center of the political controversy.

Table 5-1 shows possible combinations and indicates for each case when, in recent U.S. history, the combination prevailed.

5-1 FISCAL POLICY AND CROWDING OUT

In this section we show how changes in fiscal policy shift the *IS* curve, the curve that describes goods market equilibrium. Recall from Chapter 4 that the *IS* curve slopes downward because a decrease in the interest rate increases the demand for investment, thereby increasing aggregate demand and the level of output at which the goods market is in equilibrium. Recall also that changes in fiscal policy shift the *IS* curve.

The equation of the *IS* curve, derived in Chapter 4, is repeated here for convenience:

$$Y = \bar{\alpha}(\bar{A} - bi) \qquad \bar{\alpha} \equiv 1/[1 - c(1 - t)] \tag{1}$$

Note that $\bar{G}$, the level of government spending, is a component of autonomous spending $\bar{A}$ in (1). The income tax rate t is part of the multiplier.

TABLE 5-1 MONETARY-FISCAL POLICY MIXES

		MONETARY POLICY	
		Tightening	Easing
FISCAL POLICY	Tightening	1974, 1981	1976–1977
	Easing	1982	1982–1983

Thus both government spending and the multiplier affect the *IS* schedule. We now show in Figure 5-2 how fiscal policy changes equilibrium income and the interest rate.

AN INCREASE IN GOVERNMENT SPENDING

At unchanged interest rates, higher levels of government spending will increase the level of aggregate demand. To meet the increased demand for goods, output must rise. In Figure 5-2 we show the effect of a shift of the *IS*

FIGURE 5-2 EFFECTS OF AN INCREASE IN GOVERNMENT SPENDING. An increase in government spending raises aggregate demand at each level of the interest rate and thus shifts the *IS* schedule out and to the right to *IS′*. At point *E* there is now an excess demand for goods. Output rises, and with it the interest rate, because the income expansion raises money demand. The new equilibrium is at point *E′*. The increase in income ($Y_0' - Y_0$) is less than the amount indicated by the simple multiplier ($Y'' - Y_0$) because higher interest rates crowd out some investment spending.

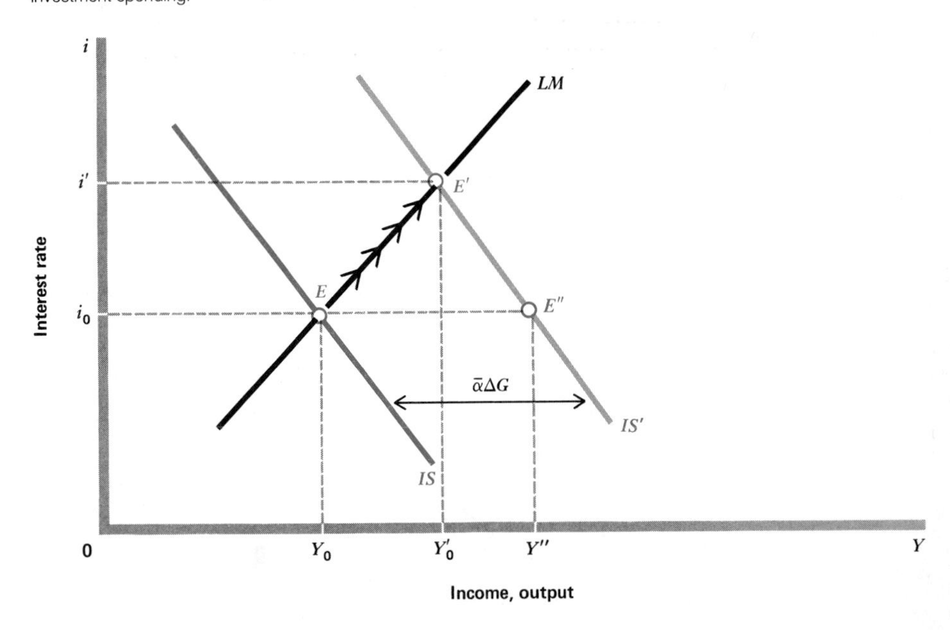

schedule. At each level of the interest rate, equilibrium income must rise by $\overline{\alpha}$ times the government spending. For example, if government spending rises by 100 and the multiplier is 2, then equilibrium income must increase at each level of the interest rate by 200. Thus the *IS* schedule shifts to the right by 200.

If the economy is initially in equilibrium at point E and now government spending rises by 100, we would move to point E'' *if the interest rate stayed constant.* At E'' the goods market is in equilibrium in that planned spending equals output. But the assets market is no longer in equilibrium. Income has increased, and therefore money demand now is higher. At interest rate i_0, the demand for real balances now exceeds the given real money supply. Because there is an excess demand for real balances, the interest rate rises. But as interest rates rise, private spending is cut back. Firms' planned investment spending declines at higher interest rates, and thus aggregate demand falls off.

What is the complete adjustment, taking into account the expansionary effect of higher government spending and the dampening effects of higher interest rates on private spending? Figure 5-2 shows that only at point E' do *both* the goods and assets markets clear. Only at point E' is planned spending equal to income and, at the same time, the quantity of real balances demanded equal to the given real money stock. Point E' is therefore the new equilibrium point.

THE DYNAMICS OF ADJUSTMENT

We continue to assume that the money market clears fast and continuously, while output adjusts only slowly. This implies that as government spending increases, we stay initially at point E, since there is no disturbance in the money market. The excess demand for goods, however, leads firms to increase output, and that increase in output and income raises the demand for money. The resulting excess demand for money, in turn, causes interest rates to be bid up, and we proceed up along the *LM* curve with rising output and rising interest rates, until the new equilibrium is reached at point E'.

The Extent of Adjustment

Comparing E' to the initial equilibrium at E, we have seen that increased government spending raises both income and the interest rate. But another important comparison is between points E' and E'', the equilibrium in the goods market at unchanged interest rates. Point E'' corresponds to the equilibrium we studied in Chapter 3 where we neglected the impact of interest rates on the economy. In comparing E'' and E' it becomes clear that the adjustment of interest rates and their impact on aggregate demand dampen the expansionary effect of increased government spending. Income, instead of increasing to the level Y'', rises only to Y'_0. This leads us to the following question: What factors determine the extent to which interest rate adjustments dampen the output expansion induced by increased government spending?

The extent to which a fiscal expansion raises income and the interest rate depends on the slopes of the *IS* and *LM* schedules and on the size of the multiplier. By drawing for yourself different *IS* and *LM* schedules you will be able to show the following:

1 Income increases more, and interest rates increase less, the flatter the *LM* schedule.
2 Income increases less, and interest rates increase less, the flatter the *IS* schedule.
3 Income and interest rates increase more the larger the multiplier $\overline{\alpha}$ and thus the larger the horizontal shift of the *IS* schedule.

To illustrate these conclusions, we turn to the two extreme cases we discussed in connection with monetary policy, the liquidity trap and the classical case.

THE LIQUIDITY TRAP

If the economy is in the liquidity trap so that the *LM* curve is horizontal, then an increase in government spending has its full multiplier effect on the equilibrium level of income. There is no change in the interest rate associated with the change in government spending, and thus no investment spending is cut off. There is therefore no dampening of the effects of increased government spending on income.

You should draw your own *IS-LM* diagrams to confirm that if the *LM* curve is horizontal, monetary policy has no impact on the equilibrium of the economy and fiscal policy has a maximal effect on the economy. Less dramatically, if the demand for money is very sensitive to the interest rate, so that the *LM* curve is almost horizontal, fiscal policy changes have a relatively large effect on output, while monetary policy changes have little effect on the equilibrium level of output.

So far, we have taken the money supply to be constant at the level $\overline{M}$. It is possible that the Fed might instead manipulate the money supply so as to keep the interest rate constant. In that case the money supply is responsive to the interest rate. We could talk of a money supply function which is elastic with respect to the interest rate. More simply, the Fed increases the money supply whenever there are signs of an increase in the interest rate, and reduces the money supply whenever the interest rate seems about to fall. If the money supply function is very elastic with respect to the interest rate, the *LM* curve will be very flat and fiscal policy will again have large impacts on the level of output.

THE CLASSICAL CASE AND CROWDING OUT

If the *LM* curve is vertical, then an increase in government spending has *no* effect on the equilibrium level of income. It only increases the interest rate. This case is shown in Figure 5-3*a*, where an increase in government spending shifts the *IS* curve to *IS′* but has no effect on income. If the demand for money

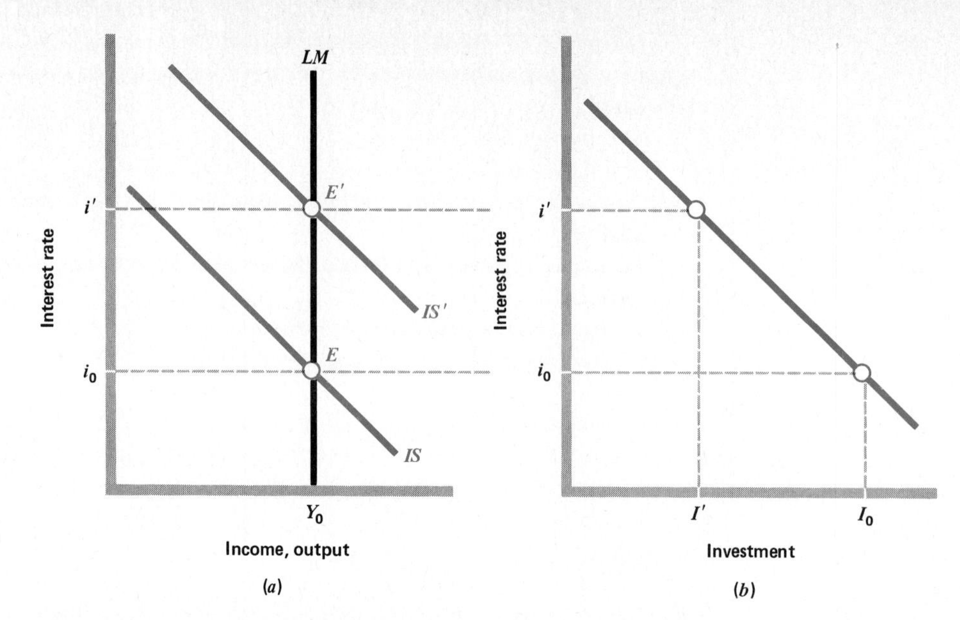

FIGURE 5-3 FULL CROWDING OUT. With a vertical *LM* schedule, a fiscal expansion, shifting out the *IS* schedule, raises interest rates, not income. Government spending displaces, or crowds out, private spending, one-for-one.

is not related to the interest rate, as a vertical *LM* curve implies, then there is a unique level of income at which the money market is in equilibrium.

Thus with a vertical *LM* curve, an increase in government spending cannot change the equilibrium level of income, but only raises the equilibrium interest rate. But if government spending is higher and output is unchanged, there must be an offsetting reduction in private spending. The increase in interest rates *crowds out* private investment spending. Crowding out, as defined earlier, is the reduction in private spending (and particularly investment) associated with the increase in interest rates caused by fiscal expansion. There will be full crowding out if the *LM* curve is vertical.[1]

In Figure 5-3 we show the crowding out in panel (*b*), where the investment schedule of Figure 4-3 is drawn. The fiscal expansion raises the equilibrium interest rate from i_0 to i' in panel (*a*). In panel (*b*), as a consequence, investment spending declines from the level I_0 to I'. Now it is easy to verify that if the *LM* schedule were positively sloped rather than vertical, interest rates would rise less with a fiscal expansion and as a result investment spending would decline less. The extent of crowding out thus depends on the slope of the *LM* curve and therefore on the interest responsiveness of money demand. The less interest-responsive is money demand, the more a fiscal expansion crowds out investment rather than raising output.

[1] Note again that, in principle, consumption spending could be reduced by increases in the interest rate, and then both investment and consumption would be crowded out.

The view that increased government spending crowds out private spending, largely or even completely, is held by most monetarists.[2] They believe money determines income or, as we saw above, that money demand does not depend on the interest rate, implying a vertical *LM* schedule. However, there is also another case where crowding out can be complete, as we shall see in Chapter 13. If the economy is at full employment so that output cannot expand, then, of course, increased purchases of goods by the government must mean that some other sector uses less goods and services. Interest rates increase to crowd out private spending by an amount exactly equal to the higher level of government spending.

BUDGET DEFICITS IN THE 1980s

By 1983 it became clear that the United States was headed for a long series of large budget deficits. For instance, the 1984 budget message of the Reagan administration projected that even with tax increases in 1985, deficits over the 6 years 1983–1988 would average 4.4 percent of GNP. This is by far the highest deficit level in any peacetime years. Even during the 6 years of largest deficits in the great depression of the 1930s, from 1931 to 1936, deficits averaged only 3.3 percent of GNP.

The large projected deficits worried the administration and outside economists because of the possibility that investment spending would be crowded out. Then the economy would not be investing in the machinery and factories that would increase output in the future. The comments of the Council of Economic Advisers in 1983 are typical of the concern:

> A succession of large deficits is likely to reduce substantially the rate of capital formation. The government's borrowing to finance such deficits would compete directly with borrowing by private business and households. With a limited amount of savings available for borrowing, high budget deficits would cause interest rates to rise until private demand for funds was reduced to the amount that remained after the government's borrowing needs were satisfied.
>
> The magnitude of the potential crowding out of private investment is immense. . . . A lower rate of capital formation would have adverse consequences because the accumulation of capital is a key determinant of future increases in productivity and economic growth and therefore of higher real wages and standards of living. . . .[3]

IS CROWDING OUT LIKELY?

How seriously must we take the possibility of crowding out? Here three points must be made. First, in an economy with unemployed resources there will *not* be full crowding out because the *LM* schedule is not, in fact, vertical. A fiscal expansion will raise interest rates, but income will also rise. Crowding out

[2] We discuss monetarism in Chap. 16.

[3] *Economic Report of the President*, 1983, p. 27.

thus, rather than being full, is a matter of degree. In terms of the above quote, the increase in aggregate demand raises income, and with the rise in income, it raises the level of saving. This expansion in saving, in turn, makes it possible to finance a larger budget deficit without *completely* displacing private borrowing or investment.

We can look at this proposition with the help of Equation (2), which states the equilibrium condition in the goods market already studied in Chapter 3[4]:

$$S \equiv I + (G + TR - TA) \tag{2}$$

Here the term $G + TR - TA$ is the budget deficit. Now from (2) it is clear that an increase in the deficit, given saving, must lower investment. In simple terms, when the deficit rises, the government has to borrow to pay for its excess spending. That borrowing "uses up" part of saving, leaving less available for firms to borrow to further their investment plans. But it is equally apparent that if saving rises with a government spending increase, because income rises, then there need not be a one-for-one decline in investment. In an economy with unemployment, crowding out is incomplete because increased demand for goods raises real income and output; savings rise and interest rates do not rise enough (because of interest-responsive money demand) to choke off investment.

The second point is that, with unemployment and thus a possibility for output to expand, interest rates need not rise at all when government spending rises, and there need not be any crowding out. This is because the monetary authorities can *accommodate* the fiscal expansion by an increase in the money supply. Monetary policy is *accommodating* when, in the course of a fiscal expansion, the money supply is increased so as to prevent interest rates from increasing. Monetary accommodation is also referred to as *monetizing budget deficits,* meaning that the Federal Reserve prints money to buy the bonds with which the government pays for its deficit.[5] When the Fed accommodates a fiscal expansion, both the *IS* and the *LM* schedule shift to the right as in Figure 5-4. Output will clearly increase, but interest rates need not rise. Accordingly, there need not be any adverse effects on investment. On some occasions, as in the 1960s, the Fed has been willing to accommodate, as we see in Section 5-3 below.

The third comment on crowding out is an important warning. So far we are assuming an economy with given prices and less than full employment. When we talk about fully employed economies in Chap. 13, crowding out becomes a much more realistic possibility, and accommodating monetary policy may turn into an engine of inflation.

[4] We have simply rearranged Eq. (1*a*) in Chap. 3, canceling consumption on both sides.

[5] The term *accommodation* is also used more generally. For instance, when oil prices increased in the 1970s, there was much discussion of whether the Fed should accommodate the higher prices by raising the money stock. This issue, and the meaning of *accommodation* in that context, are discussed in Chap. 13.

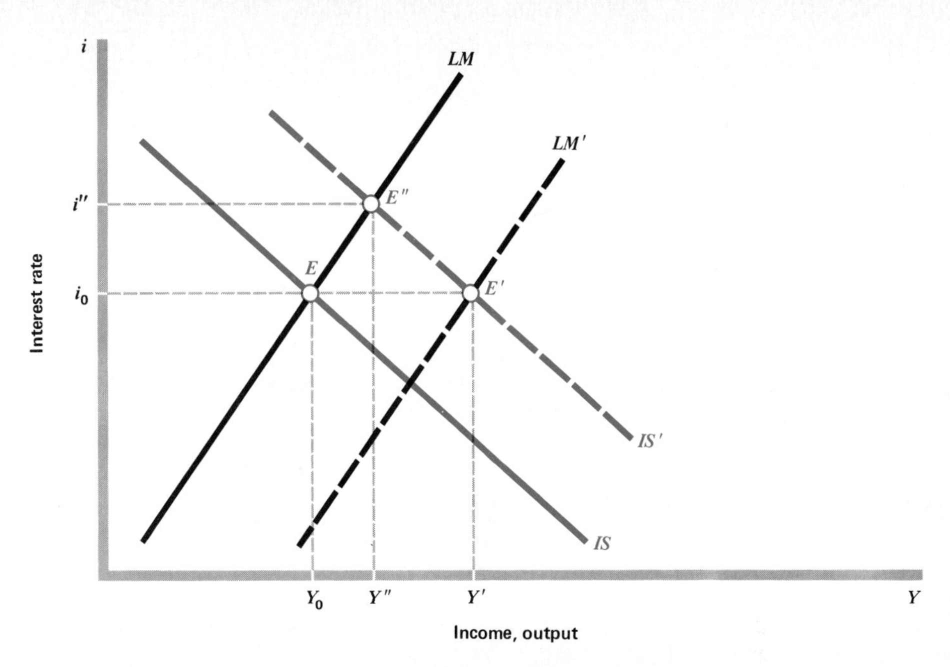

FIGURE 5-4 MONETARY ACCOMMODATION OF FISCAL EXPANSION. A fiscal expansion shifts the *IS* curve to *IS'*, and moves the equilibrium of the economy from *E* to *E''*. Because the higher level of income has increased the quantity of money demanded, the interest rate rises from i_0 to i'', thereby crowding out investment spending. But the Fed can accommodate the fiscal expansion, creating more money and shifting the *LM* curve to *LM'*, and the equilibrium of the economy to *E'*. The interest rate remains at level i_0, and the level of output rises to *Y'*.

Multipliers from Econometric Models

What about the real world? Is the situation more nearly one of the classical case or of the liquidity trap? The answer is certainly that there is some interest responsiveness of money demand. But disagreements on the magnitude of the interest response of money demand lead different experts to different conclusions about the effects of fiscal policies on the economy. This is brought out very strongly by looking at the effects of fiscal policy as predicted by different econometric models.

In Table 5-2 we show the multipliers for an increase in government spending under two assumptions: In one case monetary policy does not accommodate the fiscal expansion, so that interest rates will rise and crowd out some private spending. In the other case monetary policy accommodates the fiscal expansion, keeping interest rates constant and preventing crowding out. The difference between the two cases will be larger the more nearly we are in a world where money demand does not strongly depend on interest rates—the classical case.

One column of Table 5-2 shows forecasts of one of the well-known

TABLE 5-2 THE MULTIPLIER FOR GOVERNMENT SPENDING

	DRI	St. Louis
Nonaccommodating monetary policy	1.8	0.7
Accommodating monetary policy	2.0	6.0

Note: The multipliers refer to the impact on nominal GNP of a permanent increase in government spending after four quarters.
Source: Budget Financing and Monetary Control *(Paris: Organization for Economic Co-Operation and Development, 1982), p. 42.*

macroeconomic forecasting models, the DRI (Data Resources, Inc.) model. The forecast is that within four quarters of a $1 billion increase in government spending, output rises by $1.8 billion in the absence of accommodating monetary policy. If monetary policy accommodates, keeping interest rates constant, the expansion is somewhat larger, namely, $2 billion. In this model, clearly monetary factors do *not* play an overriding role, at least in the short-run adjustment to fiscal expansion. Certainly there is no substantial crowding out.

The next column shows the forecast of a model of the Federal Reserve Bank of St. Louis. This model assumes a central role for monetary factors and corresponds very closely to what we called the classical case above. Accordingly, fiscal expansion, unaccompanied by a monetary expansion, has only a moderate effect on nominal income. A $1 billion expansion in government spending raises income by less than a billion because already within a year the rise in interest rates chokes off a substantial amount of private spending. By contrast, a fiscal expansion accompanied by an increase in the money stock has large effects on income—the multiplier is 6. The table makes it clear that it is really important to know whether the world is more nearly described by the DRI model or by the St. Louis model. In the former case fiscal policy (without accommodating money) works well; in the latter case hardly at all. We return to these multipliers in later chapters when we take price adjustments into account.

The extreme cases of a vertical *LM* curve or a flat *LM* curve represent boundaries that are useful for reference purposes. Beyond that, their use is quite limited, since any reasonable description for policy purposes will assume the intermediate case of an upward-sloping *LM* curve, so that both monetary and fiscal policy work. As we show in Chapter 8, the demand for real balances is definitely negatively related to the interest rate.

5-2 THE COMPOSITION OF OUTPUT

We have now seen that both monetary and fiscal policy can be used to expand aggregate demand and thus raise the equilibrium level of output. Since the liquidity trap and the classical case represent, at best, extremes useful for expositional purposes, it is apparent that policy makers can use either monetary or fiscal policy to affect the level of income.

TABLE 5-3 SUMMARY: POLICY EFFECTS ON INCOME AND INTEREST RATES

Policy	Equilibrium income	Equilibrium interest rate
Monetary expansion	+	−
Fiscal expansion	+	+

Table 5-3 summarizes the effects of expansionary monetary and fiscal policy on output and the interest rate. These are the effects shown in Figures 5-2 and 5-3.

We now examine the policy choices of an economy that is in equilibrium with an output level Y_0, below the full-employment level $\bar{Y}$. What can be done to raise output? From the preceding analysis and Table 5-3, it is obvious that we could use an expansionary monetary policy. By increasing the money supply, we could shift the *LM* curve down and to the right, lower interest rates, and raise aggregate demand. Alternatively, we can use an expansionary fiscal policy to shift the *IS* curve up and to the right. Finally, we can use a combination of monetary and fiscal policy. What package should we choose?

The choice of monetary and fiscal policy as tools of stabilization policy is an important and controversial topic. In Chapter 10 we address some technical issues that deal with the flexibility and speed with which these policies can be implemented and can take effect. Here we do not discuss speed and flexibility, but rather look at what these policies do to the composition of aggregate demand.

In that respect, there is a sharp difference between monetary and fiscal policy. Monetary policy operates by stimulating interest-responsive components of aggregate demand, primarily investment spending and, in particular, residential construction. There is strong evidence that the earliest and strongest effect of monetary policy is on residential construction.

Fiscal policy, by contrast, operates in a manner that depends on precisely what goods the government buys or what taxes and transfers it changes. Here we might be talking of government purchases of goods and services such as defense spending, or a reduction in the corporate profits tax, or in sales taxes, or Social Security contributions. Each policy affects the level of aggregate demand and causes an expansion in output, except that the type of output and the beneficiaries of the fiscal measures differ. An investment subsidy, discussed below, increases investment spending. An income tax cut has a direct effect on consumption spending. Given the quantity of money, all expansionary fiscal policies have in common that they will raise the interest rate.

AN INVESTMENT SUBSIDY

Table 5-4 shows examples of the impact of different fiscal policies on key variables. One interesting case is an *investment subsidy*, shown in Figure 5-5. When the government subsidizes investment, it essentially pays part of the

TABLE 5-4 ALTERNATIVE FISCAL POLICIES

	Interest rate	Consumption	Investment	GNP
Income tax cut	+	+	−	+
Government spending	+	+	−	+
Investment subsidy	+	+	+	+

cost of each firm's investment. A subsidy to investment shifts the investment schedule in panel (*a*). At each interest rate, firms now plan to invest more. With investment spending higher, aggregate demand increases.

In panel (*b*), the *IS* schedule shifts by the multiplier times the increase in autonomous investment brought about by the subsidy. The new equilibrium is at point E', where goods and money markets are again in balance. But note now that although interest rates have risen, we see in panel (*a*) that investment is higher. Investment is at the level I_0' up from I_0. The interest rate increase thus has only dampened but not reversed the impact of the investment subsidy. Here is an example where both consumption, induced by higher income, and investment rise as a consequence of fiscal policy.

FIGURE 5-5 AN INVESTMENT SUBSIDY. An investment subsidy shifts the investment schedule in panel (*a*) at each interest rate out and to the right. The increase in planned investment shows in panel (*b*) as a shift of the *IS* curve. Equilibrium income rises to Y_0', and the interest rate increases to i_0'. At the higher interest rate, investment is still higher, I_0', than it was initially. Thus an investment subsidy raises interest rates, income, and investment.

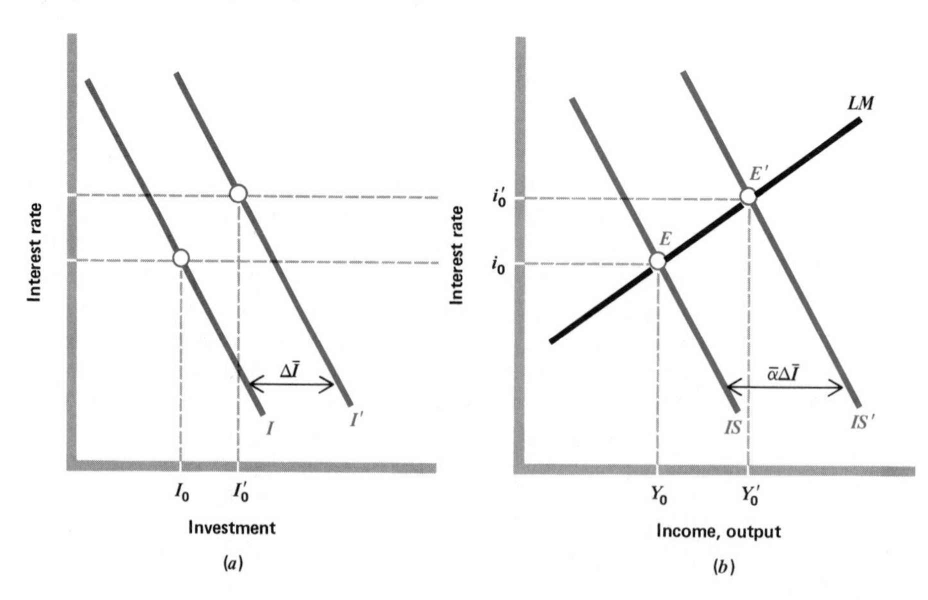

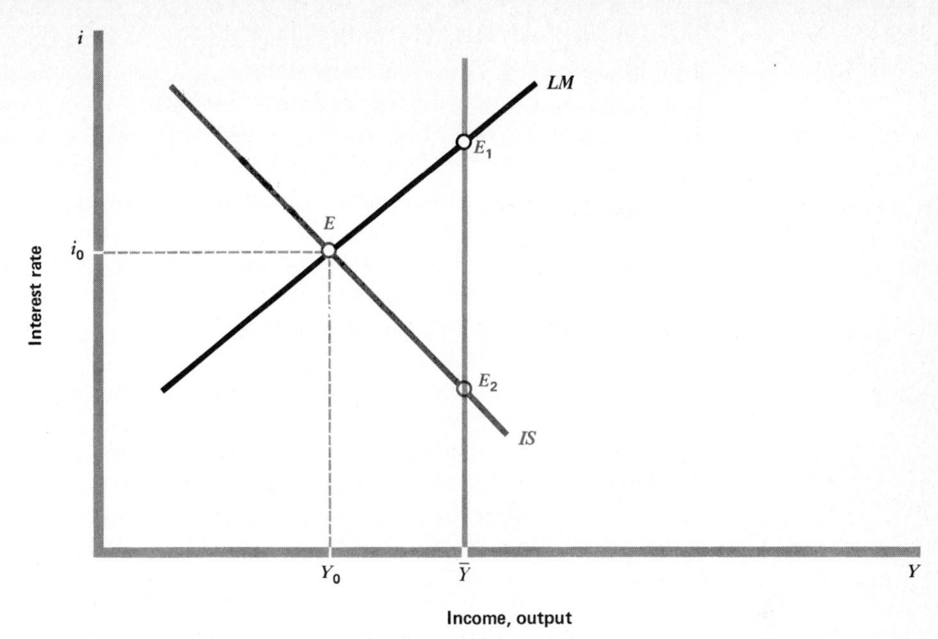

FIGURE 5-6 EXPANSIONARY POLICIES AND THE COMPOSITION OF OUTPUT. In an economy with output Y_0 below the full-employment level $\overline{Y}$, there is a choice of using monetary or fiscal expansion to move to full employment. Monetary expansion would move the *LM* curve to the right, putting the equilibrium at E_2. Fiscal expansion shifts the *IS* curve, putting the new equilibrium at E_1. The expansionary monetary policy reduces the interest rate, while the expansionary fiscal policy raises it. The lower interest rate in the case of monetary policy means that investment is higher at E_2 than it is at E_1.

THE POLICY MIX

In Figure 5-6 we show the policy problem of reaching full-employment output $\overline{Y}$ for an economy that is initially at point E with unemployment. Should we choose a fiscal expansion, moving to point E_1 with higher income and higher interest rates? Or should we choose a monetary expansion, leading to full employment with lower interest rates at point E_2? Or should we pick a policy mix of fiscal expansion and accommodating monetary policy, leading to an intermediate position?

Once we recognize that all the policies raise output but differ significantly in their impact on different sectors of the economy, we open up a problem of political economy. Given the decision to expand aggregate demand, who should get the primary benefit? Should the expansion take place through a decline in interest rates and increased investment spending, or should it take place through a cut in taxes and increased personal spending, or should it take the form of an increase in the size of government?

Questions of speed and predictability of policies apart, the issues raised above have been settled by political preferences. Conservatives will argue for a tax cut anytime. They will favor stabilization policies that in a recession cut taxes and in a boom cut government spending. Over time, given enough cycles, the government sector becomes very small, just as a conservative would want it to be. The counterpart view belongs to those who feel that there is much scope for government spending on education, environment, job training and rehabilitation, and the like, and who, accordingly, favor expansionary policies in the form of increased government spending. Growth-minded people and the construction lobby finally argue for expansionary policies that operate through low interest rates.

The recognition that monetary and fiscal policy changes have different effects on the composition of output is important. It suggests that policy makers can choose a *policy mix* that will both get the economy to full employment and also make a contribution to solving some other policy problem. We anticipate here several subsequent discussions in which we point out two other targets of policy which have been taken into account in setting monetary and fiscal policy—growth and balance of payments equilibrium.

5-3 THE POLICY MIX IN ACTION

In this section we review several episodes of monetary and fiscal policy in recent U.S. economic history. We first look at the foundations of the great economic expansion in the 1960s, originating in the 1964 tax cut. Then we look at the tax cut during the 1975 recession. We conclude with the monetary-fiscal policy mix in 1981–1982.

The 1964 Tax Cut

In the early 1960s the U.S. economy was in a recession with a GNP gap of 3.2 percent in 1963. To help the economy recover, the Kennedy-Johnson administration proposed a package of fiscal expansion. The program had two parts, a cut in the personal income tax rates and a cut in corporate profit taxes. The program, enacted in February 1964, complemented an investment subsidy that had already gone into effect in late 1962. The Revenue Act of 1964 provided for a permanent cut in income tax rates for all individual and corporate taxpayers. Personal taxes were cut by more than 20 percent and corporate taxes by about 8 percent. Before the cut, the marginal personal tax rates ranged from 20 to 91 percent; afterward, the range was 14 to 70 percent. For most corporations, the rate fell from 52 to 48 percent.

In terms of the *IS-LM* diagram the fiscal expansion moves the *IS* schedule out and to the right. Monetary policy determines the extent to which interest rates rise. Table 5-5 summarizes some of the relevant data.

We note from Table 5-5 the large fiscal expansion, visible in the decline of the full-employment surplus of 1 percent of GNP. The effects of the fiscal expansion show up in high real growth and a declining GNP gap. To judge

TABLE 5-5 THE 1964 TAX CUT

	1963	1964	1965
GNP gap, %	3.2	1.8	−0.2
GNP growth, %	4.0	5.3	6.0
Full-employment surplus, % of GNP	1.2	0.2	0.1
Interest rates, %	4.26	4.40	4.49

Source: Survey of Current Business, *April 1982, and* Economic Report of the President, *1983.*

monetary policy we look at the behavior of interest rates. Interest rates in Table 5-5 are measured by the yield on high quality corporate bonds (AAA-rated bonds). The interest rate moves up only very slightly. Thus monetary policy on balance was accommodating, keeping interest rates relatively constant. The fiscal expansion was therefore allowed to push up aggregate demand, without adverse side effects on interest rates that would lead to a decline in investment. This is precisely the policy combination shown in Figure 5-4.

Arthur Okun in commenting on the monetary-fiscal policy mix in the period summarized the experience as follows[6]:

> In short, the strong economic expansion of 1964–65 would not have taken place in the face of a highly restrictive monetary strategy. Moreover, the job could in principle have been accomplished by a very expansionary monetary strategy without a stimulative fiscal policy. But the monetary policy that was actually pursued would not in itself have quickened the pace of the economy. It supplied a good set of tires for the economy to move on, but fiscal policy was the engine of growth.

We have already seen in Chapter 4 that the monetary accommodation was only transitory, being followed already in 1966–1967 by a credit crunch. But in the period we are looking at here, monetary and fiscal policy worked in the same direction—expanding economic activity without bringing about imbalances in the composition of aggregate demand.

The 1969–1970 Contraction

The expansion of economic activity in response to stimulative fiscal policy led to a significant reduction of unemployment over the 1960s. By 1968 the unemployment rate had fallen to only 3.4 percent. At that unemployment rate, output was above its full-employment level. The boom in activity not only reduced unemployment, but also increased the inflation rate. With unemployment no longer a problem and inflation uncomfortably high—4 1/2 to 5 percent in 1968–1969, up from only 1 percent at the beginning of the 1960s—monetary and fiscal policy turned to restraint.

[6] *The Political Economy of Prosperity* (New York: Norton, 1970), p. 59.

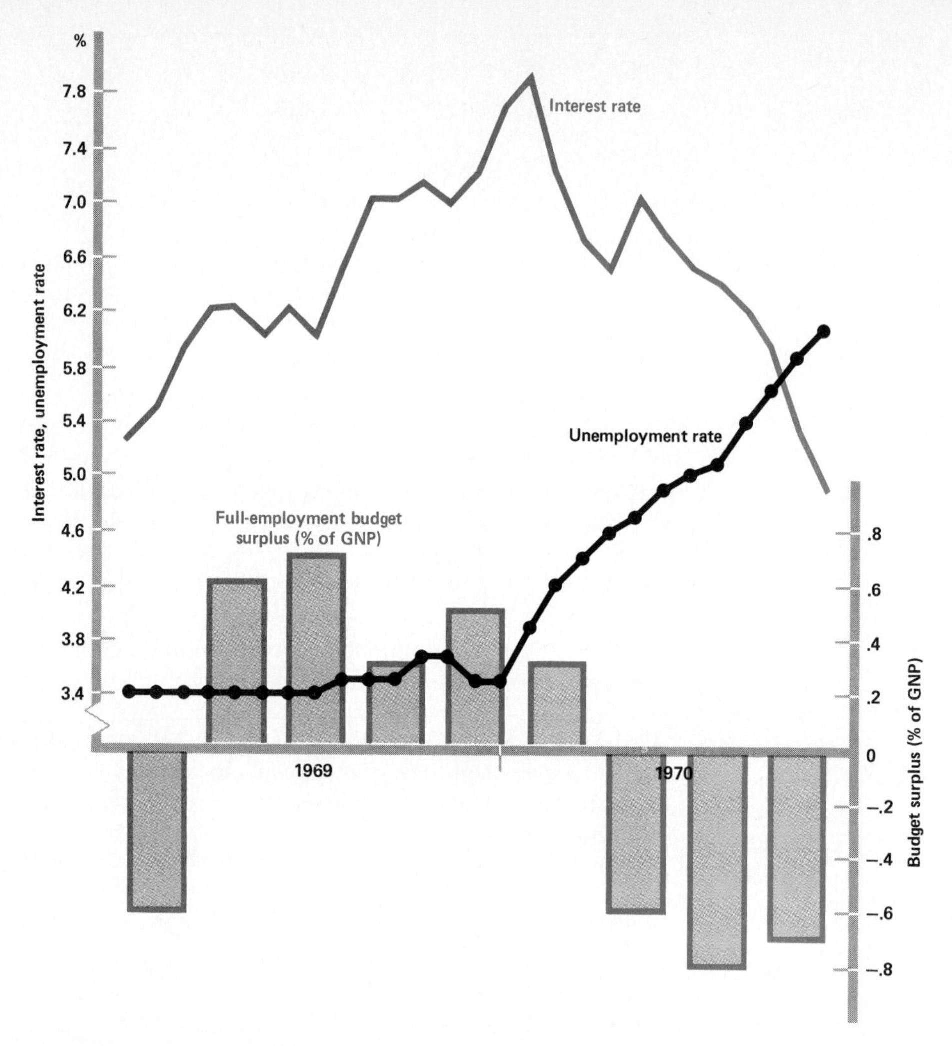

FIGURE 5-7 THE 1969–1970 CONTRACTION. The figure shows monthly data for the Treasury bill rate and the unemployment rate. Quarterly data are shown for the full-employment budget surplus, expressed as a fraction of GNP. (*Source: Business Statistics*, 1977, pp. 246 and 256; *Survey of Current Business*, April 1982, p. 27.)

Figure 5-7 shows the policy changes. Fiscal policy moved to correct the budget deficits caused by stimulative fiscal policy and the defense spending associated with the Vietnam War. Monetary policy tightened, pushing up interest rates.

The fiscal contraction, starting at the end of 1968, was a long delayed measure to help reduce the war-inflated budget deficits by increasing tax revenues. The measures that were ultimately enacted in the Revenue and

Expenditure Control Act of 1968, becoming effective in June 1968, had been recommended by the administration as early as January 1967. The chief measure was a 10 percent surtax on personal income taxes and on corporate incomes. The surtax, for example, implied that any individual who had, at a given income, previously paid $1,000 in taxes would now have to pay an extra 10 percent of those taxes, or $1,100 in taxes in total. Fiscal revenues thus increased strongly, and the budget deficit declined. These surtaxes were supplemented on the government spending side. When the Nixon administration came into power in January 1969, expenditure increases were sharply curtailed, thus further increasing the full-employment surplus.

In Figure 5-7 we show the effects of the monetary-fiscal policy mix. Tight money shows up in rising interest rates throughout 1969. The tightening of fiscal policy is indicated by the large shift in the full-employment budget. From the last quarter of 1968 to the first quarter of 1969, fiscal policy swings by a full percentage point of GNP, from a deficit of 0.6 percent to a surplus of that magnitude. If we compare annual averages (not shown in the figure), the shift is even larger: from a deficit that averaged 1.3 percent of GNP in 1968 to a surplus of 0.5 percent of GNP in 1969, which is a shift of nearly 2 percent. Clearly, fiscal policy took a decidedly restrictive course, thus complementing tight money.

Figure 5-7 also shows the unemployment rate for the period. It is interesting to observe here the lags between the restrictive policies and their effects on unemployment. Throughout 1969, the tightening of policies not withstanding, unemployment hardly changed. But by late 1969 the restraint of demand through increased taxes and high interest rates has clearly built up, and unemployment increased rapidly throughout 1970.

The business cycle timing in this recession was as follows. The longest peacetime expansion, which started in December 1961, came to an end in December 1969, the peak of the 1960s expansion. The recession, reflected in the mounting unemployment, had its trough in November 1970. From that trough a new expansion lasting exactly 3 years took place. Thus, using the business cycle dates for reference purposes, there is a very significant lag between the tightening of policies and their impact on aggregate demand.

How effective were the policies in bringing inflation to a halt? With the benefit of hindsight it is clear that the attempt at stabilization totally failed. In 1970 inflation, far from having disappeared, was even higher than in 1969. The combined monetary-fiscal tightness had put a break on economic activity, not inflation. Mounting unemployment in 1970 combined with inflation as a policy problem.

1971–1973: Expansionary Policies with Price Controls

Facing the dilemma of high inflation *and* high unemployment, the Nixon administration set out to pursue an extremely questionable policy: expanding aggregate demand vigorously while maintaining *price controls* at the same time. Price controls are government regulations that specify the rate at which firms are allowed to increase prices.

On August 15, 1971, the Nixon administration introduced its *New Eco-*

TABLE 5-6 THE 1970–1973 RECOVERY

	1970	1971	1972	1973
GNP gap	2.2	2.4	0.5	−1.6
Full-employment surplus, % of potential output	−0.5	−1.0	−1.0	−0.7
Money growth, $M1$	3.8	6.8	7.2	7.3

Source: Federal Reserve Bank of St. Louis, Survey of Current Business, *April 1982.*

nomic Policy, featuring controls on both prices and wages. Neither prices nor wages could be adjusted freely. Rather, they could rise no more than at the maximum rates set by the government. The policy was certainly successful in bringing the economy back from recession, but the target of full employment was overshot by a wide margin. With output way above normal, price controls repressed the inflation that would otherwise have emerged.

The details are shown in Table 5-6. Once again monetary and fiscal policy moved in the same direction: fiscal ease is evident in the shift of the full-employment surplus from 0.5 percent in 1969 to the deficits shown in Table 5-6. The expansionary fiscal policy was supported by a sharp increase in money growth. Thus the monetary-fiscal mix was coordinated toward expansion. The results show in the reduction of the GNP gap. Once the recovery started in 1971, the gap declined from an excess of potential over actual output of nearly 2.5 percent to a situation of overemployment. By 1973 the economy had, just as in the second part of the 1960s, overshot the full-employment mark.

The 1981–1982 Policy Mix

The three previous episodes could lead us to believe that monetary and fiscal policy always move in the same direction, be it expansion or restraint. But that is not always the case. The 1981–1982 period provides a striking example of monetary and fiscal policies at odds.

When the Reagan administration came into office at the beginning of 1981, the economy was recovering from the recession of 1980, as can be seen by the behavior of GNP in Figure 5-8. The Federal Reserve System had in 1979 instituted a new policy in which it promised to keep monetary growth low while allowing interest rates to fluctuate more than they had in the past. Thus monetary policy was expected to be contractionary.

The first priority of the new administration was a tax cut, which was promised early and went into effect in the third quarter of 1981. The effect of the tax cut can be seen in the lower panel in the decline in the full-employment budget surplus from $22 billion in the second quarter of 1981 to −$20.3 billion in the fourth quarter. This was a turnaround of $42 billion, or over 1.3 percent of GNP. Fiscal policy thus became strongly expansionary.

Accordingly, the fiscal-monetary mix was contractionary monetary policy and expansionary fiscal policy. In terms of the *IS-LM* diagram, the *LM* curve was being moved to the left and the *IS* curve to the right. The result should

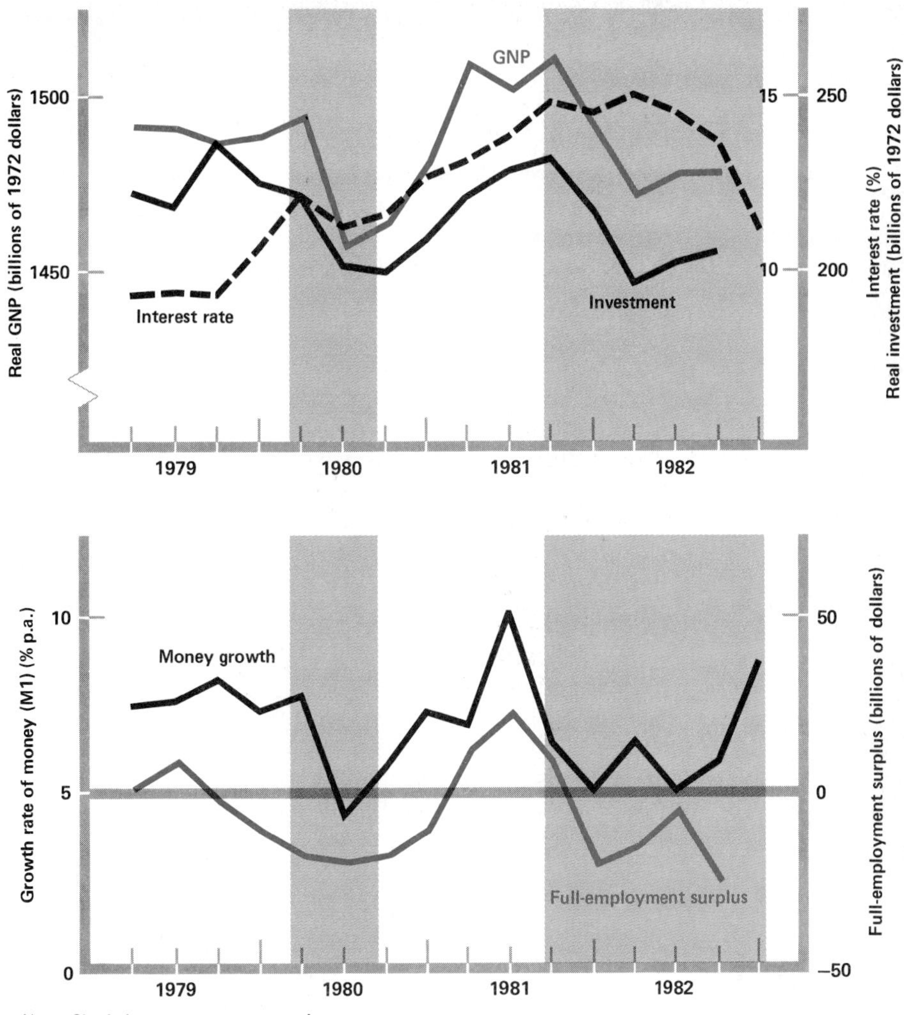

FIGURE 5-8 MACROECONOMIC VARIABLES, 1979–1982. The upper figure shows the behavior of GNP and investment, along with the corporate bond rate. Notice how the corporate bond rate continues rising well into the 1981–1982 recession, in contrast with its behavior in the previous recession. The lower panel shows monetary policy becoming more contractionary and fiscal policy more expansionary from the middle of 1981. The result is seen in the continued high interest rates and low level of investment. (*Sources: Survey of Current Business*, various issues; *Economic Report of the President*, 1983; Federal Reserve Bank of St. Louis, *Economic Indicators*, February 1983.)

have been a rise in the interest rate. The interest rate was already rising before the change in fiscal policy, but the expected effect did occur. This can be seen most clearly in Figure 5-8 from the fact that the interest rate continued rising well into the recession that began in July 1981. Normally interest rates fall after the start of a recession, but this time they stayed high for nearly a year.[7] Investment fell sharply, with much of the decline being in housing investment.

The package was thus one that, as expected, increased interest rates and reduced investment. But the package was not neutral in its effects on GNP. On balance, the contractionary monetary policy was more powerful than the expansionary fiscal policy. The economy moved into its deepest post-World War II recession.

Hopes of emerging from the recession grew at the end of 1982 when interest rates fell, helped by a rapid expansion of the stock of money. The monetary expansion at the end of 1982 was almost certainly a result of the Fed's fears that the recession could deepen even further—at a time when unemployment was already near 11 percent and bankruptcies were spreading at an alarming rate.

Two different criticisms were made of policy at the time. One was that the policy was entirely too contractionary. It was argued that the Fed should not in 1979 have changed policy so drastically. Its aim then was to reduce the inflation rate, which it ultimately did, but at great cost in unemployment. Critics argued a slower reduction of inflation would not have caused so much unemployment.

The second criticism was that the mix of policy was wrong. Critics argued for tighter fiscal policy and more expansionary monetary policy. That way investment would not have fallen so fast, and needed improvements in and additions to the capital stock could have been made. Subsequent growth of output would have been higher, the critics charged, if investment had not borne the brunt of the stabilization policy.

*5-4 A FORMAL TREATMENT OF THE *IS-LM* MODEL

Our exposition so far has been a verbal and graphical one, and has been supplemented by looking at several policy applications in recent U.S. history. We now round off the analysis with a more formal treatment that uses the equations of the *IS* and *LM* schedules to derive and discuss fiscal and monetary policy multipliers.

Equilibrium Income and the Interest Rate

The intersection of the *IS* and *LM* schedules determines equilibrium income and the equilibrium interest rate. We can derive expressions for these equilibrium values by using the equations of the *IS* and *LM* schedules. From Chapter 4 we remember the equation of the *IS* schedule or goods market equilibrium schedule as

IS schedule: $$Y = \bar{\alpha}(\bar{A} - bi) \quad (3)$$

[7] The interest rate shown is that on high-grade bonds of corporations. Similar behavior of the rate on Treasury bills is seen in Fig. 4-1.

and the equation describing money market equilibrium as[8]

LM schedule:
$$i = \frac{1}{h}\left(kY - \frac{\overline{M}}{\overline{P}}\right) \tag{4}$$

The intersection of the *IS* and *LM* schedules in the diagrams corresponds to a situation where both the *IS* and *LM* equations hold—the *same* interest rate and income levels assure equilibrium in *both* the goods and money market. In terms of the equations, that means we can substitute the interest rate from the *LM* equation (4) into the *IS* equation (3):

$$Y = \overline{\alpha}\left[\overline{A} - \frac{b}{h}\left(kY - \frac{\overline{M}}{\overline{P}}\right)\right] \tag{5}$$

Collecting terms and solving for the equilibrium level of income, we obtain

$$Y_0 = \frac{h\overline{\alpha}}{h + kb\overline{\alpha}}\overline{A} + \frac{b\overline{\alpha}}{h + kb\overline{\alpha}}\frac{\overline{M}}{\overline{P}} \tag{5a}$$

Equation (5*a*) shows the equilibrium level of income depending on two exogenous variables: autonomous spending $\overline{A}$, including fiscal policy parameters ($\overline{C}$, $\overline{I}$, $\overline{G}$, t, $\overline{TR}$) and the real money stock $\overline{M}/\overline{P}$. Equilibrium income is higher the higher the level of autonomous spending $\overline{A}$ and the higher the stock of real balances.

The equilibrium rate of interest, i_0, is obtained by substituting the equilibrium income level Y_0 from (5*a*) into the equation of the *LM* schedule, (4):

$$i_0 = \frac{k\overline{\alpha}}{h + kb\overline{\alpha}}\overline{A} - \frac{1}{h + kb\overline{\alpha}}\frac{\overline{M}}{\overline{P}} \tag{6}$$

Equation (6) shows that the equilibrium interest rate depends on the parameters of fiscal policy captured in the multiplier and the term $\overline{A}$, and on the real money stock. A higher real money stock implies a lower equilibrium interest rate.

For policy questions we are interested in the precise relation between changes in fiscal policy or changes in the real money stock and the resulting changes in equilibrium income. The *monetary* and *fiscal policy multipliers* provide the relevant information.

The Fiscal Policy Multiplier

The fiscal policy multiplier tells us how much an increase in government spending changes the equilibrium level of income, holding the real money

[8] To deal with the case where liquidity preference is not only high but at some rate, say i', *perfectly* elastic, we could rewrite the *LM* equation as $\overline{M}/\overline{P} = kY - h(i - i')$, so that real money demand depends on the excess of the interest rate above some floor level i'. With this formulation, (4) becomes $i = i' + (1/h)[kY - \overline{M}/\overline{P}]$. If h is extremely high, the interest rate is $i = i'$ or the *LM* schedule is horizontal at the level i'.

supply constant. Examine Equation (5*a*) and consider the effect of an increase in government spending on income. The increase in government spending $\Delta\overline{G}$ is a change in autonomous spending, so that $\Delta\overline{A} = \Delta\overline{G}$. The effect of the change in $\overline{G}$ is given by

$$\frac{\Delta Y_0}{\Delta\overline{G}} = \frac{h\bar{\alpha}}{h + bk\bar{\alpha}} \tag{7}$$

We note that the expression in Equation (7) is zero if h is very small and will be equal to $\bar{\alpha}$ if h approaches infinity. This corresponds, respectively, to vertical and horizontal *LM* schedules. Similarly, a large value of either b or k serves to reduce the effect on income of government spending. Why? A high value of k implies a large increase in money demand as income rises and hence a large increase in interest rates in order to maintain money market equilibrium. In combination with a high b, this implies a large reduction in private aggregate demand. Equation (7) thus presents the algebraic analysis that corresponds to the graphical analysis of Figures 5-2 and 5-3.

The Monetary Policy Multiplier

The monetary policy multiplier tells us by how much an increase in the real money supply increases the equilibrium level of income, keeping fiscal policy unchanged. Using Equation (5*a*) to examine the effects of an increase in the real money supply on income, we have

$$\frac{\Delta Y_0}{\Delta(\overline{M}/\overline{P})} = \frac{b\bar{\alpha}}{h + bk\bar{\alpha}} \tag{8}$$

The smaller h and k and the larger b and $\bar{\alpha}$, the more expansionary the effect of an increase in real balances on the equilibrium level of income. Large b and $\bar{\alpha}$ correspond to a very flat *IS* schedule. Equation (8) thus corresponds to the graphical analysis presented in Figure 4-16.

The Classical Case and the Liquidity Trap

We now turn to two special cases that demonstrate the role of the demand function for real balances in the effectiveness of monetary and fiscal policies. Consider first the possibility that money demand does not depend at all on interest rates and is simply proportional to real income. This happens if the parameter h is zero, so that real money demand is simply

$$L = kY \tag{9}$$

In this case monetary equilibrium, equating the demand and supply of money, leads to[9]

[9] The demand for real balances is $L = kY$ and the supply $\overline{M}/\overline{P}$. Thus with demand equal to supply, $\overline{M}/\overline{P} = kY$ or $Y = (1/k)\overline{M}/\overline{P}$.

$$Y = (1/k)\frac{\overline{M}}{\overline{P}} \tag{10}$$

This case is called the *classical case* because classical (that is, nineteenth century) economists did not give much emphasis to the interest response of money demand. The case is important because it has the following implication: If money demand does not depend on the interest rate and only on the level of income, as in (9), the money supply alone determines income.

In this classical case the level of nominal income, $\overline{P}Y$, is proportional to the nominal money stock. Changes in the nominal money stock lead to changes in income in the same proportion. Furthermore, while income does respond to money, it is *totally* unresponsive to fiscal policy. We also can see the point from (5*a*) by setting $h = 0$.

Interest Rates and Fiscal Policy

How is it possible that fiscal policy should have no effect at all on income? After all, if the government were to spend more, how is it possible that the increased spending should *not* raise income? The reasoning is as follows. An increase in government spending does lead to an incipient rise in aggregate demand and income, but that immediately raises the demand for money. With the money supply unchanged, interest rates will shoot up to clear the money market. But the rise in interest rates does nothing to reduce the quantity of money demanded. It does, however, have an impact on private investment spending. As interest rates rise because of the excess demand for money, investment spending declines. The fall in investment spending compensates exactly for the higher government spending, and the level of income is unchanged.

We can see this by looking at the investment equation (11), obtained by substituting in the equilibrium interest rate from (6):

$$I = \overline{I} - bi_0 = \overline{I} - \frac{bk\overline{\alpha}}{h + bk\overline{\alpha}}\overline{A} + \frac{b}{h + bk\overline{\alpha}}\frac{\overline{M}}{\overline{P}} \tag{11}$$

In the case where $h = 0$, the coefficient multiplying $\overline{A}$ in (11) is 1. This means that a \$1 increase in $\overline{A}$, given the real money stock, leads to an equal reduction of investment. That is what we call *full* crowding out. In general, with h not equal to zero, the coefficient of $\overline{A}$ is a fraction, as shown in (11). The larger h, the smaller the fraction of an extra dollar of government spending that is offset by reduced investment spending.

Liquidity Trap

The other extreme for monetary and fiscal policy is represented by a world where h is infinite. Then money and other assets are effectively perfect substitutes. In such a world, Equation (5*a*) reduces to

$$Y = \overline{\alpha}\overline{A} \tag{12}$$

This is the "multiplier world" of Chapter 3, where autonomous spending entirely determines the level of real income. It occurs if the economy is in a liquidity trap.

In the liquidity trap, money does not matter for income determination because money demand is *so* responsive to interest rates. The smallest change in interest rates is sufficient to eliminate imbalances in the money market that might arise from changes in money supply or in income. And because these corrective changes in interest rates are so small, they do not even affect aggregate demand. The interest rate effect can be verified from (11). With h extremely high, investment spending is not influenced by either monetary or fiscal policy.

5-5 SUMMARY

1 Taking into account the effects of fiscal policy on the interest rate modifies the multiplier results of Chapter 3. Fiscal expansion, except in extreme circumstances, still leads to an income expansion. However, the rise in interest rates that comes about through the increase in money demand caused by higher income dampens the expansion.
2 Fiscal policy is more effective the smaller are the induced changes in interest rates and the smaller is the response of investment to these interest rate changes.
3 In the liquidity trap, the interest rate is constant because money demand is completely elastic with respect to the interest rate. Monetary policy has no effect on the economy, whereas fiscal policy has its full multiplier effect on output—and no effect on interest rates.
4 In the classical case, the demand for money is independent of the interest rate. In that case, changes in the money stock change income. But fiscal policy has no effect on income—it affects only the interest rate. In this case there is complete crowding out of private spending by government spending.
5 Neither the liquidity trap nor the classical case applies in practice. But they are useful cases to study in order to show what determines the magnitude of monetary and fiscal policy multipliers.
6 A fiscal expansion, because it leads to higher interest rates, displaces or crowds out some private investment. The extent of crowding out is a sensitive issue in assessing the usefulness and desirability of fiscal policy as a tool of stabilization policy.
7 In an economy that is less than fully employed, crowding out need not occur. The monetary authorities can provide an accommodating monetary policy that avoids the rise in interest rates associated with the output expansion.
8 The question of the monetary-fiscal policy mix arises because expansionary monetary policy reduces the interest rate while expansionary fiscal policy increases the interest rate. Accordingly, expansionary fiscal policy

increases output while reducing the level of investment; expansionary monetary policy increases output and the level of investment.

9 Governments have to choose the mix in accordance with their objectives for economic growth, or increasing consumption, or from the viewpoint of their beliefs about the desirable size of the government.

KEY CONCEPTS

Crowding out
Monetary-fiscal policy mix
Monetary accommodation
Monetizing budget deficits
Composition of output
Investment subsidy
Price controls
Monetary policy multiplier
Fiscal policy multiplier

PROBLEMS

1 The economy is at full employment. Now the government wants to change the composition of demand toward investment and away from consumption without, however, allowing aggregate demand to go beyond full employment. What is the required policy mix? Use the *IS-LM* diagram to show your policy proposal.

2 Discuss the role of the parameters $\overline{\alpha}$, h, b, and k in the transmission mechanism linking an increase in government spending to the resulting change in equilibrium income. In developing the analysis use the following table:

(1)	(2)	(3)
Increase in $\overline{G}$ raises aggregate demand and output	The increase in income raises money demand and hence interest rates	The increase in interest rates reduces investment spending and hence dampens the output expansion

3 Suppose the government cuts income taxes. Show in the *IS-LM* model the impact of the tax cut under two assumptions: One, the government keeps interest rates constant through an accommodating monetary policy; two, the money stock remains unchanged. Explain the difference in results.

4 Discuss the circumstances in which the monetary and fiscal policy multipliers are, respectively, equal to zero. Explain in words why this can happen and how likely you think this is.

5 Consider an economy where the government considers two alternative programs for contraction. One is the removal of an investment subsidy; the other is a rise in income tax rates. Use the *IS-LM* schedule and the investment schedule, as shown in Figure 5-5, to discuss the impact of these alternative policies on income, interest rates, and investment.

*6 Suppose the parameters k and $\overline{\alpha}$ are 0.5 and 2, respectively. Assume there is an increase of $1 billion in government spending. By how much must the real money stock be increased to hold interest rates constant?

7 Discuss the circumstances where fiscal expansion leads to *full* crowding out.

8 In Figure 5-6 the economy can move to full employment by an expansion in either money or the full-employment deficit. Which policy leads to E_1 and which to E_2? How would you

expect the choice to be made? Who would most strongly favor moving to E_1? E_2? What policy would correspond to "balanced growth"?

9 "We can have the GNP path we want equally well with a tight fiscal policy and an easier monetary policy, or the reverse, within fairly broad limits. The real basis for choice lies in many subsidiary targets, besides real GNP and inflation, that are differentially affected by fiscal and monetary policies." What are some of the subsidiary targets referred to in the quote? How would they be affected by alternative policy combinations?

10 Explain why:

(*a*) A rise in interest rates reduces the quantity of real balances demanded.

(*b*) A fall in interest rates raises investment spending.

PART TWO

6

CONSUMPTION, WEALTH, AND LAGS

The *IS-LM* model developed in Chapter 4 provides a framework which enables us to understand the interaction of some of the main macroeconomic variables. Now we retrace our steps to present a more detailed and more sophisticated treatment of the key equations in the *IS-LM* model. The present chapter deals with the consumption function—since consumption purchases account for over 60 percent of aggregate demand, this is the natural place to begin. The following three chapters flesh out the behavioral equations of the *IS-LM* model and thus move us toward a more realistic and reliable understanding of the working of the economy.

Our starting point in examining consumption behavior is the consumption function we have been using in the previous chapters. Thus far, we have been assuming that consumption is a linear function of disposable income:

$$C = \overline{C} + cYD \qquad \overline{C} > 0 \qquad 1 > c > 0 \tag{1}$$

Now what does the empirical evidence show? Do the data for the post-World War II period bear out the hypothesis of a consumption function such as Equation (1)? We plot consumption and disposable income

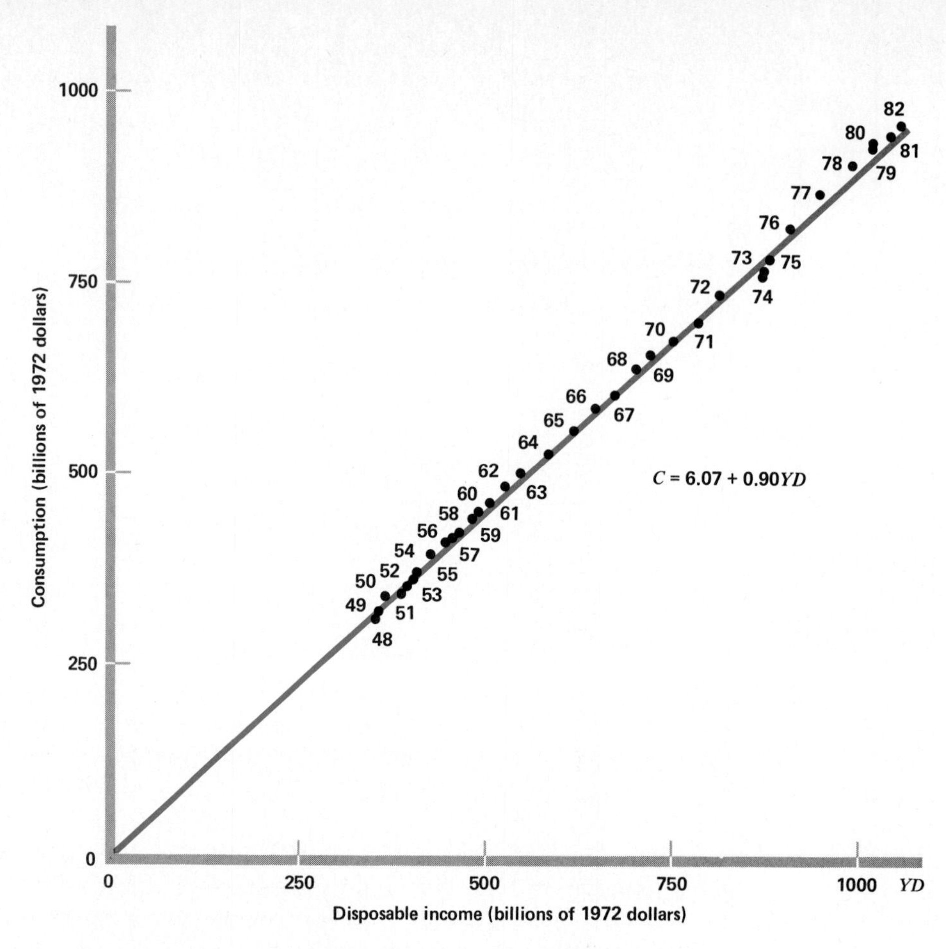

FIGURE 6-1 THE CONSUMPTION-INCOME RELATION, 1948–1982. There is a close relationship in practice between consumption spending and disposable income. Consumption spending rises on average by 90 cents for every extra dollar of disposable income. The red line is the fitted regression line that summarizes the relationship shown by the points for the individual years.

(both in 1972 dollars) for each of the years from 1948 through 1982 in Figure 6-1. The diagram clearly reveals a close positive relationship between consumption and disposable income. To find numerical estimates of the intercept ($\overline{C}$) and the marginal propensity to consume (c), we "fit" a regression line to the observations. The regression line is fitted to the data using the method of least squares, which produces the linear equation that best characterizes the relation between consumption and disposable income contained in the data.[1]

[1] It is frequently useful to summarize a relationship, such as that of Fig. 6-1, between consumption expenditures and disposable income by writing an equation such as Eq. (2), which has specific numerical values in it, rather than the more general form of Eq. (1), which does not specify numerical values of the coefficients $\overline{C}$ and c. The line drawn in Fig. 6-1 is the line

The estimated regression line is shown in Figure 6-1 as the solid line and is reported in Equation (2). The estimate of the intercept is $\overline{C} = 6.07$ (6.07 billion 1972 dollars), and the estimate of the marginal propensity to consume is 0.90.

$$C = 6.07 + 0.90YD \qquad \text{(annual data, 1948–1982)} \tag{2}$$

Two characteristics of a consumption function such as Equation (1) are borne out by the empirical equation (2). There is a positive intercept ($\overline{C} = 6.07$), and the marginal propensity to consume ($c = 0.90$) is positive and less than unity.

If we divide through by YD in Equation (2), we obtain an equation that gives the average propensity to consume (C/YD) as a function of disposable income:

$$\frac{C}{YD} = \frac{6.07}{YD} + 0.90 \tag{3}$$

Equation (3) indicates that the average propensity to consume declines as disposable income rises.[2] However, although the intercept, 6.07, is positive, it is very small relative to disposable income, which is \$1,060 billion 1972 dollars, in 1982.[3] If the intercept were actually zero, then we see from Equations (1) and (3) that consumption would be proportional to disposable income, with $C/YD = c$. The marginal and average propensities to consume would be equal. The relationship shown by Figure 6-1 and Equation (2) is essentially one of proportionality, with the average and marginal propensities to consume out of disposable income equal to each other, at about 0.91.

Inspection of the regression line in Figure 6-1 suggests that the estimated equation fits well. There are no points far off the fitted line. As a first approximation then, Equation (2) provides a reasonable summary of consumption behavior. The next step is to ask whether Equation (2) can be improved upon, and if so, to determine how.

Figure 6-2 shows the average propensity to consume, as calculated from Equation (3), the smooth line, and the actual propensity to consume in each year. The smooth line, the predicted average propensity to consume, declines slightly over time as YD rises. The actual propensity to consume jumps around a good deal, and stays above or below the predicted line for some years at a time, for example, from 1959 to 1963, or 1973 to 1975.

---

represented by Eq. (2). That line is calculated by minimizing the sum of the squares of the vertical distances of the points in Fig. 6-1 from the line, and it provides a good description of the general relationship between the two variables. [Those familiar with the method should note that we have corrected for serial correlation in calculating Eq. (2).] For further details on the fitting of such lines, called least-squares regression lines, see Robert S. Pindyck and Daniel L. Rubinfeld, *Econometric Models and Economic Forecasts*, 2d ed. (New York: McGraw-Hill, 1980).

[2] You should check a data source, such as the *Economic Report of the President*, to see how well the predicted average propensity to consume from Eq. (3) matches the actual propensity for 1983 and later years.

[3] Technically, the intercept is statistically not significantly different from zero. See Pindyck and Rubinfeld, op. cit., for the meaning of tests of significance.

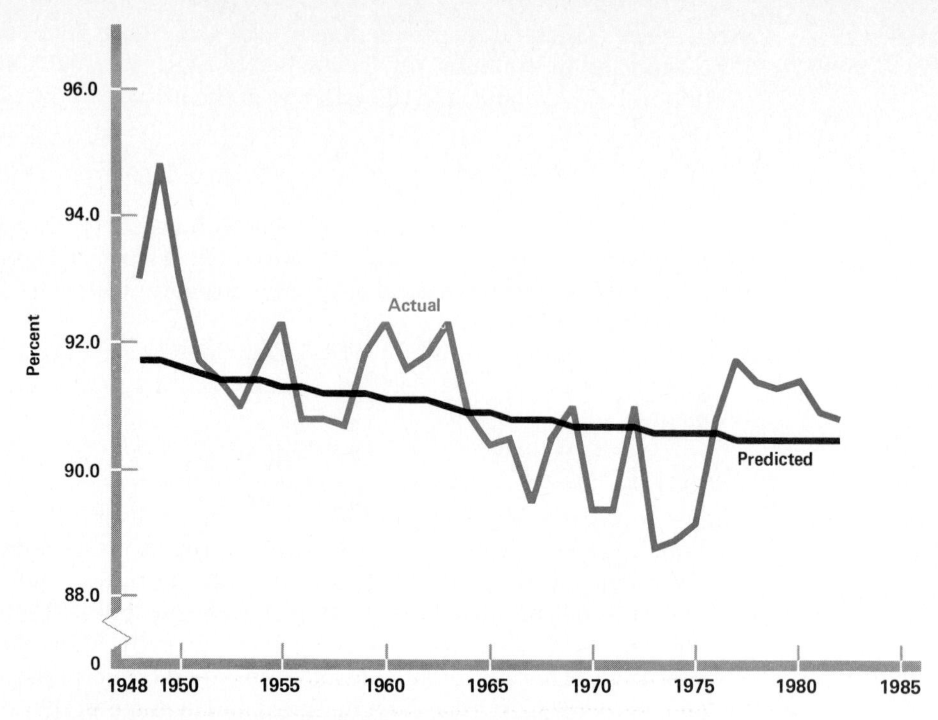

FIGURE 6-2 THE ACTUAL AND PREDICTED AVERAGE PROPENSITY TO CONSUME, 1948–1982. The average propensity to consume implied by Equation (3) is shown by the black "predicted" line. The actual average propensity to consume fluctuates more than that implied by the equation.

The deviations of the actual ratio from the predicted one raise the question of how well the equation predicts consumption behavior. For example, in 1973 the actual propensity to consume was 0.888, whereas the predicted propensity was 0.906. The error of 0.018 translates into an error in predicting consumption of almost \$16 billion, over 1 percent of GNP.[4] The differences between actual and predicted C/YD shown in Figure 6-2 suggest that the simple consumption function equation (2) can be improved upon.

In this chapter, we explore three more sophisticated formulations of the consumption function than Equation (1). These are the *life-cycle* theory of consumption, the *permanent-income hypothesis,* and the *relative-income* formulation, described in Sections 6-2 through 6-4. Before we examine those theories, though, we outline in Section 6-1 an empirical puzzle about the consumption function that was historically important in leading to the new theories of the consumption function.

[4] Disposable income in 1973 was 864.7 billion, measured in 1972 dollars.

6-1 A CONSUMPTION FUNCTION PUZZLE

The puzzle we describe consists of two types of evidence that made their appearance in the late 1940s and that were apparently in conflict. The first type of evidence came from estimates of the standard consumption function, Equation (1), using annual data for the 1929–1941 period. (No earlier data were available then.) The estimated equation (in 1972 dollars) is

$$C = 47.6 + 0.73YD \qquad \text{(annual data, 1929–1941)} \tag{4}$$

This equation implies that the average propensity to consume falls as the level of income rises. It also has a low marginal propensity to consume. If we used Equation (4) to predict today's average propensity to consume, the estimate would be 0.77, which of course is far off the actual ratio of about 0.9.

The second piece of evidence was the finding by Nobel Prize winner, Simon Kuznets, using averages of data over long periods—10 and 30 years—that there was near proportionality between consumption and income.[5] This is consistent with the intercept term in Equation (1) being zero. The average propensity to consume that he found for three overlapping 30-year periods is shown in Table 6-1. The Kuznets results suggest, using long-term averages, that there is little variation in the ratio of consumption to income and, in particular, that there is no tendency for the average propensity to decline as disposable income rises.

There is clearly a conflict between the implications of the consumption function in Equation (4) and Kuznets' findings. The Kuznets results suggest that the average propensity to consume is constant over long periods, whereas Equation (4) suggests it falls as income rises. It is also clear that the consumption function estimated in Equation (4) on the basis of the prewar data is inconsistent with the same function estimated on the basis of postwar data, that is, Equation (2).

The puzzle of the discrepancy between Kuznets' findings and Equation (4) was well known by the time the three alternative theories we outline below were developed. In resolving the puzzle, all three theories draw on the notion that consumption is related to a broader income measure than just current income. As already noted, the broader measures go under the names

[5] Simon Kuznets, *National Product Since 1869* and *National Income, A Summary of Findings* (New York: National Bureau of Economic Research, 1946).

TABLE 6-1 THE KUZNETS FINDING

	1869–1898	1884–1913	1904–1933
Average propensity	0.867	0.867	0.879

Source: Simon Kuznets, National Income, A Summary of Findings *(New York: National Bureau of Economic Research, 1946), table 16.*

of *lifetime income, permanent income,* and *relative income.* These concepts have in common the recognition that consumption spending is maintained relatively constant in the face of fluctuations of current income. Consumption spending is not geared to what we earn today, but to what we earn on average. The important question obviously is what "average" means in this context.

The theories we present all imply that there is a difference between the marginal propensity to consume in the short run and the marginal propensity to consume in the long run. The short-run consumption function—the relationship between consumption spending and *current* disposable income—is indeed quite flat. However, this consumption function shifts upward over time. These shifts in the relationship between consumption and current disposable income bring into the discussion the roles of *wealth* and *permanent income* in affecting consumer spending.[6] These considerations are taken up in the next two sections.

6-2 THE LIFE-CYCLE THEORY OF CONSUMPTION AND SAVING

The consumption function (1) is based on the simple notion that individuals' consumption behavior in a given period is related to their income in that period. The *life-cycle hypothesis* views individuals, instead, as planning their consumption and saving behavior over long periods with the intention of allocating their consumption in the best possible way over their entire lifetimes.

The life-cycle hypothesis views savings as resulting mainly from individuals' desires to provide for consumption in old age. As we shall see, the theory points to a number of unexpected factors affecting the savings rate of the economy; for instance, the age structure of the population is, in principle, an important determinant of consumption and savings behavior.

To anticipate the main results of this section, we can already state here that we will derive a consumption function of the form

$$C = aWR + cYL \tag{5}$$

where WR is real wealth, a is the marginal propensity to consume out of wealth, YL is *labor income*, and c is the marginal propensity to consume out of labor income. Labor income is the income that is earned by labor, as opposed to the income earned by other factors of production, such as the rent earned by land or the profits earned by capital.

In developing the life-cycle hypothesis of saving and consumption, we

[6] The theories of the consumption function developed hereafter are also useful for explaining another empirical puzzle that we shall not go into in detail. In *cross-sectional* studies of the relationship between consumption and income—studies in which the consumption of a sample of families is related to their income—the marginal propensity to consume out of disposable income also appears to be lower than the average propensity to consume, with the average propensity to consume falling as the level of income rises. If you are interested in the reconciliation of this evidence with the long-run evidence of Kuznets, you should look at the ingenious explanation advanced by Milton Friedman through the permanent-income hypothesis. Follow up the reference given in footnote 12.

show what determines the marginal propensities a and c in Equation (5), why wealth should affect consumption, and how the life-cycle hypothesis helps explain the Kuznets puzzle described above.

Consider a person who expects to live for NL years, work and earn income for WL years, and be in retirement for $(NL - WL)$ years. The individual's year 1 is the first year of work. We shall, in what follows, ignore any uncertainty about either life expectancy or the length of working life. We shall assume, too, that no interest is earned on savings, so that current saving translates dollar for dollar into future consumption possibilities. With these assumptions, we can approach the saving or consumption decision with two questions. First, what are the individual's lifetime consumption possibilities? Second, how will she choose to distribute her consumption over her lifetime?

Consider now the consumption possibilities. For the moment we ignore property income (income from assets) and focus attention on labor income YL. Income, YL, and consumption, C, are measured in real terms. Given WL years of working, *lifetime income* (from labor) is $(YL \times WL)$, income per working year times the number of working years. Consumption over the individual's lifetime cannot exceed this lifetime income unless she is born with wealth, which we initially assume is not the case. Accordingly, we have determined the first part of the consumer's problem in finding the limit of lifetime consumption.

We assume the individual will want to distribute consumption over her lifetime so that she has a flat or even flow of consumption. Rather than consume a lot in one period and very little in another, the preferred profile is to consume exactly equal amounts in each period.[7] Clearly, this assumption implies that consumption is not geared to *current* income (which is zero during retirement), but rather to *lifetime income.*

Lifetime consumption equals lifetime income. This means that the planned level of consumption C, which is the same in every period, times the number of years in life NL equals lifetime income:

$$C \times NL = YL \times WL \tag{6}$$

where WL is working life. Lifetime income is equal to $(YL \times WL)$. Dividing through by NL, we have planned consumption per year, C, which is proportional to labor income:

$$C = \frac{WL}{NL} \times YL \tag{7}$$

[7] Why? The basic reason is the notion of diminishing marginal utility of consumption. Consider two alternative consumption plans. One involves an equal amount of consumption in each of two periods; the other involves consuming all in one period and none in the other. The principle of diminishing marginal utility of income implies that in the latter case, we would be better off by transferring some consumption from the period of plenty toward that of starvation. The loss in utility in the period of plenty is *more* than compensated by the gain in utility in the period of scarcity. And there is a gain to be made by transferring consumption so long as there is any difference in consumption between the two periods. The principle of diminishing marginal utility of consumption conforms well with the observation that most people choose stable life-styles—not, in general, saving furiously in one period to have a big bust in the next, but rather, consuming at about the same level every period.

The factor of proportionality in Equation (7) is WL/NL, the fraction of lifetime spent working. Accordingly, Equation (7) states that in each year of working life a fraction of labor income is consumed, where that fraction is equal to the proportion of working life in total life.

NUMERICAL EXAMPLE

Suppose a person starts working at age 20, plans to work till 65, and will die at 80. The working life WL is thus 45 years (= 65 − 20) and the number of years of life, NL, is 60 years (= 80 − 20). Annual labor income YL is $20,000.

Then
$$\begin{aligned}\text{Lifetime income} &= YL \times WL \\ &= \$20{,}000 \times 45 \\ &= \$900{,}000\end{aligned}$$

This person will receive a total of $900,000 over her working lifetime.

The lifetime income, $900,000, has to be spread over the 60 years of life. The consumer wants to spread it evenly, and so

$$C = \frac{\$900{,}000}{60} = \$15{,}000 = \frac{WL}{NL} \times YL$$

$$= \frac{45}{60} \times 20{,}000$$

$$= 0.75 \times 20{,}000$$

In this example, 0.75 of labor income is consumed each year the person works. Why is the propensity to consume out of labor income in this example equal to 0.75? Because that is the fraction of lifetime that the person works.

Saving and Dissaving

The counterpart of Equation (7) is the saving function. Remembering that saving is equal to income less consumption, we have

$$S \equiv YL - C = YL\left(\frac{NL - WL}{NL}\right) \tag{8}$$

Equation (8) states that saving during the period in which the individual works is equal to a fraction of labor income, with that fraction being equal to the proportion of life spent in retirement.

Figure 6-3 shows the lifetime pattern of consumption, saving, and *dissaving*.[8] Over the whole lifetime, there is an even flow of consumption at the rate

[8] Figure 6-3 was developed by Franco Modigliani in "The Life Cycle Hypothesis of Saving, the Demand for Wealth and the Supply of Capital," *Social Research*, vol. 33, no. 2, 1966. Modigliani, together with Richard Brumberg and Albert Ando, formulated the life-cycle theory.

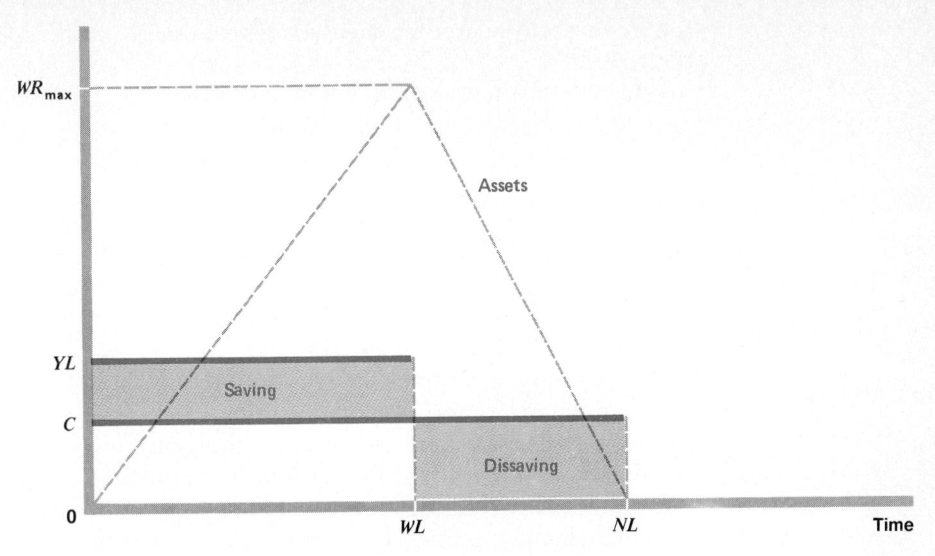

FIGURE 6-3 LIFETIME INCOME, CONSUMPTION, SAVINGS, AND WEALTH IN THE LIFE-CYCLE MODEL. During the working life, lasting WL years, the individual saves, building up assets. At the end of the working life, the individual begins to live off her assets, dissaving for the next $(NL - WL)$ years, till the end of life. Consumption is constant at level C throughout the lifetime. All assets have been used up at the end of life.

of C, amounting in total to $C \times NL$. That consumption spending is financed during working life out of current income. During retirement the consumption is financed by drawing down the savings that have been accumulated during working life. Therefore the shaded areas $(YL - C) \times WL$ and $C \times (NL - WL)$ are equal, or equivalently, saving during working years finances dissaving during retirement.

The important idea of lifetime consumption theory is apparent from Figure 6-3. It is that consumption plans are made so as to achieve a smooth or even level of consumption by saving during periods of high income and dissaving during periods of low income. This is, therefore, an important departure from consumption based on current income. It is an important difference because, in addition to current income, the whole future profile of income enters into the calculation of lifetime consumption. Before developing that aspect further, however, we return to Figure 6-3 to consider the role of assets.

During the working years, the individual saves to finance consumption during retirement. The savings build up assets, and we accordingly show in Figure 6-3 how the individual's wealth or assets increase over working life and reach a maximum at retirement age. From that time on, assets decline because the individual sells assets to pay for current consumption.

What is the maximum level that assets reach? Remember that assets are built up to finance consumption during retirement. Total consumption during retirement is equal to $C \times (NL - WL)$. All that consumption is financed out of the assets accumulated by the date of retirement, which is when assets are at their peak.

Denote the maximum level of assets by WR_{max}. Then,

$$WR_{max} = C \times (NL - WL)$$

For instance, in the numerical example above, where C was \$15,000 and $(NL - WL)$ was equal to 15, the individual would have \$15,000 × 15 = \$225,000 saved at the date of retirement. Equivalently, the person has worked for 45 years, saving \$5,000 each year. That too means she has accumulated \$225,000 at age 65.

This simple case gives the spirit of the life-cycle hypothesis of consumption and saving. People do not want to consume over their lifetimes at precisely the same times and amounts they earn income. Thus they save and dissave so as to consume their lifetime incomes in the pattern they want. Typically, the theory argues, they will save while working, and then use the savings to finance spending in their retirement years.

Introducing Wealth

The next step is to extend this model and allow for initial assets, assuming the individual is born to wealth.[9] We can draw on the previous insight that the consumer will spread any existing resources to achieve an even lifetime consumption profile. The individual who has assets in addition to labor income will plan to use these assets to add to lifetime consumption. A person who is at some point T in life, with a stock of wealth WR and labor income accruing for another $(WL - T)$ years at the rate of YL, and with a life expectancy of $(NL - T)$ years to go, will behave as follows. The person's lifetime consumption possibilities are

$$C(NL - T) = WR + (WL - T)YL \tag{9}$$

where we have included wealth WR along with lifetime labor income as a source of finance for lifetime consumption. From Equation (9), consumption in each period is equal to

$$C = aWR + cYL \qquad a \equiv \frac{1}{NL - T} \qquad c \equiv \frac{WL - T}{NL - T} \qquad WL > T \tag{10}$$

where the coefficients a and c are, respectively, the marginal propensities to consume out of wealth and out of labor income.

In the numerical example above we considered a person starting to work at age 20, who will retire at 65 and die at 80. Thus $WL = 65 - 20 = 45$; and $NL = 80 - 20 = 60$. We also assumed $YL = 20{,}000$.

[9] The individual may receive wealth early in life through gifts or bequests. In the fully developed life cycle model, the individual, in calculating lifetime consumption, has also to take account of any bequests he or she may want to leave. We discuss the role of bequests in Box 6-1.

Now suppose the person is 40 years old. Accordingly $T = 20$, meaning that the person is in the twentieth year of working life. We can calculate the propensity to consume out of wealth a and the propensity to consume out of income c from Equation (10). For this person, at age 40 (i.e., for $T = 20$):

$$a = \frac{1}{NL - T} = \frac{1}{60 - 20} = .025$$

$$c = \frac{WL - T}{NL - T} = \frac{45 - 20}{60 - 20} = .625$$

Suppose now that the individual's wealth is \$200,000. Then from the consumption function, Equation (10), we find:

$$\begin{aligned} C &= (.025 \times 200{,}000) + (.625 \times 20{,}000) \\ &= 5000 + 12{,}500 \\ &= 17{,}500. \end{aligned}$$

Note that the consumption level here is higher than in the previous example. That is because this individual has more wealth at age 40 than he would have if all his wealth came from saving out of labor income. (That amount, at age 40, would from the previous example be \$100,000—since the individual in the previous example saved \$5,000 per year, and at $T = 20$ he has been working 20 years.) We can conclude that we are dealing here with someone who inherited wealth and started out working life with some wealth.

Thus, in our model of individual lifetime consumption, we have derived a consumption function like Equation (5), where both wealth and labor income affect the individual's consumption decisions. It is important to recognize from Equation (10) that the marginal propensities are related to the individual's position in the life cycle. The closer a person is to the end of lifetime, the higher the marginal propensity to consume out of wealth. Thus, a man with 2 more years of life will consume half his remaining wealth in each of the remaining 2 years. The marginal propensity to consume out of labor income is related both to the remaining number of years during which income will be earned, $WL - T$, and to the number of years over which these earnings are spread, $NL - T$. It is quite clear from Equation (10) that an increase in either wealth or labor income will raise consumption expenditures. It is apparent, too, that lengthening working life relative to retirement will raise consumption because it increases lifetime income and reduces the length of the period of dissaving. The most basic point, however, is that Equation (10) shows both (lifetime) income and wealth as determinants of consumption spending.

To summarize where we have come so far, we note that in this form of the life-cycle model:

1 Consumption is constant over the consumer's lifetime.
2 Consumption spending is financed by lifetime income plus initial wealth.
3 During each year a fraction $1/(NL - T)$ of wealth will be consumed.

4 Current consumption spending depends on current wealth and lifetime income.

Extensions

The model as outlined makes very strong simplifying assumptions. It can be extended to remove most of the strong assumptions without affecting the underlying result of Equation (10), that consumption is related to both labor income and wealth.

First, it is necessary to take account of the possibility that saving earns interest, so that a dollar not consumed today will provide more than a dollar's consumption tomorrow. Second, the analysis has to be extended to allow for the fact that individuals are uncertain of the length of their lifetimes, and also that they sometimes want to leave bequests to their heirs. In this latter case, they would not plan to consume all their resources over their own lifetimes. Similarly, the model has to be extended to take account of the composition of the family over time, so that some consumption is provided for children before they begin to work. But, to repeat, these extensions do not change the basic results contained in Equation (10).

A final extension is very important. In practice, one never knows exactly what one's lifetime labor income will be, and lifetime consumption plans have to be made on the basis of predictions of future labor income. This, of course, raises the issue of how income is to be predicted. We do not pursue this important issue here, but leave it to the next section on permanent income, which is an estimate of lifetime income. However, *expected* lifetime labor income would be related to *current* disposable labor income, leading to a form of the consumption function like Equation (5), perhaps with other variables also included.

Indeed, it is useful to think of the life-cycle and permanent-income theories as being fundamentally the same, with the life-cycle theory developing most carefully the implications of the model for the role of wealth and other variables in the consumption function,[10] and the permanent-income theory concentrating on the best way to predict lifetime income.

Aggregate Consumption and Saving

The theory as so far outlined is strictly a theory about consumption and saving by individuals over the course of their lifetimes. How does it relate to aggregate consumption, which is, after all, the focus of macroeconomic interest in consumption? Imagine an economy in which population and the GNP were constant through time. Each individual in that economy would go through the life cycle of saving and dissaving outlined in Figure 6-3. The economy as a whole, though, would not be saving. At any one time, the saving of working people would be exactly matched by the dissaving of retired people. However, if the population were growing, there would be more

[10] The other variables indicated here will be discussed in the next paragraph.

young people than old, thus more saving in total than dissaving, and there would be net saving in the economy. Thus, aggregate consumption depends in part on the age composition of the population. It also depends on such characteristics of the economy as the average age of retirement and the presence or absence of Social Security. These surprising implications of the theory indicate the richness of the approach.

Implications

We want to return to Equation (5) to emphasize again the role of wealth. Note from Equation (5) that if there were an increase in wealth, the ratio of consumption to disposable income would rise. This has a bearing on the puzzle described in Section 6-1, where the average propensity to consume seems, on the basis of Equation (4), to decline with income, and on the basis of Kuznets' findings, to remain constant on average over long periods.

If we divide through in Equation (5) by YD, we obtain

$$\frac{C}{YD} = a\frac{WR}{YD} + c\frac{YL}{YD} \tag{11}$$

Now, if the ratio of wealth to disposable income and the ratio of disposable labor income to total disposable income are constant, then Equation (11) shows that the ratio of consumption to disposable income will be constant. However, if the ratio of wealth to disposable income is changing, the average propensity to consume will also be changing.

This suggests, as an explanation of the Kuznets puzzle, the possibility that the ratio of wealth to disposable income is roughly constant over long periods, and that it varied considerably during the 1930s, to which period the consumption function, Equation (4), applies. Similarly, Equation (11) suggests that the variability of the average propensity to consume in the short run, as seen in Figure 6-2, is explained in part by fluctuations in the ratio of wealth to disposable income. And, indeed, the ratio of wealth to disposable income is reasonably constant in the long run, but fluctuates considerably in the short run in a way that helps explain the fluctuations in the average propensity to consume shown in Figure 6-2.[11]

One further interesting implication of the life-cycle hypothesis is that it provides a route for the stock market to affect consumption behavior. The value of stocks held by the public is part of wealth and is included in WR in Equation (5). When the value of stocks is high—when the stock market is

[11] The life-cycle theory also suggests why the simple consumption function of Eq. (2) would look different when estimated over different time periods, for example, 1948–1982 and 1929–1941. Equation (2) omits a variable, wealth, which should be in the consumption function. This means that the estimates we get for the intercept and the marginal propensity to consume will depend on how wealth changes in the period for which we are fitting the line. As a difficult problem, see whether you can show that the estimated average propensity to consume will be constant if the ratio of wealth to disposable income is constant, but is omitted from the equation when it is fitted. Similarly, show that when wealth is constant but is omitted when fitting Eq. (2), the estimated average propensity to consume will decline with income.

booming—*WR* is high and tends to increase consumption, and the reverse occurs when the stock market is depressed.

We continue now to the permanent-income theory of consumption, bearing in mind that we have not yet discussed the determinants of expected lifetime labor income in Equation (10) in any detail, and recalling that the two theories should be thought of as complementary rather than competing.

6-3 PERMANENT-INCOME THEORY OF CONSUMPTION

In the long run, the consumption-income ratio is very stable, but in the short run, it fluctuates. The behavior of the propensity to consume implied by the standard consumption function, Equation (1), appears to differ when the equation is fitted over different periods. The life-cycle approach explains these observations by pointing out that people want to maintain a smooth profile of consumption even if their lifetime income profile is uneven, and thus emphasizes the role of wealth in the consumption function. Another explanation, which differs in details but entirely shares the spirit of the life-cycle approach, is the permanent-income theory of consumption.

The theory, which is the work of Milton Friedman,[12] argues that people gear their consumption behavior to their permanent or long-term consumption opportunities, not to their current level of income. A suggestive example provided by Friedman involves someone who is paid or receives her income only once a week, on Fridays. We do not expect that individual to concentrate her entire consumption on the one day on which income is received, with zero consumption on every other day. Again we are persuaded by the argument that individuals prefer a smooth consumption flow rather than plenty today and scarcity tomorrow or yesterday. On that argument, consumption on any one day of the week would be unrelated to income on that particular day but would rather be geared to average daily income—that is, income per week divided by the number of days per week. It is clear that in this extreme example, income for a period longer than a day is relevant to the consumption decision. Similarly, Friedman argues, there is nothing special about a period of the length of one quarter or one year that requires the individual to plan consumption within the period solely on the basis of income within the period; rather, consumption is planned in relation to income over a longer period.

The idea of consumption spending that is geared to long-term or average or permanent income is appealing and essentially is the same as the life-cycle theory. It leaves two further questions. The first concerns the precise relationship between current consumption and permanent income. The second question is how to make the concept of permanent income operational, that is, how to measure it.

[12] Milton Friedman, *A Theory of the Consumption Function* (Princeton, N.J.: Princeton University Press, 1957).

In its simplest form the permanent-income hypothesis of consumption behavior argues that consumption is proportional to permanent income:

$$C = cYP \tag{12}$$

where YP is permanent (disposable) income. From Equation (12), consumption varies in the same proportion as permanent income. A 5 percent increase in permanent income raises consumption by 5 percent. Since permanent income should be related to long-run average income, this feature of the consumption function is clearly in line with the observed long-run constancy of the consumption-income ratio.

ESTIMATING PERMANENT INCOME

The next problem is how to think of and measure permanent income. We define permanent income as follows:[13] *Permanent income is the steady rate of consumption a person could maintain for the rest of her life, given the present level of wealth and income earned now and in the future.*

To think about the measurement of permanent income, imagine someone trying to figure out what her permanent income is. The person has a current level of income, and has formed some idea of the level of consumption she can maintain for the rest of life. Now her income goes up. She has to decide whether that income increase represents a permanent increase, or merely a *transitory* change, one that will not persist. In any particular case, the individual may know whether the increase is permanent or transitory. A government official who is promoted one grade will know that the increase in income is likely to be maintained. Or the worker who has exceptionally high overtime in a given year will likely regard that year's increased income as transitory. But in general, a person is not so certain about what part of any change in income is likely to be maintained, and is therefore permanent, and what part is not likely to be maintained, and is therefore transitory. Transitory income is assumed not to have any substantial effect on consumption.

The question of how to infer what part of an increase in income is permanent is resolved in a pragmatic way by assuming that permanent income is related to the behavior of current and past incomes. To give a simple example, we might estimate permanent income as being equal to last year's income plus some fraction of the change in income from last year to this year:

$$\begin{aligned} YP &= Y_{-1} + \theta(Y - Y_{-1}) \qquad 0 < \theta < 1 \\ &= \theta Y + (1 - \theta)Y_{-1} \end{aligned} \tag{13}$$

where θ is a fraction and Y_{-1} is last year's income. The second line in Equation

[13] There is no standard definition of permanent income in Friedman's exposition of his theory. The definition given above is similar to average lifetime income. But it is not quite the same, because it effectively converts wealth into income in defining permanent income. Someone with no labor income, and only wealth, is defined as having permanent income equal to the amount he could consume each year by using up his wealth at a steady rate over the remainder of his life.

(13) writes permanent income as a *weighted average* of current and past income. The second formulation is, of course, equivalent to that in the first line. To understand Equation (13), assume we had a value of $\theta = 0.6$ and that this year's income was $Y = \$12,000$ and last year's income was $Y_{-1} = \$11,000$. The value of permanent income would be $YP = \$11,600 (= 0.6 \times \$12,000 + 0.4 \times \$11,000)$. Thus, permanent income is an average of the two income levels. Whether it is closer to this year's or last year's income depends on the weight θ given to current income. Clearly, in the extreme with $\theta = 1$, permanent income is equal to current income.

Some special features of Equation (13) deserve comment. First, if $Y = Y_{-1}$, that is, if this year's income is equal to last year's, then permanent income is equal to the income earned this year and last year. This guarantees that an individual who had always earned the same income would expect to earn that income in the future. Second, note that if income rises this year compared with last year, then permanent income rises by *less* than current income. The reason is that the individual does not know whether the rise in income this year is permanent. Not knowing whether the increase in income will be maintained or not, the individual does not immediately increase the expected or permanent income measure by the full amount of the actual or current increase in income.

RATIONAL EXPECTATIONS AND PERMANENT INCOME

An estimate of permanent income that uses only current and last year's income is likely to be an oversimplification. Friedman forms the estimate by looking at incomes in many earlier periods, as well as current income, but with weights that are larger for the more recent, as compared with the more distant, incomes.[14]

There is no simple theory that would tell us how expectations are or should be formed without looking at how income changes in practice. If, in practice, changes in income are typically permanent or long-run changes, then a consumer who sees a given change in his income will believe that it is mostly permanent. Such a consumer would have a high θ as in Equation (13). If the consumer's income is usually very variable, then he will not pay much attention to current changes in income in forming his estimate of permanent income. Such a consumer will have a low value of θ.[15]

This argument—that expectations are likely to be formed on the basis of the actual behavior of variables—is part of the theory of rational expectations, on which we shall focus further in Chapters 13 and 16. The theory suggests that the estimate of permanent income in Equation (13) should be based on how income in the economy actually changes over time.

At the same time, any sensible theory of expectations, including rational

[14] Friedman also adjusted permanent income by taking into account the growth of income over time.

[15] Recall that although we restricted our measure of permanent income to a 2-year average, there is no reason why the average should not be taken over longer periods. If current income is unstable, an appropriate measure of permanent income may well be an average over 5 or more years.

expectations, would emphasize that a formula like (13), based on the behavior of income in the past, cannot include all the factors that influence a person's beliefs about future income. The discovery of a vast amount of oil in a country, for instance, would raise the permanent incomes of the inhabitants of the country as soon as it was announced, even though a (mechanical) formula like Equation (13) based on past levels of income would not reflect such a change.

Permanent Income and the Dynamics of Consumption

Using Equations (12) and (13), we can now rewrite the consumption function:

$$C = cYP = c\theta Y + c(1 - \theta)Y_{-1} \tag{14}$$

The marginal propensity to consume out of *current* income is then just $c\theta$, which is clearly less than the long-run average propensity to consume, c. Hence, the permanent-income hypothesis implies that there is a difference between the short-run marginal propensity to consume and the long-run marginal (equal to the average) propensity to consume.

We shall see shortly that this implication is supported by the data. But first we explore it in more detail. The reason for the lower short-run marginal propensity to consume is that when current income rises, the individual is not sure that the increase in income will be maintained over the longer period on which she bases consumption plans. Accordingly, the person does not fully adjust consumption spending to the higher level that would be appropriate if the increase in income were permanent. However, if the increase turns out to be permanent, that is, if next period's income is the same as this period's, then the person will (next year) fully adjust consumption spending to the higher level of income. Note, though, that the adjustment here is completed in 2 years only because we have assumed, in Equation (13), that permanent income is an average of 2 years' income. Depending on how expectations of permanent income are formed, the adjustment could be much slower.

The argument is illustrated in Figure 6-4. Here we show the long-run consumption function as a straight line through the origin with slope c, which is the constant average and marginal propensity to consume out of permanent income. The lower flat consumption function is a short-run consumption function drawn for a given history of income which is reflected in the intercept $c(1 - \theta)Y_0$. Assume that we start out in long-run equilibrium with actual and permanent income equal to Y_0 and consumption therefore equal to cY_0, as is shown at the intersection of long-run and short-run consumption functions at point E. Assume next that income increases to the level Y'. In the short run, which means during the current period, we revise our estimate of permanent income upward by θ times the increase in income and consume a fraction c of that increase in permanent income. Accordingly, consumption moves up along the short-run consumption function to point E'.

Note immediately that in the short run the ratio of consumption to income declines as we move from point E to E'. Going one period ahead and assuming that the increase in income persists so that income remains at Y', we get a shift in the consumption function. The consumption function shifts

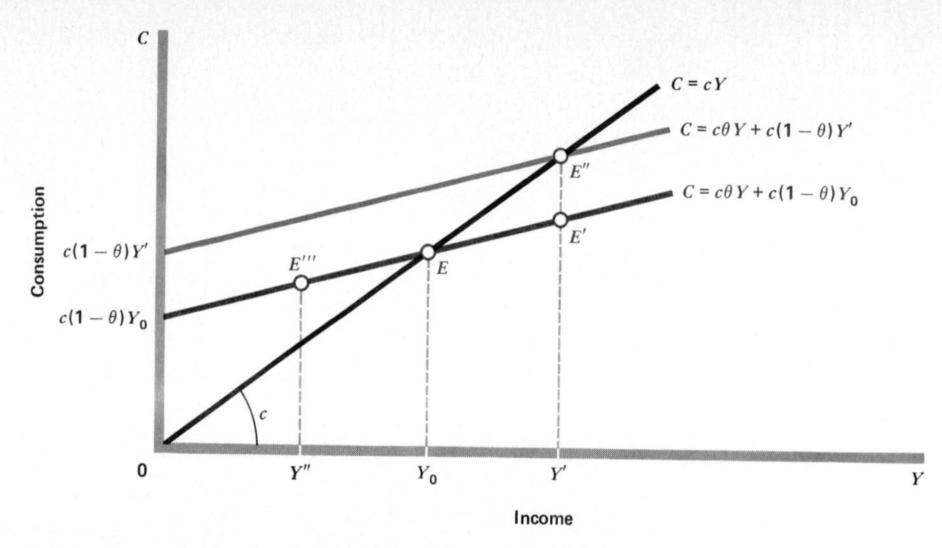

FIGURE 6-4 THE EFFECTS ON CONSUMPTION OF A SUSTAINED INCREASE IN INCOME. The short-run consumption functions, shown in red, have marginal propensity to consume of $c\theta$. The position of the short-run consumption function depends on the level of income in the previous period. The long-run consumption function is shown by the black line, and has average and marginal propensity to consume equal to c. When the level of income rises from Y_0 to Y', consumption rises only to E' in the short run, because consumers are not sure the change in income is permanent. But with income remaining at Y', the short-run consumption function shifts up and consumption rises to point E'', as consumers realize their permanent income has changed.

upward because, as of the given higher level of income, the estimate of permanent income is now revised upward to Y'. Accordingly, consumers want to spend a fraction of c of their new estimate of permanent income Y'. The new consumption point is E'', where the ratio of consumption to income is back to the long-run level. The example makes clear that in the short run, an increase in income causes a decline in the average propensity to consume because people do not anticipate that the increase in income will persist or be permanent. Once they do observe that the increase in income does persist, however, they fully adjust consumption to match their higher permanent income.

Like the life-cycle hypothesis, the permanent-income hypothesis has some unexpected and interesting implications. For instance, we noted above that an individual whose income is very unstable would have a low value of θ, whereas one whose income is more stable would have a higher value of θ. Looking at Equation (14), this means that the short-run marginal propensity to consume of someone whose income is very variable will be relatively low—because the short-run marginal propensity to consume is $c\theta$. Friedman shows that this implication is borne out by the facts. Farmers, for instance, have very variable incomes and a low marginal propensity to consume out of current income.

THE LIFE-CYCLE AND PERMANENT-INCOME HYPOTHESIS

To conclude this section, it is worth considering again the relationship between the life-cycle and permanent-income hypotheses briefly. The two hypotheses are not mutually exclusive. The life-cycle hypothesis pays more attention to the motives for saving than the permanent-income hypothesis does, and provides convincing reasons to include wealth as well as income in the consumption function. The permanent-income hypothesis, on the other hand, pays more careful attention to the way in which individuals form their expectations about their future incomes than the original life-cycle hypothesis does. Recall that current labor income entered the life-cycle consumption function to reflect expectations of future income. The more detailed analysis of the determinants of expected future income that is provided by the permanent-income hypothesis can be, and has been, included in the life-cycle consumption function.

Indeed, modern theories of the consumption function combine the expectations formation emphasized by the permanent-income approach with the emphasis on wealth and demographic variables suggested by the life-cycle approach. A simplified version of a modern consumption function would be

$$C = aWR + b\theta YD + b(1 - \theta)YD_{-1} \tag{15}$$

where YD in Equation (15) would be disposable labor income. Equation (15) combines the main features that are emphasized by modern consumption theory.[16] It also shows the role of wealth, which is an important influence on consumption spending.

Recent research on consumption has combined the two theories and has been aimed particularly at checking the implications of the permanent-income—and life-cycle—theory that transitory changes in income have little effect on consumption.[17] Some of this research is described in Box 6-1.

We end this section by repeating a warning that is important enough for us to risk overstating. An equation like (15) performs quite well on average in predicting consumption. But it is always important to remember the underlying theory when using it. Equation (15) embodies the estimate of permanent income implied by Equation (13). If we have knowledge about some particular change in income—for example, that it is transitory—then we should use that knowledge in predicting consumption. For instance, as we shall see, a temporary 1-year tax increase that reduced current disposable income would reduce current consumption by much less than a tax increase of the same size that was known to be permanent, even though Equation (15) does not show that.

[16] To fix ideas, you should draw a graph of Eq. (15) with consumption on the vertical axis and current disposable labor income on the horizontal axis. What is the intercept? How does the diagram differ from Fig. 6-4? Show the effects of (1) a transitory increase in income, (2) a sustained increase in income, and (3) an increase in wealth.

[17] See, for example, Robert E. Hall, "Stochastic Implications of the Life Cycle–Permanent Income Hypothesis: Theory and Evidence," *Journal of Political Economy*, December 1978. This is difficult reading.

BOX 6-1

MODERN CONSUMPTION FUNCTION PUZZLES

No theory explains all the facts, or is the last word to be written on a topic. Research continually turns up new questions and puzzles, which lead to further research, and to revised theories. Research of the early late 1970s and early 1980s has revealed some aspects of consumption behavior that do not fit well with the life-cycle and permanent-income theories of consumption. Over the next few years either research will show that the new facts are not quite the problem they seem now, or the existing theories will be amended.

We briefly discuss these modern consumption puzzles.

1 THE LIFE-CYCLE HYPOTHESIS, CONSUMPTION OF THE ELDERLY, AND BEQUESTS

The life-cycle hypothesis assumes that people want to smooth consumption over their lifetimes. This leads to the conclusion that people save mainly for retirement, and draw down their savings during retirement.

Two recent papers question the assumed motive for saving and the implication that people draw down their savings when old. Laurence Kotlikoff and Lawrence Summers* have made calculations suggesting that most saving is done to provide bequests rather than to provide for consumption when old. Of course, the savings are there for the old to use in retirement, but, they argue, the amount of wealth in the economy is far too large for people to have been saving only for their retirement. Rather, they conclude, people are saving mainly to pass wealth on to their descendants.

A detailed examination of the consumption propensities of the elderly by Sheldon Danziger, Jacques van der Gaag, Eugene Smolensky, and Michael Taussig† contains the remarkable conclusion that the elderly save a higher proportion of their incomes than the young. This fact is inconsistent with the simple form of the life-cycle hypothesis set out in the chapter.

How might this evidence be reconciled with existing theories? The facts are not yet definitive. For instance, the Kotlikoff-Summers argument that most of savings is undertaken to provide bequests is based on complicated calculations and assumptions that will likely be disputed by adherents of the life-cycle theory. Explanation of the consumption behavior of the elderly will probably have to take into account their increasing fears of being left alone without financial help from family, and with possibly large medical expenses, as they get older.

2 EXCESS SENSITIVITY OF CONSUMPTION TO CURRENT INCOME

Recent tests of the permanent-income hypothesis conclude that consumption is excessively sensitive to changes in current income.‡ Consumption does react more to permanent than to transitory changes in current income. But these tests show that the reaction to transitory changes is larger than the theory predicts.

Suppose the propensity to consume out of permanent income is 0.9. The permanent income theory predicts that the propensity to consume out of a change in income that is

* "The Role of Intergenerational Transfers in Aggregate Capital Accumulation," *Journal of Political Economy,* August 1981.

† In their research paper from the University of Wisconsin, "The Life Cycle Hypothesis and the Consumption Behavior of the Elderly," 1982.

expected to last only 1 year should be very small, perhaps something like 0.05. In fact, though, the propensity to consume out of transitory income is much higher, more like 0.25.

This is the puzzle that is described as the excess sensitivity of consumption to changes in income. The candidate to explain the puzzle is ***liquidity constraints***. Recall that someone with temporarily low income is supposed to use up savings to maintain the level of consumption, or else to borrow. But many people do not have the savings to draw down, nor can they borrow to finance consumption. Thus, it is argued, they cannot find the liquidity (that is, available funds) to pay for the consumption they would like. When income goes up, such people increase their consumption more than the permanent-income theory would predict, because they are no longer so constrained.

The excess sensitivity finding does not mean the permanent-income theory is irrelevant to understanding consumption behavior. It only means that there is more that determines consumption than the factors stressed by the simple permanent-income and life-cycle models.

‡ For example, Marjorie Flavin, "The Adjustment of Consumption to Changing Expectations about Future Income," *Journal of Political Economy*, October 1981.

6-4 THE 1968 TAX SURCHARGE

The importance of the distinction between transitory and permanent changes in disposable income is illustrated by the effects of the 1968 tax surcharge. During 1966 and 1967, as military spending for the Vietnam war increased, the budget went increasingly into deficit. Figure 6-5 shows both actual and full-employment deficits going increasingly into deficit during 1966 and remaining there during 1967. Note, incidentally, that in Figure 6-5 the full-employment surplus is generally less than the actual surplus. This is because the economy was operating at more than full employment.

At the same time, the rate of inflation was rising. The administration decided to ask for a tax increase. The administration argued that since spending was only temporarily high because of the war, it would only need a temporary tax increase. Therefore it asked for a temporary tax surcharge. A *tax surcharge* is a proportional increase above existing taxes. Taxes are calculated using existing tax rates, exemptions, etc., and then when the bill has been added up, a given extra percentage is added to it.

The tax surcharge was initially requested at the beginning of 1967, but was enacted only in June 1968. Its effects on both the actual and full-employment budget deficits can be seen in Figure 6-5, as the actual budget moved from a deficit of 1.4 percent of GNP in the second quarter of 1968 to balance by the end of the year, and then surplus at the beginning of 1969.

What effect should such a tax increase have on consumption and aggregate demand? In Chapter 5 we analyzed the effects of the 1964 tax cut. Perhaps we should just reverse that analysis. But there was something different about the 1968 tax surcharge: it was explicitly temporary. It was scheduled to be removed in mid-1969.

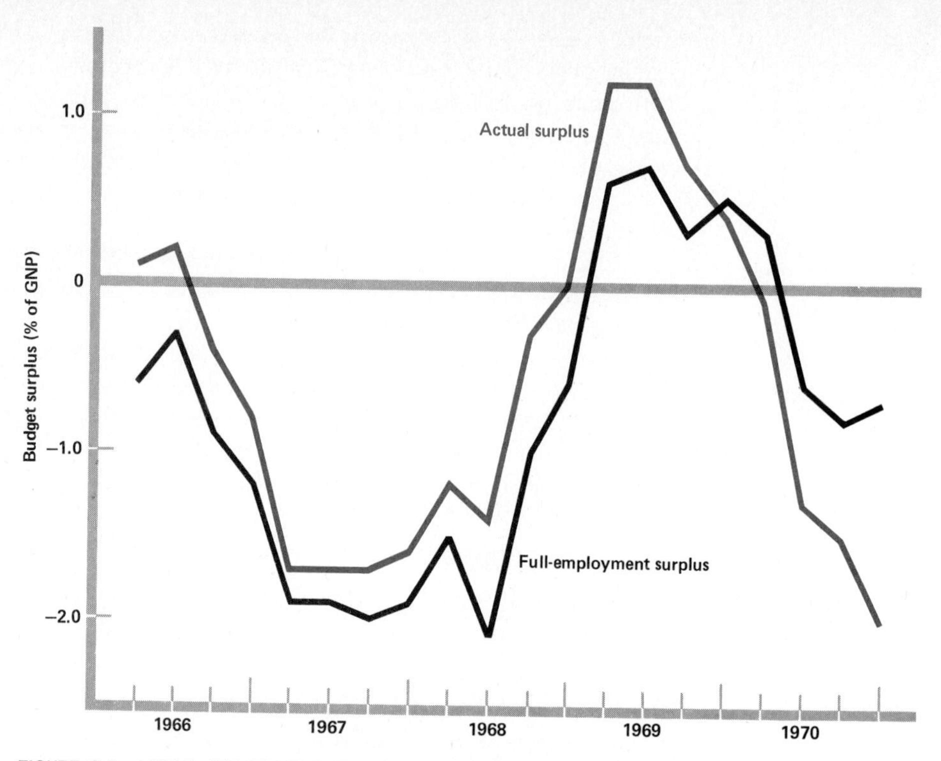

FIGURE 6-5 ACTUAL AND FULL-EMPLOYMENT BUDGET SURPLUSES, 1966–1970 (AS A PERCENT OF GNP). (*Source: Survey of Current Business*, April 1982, p. 27.)

This means, according to the permanent-income hypothesis, that individuals would reduce their consumption much less as taxes went up than they would have had the tax increase been permanent. In terms of Figure 6-4, they would move along the flatter short-run consumption function through point E in response to a temporary tax increase. In response to a permanent tax increase, we would expect them to move along the steeper long-run consumption function.

We can see the effects of the fact that the tax surcharge was temporary by looking at the behavior of the savings rate. A tax increase, of course, reduces disposable income, to level Y'' in Figure 6-4. The short-run adjustment of the consumer is to point E''', with a relatively small cut in consumption, but a larger reduction in saving.

In the short run, the ratio of consumption to income rises as we move from E to E'''. This means that the average propensity to consume rises. The average propensity to save, equal to 1 minus the average propensity to consume, therefore falls. Thus if the permanent-income theory is right, we should see a fall in the average propensity to save following the imposition of

TABLE 6-2 THE SAVING RATE IN RESPONSE TO THE 1968 TAX SURCHARGE

	1968				1969				
1967	I	II	III	IV	I	II	III	IV	1970
7.3	7.2	7.6	6.0	6.2	5.3	5.3	6.6	6.8	7.9

Source: W. L. Springer, "Did the 1968 Surcharge Really Work?" American Economic Review, *September 1975.*

the temporary tax increase. We should also expect the saving rate (as a percentage of disposable income) to increase when the surcharge is removed.

The data support this view of what happened.[18] Table 6-2 shows the saving rate in 1967 through 1970. We see the saving rate falling in the third quarter of 1968, after the tax surcharge goes into effect, and falling even more in the first quarter of 1969 when the major increase in taxes took place. Then the surcharge is lifted and the saving rate goes back to its earlier levels.

Calculations of the impact of the tax surcharge that neglected its temporary nature would have predicted a larger reduction in aggregate demand than actually occurred. And indeed, some forecasts of the effects of the tax surcharge did overpredict the effects of the tax increase, precisely because they neglected the important distinction between the effects of permanent and transitory changes in disposable income on consumption.

6-5 FURTHER ASPECTS OF CONSUMPTION BEHAVIOR

In this section we briefly review three topics in consumption behavior, starting with the relative-income hypothesis.

THE RELATIVE-INCOME HYPOTHESIS

Modern theories of the consumption function have in common the objective of explaining short-run fluctuations in the ratio of consumption to disposable income combined with virtual constancy of the ratio of consumption to disposable income in the long run. Life-cycle and permanent-income theories explain this behavior as an attempt to maintain a smooth flow of consumption that is geared to long-run consumption opportunities, as measured by lifetime income and wealth or by permanent income.

An earlier and influential theory along much the same lines is the relative-income hypothesis that was advanced by James Duesenberry.[19] The

[18] This matter is still controversial. See W. L. Springer, "Did the 1968 Surcharge Really Work?" *American Economic Review,* September 1975, and the follow-up in the *American Economic Review,* March 1977, and Alan S. Blinder, "Temporary Income Taxes and Consumer Spending," *Journal of Political Economy,* February 1981.

[19] See James Duesenberry, *Income, Savings and the Theory of Consumer Behavior* (Cambridge, Mass.: Harvard University Press, 1952).

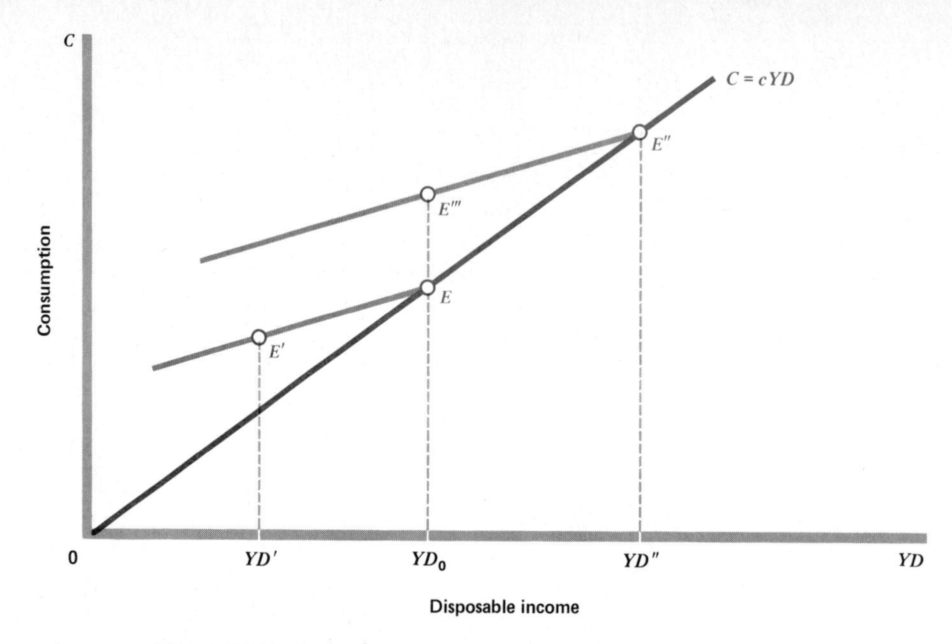

FIGURE 6-6 THE RELATIVE-INCOME HYPOTHESIS. The long-run consumption function is shown by the dark line. But previous peak levels of income or consumption affect current consumption in the short run. Thus if individuals initially are at income level YD_0, a decline in income to YD' will take them to point E'—they are reluctant to cut consumption because they have got used to the higher consumption level at E. An ***increase*** of income from YD_0 to YD'' would lead to point E'' on the long-run consumption function.

theory argues that current consumption depends not only on current income but also on the history of income. Individuals build up consumption standards that are geared to their peak income levels. If income declines relative to past income, then individuals will not immediately sacrifice the consumption standard they have adopted. There is a ratchet effect, and they will only adjust to a small extent to the decline in current income. However, there is an asymmetry, because an increase in income relative to past peaks immediately raises the consumption level.

Figure 6-6 shows consumption behavior according to the relative-income hypothesis. The dark line is the consumption function if current income is the peak level of income. Thus, if current income is YD_0 and exceeds previous levels of income, then consumption would be at point E on the consumption function $C = cYD$. If income declined from the level YD_0 to YD', then consumption would adjust along the light schedule to E'. The peak level of income YD_0 would continue to influence consumption because it determines the consumption standard that individuals seek to maintain. In the short run, therefore, saving adjusts so as to allow consumption to be maintained close to the habitual level. Assume next that income rose to the level YD''. This would be a new peak level of income, and consumption accordingly would rise to E''.

If income were then to decline to YD_0, the new peak level YD'' would continue to influence consumption, so that we would find ourselves at point E'''.

The theory is very suggestive again of the attempt to smooth consumption in the face of income fluctuations. It has an intuitive appeal in its emphasis on consumption standards geared to peak income. It lacks, perhaps, the economic richness that the later theories of the life cycle and permanent income added. Its main shortcoming is the asymmetry that suggests that a current increase in income, if it exceeds a previous peak, immediately induces a new consumption standard. Here the alternative theories are more persuasive in that they suggest a partial adjustment for both an increase and a decrease in income. But the theory does suggest that as the level of income rises over time, consumption will rise roughly in proportion, along the line $C = cYD$.

Consumption, Saving, and Interest Rates

Consumers in the United States save a lower proportion of their disposable income than consumers in many other countries, as Table 6-3 shows. One question—which we do not attempt to answer—is why the U.S. saving rate is so low. Another question is why it matters. The answer is that the amount of investment in the economy, which determines how much capital—factories and machines—is available for production, depends on the saving rate. If an economy is at full employment, then an increase in the saving rate will lead to more investment and to more future production, as we see in Chapter 17 when we discuss supply-side economics. It is thus not a coincidence that the countries with low savings rates in Table 6-3 are also the slower growing among the seven major economies listed there.

The next question is what could be done about a low saving rate? One suggestion is to make saving more worthwhile for the saver. Anyone who saves receives a return in the form of interest, or dividends and capital gains (an increase in the price) on stocks. It seems, then, that the neutral way to raise saving is to raise the return available to savers. Think of someone saving and receiving an interest rate of 5 percent each year for each dollar saved. Surely an increase in the interest rate to, say, 10 percent would make that person save more? This thinking has influenced tax policy in the United States. For instance, there are many saving schemes which exempt the interest received

TABLE 6-3 NET HOUSEHOLD SAVING AS A PERCENTAGE OF DISPOSABLE HOUSEHOLD INCOME (*Average, 1960–1980*)

United States	Japan	Germany	France	U.K.	Italy	Canada
7.6	19.0	15.3	12.8	6.7	19.5	7.7

Source: OECD Economic Outlook, Historical Statistics 1960–1980 *(Paris: Organization for Economic Co-Operation and Development, 1982), p. 65.*

on savings from the payment of taxes. This means the return received by the saver is raised compared with what it would be if taxes had to be paid on the interest received.

But should we really expect an increase in the interest rate to increase savings? It is true that when the interest rate rises, saving is made more attractive. But it is also made less necessary. Consider someone who has decided to save an amount that will ensure $10,000 per year is available for retirement. Suppose the interest rate is now 5 percent, and the person is saving $1,000 per year. Now let the interest rate rise to 10 percent. With such a high interest rate, the individual needs to save less now to provide the given $10,000 per year during retirement. It may be possible to provide the same retirement income by saving only about $650 a year. Thus an increase in the interest rate might reduce saving.

What do the facts show? Does saving rise when the interest rate increases, because every dollar of saving generates a higher return? Or does saving fall because there is less need to save to provide a given level of future income? The answer from the data is ambiguous. Many researchers have examined this question, but few have found strong positive effects of interest rate increases on saving. Typically, research suggests the effects are small and certainly hard to find.[20]

Consumption, Consumption Purchases, and Durables

The theories we have examined so far are theories about the rate at which consumers consume rather than spend on goods and services. For most consumption, such as that of eating meals, or watching movies, or using gasoline, consumption follows purchase quite closely. But for some goods, such as automobiles, or TV sets—called consumer durables because they last for a long time—the act of consumption may be separated by months or years from the purchase of the good.

The item "Consumption" in the GNP accounts and in Figure 6-1 is actually the *purchases* of consumption goods, including, for example, cars, food, refrigerators, and toasters. Obviously, though, someone who owns and uses a car is consuming automobile services in a given year even if she does not buy a new car. So there is a difference between consumption and purchases of consumption goods.

The distinction matters because the component of consumption in the GNP accounts that fluctuates most is purchases of consumer durables. It is not surprising that consumer durable purchases fluctuate more than purchases of other consumption goods, because someone whose income is temporarily low can easily make do with the same car for a short while. Thus actual consumption would fluctuate less than purchases.

This argument suggests that durable purchases may be affected more

[20] The best known study finding positive interest rate effects is that of Michael Boskin, 'Taxation, Saving, and the Rate of Interest," *Journal of Political Economy*, pt. 2, April 1978. For more typical results, see Gerald A. Carlino, "Interest Rate Effects and Intertemporal Consumption," *Journal of Monetary Economics*, March 1982.

than other components of consumers' purchases by transitory changes in income. There is indeed evidence to that effect.[21] In addition, durable purchases more than other categories of consumption spending show signs of being affected by the interest rate. In particular, high interest rates reduce automobile purchases.

6-6 CONSUMPTION AND THE *IS-LM* FRAMEWORK

In this section we discuss briefly how the more sophisticated theories of consumption we have developed in this chapter affect the *IS-LM* analysis of Chapters 4 and 5. We focus on two implications. The first is that consumption is a function of wealth, and not only income as we assumed previously. The second is that the response of consumption to various changes—for instance, in autonomous spending—may take time, as individuals gradually adjust their estimates of permanent income.

Wealth in the Consumption Function

The life-cycle hypothesis, and estimated consumption functions of a form like Equation (15), show that the rate of consumption depends on the level of wealth, as well as disposable income. This means that the position of the *IS* curve, representing equilibrium in the goods market, depends on the level of wealth.

Figure 6-7 shows how an increase in the level of wealth affects equilibrium output and the interest rate. The economy is initially in equilibrium at point E. There is then an increase in wealth: perhaps the stock market has gone up, because everyone is optimistic that the economy is recovering from a recession. The higher wealth raises consumption spending, and the *IS* curve thus shifts up to IS'. The new equilibrium is at E'.

At E', the interest rate and level of output are higher than at E. Thus an increase in wealth raises equilibrium output. Since the increase in wealth was assumed to result from expectations that the economy was recovering from a recession, we see that the expectation is partly self-fulfilling. A self-fulfilling prophecy is one which, purely as a result of being made, produces the prophesied result.

How large are such wealth effects? Estimates are that a 1 dollar increase in wealth is likely to increase consumption by about 3 cents. Households own about $1,500 billion of equities. If the value of the equities rises by 10 percent, consumption will rise by 3 percent of $150 billion, or $4.5 billion. With consumption spending at an annual rate of about $2,000 billion, this is just over 0.2 percent of consumption spending. The effect of wealth on consumption spending is thus likely to be relatively unimportant, except for very large changes in stock prices.

[21] For example, Michael Darby, "The Allocation of Transitory Income among Consumers' Assets," *American Economic Review*, December 1972.

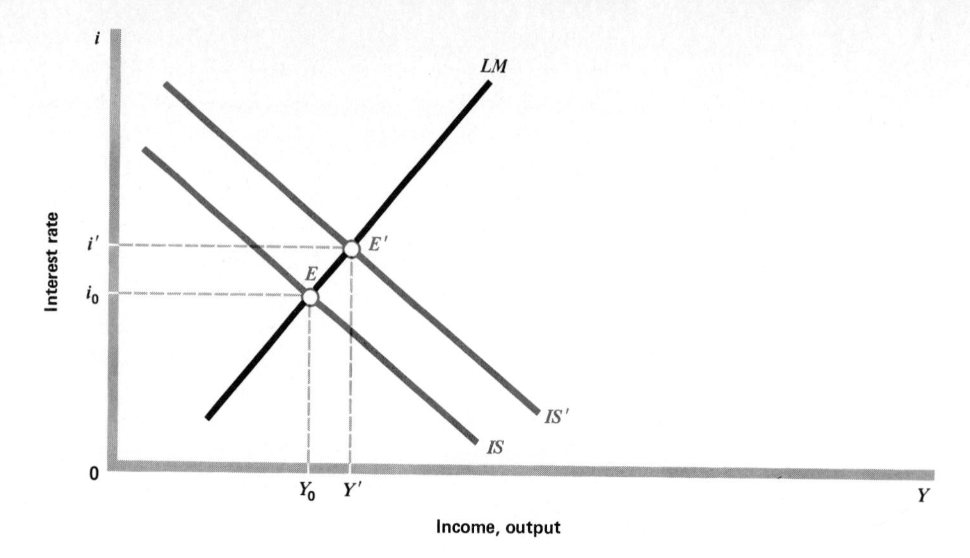

FIGURE 6-7 THE EFFECTS OF A SHIFT IN WEALTH. An increase in wealth shifts the consumption function, raising consumption demand at any level of income. Accordingly, the *IS* curve shifts to *IS'*, the level of output rises from Y_0 to Y', and the interest rate rises from i_0 to i'.

The Dynamics of Adjustment

In Section 6-3 and Figure 6-4, we examined the dynamic response of consumption spending to a shift in disposable income. Now we want to embody that dynamic adjustment in a full *IS-LM* model. The slow adjustment of consumption to a given change in disposable income will mean that income itself adjusts slowly to any given shift in autonomous spending that is not at first recognized as permanent, as we now show.

We assume here that people do not know whether the shift in autonomous demand is permanent or transitory. Rather, the only way they can figure that out is by seeing whether the change in demand persists or goes away. Figure 6-8 illustrates the effects of a permanent shift in autonomous demand, the nature of which (permanent or transitory) is not known to consumers.

Suppose that the economy is initially in equilibrium at point *E*. Now there is a shift in autonomous investment demand. In the long run, such a shift will move the *IS* curve to *IS'*. The extent of the shift is determined by the *long-run* multiplier $[1/(1 - c)]$, where c is the long-run propensity to consume. When expectations of income have fully adjusted, the economy will be at position E', with output level Y' and interest rate i'.

But in the short run the marginal propensity to consume is not c, but only $c\theta$. Thus the short-run multiplier is only $[1/(1 - c\theta)]$. In the short run, the *IS* curve shifts only to *IS"*. Thus the immediate effect of the shift in investment demand is to raise income to Y'' and the interest rate to i''.

Next period, the *IS* curve shifts again. It does not shift all the way to *IS'* though. Consumers have adjusted their estimate of permanent income up, but they have not yet adjusted it all with way to Y', because income last period was only Y'' and not Y'. (To keep the diagram simple, we do not show the *IS* curve for the second or later periods.) Income and the interest rate will rise above Y' and i', but still fall short of Y'' and i''.

This process continues, with the consumption function gradually shifting up over time, as people come to realize that their permanent incomes have risen. A single shock to autonomous demand therefore produces a slow, or *distributed lag,* effect on output. Figure 6-9 shows how income adjusts gradually to its new equilibrium level. The time pattern of changes in income caused by the increase in investment demand is called the *dynamic multiplier* of income with respect to autonomous investment.

POLICY IMPLICATIONS

Suppose we have a permanent decline in investment expenditure. As we have seen, the decline in spending would lead to a fall in output and employment, occurring over a period of time.

Suppose the government wants to offset the reduction in aggregate

FIGURE 6-8 THE DYNAMICS OF ADJUSTMENT TO A SHIFT IN INVESTMENT DEMAND. Autonomous investment demand rises by amount ΔI, but it is not known whether the shift is permanent or transitory. It is in fact permanent, so that the *IS* curve will eventually be at *IS'*, shifted by an amount $[\Delta I/(1 - c)]$ to the right, where $[1/(1 - c)]$ is the long-run multiplier. But in the first period, the *IS* curve shifts only to *IS''*, by amount $[\Delta I/(1 - c\theta)]$, determined by the short-run consumption function and multiplier. Over time, the economy moves gradually from E'' to E', as individuals come to recognize that the shift in investment demand is permanent.

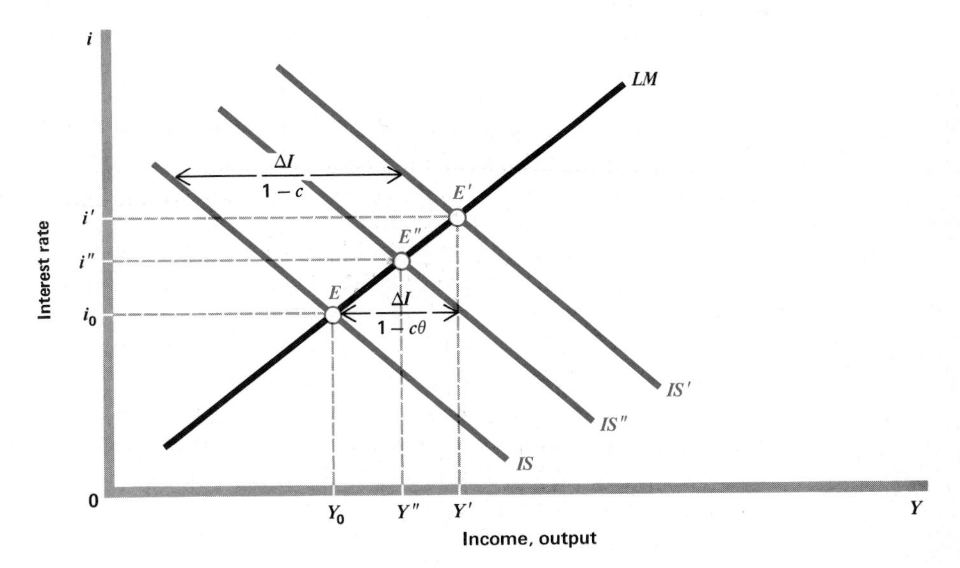

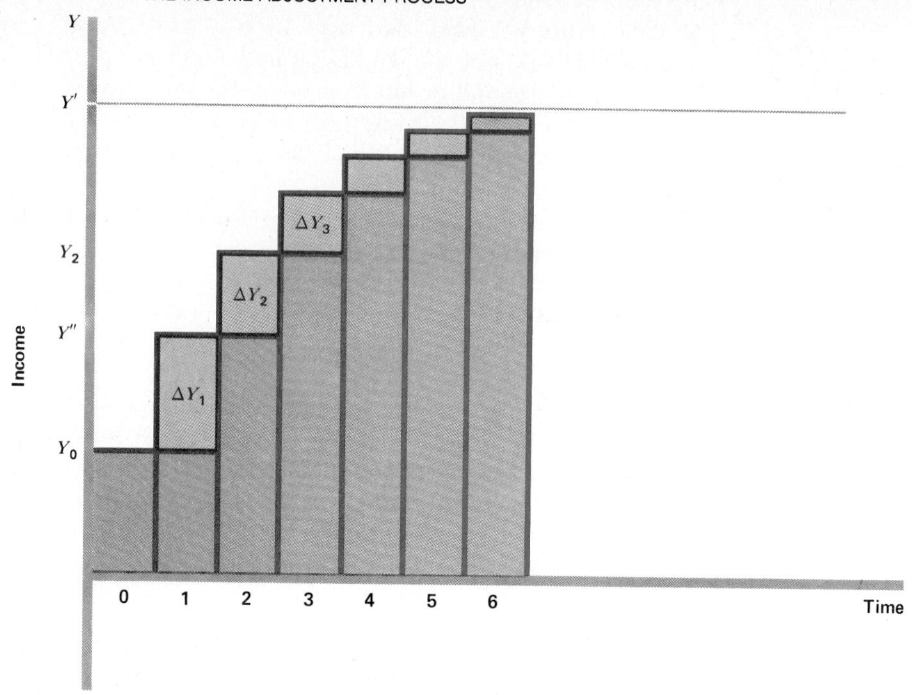

FIGURE 6-9 THE INCOME ADJUSTMENT PROCESS. The figure shows the *dynamic multiplier* of investment spending on income. This is how a given change in autonomous investment spending affects the level of output over time. Income rises in the first period from Y_0 to Y''. Then in subsequent periods it continues to rise toward its long-run equilibrium level Y'.

demand by using tax cuts to keep income at the full-employment level. Since consumption adjusts only gradually to the changes in income resulting from both the initial fall in investment and tax cuts, the policy maker who wants to stabilize output *over time* will have to know about the adjustment pattern of consumption so as not to overreact. The problems may be further complicated, as we discuss in Chapter 10, by the fact that frequently the policy maker too reacts only with a lag to changed circumstances.

In the short run, consumption does not respond fully to changes in income. Therefore it takes a relatively large tax cut to obtain a given change in consumption with which to offset the decline in investment. Over time, though, consumption adjusts to the change in disposable income, and the tax cut that was initially just sufficient to offset reduced investment now turns out to be too generous. The compensating policy must therefore be one of a tax cut that is *front-loaded* and gradually phased down to the long-run level. The difference between the short-run and long-run tax cuts is determined by the relative size of the short-run and long-run tax multipliers.

Indeed, the observant reader will recall that we assumed consumers had no special knowledge about the nature of the changes in income they experienced as a result both of the initial change in investment and of subsequent tax adjustments. Remarkably enough, if consumers knew that the investment shift was permanent, and if they could be persuaded that the change in government policy was permanent, a one-time reduction in taxes, calculated using the long-run multiplier implied by the consumption function, would precisely stabilize income. For, in that case, the response to the fall in investment would recognize the permanent nature of the change, implying the long-run multiplier is relevant, and the response to the tax change would also recognize the permanent nature of the change. Consumption would adjust immediately, rather than gradually over the course of time.

The conclusion of this section is that policy making, and understanding of the behavior of the economy, cannot be successful unless careful attention is paid to expectations formation—bearing in mind that expectations depend in part on how the policy makers are perceived to be acting. This is the message of rational expectations, to which we return in Chapters 13 and 16.

6-7 SUMMARY

1 The simple Keynesian consumption function

$$C = 6.07 + 0.90YD \tag{2}$$

accounts well for observed consumption behavior. The equation suggests that out of an additional dollar of disposable income, 90 cents is spent on consumption. The consumption function implies, too, that the ratio of consumption to income, C/YD, declines somewhat with the level of income.

2 Early empirical work on short-run consumption behavior showed that the marginal propensity to consume was lower than that found in longer-period studies. The evidence revealed also that the average propensity to consume declined with the level of income. Postwar studies, by contrast, find a relatively constant average propensity to consume of about 0.9.

3 The evidence is reconciled by a reconsideration of consumption theory. Individuals want to maintain relatively smooth consumption profiles over their lifetime. Their consumption behavior is geared to their long-term consumption opportunities—permanent income or lifetime income plus wealth. With such a view, current income is only one of the determinants of consumption spending. Wealth and expected income play a role, too. A consumption function that represents this idea is

$$C = aWR + b\theta YD + b(1 - \theta)YD_{-1} \tag{15}$$

which allows for the role of real wealth WR, current disposable income YD, and lagged disposable income YD_{-1}.

4 The life-cycle hypothesis suggests that the propensities of an individual

to consume out of disposable income and out of wealth depend on the person's age. It also suggests that aggregate saving depends on the growth rate of the economy and on such variables as the age distribution of the population.

5 The permanent-income hypothesis emphasizes the formation of expectations of future income. It implies that the propensity to consume out of permanent income is higher than the propensity to consume out of transitory income.

6 Both theories do well, in combination, in explaining aggregate consumption behavior. But there are still some consumption puzzles, including the excess sensitivity of consumption to current income and the fact that the aged do not appear to draw down their savings as they age.

7 The relative-income hypothesis argues that current consumption is related not only to current income but also to previous peak income. The argument for this is that individuals find it difficult to reduce rates of consumption to which they have become accustomed.

8 The rate of consumption, and thus of savings, could in principle be affected by the interest rate. But the evidence for the most part shows little effect of interest rates on saving.

9 Lagged adjustment of consumption to income results in a gradual adjustment of the level of income in the economy to changes in autonomous spending and other economic changes. An increase in autonomous spending raises income. But the adjustment process is spread out over time because the rising level of income raises consumption only gradually. This adjustment process is described by dynamic multipliers that show by how much income changes in each period following a change in autonomous spending (or other exogenous variables).

10 The dynamic adjustment of the economy to changes in policy variables, such as a change in government spending or transfers, creates a problem for policy making. The analysis of Section 6-6 shows that the policy maker needs detailed information about the dynamic responses of the economy, if policy is not to result in income levels that differ from the target levels. In a dynamic setting, the making of policy requires the policy maker to consider how much any particular policy action will affect income in each time period and to calculate *time paths* for policy variables that will bring about the desired performance.

KEY TERMS

Life-cycle hypothesis
Dissaving
Permanent income
Rational expectations
Liquidity constraints
Tax surcharge
Relative-income hypothesis
Dynamic multiplier

PROBLEMS

1 What is the significance of the ratio of consumption to GNP in terms of the level of economic activity? Would you expect it to be higher or lower than normal during a recession (or depression)? Do you think the ratio would be higher in developed or underdeveloped countries? Why?

The Life-Cycle Hypothesis

2 The text implies that the ratio of consumption to accumulated savings declines over time until retirement.
(*a*) Why? What assumption about consumption behavior leads to this result?
(*b*) What happens to this ratio after retirement?

3 (*a*) Suppose you earn just as much as your neighbor but are in much better health and expect to live longer than she does. Would you consume more or less than she does? Why? Derive your answer from Equation (7).
(*b*) According to the life-cycle hypothesis, what would the effect of the Social Security system be on your average propensity to consume out of (disposable) income?
(*c*) How would Equation (10) be modified for an individual who expects to receive $\$X$ per year of retirement benefits? Verify your result in 3(*b*).

4 Give an intuitive interpretation of the marginal propensity to consume out of wealth and income at time T in the individual's lifetime in Equation (10).

*5 In Equation (7), consumption in each year of working life is given by

$$C = \frac{WL}{NL} \times YL \tag{7}$$

In Equation (10), consumption is given as

$$C = aWR + cYL \qquad a \equiv \frac{1}{NL - T} \qquad c \equiv \frac{WL - T}{NL - T} \tag{10}$$

Show that Equations (7) and (10) are consistent for an individual who started life with zero wealth and has been saving for T years. [*Hint:* First calculate the individual's wealth after T years of saving at rate $YL - C$. Then calculate the level of consumption implied by Equation (10) when wealth is at the level you have computed.]

Permanent-Income Hypothesis

6 In terms of permanent-income hypothesis, would you consume more of your Christmas bonus if:
(*a*) You knew there was a bonus every year.
(*b*) This was the only year such bonuses were given out.

7 Suppose that permanent income is calculated as the average of income over the past 5 years; that is,

$$YP = \frac{1}{5}(Y + Y_{-1} + Y_{-2} + Y_{-3} + Y_{-4})$$

Suppose, further, that consumption is given by $C = 0.9YP$.

(*a*) If you have earned \$10,000 per year for the past 10 years, what is your permanent income?

(*b*) Suppose next year (period $t + 1$) you earn \$15,000. What is your new YP?

(*c*) What is your consumption this year and next year?

(*d*) What is your short-run MPC? Long-run MPC?

(*e*) Assuming you continue to earn \$15,000 starting in period $t + 1$, graph the value of your permanent income in each period using the equation above.

8 Explain why good gamblers (and thieves) might be expected to live very well even in years when they don't do well at all.

*9 The graph (below) shows the lifetime earnings profile of a person who lives for four periods and earns income of \$30, \$60, and \$90 in the first three periods of the life cycle. There are no earnings during retirement. Assume that the interest rate is 0.

(*a*) You are asked to determine the level of consumption, compatible with the budget constraint, for someone who wants an even consumption profile throughout the life cycle. Indicate in which periods the person saves and dissaves and in what amounts.

(*b*) Assume now that, contrary to 9(*a*), there is no possibility for borrowing. The credit markets are closed to the individual. Under this assumption, what is the flow of consumption the individual will pick over the life cycle? In providing an answer, continue to assume that if possible, an even flow of consumption is preferred. (***Note:*** You are assuming here that there are liquidity constraints.)

(*c*) Assume next that the person described in 9(*b*) receives an increase in wealth or nonlabor income. The increase in wealth is equal to \$13. How will that wealth be allocated over the life cycle with and without access to the credit market? How would your answer differ if the increase in wealth were \$23?

(*d*) Relate your answer to the problem of excess sensitivity of consumption to current income.

*10 Consider the consumption function in Equation (15). Assume autonomous investment spending is constant, as is government spending. The economy is close to full employment and the government wishes to maintain aggregate demand precisely constant. In these circumstances, assume there is an increase in real wealth of \$10 billion. What change in income taxes will maintain constant the equilibrium level of income in the present period? What change is required to maintain income constant in the long run?

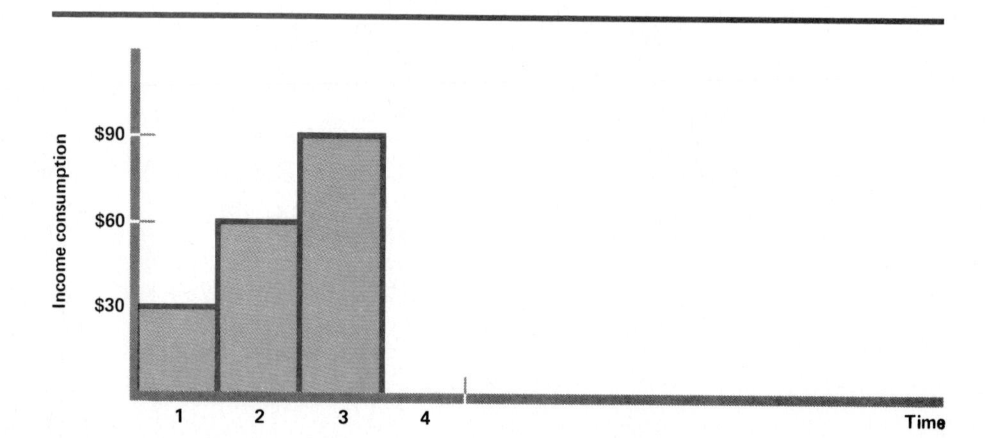

11 Equation (15) shows consumption as a function of wealth and current and lagged disposable income. To reconcile that consumption function with permanent-income expectations formation, you are asked to use Equation (13) and the consumption function

$$C = 0.045WR + 0.55YD + 0.17YD_{-1}$$

to determine the magnitude of θ and $(1 - \theta)$ that is implied by Equation (15).

12 (*a*) Explain why the interest rate might affect saving.
(*b*) Why does it matter?

*Adjustment and Dynamics

13 Here is a challenge to your ability to develop diagrams. You are asked to show short-run and long-run income determination in the 45° diagram of Chapter 3. Assume that investment demand is totally autonomous and does not respond to the interest rate. Thus you do not need to use the full *IS-LM* model.
(*a*) Draw the short-run and long-run consumption functions and the aggregate demand schedule with $I = \bar{I}$.
(*b*) Show the initial full equilibrium.
(*c*) Show the short-run and long-run effects of increased investment on equilibrium income.

7

INVESTMENT SPENDING

Consumption spending in the United States is on average about 62 percent of GNP, and thus accounts for most of aggregate demand. Investment spending is typically less than 20 percent of GNP. But investment spending fluctuates much more than consumption. Table 7-1 shows how the components of aggregate demand changed in the most recent recession, between the third quarter of 1981 and the fourth quarter of 1982. Consumption increased even though GNP fell (recall from Chapter 6 that consumption is determined by permanent or lifetime disposable income, and not by current GNP), and government purchases of goods and services increased. But GNP nevertheless fell sharply, mostly because gross investment spending declined by more than total GNP declined.[1]

Figure 7-1 shows that the major role played by the decline in investment in the most recent recession is typical. In every recession or shortly before it, the share of investment in GNP falls sharply, and then investment begins to recover as the recovery gets under way. The cyclical relationships shown in Figure 7-1 extend much further back in history: For instance, in

[1] There was also a sharp fall in net exports; this was because the exchange rate of the dollar appreciated, and American goods became more expensive relative to foreign goods. More on this in Chaps. 18 and 19.

TABLE 7-1 REAL GNP AND ITS COMPONENTS IN THE 1981–1982 RECESSION (*Billions of 1972 dollars*)

	Level, 1981 III	Level, 1982 IV	Change
GNP	1525.8	1480.7	−45.1
Consumption	962.9	979.6	+16.7
Government	286.8	299.7	+12.9
Investment	236.3	178.4	−57.9
Net exports	39.8	23.0	−16.8

Source: Data Resources, Inc.

the Great Depression, gross investment fell to less than 4 percent of GNP in both 1932 and 1933. Understanding investment, then, will go a long way in helping us understand the business cycle.

In this chapter we continue our in-depth analysis of the components of aggregate demand. We both provide a foundation for the essential component of the simple investment function of Chapter 4—that investment demand is reduced by increases in the interest rate—and go further than that investment function, by discussing the roles of output and taxes in determining investment. While much of the reason for studying investment spending is that its fluctuations help account for the business cycle, another reason is that investment spending can be significantly affected by policy. High interest

FIGURE 7-1 COMPONENTS OF INVESTMENT SPENDING AS A PERCENTAGE OF GNP.

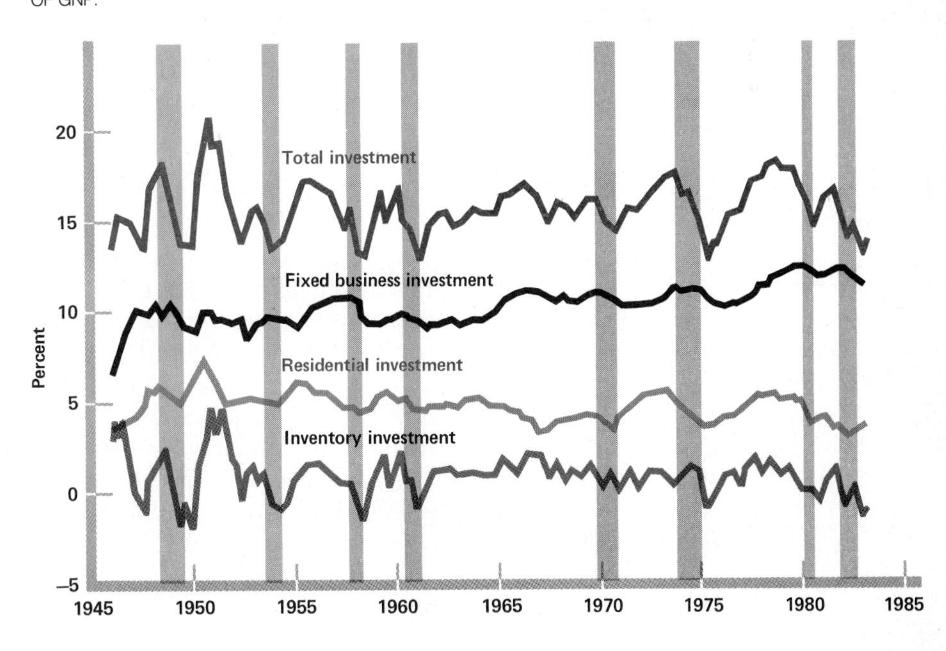

TABLE 7-2 GROSS DOMESTIC PRIVATE INVESTMENT (*Billions of 1972 dollars*)

	1982	1981 III	1982 IV	Change, 1981 III – 1982 IV
Business fixed investment	166.1	177.0	160.5	−16.5
Residential investment	37.8	43.1	40.6	− 2.5
Change in inventories	−9.4	16.1	−22.7	−38.8
	194.5	236.3	178.4	−57.9
GNP	1485.4	1525.8	1480.7	
Investment/GNP, %	13.1	15.5	12.0	

Source: Data Resources, Inc. *Components may not sum to totals, because of rounding.*

rates, caused by restrictive monetary policy and expansive fiscal policy, reduce investment spending; policies that reduce interest rates and provide tax incentives for investment can increase investment spending.

One simple relationship is vital to the understanding of investment. Investment is spending devoted to increasing or maintaining the stock of capital. The stock of capital consists of the factories, machines, offices, and other durable products used in the process of production. The capital stock also includes residential housing as well as inventories. Investment is spending that adds to these components of capital stock. Recall the distinction drawn in Chapter 2 between *gross* and *net investment.* Gross investment represents total additions to the capital stock. Net investment subtracts depreciation—the reduction in the capital stock that occurs each period through wear and tear and the simple ravages of time, equal to about 11 percent of GNP—from gross investment. Net investment thus measures the increase in the capital stock in a given period of time.

In this chapter we disaggregate investment spending into three categories. The first is *business fixed investment,* consisting of business firms' spending on durable machinery, equipment, and structures, such as factories and machines. The second is *residential investment,* consisting largely of investment in housing. And the third is *inventory investment,* some elements of which were discussed in Chapter 3.

Table 7-2 gives the levels of the three types of investment spending in 1982, along with the changes between peak and trough of the recession. Business fixed investment is the largest component of investment. Inventory investment is the component of investment that fluctuates most. It is frequently negative during recessions, when businesses decide the stocks of goods they have available for sale are too large and reduce them. But, on average, inventory investment is positive, as can be seen in Figure 7-1. Housing investment fluctuates a good deal. The fall in housing investment shown in Table 7-2 is small, but that is mainly because residential investment was at an extremely low level even before the 1981–1982 recession began, as a result of high interest rates in 1980 and 1981.

In the remainder of this chapter we develop theories and discuss evidence about the determinants of the rate of investment in each of the three major categories shown in Figure 7-1 and Table 7-2. We will develop what look like different models to explain each of the categories of investment spending. However, as we discuss in Section 7-5, the theories are essentially similar, sharing a common view of the interaction between a desired capital stock and the rate at which the economy adjusts toward that desired stock.

7-1 BUSINESS FIXED INVESTMENT: THE NEOCLASSICAL APPROACH

The machinery, equipment, and structures used in the production of goods and services constitute the *stock* of business fixed capital. Our analysis of business fixed investment in this section proceeds in two stages. First, we ask how much capital firms would like to use, given the costs and returns of using capital and the level of output they expect to produce. That is, we ask what determines the *desired capital stock*. The desired capital stock is the capital stock that firms would like to have in the long run, abstracting from the delays they face in adjusting their use of capital. However, because it takes time to order new machines, build factories, and install the machines, firms cannot instantly adjust the stock of capital used in production. Second, therefore, we discuss the rate at which firms adjust from their existing capital stock toward the desired level over the course of time. The rate of adjustment determines how much firms spend on adding to the capital stock in each period; that is, it determines the rate of investment.

The Desired Capital Stock: Overview

Firms use capital, along with labor, to produce goods and services for sale. The firms' goal is, of course, to maximize their profits. In deciding how much capital to use in production, they have to balance the contribution that more capital makes to their revenues against the cost of using more capital. The *marginal product of capital* is the increase in output produced by using one more unit of capital in production. The *rental (user) cost of capital* is the cost of using one more unit of capital in production.

To derive the rental cost of capital, we think of the firm as financing the purchase of the capital (whether the firm produces the capital itself or buys it from some other firm) by borrowing, at an interest cost i. In order to obtain the services of an extra unit of capital, in each period the firm must pay the interest cost i for each dollar of capital that it buys. Thus the basic measure of the rental cost of capital is the interest rate.[2] Later we shall go into more detail about the rental cost of capital, but for the meantime we shall think of the interest rate as determining the rental cost.

In deciding how much capital they would like to use in production, firms compare the value of the marginal product of capital with the user or rental

[2] Even if the firm finances the investment out of profits it has made in the past—retained earnings—it should still think of the interest rate as the cost of using the new capital, since it could otherwise have lent out those funds and earned interest on them, or paid them out as dividends to shareholders.

costs of capital. The value of the marginal product of capital is the increase in the *value* of output obtained by using one more unit of capital. For a competitive firm, it is equal to the price of output times the marginal product of capital. So long as the value of the marginal product of capital is above the rental cost, it pays the firm to add to its capital stock. Thus the firm will keep investing until the value of the output produced by adding one more unit of capital is equal to the cost of using that capital—the rental cost of capital. In equilibrium, we must have:

$$\text{Value of marginal product of capital} = \text{rental cost of capital} \tag{1}$$

To give content to this relationship, we have to specify what determines the productivity of capital and what determines the user (rental) cost of capital. The marginal product of capital is examined next, and then we turn to the rental cost of the capital.

The Marginal Productivity of Capital

In understanding the marginal productivity of capital, it is important to note that firms can substitute capital for labor in the production of output. Different combinations of capital and labor can be used to produce a given level of output. If labor is relatively cheap, the firm will want to use relatively more labor, and if capital is relatively cheap, the firm will want to use relatively more capital.

The general relationship among the desired capital stock (K^*), the rental cost of capital (rc), and the level of output is given by

$$K^* = g(rc, Y) \tag{2}$$

Equation (2) indicates that the desired capital stock depends on the rental cost of capital and the level of output. The lower the rental cost of capital, the larger the desired capital stock. And the greater the level of output, the larger the desired capital stock.

The relationship shown in Equation (2) makes complete sense. It says that firms want to have more capital on hand if they have to produce more output, and that they want to have more capital the cheaper it is to use capital. We now explain in more detail the factors underlying Equation (2).

As the firm combines progressively more capital with relatively less labor in the production of a *given* amount of output, the marginal product of capital declines. This relation is shown in the downward-sloping schedules in Figure 7-2. Those schedules show how the marginal product of capital falls as more capital is used in producing a given level of output. The schedule YY_1 is drawn for a level of output Y_1. The schedule YY_2 is drawn for the higher output level Y_2. The marginal product of capital, given the capital stock, say, K_0, is higher on the schedule YY_2 than on YY_1. That is because more labor is being used in combination with the given amount of capital K_0 to produce the level of output Y_2 than to produce Y_1.

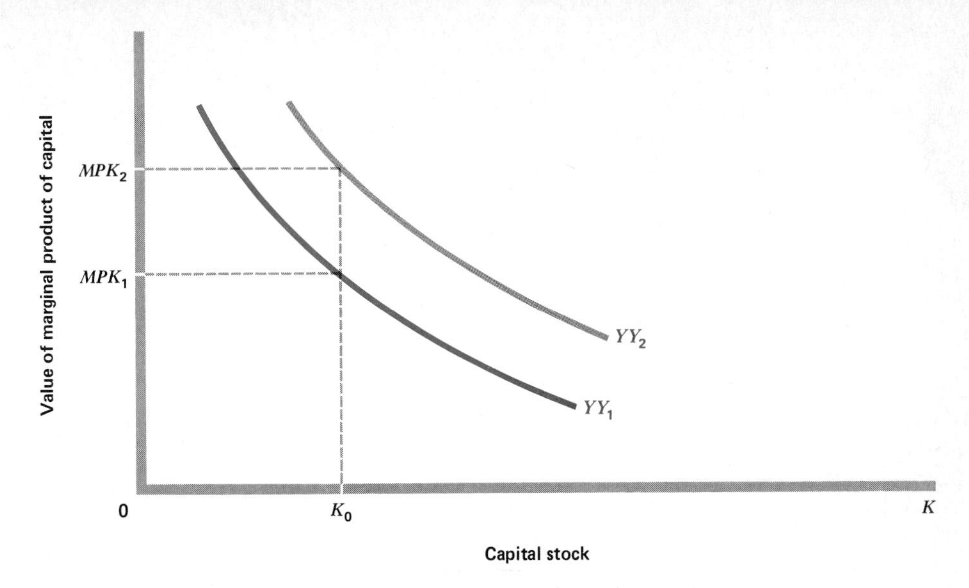

FIGURE 7-2 THE MARGINAL PRODUCT OF CAPITAL IN RELATION TO THE LEVEL OF OUTPUT AND THE CAPITAL STOCK. The marginal product of capital decreases as relatively more capital is used in producing any given level of output. Thus the schedules YY_1 and YY_2 are downward sloping. The higher the level of output, for any given capital input, the higher the marginal product of capital. Thus schedule YY_2, with output level Y_2 greater than Y_1, is above schedule YY_1.

Figure 7-2 shows the marginal product of capital in relation to the level of output and the amount of capital being used to produce that output. Figure 7-3 is a similar diagram which shows the desired capital stock as related to the rental cost of capital and the level of output. Given the level of output, say, Y_1, the firm will want to use more capital the lower the rental cost of capital—because at low rental costs of capital, it can afford to use capital even when its marginal productivity is quite low. If the rental cost of capital is high, the firm will be willing to use capital only if its marginal productivity is high—which means that the firm will not want to use very much capital and will instead substitute labor for capital. In producing a higher level of output, say, Y_2, the firm will use both more capital and more labor, given the rental cost of capital.[3] Therefore, at higher levels of output, the desired capital stock is higher.

THE COBB-DOUGLAS PRODUCTION FUNCTION

While Equation (2) provides the general relationship determining the desired capital stock, a particular form of the equation, based on the *Cobb-Douglas*

[3] Throughout this discussion, we have implicitly been assuming that the real wage paid to labor is given and does not change as the rental cost of capital changes.

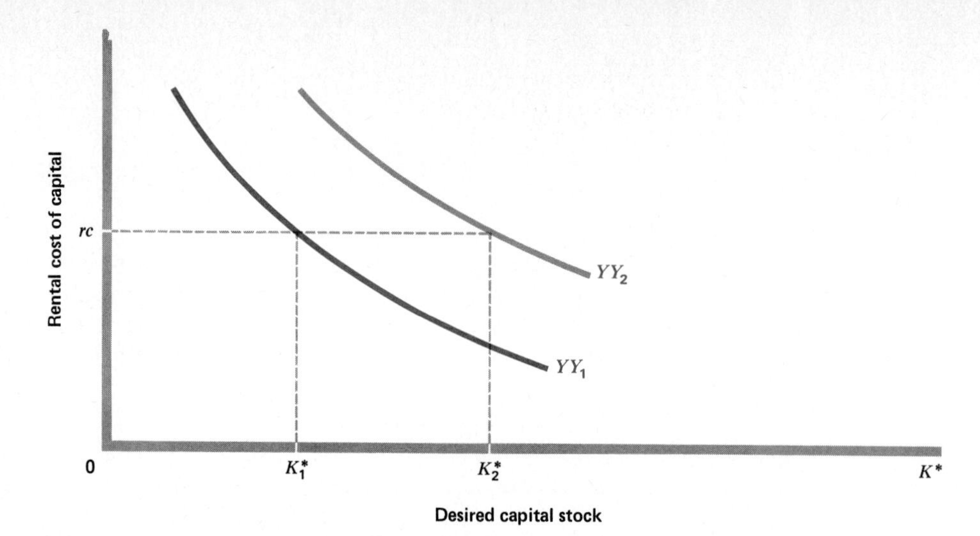

FIGURE 7-3 THE DESIRED CAPITAL STOCK IN RELATION TO THE LEVEL OF OUTPUT AND THE RENTAL COST OF CAPITAL. Firms' desired capital stock is chosen at the point at which the value of the marginal product of capital is equal to the rental cost of capital. At rental cost rc and output level Y_1, the firm's desired capital stock is K_1^*. An increase in the level of output to Y_2 raises the desired capital stock to K_2^*. An increase in the rental cost of capital (not shown) would reduce the desired capital stock at each level of output.

production function,[4] is frequently used in studies of investment behavior. The particular equation that is used is[5]

$$K^* = \frac{\gamma Y}{rc} \tag{3}$$

[4] The Cobb-Douglas production function is written in the form

$$Y = N^{1-\gamma}K^{\gamma} \qquad 1 > \gamma > 0$$

where N is the amount of labor used. This production function is particularly popular because it is easy to handle, and also because it appears to fit the facts of U.S. economic experience quite well. The coefficient γ appearing in Eq. (3) is the same as the γ of the production function. The reader trained in calculus will want to show that γ is the share of capital in total income.

[5] We draw attention here to a very subtle point: Equation (3) gives the marginal product of capital (*MPK*) when the *input of labor* is held fixed, while in Figs. 7-2 and 7-3 we work with the *MPK* when labor is being adjusted so that *output* is kept fixed. The desired capital stock that corresponds to Figs. 7-2 and 7-3 is

$$K^* = \left[\frac{\gamma w}{(1-\gamma)rc}\right]^{1-\gamma} Y \tag{3a}$$

where w is the real wage.

Equation (3*a*), like Eq. (3), implies that desired capital is proportional to Y and varies inversely with the rental cost of capital. We use Eq. (3) rather than Eq. (3*a*) in the text because it is the form that has been used in empirical studies.

where γ is a constant. In this case, the desired capital stock varies in proportion to output. Given output, the desired capital stock varies inversely with the rental cost of capital.

ESTIMATING THE RETURN TO CAPITAL

The value of the marginal product of capital is the increase in the value of output that is obtained by increasing the capital stock by one unit. If the capital stock were increased by 1 dollar today, the marginal product of capital would be the increase in the real value of output in subsequent years. An estimate of this return to capital, provided by the Council of Economic Advisers, is shown in Table 7-3.

The numbers are typically in the 10–20 percent range, meaning that 1 dollar of capital generates a return of 10 to 20 cents per year. The number varies from year to year, and according to the table has been falling, particularly since the 1960s. The return to capital is lower in recessions, so that the 1982 number is probably well below the return that will be observed in the remainder of the 1980s.[6]

The estimates of the return to capital in Table 7-3 will reappear later when we discuss the reasons for the slowdown of the real growth of the economy in the seventies and what can be done about it. One proposed remedy is to attempt, through tax policy, to increase the rate of investment. A 1-dollar increase in the capital stock would generate a return of about 10 cents or more in the form of increased output. Thus there are many who argue that one of the keys to reviving growth in the United States is to increase investment and thus the capital stock.

[6] An alternative estimate of the marginal product of capital can be obtained using the fact that the share of output received by capital is about 0.25. The share of capital in output, in turn, is equal to the marginal product of capital (*MPK*) times the capital stock, divided by the level of output:

$$\text{Share of capital} = MPK \times \frac{K}{Y}$$

With the capital output ratio (K/Y) in manufacturing at about 2 and the share of capital at 25 percent, we obtain

$$MPK = 0.25/2.0 = 12.5\%$$

This 12.5 percent confirms, in a ballpark figure way, the estimates in Table 7-3.

TABLE 7-3 RETURN TO CAPITAL, %

	1955–1959	1960–1969	1970–1979	1980–1981	1982
Average annual return	16.2	18.5	13.0	10.8	9.5

Source: Economic Report of the President, *1983, table B-88, column "Rate of return on depreciable assets" (Before Tax).*

Expected Output

In determining the desired stock, we have to specify the relevant time period for which the decision on the capital stock applies. In this section we are discussing the capital stock that the firm desires to hold at some future time. Accordingly, the level of output in Equations (2) and (3) should be the level of output which firms expect to be producing at that time. For some investments the future time at which the output will be produced is a matter of months or only weeks. For other investments—such as power stations—the future time at which the output will be produced is years away.

This suggests that the notion of permanent income (in this case, permanent output) introduced in Chapter 6 is relevant to investment as well as consumption. For longer-lived investments, the firm's capital demand is governed primarily by its views on the level of output it will be producing on average in the future. The firm's long-run demand for business fixed capital, depending on the normal or permanent level of output, is thus relatively independent of the current level of output, and depends on *expectations* of future output levels. However, it is affected by current output to the extent that current output affects expectations of permanent output.[7]

Summary on the Desired Capital Stock

It is worthwhile stepping back for a moment to summarize the main results so far:

1 The firm's demand for capital—the desired capital stock K^*—depends on the rental cost of capital, rc, and the expected level of output.
2 Firms balance the costs and benefits of using capital. The lower the rental cost of capital, the larger the optimal level of capital relative to output. This relation reflects the lower marginal productivity of capital when it is used relatively intensively. The intensive use of capital will be profitable only if the rental cost of capital is low.
3 The higher the level of output, the larger the desired capital stock.
4 The firm plans its capital stock in relation to expected future or permanent output.
5 Current output affects capital demand to the extent that it affects expectations about future output.

The Rental Cost of Capital Again

We have already introduced the notion of the rental or user cost of capital in determining the firm's desired capital stock. As a first approximation, we identified the rental cost of capital with the interest rate, on the argument that

[7] The role of permanent income in investment has been emphasized by Robert Eisner. Much of his work is summarized in his book *Factors in Business Investment* (Cambridge, Mass.: Ballinger, 1978).

firms would have to borrow to finance their use of capital. Now we go into more detail on the cost per period of using capital.

To use capital for a single period, say, a year, the firm can be thought of as buying the capital with borrowed funds and paying the interest on the borrowing. At the end of the year, the firm will still have some of the capital left. But the capital is likely to have depreciated over the course of the year. We shall assume that the firm intends to continue using the remaining capital in production in future years and that its depreciation simply represents the using up of the capital in the process of production—physical wear and tear. We now examine the rental cost, taking into account interest costs and depreciation. Later we will show that taxes also affect the rental cost of capital.

Leaving aside taxes, we now examine the two elements in the rental cost of capital in more detail. For the moment, let us write the interest cost i. Insofar as depreciation is concerned, we assume that a fixed proportion d of the capital is used up per period. The depreciation cost, per dollar of capital, is d.[8] The rental cost, or user cost, of capital, per dollar's worth of capital, which we denote by rc, is therefore

$$rc = i + d \tag{4}$$

A numerical example should help in understanding Equation (4). Suppose the interest rate is 10 percent per year and the rate of depreciation is 15 percent. That means that by the end of the year, the firm will have had to spend 15 cents per dollar of capital to maintain capital's production efficiency in the face of depreciation. The costs to the firm of using the capital for the year are then the interest cost, 10 cents per dollar of capital, and the depreciation cost, 15 cents per dollar of capital. The cost of using capital for a year is thus 25 cents per dollar's worth of capital.

The Real Rate of Interest

We have to distinguish carefully between the *real* and the *nominal* rates of interest. The *real interest rate* is the nominal (stated) rate of interest minus the rate of inflation. In general, someone borrowing at a stated nominal rate of interest, say, 10 percent, does not know what the rate of inflation over the period of the borrowing will be. Accordingly, the real rate of interest relevant when a loan transaction is entered into is the *expected* real rate of interest—the stated nominal interest rate minus the rate of inflation expected over the period of the loan.

The notion of the real rate of interest is extremely important. Suppose that the nominal interest rate, the rate stated in the loan agreement, is 10 percent. Then suppose also that prices are rising at 10 percent. Someone borrowing

[8] Why is depreciation considered as a cost? The firm continues using the capital and therefore has to devote expenditures to maintaining the productive efficiency of capital and thus offsetting wear and tear. We are assuming that, per dollar of capital, d dollars per period are required to maintain productive efficiency.

\$100 at the beginning of the year pays back \$110 at the end of the year. But those dollars in which repayment is made buy less goods than the dollars lent at the beginning of the year when the loan was made. If the inflation rate is 10 percent, then the \$110 paid at the end of the year buys the same amount of goods that could have been bought with the original \$100 at the beginning of the year. In *real* terms, in terms of the goods which the money can buy, the lender has no more at the end than at the beginning of the year. Thus the *real* interest rate actually received was zero, even though the *nominal* interest rate was 10 percent. Given the nominal interest rate, the real interest rate is lower the higher the rate of inflation becomes. In practice, nominal interest rates tend to be higher when inflation is higher.

It is the *expected real* rate of interest that should enter the calculation of the rental cost of capital. Why? The firm is borrowing in order to produce goods for sale. On average, across all firms, it is reasonable to believe that the prices of the goods the firms sell will be rising along with the general price level. Thus the value of what the firm will be producing in the future will be rising with the price level, but the nominal amount of interest it has to pay back on account of its borrowings does not rise with the price level. The real value of the debt it has incurred by borrowing will be falling over time, as a result of inflation, and it should take that reduction in the real value of its outstanding debts into account in deciding how much capital to employ.

Accordingly, we can be more precise in the way we write Equation (4) for the rental cost of capital. We write the rental cost of capital, taking account of expected inflation at the rate π^*, as

$$rc \equiv r + d \equiv i - \pi^* + d \tag{5}$$

where r is the real interest rate, i the nominal interest rate, and

$$r \equiv i - \pi^* \tag{6}$$

Equation (6) states that the real rate of interest is the nominal interest rate minus the expected rate of inflation. Implicitly, Equation (6) refers to the expected real rate of interest.[9] At the end of the period, when the rate of inflation is known, we can also state what the *actual* or realized real rate of interest for the period was—namely, the nominal interest rate i minus the actual rate of inflation.

To reiterate, it is important to note that the interest rate relevant to the firm's demand for capital is the *real* rate, and not the nominal rate. This makes it clear that the nominal rate of interest is not a good guide to the rental cost of capital. If the rate of inflation is zero and is expected to be zero and the nominal interest rate is 5 percent, then the real interest rate is 5 percent. By contrast, if the nominal interest rate is 10 percent and inflation is at the rate of

[9] Some loans to firms carry *variable* interest rates, so that the amount of interest the firm has to pay changes over time as the general level of interest rates changes. In these cases the rate i in Equation (6) would be the expected interest rate over the life of the loan.

10 percent, the real interest rate is zero. Other things equal, the desired capital stock in this example would tend to be higher with the nominal interest rate of 10 percent than with the nominal rate of 5 percent—because those rates correspond to real rates of zero and 5 percent, respectively. As you have no doubt deduced, and as we shall show, investment spending tends to be higher when the rental cost of capital is lower. But because of the distinction between real and nominal interest rates, that is *not* the same as saying that investment tends to be higher when the nominal rate of interest is lower.

Taxes and the Rental Cost as Capital

The rental cost of capital is affected by tax variables as well as by the interest rate and depreciation. The two main tax variables that affect the rental cost of capital are the corporate income tax and the investment tax credit. The corporate income tax is an essentially proportional tax on profits,[10] whereby the firm pays a proportion, say, t, of its profits in taxes. The investment tax credit allows firms to deduct from their taxes a certain fraction, say, τ, of their investment expenditures in each year. Thus a firm spending $1 million for investment purposes in a given year can deduct 10 percent of the $1 million, or $100,000, from the taxes it would otherwise have to pay the federal government.

We want to know what effects the corporate income tax and the investment tax credit have on the rental cost of capital. The easier case is the investment tax credit. The investment tax credit reduces the price of a capital good to the firm by the ratio τ, since the Treasury returns to the firm a proportion τ of the cost of each capital good. Equivalently, we can say that the rental cost is reduced by the factor τ. The investment tax credit therefore reduces the rental cost of capital.

To a first approximation, the corporate income tax, surprisingly, has no effect on the desired stock of capital. In the presence of the corporate income tax, the firm will want to equate the *after-tax* value of the marginal product of capital with the *after-tax* rental cost of capital in order to ensure that the marginal contribution of the capital to profits is equal to the marginal cost of using it.

Let us focus on the interest component of the rental cost. The basic point is that interest cost is treated as a deduction from revenues in the calculation of the corporation's taxes. Suppose there were no corporate income tax, no inflation, no depreciation, and an interest rate of 10 percent. The desired capital stock would be that level of the capital stock, say, K_0^*, such that the marginal product of capital was 10 percent. Now suppose that the corporate income tax rises to 46 percent and the interest rate remains constant. At the capital stock K_0^*, the after-tax marginal product of capital is now 5.4 percent (since 46 percent of the profits are paid in taxes). But if the interest rate stays at 10 percent and the firm gets to deduct 46 percent of its interest payments

[10] The corporate income tax reaches its maximum 46 percent at the profit level of $100,000. From the viewpoint of large firms, the tax is practically a constant proportion of profits.

from taxes, the after-tax cost of capital will be 5.4 percent too. In this case, the desired capital stock is unaffected by the rate of corporate taxation.

However, there are complexities in the tax laws, which we do not go into here, which make the total effect of the corporate income tax on the desired capital stock ambiguous. The ambiguities arise when the special tax treatment of depreciation,[11] of inflation, and of investment financing other than through borrowing is taken into account.[12]

We conclude by noting the two main points. The investment tax credit reduces the rental cost of capital and increases the desired stock of capital. The corporate income tax has ambiguous effects on the desired stock of capital.

Summary and Effects of Fiscal and Monetary Policy on the Desired Capital Stock

We summarize, using Equation (2), which gives the desired capital stock as a function of the rental cost of capital and the expected level of output, and the preceding discussion of the rental cost of capital. From Equation (2) we note that the desired capital stock increases when the expected level of output rises and when the rental cost of capital falls.

The rental cost of capital falls when the real interest rate and the rate of depreciation fall. It likewise falls when the investment tax credit rises. Changes in the rate of corporate taxation have ambiguous effects on the desired capital stock.

The major significance of these results is their implication that monetary and fiscal policy affect the desired capital stock. Fiscal policy exerts an effect through both the corporate tax rate t and the investment tax credit τ. Both these instruments are used to affect capital demand and thus investment spending.

Fiscal policy affects capital demand by its overall effects on the position of the *IS* curve, as we discussed in Chapter 5. A high tax–low government-spending policy keeps the real interest rate low and encourages the demand for capital. (At this point you want to refer to Figure 5-6.) A high government-spending–low-tax policy that produces large deficits raises the real interest rate and discourages the demand for capital.

Monetary policy affects capital demand by affecting the market interest rate.[13] A lowering of the nominal interest rate by the Federal Reserve System

[11] Internal Revenue Service counts depreciation as a business expense, but these allowances follow complicated rules and are not generally equal to the depreciation that the capital stock actually undergoes. Depreciation allowances were substantially changed by major tax acts in 1981 and 1982.

[12] Some investment is financed through the sale of equities. Part of the return to equity holders typically takes the form of dividend payments. However, dividends are not treated as a deduction from profits in the calculation of corporate income taxes. Thus the basic argument presented in the case of interest payments, that the corporate income tax does not affect the desired capital stock, would not apply for equity-financed investment.

[13] We should note that the Federal Reserve System is able to affect *nominal* interest rates directly by its sales and purchases of bonds. Its ability to control *real* interest rates is more limited.

(given the expected inflation rate), as reflected in a downward shift in the *LM* curve of Chapter 4, will induce firms to desire more capital. This expansion in capital demand, in turn, will affect investment spending, as we shall now see.

From Desired Capital Stock to Investment

We have now put more content into the general form of Equation (2) for the desired capital stock by discussing the rental cost of capital in detail. The actual capital stock will often differ from the capital stock firms would like to have. At what speed do firms change their capital stocks in order to move toward the desired capital stock? In particular, is there any reason why firms do not attempt to move to their desired capital stocks immediately?

Since it takes time to plan and complete an investment project, and because attempts to invest quickly are likely to be more expensive than gradual adjustment of the capital stock, it is unlikely that firms would attempt to adjust their capital stocks to the long-run desired level instantaneously. Very rapid adjustment of the capital stock would require crash programs by the firm which would distract management from its routine tasks and interfere with ongoing production. Thus, firms generally plan to adjust their capital stocks gradually over a period of time rather than immediately.

Capital Stock Adjustment

There are a number of hypotheses about the speed with which firms plan to adjust their capital stock over time; we single out the *gradual adjustment hypothesis* here.[14] The basic notion behind the gradual adjustment hypothesis is that the larger the gap between the existing capital stock and the desired capital stock, the more rapid a firm's rate of investment. The hypothesis is that firms plan to close a fraction λ of the gap between the desired and actual capital stocks each period. Denote the capital stock at the end of the last period by K_{-1}. The gap between the desired and actual capital stocks is $(K^* - K_{-1})$. The firm plans to add to last period's capital stock K_{-1}, a fraction λ of the gap $K^* - K_{-1}$ so that the capital stock at the end of current period, K, will be

$$K = K_{-1} + \lambda(K^* - K_{-1}) \tag{7}$$

Equation (7) states that the firm plans to have the capital stock at the end of the period (K) be such that a fraction λ of the gap (between the desired capital stock K^* and the capital stock K_{-1} that existed at the end of last period) is closed. To increase the capital stock from K_{-1} to the level of K indicated by Equation (7), the firm has to achieve an amount of net investment,

[14] The gradual adjustment hypothesis is a generalized form of the older *accelerator* model of investment, in which investment is proportional to the change in the level of GNP. The accelerator model is examined in Sec. 7-2.

$I \equiv K - K_{-1}$, indicated by Equation (7). We can therefore write net investment as

$$I = \lambda(K^* - K_{-1}) \tag{8}$$

which is the gradual adjustment formulation of net investment. Notice that Equation (8) implies that investment is larger, the larger the gap between actual and desired capital stocks.[15] With a zero gap net investment is zero.

In Figure 7-4 we show the adjustment process of capital in a circumstance where the initial capital stock is K_1 and the given desired capital stock is K^*. The assumed speed of adjustment is $\lambda = 0.5$. Starting from K_1, one-half the discrepancy between target capital and current actual capital is made up in every period. First-period net investment is therefore $0.5(K^* - K_1)$. In the

[15] Gross investment, as opposed to net investment described in Eq. (8), includes, in addition, depreciation. Thus, gross investment is $I + dK_{-1}$, where d is again the rate of depreciation.

FIGURE 7-4 THE GRADUAL ADJUSTMENT OF THE CAPITAL STOCK. The desired capital stock is K^*, and the current capital stock is K_1. The firm plans to close half the gap between the actual and the desired capital stock each period ($\lambda = 0.5$). Thus, in period one it moves to K_2, with (net) investment equal to $(K_2 - K_1)$, which in turn is equal to one half of $(K^* - K_1)$. In each subsequent period it closes half the gap between the capital stock at the beginning of the period and the desired capital stock, K^*.

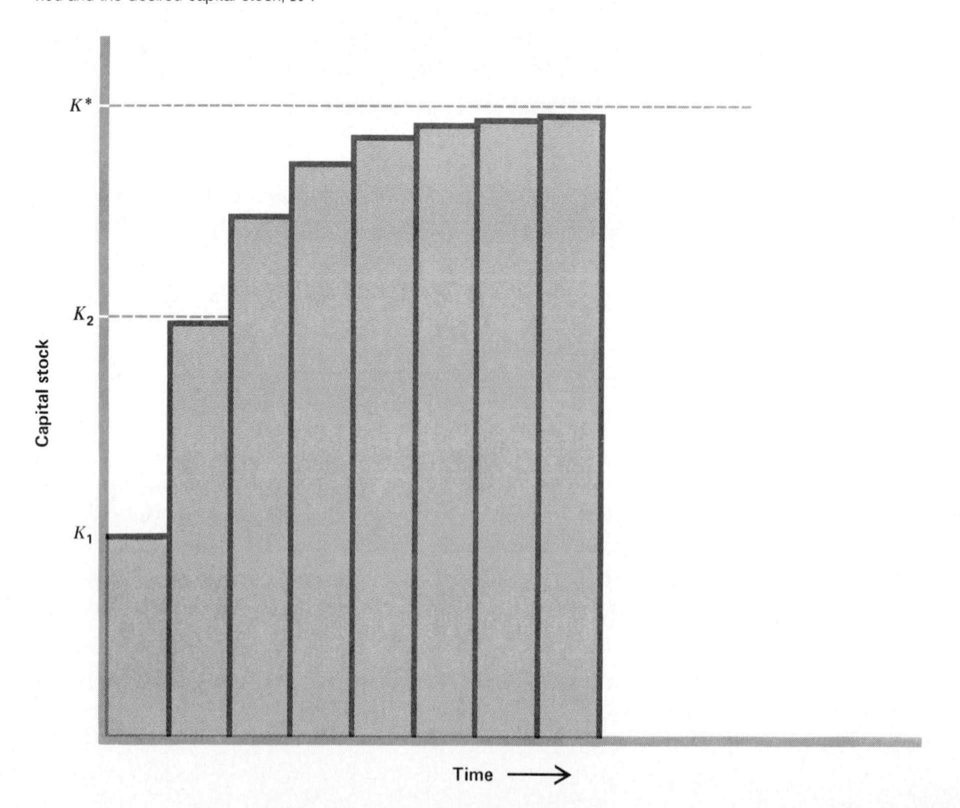

second period, investment will be less because the previous period's investment reduces the gap. Investment continues until the actual capital stock reaches the level of target capital. The speed with which this process allows actual capital to reach target capital is determined by λ. The larger λ is, the faster the gap is reduced.

In Equation (8), we have reached our goal of deriving an investment function that shows current investment spending determined by the desired stock of capital K^* and the actual stock of capital K_{-1}. According to the flexible accelerator hypothesis, any factor that increases the desired stock increases the rate of investment. Therefore an increase in expected output, or a reduction in the real interest rate, or an increase in the investment tax credit will each increase the rate of investment. We thus have derived a quite complete theory of business fixed investment that includes many of the factors we should expect to affect the rate of investment. And the theory of investment embodied in Equation (8) also contains aspects of *dynamic behavior*—that is, of behavior that depends on values of economic variables in periods other than the current period.

There are two sources of dynamic behavior in Equation (8). The first arises from expectations. The K^* term depends on the firm's estimate of future or permanent output. To the extent that the firm forms its estimates of permanent output as a weighted average of past output levels, there will be lags in the adjustment of the level of permanent output to the actual level of output. In turn, investment will therefore also adjust slowly to a change in the level of output. The second source of dynamic behavior arises from adjustment lags. Firms plan to close only a proportion of the gap between the actual and desired capital stocks each period, as shown in Figure 7-4. The adjustment lags produce lagged response of investment to changes in the variables that affect the desired capital stock.

THE TIMING OF INVESTMENT AND THE INVESTMENT TAX CREDIT

The flexible accelerator model provides a useful summary of the dynamics of investment. But it does not sufficiently emphasize the *timing* of investment. Because investment is undertaken for the long run and often requires several years to complete, there is flexibility in the dates on which the actual investment is undertaken. For example, suppose a firm wanted to have some machinery in place within 3 years. Suppose that it knew the investment tax credit would be raised substantially a year from now. Then the firm might be wise to delay the investment for a year and to make or acquire the machinery at a faster rate during the next 2 years, receiving the higher investment tax credit as the reward for waiting the extra year. Similarly, if a firm anticipated that the cost of borrowing next year would be much lower than this year, it might wait a year to undertake its investment project.

The flexibility in the timing of investment leads to an interesting contrast between the effects of the investment tax credit and the income tax on investment and consumption, respectively. We saw in Chapter 6 that a *permanent* change in the income tax has a much larger effect on consumption than a *transitory* change. However, the rate of investment *during the period* that a *temporary* investment tax credit is in effect would be higher than the rate of investment that would occur over the same period during which a *permanent* credit of the same magnitude was in effect. Why? If firms knew the investment tax credit was temporary, they would advance the timing of their planned investments in order to take advantage of the higher credit during the current period. If there were a permanent change in the investment tax credit, then the desired capital stock would rise, and there would on that account be more investment. But there would not be a bunching of investment.

It is for this reason that temporary changes in the investment tax credit have been suggested as a highly effective countercyclical policy measure. However, this is not a simple policy tool, as expectations about the timing and duration of the credit might conceivably worsen the instability of investment.

Summary on the Neoclassical Theory of Business Fixed Investment

The main conclusions of the theory of business fixed investment as developed here are:

1 Over time, net investment spending is governed by the discrepancy between actual and desired capital.
2 Desired capital depends on the rental (user) cost of capital and the expected level of output. Capital demand rises with expected output and the investment tax credit, and declines with an increase in *real* interest rates.
3 Monetary and fiscal policies exert effects on investment via the desired capital stock, although the short-run impact is likely to be minor. The longer-run effects are larger. The lags with which these investment effects occur are important to bear in mind in shaping stabilization policy.
4 Investment theory, like consumption theory, emphasizes the role of expected or permanent income or output as a determinant of capital demand.

7-2 BUSINESS FIXED INVESTMENT: ALTERNATIVE APPROACHES AND EMPIRICAL RESULTS

In this section we briefly discuss the way a firm typically approaches its investment decisions, and also describe the standard *accelerator theory of investment.* Then we go on to examine the empirical evidence on investment.

The Business Investment Decision: The View from the Trenches

Business people making investment decisions typically use *discounted cash flow analysis.* The principles of discounting are described in the Appendix to this chapter. Consider a business person deciding whether to build and equip a new factory. The first step is to figure out how much it will cost to get the factory into working order, and how much revenue the factory will bring in each year after it starts operation.

TABLE 7-4 DISCOUNTED CASH FLOW ANALYSIS AND PRESENT VALUE, $

	Year 1	Year 2	Year 3	Present discounted value
Cash or revenue	−100	+50	+80	
Present value of 1 dollar	1	1/1.15 =0.870	$(1/1.15^2)$ =0.756	
Present value of costs or revenue	−100	50 × 0.870 =43.50	80 × 0.756 =60.48	(−100 + 43.50 + 60.48) =3.98

For simplicity we consider a very short-lived project, one that costs $100 in the first year to set up and that then generates $50 in revenue (after paying for labor and raw materials) in the second year and a further $80 in the third year. By the end of the third year the factory has disintegrated.

The manager wants to know whether to undertake such a project. Discounted cash flow analysis says that the revenues received in later years should be *discounted* to the present in order to calculate their present value. As the Appendix on discounting shows, if the interest rate is 10 percent, $110 a year from now is worth the same as $100 now. Why? Because if $100 were lent out today at 10 percent, a year from now the lender would end up with $110. Thus to calculate the value of the investment project, the business person calculates its present discounted value at the interest rate at which the business can borrow. If the present value is positive, then the project is undertaken.

Suppose that the relevant interest rate is 15 percent.[16] The calculation of the present discounted value of the investment project is shown in Table 7-4. The $50 received in year 2 is worth only $43.50 today: $1 a year from now is worth $1/1.15 = 0.87 today, and so $50 a year from now is worth $43.50. The present value of the $80 received in year 3 is calculated similarly. The table shows that the present value of the net revenue received from the project is positive ($3.98) and thus that the firm should undertake the project.

Note that if the interest rate had been much higher—say, 18 percent—the decision would have been *not* to undertake the investment decision. We thus see how the interest rate affects the investment decision of the typical firm. The higher the interest rate, the less likely the firm will be to undertake any given investment project.

Each firm has at any time an array of possible investment projects, and estimates of the costs and the revenues from those projects. Depending on the level of the interest rate, it will want to undertake some of the projects and not undertake others. Taking all firms in the economy together and adding their investment demands, we obtain the total demand for investment in the economy at each interest rate.

This approach to the investment decision, which, of course, can be

[16] The interest rate here is nominal, because we are calculating the present value of dollars to be received in the future.

applied to investment projects of any duration and complexity, seems far from the description of Section 7-1 in terms of a desired capital stock and rate of adjustment.

Actually, the two approaches are quite consistent. First, we should think of the desired capital stock as being the stock of capital that will be in place when the firms have their factories and new equipment on-line. Second, the adjustment speed tells us how rapidly firms on average succeed in installing that capital.

We started with formulation in terms of the desired capital stock because the framework provides a very clear way of including the different factors that affect investment. For instance, it is easy to see how expectations of future output and taxes affect investment.

But because the two approaches are consistent, the same factors could be included using discounted cash flow analysis. The effects of expectations of future output can be analyzed using the discounted cash flow approach by asking what determines the firms' projections of their future revenues (corresponding to the \$50 in year 2 and \$80 in year 3 in the example above); expected demand for their goods and their output must be relevant. Similarly, taxes can be embodied by analyzing how taxes affect the amount of revenue the firm has left after taxes in each future year; the investment tax credit reduces the amount the firm has to lay out in the early years when it is actually building the project—because the Treasury provides a refund of part of the cost of the project through taxes.

Finally, the firm makes decisions about the speed of adjustment by considering the cash flows associated with building the project at different speeds. If the project can be built more rapidly, the firm will decide on the speed with which it wants the project brought on-line by considering the present discounted costs and revenues associated with speeding it up.

The Accelerator Model of Investment

The *accelerator model of investment* asserts that the rate of investment is proportional to the *change* in the economy's output. To derive the accelerator model of investment, assume that there is complete adjustment of the capital stock to its desired level within one period (that is, that $\lambda = 1$), so that $K = K^*$; that there is no depreciation, so that $d = 0$; and that the desired capital-output ratio is a constant, independent of the rental cost of capital:

$$K^* = vY \tag{9}$$

In Equation (9), v is a constant equal to the desired capital-to-output ratio. Substituting Equation (9) into Equation (8), setting $\lambda = 1$, and noting that $K_{-1} = K^*_{-1}$, we obtain

$$I = v(Y - Y_{-1}) \tag{10}$$

which is precisely the accelerator model of investment.

The accelerator model creates the potential for investment spending to fluctuate a good deal. If investment spending is proportional to the *change* in GNP, then when the economy is in a recovery, investment spending is positive, and when the economy is in a recession, investment will be negative.[17] Thus the accelerator model predicts that investment will fluctuate considerably, as Figure 7-1 shows it does.

Empirical Results

We now examine how the investment models we have developed, particularly the neoclassical model summarized in Equation (8), perform empirically.

To use Equation (8), it is necessary to substitute some specific equation for K^*, the desired capital stock. Frequently the Cobb-Douglas form is chosen. Using Equation (3) in Equation (8) yields a (net) investment function of the form

$$I = \lambda\left(\frac{\gamma Y}{rc} - K_{-1}\right) \tag{11}$$

The rental cost of capital, rc in Equation (11), is as in Equation (5), but adjusted for taxes.

Early empirical evidence, in particular that of Dale Jorgenson and his associates,[18] showed that an investment function including the variables in Equation (11) provided a reasonable explanation of the behavior of business fixed investment. However, the form shown in Equation (11) could be improved upon by allowing more scope for investment to respond slowly to changes in output. The empirical evidence suggests that the adjustment of investment to output takes the bell-shaped form in Figure 7-5. The major impact of a change in output on actual investment occurs with a 2-period (year) lag. The impact in the first year is less than the impact 2 years later.

There are two, not mutually exclusive, explanations for the behavior shown in Figure 7-5, corresponding to the two sources of dynamic behavior in Equation (8) that we discussed above. The first possibility is that the lag pattern of Figure 7-5 reflects the way in which expectations about future output, and thus the long-run desired capital stock, are formed. In that view, only a sustained increase in output will persuade firms that the capital stock should be increased in the long run. Figure 7-5 would then imply that it takes about 2 years for changes in the variables that determine the desired capital stock to have major impact on expectations.

The second explanation relies less on expectations and more on the physical delays in the investment process. That interpretation would be that Figure 7-5 reflects the long time it takes for a change in the desired capital

[17] The accelerator is not in practice a complete model of investment, for gross investment spending cannot be negative.

[18] See Dale W. Jorgenson, "Econometric Studies of Investment Behavior: A Survey," *Journal of Economic Literature*, December 1971.

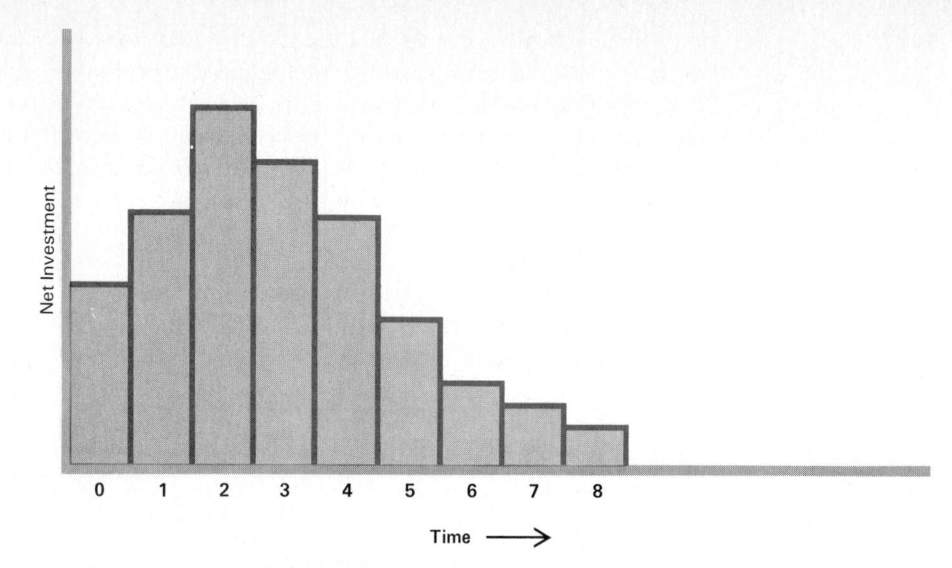

FIGURE 7-5 EFFECTS OF AN INCREASE IN OUTPUT IN PERIOD ZERO ON NET INVESTMENT IN SUBSEQUENT PERIODS (Years)

stock to be translated into investment spending. In industries in which investment can be undertaken quickly, there may be some response within a year. In other industries there may be long lags between the time machinery is ordered and the time it is ready to be delivered. In the economy as a whole, the maximum impact on investment of a change in the desired capital stock happens only 2 years after the change in the desired stock.

For many purposes, it does not matter which explanations of the form of Figure 7-5 is correct, and it is difficult to tell the explanations apart empirically. It is undoubtedly true that both explanations are relevent. The important point is that lags in the determination of the level of business fixed investment are long.

THE ACCELERATOR MODEL AGAIN

Subsequent empirical research has suggested that the accelerator model of Equation (10)—somewhat expanded—does about as good a job at explaining investment behavior as the neoclassical model.[19] The accelerator model is expanded in empirical work to make the rate of investment depend not only on the change in income this period, but also on the change in income in earlier periods. In empirical applications, this simple accelerator model differs therefore from the neoclassical model mainly in that it omits the cost of capital.

At least on evidence through 1979, it seems that the cost of capital

[19] Peter K. Clark, "Investment in the 1970's: Theory, Performance, and Prediction," *Brookings Papers on Economic Activity*, 1979:1 (Washington, D.C.: The Brookings Institution, 1979).

empirically does not much affect investment and that accordingly the simple accelerator model does as well as the neoclassical model at explaining investment. Events since 1979 should, though, provide a good test of whether the cost of capital affects investment. Real interest rates and the rental cost of capital were extremely high in 1981 and 1982, and the rate of investment fell sharply. Future empirical work is thus quite likely to confirm the importance of the rental cost of capital—as well as the level of output—in determining investment spending. Certainly, theory suggests that the rental cost should play an important role in affecting investment.

We now discuss some other aspects of investment behavior.

SALES AND PROFITS AS DETERMINANTS OF INVESTMENT

Some studies of investment find either the level of sales or total profits to be factors explaining the level of investment. The level of sales could be interpreted as affecting expectations of future output and thus affecting the desired capital stock. Note that output and sales differ by the amount of inventory accumulation.

The role of profits can be interpreted similarly. High profits may provide an indication of future demand for the firm's product, and thus of future output. Alternatively, it is often argued that firms prefer to use retained profits to finance investment, rather than borrow. The preference might result from the expense of having to raise outside funds relative to using inside funds. However, in using its retained profits to finance investment rather than borrow, the firm has also to consider the possibility of paying out its profits to the firm's owners, who can invest in other firms. Thus even when using retained earnings, firms have to take into account the level of interest rates—as a measure of the returns their owners could receive if the earnings were paid out.

Why Does Investment Fluctuate?

The facts with which we started this chapter show that investment fluctuates much more than consumption spending. The accelerator model provides one explanation of these fluctuations. There are two other basic explanations: the uncertain basis for expectations and the flexibility of the timing of investment.

UNCERTAIN EXPECTATIONS

Keynes, in the *General Theory,* emphasized the uncertain basis on which investment decisions are made. In his words, ". . . we have to admit that our basis of knowledge for estimating the yield ten years hence of a railway, a copper mine, a textile factory, the goodwill of a patent medicine . . . amounts to little and sometimes to nothing. . . ."[20] Thus, he argued,

[20] J. M. Keynes, *The General Theory of Employment, Interest and Money* (New York: Macmillan, 1936), pp. 149–150.

investment decisions are very much affected by how optimistic or pessimistic the investors feel.

The term "animal spirits" is sometimes used to describe the optimism or pessimism of investors, where "animal spirits" indicates that there may be no good basis for the expectations on which investors base their decisions. If there is no good basis for the expectations, then they could change easily—and the volume of investment along with the expectations.

3) THE TIMING OF INVESTMENT DECISIONS

The second possible reason for fluctuations in investment is that, as noted in Section 7-1, investment decisions can be delayed if the project will take a long time to come on-line. Suppose a firm has an investment project it would like to undertake, but the economy is currently in a recession and the firm is not sure when the recession will end. Further, at the current time it cannot even usefully fully employ all the capital it already has. Such a firm might choose to wait until the prospects for the economy look better—when the recovery gets under way—before deciding to start the investment project.

Either or both of these factors could help account for the substantial fluctuations that are seen in business investment spending. Indeed, they may also explain the success of the accelerator theory of investment, for if firms wait for a recovery to get under way before investing, their investment will be closely related to the change in GNP.

7-3 RESIDENTIAL INVESTMENT

We study residential investment separately from business fixed investment both because somewhat different theoretical considerations are relevant[21] and because residential investment shows large cyclical fluctuations, as can be seen in Figure 7-6.

Figure 7-6 shows residential investment spending in constant (1972) dollars for the period 1965–1982, together with the mortgage interest rate. Residential investment declines in all recessions. Thus in 1969–1970, 1973–1975, 1980, and 1981–1984, there is a dip in residential investment. The same is true for the minirecession in 1966–1967.

Theory

Residential investment consists of the building of single-family and multifamily dwellings, which we call housing for short. Housing is distinguished as an asset by its long life. Consequently, investment in housing in any one year tends to be a very small proportion—about 3 percent—of the existing stock of housing. The theory of residential investment starts by considering the

[21] In the concluding section of this chapter, we explain why slightly different theoretical models are used in explaining business fixed investment and residential investment.

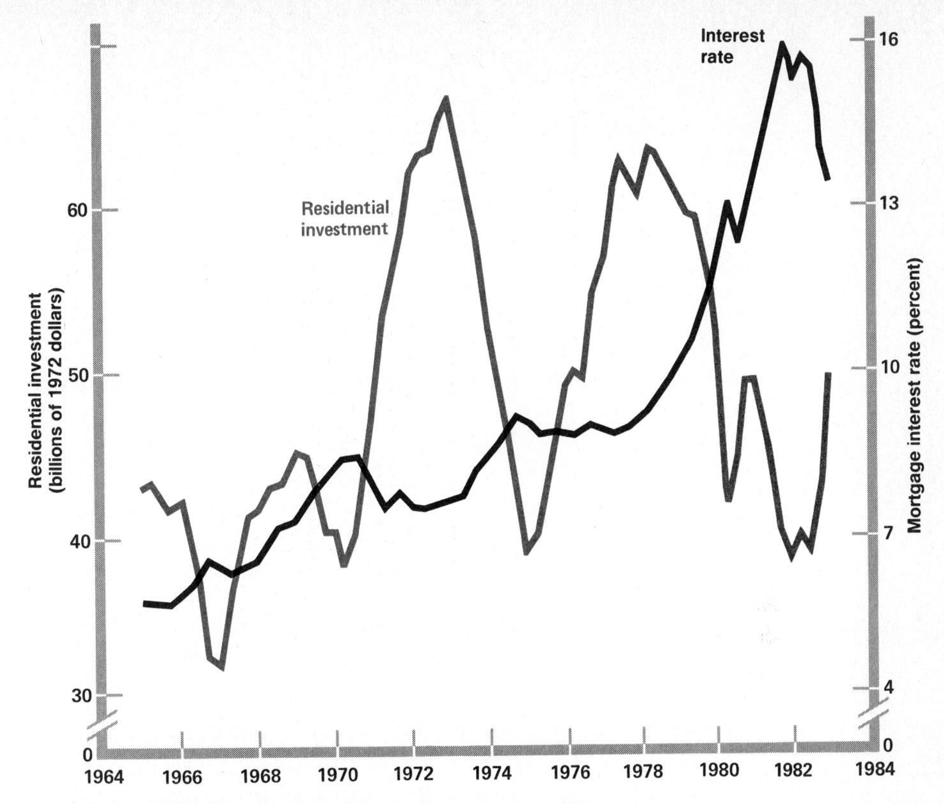

FIGURE 7-6 RESIDENTIAL FIXED INVESTMENT SPENDING VS. MORTGAGE INTEREST RATE ON NEW HOMES

demand for the existing stock of housing. Housing is viewed as one among the many assets that a wealth holder can own.

In Figure 7-7*a* we show the demand for the stock of housing in the downward-sloping DD_0 curve. The lower the price of housing (P_H), the greater the quantity demanded. The position of the demand curve itself depends on a number of economic variables. First, the greater wealth is, the greater the demand for housing. The more wealthy individuals are, the more housing they desire to own. Thus an increase in wealth would shift the demand curve from DD_0 to DD_1. Second, the demand for housing as an asset depends on the real return available on other assets. If returns on other forms of holding wealth—such as bonds—are low, then housing looks like a relatively attractive form in which to hold wealth. The lower the return on other assets, the greater the demand for housing. A reduction in the return on other assets, such as bonds or common stock, shifts the demand curve from DD_0 to DD_1.

Third, the demand for the housing stock depends on the net real return obtained by owning housing. The gross return—before taking costs into account—consists of rent, if the housing is rented out, or the implicit return

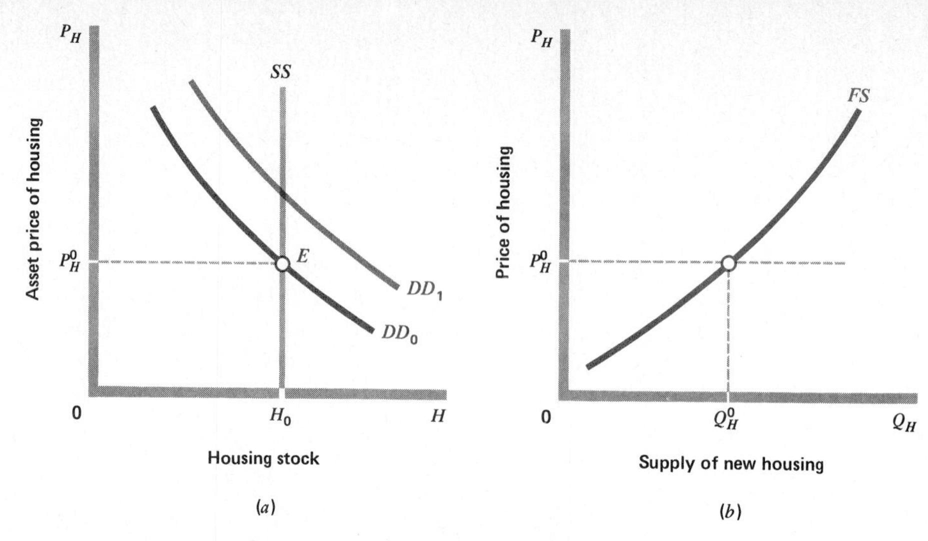

FIGURE 7-7 THE HOUSING MARKET: DETERMINATION OF THE ASSET PRICE OF HOUSING AND THE RATE OF HOUSING INVESTMENT. The supply and demand for the stock of housing determine the asset price of housing (P_H^0) in panel (*a*). The rate of housing investment (Q_H^0) is determined by the flow supply of housing at price P_H^0, in panel (*b*).

that the homeowner receives by living in the home, plus capital gains arising from increases in the value of the housing. In turn, the costs of owning the housing consist of interest cost, typically the mortgage interest rate, plus any real estate taxes, and depreciation. These costs are deducted from the gross return and, after tax adjustments, constitute the net return. An increase in the net return on housing, caused, for example, by a reduction in the mortgage interest rate, makes housing a more attractive form in which to hold wealth and shifts up the demand curve for housing from DD_0 to DD_1.

The price of housing is determined by the interaction of this demand with the stock supply of housing. At any time the stock supply is fixed—there is a given stock of housing that cannot be adjusted quickly in response to price changes. The supply curve of the stock of housing is the *SS* curve of Figure 7-7*a*. The equilibrium *asset price of housing*, P_H^0, is determined by the intersection of the supply and demand curves. The asset price of housing is the price of a typical house or apartment. At any one time, the market for the stock of housing determines the asset price of housing.

THE RATE OF INVESTMENT

We now consider the determinants of the rate of investment in housing, and for the purpose turn to Figure 7-7*b*. The curve *FS* represents the supply of new housing as a function of the price of housing. This curve is the same as the regular supply curve of any industry. The supply curve shows the amount of a good that suppliers want to sell at each price. In this case, the good being supplied is new housing. The position of the *FS* curve is affected by the costs of

Flow vs Stock supply

factors of production used in the construction industry and by technological factors affecting the cost of building.

The curve *FS* is sometimes called the flow supply curve, since it represents the *flow* of new housing into the market in a given time period. In contrast, the *stock* supply curve *SS* represents the total amount of housing in the market at a moment of time.

Given the price of housing established in the asset market, P_H^0, building contractors supply the amount of new housing, Q_H^0, for sale at that price. The higher the asset price, the greater the supply of new housing. Now the supply of new housing is nothing other than gross investment in housing—total additions to the housing stock. Figure 7-7 thus represents our basic theory of the determinants of housing investment.

Any factor affecting the demand for the existing stock of housing will affect the asset price of housing, P_H, and thus the rate of investment in housing. Similarly, any factor shifting the flow supply curve *FS* will affect the rate of investment. We have already investigated the major factors shifting the *DD* demand curve for housing, but will briefly repeat that analysis.

Suppose the interest rate—the rate potential homeowners can obtain by investing elsewhere—rises. Then the asset demand for housing falls and the price of housing falls; that, in turn, induces a decline in the rate of production of new housing, or a decline in housing investment. Or suppose that the mortgage interest rate rises: once again there is a fall in the asset price of housing and a reduction in the rate of construction.

Because the existing stock of housing is so large relative to the rate of investment in housing, we can ignore the effects of the current supply of new housing on the price of housing in the short run. However, over time, the new construction shifts the *SS* curve of the left-hand panel to the right as it increases the housing stock. The long-run equilibrium in the housing industry would be reached, in an economy in which there was no increase in population or wealth over time, when the housing stock was constant. Constancy of the housing stock requires gross investment to be equal to depreciation, or net investment to be equal to zero. The asset price of housing would have to be at the level such that the rate of construction was just equal to the rate of depreciation of the existing stock of housing in long-run equilibrium. If population or income and wealth were growing at a constant rate, the long-run equilibrium would be one in which the rate of construction was just sufficient to cover depreciation and the steadily growing stock demand. In an economy subjected to continual nonsteady changes, that long-run equilibrium is not necessarily ever reached.

Minor qualifications to the basic theoretical structure arise chiefly because new housing cannot be constructed immediately in response to changes in P_H; rather, it takes a short time for that response to occur. Thus, the supply of new housing responds, not to the actual price of housing today, but to the price expected to prevail when the construction is completed. However, the lags are quite short; it takes less than a year to build a typical house. Another qualification stems from that same construction delay. Since builders have to incur expenses before they sell their output, they need financing over the construction period. They are frequently financed at the mortgage interest rate by the thrift institutions, that is, savings and loan associations and mutual savings banks. Hence, the position of the flow supply curve is affected by the mortgage interest rate as well as the amount of lending undertaken by the thrift institutions.[22]

Monetary Policy and Housing Investment

Monetary policy has powerful effects on housing investment. Part of the reason is that most houses are purchased with the aid of mortgage financing. Since the 1930s, a mortgage has typically been a debt instrument of very long maturity, 20 to 30 years, with a fixed rate and with monthly nominal repayments which remain fixed for the 20 to 30 years to maturity.[23]

Monetary policy has powerful effects on housing investment because the demand for housing is sensitive to the interest rate. There is sensitivity to both the *real* and *nominal* interest rates. The reason for this sensitivity can be seen in Table 7-5, which shows the monthly payment that has to be made by someone borrowing $50,000 through a conventional mortgage at different interest rates. All these interest rates have existed at some time the last 25 years: 5 percent at the beginning of the sixties, 10 percent at the end of the seventies, and 15 percent in 1981 and 1982.

The monthly repayment by the borrower approximately doubles when the interest rate doubles. Thus an essential component of the cost of owning a home rises almost proportionately with the interest rate. It is therefore not surprising that the demand for housing is very sensitive to the interest rate.

The above statements have to be qualified. In the first place, there are substantial tax advantages to the homeowner who finances through a mortgage, because the interest payments can be deducted from income before calculating taxes. Second, of course, we should be concerned with the *real* and not the nominal interest cost of owning a house—and certainly much of the rise of the mortgage interest rate visible in Figure 7-6 is a result of increases in the expected rate of inflation.

But the *nominal* interest rate also affects the homeowner. The reason has to do with the form of the mortgage. The conventional mortgage makes the borrower pay a fixed amount each month over the lifetime of the mortgage.

[22] The theory of housing investment of this section is the basis of the study of the housing market undertaken by Brigham Young University's James Kearl in his 1975 MIT Ph.D. dissertation, "Inflation-Induced Distortions of the Real Economy: An Econometric and Simulation Study of Housing and Mortgage Innovation."

[23] Even though the high inflation years of the seventies saw the invention of new types of mortgages, the standard mortgage is still as described in the text.

TABLE 7-5 MONTHLY PAYMENTS ON MORTGAGES

Interest rate	5%	10%	15%
Monthly payment	$292	$454	$640

Note: The assumed mortgage is a loan for $50,000, paid back over 25 years, with equal monthly payments for those 25 years.

Even if the interest rate rises only because the expected rate of inflation has risen — and thus the real rate is constant — the payments that have to be made *today* by a borrower go up. But the inflation has not yet happened. Thus the real payments made today by a borrower rise when the *nominal* interest rate rises, even if the real rate does not rise.[24] Given the higher real monthly payments when the *nominal* interest rate rises, we should expect the nominal interest rate also to affect housing demand. And the data shown in Figure 7-6 are quite consistent with the nominal interest rate affecting housing demand.

DISINTERMEDIATION, MORTGAGE AVAILABILITY, AND REGULATION Q

Before 1978 monetary policy affected housing demand through a channel known as *disintermediation*. Mortgage financing is provided mostly by savings and loans institutions. These institutions have assets (mortgages) that have very long lives. Up to 1978 they obtained the funds they loaned out mainly from depositors, who made savings deposits in the institutions. The depositors had the right to remove their funds immediately, sometimes on payment of a penalty, or within a short time at no charge.

At that time the Fed controlled the interest rates that savings and loans (and banks and other financial institutions) could pay to their depositors.[25] The control was exercised through Regulation Q.[26] Reg Q, as it was called, in effect set the interest maximum to be paid on deposits by savings and loans at 5.5 percent. The financial institutions were generally in favor of Reg Q, since it limited the amount they had to pay to borrow.

The savings and loans in particular were concerned that the rate of interest they paid depositors should not rise. This was because they had made long-term loans (mortgages) at low interest rates. Thus they knew that they would for a long time be earning only 5 or 6 percent on the loans they had made. They could not afford to pay out more than 5 percent to their depositors.

But when market interest rates started rising, depositors limited to 5.5 percent at the financial institutions went elsewhere with their money. This is the process of disintermediation. As the depositors withdrew their deposits, for instance, buying Treasury bills instead, the savings and loans had nothing left to loan. There were no mortgages available, even though the interest rate that the savings and loans were quoting (this was the rate they would charge if they could find the money to lend) was not especially high.

Box 7-1 presents some data from the 1966–1967 period of disintermediation, known as the *credit crunch*. This shows how monetary policy affected

[24] How can the real payments rise if the real interest rate stays the same? The explanation is that today's real payments rise, but the real present value of future payments falls: the repayment stream tilts toward the present. For more on this feature, see Franco Modigliani and Donald Lessard (eds.), *New Mortgage Designs for Stable Housing in an Inflationary Environment*, Federal Reserve Bank of Boston, Conference Series #14, 1975.

[25] These controls are being phased out and should all be removed by 1986 under the terms of the 1980 Depository Institutions Decontrol and Monetary Control Act.

[26] In form, Reg Q did not directly affect savings and loans institutions. Their rates were controlled by another agency, the FHLBB (Federal Home Loan Bank Board). But the FHLBB set its rates with reference to Reg Q rates.

BOX 7-1

THE 1966 CREDIT CRUNCH: MONETARY POLICY IN ACTION

The credit crunch of the second half of 1966 was the first occasion in the post-World War II period that the Fed sharply cut back on monetary growth and caused rapid and, for the time, large increases in interest rates. Because of disintermediation, banks and other financial institutions were not able to make their normal volume of loans.

The crunch was the period of high interest rates, reduced availability of loans from financial institutions, and simple fear of financial disaster that prevailed from about August to October 1966. It was followed by a minirecession.

The crunch was set off by monetary policy in the last three quarters of 1966. In response to rising inflation, the Fed kept the money supply constant, to reduce aggregation demand and inflation. As Figure 1 shows, interest rates, measured here by the commercial paper rate (the rate large firms pay on short-term loans), rose sharply, and in particular rose above the Reg Q ceiling. Although the 6 percent interest rate is low by the standards of the seventies, it was for the mid-sixties a very high rate.

The high interest rates and disintermediation started to affect aggregate demand by late 1966. Private investment spending, as shown in Figure 2, responded dramatically to the high interest rates and credit tightness. This was particularly true for residential construction, which declined sharply under the impact of both the higher interest rates and disintermediation.* Note, too, the relative timing of reduced residential construction and the reduction in business fixed investment spending. Residential construction reacted very quickly to tightness in money and credit markets. The adjustment in business investment was considerably slower.

The credit crunch was reflected in a sharp reduction in real income growth in 1966 and early 1967. From a high rate of growth of 8 percent in 1965 the rate of increase of real output fell

FIGURE 1 INTEREST RATES AND REGULATION Q CEILING. *Source: Survey of Current Business, 1969 Supplement, and Federal Reserve Bulletin.*

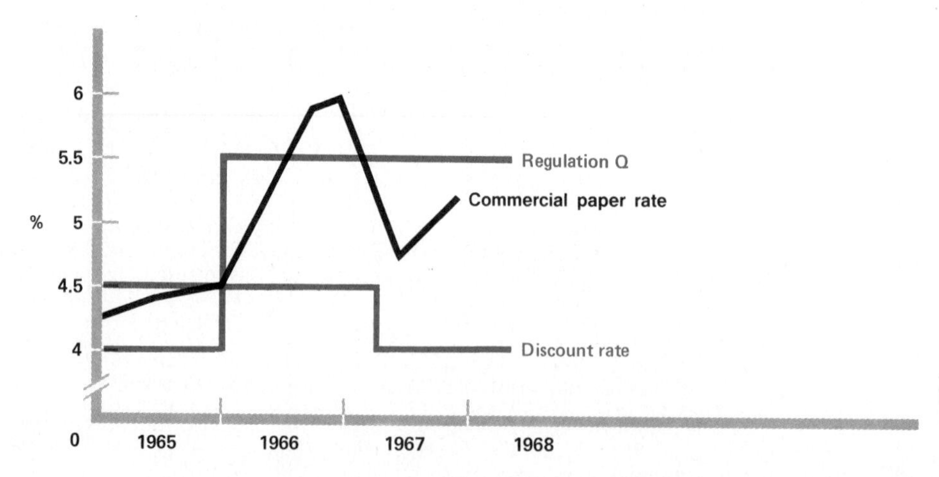

FIGURE 2 COMPONENTS OF INVESTMENT SPENDING (1965–1967)

to 1.2 percent for the first two quarters of 1967, the so-called minirecession, caused mainly by the reduction in investment in late 1966 and early 1967.

Monetary policy in this episode showed its power to reduce aggregate demand and output, operating largely by affecting investment spending.

* For further aspects, see Albert Burger, "A Historical Analysis of the Credit Crunch of 1966," *Federal Reserve Bank of St. Louis, Review*, September 1969, pp. 13–30.

investment spending. Housing investment in particular fell because there were no loans available. Disintermediation happened again in 1969–1970 and in the 1973–1975 recession. But then the savings and loans invented new ways of borrowing, and since then, monetary policy has affected housing investment directly through interest rates, rather than through the roundabout route of disintermediation.

What about the problem that the savings and loans, borrowing by paying high interest rates to depositors, would be paying out more than they were earning on the loans they had made? This was a very real problem in the late seventies and early eighties. Several savings and loans institutions failed (went bankrupt) and were bought out by other financial institutions. The hope in 1983 is that as interest rates fall, the savings and loans will get their financial affairs back in order again. One way for them to do so is not to make conventional mortgage loans in the future. The variable-rate mortgage, on which the interest payment made by the borrower varies with the general level of interest rates, is being introduced in many parts of the country. This gives protection to the savings and loans against rises in the interest rates they have to pay their depositors, but it is not very popular with the borrowers.

By the early eighties, monetary policy affected housing investment through interest rates, but not through disintermediation. Indeed, this is one reason the interest rate in the late seventies and early eighties went so high: The Fed wanted to reduce aggregate demand and had to do so through the direct interest rate route and not through the indirect disintermediation route.

7-4 INVENTORY INVESTMENT

Inventories consist of raw materials, goods in the process of production, and completed goods held by firms in anticipation of their sale. The ratio of inventories to annual final sales in the United States has been in the range of 25 to 35 percent over the past 20 years. That is, on average, firms hold inventories that constitute 3 to 4 months' worth of their final sales.

The inventories of interest to us are those held to meet future demands for goods. Firms hold such inventories because goods cannot be instantly manufactured or obtained from the manufacturer to meet demand. Some inventories are held as an unavoidable part of the production process; there is an inventory of meat and sawdust inside the sausage machine during the manufacture of sausage, for example. Inventories are also held because it is less costly for a firm to order goods less frequently in large quantities than to order small quantities frequently—just as the average household finds it useful to keep several days' supplies on hand in the house so as not to have to visit the supermarket daily.

Firms have a desired ratio of inventories to final sales that depends on economic variables. The smaller the cost of ordering new goods and the greater the speed with which such goods arive, the smaller the inventory-sales ratio. The more uncertainty about the demand for the firm's goods, given the expected level of sales, the higher the inventory-sales ratio. The inventory-sales ratio may also depend on the level of sales, with the ratio falling with sales because there is relatively less uncertainty about sales as sales increase. Finally, there is the interest rate. Since firms carry inventories over time, they must tie up money to buy and hold them. There is an interest cost involved in such inventory holding, and the desired inventory-sales ratio should be expected to fall with increases in the interest rate. However, such a link has been difficult to establish empirically.

Anticipated versus Unanticipated Inventory Investment

The most interesting aspect of inventory investment lies in the distinction between anticipated (desired) and unanticipated (undesired) investment. Inventory investment could be high in two circumstances. First, if sales are unexpectedly low, firms would find unsold inventories accumulating on their shelves; that constitutes unanticipated inventory investment. This is the type of inventory investment discussed in Chapter 3. Second, inventory investment could be high because firms plan to restore depleted inventories. The two circumstances obviously have very different implications for the behavior of aggregate demand. Unanticipated inventory investment is a result of unexpectedly low aggregate demand. On the other hand, planned inventory investment can be a response to recent, unexpectedly high aggregate demand. That is, rapid accumulation of inventories could be associated with either rapidly declining aggregate demand or rapidly increasing aggregate demand.

Inventories in the Business Cycle

Inventory investment fluctuates substantially in the business cycle—proportionately more than any other component of aggregate demand. In every post-World War II recession in the United States there has been a decline in inventory investment—the rate at which firms add to their inventories—between peak and trough. Table 7-6 gives the data on the change in the rate of inventory investment in column 2. At the end of every recession, firms have been reducing their inventories, meaning that inventory investment has been negative in the final quarter of every recession. (This information is not shown in Table 7-6 but may be visible in Figure 7-2.)

The last column of Table 7-6 gives an indication that the change in inventory investment typically plays a significant role in the decline in GNP during a recession. Column 3 of the table calculates how much less GNP grew in fact between peak and trough than it would have grown had GNP kept on growing at a trend rate of 3.2 percent per annum. That is a rough measure of the fall in output during the recession. Typically 20 to 30 percent or more of that decline is directly attributable to a decline in inventory investment.

The role of inventories in the business cycle is a result of a combination of unanticipated and anticipated inventory change. Figure 7-8 illustrates the combination using data from the most recent recessions. The behavior of sales and output for the 1981–1982 recession is the more typical. Before the recession begins, GNP is increasing rapidly, recovering from the previous recession. But from the middle of 1980 until the end of the year, sales exceed GNP. That means firms are running down their inventories. From the beginning of 1981 firms begin to accumulate inventories, as GNP exceeds their

TABLE 7-6 INVENTORY DECUMULATION IN RECESSIONS (*Billions of 1972 dollars*)

RECESSION Peak	Trough	(1) Change in real GNP	(2) Change in rate of inventory investment	(3) Change in real GNP relative to trend	(2)/(3), %
48.4	49.4	− 7.1	−12.8	− 22.7	52.9
53.2	54.2	−20.2	− 9.2	− 39.9	23.1
57.3	58.1	−23.0	−10.5	− 39.9	26.3
60.2	61.1	− 0.7	− 7.4	− 18.2	40.7
69.4	70.4	− 0.9	− 5.6	− 35.0	16.0
73.4	75.1	−61.8	−38.0	−111.3	34.1
80.1	80.3	−31.1	− 6.3	− 54.8	11.5
81.3	82.4	−33.2	−36.8	− 92.3	39.9

Source: Citibank Economic Database.
Notes:
1 Change in real GNP relative to trend is calculated by assuming GNP would have continued to grow at a quarterly rate of 0.8% from the peak level of income.
2 Dates for peaks and troughs are for years and quarters (for example, 48.4 is fourth quarter of 1948.)

sales. Firms were probably anticipating high sales in the future and decided to build up their stocks of goods for future sale. Thus there was *intended* inventory accumulation.

In the middle of 1981 there is a sharp fall in final sales, equal to aggregate demand. But GNP falls much less. In this period firms were *unanticipatedly* accumulating inventories. Inventory accumulation continued through the end of 1981, even though firms had then begun to cut back output to get inventories back in line. In the first quarter of 1982, firms have cut output way back and finally are successfully and *intentionally* reducing their inventories, as sales exceed output.

The behavior seen in the 1981 – 1982 recession explains much of the role of inventories in recessions. At the beginning of the recession there is a reduction in aggregate demand, reflected in a slowdown in sales. But output does not respond much and inventories build up unintentionally. Then firms decide to get rid of their inventories, reducing production and planning to sell out of inventories; this is *intended* inventory decumulation. In almost all post-World War II recessions there has been a stage at which output falls quite sharply as firms intentionally cut back production to get inventories back in line. And this cutback accentuated the recession.

Note that the behavior of inventories reflects the adjustment mechanism for output that we discussed in Chapter 3. When there is a fall in aggregate demand, firms unanticipatedly accumulate inventories. They cut back production in order to get output back in line with demand. As we noted in the footnotes in Chapter 3, though, in the process of reducing production to cut back inventories, firms may cause a larger reduction in GNP for a while than

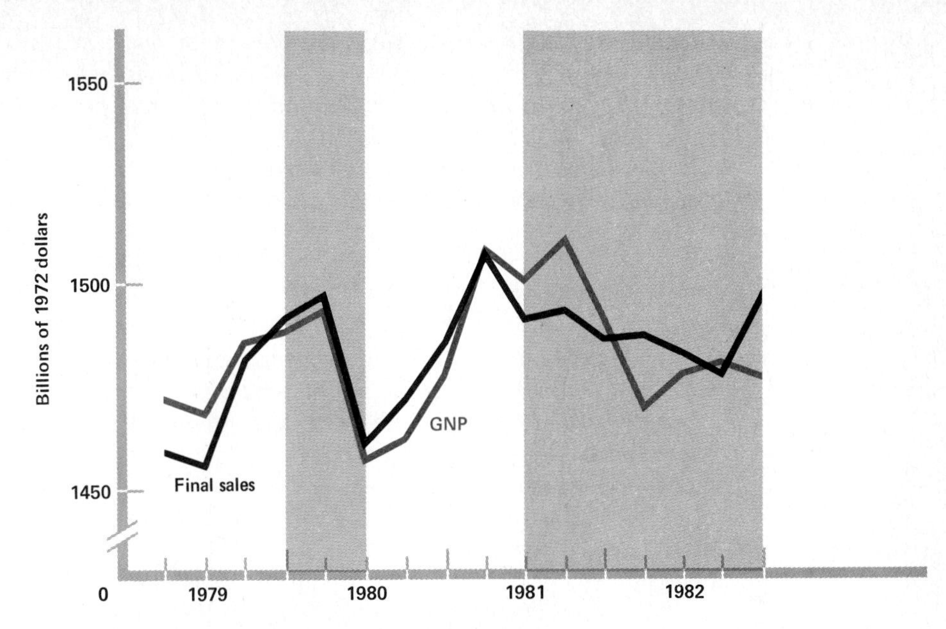

FIGURE 7-8 SALES AND OUTPUT IN THE 1980 AND 1981–1982 RECESSIONS. Note: Shaded areas indicate recessions. Before the recession begins, output exceeds sales and inventories are being accumulated. In the brief 1980 recession, inventories were being decumulated throughout. In 1981 GNP stayed well above final sales into the recession. Inventories were being unanticipatedly accumulated. Then at the end of 1981 firms begin to reduce production and decumulate inventories. Output falls particularly sharply.

would have happened had inventories not been unintentionally accumulated. This is known as the *inventory cycle.*

To understand the inventory cycle, consider the case of a hypothetical automobile dealer who sells, say, thirty cars per month, and holds an average of 1 month's sales—namely, thirty cars—in inventory. As long as sales stay steady at thirty cars per month, she will be ordering thirty cars per month from the factory. Now suppose sales drop to twenty-five cars per month, and it takes the dealer 2 months to respond to the change. During those 2 months her inventory will have climbed to forty cars. In the future she will want an inventory of only twenty-five cars on hand. Thus when she does respond to the fall in demand, she cuts her order from the factory from thirty to ten in the third month, to get the inventory back to 1 month's sales. After the desired inventory-sales ratio has been restored, she will then order twenty-five cars per month from the factory. We see in this extreme case how the drop in demand of five cars, instead of leading to a simple drop in car output of five cars per month, causes a drop in output of twenty cars in 1 month, followed by the longer-run drop in output of five cars per month.

The 1980 recession is one exception to the standard pattern of inventory behavior during a recession. In that recession there were only small movements in inventories. Sales and output basically moved together, and there is no pattern of an inventory cycle. This helps account for the brevity of the recession.

If inventories could be kept more closely in line with sales, or aggregate demand, fluctuations in inventory investment and in GNP would be reduced.

7-5 COMPARISON OF THE MODELS

We have presented several different models to explain the different categories of investment behavior in this chapter. Nonetheless, there is a basic common element in the models, the interaction of the demand for the stock of capital with investment. In each case we started by examining the determinants of the desired stock—capital or housing. The discussion of inventory investment started by examining the determinants of the desired inventory-sales ratio. Then, in each case, we went on to analyze or describe the determinants of the rate per year of that type of investment.

We come now to the question of why there is a difference between the theoretical models used to explain the level of business fixed investment and residential investment. The fundamental difference arises from the degree of standardization of the capital and the associated question of the existence of a good market for the used capital goods. Much of business fixed investment is in capital that is specifically designed for a given firm and is not of much use to other firms. It is, accordingly, difficult to establish a market price for the stock of that type of capital, and the theory used in discussing residential investment would be difficult to apply in that case. Although housing too varies a good deal, it is, nonetheless, possible to talk of a price of housing. Further, used housing is a very good substitute for new housing, whereas that is less often true for many capital goods.[27] If we disaggregated business fixed investment further than we have, we might well find that the model used to study housing investment is readily applicable for certain categories of business fixed investment, for which the capital good in question is relatively standard and has a good secondhand market.

[27] The two models look very different. However, you may be able to see a way of casting the analysis of the housing market in terms of the theory used in discussing business fixed investment. You can define the desired capital stock of housing as that stock which the economy will eventually reach when the price of housing reaches a constant level. Then the level of investment will be an increasing function of the difference between that stock and the existing stock. Similarly, the model we have used for housing investment can be transformed into a model of business fixed investment. This is the so-called *Tobin's q* theory of investment. See James Tobin, "A General Equilibrium Approach to Monetary Theory," *Journal of Money, Credit and Banking*, February 1969. Modern analysis of investment behavior frequently uses the q approach. For example, see Lawrence H. Summers, "Taxation and Corporate Investment: A q-Theory Approach," *Brookings Papers on Economic Activity*, 1981, 1. (This paper is not easy reading.)

7-6 SUMMARY

1 Investment constitutes less than 20 percent of aggregate demand, but fluctuations in investment account for a large share of business cycle movements in GNP. We analyze investment in three categories: business fixed investment, residential investment, and inventory investment.
2 Investment is spending that adds to the capital stock.
3 The neoclassical theory of business fixed investment sees the rate of investment being determined by the speed with which firms adjust their capital stocks toward their desired levels. The desired capital stock is larger the more output the firm expects to produce, and the smaller is the rental or user cost of capital. Since investment is undertaken for *future* production, it is expected future (permanent) output that determines the desired capital stock.
4 The real interest rate is the nominal (stated) interest rate minus the inflation rate.
5 The rental cost of capital is higher, the higher the real interest rate and the higher the rate of depreciation of capital. Taxes also affect the rental cost of capital, in particular through the investment tax credit. The investment tax credit is, in effect, a government subsidy for investment.
6 In practice, firms decide how much to invest using discounted cash flow analysis. This analysis gives answers that are consistent with those of the neoclassical approach.
7 The accelerator model of investment is a special case of the gradual adjustment model of investment. It predicts that investment demand is proportional to the *change* in GNP.
8 Empirical results show that business fixed investment responds with long lags to changes in output. The accelerator model, which does not take into account changes in the rental cost of capital, does almost as good a job of explaining investment as the more sophisticated neoclassical model.
9 The theory of housing investment starts from the demand for the *stock* of housing, affected by wealth, the interest rates available on alternative investments, and the mortgage rate. The latter is the cost of borrowing to buy a house. Increases in wealth increase the stock demand for housing; increases in either the interest rate on alternative assets or the mortgage rate reduce the stock demand. The price of housing is determined by the interaction of the stock demand and the given stock supply of housing available at any given time.
10 The rate of housing investment is determined by the rate at which builders supply housing at the going price.
11 Housing investment is affected by monetary policy under current conditions because housing demand is sensitive to the interest rate (real and nominal), and in the past also because of disintermediation.
12 Inventory investment fluctuates proportionately more than any other class of investment. Firms have a desired inventory-to-sales ratio. That

may get out of line if sales are unexpectedly high or low, and then firms change their production levels to adjust inventories. For instance, when aggregate demand falls at the beginning of a recession, inventories build up. Then when firms cut back production, output falls even more than did aggregate demand. This is the inventory cycle.

13 We now summarize the common elements of the different models. First, aggregate investment is the sum of the different types of investment spending. Thus any variable that affects any of the categories of investment analyzed also affects aggregate investment. Second, monetary and fiscal policy both affect investment, particularly business fixed investment and housing investment. The effects take place through changes in the real (and nominal in the case of housing) interest rates and through tax incentives for investment. Third, there are substantial lags in the adjustment of investment spending to changes in output and other determinants of investment. This is true particularly for business fixed investment and inventory investment. Such lags are likely to increase fluctuations in GNP.

KEY TERMS

Business fixed investment
Residential investment
Inventory investment
Desired capital stock
Marginal product of capital
Rental (user) cost of capital
Cobb-Douglas production function
Real interest rate
Gradual adjustment hypothesis
Discounted cash flow analysis
Accelerator model of investment
Disintermediation
Inventory cycle
Present discounted value

PROBLEMS

1 We have seen in Chapters 6 and 7 that *permanent* income and output, rather than current income and output, determine consumption and investment.
   (*a*) How does this affect the *IS-LM* model built in Chapter 4? (Refer to Figure 6-4.)
   (*b*) What are the policy implications of the use of the "permanent" measures?

2 In Chapter 4 it was assumed that investment rises during periods of low interest rates. That, however, was not the case during the 1930s, when investment and interest rates were both very low. Explain how this can occur. What would have been appropriate fiscal policy in such a case?

3 According to the description of business fixed investment in this chapter, how would you expect a firm's investment decisions to be affected by a sudden increase in demand for its product? What factors would determine the speed of its reaction?

4 It is often suggested that investment spending is dominated by "animal spirits"—the optimism or pessimism of investors. Is this argument at all consistent with the analysis of Sections 7-1 and 7-2?

5 Here are the cash flows for an investment project:

Year 1	Year 2	Year 3
−200	100	120

Should this firm undertake the project:
(*a*) If the interest rate is 5 percent?
(*b*) If the interest rate is 10 percent?

6 Is there any relation between the neoclassical theory of investment and the way firms make their investment decisions in practice?

7 Explain how the two panels of Figure 7-7 react together over time. What would happen if the demand for housing stock (*DD*) shifts up and to the right over time?

8 Trace carefully the step-by-step effects on the housing market (using Figure 7-7) of an increase in interest rates. Explain each shift and its long-run and short-run effects.

9 (*a*) Explain why the housing market usually prospers when (real) mortgage rates are low.
* (*b*) In some states, usury laws prohibit (nominal) mortgage rates in excess of a legal maximum. Explain how this could lead to an exception to the conclusion in part (*a*).
* (*c*) Could this happen in the absence of inflation? Explain.

10 In the past, restrictive monetary policy seriously hurt the housing industry in an effort to avoid excess aggregate demand. What is the mechanism by which this happened?

11 (*a*) Explain how final sales and output can differ.
(*b*) Point out from Figure 7-8 periods of planned and unplanned inventory investment and decumulation.
(*c*) During a period of slow but steady growth, how would you expect final sales and output to be related? Explain. Draw a hypothetical figure like Figure 7-8 for such a period.

12 Suppose that an explicitly temporary tax credit is enacted. The tax credit is at the rate of 10 percent and lasts only 1 year.
(*a*) What is the effect of this tax measure on investment in the long run (say, after 4 or 5 years)?
(*b*) What is the effect in the current year and the following year?
(*c*) How will your answers under (*a*) and (*b*) differ if the tax credit is permanent?

*13 For this question use the Cobb-Douglas production function and the corresponding desired capital stock given by Equation (3). Assume that $\gamma = 0.3$, $Y = 2.5$ trillion, and $rc = 0.15$.
(*a*) Calculate the desired capital stock K^*.
(*b*) Now suppose that Y is expected to rise to 3 trillion. What is the corresponding desired capital stock?
(*c*) Suppose that the capital stock was at its desired level before the change in income was expected. Suppose further that $\lambda = 0.4$ in the gradual adjustment model of investment. What will the rate of investment be in the first year after expected income changes? In the second year?
(*d*) Does your answer in (*c*) refer to gross or net investment?

*APPENDIX: INTEREST RATES, PRESENT VALUES, AND DISCOUNTING

In this Appendix we deal with the relationships among bond coupons, interest rates and yields, and the prices of bonds. In doing so, we shall introduce the very useful concept of present discounted value (*PDV*).

Section 1

We start with the case of a perpetual bond, or perpetuity. Such bonds have been issued in a number of countries, including the United Kingdom, where they are called Consols. The Consol is a promise by the British government to pay a fixed amount to the holder of the bond every year and forever. Let us denote the promised payment per Consol by Q_c, the ***coupon***.[28]

The ***yield*** on a bond is the return per dollar that the holder of the bond receives. The yield on a savings account paying 5 percent interest per year is obviously just 5 percent. Someone paying $25 for a Consol that has a coupon of $2.5 obtains a yield of 10 percent [($2.5/25) × 100%].

The yield on a Consol and its price are related in a simple way. Let us denote the price of the Consol by P_c and the coupon by Q_c. Then, as the above example suggests, the yield i is just

$$i = \frac{Q_c}{P_c} \tag{A1}$$

which says that the yield on a perpetuity is the coupon divided by the price. Alternatively, we can switch Equation (A1) around to

$$P_c = \frac{Q_c}{i} \tag{A2}$$

which says that price is the coupon divided by the yield. So, given the coupon and the yield, we can derive the price, or given the coupon and the price, we can derive the yield.

None of this is a theory of the determination of the yield or the price of a perpetuity. It merely points out the relationship between price and yield. Our theory of the determination of the yield on bonds is presented in Chapter 4. The interest rate in Chapter 4 corresponds to the yield on bonds, and we tend to talk interchangeably of interest rates and yields.

We shall return to the Consol at the end of this Appendix.

Section 2

Now we move to a short-term bond. Let us consider a bond which was sold by a borrower for $100, on which the borrower promises to pay back $108 after 1 year. This is a 1-year bond. The yield on the bond to the person who bought it for $100 is 8 percent. For every $1 lent, the lender obtains both the $1 principal and 8 cents extra at the end of the year.

Next we ask a slightly different question. How much would a promise to pay $1 at the end of the year be worth? If $108 at the end of the year is worth $100 today, then $1 at the end of the year must be worth $100/108, or 92.6 cents. That is the value today of $1 in 1 year's time. In other words, it is the present discounted value of $1 in 1 year's time. It is the present value because it is what would be paid today for the promise of money in 1 year's time, and it is discounted because the value today is less than the promised payment in a year's time.

Denoting the 1-year yield or interest rate by i, we can write that the present discounted value of a promised payment Q_1, 1 year from now, is

$$PDV = \frac{Q_1}{1+i} \tag{A3}$$

[28] The ***coupon rate*** is the coupon divided by the face value of the bond, which is literally the value printed on the face of the bond. Bonds do not necessarily sell for their face value, though customarily the face value is close to the value at which the bonds are sold when they first come on the market.

Let us return to our 1-year bond and suppose that the day after the original borrower obtained the money, the yield on 1-year bonds rises. How much would anyone *now* be willing to pay for the promise to receive $108 after 1 year? The answer must be given by the general formula (A3). That means that the price of the 1-year bond will fall when the interest rate or yield on such bonds rises. Once again, we see that the price of the bond and the yield are inversely related, given the promised payments to be made on the bond.

As before, we can reverse the formula for the price in order to find the yield on the bond, given its price and the promised payment Q_1. Note that the price P is equal to the present discounted value, so that we can write

$$1 + i = \frac{Q_1}{P} \tag{A4}$$

Section 3

Next we consider a 2-year bond. Such a bond would typically promise to make a payment of interest, which we shall denote Q_1, at the end of the first year, and then a payment of interest and principal (usually the amount borrowed), Q_2, at the end of the second year. Given the yield i on the bond, how do we compute its PDV, which will be equal to its price?

We start by asking first what the bond will be worth 1 year from now. At that stage, it will be a 1-year bond, promising to pay the amount Q_2 in 1 year's time, and yielding i. Its value 1 year from now will accordingly be given by Equation (A3), except that Q_1 in Equation (A3) is replaced by Q_2. Let us denote the value of the bond 1 year from now by PDV_1, and note that

$$PDV_1 = \frac{Q_2}{1 + i} \tag{A5}$$

To complete computing the PDV of the 2-year bond, we can now treat it as a 1-year bond, which promises to pay Q_1 in interest 1 year from now, and also to pay PDV_1 1 year from now, since it can be sold at that stage for that amount. Hence, the PDV of the bond, equal to its price, is

$$PDV = \frac{Q_1}{1 + i} + \frac{PDV_1}{1 + i} \tag{A6}$$

or

$$PDV = \frac{Q_1}{1 + i} + \frac{Q_2}{(1 + i)^2} \tag{A6a}$$

As previously, given the promised payments Q_1 and Q_2, the price of the bond will fall if the yield rises, and vice versa.

It is now less simple to reverse the equation for the price of the bond to find the yield than it was before; that is because from Equation (A6), we obtain a quadratic equation for the yield, which has two solutions.

Section 4

We have now provided the outline of the argument whereby the present discounted value of *any* promised stream of payments for any number of years can be computed. Suppose that a bond, or any other asset, promises to pay amounts $Q_1, Q_2, Q_3, \ldots, Q_n$ in future years, 1, 2, 3, . . . , n years away. By pursuing the type of argument given in Section 3, it is possible to show that the PDV of such a payments stream will be

$$PDV = \frac{Q_1}{1+i} + \frac{Q_2}{(1+i)^2} + \frac{Q_3}{(1+i)^3} + \cdots + \frac{Q_n}{(1+i)^n} \tag{A7}$$

As usual, the price of a bond with a specified payments stream will be inversely related to its yield.

Section 5

The formula (A7) is the general formula for calculating the present discounted value of any stream of payments. Indeed, the payments may also be negative. Thus in calculating the PDV of an investment project, we expect the first few payments, for example, Q_1 and Q_2, to be negative. Those are the periods in which the firm is spending to build the factory or buy machinery. Then in later years the Q_i become positive as the factory starts generating revenues.

Firms undertaking discounted cash flow analysis are calculating present values using a formula such as (A7).

Section 6

Finally, we return to the Consol. The Consol promises to pay the amount Q_c forever. Applying the formula, we can compute the present value of the Consol by

$$PDV = Q_c\left[\frac{1}{(1+i)} + \frac{1}{(1+i)^2} + \frac{1}{(1+i)^3} + \cdots + \frac{1}{(1+i)^n} + \cdots\right] \tag{A8}$$

The contents of the parentheses on the right-hand side are an infinite series, the sum of which can be calculated as $1/i$. Thus,

$$PDV = \frac{Q_c}{i} \tag{A9}$$

This section casts a slightly different light on the commonsense discussion of Section 1 of this Appendix. Equations (A8) and (A9) show that the Consol's price is equal to the PDV of the future coupon payments.

8

THE DEMAND FOR MONEY

The assets markets and the goods market receive equal billing in the *IS-LM* model we studied in Chapter 4 and 5. In the previous two chapters we concentrated on the goods market, examining the demands for consumption and investment goods. Now we move to the assets markets, starting with the demand for money.

Money is a means of payment or medium of exchange. In the United States, the basic measure of the money stock is currency plus checkable deposits, or *M*1. This is the amount that people keep in order to make payments for their purchases. *M*1 in the United States was about $480 billion at the beginning of 1983. With a population of 232 million, this means that average money holdings per person were above $2,000.

We start discussing the topic of money demand with the concept of the demand for *real balances*, introduced in Chapter 4. One of the essentials of money demand is that individuals are interested in the purchasing power of their money holdings—the value of their cash balances in terms of the goods the cash will buy. They are not concerned with their *nominal* money holdings, that is, the number of dollar bills they hold. What this means in practice is that (1) *real* money demand is unchanged when the price level increases, but *all* real variables, such as the interest rate, real income, and real wealth, remain unchanged; and (2) *nominal* money demand increases in proportion to the increase in the price level, given the constancy of the real variables just specified.[1]

We have a special name for behavior that is not affected by changes in the price level, all real variables remaining unchanged. An individual is free from *money illusion* if a change in the level of prices, holding all real variables constant, leaves real behavior, including real money demand, unchanged. By contrast, an individual whose real behavior is affected by a change in the price level, all real variables remaining unchanged, is said to suffer from money illusion.

We shall see that empirical evidence supports the theoretical argument that the demand for money is a demand for real balances—or that the demand for nominal balances, holding real variables constant, is proportional to the price level.

In Chapter 4, we also assumed that the demand for money increases with the level of real income and decreases with the nominal interest rate. Recall that the interest elasticity of the demand for money is important in determining the effectiveness of fiscal policy. Changes in fiscal variables, such as tax rates or government spending, affect the level of income if the demand for money changes when the interest rate changes—if the demand for money is interest-elastic. If the demand for money does not react at all to changes in the interest rate, increases in government spending totally *crowd out* private spending and leave the level of income unaffected.

The demand for money has been studied very intensively at both the theoretical and empirical levels. There is by now almost total agreement that the demand should, as a theoretical matter, increase as the level of real income rises and decrease as the nominal interest rate rises. Empirical work bears out these two properties of the demand-for-money function. However, a demand-for-money function based on data from the 1950s through 1973 does not explain present money demand well. Since about 1974, the money-demand function appears to have shifted in that the demand for money at given levels of income and the interest rate is less than past experience would predict. This instability in the demand-for-money function has occurred at the same time as, and is undoubtedly largely explained by, a series of changes in the financial system that we discuss below.

8-1 COMPONENTS OF THE MONEY STOCK

Money supply definitions for the United States have changed frequently in the past 5 years. The money supply concept we use in most of this chapter is *M*1, which consists of currency plus checkable deposits (including traveler's checks). Table 8-1 shows that *M*1 in March 1983 was equal to $498 billion, of which $137 billion was currency and the remaining $361 billion checkable deposits.

[1] Be sure you understand that (1) and (2) say the same thing in slightly different ways.

TABLE 8-1 COMPONENTS OF THE MONEY STOCK, MARCH 1983 (*In billions of dollars, seasonally adjusted*)

(1) Currency	(2) Checkable deposits (incl. traveler's checks)	(3) $M1 = (1) + (2)$	(4) Money market mutual funds and deposit accounts	(5) Savings and small time deposits	(6) Overnight RP's and Eurodollars	(7) $M2 = (3) + (4) + (6)$*
137.0	360.6	497.6	474.5	1056.5	48.7	2069.9

Sources: Economic Indicators and Data Resources, Inc.
* Total is seasonally adjusted, and is not equal to sum of components because (4) and (6) are not seasonally adjusted.

Currency consists of notes and coin in circulation, most of it in the form of notes. "Checkable" deposits are, as the name suggest, deposits against which checks can be written. They are held in commercial banks and thrift institutions.[2] The financial institutions referred to as thrifts are savings and loan associations, mutual savings banks, and credit unions. Before the 1980 changes in money supply definitions, only demand deposits at commercial banks were included in what was *then* called *M*1. However, because there is no obvious difference in economic function served by checkable deposits at commercial banks and other thrift institutions, the definition of *M*1 was expanded. Now *M*1 includes other checkable deposits, such as NOW accounts.[3]

We concentrate on *M*1 because it is the definition of the money supply that corresponds most closely to the role of money as a *medium of exchange*, or as the means of making payments. Payments can be made directly with coin and notes and also, for most transactions, with a check. To make a payment using a passbook savings account, it is generally necessary first to transfer money out of the savings account into a checking account and then to write the check. That is why savings and similar accounts are not included in the basic definition of the money supply.

Information on the distribution of the ownership of demand deposits is available,[4] but there are no records of the ownership of currency. About a third of demand deposits are held by consumers, with businesses holding most of the rest.

There is no very good information on the distribution of the ownership of currency because individuals are reluctant to discuss how much currency they

[2] Not all demand deposits held in U.S. banks are part of *M*1. Demand deposits held by foreign official institutions, foreign commercial banks, the U.S. government, and other commercial banks are excluded.

[3] A NOW account is an interest-bearing checking account. Box 8-1 gives details of the different types of assets.

[4] The data, available each quarter, are published in the *Federal Reserve Bulletin*.

hold when they are asked. The question sounds like the prelude to a robbery or a visit from the Internal Revenue Service. Indeed, currency holders might worry about a visit from the IRS, because the amount of currency outstanding is large, more than $500 per person in the United States. No one is sure who is holding all that currency — certainly the average person does not walk around with that much in his or her pocket. Some of the currency is held abroad, and some is used for illegal transactions. Currency is used in illegal transactions because it is much harder to trace than checks.

Although the money supply concepts have recently been revised, the present definition of *M*1 still does not correspond exactly to the role of money as a means of making payments. For instance, there is a question of whether credit cards should not be regarded as a means of making payment. If so — and the argument is certainly compelling — we should probably count the amount that people are allowed to charge by using their credit cards as part of the money stock.

Historically, there have often been changes in the type of assets which can be used as means of payment, and simultaneous disagreements about what constitutes money in those circumstances. When checks first began to be widely used in England early in the nineteenth century, there was a disagreement over whether demand deposits should be regarded as part of the money stock. Now that point is not disputed. We can expect there to be continuing changes in the financial structure over the years, with consequent changes in the definitions of the various money supply concepts.[5]

*M*2 AND OTHER MONETARY AGGREGATES

Anyone visiting a bank to make a deposit knows that there is a wide variety of ways of holding assets. Thus there are many substitutes that individuals might hold instead of the assets that make up *M*1. The major forms of monetary assets as of the beginning of 1983 are described in Box 8-1.

All the assets described in Box 8-1 are to some extent substitutes for one another. The Fed therefore publishes data for wider definitions of the money supply than *M*1. The wider definitions, from *M*2, to *M*3, to *L*, are for aggregates that are seen as increasingly less *liquid* substitutes for *M*1. An asset is liquid if it can immediately, conveniently, and cheaply be used for making payments.

*M*2 adds to *M*1 assets that are close to being usable as a medium of exchange. The largest part of *M*2 consists of savings and small (less than $100,000) time deposits at banks and thrift institutions. These can be used almost without difficulty for making payments. In the case of a savings deposit, the bank has to be notified to transfer funds from the savings deposit to a checking account; for time deposits, it is necessary to wait until the time deposit matures, or else to pay an interest penalty.

[5] Among recent changes in the definition of *M*1 is the inclusion of NOW and ATS accounts in 1980 and the subsequent inclusion of traveler's checks. See Box 8-1 for details.

BOX 8-1

COMPONENTS OF THE MONETARY AGGREGATES

A wide and growing variety of liquid assets, which can be held by individuals and businesses, are included in the monetary aggregates. We list them here, giving brief descriptions and amounts outstanding in March 1983.

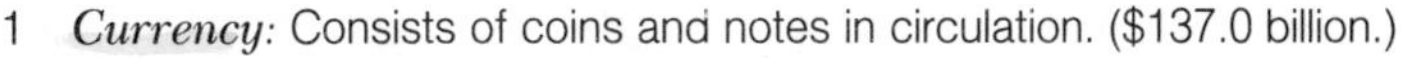

1 *Currency:* Consists of coins and notes in circulation. ($137.0 billion.)
2 *Demand deposits:* Noninterest-bearing checking accounts at commercial banks, excluding deposits of other banks, the government, and foreign governments. ($240 billion.)
3 *Traveler's checks:* The total is only of such checks issued by **nonbanks** (such as American Express). Traveler's checks issued by banks are included in demand deposits. ($4.5 billion.)
4 *Other checkable deposits:* Interest-earning checking accounts, including NOW and ATS accounts. ATS means automatic transfers from savings accounts. With ATS a deposit holder keeps assets in a savings account, and the bank transfers them automatically to the checking account when a payment has to be made. Super NOW accounts, introduced in 1983, allow unlimited checks to be written but have a high minimum balance ($2,500 in mid-1983). ($116 billion.)

$$M1 = (1) + (2) + (3) + (4)$$

5 *Overnight repurchase agreements* (RPs): Borrowing by a bank from a nonbank customer. The bank sells a security (for example, a Treasury bill) to the customer today and promises to buy it back at a fixed price tomorrow. That way the bank gets to use the amount borrowed for a day.
6 *Overnight Eurodollars:* Deposits that pay interest and mature the next day, held in Caribbean branches of U.S. banks. (Overnight RPs and Eurodollars together = $48.7 billion.)
7 *Money market mutual fund shares:* Interest-earning checkable deposits in mutual funds that invest in short-term assets. Some MMMF shares are held by institutions; these are excluded from $M2$ but included in $M3$. (MMMF shares in $M2$ = $154.0 billion.)
8 *Money market deposit accounts:* MMMFs run by banks, with the advantage that they are insured up to $100,000. Introduced at the end of 1982 to allow the banks to compete with MMMFs. ($320.5 billion.)
9 *Savings deposits:* Deposits at banks and other thrift institutions that are not transferrable by check, often recorded in a separate passbook kept by the depositor. ($322.7 billion.)
10 *Small time deposits:* Interest-bearing deposits with a specific maturity date. Before that date they can be used only if a penalty is paid. "Small" means less than $100,000. ($733.8 billion.)

$$M2 = M1 + (5) + (6) + (7) + (8) + (9) + (10)$$

11 *Large-denomination time deposits:* Interest-earning deposits of more than $100,000 denomination. The total excludes amounts held by MMMFs or MMDAs (and some other institutions) to make sure the same asset is not counted twice in the monetary aggregates. ($296.0 billion.)

12 *Term repurchase agreements:* These are RPs sold by thrift institutions, typically for longer than overnight. ($41.7 billion.)

$$M3 = M2 + (11) + (12) + \text{MMMFs held by institutions}$$

13 *Other Eurodollar deposits:* Longer-term (than overnight) Eurodollars. ($86.7 billion.)
14 *Savings bonds:* U.S. government bonds, typically sold to the small saver. ($68.8 billion.)
15 *Banker's acceptances:* These are orders to pay a specific amount at a specific time that are obligations of banks. They arise largely in international trade. ($42.0 billion.)
16 *Commercial paper:* Short-term liabilities of corporations. ($119.2 billion.)
17 *Short-term Treasury securities:* Securities issued by the U.S. Treasury that have less than 12 months to maturity. ($224.5 billion.)

$$L = M3 + (13) + (14) + (15) + (16) + (17)$$

Sources: Economic Indicators; Daniel J. Larkins, "The Monetary Aggregates: An Introduction to Definitional Issues," *Survey of Current Business,* January 1983; *Handbook of Securities of the United States Government and Federal Agencies,* First Boston Corporation; Data Resources, Inc.

The second largest category of assets in $M2$ consists of money market mutual funds and deposit accounts. A money market mutual fund (MMMF) is a fund that invests its assets in short-term interest-bearing securities, such as certificates of deposit (CDs)[6] and Treasury bills. MMMFs pay interest and permit the owner of the account to write checks (typically the checks have to be for more than $500) against the account. Money market deposit accounts (MMDAs) are MMMFs held in commercial banks. A limited number of checks can be written against MMDAs each month. Obviously MMDAs and MMMFs are close to being checkable deposits—only the limits on the size and number of checks that can be written against these accounts keep them out of $M1$.

$M2$ is an alternative definition of the money supply, whose behavior is watched almost as closely as that of $M1$. And as we shall see in Chapter 9, it is also an aggregate for which the Fed sets target levels in advance, just as it does for $M1$. Thus $M2$ receives considerable attention from the Fed and from market watchers who are trying to figure out what the Fed is doing in its monetary policy. The fact that there are $M1$ and $M2$ definitions of the money supply (and also $M3$) reflects the difficulty of defining *uniquely* a set of assets used as the medium of exchange when other assets are very close substitutes.

FINANCIAL INNOVATION

It is worth discussing briefly the reasons for the recent changes in money supply definitions. The definitional changes followed financial innovations

[6] CDs are liabilities of the banks that can be bought and sold in the open market like other securities. Typically they come in large denominations of $100,000 or more.

that changed the nature of the assets that banks and thrifts issued. For instance, thrifts, which pay interest on deposits and had been forbidden to have checkable accounts, invented NOW accounts as a way of getting around the prohibition. A NOW, a negotiable order of withdrawal, looks and smells like a check, but is not, legally speaking, a check. Banks were trying to compete with one another and thrifts by finding ways of paying interest on demand deposits, again something they were forbidden from doing. As ways around the prohibitions were found, deposits formerly called savings deposits, such as NOW accounts, became, in fact, demand deposits, and eventually the definitions changed. Similarly, money market mutual funds were invented only in 1973. Until 1982, banks were not allowed to issue money market deposit accounts, but as soon as they were permitted to do so, there was a rapid inflow of such deposits to banks: MMDA deposits rose from zero in November 1982 to $320 billion in March 1983.

In summary, there is no unique set of assets which will always constitute the money supply. At present, there are arguments for using a broader definition of the money stock than *M*1. For instance, a limited number of checks can be written against MMDAs each month; maybe they belong in *M*1. And there are even arguments for using a less broad definition—should $1,000 bills be included, for example? And over the course of time, the particular assets that serve as a medium of exchange, or means of payment, will certainly change further.

8-2 THE FUNCTIONS OF MONEY

Money is so widely used that we rarely step back to think how remarkable a device it is. It is impossible to imagine a modern economy operating without the use of money or something very much like it. In a mythical barter economy in which there is no money, every transaction has to involve an exchange of goods (and/or services) on both sides of the transaction. The examples of the difficulties of barter are endless. The economist wanting a haircut would have to find a barber wanting to listen to a lecture on economics; the peanut farmer wanting a suit would have to find a tailor wanting peanuts; and so on. Without a medium of exchange, modern economies could not operate.

Money, as a medium of exchange, makes it unnecessary for there to be a "double coincidence of wants" in exchanges. By the double coincidence, we have in mind the above examples. The wants of two individuals would have to be identically matched for the exchange to take place. For instance, the man selling peanuts would have to find a buyer whose goods he wanted to buy (the suit) while, at the same time, the woman selling suits would have to find a buyer whose goods she wanted to buy (the peanuts).

There are four traditional functions of money, of which the medium of exchange is the first.[7] The other three are store of value, unit of account, and

[7] See W. S. Jevons, *Money and the Mechanism of Exchange* (London: Routledge, Kegan, Paul, 1910).

standard of deferred payment. These stand on a different footing from the medium of exchange function.

A *store of value* is an asset that maintains value over time. Thus, an individual holding a store of value can use that asset to make purchases at a future date. If an asset were not a store of value, then it would not be used as a medium of exchange. Imagine trying to use ice cream as money, in the absence of refrigerators. There would hardly ever be a good reason for anyone to give up goods for money (ice cream) if the money were sure to melt within the next few minutes. And if the seller were unwilling to accept the ice cream in exchange for his or her goods, then the ice cream would not be a medium of exchange. But there are many stores of value other than money—such as bonds, stocks, and houses.

The *unit of account* is the unit in which prices are quoted and books kept. Prices are quoted in dollars and cents, and dollars and cents are the units in which the money stock is measured. Usually, the money unit is also the unit of account, but that is not essential. In the German hyperinflation of 1922–1923, dollars were the unit of account for some firms, whereas the mark was the medium of exchange.

Finally, as a *standard of deferred payment*, money units are used in long-term transactions, such as loans. The amount that has to be paid back in 5 or 10 years is specified in dollars and cents. Dollars and cents are acting as the standard of deferred payment. Once again, though, it is not essential that the standard of deferred payment be the money unit. For example, the final payment of a loan may be related to the behavior of the price level, rather than being fixed in dollars and cents. This is known as an indexed loan.

The last two of the four functions of money are, accordingly, functions which money *usually* performs, but not functions that it *necessarily* performs. And the store of value function is one that many assets perform.

There are fascinating descriptions of different types of money that have existed in the past that we do not have room to review here.[8] But there is one final point we want to emphasize. *Money is whatever is generally accepted in exchange.* However magnificently a piece of paper may be engraved, it will not be money if it is not accepted in payment. And however unusual the material of which it is made, anything that is generally accepted in payment is money. The only reason money is accepted in payment is that the recipient believes that it can be spent at a later time. There is thus an inherent circularity in the acceptance of money. Money is accepted in payment because it is believed that it will also be accepted in payment by others.

8-3 THE DEMAND FOR MONEY: THEORY

In this section we review the three major motives underlying the demand for money. In doing so, we will concentrate on the effects of changes in income and changes in the interest rate on money demand.

The three theories we are about to review correspond to Keynes's famous

[8] See Paul Einzig, *Primitive Money* (New York: Pergamon, 1966).

three motives for holding money[9]: (1) the transactions motive, which is the demand for money arising from the use of money in making regular payments; (2) the precautionary motive, which is the demand for money to meet unforeseen contingencies; and (3) the speculative motive, which arises from the uncertainties about the money value of other assets that an individual can hold. In discussing the transactions and precautionary motives, we are mainly discussing *M*1, whereas the speculative motive refers more to *M*2, as we shall see.

Although we examine the demand for money by looking at the three motives for holding it, we cannot separate out a particular person's money holdings, say, $500, into three neat piles of, say, $200, $200, and $100, that are being held from each motive. Money being held to satisfy one motive is always available for another use. The person holding unusually large balances for speculative reasons also has those balances available to meet an unexpected emergency, so that they serve too as precautionary balances. All three motives influence an individual's holdings of money, and as we shall see, each leads to the prediction that the demand for money should fall as the interest rate on other assets increases.

This final point is worth emphasizing. Money (*M*1) generally earns no interest (currency and some checkable deposits) or less interest than other assets. Anyone holding money is giving up interest that could be earned by holding some other asset, such as a savings deposit or a bond. The higher the interest loss from holding a dollar of money, the less money we expect the individual to hold. The demand for money will thus be higher, the greater the interest rate on money itself if interest is paid on demand deposits, and will be lower, the higher the interest rate on alternative assets. In practice, we can measure the cost of holding money as the difference between the interest rate paid on money (perhaps zero) and the interest rate paid on the most nearly comparable other asset, such as a savings deposit or, for corporations, a certificate of deposit or commercial paper.

For most of the remainder of the chapter, we shall write as if money earns no interest. This is true of much of the *M*1 stock. Further, it is easy to modify the analysis to take account of the payment of interest on other parts of *M*1. All that is necessary is to substitute the difference between the interest rate on the alternative asset and the interest rate on money in places we mention only the interest rate on the alternative asset.

The Transactions Demand

The transactions demand for money arises from the use of money in making regular payment for goods and services. In the course of each month, an individual makes a variety of payments for such items as rent or mortgage, groceries, the newspaper, and other purchases. In this section we examine how much money an individual would hold for such purchases.

[9] J. M. Keynes, *The General Theory of Employment, Interest and Money* (New York: Macmillan, 1936), chap. 13.

In analyzing the transactions demand, we are concerned with a tradeoff between the amount of interest an individual forgoes by holding money and the costs and inconveniences of holding a small amount of money. To make the problem concrete, consider a man who is paid, say, $1,200 each month. Assume that he spends the $1,200 evenly over the course of the month, at the rate of $40 per day. Now at one extreme, the individual could simply leave his $1,200 in cash (whether currency or demand deposits) and spend it at the rate of $40 per day. Alternatively, on the first day of the month the individual could take his $40 to spend that day and put the remaining $1,160 in a daily-interest savings account. Then every morning he could go to the bank to withdraw that day's $40 from the savings account. By the end of the month he would have earned interest on the money he had each day in the savings account. This would be the *benefit* of keeping his money holdings down as low as $40 at the beginning of each day. The *cost* of keeping money holdings down is simply the cost and inconvenience of the trips to the bank to withdraw the daily $40. To decide on how much money to hold for transactions purposes, the individual has to weigh the costs of holding small balances against the interest advantage of doing so.

We now study the tradeoff in more detail and derive a formula for the demand for money. Suppose the nominal monthly income[10] of the individual is Y_N. We make the simplifying assumption that Y_N is paid in to his savings account, rather than his checking account, each month. The money is spent at a steady rate over the course of the month. To spend it, the individual has to get it out of the savings account and into cash, which may be currency or a checking account. If left in the savings account, the deposit earns interest at a rate of i per month. It earns zero interest as cash. The cost to the individual of making a transfer between cash and the savings account (which we henceforth call bonds for convenience) is $\$tc$. That cost may be the individual's time, or it may be a cost that he explicitly pays someone else to make the transfer. For convenience we refer to it as a broker's fee.

THE INVENTORY APPROACH

The approach we are describing to the demand for money is known as the *inventory-theoretic approach*.[11] Although we are describing an individual's transactions demand, similar considerations apply for firms deciding how to

[10] As a reminder, nominal income Y_N is defined as real income Y times the price level P: $Y_N \equiv PY$.

[11] The approach was originally developed to determine the inventories of goods a firm should have on hand. In that context, the amount Y_N would be the monthly sales of the good, tc the cost of ordering the good, and i the interest rate for carrying the inventory. The analogy between money as an inventory of purchasing power, standing ready to buy goods, and an inventory of goods, standing ready to be bought by customers, is quite close. The inventory-theoretical approach to the demand for money is associated with the names of William Baumol and James Tobin. (William Baumol, "The Transactions Demand for Cash: An Inventory Theoretic Approach," *Quarterly Journal of Economics*, November 1952; and James Tobin, "The Interest Elasticity of Transactions Demand for Cash," *Review of Economics and Statistics*, August 1956.) The most famous result of Baumol's and Tobin's work is the *square-root law* of the demand for money, which is presented later in Eq. (4).

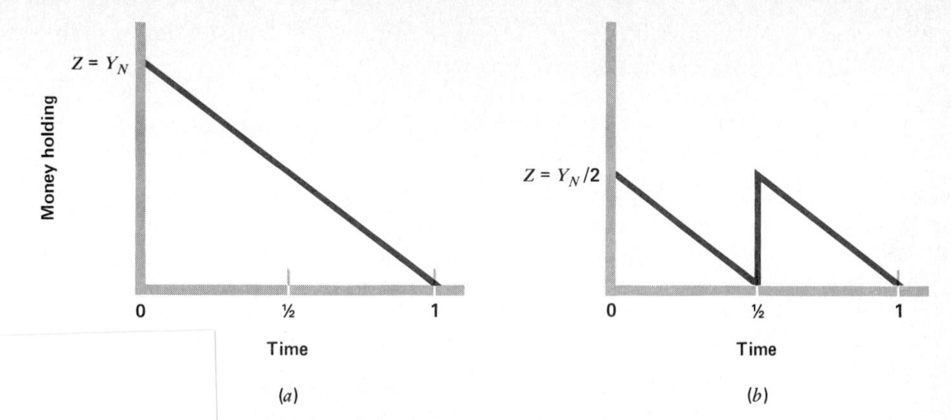

OUNT OF CASH HELD DURING THE MONTH RELATED
/ITHDRAWALS. Panel (a) shows the pattern of money
h when the individual makes just one transaction from the
during the month. At the beginning of the month he
unt to be spent, Y_N, into cash, and then spends it evenly
) shows the pattern of money holding when there are two
beginning of the month and one in the middle of the
age cash holdings for the month are $Y_N/2$; in panel (b)

oney. You should think of the inventory-theoretic approach
/ well, with small changes in terminology and assumptions, to
holds.

lual has to decide how many transactions to make between
each month. If he makes just one transaction, transferring Y_N
eginning of the month, his cash balance over the course of the
shown in Figure 8-1a. It starts at Y_N, is spent evenly over the
own to zero by the end of the month, at which time a new
eived by the individual and transferred into his checking
nakes two withdrawals from the savings account, he first
nto cash at the beginning of the month, resulting in a cash
un down to zero in the middle of the month, at which time
transferred into cash and spent evenly over the rest of the
8-1b shows the individual's cash holdings in that case.

note the size of a cash withdrawal from the bond portfolio
by Z and the number of withdrawals from the bond portfolio
he number of times the individual adds to his cash balance
during the month. If he makes n equal-sized withdrawals during the month, transferring funds from his savings account to his checking account, then the size of each transfer is Y_N/n, since a total of Y_N has to be transferred from the savings account into cash. For example, if Y_N is \$1,200, and n, the number of

[12] With simple interest being paid on the savings account, the individual's transactions between bonds and cash should be evenly spaced over the month. We leave the proof of that for the case where there are two transactions to the problem set.

transactions, is 3, then Z, the amount transferred to cash each time, is \$400. Accordingly, we can write

$$nZ = Y_N \tag{1}$$

Suppose that the amount Z is transferred from bonds to cash at each withdrawal. What then is the *average* cash balance over the course of the month? We want to find the size of the average cash balance in order to measure the interest that is lost as a result of holding cash; if that amount were not held as cash, it could be held as interest-earning bonds. In Figure 8-1*a*, the average cash balance held during the month is $Y_N/2 = Z/2$, since the cash balance starts at Y_N and runs down in a straight line to zero.[13] In the case of Figure 8-1*b*, the average cash balance for the first half of the month is $Y_N/4 = Z/2$, and the average cash balance for the second half of the month is also $Z/2$. Thus, the average cash balance for the entire month is $Y_N/4 = Z/2$. Similarly, if three withdrawals were made, the average cash balance would be $Y_N/6 = Z/2$. In general, the average cash balance is $Z/2$, as you might want to confirm by drawing diagrams similar to Figure 8-1 for $n = 3$ or other values of n.

The interest cost of holding money is the interest rate times the average cash balance, or $iZ/2$. From Equation (1), that means the total interest cost is $iY_N/2n$. The other component of the cost of managing the portfolio is the brokerage cost, or the cost in terms of the individual's time and inconvenience in managing his money. That cost is just the number of withdrawals made, n, times the cost of each withdrawal, tc, and is thus equal to $n \cdot tc$. The total cost of managing the portfolio is the interest cost plus the total brokerage cost:

$$\text{Total cost} = n \cdot tc + \frac{iY_N}{2n} \tag{2}$$

Equation (2) shows formally that the brokerage cost $n \cdot tc$ increases as the number of withdrawals (transactions between bonds and money) rises, and that the interest cost decreases as the number of withdrawals increases. It thus emphasizes the tradeoff faced in managing money, and suggests that there is an optimal number of withdrawals the individual should make to minimize the total cost of holding money to meet transactions requirements for buying goods.

To derive that optimal point, we want to find the point at which the benefit of carrying out another withdrawal is less than, or just equal to, the cost of making another transaction between bonds and money. If the benefit of making another transaction were greater than the cost, then another withdrawal should be made, and the original point could not have been optimal. The cost of making another transaction is always equal to tc. In Figure 8-2, we

[13] The average cash balance is the average of the amount of cash the individual holds at each moment during the month. For instance, if he held \$400 for 3 days and zero for the rest of the month, the average cash balance would be \$40, or one-tenth (3 days divided by 30 days) of the month times \$400.

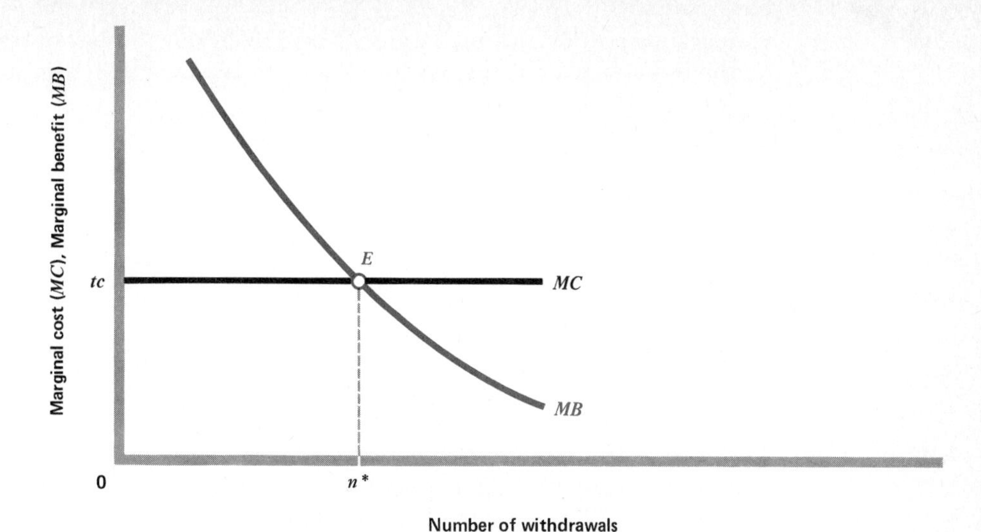

FIGURE 8-2 OPTIMAL CASH MANAGEMENT DETERMINING THE OPTIMAL NUMBER OF WITHDRAWALS. The marginal cost of making another transaction is the constant amount, tc, as shown by the MC curve. The marginal benefit of making another transaction is the amount of interest saved by holding smaller money balances. The marginal benefit decreases as the number of withdrawals from the savings account increases. Point E is the point at which the cost of managing money holdings is minimized. Corresponding to point E is n^*, the optimal number of transactions to make between the savings account and money.

show the costs of making a further transaction by the marginal cost curve MC, which is horizontal at the level tc. The financial benefit from making another transaction is represented by the MB (marginal benefit) curve in Figure 8-2, which represents the interest *saved* by making another withdrawal and thus having a smaller cash balance on average during the month.

The more transactions between money and bonds an individual makes, the lower is the total interest cost. But the reduction of the interest cost that is obtained by making more transactions falls off rapidly as the number of withdrawals increases. There is a substantial saving in interest costs by making two withdrawals rather than one, but very little saving in interest costs by making thirty-one transactions rather than thirty.

This suggests that the marginal benefit of making more withdrawals decreases as the number of withdrawals becomes large. The MB curve in Figure 8-2 is, accordingly, downward-sloping.[14]

In Figure 8-2, the optimal number of transactions is given by n^*, the number at which the marginal benefit in terms of interest saved is equal to the

[14] Two points about Fig. 8-2: First, note that we have, for convenience, drawn the curves as continuous, even though you will recognize that it is only possible to make an integral number of transactions, and not, for example, 1.6 or 7.24 transactions. Second, if you can use the calculus, try to derive the equation of the marginal benefit curve from the component of costs in Eq. (2) that is due to interest lost.

marginal cost of making a transaction. Given the number of transactions and the individual's income, we also know the average cash balance M, using the relationship between average money holdings and the size of each transfer which we derived earlier:

$$M = \frac{Z}{2} = \frac{Y_N}{2n} \tag{3}$$

PROPERTIES OF MONEY DEMAND

From Figure 8-2 we can see two important results. First, suppose the brokerage cost rises. That shifts the MC curve up, decreases the number of withdrawals n, and therefore [from Equation (3), where M is inversely related to n] *increases* the average holding of money. Second, an increase in the interest rate shifts up the MB curve, therefore increases n, and thus [again, from Equation (3)] reduces the holding of money: when the interest rate is higher, the individual is willing to make more trips to the bank to earn the higher interest now available. Figure 8-2 thus shows one of the key results we wanted to establish—that the demand for money is inversely related to the interest rate.

In the case of an increase in income, Figure 8-2 is unfortunately less useful. An increase in income shifts up the MB curve and increases the number of transactions. But from Equation (3), we see that an increase in the number of transactions accompanying an increase in income does not necessarily imply that the demand for money rises, since it seems that n could increase proportionately more than Y_N. However, more complete algebraic analysis of the individual's optimal behavior will show that the demand for money in this model rises when income rises.

The famous *square-root formula* for money demand, developed by William Baumol and James Tobin,[15] both makes the results of the graphical analysis of Figure 8-2 more precise and resolves the ambiguity about the effects of income on the demand for money. The formula gives the demand for money that is obtained as a result of minimizing the total costs in Equation (2) with respect to the number of withdrawals and then using Equation (3) to derive the cash balance.[16] The formula is

$$M^* = \sqrt{\frac{tc \cdot Y_N}{2i}} \tag{4}$$

Equation (4) shows that the transactions demand for money increases with the brokerage fee, or the cost of transacting, and with the level of income. The demand for money decreases with the interest rate.

[15] See the references in footnote 11.

[16] If you can handle calculus, try to derive Eq. (4) by minimizing total cost in Eq. (2).

MONEY DEMAND ELASTICITIES

Equation (4) also shows that an increase in income raises the demand for money proportionately less than the increase in income itself. To put the same point somewhat differently, the ratio of income to money, Y_N/M, rises with the level of income. A person with a higher level of income than another holds proportionately less money than the other person. This point is sometimes put in different words by saying that there are *economies of scale* in cash management.

Yet another way of saying the same thing is that the income elasticity of the demand for money is less than 1 [it is equal to ½ in Equation (4)]. The income elasticity measures the percentage change in the demand for money due to a 1 percent change in income.[17]

Similarly, Equation (4) implies that the elasticity of the demand for money with respect to the brokerage fee is ½, and the elasticity with respect to the interest rate is −½.

What accounts for the fact that people can somehow manage with less cash per dollar of spending as income increases? The reason is that cash management is more effective at high levels of income because the average cost per dollar of transaction is lower with large-size transactions. In turn, the lower average cost of transactions results from the fixed brokerage fee per transaction; it costs as much to transfer $10 as $10 million, so that the average cost per dollar transferred is lower for large transfers.

However, in the case of households, we should recognize that the "brokerage cost" *tc*, the cost of making withdrawals from a savings account, is in part the cost of time and the nuisance of having to go to the bank. Since the cost of time to individuals is likely to be higher the higher their income, *tc* may rise with Y_N. In that case, an increase in income would result in an increase in the demand for money by more than the income elasticity of ½ indicates because *tc* goes up together with Y_N.

THE DEMAND FOR REAL BALANCES

We started this chapter by emphasizing that the demand for money is a demand for real balances. It is worth confirming that the inventory theory of the demand for money implies that the demand for real balances does not change when all prices double (or increase in any other proportion). When all prices double, both Y_N and *tc* in Equation (4) double—that is, both nominal income and the nominal brokerage fee double. Accordingly, the demand for nominal balances doubles, so that the demand for real balances is unchanged. The square-root formula does not imply any money illusion in the demand for money. Thus we should be careful when saying the income elasticity of

[17] The income elasticity of demand is $\frac{\Delta(M/P)}{M/P} \Big/ \frac{\Delta Y}{Y}$. Similarly, the interest elasticity is $\frac{\Delta(M/P)}{M/P} \Big/ \frac{\Delta i}{i}$.

demand for money implied by Equation (4) is ½. The elasticity of the demand for *real* balances with respect to *real* income is ½. But if income rises only because all prices (including *tc*) rise, then the demand for *nominal* balances rises proportionately.

INTEGER CONSTRAINTS

So far we have ignored the important constraint that it is possible to make only an integral number of transactions, such as 1, 2, 3, etc., and that it is not possible to make 1.25 or 3.57 transactions. However, when we take account of this constraint, we shall see that it implies that many people do not make more than the essential one transaction between money and bonds within the period in which they are paid.[18] Consider our previous example of the person who received $1,200 per month. Suppose, realistically, that the interest rate per month on savings deposits is ½ percent. The individual cannot avoid making one initial transaction, since income initially arrives in the savings account. The next question is whether it pays to make a second transaction. That is, does it pay to keep half the monthly income for half a month in the savings account and make a second withdrawal after half a month? With an interest rate of ½ percent per month, interest for half a month would be ¼ percent. Half the income would amount to $600 and the interest earnings would, therefore, be $600 × ¼ percent = $1.50.

Now if the brokerage fee exceeds $1.50, the individual will not bother to make more than one transaction. And $1.50 is not an outrageous cost in terms of the time and nuisance of making a transfer from the savings to the checking account. Thus, for many individuals whose monthly net pay is below $1,200, we do not expect formula (4) to hold exactly. Their cash balance would instead simply be half their income. They would make one transfer into cash at the beginning of the month; Figure 8-1*a* would describe their money holdings. For such individuals, the income elasticity of the demand for money is 1, since their demand for money goes up precisely in proportion with their income. The interest elasticity is zero, so long as they make only one transaction, because they transfer all their income into cash immediately as they receive it.

The very strong restrictions on the income and interest elasticities of the demand for money of Equation (4) are not valid when the integer constraints are taken into account. Instead, the income elasticity is an average of the elasticities of different people, some of whom make only one transaction from bonds to money, and the elasticity is therefore between ½ and 1. Similarly, the interest elasticity is also an average of the elasticities across different individuals, being between −½ and zero.[19] Because firms deal with larger amounts of money, they are likely to make a large number of transactions between money and bonds, and their income and interest elasticities of the

[18] If we had assumed that individuals were paid in cash, it would turn out that many people would not make any transactions between money and bonds in managing their transactions balances.

[19] See Robert J. Barro, "Integer Constraints and Aggregation in an Inventory Model of Money Demand," *Journal of Finance*, March 1976.

demand for money are therefore likely to be close to the ½ and −½ predicted by Equation (4).

THE PAYMENT PERIOD

Once the integer constraints are taken into account, it can also be seen that the transactions demand for money depends on the frequency with which individuals are paid (the payment period). If one examines the square-root formula (4), the demand for money does not seem to depend on how often a person is paid, since an increase in the payments period increases both Y_N and i in the same proportion. Thus the demand for money appears unaffected by the length of the period. However, consider a person who makes only one transaction from bonds to money at the beginning of each month. Her money demand is $Y_N/2$. If such a person were paid weekly, her demand for money would be only one-quarter of the demand with monthly payments. Thus we should expect the demand for money to increase with the length of the payment period.

SUMMARY

The inventory-theoretic approach to the demand for money gives a precise formula for the transactions demand for money: The income elasticity of the demand for money is ½, and the interest elasticity is −½. When integer constraints are taken into account, the limits on the income elasticity of demand are between ½ and 1, and the limits on the interest elasticity are between −½ and zero. We have outlined the approach in terms of an individual's demand for money, but a similar approach is relevant for firms.

Some of the assumptions made in deriving the square-root formula are very restrictive. People do not spend their money evenly over the course of the month, and they do not know exactly what their payments will be. Their checks are not paid into savings accounts, and so on. It turns out, though, that the major results we have derived are not greatly affected by the use of more realistic assumptions. There is thus good reason to expect the demand for money to increase with the level of income and to decrease as the interest rate on other assets (or, generally, the cost of holding money) increases.

2)

The Precautionary Motive

In discussing the transactions demand for money, we focused on transactions costs and ignored uncertainty. In this section, we concentrate on the demand for money that arises because people are uncertain about the payments they might want to, or have to, make.[20] Suppose, realistically, that an individual did not know precisely what payments he would be receiving in the next few weeks and what payments he would have to make. He might decide to have a

[20] See Edward H. Whalen, "A Rationalization of the Precautionary Demand for Cash," *Quarterly Journal of Economics*, May 1966.

hot fudge sundae, or need to take a cab in the rain, or have to pay for a prescription. If he did not have money with which to pay, he would incur a loss. The loss could be missing a fine meal, or missing an appointment, or having to come back the next day to pay for the prescription. For concreteness, we shall denote the loss incurred as a result of being short of cash by $\$q$. The loss clearly varies from situation to situation, but as usual we simplify.

The more money the individual holds, the less likely he is to incur the costs of illiquidity (that is, not having money immediately available). But the more money he holds, the more interest he is giving up. We are back to a tradeoff situation similar to that examined in relation to the transactions demand. Somewhere between holding so little money for precautionary purposes that it will almost certainly be necessary to forgo some purchase (or to borrow in a hurry) and holding so much money that there is little chance of not being able to make any payment that might be necessary, there must be an optimal amount of precautionary balances to hold. That optimal amount will involve the balancing of interest costs against the advantages of not being caught illiquid.

Once more, we write down the total costs of holding an amount of money M.[21] This time we are dealing with expected costs, since it is not certain what the need for money will be. We denote the probability that the individual is illiquid during the month by $p(M, \sigma)$. The function $p(M, \sigma)$ indicates that the probability of the person's being illiquid at some time during the month depends on the level of money balances M being held and the degree of uncertainty σ about the net payments that will be made during the month. The probability of illiquidity is lower, the higher is M, and higher, the higher is the degree of uncertainty σ. The *expected cost* of illiquidity is $p(M, \sigma)q$—the probability of illiquidity times the cost of being illiquid. The interest cost associated with holding a cash balance of M is just iM. Thus, we have

$$\text{Expected costs} = iM + p(M, \sigma)q \qquad (5)$$

To determine the optimal amount of money to hold, we compare the marginal costs of increasing money holding by $1 with the expected marginal benefit of doing so. The marginal cost is again the interest forgone, or i. That is shown by the *MC* curve in Figure 8-3. The marginal benefit of increasing money holding arises from the lower expected costs of illiquidity. Increasing precautionary balances from zero has a large marginal benefit, since that takes care of small, unexpected disbursements that are quite likely. As we increase cash balances further, we continue to reduce the probability of illiquidity, but at a decreasing rate. We start to hold cash to insure against quite unlikely events. Thus, the marginal benefit of additional cash is a decreasing function of the level of cash holdings—more cash on hand is better than less, but at a diminishing rate. The marginal benefit of increasing cash holdings is shown by the *MB* curve in Figure 8-3.

The optimal level of the precautionary demand for money is reached

[21] This paragraph contains technical material that is optional and can easily be skipped.

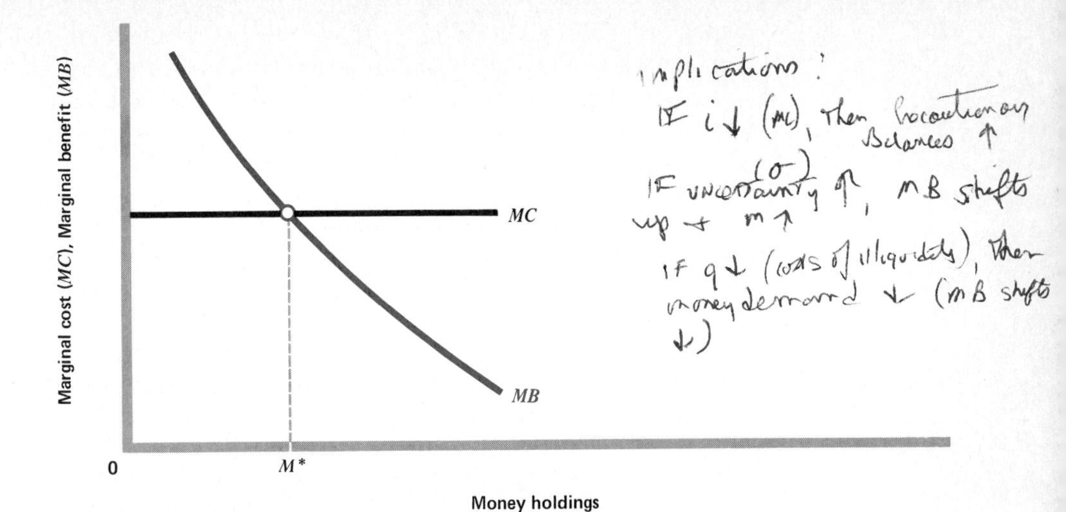

FIGURE 8-3 THE PRECAUTIONARY DEMAND FOR MONEY. The MC schedule shows the marginal cost of holding an extra dollar of money: holding an extra dollar means losing interest, and so the MC curve is horizontal at a level equal to the interest rate (or, more generally, the difference between the interest rate on money and alternative assets). The marginal benefit (MB) of holding an extra dollar is that the consumer is less likely to be short of money when it is needed. The marginal benefit declines with the amount of money held. The optimal amount of money to hold is shown by M^*, where marginal cost is equal to marginal benefit.

where the two curves intersect. That level of money is shown as M^* in Figure 8-3. Now we can use Figure 8-3 to examine the determinants of the optimal level of the precautionary demand. It is, first, apparent that precautionary balances will be larger when the interest rate is lower. A reduction in the interest rate shifts the MC curve down and increases M^*. The lower costs of holding money makes it profitable to insure more heavily against the costs of illiquidity. An increase in uncertainty leads to increased money holdings because it shifts up the MB curve. With more uncertainty about the flow of spending, there is more scope for unforeseen payments and thus a greater danger of illiquidity. It therefore pays to insure more heavily by holding larger cash balances. Finally, the lower the costs of illiquidity, q, the lower the money demand. A reduction in q moves the MB curve down. Indeed, if there were no cost to illiquidity, no one would bother to hold money. There would be no penalty for not having it, while at the same time, holding it would mean a loss of interest.

The model of precautionary demand can be applied to goods other than money. It is a broad theory that applies to any commodity inventory that is held as insurance against contingencies. For instance, cars carry spare tires. You can work out circumstances under which one would want to have more than one spare tire in a car, and even circumstances in which zero would be the optimal number. The idea of the precautionary demand for money or for goods is quite general. So, too, are the determinants of the precautionary demand: the alternative cost in terms of interest forgone, the cost of illiquidity, and the degree of uncertainty that determines the probability of illiquidity.

3) The Speculative Demand for Money

The transactions demand and the precautionary demand for money emphasize the medium of exchange function of money, for each refers to the need to have money on hand to make payments. Each theory is more relevant to the *M*1 definition of money than any other, though the precautionary demand could certainly explain part of the holding of savings accounts and other relatively liquid assets which are part of *M*2. Now we move over to the store of value function of money and concentrate on the role of money in the investment portfolio of an individual.

An individual who has wealth has to hold that wealth in specific assets. Those assets make up a *portfolio*. One would think an investor would want to hold the asset which provides the highest returns. However, given that the return on most assets is uncertain, it is unwise to hold the entire portfolio in a single *risky asset*. You may have the hottest tip that a certain stock will surely double within the next 2 years, but you would be wise to recognize that hot tips are far from infallible, and that you could lose a lot of money in that stock as well as make money. A prudent, risk-averse investor does not put all her eggs in one basket. Uncertainty about the returns on risky assets leads to a diversified portfolio strategy.

As part of that diversified portfolio, the typical investor will want to hold some amount of a safe asset as insurance against capital losses on assets whose prices change in an uncertain manner. The safe asset would be held precisely because it is safe, even though it pays a lower expected return than risky assets. Money is a safe asset in that its nominal value is known with certainty.[22] In a famous article, James Tobin argued that money would be held as the safe asset in the portfolios of investors.[23] The title of the article, "Liquidity Preference as Behavior towards Risk," explains the essential notion. In this framework, the demand for money—the safest asset—depends on the expected yields, as well as on the riskiness of the yields, on other assets. The riskiness of the return on other assets is measured by the variability of the return. Using reasonable assumptions, Tobin shows that an increase in the expected return on other assets—an increase in the opportunity cost of holding money (that is, the return lost by holding money)—lowers money demand. By contrast, an increase in the riskiness of the returns on other assets increases money demand.

[22] Of course, when the rate of inflation is uncertain, the real value of money is also uncertain, and money is no longer a safe asset. Even so, the uncertainties about the values of equity are so much larger than the uncertainties about the rate of inflation that money can be treated as a relatively safe asset.

[23] James Tobin, "Liquidity Preference as Behavior towards Risk," *Review of Economic Studies*, February 1958.

An investor's aversion to risk certainly generates a demand for a safe asset. The question we want to consider is whether that safe asset is money. That is, we want to ask whether considerations of portfolio behavior do generate a demand for money. The relevant considerations in the portfolio are the returns and the risks on assets. From the viewpoint of the yield and risks of holding money, it is clear that time or savings deposits or MMDAs have the same risks as currency or checkable deposits. However, they generally pay a higher yield. The risks in both cases are the risks arising from uncertainty about inflation. Given that the risks are the same, and with the yields on time and savings deposits higher than on currency and demand deposits, portfolio diversification explains the demand for assets such as time and savings deposits better than the demand for $M1$. We therefore regard the speculative demand as applying primarily to $M2$.

The implications of the speculative, or risk-diversifying, demand for money are similar to those of the transactions and precautionary demands. An increase in the interest rate on nonmoney assets, such as long-term bond yields or equity yields, will reduce the demand for $M2$. An increase in the rate paid on time deposits will increase the demand for time deposits, perhaps even at the cost of the demand for $M1$, as people take advantage of the higher yields they can earn on their investment portfolios to increase the size of those portfolios. One important difference between the speculative and the other two categories of demand is that here the level of wealth is clearly relevant to the demand for $M2$. The level of wealth determines the size of the total portfolio, and we expect that increases in wealth lead to increases in the demand for the safe asset, and thus in $M2$ demand.

One final point on the speculative demand. Many individuals with relatively small amounts of wealth will indeed hold part of that wealth in savings accounts in order to diversify their portfolios. But bigger investors are sometimes able to purchase other securities which pay higher interest and also have fixed (that is, risk-free) nominal values. Large CDs (in excess of \$100,000) are sometimes an example of such assets, as are Treasury bills on occasion. For such individuals or groups, the demand for a safe asset is not a demand for money.

8-4 EMPIRICAL EVIDENCE

This section examines the empirical evidence — the studies made using actual data — on the demand for money. We noted in Chapter 4, and again at the beginning of Section 8-3, that the *interest elasticity* of the demand for money plays an important role in determining the effectiveness of monetary and fiscal policies. We then showed in Section 8-3 that there are good theoretical reasons for believing the demand for real balances should depend on the interest rate. The empirical evidence supports that view very strongly. Empirical studies have established that the demand for money is responsive to the interest rate. An increase in the interest rate reduces the demand for money.

The theory of money demand also predicts that the demand for money should depend on the level of income. The response of the demand for money to the level of income, as measured by the *income elasticity* of money demand, is also important from a policy viewpoint. The income elasticity of money demand provides a guide to the Fed as to how fast to increase the money supply to support a given rate of growth of GNP without changing the interest rate.

Suppose that the aim is for GNP growth of 10 percent, 6 percent real growth and 4 percent inflation. If the Fed wants to provide a sufficient growth rate of money to prevent interest rates from rising, it has to know the income elasticity of the demand for real balances. Suppose the real income elasticity is ½. Then the Fed would have to produce monetary growth of 7 percent to prevent an increase in interest rates. Why? First, the demand for nominal money increases in proportion to the price level, since money demand is a demand for real balances. Thus 4 percent growth in money is needed to meet the increased demand from the 4 percent increase in the price level. The 6 percent growth in real income would increase the demand for real balances by 3 percent (= 6 percent × ½), given the real income elasticity of ½. Hence, the result is the needed 7 percent (= 4 + 3) growth in the nominal money supply to meet the increased demand arising from the increase in income.

LAGGED ADJUSTMENT

The empirical work on the demand for money has introduced one complication that we did not study in the theoretical section—that the demand for money adjusts to changes in income and interest rates *with a lag.* When the level of income or the interest rate changes, there is first only a small change in the demand for money. Then, over the course of time, the change in the demand for money increases, slowly building up to its full long-run change. Reasons for this lag are not yet certain. The two usual possibilities exist in this case too. The lags may arise because there are costs of adjusting money holdings, or they may arise because money holders' expectations are slow to adjust. If people believe that a given change in the interest rate is temporary, they may be unwilling to make a major change in their money holdings. As time passes and it becomes clearer that the change is not transitory, they are more willing to make a larger adjustment.

EMPIRICAL RESULTS

The standard demand-for-money function until the mid-1970s was that estimated by Stephen Goldfeld of Princeton University in a comprehensive 1973 study.[24] Goldfeld studied the demand for *M*1 using quarterly postwar data

[24] Stephen M. Goldfeld, "The Demand for Money Revisited," *Brookings Papers on Economic Activity*, 1973:3 (Washington, D.C.: The Brookings Institution, 1973). A review of other work on the demand for money is contained in the very readable book by David Laidler, *The Demand for Money: Theories and Evidence*, 2d ed. (New York: Dun-Donnelley, 1977). For a more recent survey of work on the demand for money, see John P. Judd and John L. Scadding, "The Search for a Stable Money Demand Function," *Journal of Economic Literature*, September 1982. The title of this article explains the focus of recent research.

TABLE 8-2 ELASTICITIES OF REAL MONEY DEMAND

	Y	i_{TD}	i_{CP}
Short run	0.19	−0.045	−0.019
Long run	0.68	−0.16	−0.067

Source: S. Goldfeld, "The Demand for Money Revisited," Brookings Papers on Economic Activity, 1973:3 (Washington, D.C.: The Brookings Institution, 1973), p. 602, Regression A.

and, of course, the 1973 definition of $M1$. Table 8-2 summarizes the major conclusions from that earlier empirical work. The table shows the elasticities of the demand for real balances with respect to real income Y (real GNP) and interest rates. The rate on time deposits, i_{TD}, and the rate on commercial paper, i_{CP}, are the interest rates used by Goldfeld. Commercial paper represents short-term borrowing by corporations. That interest rate is relevant to the demand for money because commercial paper is an asset which is very liquid for corporations that hold it instead of money for short periods of time.

In the short run (one quarter), the elasticity of demand with respect to real income is 0.19. This means that a 1 percent increase in real income raises money demand by 0.19 percent, which is considerably less than proportionately. The table shows that the elasticity of money demand with respect to interest rates is negative: an increase in interest rates reduces money demand. The short-run interest elasticities are quite small. An increase in the rate on time deposits from 4 percent to 5 percent, that is, a 25 percent increase ($5/4 = 1.25$), reduces the demand for money by only 1.12 percent ($= 0.045 \times 25$ percent). An increase in the rate on commercial paper from 4 to 5 percent would reduce money demand by only 0.47 percent.

The long-run elasticities exceed the short-run elasticities by a factor of more than 3, as Table 8-2 shows. The long-run real income elasticity is 0.68, meaning that in the long run the increase in real money demand occurring as a result of a given increase in real income is only 68 percent as large as the proportional increase in income. Real money demand thus rises less than proportionately to the rise in real income. The long-run interest elasticities sum to a little over 0.2, meaning that an increase in *both* i_{TD} and i_{CP} from 4 percent to 5 percent would reduce the demand for money by a little over 5 percent.

How long is the long run? That is, how long does it take the demand for money to adjust from the short-run elasticities of Table 8-2 to the long-run elasticities shown in the table? Actually, it takes forever for the full long-run position to be reached. Table 8-3, however, shows the elasticities of the demand for real balances in response to changes in the level of income and interest rates after one, two, three, four, and eight quarters. Three-fourths of the adjustment is complete within the first year, and over 90 percent of the adjustment is complete within the first 2 years.

In summary, we have so far described three essential properties of money demand, as estimated by Goldfeld:

TABLE 8-3 DYNAMIC PATTERNS OF ELASTICITIES OF MONEY DEMAND WITH RESPECT TO REAL INCOME AND INTEREST RATES

Quarters elapsed	Y	i_{TD}	i_{CP}
1	0.19	−0.045	−0.019
2	0.33	−0.077	−0.033
3	0.43	−0.100	−0.042
4	0.50	−0.117	−0.049
8	0.63	−0.148	−0.062
Long run	0.68	−0.160	−0.067

Source: S. Goldfeld, "The Demand for Money Revisited," Brookings Papers on Economic Activity, *1973:3 (Washington, D.C.: The Brookings Institution, 1973).*

1 The demand for real money balances responds negatively to the rate of interest. An increase in interest rates reduces the demand for money.
2 The demand for money increases with the level of real income. However, the income elasticity of money demand is less than 1 so that money demand increases less than proportionately with income.
3 The short-run responsiveness of money demand to changes in interest rates and income is considerably less than the long-run response. The long-run elasticities are estimated to be over three times the size of the short-run elasticities.

There is one more important question Goldfeld considered. This is the question of how money responds to an increase in the level of prices. Here Goldfeld, like other researchers before him, finds strong evidence that an increase in prices raises nominal money demand in the same proportion. We can add, therefore, a fourth conclusion:

4 The demand for nominal money balances is proportional to the price level. There is no money illusion; in other words, the demand for money is a demand for *real* balances.

THE SHIFTING MONEY-DEMAND CURVE

Since 1973, when Goldfeld first estimated the demand function for money whose properties are summarized in Table 8-2, the money-demand function has shifted. Figure 8-4 shows the errors that would be made if we used an equation such as Goldfeld's[25] to predict the quantity of money demanded

[25] Figure 8-4 is based on an equation estimated using data from 1952:II through 1973:IV, with the interest rates included in the equation being the passbook savings rate and the Treasury bill rate. A very similar pattern of errors is apparent using an equation based on data from 1959 through 1973. As a technical note, the errors in Figure 8-4 are those from a dynamic simulation, in which errors made in one period typically (but not necessarily) cumulate into larger errors for later periods.

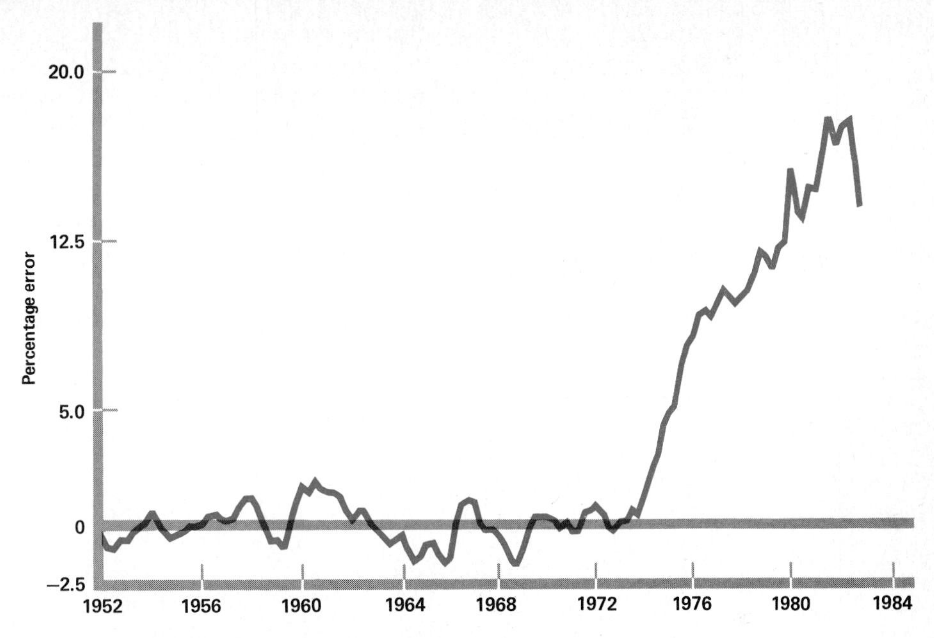

FIGURE 8-4 MONEY-DEMAND PREDICTION ERRORS. *Note:* Errors are from a dynamic simulation of the Goldfeld equation estimated on 1952–1973 data.

from the beginning of 1974 through the beginning of 1983. The errors grow rapidly from 1974 to 1976 and then stay more or less constant as a percentage of the money supply through 1980 before once again increasing rapidly. By the end of 1982 the error is nearly 20 percent of *M*1.

Thus in the 10-year period after which the money-demand equation described in Table 8-2 was estimated, the demand for *M*1 balances fell almost 20 percent compared with what would have been expected on the basis of behavior up to 1973. The big question—it is the main question that has preoccupied people studying money demand in the last 10 years—is, What happened to the missing money?[26]

There are two major explanations for the shift. The first is that the financial innovations mentioned earlier led to changes in money demand.[27] For example, in 1975 it became possible to make transfers between accounts by telephone instruction rather than by actually going to the bank. This reduces the brokerage cost, *tc*, and reduces the demand for *M*1. Similarly,

[26] The title of a paper by Goldfeld in 1976 is "The Case of the Missing Money," *Brookings Papers on Economic Activity,* 1976:3 (Washington, D.C.: The Brookings Institution, 1976). An interesting discussion, along with extensive references, is R. W. Hafer and Scott E. Hein, "The Shift in Money Demand: What Really Happened?" *Federal Reserve Bank of St. Louis Review,* February 1982. See also the references in footnote 24.

[27] See Richard Porter, Thomas Simpson, and Eileen Mauskopf, "Financial Innovation and the Monetary Aggregates," *Brookings Papers on Economic Activity,* 1979:1 (Washington, D.C.: The Brookings Institution, 1979).

during this period corporations were for the first time allowed to own savings deposits, leading them to reduce holdings of $M1$. In addition, the invention of money market mutual funds (see Section 8-1) reduced the demand for money. Such explanations do appear to account for part of the shift in money demand.

An associated explanation argues that there have been permanent shifts in money demand associated with the very high interest rates of 1973–1974 and 1978–1982. The argument here is that when interest rates became very high, firms undertook studies of how to economize on money, developing new methods of *cash management.* These are sophisticated methods for firms to reduce the amount of money held in the normal course of business.[28] Among these methods are "sweep accounts," where the bank undertakes to monitor the account and automatically invests any excess balances in short-term financial assets.

Adoption of the new methods leads to a permanent reduction in the demand for money even after interest rates have fallen from their record levels. This is because once the firm has figured out the new methods of managing its cash, it continues to use them.[29] It is clear that firms have increasingly used sophisticated methods of cash management. The explanation that centers on cash management obtains further support from two facts: First, the shift in money demand in 1974–1976 can be traced mostly to a shift in the demand for demand deposits rather than currency; and second, a substantial role in the shift can be traced to reduced demand for money by corporations.

The second main possibility is that the Goldfeld demand function omits some relevant variables. Here the leading candidate has been the long-term interest rate. It has been argued that since all assets are potentially substitutes for money in the portfolios of money holders, there is no reason why only short-term interest rates should enter the demand function for money. Inclusion of the long-term interest rate and an estimate of the return on equity does improve the fit of the money-demand function.[30]

Given the institutional changes in the financial markets during the seventies and early eighties, it should be no surprise that there have been shifts in the money-demand function. In particular, the two periods of large shifts in money demand in Figure 8-4 are the periods when several new assets were introduced. We thus put considerable weight on the roles of financial innovation and cash management in producing the shift in the money-demand function.

Finally, amid all the excitement we should remember that despite the

[28] A variety of these methods are described in Porter, Simpson, and Mauskopf, cited in footnote 27.

[29] Note, though, that the demand for money would still be higher at low interest rates than it would be at high interest rates once the new methods have been adopted.

[30] This is shown by Michael Hamburger, "Behavior of the Money Stock: Is There a Puzzle?" *Journal of Monetary Economics,* July 1977.

recent shifts in money demand, empirical work still finds that the demand for money is positively related to income and negatively related to interest rates.

8-5 THE INCOME VELOCITY OF MONEY

The *income velocity of money* is the number of times the stock of money is turned over per year in financing the annual flow of income. Thus in 1982 GNP was about $3,060 billion, the money stock ($M1$) averaged $458 billion, and velocity was therefore about 6.7. The average dollar of money balances financed $6.70 of spending on final goods and services, or the public held on average just under $0.15 of $M1$ per dollar of income. While we usually calculate velocity for the economy as a whole, we can also calculate it for an individual. For instance, for someone earning $12,000 per year, who has average money balances during the year of $1,000, the income velocity of money holdings is 12.

Income velocity (from now on we shall refer to velocity rather than income velocity) is defined, as in Section 4-8, as

$$V \equiv \frac{Y_N}{M} \tag{6}$$

the ratio of nominal income to nominal money stock. An alternative way of writing Equation (6) recognizes that Y_N, nominal GNP, is equal to the price level P times real income Y. Thus

$$M \cdot V = P \cdot Y \tag{7}$$

THE QUANTITY THEORY

Equation (7) is the famous *quantity equation*, linking the product of the price level and the level of output to the money stock. The quantity equation became the (classical) *quantity theory of money* when it was argued that both V, the income velocity of money,[31] and Y, the level of output, were fixed. Real output was taken to be fixed because the economy was at full employment, and velocity was assumed not to change much. Neither of these assumptions holds in fact, but it is, nonetheless, interesting to see where they lead. *If both V and Y are fixed, then it follows that the price level is proportional to the money*

[31] Why do we say income velocity and not plain velocity? There is another concept, transactions velocity, that is, the ratio of total transactions to money balances. Total transactions far exceed GNP for two reasons. First, there are many transactions involving the sale and purchase of assets that do not contribute to GNP. Second, a particular item in final output typically generates total spending on it that exceeds the contribution of that item to GNP. For instance, 1 dollar's worth of wheat generates transactions as it leaves the farm, as it is sold by the miller, as it leaves the baker for the supermarket, and then as it is sold to the household. One dollar's worth of wheat may involve several dollars of transactions before it is sold for the last time. Transactions velocity is thus higher than income velocity.

stock. Thus the classical quantity theory was a theory of inflation. The classical quantity theory argued that the price level was proportional to the money stock. We return to the quantity theory in Chapter 13.

VELOCITY AND POLICY

Velocity is a useful concept in economic policy making. We see how to use it by rewriting (6) as

$$Y_N \equiv VM \tag{6a}$$

Given the nominal money stock (M) and given velocity, we know the level of nominal GNP. Thus if we can predict the level of velocity, we can predict the level of nominal income, given the money stock.

Further, *if* velocity were constant, changing the money supply would result in proportionate changes in nominal income. Any policies, including fiscal policies, that did not affect the money stock would not affect the level of income. You will probably now recognize that we have previously discussed a case of constant velocity. In Chapter 5, we discussed the effectiveness of fiscal policy when the demand for money is not a function of the interest rate and the LM curve is therefore vertical. That vertical LM curve is the same as the assumption of constant velocity.

VELOCITY AND THE DEMAND FOR MONEY

The discussion of constant velocity is closely related to the behavior of the demand for money. Indeed, the notion of velocity is important because it is a convenient way of talking about money demand.

We now examine the relationship between velocity and the demand for money. Let the demand for real balances be written $L(i, Y)$, consistent with Chapter 4. Recall that Y is real income. When the supply of money is equal to the demand for money, we have

$$\frac{M}{P} = L(i, Y) \tag{8}$$

or $M = PL(i, Y)$. Now we can substitute for the nominal money supply into Equation (6) to obtain

$$V = \frac{Y_N}{PL(i, Y)} = \frac{Y}{L(i, Y)} \tag{6b}$$

where we have recognized that Y_N/P is the level of real income. Income velocity is the ratio of the level of real income to the demand for real balances.

From Equation (6*b*) we note that velocity is a function of real income and the interest rate. Consider first the effects of a change in the interest rate on velocity. An increase in the interest rate reduces the demand for real balances and therefore increases velocity: when the cost of holding money increases, money holders make their money do more work, and thus turn it over more often.

The way in which changes in real income affect velocity depends on the income elasticity of the demand for money. If the income elasticity of the demand for real balances were 1, then the demand for real balances would change in the same proportion as income. In that case, changes in real income would not affect velocity. Suppose that real income Y increased by 10 percent. The numerator Y in Equation (6*b*) would increase by 10 percent, as would the denominator, and velocity would be unchanged. However, we have seen that the income elasticity of the demand for money is less than 1. That means that velocity *increases* with increases in real income. For example, suppose that real income rose 10 percent, and the demand for real balances increased only by 6.8 percent ($= 0.68 \times 10$ percent), as Goldfeld's results suggest. Then the numerator of Equation (6*b*) would increase by more than the denominator, and velocity would rise.

The empirical work reviewed in Section 8-4 makes it clear that the demand for money and, therefore, also velocity do react systematically to changes in interest rates and the level of real income. The empirical evidence therefore decisively refutes the view that velocity is unaffected by changes in interest rates and that fiscal policy is, accordingly, incapable of affecting the level of nominal income. In terms of Equation (6*b*), and using the analysis of Chapter 4, expansionary fiscal policy can be thought of as working by increasing interest rates, thereby increasing velocity, and thus making it possible for a given stock of money to support a higher level of nominal GNP.

Velocity in Practice

The empirical evidence we reviewed in Section 8-4 is useful in interpreting the long-run, or *trend*, behavior in velocity shown in Figure 8-5. The figure shows a striking and steady increase in velocity. The velocity of $M1$ has doubled from about 3 in the mid-fifties to over 6 in 1983. The average dollar finances twice the income flow now that it did in the mid-fifties.

This increase in velocity can, of course, be explained by the same factors that explain the demand for money. Velocity has risen because income has risen (since the income elasticity of demand is less than 1) and because interest rates have risen. In addition, the financial innovations that reduced money demand in the seventies increased velocity. A look at Equation (6*b*) shows that anything which reduces the demand for money, in the denominator, for a given level of Y in the numerator, increases velocity.

VELOCITY IN 1981–1982

In contrast to the long-term trends, the importance of the behavior of velocity (or money demand) in the short run and the way in which the behavior of velocity is discussed in policy making are brought out by events in 1981 and 1982. Figure 8-6 shows the *rate of change* of velocity from quarter to quarter

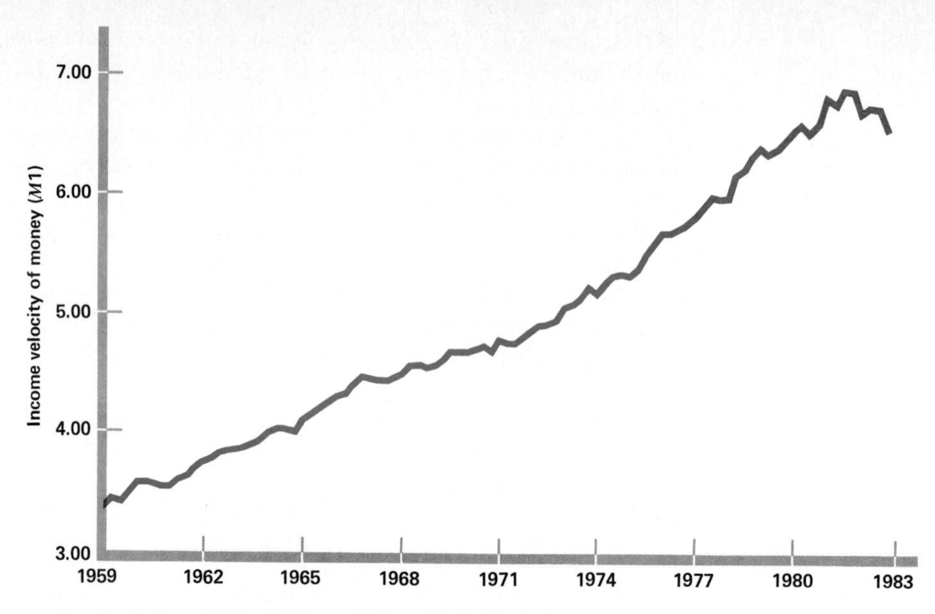

FIGURE 8-5 THE INCOME VELOCITY OF MONEY ($M1$). (*Source: Citibank Economic Database.*)

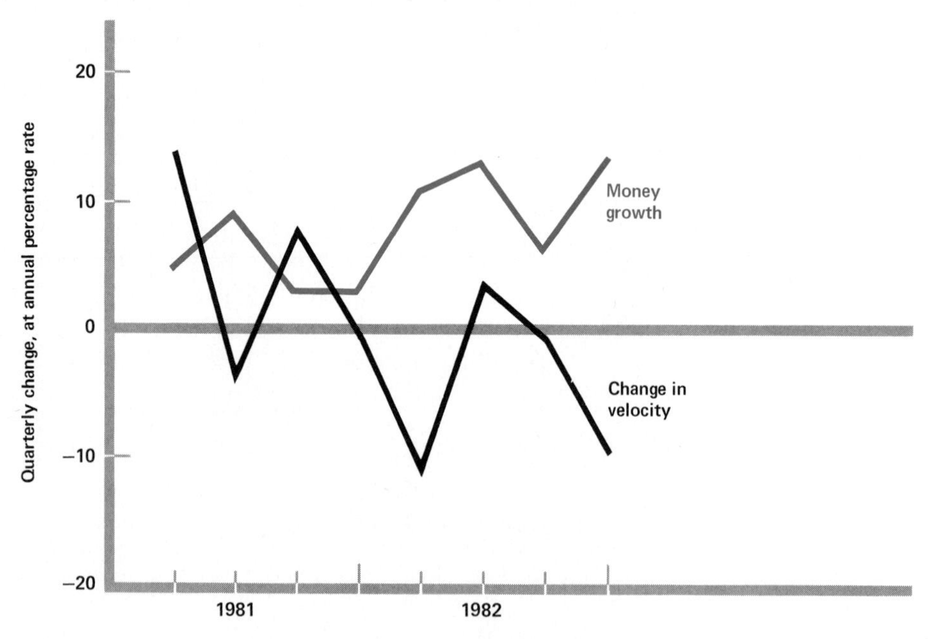

FIGURE 8-6 THE GROWTH RATE OF MONEY ($M1$) AND THE RATE OF CHANGE OF VELOCITY, 1981–1982. (*Source: Economic Report of the President, 1983.*)

in 1981 and 1982, together with the rate of growth of the ($M1$) money stock. During 1981 velocity on average increased, thus making it possible for nominal GNP to increase more rapidly than at the slow rate of money growth during the year. But in 1982 velocity fell substantially, with large declines in the first and fourth quarters outweighing small increases in the second and third quarters.

The 1983 *Economic Report of the President* notes:[32]

> The 1982 decline in the velocity of money . . . was historically atypical. Between 1961 and 1981 $M1$ velocity rose at an annual average rate of 3.2 percent [*Note:* This increase is visible in Figure 8-5]. . . . In contrast, in 1982 the velocity of $M1$ fell 4.9 percent. . . . [T]he growth of nominal GNP was well below the rate that would have prevailed if the $M1$ . . . measure of velocity had grown at [its] historic rate. . . .

The *Economic Report* then goes on to discuss the appropriate response of monetary policy to changes in velocity[33]:

> While sustained but unanticipated shifts in velocity growth can be identified in hindsight, it is nearly impossible to know at the time they occur whether unusual quarter-to-quarter changes in velocity will continue or reverse themselves. The presumption, on the basis of past experience, is that most velocity changes are temporary. Thus, increasing the rate of money growth in response to temporary declines in velocity runs the risk of providing excessive liquidity and increasing inflation, while a failure to recognize a continuing shift in . . . velocity runs the risk of providing inadequate liquidity and reducing real GNP.

The *Economic Report* is correct in suggesting that the decrease in velocity in 1982 was atypical. The report seems to be arguing also that the decrease was unrelated to monetary policy, and that policy was merely reacting to changes in velocity that occurred by accident. However, in the last half of 1982, while the Fed increased the growth rate of money, interest rates declined. We can see from Equation (6*b*) that velocity will decline when interest rates fall. The most likely interpretation of the fall in velocity at the end of 1982 is that it was not an accident, but rather that velocity fell because the Fed was expanding the money supply rapidly, thus reducing interest rates—as the *IS-LM* analysis suggests it should.

Indeed, examining Figure 8-6, we see over the 2 years 1981–1982 a systematic relationship between the growth rate of money and the rate of change of velocity. In quarters that the growth rate of money is high, velocity tends to be falling, and vice versa. There are two interpretations for this relationship. One, given by the *Economic Report*, is that the Fed attempts to compensate for changes in velocity by changing the growth rate of money. The other is that changes in the growth rate of money cause changes of velocity.

[32] Page 21.

[33] Page 22.

TABLE 8-4 CHANGES IN VELOCITY, THE GROWTH RATE OF MONEY, AND THE INTEREST RATE, 1981–1982

	1981:I	1981:II	1981:III	1981:IV	1982:I	1982:II	1982:III	1982:IV
Growth rate of $M1$	5.0	9.2	3.2	3.2	11.0	13.2	6.3	13.7
Rate of change of velocity	14.0	−3.7	7.9	−0.2	−10.8	3.5	−0.5	−9.8
Treasury bill rate	14.4	14.9	15.1	11.8	12.8	12.4	9.3	7.9

Source: *Data Resources, Inc.*
Note: Growth rate and rate of change of velocity are quarterly changes at an annual percentage rate.

How could we tell the two explanations apart? One way is to look at the behavior of interest rates. Table 8-4 shows the rate of change of velocity, the growth rate of money, and the Treasury bill rate during each quarter of 1981–1982. In those quarters in which interest rates did not change much, we can conclude that the Fed was compensating for a change in velocity. For instance, there is no change in interest rates during the first part of 1981 even though money and velocity are moving sharply in opposite directions. The same is true for the first quarter of 1982. But at the end of 1982 it is more reasonable to believe that the Fed was actively expanding the money stock, and that velocity was responding—through interest rate changes—to the Fed's monetary policy.

8-6 VELOCITY AND INFLATION

We begin to discuss inflation systematically only in Chapter 11, but we can take up here an important and fascinating aspect of inflation. The question is, How does inflation affect the demand for money? It is especially important to distinguish between the demand for *nominal* and *real* money balances. Earlier in the chapter we have seen that (1) an increase in the price level, all real variables remaining unchanged, leaves the demand for real balances unchanged and increases the demand for nominal balances in proportion to the increase in the price level, and (2) an increase in the rate of interest increases the cost of holding money and reduces the demand for real balances.

These two points are relevant in discussing the effects of expected inflation—expected continuing increases in prices—on the demand for real balances. We have seen that a one-time increase in the price level, all real variables remaining unchanged after this increase, leaves the demand for real balances unaffected. But now assume that prices increase and that the public interprets the price increases as merely the prelude to further continuing price increases. That is, the public anticipates inflation. Inflation reduces the purchasing power of money. Thus, inflation at the rate of 5 percent reduces the real value of a nominal dollar that is held for a period of 1 year by 5 percent. Inflation acts as a tax on real balances.[34] Someone holding $100 for a

[34] We explore the notion of inflation as a tax on real balances in more detail in Chap. 15, which deals with the budget.

year during which inflation is 5 percent in effect pays $5 for holding that money during the year. If she held less money, she would pay a smaller tax; if she reduced her cash holdings to $50, the tax would be only $2.50. There is thus an incentive, when increased inflation is expected, to try to reduce holdings of real balances and, instead, hold assets whose value is not as adversely affected by inflation. That is why the public reduces the demand for real balances when inflation is expected.

The effects of expected inflation on the demand for real balances have a strong influence on the behavior of the price level when money supply growth increases. Suppose that the money supply has been growing at 5 percent, that real income was constant, and that the inflation rate had been a steady 5 percent. Then let the money supply start growing more rapidly, say, at 10 percent. Ultimately, prices will increase at a 10 percent rate as well. But with 10 percent inflation expected, the demand for real balances is lower than when the expected inflation rate is only 5 percent. This means that at some stage during the process by which the economy adapts from an inflation rate of 5 percent to a rate of 10 percent, real balances have to be reduced. The only way real balances can fall is for prices to increase more rapidly than the money supply. Accordingly, at some point during the adjustment process, prices have to increase more rapidly than at 10 percent, the rate at which the nominal money supply is growing, which means that an increase in the growth rate of money to a new higher level produces, at some point, a rate of inflation higher than the rate of growth of money. The adjustment of real balances during an inflationary period will imply that prices increase more rapidly than the nominal money stock.

How does this observation link up with evidence on money demand during inflationary periods? Phillip Cagan of Columbia University studied the demand for real balances during *hyperinflations*—extremely rapid inflations—in an interesting and famous article.[35] His evidence shows that the demand for real balances declines dramatically as inflation reaches very high levels. As we noted earlier, expected inflation reduces the demand for money because it is a cost of holding money. For instance, during the Austrian hyperinflation in 1922–1923, the *monthly* rate of inflation rose from roughly zero to more than 80 percent. This extraordinary increase in inflation brought about a decline in real money demand to *one-fifth* the level that had been held at zero inflation. Velocity increased by a factor of 5. The evidence for other countries is, if anything, even more striking.

Cagan's evidence raises the question of how real money demand, or velocity, can be so flexible. How do people manage to reduce their money holdings per dollar, or crown, of income by so much? As inflation increases, the public takes more care in how it manages its cash balances. Money is spent more rapidly after it is received. Firms begin to pay their workers more frequently. Money becomes like a hot potato, with people anxious to pass it on rapidly. One can almost see the velocity of circulation increasing as people scurry to get rid of cash. These changes in payments patterns and shopping

[35] Phillip Cagan, "The Monetary Dynamics of Hyperinflation," in Milton Friedman (ed.), *Studies in the Quantity Theory of Money* (Chicago: The University of Chicago Press, 1956).

habits do impose costs on money holders that are the major costs of expected inflation, as we shall see in Chapter 14.

INFLATION AND INTEREST RATES

The adjustment of the demand for money to expected inflation is, in principle, no different from the adjustment to changes in the interest rate, which also increase the cost of holding money. Indeed, in countries with sufficiently well-developed capital markets, expected inflation is reflected in nominal interest rates. When inflation is expected, borrowers know that they will repay their debts in money that has lower purchasing power than the money they originally borrowed, and lenders know that too. Lenders, accordingly, become more reluctant to lend at any given level of the nominal interest rate, and borrowers become more anxious to borrow at a given nominal interest rate. The result is that the *nominal* interest rate rises when inflation is expected, thus compensating lenders for the loss of purchasing power of money.

The rise in the nominal interest rate that we are talking about reminds us of the distinction between *real* and *nominal* interest rates made in Chapter 7. When the expected rate of inflation rises, nominal interest rates—interest rates which specify how many dollars have to be repaid—increase. The real interest rate—the nominal interest rate minus the expected rate of inflation—need not rise and may even fall. Undoubtedly, one of the major reasons for the increase in nominal interest rates in the United States between the 1960s and 1982 was the increase in the expected rate of inflation. This relationship is investigated in more detail in Chapter 13. In some Latin American countries where inflation rates have reached 100 percent per year or more, no one is surprised by bank loan rates of, say, 80 percent.

In talking about both the expected rate of inflation itself and nominal interest rates, we raise the question of whether each is a separate influence on the demand for money. In well-developed capital markets, in which interest rates are free to move to reflect expected inflation, the nominal interest rate is the relevant opportunity cost of holding money. That is because individuals could make investments at that interest rate. In markets where interest rates are controlled and rates do not rise to reflect expected inflation, individuals begin to think of the alternative of buying goods rather than holding money when the expected rate of inflation rises. The expected inflation rate itself then becomes a separate influence on the demand for money. Franco Modigliani has offered the following useful rule of thumb to decide whether the nominal interest rate or the expected rate of inflation should be included as determining the demand for money: If the nominal interest rate exceeds the expected rate of inflation, the nominal interest rate should be thought of as the cost of holding money. If the expected inflation rate exceeds the nominal interest rate, the expected inflation rate should be thought of as the cost of holding money.

VELOCITY AND DISINFLATION

We noted above that when the growth rate of money increases and the economy moves to a higher rate of inflation, there is a period in which the rate of inflation will exceed the growth rate of money. A similar relationship holds in the opposite direction.

When the expected inflation rate and the nominal interest rate fall, there is an increase in the demand for real balances. The only way real balances (M/P) can increase is if P grows more slowly than M. Thus when the economy is disinflating, with the inflation rate coming down, there will be some period during which prices will grow less rapidly than money. Equivalently, during the disinflation there will be some period during which money grows more rapidly than prices.

During this process there may well be a fear that inflation will be reignited. For during that period, the money stock may be increasing quite fast, even though the inflation rate is low. Everyone is afraid that the higher growth rate of money will create future inflation. But maybe money is growing fast only so that people can increase their holdings of real balances.

Such a situation may help account for the behavior of velocity and money growth that we see in Table 8-4 at the end of 1982. Velocity was falling—meaning that the demand for real balances was rising relative to income. Money was growing very fast. But there was no sign of serious inflation. The reason was that during that period people began to believe that inflation was no longer a threat—as reflected in the behavior of interest rates. They therefore increased the demand for real balances, and thereby made it possible for money to grow fast without creating inflation. Indeed, if money had grown more slowly, the economy could have gone into an even worse recession than it was in already.

8-7 SUMMARY

1 The demand for money is a demand for real balances. It is the purchasing power, not the number, of their dollar bills that matters to holders of money.
2 The money supply $M1$ is made up of currency and checkable deposits. A broader measure, $M2$, includes savings and time deposits at depository institutions as well as some other interest-bearing assets.
3 The chief characteristic of money is that it serves as a means of payment.
4 There are two broad reasons why people hold money and thus forgo interest that they could earn by holding alternative assets. These reasons are transactions costs and uncertainty.
5 Transactions costs are an essential aspect of money demand. If it were costless to move (instantaneously) in and out of interest-bearing assets, nobody would hold money. Optimal cash management would involve

transfers from other assets (bonds or saving deposits) just before outlays, and it would involve immediate conversion into interest-bearing form of any cash receipts. The existence of transactions costs—brokerage costs, fees, and time costs—makes it optimal to hold some money.

6 The inventory-theoretic approach shows that an individual will hold a stock of real balances that varies inversely with the interest rate but increases with the level of real income and the cost of transactions. The income elasticity of money demand is less than unity, implying that there are economies of scale.

7 Transactions costs, in combination with uncertainty about payments and receipts, give rise to a precautionary demand for money. Money holdings provide insurance against illiquidity. Optimal money holdings are higher, the higher the variability of net disbursements and the higher the cost of illiquidity. Since holding money implies forgoing interest, optimal money holdings will vary inversely with the rate of interest.

8 Portfolio diversification involves the tradeoff between risk and return. Saving deposits form part of an optimal portfolio because they are not risky—their nominal value is constant. Saving deposits dominate currency or demand deposits, which are also safe nominal assets, because they bear interest. Thus the speculative portfolio demand for money is a demand for saving or time deposits.

9 The empirical evidence provides strong support for a negative interest elasticity of money demand and a positive income elasticity. Because of lags, short-run elasticities are much smaller than long-run elasticities. The long-run income elasticity is about 0.7, and the long-run interest elasticity is about −0.2.

10 Over the decade 1974–1983 the demand for money shifted; less money ($M1$) was demanded than should have been demanded according to the standard demand-for-money equation. The reduction in money demand was a result of both the introduction of new assets and improvements in cash management methods.

11 The income velocity of money is defined as the ratio of income to money or the rate of turnover of money. Since the fifties, velocity has doubled to a level in excess of 6.

12 The empirical evidence implies that an increase in real income raises velocity, as does an increase in the rate of interest. At higher levels of income or at higher interest rates, there is a lower demand for money in relation to income. Higher interest rates lead people to economize on cash balances.

13 Inflation implies that money loses purchasing power, and inflation thus creates a cost of holding money. The higher the rate of inflation, the lower the amount of real balances that will be held. Hyperinflations provide striking support for this prediction. Under conditions of very high expected inflation, money demand falls dramatically relative to income. Velocity rises as people use less money in relation to income.

KEY TERMS

Real balances
Money illusion
$M1$
$M2$
Liquidity
Medium of exchange
Store of value
Unit of account
Standard of deferred payments
Transactions demand
Inventory-theoretic approach
Square-root formula
Precautionary demand
Speculative demand
Income velocity of money
Quantity equation
Quantity theory of money
Hyperinflation

PROBLEMS

1 To what extent would it be possible to design a society in which there was no money? What would the problems be? Could currency at least be eliminated? How? (Lest all this seems too unworldly, you should know that some people are beginning to talk of a "cashless economy" in the next century.)

2 Evaluate the effects of the following changes on the demand for $M1$ and $M2$. Which of the functions of money do they relate to?
  (*a*) "Instant cash" machines which allow 24-hour withdrawals from savings accounts at banks
  (*b*) The employment of more tellers at your bank
  (*c*) An increase in inflationary expectations
  (*d*) Widespread acceptance of credit cards
  (*e*) Fear of an imminent collapse of the government
  (*f*) A rise in the interest rate on time deposits

3 (*a*) Do you think credit card credit limits should be counted in the money stock?
  (*b*) Should MMDAs be part of $M1$?

4 (*a*) Determine the optimal strategy for cash management for the person who earns $1,600 per month, can earn 0.5 percent interest per month in a savings account, and has a transaction cost of $1.
  (*b*) What is the individual's average cash balance?
  (*c*) Suppose her income rises to $1,800. By what percentage does her demand for money rise? (Pay attention to the integer constraints.)

5 Discuss the various factors that go into an individual's decision regarding how many traveler's checks to take on a vacation.

6 In the text, we said that the transactions demand-for-money model can also be applied to firms. Suppose a firm sells steadily during the month and has to pay its workers at the end of the month. Explain then how it would determine its money holdings.

7 In the text we argued that the demand for money fell when corporations received permission to hold savings accounts.
  (*a*) For which money-demand concept is this true? For which is it false?
  (*b*) Explain why this change would have been more important for small firms than for large ones.

8 Explain why the demand-for-money function shifted during the seventies and early eighties.

9 (*a*) Is V high or low relative to trend during recessions? Why?

(*b*) How can the Fed influence velocity?

10 In the text it is argued that during a process of disinflation there may be a period in which the money stock grows more rapidly than prices. Explain.

11 This chapter emphasizes that the demand for money is a demand for real balances. Thus the demand for nominal balances rises with the price level. At the same time, inflation causes the real demand to fall. Explain how these two assertions can both be correct.

12 "Muggers favor deflation." Comment.

*13 The assumption was made in the text that in the transactions demand for cash model, it is optimal to space transactions evenly throughout the month. Prove this as follows in the case where $n = 2$. Since one transaction must be made immediately, the only question is when to make the second one. For simplicity, call the beginning of the month $t = 0$ and the end of the month $t = 1$. Then consider a transaction strategy which performs the second transaction at the time t_0. If income is Y_N, then this will require moving $t_0 Y_N$ into cash now and $(1 - t_0)Y_N$ at time t_0. Calculate the total cost incurred under this strategy, and try various values of t_0 to see which is optimal. (If you are familiar with calculus, prove that $t_0 = ½$ minimizes total cost.)

*14 For those students familiar with calculus, derive Equation (4) from Equation (2) by minimizing total costs with respect to n.

9

THE MONEY SUPPLY AND THE FED

We have so far taken the money supply to be given and determined by the Federal Reserve System. By and large, the Fed is able to determine the money supply quite accurately, but it does not set it directly. In this chapter we study the way in which the actions of the Fed, financial institutions, and the public interact to determine the stock of money.

In conducting monetary policy, the Fed pays attention to the behavior of both interest rates and the money stock. Some monetarist critics of the Fed argue that this practice makes monetary policy wrong. They claim the Fed is continually distracted from its main task of keeping the money stock growing steadily by its habit of worrying about changes in interest rates. Other critics argue that the Fed *should* worry more about the behavior of interest rates, and not slavishly follow announced target paths for the money stock.

We start this chapter with the mechanics of money supply determination. Then we go on to discuss monetary policy: both how the Fed conducts monetary policy and controversies about how it should conduct monetary policy.

9-1 DEFINITIONS

We noted in Chapter 8 that the money stock $M1$ is the sum of checkable deposits CD plus currency held by the public, CU.

$$M1 = CD + CU \tag{1}$$

A broader measure of the money supply is $M2$, which adds MMMF shares, MMDAs, and time and savings and other deposits to $M1$ (see footnote 1):

$$M2 = M1 + LD \tag{2}$$

Figure 9-1 shows the history of these aggregates and their components. (Currency is not shown but is the difference between $M1$ and checkable deposits.) Because time and savings deposits, and especially MMDAs and MMMFs, have been growing more rapidly than the other components of the money supply, $M2$ has grown more rapidly than $M1$. Over the 1972–1982 period, $M1$ grew at 6.6 percent per annum and $M2$ at 9.3 percent. The 6.6 percent growth rate of $M1$ from 1972 to 1982 is well above the average rate of growth of $M1$ of 4.9 percent from 1960 to 1972.

Table 9-1 reproduces part of Table 8-1 and shows the March 1983 components of the money stock. $M1$ is about \$500 billion, more than a quarter of that consisting of currency. The difference between $M2$ and $M1$ of \$1,572 billion is composed chiefly of time and savings deposits.

For simplicity, we shall now ignore the distinction between checkable deposits and the assets grouped in column (4) in Table 9-1 and consider the money supply process as if there were only a uniform class of deposits D. Using that simplification, we define money as deposits plus currency:

$$M \equiv CU + D \tag{3}$$

Starting from Equation (3), we now begin to develop the details of the process of money stock determination. It is apparent from Equation (3) that both the public and the depository institutions (which we shall refer to simply as banks in the rest of this chapter) have an influence on the determination of the money supply. The public has a role because its demand for currency affects the currency component CU. The banks have a role because the other component of the money stock, deposits D, is a liability of the banks, that is, a debt the banks owe their customers. We know too that the Fed has a part (the most important) in determining the money supply. The interactions among the actions of the public, the banks, and the Fed determine the money supply. We shall summarize the behavior of the public, the banks, and the Fed in the money supply process by three separate variables.

[1] We are using CD to stand for "checkable deposits" and LD for "liquid deposits"; there is no generally accepted term as yet for the sum of the assets we are calling LD.

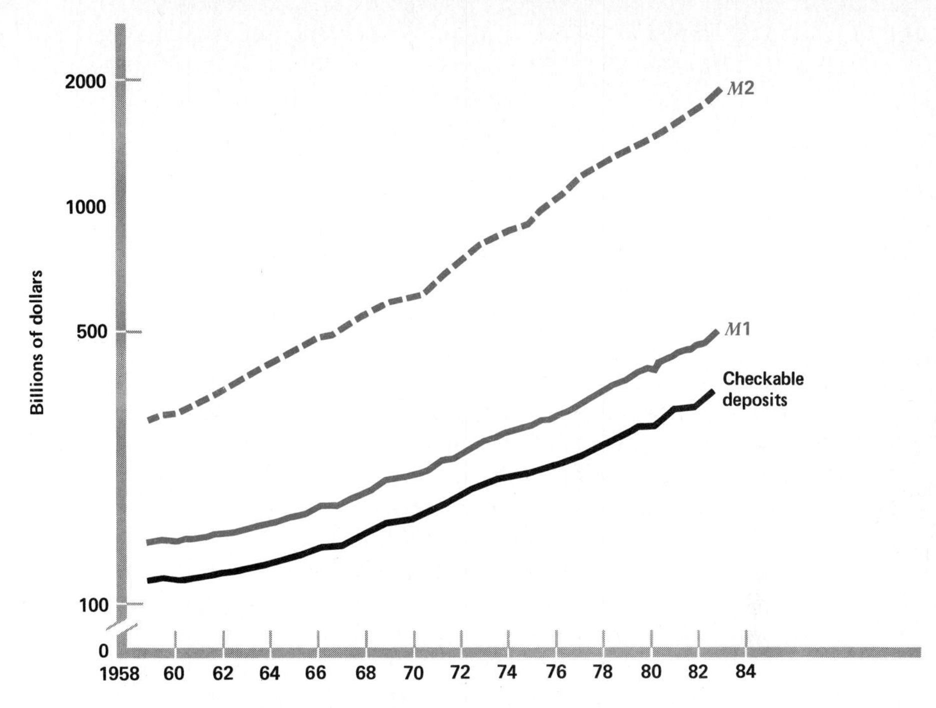

FIGURE 9-1 MONETARY AGGREGATES. (*Source:* Data Resources, Inc.) *Note:* Scale is logarithmic.

THE PUBLIC

From the viewpoint of money supply determination, the variable on which we concentrate as representing the behavior of the public is the *currency-deposit ratio,* that is, the ratio of the public's holdings of currency to their holdings of deposits. In early 1983, that ratio was 0.38 (= $137 billion cur-

TABLE 9-1 COMPONENTS OF THE MONEY STOCK, MARCH 1983 (*In billions of dollars, seasonally adjusted*)

(1) Currency	(2) Checkable deposits	(3) $M1 = (1) + (2)$	(4) Time and savings deposits, MMMFs, MMDAs, etc.	(5) $M2 = M1 + (4)$
137.0	360.6	497.6	1,572.3	2,069.9

Source: Data Resources, Inc.

rency ÷ $360.6 billion of checkable deposits), using the $M1$ definition of the money stock. We denote the currency-deposit ratio CU/D by cu.

THE BANKS

The behavior of the banks is summarized by the *reserve-deposit ratio. Reserves* are assets held by the banks to meet (1) the demands of their customers for cash and (2) payments their customers make by checks which are deposited in other banks. Reserves consist of notes and coin held by the banks—*vault cash*—and also of deposits held at the Fed.

Banks that have accounts at the Fed can use them to make payments among themselves. Thus, when my bank has to make a payment to your bank because I paid you with a check drawn on my bank account, it makes the payment by transferring money from its account at the Fed to your bank's account at the Fed.

We examine the determinants of the banks' demand for reserves, RE, in more detail in Section 9-5, but in the meantime we summarize that behavior by the reserve-deposit ratio $RE/D \equiv re$.[2] The reserve ratio is less than 1, since banks hold assets other than reserves, such as loans they make to the public and securities, in their portfolios. Banks in early 1983 held about $41 billion of reserves. With checkable deposits of $360.6 billion, the reserve-deposit ratio was $re = 11.4$ percent.

THE FED

The Fed's behavior is summarized by the stock of *high-powered money*, or the *monetary base, H*. High-powered money consists of currency (notes and coin) and banks' deposits at the Fed. Part of the currency is held by the public—that is, the $137 billion previously referred to. The remaining currency, about $20 billion, is held by banks as vault cash. The notes that constitute most of the outstanding stock of currency are issued by the Fed[3] and the reserves held by member banks as Fed deposits are a liability of the Fed—that is, a debt of the Fed to the member banks.

[2] Until the Depository Institutions Decontrol Act and Monetary Control Act of 1981, the Fed had more power to control the behavior of member banks of the Federal Reserve System than it had over nonmembers. In particular, the Fed could set reserve requirements for members but not for nonmembers. In return, members had access to services, such as borrowing from the Fed and using the Fed's check-clearing system, that nonmembers did not have. The new law allowed the Fed to impose reserve requirements on *all* deposit-issuing financial institutions. The Fed now is supposed to supply its services on equal terms to all banks, members or not. There is thus little to choose for a bank between belonging or not belonging to the Fed, since both reserve requirements and the ability to use the Fed's services are independent of whether a bank belongs to the Federal Reserve System.

[3] Coins are minted by the Treasury and sold to the Fed by the Treasury. This detail complicates the bookkeeping but is of no real importance to the process of money supply determination.

In this section we develop a simple approach to money stock determination. The approach is organized around the supply of and the demand for *high-powered money*. The Fed can control the *supply* of high-powered money. The total *demand* for high-powered money comes from the public, who want to use it as currency, and the banks, who need it as reserves. Because the public has a preferred ratio of currency to deposits and because the banks have a desired ratio of reserves to deposits, we can calculate the total money stock that can be supported by any given stock of high-powered money.

Before we go into the details, we want to think briefly about the relationship between the money stock and the stock of high-powered money. Figure 9-2 illustrates the relationship. At the top of the figure we show the stock of high-powered money. At the bottom we show the stock of money. They are related by the *money multiplier*. The money multiplier is the ratio of the stock of money to the stock of high-powered money.

The money multiplier is larger than 1. It is clear from the diagram that the multiplier is larger the larger are deposits as a fraction of the money stock. That is because currency uses up 1 dollar of high-powered money per dollar of money. Deposits, by contrast, use up only amount *re* of high-powered money (in reserves) per dollar of money stock. For instance, if the reserve ratio *re* is 11 percent, every dollar of the money stock in the form of deposits uses up only 11 cents of high-powered money.

It is thus clear that (1) *the money multiplier is larger, the smaller is the reserve ratio re*. In addition, (2) *the money multiplier is larger, the smaller is the currency deposit ratio cu*. That is because the smaller is *cu*, the smaller the proportion of the high-powered money stock that is being used as currency (which translates high-powered money only one for one into money) and the

FIGURE 9-2 THE MONEY MULTIPLIER. The money multiplier is the ratio of the money stock (the base of the diagram) to high-powered money. The multiplier is larger than 1. It is larger, the smaller the ratio of currency to deposits and the smaller the ratio of reserves to deposits.

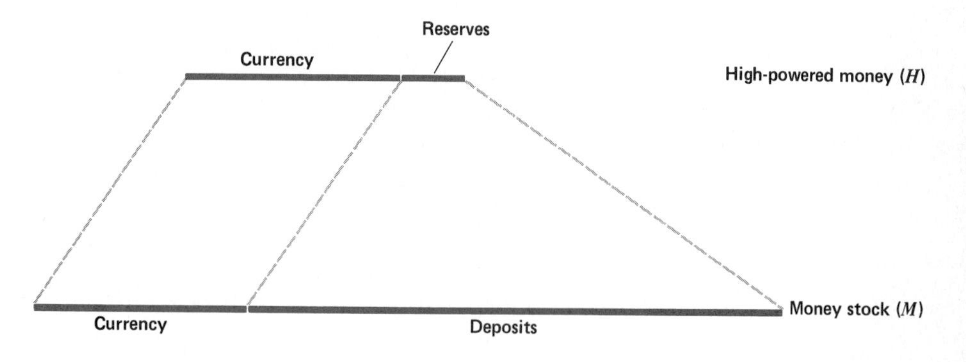

larger the proportion that is available to be reserves (which translate much more than one for one into money).

The precise relationship between the money stock M, the stock of high-powered money H, the reserve-deposit ratio re, and the currency-deposit ratio cu is derived in the Appendix to this chapter. Here we present the resulting expression for the money supply expressed in terms of its principal determinants, re, cu, and H:

$$M = \frac{1 + cu}{re + cu} H \equiv mm \cdot H \tag{4}$$

where mm is the money multiplier given by

$$mm \equiv \frac{1 + cu}{re + cu} \tag{5}$$

Careful examination of the formula for the money multiplier (5) shows that the multiplier is higher the smaller the reserve ratio and the smaller the currency-deposit ratio—as our earlier discussion suggested.

EXAMPLE

We can calculate the money multiplier as given by Equation (5) using the actual values of the currency-deposit ratio, $cu = 0.38$, and the reserve ratio, $re = 0.114$, that existed at the beginning of 1983. That gives

$$mm = \frac{1 + 0.38}{0.114 + 0.38} = 2.794$$

You should confirm that you get the same result using the definition that the money multiplier is the ratio of money stock to high-powered money. (In March 1983, the money stock was \$497.6 billion, reserves were \$41 billion, and currency was \$137 billion.)

GRAPHICAL ANALYSIS

Figure 9-3 shows graphically how the money multiplier works. The supply of high-powered money, $\overline{H}$, is shown by the horizontal black line. The demand for high-powered money, HD, is an upward-sloping line with slope equal to 1 over the money multiplier. The intersection point E is the point at which the demand for high-powered money is equal to the supply. The corresponding money supply is shown by M_0.

Now suppose the stock of high-powered money increases to H'. The $\overline{HH}$ schedule moves up by amount $\Delta\overline{H}$ to $\overline{HH}'$. The money supply increases until we reach point E', with new money stock M'. Because the slope of the HD schedule is less than 1, the distance between M_0 and M' is greater than $\Delta\overline{H}$.

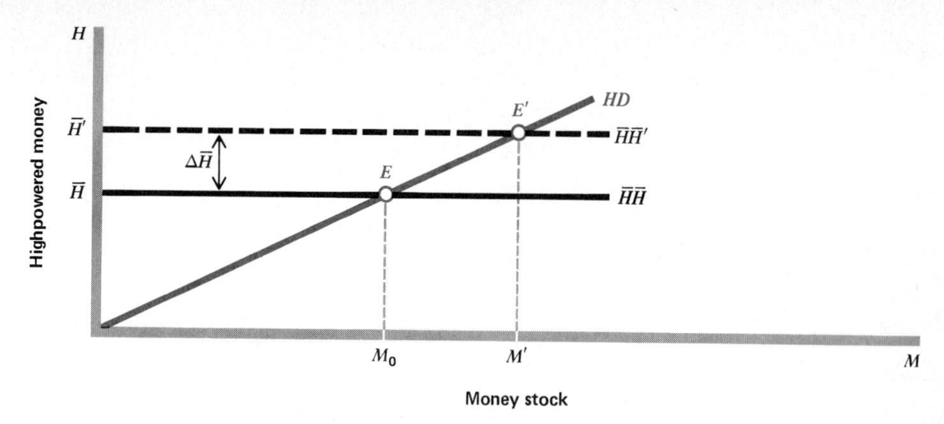

FIGURE 9-3 THE MONEY MULTIPLIER AND AN INCREASE IN THE MONETARY BASE. The *HD* schedule shows the demand for high-powered money, as related to the money stock *M*. The slope of the *HD* schedule is 1 over the money multiplier [see Equation (4)]. The supply of high-powered money is shown by the $\overline{HH}$ schedule. At point *E* the demand for high-powered money is equal to supply. The corresponding money supply is M_0. An increase in the stock of high-powered money by $\Delta\overline{H}$ shifts the $\overline{HH}$ schedule up to $\overline{HH}'$, resulting in a new equilibrium money stock M'. The ratio of the distance $(M' - M_0)$ (the increase in the money stock) to $\Delta\overline{H}$ (the increase in the base) is equal to the money multiplier.

Indeed, the ratio of the distance $(M' - M_0)$, which is the increase in the money stock, to $\Delta\overline{H}$ is equal to the money multiplier.[4]

THE MULTIPLIER IN PRACTICE

Since the Fed controls $\overline{H}$, it would be able to control the money stock *M* exactly if the multiplier were constant or fully predictable. Actual data for the money multiplier are shown in Figure 9-4. It is clear that the money multiplier is far from constant. Further, it is not possible for the Fed to predict the money multiplier exactly.[5] This means that the Fed cannot exactly determine the money stock in any period by setting the base at a specific level. For instance, suppose it wants the money stock to be \$520 billion, and therefore sets the base at \$186.1 billion (= \$520 billion/2.794, which is the value of the multiplier we calculated above). The multiplier might turn out to be 2.83. Then the money stock would be \$526.7 billion (2.83 × 186.1), which means that the money stock would differ by more than 1 percent from the value the Fed intended.

[4] In problem 1, we ask you to use Fig. 9-3 to show the effects of increases in the currency-deposit ratio (*cu*) and the reserve-deposit ratio (*re*) on the money multiplier and the money stock. Changes in these ratios change the slope of the *HD* line in Fig. 9-3.

[5] A sophisticated method of predicting the money multiplier is presented in James M. Johannes and Robert H. Rasche, "Predicting the Money Multiplier," *Journal of Monetary Economics*, July 1979.

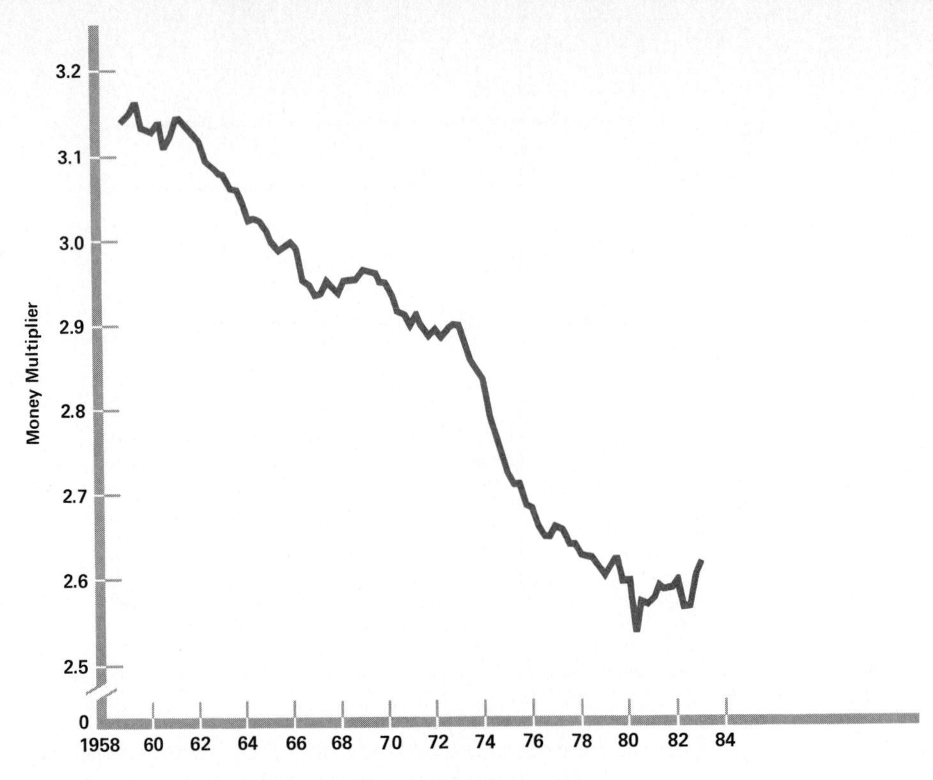

FIGURE 9-4 THE *M*1 MONEY MULTIPLIER (1959–1983). (*Source:* Data Resources, Inc.)

In much of the remainder of this chapter we take a closer look at the reasons the money multiplier varies. To do that we examine more closely the process by which the Fed determines $\overline{H}$, and the portfolio behavior of households and banks.

9-3 THE STOCK OF HIGH-POWERED MONEY

Table 9-2 shows a highly simplified form of the Fed's balance sheet, designed to illustrate the sources of the monetary base—the way the Fed creates high-powered money—and the uses of, or demand for, the base. The Fed's main assets appear on the left-hand side and its liabilities appear on the right.[6]

The fundamental reason for examining the Fed's balance sheet is this: High-powered money is created when the Fed acquires assets and pays for

[6] We have simplified the balance sheet by lumping together a number of assets in the entry "Net other assets." More detail on the Fed's balance sheet and the monetary base can be obtained by examining the tables in the *Federal Reserve Bulletin*.

TABLE 9-2 SIMPLIFIED FORM OF THE FED BALANCE SHEET, SHOWING SOURCES AND USES OF HIGH-POWERED MONEY, MARCH 1983 (*In billions of dollars*)

Assets (sources)			Liabilities (uses)		
Gold and foreign exchange		$ 15.7	Currency		$153.2
Federal reserve credit		161.0	Held by the public*	$133.7	
Loans and discounts	$ 0.9		Vault cash	19.5	
Government securities	144.1		Bank deposits at Fed		22.5
Net other credit	16.0				
Plus					
Net other assets		− 1.0			
Monetary base (sources)		$175.7	Monetary base (uses)		$175.7*

* These data are not seasonally adjusted. Thus they differ from data in Section 9-2, which show the currency held by the public as $137.0 billion and the monetary base as $178 billion.
Source: Federal Reserve Bulletin, *April 1983.*

these assets by creating liabilities. The two main classes of liabilities, or *uses* of the base, are currency and member bank deposits.

AN OPEN MARKET PURCHASE

The operation by which the Fed most often changes the stock of high-powered money is an open market operation. We examine the mechanics of an open market *purchase,* an operation in which the Fed buys, say $1 million of government bonds from a private individual. An open market purchase *increases* the monetary base.

The accounting for the Fed's purchase is shown in Table 9-3. The Fed's ownership of government securities rises by $1 million, which is reflected in the "Government securities" entry on the assets side of the balance sheet. How does the Fed pay for the bond? It writes a check on itself. In return for the bond, the seller receives a check instructing the Fed to pay (the seller) $1 million. This individual takes the check to his bank, which credits the depositor with the $1 million, and then deposits the check at the Fed. That bank has an account at the Fed, which is credited for $1 million, and the bank deposits entry on the "Liabilities" side of the balance sheet rises by $1 million. The

TABLE 9-3 EFFECTS OF AN OPEN MARKET PURCHASE ON THE FED BALANCE SHEET

Assets (millions of dollars)		Liabilities (millions of dollars)	
Government securities	+1	Currency	0
All other assets	0	Bank deposits at Fed	+1
Monetary base (sources)	+1	Monetary base (uses)	+1

commercial bank has just increased its reserves by $1 million, held in the first instance as a deposit at the Fed.[7]

The only strange part of the story of the open market purchase is that the Fed can write checks on itself. The check instructs the Fed to pay $1 million to the order of the seller of the bond. The payment is made by giving the eventual owner of the check a deposit at the Fed. That deposit can be used to make payments to other banks, or it can be exchanged for currency. Just as the ordinary deposit holder at a commercial bank can obtain currency in exchange for deposits, the bank deposit holder at the Fed can acquire currency in exchange for its deposits. When the Fed pays for the bond with a deposit at the Fed, it creates high-powered money with a stroke of the pen. Further, since it is the issuer of currency, it also creates high-powered money with the printing press. In either event, the Fed can create high-powered money at will merely by buying assets, such as government bonds, and paying for them with its liabilities.

THE FED BALANCE SHEET

We return now to the balance sheet, starting by examining the assets. The purchase of assets generates high-powered money. The gold and foreign exchange that the Fed owns were acquired in the past, when the Fed paid for them by writing checks on itself. There is, accordingly, almost no difference between the way in which an open market purchase of gold affects the balance sheet and the way in which an open market purchase of bonds affects the balance sheet. The Fed's 1983 holdings of gold were about $11 billion, valued at $42 an ounce. The market value of the gold is much higher, since the market price of gold is far above $42 per ounce.[8]

FOREIGN EXCHANGE AND THE BASE

Table 9-2 points to the effects of Fed purchases of foreign exchange on the monetary base. As we shall see in Chapter 18, the Fed sometimes buys and sells foreign currencies in an attempt to affect exchange rates. These purchases and sales of foreign exchange—*foreign exchange market intervention*—affect the base. Note from the balance sheet that if the central bank buys gold or foreign exchange, there is a corresponding increase in high-powered money, as the Fed pays with its own liabilities for the gold or foreign exchange that is purchased. The first point to note, then, is the direct impact of foreign exchange market operations on the base.[9]

The second point concerns *sterilization*. By that term we denote attempts

[7] In problem 2 we ask you to trace through the effects of an open market sale that reduces $\overline{H}$.

[8] In the problem set, you are asked to show how the balance sheet would be affected if the Fed decided to value its gold at the free market price. For that purpose you will have to adjust the item "Net other assets" appropriately.

[9] Details of this impact may be complicated by the fact, which we shall not pursue, that the Fed and the Treasury usually cooperate in foreign exchange intervention.

by the Fed to neutralize the effects of its intervention in the foreign exchange market, outlined above, on the base. What the Fed does here is to conduct an open market operation that offsets the effects of its intervention *on the base.* For instance, if the Fed sells foreign exchange (thereby reducing the monetary base when purchasers of foreign exchange pay the Fed), it, at the same time, makes an open market purchase of bonds (thereby restoring the base to its original level.) The net effect, therefore, is to leave the base unchanged but to change the portfolio composition of the Fed's balance sheet. There will be an increase in the gold and foreign exchange entry and an offsetting reduction in Federal Reserve credit. Thus, by sterilization, the Fed breaks the link between foreign exchange operations and the money supply.

THE DISCOUNT RATE

The Fed's role as a lender is reflected by the "Loans and discounts" item in Table 9-2. The Fed provides high-powered money to banks that need it by lending to them (crediting their account at the Fed) against the collateral of government securities. The rate at which the Fed typically lends is called the *discount rate,* and it is a rate set by the Fed. If a bank is short of reserves, it can try to borrow from the Fed. The Fed does not automatically lend to banks that want to borrow, even if they are willing and able to pay the discount rate for the borrowing, in part because it does not want banks to use the Fed habitually as a source of reserves. The willingness of banks to borrow from the Fed is partially affected by the rate the Fed charges, and the discount rate accordingly influences the volume of borrowing. Since borrowed reserves are also part of high-powered money, the Fed's discount rate has some effect on the monetary base.[10]

THE TREASURY AND THE FED

The balance sheet of Table 9-2 conceals one important item in the "Net other assets" entry. Among those net assets are deposits that the Treasury holds at the Fed. (Actually, Treasury deposits are Fed *liabilities,* which are negative net assets.) The Treasury makes almost all its payments for the purchases of goods and services and repays maturing government debt out of its accounts at the Fed. That has the interesting implication that Treasury purchases affect the stock of high-powered money. For instance, suppose the Treasury, to buy weapons, makes a payment of $1 billion out of its Fed account by writing a check on that account. Such a check would look much like any other check, except that it would instruct the Fed, rather than a commercial bank, to pay $1 billion to the bearer of the check. The seller of the weapons deposits the check in a commercial bank, which, in turn, presents it to the Fed. The Fed

[10] At one time, the discount rate had considerable importance as a signal of the Fed's intentions with regard to the behavior of interest rates. More recently, the Fed has tended to use discount policy passively, letting the discount rate adjust occasionally as the general level of interest rates changes.

then credits the commercial bank account at the Fed for $1 billion. Member bank deposits have risen. We show these changes in the balance sheet in Table 9-4.

Because payments by the Treasury from its Fed accounts affect the stock of high-powered money, the Treasury attempts to prevent those accounts from fluctuating excessively. For that purpose, it also keeps accounts at commercial banks, the so-called *tax and loan accounts*. When the Treasury receives tax payments, it typically deposits them in commercial banks, rather than the Fed, so that it does not affect the stock of high-powered money; then, before it has to make a payment, it moves the money from the commercial bank to the Fed. If the payment is made fairly soon after the money is moved into the Fed, the stock of high-powered money is only temporarily affected by the Treasury purchase. The Treasury's degree of concern over the effects of its operations on the stock of high-powered money has varied over the years.

The relationship between the Fed and the Treasury is important also in understanding the financing of government budget deficits. Such deficits can be financed by the Treasury's borrowing from the public. In that case, the Treasury sells bonds to the public. The public pays for the bonds with checks, which are deposited in a tax and loan account. This, accordingly, does not affect the stock of high-powered money. When the Treasury makes payment, it moves the money in and out of its Fed account, leaving the monetary base the same after it has made its payments as it was before the money was transferred into the Fed from the tax and loan account. Thus, Treasury deficit financing through borrowing from the public has only a temporary effect on the monetary base, and no effect on the base after the Treasury has used the borrowed funds to make the payments for which the funds were raised.

Alternatively, the Treasury can finance its deficit by borrowing from the Fed. It is simplest to think of the Treasury's selling a bond to the Fed instead of to the public. When the bond is sold, the Fed's holdings of government securities increase, and simultaneously the asset "Net other assets" falls because Treasury deposits, a liability of the Fed, have risen. But then when the Treasury uses the borrowed money to make a payment, the stock of high-powered money rises, just as in Table 9-4. Accordingly, when a budget deficit is financed by Treasury borrowing from the Fed, the stock of high-powered money is increased. We sometimes talk of central bank financing of

TABLE 9-4 FED BALANCE SHEET: EFFECT OF TREASURY PAYMENT (*In billions of dollars*)

Assets		Liabilities	
Net other assets*	+1	Currency	0
Other assets	0	Bank account at Fed	+1
Monetary base (sources)	+1	Monetary base (uses)	+1

* The Treasury's payment *reduces* Fed liabilities by $1 billion, therefore *increasing* assets by $1 billion.

government deficits as financing through the printing of money. It is not necessarily true that the deficit is literally financed by the central bank through the printing of money, but it is true that central bank financing increases the stock of high-powered money, which comes to much the same thing.

SUMMARY

1 The main point of this section is that the Fed controls the stock of high-powered money primarily through open market operations.
2 The Fed has some influence over the stock of high-powered money through the indirect route of changing the discount rate and thereby affecting the volume of member bank borrowing.
3 Treasury financing of its deficits through borrowing from the public leaves the stock of high-powered money unaffected, whereas Treasury financing by borrowing from the Fed increases the monetary base.
4 The Fed does not *have* to finance Treasury borrowing. Thus it still retains its ability to control the stock of high-powered money even when the Treasury is running a budget deficit.

9-4 THE CURRENCY-DEPOSIT RATIO

The next element in the money multiplier formula (5) is the currency-deposit ratio, which reflects the behavior of the public. The currency-deposit ratio is determined primarily by payment habits and has a strong seasonal pattern; it is highest around Christmas. The ratio increases when the ratio of consumption to GNP increases, since currency demand is more closely linked to consumption than GNP, while deposit demand is more closely linked to GNP.

The currency-deposit ratio has been increasing, as can be deduced from the behavior of currency and demand deposits since 1970, as shown in Figure 9-1. The increase in the currency-deposit ratio accounts for some of the decline in the money multiplier shown in Figure 9-4. For the remainder of the chapter we shall treat the currency-deposit ratio as independent of interest rates and constant.

9-5 THE RESERVE-DEPOSIT RATIO

The banking system affects the supply of money through the reserve-deposit ratio re. The reserve-deposit ratio is determined by two sets of considerations. First, the banking system is subject to Fed regulation in the form of *minimum reserve requirements.* The reserve requirements vary by type of deposit and also by bank size and location. The reserve requirements against time deposits are lower than those against demand deposits; reserve requirements are lower for smaller banks than for larger banks, and so on. The variety of the reserve requirements creates some difficulties for control of the money stock because shifts of deposits between different categories of deposits change the level of required reserves even if the level of deposits is unaffected. There is no compelling logic to the way in which the reserve requirements have evolved, and we shall not discuss them further.[11]

Second, banks may want to hold *excess reserves* beyond the level of required reserves. In deciding how much excess reserves to hold, a bank's economic problem is very similar to the problem of the individual in deciding on a precautionary demand for money. Banks hold reserves to meet demands on them for cash or payments to other banks.[12] If they cannot meet those demands, they have to borrow, either from the Fed or from other banks that happen to have spare reserves.

The explicit cost of borrowing from the Fed is the discount rate, while the implicit cost is Fed disapproval of the bank's imprudent behavior (if it is short of reserves frequently) and possible future refusal of the borrowing privilege. The cost of borrowing from other banks is the *federal funds rate.* Federal funds are simply reserves that some banks have in excess and other need. The federal funds rate varies with the overall availability of reserves to the banking system, and can be affected by the Fed through open market operations. When the Fed buys assets in the open market, it increases the availability of reserves and reduces the federal funds rate. In brief, there is a cost to a bank of being short of reserves, and that cost is affected by the Fed's actions.

There is also a cost to a bank of holding reserves. Reserves do not earn interest. By holding smaller reserves, a bank is able to invest in interest-earning assets and increase its profits. A simplified commercial bank balance sheet is shown in Table 9-5. By reducing its reserves, the bank is able to increase its loans or investments on which it earns interest. There is thus a tradeoff of the sort examined in Chapter 8 in discussing the precautionary demand for money. The more reserves a bank holds, the less likely it is to have to incur the costs of borrowing. But the more reserves it holds, the more interest it forgoes.

The bank's choice of reserve ratio therefore depends on three factors in addition to the required reserve ratio, which we denote r_R. The first is the uncertainty of its net deposit flow. The more variable the inflows and outflows of cash a bank experiences, the more reserves it will want to hold. The second is the cost of borrowing when the bank runs short of reserves. We shall take the discount rate i_D to be the cost of borrowing. The third factor is the interest forgone by holding reserves, which we shall take as the market interest rate i. We can therefore write the bank's reserve-deposit ratio re as a function of the market interest rate, the discount rate, the required reserve ratio r_R, and σ:

[11] Reserve requirements are published in the *Federal Reserve Bulletin.* In March 1980, the Congress passed the important Depository Institutions Deregulation and Monetary Control Act, which among other things requires all depository institutions to hold the same reserve ratios. Before March 1980, reserve requirements varied, depending on whether a bank belonged to the system or was instead state-chartered.

[12] Many banks, particularly small ones, hold deposits at other banks to facilitate transactions of this sort. These *interbank deposits* serve the same function as reserves but are not included in our measure of reserves. They are excluded from the definitions of the money stock.

TABLE 9-5 COMMERCIAL BANK BALANCE SHEET

Assets	Liabilities
Reserves	Deposits
Commercial bank credit	
Loans	
Investments	
Less:	
Borrowing from Fed	
Borrowing in the Fed funds market (net)	

$$re = r(i, i_D, r_R, \sigma) \tag{6}$$

where σ indicates the uncertainty characteristics of the bank's deposit inflows and outflows.

How does each of the factors in Equation (6) affect the reserve ratio? An increase in the market interest rate on earnings assets decreases the reserve ratio, since it makes reserves more costly to hold. An increase in the discount rate increases the ratio, since it raises the cost of running short of reserves. And an increase in the required reserve ratio increases the actual reserve ratio. We thus see that the reserve ratio is a function of market interest rates, which suggests that the supply of money itself may also be a function of market interest rates.

EXCESS RESERVES

Excess reserves in the last 10 years have averaged less than 1 percent of total reserves. Indeed, in the entire postwar period, they have been small compared with levels reached in the 1930s. The thirties were a period of great economic uncertainty, during which there were many bank failures: that is, banks were unable to meet the demands of their depositors for cash. If you have a deposit in a failed bank, you cannot "get your money (currency) out."

In the thirties, it became necessary for banks to hold large reserves. The reason is that a bank that holds relatively few reserves, with most of its assets in loans or securities, cannot quickly meet its depositors' demands for currency. Banks that hold low reserves are exposed to the risk that a run by depositors—an attempt to convert their deposits into currency—will drive the bank into default. But it is precisely when depositors are afraid that a bank is in danger of defaulting that they are likely to attempt to withdraw their money from that bank before it is too late. That is to say that a run may occur on a bank precisely because its depositors believe that a run on the bank is likely to occur.

In a general atmosphere of instability—such as prevailed in the thirties—it therefore became important for banks to demonstrate their ability to meet cash withdrawals by holding large reserves, that is, by holding excess reserves. Only by being in a position to meet large cash demands could the banks avoid their depositors actually making those demands. The massive bank failures of the thirties, as a consequence of runs on banks, gave rise to an important institutional reform, the creation of the *Federal Deposit Insurance Corporation* (FDIC). That institution insures bank deposits, so that depositors get paid even if a bank fails.

There are three main reasons why excess reserves are now so small. First, bank deposits are now insured, mainly through the FDIC. Individual depositors now know that their deposit will ultimately be paid back. The threat of runs on banks is accordingly much reduced, and banks do not have to hold large reserves to guard against runs.[13] Second, the development of financial markets and communications has reduced the cost to banks of managing their balance sheets in such a way as to keep excess reserves small. Third, the relatively high level of interest rates makes it costly for banks to hold idle reserves rather than earning assets.

9-6 COMMERCIAL BANKS AND THE MONEY MULTIPLIER

Now that we have seen the typical balance sheet of a commercial bank in Table 9-5, we can present another way of thinking about the money multiplier. We show that the money multiplier reflects in part the lending activity of banks, and that part of the money stock results from bank lending.

Suppose the stock of high-powered money has been increased by 1 dollar, say through an open market purchase. We start by considering the individual who sold the bond to the Fed. She is paid with a check, which she takes to her bank. But she, like all portfolio holders, has a currency-deposit ratio of cu. Therefore, of the 1 dollar she has received from the Fed, she wants to keep the fraction $[cu/(1 + cu)]$ as currency. For instance, with cu equal to 0.38, she keeps 27.5 cents ($= 0.38/1.38$ dollars) as currency and deposits 72.5 cents.

At this stage the money stock has increased by only 1 dollar as a result of the increase in the stock of high-powered money. The effect of the deposit on the bank's balance sheet is shown in Table 9-6*a*. The bank has increased its reserves by 72.5 cents. This is a result of its depositing at the Fed the check it

[13] See Milton Friedman and Anna Schwartz, *A Monetary History of the United States* (Princeton, N.J.: Princeton University Press, 1963); and Thomas Mayer, *Monetary Policy in the United States* (New York: Random House, 1968).

TABLE 9-6 A BANK LOAN*

(*a*) Assets		(*a*) Liabilities		(*b*) Assets		(*b*) Liabilities	
Reserves	72.5¢	Deposits	72.5¢	Reserves	8.26¢	Deposits	72.5¢
				Loans	64.24¢		

* In (*a*), reserves and deposits both increase by $(1/1 + *cu*).
In (*b*), the bank lends out fraction (1 − *re*) of the reserves.
cu = 0.38; *re* = 0.114.

received from its customer, which increased reserves by 1 dollar, and then paying out 27.5 cents in currency—leaving it with an extra 72.5 cents of reserves.

Now comes the crucial stage. The bank does not want to hold the *entire* extra 72.5 cents as reserves. The bank's reserve ratio is only *re*, which means that it wants to hold only *re* of every extra dollar of assets it receives in the form of reserves. It wants to hold the rest $(1 - re)$ in some other form. For instance, if *re* is equal to 0.114, it wants to hold 11.4 cents of every dollar of its portfolio as reserves and 88.6 cents in some other form. As we see from Table 9-5, the bank's other assets are loans and securities. We assume the bank wants to loan out 88.6 cents of every extra dollar of assets it receives. When it has received 72.5 cents, it will want to loan out 64.24 cents $(= 0.886 \times 72.5$ cents).

This loan is shown in Table 9-6*b*. For simplicity we think of the borrower receiving the loan in the form of currency. The loan is equal to 64.24 cents. *It is at this stage that the bank's lending activities have increased the money stock by more than the increase in high-powered money.* Why? The person who sold the bond to the Fed has 1 more dollar in money—27.5 cents in currency and the rest in deposits. But the person who took a loan from the commercial bank also has more money holdings—the 64.24 cents lent by the bank. The money stock is up by $1.6424, which is, of course, more than 1 dollar.

The person taking the loan probably wanted to spend it. Thus assume the 64.24 cents is spent. The person receiving the 64.24 cents now wants to hold a fraction $(cu/1 + cu)$ as bank deposits. But of that amount deposited in that person's bank, the bank will want to lend out a fraction $(1 - re)$. Clearly the process can keep going for a long time.

Table 9-7 shows the successive steps by which the money multiplier builds up as a result of the decisions of individuals to deposit part of their increased money holdings in the banks, and the decision of the banks to make loans (or buy securities). Round 1 is the process described in Table 9-6, ending with the bank making a loan. Round 2 starts when the borrower spends the loan, and the person receiving the proceeds holds some of that amount as currency and deposits the rest in a bank. Round 2 ends once again with a bank loan, and so forth.

We can now add up the increases in currency, deposits, reserves, and bank credit occurring over all the rounds together, that is, during the entire process. As in the Appendix to Chapter 7, we are now dealing with the sum of an infinite series, denoted here as *SUM*. That sum is given by[14]

[14] *Technical note:* The formula for the sum of a geometric series, which can in general be written

$$SUM = 1 + a + a^2 + \cdots$$

where a is a number between minus and plus 1, is

$$SUM = \frac{1}{1 - a}$$

If you have not met geometric series before, you may want to take an example, say, $a = 1/4$, and start adding the terms in the first formula in the footnote. You will soon find your answer coming close to $4/3$, which is the answer given by the second formula in the footnote.

$$SUM = 1 + \left(\frac{1 - re}{1 + cu}\right) + \left(\frac{1 - re}{1 + cu}\right)^2 + \left(\frac{1 - re}{1 + cu}\right)^3 + \cdots$$
$$= \frac{1 + cu}{cu + re} \tag{7}$$

We use Equation (7) in arriving at the bottom row of Table 9-7, which shows that currency increases by the fraction $[cu/(cu + re)]$ of \$1 following the increase in H of \$1, that deposits increase by $[1/(cu + re)]$, that reserves increase by $[re/(cu + re)]$, and finally, that credit increases by $[(1 - re)/(cu + re)]$.

Adding the increases in currency and deposits, we discover that the two together have risen by the amount $[(1 + cu)/(cu + re)]$, which is nothing other than the money multiplier. Table 9-7 thus provides another way of thinking about the money multiplier. The table also shows how, and by how much, the banking system creates loans (or buys securities) when the Fed increases high-powered money.

EXAMPLE

With cu equal to 0.38 and re equal to 0.114, we have currency increasing by \$0.77 $(cu/cu + re)$, deposits by \$2.02 $(1/cu + re)$, reserves by \$0.23 $(re/cu + re)$, and bank loans by \$1.79 $(1 - re)(cu + re)$. The money stock increases by \$2.79, or 2.79 times the increase in the stock of high-powered money. This is the value of the money multiplier calculated earlier.

TABLE 9-7 MULTIPLE EXPANSION OF BANK DEPOSITS, BANK LOANS, AND THE MONEY MULTIPLIER

Increase in H	Increase in currency	Increase in deposits	Increase in reserves	Increase in bank loans	Stage
1	$\frac{cu}{1+cu}$	$\frac{1}{1+cu}$	$\frac{re}{1+cu}$	$\frac{1-re}{1+cu}$	Round 1
	$\frac{cu}{1+cu}\left(\frac{1-re}{1+cu}\right)$	$\frac{1}{1+cu}\left(\frac{1-re}{1+cu}\right)$	$\frac{re}{1+cu}\left(\frac{1-re}{1+cu}\right)$	$\frac{1-re}{1+cu}\left(\frac{1-re}{1+cu}\right)$	Round 2
	$\frac{cu}{1+cu}\left(\frac{1-re}{1+cu}\right)^2$	$\frac{1}{1+cu}\left(\frac{1-re}{1+cu}\right)^2$	$\frac{re}{1+cu}\left(\frac{1-re}{1+cu}\right)^2$	$\frac{1-re}{1+cu}\left(\frac{1-re}{1+cu}\right)^2$	Round 3
	$\frac{cu}{1+cu}\left(\frac{1-re}{1+cu}\right)^n$	$\frac{1}{1+cu}\left(\frac{1-re}{1+cu}\right)^n$	$\frac{re}{1+cu}\left(\frac{1-re}{1+cu}\right)^n$	$\frac{1-re}{1+cu}\left(\frac{1-re}{1+cu}\right)^n$	Round $n + 1$
	$\frac{cu}{1+cu} SUM$	$\frac{1}{1+cu} SUM$	$\frac{re}{1+cu} SUM$	$\frac{1-re}{1+cu} SUM$	Total*
	$\frac{cu}{cu+re}$	$\frac{1}{cu+re}$	$\frac{re}{cu+re}$	$\frac{1-re}{cu+re}$	After substituting for SUM from Equation (7)

* SUM is defined by Equation (7).

MULTIPLE EXPANSION OF BANK DEPOSITS

Table 9-7 illustrates the process known as the *multiple expansion of bank deposits.* It shows how an increase in deposits leads to further deposits, and therefore how the money multiplier works. There is one further interesting aspect of the results shown in Table 9-7. It is possible to say that the banking system creates money in the sense that if there were not a banking system, a \$1 increase in H would increase the money stock only by \$1. With the banking system, the \$1 increase in H leads to more than a \$1 increase in M.[15]

The interesting point is that at each stage of the process, no one bank believes it is, or can be said to be, creating money. At each stage, each bank in the process is only lending out money that has been deposited with it. Each bank manager would rightly, and no doubt vehemently, deny that the bank is creating money. The system as a whole, though, is creating money through the successive rounds of loans and subsequent further bank deposits.

9-7 THE MONEY SUPPLY FUNCTION AND THE INSTRUMENTS OF MONETARY CONTROL

We have, in Sections 9-3 to 9-5, gone behind formula (4) for the determinants of the money supply and studied the behavior of the three variables in that formula. We now return to Equation (4) to summarize the implications of Sections 9-3 to 9-5 by writing a *money supply function* that takes account of the behavior of the banking system and the public:

$$M = \frac{1 + cu}{cu + re}\overline{H}$$
$$= mm(i, i_D, r_R, cu, \sigma)\overline{H} \tag{8}$$

In Equation (8) we have written the money multiplier *mm* as a function of interest rates, the discount rate, required reserves, the currency-deposit ratio, and the variability of deposit flows.

Given the stock of high-powered money, the supply of money increases with the money multiplier *mm*. The multiplier, in turn, increases with the level of market interest rates and decreases with the discount rate, the required reserve ratio, and the currency-deposit ratio. We refer to Equation (8) as a supply *function* because it describes the behavior that determines the money supply, given $\overline{H}$. Note that the Fed affects the money supply through three routes: $\overline{H}$, controlled primarily through open market operations; the discount rate i_D; and the required reserve ratio r_R.

Of these three *instruments of monetary control,* open market operations are the most frequently used. There is a fourth instrument of monetary control

[15] Bank loans and purchases of securities are described as *bank credit.* It is the existence of bank credit that makes the money stock larger than the stock of high-powered money. If banks did not extend credit (that is, did not make loans or buy securities), the entire multiple expansion process would never get off the ground, and we would have $M = H$.

that we have not emphasized in Equation (8). The currency-deposit ratio is affected by the interest rate paid on deposits, and that interest rate is controlled by the Fed's Regulation Q.[16] By raising the permissible interest rate on deposits, the Fed can reduce cu and increase the money multiplier. Thus the four major instruments of monetary control are open market operations, the required reserve ratio, the discount rate, and interest rates on bank deposits.

Why can the Fed not control the money stock exactly? The reasons emerge by looking at the money multiplier formula in Equation (8). We have assumed cu is constant—but in fact cu varies from month to month, and the Fed does not know in advance exactly what its value will be. The public does not keep an exactly constant ratio of currency to deposits. Similarly, the reserve ratio re varies, both because deposits move among banks with different reserve ratios and because banks change the amount of excess reserves they want to hold.

In brief, the Fed cannot control the money stock exactly because the money multiplier is not constant, nor is it fully predictable.

9-8 EQUILIBRIUM IN THE MONEY MARKET

We can now combine the money supply function in Equation (8) with the money demand function developed in Chapter 8 to study money market equilibrium. For that purpose we will continue to assume, as we generally have so far, that the price level is given at the level $\bar{P}$. Furthermore, for the purposes of this section, we will take the level of real income as given, $Y = Y_0$. With both the price level and level of income fixed, money demand depends only on the interest rate, while the money market equilibrium will determine the equilibrium interest rate and quantity of money for given $\bar{P}$ and Y_0.

The equilibrium condition in the money market is that the real money supply M/P equals the demand for real balances, or

$$\frac{M}{P} = L(i, Y) \tag{9}$$

Substituting expression (8) for M in the money market equilibrium condition (9), and noting $P = \bar{P}$ and $Y = Y_0$ by assumption, we obtain

$$mm(i, i_D, r_R, cu, \sigma)\frac{\bar{H}}{\bar{P}} = L(i, Y_0) \tag{10}$$

We now have the money market equilibrium condition in terms of interest rates and the other variables affecting the supply of, and demand for, money.

In Figure 9-5 we show the real money demand function (LL) as a downward-sloping schedule, drawn for a given level of real income. The real

[16] Regulation Q is being phased out over a period of 6 years starting in March 1980.

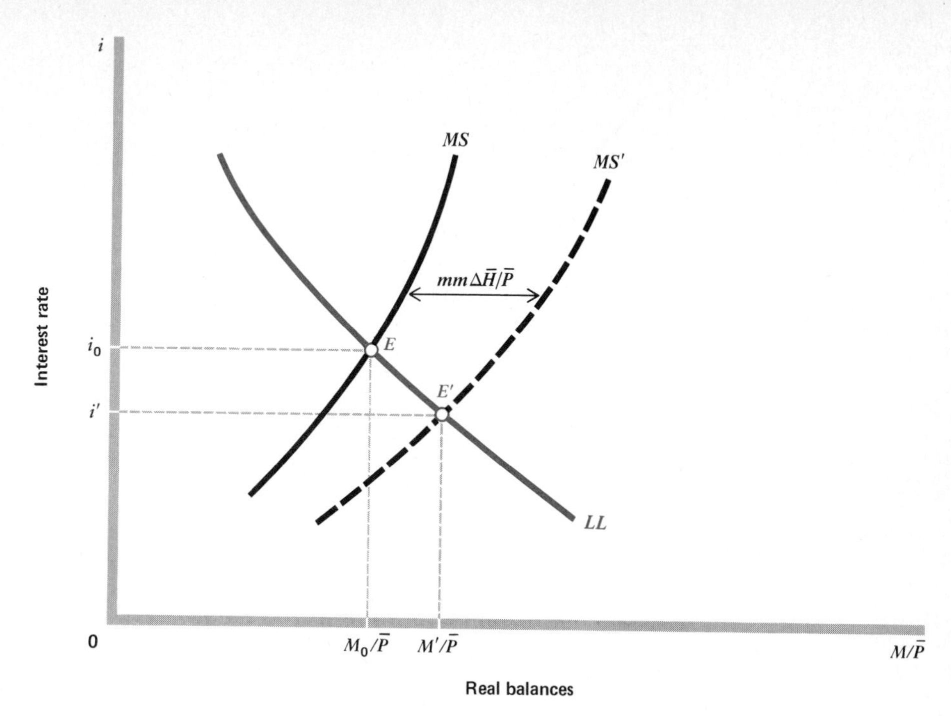

FIGURE 9-5 EQUILIBRIUM IN THE MONEY MARKET. The downward-sloping curve is the demand for money. The quantity of money demanded is greater the lower the interest rate. The upward-sloping curve is the money supply function. This slopes up because, given the quantity of high-powered money, banks reduce their demand for excess reserves when the interest rate rises. Thus the reserve ratio is lower and the money multiplier bigger at higher interest rates. The equilibrium interest rate and stock of money are determined at the intersection point E. An increase in the stock of high-powered money shifts the money supply curve out to the right, with a new equilibrium at E'. The money stock increases, and the interest rate decreases.

money supply function (*MS*), given $\overline{P}$, σ, cu, i_D, and r_R, is upward-sloping and is drawn for a given stock of high-powered money $\overline{H}$. The positive slope of *MS* reflects the fact that at higher interest rates, banks prefer to hold fewer reserves, so that the money multiplier is higher.[17] The equilibrium money supply and interest rate are jointly determined at point *E*.

Figure 9-5 studies the effects of monetary policy on interest rates, given the price level and the level of income. An increase in the monetary base of $\Delta\overline{H}$ shifts the *MS* curve to the right to *MS'*, increasing the money stock and reducing the interest rate. Because the interest rate falls, the money multiplier declines as a result of the increase in $\overline{H}$. But there is no question, despite the decline in the interest rate, that the money stock increases.

[17] At sufficiently high interest rates, the money supply schedule becomes vertical. This is because excess reserves become zero at very high interest rates and the banks cannot squeeze out any more loans on the basis of the reserves they have.

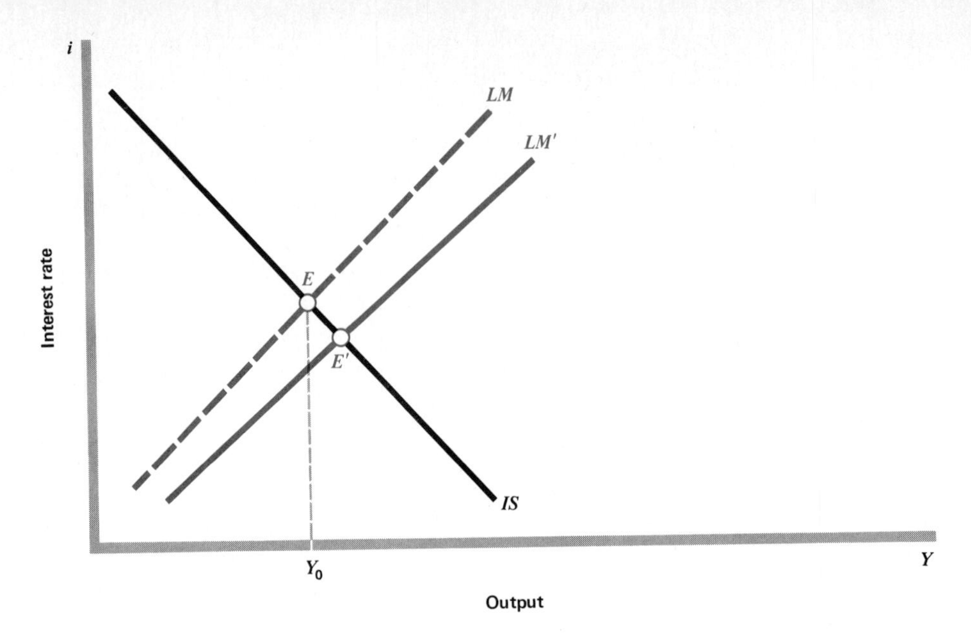

FIGURE 9-6 THE EFFECTS OF AN INCREASE IN THE STOCK OF HIGH-POWERED MONEY. As Figure 9-5 shows, an increase in the stock of high-powered money reduces the interest rate at which the money market is in equilibrium, for any given level of output. That means the *LM* curve shifts down when $\overline{H}$ is increased. The equilibrium interest rate falls and the level of output rises as the economy moves from E to E'.

In Figure 9-5, we, in effect, look at the effects of a change in the stock of high-powered money on the *LM* curve. Figure 9-6 shows the *IS-LM* curves familiar from Chapter 4. The *LM* curve represents the combinations of income levels and the interest rate at which the money market is in equilibrium. What happens to the *LM* curve when the stock of high-powered money is increased? In Figure 9-5 we saw that for any given level of income (Y_0), an increase in $\overline{H}$ reduces the equilibrium interest rate. That means that the *LM* curve in Figure 9-6 shifts down to *LM'* when $\overline{H}$ increases. The equilibrium shifts from E to E', with output rising and the interest rate falling. Thus our analysis confirms that the Fed, by increasing the stock of high-powered money, can reduce the interest rate and increase the level of income.

This is basically what we concluded in Chapter 4, except there we assumed the Fed controlled the money supply directly. Now we know the Fed does not have such direct control; nonetheless it can shift the *LM* curve and affect output and the interest rate.

CHANGES IN THE DISCOUNT RATE

We can also analyze the effects of an increase in the discount rate on the position of the *LM* curve and thus on the interest rate and output. We know from our analysis of the demand for reserves that banks will hold higher reserves when the discount rate rises, because it is more expensive to run short of reserves when the cost of borrowing to cover the shortage is higher.

An increase in the discount rate therefore reduces the money multiplier. Figure 9-7 shows in terms of the money market, at a given level of income, that the money supply curve shifts up to *MS′*. The interest rate rises at the given level of income. In terms of the *IS-LM* analysis, the *LM* curve would therefore move to the left (we do not show this here, but ask you to do so in problem 13), the interest rate would rise, and output would fall. Thus an increase in the discount rate is a contractionary monetary policy.

9-9 CONTROL OF THE MONEY STOCK AND CONTROL OF THE INTEREST RATE

We make a simple but important point in this section: The Fed cannot simultaneously set both the interest rate and the stock of money at any given target levels that it may choose. If the Fed wants to achieve a given interest rate target, such as 5 percent, it has to supply the amount of money that is demanded at that interest rate. If it wants to set the money supply at a given

FIGURE 9-7 THE EFFECTS OF AN INCREASE IN THE DISCOUNT RATE. An increase in the discount rate increases the amount of reserves that banks want to hold at each level of market interest rates ***i***. Thus the money multiplier is reduced, and the money supply function shifts from *MS* to *MS′*. Accordingly, the market interest rate rises, and the quantity of real balances falls. An increase in the discount rate is a contractionary monetary policy.

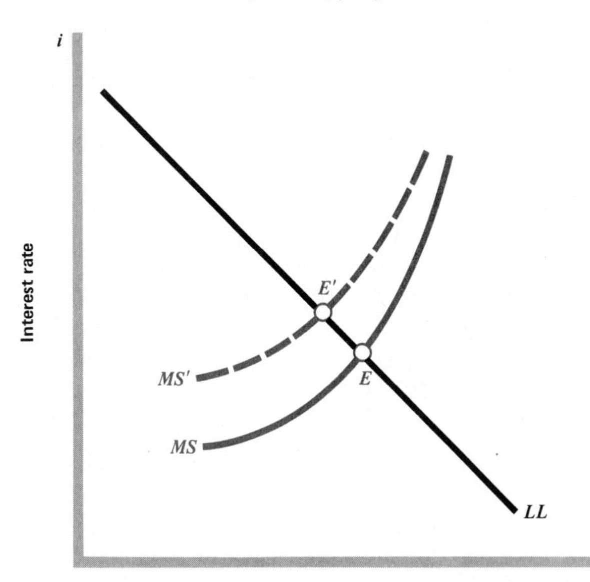

BOX 9-1

THE DEREGULATED BANKING SYSTEM

From the time of the great depression to 1980, the Fed directly controlled the maximum interest rates that banks could pay their depositors. By 1986, the controls on interest rates will be gone. Here we ask how the monetary system will work without controls on the interest rates banks can pay their depositors.

We assume that competition will ensure that banks pay depositors interest rates that move closely with market interest rates, such as the rate on Treasury bills and commercial paper. This means that changes in the market interest rate i will have little effect on the demand for deposits. If deposits are earning zero interest, then a change in the interest rate on alternative assets from, say, 5 to 6 percent will cause people to shift out of deposits to other assets. But if deposits are earning 1 percent less than other assets, then when the interest rate on those other assets goes up from 5 to 6 percent, that on deposits rises from 4 to 5 percent. There is not likely to be much substitution out of deposits to other assets.

The reforms will thus make the demand for deposits less interest-sensitive. At the same time, the demand for currency would become *more* interest-sensitive, because now currency earns zero interest while deposits earn interest that moves with the general level of interest rates.

FIGURE 1 EFFECTS OF DEREGULATION OF INTEREST RATES. Deregulation of interest rates that banks can pay their depositors will make the LL curve more nearly vertical, shifting it from LL to a shape more like LL', The supply of money MS will become more elastic, shifting to MS', because currency demand will become more elastic. For simplicity we show the curves changing by pivoting around point E, though that need not happen. Given the new money supply curve MS', an increase in H will still shift MS' down and reduce the market interest rate. Thus the LM curve would shift, and monetary policy would retain its ability to affect the economy.

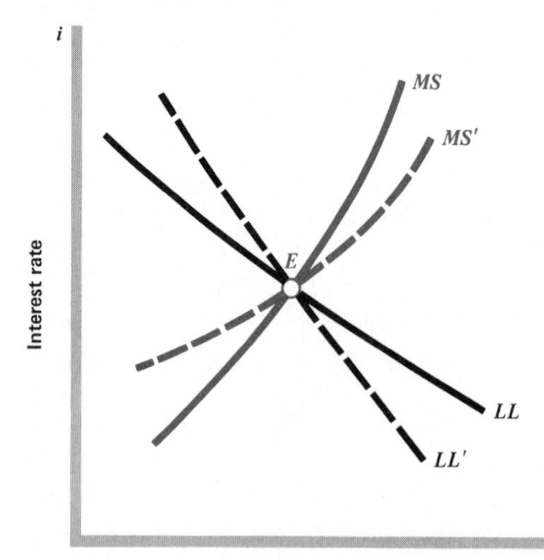

Now when the interest rate rises, people tend to hold more deposits and less currency. The demand for one part of the money stock (currency) would be made more interest-elastic and the other (deposits) less interest-elastic as a result of the reforms. On balance, we assume, the demand becomes less elastic, and thus the *LL* curve in Figure 1 becomes steeper (*LL'*).

The *MS* curve would become more elastic, or flatter, as a result of the monetary deregulation. That is again because the money multiplier becomes more interest-sensitive since the demand for currency is more interest-elastic. As the interest rate rises, people reduce their holdings of currency, leaving more high-powered money available for reserves, which can support a larger money stock per dollar of high-powered money. The new *MS'* curve is shown in Figure 1.

An increase in *H* still moves the *MS* curve down and reduces the interest rate. The *LM* curve in an *IS-LM* model would shift to the right as before, the interest rate would fall, and the level of output would rise. But the slope of the *LM* schedule is also affected.

We have argued that the monetary reform would make the demand for money less interest-elastic, thus tending to make the *LM* curve more nearly vertical. But there is an offsetting effect from money supply. The money supply function becomes *more* elastic as a result of the reform, tending to make the *LM* curve flatter.

We cannot say in advance which effect will be more important—whether the *LM* curve will become steeper or flatter. The result depends on whether the increased supply elasticity outweighs the reduced demand elasticity. On balance then, the monetary changes need not have a major effect on the way in which open market operations of the Fed affect the economy. An open market purchase will still reduce interest rates and shift the *LM* curve down, thus tending to increase the level of output.

level, say, $550 billion in the month of June 1985, it has to allow the interest rate to adjust to equate the demand for money to that supply of money.

Figure 9-8 illustrates the point. Suppose that the Fed, for some reason, decides that it wants to set the interest rate at a level i^* and the money stock at a level M^*, but that the demand-for-money function is as shown in *LL*. The Fed is able to move the money supply function around, as in Figure 9-6, but it is not able to move the money demand function around. It therefore has to accept that it can set only the combinations of the interest rate and the money supply that lie along the money demand function. At the interest rate i^*, it can have the money supply $M_0/\overline{P}$. At the target money supply $M^*/\overline{P}$, it can have the interest rate i_0. But it cannot have both $M^*/\overline{P}$ and i^*.

The point is sometimes put more dramatically as follows. When the Fed decides to set the interest rate at some given level and keep it fixed—a policy known as *pegging* the interest rate—it loses control over the money supply. It has to supply whatever amount of money is demanded at that interest rate. If the money demand curve were to shift, because of income growth, say, the Fed would have to increase the stock of high-powered money to increase the money supply.

As an operational matter, the Fed, in its day-to-day operations, can more

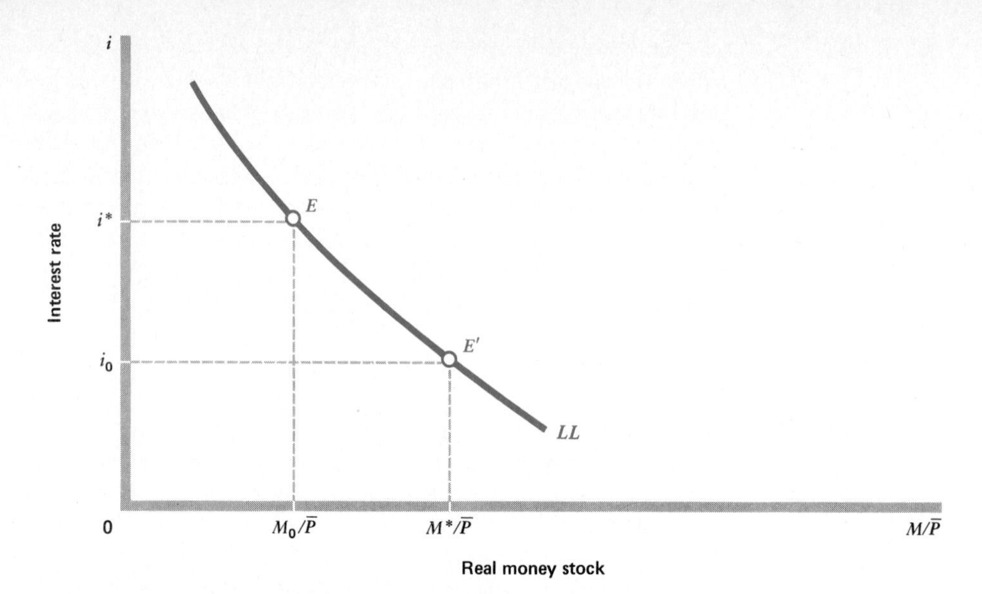

FIGURE 9-8 CONTROLLING THE MONEY STOCK AND INTEREST RATES. The Fed cannot simultaneously set both the interest rate and the money stock levels it wants. Suppose it wanted the interest rate to be i^* and the money stock to be M^*. These two levels are inconsistent with the demand for money, *LL*. If the Fed insists on the interest rate level i^*, it will have to accept a money stock equal to M_0. If instead the Fed wants to set the money stock at M^*, it will end up with an interest rate equal to i_0.

easily control interest rates exactly than it can control the money stock exactly. The Fed buys and sells government securities—primarily Treasury bills—from its *open market desk* in the New York Fed every day. If the Fed wanted to raise the price of government securities (lower the interest rate), it would have to buy the securities at the price it wanted. If it wanted to reduce prices of government securities (raise the interest rate), it would sell a sufficient amount of securities from its large portfolio. Thus, on a day-to-day basis, the Fed can determine interest rates quite accurately.[18]

However, the Fed cannot determine the money supply precisely on a day-to-day basis. For one thing, there is a lag in obtaining data on the money stock. Some time must pass before reasonably good money supply data for a given date become available. That would not affect the Fed's ability to control the money stock if the money multiplier were constant, for then it would be able to deduce, from the behavior of the monetary base, what the money stock was. But as we have seen earlier, the multiplier is not constant. It varies as a result of changes in the currency-deposit and reserve-deposit ratios.

These are *technical* reasons the Fed cannot control the money supply exactly in the sense that the Fed cannot hit the target stock of money exactly even if it wants to. But over a slightly longer period, the Fed can determine

[18] For a description of techniques of monetary control, see Paul Meek, *U.S. Monetary Policy and Financial Markets*, Federal Reserve Bank of N.Y., 1982.

the money supply fairly accurately. As data on the behavior of the money stock and the money multiplier become available, the Fed can make mid-course corrections to its setting of the base. For example, if the Fed were aiming for monetary growth of 5 percent over a given period, it might start the base growing at 5 percent. If it found halfway into the period that the multiplier had been falling, and the money stock therefore growing less than 5 percent, it would step up the growth rate of the base to compensate.

The main reason the Fed does not hit its money growth targets are not technical, but rather have to do with its having both interest rate *and* money stock targets, and as we have seen in this section, it cannot hit them both at the same time.

9-10 MONEY STOCK AND INTEREST RATE TARGETS

Over the period since the 1950s, the Fed has moved from an emphasis on the interest rate as a target of monetary policy to a much greater emphasis on the money stock as the variable it tries to control. Indeed, it was not until 1959 that the Fed even began to publish money stock data. In this section we discuss the issues involved in the choice between interest rate and money stock targets.

Making Monetary Policy

Monetary policy is made by the Fed's Open Market Committee, which meets about every 6 weeks and also holds frequent consultations between meetings. At these meetings the Fed issues a *monetary policy directive* to the open market desk in New York describing the type of monetary policy it wants.

In recent years, the directive has instructed the open market desk to conduct open market operations to produce monetary growth or money stock growth within given target ranges. The target ranges for several years, for $M1$ and $M2$, are given in Table 9-8.[19] In addition, the Committee specifies a wide

[19] The Fed specifies, in addition, target ranges for $M3$ and, since 1982, for total nonfinancial debt in the economy. This latter total is the amount of lending to spending units in the economy.

TABLE 9-8 TARGET AND ACTUAL GROWTH RATES OF MONEY*

Period:	1976	1977	1978	1979	1980	1981	1982	1983
$M1$ target range	4.5–7.5	4.5–6.5	4–6.5	1.5–4.5	4–6.5	3.5–6	2.5–5.5	4–8
$M1$ actual	5.8	7.9	7.2	5.5	7.2	5.1	8.5	
$M2$ target range	7.5–10.5	7–10	6.5–9	5–8	6–9	6–9	6–9	7–10
$M2$ actual	10.9	9.8	8.7	8.3	9.0	9.4	9.2	

* Money definitions are those in effect at the time targets were set. Growth rates are for a 1-year period ending in the fourth quarter of the specified year.
Source: Various Federal Reserve Bulletins, *and Federal Reserve Board,* Monetary Policy Objectives 1982 and 1983.

range within which it expects interest rates to be during the period until the next meeting. If interest rates threaten to move outside the range, the Committee members will typically consult (on the telephone) and decide whether to change the instructions to the open market desk.

Interest Rate or Money Targets?

There are two levels on which the discussion of interest rate versus money targets proceeds. (1) The first is at the technical level of the open market desk. The question here is whether a given target level of the money stock can be attained more accurately by holding the interest rate fixed or by fixing H. (2) The second level is that of the economy as a whole. The question here is whether the Fed makes the economy more stable by aiming for a particular money stock or for a particular interest rate.

The analyses for evaluating these questions are similar. We start with and discuss in more detail the second issue.

THE BROAD VIEW

We assume that the Fed aims for the economy to reach a particular level of output. The question is whether it can do that more accurately by targeting the money stock or by fixing interest rates. We should think of the analysis as applying to a reasonably short period such as 3 to 9 months.[20]

Figure 9-9*a* starts with the *IS* and *LM* curves. Recall that the *LM* curve shows combinations of the interest rate and output at which the money market is in equilibrium. The *LM* curve labeled *LM(M)* is the *LM* curve that exists when the Fed fixes the money stock. The *LM* curve labeled *LM(i)* describes money market equilibrium when the Fed fixes the interest rate. It is horizontal at the chosen level of the interest rate i^*.

The problem for policy is that the *IS* and *LM* curves shift in ways that cannot be predicted. When they shift, output ends up at a level different from the target level. In Figure 9-9*a* we show two alternative positions for the *IS* curve, IS_1 and IS_2. We assume that the Fed does not know in advance which *IS* curve will obtain: the position depends, for instance, on investment demand, which is difficult to predict. The Fed's aim is to have income come out as close as possible to the level Y^*.

In Figure 9-9*a* we see that the level of output stays closer to Y^* if the *LM* curve is *LM(M)*. In that case the level of output will be Y_1 if the *IS* curve is IS_1 and Y_2 if the *IS* curve is IS_2. If policy had kept the interest rate constant, we would in each case have a level of income that is further from Y^* : Y_1' instead of Y_1, and Y_2' instead of Y_2.

Thus we have our first conclusion: If output deviates from its equilibrium level mainly because the *IS* curve shifts about, then output is stabilized by

[20] The analysis we are presenting here is based on William Poole, "Optimal Choice of Monetary Policy Instruments in a Simple Stochastic Macro Model," *Quarterly Journal of Economics*, May 1970.

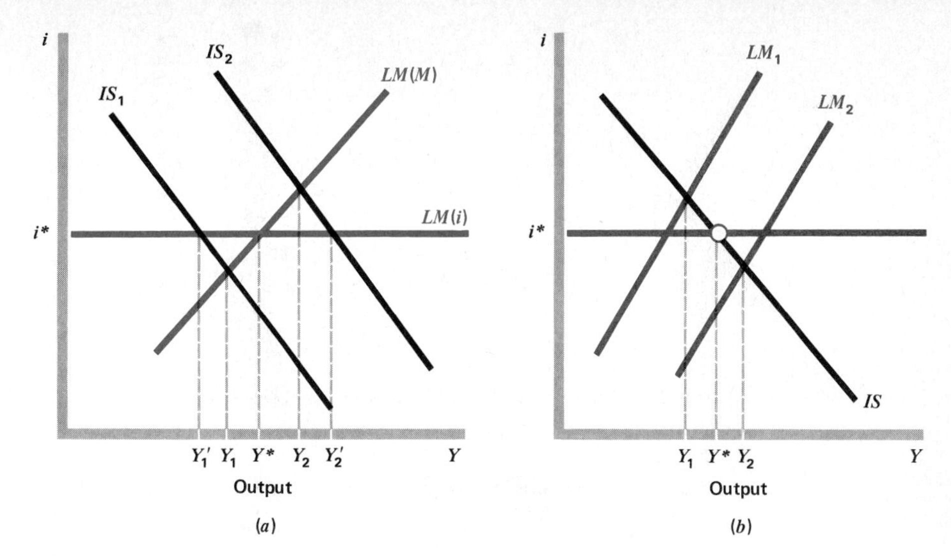

FIGURE 9-9 MONEY AND INTEREST RATE TARGETS. In panel (*a*), the *IS* curve shifts. If the Fed targets the money stock, the *LM* curve is shown by *LM(M)*. *LM(i)* is the *LM* curve when the interest rate is held constant. The aim of policy is to hit output level Y^*. If the *LM* curve is *LM(M)*, the output levels will be either Y_1 or Y_2, depending on where the *IS* curve turns out to be. In the case of an interest rate target, the corresponding levels of output are Y_1' and Y_2', both further from the desired level of output Y^*. Thus monetary targeting leads to more stable output behavior. In panel (*b*) it is the *LM* curve that is shifting, because of shifts in the demand for money. With *LM* shifting and the *IS* curve stable, output will be at the target level Y^* if the interest rate is held constant at i^*, but will be at either Y_1 or Y_2 if the money stock is held constant. Therefore the Fed should target the interest rate if the demand-for-money function is unstable.

keeping the money stock constant. The Fed should, in this case, have monetary targets.

We can see from Figure 9-9*a* why it is more stabilizing to keep *M* than *i* constant. When the *IS* curve shifts to the right and the *LM(M)* curve applies, the interest rate rises, thereby reducing investment demand and moderating the effect of the shift. But if the *LM(i)* curve applies, there is no resistance from monetary policy to the effects of the *IS* shift. Monetary policy is thus automatically stabilizing in Figure 9-9*a* when the *IS* curve shifts, and the money stock is held constant.

In Figure 9-9*b* we assume that the *IS* curve is stable. Now the uncertainty about the effects of monetary policy results from shifts in the *LM* curve. Assuming that the Fed can fix the money stock, the *LM* curve shifts because the money demand function shifts. The Fed does not know when it sets the money stock what the interest rate will be. The *LM* curve could end up being either LM_1 or LM_2. Alternatively the Fed could simply fix the interest rate at level i^*. That would ensure that the level of output is Y^*.

If the Fed were to fix the money stock, output could be either Y_1 or Y_2. If it fixes the interest rate, output will be Y^*. Thus we have our second conclusion: If output deviates from its equilibrium level mainly because the demand-for-money function shifts about, then the Fed should operate monetary policy by fixing the interest rate. That way it automatically neutralizes the effects of the shifts in money demand. In this case the Fed should have interest rate targets.

It is important to note that the argument discusses Fed targeting over short periods. The Fed should readjust its targets in light of the changing behavior of the economy. It is *not* to be thought of as announcing or desiring that the interest rate will be, say, 5 percent forever. Rather, the target interest rate might be 5 percent at the bottom of a recession and 15 percent when the economy is overheating. Similarly, the money growth targets could also be adjusted in response to the state of the economy.

THE SHORT RUN AND THE LONG RUN

This analysis describes well the reasons why the Fed might choose either the money stock or the interest rate as a target at which to aim over a period of less than a year. In particular, at a time when money demand is shifting a lot—as it did in the seventies and early eighties—the Fed should pay attention to the behavior of interest rates. The reason is that when money demand is shifting, it is hard to evaluate the meaning of money stock data.

Suppose the Fed is aiming for nominal GNP to increase only 2 percent and we find ourselves in a recession. How could we tell things are going wrong? By looking at interest rates. If there has been a shift in money demand, increasing the quantity demanded at any interest rate, the interest rate will rise. If the Fed were paying attention to the behavior of the interest rate, it would automatically adjust the money stock to account for that shift in money demand. That is why interest rate targets are useful.

But monetarist proponents of money stock targeting have another argument in favor of targeting the money stock. They might concede that in the short run the Fed may do better targeting interest rates. But, they say, a policy of targeting interest rates can over long periods lead to big trouble, by steadily raising the growth rate of money. They point, rightly, to the fact that changes in monetary policy take a long time to affect the economy. They argue that increases in the money stock lead eventually to inflation, and that the only way to avoid inflation in the long run is by keeping money growth moderate. The problem with focusing on interest rates, they suggest, is that while the Fed keeps its eye on interest rates, the growth rate of money and the inflation rate increase.[21] This argument appears to fit the facts of the 1960s and 1970s well.

It is for that reason that the Fed moved to a two-track targeting system. It has *long-run* targets for money growth. Thus it has continually to worry

[21] Another argument for money targeting arises from the distinction between real and nominal interest rates. The nominal interest rate can rise because inflation is expected. If the Fed fights this increase in the nominal rate by increasing the money stock, it is only feeding the inflation. We examine this argument in more detail in Chap. 13.

whether it is following monetary paths consistent with desired low rates of inflation.[22] At the same time it pays attention to interest rates in case its monetary targets lead in the short run to recession or inflation if there are shifts in money demand.

By "pays attention" we mean that the Fed has target ranges for both money and interest rates. When either moves close to the limits of the range, the Fed has a meeting to discuss why this is happening. And then it gives fresh instructions to the open market desk. Typically these instructions are to compromise on both targets. For instance, if the interest rate is very high, the Fed would allow the growth rate of money to increase slightly. Or if the growth rate of money is high, the Fed would increase the target range for the interest rate.

At some times, for instance, at the end of 1982, the Fed paid less attention to its money targets than to others. It does that when it is not certain whether the demand function for money is shifting. At the end of 1982 MMDAs and Super-NOW accounts were being introduced (as discussed in Chapter 8), and it was not obvious what effect these changes were having on the demand for money. In those circumstances, the Fed paid closer attention to interest rates and less attention to the money stock.

MONETARY CONTROL

We noted at the beginning of this section that there were two levels at which the issue of interest rates versus money targets arose. We have already discussed the economywide issue. There is also a much narrower question: If the Fed has already decided that it wants to target the money stock, will it come closer to target by setting the interest rate at a given level, or will it do better by fixing H? Here the horizon is a very short one, of a few weeks—about the period between meetings of the Open Market Committee.

We do not go into the full analysis, but sketch the arguments, which rely on a diagram like Figure 9-5, and an analysis very similar to that used in Figure 9-9. The result of such an analysis involves the relative stability of money demand and the money multiplier and shows the following:

1 If the demand-for-money function is stable, then fixing interest rates ensures that the Fed will come closest to hitting the target money stock.
2 If the demand-for-money function is relatively unstable (compared with the money multiplier), then the Fed should target H if it wants to hit its target level of the money stock most closely.

Note again that we are talking about a very short period. In this context, the Fed may want to target an interest rate in the short run *in order to hit the target money stock most closely.* More generally, this analysis suggests again

[22] A comprehensive discussion of monetary policy and the Fed's operating procedures, generally critical of monetary targeting, is presented in Ralph C. Bryant, *Controlling Money. The Federal Reserve and Its Critics*, The Brookings Institution, 1983.

why the Fed should pay attention to the behavior of both interest rates and the money stock. Shifts in money demand may reveal themselves first in movements in interest rates — and if the Fed wants to stabilize the economy, it should respond to shifts in money demand.

The New Monetary Policy of 1979

On October 6, 1979, at a special Sunday meeting, the Fed's Open Market Committee decided on a major change in the methods of monetary policy. The Fed announced that it was henceforth going to stay close to its target path for monetary policy and allow interest rates to fluctuate more than in the past. The change was made at a time of high inflation (the CPI inflation rate over 1979 was more than 13 percent).

The Fed made the change as part of its program to fight inflation. It wanted to get the inflation rate down, and it wanted everyone to understand that it was committed to doing so, even if that meant interest rates had to reach very high levels.

The change in monetary policy was most evident in the increase in the ranges the Fed presented for target levels of the interest rate. Figure 9-10 shows the changes. Up to the end of 1979, the Fed had specified narrow ranges in which the interest rate could move. As can be seen, the interest rate stayed within these ranges. After the monetary policy reform, the ranges for the interest rate widened. The range increased from about ½ of a percentage point to 5 percent. And not only that — interest rates fluctuated substantially after the change. Thus the change in Fed operating procedure certainly was followed by much larger interest rate fluctuations than before.

But the change did not lead to more stable monetary growth. Figure 9-11 shows target ranges of the money stock in the prereform and postreform period. There is no marked increase in the stability of monetary growth. That is, there is no evidence that after the reform the Fed kept closer to its target path for the money stock than it had before. We also note that the money stock typically, toward the end of the year, approaches or exceeds the upper range.

Was the reform a failure? After all, interest rates became more unstable while there was no improvement in the Fed's aim at money growth. Opinions differ, depending on the interpretation of the reasons for the greater instability of money growth after the reform. One view is that, because of financial innovations, the Fed was dealing with a much more unstable environment, and therefore did well to maintain money growing as close to target paths as it had in the past. Proponents of this view argue that without the increase in interest rate movements, the money stock would have fluctuated more in the 1979–1983 period than it did.

The monetarist view blames the Fed for most of the instability that followed the reform. Their argument is that the Fed permitted wide swings in the money supply (these can be seen in Figure 9-11) because it was still worried about the level of interest rates. Other critics argue that technical

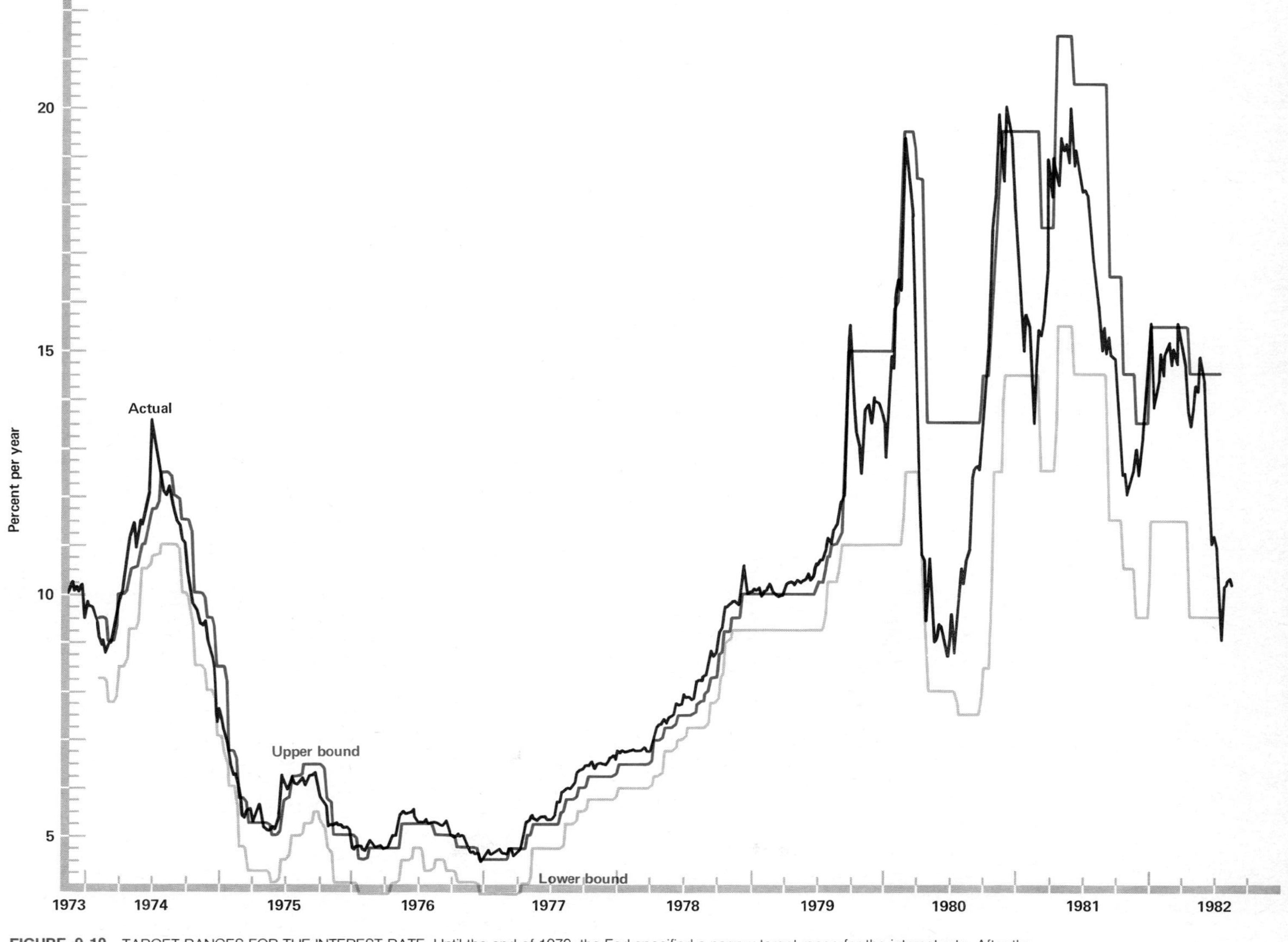

FIGURE 9-10 TARGET RANGES FOR THE INTEREST RATE. Until the end of 1979, the Fed specified a narrow target range for the interest rate. After the monetary policy change in October 1979, the range was widened. Interest rates have fluctuated much more since then than they did earlier. (*Source:* Ralph C. Bryant, *Controlling Money*, Brookings Institution, 1983.)

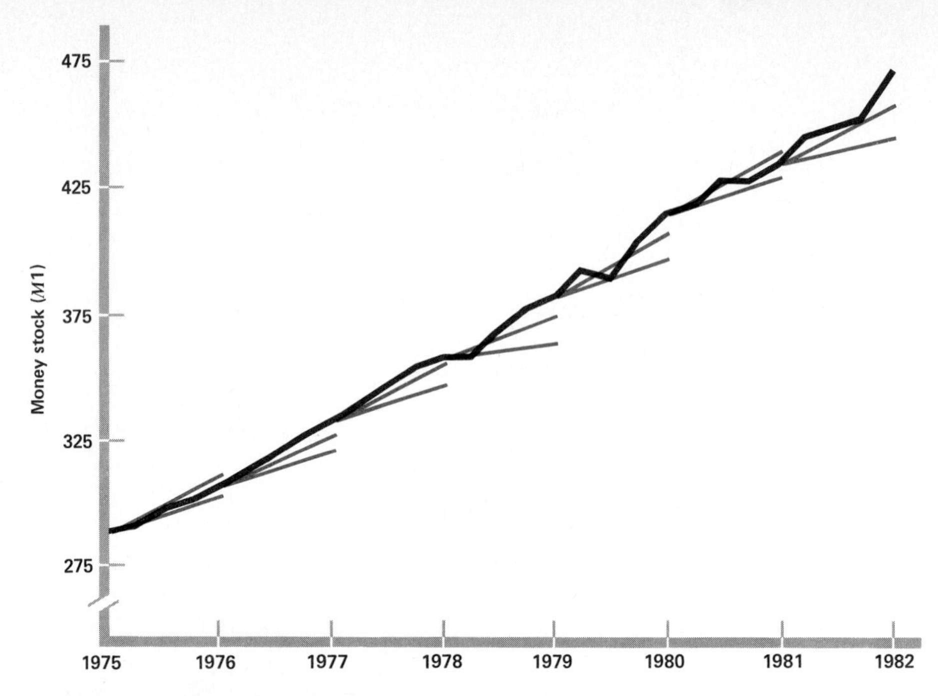

FIGURE 9-11 TARGET AND ACTUAL MONEY STOCK ($M1$), 1975–1982. (*Source:* Various issues of the *Federal Reserve Bulletin.*) *Notes:* (1) Money stocks and targets are as of definitions of M1 when target was set. (2) Target ranges for money stock are shown in red, and the actual path of money stock is shown in black. Target ranges are set at the end of one year to apply 1 year later. New targets are set each year.

details of the Fed's operating procedure in attempting to control the money stock produced the instability.[23]

A final verdict on this topic is not in. Some further considerations are presented in Chapter 10, where we discuss the difficulties of policy making in general. Our own view is that rigid commitment to monetary targets is unwise in light of shifts in the money demand function, and that the Fed should target interest rates as well as the stock of money. We note also that on a year-to-year basis the Fed has maintained quite stable monetary growth—much more stable than that of other leading countries, such as Japan and Germany. The Fed thus does not let money growth get out of hand: if the growth rate is very

[23] William Poole, in "Federal Reserve Operating Procedures: A Survey and Evaluation of the Historical Record since October 1979," *Journal of Money, Credit, and Banking,* November 1982 (part 2), makes this argument. For some counterarguments, see, in the same issue, the Comment by John Paulus.

high for a short time — as in Figure 9-11 — the growth rate will typically later be reduced to compensate for the high growth and bring the money stock closer to target.

9-11 SUMMARY

1 The stock of money is determined by the Fed through its control of the monetary base (high-powered money); the public, through its preferred currency-to-deposit ratio; and the banks, through their preferred reserve holding behavior.
2 The money stock is larger than the stock of high-powered money because part of the money stock consists of bank deposits, against which the banks hold less than 1 dollar of reserves per dollar of deposits.
3 The money multiplier is the ratio of the money stock to high-powered money. It is larger the smaller the reserve-deposit ratio and the smaller the currency-deposit ratio.
4 The Fed creates high-powered money when it buys assets (for example, Treasury bills, gold, foreign exchange) by creating liabilities on its balance sheet. Purchases of these assets by the Fed increase banks' reserves held at the Fed and lead through the multiplier process to a larger increase in the money stock.
5 The money multiplier builds up through an adjustment process in which banks make loans (or buy securities) because deposits have increased their reserves to more than desired levels.
6 The Fed has 3½ basic policy instruments: open market operations, the discount rate, its ability to fix reserve requirements for the banks, and (the half — expiring in 1986) the right to fix the interest rate that banks can pay on their deposits.
7 Because the desired reserve-deposit ratio of banks decreases as the interest rate rises, the supply-of-money function is interest-elastic. A second reason for the supply-of-money function (based on a constant stock of high-powered money) to be interest-elastic is that the demand for currency may become interest-elastic when controls on deposit interest rates are removed.
8 The Fed cannot control both the interest rate and the money stock exactly. It can only choose combinations of the interest rate and money stock that are consistent with the demand-for-money function.
9 The Fed operates monetary policy by specifying target ranges for both the money stock and the interest rate. In order to hit its target level of output, the Fed should concentrate on its money targets if the *IS* curve is unstable or shifts about a good deal. It should concentrate on interest rate targets if the money demand function is the major source of instability in the economy.
10 The Fed announced a major change in policy in 1979. The new policy allowed for wider fluctuations in interest rates and more emphasis on

money targets than before. Since then, interest rates have fluctuated more than before the new policy, but money growth has not been noticeably smoother. There is considerable controversy about the reasons for this outcome.

KEY TERMS

Currency-deposit ratio
Reserve-deposit ratio
High-powered money (monetary base)
Money multiplier
Discount rate
Excess reserves
FDIC
Multiple expansion of bank deposits
Money supply function
Money stock and interest rate targets

PROBLEMS

1. Use Figure 9-3 to show how (*a*) an increase in the currency-deposit ratio and (*b*) an increase in the reserve-deposit ratio affect the money stock, given the monetary base.
2. Show how an open market sale affects the Fed's balance sheet and also the balance sheet of the commercial bank of the purchaser of the bond sold by the Fed.
3. When the Fed buys or sells gold or foreign exchange, it automatically offsets or sterilizes the impact of these operations on the monetary base by compensating open market operations. Show the effects on the Fed balance sheet of a purchase of gold and a corresponding sterilization through an open market operation.
4. How much do bank loans and security purchases increase when the Fed increases the monetary base by $1. Give the answer in terms of cu and re. (You may want to use Table 9-7.)
5. Explain how the Fed's balance sheet would be affected if it valued gold at the market price.
6. A proposal for "100 percent banking" involves a reserve-deposit ratio of unity. Such a scheme has been proposed for the United States in order to enhance the Fed's control over the money supply.
   (*a*) Indicate why such a scheme would help monetary control.
   (*b*) Indicate what bank balance sheets look like under this scheme.
   (*c*) Under 100 percent money, how would banking remain profitable?
7. Discuss the impact of credit cards on the money multiplier.
8. By using Figures 9-5 and 9-6 show the effect of an increase in required reserves on:
   (*a*) The equilibrium money supply
   (*b*) Interest rates
   (*c*) The equilibrium level of income
9. The Federal Deposit Insurance Corporation insures commercial bank deposits against bank default. Discuss the implications of that deposit scheme for the money multiplier.
10. Assume required reserves were zero. Would banks hold any reserves?
11. Under what circumstances should the Fed conduct monetary policy by targeting mainly (*a*) interest rates or (*b*) the money stock?
12. Why does the Fed not stick more closely to its target paths for money?
13. Show the effect of a discount rate increase (*a*) on the money supply and (*b*) on income and interest rates.

APPENDIX

We derive the equilibrium money stock and the multiplier by looking at the demand and supply of money and of high-powered money. Consider, first, equilibrium between the supply of money and the demand for money, which, in turn, equals currency plus deposits:

$$M = CU + D \equiv (cu + 1)D \tag{A1}$$

where we have substituted for $CU = cuD$, noting the public's desired ratio of currency to deposits cu.

Equilibrium between the supply of high-powered money and the demand for high-powered money which equals currency plus reserves implies:

$$\overline{H} = CU + RE \equiv (cu + re)D \tag{A2}$$

Again we have expressed the demand side in terms of the desired ratio of currency to deposits and of the banks' desired reserve-deposit ratio re. When (A1) and (A2) both hold, we are in monetary equilibrium because people hold the composition of their money balances in the preferred ratio and banks hold just the right ratio of reserves to deposits.

Dividing (A2) by (A1) yields an expression for the money multiplier:

$$M/\overline{H} = mm \equiv \frac{1 + cu}{cu + re} \tag{A3}$$

The money multiplier thus depends on the cu ratio and the re ratio. We can also use (A3), multiplying both sides by $\overline{H}$, to obtain the money supply in terms of the principal determinants mm and $\overline{H}$:

$$M = mm\,\overline{H} \tag{A4}$$

In writing (A4) we remember that mm is dependent on the currency-deposit preferences of the public and the reserve-deposit preferences of banks. It thus takes into account preferences about the composition of balance sheets.

10

PROBLEMS OF STABILIZATION POLICY

This is the first of two chapters that discuss the problems of macroeconomic policy making. An understanding of the general difficulties of carrying out successful stabilization policies — policies to reduce the fluctuations of the economy — helps explain past economic performance. Figure 10-1, which shows the unemployment rate over the period 1926–1982, gives the clear impression that stabilization policy has left something to be desired. Particularly in 1974–1975 and 1980–1982, unemployment in the post-World War II period has frequently been high, although the disaster of the great depression years has fortunately not been repeated.

The reason for discussing the problems of stabilization policy here is that the preceding chapters have laid out a clear body of theory that seems to show exactly the policy measures that can be used to maintain full employment. We saw that high unemployment, or a large GNP gap, can be reduced by an expansion in aggregate demand. An increase in aggregate demand, in turn, can be achieved by expansionary monetary or fiscal policies: an increase in the money supply, a reduction in taxes, an increase in government spending, or an increase in transfers. Similarly, a boom can be contained by restrictive monetary or fiscal policies.

The policies needed to prevent the fluctuations in unemployment shown in Figure 10-1 accordingly appear to be simple and obvious. The policy maker knows the full-employment level of output. If there is unemployment, she can use a model, such as the *IS-LM* model, to calculate the

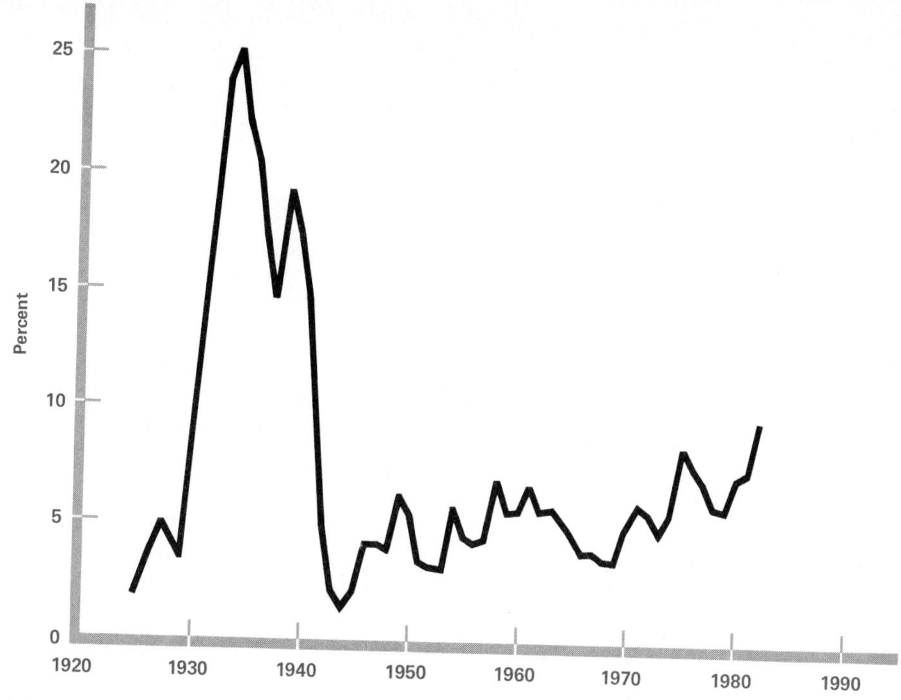

FIGURE 10-1 THE CIVILIAN UNEMPLOYMENT RATE IN THE UNITED STATES, 1926–1982. (*Sources:* Data Resources, Inc. and *Historical Statistics of the United States,* Bureau of the Census, 1976.)

level of government spending or taxes needed to get income to the full-employment level. But if it is so simple, how did the fluctuations in Figure 10-1 occur? The answer must be that policy making is far from simple. Part of the difficulty arises from the possible *conflict between the maintenance of full employment and the target of low inflation.* That important issue is discussed in Chapters 13 and 14. Other difficulties are described in this chapter.

We begin by discussing the types of disturbance that cause the economy to move away from the full-employment level of output in the first place. Then we briefly describe *econometric models,* models of the economy with specific numerical values for parameters and multipliers, that can be used to assist policy making. The bulk of the chapter is taken up by a discussion of three factors that in large measure account for the failure of policy continually to achieve its targets. The three *handicaps of policy making are:*

1 Lags in the effects of policy
2 The role of expectations in determining private sector responses to policy
3 Uncertainty about the effects of policy

In a nutshell, we are going to argue that a policy maker who (1) observes a disturbance, (2) does not know whether it is permanent or not, and (3) takes time to develop a policy which (4) takes still more time to affect behavior and (5) has uncertain effects on aggregate demand, is very poorly equipped to do a perfect job of stabilizing the economy.

10-1 ECONOMIC DISTURBANCES

Before identifying in detail the obstacles in the way of successful policy making, we discuss economic disturbances in terms of their sources, persistence, and importance for policy. Disturbances are shifts in aggregate demand or aggregate supply, or shifts in money demand or money supply, that cause output, interest rates, or prices to diverge from their target paths.

We return to the *IS-LM* model as the framework for the discussion of economic disturbances in this chapter. In Figure 10-2 we show the *IS* and *LM* schedules and also the full-employment level of output, $\bar{Y}$. The economy is initially at full emplyment at point *E*. What disturbances might cause the economy to move away from full employment? Obviously, anything that shifts the *IS* and/or *LM* curves would disturb the economy and move it away from *E*.

In terms of overall economic impact, the major disturbances to the economy—the forces moving *IS* and *LM* curves—have typically been wars. The effects of the increases in government spending associated with World War II, the Korean war, and the Vietnam war can be seen in Figure 10-1 in the very low unemployment rates in those period. Of these, World War II had the largest impact on the economy. At the height of the war, in 1944, federal government spending exceeded 40 percent of GNP.

As shown in Figure 10-2, an increase in government spending would shift the *IS* schedule upward and therefore lead to an excess demand for goods. To contain aggregate spending to the full-employment level of output, increased government spending would have to be offset by a reduction in private demand, that is, a reduction in investment and/or consumption spending. Investment spending can be reduced by allowing the interest rate to rise, and consumption spending can be reduced by increasing income taxes. These conventional economic policies may not be sufficient in wartime, however. In World War II more direct methods of reducing investment and consumption were used. A system was set up in which investment projects had to be licensed. That system served to reduce the overall rate of private investment and also to direct investment toward areas helpful for the war effort. There was also some rationing of consumption goods, which reduced consumption expenditure as some of the rationed demand spilled over into increased saving rather than being diverted toward other goods. Thus, the aggregate level of consumption spending was reduced by using rationing to reduce the consumption of various goods essential for the war effort (gasoline, tires, meat, shoes, etc.).[1]

[1] In passing, it is worth considering for a moment why partial rationing might work as a macroeconomic policy, that is, as a policy reducing aggregate demand. The reason must be that part of the expenditure that is precluded by rationing does not shift to other goods but, instead, increases saving, that is, future consumption.

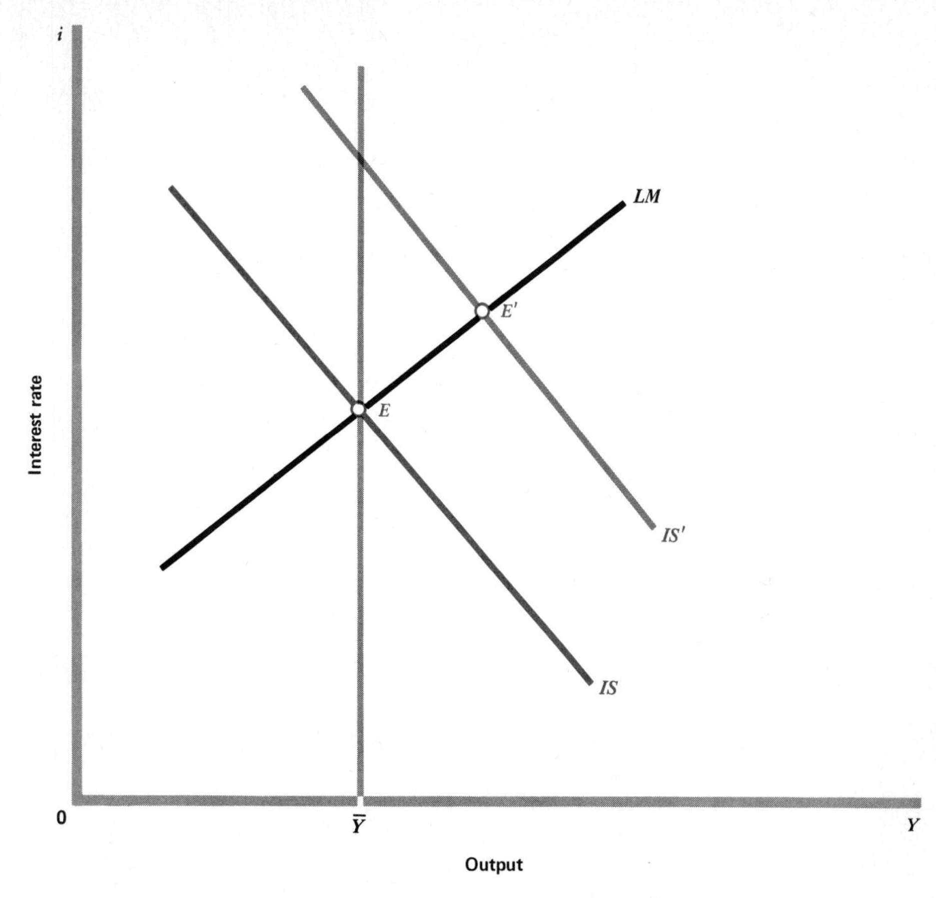

FIGURE 10-2 AN AGGREGATE DEMAND DISTURBANCE. The economy is initially in equilibrium at point E, with level of output $\overline{Y}$. An increase in government spending (for example, for defense) shifts the IS curve to IS'. This disturbance tends to raise the level of output above the full-employment level. Monetary and/or fiscal policy, or even rationing, may be used to keep the level of demand in check, shifting the IS' curve back to IS and/or shifting the LM curve up and to the left.

Changes in government spending or tax policies not connected with wars may also constitute economic disturbances. Government spending or taxes may be increased or reduced for reasons which have to do with the government's view of desirable social policies. Those changes too may affect the level of aggregate demand if not accompanied by appropriate monetary and fiscal policies.

Other economic disturbances that lead to changes in aggregate demand, which originate in the private sector, are shifts in the consumption or investment function. If consumers decide to consume more out of their disposable income at any given level of income, the *IS* curve of Figure 10-2 shifts upward, tending to increase the level of income. If there is no economic explanation for the shift in the consumption function, then it is attributed to a change in the tastes of consumers between consumption and saving. In such a case, we describe the shift as a disturbance.

Similarly, if investment spending increases for no apparent economic reason, then we attribute the increase to an unexplained change in the optimism of investors about the returns from investment. Again, we regard that change in investment behavior as a disturbance to the system. Changes in the optimism of investors are sometimes described as changes in their *animal spirits*—a term that suggests that there may be little rational basis for those spirits.[2] Some shifts in the investment function are caused by new inventions that require large amounts of investment for their successful marketing, such as the development of the railroads in the nineteenth century and the spread of the automobile in the 1920s.

Shifts in the demand for money may affect the interest rate, and thus indirectly affect the rate of investment; they, too, constitute a possible source of private sector economic disturbances.

Disturbances that we have not yet incorporated in our basic theoretical framework also affect the level of income. These include increases in exports, caused by changes in foreigners' demand for our goods, which tend to increase the level of income. Changes in supply conditions, such as the oil price increases of 1973–1974 and 1979–1980, will affect the level of income and are discussed in Chapter 12. In Chapter 13, we also discuss the possibility that the behavior of wages may constitute a source of economic disturbances.

Finally, there is the interesting and important possibility that disturbances may be caused by the policy makers themselves. There are two different arguments concerning this possibility. First, since policy making is difficult, it is entirely possible that the attempts of policy makers to stabilize the economy could be counterproductive. Indeed, a forcefully stated and influential view of the causes of the great depression[3] argues that an inept monetary policy by the Federal Reserve System was chiefly responsible for the severity of the depression. The argument of Friedman and Schwartz is basically that the officials in charge of the Federal Reserve System in the early 1930s did not understand the workings of monetary policy and therefore those officials carried out a policy that made the depression worse rather than better.

The second argument that policy makers themselves may be responsible for economic disturbances arises from the relationship between election

[2] As we noted in Chap. 7, Keynes, in particular, argued that shifts in the investment function were a major cause of fluctuations in the economy. See J. M. Keynes, *The General Theory of Employment, Interest and Money* (New York: Macmillan, 1936), Chap. 22.

[3] See Milton Friedman and Anna J. Schwartz, *The Great Contraction* (Princeton, N.J.: Princeton University Press, 1965).

results and economic conditions in the period before the election.[4] It appears that incumbents tend to be reelected when economic conditions, primarily the unemployment rate, are improving in the year before the election. Accordingly, it is tempting for incumbents to try to improve economic conditions in the period before the election; their efforts may involve tax reductions or increases in government spending. It is now quite common to talk of the *political business cycle.* The political business cycle consists of economic fluctuations produced by economic policies designed to help win elections.

It has been argued that election results are significantly affected by the *growth rate,* rather than the level, of income, in the year leading up to an election. If that is so, then it is tempting indeed for governments to start an expansion in an election year. Despite the difficulties of policy making, it is always easy, by cutting taxes, increasing government spending, and easing monetary policy, to start an economic expansion in the short run—though not to control it later when its inflationary consequences appear. While some evidence supports the notion of a political business cycle, the argument should be regarded as tentative because the link between economic conditions and election results is not yet firmly established.

We proceed next to discuss econometric models and the three factors that make the task of policy makers far more difficult than an overliteral interpretation of the simple *IS-LM* model in Figure 10-2 might suggest.

10-2 ECONOMETRIC MODELS FOR POLICY MAKING AND FORECASTING

In Figure 10-3 we show the typical situation facing economic policy makers. Something has happened that created a recession. Output is at level Y_0 rather than full-employment level $\overline{Y}$. How should policy makers react if they want to get output back to the full-employment level? The *IS-LM* model gives a number of choices. One possibility is to increase the money stock. Or taxes could be reduced, or government spending increased.

Suppose the decision has been made to attempt to return to full employment at point E^*, with the interest rate remaining at i^*. Suppose also that the plan is to do this by increasing government spending and at the same time expanding the money supply. The *IS* curve has to be shifted to *IS′* and the *LM* curve to *LM′*.

Such plans are, however, not detailed enough. The policy makers need to know not only in what direction to shift government spending and the money stock, but also *how much* to change them. If government spending should be increased by $50 billion, it will not do much good to increase it by $5 billion. But if it should be increased by only $5 billion, an increase in government spending of $50 billion will push the economy well beyond the point of full

[4] See, for example, Edward R. Tufte, *Political Control of the Economy* (Princeton, N.J.: Princeton University Press, 1978).

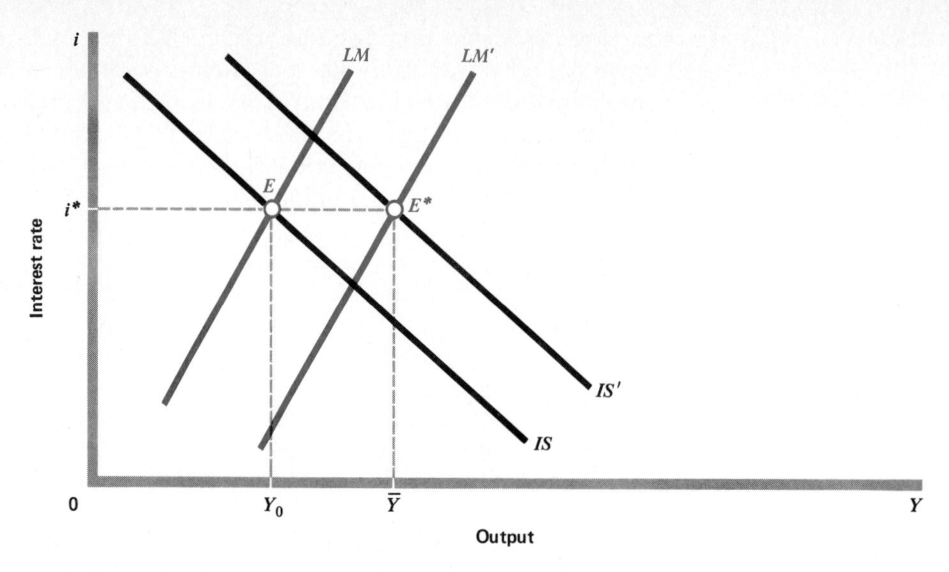

FIGURE 10-3 POLICIES TO END A RECESSION. The economy is in a recession at point E. Policy makers plan to return to full-employment output at the interest rate i^*, at point E^*. The IS curve has to be shifted to IS' and the LM curve to LM'. This requires expansionary fiscal and monetary policy. The precise amounts to increase government spending and the money stock can be calculated from the government spending and monetary policy multipliers.

employment and create inflationary pressures. The policy makers have to know not only the medicines to prescribe, but also the right doses.

In other words, they have to know the *multipliers*, associated with monetary and fiscal policy. To calculate these multipliers, they typically rely on *econometric models*. An econometric model is an equation or a set of equations with numerical values for parameters, based on the past behavior of the economy, describing the behavior of some specific sectors of the economy or the economy as a whole.

Figure 10-4 shows estimates of the effects of monetary policy in the DRI (Data Resources, Inc.) model. The monetary policy change permanently increases the amount of unborrowed reserves held by the banks by $1 billion in period zero. The figure shows the resultant changes in GNP in subsequent periods. (The changes in GNP are measured as a percent of GNP.) There is very little change in GNP in period 1, but then the effect builds up, reaching a peak after 2 years before falling again.

Figure 10-4 presents a *dynamic multiplier*, with the effects of monetary policy on real GNP first building up and then dying away.[5] The monetary policy multiplier in Figure 10-4 seems to be exactly what is needed for policy making. We thus want to look more closely at econometric models.

Econometric models that describe the entire economy are, as we should

[5] Dynamic multipliers were defined in Chap. 6.

expect, called *macroeconometric models.*[6] Macroeconometric models differ enormously in size. The smallest model may be a single equation that estimates how the level of real GNP depends on the money stock and fiscal policy variables. By contrast, the WEFA (Wharton Econometric Forecasting Associates, Inc.) model attempts to predict 10,000 variables, among them the level of GNP, the inflation rate, interest rates, and prices and output levels in particular industries.[7]

THE BIG MODELS

Many econometric models are owned by corporations, which sell the forecasts and analyses produced by the models. The best known large commercial macroeconometric models are the DRI model, the CHASE (Chase Econometric Associates Inc.) model, and the WEFA model. Customers receive the forecasts of the model for the behavior of the economy over the next few

[6] We do not describe the statistical methods of estimating such models. For an introduction to the statistical methods, see Robert S. Pindyck and Daniel L. Rubinfeld, *Econometric Models and Economic Forecasts,* 2d ed. (New York: McGraw-Hill, 1981).

[7] Stephen K. McNees, in "The Recent Record of Thirteen Forecasters," *New England Economic Review,*" September/October 1981, provides some details on several models used for macroeconometric forecasting.

FIGURE 10-4 MONETARY POLICY MULTIPLIER FROM THE DRI MODEL. (*Source: The Data Resources Review of the U.S. Economy,* April 1983, p. 1.18.) The figure shows the dynamic multiplier for a one-time increase in unborrowed reserves, which corresponds to an open market purchase by the Fed. The increase takes place in period zero, and the figure shows how much higher GNP would be as a result in subsequent periods. The effects of the open market purchase increase over time. After the end of the first year, we show the effects of the increase in reserves on GNP only for every fourth quarter, to keep the figure from being too cluttered.

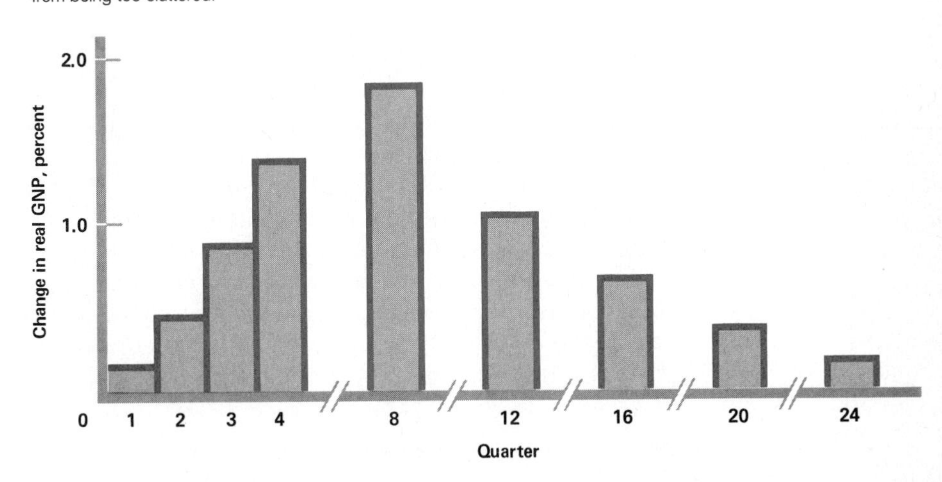

quarters and years.[8] These forecasts are based on assumptions about future economic policy and also about such important factors as future oil prices.

Macroeconometric models are also used by the government. The Federal Reserve Board in Washington uses a model it originally helped develop, now called the MPS (MIT-Penn-SSRC) model to predict the effects of different policy choices. The Department of Commerce maintains and uses the BEA (Bureau of Economic Analysis) model.

The models mentioned rely for the modeling of aggregate demands on an extended *IS-LM* framework. They estimate equations for the components of aggregate demand, consumption, different categories of investment, exports, and state and local government spending. The consumption function, for instance, would be similar to the sophisticated consumption function we discussed in Chapter 6. In modeling the financial markets, the models will typically include a money demand function similar to that which we presented in Chapter 8. They may also include a money supply *function* like that of Chapter 9, relating the stock of money to the supply of high-powered money. In brief, we can think of the aggregate demand side of most of the larger econometric models as attempts to describe statistically the extended *IS-LM* framework outlined in Chapters 4 and 5 and developed in Chapters 6 through 9.

There are, in addition, many smaller models with much less detail. Among these is the St. Louis model, produced by the St. Louis Federal Reserve Bank, which starts from an equation that links the behavior of nominal GNP to monetary and fiscal policy. It thus leaves out the details of the way in which policy affects the economy, and looks only at the final effects of policy. Four additional equations allow the model to predict the level of real as well as nominal GNP (and thus the GNP deflator and the inflation rate) and also to predict interest rates.

To be useful for policy making, and for selling forecasts to the public, the models, of course, have to predict the rate of inflation as well as the level of output. For this purpose the large models include an aggregate supply sector. The outlines of the theory of aggregate supply will be described in Chapters 11 to 13.

FORECAST ACCURACY

How accurate are the models? There are many different models, none of them predicting exactly the same set of variables, and none of them predicting better than all the other models on all occasions. There is thus no simple answer to the question of how well econometric models in general predict.

Table 10-1 gives some idea of the accuracy of econometric forecasts. In November and December each year the Federal Reserve Bank of Richmond collects forecasts for the next year from a large number of different forecasters. At the end of 1982, for instance, the Richmond Fed collected forty forecasts. Table 10-1 shows the median forecasts for the growth rate of real

[8] Customers also typically obtain access to computer programs and data associated with the models.

TABLE 10-1 ECONOMETRIC FORECASTS*

	REAL GNP (% CHANGE)			INFLATION RATE (GNP DEFLATOR)		
Year	Actual	Predicted	Error	Actual	Predicted	Error
1978	5.3	4.2	−1.1	8.5	5.9	−2.6
1979	1.7	1.5	−0.2	8.1	7.1	−1.0
1980	−0.3	−0.8	−0.5	9.8	8.2	−1.6
1981	0.9	2.4	1.5	8.9	9.1	0.2
1982	−1.2	2.8	4.0	4.5	7.1	2.6
Average error (1971–1982)			1.7			1.7
1983	?	2.5		?	5.1	

* These are the median forecasts from those collected.
Source: Federal Reserve Bank of Richmond, *Business Forecasts 1983*, p. 7; forecast for 1983 from p. 5.

GNP and the inflation rate collected since 1978. We show, in addition, the average error made by the median forecasts over the period 1971–1982.[9] Also, we give what the Richmond Fed describes as typical forecasts for 1983. Since the final data for 1983 will be available only after this book is published, you will have to fill in for yourself in the table how well or badly the forecasters did in 1983.

It is quite clear from Table 10-1 that econometric forecasting is not perfect. But it is not random either. For the years 1978–1980 the forecasts of real GNP growth are reasonably accurate. Inflation for 1978–1980 was substantially underpredicted. The 1982 recession obviously caught the forecasters by surprise. Instead of the predicted real growth of 2.8 percent, we had negative real growth, of minus 1.2 percent. Inflation too was substantially overpredicted.

Why do the forecasters make mistakes? One reason is that unexpected events happen over the next year; for instance, economic policy may be different than the forecasters expected when they made their predictions, or the price of oil may rise—or for that matter fall—unexpectedly. But this is not the only reason. A second reason is that the models themselves are not accurate. That is, even when the actual values of government spending, the money stock, the price of oil, etc., are fed into a model, it does not respond with the actual values of real GNP, or the inflation rate, or the unemployment rate. Why? Because we do not know accurately how the economy works.[10]

With this description of econometric models as background, we are ready

[9] Two definitions are needed. First, the *median forecast* for each variable is the middle forecast when the forecasts are lined up in order. Second, the average error in Table 10-1 is the *average absolute error*—the average difference between the forecast and the actual value of the variable, whether positive or negative. For instance, if there are three forecasts, with errors of −3, −1, and 5, the average absolute error is 3 [= (3 + 1 + 5)/3].

[10] Indeed, one of the most useful pieces of statistical information that comes with econometric model estimates is a measure of the confidence that can be attached to estimates of parameters and also multipliers.

to discuss the three handicaps of policy making: lags, expectations, and uncertainty about the effects of policy.

10-3 LAGS IN THE EFFECTS OF POLICY

Suppose that the economy was at full employment and has been affected by an aggregate demand disturbance that reduces the equilibrium level of income below full employment in Figure 10-3 toward point E. Suppose further that there was no advance warning of this disturbance and that, consequently, no policy actions were taken in anticipation of its occurrence. Policy makers now have to decide *whether at all* and *how* to respond to the disturbance.

The first concern—and the first difficulty—should be over the permanence of the disturbance and its subsequent effects. Suppose the disturbance is only transitory, such as a one-period reduction in consumption spending. When the disturbance is transitory so that consumption rapidly reverts to its initial level, the best policy may be to do nothing at all. Provided suppliers or producers do not mistakenly interpret the increase in demand as permanent but, rather, perceive it as transitory, they will absorb it by production and inventory changes rather than capacity adjustments. The disturbance will affect income in this period but will have very little permanent effect. Policy actions generally do not affect the economy immediately. Any policy actions taken to offset the disturbance this period, for example, a tax reduction, will have their impact on spending and income only over time. In later periods, however, the effects of the initial fall in demand on the level of income will be very small, and without the policy action the economy would tend to be very close to full employment. The effects of a tax cut, therefore, would be to raise income in later periods and move it away from the full-employment level. Thus, if the disturbance is temporary and it has no long-lived effects and policy operates with a lag, then the best policy is to do nothing.

Figure 10-5 illustrates the main issue. Assume an aggregate demand disturbance reduces output below potential, starting at time t_0. Without active policy intervention output declines for a while but then recovers and reaches the full-employment level again at time t_2. Consider next the path of GNP under an active stabilization policy, but one that works with the disadvantage of lags. Thus, expansionary policy might be initiated at time t_1 and start taking effect some time after. Output now tends to recover faster as a consequence of the expansion and, because of poor dosage and/or timing, actually overshoots the full-employment level. By time t_3, restrictive policy is initiated, and some time after, output starts turning down toward full employment and may well continue cycling for a while. If this is an accurate description of the potency or scope of stabilization policy, then the question must seriously arise whether it is worth trying to stabilize output or whether the effect of stabilization policy is, in fact, to make things worse. Stabilization policy may actually *destabilize* the economy.

One of the main difficulties of policy making is in establishing whether or not a disturbance is temporary. It was clear enough in the case of World War II that a high level of defense expenditures would be required for some years.

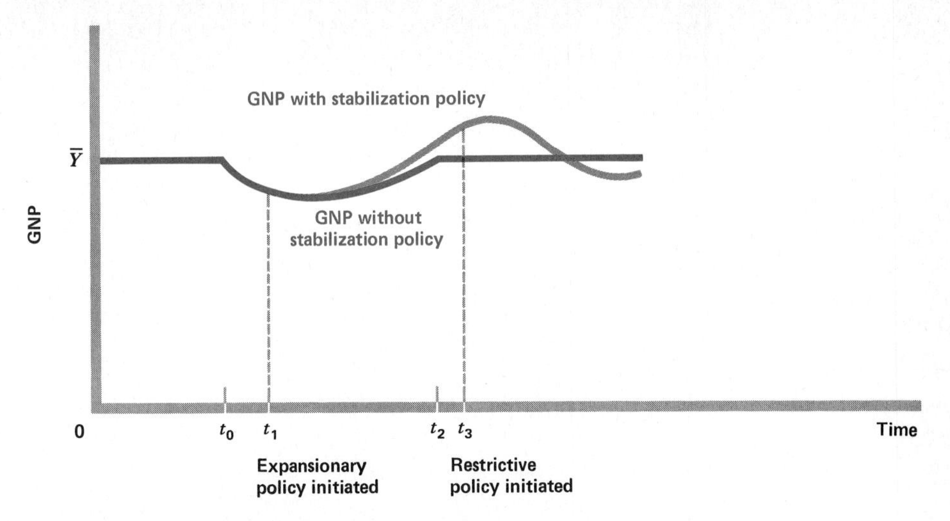

FIGURE 10-5 LAGS AND DESTABILIZING POLICY. A disturbance at time t_0 reduces output below the full-employment level. It takes until t_1 before policy responds, and there is a further lag until the policy starts working. By the time the full effects of the policy are evident, output would already have returned to the full-employment level even without policy. But because a policy action has been taken, output now rises *above* the full-employment level and then fluctuates around $\overline{Y}$. The lags in policy thus have made policy a source of fluctuations in output that would not otherwise have happened.

However, in the case of the Arab oil embargo of 1973–1974, it was not clear at all how long the embargo would last or whether the high prices for oil that were established in late 1973 would persist. At the time, there were many who argued that the oil cartel would not survive and that oil prices would soon fall—that is, the disturbance was temporary. That did not turn out to be true. Let us suppose, however, that it is known that the disturbance will have effects that will last for several quarters, and that the level of income will, without policy, be below the full-employment level for some time. What lags do policy makers encounter?

We now consider the steps required before a policy action can be taken after a disturbance has occurred, and then the process by which that policy action affects the economy. There are delays, or lags, at every stage. It is customary and useful to divide the lags into an *inside* lag, which is the time period it takes to undertake a policy action—such as a tax cut, or an increase in the money supply—and an *outside* lag, which describes the timing of the effects of the policy action on the economy. The inside lag, in turn, is divided into recognition, decision, and action lags.

The Recognition Lag

The *recognition lag* is the period that elapses between the time a disturbance occurs and the time the policy makers recognize that action is required. This lag could, in principle, be *negative* if the disturbance could be predicted and appropriate policy actions considered *before* it even occurs. For example, we know that seasonal factors affect behavior. Thus it is known that at Christmas the demand for currency is high. Rather than allow this to exert a restrictive effect on the money supply, the Fed will accommodate this seasonal demand by an expansion in high-powered money.

In other cases the recognition lag has been positive, so that some time has elapsed between the disturbance and the recognition that active policy was required. This was true, for example, of the 1974–1975 recession. The unemployment rate started increasing very rapidly in the third, and particularly in the fourth, quarter of 1974. It is now clear that expansionary action was required no later than September 1974. Yet, in October 1974, the administration was still calling for a tax *increase* to reduce aggregate demand and inflation. By December, a sharp increase in the unemployment rate led forcefully to the recognition by most economists that there was need for expansionary action. Only in January, in his State of the Union address, did the President call for a tax reduction, which was implemented in the Tax Reduction Act of 1975. Solow and Kareken have studied the history of policy making and have found that on average the recognition lag is about 5 months.[11] That lag was found to be somewhat shorter when the required policy was expansionary and somewhat longer when restrictive policy was required. The speed with which tax cuts follow sharp increases in unemployment was clearly evident in both 1975 and 1980.

The major reason that there is any recognition lag at all, apart from the delay in collecting statistical data, is that it is never certain what the consequences of a disturbance will be. That uncertainty, in turn, is a result of economists' lack of knowledge of the workings of the economy (which was discussed above) as well as political uncertainties.

The Decision and Action Lags

The recognition lag is the same for monetary and fiscal policy. The Federal Reserve Board, the Treasury, and the Council of Economic Advisers are in constant contact with one another and share their predictions about the future course of the economy. For the *decision lag*—the delay between the recognition of the need for action and a policy decision—by contrast there is a difference between monetary and fiscal policy. The Federal Reserve System's Open Market Committee meets frequently to discuss and decide on policy. Thus, once the need for a policy action has been recognized, the decision lag for monetary policy is short. Further, the *action lag*—the lag between the policy decision and its implementation—for monetary policy is also short.

[11] See John Kareken and Robert Solow, "Lags in Monetary Policy," in *Stabilization Policies*, prepared for the Commission on Money and Credit (Englewood Cliffs, N.J.: Prentice-Hall, 1963). See, too, the review of the evidence in Thomas Mayer, *Monetary Policy in the United States* (New York: Random House, 1968), Chap. 6, and Michael J. Hamburger, "The Lag in the Effect of Monetary Policy: A Survey of the Recent Literature," Federal Reserve Bank of New York, *Monthly Review*, December 1971. This question has not, so far as we know, been reexamined recently.

The major monetary policy actions, we have seen, are open market operations and changes in the discount rate. These policy actions can be undertaken almost as soon as a decision has been made. Thus, under the existing arrangements for the Federal Reserve System, the decision lag for monetary policy is short and the action lag practically zero.

However, fiscal policy actions are less rapid. Once the need for a fiscal policy action has been recognized, the administration has to prepare legislation for that action. Next, the legislation has to be considered and approved by both houses of Congress before the policy change can be made. Depending on the degree of agreement between the administration and the Congress, that may be a lengthy process. Even after the legislation has been approved, the policy change has still to be put into effect. If the fiscal policy takes the form of a change in tax rates, it may be some time before the changes in tax rates begin to be reflected in paychecks—that is, there may be an action lag. On occasion, though, as in early 1975 when taxes were reduced, the fiscal decision lag may be short; in 1975 it was about 2 months.

The lengthy legislative process for fiscal policy in the United States has led to repeated suggestions that the President be granted the authority to undertake certain fiscal actions without legislation. One proposal is that the President should be allowed to vary tax rates by limited amounts in either direction without first obtaining specific authorization from Congress but subject to congressional veto.[12] This proposal would reduce the decision lag. Whether such a change is desirable from the economic viewpoint depends obviously on whether the President would, on average, make changes in tax rates that tend to offset disturbances to the economy. Do remember, though, the political business cycle.

BUILT-IN STABILIZERS

The existence of the inside lag of policy making focuses attention on the built-in or automatic stabilizers that we discussed in Chapter 3. One of the major benefits of automatic stabilizers is that their inside lag is zero. Recall from Chapter 3 that the most important automatic stabilizer is the income tax. It stabilizes the economy by reducing the multiplier effects of any disturbance to aggregate demand. The multiplier for the effects of changes in autonomous spending on GNP is inversely related to the income tax rate. The higher the tax rate, the smaller the effects of any given change in autonomous demand on GNP. Similarly, unemployment compensation is another automatic stabilizer. When workers become unemployed and reduce their consumption, that reduction in consumption demand tends to have multiplier effects on output. Those multiplier effects are reduced when a worker receives unemployment compensation and her disposable income is reduced by less than the loss in earnings.

Figure 10-6 therefore shows the practical importance of automatic stabilizers (and active fiscal policy) in the U.S. economy. The figure shows personal

[12] Report of the Commission on Money and Credit, *Money and Credit—Their Influence on Jobs, Prices and Growth* (Englewood Cliffs, N.J.: Prentice-Hall, 1961), pp. 133–137.

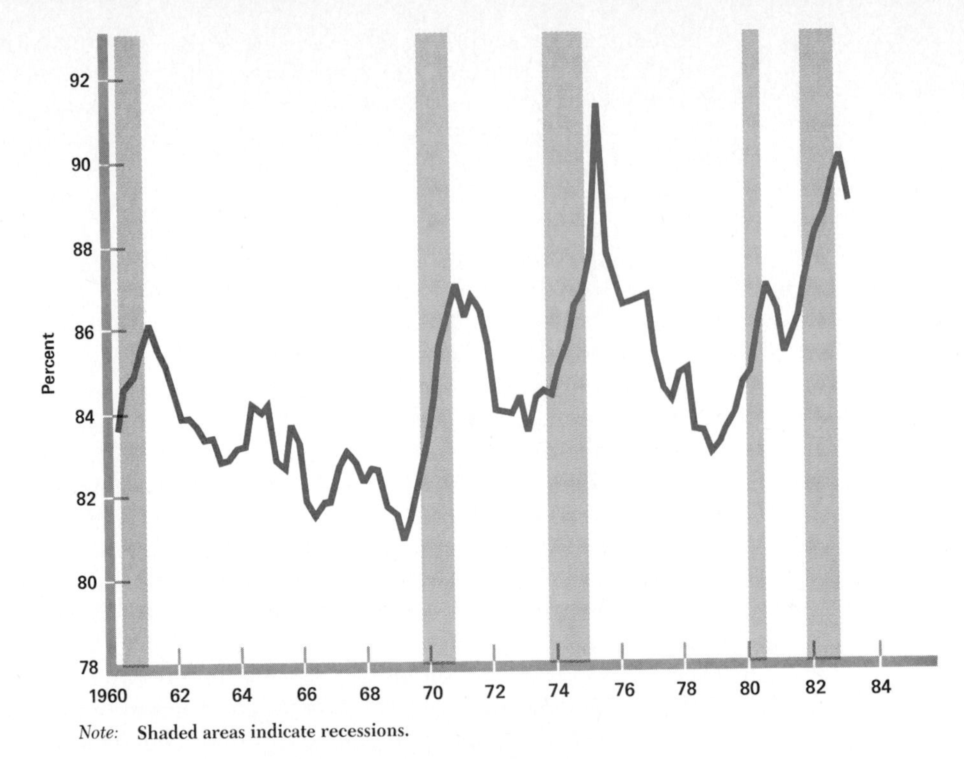

Note: **Shaded areas indicate recessions.**

FIGURE 10-6 AUTOMATIC STABILIZERS: THE RATIO OF PERSONAL DISPOSABLE INCOME TO NATIONAL INCOME. (*Source:* Data Resources, Inc.)

disposable income as a fraction of national income. Personal disposable income, as you will remember from Chapter 2, is the income that actually accrues to households after all taxes and inclusive of all transfers. The figure brings out the fact that during periods of a high GNP gap—the early sixties, the 1969–1971 period, 1974–1975, and 1981–1982—personal disposable income rises relative to national income. In these periods, transfer payments rise and the growth in income tax collection slows down. For the whole period 1960–1982, the ratio of personal disposable income to national income was, on average, 85 percent. In a recession such as 1974–1975, however, the ratio increases sharply, whereas during a period of high aggregate demand and expansion such as in 1965–1969, the ratio declines below average.[13] In problem 6 we ask you what the counterpart of the increase in the ratio of personal disposable income to national income is in a recession. We also ask what ratio you would expect to decline sharply when the ratio of personal disposable income to national income rises.

Although built-in stabilizers have desirable effects, they cannot be carried too far without also affecting the overall performance of the economy.

[13] To be precise, the chart reflects both automatic stabilizers and discretionary changes in taxes and transfers. Thus the increase in the ratio in 1975 reflects not only automatic transfers but also the tax rebate of early 1975. The data that would separate out the automatic stabilizers are not conveniently available.

The multiplier could be reduced to 1 by increasing the tax rate to 100 percent, and that would appear to be a stabilizing influence on the economy. But with 100 percent marginal tax rates, the desire to work, and consequently the level of GNP, would be reduced. Thus there are limits on the extent to which automatic stabilizers are desirable.[14] Nonetheless, automatic stabilizers play an important role in the economy; it has been argued that the absence of significant unemployment compensation in the 1930s was one of the major factors that made the great depression so severe, and that the existence of the stabilizers alone makes the recurrence of such a deep depression unlikely.

The Outside Lag

The inside lag of policy is a discrete lag in which policy can have no effect on the economy until it is implemented. The outside lag is generally a distributed lag: once the policy action has been taken, its effects on the economy are spread over time. There is usually a small immediate effect of a policy action, but other effects occur later.

The idea that policy operates on aggregate demand and income with a distributed lag was already shown in Figure 10-4. There we showed the effects of a once-and-for-all increase in bank reserves in period zero. This increase in bank reserves, by affecting interest rates and therefore aggregate spending, changes the level of income in subsequent quarters by the amounts indicated in Figure 10-4. The height of the bars shows the percentage amount by which GNP exceeds the level that it would have reached in the absence of the policy change. The main point to be made is that monetary or fiscal policies taken now affect the economy over time, with most of the effects typically not occurring in the first quarter.

Figure 10-4 makes it clear that the impact of an increase in bank reserves (corresponding to an open market purchase by the Federal Reserve) is initially very small, and that it continues to increase over a long period of time. Thus, if it were necessary to increase the level of employment rapidly to offset a demand disturbance, a large open market purchase would be necessary. But in later quarters, the large initial open market purchase would build up large effects on GNP, and those effects would probably overcorrect the unemployment, leading to inflationary pressures. It would then be necessary to reverse the open market purchase and conduct open market sales to avoid the inflationary consequences of the initial open market purchase.

It should thus be clear that when policy acts slowly, with the impacts of policy building up over time, considerable skill is required of policy makers if their own attempts to correct an initially undesirable situation are not to lead to problems that themselves need correcting. Recall also that we have been talking here about the outside lag, and that the policy action we are considering would be taken only 6 months after the initial disturbance if the inside lag is 6 months long.

[14] For a discussion of the history of automatic stabilizers, see Herbert Stein, *The Fiscal Revolution in America* (Chicago: The University of Chicago Press, 1969).

Why are there such long outside lags? We have already discussed some of the reasons for these lags in Chapter 6 on the consumption function, where current consumption depends on lagged income, and also in Chapter 7 on investment, where the accelerator models imply that investment depends on lagged and current income. Similar lags are also present in the financial sector of the economy, where the demand for money depends on lagged income. Each of these sources of lags creates an outside lag, and their interaction generally produces longer lags than each of the underlying lags.

Because the point is so important, let us describe in more detail how the lags of monetary policy arise. Suppose the Fed conducts an open market purchase. Because aggregate demand depends heavily on lagged values of income, interest rates, and other economic variables, the open market purchase initially has effects mainly on short-term interest rates and not on income. Short-term interest rates, such as the Treasury bill rate, affect long-term interest rates with a lag. The long-term interest rates, in turn, affect investment with a lag, and also affect consumption by affecting the value of wealth.[15] Then when aggregate demand is affected by the initial open market purchase, the increase in aggregate demand itself produces lagged effects on subsequent aggregate demand through the fact that both consumption and investment depend on past values of income. So the effects of an initial open market purchase will be spread through time, as in Figure 10-4.

Monetary versus Fiscal Policy Lags

The discussion of the previous paragraph suggests that fiscal policy and certainly changes in government spending, which act directly on aggregate demand, may affect income more rapidly than monetary policy. This is indeed the case. However, the fact that fiscal policy acts faster on aggregate demand than monetary policy must not lead us to overlook the fact that fiscal policy has a considerably longer inside lag. Moreover, the inside lag for government spending is longer than that for taxes because when the government purchases goods and services, it has to decide what goods to buy, have bids for the sale of those goods submitted by the private sector, and then decide on the award of the contracts. In summary, therefore, fiscal policy is attractive because of the short outside lag, but that advantage is more than offset by a potentially long inside lag.

Our analysis of lags indicates clearly one difficulty in undertaking stabilizing short-term policy actions: it takes time to set the policies in action, and then the policies themselves take time to affect the economy. But that is not the only difficulty. Further difficulties considered in Sections 10-4 and 10-5 arise from uncertainty about the exact timing and magnitude of the effects of policy.

[15] Recall that in Chap. 6 we discussed the life-cycle model of consumption demand, in which consumption is affected by the level of wealth. Part of wealth is the value of stock market assets; the value of stock market assets rises when the long-term interest rate falls. Thus, interest rates affect consumption through a wealth effect.

We have discussed the two basic sources of lags in economic behavior in earlier chapters. The first source is the cost of rapid adjustment. For example, in Chapter 7 we showed how the costs of adjusting the actual capital stock to the desired capital stock led to lags in the investment function. The second source of lags is expectations. In this section we focus on expectations, their formation, and the effects they have on policy and its effectiveness.

While it is undoubtedly true that the past behavior of a variable influences expectations about its future behavior, it is also true that consumers and investors will sometimes use more information than is contained in the past behavior of a variable when trying to predict its future behavior.

Consider, for example, forecasts of permanent income — long-run average income. In Chapter 6, as in Friedman's original work on the consumption function, permanent income is estimated as an average of income in the recent past. Suppose, however, that you were a resident of a small country that had just discovered vast gold deposits. You would then take the information about the gold discovery into account in forming an estimate of your permanent income. You would immediately estimate a permanent income substantially higher than your historical average income. Or suppose that you have been estimating the expected rate of inflation as an average of past rates of inflation at a time when the inflation rate is high and a new government is elected on a strictly anti-inflationary platform. You would lower your estimate of the inflation rate; that is, you would use more information in predicting it than is contained solely in its past behavior. It should be clear that it is, in general, very difficult to incorporate all relevant information that is used by economic agents within a simple econometric model. That means that there will inevitably be errors in what the models predict for the consequences of various policy actions, meaning, in turn, that it is difficult to control the economy precisely.

THE 1968 TAX SURCHARGE

Reliance on models in which expectations are based on past behavior can easily lead to policy mistakes, as was the case with the 1968 tax surcharge, discussed in Section 6-4. Recall that the administration decided to ask for a tax increase in the form of a 10 percent surcharge on personal and corporate income taxes, to counteract a rising inflation rate. Every taxpayer would have to pay 10 percent more tax on the same income than in the past year.

To predict the effects of the policy, it was obviously necessary to consider the effects of the tax surcharge on consumer spending and thus on the level of income. This was done using a consumption function that related the level of consumption to current and past levels of disposable income, as in our formulation of the permanent-income consumption function. Predictions were that the tax increase would have a substantial direct and induced effect on the level of aggregate demand and income — so much of an impact that the

Federal Reserve System decided to undertake an expansionary monetary policy to offset part of the contractionary effects of the tax increase. However, the combined contractionary fiscal policy and expansionary monetary policy did not reduce the rate of inflation.

What went wrong? As we argued in Chapter 6, the major clue is that the tax increase was explicitly stated to be a temporary tax surcharge that was supposed to last only 1 year. A 10 percent increase in taxes in 1 year has a much smaller effect on lifetime income than a permanent 10 percent tax increase. Thus, if a tax increase is expected to be temporary, as was the 1968 tax increase, its effects on consumption will be smaller than if the increase is expected to be permanent.

It is now clear that calculation of the effects of the tax surcharge should have taken account of its temporary nature. Does the lesson that economists learned from the 1968 experience guarantee that similar mistakes will not be made in the future? Unfortunately, there is no such guarantee. Expectations enter economic models in many places, and in order to estimate the models using actual data, it is necessary to include some method of calculating the expectations, such as permanent income, or the expected rate of inflation. A careful user of an econometric model will no doubt try to check for the reasonableness of the expectations that it includes, but because there are so many places in which expectations matter, it is unlikely that they will always be treated appropriately.

EXPECTATIONS AND POLICY

It is particularly important to consider the effects of a given policy action itself on expectations, since it is possible that a new type of policy will affect the way in which expectations are formed.[16] Suppose that the Federal Reserve System announced a new monetary policy designed to stabilize the average level of income and avoid booms and recessions. The new policy would be to increase the money supply whenever the income level fell. Such a countercyclical rule has implications for expectations. Clearly, it would be inappropriate in the presence of such monetary policy to use an expectations mechanism that implies that an increase in income will persist. The monetary policy rule implies that the money supply should be reduced following an increase in income, and one expects the reduction in money to exert at least a dampening effect on income.

While correct expectations mechanisms must therefore use information about policy responses to disturbances, such care is difficult to apply in practice. Most expectations mechanisms embodied in econometric models of the U.S. economy and used for the assessment of policies assume that expec-

[16] The role of expectations in economics and the interaction between policy and expectations in particular have been the subject of much recent research. See, for example, Thomas J. Sargent and Neil Wallace, "Rational Expectations and the Theory of Economic Policy," *Journal of Monetary Economics*, April 1976. See also our discussion in Chap. 16. The rational expectations approach, described in Chap. 16, became increasingly influential within the economics profession in the late 1970s and early 1980s.

tations affecting consumption and investment spending are based entirely on past values.

ECONOMETRIC POLICY EVALUATION

The preceding example of the effects of a change in policy on expectations is part of a wider *econometric policy evaluation critique* formulated by Robert E. Lucas, of the University of Chicago, intellectual leader of the rational expectations approach to macroeconomics.[17] Lucas argues that existing macroeconometric models cannot be used to study the effects of policy changes *because the way private agents (firms and consumers) respond to changes in income and prices depends on the types of policy being followed.*

For example, suppose there is a change in income this period. How does consumption react? If policy is successful in keeping income always very close to potential, the change in income will be viewed as transitory, and there will be almost no change in consumption. But if policy is such that deviations of output from potential are typically prolonged, the change in income will be regarded as more permanent and the consumption response will be large. The key point is that the consumption response to changes in income depends on the types of policy being followed. Therefore one cannot use a consumption function which does not allow for this change in behavior to examine the effects of policy changes.

Lucas argues that problems of this sort are pervasive in macroeconometric models. He does not argue that it will never be possible to use econometric models to study policy—only that existing models cannot be used for that purpose.

Accordingly, the Lucas critique is not one that rules out the use of econometric models. It suggests rather that very careful modeling of the responses of consumers and firms to changes in income and prices is necessary. For instance, the consumption example above would not be impossible to handle, so long as permanent income were estimated as a weighted average of past incomes that changed appropriately as the behavior of income itself changed with policy.

SUMMARY

This section has made two important points about the role of expectations in explaining the difficulties of policy making. First, the general point is that the difficulties of modeling the way in which expectations are formed will inevitably lead to errors in economists' forecasts of the effects of particular policy actions on the economy. The second point, a particular one, is that expectations themselves are likely to be affected by policy measures, and that failure to take account of the effects of policy on expectations will lead to mistaken predictions of the effects of those policies.

[17] See "Econometric Policy Evaluation: A Critique," in R. E. Lucas, Jr., *Studies in Business Cycle Theory* (Cambridge, Mass.: M.I.T. Press, 1981).

10-5 UNCERTAINTY AND ECONOMIC POLICY

So far in this chapter we have described the disturbances that affect the economy, econometric models that are used in policy making, the difficulties of making policy when there are long lags in the effects of policy, and the problem of modeling expectations. We can summarize most of the implied problems for policy making by saying that it is impossible to predict the effects of any given policy action exactly.

How should a policy maker react in the face of these uncertainties? We want to distinguish here between uncertainty about the correct model of the economy and uncertainty about the precise values of the parameters or coefficients within a given model of the economy, even though the distinction is not watertight.

First, there is considerable disagreement and therefore uncertainty about the correct model of the economy, as evidenced by the large number of macroeconometric models. Reasonable economists can and do differ about what theory and empirical evidence suggest are the correct behavioral functions of the economy. Generally, each economist will have reasons for favoring one particular form and will use that form. But, being reasonable, the economist will recognize that the particular formulation being used may not be the correct one, and will thus regard its predictions as subject to a margin of error. In turn, policy makers will know that there are different predictions about the effects of a given policy, and will want to consider the range of predictions that are being made in deciding on policy.

Second, as we noted in Section 10-2, even within the context of a given model there is uncertainty about the values of parameters and multipliers. The statistical evidence does allow us to say something about the likely range of parameters or multipliers,[18] so that at least we can get some idea of the type of errors that could result from a particular policy action.

Uncertainty about the size of the effects that will result from any particular policy action is known as *multiplier uncertainty.* For instance, our best estimate of the multiplier of an increase in government spending might be 1.2. If GNP has to be increased by \$60 billion, we would increase government spending by \$50 billion. But the statistical evidence might be better interpreted as saying only that we can be quite confident the multiplier is between 0.9 and 1.5. In that case, when we increase government spending by \$50 billion, we expect GNP to rise by some amount between \$45 and \$75 billion.

What is optimal behavior in the face of such multiplier uncertainty? The more precisely policy makers are informed about the relevant parameters, the more activist the policy can afford to be. Conversely, if there is a considerable range of error in the estimate of the relevant parameters—in our example, the multiplier—then policy should be more modest. With poor information,

[18] We are discussing here confidence intervals about estimates of parameters; see Robert S. Pindyck and Daniel L. Rubinfeld, *Econometric Models and Economic Forecasts,* 2d ed. (New York: McGraw-Hill, 1980), for further discussion. This is the point made in footnote 10.

POLICY MAKING UNDER UNCERTAINTY: 1980

In October 1979, in response to the high and rising inflation, the Fed changed its policies with the intention of keeping money growth under control to fight inflation. (This change was discussed in Chapter 9; inflation is analyzed in Chapters 11 to 13.)

In the beginning of 1980 the inflation news was all bad, as Table 1 shows. From month to month the inflation rate was at an annual rate of about 18 percent. Much of this increase was due to higher oil prices, but the Fed and the administration, nonetheless, were deeply concerned over rising prices. Although a recession had been expected, and would reduce inflation if it happened, the unemployment rate hardly increased in early 1980. At the same time, the demand for loans in the economy was very high; firms and consumers were doing a lot of borrowing despite record high interest rates, which suggested that the demand for investment and consumer durables would be high—thus also suggesting that there would not be a recession.

Although interest rates were at record highs, monetary growth data presented a mixed picture. This was a period when the money stock measures were being redefined. $M1$ (there were then two versions) was growing reasonably slowly, while $M2$ was growing more rapidly. Thus judging from interest rates, monetary policy was restrictive, while judging from money growth, it was uncertain what was happening.

In March the administration acted. Worried by the continuing inflation and continuing high level of borrowing, the President announced a program of credit controls. Limits were placed on the amount of loans banks could make, and other steps were taken to reduce the growth of assets that were close substitutes for money, such as money market mutual funds. The growth rate of money ($M1$) had already started falling in March and was negative also for the next 2 months. Interest rates came down sharply in May and June.

The second quarter of 1980 saw the sharpest decline in GNP in a single quarter in the

TABLE 1 ECONOMIC DATA, JANUARY–JUNE 1980*

Month	Inflation rate (CPI), % per annum	Civilian unemployment rate	Money growth rate ($M1B$) % per annum	Money growth rate ($M2$), % per annum	Treasury bill rate
January	18.7	6.2	5.4	7.3	12.0
February	17.8	6.2	10.4	10.0	12.8
March	18.7	6.3	−0.3	5.1	15.5
April	14.4	6.9	−13.2	−2.4	14.0
May	12.5	7.6	−1.2	9.9	9.2
June	14.1	7.5	15.6	19.7	7.0

* Inflation and money growth rates are one-month changes at annual rates.
Source: Economic Report of the President, 1981.

post-World War II period. The unemployment rate increased sharply from March to April and from April to May. The recession that had been widely expected was now fully visible. Indeed, the National Bureau of Economic Research later decided that the recession had begun in January 1980. Thus the credit controls were put in place after the recession had begun.

Most likely the credit controls were overkill. The economy was already into a recession when they were imposed. But policy makers and outside observers did not know that then. And the signs in early 1980 were, indeed, very mixed. The problem of policy making is that it cannot be done with the benefit of hindsight. But with the benefit of hindsight we can see that the policy makers in March 1980 were wrong about the current economic situation and the likelihood of recession. Of course uncertainties about both the current situation and the future are certain to be with us always, and to complicate the policy-making task.

very active policy runs a large danger of introducing unnecessary fluctuations in the economy.

10-6 ACTIVIST POLICY

We started this chapter by asking why there are any fluctuations in the American economy when the policy measures needed to iron out those fluctuations seem to be so simple. The list of difficulties in the way of successful policy making that we have outlined may have raised a different question: Why should one believe that policy can do anything to reduce fluctuations in the economy?

Indeed, considerations of the sort spelled out in the previous four sections have led Milton Friedman and others to argue that there should be no use of active countercyclical monetary policy,[19] and that monetary policy should be confined to making the money supply grow at a constant rate. The precise value of the constant rate of growth of money, Friedman suggests, is less important than the fact that monetary growth be constant and that policy should *not* respond to disturbances. At various times, he has suggested growth rates for money of 2 or 4 or 5 percent. As Friedman has expressed it, "By setting itself a steady course and keeping to it, the monetary authority could make a major contribution to promoting economic stability. By making that course one of steady but moderate growth in the quantity of money, it would make a major contribution to avoidance of either inflation or deflation of prices."[20] Friedman thus advocates a simple monetary rule in which the Fed does not respond to the condition of the economy. Policies that respond to the current or predicted state of the economy are called *activist policies.*

In discussing the desirability of activist monetary and fiscal policy, we want to distinguish between policy actions taken in response to major distur-

[19] See Milton Friedman, *A Program for Monetary Stability* (New York: Fordham University Press, 1959).

[20] Milton Friedman, "The Role of Monetary Policy," *American Economic Review,* March 1968.

bances to the economy and *fine tuning,* in which policy variables are continually adjusted in response to small disturbances to the economy. We see no case for arguing that monetary and fiscal policy should not be used actively in the face of major disturbances to the economy. Most of the considerations of the previous sections of this chapter indicate some uncertainty about the effects of policy, but there are still clearly definable circumstances in which there can be no doubt that the appropriate policy is expansionary or contractionary. An administration coming to power in 1933 should not have worried about the uncertainties associated with expansionary policy that we have outlined. The economy does not move from 25 percent unemployment to full employment in a short time (precisely because of those same lags that make policy difficult). Thus, expansionary measures, such as a rapid growth of the money supply, or increased government expenditures, or tax reductions, or all three, would have been appropriate policy since there was no chance they would have an impact only after the economy was at full employment. Similarly, contractionary policies for private demand are called for in wartime. Early in 1975, with unemployment at 8.2 percent and rising rapidly and forecasts of unemployment for the next 2 years being very high, policies designed to reduce unemployment were appropriate.[21] In the event of large disturbances in the future, activist monetary and/or fiscal policy should once again be used.[22]

Fine tuning presents more complicated issues. The basic question is whether policy variables should be adjusted at frequent intervals to attempt to smooth out minor disturbances to the economy. For example, should an increase of 0.5 percent in the unemployment rate lead to a small tax reduction, or a small increase in the rate of growth of the money supply, or should policy simply not respond to such disturbances? One possibility is that the initial increase in the unemployment rate is transitory and that policy action is therefore inappropriate; the other is that the initial disturbance is permanent and perhaps even the first sign of a major disturbance, in which case a policy reaction is suitable. If the disturbance is permanent, the appropriate policy response to a small disturbance is a small change in the course of policy. Thus, even if it turned out that the policy action was inappropriate because the disturbance was transitory, the (undesirable) consequences of the policy action would be limited because only a small adjustment had been made. Accordingly, we believe that fine tuning is appropriate provided that policy responses are always kept small in response to small disturbances.

However, we should emphasize that the argument for fine tuning is a controversial one. The major argument against it is that in practice policy makers cannot behave as suggested—making only small adjustments to small disturbances. Rather, it is argued, they tend to try to do too much, if allowed

[21] Because the inflation rate was high in early 1975, policy making then required some judgment about the costs of inflation compared with those of unemployment, a topic discussed in Chap. 14. Policy making in early 1975 was thus more difficult than policy making in 1933. Policy decisions in 1980 through 1982, with rising unemployment and very high inflation, were also very tough.

[22] Interestingly, in the article cited in footnote 20, Friedman argues for the use of active policy in the face of major disturbances.

to do anything. Instead of merely trying to offset disturbances, they attempt to keep the economy always at full employment and therefore undertake inappropriately large policy actions in response to small disturbances.

The major lesson of the previous sections is not that policy is impossible, but that policy that is too ambitious in trying to keep the economy always at full employment (with zero inflation) is impossible. The lesson is to proceed with extreme caution, always bearing in mind the possibility that policy itself may be destabilizing. We see no reason why the Federal Reserve System should try to keep the money supply always growing at the same rate; we believe, on the contrary, that the stability of the economy would be improved by its following a careful countercyclical policy. Similarly, if fiscal policy were not subject to a long inside lag, we would believe it possible for cautiously used fiscal policy to be stabilizing.

Rules versus Discretion

Finally, in this chapter, we want to discuss an issue that has perhaps had more attention in the economics literature than it deserves. This is the issue of "rules versus discretion." The issue is whether the monetary authority and also the fiscal authority should conduct policy in accordance with a preannounced rule that describes precisely how their policy variables will be determined in all future situations, or whether they should be allowed to use their discretion in determining the values of the policy variables at different times.

One example is the rule establishing the constant growth rate, say, at 4 percent, for monetary policy. The rule is that no matter what happens, the money supply will be kept growing at 4 percent.[23] Another example would be a rule stating that the money supply growth rate will be increased by 2 percent per year for every 1 percent unemployment in excess of, say, 5 percent. Algebraically, such a rule would be expressed as

$$\frac{\Delta M}{M} = 4.0 + 2(u - 5.0) \tag{1}$$

where the growth rate of money $\Delta M/M$ is at an annual percentage rate, and u is the percentage unemployment rate.

The activist monetary rule of Equation (1) is shown in Figure 10-7. On the horizontal axis, we show the unemployment rate, and on the vertical axis, the growth rate of the money stock. At 5 percent unemployment, monetary growth is 4 percent. If unemployment rises above 5 percent, monetary growth is *automatically* increased. Thus, with 7 percent unemployment, monetary growth would be 8 percent. Conversely, if unemployment dropped below 5 percent, monetary growth would be lowered below 4 percent. The rule therefore gears the amount of monetary stimulus to an indicator of the business cycle. By linking monetary growth to the unemployment rate, an

[23] Recall from Chap. 9 that although the monetary authority cannot control the money supply and its growth rate exactly, it is able to control the high-powered money stock with considerable accuracy.

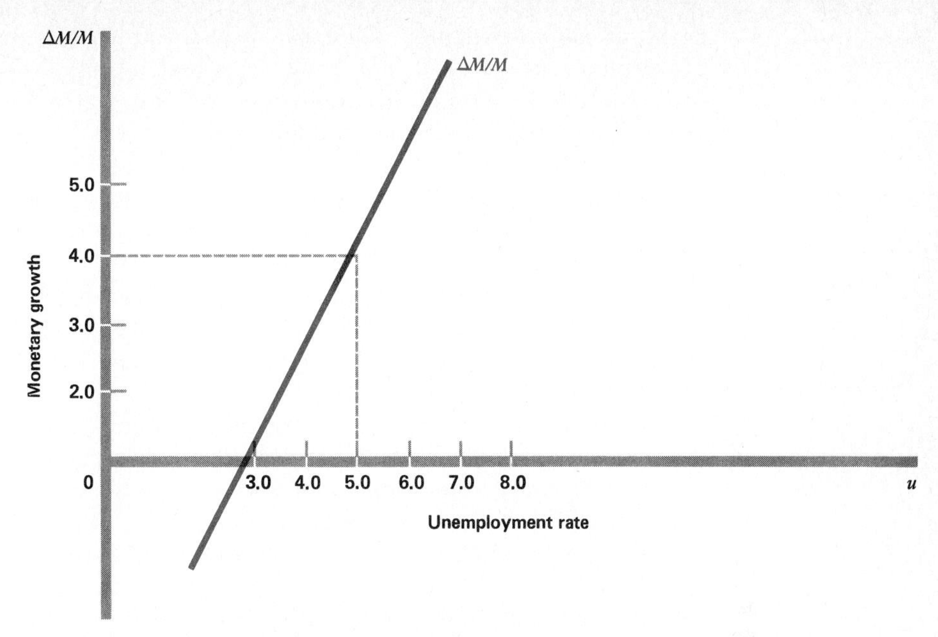

FIGURE 10-7 AN ACTIVIST MONETARY RULE. The figure describes an activist monetary rule. The growth rate of money is high when the unemployment rate is high and is low when unemployment is low. That way monetary policy is expansionary at times of recession and contractionary in a boom.

activist, anticyclical monetary policy is achieved, but this is done without any discretion.

The issue of rules versus discretion has been clouded by the fact that most proponents of rules have been nonactivist, whose preferred monetary rule is a constant growth rate rule.[24] Consequently, the argument has tended to center on whether activist policy is desirable or not. The fundamental point to recognize is that we can design *activist rules*. We can design rules that have countercyclical features without at the same time leaving any discretion in their actions to policy makers. The point is made by Equation (1), which is an activist rule because it expands money when unemployment is high and reduces it when unemployment is low. It leaves no room for policy discretion and in this respect is a rule.

Given that the economy and our knowledge of it are both changing over time, there is no economic case for stating permanent policy rules that would tie the hands of the monetary and fiscal authorities permanently. The practical issue in rules versus discretion then becomes that of whether the policy makers should announce in advance what policies they will be following for the foreseeable future. Such announcements would seem to be a desirable

[24] An assessment of the issues is provided in Arthur Okun, "Monetary-Fiscal Activism: Some Analytical Issues," *Brookings Papers on Economic Activity*, 1972:1 (Washington, D.C.: The Brookings Institution, 1972).

development in that they would aid private individuals in forecasting the future course of policy. In fact, as we described in Chapter 9, the chairperson of the Fed has been required to announce to Congress the Fed's target growth rate for the money stock over the next year.

10-7 SUMMARY

1 Despite the apparent simplicity of policies needed to maintain continuous full employment, the historical record of the behavior of unemployment, shown in Figure 10-1, implies that successful stabilization policy is difficult to carry out.
2 Many of the complications in the execution of stabilization policy are a result of the tradeoff between inflation and unemployment in the short run. This important topic is deferred to Chapter 13. The present chapter concentrates on other sources of difficulty for stabilization policy.
3 The potential need for stabilizing policy actions arises from economic disturbances. Some of these disturbances, such as changes in money demand, consumption spending, or investment demand, arise from within the private sector. Others, such as wars, may arise for noneconomic reasons.
4 Inappropriate economic policy may also tend to move the economy away from full employment. Policy may be inappropriate because policy makers make mistakes or because policy is manipulated for political reasons, leading to the political business cycle.
5 Policy makers work with econometric models in predicting the effects of their policy actions. Econometric models are typically statistical descriptions of the types of model we have worked with in earlier chapters and also include an aggregate supply section. The models do not forecast with perfect accuracy, partly because they cannot forecast policy and disturbances such as the increase in the price of oil. But, in addition, their forecasts are inaccurate because we do not have accurate knowledge of the workings of the economy.
6 The first difficulty of carrying out successful stabilization policy is that policy works with lags. The inside lag—divided into recognition, decision, and action lags—is the period between which an action becomes necessary and when it is taken. The outside lag is the period between which a policy action is taken and when it affects the economy. The outside lag is generally a distributed lag: the effects of a policy action build up over the course of time.
7 The behavior of expectations is a further source of difficulty for policy making. First, it is difficult to know exactly what determines expectations and to capture those factors in a simple formula. Second, policy actions themselves are likely to affect expectations.
8 More generally, there is always uncertainty about the effects of a given policy action on the economy. Economists are not agreed on the "correct" model of the economy, and evidence is not likely to be at hand soon

to settle decisively disagreements over some behavioral functions—such as the consumption function. And even if we did know the form of the behavioral functions, the statistical evidence would be insufficient to pinpoint the values of the relevant parameters.

9 There are clearly occasions on which active monetary and fiscal policy actions should be taken to stabilize the economy. These are situations in which the economy has been affected by major disturbances.

10 Fine tuning—continuous attempts to stabilize the economy in the face of small disturbances—is more controversial. If fine tuning is undertaken, it calls for small policy responses in an attempt to moderate the economy's fluctuations, rather than to remove them entirely. A very active policy in response to small disturbances is likely to destabilize the economy.

11 The real issue in rules versus discretion is whether policy actions should be announced as far in advance as possible. Such announcements are desirable in that they aid private individuals in forecasting the future behavior of the economy.

KEY TERMS

Economic disturbances
Political business cycle
Econometric models
Macroeconometric models
Inside lag
Recognition lag
Decision lag
Action lag
Outside lag
Econometric policy evaluation critique
Multiplier uncertainty
Activist policy
Fine tuning
Rules versus discretion

PROBLEMS

1 Suppose that GNP is $40 billion below its potential level. It is expected that next period GNP will be $20 billion below potential, and two periods from now it will be back at its potential level. You are told that the multiplier for government spending is 2, and that the effects of the increased government spending are immediate. What policy actions can be taken to put GNP back on target each period?

2 The basic facts about the path of GNP are as above. But there is now a one-period outside lag for government spending. Decisions to spend today are translated into actual spending only tomorrow. The multiplier for government spending is still 2 in the period that the spending takes place.
(*a*) What is the best that can be done to keep GNP as close to target as possible each period?
(*b*) Compare the path of GNP in this question with the path in problem (1), after policy actions have been taken.

3 Life has become more complicated. Government spending works with a distributed lag. Now when $1 billion is spent today, GNP increases by $1 billion this period and $1.5 billion next period.

(*a*) What happens to the path of GNP if government spending rises enough this period to put GNP back to its potential level this period?
(*b*) Suppose fiscal policy actions are taken to put GNP at its potential level this period. What fiscal policy will be needed to put GNP on target next period?
(*c*) Explain why the government has to be so active in keeping GNP on target in this case.

4 Suppose that you knew that the multiplier for government spending was between 1 and 2.5, but that its effects were all over in the period that spending was increased. How would you run fiscal policy if GNP would, without policy, behave as in problem 1?

5 Explain why monetary policy works with a distributed lag, as in Figure 10-4.

6 In Figure 10-6 we show how the ratio of disposable personal income to national income changes between booms and recessions. Go back to Table 2-6 and then explain:
(*a*) What component of the adjustment between national income and personal income moves with automatic stabilizers to produce the cyclical behavior seen in Figure 10-6?
(*b*) What other component in that table is likely to fall sharply during recessions?

7 (*a*) Check the *Economic Report of the President* for 1984 or some other publication (for example, *Survey of Current Business, Economic Indicators*) to see how accurate the typical forecast in Table 10-1 was for 1983.
(*b*) Explain why econometric forecasts are not totally accurate.

8 Evaluate the argument that monetary policy should be determined by a rule rather than discretion. How about fiscal policy?

9 Evaluate the arguments for a constant growth rate rule for money.

10 (*a*) What is the unemployment rate at the time you are reading this?
(*b*) Should either fiscal or monetary policy be changed to enable the economy to return more rapidly to full employment?

PART THREE

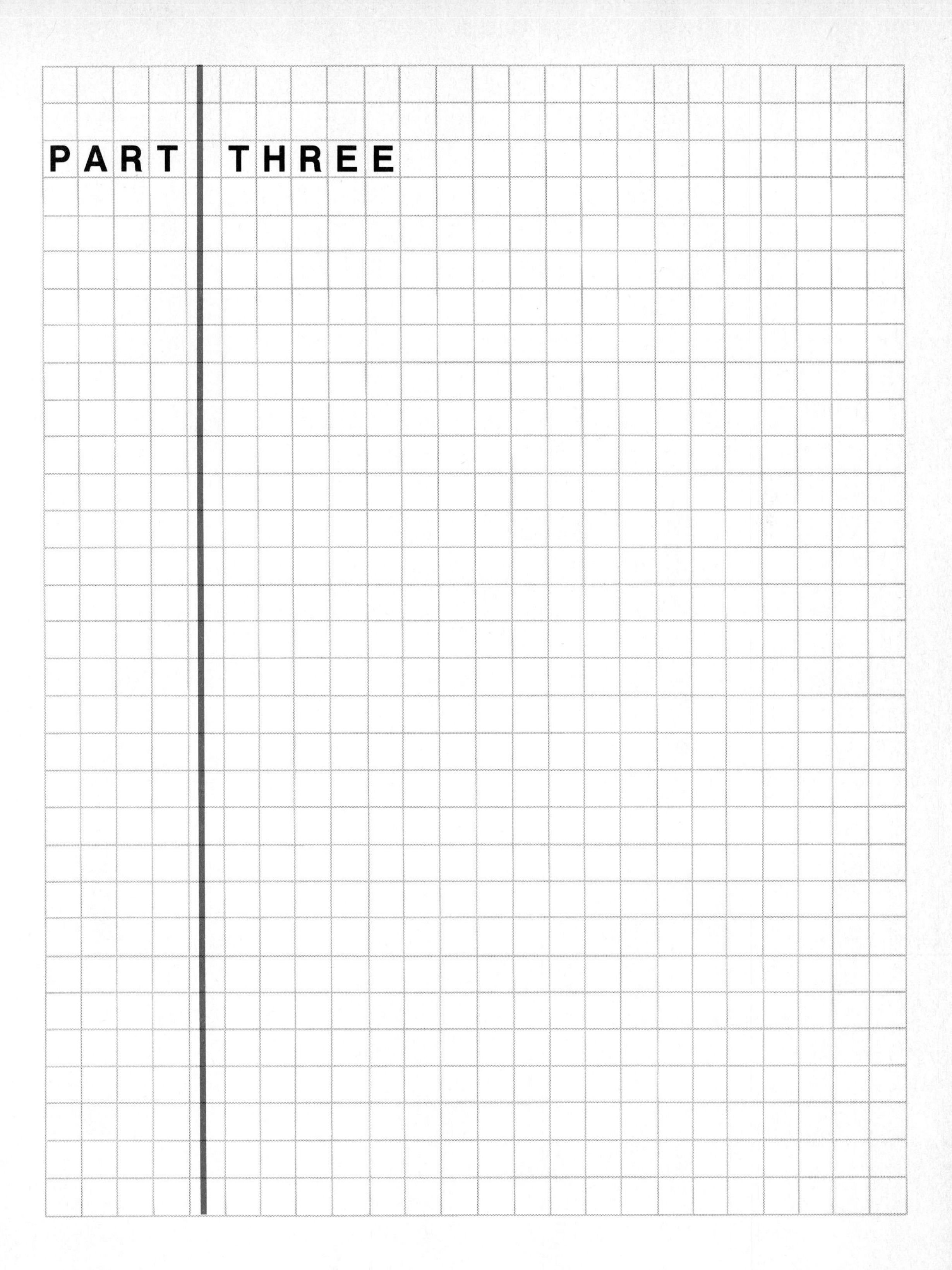

11

AGGREGATE SUPPLY AND AGGREGATE DEMAND: AN INTRODUCTION

So far our analysis of the behavior of the economy has assumed that the price level is fixed. We studied the impacts of changes in the money supply, or of taxes, or of government spending, assuming that whatever amount of goods was demanded would be supplied, *at the existing price level.*

To put the same point in different words, we have not yet analyzed *inflation.* But, of course, inflation is one of the major concerns of macroeconomists, citizens, and policy makers. The time has therefore come to bring the price level and the inflation rate — the rate of change of the price level — into the center of our analysis of the economy. We have to study the determination of both the level of output — on which we have concentrated thus far — and the price level.

Figure 11-1 shows the model of *aggregate demand and supply* that we shall use to study the joint determination of the price level and the level of output. The aggregate demand curve *AD*, which is downward-sloping, is based entirely on the material of the earlier chapters, in particular Chapters 4 and 5. We define the aggregate demand curve in this chapter, and show why it slopes down and what causes it to shift. The aggregate supply curve will be introduced in this chapter and developed further in Chapter 12. The intersection of the *AD* and *AS* schedules at *E* determines

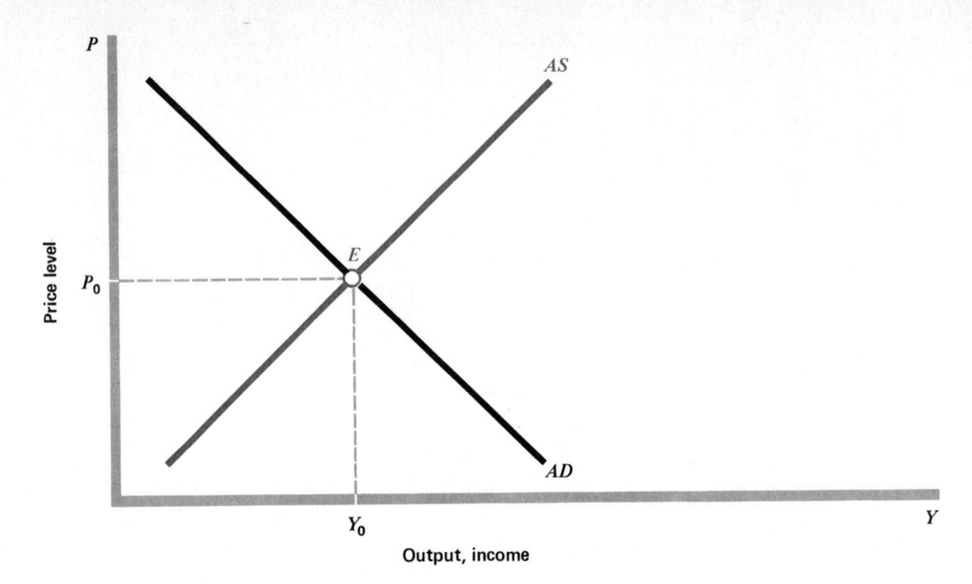

FIGURE 11-1 AGGREGATE SUPPLY AND DEMAND. The diagram shows the complete model of aggregate demand and supply that is developed in this and the next chapter to explain the joint determination of the levels of output and prices. The aggregate demand curve, *AD*, is based on the *IS-LM* model studied in earlier chapters. The aggregate supply curve *AS* is developed in this and the next chapter. Their intersection at point *E* determines the level of output Y_0 and the price level P_0.

the equilibrium level of output, Y_0, and the equilibrium price level P_0. Shifts in either schedule cause the price level and the level of output to change.

The aggregate demand-supply model is the basic macroeconomic model for studying output and price level determination—just as in microeconomics, demand and supply curves are the essential tools for studying output and price determination in a single market. But the aggregate demand and supply curves are not as simple as the microeconomic demand and supply curves, for there is more going on in the background of the aggregate curves than there is in that of the microeconomic curves. That is why it will take us two chapters to develop the aggregate curves.[1]

11-1 INTRODUCING AGGREGATE DEMAND AND SUPPLY

Before we go deeply into the factors underlying the aggregate demand and supply curves, we show how the curves will be used. Suppose that the money

[1] The aggregate demand curve is sometimes referred to as the *macroeconomic demand curve*, both to emphasize that it is different from a regular demand curve in microeconomics and to distinguish it from the aggregate demand schedule in Chap. 3. We stay with the same name *AD* here after warning that the present *AD* schedule represents an extension of that in Chap. 3 since it makes interest rates endogenous along the curve.

supply is increased. What effects will that have on the price level and output? In particular, does an increase in the money supply cause the price level to rise, thus producing inflation? Or does the level of output rise, as it did in the analysis of earlier chapters? Or do both output and the price level rise?

Figure 11-2 shows that an increase in the money supply shifts the aggregate demand curve *AD* to the right, to *AD*′. We see later in this chapter why that should be so. The shift of the aggregate demand curve moves the equilibrium of the economy from *E* to *E*′. The price level rises from P_0 to P', and the level of output from Y_0 to Y'. Thus the answer to the questions we asked at the end of the previous paragraph is that an increase in the money stock causes both the level of output and the price level to rise.

THE SLOPE OF THE AGGREGATE SUPPLY CURVE

What determines how much the price level rises and how much output increases? Looking at Figure 11-3*a* we see that if the aggregate supply curve is relatively flat, a shift in the *AD* curve raises output a lot and prices very little. By contrast, in Figure 11-3*b* we see that when the aggregate supply curve is nearly vertical, an increase in the money supply mainly causes prices to rise and hardly increases output at all.

If the aggregate supply curve is vertical, or nearly so as in Figure 11-3*b*, then the analysis of the earlier chapters that showed an increase in the money stock raising output could be very misleading. For example, if the aggregate

FIGURE 11-2 THE EFFECTS OF AN INCREASE IN THE NOMINAL MONEY STOCK. An increase in the money stock shifts the aggregate demand curve from *AD* to *AD*′. The equilibrium moves from *E* to *E*′, resulting in higher levels of both prices and output. Thus an increase in the money stock in part results in higher prices, and not entirely in higher output.

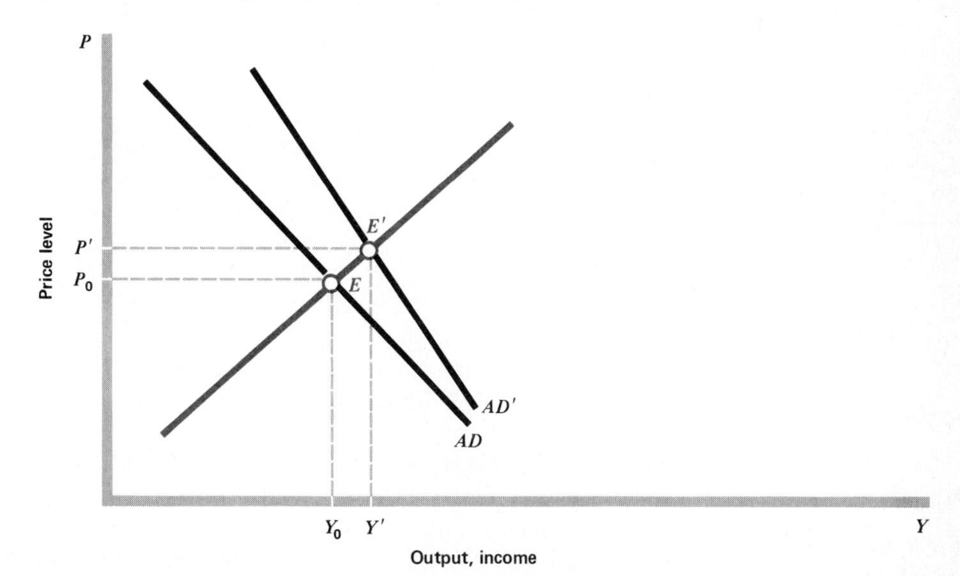

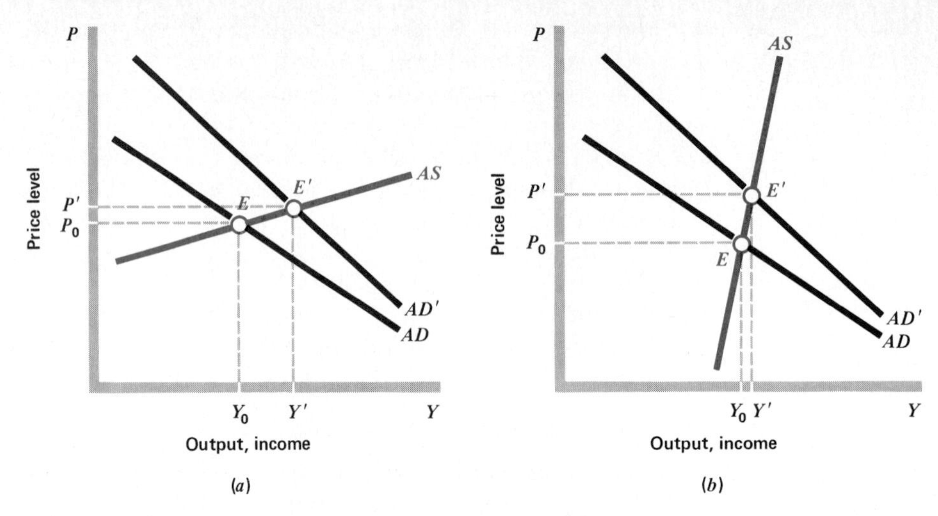

FIGURE 11-3 THE INTERACTION OF AGGREGATE SUPPLY AND DEMAND. The effects of a shift in the aggregate demand curve from AD to AD' depend on the slope of the aggregate supply curve. If the AS curve is relatively flat, as in Figure 11-3*a*, the shift in the aggregate demand curve results mainly in an increase in output. By contrast, in Figure 11-3*b*, the shift in the aggregate demand curve results almost entirely in an increase in the price level and very little in an increase in output.

supply curve is vertical, an increase in the money stock will lead only to higher prices, not to more output. Thus one of the key questions on which we shall concentrate is what determines the shape of the aggregate supply curve. When is it vertical, or nearly so as in Figure 11-3*b*? When is the aggregate supply curve more nearly horizontal as in Figure 11-3*a*?

Fully developing the answers will take the next two chapters. We start here by defining aggregate demand and supply.

Aggregate Demand and Supply Defined

The *aggregate demand curve* shows the combinations of the price level and level of output at which the goods and assets markets are simultaneously in equilibrium. At any point on the aggregate demand curve, for instance point B in Figure 11-4, we see that for the given price level, P_B in this case, the level of output at which the goods and assets markets are in equilibrium is Y_B.

We can already give a preliminary explanation of why the aggregate demand curve slopes down, based on the discussion of monetary policy in Chapter 4. Suppose that the goods and assets markets are in equilibrium at a level of output like Y_B, with given price level P_B. Now suppose the price level falls. With a given nominal stock of money, a fall in the price level creates an increase in the quantity of *real balances*. We recall from Chapter 4 that an increase in the quantity of real balances reduces interest rates, increases investment demand, and therefore increases aggregate spending. Accordingly, when the price level falls, the equilibrium level of output rises; therefore the AD curve slopes down. We go into the details in Section 11-3.

We can also see, from the definition of the aggregate demand curve, why the analysis of the previous ten chapters is not at all wasted. The aggregate demand curve describes the joint equilibrium of the goods and assets markets. That is precisely what the *IS-LM* analysis describes. Thus the material we studied in earlier chapters is an essential part of the aggregate demand and supply model we shall use to analyze the simultaneous determination of the levels of output and prices.

The *aggregate supply curve* describes the combinations of output and the price level such that firms are willing, at the given price level, to supply the given quantity of output. For instance, at point C in Figure 11-4, with price level P_C, firms are willing to supply output equal to Y_C. The amount of output firms are willing to supply depends on the prices they receive for their goods and the amounts they have to pay for labor and other factors of production. Accordingly, the aggregate supply curve reflects conditions in the factor markets—especially the labor market—as well as the goods markets.

11-2 AGGREGATE SUPPLY: TWO SPECIAL CASES

In this chapter we concentrate on two special cases in discussing aggregate supply. The first, the *Keynesian case*, shown in Figure 11-5*a*, is a horizontal aggregate supply curve. The *Keynesian aggregate supply curve* is horizontal,

FIGURE 11-4 AGGREGATE DEMAND AND SUPPLY CURVES DEFINED. At any point on the aggregate demand curve, such as point B, both the goods and assets markets are in equilibrium. This is the equilibrium described by the intersection of *IS* and *LM* curves in Chapter 4. For instance, with price level P_B, the level of output at which both goods and assets markets are in equilibrium is Y_B. The aggregate supply curve *AS* describes the relation between the price level and the amount of output firms wish to supply. For instance, at price level P_C, firms want to supply output Y_C.

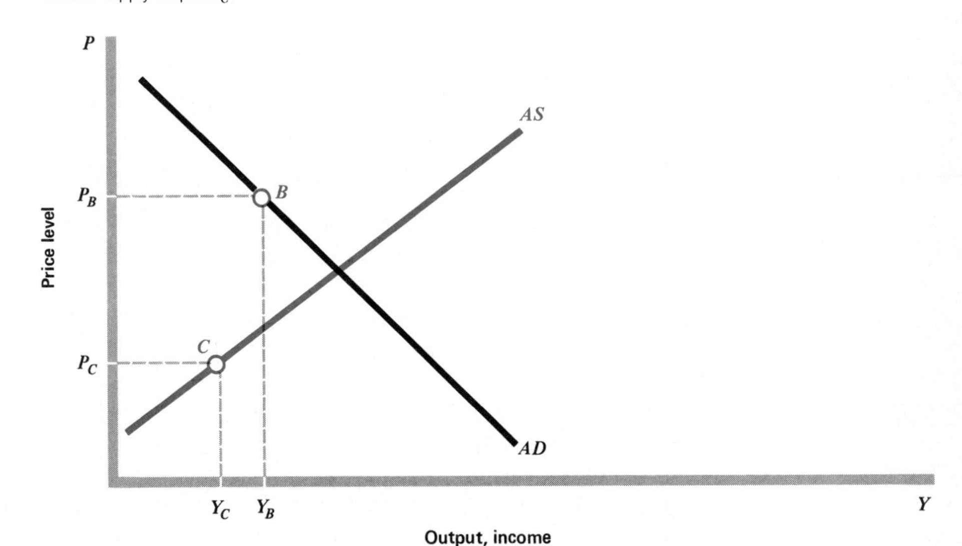

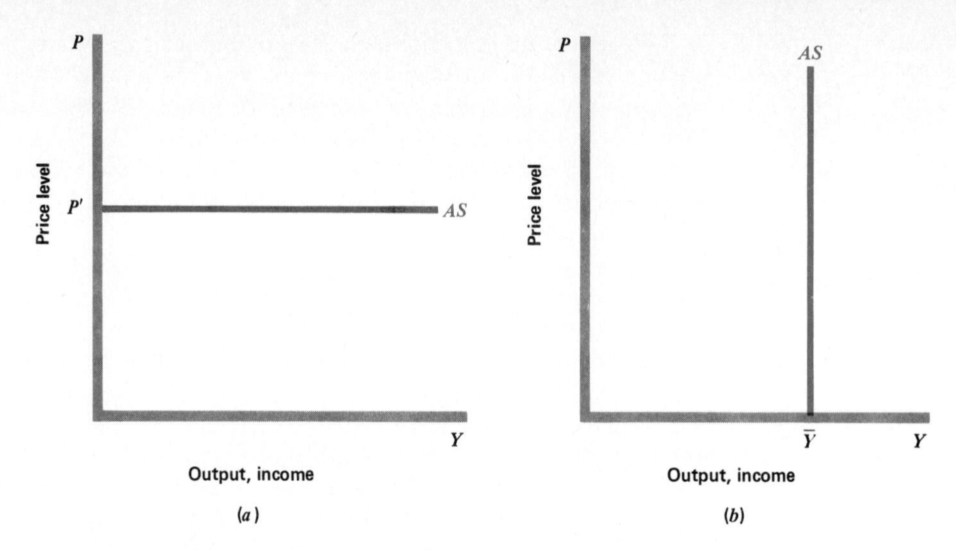

FIGURE 11-5 KEYNESIAN AND CLASSICAL SUPPLY FUNCTIONS. The Keynesian aggregate supply curve is horizontal, implying that any amount of output will be supplied at the existing price level. This is shown in panel (*a*), where the *AS* curve is horizontal at price level P'. The classical supply function is based on the assumption that there is always full employment of labor, and thus that output is always at the level of output corresponding to full employment of labor, $\overline{Y}$, and *independent of the price level.* This is shown by the vertical aggregate supply curve in panel (*b*).

indicating that firms will supply at the existing price level whatever amount of goods is demanded.

The idea underlying the Keynesian aggregate supply curve is that because there is unemployment, firms can obtain as much labor as they want at the current wage. Their average costs of production therefore are assumed not to change as their output levels change, and they are accordingly willing to supply as much as is demanded at the existing price level.

The Classical Supply Curve

Figure 11-5*b* shows the opposite extreme, of a vertical supply curve. In the *classical* case, the *aggregate supply curve* is vertical, indicating that the same amount of goods will be supplied whatever the price level.

The classical supply curve is based on the assumption that the labor market is always in equilibrium with full employment of the labor force. If the entire labor force is being employed, then output cannot be raised above its current level even if the price level rises. There is no more labor available to produce any extra output. Thus the aggregate supply curve will be vertical at a level of output corresponding to full employment of the labor force, $\overline{Y}$ in Figure 11-5*b*.

Underlying the assumption that the labor market is always in equilibrium is another assumption—that the wage adjusts rapidly to maintain equilibrium. For example, suppose that the economy is in equilibrium and the aggregate demand curve shifts to the right, as in Figure 11-2. At the existing price level, the quantity of goods demanded increases.

Now firms try to obtain more labor. Each firm attempts to hire more labor, offering to pay higher wages if necessary. But there is no more labor available in the economy, and so firms are unable to obtain more workers. Instead, in competing against each other for workers, they merely bid up wages. Because wages are higher, the prices the firms charge for their output will also be higher. But output will be unchanged.

The essential difference in assumptions between the classical and Keynesian aggregate supply curves is that the classical supply curve is based on the belief that the labor market works smoothly, always maintaining full employment of the labor force. Movements in the wage are the mechanism through which full employment is maintained. The Keynesian aggregate supply curve is instead based on the assumption that the wage does not change much or at all when there is unemployment, and thus that unemployment can continue for some time.

These two cases—the classical, representing continuing labor market equilibrium, and the Keynesian, assuming wages do not adjust—are the two extremes. In the next chapter we show what determines the slope of the aggregate supply curve and discuss when it will be more like the classical extreme and when it will be more like the Keynesian extreme.

11-3 THE AGGREGATE DEMAND SCHEDULE

As noted earlier, the aggregate demand curve, or schedule, shows, for each price level, the level of output at which the goods and assets markets are simultaneously in equilibrium. At any given price level, we use the *IS-LM* model to determine the level of output at which the goods and assets markets are in equilibrium.

In Figure 11-6 we show the *IS-LM* model. The position of the *IS* curve depends on fiscal policy. The *LM* schedule is drawn for a given nominal money stock M and a given price level P_0 and thus for a given real money stock M/P_0. The equilibrium interest rate is i_0, and the equilibrium level of income and spending is shown as Y_0.

A CHANGE IN THE PRICE LEVEL

Consider the effect of a fall in the price level from P_0 to P'. This reduction in the price level increases the real money stock from M/P_0 to M/P'. To clear the money market with an increased real money stock, either interest rates must fall, inducing the public to hold more cash balances, or output must rise, thus increasing the transactions demand for money.

Accordingly, the *LM* curve shifts down and to the right, to *LM′*. The new equilibrium is shown at point E', where once again both the money market

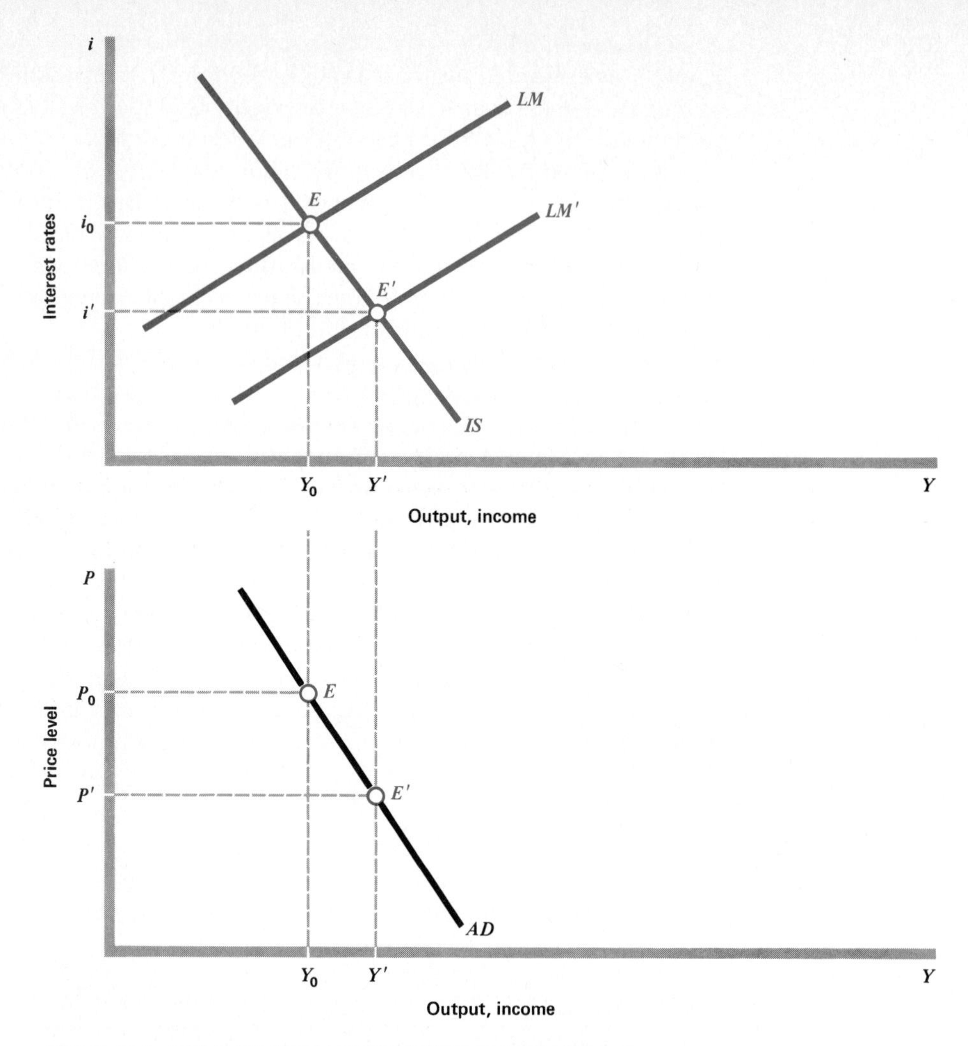

FIGURE 11-6 DERIVATION OF THE AGGREGATE DEMAND SCHEDULE. The upper panel shows the IS schedule and the initial LM schedule drawn for the real money stock M/P_0. Equilibrium is at point E. In the lower panel we record that at a price level P_0 the equilibrium level of income and spending is Y_0. This is shown by point E. At a lower level of prices, say, P', the real money stock is M/P', and therefore the LM schedule shifts to LM'. Equilibrium income now is Y'. Again in the lower panel we show at point E' the combination of the price level P' and the corresponding equilibrium level of income and spending Y'. Considering different levels of prices and connecting the resulting points such as E and E', we derive the aggregate demand schedule AD. The schedule shows the equilibrium level of spending at each level of prices, *given* the nominal money stock and fiscal policy.

clears—because we are on the LM curve—and the goods market clears—because we are on the IS curve. The new equilibrium level of output is Y', corresponding to the lower price level P'. Thus a reduction in the price level, *given the nominal quantity of money*, results in an increase in equilibrium income and spending. The derivation of the *AD* schedule can be seen in Figure 11-6. The economy is initially in equilibrium at points *E* in both the upper and lower panels. The equilibrium interest rate is i_0, the level of output is Y_0, and the corresponding price level is P_0. Now the price level drops to P'. In the upper panel, the equilibrium moves to E', as a result of the shift of the *LM* curve to *LM'*. Corresponding to point E' in the upper panel is point E' in the lower panel, at price level P' and level of income and output Y'.

Thus *E* and E' in the lower panel are both points on the *AD* schedule. We could now consider all possible price levels and the corresponding levels of real balances. For each level of real balances there is a different *LM* curve in the upper panel. Corresponding to each *LM* curve is an equilibrium level of income, which would be recorded in the lower panel at the price level that results in the *LM* curve in the upper panel. Connecting all these points gives us a downward-sloping aggregate demand curve *AD*, as shown in Figure 11-6.

The *AD* curve is downward-sloped because there is a definite relation between equilibrium spending and the price level: the higher the price level, the lower are real balances, and hence the lower the equilibrium level of spending and output.

Properties of the *AD* Schedule

The *AD* schedule shows how the level of real spending changes with the level of prices, given fiscal policy, the quantity of money, and autonomous private spending. What are the precise properties of the *AD* schedule? We start with the slope, which tells us how much real spending changes in response to a change in the level of prices.

THE SLOPE OF THE *AD* SCHEDULE

In Figure 11-6 we derived the *AD* schedule by considering the effect of changes in the price level, and hence in real balances, on the *LM* schedule and hence on equilibrium income and spending. The slope of the *AD* curve therefore reflects the extent to which a change in real balances changes the equilibrium level of spending, taking both assets and goods markets into account.

But we have already examined the effects of a change in the stock of real balances on the level of output that equilibrates the goods and assets markets. In Chapters 4 and 5 we showed the effect of an increase in the nominal stock of money on equilibrium spending and output, with the price level given. Now we ask what is the effect of a change in real balances due to lower prices, given nominal money.

In discussing monetary policy in Chapters 4 and 5 we showed the following results using the *IS-LM* schedules:

> An increase in real balances leads to a larger increase in equilibrium income and spending, the smaller the interest response of money demand and the higher the interest response of investment demand.

An increase in real balances leads to a larger increase in equilibrium income and spending, the larger the multiplier and the smaller the income response of money demand.

Because the slope of the AD *curve is determined by the effect of a change in real balances on equilibrium spending and output, the same factors that determine the effects of a change in the stock of money on equilibrium output and spending also determine the slope of the* AD *curve.* If a given change in real balances has a large impact on equilibrium spending, then the *AD* curve will be very flat—because a small change in the price level creates a large change in equilibrium spending. But if a given change in real balances has a small effect on equilibrium spending and output, then the *AD* curve will be steep: in that case it takes a large change in the price level to create a small change in spending and output.

Accordingly, we see that:

1 The *AD* curve is flatter (*a*) the smaller the interest responsiveness of the demand for money, and (*b*) the larger the interest responsiveness of investment demand.
2 The *AD* curve is flatter (*a*) the larger the multiplier, and (*b*) the smaller the income responsiveness of the demand for money.

To fix ideas further, it is useful to think for a moment about the *AD* schedule in terms of the extreme classical and liquidity trap cases that we learned about in Chapter 4. In the classical case, where money demand is entirely unresponsive to interest rates and the *LM* curve is vertical, changes in real balances have a big effect on income and spending. In Figure 11-7 that corresponds to a very flat *AD* schedule, such as *AD′*, as we should expect based on point 1 (*a*) above. Conversely, in the liquidity trap case, where the public is willing to hold any amount of real balances at unchanged interest rates, a fall in prices and a rise in the real money stock have very little effect on income and spending.[2] In Figure 11-7 that would correspond to an almost vertical *AD* curve, as suggested again by point 1 (*a*) above. A vertical *AD* curve means that the planned level of spending is unresponsive to the price level.

You should now experiment with alternative *IS* and *LM* schedules to see how the effects of a change in the price level depend on the slopes of the *IS* and *LM* curves and the factors underlying those slopes. In doing so you will confirm the points summarized under 1 and 2 above. In problem 4 at the end of the chapter, we ask you to demonstrate these links.

Next we consider the factors that determine the position of the *AD* curve.

[2] The reason a reduction in prices increases output in this case is the *real balance effect:* with lower prices, the value of real balances held by the public is higher, their wealth is accordingly higher, and therefore their consumption spending and output are higher. See footnote 13 in Chap. 4 for a related point. The real balance effect is central to monetary theory as developed in the classical treatise by Don Patinkin, *Money, Interest and Prices* (New York: Harper & Row, 1965).

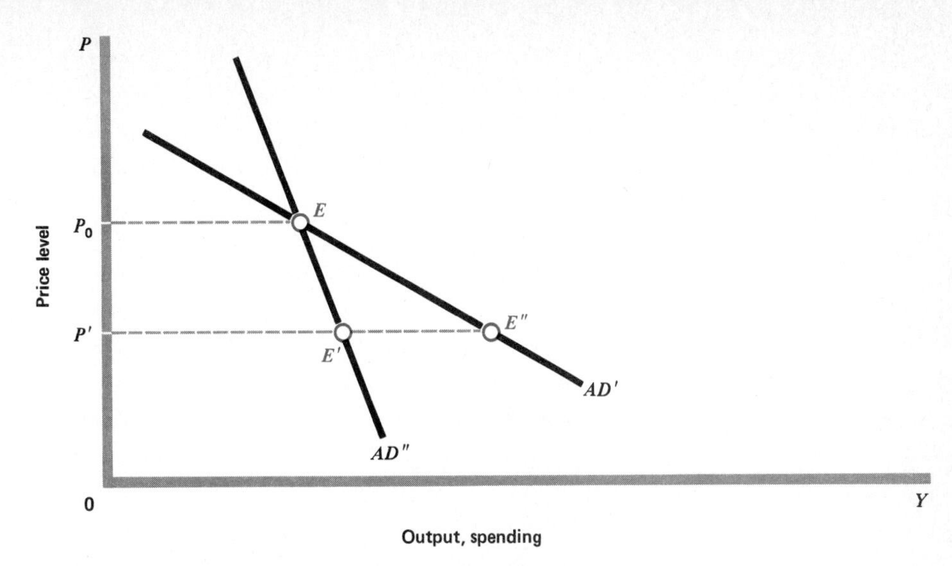

FIGURE 11-7 THE SLOPE OF THE AD SCHEDULE. The diagram shows two possible *AD* schedules. Along *AD''* a change in prices from P_0 to P' has a smaller effect on spending than along *AD'*. The former corresponds to the case where changes in real balances have little impact on equilibrium income and spending; the latter to the case where real balance changes exert significant effects.

THE EFFECT OF A FISCAL EXPANSION

We noted above that the same factors that determine the positions of the *IS* and *LM* schedules also determine the position of the *AD* curve. We now show how changes in fiscal and monetary policy shift the *AD* curve, starting with a fiscal expansion.

In Figure 11-8 the initial *LM* and *IS* schedules correspond to a given nominal quantity of money and the price level P_0. Equilibrium obtains at point *E*, and there is a corresponding point on the *AD* schedule in the lower panel.

Now the government increases the level of spending, say, on defense. As a consequence, the *IS* schedule shifts out and to the right. At the initial price level there is a new equilibrium at point *E'* with higher interest rates and a higher level of income and spending. Thus at the initial level of prices, P_0, equilibrium income and spending now are higher. We show this by plotting point *E'* in the lower panel. Point *E'* is a point on the new schedule *AD'* reflecting the effect of higher government spending.

Of course, we could have started with any other point on the original *AD* curve, and would then have shown how in the lower panel the rise in government spending leads to a higher equilibrium level of output at each price level. In that way we trace out the entire *AD'* schedule, which lies to the right of *AD*.

In fact, we can say more: At each level of prices, and hence of real

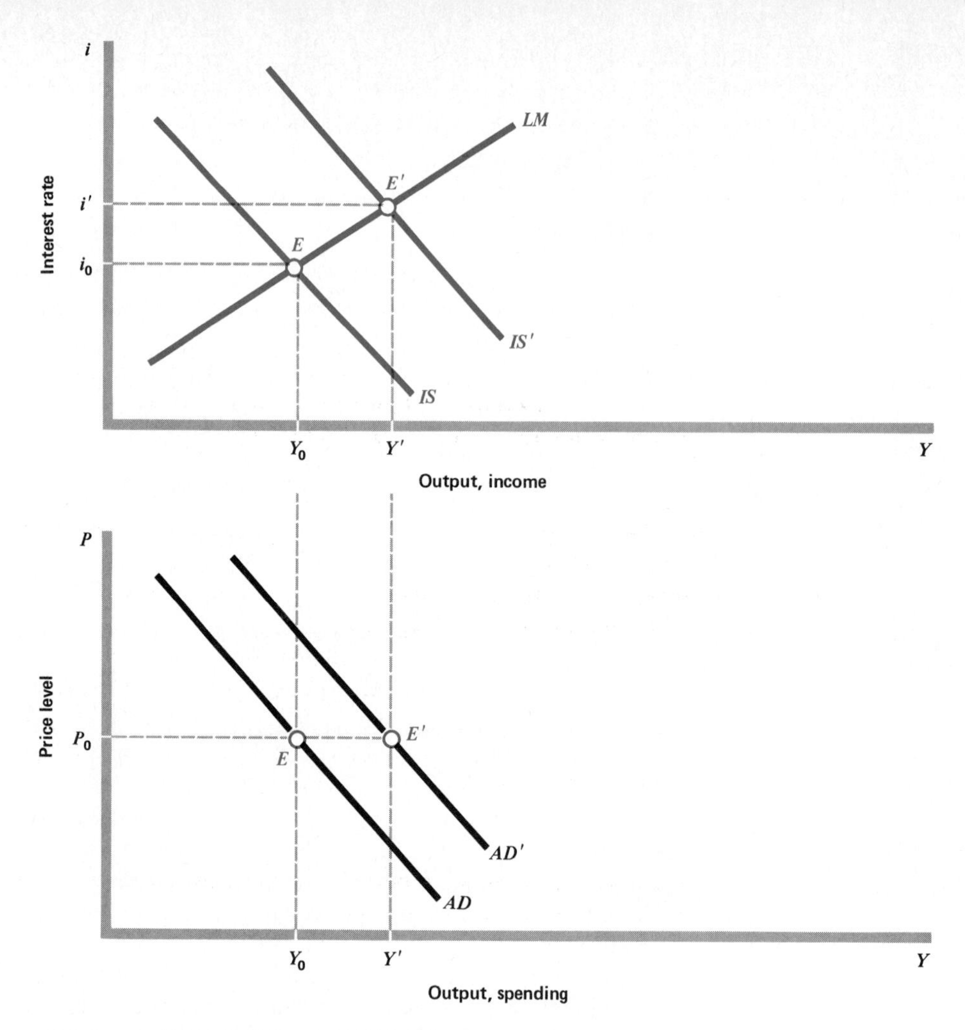

FIGURE 11-8 THE EFFECT OF A FISCAL EXPANSION ON THE AD SCHEDULE. A fiscal expansion, such as an increase in government spending, shifts the *IS* curve in the upper panel to *IS*′. At any given price level, such as P_0, the equilibrium in the upper panel shifts to *E*′, with higher level of output *Y*′ and higher interest rate *i*′. Point *E*′ in the lower panel is a point on the new aggregate demand schedule *AD*′ corresponding to price level P_0. We could similarly trace the effect of increased government spending on the equilibrium level of output and spending in the lower panel for every price level, and thus show that the *AD* curve shifts out to *AD*′ when fiscal policy is expansionary.

balances, the *AD* schedule shifts to the right by an amount indicated by the fiscal policy multiplier developed in Chapter 5. As we saw there, a fiscal expansion leads to a higher level of income and spending, the larger the interest response of money demand, the smaller the interest response of aggregate demand, and the larger the marginal propensity to consume.

Thus if the fiscal policy multiplier derived in Chapter 5 was, for example,

1.5, then a $1 (billion) dollar increase in government spending would increase equilibrium income and spending by $1.5 billion, at the given price level. In response to any change in government spending, the *AD* schedule would shift to the right by 1.5 times the increase in G.[3]

THE EFFECT OF A MONETARY EXPANSION ON THE *AD* SCHEDULE

An increase in the nominal money stock implies, at each level of prices, a higher real money stock. In the assets markets interest rates decline to induce the public to hold higher real balances. That decline in interest rates, in turn, stimulates aggregate demand and thus raises the equilibrium level of income and spending. In Figure 11-9 we show that an increase in the nominal money stock shifts the *AD* schedule up and to the right.

The extent to which an increase in nominal money shifts the *AD* schedule to the right depends on the monetary policy multiplier. If the monetary policy multiplier is large, say, because money demand is not very interest elastic and goods demand is, the *AD* schedule will shift a lot. Conversely, if the *LM* schedule is nearly flat, in which case we know monetary policy is ineffective, the *AD* schedule will shift very little.

We can also ask about the *upward* shift of the schedule. Here an interesting and important point emerges. Recall that what matters for equilibrium income and spending is the *real* money supply M/P. If an increase in nominal money is matched by an equiproportionate increase in prices, M/P is unchanged, and hence interest rates, aggregate demand, and equilibrium income and spending will remain unchanged. This gives us the clue to the vertical shift of the *AD* schedule.

An increase in the nominal money stock shifts the AD *schedule up exactly in proportion to the increase in nominal money.* Thus if, starting at point E in the lower panel of Figure 11-9, we have a 10 percent increase in M, real spending will be unchanged only if prices also rise by 10 percent, thus leaving real balances unchanged. Therefore the *AD* schedule shifts upward by 10 percent. At point K in Figure 11-9, *real* balances are the same as at E, and therefore interest rates and equilibrium income and spending are the same as at E.

We now have completed the derivation of the aggregate demand schedule. The important points to recall are that the *AD* schedule is shifted to the right both by increases in the money stock and by expansionary fiscal policy. In the remainder of this chapter we show how to use this tool to discuss the effects of monetary and fiscal policy *on both the level of output and the price level* under alternative assumptions about the supply side. We thus begin to consider how the price level and the rate of inflation are determined and affected by monetary and fiscal policy. The discussion continues, again using the *AD* schedule, in the next chapter, where we look at macroeconomic adjustment over time.

[3] In Chap. 5 we showed that the fiscal policy multiplier is given by the expression $\beta \equiv h\bar{\alpha}/(h + kb\bar{\alpha})$, where h is the interest responsiveness of money demand, $\bar{\alpha}$ the simple Keynesian multiplier, k the income response of money demand, and b the interest response of investment demand.

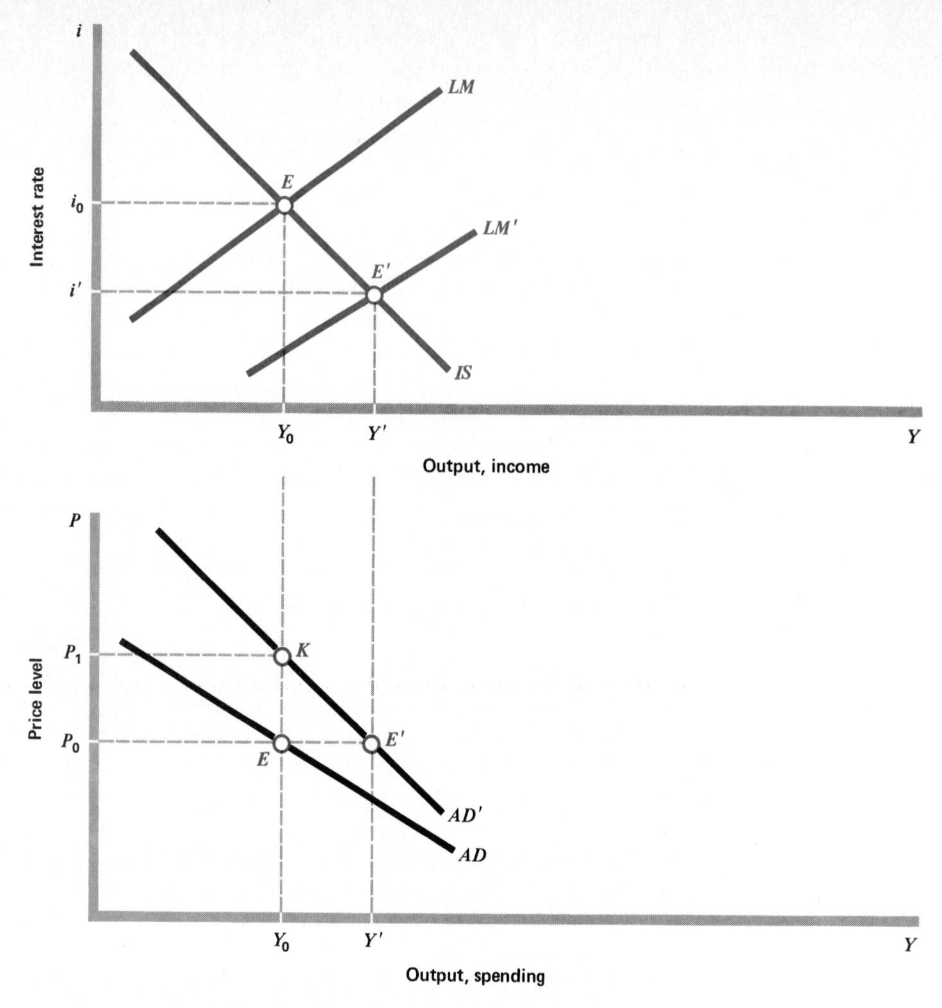

FIGURE 11-9 THE EFFECTS OF AN INCREASE IN THE MONEY STOCK ON THE AD SCHEDULE. An increase in the money stock shifts the LM curve to LM' in the upper panel. The equilibrium level of income rises from Y_0 to Y' at the initial price level P_0. Correspondingly, the AD curve moves out to the right, to AD', with point E' in the lower panel corresponding to E' in the upper panel. The AD curve shifts *up* in exactly the same proportion as the money stock increases. For instance, at point K the price level P_1 is higher than P_0 in the same proportion that the money supply has risen. *Real balances* at K on AD' are therefore the same as at E on AD.

11-4 MONETARY AND FISCAL POLICY UNDER ALTERNATIVE SUPPLY ASSUMPTIONS

In Figure 11-2 we showed how the aggregate supply and demand curves together determine the equilibrium level of income and prices in the economy. Now that we have shown how the aggregate demand curve is derived, and how it is shifted by policy changes, we use the aggregate demand and supply model to study the effects of monetary and fiscal policy in the two extreme supply cases—Keynesian and classical.

We should expect that the conclusions we reach in the Keynesian supply case are precisely the same as those reached in Chapters 4 and 5. In those chapters, in developing the *IS-LM* model, we assumed that whatever amount of goods was demanded would be supplied at the existing price level. And of course, as Figure 11-5*a* shows, the Keynesian supply curve implies that any amount of goods demanded will be supplied at the existing price level.

The Keynesian Case

In Figure 11-10 we combine the aggregate demand schedule with the Keynesian aggregate supply schedule. The initial equilibrium is at point *E*, where *AS* and *AD* intersect. At that point the goods and assets markets are in equilibrium.

Consider now a fiscal expansion. As we have already seen, increased government spending, or a cut in tax rates, shifts the *AD* schedule out and to the right from *AD* to *AD'*. The new equilibrium is at point *E'*, where output has increased. Because firms are willing to supply *any* amount of output at the level of prices P_0, there is no effect on prices. The only effect of higher government spending in Figure 11-10 is to increase output and employment. In addition, as we know from the *IS-LM* model that lies behind the *AD* schedule, the fiscal expansion will raise equilibrium interest rates. Because

FIGURE 11-10 A FISCAL EXPANSION: THE KEYNESIAN CASE. In the Keynesian case, with output in perfectly elastic supply at a given price level, a fiscal expansion increases equilibrium income from *Y* to *Y'*. This is exactly the result already derived with *IS* and *LM* schedules.

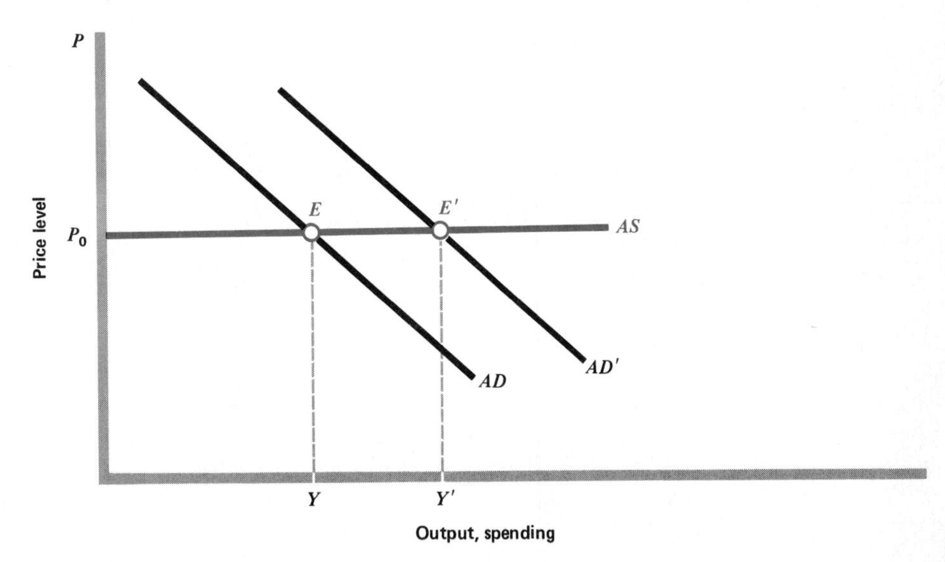

interest rates do increase, the fiscal expansion raises output less than suggested by the simple multiplier of Chapter 3.

We leave it to you to show that in the Keynesian case an increase in the nominal quantity of money likewise leads to an expansion in equilibrium output. With a horizontal *AS* schedule there is again no impact on prices. The magnitude of the output expansion then depends, in this Keynesian case, only on the monetary policy multiplier that determines the extent of the horizontal shift of the *AD* schedule.

Thus, as we expected, all our conclusions about the effects of policy changes in the Keynesian supply case are those of the simple *IS-LM* model.

The Classical Case: Fiscal Policy

In the classical case the aggregate supply schedule is vertical at the full-employment level of output. Firms will supply the level of output $\overline{Y}$ whatever the price level. Under this supply assumption we obtain results very different from those reached using the Keynesian model. Now the price level is not given, but rather depends on the interaction of supply and demand.

In Figure 11-11 we study the effect of a fiscal expansion under classical supply assumptions. The aggregate supply schedule is *AS*, with equilibrium

FIGURE 11-11 A FISCAL EXPANSION: THE CLASSICAL CASE. The supply of output is perfectly inelastic at the full-employment level of output, $\overline{Y}$. A fiscal expansion raises equilibrium spending, at the initial price level P_0, from E to E'. But now there is an excess demand because firms are unwilling to supply that much output. Prices increase, and that reduces real balances until we reach point E''. At E'' government spending is higher, but the higher price level means lower real balances, higher interest rates, and hence reduced private spending. At E'' increased government spending has crowded out an equal amount of private spending.

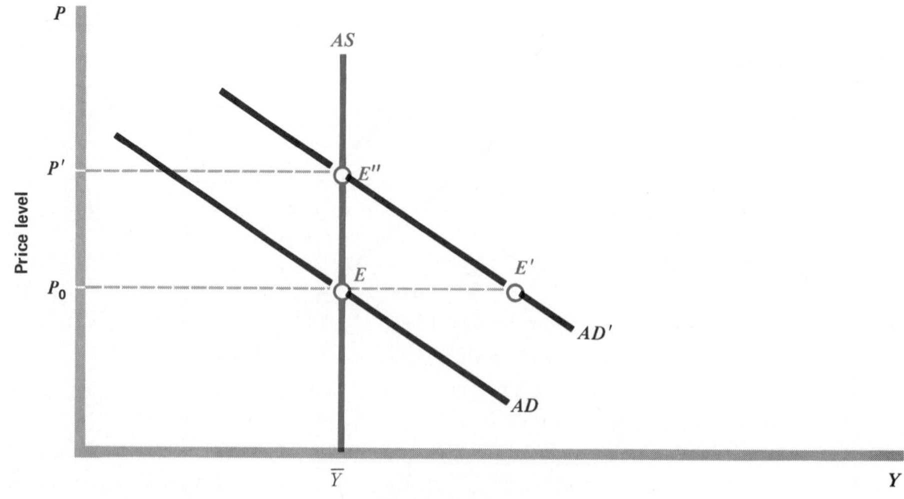

initially at point E. Note that at point E there is full employment because, by assumption, firms supply the full-employment level of output at any level of prices.

The fiscal expansion shifts the aggregate demand schedule from AD to AD'. At the initial level of prices, P_0, spending in the economy rises to point E'. At price level P_0 the demand for goods has risen. But firms cannot obtain the labor to produce more output, and output supply cannot respond to the increased demand. As firms try to hire more workers, they only bid up wages and their costs of production, and therefore they charge higher prices for their output. The increase in the demand for goods therefore leads only to higher prices, and not to higher output.

The increase in prices reduces the real money stock and leads to an increase in interest rates and a reduction in spending. The economy moves up the AD' schedule until prices have risen enough, and real balances have fallen enough, to raise interest rates and reduce spending to a level consistent with full-employment output. That is the case at a price level P'. At point E'' aggregate demand, at the higher level of government spending, is once again equal to aggregate supply.

CROWDING OUT AGAIN

Note what has happened in Figure 11-11: output is unchanged at the full-employment level $\bar{Y}$, but government spending is higher. That must imply less spending by the private sector. There is thus *full*, or complete, *crowding out.* Recall from Chapter 5 that crowding out occurs when an increase in government spending results in less spending by the private sector. Typically, as we showed in Chapter 5, government spending crowds out investment. In the case shown in Figure 11-11, with a classical supply curve, every dollar increase in real government spending is offset by a dollar reduction in private spending, so that crowding out is complete.

We thus reach the following important result: *In the classical case increased real government spending leads to full crowding out.* We now explain the mechanism through which crowding out occurs.

Figure 11-12 shows the IS-LM diagram, augmented with the line $\bar{Y}$ at the full-employment level of output. The initial equilibrium is at point E, where the money market clears and planned spending equals output. The fiscal expansion shifts the IS schedule to IS'. At an unchanged price level, and assuming firms were to meet the increase in demand by expanding production, we would move to point E'. But this is not possible under classical supply assumptions. Faced with an excess demand for goods, firms end up raising prices rather than output. The price increase, in turn, reduces real balances and therefore shifts the LM schedule up. Prices will increase until the excess demand has been eliminated. That means the LM schedule shifts up and to the left until we reach a new equilibrium at point E''.

At E'' the goods market clears at the full-employment level of output. Interest rates have increased compared with the initial equilibrium at E, and that increase in interest rates has reduced private spending to make room for

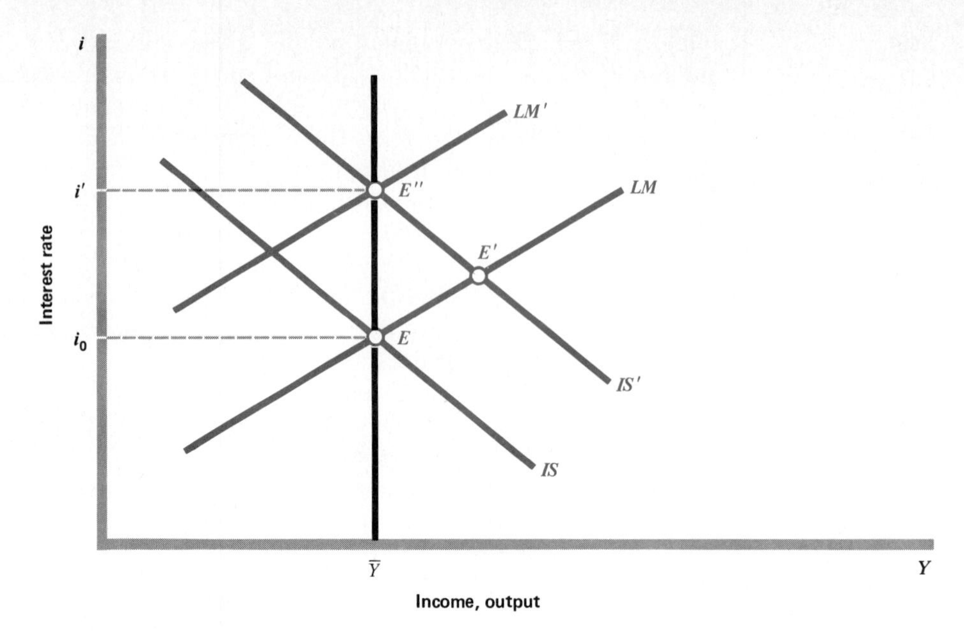

FIGURE 11-12 CROWDING OUT IN THE CLASSICAL CASE. A fiscal expansion in the classical case leads to full crowding out. The fiscal expansion shifts the IS schedule to IS'. At the initial price level the economy would move to point E', but there is excess demand since firms only supply $\overline{Y}$. Prices increase, shifting the LM schedule up and to the left until LM' is reached. The new equilibrium is at point E'', where interest rates have risen enough to displace an amount of private spending equal to the increased government demand.

increased government purchases. Note that the money market is also in equilibrium. Output and income are the same as at point E. The higher interest rate reduces the demand for real balances, matching the decline in the real money stock.

Note that we have now seen two mechanisms that produce full crowding out. In Chapter 5, crowding out is complete if the LM curve is vertical. In that case, crowding out occurs because money demand is interest inelastic. In this chapter, full crowding out occurs because aggregate supply limits total output. In brief, in Chapter 5 crowding out is a demand phenomenon; here it is a supply phenomenon.

We summarize in Table 11-1 the effects of a fiscal expansion in the cases of classical and Keynesian supply conditions. In each case we show what happens to output, interest rates, and the price level.

The table reinforces our understanding of the two models: in one case only prices adjust; in the other case only output. These models are clearly extremes, and we would expect that often adjustment occurs in both output and prices. That is the adjustment process we study in the next chapter. We shall see there that the Keynesian case comes close to describing the short-run effects of a fiscal expansion, while the classical case more accurately predicts what happens in the long run after all adjustments have taken place.

TABLE 11-1 THE EFFECTS OF A FISCAL EXPANSION

Aggregate supply	Output	Interest rate	Prices
Keynesian	+	+	0
Classical	0	+	+

Monetary Expansion Under Classical Conditions

We have already seen the impact of monetary policy under Keynesian supply conditions: with prices given, a rise in the nominal money stock is a rise in the real money stock. Equilibrium interest rates decline as a consequence, and output rises. Consider now the adjustments that occur in response to a monetary expansion when the aggregate supply curve is vertical and the price level is no longer fixed.

In Figure 11-13 we study an expansion in the nominal money stock under classical supply conditions. The initial full-employment equilibrium is at point

FIGURE 11-13 THE EFFECT OF A MONETARY EXPANSION UNDER CLASSICAL SUPPLY ASSUMPTIONS. Starting from the full-employment equilibrium at point E, an increase in the nominal money stock shifts the aggregate demand schedule to AD'. At the initial price level there is now an excess demand for goods. Prices increase, and thus the real money stock declines toward its initial level. Price increases continue until the economy reaches point E''. Here the *real* money stock has returned to its initial level, and with output unchanged, interest rates are again at their initial level. Thus a monetary expansion only affects prices, not output or interest rates.

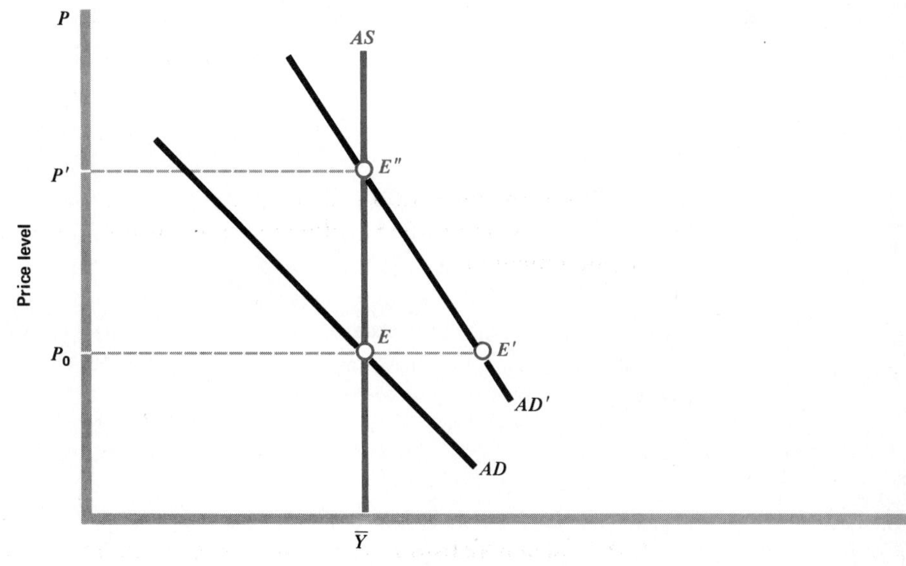

E, where the AD and AS schedules intersect. Now the nominal money stock is increased, and accordingly, the aggregate demand schedule shifts up and to the right to AD'. If prices were fixed, the economy would move to E', the Keynesian equilibrium. But now output is in fixed supply. The increase in aggregate demand leads to an excess demand for goods. Firms that attempt to expand, hiring more workers, bid up wages and costs. Prices increase in response to the excess demand, and that means real balances fall back toward their initial level. In fact prices keep rising until the excess demand for goods disappears. Thus they must increase until the economy reaches point E'', where AS intersects the new aggregate demand schedule AD'. Only when aggregate demand is again equal to full-employment supply does the goods market clear and the pressure for prices to rise disappear.

Consider now the adjustment that takes place in moving from E to E''. There is no change in output, only a change in the price level. Note, moreover, that prices rise in exactly the same proportion as the nominal quantity of money.[4] This we know because we saw earlier that in response to an increase in nominal money the AD schedule shifts upward in the same proportion as the increase in money. Thus at point E'' the real money stock M/P is back to its initial level. At E'' both nominal money and the price level have changed in the same proportion, leaving real money and hence interest rates and aggregate demand unchanged. We thus have an important implication of the classical model: *Under classical supply conditions an increase in nominal money raises the price level in the same proportion, but leaves interest rates and real output unchanged.*

In Table 11-2 we summarize the effects of an increase in the nominal money stock under Keynesian and classical supply conditions. Once again we look at the effects on output, prices, and interest rates. In addition we show the effect on real balances M/P. The table brings out the fact that under classical supply conditions, none of the *real* variables, such as output, interest rates, or real balances, are affected by a change in the nominal money stock. Only the price level changes.

11-5 THE QUANTITY THEORY AND THE NEUTRALITY OF MONEY

The classical model of supply, in combination with the *IS-LM* model describing the demand side of the economy, has extremely strong implications. Because, by assumption, output is maintained at the full-employment level by full price flexibility, monetary and fiscal policy do not affect output. Fiscal policy affects interest rates and the *composition* of spending between the government and the private sector and between consumption and investment. Monetary policy only affects the price level.

These implications about the effects of monetary policy on output are consistent with the *quantity theory of money*. The quantity theory of money in

[4] In problem 7 we ask you to use the *IS* and *LM* curves to show how the change in the money supply works. To answer the problem you have to use Fig. 11-9 along with the fact that the *LM* schedule shifts as the price level changes.

TABLE 11-2 THE EFFECTS OF AN INCREASE IN THE NOMINAL MONEY STOCK

Aggregate supply	Output	Interest rate	Prices	Real balances
Keynesian	+	−	0	+
Classical	0	0	+	0

its strongest form asserts that the price level is proportional to the stock of money. For instance, in the case of the classical supply curve, an increase in the quantity of money produces, in equilibrium, a proportional increase in the price level. In this case, money is *neutral.*

THE NEUTRALITY OF MONEY

Money is *neutral* when changes in the money stock lead only to changes in the price level, with no real variables (output, employment, and interest rates) changing. For instance, money is neutral in the second row of Table 11-2, where in response to a change in the money stock, only the price level changes, with output, interest rates, and real balances remaining unchanged.

We saw above that the classical supply curve has the powerful and important implication that fiscal policy cannot affect output. The neutrality of money likewise has strong policy implications. For instance, if money were neutral, there would be an easy way to reduce the inflation rate if we ever wanted to do that. All we would have to do would be to reduce the rate at which the money stock is growing.

In practice, it is very difficult to change the inflation rate without producing a recession, as for instance in the period 1979–1983 in the United States. When a lower growth rate of money leads first to unemployment, and only later to lower inflation, as it did in the recession in 1982, then we know that money is not neutral. Changes in the quantity of money then have real effects—monetary policy affects the level of output. This means that the aggregate supply curve cannot be vertical in the short run. In the next chapter we develop the aggregate supply curve, showing why in the short run it is quite flat, whereas over longer periods it is more nearly vertical.

The Modern Quantity Theory: Monetarism

We defined the strict quantity theory as asserting that the price level is proportional to the quantity of money. Although the quantity theory is centuries, and perhaps millennia, old, few have believed in the strict quantity theory. That is, few have believed that the price level is strictly proportional to the money stock, or that money is the *only* factor affecting the price level. Rather, quantity theorists argued and argue that the money stock is, in practice, the single most important factor producing inflation.

Box 11-1 presents quotations from Irving Fisher (1867–1947), widely thought to be the greatest American economist of his time, and from Milton

BOX 11-1

THE QUANTITY THEORY OF MONEY

Irving Fisher (1867–1947) and Milton Friedman (born 1912) are two of the foremost monetary economists in the United States in this century. Both strongly advocated the quantity theory of money as the right model of price level determination.

Fisher stated*:

> In recent popular discussions a great variety of reasons have been assigned for the "high cost of living," *e.g.*, "profiteering"; speculation; hoarding; the middleman; . . . the tariff; cold storage; longer hauls on railroads; marketing by telephone; the free delivery system; the individual package; the enforcement of sanitary laws; the tuberculin testing of cattle; the destruction of tainted meat; sanitary milk; the elimination of renovated butter and of "rots" and "spots" in eggs; food adulteration; advertising; unscientific management; extravagance; higher standards of living; the increasing cost of government; the increasing cost of old-age pensions, and of better pauper institutions, hospitals, insane asylums, reformatories, jails and other public institutions; . . .
>
> I shall not discuss in detail this list of alleged explanations. While some of them are important factors in raising particular prices, none of them . . . has been important in raising the *general* scale of prices. . . .
>
> The ups and downs of prices roughly correspond with the ups and downs of the money supply. Throughout all history this has been so. For this general broad fact the evidence is sufficient even where we lack the index numbers by which to make accurate measurements. Whenever there have been rapid outpourings from mines, following discoveries of the precious metals used for money, prices have risen with corresponding rapidity. This was observed in the sixteenth century, after great quantities of the precious metals had been brought to Europe from the New World; and again in the nineteenth century, after the Californian and Australian gold mining of the fifties; and, still again, in the same century after the South African, Alaskan, and Cripple Creek mining of the nineties. Likewise when other causes than mining, such as paper money issues, produce violent changes in the quantity or quality of money, violent changes in the price level usually follow.

Friedman wrote†:

> Since men first began to write systematically about economic matters they have devoted special attention to the wide movements in the general level of prices that have intermittently occurred. Two alternative explanations have usually been offered. One has attributed the changes in prices to changes in the quantity of money. The other has attributed the changes in prices to war or to profiteers or to rises in wages or to some other special circumstance of the particular time and place and has regarded any accompanying change in the quantity of money as a common consequence of the same special circumstance. The first explanation has generally been referred to as the quantity theory of money, although that designation conceals the variety of forms the explanation has taken, the different levels of sophistication on which it has been developed, and the wide range of the claims that have been made for its applicability. . . .
>
> In its most rigid and unqualified form the quantity theory asserts strict proportionality

* Irving Fisher, *Stabilizing the Dollar* (New York: Macmillan, 1920), pp. 10–11 and 29.

† Milton Friedman, "Money: The Quantity Theory," in *The International Encyclopedia of the Social Sciences*, Vol. X, 1968, pp. 432–447.

between the quantity of what is regarded as money and the level of prices. Hardly anyone has held the theory in that form, although statements capable of being so interpreted have often been made in the heat of argument or for expository simplicity. Virtually every quantity theorist has recognized that changes in the quantity of money that correspond to changes in the volume of trade or of output have no tendency to produce changes in prices. Nearly as many have recognized also that changes in the willingness of the community to hold money can occur for a variety of reasons and can introduce disparities between changes in the quantity of money per unit of trade or of output and changes in prices. What quantity theorists have held in common is the belief that these qualifications are of secondary importance for substantial changes in either prices or the quantity of money, so that the one will not in fact occur without the other.

Friedman, the leading exponent of the quantity theory and the importance of money in the modern era. The two differ in emphasis: Fisher comes close to asserting that only changes in the quantity of money affect the price level; Friedman is more clear in arguing that other factors can affect the price level, but that these other factors are of secondary importance.

Friedman is the recognized intellectual leader of an influential group of economists, called *monetarists*, who emphasize the role of money and monetary policy in affecting the behavior of output and prices. Leading monetarists include Professors Karl Brunner of the University of Rochester, Allan Meltzer of Carnegie-Mellon University, Thomas Mayer of the University of California at Davis, David Laidler and Michael Parkin of the University of Western Ontario, and other scholars, both in the United States and other countries. There is more to monetarism than the argument that money is the most important determinant of macroeconomic performance, but we leave the other tenets of monetarism for further discussion in Chapter 16.

A FORMAL STATEMENT

We can discuss the quantity theory more formally by drawing on the definition of the income velocity of money V presented in Chapter 8. Income velocity times the stock of money M is equal to nominal income, which in turn is equal to the price level P times real income Y:

$$MV = PY \tag{1}$$

or, dividing by real output Y,

$$P = \frac{MV}{Y} \tag{2}$$

Suppose that output is fixed at the full employment level $\bar{Y}$. Suppose also that the velocity of money is fixed. Then it follows from Eq. (2) that changes in the money stock will cause proportionate changes in the price level. Thus, if

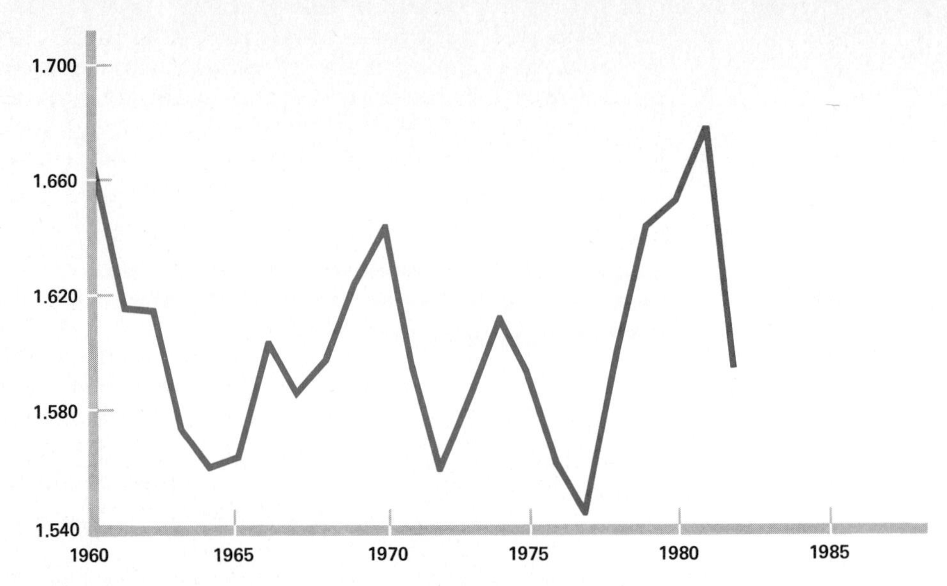

FIGURE 11-14 THE INCOME VELOCITY OF MONEY ($M2$). (*Source:* Citibank Economic Database.)

(1) output is at the full employment level, and (2) velocity is constant, the *strict* quantity theory holds.

Figure 11-14 shows the income velocity of money ($M2$) over the period since 1960. The data make it clear that the income velocity of money is far from constant and thus that the strict quantity theory does not hold.

We can also use (2) to see why modern quantity theorists argue, as does Friedman, that factors other than the quantity of money may affect prices. Most important, and as the data in Figure 11-14 confirm, the income velocity of money may change.

Recall from Chapter 8 that the income velocity of money is closely related to the demand for money. The more money people hold in relation to their income, the lower the income velocity of money. For instance, if people on average hold money balances equal to 2 months of their income, the income velocity of money (the ratio of annual income to the money stock) will be 6. We know that the lower the interest rate, the more real balances people hold. Thus we certainly expect velocity to be affected by interest rates: the higher the interest rate, the higher the velocity because the less real balances people will hold relative to their incomes.

Modern quantity theorists or monetarists recognize that interest rate movements do affect velocity. Similarly, velocity is affected by changes in the banking system that make it easier to economize on the holding of money. But in practice, monetarists assert, changes in interest rates and the structure of the banking system are not important enough to obscure the main message: The most important factor changing the price level is the quantity of money.

We return to monetarism and the evidence supporting it in Chapters 13 and 16.

FISCAL POLICY AND THE PRICE LEVEL

We can use Equation (2) to show how a change in fiscal policy affects the price level in the classical case. Assuming that the economy is at the full-employment level of output, we know that expansionary fiscal policy increases the interest rate. That means velocity rises. From Equation (2) we see that the price level must rise, given the nominal money stock M. This confirms the conclusion we reached in Figure 11-11 in discussing fiscal policy in the classical case.

THE LONG RUN AND THE SHORT

Modern quantity theorists differ also from the strict quantity theory in not believing that the supply curve is vertical in the short run. Monetarists such as Milton Friedman argue that a reduction in the money stock does in practice *first* reduce the level of output, and only later have an effect on prices.

Thus Friedman and other monetarists make an important distinction between the short- and long-run effects of changes in money. They argue that in the long run money is more or less neutral. Changes in the money stock, after they have worked their way through the economy, have no real effects and only change prices: the quantity theory and the neutrality of money are, from this long-run perspective, not just theoretical possibilities, but instead a reasonable description of the way the world works. But in the short run, they argue, monetary policy and changes in the money stock can and do have important real effects.

The short-run versus long-run distinction is pursued in the next chapter, where we go more deeply into the aggregate supply curve.

11-7 SUMMARY

1. The aggregate supply and demand model is used to show the determination of the equilibrium levels of *both* output and prices.
2. The aggregate supply schedule *AS* shows at each level of prices the quantity of real output or GNP firms are willing to supply.
3. The Keynesian supply schedule is horizontal, implying that firms supply as much goods as are demanded at the existing price level. The classical supply schedule is vertical. It would apply in an economy that has full price and wage flexibility. In such a frictionless economy, employment and output are always at the full-employment level.
4. The aggregate demand schedule *AD* shows at each price level the level of output at which the goods and assets markets are in equilibrium. This is the quantity of output demanded at each price level. Along the *AD* schedule fiscal policy is given, as is the nominal quantity of money. The *AD* schedule is derived using the *IS-LM* model.
5. Moving down and along the *AD* schedule, lower prices raise the real

value of the money stock. Equilibrium interest rates fall, and that increases aggregate demand and equilibrium spending.

6 A fiscal expansion or an increase in the nominal quantity of money shifts the *AD* schedule out and to the right.
7 Under Keynesian supply conditions, with prices fixed, both monetary and fiscal expansion raise equilibrium output. A monetary expansion lowers interest rates, while a fiscal expansion raises them.
8 Under classical supply conditions a fiscal expansion has no effect on output. But a fiscal expansion raises prices, lowers real balances, and increases equilibrium interest rates.
9 Under classical supply conditions there is full crowding out. Private spending declines by exactly the increase in government demand.
10 A monetary expansion, under classical supply conditions, raises prices in the same proportion as the rise in nominal money. All real variables, specifically output and interest rates, remain unchanged. When changes in the money stock have no real effects, money is said to be *neutral.*
11 The strict quantity theory of money states that prices move in proportion to the nominal money stock. The strict quantity theory holds if velocity is constant and if output remains at the full-employment level. Neither of these conditions obtains in practice.
12 Modern quantity theorists or monetarists accept that there is no exact link between money and prices, but argue that changes in the money stock are, in practice, the most important single determinant of changes in the price level. They note, also, that changes in the money stock have real effects in the short run, but, they argue, money is approximately neutral in the long run.

KEY TERMS

Aggregate supply curve
Aggregate demand curve
Keynesian aggregate supply curve
Classical aggregate supply curve
Full crowding out
Quantity theory of money
Neutrality of money
Monetarism

PROBLEMS

1 Define the aggregate demand and supply curves.
2 Explain why the classical supply curve is vertical and explain the mechanisms that ensure continued full employment of labor in the classical case.
3 Discuss, using the *IS-LM* model, what happens to interest rates as prices change along a given *AD* schedule.
4 Show graphically that the *AD* curve is steeper (*a*) the larger the interest responsiveness of the demand for money and (*b*) the smaller the multiplier.

5 Suppose full-employment output increases from $\overline{Y}$ to $\overline{Y}'$. What does the quantity theory predict will happen to the price level?

6 In goods market equilibrium, $S + T = I + G$. Use this equation to explain why, in the classical case, a fiscal expansion must lead to full crowding out.

7 Show, using *IS* and *LM* curves, why money is neutral in the classical supply case. (Refer to footnote 4 for hints.)

8 Suppose the government reduces the personal income tax rate from t to t'.
   (*a*) What is the effect on the *AD* schedule?
   (*b*) What is the effect on the equilibrium interest rate?
   (*c*) What happens to investment?

9 Suppose there is a decline in the demand for money. At each output level and interest rate the public now wants to hold lower real balances.
   (*a*) In the Keynesian case, what happens to equilibrium output and to prices?
   (*b*) In the classical case, what is the effect on output and on prices?

10 In question 9, use the quantity theory of money to explain the effect of the money demand shift on prices.

11 Suppose the government undertakes a balanced budget increase in spending. Government spending rises from G to G', and there is an accompanying increase in tax rates so that at the initial level of output the budget remains balanced.
   (*a*) Show the effect on the *AD* schedule.
   (*b*) Discuss the effect of the balanced budget policy on output and interest rates in the Keynesian case.
   (*c*) Discuss the effect in the classical case.

12 (*a*) Define the strict quantity theory.
   (*b*) Define monetarism.
   (*c*) What type of statistical evidence would you need to collect to support or refute the major argument of monetarism presented in this chapter?

12

AGGREGATE SUPPLY: WAGES, PRICES, AND EMPLOYMENT

In this chapter we develop the aggregate supply side of the economy. We show the links between wages, prices, and employment and the adjustment process to disturbances in aggregate demand — monetary or fiscal policy changes or autonomous changes in spending. The development of the aggregate supply side of the economy also allows us to study the adjustment to supply shocks such as the increase in oil prices of 1973–1974 and 1979–1980 or the decline in oil prices in 1982–1983. The supply side of the economy is an essential part of the *dynamics* of prices (inflation) and output, that is, of the adjustment of prices and output over time when the economy is hit by a disturbance. For that reason we spend an entire chapter on the topic. The investment of time on this topic is worthwhile also because an understanding of aggregate supply is essential if we are to grasp the policy dilemma, described in later chapters, that comes from the short-run tradeoff between inflation and unemployment.

We start, in Section 12-1, with the *frictionless classical model* of output, prices, wages, and employment. This model provides a sensible general framework of analysis. But because the model makes a number of extremely strong assumptions about the working of goods and labor markets — in particular, *full* wage and price flexibility — it cannot explain recessions and booms.

We therefore move on, in Sections 12-2 and 12-3, to develop a more realistic framework that leads to an upward-sloping supply schedule such as the one in Chapter 11. But we do not lose sight of the classical model because we also show that the supply schedule does not stay put, but rather moves over time in response to changes in wages which come about because of overemployment or underemployment. Three points emerge from that analysis:

- Changes in aggregate demand lead in the short run to changes in both output and prices in the same direction. The extent to which the price level changes depends on the slope of the aggregate supply curve.
- The extent to which changes in demand are met by changes in output as opposed to prices depends on the response of costs to an expansion in output and employment. If wage costs are very unresponsive in the short run, the supply curve is quite flat, and shifts in demand are met at essentially constant prices.
- An expansion of output above normal will bring about overemployment and therefore rising wages and costs. Firms will pass on these cost increases by increasing their prices. The aggregate supply schedule shifts upward, thereby raising equilibrium prices and reducing equilibrium output along the aggregate demand schedule. The process continues until output declines to the level of full employment. There is, of course, a parallel story for a decline in demand.

The last point means that the classical model describes well the long-run response of output, employment, and prices to disturbances. It is thus an essential part of our understanding of the workings of the economy. But the frictionless model does not do a good job of explaining short-run responses of prices and output to disturbances. That is why we have to go beyond the classical model in this chapter.

Once the aggregate supply framework is developed, we use it to study the economy's adjustment to a change in monetary and fiscal policy. We show that both monetary and fiscal expansion in the short run lead to higher output and higher prices, just as in Chapter 11. In the long run, however, the economy returns to full employment. The chapter concludes with a discussion of the adjustment to supply shocks and some finer points of aggregate supply.[1]

12-1 THE FRICTIONLESS CLASSICAL MODEL

The relationship among wages, prices, and employment and between employment and output will now be studied in an idealized *frictionless* case. That

[1] The theory of aggregate supply is more difficult, less settled, and more controversial than the theory of aggregate demand. The student not concerned with the more difficult points can acquire the essentials of the theory by reading Sections 12-1 through 12-4.

is the case where wages and prices are *fully* flexible, where there are no costs either to workers in finding jobs or to firms in increasing or reducing their labor force, and where firms behave competitively and expect to sell all they produce at prevailing prices. That case both serves as a benchmark for the discussion of more realistic cases, and also allows us to introduce such useful concepts as the production function and the demand for labor. Throughout, we assume that labor is the only variable factor of production in the short run and that the capital stock is given.

The Production Function

A production function provides a relation between the quantity of factor inputs, such as the amount of labor used, and the maximum quantity of output that can be produced using those inputs.[2] The relation reflects only technical efficiency. In Equation (1) we write the production function

$$Y = F(N, \ldots) \tag{1}$$

where Y denotes real output, N is labor input, and the dots denote other cooperating factors (capital, for example) that are in short-run fixed supply. The production function is shown in Figure 12-1. The production function exhibits *diminishing returns* to labor, which means that the increase in output resulting from the employment of one more unit of labor declines as the amount of labor used increases.

Diminishing returns are shown in the production function by the fact that it is not a straight line through the origin (constant returns) or an upward-curling line (increasing returns). Diminishing returns are explained by the fact that as employment increases and other inputs remain constant, each laborer on the job has fewer machines with which to work and therefore becomes less productive. Thus, increases in the amount of labor progressively reduce the addition to output that further employment can bring. An increase in the labor force will always raise output, but progressively less so as employment expands. The marginal contribution of increased employment is indicated by the slope of the production function, $\Delta Y/\Delta N$. It is readily seen that the slope flattens out as we increase employment, thus showing that increasing employment makes a diminishing, but still positive, contribution to output.

Labor Demand

From the production function we proceed to the demand for labor. We are asking how much labor a firm would want to hire. The rule of thumb is to hire additional labor and expand production as long as doing so increases profits. A firm will hire additional workers as long as they will bring in more in revenue than they cost in wages.

The contribution to output of additional labor is called the *marginal product of labor*. It is equal, in Figure 12-1, to the slope of the production

[2] The production function was introduced in Chap. 7.

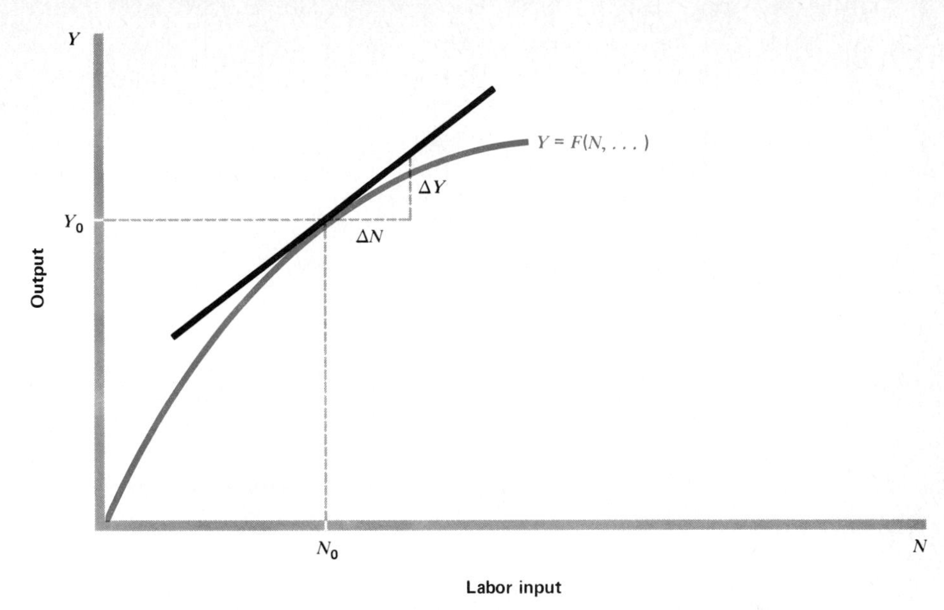

FIGURE 12-1 THE PRODUCTION FUNCTION AND THE MARGINAL PRODUCT OF LABOR. The production function links the amount of output produced to the level of labor input, given other factors of production such as capital. The schedule shows diminishing returns. Successive increases in labor yield less and less extra output. The marginal product of labor is shown by the slope of the production function, $\Delta Y/\Delta N$, that is, the increase in output per unit increase in employment. The flattening of the slope shows that the marginal product of labor is declining.

function. The marginal product, as we have seen, is both positive—additional labor is productive—and diminishing, which means that additional employment becomes progressively less productive. *A firm will employ additional labor as long as the marginal product of labor, MPN for short, exceeds the cost of additional labor.* The cost of additional labor is given by the real wage, that is, the nominal wage divided by the price level. The real wage measures the amount of real output the firm has to pay each worker. Since hiring one more worker results in an output increase of *MPN* and a cost to the firm of the real wage, firms will hire additional labor if the *MPN* exceeds the real wage. This point is formalized in Figure 12-2, which looks at the labor market.

The downward-sloping schedule in Figure 12-2 is the demand for labor schedule, which is the *MPN* schedule; firms hire labor up to the point at which the *MPN* is equal to the real wage. The *MPN* schedule shows the contribution to output of additional employment. It follows from our reasoning that the *MPN* is positive but that additional employment reduces it, so that the *MPN* schedule is negatively sloped.

Now consider a firm that currently employs a labor force, N_1, and assume the real wage is $(w/P)_0$, where w is the money wage and P the price of output. At an employment level N_1 in Figure 12-2, the firm is clearly employing too

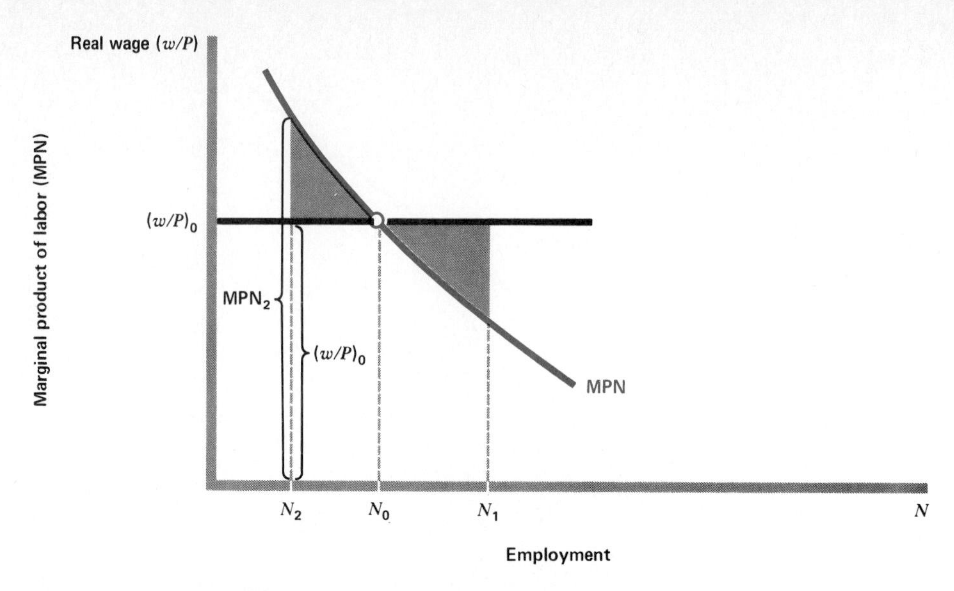

FIGURE 12-2 THE OPTIMAL EMPLOYMENT CHOICE FOR A GIVEN REAL WAGE. The marginal product of labor *MPN* is a declining function of the level of employment because of diminishing returns. Given a real wage $(w/P)_0$, the optimal employment choice is N_0. At N_1 the marginal product of labor is less than the real wage, so that the firm would save by reducing employment. Conversely, at N_2 the marginal product exceeds the real wage, so that the firm would gain by hiring an additional worker.

much labor since the real wage exceeds the *MPN* at that level of employment. What would happen if the firm should reduce employment by one unit? The reduction in employment would decrease output by the *MPN*, and therefore reduce revenue to the firm. On the other side of the calculation, we have the reduction in the wage bill. Per unit reduction in employment, the wage bill would fall at the rate of the real wage $(w/P)_0$. The net benefit of a reduction in the employment level is thus equal to the vertical excess of the real wage over the *MPN* in Figure 12-2. It is apparent that at the level of employment N_1, the excess is quite sizable, and it pays the firm to reduce the employment level. Indeed, it pays to reduce employment until the firm gets to point N_0. Only at that point does the cost of additional labor—the real wage—exactly balance the benefit in the form of increased output.

The same argument applies to the employment level N_2. Here employment is insufficient because the contribution to output of additional employment, MPN_2, exceeds the cost of additional employment, and it therefore pays to expand the level of employment. It is readily seen that with a real wage $(w/P)_0$, the firm's profits are maximized when employment is N_0. In general, given *any* real wage, the firm's demand for labor is shown by the *MPN* curve.

The firm's optimal employment position is formalized in Equation (2). At the optimal employment level the marginal product of labor (which is a declining function of employment) $MPN(N)$ is equal to the real wage:

$$MPN(N) = w/P \tag{2}$$

Equilibrium in the Labor Market

We have now developed the relation between output and employment (the production function) and the optimal employment choice for a given real wage that is implied by the demand for labor. It remains to consider the determination of the real wage as part of labor market equilibrium. What we have not yet dealt with is the supply of labor.

We make a quite simple assumption concerning labor supply. We assume that the supply of labor is fixed at $\overline{N}$ and that it is independent of the real wage.[3] This is shown in Figure 12-3 as the vertical schedule, $\overline{NN}$. The equilibrium real wage is clearly $(w/P)_0$.

[3] The exposition of this chapter would be little affected if we assumed that labor supply increased as the real wage increased. The major change then would be that the full-employment level of employment would depend on the level of the real wage. You might want to experiment with an upward-sloping labor supply curve as you continue reading. The quantity of labor supplied does appear to increase with the real wages because new workers—particularly women—come into the labor force as the wage increases.

FIGURE 12-3 EQUILIBRIUM IN THE LABOR MARKET. The labor supply is $\overline{N}$ and is independent of the real wage. The demand for labor is the marginal product schedule MPN. Labor market equilibrium obtains at a real wage $(w/P)_0$. At that real wage the demand for labor equals the quantity of labor supplied. At a lower real wage there is an excess demand for labor; at a higher real wage there is an excess supply or unemployment.

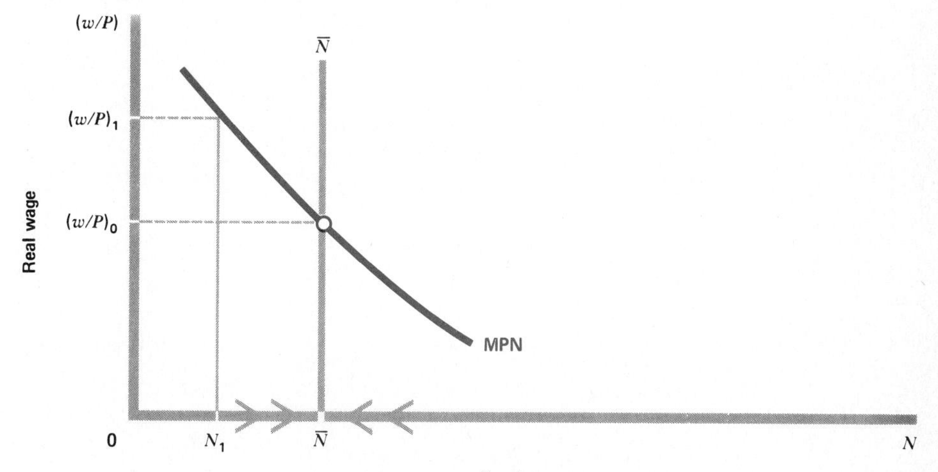

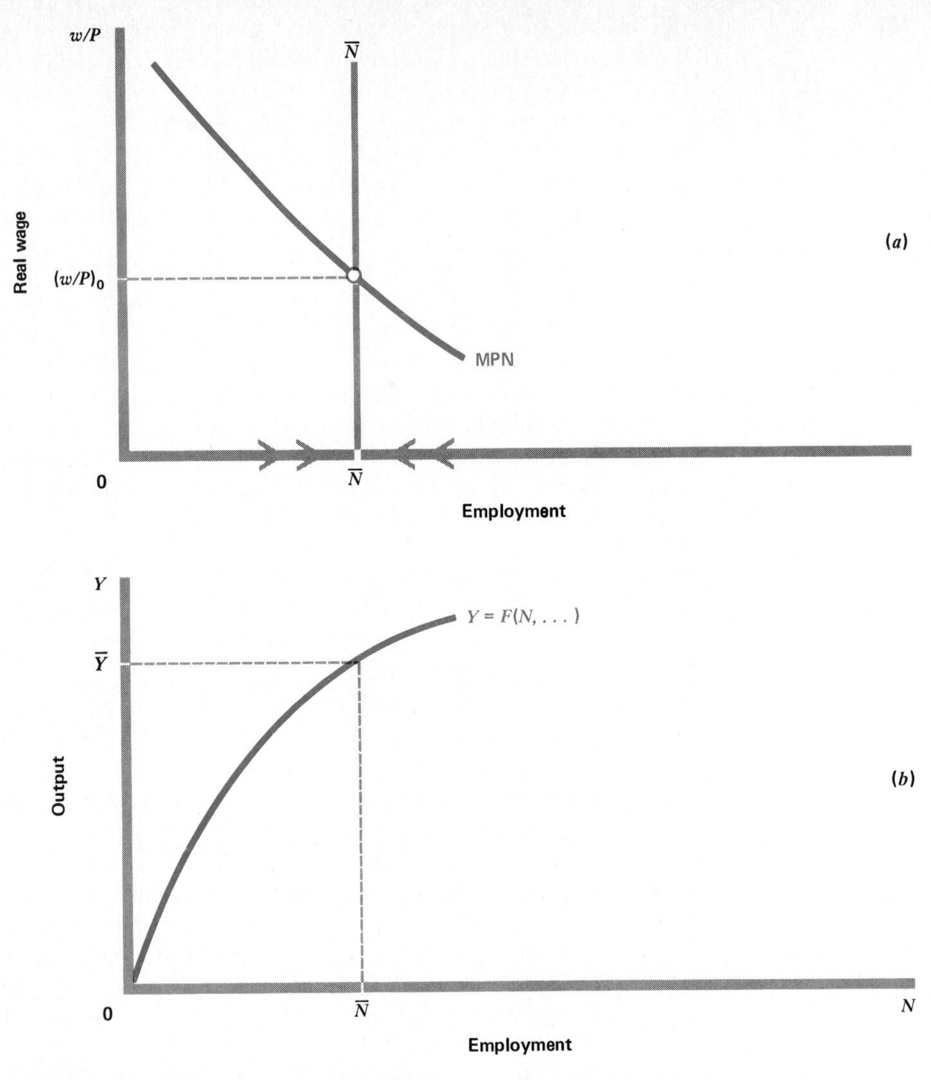

FIGURE 12-4 EQUILIBRIUM IN THE LABOR MARKET AND FULL-EMPLOYMENT OUTPUT. Part (*a*) of the diagram repeats the labor market equilibrium of Figure 12-3. Part (*b*) shows the production function. The equilibrium employment level $\overline{N}$, also the full-employment level, leads to an output $\overline{Y}$, which is the full-employment level of output.

How would the labor market get to that equilibrium? Suppose that the real wage fell whenever there was an excess supply of labor and that it rose whenever there was an excess demand. In terms of Figure 12-3 this would mean that the real wage would decline whenever it was above $(w/P)_0$. At $(w/P)_1$, for example, labor demand is only N_1 and thus falls short of the labor supply. This would put downward pressure on the real wage, cause the real wage to fall, and make it profitable to expand employment. Exactly the reverse argument holds for real wages lower than $(w/P)_0$, where there is an excess demand for labor.

From Figure 12-3 we see that adjustment of the real wage would bring the labor market into full-employment equilibrium at a real wage $(w/P)_0$ and an employment level equal to the given labor supply $\bar{N}$. Figure 12-4 summarizes the complete equilibrium in the labor market and the corresponding level of *full-employment output* $\bar{Y}$, which is the level of output associated with employment equal to the given labor supply.

Classical Goods and Labor Market Equilibrium

We have now derived the full-employment supply of output and the corresponding *real* wage, and have to complete the classical model by asking how *money* wages and prices are determined. How can we be sure that goods produced can be sold? Here we make two important assumptions: (1) goods prices will rise or fall instantaneously to clear the goods market, and (2) money wages will instantaneously rise or fall to clear the labor market. How will those adjustments work?

In the labor market, the flexibility of money wages ensures that at each price level the money wage rises or falls to achieve the necessary level of the real wage. We are therefore continuously in labor market equilibrium, and whatever the level of prices, firms will employ the full-employment labor force $\bar{N}$ and supply the corresponding level of output $\bar{Y}$. This is shown in Figure 12-5 in the aggregate supply curve *AS*. The aggregate supply schedule is vertical to show that the equilibrium level of output supplied—when the labor market is in equilibrium—is independent of the price level. If prices rose relative to wages, firms would be making profits. In an attempt to secure even larger profits, they would attempt individually to expand their employment level at the going money wage. In the aggregate, though, all they would do would be to compete for the given labor force and drive up the money wage until it had risen in proportion to the increase in prices, thus leaving real output unchanged.

Figure 12-5 includes an aggregate demand curve *AD* along with the vertical classical aggregate supply function. Recall from Chapter 11 that the aggregate demand curve slopes downward because increases in the price level reduce real balances, increase the interest rate, and reduce aggregate demand. Aggregate demand and supply jointly determine the equilibrium price level P_0. We need not be concerned yet with a full understanding of the details of the adjustment process of the price level in response to shifts in aggregate supply or demand. We need only recognize that it is plausible that the economy will converge to a full-employment equilibrium with all markets in equilibrium. Given the equilibrium price level P_0, the nominal wage will adjust so that the real wage is $(w/P)_0$. Furthermore, *if* wages and prices adjust

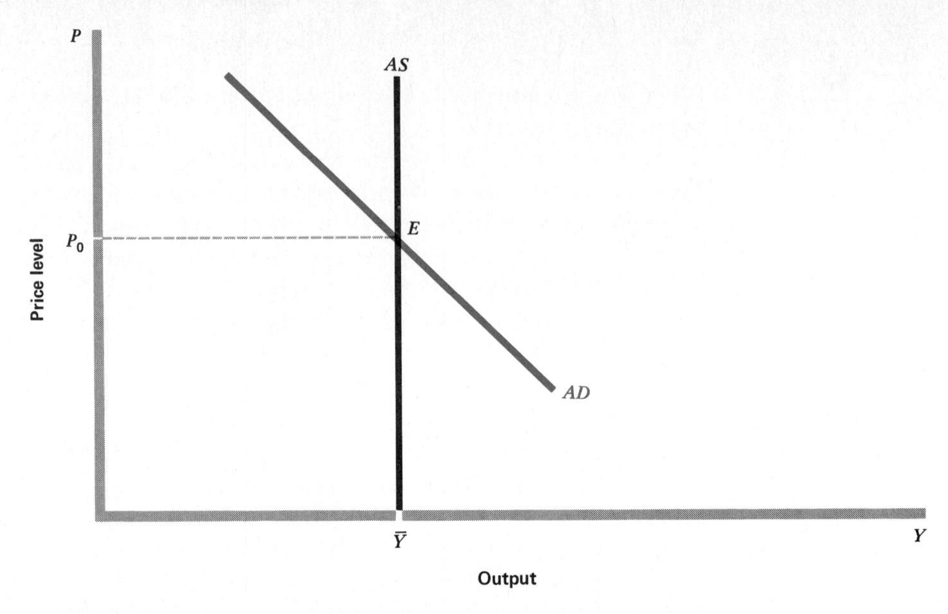

FIGURE 12-5 AGGREGATE DEMAND, AGGREGATE SUPPLY, AND THE EQUILIBRIUM PRICE LEVEL. The labor market equilibrium leads to an employment level $\bar{N}$ and implies an output level $\bar{Y}$. This is the full-employment output level shown by the vertical supply schedule *AS*. Aggregate demand is shown by the downward-sloping schedule *AD*. Equilibrium in the goods market obtains at a price level P_0. At that price level, demand for output equals the full-employment supply. Price and wage flexibility ensures that the economy reaches the equilibrium at point *E*.

rapidly, and *if* firms respond rapidly in their production decisions to changing conditions, and *if* labor moves rapidly between jobs as some firms expand and others contract, we would expect to be in full-employment equilibrium continuously. Any disturbance, such as an increase in the nominal money supply or an improvement in technology, would immediately be reflected in changes in wages and prices that would restore the full-employment equilibrium.

The classical full equilibrium is a useful reference point for the study of more realistic descriptions of macroeconomics. We should expect to converge to the classical equilibrium in the long run. But in the short run, transactions costs and information problems associated with finding and taking jobs, together with simple stickiness of wages and prices due to contractual arrangements, will affect the adjustment process. If, for example, prices do not fall fast enough in response to a decline in the nominal quantity of money, we would expect to get transitory disequilibrium and unemployment. Such unemployment would not occur in the classical model. It is exactly the range of issues such as short-run adjustment and unemployment with which the macroeconomics of the short run is concerned. We therefore retain the classical analysis as a reference point and turn next to a discussion of the adjustment process under less ideal conditions.

We have seen that the classical model assumes fully flexible wages and prices which imply continual full employment. The classical model therefore cannot explain unemployment. A popular modification of the classical model that goes some way toward a satisfactory model is the *wage floor assumption*. The wage floor assumption states that in the short run money wages are *completely* rigid downward, but *fully* flexible upward.

In Figure 12-6 we show labor supply as a function of the *money* wage. Below full employment $\overline{N}$, the supply schedule is flat at the level of wages w_0. Whatever the level of unemployment, workers will not work for less. But the wage is fully flexible upward. Therefore, if more than $\overline{N}$ of labor were demanded, wages would immediately increase, moving up to the point where the quantity of labor demanded were again equal to the full-employment supply.

AGGREGATE SUPPLY

How does the wage floor assumption modify the aggregate supply function *AS* of Figure 12-5? To answer that question we look in Figure 12-6 at the labor market and the production function. We show two labor demand schedules corresponding to two price levels, P' and a lower level P'', respectively. At a price level P', given the wage floor w_0, the value of the marginal product of labor at full employment, $P' \cdot MPN(\overline{N})$, far exceeds the wage floor. Equilibrium in the labor market obtains at point E' with a money wage w'. The corresponding levels of employment and output are $\overline{N}$ and $\overline{Y}$.

Suppose next that the price level were much lower, for example, P''. At each wage rate the demand for labor would be much lower. At any given level of employment, the value of the marginal product of labor is correspondingly lower. Thus at the wage rate w_0, the demand for labor is only N'', and accordingly, the amount of output produced and supplied is only Y'', less than the full-employment supply. How much less depends on the curvature of the production function, that is, on the extent of diminishing returns. If returns are nearly constant (a nearly straight production function), output declines by quite a bit. If returns are strongly diminishing, then a reduction in employment costs relatively little in terms of output lost. We thus find that if the price level falls below a certain level (the level at which the labor demand schedule passes through the kink at $\overline{N}$), prices are too low relative to the wage floor, and therefore employment and output decline. The lower are prices, the lower is output.[4]

In Figure 12-7 we show the aggregate supply schedule that embodies the wage floor assumption. Just as in the classical model, the aggregate supply schedule becomes vertical at the full-employment level of output $\overline{Y}$. This

[4] Here is a more technical version of the argument. The firm maximizes profits when it chooses an employment level such that $w/P = MPN(N)$. From this equation there is a level of employment that corresponds to each wage and price level, $N = N(w/P)$. Using the production function, there is a level of output for each price level, given the wage floor. The higher the price level, the more output that is supplied, up to the level $\overline{Y}$.

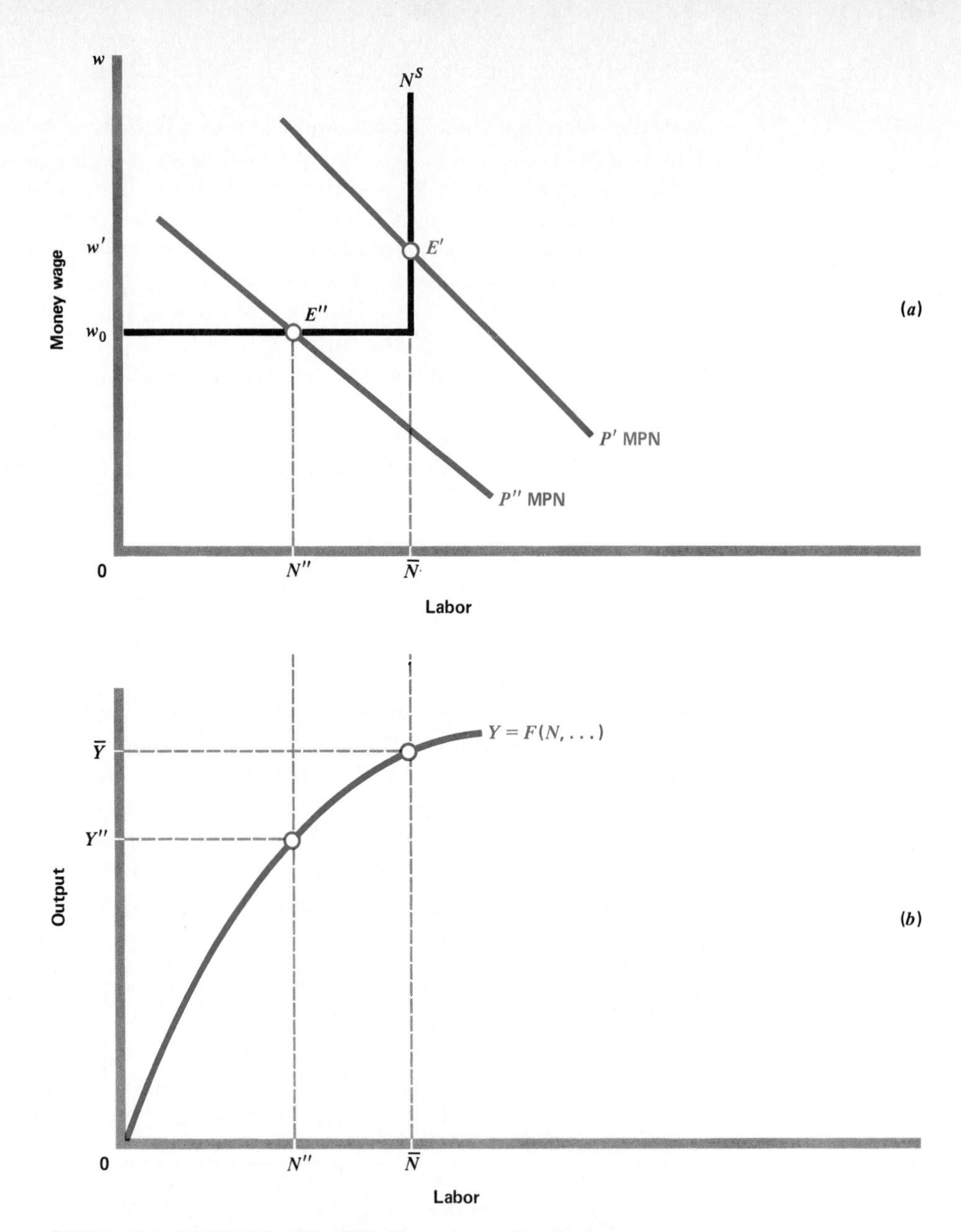

FIGURE 12-6 THE WAGE FLOOR MODEL. The upper part of the diagram shows the labor supply as a function of the *money* wage. Up to $\bar{N}$, any amount of labor is supplied at a given wage w_0. At $\bar{N}$, labor supply becomes completely unresponsive to the money wage, and the money wage is fully flexible upward. Labor demand schedules, the value of the marginal product ($P \cdot MPN(N)$), are shown for alternative price levels. At a price level P', the equilibrium wage is w', above the wage floor, and employment and output correspond to full employment. But at a lower price level P'', firms only hire N'' of labor, and accordingly, output supplied is only Y'', less than full-employment output $\bar{Y}$.

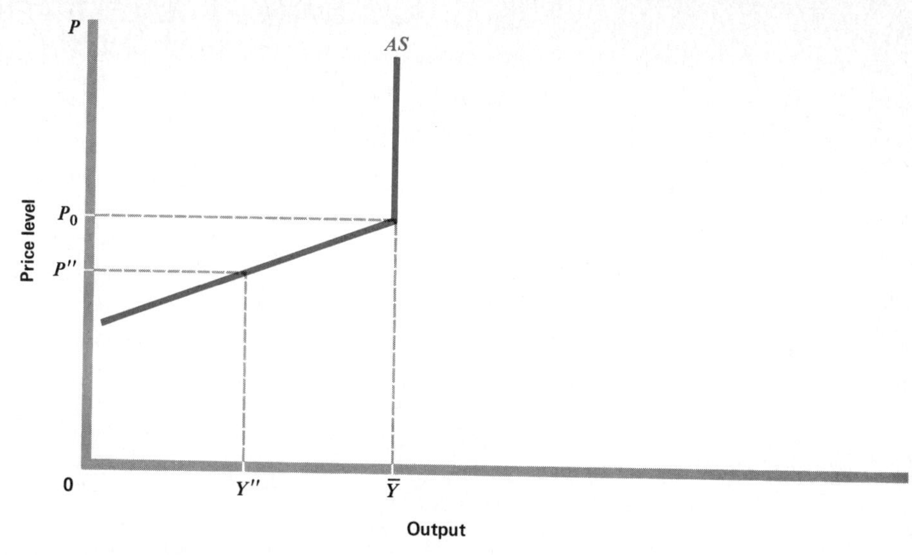

FIGURE 12-7 AGGREGATE SUPPLY IN THE WAGE FLOOR MODEL. With a wage floor w_0 the aggregate supply schedule has a kink. At high enough prices the value of the marginal product of labor exceeds the wage floor, and labor demand therefore is equal to the full-employment level. Thus the aggregate supply schedule, at high enough prices, becomes vertical just as in the classical case. But for lower prices firms find it profitable to hire less than the full-employment labor force. Output therefore is at Y'', below the full-employment $\bar{Y}$. The extent to which a reduction in prices leads to a reduction in output supplied depends on the production function.

is because the wage is fully flexible upward. Any attempt by firms to produce more than $\bar{Y}$ would require a labor input in excess of $\bar{N}$, and that would make wages rise.

But now the aggregate supply schedule has a kink. The level of that kink, P_0, depends on the given money wage floor w_0. If prices fall below P_0, say, to P'', the value of the marginal product of labor at full employment, $P'' \cdot MPN(N)$, is less than the given wage w_0. Firms therefore reduce employment because, at the margin, workers cost more than they add to the firms' revenue. With full wage flexibility the resulting unemployment would immediately lead to lower wages, and that would restore full employment. But now wages are entirely rigid downward. Thus when prices decline below P_0, firms must cut employment enough to restore profitability. Cutting employment does so, because as employment falls, the marginal product of labor rises. Therefore firms can afford to pay the same nominal wage, w_0, even though the price level is below P_0.

The upward-sloping segment of the aggregate supply schedule thus shows the supply of output in the unemployment region. Because the firm faces a given money wage, it cannot profitably supply the output level $\bar{Y}$, at *any* level of prices. Prices have to be high enough to pay the labor costs of producing the output. The lower the level of prices (relative to the given money wage), the less output can be profitably produced.

Effects of a Demand Disturbance

Consider now how the wage floor model affects our analysis of demand disturbances, say, a change in government spending. In Figure 12-8 we start in a full-employment equilibrium at point E. We look at two alternatives: an increase in government spending, leading to a rightward shift of the aggregate demand schedule to AD', and a reduction in spending, shifting the schedule to AD''. When demand increases, we observe the same result as in the classical model. Wages increase as firms compete in the labor market for the scarce labor supply. Prices increase because buyers are competing for the limited supply of goods. Equilibrium output and employment do not change, and the rise in prices, by reducing real balances and raising interest rates, leads to crowding out that restores aggregate demand to the full-employment level.

But consider now a reduction in government spending. The decline in demand leads to a new equilibrium at point E''. Both output and prices decline. The fall in demand means that firms cannot sell the full-employment

FIGURE 12-8 DEMAND DISTURBANCE IN THE WAGE FLOOR MODEL. The economy starts at an initial full-employment equilibrium at E. An increase in government spending shifts the aggregate demand schedule to AD' and leads to higher prices but no increase in output, just as in the classical case. However, a fall in demand shifts the aggregate demand schedule to AD'' and brings about an unemployment equilibrium at E''. There is some fall in prices and a decline in employment and output. Because wages are totally rigid, prices cannot fall enough to restore demand to the full-employment level.

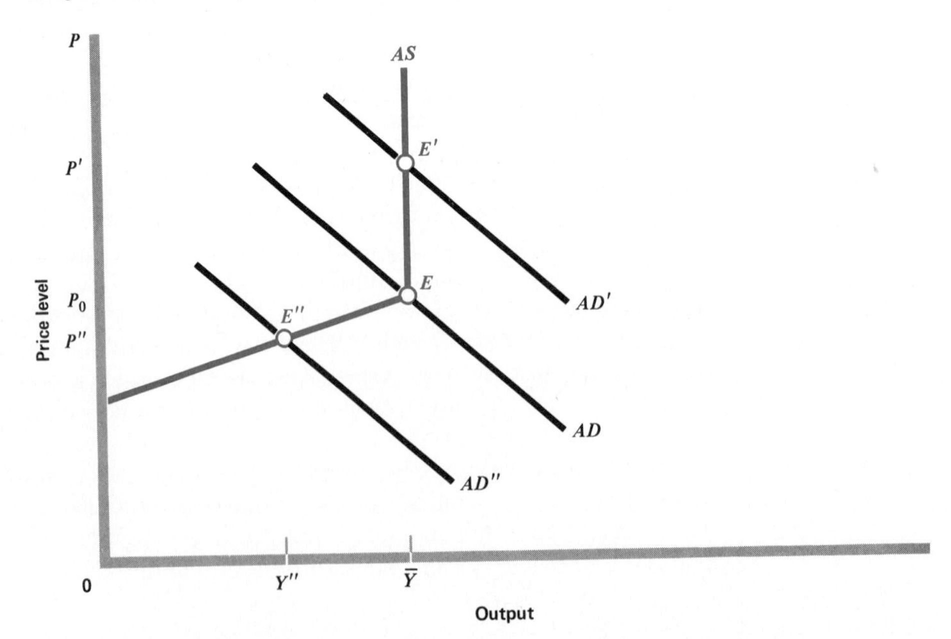

level of output, and they therefore cut down on employment. But the fall in employment does not now lead to lower wages. Wages are rigid, and therefore, unlike in the classical case, we end up with some unemployment. It is no longer the case that wages and prices decline enough to raise real balances and lower interest rates to the point where private spending has risen enough to make up for reduced government spending. Wage stickiness, when demand declines, is therefore clearly a cause of unemployment.

EVALUATION OF THE WAGE FLOOR MODEL

The wage floor model is successful in explaining how a reduction in demand can lead to unemployment. In providing that explanation it is an important modification of the classical model, bringing the analysis much closer to realism. But the model is not quite realistic yet.

The main objection is to the overly sharp asymmetry between the behavior of wages at full employment and below full employment. It is not in fact the case that the wage is fully flexible when labor demand exceeds the full-employment level. Output can be above the full-employment level $\bar{Y}$, for instance if labor works overtime. It is also not the case that money wages are totally rigid downward, whatever the level of unemployment.

Under the wage floor assumption nothing further happens once the economy is caught in an unemployment situation such as E'' in Figure 12-8. Specifically there is no link between unemployment and *changes* in wages.

What is more nearly the case, as we see in the next section, is that wages rise gradually when there is overemployment or fall gradually when there is unemployment. Our analysis will therefore use a model of *sticky* wages rather than the extreme right-angled labor supply schedule of Figure 12-6.

A second objection concerns the behavior of real wages, w/P, that is implied by the wage floor model. This model assumes that when aggregate demand and output decline, for example, from E to E'' in Figure 12-8, prices fall but money wages remain unchanged. Therefore in a recession *real* wages rise. Conversely, in moving from a point like E'' to E, prices rise, and with unchanged money wages, that means real wages decline in an expansion.

The wage floor model thus implies that real wages move *countercyclically,* that is, they fall in an expansion and rise in a recession. Keynes originally advanced this idea, and it has been explored with U.S. data in numerous studies. The conclusion that emerges from all this work is that there is no clearcut evidence in support of the hypothesis of a significant cyclical behavior of real wages. Some studies find that wages are mildly procyclical; others that wages are mildly countercyclical. There is no evidence that real wages move in a strongly countercyclical fashion. The facts thus do not support a key implication of the wage floor model.[5]

[5] A study suggesting that wages and employment essentially are independent over the cycle, based on data from twelve countries, is "The Employment–Real Wage Relationship: An International Study, "*Journal of Political Economy,* August 1982, by P. T. Geary and J. Kennan, Geary and Kennan also discuss why different researchers have come to different conclusions. A large part of the reason is that they measure the real wage w/P using different measures for w (for example, average hourly wage versus average hourly wage excluding overtime) and different measures for P (for example, producer price index, consumer price index, GNP deflator).

12-3 WAGES, EMPLOYMENT, AND OUTPUT

The wage floor model represents a significant modification of the classical model because it does at least allow the possibility of unemployment. Both the wage floor and the classical models build on two components, as can be seen in Figures 12-4 and 12-6. Those components are the production function, linking output to employment, and a relationship between employment and the wage. In the wage floor model, that is the labor supply curve N^S.

In this section we develop a theory of aggregate supply that builds on the same two elements. We examine first the link between output and employment in the short run, equivalent to the production function in Figures 12-4 and 12-6. And second we present a modified view of the relationship between employment and the wage rate. In particular we look at how unemployment causes wages to change, and thus study the link between wages and employment over time.

We start with the cyclical relationship between employment and output.

Employment and Output in the Short Run

Estimates of the production function typically do not show diminishing returns to labor, of the type seen in the production function in Figure 12-1. If anything, there seem to be constant returns to labor or even increasing returns over the cycle. The key to the short-run relationship between output and employment is found in the cyclical behavior of capacity utilization.

THE CYCLICAL BEHAVIOR OF EMPLOYMENT AND CAPACITY UTILIZATION

The employment rate is defined as the fraction of the labor force that is currently employed. (More on the definition is given in Chaper 14.) The rate of capacity (capital) utilization is measured similarly. The rate of capacity utilization represents the fraction of the capital stock that is currently being used. The series for these two variables are shown in Figure 12-9. The striking point is the extent to which both series move together. In an expansion such as the one that occurred in the 1960s or 1975–1979, the employment rate and capacity utilization both rise; in a contraction such as the one in 1980–1982 they both fall.[6]

Figure 12-9 shows that over the business cycle capital and labor input move together. This differs sharply from the assumption in the wage floor model that capital is given and fully utilized but employment varies. Here,

[6] The two series are drawn on different scales. The average rate of capacity utilization in 1960–1982 was only 82.3 percent; that of labor was much higher and equal to 94 percent. The difference reflects the fact that the labor force measure excludes old people. In the capital stock, however, firms that report the utilization data include even machinery that has not been used for years and may never be used again. Our interest here is only in the fact that the two series move together.

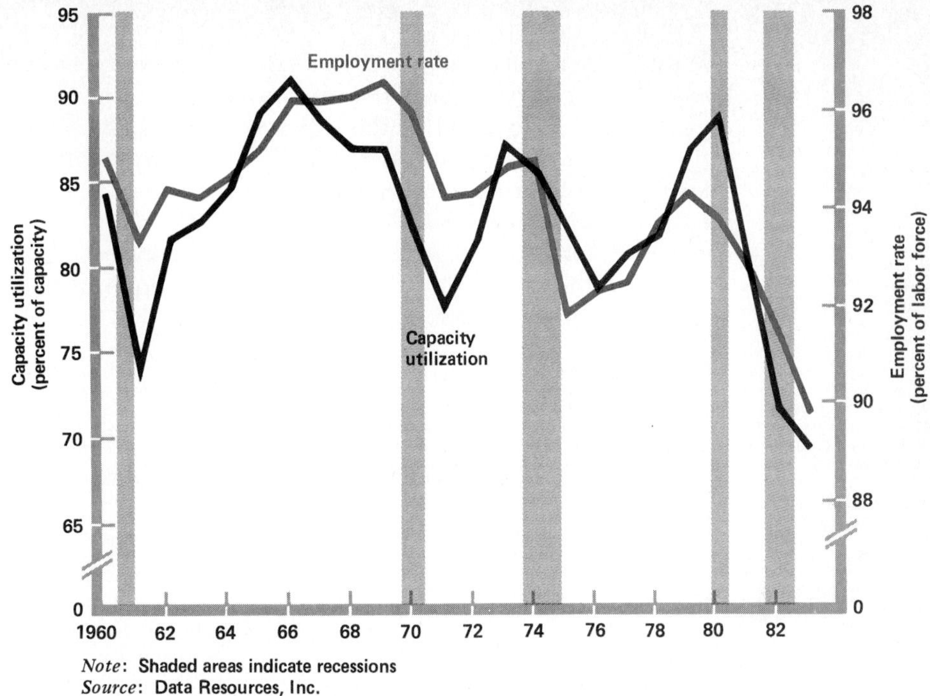

FIGURE 12-9 EMPLOYMENT OF LABOR AND CAPACITY UTILIZATION.
(*Source: Economic Report of the President,* 1983.)

with both inputs moving in the same direction, the ratio of capital to labor employed moves much less if at all. *Accordingly the marginal product of labor also is less variable, and with it so is the real wage.* The behavior of capacity utilization thus explains why there is no consistent cyclical pattern of the real wage. The amount of capital *used* per worker is *not* higher in recessions than in booms; thus the marginal product of labor is not necessarily higher in recessions, and therefore the real wage should not be expected to be higher.

The observation that capital utilization and employment vary together leads to a quite different way of looking at the cyclical behavior of employment. We now place less emphasis on the real wage as a determinant of cyclical employment and place more emphasis on the link between the demand for output and the level of employment.

In passing we note that the large variation in capacity utilization comes as a bit of a surprise. If firms own capital and it costs nothing (or little) to use, why do they not use it to full capacity at all times and thus save some on labor costs? A large part of the answer is that in the short run technology does not permit a lot of capital-labor substitution. For example, it takes a certain number of people to run a steel mill or to drive a truck. When demand declines, firms will work the plant for fewer shifts or even close down some plants for a time.

With the real wage and the capital-labor ratio both being relatively constant over the cycle, we cannot rely on movements in the real wage to generate changes in employment. Rather we now assume that the amount of labor that firms hire is determined by the amount of output that they produce. We assume that to produce a level of output Y, the firm needs an amount of labor aY.[7] The coefficient a denotes the labor requirement per unit of output. For example, if $a = 2$, it takes 2 hours of labor to produce 1 unit of output.[8]

With the assumption of a given unit labor requirement a, there is a direct link between employment and output:

$$N = aY \tag{3}$$

Equation (3) states that employment (or the demand for labor) is proportional to the level of output. The factor of proportionality is the unit labor requirement.

Equation (3) implies that employment varies one for one with the level of

[7] At the end of the chapter we refine the analysis of the output-employment link. For the moment nothing is lost by assuming there is a tight proportional relationship between output and employment.

[8] The unit labor requirement is related to the average product of labor, or *labor productivity* for short. Labor productivity is defined as the ratio of output to labor input. The more productive is labor, the smaller is the labor requirement to produce a unit of output. In fact, labor productivity is simply the ratio of output to labor use, or $1/a$. We discuss labor productivity in more detail in Section 12-8.

FIGURE 12-10 THE SHORT-RUN PRODUCTION FUNCTION. In the short run, the relationship between output and employment does not show diminishing returns. The short-run production function is assumed to have constant returns, with output proportional to the input of labor. The factor of proportionality is $1/a$, where a is the amount of labor needed to produce one unit of output. In the background, capital utilization is varying along with employment, as in Figure 12-9.

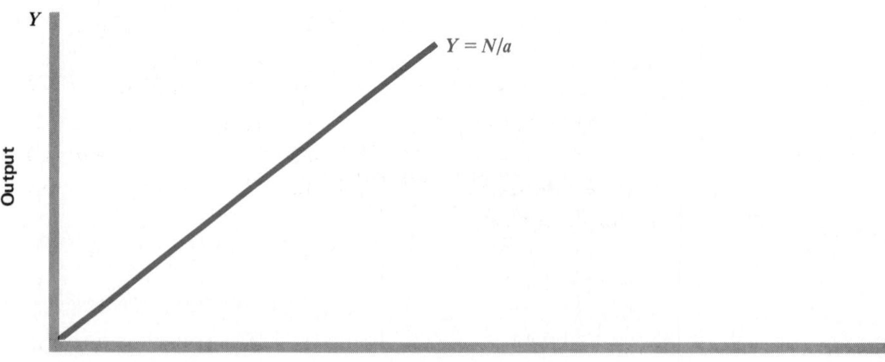

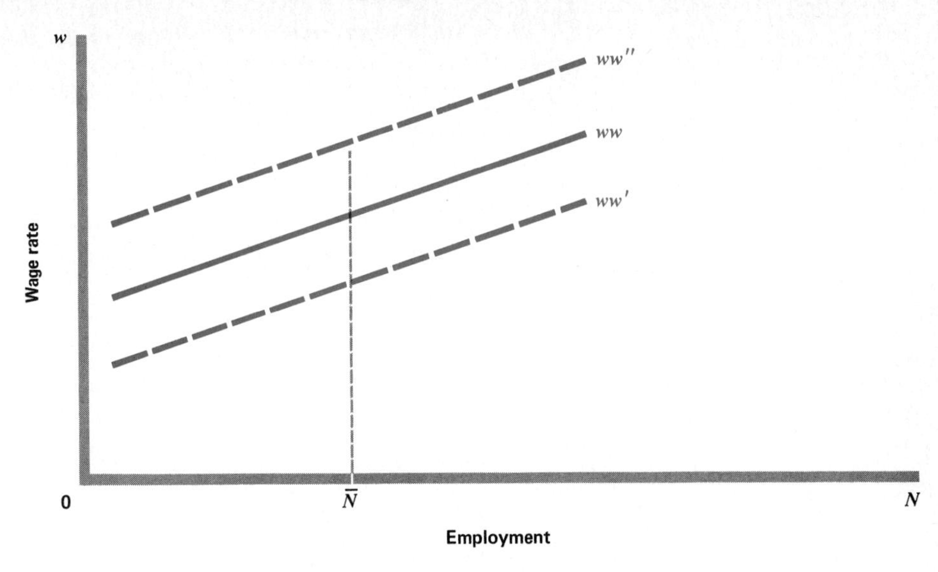

FIGURE 12-11 THE WAGE-EMPLOYMENT RELATIONSHIP. The short-run relationship between the wage rate and employment is shown by *ww*. The higher the level of employment this period, the higher the wage rate. In addition, there is a dynamic relationship between employment this period and the wage rate in the future. If output this period is below $\bar{N}$ (if there is unemployment this period) the *ww* curve shifts down to *ww'* next period. Thus unemployment reduces the wage over time. Similarly, if employment this period is above $\bar{N}$, the *ww* curve shifts up to *ww''*. Overemployment this period increases the wage over time. If unemployment continues from period to period, the *ww* curve keeps falling.

production. The implied short-run production function is shown in Figure 12-10. This is a simplified view of the employment-production link, but it takes us far in understanding the supply side. Some qualifications follow at the end of the chapter. Until then, we maintain this useful simplification.

Employment and Wages

The second critical departure from the wage floor model comes with our assumptions about the behavior of money wages. We reject the sharp asymmetry of the wage floor model and assume instead that money wages rise when there is overemployment and fall when there is unemployment. But, and this is critical, wages do not adjust rapidly. *Money wages move over time in response to disequilibrium in the labor market. They are neither totally rigid nor fully flexible.*

Wage behavior is shown in Figure 12-11. We assume that money wages increase with current employment. Hence the *ww* curve, showing the wage-employment relationship, is upward-sloping. But we add a second, *dynamic,* element to the relationship. We assume that the *ww* curve *shifts* over time. If there is unemployment this period—if employment is less than $\bar{N}$—then next period at any given employment level, the wage will be lower than it is this period. The dynamic assumption is that unemployment forces wages down over time. In terms of Figure 12-11, if there is unemployment this period, the ww curve shifts to ww' next period. If there is overemployment this period, the ww curve shifts to ww'' next period.

Figure 12-11 shows two implications of our assumptions about wage behavior. First, to each level of employment today there is a corresponding money wage. Second, the present level of employment affects next period's wages. If there is unemployment, wages *keep falling;* if there is overemployment, wages *keep rising.*

These assumptions about wage behavior are partway between the classical model of Section 12-1 and the wage floor model of Section 12-2. In the classical model wages adjust instantaneously in response to overemployment or unemployment. In the wage floor model wages do not fall at all in response to unemployment. In the model we are developing now—and in the real world—they are neither fully flexible nor totally rigid. Rather they adjust over time.

We formalize wage behavior in Equation (4). The wage this period is equal to the wage that prevailed last period (say, last quarter), but with an adjustment for the state of employment:

$$w = w_{-1}[1 + \epsilon(N/\overline{N} - 1)] \tag{4}$$

where w_{-1} is the wage that prevailed last period. The adjustment is shown by the term in brackets, which involves the ratio of employment N to the full-employment labor force $\overline{N}$. At full employment $N = \overline{N}$, and therefore wages do not change over time and the ww schedule does not shift. But when there is unemployment, $N/\overline{N}$ is less than 1. In that case the second term in Equation (4) is negative and wages today are less than they were last period. Further, because today's wage is below last period's, *next* period the ww schedule will be below this period's ww schedule. This Equation (4) implies that when there is unemployment, the ww schedule shifts down from period to period.

The extent to which wages respond to employment depends on the parameter ϵ. If ϵ is large, unemployment has a strong effect on wages. Conversely if ϵ is very small, wages are very sticky. The model of wage adjustment also implies that overemployment (unusually large amounts of overtime) leads to rising wages. The larger the adjustment coefficient ϵ, the more rapidly wages rise.

WHY WAGES ARE STICKY

Wages are said to be sticky, or wage adjustment sluggish, when wages move slowly, over time, rather than being fully and immediately flexible so as to assure full employment at every point in time. The stickiness of wages is a well-established fact, but the reasons for that stickiness are much less established and remain the subject of intense research.

The central element in any explanation, however, is the following fact. The labor market involves long-term relations between firms and workers and an important role for *reputations.* These *long-term labor market relations* mean that one party will not take advantage of the other, because each gains from continuing reasonably trouble-free relations.[9] Workers who stay in the same job save themselves the trouble of quitting and searching for new jobs; firms save the costs of locating, screening, and training new workers. Each benefits if they can get on together.

In such a setting firms will not aggressively cut wages when there is unemployment, threatening workers with dismissal unless they take a cut. In turn, workers cannot threaten management with walkouts unless they immediately receive wage increases anytime the economy is doing well.

Of course there is *some* competition for a workplace between the unemployed and those who hold jobs. But that competition is *very* moderate. A firm that tries to cut its wage bill by threatening workers with unemployment gets a bad reputation and will lose workers the moment the economy improves. In the meantime work morale may deteriorate.

On the other side, to retain their labor force firms must be sure that the wages they pay match those that can, *on average,* be gotten elsewhere in the market. A worker who expects to come out, on average, as well in her current job as in another will not quit the job merely because the wage this month is below that in another firm. In the market for fresh fish the price must clear the market every day. The labor market is very different. It is not day-to-day fluctuations in the money wage that "clear" the labor market; rather, it is explicit or implicit long-term arrangements between firms and their work forces.

Another fact reinforces the slow adjustment of wages. Workers who are unemployed will receive benefits that allow them for some time to *search* for a job rather than just accept *any* kind of work to avoid starvation. They can wait for an opportunity that matches their skills. Thus competition from the unemployed is dampened by institutions that make unemployment less difficult to bear. If the unemployed were willing to accept work at any wage, however small, we would not observe unemployment for any length of time. But that clearly is not the case.

The implication of this view of the labor market is that wages move slowly. Unemployment leads only gradually to declining wages. High employment or overemployment leads only gradually to rising wages. There is a lot of inertia or stickiness in wages even if adjustment does take place over time. Both aspects of wage behavior are central to modern macroeconomics. The short-run stickiness means that in the short run changes in aggregate demand lead to changes in output and employment. The long-run adjustments imply that these output and employment changes are only transitory.

The Phillips Curve

The *Phillips curve* relates the rate of change of wages to the level of unemployment (see Box 12-1). The lower the unemployment rate, the more rapid the rate of wage increase.

[9] For an introduction to the literature see A. Okun, *Prices and Quantities,* (Washington, D.C.: The Brookings Institution, 1981), and R. M. Solow, "On Theories of Unemployment," *American Economic Review,* March 1980.

BOX 12-1

THE PHILLIPS CURVE

> When the demand for a commodity or service is high relatively to the supply of it we expect the price to rise, the rate of rise being greater the greater the excess demand. Conversely when the demand is low relatively to the supply we expect the price to fall, the rate of fall being greater the greater the deficiency of demand. It seems plausible that this principle should operate as one of the factors determining the rate of change of money wage rates, which are the price of labour services.

This quote reproduces the opening lines to one of the most famous papers in macroeconomics. In 1958 A. W. Phillips, a professor at the London School of Economics, published a comprehensive study of wage behavior in the United Kingdom for the period 1861–1957.* The main finding is summarized in Figure 1 reproduced from his article: The higher the rate of unemployment, the lower the rate of increase of money wages, or in other words, there is a tradeoff between wage inflation and unemployment.

* A. W. Phillips, "The Relation between Unemployment and the Rate of Change of Money Wages in the United Kingdom, 1861–1957," *Economica*, November 1958.

FIGURE 1 THE ORIGINAL PHILLIPS CURVE FOR THE UNITED KINGDOM.

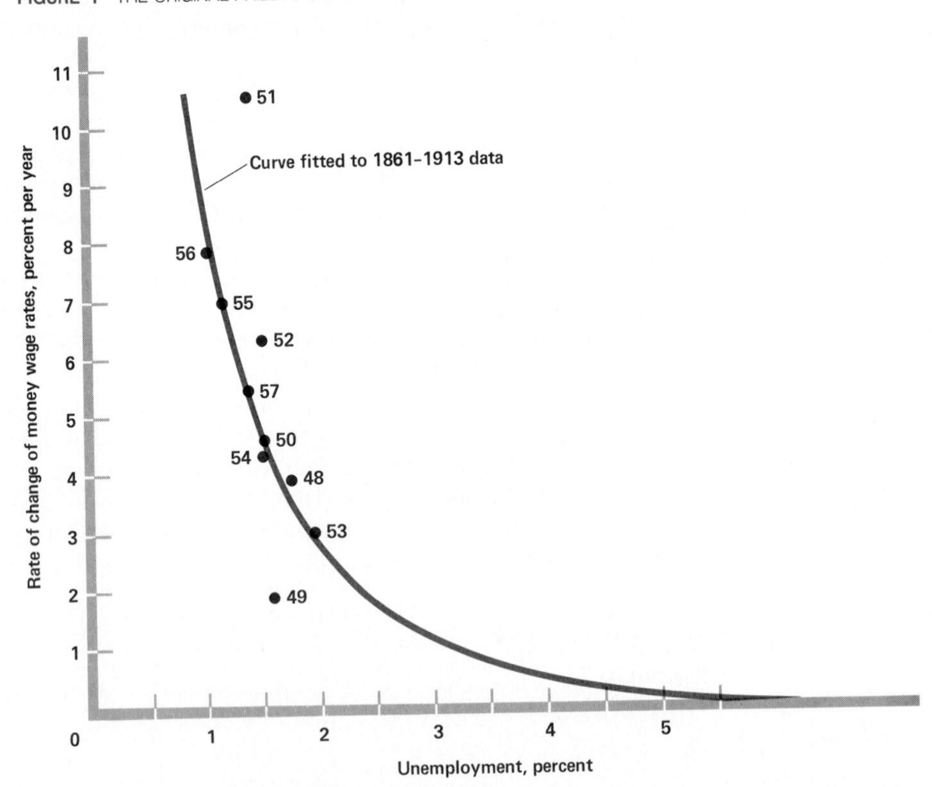

Today we call such a relation the ***Phillips curve***. The Phillips curve very rapidly became a cornerstone of macroeconomic policy analysis. It suggested that policymakers could choose different combinations of unemployment and rates of wage inflation. For instance, they could have low unemployment so long as they recognized that meant high wage inflation. Or they could have low wage inflation if they were willing to put up with high unemployment. Moreover, there appeared to be the possibility of improving the tradeoff. Specific policies (retraining, job banks, etc.) could make the labor market more efficient, thus shifting the Phillips curve in a way that reduced the rate of wage increases at each unemployment rate.

Economic policies in the United States in the 1960s led to a sustained expansion of activity, falling unemployment, and gradually rising inflation, as if the economy were moving up and along a Phillips curve. But attempts to reverse the inflation in the 1970s showed that there was much more to the inflation process than the simple Phillips curve suggests. Inflationary expectations in particular, as we shall see in Chapter 13, play a critical role. By the early 1970s the profession by and large recognized the proposition advanced by Milton Friedman and Edmund Phelps: *In the long run* there is no tradeoff between inflation and unemployment.† In other words, in the long run the economy moves to the full-employment rate of unemployment, whatever the rate of change of wages and prices.

† Milton Friedman, "The Role of Monetary Policy," *American Economic Review*, March 1969, and Edmund Phelps, *Inflation Policy and Unemployment Theory* (New York: Norton, 1972).

The link between wage changes and unemployment for nearly 100 years was documented for the United Kingdom in an important article written by A. W. Phillips in 1958. In some form or other, it has since become a cornerstone of modern macroeconomics. Our wage-employment model summarized in Equation (4) implies a Phillips curve. To derive the Phillips curve relation we use the definition of the unemployment rate as the percentage of the labor force that is not employed, $u \equiv 1 - N/\bar{N}$, in (4) to obtain:

$$w = w_{-1}[1 - \epsilon u] \tag{4a}$$

In the form of (4*a*), the wage equation states that wages are falling when there is unemployment and rising when there is overemployment (when the unemployment rate is negative).[10]

Wages and Output

In Figure 12-10 we show the relationship between output and employment. Figure 12-11 links the wage rate with employment. Putting the two relationships together in Figure 12-12, we obtain the wY relationship between money wages and output. The wage in the current period is higher, the higher

[10] The measured unemployment rate is never negative. We must therefore interpret the unemployment rate in (4*a*) as the deviation of the unemployment rate from the unemployment rate at full employment, say, 6 percent. For further discussion see Chapter 14.

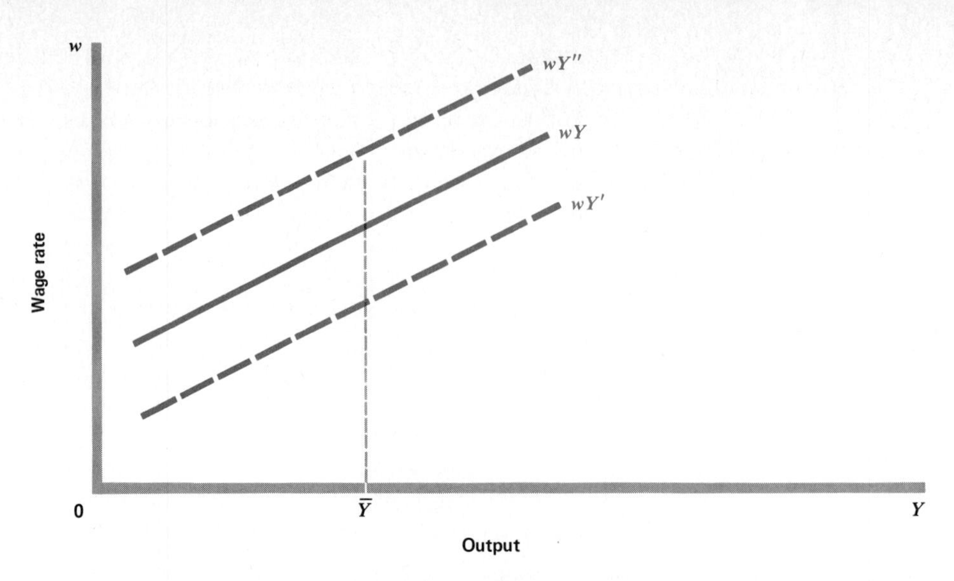

FIGURE 12-12 THE RELATIONSHIP BETWEEN WAGES AND OUTPUT. The relationship between the wage rate and output is derived from Figures 12-10 and 12-11. Because the wage rate rises with employment, and employment rises with output, the wage rate rises with output. Thus the wY curve is upward sloped. The wY curve shifts over time. If output is above the full-employment level this period, wY shifts next period to wY''. Similarly, if output is below $\bar{Y}$ this period, the wY curve will shift to a position like wY' next period.

the level of output. And if output this period is above the full-employment level, the wY curve shifts up to wY'' next period. Similarly, if output this period is below full employment, the wY curve will shift down to wY' next period.

We can formalize the link using Equations (3) and (4). Equation (3) states that $N = aY$. In particular, at the full-employment level we have $\bar{N} = a\bar{Y}$. Substituting for N and $\bar{N}$ in Equation (4) gives us the link between wages and output:

$$w = w_{-1}[1 + \epsilon(Y/\bar{Y} - 1)] \tag{5}$$

Equation (5) describes the wY curve in Figure 12-12. It states that wages increase when output is above the full-employment level and fall when output is below full employment. Thus Equation (5), like (4) and (4a), states that wages are rising or falling depending on the state of the business cycle.[11] Figure 12-12 [or Equation (5)] is one of the building blocks of the aggregate supply curve. We thus summarize the derivation of the wY schedule. It is

[11] Indeed, we can make the relationship between wage behavior and the cycle even clearer by noting that $(Y/\bar{Y} - 1)$ is equal to the output gap. Then we can write:

$$w = w_{-1}[1 + \epsilon \text{ gap}] \tag{5a}$$

based on the assumptions that labor input increases with the level of output (Figure 12-12), and that the wage both (*a*) increases in the current period with the level of output and (*b*) falls over time if there is unemployment or rises if there is overemployment.

12-4 THE AGGREGATE SUPPLY CURVE

Firms base the prices at which they sell on the costs of production, including a profit margin that constitutes the return to capital. We assume that the relation between prices and costs takes the simple *markup* form where price is equal to the unit labor cost plus a profit margin, z:

$$P = aw(1 + z) \tag{6}$$

The term aw represents the labor costs of producing a unit of output. If it takes a hours of labor to produce a unit of output, the labor cost is a hours of labor times the wage per hour, or aw. For example, let $a = 2$ and $w = \$10$ per hour. Then the unit labor cost of the good is \$20. Price exceeds unit labor cost because the firm must also earn a competitive rate of return on the capital that is employed. Therefore a markup over cost of z percent is charged.[12] We take the markup to be constant and given. If the markup is 15 percent or $z = 0.15$, then the firm would charge \$23 (= \$20 × 1.15) per unit of output.

The markup pricing assumption singles out three determinants of prices: the money wage; the unit labor requirement or its reciprocal, labor productivity[13]*; and the markup rate.* A rise in any of these three determinants will increase the price that firms set for their output. Conversely, a decline in wages, a rise in productivity, or a fall in the markup rate will lower costs and therefore lower prices.

We now are ready to derive the aggregate supply equation, by combining wage behavior and the price equation. Substituting in (6) for the wage rate, using (5), we obtain the following equation:

AS equation

$$P = a(1 + z)w_{-1}[1 + \epsilon(Y/\bar{Y} - 1)] \tag{7}$$

This equation can be simplified to arrive at our basic supply curve by noting from (6) that $a(1 + z)w_{-1} = P_{-1}$ because last period, too, prices were set on the

[12] Microeconomic theories of the competitive firm show that in equilibrium price is equal to marginal cost. With constant returns marginal and average cost are equal, so that price is equal to average cost. Similar relations, with an adjustment for the degree of monopoly, apply to noncompetitive firms. Thus the markup equation is fully consistent with microeconomic theory of pricing.

Note also that in (6) the real wage w/P is equal to $1/a(1 + z)$. If z is constant, this implies a constant real wage over the cycle. But if z increases with output, then the real wage is lower the higher the level of output. This is consistent with the classical model that predicts an inverse relationship between output and real wages.

[13] See footnote 8.

basis of the same markup pricing. Thus replacing the first term in (7) by P_{-1} we have arrived at the aggregate supply equation:

$$P = P_{-1}[1 + \epsilon(Y/\bar{Y} - 1)] \tag{8}$$

Figure 12-13 shows the aggregate supply function implied by equation (8). The supply curve is upward-sloping. Like the *ww* and *wY* schedules on which it is based, the *AS* curve shifts over time. If output this period is above the full-employment level, then next period the *AS* schedule will shift up to *AS″*. If output this period is below full employment, next period the *AS* schedule will shift down to *AS′*. Thus the properties of the *AS* curve are those of the *wY* curve. This is so because with the markup fixed at *z*, the price is just proportional to the money wage.

Equation (8) is an aggregate supply equation because it shows the price at which each level of output will be supplied. The aggregate supply equation (8) (and the *AS* schedule in Figure 12-13) shows a direct relation between prices today, prices last period, and the level of output. Prices today are equal to last period's prices with an adjustment for cyclical conditions. In a boom they exceed last period's prices; in a recession they fall below last period's price.

The *AS* curve is the aggregate supply curve of a world where wages are less than fully flexible. Prices increase with the level of output because

FIGURE 12-13 THE AGGREGATE SUPPLY CURVE. The aggregate supply curve is obtained from the wage-output curve *wY* of Figure 12-12, and from the assumption that the price level is a constant markup on the wage rate. *AS* is the aggregate supply curve in the current period. If output this period is above $\bar{Y}$, then next period the aggregate supply curve will shift to *AS″*. If output is below the full-employment level this period, then next period the aggregate supply curve will shift down to *AS′*.

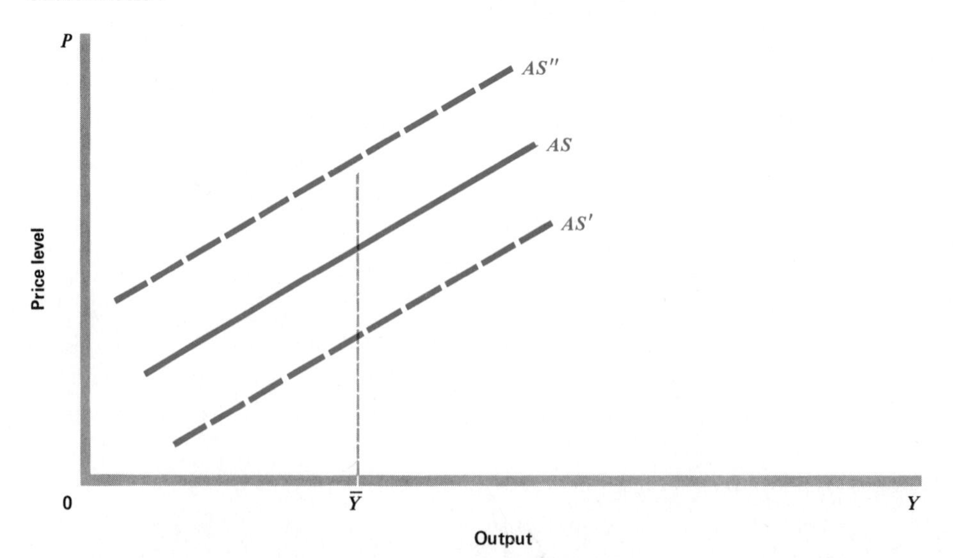

increased output implies increased employment, reduced unemployment, and therefore increased labor costs. The fact that prices rise with output is entirely a reflection of the adjustments in the labor market where higher employment increases wages. Firms pass on these wage increases by raising prices, and for that reason prices rise with the level of supply.

Properties of the Aggregate Supply Curve

We now have derived the aggregate supply schedule *AS* used in Chapter 11 and can, with the help of (8), explore its properties more closely. We want to develop three points:

1 The aggregate supply schedule is flatter the smaller is the impact of output and employment changes on wages. If wages respond only slowly to unemployment, then the *AS* schedule in Figure 12-13 will be very flat. Conversely, if wages are highly responsive to unemployment, then a small change in unemployment will induce large wage changes and therefore price changes. The coefficient ϵ in Equations (5) and (8) captures this employment-wage change linkage.

2 The position of the aggregate supply schedule depends on the past level of prices. The schedule passes through the full-employment output level $\overline{Y}$ at $P = P_{-1}$. For higher output levels there is overemployment, and hence prices today exceed prices last period. Conversely, when there is unemployment, prices today are less than those of last period.

3 The aggregate supply schedule shifts over time. If output is maintained above the full-employment level $\overline{Y}$, then over time wages rise and the wage increases are passed on into increased prices.

Rather than discuss these three points in the abstract, we use the aggregate supply curve to examine the effects of a monetary expansion in Figure 12-14. This will give us a full understanding of both the short-run and long-run implications of our wage-price model.

12-5 THE EFFECTS OF A MONETARY EXPANSION

In Figure 12-14 we show the economy in full-employment equilibrium at point *E*. The aggregate supply schedule *AS* is drawn for a given past price level P_{-1}. It passes through the full-employment output level $\overline{Y}$ at the price level P_{-1} because when output is at the full-employment level, there is no tendency for wages to change, and hence costs and prices too are constant from period to period. The aggregate supply schedule is drawn relatively flat, suggesting a small effect of output and employment changes on wages.

SHORT-RUN EFFECTS

Suppose now that the nominal money stock is increased. At each price level real balances are higher, interest rates are lower, and hence the demand for

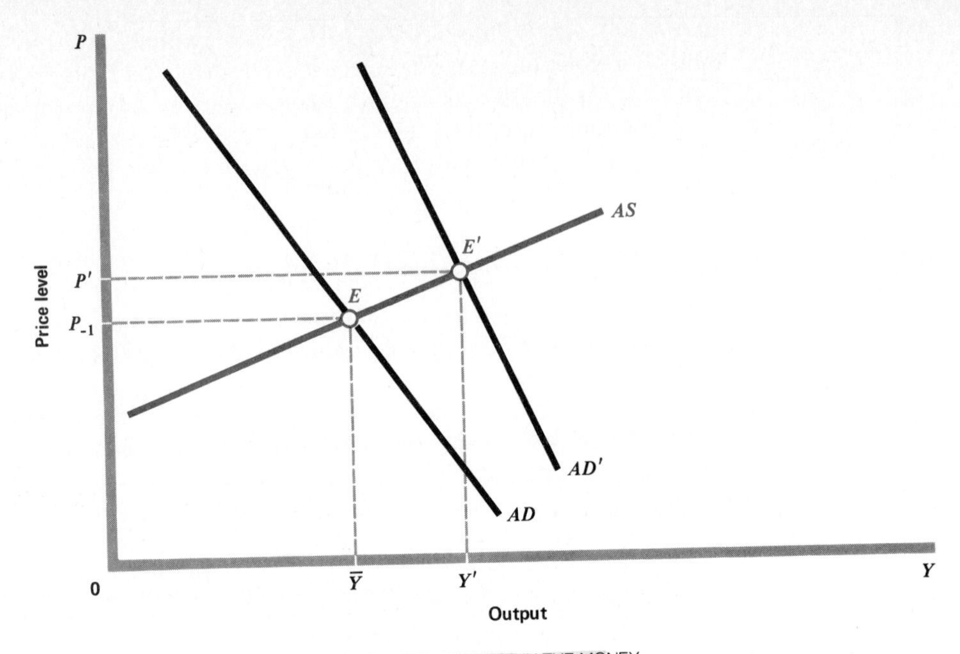

FIGURE 12-14 THE SHORT-RUN EFFECT OF AN INCREASE IN THE MONEY STOCK. The aggregate supply schedule AS is positively sloped and passes through the full-employment output level $Y = \overline{Y}$ at a price level equal to that prevailing last period, $P = P_{-1}$. The initial full-employment equilibrium at E is disturbed by an increase in the money stock that shifts aggregate demand to AD'. Short-run equilibrium is at point E' where *both* output and prices have increased. Prices are higher because the output and employment expansion have increased wages, and firms pass these cost increases into higher prices. The AS schedule is drawn quite flat, reflecting the assumption that wages are very sticky. Under these conditions prices rise little and most of the short-run effect is on output.

output rises. The AD schedule shifts up and to the right, to AD'. At the initial price level $P = P_{-1}$ there is now an excess demand for goods. Firms find that their inventories are running down and accordingly hire more labor and raise output until point E', the short-run equilibrium, is reached. Note that at E' both output and prices have risen. A monetary expansion has led to a short-run increase in output. The rise in prices is due to the increase in labor costs as production and employment rise.

Compare now the short-run result with the Keynesian and classical models of Chapter 11. Our new equilibrium at E' has a feature of each: output is higher, and prices have risen. Whether we are more nearly in the classical or Keynesian situation depends entirely on the slope of the aggregate supply schedule, that is, on the coefficient ϵ that translates employment changes into wage changes.

In moving from E to E' *real* balances have increased less than in a world where prices do not change. Therefore at E' output will have increased less than in the Keynesian case, though of course more than in the classical case, where output remains at the full-employment level and all adjustment takes place through prices.

MEDIUM-TERM ADJUSTMENT

The short-run equilibrium at point E' is not the end of the story. At E' output is above normal. Therefore, from (8) prices *will keep on rising.* Consider now in Figure 12-15 what happens in the second period. Once we are in the second period, looking back, the price in the preceding period was P' at point E'. Therefore the second-period supply curve passes through the full-employment output level at a price equal to P'. We show this by shifting the aggregate supply schedule up to AS', reflecting the increase in wages that has taken place since last period in response to the high level of employment.

With the new aggregate supply schedule AS', and with the aggregate demand schedule unchanged at the higher level AD', the new equilibrium is

FIGURE 12-15 THE MEDIUM-TERM EFFECT OF AN INCREASE IN MONEY. The monetary expansion has led to a short-run equilibrium at point E'. But at E' output is above normal, and therefore wages are rising. The increase in wages shifts the AS schedule upward. Prices in the second period would be equal to those at E' if the economy were back at full employment. Thus AS shifts up to AS' and we have a new equilibrium at E''. Output falls somewhat compared to E', and prices rise further. The adjustment from E' to E'' reflects cost pressures that arise in an overemployed economy. As these cost increases are passed on into higher prices, real balances fall, interest rates rise, and equilibrium income and spending fall.

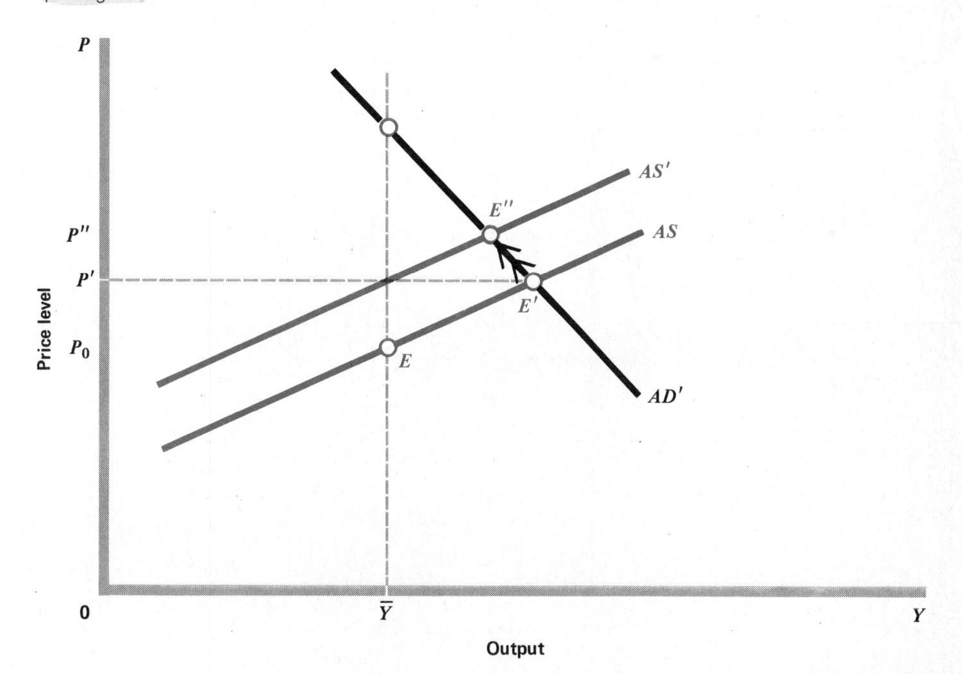

at E''. Comparing E' and E'' we note that output now has fallen compared with the first period and prices have risen further. The increase in wages has been passed on by firms as an upward shift of the *AS* schedule, and the resulting price increase reduces real balances, raises interest rates, and lowers equilibrium income and spending. Thus, starting in the second period, we enter a phase of the adjustment process in which the initial expansion begins to be reversed. We continue this process by looking at the long-term adjustment.

LONG-TERM ADJUSTMENT

As long as output is above normal, employment is above normal, and therefore wages are rising. Because wages are rising, firms experience cost increases, and these are passed on, at each output level, as an upward shift of the aggregate supply schedule. As long as the short- and medium-term equilibrium positions of the economy (points E', E'', etc.) lie to the right of $\overline{Y}$, the *AS* schedule is shifting up and to the left. As a result, output will be declining toward the full-employment level and prices will keep rising. This adjustment is shown in Figure 12-16.

FIGURE 12-16 THE FULL ADJUSTMENT TO AN INCREASE IN THE MONEY STOCK. As long as output is above $\overline{Y}$, wages, costs, and equilibrium prices will be rising. From the short-run equilibrium at E', the upward-shifting aggregate supply schedule leads to declining output and rising prices as shown by the arrows. The adjustment continues until at E''' prices have risen in proportion to the increase in the money stock. At this point, output and employment have returned to the full-employment level. In the long run, therefore, a monetary expansion has no real effects.

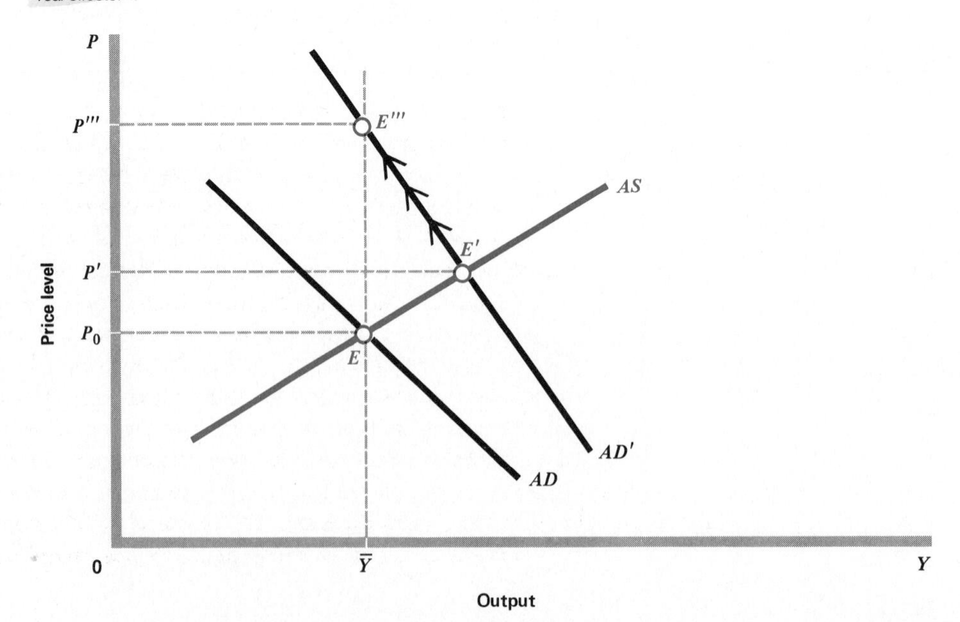

Figure 12-16 shows that the upward-shifting *AS* schedule gives us a series of equilibrium positions on the *AD* schedule, starting with E' and moving up toward E'''. During the entire adjustment process, output is above the full-employment level, and prices are rising. But there is a long-run equilibrium at E''' in which the economy has returned to full employment.

Once prices have risen in the same proportion as the nominal money stock, the real money stock M/P is again at the initial level. This happens at E'''. When real balances and therefore interest rates are again at the initial level, so are aggregate demand, output, and employment. In the long run, once wages and prices have had time to adjust fully, the model has the same predictions as the classical case of Chapter 11 and Section 12-1. *The difference is only in the adjustment process.* In the classical case a monetary expansion leads immediately to an equiproportionate rise in prices with no real expansion. Here output and prices *both* rise in the short and medium term, and only in the long run do we reach the classical case. In the short run the predictions of our model more closely resemble the Keynesian case, and the more slowly that wages adjust to changes in employment, the greater the resemblance.

Because the adjustments of wages and prices are in fact quite slow, the short- and medium-term adjustments are an important aspect of macroeconomics.

12-6 ADJUSTMENT TO A DECLINE IN SPENDING

In Figure 12-17 we provide another application of the model. This time we look at a fall in autonomous spending, say, a reduction in investment due to a loss of business confidence. We start in full-employment equilibrium at E, with no tendency for prices to be changing because the labor market is in full-employment equilibrium and therefore exerts no cost pressures through changing wages.

The equilibrium is now disturbed by a decline in autonomous spending, shifting the aggregate demand schedule down from *AD* to *AD'*. Output and prices both fall as the economy moves from E to E' in the short run. Because wages are not fully flexible and firms set prices on the basis of costs, the price level cannot fall fast enough to raise real balances, lower interest rates, and thus restore full employment immediately. Now the economy is in recession at E'.

Unemployment at point E' implies that wages are falling. Therefore the aggregate supply schedule will start shifting down and to the right. Over time prices decline. The resulting rise in real balances gradually lowers interest rates and encourages aggregate demand. The process continues, with falling unemployment, until the economy reaches $\bar{Y}$ again.

In the long run, once again, the model has classical predictions. A decline in demand leads to a fall in prices, lower interest rates, and full employment. But in the short run the economy behaves very differently. Sluggish or slowly adjusting wages are an obstacle to continuing full employment. Only by going through a recession and unemployment can the price level be brought down.

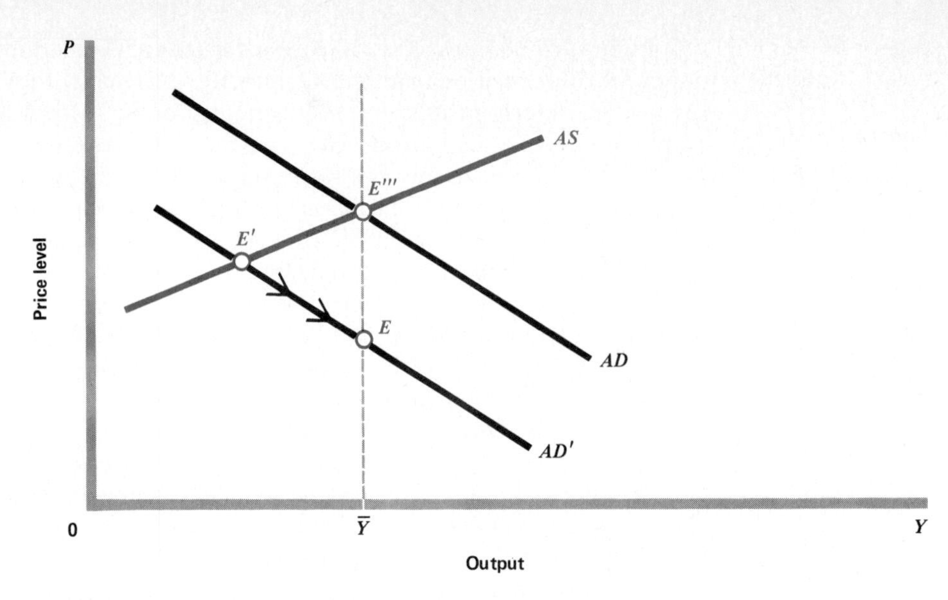

FIGURE 12-17 THE ADJUSTMENT TO A DECLINE IN AUTONOMOUS SPENDING. The initial equilibrium at E is disturbed by a decline in autonomous spending shifting the aggregate demand schedule to AD'. In the short run, both output and prices decline at point E'. Wage stickiness precludes an immediate return to full employment. Only as the recession and unemployment persist do wages decline, leading the supply schedule to shift down. Output recovers along with falling prices, as shown by the arrows. In the long run, the price level falls enough to lower interest rates and raise real spending back to the full-employment level.

SUMMARY

At the end of Section 12-4 we noted three features of the aggregate supply schedule: its slope, its position, and its movement over time. The description of the adjustment process to monetary changes or changes in autonomous demand has brought these three points into focus. Each plays an important role in determining how the sticky wage model compares with the two extremes of a fixed-price Keynesian model and a fully flexible-price classical model.

The flatter the *AS* schedule, the more Keynesian the model in the short run. But in the long run, that is, given enough time, the economy has fully flexible wages and prices and therefore *ultimately* reaches the classical full-employment equilibrium. However, because that adjustment can take a long time, there may be room for monetary and fiscal policy to help keep the economy more nearly at full employment.

12-7 SUPPLY SHOCKS

The macroeconomic story of the 1970s was largely a story of *supply shocks*. A supply shock is a disturbance to the economy whose first impact is to shift the

BOX 12-2

NUMERICAL ESTIMATES OF THE ADJUSTMENT PROCESS

How long does it take for policy changes to translate mainly into prices rather than output adjustments. The *DRI model*, one of the largest and best-known econometric models (see Chapter 10) provides estimates of the adjustment path when the economy is disturbed by a monetary expansion. These estimates correspond to the analysis of Figures 12-14 to 12-16.

The estimates are obtained by first calculating how the economy would behave for a given path of policy variables. Then a particular policy instrument is changed, and the resulting changes in the time path of output, prices, interest rates, etc., are calculated. This is called a policy *simulation*.

A MONETARY EXPANSION

In Table 1 we show the results of a simulation of the DRI model for a change in monetary policy. Here we look at the real GNP multiplier and the price level effects associated with an increase in bank reserves. The particular policy experiment can be thought of as an open market operation (or a series of them) that raises bank reserves and therefore high-powered money.

The increase in bank reserves and high-powered money leads over time to a multiple expansion of the money stock. That, in turn, raises real balances (while prices have not yet caught up), lowers interest rates, and causes output to expand. But the expansion leads to overemployment, rising wages, and rising prices. Over time the real money stock therefore first rises and then declines. The multipliers in Table 1 mirror the behavior of the real money stock.

TABLE 1 EFFECTS OF AN INCREASE IN MONEY ON REAL GNP AND PRICES IN THE DRI MODEL

	QUARTERS AFTER POLICY IS INITIATED				
	1	4	8	12	24
Increase in real GNP per dollar increase in bank reserves.	1.9	17.9	24.8	15.0	2.3
% change in prices per % change in money	0.02	0.15	0.33	0.57	1.26

Source: The Data Resources Review of the U.S. Economy, April 1983, p. 1.18.

In the very short run a rise in high-powered money changes the money stock very little and therefore has only a small impact on real GNP. But within a year, and peaking at 2 years, the monetary expansion builds up, and the decline in interest rates leads to a large increase in real output. Then the resulting price increases take over. The second row shows the price response, which starts off negligibly and then builds up to become equal to the growth in money. The simulation results thus mirror our analysis in Figures 12-14 to 12-16. In the long run (which in this model is more than 6 years) the economy is entirely classical, but in the short run and in the medium run the economy as represented by the DRI model is quite Keynesian.

Caution: As we discussed in Chapter 10, no econometric model gives totally accurate predictions of the future or estimates of the effects of policies. Thus the multipliers shown above should only be regarded as illustrating the general adjustment pattern.

aggregate supply curve. The two major supply shocks in the 1970s were the increases in the price of oil in 1973–1974 and 1979–1980. The first OPEC shock helped push the economy into the 1973–1975 recession, up to then the worst recession of the post-World II period. And the second OPEC price increase sharply accelerated the inflation rate. The high inflation led to tough monetary policy to fight inflation—with the eventual result that the economy went into an even deeper recession than in 1973–1975. So there is no doubt that supply shocks matter.

An Adverse Supply Shock

An *adverse supply shock* is one that shifts the aggregate supply curve up. Figure 12-18 shows the effects of such a shock. The *AS* curve shifts up to *AS′*, and the equilibrium of the economy moves from *E* to *E′*. The immediate effect of the supply shock is thus to raise the price level and reduce the level of output. An adverse supply shock is doubly unfortunate: it causes *higher* prices and *lower* output.

There are two points to note about the impact of the supply shock. First, the shock is best thought of as an increase in the price of a raw material used in production. The *AS* curve shifts up because it now costs firms more to produce each unit of output. Second, we are assuming that the supply shock does not affect the level of potential output, which remains at $\bar{Y}$.[14]

What happens after the shock has hit? In Figure 12-18, the economy moves, from *E′* back to *E*. The unemployment at *E′* forces wages and thus the price level down. The adjustment is slow because wages are slow to adjust. The adjustment takes place along the *AD* curve, with wages falling until *E* is reached.

At *E* the economy is back at full employment, with the price level the same as it was before the shock. But the nominal wage rate is lower than it was before the shock, because the unemployment in the meantime has forced the wage down. Thus the *real* wage too is lower than it was before the shock: the adverse supply shock reduces the real wage.

1973–1974

Table 12-1 shows data for the 1973–1974 oil price increase.[15] From 1973 to 1974 the oil price increased by 25 percent more than other prices and then increased further in 1975. The GNP deflator increased rapidly in both 1974 and 1975. Real GNP fell, as we should expect from Figure 12-18. And the real wage fell in both years.

Thus the analysis presented in Figure 12-18 describes well the economy's responses to the first OPEC shock.

[14] The increase in the price of oil in the seventies both shifted up the *AS* curve and reduced the level of potential output because firms reduced their use of oil and could not use capital as efficiently as before. But we are assuming in Figure 12-18 that the supply shock does not affect $\bar{Y}$.

[15] In 1973–1974 prices of other raw materials, such as copper, also increased sharply. These increases had the same type of impact as the oil price shock and are not shown separately.

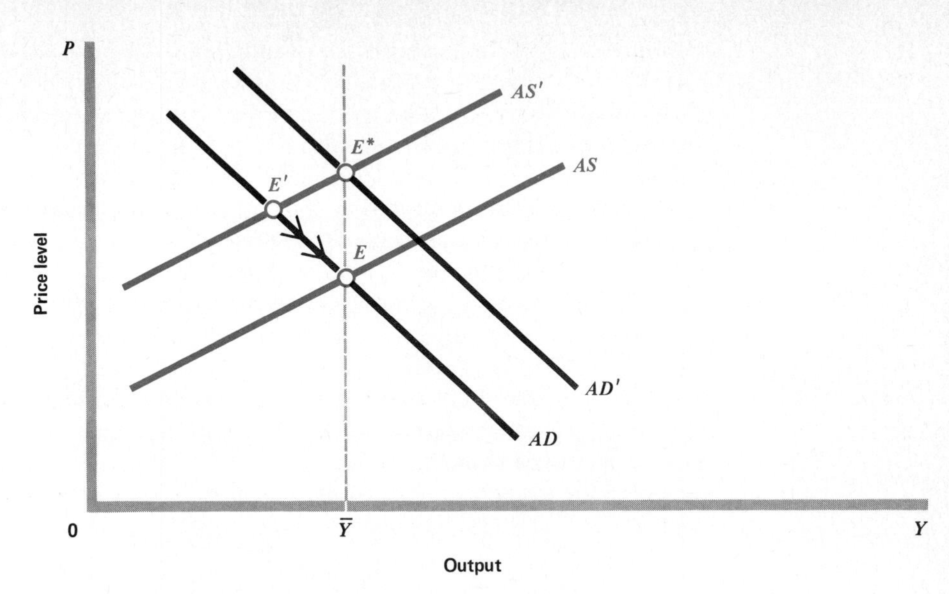

FIGURE 12-18 AN ADVERSE SUPPLY SHOCK. An increase in the real price of oil shifts the aggregate supply schedule up and to the left. The costs of production are higher at each level of output, and therefore *AS* shifts to *AS'*. In the short run, because wages do not decline enough, the economy moves into an unemployment equilibrium at *E'*. Prices are higher and output is lower because of the reduction in real balances. Over time, wages decline because of unemployment and the economy returns to the initial equilibrium at *E'*. Accommodating monetary or fiscal policies could shift the *AD* schedule to *AD'*, reducing the unemployment effects of the supply shock but increasing the inflationary impact.

ACCOMMODATION OF SUPPLY SHOCKS

In 1975–1976 stimulatory fiscal and monetary policy helped the economy recover from the recession more rapidly than it otherwise would have. But why were such policies not used earlier?

To answer that question, we look at Figure 12-18. If the government had, at the time of the oil price increase, increased aggregate demand enough, the

TABLE 12-1 THE 1973–1974 OIL PRICE SHOCK

	1974	1975
Real fuel price (1973 = 100)	122.6	138.8
GNP deflator (1973 = 100)	108.8	118.9
Real GNP growth (% per year)	−0.6	−1.2
Real wage change* (% per year)	−2.8	−0.8

* Real wage is adjusted hourly earnings in the private nonagricultural sector.
Source: Economic Report of the President, 1983.

economy could have moved to E^* rather than E'. Prices would have risen by the full extent of the upward shift in the aggregate supply curve. Money wages would have remained unchanged, and the economy would have stayed at full employment. Of course, the real wage would have been lower, but in the end it is lower anyway.

The monetary and fiscal policies that shift the *AD* curve to *AD'* in Figure 12-18 are known as *accommodating* policies. There has been a disturbance that requires a fall in the real wage. Policy is adjusted to make possible, or accommodate, that fall in the real wage *at the existing nominal wage.*

So the question now is why accommodating policies were not undertaken in 1973–1975. The answer is that there is a tradeoff between the inflationary impact of a supply shock and its recessionary effects. The more accommodation there is, the greater the inflationary impact of the shock and the smaller the unemployment impact. The policy mix actually chosen resulted in an intermediate position—some inflation (quite a lot) and some unemployment.

*Incorporating Materials Prices in the Analysis

In Equation (6) labor costs (and the markup) were the only determinants of output prices. Materials such as energy or copper or cotton were entirely neglected. But clearly the manufacturing sector does use these inputs whose prices have an impact on the prices of final goods.

We incorporate materials prices in our analysis by modifying the price equation to include not only labor costs and the markup, but also *materials prices,* which we denote by P_m:

$$P = aw(1 + z) + \lambda P_m \tag{9}$$

In (9) the term λ denotes the material requirement per unit output, and hence λP_m is the component of unit costs that comes from materials inputs.

The wage rate, we recall, increases with the level of output. Hence from Equation (9) we get an upward-sloping supply curve. Further, any increase in the price of materials will increase the price level as of a given w. Thus an increase in P_m shifts the *AS* curve up, as in Figure 12-18.

We can alternatively write the price equation in terms of the *relative* or *real* price of materials, which we denote by the lower case p_m. The relative price is given by

$$p_m = P_m/P \tag{10}$$

Substituting from (10) in (9) gives us a modified equation linking wages and prices[16]:

$$P = [a(1 + z)/(1 - \lambda p_m)]w \qquad 1 > \lambda p_m \tag{11}$$

[16] The analysis is easily extended to recognize the fact that the real price of commodities is *highly* cyclical. To do so we simply write $p_m = \bar{p}_m + \gamma$ gap, where γ denotes the cyclical response of the real commodity price and $\bar{p}_m$ is the full-employment real price.

Equation (11) shows that for given wages, profit margins, and labor productivity, a change in the real price of commodities will increase prices simply because it raises costs. The impact of a change in real commodity prices therefore is to shift the aggregate supply schedule upward at each level of output, as in Figure 12-18.

12-8 THE CYCLICAL BEHAVIOR OF PRODUCTIVITY

In developing the sticky wage macroeconomic model we made a strong assumption about the link between output and employment, namely, $N = aY$. According to our assumption, labor productivity Y/N is equal to a constant $1/a$.

That assumption is readily testable by looking at the data for labor productivity or output per worker, Y/N. The data are shown in Figure 12-19. It is immediately clear that productivity varies over time—it grows over time, as we shall see in Chapter 17—but it also moves cyclically.

Figure 12-19 shows that as or shortly before the economy moves into a recession, productivity declines, while productivity begins to grow again some time after the recession starts. How do we explain these facts, and what implications do they have for our model? As we noted above, firms maintain long-term relations with their labor force. Part of that long-term relation is that during recessions firms are slow to dismiss personnel, especially highly

FIGURE 12-19 THE PRODUCTIVITY OF LABOR, 1960–1983.

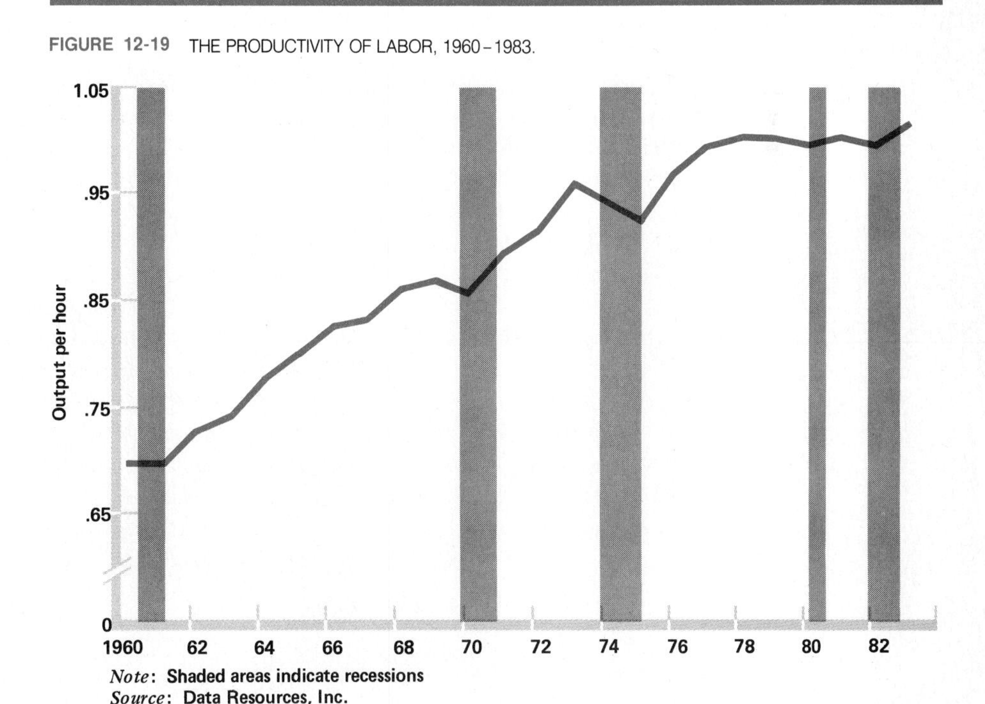

Note: Shaded areas indicate recessions
Source: Data Resources, Inc.

specialized workers whom the firm does not want to risk losing permanently. This applies also to managers, because even if the firm produces only half the normal level of output, it is difficult to cut a manager in half.

Thus employment tends to fluctuate *less* than output or production. During a recession output falls, but employment falls relatively less. Hence productivity—the ratio of output to employment—falls. Conversely, in a recovery production rises, but because the firm has kept on or *hoarded* a lot of the work force, employment increases less. Thus productivity rises in a recovery.

The effects we have just described are reinforced by the fact that the firm bases its hiring and firing on expectations about future production. A firm will hire more workers and incur the expense of increasing employment only if there is an expectation that production and output will be higher for some time. Otherwise, paying overtime to the existing labor force would be a cheaper solution. Conversely, firms will lay off or dismiss workers only if they believe the decline in demand will last some time. Here then is another source of discrepancy between current employment and current production. Current production may be low but employment high because firms believe demand has declined only transitorily.

By assuming a tight link between output and employment, our model thus simplifies the complex relationships between a firm's production decisions and its employment decisions. For purposes of understanding aggregate supply, the simplification is justifiable, since output and employment do, in practice, move in the same direction, even if not exactly in lockstep.

12-9 SUMMARY

This chapter has covered a lot of hard ground. The major point to be established was that output variations along the short-run aggregate supply schedule are accompanied by only moderate price changes. In the short run, the price level varies little with the level of output. Over time, however, wages, costs, and prices will keep rising if output is above normal and keep falling if output is below normal.

We summarize the contents of the chapter as:

1 The classical theory of the demand for labor relates labor demand only to the real wage, given the quantity of other factors the firm is using. Competitive firms that are free to change the quantity of labor they use, costlessly and immediately, will hire labor up to the point where the real wage is equal to the marginal product of labor (*MPN*).
2 With wages and prices freely flexible, the equilibrium level of employment is determined in the labor market. The labor market is continuously in equilibrium at the full-employment level, and aggregate supply will

therefore be the amount of output which that amount of labor produces. Given that the labor market is in equilibrium, the aggregate supply curve is vertical at the level of potential output — the aggregate supply curve is independent of the price level.

3 The wage floor model assumes that money wages are totally rigid downward, but entirely flexible upward. This leads to a kinked aggregate supply schedule. A rise in aggregate demand raises prices, but not output. A fall in aggregate demand reduces both prices and output.
4 The wage floor model is unrealistic with its emphasis on the asymmetry between an increase and decrease in demand. It also fails with its prediction about the cyclical behavior of real wages.
5 Firms and workers share an interest in stable long-term employment relations. Neither party benefits on average from frequent changes in employment and employment conditions. This environment makes for sluggish wage adjustment.
6 Nominal wages change in accordance with the state of excess demand in the labor market. When there is unemployment, wages fall, and when there is negative unemployment, wages rise. In this connection, it should be recalled that we abstract in this chapter from the existence of frictional unemployment.
7 Firms base the prices they charge on their costs of production. Thus, when wages rise because the level of employment is above the full-employment level, prices are increased too.
8 To assemble these elements: An increase in output is accompanied by an increase in prices. An increase in output resulting, say, from an increase in aggregate demand affects expected output, leading to an increase in employment. The increase in employment increases the nominal wage, which leads to some increase in the prices firms charge.
9 The full impact of changes in aggregate demand on prices occurs only over the course of time. A permanent increase in aggregate demand feeds slowly into an increased demand for labor, which in turn means wages rise slowly, which in turn means that prices are adjusted only over the course of time. If employment is somehow held above the full-employment level, wages and prices will continue to rise without end.
10 Materials prices, along with wages, are a determinant of costs and prices. Changes in materials prices are passed on as changes in prices and therefore changes in real wages. Materials price changes have been an important source of aggregate supply shocks.
11 Supply shocks, such as a material price increase, pose a difficult problem for macroeconomic policy. They can be accommodated through an expansionary aggregate demand policy with the effect of increased prices but stable output. Alternatively, they can be offset so that prices remain stable because of deflationary aggregate demand policy, but then output falls.

KEY TERMS

Frictionless classical model
Marginal product of labor
Wage floor assumption
Labor productivity
Long-term labor market relations
Sluggish wage adjustment
Phillips curve
Unit labor cost
Adverse supply shock
Accommodation of supply shocks
Real materials prices

PROBLEMS

1 Using Figures 12-14 to 12-16, analyze the effects of a reduction in the money stock on the price level and on output.
2 In problem 1, what happens to the level of real balances as a result of a reduction in the nominal money stock?
3 Suppose a new method of production is invented which increases the marginal product of labor at each level of employment.
   (*a*) What effect does this have on the (classical) demand for labor?
   (*b*) What effect does it have on the equilibrium real wage if the supply of labor is fixed and independent of the real wage?
   (*c*) How would your answer to (*b*) be affected if the supply of labor increased with the real wage?
4 Discuss the short-run and long-run adjustments to an increase in government spending using diagrams similar to Figures 12-14 to 12-16.
5 Suppose the economy is in a recession. How can monetary and fiscal policies speed up the recovery? What would happen in the absence of these policies?
6 The government increases income taxes. What are the effects on output, prices, and interest rates:
   (*a*) In the short run?
   (*b*) In the long run?
7 Consider a cut in aggregate demand because of reduced autonomous investment. Compare the effects in the sluggish wage model of Figure 12-17 with the wage floor model. Describe in detail what you see as the important differences.
8 Discuss why wages only move sluggishly.
9 Use the aggregate supply and demand framework to show the effect of a decline in the real price of materials. Show the effects:
   (*a*) In the short run
   (*b*) In the long run
10 Suppose a policy could be found to shift the *AS* curve down.
   (*a*) What are the effects?
   (*b*) Why do you think there is great interest in such policies? [In Chapter 16 we discuss TIP (tax-based incentive programs) that are intended to shift the *AS* schedule down.]
*11 Suppose that an increase in materials prices is accompanied by a fall in the level of potential output. There is no change in monetary or fiscal policy, and so the *AD* curve does not shift.
   (*a*) What is the long-run effect of the disturbance on prices and output? Compare the effect with the case in the text where potential output does not fall.
   (*b*) Assume the upward shift of the *AS* schedule leads initially to a decline in output below the new potential output level. Then show the adjustment process by which output and prices reach the new long-run equilibrium.

*12 Why does productivity move procyclically?

*13 Determine, using Equation (11), the long-run effect of an increased real price of materials on the real wage w/P. What effect would an energy conservation program have?

13

INFLATION AND UNEMPLOYMENT

I know of no example of a country that has cured substantial inflation without going through a transitional period of slow growth and unemployment.

Milton Friedman, 1979

The Fed announces lower monetary targets and promises to lower them further until they accord with zero (not 4%) inflation. The specter of collision between those targets and the economy's inflationary momentum hangs over the recovery. When and if they collide, everyone knows in his bones, it is output not prices that will give way.

James Tobin, 1977

One of the many things Arthur Okun drummed into my head was that the inertia of wages was not necessarily related to expectations. . . . If inertia comes from some other source, the current emphasis on the credibility of anti-inflation policy may be misplaced. Until inertia is better understood, we should be cautious in advocating aggressive anti-inflation policies.

Robert E. Hall, 1983

From the late 1950s through the end of the 1970s the inflation rate in the United States increased in every successive business cycle. During a recession inflation would fall below its past trend, but in the following recovery it would rise again and before long exceed its past level. Figure 13-1 shows that pattern of an ever-increasing inflation rate from just above 2 percent in the early 1950s to well above 10 percent in 1979–1980. In late 1979 the Fed made a dramatic decision: monetary policy was to be changed in a decisive way to stop inflation from rising and to force it back down to the level of the 1950s.

The decision was dramatic because there was very little doubt among economists of widely different macroeconomic persuasions that the move toward tight money would not bring about an instant reduction in inflation without severe costs in terms of reduced output and employment. Indeed, as the quotes above show, the leaders of the monetarist and Keynesian schools of thought (Friedman and Tobin, respectively) agreed: stopping

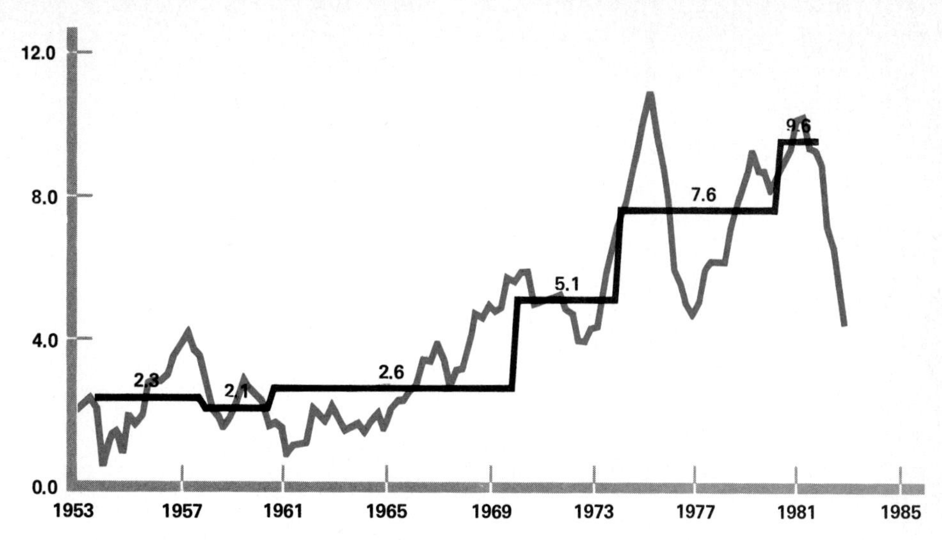

FIGURE 13-1 CYCLICAL AVERAGE INFLATION RATES (GNP DEFLATOR, PEAK TO PEAK).

inflation will create unemployment. Moreover, that view was shared by many of the younger generation of macroeconomists who accept much of the spirit of the rational expectations school, as Robert Hall's quote makes clear.[1]

Even though the consequences of tight money for unemployment were well understood and uncontested — except by a small, vocal group of supply-siders — the Fed went ahead with the tight money policy. It did not openly discuss the unemployment-inflation tradeoff, but it certainly was aware of the consequences of the policies it was undertaking. Figure 13-2 shows the results. By 1983 the fight against inflation had indeed been successful, but the cost in terms of unemployment was stunning. In February 1983 the chairman of the Fed, Paul Volcker, told Congress:

> I am also acutely aware that the recent gains against inflation have been achieved in a context of serious economic hardship. The present state of affairs must not continue. Millions of workers are unemployed, many businesses are hard pressed to maintain profitability and business bankrupticies are at a postwar high. But in coping with inflation I also firmly belive we have laid much of the foundation for a long period of noninflationary expansion.[2]

The big question of 1983 was whether the war against inflation had been won or whether recovery to high employment would rapidly rekindle inflation as had happened repeatedly in the past thirty years.

[1] The references are from M. Friedman, *Bright Promises, Dismal Performance* (New York: Harcourt, Brace, Jovanovich, 1983), p. 202; J. Tobin, "Is Keynes Dead?" in his *Essays in Economics: Theory and Policy* (Cambridge, Mass.: MIT Press, 1982), p. 89; and "Comment by Robert E. Hall," in J. Tobin (ed.), *Macroeconomics: Prices and Quantities* (Washington, D.C.: The Brookings Institution, 1983), p. 77.

[2] *Federal Reserve Bulletin,* February 1983, p. 80.

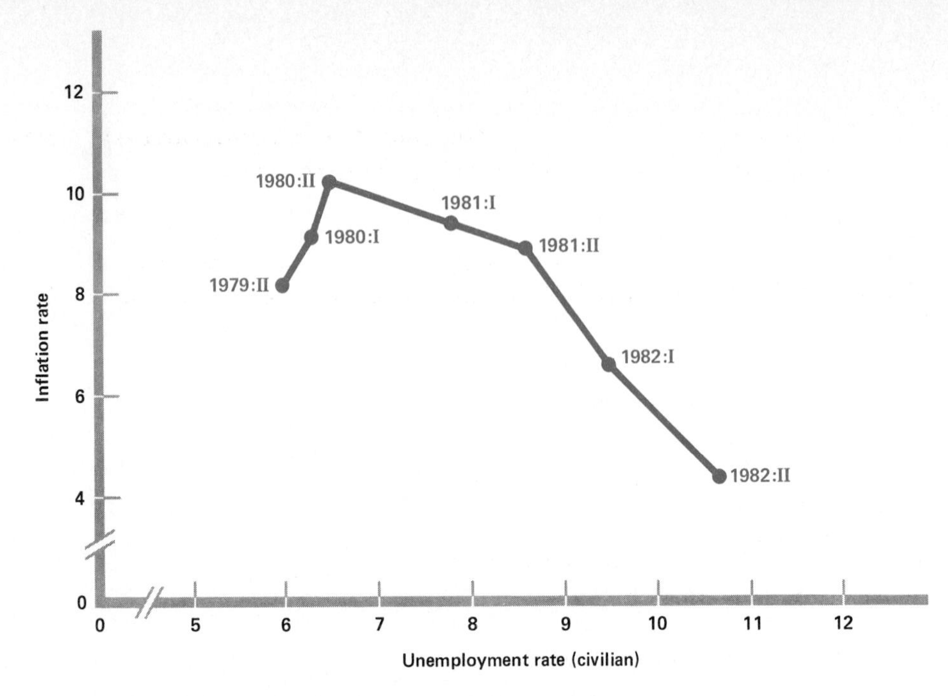

FIGURE 13-2 THE PHILLIPS CURVE: RECENT EVIDENCE (SEMIANNUAL: 1979-1983). (*Source:* Data Resources, Inc.)

In this chapter we address the problem of inflation and unemployment, extending the analysis of Chapter 12. We ask why it is apparently inevitable that inflation stabilization should bring about unemployment. This question leads us to a distinction between short-run and long-run inflation-unemployment tradeoffs. In the short run, inflation cannot be reduced without creating unemployment; in the long run, though, the inflation rate is essentially independent of the rate of unemployment.

In Section 13-4 we explore the link between inflation and money growth. We concentrate on the question of whether money is all that matters for inflation, even in the short run. We reject that view and therefore, in Section 13-5, analyze other factors that play a role in determining short-run inflation. In the final section we address the policy question of alternative strategies for reducing inflation. The question is whether it is necessary to throw the economy into a deep recession to reduce inflation, as was done in the early 1980s, or whether there are other policy options to cope with the inflation problem.

13-1 THE PHILLIPS CURVE AND THE AGGREGATE SUPPLY CURVE

In Chapter 12 we introduced the aggregate supply curve and the Phillips curve. The Phillips curve made famous by A. W. Phillips, as described in Box

12-1, is a relationship between the rate of change of wages and the unemployment rate. The term *Phillips curve* is now used mainly to refer to a relationship between the rate of change of *prices* (the inflation rate) and the unemployment rate. We therefore refer to the Phillips curve as the *inflation*-unemployment relation unless we specify otherwise.

In this section we first show how the inflation-unemployment Phillips curve is derived. Then we show that *the Phillips curve and the aggregate supply curve are fully consistent with each other. The Phillips curve is a form of the aggregate supply curve that is convenient for studying ongoing inflation.*

The Phillips Curve

Our derivation of the aggregate supply curve in Chapter 12 started from the relation between the rate of wage change and unemployment. We argued—as did Phillips in 1958—that wages increase more rapidly the lower the unemployment rate. When unemployment is low, firms find it difficult to obtain the labor they demand, and accordingly offer higher wages to attract workers. Thus wages rise more rapidly when unemployment is low. On the other side, when unemployment is high, jobs are difficult to find, and firms can fill any vacancies they might have without raising wages—indeed wages may even be falling as workers compete for scarce jobs.

We briefly review the link between wages, prices, and the cyclical position of the economy. This time we look at unemployment rather than the GNP gap $Y/\bar{Y}$, but the analysis is entirely the same. In Chapter 12 we formalized wage behavior by an equation that links current wages w to past wages w_{-1}, and the deviation of unemployment from the natural rate, $u - \bar{u}$.[3]

$$w = w_{-1}[1 - \epsilon(u - \bar{u})] \tag{1}$$

We also had a relation between wages and prices, $P = aw(1 + z)$, which in combination with (1) implies a link between prices today, past prices, and unemployment[4]:

$$P = P_{-1}[1 - \epsilon(u - \bar{u})] \tag{2}$$

Equation (2) states that prices today are above or below those last period, depending on the unemployment rate. When unemployment is high, prices are falling; when unemployment is low (relative to the natural rate), prices are rising.

[3] We discuss the natural rate of unemployment, $\bar{u}$, in Chapter 14. In Chapter 12 we omitted the natural rate of unemployment, $\bar{u}$, noting in footnote 10 that we were measuring the unemployment rate relative to the full employment rate. Now we put in the natural or full employment rate because it begins to play an important role in the analysis.

[4] To get from Eq. (1) to Eq. (2) in this chapter, you can follow the same steps that took us from Eq. (6) to Eq. (8) in Chap. 12.

In the last chapter we were interested in the level of prices and looked at the determination of output and prices over the adjustment period. In this chapter we examine the adjustment path further, looking at inflation, or a process of ongoing price increases. We can analyze inflation here because Equation (2) describes the inflation rate. Remember that the inflation rate is defined as the percentage increase in prices from one period to the next. With that definition in mind we can write

$$\text{Inflation rate} \equiv P/P_{-1} - 1 = gp \tag{3}$$

where gp is the growth rate of prices, or inflation. To fix ideas about calculating the inflation rate, suppose this period the price level index is 107 and last period it was 101. Then the inflation rate, using (3), is $gp = 5.9$ percent $[= (107 - 101)/(101) \times 100$ percent$]$.

It is immediately clear from (2) and (3) that we already have a model of inflation. Dividing (2) by P_{-1} and subtracting 1 from both sides yields

$$gp = P/P_{-1} - 1 = -\epsilon(u - \bar{u}) \tag{2a}$$

This model of inflation, $gp = -\epsilon(u - \bar{u})$, states that there is inflation when unemployment is below the natural rate, and there is deflation (falling prices)

FIGURE 13-3 THE PHILLIPS CURVE. The Phillips curve is a negative relationship between the inflation rate and the unemployment rate. The Phillips curve PC shows a zero rate of inflation when unemployment is at the full-employment, or natural, rate $\bar{u}$. At higher unemployment rates, such as at point A, the inflation rate is negative. At lower unemployment rates, for example at point B, the inflation rate is positive. The slope of PC is equal to $-\epsilon$, which is the sensitivity of the rate of wage change to unemployment.

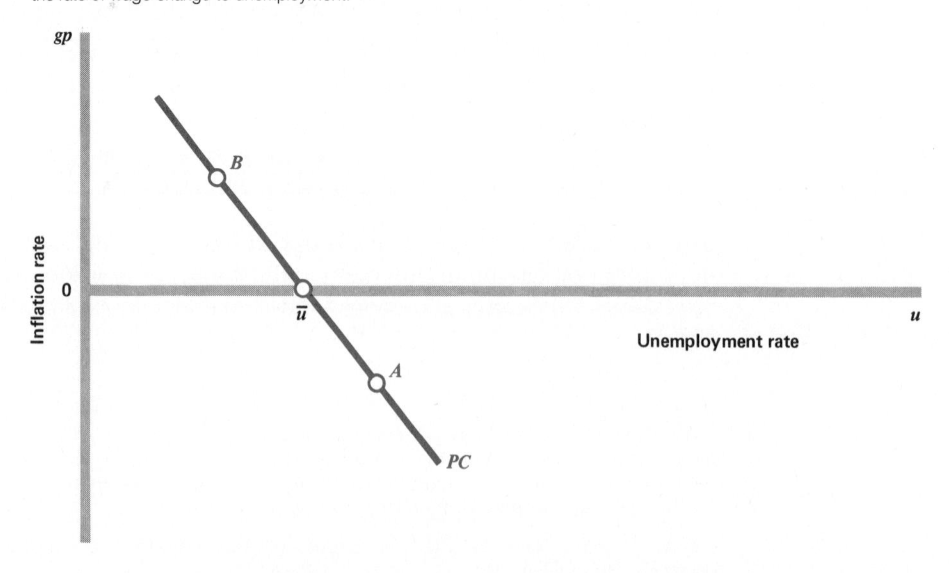

when unemployment exceeds the natural rate. Equation ($2a$) is the Phillips curve, and it is shown in Figure 13-3.

The Phillips Curve

Figure 13-3 shows the relation between the rate of inflation and the rate of unemployment as the schedule labeled *PC*. The Phillips curve has three properties that we want to draw out. First, the schedule is negatively sloped. When the slope is negative, lower unemployment rates imply higher inflation rates. This negative slope leads to the notion of a tradeoff: to have lower inflation we have to accept an increase in unemployment. This notion of a tradeoff occupies us in much of the chapter.

The second point concerns the intercept on the horizontal axis. The Phillips curve shows that at the natural rate of unemployment, $\bar{u}$, inflation is zero. At higher unemployment rates, prices are falling, or there is deflation. At lower unemployment rates, prices are rising, or there is inflation; the higher inflation, the lower is unemployment.

Finally, the schedule shows how responsive inflation is to the unemployment rate. A very flat Phillips curve implies that a given change in unemployment leads to only a small change in inflation. By contrast, a very steep Phillips curve implies that small unemployment changes have a major impact on the inflation rate.

The slope of the Phillips curve corresponds to the coefficient ϵ in (1) and ($2a$), which we remember as the parameter that tells us how responsive wages, and hence prices, are to unemployment. Highly sensitive wages imply a very steep Phillips curve; highly sluggish wages imply a very flat Phillips curve.

This is a good point to see the link between the aggregate supply schedule of Chapter 12 and the Phillips curve. In Chapter 12 a very flat aggregate supply curve meant that changes in aggregate demand have a big effect on output and little short-run effect on prices. Exactly the same can be said here in terms of the Phillips curve. If wages are highly sticky, so that the aggregate supply schedule is very flat, then the Phillips curve, too, is very flat. They are simply alternative ways of stating the link between wages and prices over time and the cyclical position of the economy.

Adjustment to a Fall in the Money Stock

We now use an example to show the precise link between the aggregate demand and supply analysis and the Phillips curve analysis of this chapter. We take the example of a reduction in the nominal money stock. The economy is initially in equilibrium with full employment and unchanging prices. Now the Fed reduces the nominal money stock through an open market operation. The impact effect, as we know from Chapter 12, is to reduce both prices and output.[5] In the short run, wages and hence prices are sluggish, and thus a recession results.

[5] It will be a good exercise for you and refresh your memory to draw the *AD* and *AS* schedules as you work through the argument.

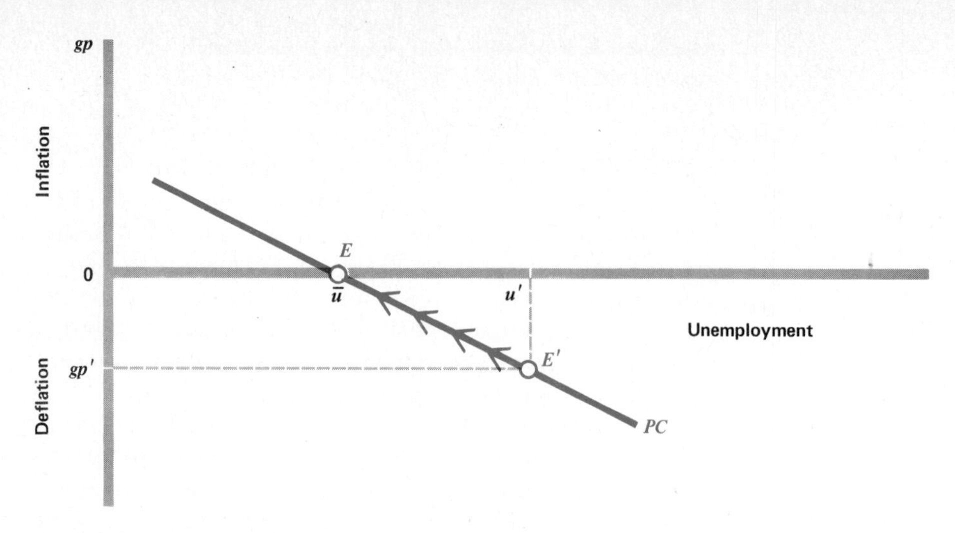

FIGURE 13-4 THE ADJUSTMENT TO A FALL IN THE NOMINAL MONEY STOCK. A reduction in the nominal money stock leads immediately to a recession because wages and prices are not fully flexible. The economy moves from E to a position like point E' where we have unemployment and falling wages and prices. The unemployment rate is u' and the rate of deflation is gp'. Over time, deflation or falling prices raises the *real* money stock and therefore lower interest rates, increasing spending and employment. Through that adjustment process the economy moves with falling unemployment from E' back to E. The process is complete when prices have fallen far enough to restore the initial stock of real balances and hence spending and employment.

In Figure 13-4 we show the impact effect of the reduction in the nominal money stock which moves the economy from zero inflation at the natural rate to point E'. At point E' there is now excess unemployment, and therefore wages and prices are falling. Next we have to ask how the falling prices help restore full-employment equilibrium. This is easy to see.

The nominal money stock remains constant. Therefore falling prices imply that the *real* money stock moves back up over time. This, in turn, means interest rates are falling and aggregate demand is rising. Rising aggregate demand leads to rising output and employment, or to falling unemployment. Thus over time the economy moves from E' toward the full-employment equilibrium E. Prices will continue falling until they have declined enough to restore the *real* money stock to the initial level. At that point interest rates, spending, output, and employment all have returned to the initial level, and the economy is back at $\bar{u}$. Thus movements along the Phillips curve represent the same adjustment process that we saw before in terms of the *AS* and *AD* schedules. Of course, without understanding the details of the earlier analysis we could not understand the present argument.

To round out the analysis we can also talk about the speed with which the economy returns to full employment. This depends simply on the slope of the Phillips curve. If wage changes and inflation are highly unresponsive to unemployment (a very flat Phillips curve), then the adjustment takes a long time, because prices are slow to fall and therefore have to fall for a long time. Conversely, if wage and price changes are extremely sensitive (a very steep Phillips curve), adjustment will be very rapid.

We can develop the same kind of analysis, using a diagram like Figure 13-4, to study the adjustment process, for example, to a fiscal expansion. Initially the expansion leads to a rise in employment, or a fall in unemployment, to a point on the Phillips curve to the left of the natural rate $\bar{u}$. There is now inflation. Given the nominal money stock, *real* balances will be falling, interest rates will be increasing, and thus crowding out takes place. As demand and employment decline, unemployment rises back up to the natural rate. The speed of adjustment of the process depends once again on the sensitivity of wages to unemployment, that is, on the slope of the Phillips curve.

The Phillips Curve as a Tradeoff

The adjustment process to monetary or real disturbances has been described in terms of movements along the Phillips curve. But we can also think of the Phillips curve as showing a tradeoff between inflation and unemployment. Policy makers, with this view, could pick monetary and fiscal policies to put the economy on a particular point on the Phillips curve, *and keep it there.* This tradeoff view of the Phillips curve was in the mind of policy makers in the early 1960s, and we now discuss why it had to be totally revised.

13-2 EXPECTATIONS AND SHORT-RUN PHILLIPS CURVES

After the appearance of Phillip's article in 1958, it was widely assumed that a Phillips curve such as *PC* in Figure 13-3 presented policy makers with a menu of inflation and unemployment rates from which to choose. Policy makers could choose a low unemployment–high inflation combination, such as point *B*, or if they preferred, they could be at a point such as *A*, with low inflation but high unemployment. Their choice between points such as *A* and *B* would depend on their estimates of the costs of inflation and unemployment.

Inflation and unemployment rates for the U.S. economy during the 1960s are shown in Figure 13-5. These certainly display a Phillips curve tradeoff: over that decade policy makers seemed to be choosing to trade off ever-higher inflation for lower unemployment. Indeed, the U.S. data from the 1960s even show the curved shape of the original Phillips curve of Box 12-1.

The Friedman-Phelps Argument

In 1967 and 1968, Edmund Phelps, of Columbia University, and Milton Friedman independently argued that a Phillips curve such as *PC* in Figure 13-3 did *not* represent a stable long-run relationship that could be used by

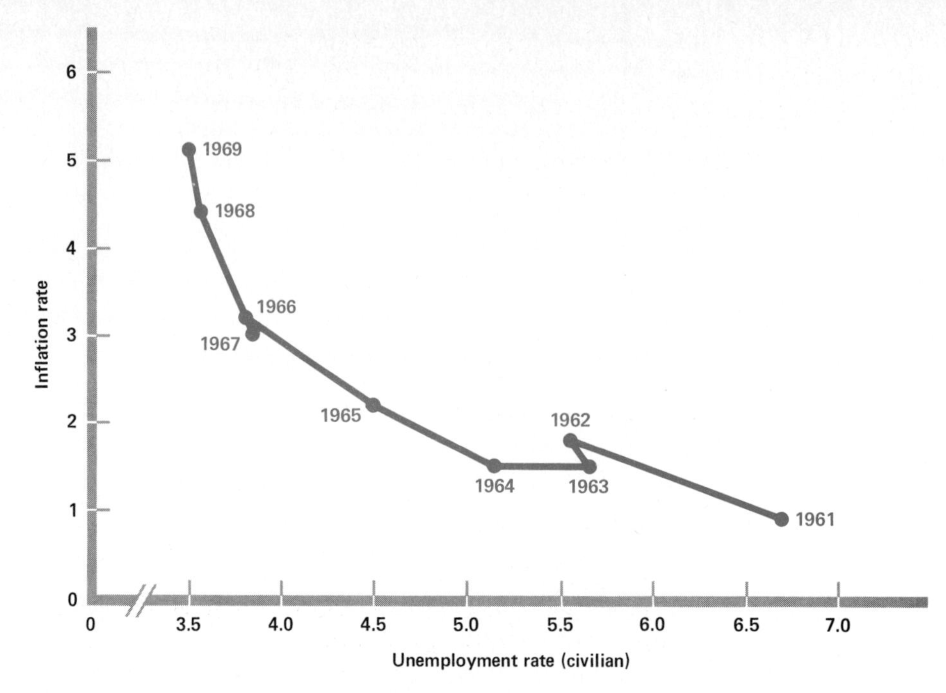

FIGURE 13-5 THE PHILLIPS CURVE IN THE 1960s. (*Source:* Data Resources, Inc.)

policy makers. They predicted that a Phillips curve such as *PC* would *shift* upward if policy makers tried to keep the unemployment rate below the natural rate, and would shift downward if the unemployment rate were above the natural rate.

Their argument started from the same point as that of Phillips, by discussing the adjustment of wages. Phillips, we recall, assumed that nominal wages rise more rapidly when the unemployment rate is low and less rapidly when the unemployment rate is high. But, argued Friedman and Phelps, neither workers nor firms are concerned with *nominal* wages. Rather, both workers, in supplying labor, and firms, in demanding labor, are concerned with the *real* wages they will be receiving and paying, respectively.

When firms and workers bargain over the nominal wages to be paid for the next several years, they take into account the inflation they expect during that period. For instance, suppose both firms and workers expect prices to be rising at 10 percent per year over the next 3 years. In fixing the nominal wage rates to be paid during those years, they adjust for the inflation they expect. With prices rising at 10 percent, wages are settled now to rise at 10 percent too in order to keep the *real* wage constant.

Accordingly, argued Friedman and Phelps, the rate of wage change should reflect two factors: (1) As in the regular Phillips curve, the lower the unemployment rate, the more rapidly nominal wages rise. (2) The higher the expected inflation, the more rapidly nominal wages rise.

It is, of course, the second factor—the effects of expected inflation on the rate of wage change—that is the novel element in the Friedman-Phelps analysis of wage setting. It is clear why workers want wages to rise more rapidly when inflation is expected. Higher prices will reduce their real wages unless the nominal wage increases along with inflation. But what about the other side of the deal? Why do firms agree to raise wages more rapidly when they expect inflation? The reason is that they can afford to pay higher wages if the price of their output is rising. Indeed, when wages and prices are rising at the same rate, the real wage is constant. Both workers and firms are in the same position as they would be if there were no inflation and the real wage were constant.

Expected Inflation and the Phillips Curve

We modify the Phillips curve to include expected inflation by writing:

$$gp = gpe - \epsilon(u - \bar{u}) \tag{4}$$

In Equation (4), gpe is the expected rate of inflation. Equation (4) is known as the *expectations-augmented Phillips curve,* meaning simply that it is the standard Phillips curve with expectations of inflation added.

According to the expectations-augmented Phillips curve, if unemployment is above the natural rate, inflation is below the expected rate, and vice versa. Or to put the argument the other way around, the only way the unemployment rate can be reduced below the natural rate is by causing more inflation than was expected.

The link between the Friedman-Phelps arguments about wage behavior and the Phillips curve equation (4) is again markup pricing. With unemployment at the natural rate, wages are rising at the expected rate of inflation. Prices, in turn, are based on wages, and are rising at the same rate as wages—equal to the expected rate of inflation. Thus with unemployment at the natural rate, prices are rising at the rate at which they were expected to rise. Similar arguments explain why prices rise more rapidly than expected when the unemployment rate is below the natural rate, and more slowly than expected when unemployment is above the natural rate.

Short-Run Phillips Curves

In Figure 13-6 we show how the inclusion of expectations of inflation affects the Phillips curve. On PC'', the expected inflation rate is 8 percent. We can tell that by the fact that when u is equal to $\bar{u}$, the natural rate, the inflation rate on PC'' is equal to 8 percent (point A). On the Phillips curve PC', the expected inflation rate is 3 percent. And on the Phillips curve PC, the expected inflation rate is zero.

Each of the three Phillips curves in Figure 13-6 is a *short-run Phillips curve.* The short-run Phillips curve shows the relationship between the inflation and unemployment rates when the expected inflation rate is held constant.

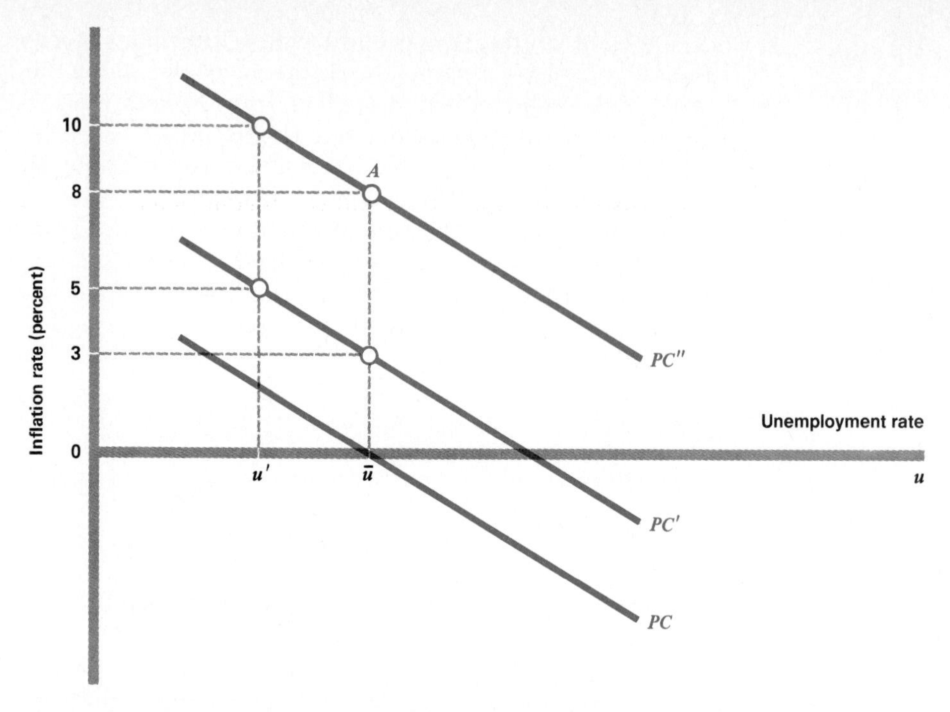

FIGURE 13-6 SHORT-RUN PHILLIPS CURVES. There is a short-run Phillips curve corresponding to each expected rate of inflation. For instance, on PC'', the expected rate of inflation is 8 percent. On PC' the expected inflation rate is only 3 percent, whereas on PC it is zero. If unemployment is at the natural rate, inflation is only 3 percent on PC', but 8 percent on PC''. If the unemployment rate were lower, at u', the inflation rate would be 5 percent on PC' but 10 percent on PC''.

The slope of the short-run Phillips curve represents the short-run tradeoff that can be made between inflation and unemployment. In the short run, by which we mean the length of time it takes for expectations to adjust to inflation, the economy moves along a given short-run Phillips curve, such as PC''. On such a curve, the only way to reduce inflation is to have more unemployment. That is precisely the type of tradeoff that was chosen by U.S. policy makers from 1979 to 1983, as seen in Figure 13-2.

The short-run Phillips curves in Figure 13-6 are quite flat. This reflects the evidence that in the short run of a few years, it typically takes a large amount of extra unemployment to produce just a small reduction in inflation. In Section 13-3, we examine the long-run tradeoff between inflation and unemployment.

Determinants of Expectations

We have already discussed the role of expectations in the context of the consumption function—where permanent income is a measure of expected income—and the investment function—where the rate of investment depends on expectations of future output. Now we need to discuss inflation expectations because of their role in the expectations-augmented Phillips curve.

How do people form expectations of inflation? Probably most of the time they base their expectations on the recent behavior of the inflation rate. If the inflation rate has been around 10 percent for a while, then people are quite likely to believe it will continue at around 10 percent. Accordingly, economists frequently assume that expectations of inflation are equal to an average of inflation rates in the recent past. In normal times this is a good assumption.

But we cannot assume that expected inflation is always equal to an average of recent rates of inflation. For instance, if a new government comes to power committed to pursuing highly inflationary policies, expectations of inflation will rise because people expect economic policies to change. In this case the expected rate of inflation will change on the basis of expectations about economic policy—even if there has been no change in actual inflation rates.

RATIONAL EXPECTATIONS

The *rational expectations* hypothesis is the assumption that people base their expectations of inflation (or any other economic variable) on all the information available about the future behavior of that variable.

The rational expectations approach to macroeconomics, associated primarily with the names of Robert Lucas of the University of Chicago and Thomas Sargent of Minnesota, was extremely influential in the 1970s. As we shall see in Chapter 16, the approach developed by Lucas, Sargent, and others involves much more than merely a theory of expectations. For now, though, we concentrate on the expectations part of the theory.

The rational expectations hypothesis implies that people do not make *systematic* mistakes in forming their expectations. Systematic mistakes—for instance, always underpredicting inflation—are easily spotted. According to the rational expectations hypothesis, people correct such mistakes and change the way they form expectations accordingly. On average, according to the rational expectations hypothesis, expectations are correct, because people understand the environment in which they work. People, of course, make mistakes from time to time, but they do not make *systematic* mistakes.

According to the rational expectations hypothesis, any policy that relies on people failing to understand what is happening in the economy is bound to fail eventually. Perhaps policy makers can fool people once, by doing something unexpected. But policy makers cannot repeatedly fool people by doing the same thing. In the context of the expectations-augmented Phillips curve, this means that any policy that relies for its effects on systematic differences between the actual and the expected inflation rates will not work very long.

The expectations that underlie the position of the short-run Phillips curve are not just the expectations that people have today about the inflation rate for the next year. Rather, expected rates of change of prices of the past few years are embodied in all the contracts, formal and informal, entered into in the past and in existence now. For instance, 3-year labor contracts specify wages to be paid over the next 3 years. Typically such contracts build in an increase in the wages to be paid each year. The increase in the wage rate year to year would have been 4 to 5 percent in the late fifties, but 9 to 10 percent in the late seventies. The difference results from the higher inflation expected in the seventies.

Thus the expected inflation rate term *gpe* in the expectations-augmented Phillips curve equation (4) has to be interpreted carefully. It represents expectations of inflation, *current and past,* that are present in existing contracts and affect today's economy. Shifts in the expected inflation rate *gpe* shift the short-run Phillips curve. But the curve does not shift quickly. This is the inertia of wages referred to by Stanford's Robert Hall in the quote at the beginning of this chapter.

The Shifting Short-Run Phillips Curve

Friedman and Phelps argued that the Phillips curve would shift over time during the 1960s, when the experience seen in Figure 13-5 seemed to confirm that there was a stable Phillips curve. But subsequent events, shown in Figure 13-7, provided strong support for the Friedman-Phelps view. There are periods of rising inflation combined with rising unemployment, and then from 1976 to 1979 a period that once again looks like the 1960s' tradeoff, except that this time the tradeoff is taking place at a much higher rate of inflation.

What happened? As predicted by Friedman and Phelps, the short-run Phillips curve shifted. In the early 1960s, after a long period of low inflation, the expected inflation rate cannot have been more than 3 percent. Accordingly, in the early 1960s the U.S. economy was on a short-run Phillips curve such as PC' in Figure 13-6, with expected inflation rate equal to 3 percent. By the mid-1970s, after a decade of rising inflation, the expected inflation rate was closer to 7 to 8 percent. At that stage the economy was on a short-run Phillips curve such as PC'' in Figure 13-6, with an expected inflation rate of 8 percent. Between the early 1960s and the late 1970s, the short-run Phillips curve shifted up as expectations of inflation changed and became embodied in the structure of contracts in the economy.

The shifts of the short-run Phillips curve meant that there was a higher inflation rate corresponding to a given rate of unemployment in the 1970s than in the early 1960s. For instance, with the unemployment rate at u', below the natural rate $\bar{u}$, the inflation rate in the late 1970s would have been 10 percent but in the early 1960s would have been only 5 percent. That is why the inflation rate corresponding to any given unemployment rate in the late

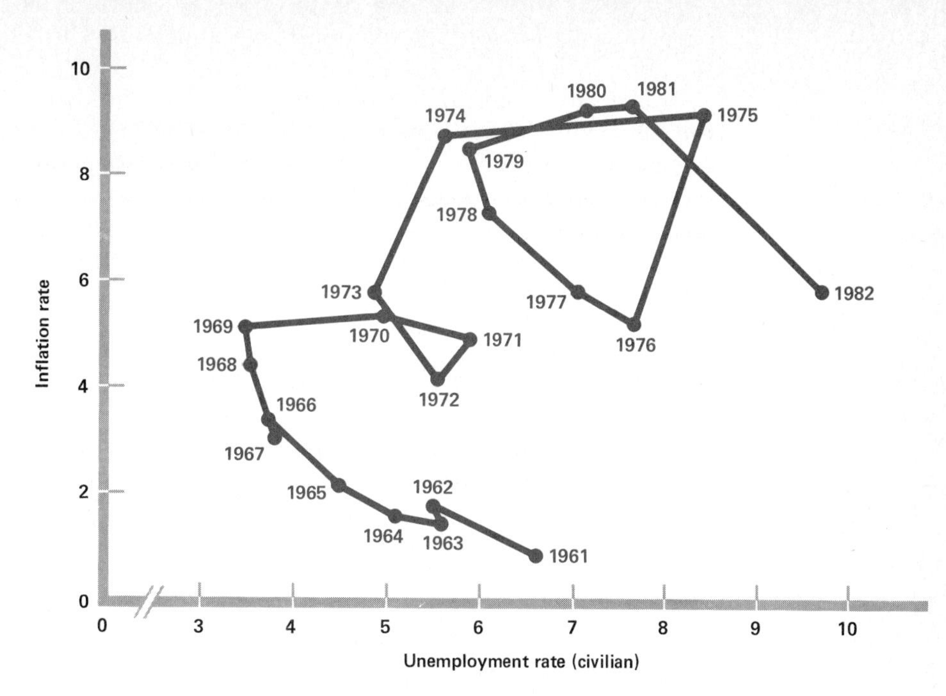

FIGURE 13-7 THE PHILLIPS CURVE 1961 – 1982. (*Source:* Data Resources, Inc.)

seventies was higher than the inflation rate corresponding to the same unemployment rate in the early sixties.[6]

The conclusion of this section is the most important lesson economists and economic policy makers learned in the last 20 years. *The short-run Phillips curve shifts with the expected rate of inflation. The inflation rate corresponding to any given unemployment rate therefore changes over time as the expected inflation rate changes. The higher the expected inflation rate, the higher the inflation rate corresponding to a given unemployment rate.* This explains why we can have both higher inflation and more unemployment.

13-3 THE LONG-RUN PHILLIPS CURVE

Suppose that the expected inflation rate is initially 3 percent, as in the late fifties and early sixties. Then expansionary monetary and fiscal policies push the inflation rate up over the next 15 years to an average of 7 to 8 percent. The

[6] The experience shown in Figure 13-7 reflects more than changes in the expected rate of inflation. During this period there were also (1) supply shocks that shifted the short-run Phillips curve, (2) increases in the natural rate of unemployment, and (3) attempts to reduce the inflation rate by restrictive monetary policy. Later in this chapter and in the next we show how these other events affect the inflation and unemployment rates.

expected inflation rate too will be 7 to 8 percent after the actual inflation rate has been in that range for several years.

Thus after a period of years, the expected inflation rate will catch up to the actual inflation rate. *In the long run, the actual and expected inflation rates are equal.* Accordingly, we define the *long-run Phillips curve* as follows: The long-run Phillips curve describes the tradeoff, if any, between inflation and unemployment when the actual and expected inflation rates are equal. In working with this definition of the long-run Phillips curve, recall that the expectations embodied in the Phillips curve are expectations about inflation, current and past, that affect contracts currently in force in the economy.

What does the long-run Phillips curve look like? We can find that out using Equation (4), the expectations-augmented Phillips curve.

$$gp = gpe - \epsilon(u - \bar{u}) \tag{4}$$

In the long run, the actual and expected inflation rates are equal, and so $gp = gpe$. Thus in the long run

$$0 = -\epsilon(u - \bar{u})$$

or

$$u = \bar{u} \tag{5}$$

Equation (5) implies that *in the long run, the actual unemployment rate is equal to the natural rate, whatever the rate of inflation.* In other words, *in the long run, there is no tradeoff between inflation and unemployment.* When expected inflation is equal to actual inflation, the unemployment rate is equal to the natural rate of unemployment.

Figure 13-8 shows the relationship between the short- and long-run Phillips curves. In the short run of a year or less, the economy moves along a short-run Phillips curve, such as PC', with a given expected inflation rate. In the long run, though, expectations catch up to the actual inflation rate, and the economy will be at a point at which the actual and expected inflation rate are equal. That happens only along the vertical line LPC, the long-run Phillips curve.

Adjusting to a Higher Inflation Rate

Our understanding of the long-run Phillips curve is increased by asking how the economy moves over time from one long-run inflation rate to another. In Figure 13-9 the economy is initially at point E, with unemployment at the natural rate $\bar{u}$ and an inflation rate of 3 percent. Now monetary and fiscal policies become expansionary, moving the economy to a point such as E' on the short-run Phillips curve PC'. Because PC' is quite flat, there is only a small increase in the inflation rate and a substantial decline in the unemployment rate, to u'.

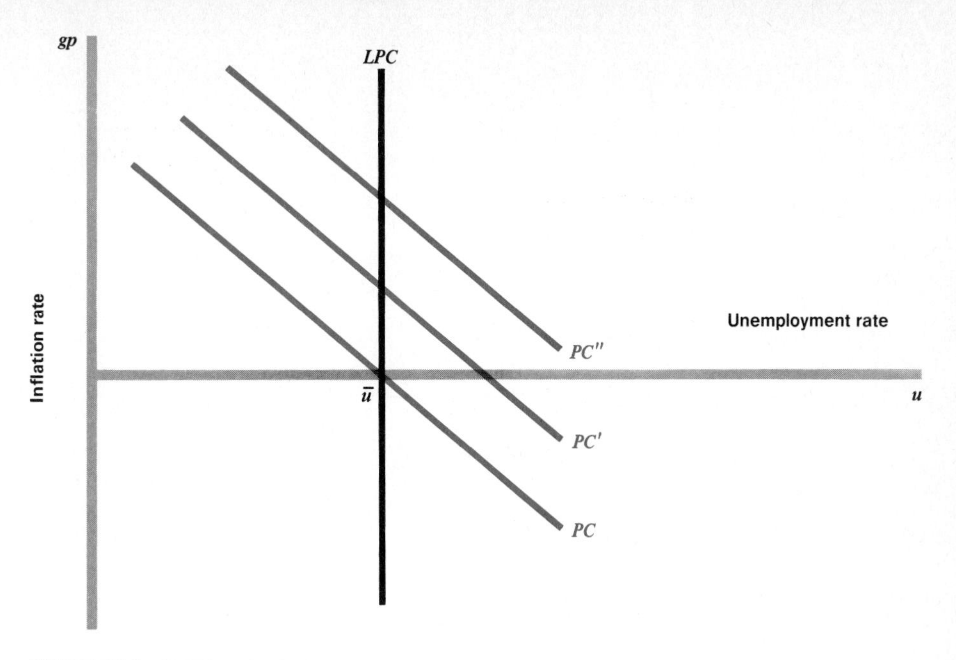

FIGURE 13-8 SHORT- AND LONG-RUN PHILLIPS CURVES. In the short run the economy moves along one of the short-run Phillips curves, such as *PC′*. The expected rate of inflation is constant on each of the short-run curves. In the long run, though, the expected rate of inflation is equal to the actual rate, and unemployment is at the natural rate $\bar{u}$. In the long run the economy moves along *LPC*, with no tradeoff between inflation and unemployment.

But now expectations of inflation begin to adjust. Wage increases in existing contracts were based on the assumption that the inflation rate would be 3 percent. But it is actually 5 percent. Workers adjust their expectations of inflation, say, to 5 percent, and that rate of wage increase is built into labor contracts.

The short-run Phillips curve moves up to a position such as *PC‴*. The expected inflation rate is 5 percent, and wages rise at a rate reflecting the higher expected inflation. The expansionary monetary and fiscal policies now show up more in higher inflation and less in lower unemployment, as the economy moves to a position such as *E‴*.

Once again expectations of inflation adjust, they become embodied in wages, and the short-run Phillips curve shifts up. We do not show how the short-run Phillips curve shifts from *PC‴*, to avoid cluttering the diagram. Eventually, though, expected and actual inflation are equal, and the economy is on both *PC″* and *LPC* at point *E″*. The path the economy takes to *E″* is shown by the arrows in Figure 13-9.

Eventually, then, expansionary aggregate demand policies produce a higher inflation rate and no reduction in the unemployment rate. But in the process of adjusting to the new inflation rate, there is a period in which output is higher than normal and unemployment is below the natural rate.

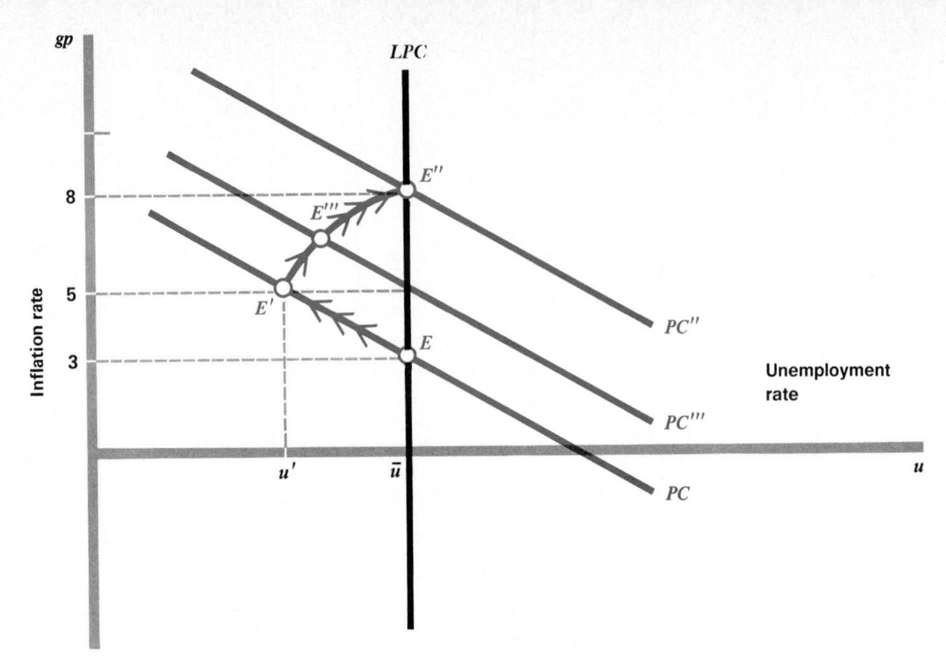

FIGURE 13-9 ADJUSTING TO HIGHER LONG-RUN INFLATION. The economy is initially at point E, with 3 percent inflation and unemployment at the natural rate $\bar{u}$. Expansionary monetary and fiscal policies move the economy in the short run to point E', on the short-run Phillips curve PC'. The unemployment rate drops to u', and the inflation rate increases to 5 percent. As a result of the higher inflation, expectations of inflation increase, shifting the short-run Phillips curve to PC'''. From E' the economy moves to E''', with higher inflation and more unemployment. Gradually, as expectations of inflation adjust, the short-run Phillips curve keeps shifting, and the economy moves to point E'', which is on both PC'' and LPC. The economy is back in equilibrium with a higher inflation rate and the same unemployment rate at which it started, $\bar{u}$. The adjustment process is shown by the arrows.

STAGFLATION

Note that as the economy moves from E to E'', we first see the inflation rate rising as the unemployment rate falls. Then, as expectations adjust to the higher inflation, the inflation rate and the unemployment rate increase together. That is, in the adjustment process of the economy to a higher inflation rate, there will be a period in which the inflation rate and the unemployment rate increase together.

A period of rising inflation together with rising unemployment is known as *stagflation*. Examining Figure 13-7, we see stagflationary episodes in 1973–1975 and 1979–1981. It is often believed that the Phillips curve implies that inflation and unemployment cannot increase together. That is not necessarily true, so long as we realize that the short-run Phillips curve can shift, and that in periods in which the short-run Phillips curve is shifting, the inflation rate and unemployment rate might well be moving in the same direction.[7]

ANTI-INFLATIONARY POLICIES

The description in this section of how the economy moves from a lower to a higher inflation rate applies to the increasing inflation experienced by the United States from the early sixties to the late seventies. A very similar analysis, moving in the opposite direction, applies when an attempt is made to reduce the inflation rate through tight monetary policy. In that case the restrictive policies first produce a sharp rise in the unemployment rate with little reduction in inflation. Later the inflation rate begins to fall, and eventually the economy starts moving back to full employment, with a lower rate of inflation. This was the story in the United States from 1979 to 1983.[8]

Is the Long-Run Phillips Curve Really Vertical?

The view that the long-run Phillips curve is vertical was initially controversial. Some economists argued that there was a long-run Phillips curve, steeper than the short-run curves, but not necessarily vertical. Curve *LPC′* in Figure 13-10 is an example. Part of the controversy arose because a curve such as *LPC* appears to suggest that *nothing* can be done about long-run unemployment, which will settle down to the rate $\bar{u}$ whatever aggregate demand policies are followed. *LPC′* does give a long-run tradeoff, leaving room for expansionary aggregate demand policies.

However, whether the long-run Phillips curve is vertical or negatively sloped, it may be possible to reduce the natural rate $\bar{u}$ through policies designed to make the labor market more efficient. Such policies would include, for instance, setting up job banks designed to improve the information available to both workers and employers about jobs and the workers available to fill them. Retraining programs for workers whose industries are in decline would be another example. In terms of Figure 13-10, these policies would shift the *LPC* curve to the left. They would also shift *LPC′* to the left, implying a lower rate of inflation at any given unemployment rate. Indeed, the idea of shifting the Phillips curve was discussed long before the issue of long-run vertical versus downward-sloping curves arose.

While there is now considerable agreement on a long-run vertical Phillips

[7] In both 1973–1975 and 1979–1981 the short-run Phillips curve was shifting up for two reasons: first, expectations of inflation were increasing, catching up to past inflation; and second, there were supply shocks.

[8] In the problem set we ask you to show how a strongly anti-inflationary monetary policy affects the inflation and unemployment rates in the short and long runs. We also examine alternative stabilization policies in the last section of this chapter.

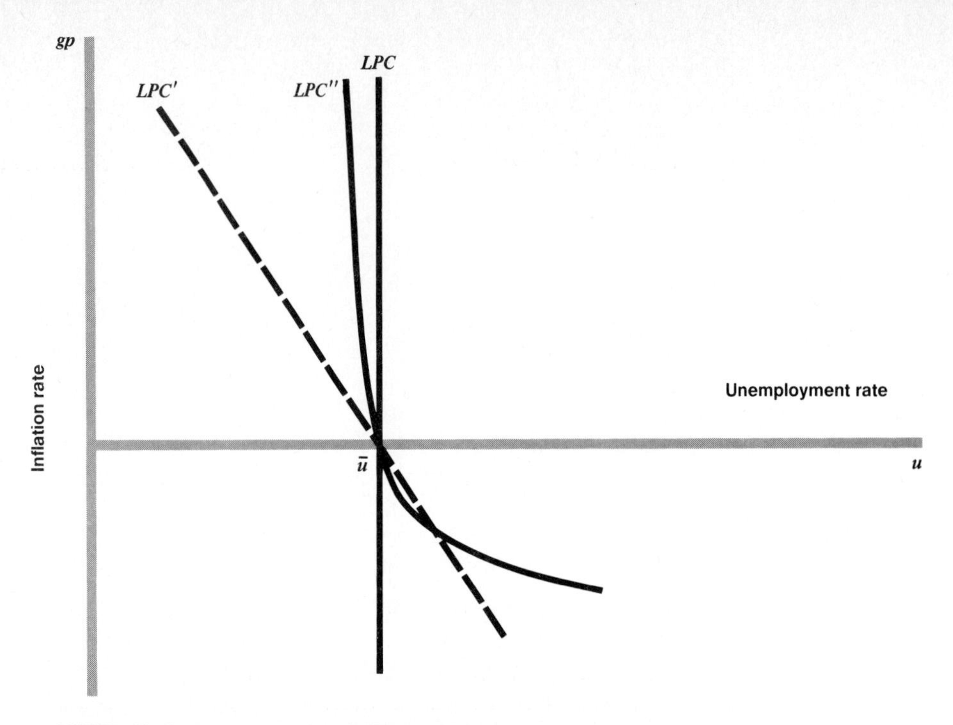

FIGURE 13-10 LONG-RUN PHILLIPS CURVES. *LPC* is the vertical long-run Phillips curve discussed earlier. In the sixties and early seventies some economists believed there was a long-run tradeoff between inflation and unemployment, as on *LPC′*, which is steeper than the short-run Phillips curves in earlier figures. This view is no longer widely held. A third possibility is that the long-run Phillips curve is practically vertical at positive rates of inflation, but quite flat at negative inflation rates, as on *LPC″*. This would be a result of downward wage stickiness. Because our experience since World War II is limited to positive rates of inflation, it is difficult to choose between *LPC* and *LPC″* on the basis of recent evidence.

curve, that agreement is not unanimous.[9] Nor, for that matter, do we feel completely confident that the Phillips curve is vertical at *all* rates of inflation. We would not be surprised if the long-run Phillips curve has a shape such as that of *LPC″* in Figure 13-10. At positive rates of inflation (which are essentially what we have experienced since 1945), the curve is, for all practical purposes, vertical. At negative rates of inflation, it may well be virtually horizontal.

The basis for the long-run Phillips curve *LPC″* is the suggestion that money wage behavior is asymmetrical. Wages rise in the face of excess demand for labor, or expected inflation, but do not fall at the same rate in the

[9] See, for example, Robert Solow, "Down the Phillips Curve with Gun and Camera," in David A. Belsley et al. (eds.), *Inflation, Trade and Taxes* (Columbus: Ohio State University Press, 1976). James Tobin, in "Stabilization Policy Ten Years After," *Brookings Papers on Economic Activity*, 1:1980, asks whether the natural rate of unemployment might not respond to recent unemployment experience, rather than being a constant or a slowly moving rate. We discuss the natural rate in Chapter 14.

face of even heavy unemployment or expected deflation. There is some evidence for that view, and if it is correct, the long-run Phillips curve might well be kinked, like *LPC*″.

But even if *LPC*″ did describe long-run tradeoffs, it offers little hope for manipulating the unemployment rate in the long run through changes in the inflation rate. Even on *LPC*″, any attempts to reduce the unemployment rate through expansionary aggregate demand policies soon produce inflation, rather than any further reductions in unemployment. The experience of the last 20 years in the United States and abroad suggests two basic Phillips curve lessons: (1) In the short run, aggregate demand policies can reduce the unemployment rate, (2) but such policies cannot produce sustained reductions in the unemployment rate. For all practical purposes, the long-run Phillips curve is vertical.

13-4 MONEY AND INFLATION IN THE LONG RUN

In the previous section we discussed how the economy moves from a low to a higher inflation rate, from point *E* to *E*″ in Figure 13-9. We suggested that expansionary aggregate demand policies would produce such a shift, but did not say precisely what sort of policies could produce an increase in the inflation rate in the long run.

It is often asserted, particularly by monetarists, that inflation is a monetary phenomenon. The claim that inflation is a monetary phenomenon means that sustained high rates of money growth produce high inflation, and that low rates of money growth will eventually produce low rates of inflation. Further, the statement that inflation is a monetary phenomenon means that high rates of inflation cannot long continue without high rates of money growth. The view that inflation is a monetary phenomenon is the implication of the quantity theory of money (described in Chapter 9), which is the backbone of monetarist macroeconomics. In this section we analyze the sense in which inflation is a monetary phenomenon, concentrating on long-run inflation.

Figure 13-11 presents evidence from the United States over the period since 1950, showing that the inflation rate and the growth rate of money have, more or less, moved together. The inflation rate and the rate of money growth in the figure are each average rates over the past 4 years. The averaging removes much of the short-term variation in both money growth and the inflation rate. Although the relationship in Figure 13-11 is clearly positive, it is also obvious that the link between money growth and inflation is not precise. We examine the reasons the link is not precise in the next section.

The reason to expect a link between inflation and money growth derives from the fact that the demand for money is a demand for *real balances*. We write the demand function for real balances as

$$\frac{M}{P} = L(i, Y) \tag{6}$$

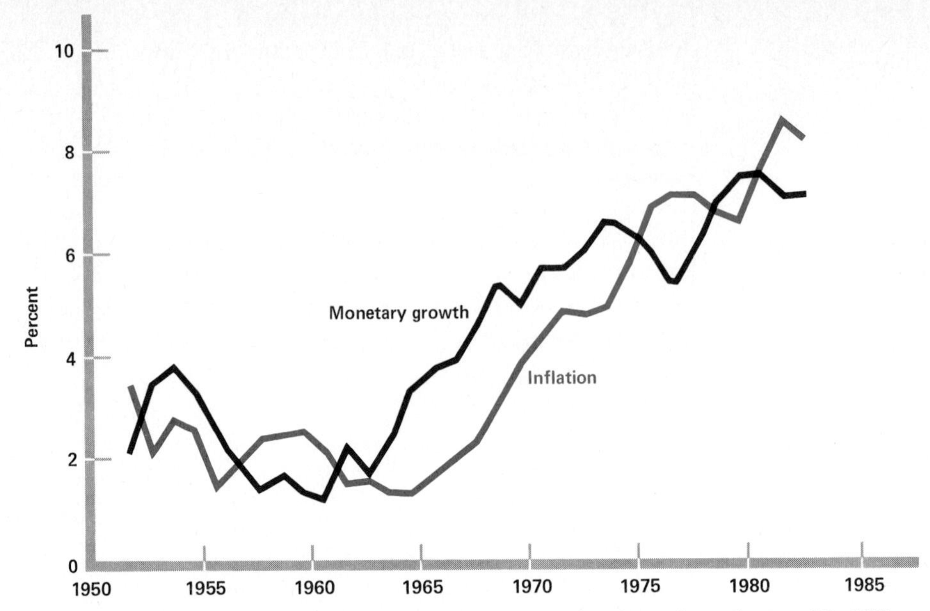

Note: **Inflation and monetary growth are 4-year moving average of annual growth rates of the GNP deflator and of M1.**

FIGURE 13-11 LONG-TERM INFLATION AND MONETARY GROWTH. (*Source:* Data Resources, Inc.)

The demand function for real balances states that the demand depends on the nominal interest rate, i, and on real GNP, Y.

The long run is defined as the period in which the actual and the expected inflation rates are equal. In the long run, unemployment is at the natural rate $\bar{u}$, and thus output is at the full-employment level $\bar{Y}$. (For the moment assume that there is no growth in potential output, and so $\bar{Y}$ is constant over time.) Further, in the long run, when the economy is in equilibrium, the nominal interest rate is at some long-run equilibrium level, say, i^*. Thus in long-run equilibrium, both i and Y are at their constant equilibrium levels, i^* and $\bar{Y}$, respectively. Accordingly, *in long-run equilibrium in an economy in which potential output is constant, real balances are constant.*

When real balances are constant, the ratio M/P is constant. That means the nominal money stock M and the price level P are growing at the same rate. For instance, if the money stock is growing at 8 percent so are prices. Thus we conclude that *in long-run equilibrium (with output constant), the inflation rate is equal to the growth rate of money* (gm). We write this long-run relationship as

$$gp = gm \tag{7}$$

The basic argument that in the long run inflation is a monetary phenomenon thus comes from the recognition that in long-run equilibrium, real money demand and hence real balances will be constant if potential output is not growing. But there are several qualifications to the strong statement of Equation (7).

Output Growth and Inflation in the Long Run

Suppose that output, instead of being constant, grows in the long run at the growth rate of potential output, gy^*. In the United States gy^* has been about 3 percent. Some money growth is needed just to meet the increasing demand for real balances arising from growing income. Accordingly, the money growth rate will exceed the inflation rate in the long run.

The difference between money growth and inflation arises from the amount of money growth needed to meet the demand increases resulting from steadily rising income. How much money growth is that? Suppose the income elasticity of money demand is 0.7. Then for every 1 percent that income rises, the demand for real balances rises 0.7 percent. The 3 percent growth in potential output thus increases the demand for real balances by 2.1 percent a year.

If real money demand is rising—say, at the rate of 2.1 percent per year—as a result of income growth, then monetary equilibrium requires that the real money supply increase at the same rate. The growth rate of the real money stock is just the difference between the growth rate of the nominal money stock and the rate of inflation. For instance, if the nominal money stock is increasing at 10 percent and the rate of inflation is 7.9 percent, the real money stock is increasing at 2.1 percent per year.

If the real money supply has to be growing at 2.1 percent per year to maintain monetary equilibrium, then the rate of inflation has to be 2.1 percent less than the rate of money growth, or, in symbols, $gp = gm - 2.1$.

More generally, with gy^* as the growth rate of potential output and η as the income elasticity of the demand for real balances, the relationship among the inflation rate, the growth rate of money, and the growth rate of output is

$$gp = gm - \eta gy^* \tag{8}$$

Changes in Velocity and Inflation

Table 13-1 shows the inflation rate, the growth rate of $M1$, and the growth rate of real GNP for six countries over the period 1953–1982. According to Equation (8), we should find that

$$gp - (gm - \eta gy) = 0 \tag{8a}$$

In column (4) of Table 13-1 we calculate $gp - (gm - gy)$, an amount which should be zero if the income elasticity of money demand is unity. Column (5) shows a similar calculation, assuming the income elasticity of money demand is 0.7.

TABLE 13-1 MONEY GROWTH AND INFLATION, 1953–1982

Country	(1) Inflation rate (CPI), gp	(2) Growth rate of $M1$, gm	(3) Growth rate of real GNP (or GDP), gy	(4) $gp - (gm - gy)$	(5) $gp - (gm - 0.7gy)$
Canada	4.8	7.7	4.0	1.1	−0.1
Germany	3.4	8.6	4.5	−0.7	−2.1
Italy	7.7	14.3	4.5	−2.1	−3.4
Japan	5.8	13.7	7.7	−0.2	−2.5
United Kingdom	7.3	6.9	2.3	2.7	2.0
United States	4.5	4.5	3.0	3.0	2.1

Source: International Financial Statistics.

Whichever estimate of the income elasticity of demand for money is used, the inflation experienced by the countries does not exactly match that predicted by Equation (8*a*). In the United Kingdom and the United States, inflation has been, on average, faster than predicted using Equation (8*a*). In Italy, and, depending on the correct income elasticity, perhaps Japan and Germany, inflation has been, on average, slower than predicted by Equation (8*a*).

The deviations of the inflation rate from the quantity theory predictions in Table 13-1 are a result of shifts in the demand for money over the last 30 years. In particular, the downward shifts of the demand function for $M1$ in the United States have reduced the amount of real balances individuals want to hold. If M/P demand falls, then P will rise, in the adjustment process, faster than M. That is why the inflation rate has exceeded the rate we would predict from knowledge of the growth rate of $M1$ and the growth rate of income.

BOX 13-1

EXPECTATIONS, INTEREST RATES, AND INFLATION: THE FISHER EQUATION

Table 1 shows interest rates for several countries in 1980. The rates differ widely, ranging from under 5 percent in Switzerland to above 30 percent in Brazil and Colombia. Also shown in the table are inflation rates for these countries for the preceding 4 years. This is a rough measure of the expected inflation rate in each country.

The table shows a very strong relationship between the interest rate in a country and the expected inflation rate. Figure 1 looks at the same relationship over the period 1952–1982 in the United States. There is again a definite positive relationship, with interest rates rising as inflation increases. The positive relationship between expected inflation and the nominal interest rate is called the ***Fisher equation***. It is named after Irving Fisher, the foremost American macroecono-

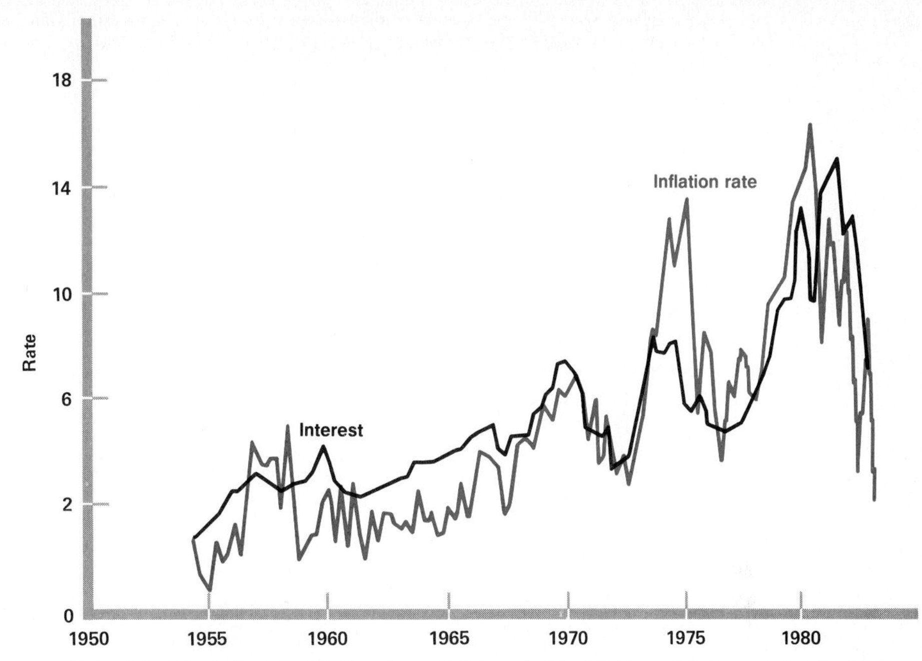

Note: **Interest rate is market yield on 3-month Treasury bills. Inflation rate is the growth rate of the CPI over the following quarter.**

FIGURE 1 INTEREST AND INFLATION

mist of the late nineteenth and first half of this century.* The Fisher equation is based on the distinction between the real and nominal interest rates:

Nominal interest rate = real interest rate + expected inflation rate†

Fisher argued that the real interest rate is roughly constant in long-run equilibrium. He regarded it as determined by the real factors in the economy, particularly the productivity of capital. ***With the real interest rate approximately constant in the long run, and with expectations of inflation adjusting to actual inflation in the long run, the nominal interest rate adjusts with the inflation rate.*** This is what we see in Table 1 and in Figure 1.

How does expected inflation get built into the interest rate? The reasoning is almost identical to that explaining how the expected inflation rate gets built into the rate of wage increase. Anyone making a loan when inflation is expected knows that she will be repaid in dollars of lower real value. For instance, suppose the expected inflation rate is 10 percent. Prices a year from now will be 10 percent above the price level today. One dollar will buy 10 percent

* Fisher (1867–1947) taught at Yale, and was an effective and sophisticated developer of the quantity theory of money. (See Box 11-1.) He had other interests too; he was the inventor of the card index file still used for keeping addresses, and was a health food enthusiast who wrote several books on the subject. Fisher was an early, if long forgotten, discoverer of the Phillips curve. See the reprinted version of his 1926 article "A Statistical Relation between Unemployment and Price Changes," under the heading "Lost and Found," *Journal of Political Economy*. March/April 1973, pp. 496–502.

† Irving Fisher, *The Theory of Interest* (New York: A. M. Kelly Publishers, 1965, reprint of 1930 edition), p. 427.

TABLE 1 INTEREST RATES AND EXPECTED INFLATION, 1980*

Country	Interest rate % per annum	Average inflation rate, 1976–1980
Australia	11.5	9.9
Brazil	33.0	53.6
Canada	12.8	9.1
Colombia	30.0†	25.4
France	11.9	10.6
Germany	9.1	4.0
Italy	17.2	16.2
Switzerland	4.8‡	2.5
United Kingdom	15.1	13.8
United States	11.6	9.7

* Interest rates are short-term market rates except as noted. The expected inflation rate is assumed to be the average of inflation rates over the previous 4 years.
† Central bank discount rate.
‡ Government bond yield.
Source: International Financial Statistics.

less a year from now than a dollar buys today. Accordingly, the lender will want to be compensated by an extra 10 percent per year to adjust for the expected decline in the value of money. Someone lending at 3 percent when there is no inflation is effectively in the same situation as someone lending at 13 percent when there is 10 percent inflation.

But how can the borrower afford to pay the extra 10 percent? Suppose the borrower is a businessperson who plans to invest in machinery to produce goods for sale a year from now, and to repay the loan out of the proceeds. If prices are expected to rise by 10 percent, then the borrower will be able to sell the goods for 10 percent more next year than he could sell them if there were zero inflation. Thus the borrower will be willing to pay the extra 10 percent. He too will be in the same position with a 13 percent interest rate and 10 percent inflation as he would have been at 3 percent interest and zero inflation.

We make two points about the Fisher equation:

1 The real interest rate is not constant. It has, in particular, been extremely high in the United States and other countries in the period since 1980. In Chapter 15 we examine the Fisher equation and variations in the real interest rate in more detail.
2. Fisher believed that it took a long time for the economy to adapt to a new rate of inflation. His estimate was that it was 30 years before the interest rate fully adapted to higher inflation.

Is Inflation a Monetary Phenomenon in the Long Run?

The answer to the question whether inflation is a monetary phenomenon in the long run is yes. No major inflation can take place without rapid money growth, and rapid money growth will cause rapid inflation. Further, any policy that determinedly keeps the growth rate of money low will lead eventually to a low rate of inflation.

But at the same time the long-run link between money growth and inflation is not precise, as the data of Table 13-1 show. There are two reasons for that. First, increases in output increase the demand for real balances and reduce the inflation rate corresponding to a given rate of money growth. And second, financial institutions change, the definition of money changes, and the demand for money may shift over time. Those are the reasons that the United States, which has the lowest average growth rate of $M1$ in Table 13-1, does not have the lowest average inflation rate.

The role of money growth in determining long-run inflation is well summarized in a passage from the *1983 Economic Report of the President* (p. 20):

> Over short periods of time a variety of factors influence the rate of inflation. One important factor in the 1970s was supply-determined changes in commodity prices resulting from fluctuations in harvests and disruptions in the supply of foreign oil. Another important factor was the increasing level of expected inflation. Once the expectation of continuing inflation has become firmly entrenched, prices and wages may continue to rise even in the face of declining demand, and the cost of reducing inflation may increase.
>
> These factors, however, only affect the rate of inflation for a limited time. The popular axiom that attributes inflation to "too much money chasing too few goods" reflects a basic truth: it is difficult to imagine a sustained inflation that is not supported by excessive money growth. Over long periods of time, an additional percentage point in the rate of growth of the money stock will tend to produce an additional percentage point of growth of nominal GNP, that is, GNP measured at current prices. If the rate of real GNP growth does not change, the entire increase in nominal GNP growth will take the form of increased inflation. Although the relations between money growth, nominal GNP growth, and inflation are considerably more variable over shorter periods than they are in the long run, the impact of money growth on nominal income and inflation remains powerful even in the short run.

Having recognized now the special role of money growth in setting long-run inflation trends, we turn to the other factors mentioned in the above quote that can, *in the short run*, also influence the inflation rate.

13-5 OTHER CAUSES OF INFLATION

Figure 13-12 shows two short-run Phillips curves, PC' and PC''. We have already seen that expansionary monetary policy can move the economy from one Phillips curve to another. When the growth rate of money first increases, the economy moves from E to a position such as E', moving along a short-run Phillips curve. But then, provided the money growth continues, expectations and contracts adjust, and the short-run Phillips curve moves up to PC''. If the new higher rate of money growth is maintained, the economy will end up with a higher inflation rate back at the natural rate of unemployment.

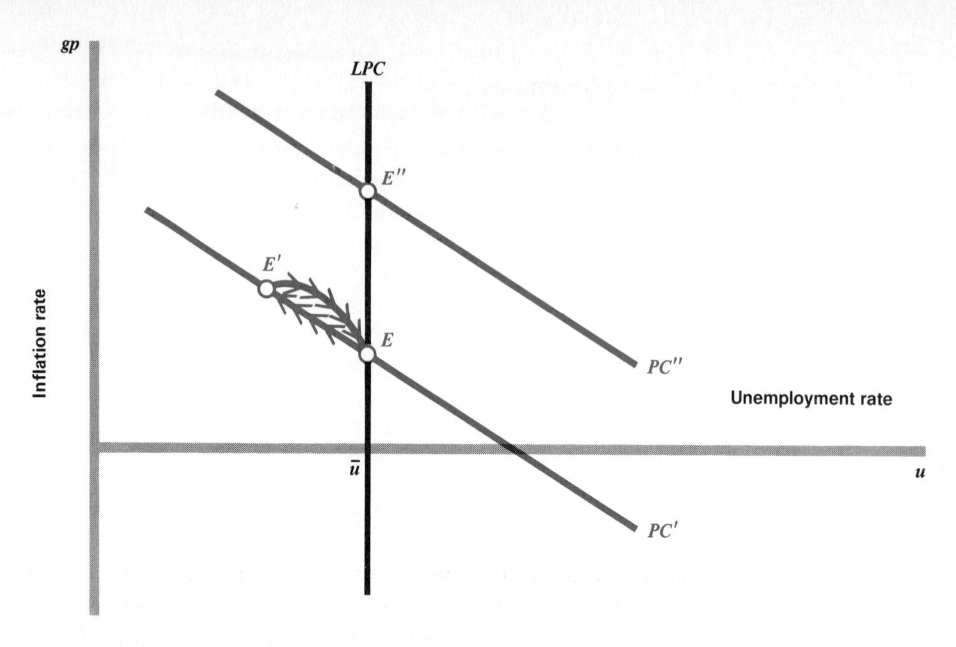

FIGURE 13-12 ADJUSTMENT TO A PERMANENT INCREASE IN GOVERNMENT SPENDING. A permanent increase in government spending shifts the economy in the short run along PC', to point E'. Thus the initial impact of the fiscal expansion is to increase inflation and reduce unemployment. If expectations of inflation increase, the PC' curve may shift up (not shown). But eventually the economy returns to point E on LPC. This is because the fiscal expansion took place without any change in the growth rate of money—and in the long run the economy therefore has to come back to the same inflation rate from which it started. Curve PC'' is included in the diagram to remind us of the contrast between the long-run effects of fiscal and monetary expansion on the inflation rate. (Figure 13-9 shows the long-run effects of an increase in the growth rate of money.)

Increased money growth thus causes more inflation in both the short and the long run. But money growth is not the only source of inflation in the short run. In this section we briefly review three other potential sources of inflation in the short run: (1) expansionary fiscal policy, (2) supply shocks, and (3) wage disturbances. None of these can produce inflation *in the long run* unless money growth also increases. But here we are concentrating on the short run, not the long run.

Expansionary Fiscal Policy

Suppose there is an increase in government spending to a new higher level. In the short run, with wages and prices quite sticky, the increase in aggregate demand increases real output and reduces unemployment. The economy moves along a short-run Phillips curve such as PC' in Figure 13-12, to a position such as E'.

If people believe the increase in inflation caused by the expansionary fiscal policy is merely temporary, expectations will not adjust, and the economy will move back down the PC' curve. The adjustment after the initial expansion will involve a falling inflation rate and an unemployment rate that is still below the natural rate, but rising. Eventually the economy returns to the original inflation rate and the natural rate of unemployment.

However, people might believe that the new fiscal policy will have prolonged inflationary effects. In that case, because of inflationary expectations, the short-run Phillips curve will shift up after the move to point E'. From E' the inflation rate will increase while unemployment rises. But eventually the inflation rate will fall back to its original level as the economy moves back to the natural rate of unemployment. The arrows in Figure 13-12 show the adjustment path of the economy to the increase in government spending.

SOME EVIDENCE

Our analysis of the effects of fiscal expansion suggests that a permanent increase in real government spending first reduces unemployment (and increases output) but then gradually loses its effectiveness. In other words, the analysis suggests there is full *crowding out* in the long run, but not in the short run.

Table 13-2 presents fiscal multipliers from the DRI macroeconometric model. These are the estimated effects on real GNP of a permanent $1 billion increase in real government spending. Money growth is maintained constant. In the first quarter, the impact of the increased government spending is to increase real output. The output rises a bit more through the end of the first year. Then in each successive year, the expansionary impact of the fiscal expansion falls. After 6 years the real effects of the fiscal expansion have almost disappeared. Both output and the unemployment rate are back to the levels at which they started. This is what the analysis of Figure 13-12 implies.

The inflation rate initially rises with the increase in government spending, but eventually the inflationary effect of the increase in government spending disappears. But the adjustment process takes a long time. Thus our analysis shows that a *permanent* increase in government spending has only *transitory* real expansionary and inflationary effects.

Table 13-3 summarizes the short- and long-run effects both of changes in

TABLE 13-2 GOVERNMENT SPENDING MULTIPLIER*

Quarters after policy change	1	4	8	12	24
Multiplier	1.04	1.24	0.96	0.75	0.12

* This is a dynamic multiplier showing the increase in real GNP per dollar permanent increase in government spending over successive quarters following the policy change.
Source: Data Resources, Inc.

TABLE 13-3 THE EFFECTS OF INCREASED MONEY GROWTH AND PERMANENT FISCAL EXPANSIONS

	Inflation		Output	
	Short run	Long run	Short run	Long run
Increased money growth	+	+	+	0
Fiscal expansion	+	0	+	0

the growth rate of money and of a fiscal expansion on output and on inflation. It serves to review the results we have derived so far. Note that the effects on unemployment are just the opposite of those on output.

Table 13-3 shows that neither increased money growth nor fiscal expansion can, in the long run, sustain output above full employment or reduce unemployment permanently below the natural rate. The table also shows that increased money growth permanently increases inflation, while fiscal expansion only transitorily raises inflation until the real money stock has declined enough to lead to full crowding out. In Chapters 15 and 16 we return to a discussion of the long-run effects of fiscal policy in the context of long-run supply-side issues.

Supply Shocks

In Figure 13-13 we examine the effects of a supply shock. Suppose the price of oil rises. An increase in a key material price, such as that of oil, takes time to be built into the prices charged by all the firms in the economy. While that adjustment is taking place, the short-run Phillips curve shifts up, for instance, from *PC* to *PC′*. There is a higher inflation rate corresponding to any given unemployment rate. If there is no change in monetary or fiscal policy, aggregate demand does not change. With prices higher, output has to fall, and unemployment therefore rises. The economy moves to *E′* on *PC′*. In the short run, inflation and unemployment increase together. This is exactly the pattern seen in Figure 13-7 in the 1973–1975 and 1979–1980 periods when the economy was hit by oil price shocks.

If the inflationary effects of the oil price shocks are slow in working their way into prices of all goods, then the short-run Phillips curve may stay at *PC′* for some time. Indeed, the short-run Phillips curve might even move up to a position such as *PC″* if expectations of inflation adjust, and workers begin to ask for higher rates of wage increase to compensate for the higher inflation they expect. With aggregate demand unchanged, this will lead to more unemployment along with the higher inflation.

Eventually though, the pressure of unemployment reduces the rate of increase of wages, the short-run Phillips curve begins to drop back toward *PC′* and then to *PC*, and the economy returns to full employment and lower

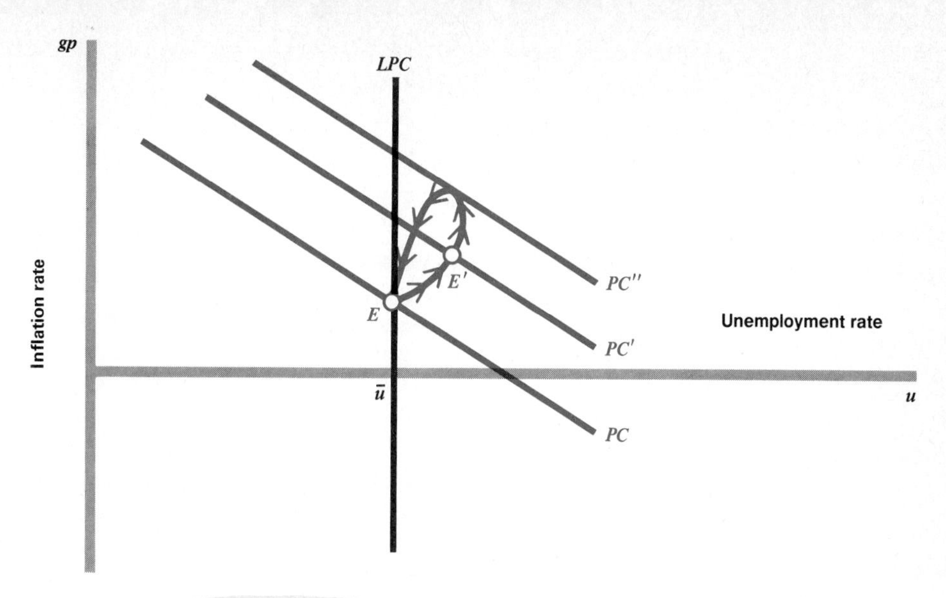

FIGURE 13-13 THE EFFECTS OF A SUPPLY SHOCK. A supply shock initially moves the short-run Phillips curve up, from *PC* to *PC'*. Because aggregate demand has not changed, the higher prices will force output down, thus causing unemployment. The economy moves in the short run from *E* to *E'*. From *E'* the short-run Phillips curve may shift up if workers demand higher rates of wage increase to compensate for the higher inflation. Eventually, though, the economy returns to point *E*. The arrows show the adjustment path followed after the supply shock.

inflation. But in the meantime, the economy has been through a recession caused by the supply shock.

Wage Push and the Policy Dilemma

Suppose that the economy was in a steady state and that workers ask for higher wages. A *wage push* takes place if workers claim wage increases that exceed those implied by the ongoing inflation rate on the short-run Phillips curve. A wage push might take place, for instance, in an economy which has large trade unions that have decided to mount a major campaign to increase wages.

The economic effects of a wage push are the same as those of any supply shock. If there is no response from monetary and fiscal policy, the inflation rate and unemployment rate will both rise in response to the wage push. Employed workers will get higher nominal wages. But because monetary and fiscal policy do not react, output falls as the price level rises. As a result of the higher unemployment, some workers who started out pushing for higher wages are out of a job and have lower rather than higher income.

If there were no response whatsoever from monetary and fiscal policy, the inflation rate and the unemployment rate would eventually return to their initial levels, as in Figure 13-13. But in the meantime the economy has been through a period of unemployment.

ACCOMMODATION

In both the case of a supply shock and the case of a wage push, the policy makers face the issue of whether to accommodate the inflation.[10] Policy makers *accommodate* supply shocks when they increase the growth rate of money to prevent unemployment that would otherwise occur as a result of a supply disturbance that shifts the short-run Phillips curve.

Accommodation of supply shocks results in higher inflation but has the benefits of reducing the unemployment rate. Since we have not yet examined the costs of inflation and unemployment, we are not in a position to evaluate the costs and benefits of accommodation.[11]

But there is one important point to make about accommodation. We make it using the example of the wage push. Suppose that workers push for higher nominal wages, and that policy makers expand aggregate demand to accommodate that. The accommodation will produce an inflation rate above that expected by workers, and thus give them lower real wages than they expected. If their push is for higher *real* wages, next period they will push for yet higher increases in nominal wages to compensate for the greater inflation they expect. If policy makers try to accommodate real disturbances of this type, they end up in a process of ever-increasing inflation.

In Chapter 12 we discussed accommodation of an oil price shock that required a fall in the real wage. We argued there that the economy could adjust more easily to a shock of that type if monetary policy were expansionary. That would make it possible for the real wage to fall without the nominal wage having to fall. In that case accommodation would work, *because it is not attempting permanently to counteract a real change that the economy has to make.* Rather, it is helping the economy make the appropriate real adjustments more smoothly, by adjusting for the stickiness of nominal wages.

What is the general point about accommodation? It is that accommodation works when it is used to help move the economy toward the real adjustments it has to make to disturbances. Accommodation will not succeed if it tries to prevent real adjustments to real disturbances.

13-6 ALTERNATIVE STRATEGIES TO REDUCE INFLATION

Suppose the inflation rate in the economy is 10 percent, and concerned policy makers decide to fight inflation and return to inflation rates of only around 2 to 3 percent. This is the decision that was made in the United States at the end of 1979. How fast should they aim to reduce inflation?

[10] In Chapter 5 we discussed accommodation through fiscal policy where the monetary authorities prevent an increase in the interest rate and crowding out by allowing the money stock to rise in the course of a fiscal expansion.

[11] We discuss the costs of inflation and unemployment in Chap. 14.

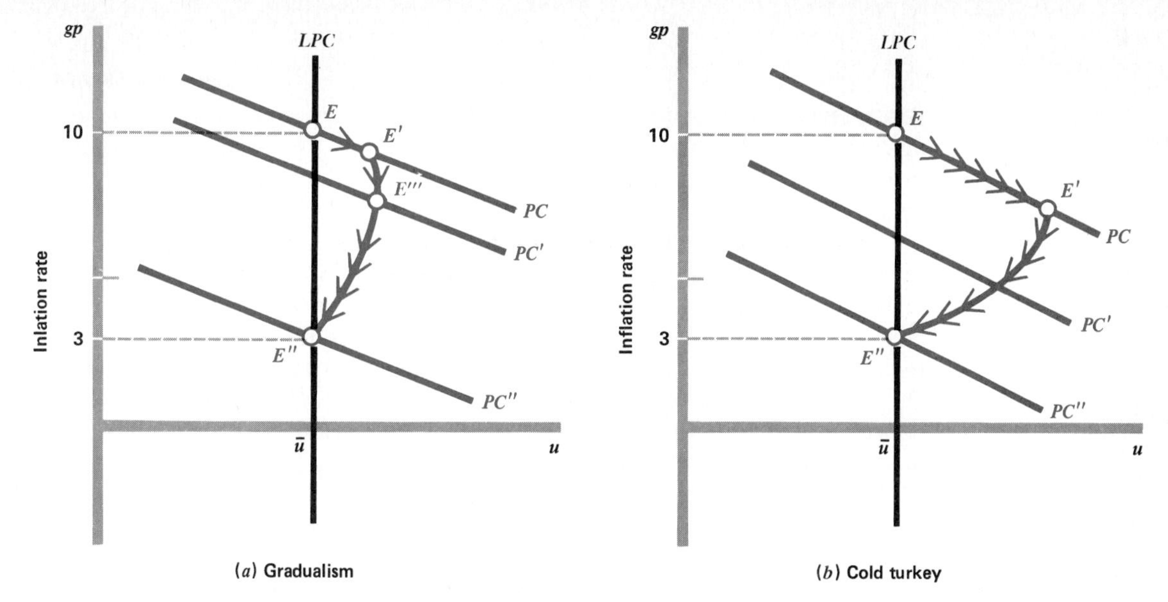

FIGURE 13-14 STRATEGIES TO REDUCE INFLATION. Under the gradualist strategy, the growth rate of money is reduced slowly, so that the unemployment rate does not increase much. The economy gradually moves from *E* to *E″*, with the growth rate of money being cut all the way down, and the short-run Phillips curve slowly moving down from *PC* to *PC″*. The cold turkey strategy, by contrast, starts with a large cut in the growth rate of money. The economy moves initially from *E* to *E′* on *PC*. There is a lot of unemployment and not much reduction in the inflation rate. But then the short-run Phillips curve moves down faster than it does under the gradualist strategy. The economy reaches *E″* more rapidly than it would under gradualism, but with higher unemployment on the way.

GRADUALISM

Figure 13-14 shows the choices. A policy of *gradualism* (in the left panel) attempts a slow steady return to low inflation. The policy begins with a small reduction in the money growth rate that shifts the economy a little way along the short-run Phillips curve *PC*, from *E* to *E′*. The increased unemployment at *E′* causes the short-run Phillips curve to move from *PC* to *PC′*. Policy makers then make a further small cut in the growth rate of money, moving to *E‴*. In response to the slightly higher unemployment, and because the expected inflation rate is falling, the short-run Phillips curve again shifts down (not shown in the figure). The policy continues, with policy makers gradually cutting the growth rate of money as the short-run Phillips curve slowly moves down in response to both unemployment and the falling inflation rate that reduce the expected rate of inflation.

Eventually the economy returns to low inflation with full employment at point *E″*. There has not been any massive unemployment during the adjustment process, although unemployment has remained above normal.

COLD TURKEY

The right panel of Figure 13-14 shows the alternative. The *cold turkey strategy* tries to cut the inflation rate fast. The strategy starts with an immediate sharp cutback in money growth, creating a large recession as the economy moves from E to E'. Even so, the reduction in inflation is small to begin with, because the short-run Phillips curve is flat.

By creating massive unemployment immediately, though, the cold turkey strategy causes the short-run Phillips curve to shift down rapidly. The PC' curve in the right panel of Figure 13-14 is lower than PC' under gradualism. That is because the much bigger recession of the cold turkey strategy drives down the rate of wage increase more quickly than happens under gradualism. The cold turkey strategy keeps up the pressure, by holding the rate of money growth low. Eventually the rate of inflation falls sufficiently that output and employment begin to recover. The economy returns to point E'' with full employment and a lower rate of inflation.[12]

Gradualism versus Cold Turkey

Figure 13-15 presents the gradualist and cold turkey strategies in an alternative form. In the gradualist strategy the growth rate of money is initially reduced only slightly, and the economy never strays very far from the natural rate of unemployment. But the inflation rate comes down only slowly. The cold turkey strategy, by contrast, starts with a massive cut in the growth rate of money and a large recession. The unemployment rate is much higher than it ever is in the gradualist strategy, but the reduction in inflation is more rapid.

Which strategy should be chosen? Is moderate unemployment with higher inflation preferable to high unemployment with lower inflation? We cannot answer that before discussing the costs of inflation and unemployment in Chapter 14. United States policy makers in 1979 chose a policy closer to cold turkey than to gradualism.

CREDIBILITY

The cold turkey strategy has one major point in its favor, though. It is clear in the case of cold turkey that a decisive policy change has been made, and that policy has the firm aim of driving down the inflation rate. The gradualist strategy, which takes a long time to be implemented, is more likely to be abandoned if it seems to be producing more unemployment than expected, or if the policy-making team changes.

Thus people forming their expectations rationally will be more likely to believe policy has changed under the cold turkey strategy than under gradualism. A belief that policy has changed will by itself drive down the expected

[12] It is possible that the economy does not return directly to equilibrium but rather overshoots the new equilibrium, with the inflation rate falling below the new equilibrium rate and perhaps fluctuating before settling down. For simplicity we concentrate on the paths shown in Figure 13-14.

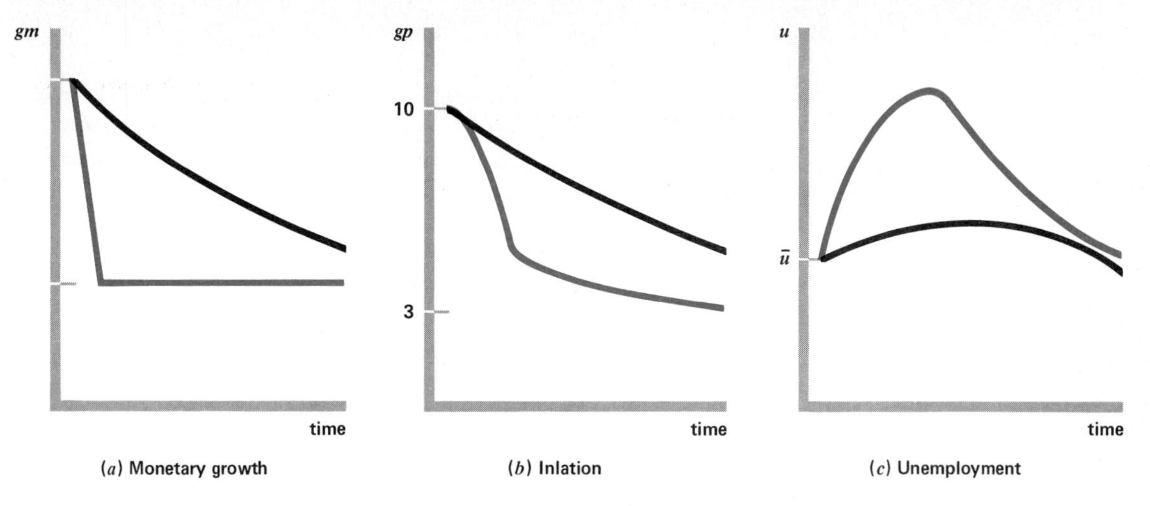

FIGURE 13-15 COLD TURKEY VERSUS GRADUALISM. This is an alternative way of comparing the two strategies. Cold turkey (red curves) cuts the growth rate of money immediately to its new steady-state level, producing a massive recession and relatively rapid reduction in the inflation rate. The gradualist strategy (black curves) produces less unemployment, but also a much less rapid reduction in the inflation rate.

rate of inflation, and for that reason cause the short-run Phillips curve to shift down. A credible policy is one that the public believes will be kept up and succeed. The cold turkey policy gets a *credibility bonus* that gradualism does not.

CREDIBILITY AND RAPID DEFLATION

Throughout the period of deflation, starting with the Fed's change in policy in October 1979, there has been strong emphasis on the credibility of policy. Some proponents of rational expectations even believed that if only policy could be made credible, it would be possible to disinflate without causing practically any recession at all.

The argument went like this. The expectations-augmented Phillips curve equation (4) is

$$gp = gpe - \epsilon(u - \overline{u}) \qquad (4)$$

If policy is credible, people immediately adjust their expectations of inflation to the new policy, with its lower rate of growth of money. Thus the short-run Phillips curve will move down immediately when the new policy is announced. Accordingly, it is possible to move immediately from point E in Figure 13-14 to E''. In brief, the argument is that if policy is credible and if expectations are rational, the economy can move to a new long-run equilibrium immediately when there is a change in policy.

The experience of the United States in the early 1980s, seen in Figure 13-2, and even more the experience of Britain in the same period when the

Thatcher government was pursuing a resolute anti-inflationary policy that led to a 13 percent unemployment rate, casts doubt on this optimistic scenario. The reason the extreme credibility–rational expectations argument does not work is that it is not enough for people to believe a new policy will reduce the inflation rate. The expectations must also be incorporated into wage and other long-term contracts. The economy at any time has an overhang of past contracts, embodying past expectations, and it takes time for those to be renegotiated. Thus a rapid return to lower inflation in economies experiencing inflation rates in the 10 to 20 percent range is unlikely.

It remains true, though, that the more credible a policy that aims to disinflate the economy is, the more successful that policy will be.[13]

CONTRACTS AND DISINFLATION

However credible a policy is, it will not lead to instant disinflation in an economy that has long-term wage contracts, that is, contracts that run for a year or even 3 years. In the United States, for example, even with an unemployment rate of 10 percent in 1982, very few wage contracts were renegotiated before the normal time. The bulk of contracts were not revised in response to the high unemployment.

Disinflation is somewhat easier if contracts specify *indexation* of wages than if future nominal wage changes are set ahead of time. The wage (or any other payment) is indexed when the nominal amount to be paid is fixed with reference to a price index. In the United States wages are sometimes indexed through COLAs (cost of living allowances). For instance, the wage might be specified to equal $10 per hour in real terms, using the CPI of June 1979 as the base. If by December 1979 the CPI is 6.1 percent higher, the wage is *automatically* raised to $10.61.

When contracts are indexed, disinflation is more rapid, because any success at reducing inflation translates automatically into reduced rates of wage and cost increases. To see this, compare two contracts. One is nominal, with the wage scheduled to rise automatically by 10 percent at the beginning of each of the next 2 years. The other is indexed, and the wage is scheduled to grow by 2 percent plus the rate of inflation that actually occurred during the past year. If the inflation rate were 8 percent, the two contracts would imply the same wage increases. But if a disinflation program succeeds in reducing the rate of inflation to 5 percent, wages in the indexed contracts will rise by only 7 percent in the following year, while in the other contract the increase is unaffected. In the latter case firms would suffer severe losses, and that would tend to reduce the willingness and ability of the authorities to implement rapid disinflation. By contrast, with indexation, reduced wage inflation allows still further rounds of inflation reduction in rapid succession.[14]

[13] The credibility issue is treated in several interesting papers in "Anti-inflation Policies and the Problem of Credibility," *American Economic Review* (Papers and Proceedings), May 1982.

[14] Of course, indexed contracts allow the inflation rate to increase much more rapidly than would be the case with contracts fixed in nominal terms. This is a particularly severe problem in the context of supply shocks.

It is easiest to change the inflation rate when there are no long-term contracts in the economy. There will be few contracts of that kind if inflation is high and variable. Under such conditions no one will want to sign agreements in nominal terms because they will be gambling too much on the future behavior of the price level. And because there are delays in producing the price index, even indexed contracts become risky. At high and variable rates of inflation, long-term contracts disappear, and wages and prices are frequently reset. A credible policy will have rapid effects. But such rapid success cannot be expected in an economy where the structure of contracts has not yet been destroyed by extreme inflation.

Is There a Better Way?

The treatments for the inflation disease summarized in Figure 13-15 are painful, and have led to a search for better ways. In this section we briefly describe two other anti-inflationary policies, incomes policy and tax incentive plans.

INCOMES POLICY

Inflation stabilization takes time and involves unemployment because that is what is needed to get the rate of wage change down. Incomes policies try to short-circuit that slow process by getting the rate of wage change down fast, either by law (wage-price controls) or by persuasion. *Incomes policies* are policies that attempt to reduce the rate of wage and price increases by direct action. Either wages and prices are controlled, or the government tries to persuade labor leaders and business to raise wages and prices more slowly than they otherwise would. Incomes policies, if successful, shift the short-run Phillips curve down.

Wage and price controls are typically used in wartime in many countries and were used in the United States in the period 1971–1974. The 1971 controls were imposed in an effort to break the back of an inflation that for 2 years had shown little sign of responding to restrictive monetary and fiscal policy. The controls began with a 90-day wage-price *freeze.* For 3 months firms were forbidden to raise prices or pay higher wages. The freeze applied to the prices of most goods, with some exceptions, for example, for agricultural goods.

A wage-price freeze certainly brings the inflation rate down. So why not get rid of inflation that way? The reason is that wages and prices have to change if resources are to be allocated efficiently in the economy. Anti-inflationary policy has to try to reduce the average rate of price increase without interfering with the role of prices in allocating resources.

Over a short period, misallocations of resources from frozen wages and prices will be small and not costly. But if wages and prices are kept fixed for a long time, shortages of labor and particular goods will develop. The problem then is to find a way out of controls that does not reignite inflation. The United States did not avoid that problem when, after many policy shifts, controls were lifted in 1973–1974—at the time the oil price shock hit the economy.

Less formal income policies, for instance, trying to persuade labor union leaders that they should moderate their wage claims, should work in the same way as wage-price controls. But such policies have rarely been successful in bringing down the inflation rate over any prolonged period.

One reason incomes policies have rarely if ever succeeded is that they have not been combined with appropriate aggregate demand policies. The long-run inflation rate cannot be reduced if the short-run Phillips curve is shifted down while the rate of money growth stays high. That will reduce the inflation rate in the short run, but will also reduce unemployment. Then wages will again start increasing more rapidly, and eventually the incomes policy will break down and the economy move right back to where it started.

For incomes policies to have a chance of reducing the inflation rate in a lasting way, they have to be accompanied by restrictive aggregate demand policies. That rarely happens. Indeed, many observers argue that governments turn to incomes policies when they are not serious about reducing the inflation rate. They hope to get the inflation rate down in the short run without doing anything about the long-run rate of inflation.

It is entirely possible that incomes policy could help reduce the unemployment costs of an anti-inflationary program, so long as the incomes policy is indeed combined with restrictive aggregate demand policies.

TIP

Tax incentive plans (*TIP*) to reduce the inflation rate encourage workers and firms to keep wage and price increases low by providing tax incentives to do so.[15]

For instance, TIP might set a baseline rate of wage increase of 5 percent. Any firm that pays a higher rate of wage increase to its employees has its taxes increased. Any firm paying a lower rate of wage increase receives a tax break. Or the penalties and rewards might be placed directly on the workers. Any worker receiving an increase in excess of 5 percent would have her tax rate increased, and so forth.

The major problem with TIP is that it would be very difficult to administer.[16] The aim is to discourage wage or price increases that are being made only to compensate for inflation. We would not, for instance, want to penalize a worker who has a large wage increase because she has worked hard and has been promoted. But how can the law discriminate between these two cases? If the law says anyone who is promoted is not penalized for receiving a rate of wage increase above the baseline rate, firms and workers who find it in their joint interest to raise the wage will do so by promoting people.

Both incomes policies and TIP run into the same difficulty. The difficulty is that relative wages and prices in the economy do have to change if the price

[15] The *Brookings Papers on Economic Activity*, 2: 1978, contains several articles and discussions of TIP.

[16] TIP has not been implemented, though the Carter administration did in 1978 propose a form of TIP that the Congress rejected.

mechanism is to work. Policies that operate directly on wages and prices have to try to prevent the overall price level from rising while relative prices are permitted to change. This is either impossible or extremely difficult over any extended period.

Is There Hope?

By the middle of 1983 the tough monetary policy pursued in the United States since 1979 had driven the inflation rate down from more than 10 percent to only 3 to 4 percent. But the unemployment rate was more than 10 percent.

Is it possible to come out of such a recession without reigniting inflation? The answer is yes, provided that aggregate demand policies do not become too expansive. But the inflation rate cannot be kept continually at 3 percent. The economy is certain to be hit by supply shocks at one time and shifts in aggregate demand at another. These shocks can increase the inflation rate. Restrictive, nonaccommodating policies can keep the inflationary shocks from shifting the inflation rate from a basic 3 to 4 percent range to a higher range such as 9 to 10 percent.

13-7 SUMMARY

1. The inflation-unemployment Phillips curve is an alternative form of the aggregate supply curve introduced in Chapter 12. The choice of which to use is purely a matter of convenience.
2. The adjustment along a Phillips curve, given the nominal money stock, involves price changes, changes in real balances, and therefore changes in spending output and employment. In the long-run the economy will converge to the natural rate of unemployment unless policy makers attempt to maintain a different position.
3. Friedman and Phelps argued that the wage-unemployment Phillips curve would shift with the expected rate of inflation, as workers and firms adjust wages for the inflation expected over the period during which the wages will be paid. This leads to the expectations-augmented Phillips curve, which argues that the rate of price increase increases with the expected inflation rate and declines with the unemployment rate.
4. The expected inflation rate is constant on a short-run Phillips curve. The short-run Phillips curve is quite flat, reflecting the stickiness of wages and prices in the short run.
5. The expected rate of inflation in the Phillips curve should be interpreted as the inflation, current and past, that was expected when contracts relevant to current wages and prices were made.
6. The short-run Phillips curve shifts with the expected rate of inflation. The higher the expected rate of inflation, the higher the inflation rate corresponding to any given unemployment rate.

7 In the long run, expectations catch up with actual inflation. The long-run Phillips curve describes the tradeoffs, if any, between inflation and unemployment when the actual and expected inflation rates are equal. The long-run Phillips curve is essentially vertical, implying that the unemployment rate in the long run is equal to the natural rate, whatever the inflation rate.
8 Inflation is a monetary phenomenon in the sense that prolonged rapid inflation is impossible without high rates of money growth and that low rates of money growth will eventually reduce the inflation rate. The link between money growth and long-run inflation is not exact because of long-run growth in output and shifts in the demand for money.
9 The Fisher equation predicts that nominal interest rates are higher the higher the expected inflation rate.
10 Changes in monetary policy cause the inflation rate to change in both the short run and the long run. Fiscal policy changes and supply shocks change the inflation rate in the short run. A supply shock or a wage push creates a policy dilemma by raising the question of whether the inflation should be accommodated through expansionary monetary policy. Accommodation will be successful only when it helps the economy make real adjustments that would otherwise be impeded by wage and price stickiness.
11 There are alternative approaches to reducing the inflation rate. A gradualist policy tries to keep unemployment low by reducing the inflation rate slowly. A cold turkey policy attempts to get the inflation rate down rapidly by creating a big recession to begin with. The cold turkey policy has the advantage that it is more credible.
12 Alternative policies to reduce inflation include incomes policies (wage-price controls and less formal approaches) and tax incentive plans. They have not been implemented successfully.

KEY TERMS

Expectations-augmented Phillips curve
Short-run Phillips curve
Rational expectations
Long-run Phillips curve
Stagflation
Fisher equation
Wage push
Accommodation
Gradualism
Cold turkey strategy
Credibility
Indexation
Incomes policies
TIP

PROBLEMS

1 Use Figure 13-4 to discuss the adjustment process to a reduction in personal income tax rates. Specifically, use the insights gained from the aggregate demand and supply framework to determine the effects on the time path of unemployment and inflation.

2 Explain in words why the expected rate of inflation affects the position of the wage-unemployment Phillips curve.

3 (*a*) What determines the position and slope of the short-run Phillips curve?
(*b*) Why does the short-run Phillips curve not shift immediately when a new policy to reduce inflation is introduced?

4 (*a*) In Figure 13-9 we show how the economy reaches a higher rate of inflation. Starting at an 8 percent inflation rate, show how the economy would shift back to 3 percent if the right policies were used.
(*b*) What sort of policy would be needed to reduce the inflation rate from 8 to 3 percent?

5 (*a*) Define the long-run Phillips curve.
(*b*) Explain why, according to the expectations-augmented Phillips curve, the long-run Phillips curve is vertical.

6 Suppose we have an economy where real output grows at the rate of 6 percent per year. The nominal quantity of money grows at the rate of 5 percent. The income elasticity of money demand is 0.5.
(*a*) What is the rate of inflation in long-run equilibrium?
(*b*) What is the rate of growth of nominal income? (Remember that nominal income can grow because prices increase, real output rises, or both.)
(*c*) How would your answers to (*a*) and (*b*) change if the income elasticity of money demand was unity?

7 Figure 13-11 shows the long-run growth rate of $M1$ and the inflation rate in the United States from 1951 to 1982. The inflation rate differs from the growth rate of money (*a*) as a result of output growth, (*b*) when there are supply shocks, (*c*) when the demand function for money shifts. Discuss what parts of the relationship seen in Figure 13-11 can be explained using each of these factors.

8 (*a*) Show how a permanent increase in the price of oil affects inflation and unemployment in the short run.
*(*b*) An increase in the price of oil results in a price level that is higher than it would otherwise have been. Explain. (***Hint:*** During a period of higher than normal inflation, the price level is increasing relative to the level it would otherwise had been. Examine the adjustment path to the oil price shock and compare inflation rates with and without the shock.)

9 When would it be useful to accommodate a supply shock?

10 (*a*) Explain the Fisher equation that describes the relationship between the nominal interest rate and expected inflation.
(*b*) Use Figure 1 to show that the real interest rate was very high in the early 1980s.

11 (*a*) Explain how the U.S. economy moved from low to high inflation between 1961 and 1980.
(*b*) Explain how the U.S. economy moved from high to low inflation between 1979 and 1983.
(*c*) In your view, was there any better way of reducing the inflation rate?

14

THE TRADEOFFS BETWEEN INFLATION AND UNEMPLOYMENT

In 1982 the U.S. economy reached the highest unemployment rate since the great depression. More than 1 person in 10 in the labor force was unemployed. Yet even with such high unemployment, concern was voiced lest the recovery should be too rapid. The Council of Economic Advisors stated in the 1983 *Economic Report of the President,* under the heading "the limits of macroeconomic policy":

> The only way to reduce current high levels of cyclical unemployment is for the United States to achieve a sound recovery from the recent recession. Avoiding future recurrences of high cyclical unemployment requires avoiding an expansion so rapid as to lead to rapidly increasing inflation. Historical experience suggests that the change in the rate of inflation depends both on the rate at which economic activity is expanding and on the level of economic slack. If the slack in the economy declines too rapidly, or capacity utilization is held at too high a level, inflation will tend to increase. [p. 37]

The statement conveys the idea of a tradeoff: a more rapid recovery and therefore lower unemployment today implies the risk of higher inflation *and* higher unemployment in the future. Economic slack today is an investment in future stability. Further, the statement implies we *should* trade off more unemployment today for less inflation in the future. In this chapter we discuss the inflation-unemployment tradeoff and the cost-benefit analysis that policy makers must bear in mind when designing stabilization policy.

We start with a discussion of unemployment. The main point of the discussion is to distinguish between *cyclical* and *structural* unemployment and to develop the concept of the natural rate of unemployment. The discussion proceeds from there to the costs of inflation and to the cost-benefit analysis of inflation stabilization.

14-1 THE ANATOMY OF UNEMPLOYMENT

An unemployed person is defined as one who is out of work *and* who (1) has actively looked for work during the previous 4 weeks, or (2) is waiting to be recalled to a job after having been laid off, or (3) is waiting to report to a new job within 4 weeks. The requirement of having looked for a job in the past 4 weeks is included to try to ensure that the person is actively interested in a job, and not merely expressing an interest if a job should happen to show up.

In April 1983, 10.1 percent of the total or 10.4 percent of the civilian labor force (excluding resident armed forces) were unemployed. Table 14-1 presents some details of unemployment rates at that time for different groups in the population.

The table reveals extraordinary differences in the unemployment rates for the four groups. Nearly 1 in every 2 black teenagers was unemployed, but "only" 1 in 5 white teenagers, and less than 1 in 10 white adults. These differences in group unemployment rates are an important part of understanding unemployment in the United States, as we shall see shortly. But before that we want to make the distinction between the part of unemployment that is cyclical and the part that is called noncyclical, or structural.

Table 14-2 shows data for two different periods—1978:IV, a time when unemployment was at the lowest level in the last 10 years, and 1983:I, when unemployment was at the highest level since the 1930s. The data bring out two important contrasts. In both periods unemployment rates for teenagers are much higher than they are for people 20 years and over. Second, unemployment rates for whites are much lower than they are for blacks.

The unemployment rate in the first row of Table 14-2 corresponds, roughly, to structural unemployment. *Structural unemployment* is the unem-

TABLE 14-1 UNEMPLOYMENT RATES BY AGE AND RACE, APRIL 1983 (*Percentage of group unemployed*)

	Black	White
16–19 years	47.8	20.3
20 years and over	18.4	7.9

Source: Employment and Earnings, *May 1983.*

TABLE 14-2 SELECTED UNEMPLOYMENT INDICATORS (*Percentage of group unemployed*)

	Total	20 YEARS+ Men	Women	16–19 years	White	Black and other
1978:IV	5.9	4.1	5.7	16.3	5.1	11.5
1983:I	10.4	9.7	8.9	22.8	9.1	18.5

Source: Employment and Earnings.

NOT FRICTIONAL?

ployment that exists when the economy is at full employment. Structural unemployment corresponds to the *natural rate of unemployment.* Structural unemployment results from the structure of the labor market—from the nature of jobs in the economy and from the labor force participation patterns of workers. We discuss the determinants of structural unemployment in more detail below when we examine the natural rate of unemployment. *Cyclical unemployment* is unemployment in excess of structural unemployment, and occurs when output is below its full-employment level. Cyclical unemployment for 1983:I was the excess of unemployment in the second row of Table 14-2 above that in the first row.

CHARACTERISTICS OF U.S. UNEMPLOYMENT

The anatomy of unemployment is built around three central facts of U.S. unemployment behavior:

1. There are substantial flows of individuals in and out of unemployment each month, and most people who become unemployed in any given month remain unemployed for only a short time.
2. Much of U.S. unemployment is constituted of people who will be unemployed for quite a long time.
3. There is considerable variation of unemployment rates across different groups in the labor force (as can be seen in Tables 14-1 and 14-2).

The first and second facts may seem contradictory. A numerical example should make it clear that there is no necessary contradiction. Suppose that the labor force consists of 100 (million) people and that 5 people become unemployed each month. Suppose that four of those people are unemployed for precisely 1 month, and one person will be unemployed for 6 months. Suppose also that the economy is in a steady state, so that this situation has repeated itself every month for years.

We ask first how many people are unemployed at any one time, say, September 30. There will be five people who became unemployed September 1, one person who became unemployed August 1 (and who has been unemployed for 2 months), and so on, back to the person who became unemployed April 1, and whose 6 months of unemployment will end the next day, on October 1. In total, there will be ten people unemployed, so the unemployment rate is 10 percent. Of the ten, six will suffer a 6-month spell of unemployment before they again become employed. This is consistent with the second fact. But remember that we started with five people becoming unemployed each month, four of whom remain unemployed for only a month. And that is consistent with the first fact, that most people who become unemployed within a given month remain so for only a short time. We return to this example later in this section.

The third fact, variation of unemployment rates across different groups in the labor force, can be examined using the relationship between the overall unemployment rate u and the unemployment rates u_i of groups within the labor force. The overall rate is a weighted average of the unemployment rates of the groups:

$$u = w_1u_1 + w_2u_2 + \cdot \cdot \cdot + w_nu_n \tag{1}$$

The weights w_i are the fraction of the civilian labor force that falls within the specific group, say, black teenagers.

Equation (1) makes it clear that the overall unemployment rate either could be made up of unemployment rates that are much the same for different groups in the labor force or could conceal dramatic differences in unemployment rates among groups categorized, say, by age, race, and sex. Fact 3 is that the aggregate rate does conceal substantial differences in unemployment rates. For instance, in April 1983, the aggregate unemployment rate averaged 10.4 percent: white unemployment was 9.1 percent, and nonwhite unemployment was 18.5 percent. In terms of Equation (1), we have

$$10.4\% = (0.87)9.1\% + (0.13)18.5\% \tag{1a}$$

where the shares of the two groups in the labor force are 87 percent and 13 percent, respectively.

We now turn to a more detailed examination of the three central facts about the anatomy of unemployment.

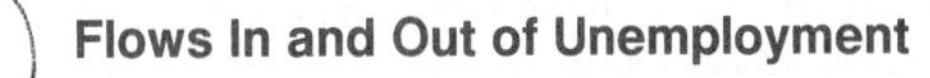

Flows In and Out of Unemployment

Figure 14-1 shows how people enter and leave the *unemployment pool.* A person may become unemployed for one of four reasons: (1) The person may be a new entrant into the labor force, looking for work for the first time, or else be a reentrant—someone returning to the labor force after not having looked for work for more than 4 weeks. (2) A person may quit a job in order to look for other employment and register as unemployed while searching. (3) The person may be laid off. The definition of *layoff* is a suspension without pay lasting or expected to last more than 7 consecutive days, initiated by the employer "without prejudice to the worker." The latter qualification means

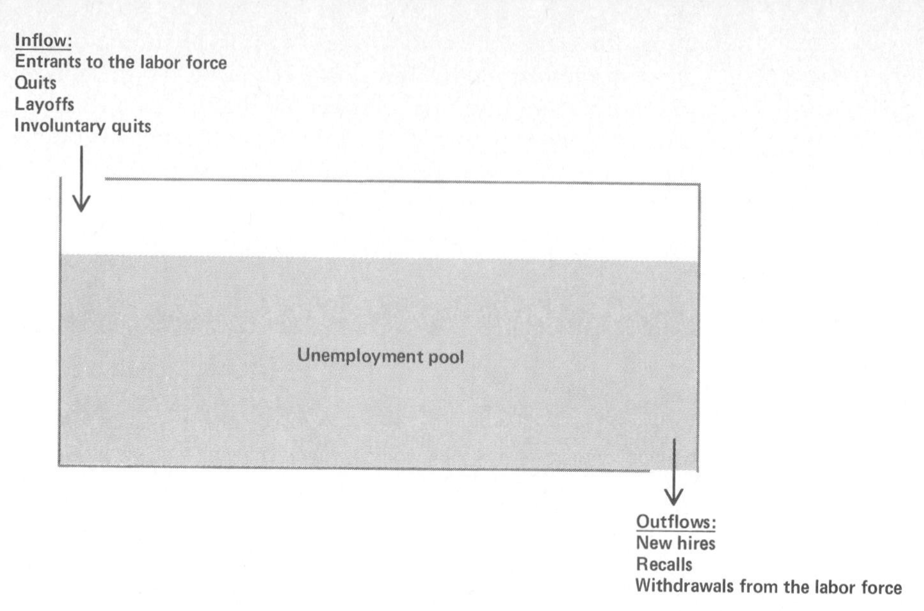

FIGURE 14-1 FLOWS IN AND OUT OF THE UNEMPLOYMENT POOL.

that the worker was not fired but rather will return to the old job if demand for the firm's product recovers. A firm will typically adjust to a decline in product demand by laying off some labor. A firm may also rotate layoffs among its labor force so that the individual laid-off worker may expect a recall even before product demand has fully recovered. In manufacturing, it appears that over 75 percent of laid-off workers return to jobs with their original employers.[1] (4) A worker may lose a job to which there is no hope of returning, either because he is fired or because the firm closes down. This last way of becoming unemployed is referred to as *involuntary quits*.

These sources of inflow into the pool of unemployment have a counterpart in the outflow from the unemployment pool. There are essentially three ways of moving out of the pool of unemployment. (1) A person may be hired into a new job. (2) Someone laid off may be recalled. (3) An unemployed person may stop looking for a job and thus, by definition, leave the labor force. Such a person may plan to look for a job again soon.

Table 14-3 shows the average of monthly flows in 1981 into and out of employment. These data, which unfortunately are no longer collected, show the movement, or *turnover*, in the labor market by splitting net employment changes into the different components. They support our conclusion about large flows in and out of the pool of unemployment.

[1] See Martin Feldstein, "Temporary Layoffs in the Theory of Unemployment," *Journal of Political Economy*, October 1976.

TABLE 14-3 LABOR TURNOVER RATES IN MANUFACTURING IN 1981 (*Per 100 employees, average of monthly data*)

ACCESSIONS			SEPARATIONS			
Total	New hires	Recalls	Total	Quits	Layoffs	Other
3.2	2.0	1.0	3.6	1.3	1.6	0.7

Note: Components do not add to totals due to averaging and rounding. "Other" includes involuntary separations.
Source: Employment and Earnings, *March 1982.*

Research has concentrated on the flows into and out of unemployment.[2] The research starts from the recognition that the flows are large relative to the average level of unemployment. A first way of looking at the flows in and out of unemployment is by obtaining direct estimates of the rate at which the labor force turns over in manufacturing establishments. *Accessions* are names added to the payroll of a company in a given month. Thus, in 1981, manufacturing companies on average added 3.2 names to their payrolls per 100 employees. *Separations* are names removed from the payrolls during the month. In 1981 manufacturing companies each month on average removed 3.6 names from their payrolls per 100 employees. Note first that the levels of accessions and separations (per 100 employees) are consistently high, each above 3 percent *per month.* Second, note that even though the unemployment rate was at 7.6 percent, accessions were equal to 3.2 percent of the manufacturing work force. Firms were hiring new people and calling back workers who had earlier been laid off, despite the high unemployment rate. Perhaps even more surprising, 1.3 percent of the workers in manufacturing quit their jobs voluntarily. Table 14-3 presents a remarkable picture of movement in the labor force. People are taking *and* leaving jobs even during times of high unemployment.

DURATION OF UNEMPLOYMENT

A second way of looking at flows in and out of unemployment is to consider the *duration of spells of unemployment.* A spell of unemployment is defined as a period in which an individual remains continuously unemployed. Given the unemployment rate, the shorter the average spell of unemployment—the time the individual is unemployed—the larger the flows. For instance, in the example at the beginning of this section we had a 10 percent unemployment

[2] Robert E. Hall, "Why Is the Unemployment Rate So High at Full Employment?" *Brookings Papers on Economic Activity.* 3:1970 (Washington, D.C.: The Brookings Institution); Stephen T. Marston, "Employment Instability and High Unemployment Rates," *Brookings Papers on Economic Activity,* 1:1976 (ibid.); and Kim B. Clark and Lawrence H. Summers, "Labor Market Dynamics and Unemployment: A Reconsideration," *Brookings Papers on Economic Activity,* 1:1979 (ibid.).

TABLE 14-4 CHARACTERISTICS OF COMPLETED SPELLS OF UNEMPLOYMENT, BY DEMOGRAPHIC GROUP, 1974, AND FOR ALL GROUPS, 1969 AND 1975

	1974					1969	1975
	MALES		FEMALES				
Characteristic	16–19	20 and over	16–19	20 and over	All groups	All groups	All groups
Proportion of spells ending within one month	0.71	0.47	0.70	0.60	0.60	0.79	0.55
Mean duration of a completed spell (months)	1.57	2.42	1.57	1.91	1.94	1.42	2.22
Proportion of spells ending in withdrawal from the labor force	0.46	0.26	0.58	0.55	0.45	0.44	0.46

Source: Kim B. Clark and Lawrence H. Summers, "Labor Market Dynamics and Unemployment: A Reconsideration," Brookings Papers on Economic Activity, *1:1979 (Washington, D.C.: The Brookings Institution, 1979). Copyright © 1979 by the Brookings Institution, Washington, D.C.*

rate with five people becoming unemployed each month. We could also have a 10 percent unemployment rate if ten people became unemployed each month and each one remained unemployed for exactly 1 month. In the earlier example, the average spell is longer than a month since four out of five spells end in a month, but one out of five lasts 6 months. (The average spell is thus 2 months.) The shorter the average duration, the larger the flows of labor through the unemployment pool, given the overall unemployment rate.

As Table 14-4 shows, in 1974, a year in which unemployment was 5.6 percent, or about the natural rate, 60 percent of all spells ended within a month, and the average completed spell of unemployment lasted less than 2 months. Again, the suggestion is one of considerable movement of labor in and out of unemployment. We should note, though, one perhaps surprising feature in Table 14-4, which is that almost half the spells of unemployment ended in withdrawal from the labor force, rather than in employment in a new job. Indeed, recent research[3] suggests that the distinction between being unemployed and being out of the labor force is not a very sharp one, and that individuals move quite easily in both directions—between being unemployed (meaning essentially that they looked for a job in the past 4 weeks) and being out of the labor force.

Now that we have a picture of the labor market as being in a constant state of movement, we can ask about the factors changing the rate of unemployment and those determining the overall level of unemployment. Figure 14-1 makes it clear that unemployment increases when the flow into unemploy-

[3] See for example, the Clark and Summers article cited in footnote 2.

ment exceeds that out of the pool. Thus, increases in quits and layoffs increase unemployment, as does an increase in the flow of new entrants into the labor market, since new entrants typically take time to find a job once they decide to become employed. Unemployment is reduced by increases in hiring rates and by unemployed workers leaving the labor force.

Table 14-5 provides some information about the breakdown of the reasons for unemployment. The categories in this table show the importance of variations in the rate of job loss, as well as the reentry rate, in affecting the overall rate of unemployment. When unemployment was very high, as in 1983, job loss was by far the most important reason for unemployment. The data also show the importance of the reentrant category, which is consistent with the earlier comment that flows both from unemployment to "out of the labor force" and in the reverse direction are large.

The Unemployment Rate and the Time Unemployed

We turn now to the second fact to be established in this section. We noted earlier that the average duration of a spell of unemployment is quite short—under 2 months—and that most spells of unemployment end within a month. But as the example with which we started this section showed, it is still possible that much of unemployment can be traced to people who are unemployed for long spells. Indeed, given the fact that a spell of unemployment ends when someone either withdraws from the labor force or finds a job, it is possible for a person to have several spells of unemployment within the year and not actually work at all that year.

Table 14-6 provides information about the proportion of unemployment that consists of people who are unemployed for different lengths of time within the year.[4] In 1974, only 4.2 percent of total unemployment within the year was accounted for by people who were unemployed for 1 to 4 weeks, even though most spells of unemployment ended within a month. Nearly 42 percent of unemployment (the sum of the last two rows in Table 14-6) was accounted for by people who were unemployed for 27 or more weeks, or more than 6 months.

If instead of looking at unemployment we looked at nonemployment

[4] The *total* amount of time unemployed (over all spells of unemployment) is counted for an individual who experiences more than one spell of unemployment.

TABLE 14-5 UNEMPLOYMENT BY REASON FOR UNEMPLOYMENT (*Percentage of unemployed persons*)

	JOB LOSERS				
	Layoff	Other	Job leavers	Reentrants	New entrants
1978:IV	12.1	29.1	14.3	30.3	14.2
1983:I	19.2	38.3	8.8	22.9	10.7

Source: Employment and Earnings, *May 1983, and* Employment and Training Report of the President, *1981.*

TABLE 14-6 PERCENTAGE OF UNEMPLOYMENT ACCOUNTED FOR BY THE UNEMPLOYED (*Per unemployed person*)

All groups	1974	1975
Weeks of unemployment		
1-4 weeks	4.2	2.6
5-14 weeks	22.4	15.6
15-26 weeks	31.7	27.0
27-39 weeks	21.1	22.3
40 weeks or more	20.7	32.5
	100.0	100.0

Source: Adapted from Kim B. Clark and Lawrence H. Summers, "Labor Market Dynamics and Unemployment: A Reconsideration," Brookings Papers on Economic Activity, *1:1979 (Washington, D.C.: The Brookings Institution, 1979). Copyright © 1979 by The Brookings Institution, Washington, D.C.*

data—adding together the time individuals are unemployed and the time they are not in the labor force—we would find long-term *nonemployment* to be even more important than long-term unemployment. For instance, in 1974, over 50 percent of total time not employed of all individuals taken together could be attributed to those not employed for 40 or more weeks.

These data establish that despite the substantial flows in and out of unemployment, much of aggregate unemployment is accounted for by people who remain unemployed for a substantial time. Thus, if one believes that unemployment is a more serious problem when it affects only a few people intensely, rather than many people a little, these data suggest that unemployment is a more severe problem than the aggregate unemployment rate indicates.[5] The next set of data we review, those on the distribution of unemployment by age, race, and sex groups, supports that view.

The Distribution of Unemployment

The third important fact about the anatomy of unemployment is that unemployment is distributed very unevenly across the population. Tables 14-1 and 14-2 already showed unemployment rates by age, sex, and race categories. The message from the data is clear. First, there are some differences in unemployment rates between males and females, given age and race. However, these differences are relatively small. Second, nonwhite unemployment is substantially higher than white unemployment, with the unemployment rate for black teenagers (not shown in the table) being twice the corresponding rate for white teenagers. In fact, in all age and sex groups, black unemployment rates are at least 1½ times as large as white unemployment rates.

[5] This finding applies to teenagers as much as to older workers. For example, 54 percent of total male teenage unemployment is accounted for by people unemployed more than 6 months of the year. See Kim B. Clark and Lawrence H. Summers, "The Dynamics of Youth Unemployment," in Richard B. Freeman and David A. Wise (ed.), *The Youth Labor Market Problem: Its Nature, Causes, and Consequences* (Chicago: University of Chicago Press, 1982).

TABLE 14-7 DIFFERENCES BETWEEN TEENAGE AND ADULT UNEMPLOYMENT: REASONS FOR UNEMPLOYMENT (*Percentage of group unemployed, April 1983*)

	Job losers	Job leavers	Reentrants	New entrants
16–19 years	21.9	5.4	25.7	47.0
20 Years +				
Men	80.1	5.4	12.8	1.9
Women	52.8	10.0	31.3	6.0

Source: Employment and Earnings, *May 1983.*

And third, unemployment rates fall as age rises.[6]

The difference between the unemployment behavior of teenagers and that of adult workers is evident in Table 14-7. Here we observe that older workers suffered unemployment primarily as a consequence of job losses. Teenagers, by contrast, were either entering the labor force looking for a job or reentering after a period out of the labor market.

Table 14-4 presents data on the duration of unemployment spells by age and sex characteristics. The duration of unemployment differs across groups in the labor force, lengthening particularly with age.[7] Table 14-4 also shows data on the proportion of spells of unemployment ending in withdrawal from the labor force. Spells of unemployment are more likely to end in withdrawal from the labor force among young males than among older males; this difference does not exist between younger and older females.

Despite the greater movement of the young workers among jobs, unemployment, and being out of the labor force, a significant part of teenage unemployment is accounted for by long-term unemployment, just as it is for older workers.[8]

The evidence tells an unambiguous story. Unemployment is much higher among the young than among the older. But the nature of the unemployment is different. The young tend to be unemployed more often and for short spells, whereas older workers are unemployed less often but for longer periods. It should also be noted that about half the teenage unemployed are, in fact, at school and looking for part-time work.

[6] For details see *Monthly Labor Review*, which regularly gives unemployment data by age, sex, and race.

[7] *Technical note:* If you consult one of the sources of labor market data, such as *Monthly Labor Review* or *Employment and Earnings*, you will find figures on the duration of unemployment by characteristic, along with overall rates of unemployment. These duration data refer to the length of time the individual has been unemployed to date, *not* to the length of a *completed spell* of unemployment. Going back to our example at the beginning of this section, the duration data in the official sources would show 5 people who have been unemployed 1 month, 1 person unemployed 2 months, and 1 each unemployed for 3, 4, 5, and 6 months. The average duration would be computed as $[(5 \times 1) + (1 \times 2) + (1 \times 3) + \cdots + (1 \times 6)]/10 = 2.5$ months. Of course, the duration as reported in the official sources would increase together with the duration of completed spells. Thus the comparative duration rates shown in the official sources agree fully with the statements here, and are well worth examining.

[8] See footnote 5.

We have now reviewed the three central facts about U.S. unemployment experience:

1 There are substantial flows through the pool of unemployment each month.
2 Nonetheless, most unemployment is accounted for by people who will be unemployed for several months during the year.
3 There are substantial variations in unemployment rates across different labor force groups.

We turn next to the natural rate of unemployment.

14-2 THE NATURAL RATE OF UNEMPLOYMENT

The *natural rate of unemployment* is also called the full-employment level of unemployment, or the long-run equilibrium level of unemployment, or the structural unemployment rate. In this section, we discuss the determinants of the natural rate of unemployment, then examine estimates of changes in the natural rate since the fifties, then consider proposals for reducing it.

Figure 14-1 points to the factors causing the unemployment rate to change. Increases in the rate of entry to the labor force, or quits, or layoffs, or involuntary quits cause the unemployment rate to rise. Increases in hiring, or recalls, or withdrawals from the labor force cause the unemployment rate to fall. Each of these factors is in part determined by economic variables, such as the level of aggregate demand and the actual and expected real wage rate. When aggregate demand rises (at a given real wage), firms increase their hiring. When aggregate demand falls, firms lay off workers. Thus there is an immediate link between the factors emphasized in Figure 14-1 and aggregate demand. However, it should be noted that the relationship between aggregate demand and the variables affecting the rate of unemployment is not unambiguous. For instance, an increase in the demand for labor increases quits at the same time as it reduces layoffs. A person thinking of leaving a job to search for another would be more likely to quit when the job market is good and demand is high than when there is heavy unemployment and the prospects of finding a good job quickly are low. In fact, it can be seen from Table 14-5 that quits and layoffs move in the opposite direction.

When the unemployment rate is constant, flows in and out of unemployment just balance each other. These flows can match at any level of unemployment. The *natural rate of unemployment,* however, is that rate of unemployment at which flows in and out of unemployment just balance,[9] *and* at which expectations of firms and workers as to the behavior of prices and wages are correct.

[9] We should recognize that when the labor force is growing and the unemployment rate is constant, the pool of unemployed grows over time. For example, with a labor force of 90 million and 5 percent unemployment, total unemployment is 4.5 million people. With a labor force of 100 million and 5 percent unemployment, there are 5 million unemployed, and the unemployment pool has grown by a half-million people.

The determinants of the natural rate of unemployment can be thought of in terms of the duration and frequency of unemployment. The *duration* of unemployment is the average length of time a person remains unemployed. The duration depends on (1) the organization of the labor market, in regard to the presence or absence of employment agencies, youth employment services, etc.; (2) the demographic makeup of the labor force, as discussed above; (3) the ability and desire of the unemployed to keep looking for a better job; and (4) the availability and types of jobs. If all jobs are the same, an unemployed person will take the first one offered. If some jobs are better than others, it is worthwhile searching and waiting for a good one. If it is very expensive to remain unemployed, say, because there are no unemployment benefits, an unemployed person is more likely to accept a job offer than to continue looking for a better one. If unemployment benefits are high, then it may be worthwhile for the unemployed person to continue looking for a better job rather than to accept a poor job when one is offered.

The behavior of workers who have been laid off is also important when considering the duration of unemployment. Typically, a worker who has been laid off returns to the original job and does not search for another job. The reason is quite simple: once a worker has been with a firm for a long time, she has special expertise in the way that firm works which makes her valuable to that firm but is not of great benefit to another employer. In addition, she may have built up seniority rights, including a pension. That means that such an individual could not expect to find as good a job if she searched for a new one. Her best course of action may be to wait to be recalled.

FREQUENCY OF UNEMPLOYMENT

The *frequency of unemployment* is the average number of times, per period, that workers become unemployed. There are two basic determinants of the frequency of unemployment. The first is the variability of the demand for labor across different firms in the economy. The second determinant is the rate at which new workers enter the labor force: The more rapidly new workers enter the labor force—the faster the growth rate of the labor force—the higher the natural rate of unemployment. Even when aggregate demand is constant, some firms are growing and some are contracting. The contracting firms lose labor and the growing firms hire more labor. The greater this variability of the demand for labor across different firms, the higher the unemployment rate. Further, the variability of aggregate demand itself will affect the variability of the demand for labor.

The four factors affecting duration and the two factors affecting frequency of unemployment are the basic determinants of the natural rate of unemployment.

You should note that the factors determining the level of the natural rate of unemployment are not immutable. The structure of the labor market and the labor force can change. The willingness of workers to remain unemployed while looking for, or waiting for, a new job can change. The variability of the demand for labor by different firms can shift. As Edmund Phelps has noted, the natural rate is not "an intertemporal constant, something like the speed of light, independent of everything under the sun."[10] Indeed, the natural rate is difficult to measure, and estimates of it have changed over the past few years from about 4 percent in the 1960s to near 5.5, or even 6, in the early 1980s.

Estimates of the Natural Rate of Unemployment

Estimates of the natural rate of unemployment typically try to adjust for changes in the composition of the labor force, and perhaps for changes in the natural rate of unemployment of the various groups in the labor force. We can write an equation very similar to Equation (1) for the natural rate $\bar{u}$:

$$\bar{u} = w_1\bar{u}_1 + w_2\bar{u}_2 + \cdot \cdot \cdot + w_n\bar{u}_n \tag{2}$$

Equation (2) says that the natural rate is the weighted average of the natural rates of unemployment of the subgroups in the labor force.

Estimates of the natural rate generally start from some period when the labor market was thought to be in equilibrium and when the aggregate unemployment rate and the unemployment rates of the groups in Equation (2) were at their natural levels. This period is usually taken to be the mid-1950s, and the aggregate natural rate for that period is assumed to be 4 percent. The natural rate estimated for each group will differ from 4 percent: for teenagers it will be much higher, for prime-age males it will be lower, and so on.

The first adjustment made to the 4 percent rate follows from the fact that the composition of the labor force has been changing since the mid-1950s. The weight of teenagers and women in the labor force has been rising. Holding the $\bar{u}_i$ constant, the changing composition of the labor force is taken into account by changing the weights w_i in Equation (2) to reflect the current composition of the labor force rather than that of the mid-fifties. The result is a rise in the natural rate.

The second adjustment that is typically undertaken is to assume that the natural rate for each group may depend on the relative size of that group in the labor force, that is, on the weight w_i. The idea here is that one type of labor is not a perfect substitute for another, and that the more of some type of labor there is, the higher the unemployment rate for that group.[11] There are other estimates of the natural rate; they differ in their method of calculation, but they all include adjustments for the composition of the labor force, and they all show the natural rate rising substantially since the fifties.[12]

[10] See E. Phelps, "Economic Policy and Unemployment in the Sixties," *Public Interest*, Winter 1974.

[11] For details of the method of adjustment, see Peter K. Clark, "Potential GNP in the United States, 1948–1980," in *U.S. Productive Capacity: Estimating the Utilization Gap*, Working paper 23 (St. Louis: Washington University, Center for the Study of American Business, 1977). Clark was then on the Council of Economic Advisers, and his paper describes the method used by the Council to arrive at measures of the full-employment unemployment rate. In 1982 the Council of Economic Advisors stopped calculating potential output and the natural rate of unemployment.

[12] See, for instance, George L. Perry, "Potential Output and Productivity," *Brookings Papers on Economic Activity*, 1977:1 (Washington, D.C.: The Brookings Institution, 1977), and Jeffrey Perloff and Michael Wachter, "A Production Function—Nonaccelerating Inflation Approach to Potential Output," in Karl Brunner and Allan Meltzer (eds.), *Carnegie-Rochester Conference Series*, vol. 10 (Amsterdam: North-Holland).

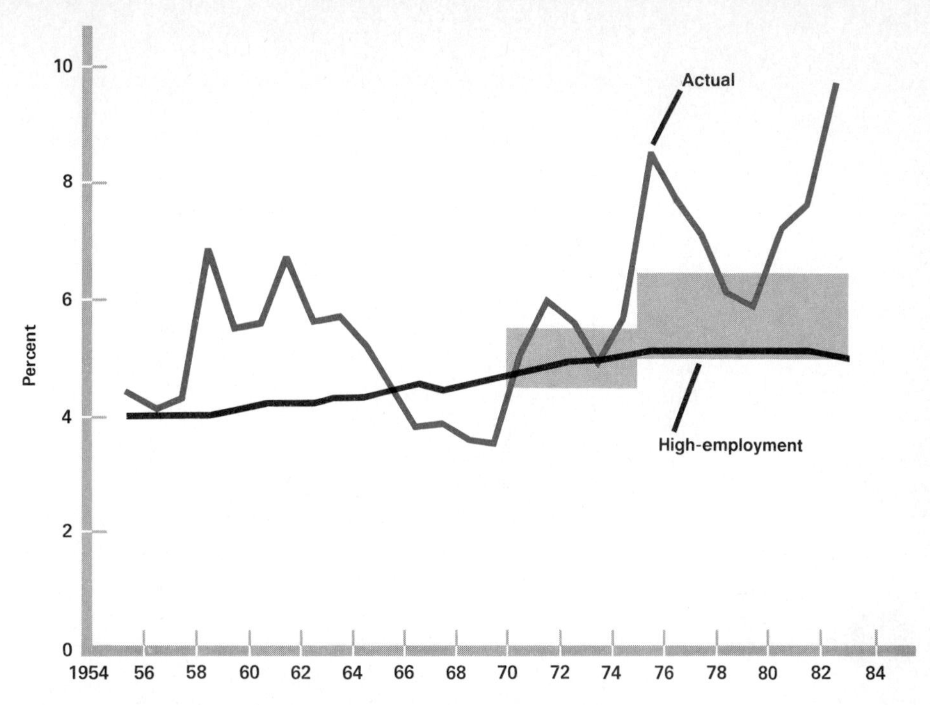

FIGURE 14-2 ACTUAL AND HIGH-EMPLOYMENT UNEMPLOYMENT RATES (1955 TO 1983). (*Sources: Survey of Current Business*, November 1980 and April 1983, and Data Resources, Inc.)

In Figure 14-2 we show the actual unemployment rate for the period 1955–1982, as well as the official full-employment rate of unemployment that was used until recently. The two series coincide in the assumed full-employment years 1954 and 1973. The upward drift of the natural rate reflects only changes in the composition of the labor force. Adjusted for these changes, the 4.9 percent of 1973 represents the same unemployment as the 4 percent for 1954. We note also that with the exception of a brief period in the 1960s, actual unemployment rates are always above the official bench-mark full-employment rate.

It is doubtful whether the official 5 percent bench-mark rate is meaningful once we recognize that unemployment has not been that low since 1969. We therefore indicate a range that is suggestive of where the full-employment rate may lie. A new, provisional assumption of the Congressional Budget Office places the bench-mark full-employment rate at 6 percent; other estimates are in the 5.0 to 6.5 percent range which we indicate for the early 1980s. It may well be the case, as the figure suggests, that extended periods of high unemployment raise the natural rate, making it difficult to reach the previous low.[13]

[13] See James Tobin, "Stabilization Policy Ten Years After," *Brookings Papers on Economic Activity*, 1:1980 (Washington, D.C.: The Brookings Institution, 1981), especially pp. 61–62; and Joseph Pechman (ed.), *Setting National Priorities*, (Washington, D.C.: The Brookings Institution, 1983). The official estimates are in F. deLeeuw et al., "The High Employment Budget: New Estimates," *Survey of Current Business*, November 1980.

Reducing the Natural Rate of Unemployment

Discussion of methods for reducing the natural rate of unemployment tends to focus on the high unemployment rates of teenagers, and on the very high proportion of total unemployment accounted for by the long-term unemployed.[14]

We start with teenage unemployment. We have pointed out earlier that teenagers are unemployed more frequently than others. Reasons for their unemployment may be examined with the help of Table 14-8. It can be seen that many of the unemployed teenagers are new entrants to the labor force, and also that more teenagers than adult males are reentrants to the labor force. The unemployment among teenagers could be reduced if the length of time teenagers take to find a first job were reduced, and also if their entry and exit from the labor force were made less frequent. In order to reduce delays in the finding of jobs, it has been suggested that a Youth Employment Service be set up to help those who leave school locate jobs.

One of the main reasons teenagers enter and leave the labor force often is that the jobs they hold when they are working are not particularly attractive. It is a matter of some controversy as to how to improve existing jobs. Martin Feldstein has suggested that part of the reason jobs are unappealing is that the minimum wage is too high to make it worthwhile for employers to spend more money training the labor they hire in order to make their employees more skilled in their line of work.[15] He points to the apprentice system in other countries, in which young workers either receive very low pay or else pay to get jobs while they are learning skills. He argues that a reduction in the minimum wage would help make such on-the-job training more attractive to employers in the United States. He also suggests that there should be a system of scholarships for this type of training, since he doubts that a lower minimum wage by itself would be sufficient to encourage the right amount of on-the-job

[14] See the *Economic Report of the President,* 1983, Chap. 2.

[15] Martin Feldstein, "The Economics of the New Unemployment," *Public Interest,* 33, Fall 1973.

TABLE 14-8 UNEMPLOYED PERSONS BY REASON FOR UNEMPLOYMENT BY SEX, AGE, AND RACE, APRIL 1983 (*In percent*)

	Males, 20+	Females, 20+	Both sexes, 16–19	White	Nonwhite	Total
Total unemployed (percentage distribution)	100	100	100	100	100	100
Job losers	80.1	52.8	21.9	64.6	59.0	62.3
Job leavers	5.4	10.0	5.4	7.4	1.0	6.9
Reentrants	12.6	31.3	25.7	27.1	27.4	20.6
New entrants	1.9	6.0	47.0	9.5	12.6	10.2

Source: Employment and Earnings, *May 1983.*

training. Similarly, there might be a case for the payment of wage subsidies to encourage firms to hire teenagers who might otherwise be unemployed.

TARGETED PROGRAMS

In 1983 the administration proposed two programs to deal specifically with youth unemployment. One measure was a "summer special," reducing the minimum wage by 25 percent during the May 1 – September 30 period. This program, being geared with its timing to favor the hiring of young people, not only would provide increased summer employment, but also would go further by providing teenagers access to jobs and therefore better long-run chances in the labor market.[16]

Other measures include tax credits that act as an incentive for firms to employ teenagers from economically disadvantaged groups during the summer. Under this program employers can hire eligible young people and pay them the minimum wage, but at a cost to the firm of only 50 cents per hour. Each of the programs is *targeted* to cope specifically with the program of youth employment.

THE SECONDARY LABOR MARKET

Peter Doeringer and Michael Piore[17] doubt that measure such as reducing the minimum wage will do much to improve the nature of jobs in what they call the *secondary labor market.* They suggest that there are a host of noneconomic factors affecting the kinds of jobs that are typically available in the economy. The major economic variables they cite as determining the nature of jobs are the stability and level of aggregate demand. They argue that the instability of aggregate demand is the major reason firms rely on temporary labor and subcontracting to meet high levels of demand. If demand were maintained at a high *and* stable level, firms would have more incentive to create good stable jobs for their entire work force.

When we move away from teenage unemployment to other categories of unemployment, it is clear from Table 14-8 that reentry rates into the labor force are much higher for all categories other than mature males. This suggests that these other groups, too, move in and out of the labor force frequently. Thus the same policies that might increase the stability of teenage employment should be expected to work for these groups. These would include policies to provide such workers with more training, perhaps in government training schemes. There have been many such programs, the

[16] In the problem set we ask you to discuss whether this program is just a way of cheating young people out of their summer income. For a review of the effects of minimum wage legislation see J. P. Martin, "Effects of the Minimum Wage on the Youth Labor Market in North America and France," *Occasional Papers,* OECD, June 1983.

[17] Peter B. Doeringer and Michael J. Piore, "Unemployment and the 'Dual Labor Market,'" *Public Interest,* 38, Winter 1975.

success of which is difficult to evaluate.[18] They would also include attempts to create "job banks" which would make it possible to match the characteristics of available jobs with those of workers looking for jobs. Better day-care facilities would also contribute to more stable labor market participation.

UNEMPLOYMENT BENEFITS

We come next to the implication of unemployment benefits for unemployment. Unemployment benefits affect the unemployment rate. Table 14-9 shows an index of relative family incomes for families that differ in unemployment experience and the number of family members working. Incomes are measured relative to the median income of families in which both the husband and wife work and which suffered no unemployment during the year. For example, suppose only the husband works. When he is working, the family earns 79 percent of the amount earned by a family in which both husband and wife work. If he becomes unemployed, for less than 26 weeks, his family earns 52 percent of the amount earned by the family with both partners at work. In this case, the family receives 66 percent [equals (52/79) × 100 percent] off its normal income when the worker in the family loses his job.

Note that as long as unemployment does not last more than 26 weeks, almost half of income is maintained even when the family suffers some unemployment. But, of course, disposable income falls dramatically when the family's worker(s) is unemployed for a long period.

Unemployment benefits add in three separate ways to the *measured* rate of unemployment. First, the presence of unemployment benefits allows longer job search. A high level of unemployment benefits makes it less urgent for an unemployed person to obtain a job. Further, the fact that a laid-off worker will not suffer a large loss from being unemployed makes it more attractive for an employer to lay off workers temporarily than to attempt to keep them on the job.

The second channel through which unemployment benefits raise the *measured* unemployment rate is through *reporting effects*. To collect unemployment benefits people have to be "in the labor force," looking for work even if they do not really want a job. They therefore get counted as unem-

[18] See the paper by Hall referred to in footnote 2.

TABLE 14-9 UNEMPLOYMENT AND RELATIVE MEDIAN FAMILY INCOMES IN 1981

	DURATION OF UNEMPLOYMENT		
Normal work status	None	Less than 26 weeks	More than 26 weeks
Husband and wife both work	100	73	57
Only husband works	79	52	32
Only wife works	60	48	35

Source: Economic Report of the President, *1983, p. 30.*

ployed. In the absence of unemployment benefits some people might not be in the labor force, and hence measured unemployment rates would be lower. A recent estimate (using 1978 data) suggests that elimination of unemployment insurance would have reduced the unemployment rate by more than one-half percentage point below the 6 percent level of that year. The employment ratio would have risen by one-half percentage point, and the nonparticipation rate would have increased by more than a full percentage point.[19]

The third channel is *employment stability*. With unemployment insurance, the consequences of being in and out of jobs are less severe, and accordingly, workers and firms do not find it as much in their interest to create highly stable employment.

There seems to be little doubt that unemployment compensation does add to the natural rate of unemployment. This does not imply, though, that unemployment compensation should be abolished. What is appropriate is a scheme that will create less incentive for firms to lay off labor while at the same time ensuring that the unemployed are not exposed to economic distress.[20] This is obviously a difficult trick to carry off.

It has become fashionable to argue that unemployment does not present a serious social problem because the unemployed choose to be unemployed and live off unemployment compensation. This argument is wrong in assuming that all unemployment is covered by unemployment benefits. In fact, insured unemployment is less than two-thirds of total unemployment.

14-3 THE COSTS OF UNEMPLOYMENT

The costs of unemployment are so obvious that this section might seem superfluous. Society on the whole loses from unemployment because total output is below its potential level. The unemployed as individuals suffer both from their income loss while unemployed and from the low level of self-esteem that long periods of unemployment cause.[21]

This section provides some estimates of the costs of forgone output resulting from unemployment, and clarifies some of the issues connected with the costs of unemployment and the potential benefits from reducing unemployment. We distinguish between cyclical unemployment, associated with short-run deviations of the unemployment rate from the natural rate, and "permanent" or structural unemployment that exists at the natural rate.

[19] See K. Clark and L. Summers, "Unemployment Insurance and Labor Market Transitions," in M. Bailey (ed.), *Workers, Jobs and Inflation* (Washington, D.C.: The Brookings Institution, 1982), pp. 314–315.

[20] Unemployment insurance rates charged to firms are *experience-rated*. This means that firms that frequently fire workers must pay higher unemployment insurance rates than those with records of infrequent firings. Firms are thus discouraged from excessive firings.

[21] See "Despair among Jobless Is on Rise, Studies Find," in the *New York Times*, Apr. 2, 1983, p. 25. See also Robert J. Gordon, "The Welfare Cost of Higher Unemployment," *Brookings Papers on Economic Activity*, 1:1973 (Washington, D.C.: The Brookings Institution, 1973); and Edmund S. Phelps, *Inflation Policy and Unemployment Theory* (New York: Norton, 1972).

The Costs of Cyclical Unemployment

We now discuss the costs that arise from cyclical unemployment. The problem here is to identify the costs to society of the output forgone because the economy is not operating at full employment. A first measure of the cost is provided by a calculation using Okun's law.

OKUN'S LAW

There is a close link between the percentage unemployment rate and the GNP gap, or the deviation of output from full employment. Arthur Okun established the relationship, now called *Okun's law*, which quantifies that link. Okun's law states that for every one percentage point reduction in the unemployment rate, real GNP will rise by 2.5 percent.[22] The "law" is a convenient way of moving from the unemployment rate to the level of real GNP.

Okun's law was initially a 3 : 1 relation, meaning that every extra point of unemployment cost 3 percent in real GNP forgone. In the 1970s the relation has been revised downward to the 2.5 to 2.7 range. The relation can also be used to calculate the GNP gap. For every 1 percentage point that unemployment is above the natural rate, there is a 2.5 percentage point GNP gap.

The link between changes in unemployment and changes in real GNP that is summarized in the 2.5 : 1 rule reflects three separate channels through which the business cycle affects real GNP. Two of these channels work through reduced labor input. First, there is a reduction in labor hours through a reduced workweek. Second, a fall in real GNP leads to a reduction in the number of people employed. The third channel is a reduction in the productivity of those who remain employed but produce less than normal output. The contribution of the three channels is relatively stable and can therefore be quantified by the convenient 2.5 : 1 unemployment-real GNP gap link.

Consider now how to use the 2.5 : 1 rule to calculate the cost of output forgone. In 1983 the unemployment rate was about 9.5 percent. With a natural rate of unemployment equal to 6 percent the excess is 3.5 percentage points. The GNP gap due to the recession therefore amounts to 8.75 percent (= 3.5 percent × 2.5). At the level of GNP of $3,300, this is equal to $288 billion, a huge number. Another way of looking at the cost of unemployment is to ask how much extra GNP would be made available if the unemployment rate were brought down more rapidly. Suppose in 1983 a more expansionary policy had reduced unemployment to 9.0 percent instead of 9.5 percent. The extra half point reduction would have yielded an extra $40 billion in income.[23]

[22] See Arthur Okun, "Potential GNP: Its Measurement and Significance," American Statistical Association, *Proceedings of the Business and Economics Statistics Section*, 1962, reprinted in M. Bailey and A. Okun (eds.), *The Battle against Inflation and Unemployment* (New York: Norton, 1983); and J. Pechman (ed.), *Setting National Priorities* (Washington, D.C.: The Brookings Institution, 1983).

[23] The number is obtained as follows: 0.5% × 2.5 × $3,300 = $41.25 billion

OTHER COSTS AND BENEFITS

Are there any other costs of unemployment or, for that matter, offsetting benefits? It is possible to imagine offsetting benefits. We do not discuss here the benefit arising from a temporary reduction in the inflation rate accompanying a temporary increase in unemployment, but rather focus on the costs of unemployment taken by itself. A possible offsetting benefit occurs because the unemployed are not working and have more leisure. However, the value that can be placed on that leisure is small. In the first place, much of it is unwanted leisure.

Second, there is a fairly subtle issue that we shall have to explore. If a person were free to set her hours of work, she would work up to the point at which the marginal value of leisure to her was equal to the marginal return from working an extra hour. We would then be able to conclude that if her workday were slightly reduced, the overall loss to her would be extremely small. The reason is that she acquires extra leisure from working less, at the cost of having less income. But she was previously at the point where the marginal value of leisure was equal to the after-tax marginal wage, so that the benefit of the increased leisure almost exactly offsets the private loss of income. However, the net marginal wage is less than the value of the marginal product of an employed person to the economy. The major reason is that society taxes the income of the employed person, so that society as a whole takes a share of the marginal product of the employed person. When the employed woman in our example stops working, she loses for herself only the *net* of tax wage she has been receiving. But society also loses the taxes she has been paying. The unemployed person values her leisure at the net of tax wage, and that value is smaller than the value of her marginal product for society as a whole. Therefore, the value of increased leisure provides only a partial offset to the Okun's law estimate of the cost of cyclical unemployment.

Note that we do not count both the individual's personal loss of income and the Okun's law estimate of forgone output as part of the cost of unemployment. The reason is that Okun's law estimate implicitly includes the individual's own loss of income—it estimates the total loss of output to the economy as a whole as a result of the reduction of employment. That loss could in principle be distributed across different people in the economy in many different ways. For instance, one could imagine that the unemployed person continues to receive benefit payments totaling close to her or his previous income while employed, with the benefit payments financed through taxes on working individuals. In that case, the unemployed person would not suffer an income loss from being unemployed, but society would still lose from the reduction in total output available.

However, the effects of an increase in unemployment are, in fact, borne heavily by the unemployed themselves. There is thus an extra cost to society of unemployment that is very difficult to quantify. The cost arises from the uneven distribution of the burden of unemployment across the population. Unemployment tends to be concentrated among the poor, and that makes the distributional aspect of unemployment a serious matter. It is not one we can easily quantify, but it should not be overlooked. Further, there are many reports of the adverse psychic effects of unemployment that, again, are not easy to quantify but should not be ignored.[24]

"Structural" Unemployment

The benefits of reducing the natural rate of unemployment are more difficult to estimate than the costs of cyclical unemployment. It is clear that the Okun's law estimate of a 2.5 percent change in output resulting from a change of one percentage point in the unemployment rate is not appropriate here. The reason is that the increase in output associated with cyclical changes in unemployment results in part from the fact that the labor put back to work in the short run is able to use capital that has not been fully utilized when unemployment was high. However, in the long run, which is relevant when considering a reduction in the natural rate of unemployment, it would be necessary to invest to provide for the capital with which the newly employed would work. The Okun 2.5 : 1 ratio is therefore too high for the long-run benefits of reducing the natural rate of unemployment. One estimate of benefit is that a reduction of one percentage point in the natural unemployment rate would increase long-run output by only 0.76 percent.[25]

The available estimates of the social benefits of a reduction in long-run unemployment cannot be narrowed down to very solid numbers. Even more difficult is the estimate of an "optimal" long-run unemployment rate. Here we ask the question whether any—and, if so, how much—unemployment is desirable in the long run. A first guess at the answer to that question is that all unemployment is wasteful, since the unemployed labor could usefully be employed. However, that answer is not right. Those people who are unemployed in order to look for a better job are performing a valuable service not only for themselves. They are also performing a service for society by attempting to put themselves into a position in which they earn the most and are the most valuable.

Because the composition of demand shifts over time, we can expect always to have some firms expanding and some contracting. This is true even with a stable level of aggregate demand. Those who lose their jobs will be unemployed, and they benefit both society and themselves by not taking the very first job that comes along, but rather searching for the optimal employment. Accordingly, we can conclude that some unemployment is a good thing in an economy in which the composition of demand changes over time. It is one thing to recognize this and quite another to pin down the optimal rate of unemployment numerically.

[24] See Harry Maurer, *Not Working* (New York: Holt, Rinehart and Winston, 1979), and Kay L. Schlozman and Sidney Verba, *Injury to Insult* (Cambridge, Mass.: Harvard University Press, 1979). See also the *New York Times* article referred to in footnote 21.

[25] See Robert J. Gordon, cited in footnote 21. Can you see how a number like this would emerge if the economy's production function is Cobb-Douglas with a labor share of about ¾? See Chap. 17 where we discuss the link between employment growth and output.

The costs of inflation are much less obvious than those of unemployment. There is no direct loss of output from inflation, as there is from unemployment. In studying the costs of inflation, we again want to distinguish the short run from the long run. In the case of inflation, though, the relevant distinction is between inflation that is *perfectly anticipated,* and taken into account in economic transactions, and *imperfectly anticipated,* or unexpected inflation. We start with perfectly anticipated inflation because that case provides a useful bench-mark against which to judge unanticipated inflation.

Perfectly Anticipated Inflation

Suppose that an economy has been experiencing a given rate of inflation, say, 5 percent, for a long time, and that it is correctly anticipated that the rate of inflation will continue to be 5 percent. In such an economy, all contracts would build in the expected 5 percent inflation. Borrowers and lenders will both know and agree that the dollars in which a loan will be repaid will be worth less than the dollars which are given up by the lender when making the loan. Nominal interest rates would be 5 percent higher than they would be in the absence of inflation. Long-term wage contracts will increase wages at 5 percent per year to take account of the inflation, and then build in whatever changes in real wages are agreed to. Long-term leases will take account of the inflation. In brief, any contracts in which the passage of time is involved will take the inflation into account. In that category we include the tax laws, which we are assuming would be indexed. That is, as discussed further in Chapter 15, the tax brackets themselves would be increased at the rate of 5 percent per year.[26] Inflation has no real costs in such an economy, except for a minor qualification.

That qualification arises because the interest rate that is paid on money might not adjust to the inflation rate. No interest is paid on currency—notes and coins—throughout the world, and no interest is paid on demand deposits in many countries. It is very difficult to pay interest on currency, so that it is likely that the interest rate on currency will continue to be zero, independent of the perfectly anticipated inflation rate. Interest can be paid on demand deposits. Thus it is reasonable to expect that in a fully anticipated inflation, interest would be paid on demand deposits, and the interest rate paid on demand deposits would adjust to the inflation rate. If so, the only cost of perfectly anticipated inflation is that the inflation makes it more costly to hold currency.

The cost to the individual of holding currency is the interest forgone by not holding an interest-bearing asset. When the inflation rate rises, the nominal interest rate rises, the interest lost by holding currency increases, and the cost of holding currency therefore increases. Accordingly, the demand for

[26] The taxation of interest would have to be on the *real* (after-inflation) return on assets for the tax system to be properly indexed.

currency falls. In practice, this means that individuals economize on the use of currency by carrying less in their wallets and making more trips to the bank to cash smaller checks than they did before. The costs of these trips to the bank are often described as the "shoeleather" costs of inflation. They are related to the amount by which the demand for currency is reduced by an increase in the anticipated inflation rate, and they are small.

We should add that throughout this discussion, we are assuming inflation rates that are not too high effectively to disrupt the payments system. This disruption was a real problem in some instances of hyperinflation, but it need not concern us here. We are abstracting, too, from the cost of "menu change." This cost arises simply from the fact that with inflation—as opposed to price stability—people have to devote real resources to marking up prices and changing pay telephones and vending machines as well as cash registers. These costs are there, but one cannot get too excited about them. On balance, the costs of fully anticipated inflation are small.

The notion that the costs of fully anticipated inflation are small does not square well with the strong aversion to inflation reflected in policy making and politics. The most important reason for that aversion is probably that inflations in the United States have not been steady, and that the inflationary experience of the United States is one of imperfectly anticipated inflation, the costs of which are substantially different from those discussed in this section.

There is a further line of argument that explains the public aversion to inflation, even of the fully anticipated, steady kind we are discussing here. The argument is that such a state is not likely to exist, that it is a mirage to believe that policy makers could and would maintain a steady inflation rate at any level other than zero. The argument is that policy makers are reluctant to use restrictive policy to compensate for transitory increases in the inflation rate. Rather than maintain a constant rate of inflation in the face of inflation shocks, the authorities would accommodate these shocks and therefore validate them. Any inflationary shock would add to the inflation rate rather than being compensated by restrictive policy. In this manner, inflation, far from being constant, would, in fact, be rising as policy makers validate any and every disturbance rather than use policy to rigidly enforce the inflation target. Zero inflation, it is argued, is the only target that can be defended without this risk.[27]

Although there are many examples of countries with long inflationary histories, there does not appear to be any tendency for the inflation rate of those countries to increase over time. The argument thus seems weak. However, it is true that the inflation rate has been more stable in countries with low rates of inflation than in countries with inflation rates that are on average higher,[28] perhaps providing a germ of validity to the notion.

[27] See William J. Fellner, introductory essay in William J. Fellner (ed.), *Contemporary Economic Problems* (Washington, D.C.: American Enterprise Institute, 1973).

[28] Arthur M. Okun, "The Mirage of Steady Inflation," *Brookings Papers on Economic Activity,* 2:1971 (Washington, D.C.: The Brookings Institution, 1971).

Imperfectly Anticipated Inflation

The idyllic scene of full adjustment to inflation painted here does not describe economies that we know. Modern economies include a variety of institutional features representing different degrees of adjustment to inflation. Economies with long inflationary histories, such as those of Brazil and Israel, have made substantial adjustments to inflation through the use of indexing. Others in which inflation has been episodic, such as the U.S. economy, have made only small adjustments for inflation.

One of the important effects of inflation is to change the real value of assets fixed in nominal terms. A tripling of the price level, such as the United States experienced in the period from 1960 to 1984, cuts the purchasing power of all claims or assets fixed in money terms to one-third. Thus, someone who bought a 20-year government bond in 1960 and expected to receive a principal of, say, $100 in constant purchasing power at the 1984 maturity date actually winds up with a $100 principal that has purchasing power of $30 in 1960 dollars. The more than tripling of the price level has transferred wealth from creditors—holders of bonds—to debtors. This effect operates with respect to all assets fixed in nominal terms, in particular, money, bonds, savings accounts, insurance contracts, and some pensions. Obviously, it is an extremely important effect since it can wipe out the purchasing power of a lifetime's saving that is supposed to finance retirement consumption. In 1979 the total value of assets fixed in nominal terms was about $7 trillion, or about $30,000 per head. An increase of one percentage point in the price level would reduce the real value of these assets by $70 billion, or an amount equal to 3 percent of GNP.

Those figures by themselves seem to explain the public concern over inflation. There appears to be a lot riding on each percentage-point change in the price level. That impression is slightly misleading. Many individuals are both debtors and creditors in nominal assets. Almost everyone has some money and is thus a creditor in nominal terms. Many of the middle class own housing, financed through mortgages whose value is fixed in nominal terms. Such individuals benefit from inflation because it reduces the real value of their mortgage. Other individuals have borrowed in nominal terms to buy consumer durables, such as cars, and to that extent have their real indebtedness reduced by inflation.

Table 14-10 shows the net position of different sectors in the economy in terms of the amounts of nominal assets they own or owe. In other words, the table shows the net debtor or creditor status in terms of nominal or "monetary" assets and liabilities.[29] The household sector shows up as a net monetary creditor, with the government the offsetting major monetary debtor. Nonfinancial corporations are to a large extent monetary debtors reflecting their debt-financed capital structure. Similarly, financial corporations are net monetary debtors. For example, the banks' net debtor position is reflected by their

[29] Table 14-10 is an updated version of a similar table in G. L. Bach and James B. Stephenson, "Inflation and the Distribution of Wealth," *Review of Economics and Statistics,* February 1974.

TABLE 14-10 NET DEBTOR OR CREDITOR STATUS IN NOMINAL ASSETS OF MAJOR ECONOMIC SECTORS (*in billions of dollars*)

	1960	1970	1980
Households	+350	+696	+1803
Unincorporated businesses	−23	−108	−438
Nonfinancial corporations	−57	−172	−356
Financial corporations	+24	−18	−81
Governments	−250	−341	−750

Note: A plus sign indicates a net monetary creditor.
Source: Federal Reserve Flow-of-Funds. Accounts Assets and Liabilities Outstanding.

liabilities in the form of debt and deposits, while their assets include some real assets like land and structures.

The important point about Table 14-10 is the recognition that a change in the price level brings about a major *redistribution of wealth* between sectors. Thus an inflation rate of 10 percent in 1980 would have resulted in a transfer of $75.0 billion from the household sector to the government. Obviously, we must be careful in assessing the implications of that statement. A redistribution of wealth from corporations to the household sector, for example, means that as a household the average person has gained, but as an owner of a corporate stock, the average household has lost. This singles out transfers between the government and the private sector as particularly important because here the offset is much less immediate.

We are talking here about inflation because that is the current issue. It should be apparent, though, that much the same problems arise with deflation or falling prices. Thus, from 1929 to 1933, the consumer price index fell by almost 25 percent, and that decline meant an extremely large increase in the real value of liabilities, in particular, the real debt of farmers. Inflation redistributes wealth within society from creditors to debtors, and deflation redistributes wealth from debtors to creditors.

However, we must go beyond Table 14-10 in two respects. First, that table really indicates the vulnerability of different sectors to inflation. It does not tell us to what extent inflation was anticipated when the contracts behind the figures in Table 14-10 were drawn. The 10 percent inflation referred to above might have been correctly anticipated, so that the wealth transfers occurring as a result of the inflation would not cause any surprises. However, that does not mean that the creditors would not benefit from higher rates of inflation, and the debtors from lower rates. Second, the gains and losses from these wealth transfers basically cancel out over the economy as a whole. When the government gains from inflation, the private sector may have to pay lower taxes later. When the corporate sector gains from inflation, owners of corporations benefit at the expense of others. If we really did not care about the distribution of wealth among individuals, the costs of unanticipated inflation would be negligible. Included in the individuals of the previous sentence are those belonging to different generations, since the current owners of the national debt might be harmed by inflation—to the benefit of future taxpayers.

The costs of unanticipated inflation are thus largely distributional costs. There is some evidence[30] that the old are more vulnerable to inflation than the young in that they own more nominal assets. Offsetting this, however, is the fact that Social Security benefits are indexed, so that a substantial part of the wealth of those about to retire is protected from unanticipated inflation. There appears to be little evidence supporting the view that the poor suffer unduly from unanticipated inflation.

Inflation redistributes wealth between debtors and creditors because changes in the price level change the purchasing power of assets fixed in money terms. There is room, too, for inflation to affect income positions by changing the distribution of income. A popular line of argument has always been that inflation benefits capitalists or recipients of profit income at the expense of wage earners. Unanticipated inflation, it is argued, means that prices rise faster than wages and therefore allow profits to expand.[31] For the United States in the postwar period, there is no persuasive evidence to this effect. There is evidence that the real return on common stocks—that is, the real value of dividends and capital gains on equity—is reduced by unanticipated inflation. Thus, equity holders appear to be adversely affected by unanticipated inflation.[32]

The last important distributional effect of inflation concerns the real value of tax liabilities. We show in Chapter 15 that a failure to index the tax structure implies that inflation moves the public into higher tax brackets and thus raises the real value of its tax payments or reduces real disposable income. Inflation acts as though Congress had voted an increase in tax schedules.

The fact that unanticipated inflation acts mainly to redistribute wealth, the net effects of which redistribution should be close to zero, has led to some questioning of the reasons for public concern over inflation. The gainers, it seems, do not shout as loudly as the losers. Since some of the gainers (future taxpayers) have yet to be born, this is hardly surprising. There is also a notion that the average wage earner is subject to an illusion when both the nominal wage and the price level increase. Wage earners are thought to attribute

[30] See Bach and Stephenson, cited in footnote 29.

[31] Louis De Alessi, "Do Business Firms Gain from Inflation? Reprise," *Journal of Business*, April 1975. See also Nancy Jianakoplos, "Are You Protected from Inflation?" Federal Reserve Bank of St. Louis, *Review*, January 1977.

[32] See Charles R. Nelson, "Inflation and Rates of Return on Common Stocks," *Journal of Finance*, May 1976. See also Franco Modigliani and Richard Cohn, "Inflation, Rational Valuation and the Market," *Financial Analysts Journal*, March–April 1979, for a controversial view of the reasons why inflation affects the stock market.

increases in nominal wages to their own merit rather than to inflation, while the general inflation of prices is seen as causing an unwarranted reduction in the real wage they would otherwise have received. It is hard to know how to test the validity of this argument.

It does appear that the redistributive effects of unanticipated inflation are large, and that, accordingly, some parts of the population could be seriously affected by unanticipated inflation. It is difficult to be more precise in discussing this complicated question, which, like others in this chapter, remains the subject of ongoing research.

14-5 INFLATION, INTEREST RATES, AND WAGE INDEXATION

In this section we look at two kinds of contracts that are especially affected by inflation. These are long-term loan contracts and wage contracts. In each case payments are fixed in nominal terms over some length of time ahead. But the future price level is not known ahead of time, and hence the *real* value of the payments can turn out to be very different from what borrowers and lenders, or workers and firms, had anticipated.

Inflation and Interest Rates

One of the areas where inflation plays an important role is the capital market. Here borrowers and lenders make loan contracts that specify fixed dollar payments. For example, a firm may sell 20-year bonds in the capital markets at an interest rate of 12 percent per year. Whether the real interest rate on the bonds turns out to be high or low depends on what the inflation rate will be over the next 20 years. The borrower and lender will each have some idea of what inflation will be. They may even agree, but they may also turn out to be wrong. Inflation has major effects particularly in the area of home financing, where loans are made for 25 to 35 years.

INFLATION AND HOUSING

Investment in housing is one of the areas where errors in inflation expectations can bring about large redistributions between borrowers and lenders. The typical household buys a home by borrowing from a bank or savings and loan institution. The mortgage — this is the term for the home loan — used to be a fixed nominal interest rate loan for a duration of 25 or 30 years. The interest payments are deductible in calculating federal income taxes, and accordingly, the effective cost of the loan is less than the actual interest by an amount that depends on the household's marginal tax rate. Suppose the marginal tax rate is 30 percent; then the nominal interest cost is 70 percent of the actual mortgage rate.

Now consider the economics of investing in a home, comparing the interest cost with the capital gains that arise from inflation. With inflation, the

TABLE 14-11 HOME PRICE INFLATION AND MORTGAGE RATES (*Average percentage rate per year*)

	Home price inflation rate	Mortgage rate	After-tax real differential*
1963–1982	5.76	5.89	1.64
1973–1982	8.36	7.60	2.86
1977–1982	9.0	9.02	2.87
1981–1982	5.19	14.70	−5.10

* The differential is calculated as the difference between the home price inflation and 0.7 times the mortgage rate.
Source: Economic Report of the President, *1983*.

value of the home rises over time. Therefore if the interest cost falls short of the capital gains, investing in a house is a good idea, even leaving aside noneconomic considerations of owning versus renting.

Consider, for example, someone buying a home in 1963. At that time the mortgage rate was 5.89 percent for a long-term loan. Looking now at the 1963–1982 period, we see that housing prices increased roughly at the same rate as the mortgage rate. Without including the tax deductions for interest payments, the borrower in 1962 over the next 20 years paid *real* interest of essentially zero because the rate of inflation of housing prices was almost equal to the interest rate. When the interest deductibility is figured in, capital gains exceed the tax-adjusted interest cost, as the last columns of Table 14-11 shows. This is even more the case for an investment starting in the 1970s and especially in the late 1970s. Nominal interest rates are higher, but the rate of increase of housing prices is higher too. The differential including the tax treatment now makes the purchase of a house especially favorable because the after-tax interest cost rises much less than the capital gains. But housing is not a sure bet. For example, someone who bought in 1981 with a high 14.70 percent mortgage rate and had to sell in 1982 would have lost 5 percent, even taking into account tax treatment of the loan.[33]

What is the calculation for someone investing in, say, 1983? The mortgage rate was about 13 percent or 9.1 percent taking into account the tax treatment of interest. Could an investor expect housing prices over the next 20 years to rise enough to keep the real interest cost small? The answer is uncertain. Uncertainty about the outlook for inflation was one of the reasons why a new financial instrument made its appearance: *the floating-rate mortgage.* These are long-term loans with an interest rate that is periodically (every 3 years, for example) adjusted in line with prevailing short-term interest rates. To the extent that nominal interest rates roughly reflect inflation trends, *floating-rate mortgages* reduce the effects of inflation on the long-term costs of financing home purchases. There will not be large unanticipated capital gains, nor will there be persistent capital losses.

[33] For a further discussion see L. Summers, "Inflation, the Stock Market and Owner-Occupied Housing," *American Economic Review*, May 1981.

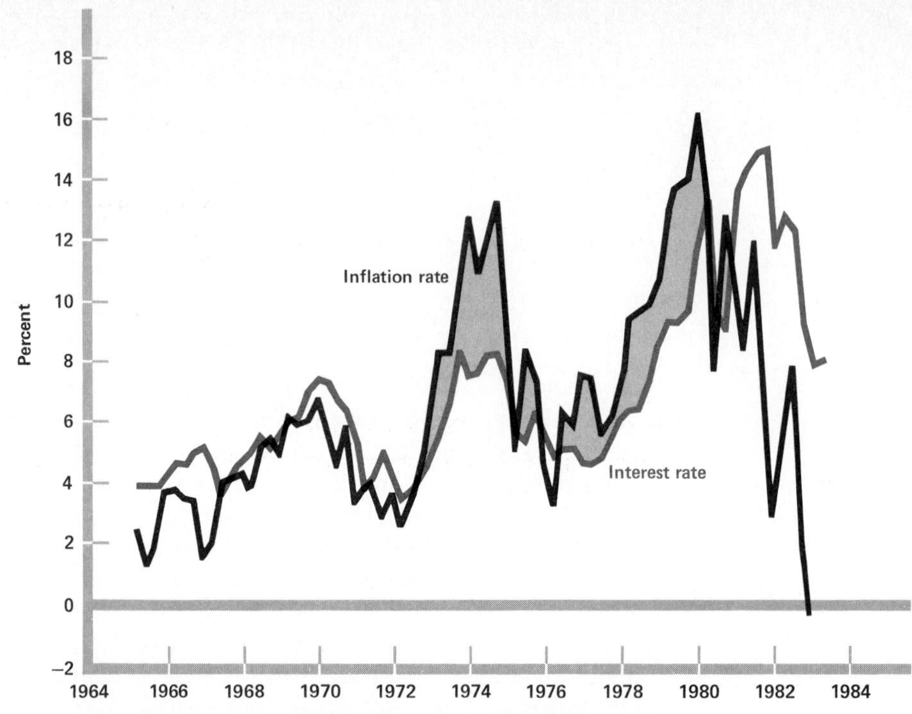

Note: **Interest rate is the quarterly average of the market yield on 3-month Treasury bills. Inflation rate is annualized percent change in the CPI over the following quarter.**

FIGURE 14-3 INFLATION AND THE INTEREST RATE, 1965–1983. (*Source:* Data Resources, Inc.)

THE FISHER EQUATION AGAIN

The Fisher equation introduced in Chapter 13 implies that expected inflation will be reflected one for one in nominal interest rates. We repeat that equation here:

$$\text{Nominal interest rate} = \text{real interest rate} + \text{expected inflation rate} \quad (3)$$

In Figure 14-3 we show the nominal interest rate on 3-month Treasury bills and the *actual* rate of inflation over the subsequent 3 months. The shaded areas represent periods where inflation exceeds the nominal interest rate so that real rates are negative. During the early 1970s, when inflation accelerated, negative real rates were not infrequent.

The early 1980s stand out as a period of high real interest rates. Inflation in 1982–1983, for example, declined much more than nominal interest rates, and hence real rates were strongly positive. There used to be a belief that expected real interest rates are roughly constant. There is now little left of that belief: the experience of the early 1980s shows that real rates of interest can change substantially as a result of monetary and fiscal disturbances.[34]

Indexation of Wages

In Chapter 13 we discussed the role of automatic cost of living adjustment (COLA) provisions in wage contracts. COLA provisions link increases in money wages to increases in the price level. The adjustment may be complete — 100 percent indexation — or only partial. Partial indexation takes one of two forms. There may be a *threshold* or a *cap*. A threshold specifies a minimum increase in the price level before indexation comes into play. This implies that small price increases are not compensated, while larger ones are. A cap puts a limit on the extent to which price increases are compensated, say, 10 percent per year. COLA clauses are designed to allow workers to recover purchasing power lost through price increases.

WHY INDEXATION?

Indexation in some form is a quite common feature of labor markets in many countries. Indexation strikes a balance between the advantages of long-term wage contracts and the interests of workers and firms in not having *real* wages get too far out of line. Bargaining for wages is costly because workers (unions) and the firm have to devote time and effort to arrive at a settlement and often work is disrupted through strikes. It is in the common interest of workers and firms therefore to hold to a minimum the number of times these negotiations take place.

Thus wages are not negotiated once a week or once a month, but rather they are negotiated in the form of 2- or 3-year contracts. But over the term of these contracts the evolution of prices — consumer prices and the prices at which firms sell their output — is not known with certainty. Therefore real wages paid by firms or received by workers are not known even if money wages are. To remedy this uncertainty, some provision is made to adjust wages for inflation. Broadly, there are two possibilities. One is to index wages to the CPI and in periodic reviews, say, quarterly, increase wages by the increase in prices over the period. The other is to schedule periodic, preannounced wage increases based on the expected rate of price increase. If inflation were known with certainty, the two methods would come to the same thing. But since inflation can differ from expectations, there will be discrepancies. Prefixed wage increases may turn out to be high or low relative to actual inflation. On that account indexation on the basis of actual inflation offers

[34] The initial argument is due to Eugene Fama, "Short-Term Interest Rates as Predictors of Inflation," *American Economic Review*, 1975. For subsequent discussion see David Begg, *The Rational Expectations Revolution in Macroeconomics* (Baltimore: Johns Hopkins University Press, 1982), and Frederic Mishkin, *A Rational Expectations Approach to Macroeconomics* (Chicago: University of Chicago Press, 1983).

greater assurance of stable real wages for workers than do scheduled increases.

SUPPLY SHOCKS AND INDEXATION

Suppose real material prices increase, and firms pass these cost increases on into higher prices of final goods. Consumer prices will rise, and under a system of 100 percent indexation, wages would rise. This leads to further price and material costs, and wage increases. Indexation here leads to an inflation spiral that would be avoided under a system of prefixed wage increases because then real wages could fall as a consequence of higher material prices.

The example makes it clear that we must distinguish two possibilities in considering the effects of wage indexing, monetary disturbances and real disturbances. In the case of a monetary disturbance (a shift in the *LM* schedule), there is a "pure" inflation disturbance, and firms can affort to pay the same real wages and therefore would not mind 100 percent indexation. In the case of adverse real disturbances, however, real wages must fall, and full indexation is entirely the wrong system because it stands in the way of downward real wage flexibility.

From the two cases it is apparent that neither completely prefixed wage increases nor complete indexation is likely to be optimal. The best arrangement will depend on the relative importance of monetary and real shocks. Countries that had practiced 100 percent indexation—for example, Italy and Brazil—have found in the 1970s that it is difficult to adjust to real shocks and that the indexation leads to a wage-price spiral that pushes up inflation with great speed.

WAGE INDEXATION IN THE UNITED STATES

In the U.S. economy more than 50 percent of workers who are covered in major collective bargaining agreements have contract provisions for automatic cost-of-living provisions. Table 14-12 shows that these provisions are much more common in the last 10 years than they had been in the previous 10 years. The increase in the level and variability of the rate of inflation is the explanation.

Table 14-12 might give the impression that indexation is a very common feature of the U.S. labor market. But that is not the case once we note that

TABLE 14-12 INFLATION AND COLA PROVISIONS (*In percent*)

Rate	Average inflation rate	Workers with COLA coverage*
1963–1972	3.5	26.7
1973–1982	8.2	54.6

* Percentage of all workers covered in major collective bargaining agreements.
Source: Monthly Labor Review, *various issues, and* Economic Report of the President.

major bargaining agreements cover only a small part of the labor force. In 1982 about 10 million workers of a total labor force pool of 100 million were covered by COLA provisions.

The role of indexation is further limited because 100 percent indexation is not the rule. For example, a common rule in 1981 was an adjustment of $0.01 per hour for each 0.3 percent, or in some cases 0.2 percent, increase in the CPI. With an hourly wage of $10 and an inflation rate of 10.4 percent, the adjustment is $0.35 (= $0.01 × 10.4 percent/0.3) per hour, or 3.5 percent (= $0.35/$10). Under this rule, indexation is thus far from 100 percent since 10 percent inflation leads to less than 4 percent wage increases.

We noted above that a system of 100 percent indexation is difficult to manage when there are supply shocks such as occurred in the 1970s. The U.S. system is clearly very far from full indexation. Some observers see in this fact the reason that the U.S. economy has more easily adjusted to the oil shock than have countries in Europe where full indexation is more common.[35]

14-6 THE POLITICAL ECONOMY OF INFLATION AND UNEMPLOYMENT

We have seen the costs of unemployment and the problems that arise from inflation. The final question is how policy makers strike a balance, deciding how much unemployment to live with and how much inflation to accept. It is clear from the outset that the best of all worlds is one without either inflation or excess unemployment. But disturbances in the economy do occur, and in the absence of full wage-price flexibility, it will not be possible to restore full employment with stable prices instantly. Policy makers therefore face a tradeoff: Should they try to maintain the economy close to or at full employment, even if that involves risks of inflation bursts when shocks do occur? Or should they opt for policies that are much less accommodating and therefore involve larger swings in unemployment but more stable prices?

ALTERNATIVE POLICY PATHS

What should be done when a disturbance, say, a supply shock, creates both high unemployment and inflation? Should the return to full employment be rapid, even at the cost of high inflation? Or should stopping inflation be the first priority even if that means an extended period of unemployment? Policy makers must make these decisions. Even if their control of the economy is not perfect, for the reasons discussed in Chapter 10, there is still a need to set policy instruments to move the economy in the desired direction.

Figure 14-4 shows the long-run Phillips curve *LPC*, which indicates that in the long run there is no tradeoff between inflation and unemployment. Suppose now that as a consequence of a disturbance, say, an oil shock, the

[35] See J. Sachs, "Wages, Profits, and Macroeconomic Adjustment: A Comparative Study," *Brookings Papers on Economic Activity*, 2:1979 (Washington, D.C.: The Brookings Institution, 1979).

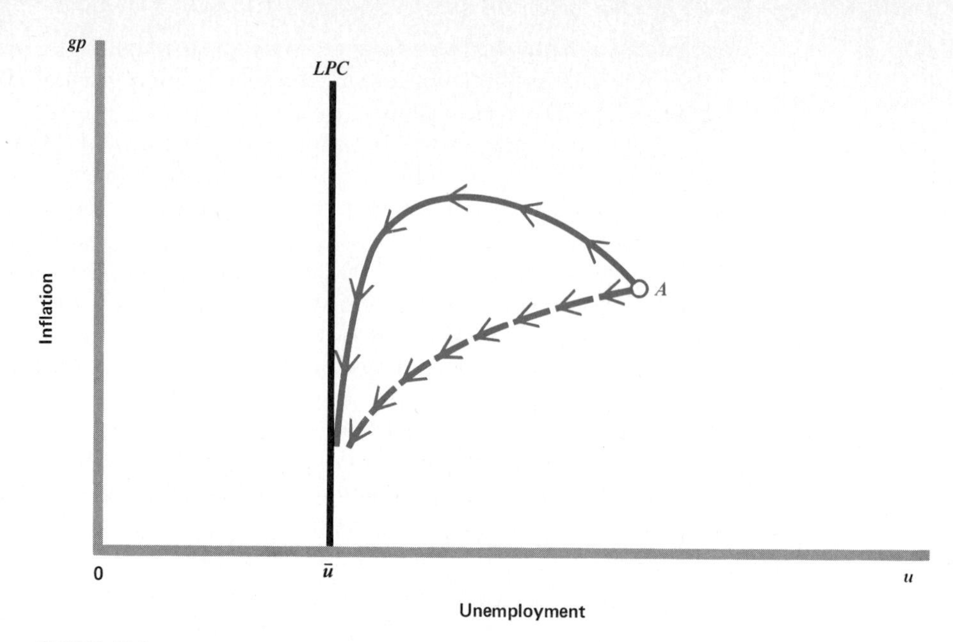

FIGURE 14-4 ALTERNATIVE PATHS OF INFLATION AND UNEMPLOYMENT. A disturbance moves the economy to point A, where there is high unemployment and inflation. There are alternative paths of recovery toward full employment and zero inflation to choose from. The lower path results from a slow reduction in unemployment to gain more rapid disinflation. The upper path emphasizes a rapid elimination of unemployment.

economy finds itself at point A with high inflation and high unemployment. We show two possible adjustment paths. The solid path shows higher inflation rates in the transition and corresponds to a policy choice of rapid restoration of low unemployment levels and then a long period of decelerating inflation. An alternative is the dashed path along which there is an immediate reduction in inflation. Along this path inflation is falling, but the cost is that the reduction in unemployment is more gradual.

Figure 14-4 makes the point that policy makers do not choose between inflation and unemployment, but rather between *adjustment paths* that differ in the inflation-unemployment mix. A path that maintains high initial unemployment promotes a more rapid and certain disinflation. A path that tries to restore full employment rapidly involves more inflation.

*THE EXTENDED PHILLIPS CURVE

To see more precisely the options open to policy makers, we look at the expectations-augmented Phillips curve in (4), which is already familiar from Chapter 13,

$$gp = gpe - \epsilon(u - \bar{u}) \tag{4}$$

where, as a reminder, *gp* denotes the inflation rate and *gpe* the trend or expected inflation rate. In this form the Phillips curve states that inflation will decline relative to the previous trend if the actual unemployment rate exceeds the natural rate $\bar{u}$. But often it is argued that the rate of inflation depends not only on the trend inflation rate *gpe* and on the *level* of the unemployment rate but also on the *change* in the unemployment rate. The argument is that at the same level of the unemployment rate, inflation will be different depending whether unemployment is rapidly falling or sharply increasing. Suppose the unemployment rate is 8 percent, and there are two possibilities. In one case unemployment is declining by 2 percent per year; in another it is not declining at all. We would expect higher inflationary pressure or less rapidly falling inflation in the former case than in the latter.

This extension is shown in Equation (5), where we add another term $\beta(u - u_{-1})$ to the Phillips curve. The coefficient β measures the extent to which changing unemployment $(u - u_{-1})$ affects inflation. The larger is β, the more important is the effect of changing unemployment on the inflation rate. In this extended form high unemployment still exerts dampening effects on inflation, but they are now modified by the change in unemployment effect.

$$gp = gpe - \epsilon(u - \bar{u}) - \beta(u - u_{-1}) \tag{5}$$

Equation (5) is immediately useful for policy decisions because it suggests that there is a concrete tradeoff. The more rapid the reduction in unemployment, the less disinflation is achieved at each unemployment level. Even if unemployment is very high, inflation falls little if the economy is moving too rapidly out of the recession. Conversely, a slow recovery reinforces the inflation dampening effects of high unemployment.

OKUN'S LAW AGAIN

We saw Okun's law as a link between the unemployment rate and the GNP gap. Now we look at a different version of the same law that links the behavior of real output growth and changes in unemployment over time. In this alternative form the "law" draws attention to the fact that over time the labor force grows and unemployment would rise unless real output, and with it employment, grows sufficiently fast. In fact, just to keep unemployment constant, output must grow to compensate for the increasing labor force and the reduction in labor requirements that come from productivity growth.

In this growth form, Okun's law establishes a simple numerical link between the growth rate of output and the change in unemployment. The law states that the unemployment rate declines by 0.4 (= 1/2.5) percentage point for every 1 percentage point of annual real GNP growth above trend. Thus if output grows 3 percentage points above trend, the unemployment rate declines by 1.2 percentage points (= 0.4 × 3), but if output growth were, say, 2 percent below trend, unemployment would rise by 0.8 percentage point. The trend growth rate of output, discussed further in Chapter 17, is between 2.5 and 2.9 percent in the early 1980s. For concreteness we assume it is 2.7

percent. With this assumption Okun's law linking real growth and the change in unemployment reads as follows:

$$u = u_{-1} - 0.4(gy - 2.7) \tag{6}$$

From (6) unemployment exceeds or falls short of last period's unemployment as the growth rate of output, *gy*, exceeds or falls short of trend growth. Every extra point of output growth buys a reduction of unemployment of 0.4 percent, or every 2.5 percent extra growth, sustained for a year, reduces unemployment by a whole percentage point.

Once again it is necessary to emphasize that Okun's law summarizes an empirical relation between growth and unemployment, not an immutable law. In particular, the numerical estimates of trend growth and the growth-unemployment linkage have changed over time. But even with that qualification in mind, the relation is an extremely useful tool for macroeconomic planning. An example will make this point.

In 1983 the unemployment rate at the beginning of the year was 10 percent. How many years would it take for the economy to return to an unemployment rate of 6.5 percent? The answer, using Okun's law, depends on the growth rate of output. In Table 14-13 we show a calculation for a specified path of output growth.

It is striking that even by the late 1980s the unemployment rate will not have come down to the level of the natural rate. Growth does lower unemployment, but a much more rapid expansion than that shown in Table 14-13 would be needed to get the unemployment rate down rapidly from 10.2 percent to the natural rate.[36]

THE POLICY TRADEOFF

We can now return to the policy problem posed in Figure 14-4. The problem is to reduce unemployment but at the same time produce a long-run reduction in inflation. Okun's law suggests that reducing unemployment requires a sustained high-growth strategy. But the extended Phillips curve in Equation (5) shows that a strategy of rapidly reducing unemployment will tend to

[36] In the problem set we ask you to look at a high-growth scenario and show the path of unemployment. The calculation of each step in Table 14-13 is to take the initial unemployment rate and subtract $0.4(gy - 2.7)$ to get the unemployment rate in the next column. For *gy* we fill in the growth rate of output for the year.

TABLE 14-13 GROWTH AND UNEMPLOYMENT

	1983	1984	1985	1986	1987
Growth	5.5%	4.8%	4.0%	4.0%	4.0%
Unemployment rate	10.2%	9.08%	8.24%	7.72%	7.2%

increase the inflation rate. There is a choice to be made between a *high-growth recovery* that rapidly reduces unemployment and a *slow-growth recovery* that cuts into inflation, but at the cost of sustained high unemployment.[37]

Okun's law and the extended Phillips curve have another implication. High unemployment exerts a strong dampening effect on inflation, making deceleration possible even in the presence of rapidly falling unemployment. But following such a strategy over time, the level of the unemployment rate declines, and hence the dampening effects on inflation become smaller. To achieve continuing deceleration of inflation, growth of output and the decline in unemployment must slow down. The second implication of the combined tools—Okun's law and the extended Phillips curve—is that growth can be fast at high rates of unemployment without reigniting inflation.

What Do Policy Makers Do?

We have now seen the menu of growth-unemployment-inflation from which policy makers must choose their path. How do they decide, and what typically is the choice? There are two ways of thinking about this problem. One is to assume that policy makers act in the interest of society. They form estimates of the social costs associated with alternative paths of inflation and unemployment and choose the one that minimizes the total cost of stabilization to society. This is the approach a benevolent dictator would choose.

In a democracy, policy makers respond to the electorate and choose policies that will maximize their chances of being kept in office. This may or may not result in policy makers choosing the socially optimal path. This second approach has given rise to an extensive literature in economics and political science that is classified as the political business cycle.

THE POLITICAL BUSINESS CYCLE

Policy makers who hold office in a democracy choose policies that contribute to their reelection. It is therefore important for them to determine the issues that voters are concerned with, their relative importance, and the ease and degree of risk or certainty with which macroeconomic policy can be used to help secure reelection. The theory of the *political business cycle* predicts that the path of the macroeconomy mirrors the timetable of the election cycle. We now review the building blocks of that theory.[38]

We have already discussed the first building block: the tradeoffs from which a policy maker can choose. There are two more building blocks: first,

[37] We can derive the exact tradeoff by substituting $u - u_{-1}$ from Equation (6) into Equation (5) to obtain $gp = gpe - \epsilon(u - \overline{u}) + 0.4\beta\,(gy - 2.7)$. This equation shows that inflation is higher, given gpe and u, the higher the growth rate of output. To achieve a reduction in inflation below trend, growth must be sufficiently slow, the more so the lower the level of the unemployment rate.

[38] See Bruno Frey, *Modern Political Economy* (New York: Wiley, 1978), Edward Tufte, *Political Control of the Economy* (Princeton, N.J.: Princeton University Press, 1978), and D. Golden and James Poterba, "The Price of Popularity: The Political Business Cycle Reexamined," *American Journal of Political Science*, November 1980.

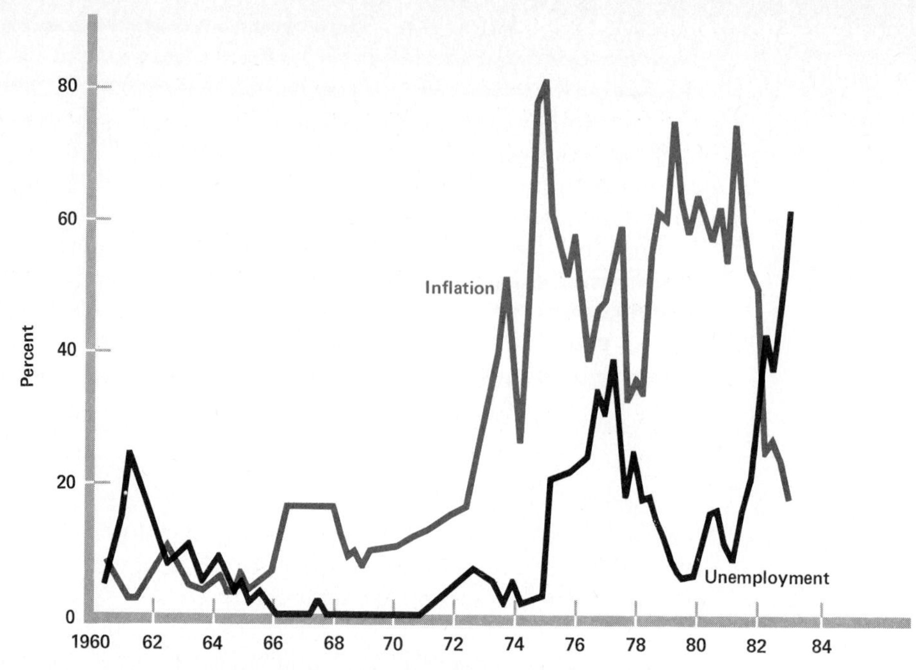

FIGURE 14-5 INFLATION, UNEMPLOYMENT AS THE NATION'S MOST IMPORTANT PROBLEM—THE GALLUP REPORT. (*Source: The Gallup Opinion Index,* June 1979 and *The Gallup Report,* various issues, 1980–1982)

how do voters rate the issues—inflation versus unemployment—and second, what is the optimal timing to influence election results?

OPINION POLLS

Voters are concerned with both inflation and unemployment. Figure 14-5 shows responses to the Gallup opinion poll. In virtually every poll since 1973 more than 50 percent of the respondents rated either inflation or unemployment as the most serious problem facing the country. The same pattern emerges from virtually all public opinion polls.

There is an important further lesson to be drawn from opinion polls: the public is concerned less with the level of unemployment than with the direction of change. *Rising* unemployment brings about sharply increased concern over unemployment. Concern over inflation depends on the expectation of rising inflation, as well as on the level of inflation.

The evidence is thus that voters worry about both the *level* and the *rate of change* of the inflation and unemployment rates. For instance, the public is less worried about a high but *falling* unemployment rate than it is about a medium but constant unemployment rate. These facts will influence the types of policies politicians will choose.

THE TIMING ISSUE

The policy maker thus wants to be sure that at election time the economy is pointed in the right direction to yield a maximum of voter approval. The inflation rate and unemployment rate should be falling if possible—and should not be too high if that can be managed. The problem is how to use the period from inauguration to election to bring the economy into just the right position.

The answer of the political business cycle hypothesis is that politicians will use restraint early in an administration, raising unemployment but reducing inflation. The need for restraint can often be blamed on a previous administration. But as the election approaches, expansion takes over to assure that falling unemployment brings voter approval even while the level of unemployment still checks inflation. In this hypothesis then there is a systematic cycle in unemployment, rising in the first part of a presidential term and declining in the second. There is a matching cycle, of course, in the policy instruments. Thus in the first part of the term, fiscal policy would tighten to create slack and disinflation; in the second part expansion takes over to reduce unemployment.

The empirical evidence on the political business cycle remains mixed. There does not appear to be in the U.S. data a very obvious behavior of the key variables over the 4-year presidential cycle in the United States, as the theory would lead us to expect.[39] Every now and then, though, as in 1969–1972 and 1981–1984, the facts seem in accord with the theory.

In any event, there are factors that work against the political business cycle. One is that the President cannot use the business cycle fully because of midterm congressional elections. The second is that a President cannot indulge too openly in staging recession and recoveries timed solely with a view to the election. There are risks to being caught in a cynical application of macroeconomic policies. Third, large macroshocks—oil shocks and wars—may on occasion overshadow the election cycling. Finally, the executive does not control the full range of instruments. Specifically the Fed, in principle at least, is independent and therefore need not accommodate an attempt to move the economy on an election cycle. In fact, though, the Fed, has not always spoiled the game.[40] At least on one occasion, in 1972, the Fed very obviously provided expansion just at the right time.

The difficulty in finding striking evidence in the data does not mean the hypothesis should be entirely dismissed. For instance, other things equal, we should be surprised to see an administration staging a recession in an election year or allowing inflation to increase sharply just as the voters go to the poll. On occasion economics may be the overriding issue and a perfect election cycle is being played—1984?—on other occasions noneconomic issues may take precedence.

[39] See Golden and Poterba cited above.

[40] L. Laney and T. Willett, "Presidental Politics, Budget Deficits, and Monetary Policy in the United States, 1960–76," *Public Choice,* 1, 1983.

BOX 14-1

REAL WAGES AND UNEMPLOYMENT

Unemployment rates in the United States and in Europe in the early 1980s were far higher than they had been in the 1960s or even in the 1970s. Table 1 shows the data for different subperiods.

The high unemployment rates led to a discussion, especially in Europe, of whether excessively high real wages or insufficient aggregate demand was the chief source of the problem. Figure 1 helps sort out the issues. The figure shows the labor demand schedule — the marginal product of labor — with the real wage on the vertical axis and $\overline{N}$ as the full-employment labor supply. The full-employment real wage is $(w/P)_0$.

One interpretation of the unemployment problem of the early 1980s was that the economy was at a point such as A at a real wage $(w/P)'$. At point A firms hire only an amount of labor N' which falls short of full employment because the real wage is too high. The economy suffers from ***classical*, or *real wage, unemployment***. The cure is either a reduction in the real wage to $(w/P)_0$ or else productivity growth or increased investment that shifts the MPN schedule out and to the right and thus reduces unemployment.

An alternative interpretation is that the economy was at a point such as A'. Again there is unemployment, but this time the real wage is not the problem. Firms are not willing to hire more workers than N' because they cannot sell the output. Aggregate demand is insufficient to absorb more output than is produced by an employment level N'. Therefore firms do not hire more workers, and accordingly, there is ***Keynesian unemployment***. The cure, in this case, is not a cut in real wages but rather an expansion in aggregate demand through monetary or fiscal stimulus.

In both cases there is unemployment. In both cases it is unprofitable for firms to hire more labor than N'. In one case the problem is that labor is too expensive; in the other there is no market for the increased output. But it is essential to identify what kind of unemployment the economy faces before designing policy action. Because we do not know the equilibrium real wage, there is no direct way to decide whether unemployment is Keynesian or classical.

In all likelihood in the early eighties, there was some classical unemployment in Europe, because real wages had not adjusted enough in response to the increased price of oil and reduced productivity growth. But in addition a dose of Keynesian unemployment was superimposed between 1980 and 1982, so that the economy was to the left of point A. In that case expansionary aggregate demand policies would have gone some way toward reducing unemployment, but there was also a need to cut labor costs relative to labor productivity.

TABLE 1 UNEMPLOYMENT RATES IN THE UNITED STATES AND IN EUROPE

	1970–1974	1975–1980	1980–1982
European community	2.5	5.3	7.9
United States	5.4	7.1	8.1

Source: European Economy *and* Economic Report of the President, *1983.*

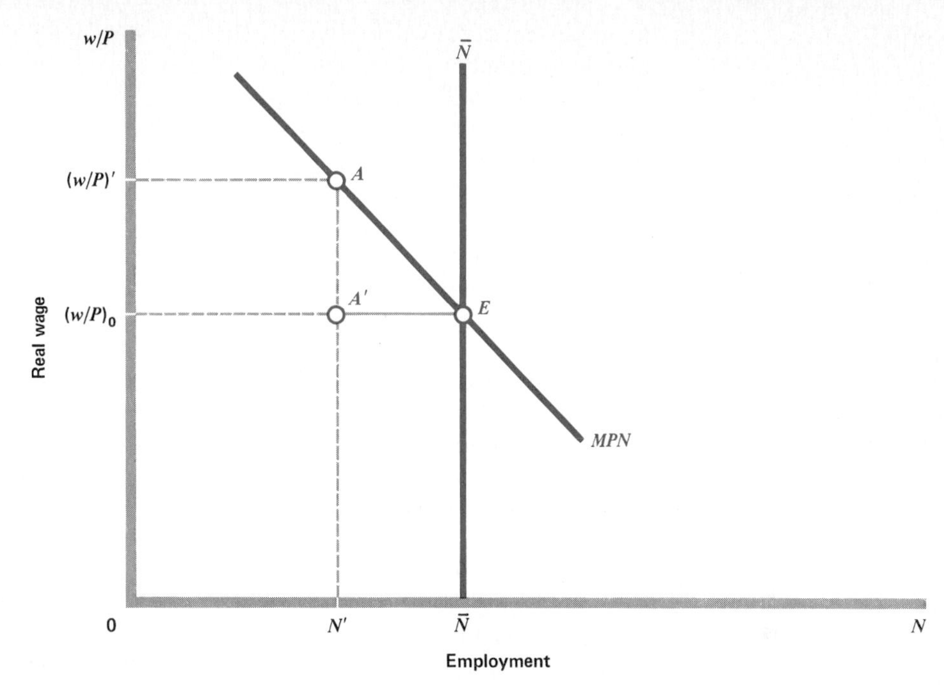

FIGURE 1 CLASSICAL OR KEYNESIAN UNEMPLOYMENT? The schedule MPN is the marginal product of labor or the demand curve for labor. The full-employment labor supply is $\overline{NN}$. At a real wage $(w/P)'$ there is "high real wage" unemployment because firms only want to hire a labor force of N', which falls short of the supply $\bar{N}$. But it is also possible that even at the lower wage $(w/P)_0$ firms only want to hire N' of labor because they cannot sell the output that would be produced by a larger labor force. The question is to know whether the unemployment results from high real wages, as at point A, or from insufficient aggregate demand, as at point A'.

14-8 SUMMARY

1 The anatomy of unemployment for the United States reveals frequent and short spells of unemployment. Nonetheless, a substantial fraction of U.S. unemployment is accounted for by those who are unemployed for a large portion of the time.
2 There are significant differences in unemployment rates across age groups and race. Unemployment among black teenagers is highest, and that of white adults is lowest. The young and minorities have significantly higher unemployment rates than middle-aged whites.
3 The concept of the natural or structural rate of unemployment singles out that part of unemployment which would exist even at full employment. The unemployment arises in part because of a high frequency of job changes, in particular for teenagers. The high frequency of teenage

unemployment is explained partly by the poor quality of jobs available to people without training. The natural rate of unemployment is hard to conceptualize and even harder to measure. The consensus is to estimate it around 6 percent, up from the 4 percent of the mid-fifties.

4 Policies to reduce the natural rate of unemployment involve labor market and aggregate demand policies. The economy needs a stable, high level of aggregate demand. Disincentives to employment and training, such as minimum wages, and incentives to extended job search, such as untaxed unemployment benefits, also tend to raise the natural rate.

5 The cost of unemployment is the psychic and financial distress of the unemployed as well as the loss of output. The loss of output is little compensated for by the unemployed's enjoying leisure. For one thing, a large part of unemployment is involuntary. For another, the social product of labor exceeds the wage rate because of income taxes.

6 The economy can adjust to perfectly anticipated inflation by moving to a system of indexed taxes and to nominal interest rates that reflect the expected rate of inflation. In the absence of regulations that prevent these adjustment (such as usury laws or interest rate ceilings), there are no important costs to perfectly anticipated inflation. The only costs are those of changing price tags periodically and the cost of suboptimal holdings of currency.

7 Imperfectly anticipated inflation has important redistributive effects among sectors. Unanticipated inflation benefits monetary debtors and hurts monetary creditors. The government gains real tax revenue, and the real value of government debt declines.

8 In the U.S. housing market, unanticipated increases of inflation, combined with the tax deductibility of interest, made housing a particularly good investment over the 1960–1980 period.

9 In the U.S. economy, wage indexation is neither very widespread nor complete. This absence of strong indexation probably eased the adjustment to supply shocks.

10 Stabilization policy involves choosing an optimal path of inflation and unemployment. The choice is between more or less rapid paths of recovery. The more rapid path reduces unemployment rapidly but does so without making large inroads on inflation. To reduce inflation quickly, unemployment must be high and/or recovery slow.

11 The political business cycle hypothesis emphasizes the direction of change of the economy. For incumbents to win an election, the unemployment rate should be falling and the inflation rate not worsening.

KEY TERMS

Unemployment pool
Layoffs
Involuntary quits
Accessions
Separations
Duration of spells of unemployment
Natural rate of unemployment
Frequency of unemployment

Targeted programs
Costs of cyclical unemployment
Okun's law
Anticipated inflation
Redistribution of wealth
Fisher equation
Indexation
COLA
Extended Phillips curve
Political business cycle

PROBLEMS

1 Discuss strategies whereby the government (federal, state, or local) could reduce unemployment in or among:
   (*a*) Depressed industries
   (*b*) Unskilled workers
   (*c*) Depressed geographical regions
   (*d*) Teenagers
   Include comments on the ***type*** of unemployment you would expect in these various groups (that is, relative durations of unemployment spells).
2 Discuss how the following changes would affect the natural or structural rate of unemployment. Comment also on the side effects of these changes.
   (*a*) Elimination of unions
   (*b*) Increased participation of women in the labor market
   (*c*) Larger fluctuations in the ***level*** of aggregate demand
   (*d*) An increase in unemployment benefits
   (*e*) Elimination of minimum wages
   (*f*) Larger fluctuations in the ***composition*** of aggregate demand
3 Discuss the differences in unemployment between adults and teenagers. What does this imply about the types of jobs (on average) the different groups are getting?
4 Some people say that inflation can be reduced in the long run without an increase in unemployment, and so we should reduce inflation to zero. Others say a steady rate of inflation at, say, 6 percent is not so bad, and that should be our goal. Evaluate these two arguments and describe what, in your opinion, are good long-run goals for inflation and unemployment. How would these be achieved?
5 The following information is to be used for calculations of the unemployment rate. There are two major groups, adults and teenagers. Teenagers account for 10 percent of the labor force and adults for 90 percent. Adults are divided into men and women. Women account for 35 percent of the adult labor force. The following table shows the unemployment rates for the groups.

Group	Unemployment rate, u
Teenagers	20%
Adults:	
Men	9%
Women	8.5%

   (*a*) How do the numbers in this table compare (roughly) with the numbers for the U.S. economy?
   (*b*) Calculate the aggregate unemployment rate.
   (*c*) Assume the unemployment rate for teenagers rises from 20 to 30 percent. What is the effect on

female unemployment? (Assume 60 percent of the teenagers are men.) What is the effect on the aggregate unemployment rate?

(*d*) Assume the share of women in the adult labor force increases to 40 percent. What is the effect on the unemployment rate? What is the effect on the aggregate unemployment rate?

(*e*) Relate your answers to methods of estimating the natural rate of unemployment.

6 Use the *Economic Report of the President* to find the unemployment data for the years 1975, 1979, and 1982. Use, as labor force groups, males and females, 16 to 19 years of age and 20 and over (that is, four groups). Calculate what 1975 and 1982 unemployment would have been if each group in 1975 and 1982 had the unemployment rate of the group in 1979. What does the answer tell you?

7 In the *Economic Report of the President*, you will find data on the duration of the unemployment. Compare the distribution of unemployment by duration in 1978 and 1982. What relationship do you find between duration and the overall unemployment rate?

8 (*a*) What are the economic costs of inflation? Distinguish between anticipated and unanticipated inflation.

(*b*) Do you think anything is missing from the list of costs of inflation that economists present? If so, what?

9 A reduction in minimum wages during summer months reduces the cost of labor to firms, but it also reduces the income per hour that a teenager receives.

(*a*) Who benefits from the measure? Firms who have access to cheaper labor, teenagers who otherwise would not have a job, or both?

(*b*) Who "pays" for the program? Teenagers who would have a job anyway but who now receive less pay than they would have, and/or other workers who are displaced by the cheaper labor on reduced minimum wages? Spell out what you think is the answer to these questions and decide whether you think the program is a good idea.

10 Consider Table 14-13 which shows the link between output growth and the path of unemployment.

(*a*) Suppose the trend growth rate of output is 2.0 percent. Use the data in Table 14-13 to show the time path of unemployment under this assumption, using the actual growth rates given in the table.

(*b*) Suppose growth rates were 6.0, 5.5, 4.5, and 4.4. What would the unemployment rate be in 1987?

11 Evaluate the following argument that attempts to dispose of the notion of the political business cycle. "The public is too sophisticated to think that it makes much difference which party is running the economy. Both the Democrats and Republicans want the economy to boom, and want to keep inflation low. Both have access to the best economists available. Why would anyone think economic performance would be different with one party than with the other?"

15

BUDGET DEFICITS, INFLATION, AND THE PUBLIC DEBT

> The scary thing is what happens if you look ahead. It is a very different situation from what budgeteers have ever faced before. . . . We have this enormous problem that, if policy is not changed, we will be financing a very, very large government deficit relative to anything. . . .
>
> Alice Rivlin, Director of the Congressional Budget Office[1]

In 1983 the U.S. economy faced the prospect of budget deficits expected to average more than 5 percent of GNP over the next 5 years, by far the highest peacetime deficits ever. Except during the great depression, the pre-World War II federal budget was typically in surplus during peacetime and in deficit during wartime. Table 15-1 sets the prospective deficits in post-World War II perspective. The deficit has been increasing as a percentage of GNP over most of the period since 1950. Even so, the projected deficits of 5.6 percent of GNP through 1988 are well outside the range of peacetime experience.

[1] In W. Craig Stubblebine and Thomas D. Willett (eds.), *Reaganomics: A Midterm Report*, Institute for Contemporary Studies, San Francisco, 1983, pp. 136–137.

TABLE 15-1 FEDERAL BUDGET DEFICITS (*As a percentage of GNP*)

1950–1959	1960–1969	1970–1982	1983–1988*
0.4	0.8	2.1	5.6

* Projection. Data are averages for period shown.
Sources: Economic Report of the President, *1983, and* Reducing the Deficit: Spending and Revenue Options, *Congressional Budget Office, February 1983.*

What are the implications of such deficits? A major concern is *crowding out.* The government will have to borrow to pay for its spending. The fear is that massive government borrowing will cause interest rates to rise, which will crowd out private investment, thereby reduce productivity growth, and hence slow down the long-run growth in the standard of living. An alternative possibility is that the higher interest rates caused by the deficits will lead to Federal Reserve intervention to try to keep rates from rising too high. The Fed, some fear, will intervene by buying government debt, thereby creating more money, and causing inflation.

The projected budget deficits are a result of a fiscal revolution created by the Reagan administration in 1981–1982. In 1981 the Congress passed a three-stage program of tax cuts, which reduced personal income tax rates by 25 percent, starting with a 5 percent cut in 1981, a 10 percent reduction in July 1982, and a third cut effective July 1983. At the same time, taxation of corporations was reduced, with the announced aim of encouraging investment and growth. The tax cuts produced the deficits that are expected for the eighties.

The tax cuts were introduced because the Reagan administration believed that the federal government was taking too large a share of resources. Evaluation of the tax cuts thus involves fundamental questions of the proper size and activities of the government in the economy, and the balance between the need for raising revenue against the disincentive effects of taxation.

At the time the tax cuts were introduced, the Reagan administration and an associated group of *supply-side economists* argued that the tax cuts would not create any deficits. They argued that the tax cuts would be self-financing because lower tax rates would cause people to work harder, so much harder that total income taxes would rise. Similarly, it was argued, the increase in investment would lead to higher output, and again to higher total revenue received by the government despite the reduction in tax rates. In other words, this group argued that tax cuts would *increase* total government tax revenue. Moreover, they argued, problems of crowding out would not occur because the tax cuts would induce people to save more.

The tax cuts of 1981–1982 and the prospects for unprecedented deficits in the eighties raise many questions that we have not yet analyzed. This chapter therefore continues and extends the discussion of fiscal policy in Chapters 3 and 5. We examine the linkages among deficits, money creation, inflation, and interest rates. We discuss the size and significance of the public debt, study the relationship between changes in tax rates and the amount of revenue received by the government, and briefly take up the issue of the size and role of government in the economy.

15-1 THE MECHANICS OF FINANCING THE BUDGET

In this section we examine how the federal government finances its spending. We are particularly interested in the relationship between the federal government's deficit and changes in the stocks of money and government debt.

How does the government pay for its spending? Directly, it pays for most of its spending with checks, drawn on a Federal Reserve bank. Aside from the fact that the checks are drawn on a bank in which private individuals do not have accounts, payments made by the government looks much like check payments made by anyone else. Like an individual, the federal government must have funds in the accounts on which it writes checks. So the question of how the federal government finances its spending is the same as the question of how it makes sure that it has funds in the bank accounts (at the Federal Reserve System) on which it writes its checks.

The Treasury is the agency of the federal government that collects government receipts and makes payments for the government. The government's accounts at the Federal Reserve System are held and operated by the Treasury. The Treasury receives the bulk of its receipts from taxes.

How does the Treasury make payments when its tax receipts are insufficient to cover its expenditures, in other words, when there is a budget deficit? The answer is that it has to borrow. In describing how the Treasury borrows to finance its deficit, we shall step back a moment from the particular institutional arrangements of the U.S. economy and talk in general terms of a treasury financing its budget deficit by borrowing either from the public or from its central bank. We shall talk as if the Treasury can borrow directly from the central bank by selling it securities. Alternatively, it can sell securities (debt) to the public.[2]

DEBT-FINANCED DEFICITS

When the Treasury finances its deficit by borrowing from the private sector, it is engaged in debt financing. In this case the Treasury sells Treasury bonds or bills to the private sector. Individuals and firms (including banks) pay for the securities with checks. The checks are deposited either in Treasury accounts at private banks ("tax and loan accounts") or at the central bank. The funds can then be spent by the Treasury in the same way as tax receipts.

MONEY-FINANCED DEFICITS

When the Treasury borrows from the central bank to finance its deficit, it is engaged in money financing. In the case of money financing, the central bank purchases some of the debt of the Treasury.

[2] Foreign central banks, financial institutions, and individuals buy some U.S. Treasury securities and thus help finance the deficit. We treat sales of securities to foreigners as sales to the public.

There is a major difference between the Treasury's borrowing from the public and its borrowing from the central bank. When the central bank buys Treasury debt, it pays for the debt by giving the Treasury a check on the central bank—that is, by creating high-powered money. When the Treasury spends the deposit it has received at the central bank in exchange for its debt, it leaves the private sector with larger holdings of high-powered money. By contrast, when the Treasury borrows from the public, it receives and then spends high-powered money, thus leaving the amount of high-powered money in the hands of the public unchanged—except for a brief transition period between the sale of securities and expenditures by the Treasury. Since the stock of high-powered money is an important macroeconomic variable, the distinction between selling debt to the public and selling it to the central bank is essential.

The distinction between money and debt financing can be further clarified by noting that Treasury sales of securities to the central bank are referred to as monetizing the debt, meaning that the central bank creates (high-powered) money to finance the debt purchase. Yet another way of looking at the difference between sales to (borrowing from) the central bank and sales to the public is to ask, What is the net change in the private sector's portfolio after the Treasury has made and financed its expenditures? Consider first the case of borrowing from the public, or selling debt to the public. In this case, the public holds more debt, having bought the Treasury offering, and holds an unchanged quantity of high-powered money, since the Treasury spends the money it obtains from the debt sale to cover its deficit. Consider next the case where the deficit is financed by sale of debt to the central bank. Here, the private sector's debt holding is unchanged, while its holding of high-powered money is increased. The reason is that Treasury expenditures were financed by the creation of high-powered money by the central bank.

The government deficit can thus be financed in two ways: by selling debt to the private sector and by borrowing from the central bank. Let ΔB_p be the value of sales of government bonds to the private sector and ΔB_f be the value of sales of bonds to the central bank. Let H be the stock of high-powered money, and recall that BD is the budget deficit, measured in *real* terms. P is the price level. We have just seen that[3]

$$P \cdot BD = \Delta B_f + \Delta B_p \simeq \Delta H + \Delta B_p \tag{1}$$

Equation (1) is called the government's budget constraint. It states that the nominal budget deficit is financed by borrowing either from the central bank (ΔB_f) or from the private sector (ΔB_p). The change in the central bank's holdings of Treasury debts causes a corresponding change in high-powered money (ΔH), so that we can say that the budget deficit is financed either by

[3] As we saw in Chap. 9, the stock of high-powered money may change for reasons other than open market operations. For that reason we use the symbol for "approximately equal to" ($\simeq$) in Eq. (1). The change in the central bank's holdings of government bonds is only approximately equal to the change in high-powered money.

selling debt to the public or by increasing the stock of high-powered money. It is in this sense that the central bank "monetizes" the debt.[4]

The view that the deficit is financed either by selling debt to the public or by increasing the stock of high-powered money looks at the government sector as a whole, including, or "consolidating," the central bank with the Treasury in the government sector. When one thinks of the government sector as a whole, relative to the private sector, the transactions in which the central bank buys debt from the Treasury or lends to the Treasury are seen as mere bookkeeping entries within the government sector.

THE FED AND THE TREASURY

In many countries it is useful to think of the government sector as a whole, without bothering to distinguish between the actions of the treasury and the central bank. However, in the United States the Fed retains considerable power and independence. Indeed, the Fed does not generally buy debt directly from the Treasury, and so does not directly finance the deficit in the way just described. The great bulk of Fed purchases of debt are made directly from the public. However, that should be thought of as only an institutional detail. For although the Fed by and large does not buy directly from the Treasury, it can do so indirectly by buying securities from the public. Suppose that the Fed is conducting open market purchases at the same time as the Treasury is selling debt to the public. The net effect of the combined Treasury sale of debt and Fed open market puchase is that the Fed ends up holding more Treasury debt, which is precisely what would happen if it bought directly from the Treasury.

In the United States the Fed is largely responsible for the division of the total deficit, *BD* in Equation (1), between the change in high-powered money and the change in government debt held by the private sector. There is no necessary association between the size of the government deficit in the United States and increases in the stock of high-powered money. If the Fed does not choose to conduct open market purchases when the Treasury is borrowing, the stock of high-powered money is not affected by the Treasury's deficit.

Nonetheless, there have been occasions in the past when there was a more or less automatic association between Fed open market purchases and Treasury borrowing. This link was most direct when the Fed was committed to maintaining constant the nominal interest rates on government bonds, in the period from 1941 to 1951. As we saw in Chapter 5, an increase in the government deficit tends to increase the nominal interest rate. If the Fed were committed to maintaining constant the nominal interest rate, an increase in the deficit would force it to conduct an open market purchase to keep the nominal interest rate from rising. Thus there would be a link between Treasury borrowing and Fed open market purchases.

[4] Note that the government budget constraint, Eq. (1), also shows that for a given value of the deficit, changes in the stock of high-powered money are matched by offsetting changes in the public's holdings of government debt. A positive ΔH matched by a negative ΔB_p is nothing other than an open market purchase.

The Fed's commitment to maintain constant nominal interest rates on government bonds ended formally in 1951 in the "Accord" between the Fed and the Treasury. Even though, after 1951, the Fed had no formal commitment to maintain constant nominal interest rates, its long-time policy of having target nominal interest rates—which could change from time to time—also led to an association between deficits and Fed open market purchases. Given the Fed's target interest rates, Treasury borrowing which would have led to interest rate increases triggered Fed open market purchases to keep the interest rate from rising above its target level. Thus, for much of the fifties and sixties, there was a link between increased Treasury borrowing and Fed open market purchases.

Recently, the Fed has moved over to policies which concentrate more on the behavior of the nominal money stock. A Fed commitment to producing a given money stock breaks the link between government deficits and the creation of high-powered money. Now the Fed creates high-powered money at a rate that should result in money's growing at the target rate, and the change in the stock of high-powered money is therefore not necessarily directly associated with the size of the government deficit.

DEFICITS AND THE NATIONAL DEBT

It follows from Equation (1) that when the budget is not balanced, the Treasury changes the net amount of claims on it held by the private sector and the Fed. Those claims are the securities the Treasury sells to the private sector and (indirectly) the Fed, and they represent claims for future interest payments. The total stock of government bonds (or claims on the government) outstanding constitutes the *national*, or *public*, debt. When the budget is in deficit, the national debt increases—the stock of claims against the Treasury increases. When the budget is in surplus, the national debt decreases. The Treasury takes in more taxes than it pays out, and can use the excess to retire (or buy back) previously issued debt.

The national debt is a direct consequence of past deficits in the federal budget. The national debt increases when there is a budget deficit and decreases when the budget is in surplus. The way the national debt is divided between private sector claims on the Treasury and high-powered money depends on past monetary policy. If the Fed has financed a large proportion of each deficit in the past, then the ratio of high-powered money to the national debt is large. If the Fed has financed only a small part of each deficit in the past, then the ratio of high-powered money to national debt is small.

Table 15-2 shows the stock of public debt outstanding, the holders of the public debt, and the monetary base. During 1982 the public debt increased by $162.3 billion. Of this increase only $8.3 billion was bought by the Fed. The remainder was bought by the private sector, that is, individuals, banks and other financial institutions, corporations, and foreign governments or investors.

TABLE 15-2 THE PUBLIC DEBT AND THE MONETARY BASE (*December 31, billion dollars*)

	1981		1982		Change	
Public debt outstanding	825.4		987.7		162.3	
Held by:						
Federal Reserve		131.0		139.3		8.3
Private sector		694.4		848.4		154.0
Monetary base	173.8		179.3		5.5	

Note: Public debt outstanding is defined as gross public debt less holdings by U.S. government agencies and trust funds. Private sector includes the rest of the world.
Source: Federal Reserve Bulletin, *May 1983.*

The table also shows the change in the monetary base, which was $5.5 billion and thus less than the Fed purchases of public debt. Accordingly, other items in the Fed balance sheet declined over the period, thus reducing the increase in the monetary base below the amount implied by the purchases of public debt.

The Treasury sells securities more or less continuously. There is, for instance, a weekly Treasury bill auction, at which prospective buyers of Treasury bills (lenders to the federal government) submit sealed bids specifying how much they are prepared to lend at different interest rates. The Treasury sells the amount of Treasury bills it has offered at the auction to the bidders who offer the highest prices, or the lowest interest rates.[5] Longer-term debt issues are less frequent. Issues of Treasury debt are not all made for the purpose of financing the budget deficit. Most debt issues are made to refinance parts of the national debt that are maturing. For example, 6 months after a 180-day Treasury bill is issued, the Treasury has to pay the face amount of the Treasury bill to the holder. Typically, the Treasury obtains the funds to make those payments by further borrowing. The process by which the Treasury (with the help and advice of the Fed) finances and refinances the national debt is known as *debt management.* Only part of debt management is concerned with financing the current budget deficit. Most of it is concerned with the consequences of past budget deficits.

We have discussed in this section the financing of budget deficits. The same principles apply in the case of a budget surplus. When the government has an excess of tax revenues over outlays, there is a surplus. Rather than having to borrow, the Treasury is in a position to *retire debt.* Practically, what happens is the following: The excess of tax receipts over outlays means that the government's tax and loan accounts and accounts at the Fed are building

[5] Technically, no interest is paid on Treasury bills. Instead, a Treasury bill is a promise by the Treasury to pay a given amount on a given date, say, $100 on June 30. Before June 30, the Treasury bill sells for a discount at less than $100, with the discount implying a rate of interest. For instance, if the Treasury bill just described sold for $97.50 on January 1, the holder of the bill for 6 months would earn a little more than 5 percent per annum, or 2.5 percent for 6 months.

up. The Treasury responds by not renewing maturing debt, but rather by paying off bonds or Treasury bills that are coming due. Thus the stock of public debt outstanding declines.

Summary

Five main points have been made in this section.

1 Federal government spending is financed through taxes and through borrowing, which is necessary when the budget is in deficit.
2 Borrowing may be from the private sector or indirectly from the Federal Reserve System.
3 Lending by the Fed to the Treasury changes the stock of high-powered money, whereas lending by the private sector to the Treasury does not affect the stock of high-powered money.
4 The stock of claims held by the Fed and the private sector against the Treasury—the national debt—changes with the budget deficit. The national debt increases when there is a budget deficit and decreases when there is a budget surplus.
5 Because the deficit can be financed in two ways, there is no *necessary* connection between the budget deficit and changes in the stock of high-powered money. Equation (1), the government budget constraint, says only that the *sum* of changes in the stock of debt and changes in high-powered money is approximately equal to the budget deficit.

15-2 BUDGET FACTS

In this section we review the main facts about government spending and receipts, starting with the federal government.

Receipts

Table 15-3 shows the sources of federal revenues. Data are presented as a percentage of GNP.

TABLE 15-3 FEDERAL REVENUES BY SOURCE (*Unified budget, fiscal years, as a percentage of GNP*)

Source	1965	1970	1975	1980	1981	1982	1983*
Individual income taxes	7.4	9.3	8.3	9.5	10.0	9.8	8.9
Corporate income taxes	3.9	3.4	2.7	2.5	2.1	1.6	1.3
Social insurance taxes	3.4	4.6	5.7	6.1	6.4	6.6	6.6
Excise taxes	2.2	1.6	1.1	0.9	1.4	1.2	1.2
All other	0.9	1.0	1.0	1.0	1.0	1.1	1.0
Total	17.8	19.9	18.8	20.0	20.9	20.3	19.0

* Predicted.
Source: Reducing the Federal Deficit, *Congressional Budget Office, February 1982 and February 1983.*

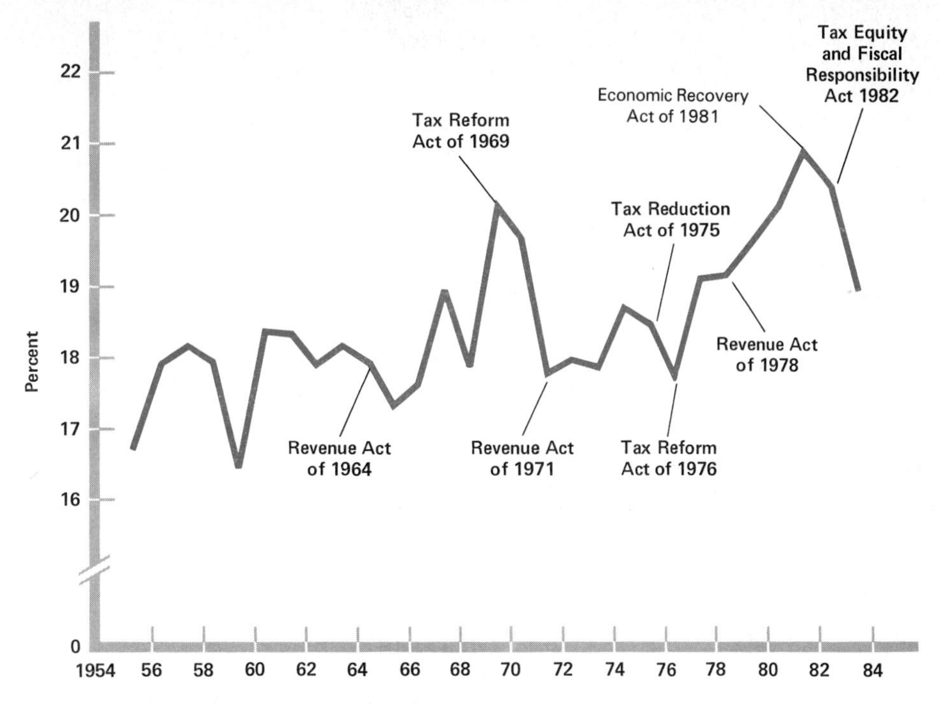

FIGURE 15-1 FEDERAL REVENUES AS A PERCENTAGE OF GNP (fiscal years, unified budget). (*Sources: The Budget of the United States, 1983* and Data Resources, Inc. Estimate for 1983 from the Congressional Budget Office)

The first point to note is that federal budget revenues for the past 20 years have been in the range of 17.5 to 21 percent of GNP. In that range 1981 represents a high and 1965 a low. Figure 15-1 shows revenues as a fraction of GNP since 1955, and indicates the major tax acts that have affected revenues. The figure shows a rising revenue share from 1975 to 1981, which is now being drastically reversed by the combined effects of the 1981–1982 legislation, the *Economic Recovery Act (ERTA)* of 1981, and the *Tax Equity and Fiscal Responsibility Act (TEFRA)* of 1982. ERTA is largely responsible for the prospective deficits seen in Table 15-1.

Consider next the composition of revenues. The chief point is that personal income taxes have since 1970 accounted for almost half of total revenues. Although income tax rates were sharply reduced by the 1981 tax cuts, the individual income tax will continue to be the largest single source of revenue.

Aside from the personal income tax, there are two other important sources of revenue, corporate income taxes and social insurance taxes. Social insurance taxes are taxes on labor income levied on employers and employees. The tax is paid by workers and employers and finances retirement benefits through the Social Security system. Social Security taxes have risen sharply in the past 20 years and are now the second largest source of government revenue. Corporate income taxes show an opposite trend. The corporate income tax is becoming a relatively small source of revenue, while social insurance taxes have become a very large part.

The excise tax entry reflects federal taxes on particular goods such as liquor, tobacco, gasoline, and airline tickets. The item "All other" includes a vast variety of revenues, from estate taxes to custom duties.

Outlays

Federal outlays as a fraction of GNP, and the composition of these outlays, are shown in Table 15-4. Note that the share of government outlays in GNP shows a *steeply* rising trend, from 17.8 percent in 1965 to 25.1 percent in 1983. With revenues at about 20 percent of GNP, the magnitude of the deficit problem is obvious.

Consider now the *composition* of government outlays. Nearly half of government spending finances *entitlements.* An entitlement program is one that sets requirements that have to be met by recipients of the government spending, but spending is otherwise automatic. For instance, unemployment benefits are paid automatically to those who have been unemployed for the necessary amount of time. Similarly, eligible hospital bills are paid by the Medicare program. In these programs, once the law has established eligibility, demand determines outlays in the sense that anyone who qualifies can ask for payment. Because entitlement to the benefit determines spending, these programs can show large swings in outlays. In a recession entitlements are high, and therefore outlays are high. These programs, as is apparent from

TABLE 15-4 COMPOSITON OF FEDERAL SPENDING, 1965–1983 (*As a percentage of GNP*)

Category	1965	1970	1975	1980	1982	1983*
National defense	7.2	8.1	5.8	5.3	6.2	6.7
Entitlements and other mandatory spending						
Social Security benefits	2.6	3.0	4.2	4.5	5.0	5.3
Medicare and Medicaid	†	1.0	1.5	1.9	2.2	2.4
Farm price supports	0.4	0.4	‡	0.1	0.4	0.6
Other entitlements	2.1	2.2	4.5	4.0	3.7	3.9
Subtotal	5.1	6.6	10.2	10.5	11.3	12.2
Nondefense discretionary spending and other	4.2	3.9	4.3	4.7	3.7	3.5
Net interest	1.3	1.5	1.6	2.0	2.8	2.7
Total	17.8	20.1	21.9	22.5	24.1	25.1

* Predicted.
† Predecessor programs counted elsewhere.
‡ Less than 0.1 percent.
Note: Details may not add to totals because of rounding.
Source: Congressional Budget Office.

Table 15-4, have been growing rapidly over the last 15 years. *Indeed as Table 15-4 shows, almost all the increase in federal outlays between 1965 and 1983 is accounted for by increases in entitlement spending.*

Along with entitlements and mandatory programs, national defense expenditures and nondefense discretionary spending (programs such as the National Science Foundation; national parks; and federal functions such as justice, education, or the FBI) are the major outlay areas. These programs are approved year by year, and every year budget funds are allocated. The programs thus differ from entitlements where eligibility determines spending. Here budget allocation determines outlays. Table 15-4 shows how defense spending fell as a percentage of GNP through 1980 and then began to grow rapidly.

The entry to which we want to draw attention is "Net interest." This represents the interest payments on the public debt outstanding, net of interest receipts by the government. Net interest by 1982 accounted for over 10 percent of total federal government outlays. The rapid growth of the share of net interest from 1975 to 1982 was at the center of concern in some discussions of debt-financed budget deficits, as we shall see in Section 15-4 of this chapter.[6]

State and Local Government Spending and Financing

Figure 15-2 shows state and local government expenditure (on purchases of goods and services and transfers) as a percentage of GNP. State and local government expenditure has increased markedly as a percentage of GNP over the period since 1955. In 1982 the share was about 13.3 percent compared with 25.1 percent for the Federal government.

Most state and local government spending is on purchases of goods and services and constitutes an important component of aggregate demand. In fact, state and local governments purchase more goods and services than the federal government does. In 1982, state and local governments spent $390 billion on goods and services, compared with $258 billion for the federal government. The rapid increase in state and local government purchases relative to federal purchases of goods and services began in the late sixties. The goods and services that state and local governments buy are typically education, highways, hospitals, fire protection, garbage removal, and police protection. State and local governments spend relatively small amounts on transfer payments. With regard to interest payments, state and local govern-

[6] There is a complicated issue about the right measurement of interest payments in the budget. We have seen from the Fisher equation that nominal interest rates rise when the inflation rate is high. The high interest rate corresponds to the loss in value of the dollars in which debts are paid off. It is argued (correctly) that if we count all interest payments as an expense to the government, then we should add in the amount the government gains because the value of its debt is falling as a result of inflation. In effect, this implies that we should compute interest payments in the government budget by multiplying the amount of debt by the *real* and not the nominal interest rate. Although this would be a better procedure, we do not adopt it here, rather remaining with the budget as it is published by the government—for ease of reading. This correction would *reduce* the measured budget deficit, the more so, the higher the inflation rate.

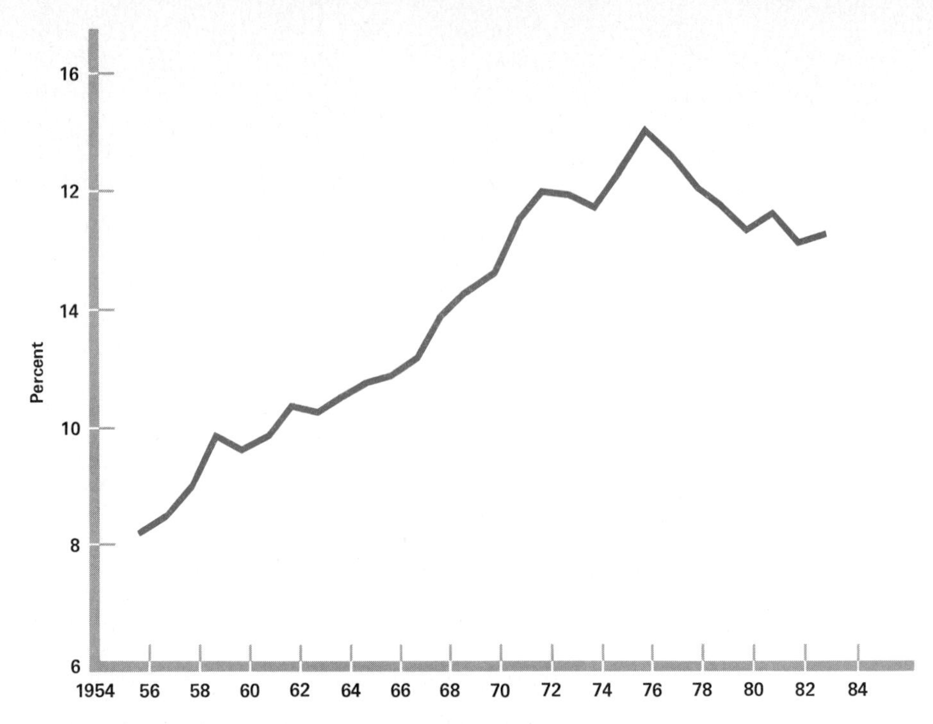

FIGURE 15-2 STATE AND LOCAL GOVERNMENT EXPENDITURES AS A PERCENTAGE OF GNP. (*Source:* Data Resources, Inc.)

ments actually, on balance, receive more interest than they pay out. This is a result of the budget surpluses they have been running which have enabled them, taken together, to purchase federal securities. Although many state and local governments run deficits (for example, New York City) and have to borrow, thus accounting for the existence of state and local government securities, others run surpluses and purchase securities.

The major sources of state and local government revenues are indirect taxes, primarily the sales tax. Other large sources of funds are state income taxes, property taxes, and grants-in-aid from the federal government.

State and local government financing differs from federal financing mainly in that the state and local governments cannot borrow from the Fed. Thus, when a state or local government runs a deficit, it has to borrow by selling securities to the private sector.

Two major questions arise in connection with the role of state and local governments in the economy. The first concerns the determinants of state and local government spending. In large part, this is determined through the political process. Although state and local spending as a proportion of GNP has been rising, it would not be wise to assume that this trend will continue. The political reaction to increasing taxes, especially at the local level, may well reverse, or at least halt, the trend shown in Figure 15-2, as indeed appears to be happening in the figure in the early eighties.

The second question concerns the effects of state and local government spending on the economy. Here the analysis of federal government spending and taxing presented in earlier chapters is relevant. There are multiplier effects for changes in state and local spending, just as there are for changes in federal spending.

15-3 THE 1981 TAX CUTS AND DEFICIT PROSPECTS FOR THE EIGHTIES

Table 15-1 summarizes post-World War II deficit experience, which is shown in more detail in Figure 15-3. It is apparent from the figure that the actual deficit is very strongly cyclical. When the economy is in a recession, revenues are low and outlays are high. Conversely, when the economy is booming, as in 1973, for example, the deficit is reduced or the surplus increased.

Aside from the strongly cyclical pattern of the budget we also note from both Table 15-1 and Figure 15-3 that there has been an unmistakable tendency toward larger deficits. In the 1950s surpluses and deficits alternated. In

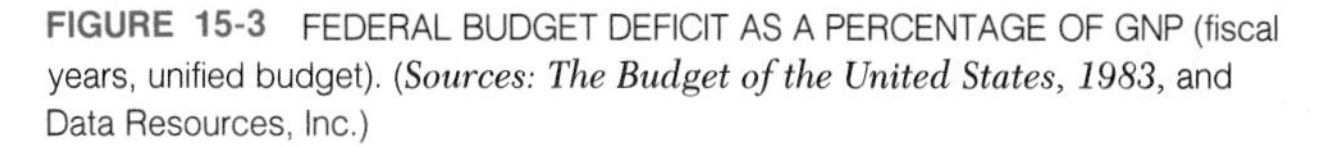

FIGURE 15-3 FEDERAL BUDGET DEFICIT AS A PERCENTAGE OF GNP (fiscal years, unified budget). (*Sources: The Budget of the United States, 1983,* and Data Resources, Inc.)

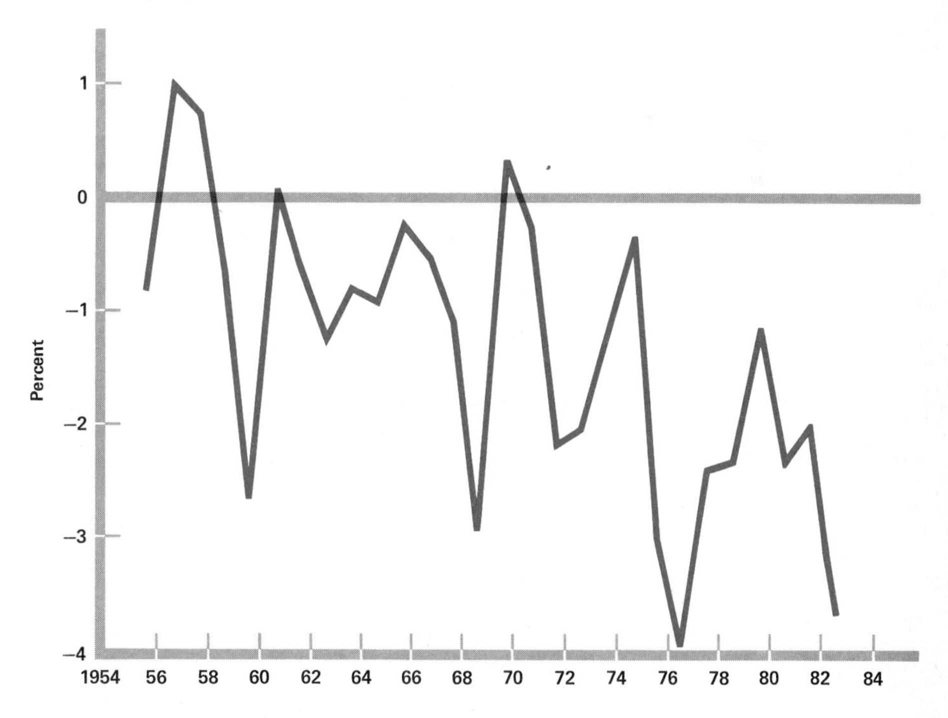

the 1960s there were still occasional surpluses. But since 1969 the Federal budget has been in deficit every year, and increasingly so. And, of course, the prospect is for even larger deficits for the remainder of the eighties. What caused those deficits?

The Deficit of the Mid-1980s

The growing deficit since 1981 reflects a combination of *cyclical deficits* and *structural deficits*. The structural, or full-employment,[7] deficits result from net reductions in tax rates. Table 15-5 shows a breakdown of the sources of the budget deficit. For example, in fiscal 1984 the budget deficit is predicted to be 5.6 percent of GNP. In the absence of the 1981–1982 tax reductions the deficit would be a full 2.9 percent of GNP less. If the economy were at full employment, given the new tax structure, the deficit would be an extra 2.9 percent less. Thus without the tax cuts and at full employment the budget would show a surplus.

These calculations are only approximate because the estimation of outlays and receipts under different tax structures or at different unemployment rates is not entirely precise, and estimates therefore differ among various agencies. But the calculations do help to show the two large sources of deficit in the early 1980s—the low level of activity and the 1981–1982 tax cuts.[8]

[7] In the early 1980s the term "full-employment deficit" began to drop out of official administration use, to be replaced by the "structural deficit." There are probably two reasons for this change. First, after the many economic shocks of the 1970s, it was no longer so clear what was the appropriate unemployment rate to use in calculating the full-employment budget. And second, use of the "full-employment deficit" would be a constant reminder of how far the economy was in the early eighties—particularly in 1982–1983—from full employment.

[8] The 1983 *Economic Report of the President* uses the rule of thumb of an extra $25 billion deficit in fiscal 1983 per extra point of unemployment. Therefore with unemployment of 10.5 percent and a full-employment rate of 6.5 percent, the cyclical effect is $100 billion. The Bureau of Economic Analysis of the Department of Commerce estimates a cyclical effect, with the same 6 percent full-employment bench-mark, of $109 billion. See *Economic Report of the President*, 1983, p. 26, and *Survey of Current Business*, April 1983, pp. 25–26. See also F. de Leeuw and T. Holloway, "The High-Employment Budget: Revised Estimates and Automatic Inflation Effects," *Survey of Current Business*, April 1982. For an international comparison of budget deficits, see "Public Sector Deficits: Problems and Policy Implications," *Occasional Papers*, OECD, June 1983.

TABLE 15-5 THE BUDGET DEFICIT OF THE MID-1980s (*Unified budget, fiscal years, percentage of GNP*)

	1981	1982	1983*	1984*	1985*
Actual deficit	2.0	3.6	6.1	5.6	5.6
Due to:					
1981–1982 tax bills	—	1.3	2.0	2.9	3.3
Economic slack	1.4	2.8	3.8	2.9	2.3

* Predicted.
Note: The contribution of the recession is calculated as the difference between the actual deficit and the high-employment deficit.
Source: Calculated from The Outlook for Economic Recovery, *Congressional Budget Office, February 1983, and* Reducing the Deficit, *February 1983.*

The unusual aspect of the budget prospects for the 1980s is that the deficit is not expected to disappear as the economy returns to full employment. This is the first time that budget deficits of this magnitude have been expected in peacetime in the United States. The Reagan administration in its 1984 budget proposed standby taxes, which would go into effect in 1985 if budget deficits were still high. This would effectively remove the threat of massive budget deficits. But the Congress did not show much sign of voting for such a standby tax. Many observers in 1983 believed that there would, in any event, be a tax increase in 1985, after the 1984 elections, and that the budget deficits shown in Table 15-5 would not happen. But we will, nonetheless, have to ask in the next section what would happen if there were such large deficits.

Tax Cuts, Deficits, and Government Spending

No political candidate or officeholder is in favor of deficits. How, then, did the tax cuts of 1981 pass when they resulted in such large deficits? There are two explanations. The first is that supply-side economists argued that the tax cuts would produce *more,* not less, revenue for the government. The other is an argument of political economy that says that Congress will spend whatever revenue it receives and that therefore the only way to get it to cut spending is to cut its revenues. We take up the two arguments in turn.

TAX CUTS AND GOVERNMENT REVENUE

Much of the controversy surrounding the 1981 tax cuts centered on a highly unusual proposition advanced by supply-side economists: a *cut* in income tax rates will *raise* tax revenues. The idea was highly controversial because it had until then been accepted that lower tax rates usually mean lower government revenues. For example, we saw in Chapter 3 that a tax cut would increase the budget deficit, even when we took into account the expansion in output induced by lower taxes.

But the supply-side economists, some of whom were installed in the U.S. Treasury by the Reagan administration, were certainly not thinking in terms of the simple Keynesian analysis of Chapter 3. Rather they were concentrating on the *incentive effects* of tax cuts. Take the income tax as an example. Anyone who is taxed, say, at 25 percent marginal rate, on income earned receives only 75 percent of the wage for working an extra hour. Supply-siders argued that a cut in income taxes, say, from 25 to 15 percent, would encourage such a person to work harder. For instance, suppose the wage rate is $10 per hour. Before the tax cut a person working 1 extra hour earns, after tax, $7.50; after the tax cut the same extra hour brings in $8.50. Surely, supply-siders argued, such a person would want to work more hours.

Up to this point the analysis is relatively uncontroversial. There is some question whether cuts in tax rates encourage people to work more, because conflicting effects are operating. The cut in the tax rate raises the after-tax wage and therefore makes work more desirable, relative to leisure. But with a higher after-tax wage, a worker needs to work less to support the same

BOX 15-1

THE LAFFER CURVE

Arthur Laffer, of the University of Southern California, is among the best known of the supply-side economists. Figure 1 shows the *Laffer curve,* relating tax revenues to the tax rate. The curve shows total tax revenue first increasing as the tax rate rises and then eventually decreasing.

The argument supporting the shape of the curve is as follows. Assume that we are discussing the income tax rate. When the tax rate is zero, government tax revenue is certainly zero. Hence we have point A on the curve. Further, suppose the tax rate were 100 percent. Then the government would be taking all the income that people earn. There would be no point in working if the government took all earnings, and so income in that case too would be zero. Then tax revenue would also be zero. Accordingly, point B is also a point on the Laffer curve.

Between A and B, though, the government certainly takes in some revenue from taxes. Thus we expect the curve to start to rise from point A as the tax rate is increased from zero to some very small rate, such as 3 percent. Eventually, though, the curve has to come back down to B. Thus at some point it will turn around—perhaps at a tax rate of 60 percent, as shown in Figure 1. Point C is the dividing line: at tax rates below 60 percent, any increase in the tax rate *raises* total tax revenue. At tax rates above 60 percent, any increase in the tax rate *reduces* total revenue. Looking at the same relationship in the opposite direction, we find that at any tax rate above 60 percent, a *cut* in the tax rate will *increase* total tax revenue.

Supply-siders were thus arguing in 1981 that the American economy was to be right of the point where the Laffer curve turns down—say, at some point such as D. There was no evidence to support this assertion, and it does not appear to have been right. But it is a theoretical possibility.

Supply-siders made a similar claim about the effects of cuts in taxes on saving. When tax

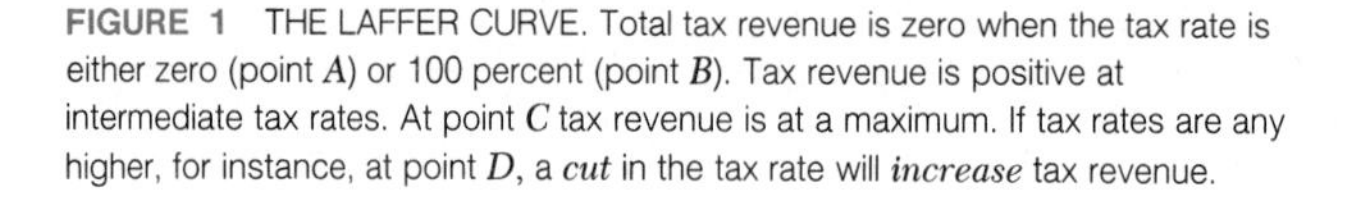

FIGURE 1 THE LAFFER CURVE. Total tax revenue is zero when the tax rate is either zero (point A) or 100 percent (point B). Tax revenue is positive at intermediate tax rates. At point C tax revenue is at a maximum. If tax rates are any higher, for instance, at point D, a *cut* in the tax rate will *increase* tax revenue.

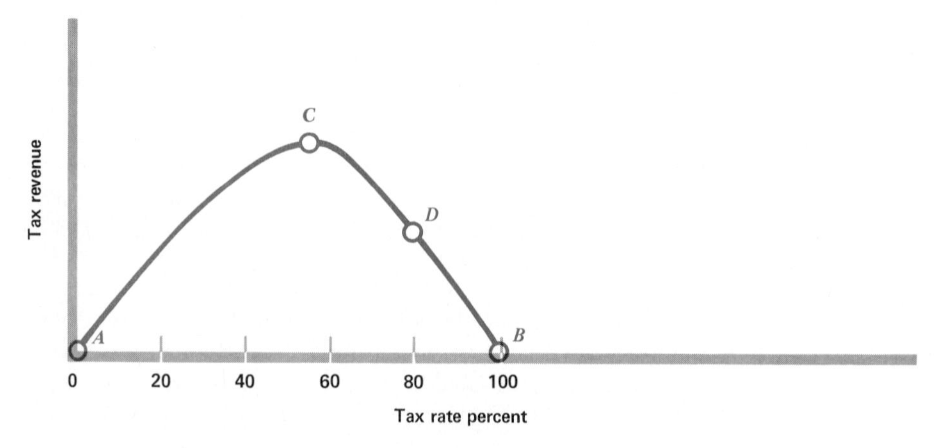

rates on saving are cut, the after-tax rate of return rises. For instance, suppose someone is earning 9 percent before tax on her savings. The tax rate is 25 percent, implying an after-tax rate of return on savings of 6.75 percent (= 0.75 × 9 percent). Now suppose the tax rate is cut to 20 percent. The after-tax rate of return rises to 7.2 (= 0.8 × 9 percent). Surely, supply-siders argued, such a person will save more.* Then there will be more investment, a larger capital stock, and higher output. With output higher, total tax revenue could be higher despite the cut in the tax rate.

Whatever the theoretical possibilities, the 1981 tax cuts did not lead to an increase in government revenue, as Table 15-5 shows. Even if we concentrate on the full-employment budget, we do not see in Table 15-5 an increase in government revenue resulting from the tax cuts. This excessively optimistic element in supply-side economics was never believed by any but a small minority of economists, and is now totally dismissed.† The emphasis on the role of incentives, though, is a valuable component of supply-side analysis and is discussed further in Chapter 17.

* There are conflicting income and substitution effects at work in this case too, and the theoretical effect of the cut in the tax rate on saving is uncertain.
† On the supply-side story, see Michael Evans, *The Truth about Supply-Side Economics* (New York: Basic Books, 1983), and Jude Wanniski, *The Way the World Works* (New York: Touchstone, 1978). For a critical view, see Robert Lekachman, *Greed Is Not Enough: Reganomics* (New York: Pantheon, 1982).

standard of living. Perhaps when the after-tax wage rises, the response is to work less, earn more income, and have more leisure. For example, suppose someone is working 40 hours at an after-tax wage of $7.50, earning $300 per week. Now the after-tax wage rises to $8.50. By working 38 hours, the worker earns $323 per week—income and leisure have both risen.[9] However, empirical evidence, discussed in Chapter 17, suggests that a given worker will work more when the after-tax wage rises. Further, there is an unambiguous increase in the number of people working when wages rise—people who used to stay home now enter the labor force to find work. So on balance a cut in tax rates will increase output through supply-side incentive effects.

But the supply-side claim was stronger than a claim that a cut in income tax rates would motivate people to work more. The supply-side claim was that, despite the cut in the tax rate, total tax revenue would rise because a lot more work would be done. To see the point, we use the simple formula

$$\text{Income tax revenue} = \text{income tax rate} \times \text{income} \tag{2}$$

The supply-side claim was that when the tax rate fell, income would rise enough that total income tax revenue would increase. For instance, suppose the tax rate was cut from 20 to 15 percent. Suppose income was originally

[9] If you have taken a course in microeconomics, you will recognize that the substitution effect of the increase in the after-tax wage causes the worker to work more, while the income effect reduces work. The net effect is therefore ambiguous.

equal to $2 trillion. Taxes would thus be $400 billion to begin with. With a tax rate of 15 percent, income would have to rise to $2,667 billion for total revenue from the income tax to increase. It is rare, indeed, that income rises by one-third within a short time—but that is the size of the increase that would be needed if taxes were cut by one-quarter, as in the example of this paragraph.

TAX CUTS AND GOVERNMENT SPENDING

Quite another motive than supply-side arguments also led the Reagan administration to cut tax rates in 1981, despite the high deficits that would probably result over the next few years. That was the argument that the only way to get Congress to cut government spending is to reduce the revenue it receives.

The administration believed that unless tax rates were cut, and tax revenues reduced, the Congress would continue to spend. One of the major aims of the Reagan administration was to cut government spending, and so it was willing to have deficits for some time to put pressure on the Congress to reduce spending.

The final outcome of that strategy remains to be seen. In 1982 Congress increased taxes, with the support of the administration, to contain the deficits. And it is widely expected that in 1985 taxes will be increased again to deal with the deficit. Thus the Reagan administration did not succeed in forcing spending down to the low levels (as a percentage of GNP) that it had hoped when it proposed its tax cuts. But it does seem true that the massive deficits put pressure on Congress that kept government spending lower than it would otherwise have been.

Inflation and Bracket Creep

The large budget deficits that seem to lie ahead arise in part from an important change in the U.S. tax code, namely, *indexation of tax brackets.* The indexation, due to go into effect in 1985, will automatically adjust tax brackets so that inflation does not increase the share of government revenue in GNP. In other words, indexation will end *bracket creep.* Bracket creep occurs when inflation interacts with progressive taxation of nominal income to move people over time automatically into higher income tax brackets.

How does bracket creep work? With progressive income taxes, the higher the income, the larger the share of income on which taxes are paid. Table 15-6 illustrates. We compare two people, both in the same year. One earns $20,000, and the other earns $40,000. With progressive taxation, the person earning $40,000 pays a larger *share* of income in taxes than the other person. Thus the $20,000 earner pays 35 percent of income in taxes ($7,000), while the $40,000 earner pays 50 percent of income in taxes ($20,000).

So far we have been comparing two people at the same time. Now suppose we compare one person at two different times, with two different price levels. Initially the person earns $20,000, with the price level equal to 100. After-tax real income is $13,000. Now the price level doubles to 200, while pretax real income remains constant. That means pretax nominal in-

TABLE 15-6 EFFECTS OF INFLATION ON AFTER-TAX INCOME

Price level	Pretax income, nominal	Taxes, nominal	After-tax income, nominal	After-tax income, real
100	$20,000	$ 7,000	$13,000	$13,000
200	40,000	20,000	20,000	10,000

come rises from $20,000 to $40,000. Before taxes, the person has the same real income with $40,000 now that he had with $20,000 when the price level was at 100. But because of progressive taxation, the after-tax income situations are different. Now taxes take 50 percent of the person's income, leaving him with only $20,000 nominal, worth only $10,000 in real terms. Thus the share of income taken by the government has risen as a result of the inflation.[10]

After the move to indexation, tax revenues that otherwise would have been generated automatically as a result of inflation will no longer be available to the government. It will then be necessary to make an explicit change in the tax code to generate more tax revenue.

How important is bracket creep in practice? The Congressional Budget Office estimates that even over the period 1983–1985, bracket creep could generate between 0.6 and 1.2 percent of GNP in extra government revenue. Bracket creep is a potentially important source of government revenue, especially when the inflation rate is high.

It is because bracket creep generates revenue without tax rates being raised *explicitly*, and because it can generate substantial amounts of revenue, that one of the most likely ways the large deficits of the mid-eighties will be handled is through repeal or delay of the introduction of tax indexing. A delay, say, to 1988, of tax indexation would imply that in the meantime, with inflation still around, bracket creep would increase tax rates, thus undoing part of the 1981 tax cuts. By the time indexation became effective, tax rates would have risen somewhat further and thus helped reduce the deficit.

This discussion highlights the great convenience of bracket creep for the Congress—tax rate increases just happen. Bracket creep worked strongly throughout the high inflation of the seventies. Congress never had to raise taxes explicitly, and indeed could even cut tax rates occasionally. Once tax brackets are indexed, more fiscal discipline in matching spending and taxes is required of the Congress.

15-4 DEFICITS, INFLATION, AND INSTABILITY

This is the section where we finally discuss the consequences of deficits. The main question is, What, if anything, is wrong with running budget deficits? The common beliefs are that deficits are inflationary and that they crowd out

[10] The name "bracket creep" comes from the "tax brackets" for which income tax rates are specified. The tax rate rises with income. Indexation works by specifying tax brackets in real terms.

investment. We will see that the inflationary impact of a deficit depends on how it is financed. The impact of deficits also depends on whether they are short-lived or permanent.

We draw on the discussion of money and inflation in Chapter 13 to make the first point. *Inflation, in the long run, is determined by the rate of money growth. If the budget deficit does not affect long-run money growth, then it will not affect long-run inflation. If the method of financing the deficit does lead to higher money growth in the long run, it also leads to higher inflation.*

In those cases where the method of financing the deficit does not affect the long-run rate of money growth, the deficit does not lead to higher *long-run* inflation. For instance, if the deficit is short-lived, it will not affect the long-run rate of growth of the money stock, and will not lead to long-term inflation. It will, though, lead to higher inflation in the short run through the normal channels of fiscal expansion.

In this section we concentrate on money-financed deficits. We ask to what extent deficits can be financed through the printing of money, and what happens when not enough money can be printed to cover a given deficit. We start with a temporary budget deficit.

Money-Financed Transitory Deficits

The first case we consider is that of a deficit, say, due to a temporary cut in taxes, that is transitory and financed by money creation. The Fed buys the debt that the Treasury issues to cover its deficit. The deficit is known to be temporary.

In Figure 15-4 we show a short-run Phillips curve *PC* and the vertical long-run Phillips curve *LPC*. Suppose now that the government cuts taxes and that there is consequently a budget deficit. The immediate impact of the reduction in taxes is to increase aggregate demand, shifting the economy up along the short-run Phillips curve *PC* to point *E′* from *E*.

As long as the deficit lasts, the Fed is increasing the money stock by buying debt. The rising money stock keeps aggregate demand rising. While the money stock is rising, inflation expectations increase, and aggregate demand expands because the money creation lowers interest rates and raises investment spending relative to the level that would obtain if the money supply were kept constant. But in the long run, by assumption, the deficit disappears. There is no further need for increasing the money stock, and inflation disappears along with the deficit. The economy therefore will follow a cycle as shown in Figure 15-4, with inflation above trend and unemployment below trend.

In the long run, inflation returns to its original level. The only effect of the transitory deficit is that it raises the money stock and the price *level.* Thus so long as a deficit is going to be transitory, it can be financed through the printing of money without any long-run effect on the inflation rate—though, of course, the increase in the money stock during the period of the deficit does result in a temporarily higher inflation rate.

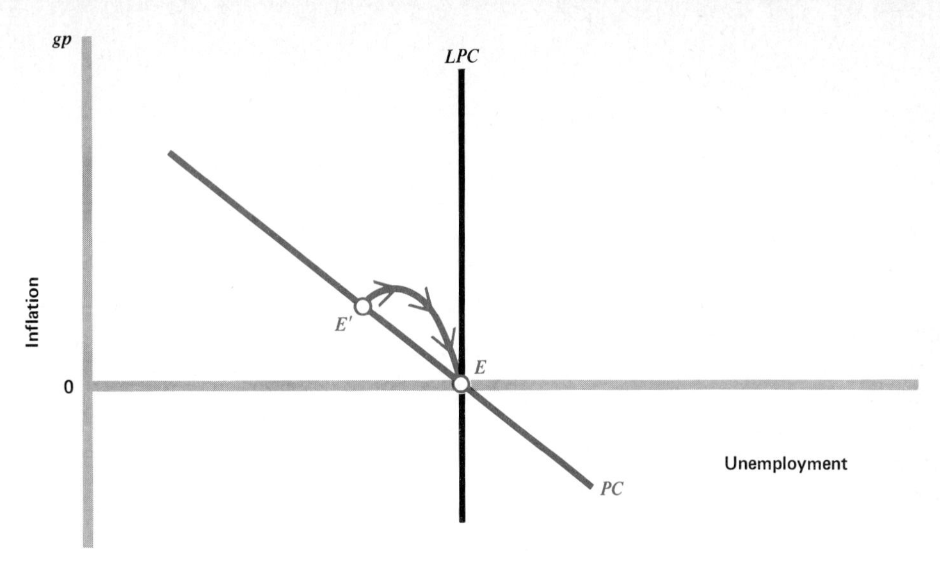

FIGURE 15-4 THE EFFECTS OF A TRANSITORY, MONEY-FINANCED DEFICIT. Initial equilibrium is at point E with zero inflation and unemployment at the natural rate. A transitory fiscal expansion raises aggregate demand, and this effect is reinforced by the money creation that finances the budget. The economy moves in the short run to E' with higher inflation and less unemployment. Once the government spending declines again, the economy returns to E. In the long run the only effect is the cumulative increase in the money stock and hence a cumulative increase in the level of prices.

Money-Financed Permanent Deficits

Permanent deficits financed by money creation necessarily affect the long-run inflation rate. We show now the relationship between the budget deficit and the inflation rate, using a diagram that looks much like the Laffer curve described in Box 15-1. The schedule *AA* in Figure 15-5 shows the long-run relationship between deficits and inflation, which we now derive.

THE INFLATION TAX

When the government finances a deficit by creating money, it in effect keeps printing money, period after period, which it uses to pay for the goods and services it buys. This money is absorbed by the public. But why would the public choose to increase its holdings of nominal money balances period after period?

The only reason, real income growth aside, that the public would be adding to its holdings of nominal money balances is to offset the effects of inflation. Assuming there is no real income growth, in the long run the public will hold a constant level of *real* balances. But if prices are rising, the purchasing power of a given stock of *nominal balances* is falling. To maintain

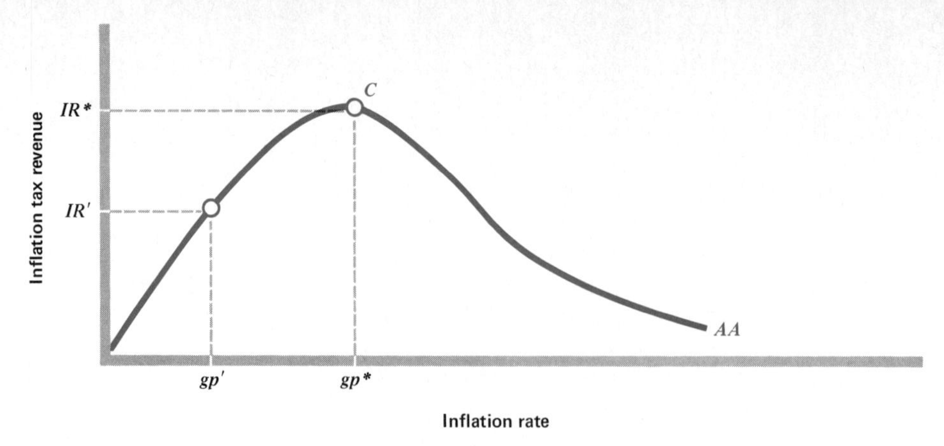

FIGURE 15-5 THE INFLATION TAX. At a zero inflation rate, the inflation tax revenue is zero. As the inflation rate rises, the government receives more revenue from inflation, up to point C, where the tax revenue reaches its maximum of IR^*. The corresponding inflation rate is gp^*. Beyond point C the demand for real balances is falling so much as the inflation rate increases that total tax revenues decline.

the real value of its money balances constant, the public has to be adding to its stock of nominal balances, exactly at the rate that will offset the effects of inflation.

When the public is adding to its stock of nominal balances in order to offset the effects of inflation on holdings of real balances, it is using part of its income to increase holdings of nominal money. For instance, suppose someone has an income of \$20,000 (nominal) this year. Over the course of the year, inflation reduces the value of her real balances. She therefore has to add, say, \$300, to her bank account just to maintain the real value of her money holdings constant. That \$300 is not available for spending. The person seems to be saving \$300 in the form of money holdings, but in fact in real terms she is not increasing her wealth by adding the \$300 to her nominal balances. All she is doing is preventing her wealth from falling as a result of inflation.

Inflation acts just like a tax because people are forced to spend less than their income and pay the difference to the government in exchange for extra money.[11] The government thus can spend more resources, and the public less, just as if the government had raised taxes to finance extra spending. When the government finances its deficit by issuing money, which the public adds to its holdings of nominal balances to maintain the real value of money balances constant, we say the government is financing itself through the inflation tax.[12]

[11] There is one complication in this analysis. The amount that is received by the government is the increase in the stock of *high-powered* money, because the Fed is buying Treasury debt with high-powered money. But the public is increasing its holdings of both bank deposits and currency, and thus part of the increase in the public's holdings of money does not go to the government to finance the deficit. This complication in no way changes the essence of the analysis.

How much revenue can the government collect through the inflation tax? By analogy with Equation (2), the amount of revenue produced by the inflation tax is the product of the tax rate (the inflation rate) and the object of the taxation (in this case the stock of real balances). When real output is constant, inflation tax revenue is given by

$$\text{Inflation tax revenue} = \text{inflation rate} \times \text{real balances} \tag{3}$$

Now we can explain the shape of the curve *AA* in Figure 15-5. When the inflation rate is zero, the government gets no revenue from inflation. As the inflation rate rises, the amount of inflation tax received by the government increases. But, of course, as the inflation rate rises, people reduce their holdings of real balances—because it is becoming increasingly costly to hold money.[13] Eventually the quantity of real balances falls so much that the total amount of inflation tax revenue received by the government falls. Beyond point *C* the amount of inflation tax revenue actually falls as the inflation rate rises. This means that there is a maximum amount of revenue the government can raise through the inflation tax: it is shown as amount IR^* in Figure 15-5. There is a corresponding inflation rate, denoted gp^*, at which the inflation rate is at its maximum.

We can now turn to Figure 15-6 to study the long-run effects of money-financed deficits. We start at point *E* on the short-run Phillips curve *PC*. Now the government cuts taxes and finances the deficit by printing money. We assume the deficit is equal to amount IR' (in Figure 15-5), which is less than IR^* and thus can be financed entirely through the inflation tax. The tax cut moves us, in the short run, to point E'. But now money growth has been permanently increased, and inflation will in the long run move to the rate gp', corresponding to the inflation tax revenue IR'.

The new steady-state inflation rate gp' is shown by the horizontal line in Figure 15-6. In the long run the economy reaches point E''. In that equilibrium expectations have fully adjusted to the inflation, and unemployment is back at the natural rate. Inflation equals the growth rate of money, and the inflation rate depends on the size of the deficit. The larger the deficit, the higher the inflation rate. Of course, it is even possible that the maximum amount that can be raised through the inflation tax is smaller than the budget deficit—and thus that long-run money financing of the deficit is impossible.

Hyperinflation

Money-financed deficits are inevitably part of the extreme inflations of 50 or 100 percent or more that we see on occasion in Latin America or Israel. They

---

[12] Inflation is often referred to as the "cruelest tax." This does not refer to the above analysis of the inflation tax, but rather to the redistributions of wealth and income associated with unanticipated inflation, discussed in Chap. 14.

[13] If bank deposits pay interest, then the interest rate on such deposits will rise with inflation, and the quantity of deposits demanded will not necessarily fall as the inflation rate increases. But no interest is paid on currency, and the quantity of currency demanded will fall as the inflation rate rises.

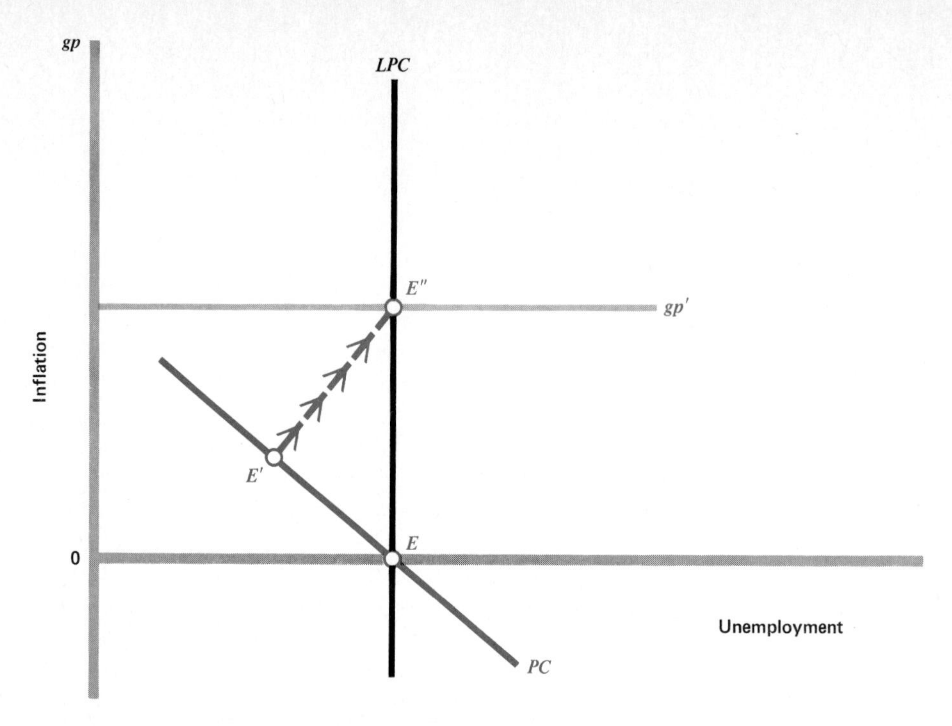

FIGURE 15-6 THE EFFECTS OF A PERMANENT MONEY-FINANCED DEFICIT. The long-run vertical Phillips curve is *LPC*. The schedule *gp'* shows the inflation rate required to finance the given real budget deficit. Starting from a zero deficit and long-run equilibrium at *E*, a permanent money-financed deficit first expands aggregate demand and leads the economy to *E'*. But over time, inflationary expectations adjust, and the economy returns to full employment at the permanently higher inflation rate *gp'*.

are also part of the even more extreme cases of *hyperinflation*. Hyperinflations are periods of very rapid inflation, in excess of 1,000 percent per year.

Suppose that the government is running a deficit larger than IR^* in Figure 15-5. This means it cannot raise enough revenue through inflation to cover the deficit. Suppose also that whenever it finds itself unable to pay for what it buys, it prints more high-powered money. In this case the inflation rate will keep on increasing. The public and the government will be competing for goods, with the government printing money, and the public trying to reduce its holdings of real balances and thereby driving up the inflation rate. Eventually the economy will experience a hyperinflation. For instance, in the German hyperinflation of 1922–1923, the average inflation rate was 322 percent *per month*. In October 1923, just before the end of the hyperinflation, prices rose by over 29,000 percent.[14] In dollars, that means that something that cost $1 at the beginning of the month would have cost $290 at the end of the month.

[14] Data based on C. L. Holtferich, *Die Deutsche Inflation, 1914–1923* (New York: Walter de Gruyter, 1980).

Keynes, in a masterful description of the hyperinflation process in Austria after World War I, tells of how people would order two beers at a time because they grew stale at a rate slower than their price was rising.[15] Other stories include those of a woman who carried her (almost worthless) currency in a basket and found that when she set down the basket for a moment, it was stolen, but the money was left.

To return now to the budget deficit, the basic point is that there are real deficits that simply cannot, in the long run, be financed by borrowing from the central bank, that is, by the issuing of high-powered money. Attempts to finance in that way would lead to hyperinflation. The fear that hyperinflation will result from large budget deficits may be one of the arguments in the minds of those most concerned over the budget deficit. But it is foolish to assume that any budget deficit, however small, will lead to a hyperinflation, even if it is financed by borrowing from the Fed.

The analysis of the inflation tax is not of great importance for the United States, with its well-functioning tax system and independent central bank. In other countries, with less well-developed tax systems, the printing of money may be one of the few ways the government has of obtaining resources. To put it differently, in some countries, large parts of government spending are financed by borrowing from the central bank and thus by inflation.

15-5 DEBT-FINANCED DEFICITS

The alternative to money financing of the deficit is debt financing. In this section we examine the effects of debt financing of deficits, once again distinguishing between transitory and permanent deficits.

A Debt-Financed, Transitory Deficit

Figure 15-7 presents the aggregate demand and supply diagram of Chapter 12. We are once again considering the effects of a tax cut. The tax cut is temporary, and the budget deficit is financed by the selling of debt to the private sector. The initial effect of the cut in taxes is to shift the aggregate demand curve out from AD to AD_1. Because the private sector is buying bonds during the period of the deficit, it ends up holding a higher stock of government bonds. What effect does that higher stock of government debt held by the private sector have on aggregate demand?

Individuals holding government bonds regard those bonds as part of their wealth. Thus it would seem that given the level of income, aggregate demand should rise when the stock of government bonds rises, because individuals holding those bonds have higher wealth. The higher wealth increases con-

[15] See John Maynard Keynes, *A Tract on Monetary Reform* (New York: Macmillan, 1923), which remains one of the most readable accounts of inflation. See also Phillip Cagan, "The Monetary Dynamics of Hyperinflation," in Milton Friedman (ed.), *Studies in the Quantity Theory of Money* (Chicago: The University of Chicago Press, 1956). Cagan's article contains data on inflation rates in seven hyperinflations.

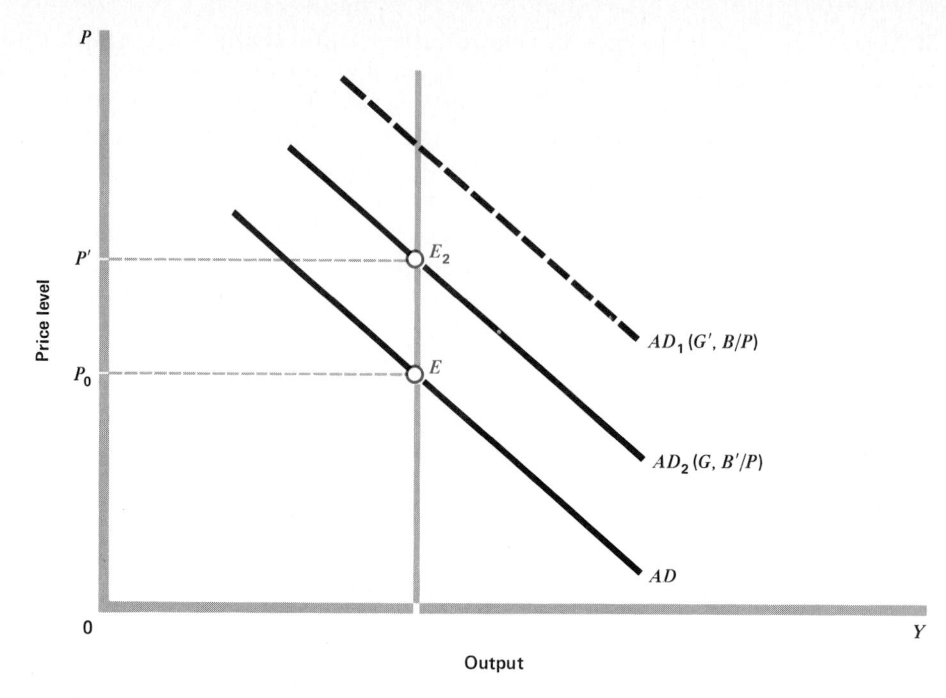

FIGURE 15-7 A TRANSITORY, DEBT-FINANCED DEFICIT. A cut in taxes shifts the aggregate demand curve from AD to AD_1. In the short run, aggregate demand expands. Because the deficit is transitory, the tax cut is later reversed. The rise in public debt that financed the transitory deficit raises the wealth of the debt holders. Once the deficit has returned to normal, the effect of increased debt outstanding implies higher aggregate demand. AD_1 shifts back only to AD_2 rather than to AD. There is a permanent increase in the price level and, given nominal money, a rise in interest rates.

sumption demand.[16] Accordingly, the aggregate demand curve would shift out to the right as a result of the increase in privately held wealth. Hence, we show the final aggregate demand curve—after government spending has returned to its original level—at AD_2 above the initial AD curve. The difference between the two aggregate demand schedules AD and AD_2 arises from the higher stock of government bonds B', compared with $\overline{B}$ on the initial aggregate demand curve. Since the effects of the higher wealth on consumption demand are likely to be small, we show the final aggregate demand curve AD_2 below the aggregate demand curve AD_1.

There are two complications to this analysis. The first is that the existence of the higher stock of debt raises the amount of interest payments in the federal budget. If the budget was originally balanced at point E, it may not be balanced at E_2. Of course, since the price level at E_2 is higher than at E, tax recipts may have risen at E_2 compared with E, and perhaps the budget would be balanced. But it need not be. If it were not, then further financing of the

[16] Recall the discussion of wealth as a factor in consumption spending in Chap. 6.

deficit would have to be undertaken, and that would have subsequent effects on the equilibrium.

ARE BONDS WEALTH?

The second complication is related to the first. It is possible that individuals in the economy calculate their wealth taking into account the tax payments they will have to make in the future. Suppose that everyone believed that the national debt would eventually be paid off. Then everyone would know that at some point in the future the federal government would have to run a surplus. Individuals might think the federal government would at some future date have to raise taxes in order to pay off the debt. In this case an increase in the debt would increase their wealth and at the same time suggest to them that their taxes would be higher in the future. The net effect on aggregate demand might then be zero.[17] The issue raised by this argument is sometimes posed by the question, Are government bonds wealth?

There is another way of looking at this argument. Instead of concentrating on wealth, we concentrate on disposable income. An increase in the debt raises disposable income for the private sector because it raises the interest payments the private sector receives. The federal government has to finance those interest payments in some way. Suppose that it financed them by raising taxes or reducing other transfer payments. Then disposable income would be unaffected, despite the higher debt. Consumption demand in this case would be little affected by the increase in the national debt. With such a combined change in the debt and taxes that leaves the budget balanced in the long run, the aggregate demand curve would return to its initial position at *AD*. There would be no (or little) long-run effect from the higher debt if the higher debt did not result in an unbalanced budget.

The theoretical and empirical issue of whether an increase in the national debt increases aggregate demand is not yet settled. It is difficult to isolate the effects of changes in the debt on consumption demand in empirical studies of consumption. The theoretical arguments we have are not conclusive. We are not certain whether individuals do take account of their future tax liabilities when they calculate their wealth. Thus we have to leave this question in an unresolved state.

MONEY AND DEBT FINANCING

There is one important difference between debt financing and money financing of a given short-run budget deficit. Money financing of the deficit tends to reduce the interest rate in the short run compared with debt financing. That is because money financing increases the nominal money stock (shifting up the *LM* curve in the *IS-LM* model), whereas debt financing does not. In the short

[17] For an eclectic, but difficult, view of this argument, see Robert J. Barro, "Are Government Bonds Net Wealth?" *Journal of Political Economy*, December 1974. See, too, the discussion in the *Journal of Monetary Economics*, August 1978.

run, then, debt financing reduces the level of investment compared with money financing. That is an issue connected with the crowding-out question.

We want also to compare the effects on the price level of money and debt financing of a temporary increase in government spending. The price level is higher with money financing than with debt financing. There are two reasons. First, money financing increases the money stock, and debt financing does not. The higher the money stock, the greater the aggregate demand at any given price level. Second, we attributed a price level rise in the case of debt financing to the wealth effect of a greater stock of debt on consumption. While there is some argument about whether bonds are wealth, there is no question that money is wealth. So the wealth effect on consumption is larger in the case of money financing than debt financing. That, too, means that aggregate demand at any given price level will be higher with money than with debt financing.

We now summarize the effects of a temporary budget deficit financed by debt creation. Such financing probably increases aggregate demand, but because of the possible effects of anticipated future tax liabilities on consumption, that is not certain. Debt financing, starting from a balanced budget and if not compensated for by higher taxes or reductions in other transfer payments, leads to a permanent deficit in the budget because interest has to be paid on the debt. Debt financing raises the interest rate and reduces investment in the short run as compared with the effects of money financing.

Debt-Financed Permanent Deficits

We turn now to a permanent real deficit. Suppose, to begin with, that the economy is not growing. Then any attempt to run a permanent real deficit, financed by debt, will fail. For as the debt accumulates over time, interest payments on the debt increase. These rising interest payments can initially be handled by reducing other government expenditures, or by raising taxes. But eventually there are no other government expenditures to cut, and no more taxes to raise, and the ever-increasing interest payments cannot be paid by the government. Thus attempts to finance a given real deficit purely through debt financing cannot be viable in the long run in an economy that is not growing.[18]

DEBT, GROWTH, AND INSTABILITY

The impossibility of running a permanent debt-financed deficit in a nongrowing economy is a dramatic conclusion, which certainly seems to justify concern over the massive deficits the U.S. economy faces for the next decade. It is therefore worth emphasizing what the problem is, and also showing why the problem is less serious in a growing economy.

[18] The long-run effects of debt-financed changes in government spending are analyzed in a well-known paper by Alan Blinder and Robert Solow, "Analytic Foundations of Fiscal Policy," in A. S. Blinder et al., *The Economics of Public Finance* (Washington, D.C.: The Brookings Institution, 1974).

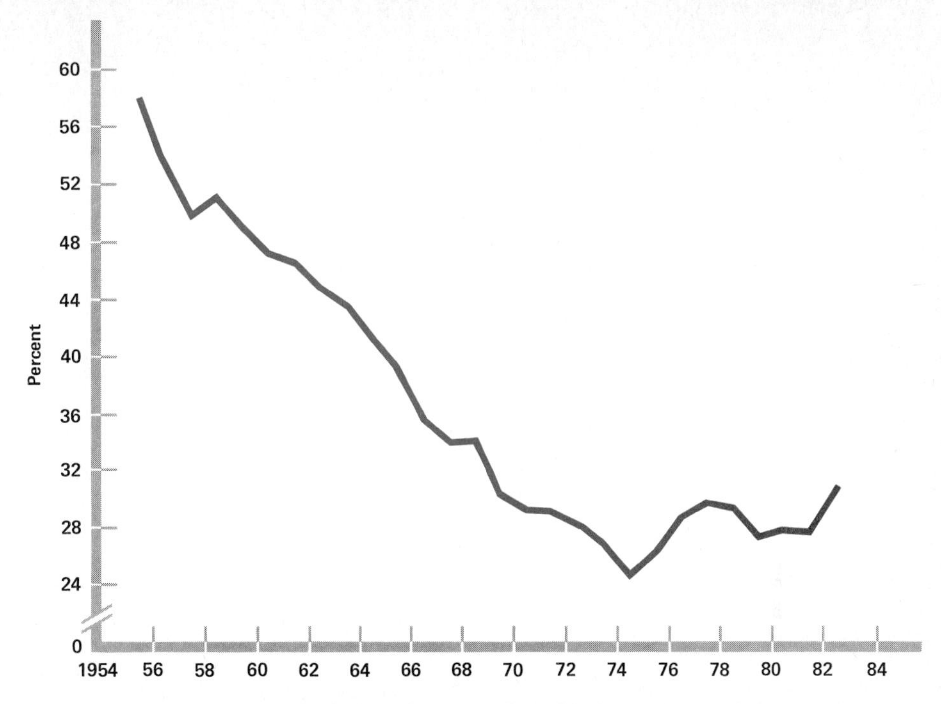

Note: **Public debt outstanding is defined as gross public debt less holdings by U.S. government agencies. It comprises holdings by the Federal Reserve and by private investors including the rest of the world.**

FIGURE 15-8 FEDERAL BUDGET DEFICIT AS A PERCENTAGE OF GNP (fiscal years, unified budget). (*Sources: The Budget of the United States, 1983,* and Data Resources, Inc.)

Suppose the economy is not growing and the government is running a budget deficit. It can finance the deficit by issuing debt. But next period it has to pay interest on all the debt that existed in the past, *and also on the new debt that it issued to cover last period's deficit.* How can it pay this interest? One way is to borrow some more. But then next period the interest needed to service the debt is even larger, and hence even more debt needs to be issued, and so on.

The national debt in the United States has typically risen year after year for the past 50 years. Does that mean the government budget is bound to get out of hand, with interest payments rising so high that taxes have to keep rising, until eventually something terrible will happen? The answer is no, because the economy has been growing.

Figure 15-8 shows the ratio of the national debt in the United States to GNP. Over most of the period since World War II until 1974 the ratio of the debt to nominal GNP was falling *even though the debt itself was rising as a result of budget deficits.* How could this happen? The answer is that *the ratio of debt to GNP falls when nominal GNP grows more rapidly than the debt.*

To see this point it is useful to look separately at the numerator and denominator of the debt-GNP ratio. The numerator, the debt, grows because of deficits. The denominator, nominal GNP, grows as a result of both inflation and real GNP growth. If the debt is growing more rapidly than GNP, the debt-GNP ratio is rising. If the debt is growing less rapidly than GNP, the debt-GNP ratio is falling.

Consider two examples. First, the stock of debt is \$500 billion, and the debt-financed budget is \$20 billion. Therefore the growth rate of debt is 4 percent [= (20/500 × 100) percent]. Suppose inflation is 3 percent and real growth 4 percent, and therefore nominal GNP growth is equal to 7 percent. With nominal income growth exceeding debt growth the debt-GNP ratio decreases. Alternatively, suppose the stock of debt is \$1,000 billion and the deficit is \$150 billion. The debt is growing at 15 percent. Suppose inflation is 5 percent and real growth 4 percent, so that GNP growth is 9 percent. With debt growing faster than income, the debt-to-income ratio is rising.

Why is it useful to look at the ratio of debt to income rather than at the absolute value of the debt? The reason is that GNP is a measure of the size of the economy, and the debt-GNP ratio is thus a measure of the magnitude of the debt relative to the size of the economy. A national debt of \$1 trillion would have been overwhelming in 1929 when U.S. GNP was about \$100 billion—even if the interest rate had been 2 percent, the government would have had to raise 20 percent of GNP in taxes to pay interest on the debt. But when GNP is more than \$3 trillion, a \$1 trillion debt is not so overwhelming.

If the debt-GNP ratio starts out at a reasonably low level, government deficits that are small enough to ensure that the debt is not growing more rapidly than GNP are sustainable. But if the deficit is so large that the debt-GNP ratio is growing, with no obvious signs of the situation turning around, then there will be concern over the size of the deficit.

What would happen if the deficit were too large, so that debt grows relative to income seemingly without bounds? Such a process can really not go on forever. Ultimately the public debt totally overshadows and displaces other assets, and crowding out becomes so pervasive that the public comes to expect *some* action to balance the budget. This might involve either inflation or special taxes to balance the budget.[19]

How does inflation help solve the deficit problem? First, the inflation tax can make some small contribution to financing the deficit. But more importantly, a large *unanticipated* inflation will reduce the real value of the outstanding stock of government debt. The national debt in most countries is *nominal*, meaning that the government is obliged only to pay a certain number of dollars to the holders of the debt. A policy that raises the price level thus reduces the real value of the payments the government is obliged to make.

[19] See T. Sargent and N. Wallace, "Some Unpleasant Monetarist Arithmetic," Federal Reserve Bank of Minnesota, *Quarterly Review*, Fall 1981. As the title suggests, the treatment is technical. The main point the authors make is that debt problems ultimately become inflation problems.

The debt can therefore virtually be wiped out by a large enough unanticipated inflation — so long as the debt is a nominal debt.

The potential instability brought about by ever-growing debt means that ultimately some policies will be undertaken to handle the deficit problem. There may be tax increases, or reductions in government spending, or inflation, or all three.

It is important to have some perspective on the relevance of these extreme conditions to the world today. They are in no way relevant to the U.S. economy of the mid-1980s. There is no massive "debt problem," and there is no threat of instability even if deficits are large for some years. Figure 15-8 shows that the debt-income ratio is still well below its 1955 level.

But there is little doubt that there are a number of countries even today where many years of deficits have cumulated into a large public debt that ultimately becomes unmanageable. Often that outcome is clearly visible ahead of time, but on occasion a sharp increase in real interest rates together with a major loss in tax revenues, perhaps because of a world recession, can suddenly make the debt problem much more immediate.

Summary

Table 15-7 summarizes the effects of alternative deficit scenarios. The table makes it clear that the really serious problems arise only when deficits are large and persistent. In that case inflation and possibly, in extreme cases, hyperinflation or instability are possible. Moderate deficits and especially small, temporary deficits do not pose a macroeconomic problem. In fact, over the business cycle it is entirely appropriate that there should be (larger) deficits during recessions offset by smaller deficits or surpluses during booms.

The problems of the 1980s are budget deficits, but we could likewise talk about problems arising from budget surpluses. What would happen if the government embarked on a permanent tax increase leading to a surplus? Either debt would be retired until none was left, or the money stock would be declining without limit, causing prices to fall. At present the risk of persistent surpluses is not a realistic problem.

TABLE 15-7 EFFECT OF BUDGET DEFICITS ON LONG-RUN INFLATION AND PRICE LEVEL

	Permanent deficit	Transitory deficit
Money-financed	Higher inflation Huge deficits lead to hyperinflation	Higher price level
Debt-financed	Leads to instability, except for moderate deficits	Small long-run effects

15-6 DEFICIT FINANCING IN PRACTICE

We have now discussed the two extreme cases of financing of the deficit purely through the creation of high-powered money and purely through borrowing. In practice, neither of these extremes is followed.

Figure 15-9 shows the growth rate of the public debt outstanding and the growth rate of the monetary base. It is clear that both rates tend to be positive, meaning that the base and debt both are growing over time. It is also the case that they occasionally increase sharply together.

Empirical evidence suggests that the Fed does systematically monetize part of the deficit.[20] But the Fed has not habitually financed the entire deficit, or even some fixed share of it. The evidence is that the Fed *reduces* the amount of money financing of the deficit when the inflation rate is high or when government spending is rising rapidly. This suggests that the Fed is well aware of the potential inflationary consequences of money financing of deficits, and has followed policies that avoid these consequences. Further, whatever the Fed has done in the past, it can always change policies, entirely breaking the link between the deficit and money growth if it so wishes.

The conclusions we draw about deficit financing and its dangers are:

1. There is no automatic link between money growth and the deficit.
2. Small deficits can be financed through borrowing, without causing the ratio of debt to GNP to increase.
3. Money financing of deficits is inflationary. Further, there are limits on the size of the deficit that can be financed through the inflation tax.
4. Similarly, extremely large permanent deficits cannot be financed. There is a limit to the amount of inflation tax revenue that can be raised, and a rapidly growing debt means rapidly growing interest payments. Something ultimately has to give, to reduce the deficit. The something could be taxes, or spending, or inflation.
5. We have not in this chapter analyzed the crowding out associated with deficits in any detail. But deficits do create crowding out of investment spending, the more so if they are debt-financed.

The overall conclusion is that deficits are indeed to be worried about, particularly if they are very large and long-lasting. But small deficits can easily be handled through borrowing—and as noted in Section 15-5, cyclical changes in the deficit are desirable to help smooth the trade cycle.

15-7 THE BURDEN OF THE DEBT

As deficits continue, the national debt piles up. The U.S. national debt now exceeds $1 trillion, an amount that is enough to get anyone worried. In per capita terms, the national debt now exceeds $4,000 per person in the United

[20] Alan S. Blinder, "On the Monetization of Deficits," Working Paper No. 1052, National Bureau of Economic Research, 1982.

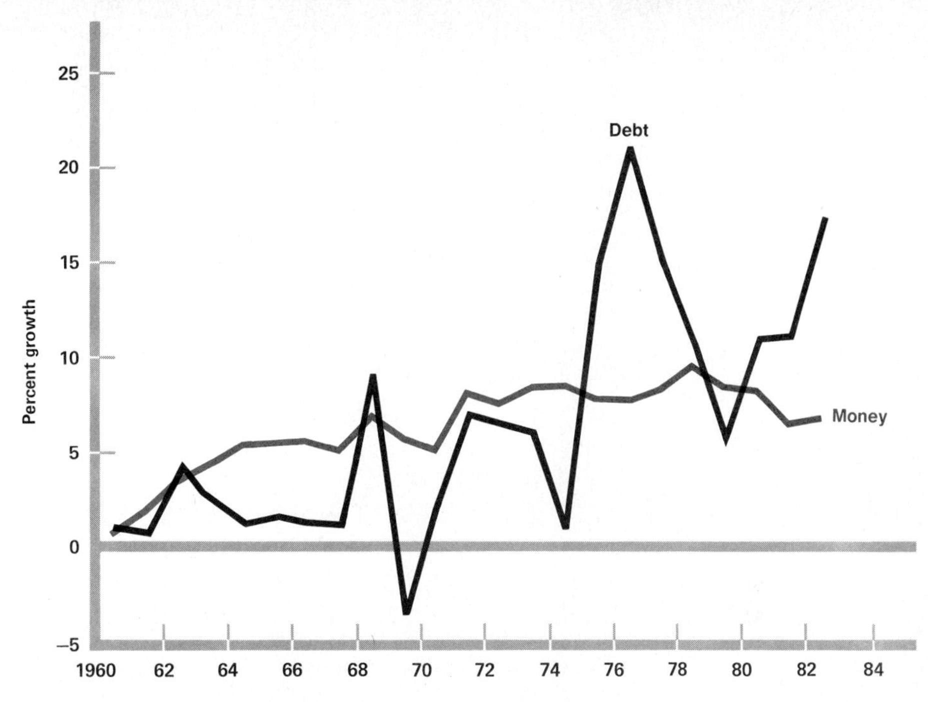

FIGURE 15-9 THE GROWTH RATE OF PUBLIC DEBT OUTSTANDING AND THE GROWTH RATE OF HIGH-POWERED MONEY. (*Sources: The Budget of the United States, 1983,* and Data Resources, Inc.)

States. That seems to be a heavy debt for each individual to bear. It is the notion that every person in the country has a large debt that makes the existence of the debt seem so serious.

However, we should realize that corresponding to the debt that individuals each have as their share of the national debt, there are Treasury bonds and bills that every person on average has. By and large, we owe the national debt to ourselves. Each individual shares in the public debt, but many individuals own claims on the government that are the other side of the national debt. If there is a debt for individuals taken together, it arises from prospective taxes to pay off the debt. The taxes that different individuals would pay to retire the debt would also vary among the population. To a first approximation, one could think of the liability that the debt represents as canceling out the asset that the debt represents to the individuals who hold claims on the government.

You will recognize that we are now discussing the question of whether the debt is counted as part of wealth for the population as a whole. Earlier, we started from the view that the government bonds and Treasury bills that individuals hold are part of their wealth. We then asked whether the possibility that all individuals consider the future tax liabilities connected with the hypothetical paying off of the debt at some future date meant that on balance the debt was not part of the wealth. In this section we started from the other side: we first talked of the national debt as a debt, and then pointed out that there were assets held by individuals corresponding to that debt. We pointed out earlier that it was not yet certain whether individuals taken together in fact count the national debt as a part of wealth. There certainly does not seem to be any argument that the liability represented by some possible paying off of the debt at some unknown future time outweighs the value of the assets that individuals hold at present. At this level, then, there is no persuasive argument that the debt is a burden in the sense that the economy as a whole regards the national debt as a reduction in its wealth.

The only factor ignored in the previous paragraph is that part of the debt is owned by foreigners. In that case, for the U.S. economy as a whole, part of the asset represented by the debt is held by foreigners, while the future tax liability accrues entirely to residents. Then that part of the debt held by foreigners might represent a net reduction in the wealth of U.S. residents.

Although the debt is not a burden in the fairly crude sense in which one asks whether individuals regard themselves as being poorer because of the existence of the debt (leaving aside the part of the debt owned by foreigners), there are more sophisticated senses in which it might be a burden. The most important sense in which there is a possible burden arises from the potential long-run effects of the debt on the capital stock. We saw earlier that debt financing increases the interest rate and reduces investment. That would mean that the capital stock would be lower with debt financing than otherwise. If individuals regard the debt as part of their wealth, then they tend to increase their consumption at a given level of income, which results in a smaller proportion of GNP being invested, in a lower capital stock, and thus lower output. This is a real burden.

Further, the debt might be a burden because debt servicing in the long run could require higher tax rates. If those tax rates have adverse effects on the amount of work that individuals do, then real output would be reduced.

Thus, if the debt is a burden, it is a burden for reasons very different from those suggested by the statement that every person in the United States has a debt of $4,000 as a share of the national debt. The major possible source of burden arises from the possible effects of the national debt on the capital stock.

15-8 THE SIZE OF GOVERNMENT CONTROVERSY

There has been a worldwide trend over the last 25 years toward an increased share of government in GNP. Figure 15-10 shows the share of government outlays (all levels of government) in GNP for the United States and for the group of industrialized countries. In 1980 the share was significantly higher than it had been in 1960 in the United States, and even more so abroad. This increase reflects in large measure the broadening of government social pro-

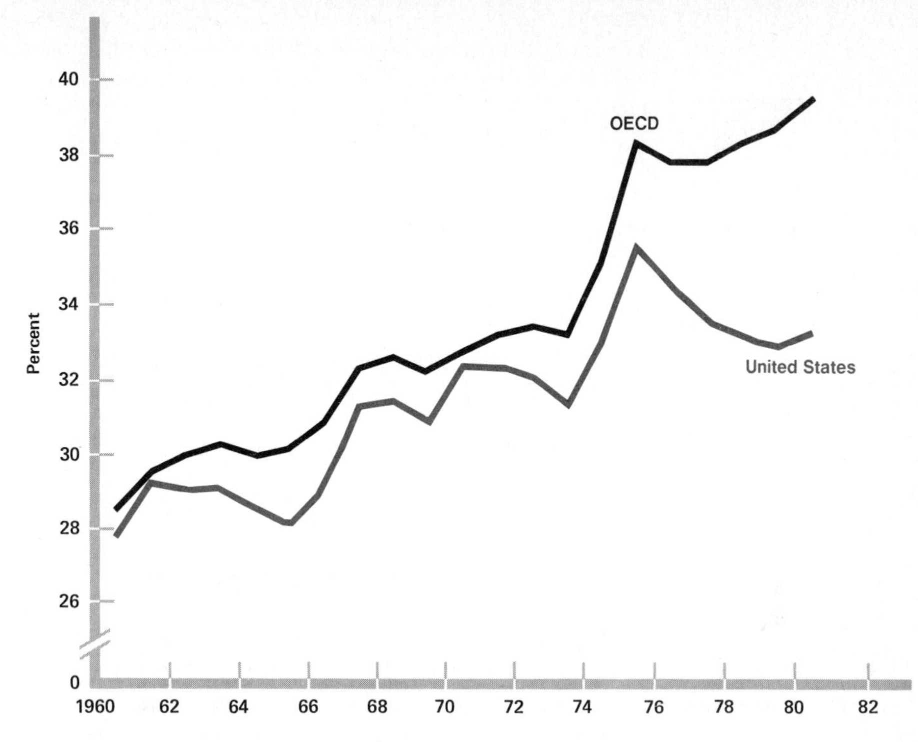

FIGURE 15-10 THE SHARE OF GOVERNMENT SPENDING IN GNP IN THE UNITED STATES AND IN INDUSTRIALIZED COUNTRIES. (*Source: Economic Outlook*, OECD, December 1982.)

grams, especially the growth of transfer programs discussed above. Today that growth in spending is under sharp attack.

A vocal part of the electorate and the government argues that much of government spending is wasteful, that the tax burden is excessive, and that the role of government in the economy should be reduced. In the United States the response to the growth of government has been a tax revolt, leading to limitations on taxes in several states, and an attempt to secure a constitutional amendment that would both prevent government spending from rising and require budgets to be balanced, or almost so. The balanced budget amendment has had the support of the Reagan administration, despite the administration's introducing extremely unbalanced budgets.

A CONSTITUTIONAL AMENDMENT

In 1982 a Senate resolution, supported by the administration, proposed a constitutional amendment from which we quote here:

> SECTION 1. Prior to each fiscal year, the Congress shall adopt a statement of receipts and outlays for that year in which total outlays are no greater than total

receipts. The Congress may amend such statement provided revised outlays are no greater than revised receipts. Whenever three-fifths of the whole number of both Houses shall deem it necessary, Congress in such statement may provide for a specific excess of outlays over receipts by a vote directed solely to that subject. The Congress and the President shall, pursuant to legislation or through exercise of their powers under the first and second articles, ensure that actual outlays do not exceed the outlays set forth in such statement.

SECTION 2. Total receipts for any fiscal year set forth in the statement adopted pursuant to this article shall not increase by a rate greater than the rate of increase in national income in the year or years ending not less than six months nor more than twelve months before such fiscal year, unless a majority of the whole number of both Houses of Congress shall have passed a bill directed solely to approving specific additional receipts and such bill has become law.

The Balanced Budget

The constitutional amendment has two main sets of provisions. First, it essentially requires a balanced budget. It thus limits the government's ability to run deficits. Under the proposed amendment, unbalancing of the budget requires a three-fifths majority of the Congress. The presumption will be that the budget should be balanced, even in a recession. Fiscal policy thus loses flexibility to deal with the business cycle. By requiring annual budget balance, the amendment ensures that even automatic stabilizers are neutralized—for if the budget is going into deficit because of automatic stabilizers, it takes a three-fifths majority to permit that deficit. Otherwise taxes have to be raised or other spending cut. This feature of the amendment is widely believed to be a setback.

THE SIZE OF GOVERNMENT

The second set of provisions, and the more significant, deals with the size of government. Government spending is to be reduced to 20 percent of GNP. Only real growth of the economy will permit government spending to increase. The balanced budget amendment would make the 1960–1980 pattern of a growing share of government in GNP impossible.[21]

How large should the government be? That is, of course, a difficult question. Clearly, some government programs are widely regarded as desirable: for instance, few dispute the need for an adequate national defense. Other programs, such as the Social Security program, also command wide assent, though just how large such programs should be is controversial.

But there is no simple test that will tell us whether we get our money's worth from government spending in general. There have been a number of studies of particular government programs showing that they work less effectively than was originally expected, perhaps very badly, and arguing that it would be better if the programs were abandoned and the problem left to the

[21] See the study by the Congressional Budget Office, *Balancing the Federal Budget and Limiting Federal Spending: Constitutional and Statutory Approaches*, September 1982.

free market to handle. Even the Social Security system and the food stamp program have received substantial criticism. The approach that looks at individual programs to examine their success and suggest changes is clearly the most careful way to evaluate government spending.

The evaluation of individual programs has also to take into account the costs of financing such programs. Raising taxes creates disincentives to work and save that are properly counted as part of the cost of government spending. There is no getting away from the fact that resources are not free (except in a recession) and that resources that are used by the government could also have been used in other ways by the private sector.

There is no reason to think that a careful analysis of the costs and benefits of government programs would conclude that the share of government in GNP should be some fixed number, such as 20 percent. Richer societies may want to spend a greater share of GNP through the government, to finance programs that provide support for the poor. Or richer societies may feel that there are so many good opportunities in the private economy that people should look after themselves.

In practice, of course, the issue of how much government spending there should be is handled by the political process. In the 1930s and in the 1960s the rules and traditions of fiscal policy were changed by activist government policy in pursuit of full employment and widening social objectives. Today there is a widespread sentiment that things have gone too far and need to be brought under control by a return to "sound fiscal policy." We have seen that long-run control of deficits is, indeed, necessary for macroeconomic stability. The rest of the fiscal revolt reflects a disagreement in society on how best to use resources.

15-9 SUMMARY

1 Federal government expenditures are financed through taxes and borrowing. The borrowing takes place directly from the public, and may be indirectly from the Fed.
2 Under present institutional arrangements, there is no necessary link between Treasury borrowing and changes in the stock of high-powered money. Federal Reserve financing of the deficit increases the stock of high-powered money.
3 When the Fed tries to control the level of interest rates, it creates an automatic link between Treasury borrowing and the creation of high-powered money.
4 Federal government receipts come chiefly from the individual income tax and social insurance taxes and contributions. The share of the last category has increased rapidly in the postwar period, especially since 1965.
5 Federal government expenditures are chiefly on defense and transfer payments to individuals. The share of defense in federal expenditure has fallen over the past 25 years, while the share of transfers has risen.

6 A temporary increase in government spending financed by an increase in the stock of high-powered money increases the price level permanently.
7 A permanent increase in government spending financed by money creation results in a permanent increase in the inflation rate.
8 Inflation can be regarded as a tax on real balances. The federal government collects the tax through the issue of high-powered money that it provides during inflation to meet the increased demand for high-powered money. There is a maximum revenue that can be raised through the inflation tax.
9 A temporary increase in government spending financed by debt creation increases the price level permanently.
10 Debt financing of a permanent increase in government spending is not viable if the economy is not growing. The interest payments on the debt would continually increase, making for a rising deficit that has to be funded by ever-increasing borrowing. In a growing economy, small deficits can be run permanently without causing the debt-GNP ratio to rise.
11 The major sense in which the national debt may be a burden is that it may lead to a decline in the capital stock in the long run.
12 The increase in government spending in the 1960–1980 period led to the imposition of limits on taxes and spending in several states and a proposed constitutional amendment in the United States to require a balanced budget and limits on government spending as a share of GNP.

KEY TERMS

Bracket creep
Hyperinflation
Budget deficit
Debt problem
Burden of the debt
Entitlement spending
Discretionary spending
Balanced budget amendment
Debt-financed deficits
Money-financed deficits
National (public) debt
Debt management
Structural deficits
Cyclical deficits
Supply-side economics
Laffer curve
Indexation of tax brackets
Inflation tax

PROBLEMS

1 What effect does a federal government surplus have on the stock of money and the stock of debt? Explain in detail the mechanics of how the stocks of money and bonds are affected.
2 Suppose the Treasury issues $1 billion in Treasury bills which are bought by the public. Then the Fed conducts open market purchase of $300 million. Effectively, how has the debt been financed?

3 Under what circumstances are fiscal and monetary policy related rather than existing as two completely independent instruments in the hands of the government?
4 In some countries there is virtually no capital market in which the government can borrow, and only a rudimentary tax system, so that taxes produce only very small revenues.
   (*a*) What is the relationship between monetary and fiscal policy in such countries?
   (*b*) What does the inflation tax analysis imply about the ability of the government in such a country to spend a large share of GNP permanently?
5 Analyze the difference in the impact on the interest rate, investment, and the price level of a temporary change in government spending, financed by money creation and borrowing, respectively.
6 What would be the effect of inflation on real income taxes if income taxation was:
   (*a*) Regressive?
   (*b*) Proportional?
   (*c*) Indexed?
7 Analyze the effects on the economy of a permanent increase in the level of government spending financed by money creation.
8 Trace the path the economy follows when there is a permanent increase in government spending that is financed by borrowing from the public. Assume the economy is growing.
9 Evaluate the argument that the budget should be balanced every period.
10 Some people say that a huge government debt is a burden in that individuals on average owe over $4,000 as their share of the debt. Others point out that a large debt means individuals own large amounts of government securities and thus are wealthy. Who is right?
11 Should there be a limit on government spending?

16

THE THIRTIES TO THE EIGHTIES: THE INTERACTION OF EVENTS AND IDEAS

The ideas of economists and political philosophers, both when they are right and when they are wrong, are more powerful than is commonly understood. Indeed, the world is ruled by little else.

—John Maynard Keynes, 1936

. . . I believe that the original hope of the New Economics can be fulfilled. That is, active fiscal and monetary policies, dedicated to economic ends, and liberated from extraneous taboos, can keep the economy growing within a narrow band of full employment. . . . But we are fooling ourselves if we think that chronic inflation can be altogether avoided.

—James Tobin, 1974

As an advice-giving profession we are in way over our heads.

—Robert E. Lucas, Jr., 1980[1]

Macroeconomics, more than microeconomics, seems to be subject to changing fashions and beliefs. As late as 1971 President Nixon announced, "I am a Keynesian." Within the next decade, monetar-

[1] The quotes are from J. M. Keynes, *The General Theory of Employment, Interest and Money* (London: Macmillan, 1936), p. 383; James Tobin, *The New Economics One Decade Older* (Princeton, N.J.: Princeton University Press, 1974); and Robert E. Lucas, "Rules, Discretion, and the Role of the Economic Adviser," in his book *Studies in Business Cycle Theory* (Cambridge, Mass.: MIT Press, 1981).

ism, rational expectations, supply-side economics, and Reaganomics all, at one time or another, were confidently prescribed as the solution for the economy's problems. And during that same period, none of the different approaches delivered what it promised.

Any student may wonder about a field where opinions and policy prescriptions change so often. And he should worry too about the differences of views among macroeconomists at a given time. For instance, what should you conclude when one economist says that the budget deficit is the biggest problem facing the economy in the 1980s, and another says that it is better to pay for government spending by borrowing (that is, by deficits) than by taxing?

In this chapter we describe the major currents of thought in macroeconomics in the period since the 1930s. We start with the 1930s because it is that period of the great depression, together with the prolonged high unemployment in Britain in the 1920s, which gave birth to the Keynesian revolution. Keynesian economics remained the mainstream of macroeconomic theory until inflation began to get out of hand in the late 1960s. Since then, macroeconomic theory has struggled with the problem of inflation, analyzing the roles of the money stock, expectations, and the supply side in determining the levels of output and prices.

Throughout the period since the early 1960s there has been a close interaction between policy and ideas. The apparent success of a policy action based on a particular theory strengthened confidence in that theory—as the 1964 tax cut did for Keynesianism. The apparent failure of a policy based on a particular theory weakened support for that theory—as the 1969–1971 failure of slow money growth to stem inflation did for monetarism. In the early eighties there is a question of what the 1981–1982 recession will mean for the acceptance of supply-side economics. In 1980 supply-siders promised that disinflation was possible without unemployment. After the recession, some supply-siders argued that their theories were never given a chance, because monetary policy in 1981–1982 was more restrictive than it should have been.

Because policy and ideas are so intertwined, we shall, in discussing the main macroeconomic currents, refer also to economic events of the time. We show how theories influence policies, and how the results of policies influence views about theory. It is entirely appropriate that we change our views of the way the economy works on the basis of experience. There is never certainty about the way the world works, and any worthwhile field of study develops over time as new evidence comes in.

It is also true that the disagreements among economists, and the distinguishing features of different points of view, are systematically exaggerated by the media. Macroeconomic controversies are always in the newspapers because macroeconomics concerns some of the most important issues of daily life—whether jobs are hard or easy to find, whether prices are rising slowly or fast, whether living standards will rise fast or hardly at all. The disagreements are systematically exaggerated because disagreements are news.

Behind the rapidly changing macroeconomic fashions of the media is a more balanced macroeconomic analysis that addresses current economic

FIGURE 16-1 OUTPUT AND PRICES IN THE GREAT DEPRESSION. (*Sources:* U.S. Department of Commerce, The National income and Product Accounts of the United States, 1929–1974, and Economic Report of the President, 1957.)

problems while at the same time weighing carefully evidence that leads to changes—mostly small, but sometimes large—in macroeconomic theories.

16-1 THE GREAT DEPRESSION

The great depression of the 1930s is the event that shaped both many institutions in the economy, including the Fed, and modern American macroeconomics. The essential facts about the depression are shown in Figure 16-1 and in Table 16-1. Between 1929 and 1933, GNP fell by nearly 30 percent. Over the same period, the unemployment rate rose from 3 to 25 percent. For the 10 years 1931 to 1940, the unemployment rate averaged 18.8 percent, ranging between a low of 14.3 percent in 1937 and a high of 24.9 percent in 1933. By contrast, the post-World War II high, reached in 1982, was under 11 percent. Investment collapsed in the great depression; indeed, net investment was negative from 1931 to 1935. The consumer price index fell nearly 25 percent from 1929 to 1933; the stock market fell 80 percent between September 1929 and March 1933. From 1933 to 1937, real GNP grew fast, at an annual rate of nearly 9 percent, but even that did not get the unemployment rate down to normal levels. Then, in 1937–1938 there was a major recession within the depression, pushing the unemployment rate back up to

TABLE 16-1 ECONOMIC STATISTICS OF THE GREAT DEPRESSION

Year	GNP (billion 1972 $)	I/GNP (%)	G (billion 1972 $)	Unemployment rate (%)	CPI (1929 = 100)	Commercial paper rate (%)	AAA rate (%)	Stock market index	$M1$ (1929 = 100)	Full-employment surplus/$\overline{Y}$ (%)
1929	314.7	17.8	40.9	3.2	100	5.9	4.7	83.1	100	−0.8
1930	285.2	13.5	44.6	8.7	97.4	3.6	4.6	67.2	96.2	−1.4
1931	263.3	9.0	46.2	15.9	88.7	2.6	4.6	43.6	89.4	−3.1
1932	226.8	3.5	44.0	23.6	79.7	2.7	5.0	22.1	78.0	−0.9
1933	222.1	3.8	42.8	24.9	75.4	1.7	4.5	28.6	73.5	1.6
1934	239.4	5.5	48.7	21.7	78.0	1.0	4.0	31.4	81.4	0.2
1935	260.8	9.2	49.8	20.1	80.1	0.8	3.6	33.9	96.6	−0.1
1936	296.1	10.9	58.5	16.9	80.9	0.8	3.2	49.4	110.6	−1.1
1937	309.8	12.8	56.3	14.3	83.8	0.9	3.3	49.2	114.8	1.8
1938	297.1	8.1	61.3	19.0	82.3	0.8	3.2	36.7	115.9	0.6
1939	319.7	10.5	63.8	17.2	81.0	0.6	3.0	38.5	127.3	−0.1

Note: Stock market index is the Standard & Poor's composite index, which includes 500 stocks. September 1929 set equal to 100. $\overline{Y}$ denotes full-employment output.

Sources:

Cols. 1, 2, 3: The National Income and Product Accounts of the United States. 1929–1974, *U.S. Department of Commerce.*

Col. 4: Revised Bureau of Labor Statistics data taken from Michael Darby, "Three-and-a-Half Million Employees Have Been Mislaid: Or, an Explanation of Unemployment, 1934–1941," Journal of Political Economy, *February 1976.*

Cols. 5, 6, and 7: Economic Report of the President, 1957.

Col. 8: Security Price Index Record, *1978, Standard & Poor's Statistical Service.*

Col. 9: Milton Friedman and Anna J. Schwartz, A Monetary History of the United States, 1867–1960 (*Princeton, N.J.: Princeton University Press, 1963*), *table A1, col. 7.*

Col. 10: E. Cary Brown, "Fiscal Policy in the Thirties: A Reappraisal," American Economic Review, *December 1956, table I, cols. 3, 5, and 19.*

nearly 20 percent. In the second half of the decade, short-term interest rates, such as the commercial paper rate, were near zero.

Facts such as those in Table 16-1 raise a host of questions. The two most important are, Why did this happen? and, Could it have been prevented? Underlying these questions is one that many economists are asked whenever the economy is in recession, and that they ask themselves in their bad moments: Could it happen again?

The depression and the stock market crash of October 1929 are popularly thought of as almost the same thing. In fact, the economy started turning down before the stock market crash. The peak of the business cycle is estimated to have been in August 1929, and the stock market itself peaked in September 1929. Standard & Poor's composite stock price index, which was calculated using September 1929 as the base period, fell from 100 in September to 66 in November. It rose again through March 1930, but then the collapse continued until the index fell to 15 in June 1932.

By early 1931, the economy was suffering from a very severe depression, but not one that was out of the range of the experience of the previous century.[2] It was in the period from early 1931 until Franklin Roosevelt became President in March 1933 that the depression became "great."

ECONOMIC POLICY

What was economic policy during this period? The money stock fell from 1929 to 1930, and then fell rapidly in 1931 and 1932 and continued falling through April 1933. At the same time, the composition of the money stock changed. In March 1931 the currency-demand deposit ratio was 18.5 percent; 2 years later, it was 40.7 percent.

The fall in the money stock was the result of large-scale bank failures. Banks failed because they did not have the reserves with which to meet customers' cash withdrawals, and in failing they destroyed deposits and hence reduced the money stock. But the failures went further in reducing the money stock, because they led to a loss of confidence on the part of depositors and hence to an even higher desired currency-deposit ratio. Furthermore, banks that had not yet failed adjusted to the possibility of a run by holding increased reserves relative to deposits. The rise in the currency-deposit ratio and the reserve-deposit ratio reduced the money multiplier and hence sharply contracted the money stock.

The Fed took very few steps to offset the fall in the money supply; for a few months in 1932 it did undertake a program of open market purchases, but otherwise it seemed to acquiesce in bank closings and certainly failed to understand that the central bank should act vigorously in a crisis to prevent the collapse of the financial system.[3]

[2] Milton Friedman and Anna J. Schwartz, in *A Monetary History of the United States 1867–1960* (Princeton, N.J.: Princeton University Press, 1963), give a very detailed account of the great depression, comparing it with other recessions and emphasizing the role of the Fed. For a more general economic history of the period, see Robert A. Gordon, *Economic Instability: The American Record* (New York: Harper & Row, 1974), chap. 3.

[3] Friedman and Schwartz speculate on the reasons for the Fed's inaction; the whodunit or "who didn't do it" on pp. 407 to 419 of their book (cited in footnote 1) is fascinating.

TABLE 16-2 GOVERNMENT SPENDING AND REVENUE, 1929–1939 (*In percent*)

	TOTAL GOVERNMENT		FEDERAL GOVERNMENT		TOTAL GOVERNMENT
Year	Expenditure/ GNP	Actual surplus/ GNP	Expenditure/ GNP	Actual surplus/ GNP	Full employment surplus/ $\bar{Y}$*
1929	10.0	1.0	2.5	1.2	−0.8
1930	12.3	−0.3	3.1	0.3	−1.4
1931	16.4	−3.8	5.5	−2.8	−3.1
1932	18.3	−3.1	5.5	−2.6	−0.9
1933	19.2	−2.5	7.2	−2.3	1.6
1934	19.8	−3.7	9.8	−4.4	0.2
1935	18.6	−2.8	9.0	−3.6	−0.1
1936	19.5	−3.8	10.5	−4.4	−1.1
1937	16.6	0.3	8.2	0.4	1.8
1938	19.8	−2.1	10.2	−2.5	0.6
1939	19.4	−2.4	9.8	−2.4	−0.1

* $\bar{Y}$ = potential output.
Sources:
Cols. 1, 2, 3, 4: Economic Report of the President, 1972, *tables B1 and B70.*
Col. 5: E. Cary Brown. "Fiscal Policy in the Thirties: A Reappraisal," American Economic Review, *December 1956, table 1, cols. 3, 5, and 19.*

Fiscal policy too was not vigorous. The natural impulse of politicians then was to balance the budget in times of trouble, and much rhetoric was devoted to that proposition. The presidential candidates in 1932 campaigned on balanced budget platforms. In fact, as Table 16-2 shows, the federal government ran enormous deficits, particularly for that time, averaging 2.6 percent of GNP from 1931 to 1933 and even more later. (These actual deficits are lower as a percentage of GNP than those projected for the mid-eighties.) The belief in budget balancing was more than rhetoric, however, for state and local governments raised taxes to match their expenditures,[4] as did the federal government, particularly in 1932 and 1933. President Roosevelt tried seriously to balance the budget—he was no Keynesian. The full-employment surplus shows fiscal policy (combined state, local, and federal) as most expansionary in 1931, and moving to a more contractionary level from 1932 to 1934. In fact, the full-employment surplus was positive in 1933 and 1934, despite the actual deficits.[5] Of course, the full-employment surplus concept had not been invented in the 1930s.

Economic activity recovered in the period from 1933 to 1937, with fiscal policy becoming more expansionary and the money stock growing rapidly. The growth of the money stock was based on an inflow of gold from Europe. This provided high-powered money for the monetary system. It was in the thirties that the Fed acquired most of its current holdings of gold.[6]

[4] You can calculate the surplus of state and local governments as a percentage of GNP by subtracting column 4 in Table 16-2 from column 2.

[5] Note that in this chapter, unlike Chapter 3 and elsewhere in the book, the full-employment deficit includes federal, state, and local governments.

[6] For details of the way in which the Fed acquired the gold, see Friedman and Schwartz, op. cit., p. 506.

The period from 1933 to 1937 also saw substantial legislative and administrative action—the *New Deal*—from the Roosevelt administration. The Fed was reorganized, and the Federal Deposit Insurance Corporation (FDIC) was established, as were a variety of regulatory agencies and the Social Security Administration.

The FDIC insures deposits in participating banks, thus assuring depositors that their funds (up to a maximum that is raised periodically) can be obtained even if the bank fails. Deposit insurance both reduces the likelihood that depositors will cause a run on a bank and ensures that depositors do not lose wealth if banks do fail. Regulation Q, forbidding the payment of interest on demand deposits, was instituted, based on the belief that excessive competition among banks in the late twenties had caused them to offer depositors higher interest rates than were wise, and thus had caused bank failures.

A number of regulatory agencies were also created, most notably the Securities and Exchange Commission, which regulates the securities industry. Its purpose was to prevent speculative excesses that were thought largely responsible for the stock market crash. The Social Security Administration was set up so that the elderly would not in the future have to rely on their own savings to ensure themselves a minimally adequate standard of living in retirement. The Roosevelt administration also believed that the route to recovery lay in increasing wages and prices, so it encouraged trade unionization, and price-raising and price-fixing schemes by business, through the National Recovery Administration.

INTERNATIONAL ASPECTS

Another important aspect of the depression deserves mention: it was virtually worldwide. To some extent, this was the result of the collapse of the international financial system.[7] It resulted too from the mutual adoption of high tariff policies by many countries (including the United States), keeping out foreign goods to protect domestic producers. And, of course, if each country keeps out foreign goods, the volume of world trade declines, providing a contractionary influence on the world economy.

The experience of the thirties varied internationally. Sweden suffered its depression in the twenties and benefited from expansionary policies in the thirties. Britain's economy too suffered more in the twenties than in the thirties. Germany grew rapidly after Hitler came to power and expanded government spending. China escaped the recession until after 1931, essentially because it had a floating exchange rate. As always, there is much to be learned from the exceptions.

In 1939, real GNP in the United States rose above its 1929 level for the

[7] This aspect of the depression is emphasized by Charles Kindleberger, *The World in Depression, 1929–1939* (Berkeley: University of California Press, 1973), and Gottfried Haberler, *The World Economy, Money and the Great Depression,* (Washington, D.C.: American Enterprise Institute, 1976).

first time in the decade. But it was not until 1942, after the United States formally entered World War II, that the unemployment rate finally fell below 5 percent.

16-2 THE GREAT DEPRESSION: THE ISSUES AND IDEAS

In Section 16-1 we asked what caused the great depression, whether it could have been avoided, and whether it could happen again. The question of what caused the depression seems purely academic, but it is much more than that. The depression was the greatest economic crisis the Western world had experienced.

The classical economics of the time had no well-developed theory that would explain persistent unemployment, nor any policy prescriptions to solve the problem. Many economists of the time did, in fact, recommend government spending as a way of reducing unemployment, but they had no macroeconomic theory by which to justify their recommendations.

Keynes wrote his greatest work, *The General Theory of Employment, Interest and Money* in the 1930s, after Britain had suffered during the 1920s from a decade of double-digit unemployment and while the United States was in the depths of its depression. He was fully aware of the seriousness of the issues. As Don Patinkin of the Hebrew University puts it[8]:

> . . . the period was one of fear and darkness as the Western world struggled with the greatest depression that it had known. . . . [T]here was a definite feeling that by attempting to achieve a scientific understanding of the phenomenon of mass unemployment, one was not only making an intellectual contribution, but was also dealing with a critical problem that endangered the very existence of Western civilization.

Keynesian theory explained what had happened, what could have been done to prevent the depression, and what could be done to prevent future depressions. The explanation soon became accepted by most macroeconomists, in the process described as the Keynesian revolution. The Keynesian revolution did not have much impact on economic policy making in the United States until the 1960s, but it affected macroeconomics much earlier than that.

The Keynesian Explanation

The essence of the Keynesian explanation of the great depression is based on the simple aggregate demand model developed in Chapter 3. Growth in the twenties, in this view, was based on the mass production of the automobile and

[8] In "The Process of Writing *The General Theory:* A Critical Survey," in Don Patinkin and J. Clark Leith (eds.), *Keynes, Cambridge and the General Theory* (Toronto: University of Toronto Press, 1978), p. 3. For a short biography of Keynes, see D. E. Moggridge, *John Maynard Keynes* (New York: Penguin Books, 1976).

radio and was fueled by a housing boom. The collapse of growth in the thirties resulted from the drying up of investment opportunities and a downward shift in investment demand. The collapse of investment, shown in Table 16-1, fits in with this picture. Some researchers also believe there was a downward shift in the consumption function in 1930.[9] Poor fiscal policy, as reflected in the perverse behavior of the full-employment surplus from 1931 to 1933, shares the blame, particularly for making the depression worse.

What does this view have to say about the monetary collapse? The Fed argued in the thirties that there was little it could have done to prevent the depression, because interest rates were already as low as they could possibly go. A variety of sayings of the type, "You can lead a horse to water but you can't make it drink," were used to explain that further reductions in interest rates would have had no effect if there was no demand for investment. Investment demand was thought to be very unresponsive to the rate of interest — implying a very steep *IS* curve. At the same time, the *LM* curve was believed to be quite flat, though not necessarily reaching the extreme of a liquidity trap. In this situation, as we saw in Chapter 4, monetary expansion would be relatively ineffective in stimulating demand and output.

It was also widely believed that the experience of the depression showed that the private economy was inherently unstable in that it could self-depress with no difficulty if left alone. The experience of the thirties, implicitly or explicitly, was the basis for the belief that an active stabilization policy was needed to maintain good economic performance.

The Keynesian model not only offered an explanation of what had happened, but also suggested policy measures that could have been taken to prevent the depression, and that could be used to prevent future depressions. Vigorous use of countercyclical fiscal policy was the preferred method for reducing cyclical fluctuations. If a recession ever showed signs of deteriorating into a depression, the cure would be to cut taxes and increase government spending. And those policies would, too, have prevented the depression from being as deep as it was.

There is nothing in the *IS-LM* model developed in Chapter 4 that suggests fiscal policy is more useful than monetary policy for stabilization of the economy. Nonetheless, it is true that until the 1950s, Keynesians tended to give more emphasis to fiscal than to monetary policy.

The Monetarist Challenge

The Keynesian emphasis on fiscal policy, and its downplaying of the role of money, was increasingly challenged by Milton Friedman and his coworkers[10] during the 1950s. During this period Friedman was developing much of the analysis and evidence that provided the basis for monetarism, which we describe in detail in Section 16-5. The main thrust was a heavy emphasis on

[9] Peter Temin, *Did Monetary Forces Cause the Great Depression?* (New York: Norton, 1976).

[10] See, in particular, Milton Friedman (ed.), *Studies in the Quantity Theory of Money* (Chicago: University of Chicago Press, 1956).

the role of monetary policy in determining the behavior of both output and prices.

If monetary policy was to be given an important role, though, it was necessary to dispose of the view that monetary policy had been tried in the great depression and had failed. In other words, the view that "You can lead a horse to the water, etc.," had to be challenged.

The view that monetary policy in the thirties had been impotent was attacked in 1963 by Friedman and Schwartz in their *Monetary History*. They argued that the depression, far from showing that money does not matter, "is in fact a tragic testimonial to the importance of monetary factors."[11] They argued, with skill and style, that the failure of the Fed to prevent bank failures and the decline of the money stock from the end of 1930 to 1933 was largely responsible for the recession being as serious as it was. This monetary view, in turn, came close to being accepted as the orthodox explanation of the depression.[12]

Synthesis

Both the Keynesian and the monetarist explanations of the great depression fit the facts, and both provide answers to the question of why it happened, and how to prevent it from happening again. Inept fiscal and monetary policies both made the great depression severe. If there had been prompt, strong, expansive monetary and fiscal policy, the economy would have suffered a recession but not the trauma it did.

On the question of whether it could happen again, there is agreement that it could not, except, of course, in the event of truly perverse policies. But these are less likely now than they were then. For one thing, we have history to help us avoid its repetition. Taxes would not again be raised in the middle of a depression, nor would attempts be made to balance the budget. The Fed would seek actively to keep the money supply from falling. In addition, the government now has a much larger role in the economy than it did then. The higher level of government spending, which is relatively slow to change, and automatic stabilizers, including the income tax,[13] unemployment insurance, and Social Security, give the economy more stability than it had then.[14]

There is no inherent conflict between the Keynesian and monetarist explanations of the great depression. The *IS-LM* model, augmented by the supply-side analysis of wage and price adjustment in Chapters 11 to 13, easily combines both explanations. Why, then, has there been controversy over the causes of the great depression? The reason is that the thirties are seen as the

[11] Friedman and Schwartz, op. cit., p. 300.

[12] Ben Bernanke, in "Nonmonetary Effects of the Financial Crisis in the Propagation of the Great Depression," *American Economic Review*, June 1983, takes issue with the monetary view, arguing instead that the destruction of the financial system made it difficult for borrowers to obtain funds needed for investment.

[13] Recall from Chap. 3 that a proportional income tax reduces the multiplier.

[14] See Martin Baily, "Stabilization Policy and Private Economic Behavior," *Brookings Papers on Economic Activity*, 1978:1, (Washington, D.C.: The Brookings Institution, 1978).

period that set the stage for massive government intervention in the economy. Those opposed to an active role for government have to explain away the debacle of the economy in the thirties. If the depression occurred because of, and not despite, the government (particularly the Fed), the case for an active government role in economic stabilization is weakened. Further, the thirties are a period in which the economy behaved in such an extreme way that competing theories have to be subjected to the test of whether they can explain that period. Those are the main reasons the dispute over the causes of the great depression continues more than 50 years after it began.[15]

16-3 THE NEW ECONOMICS

Keynesian economics was rapidly accepted by most macroeconomists, but it affected policy less rapidly. The budget was used in Britain as a countercyclical policy tool in the entire post-World War II period. In the United States, the Employment Act of 1946 imposed on the government the obligation to follow policies that would produce high employment. Nonetheless, it was not until the Kennedy administration in the early 1960s that an administration began to follow avowedly Keynesian policies.

The approach was described as the *New Economics.* The analytical approach consists basically of the tools we have outlined in Chapters 3 through 9. The philosophy characterizing that approach to economics is a mix of activism and optimism. It is well characterized by an excerpt from the 1962 *Economic Report of the President* (page 68)[16]:

> Insufficient demand means unemployment, idle capacity, and lost production. Excessive demand means inflation—general increases in prices and money incomes, bringing forth little or no gains in output and real income. The objective of stabilization policies is to minimize these deviations, i.e., to keep over-all demand in step with the basic production potential of the economy.
>
> Stabilization does not mean a mere leveling off of peaks and troughs in production and employment. It does not mean trying to hold over-all demand for goods and services stable. It means minimizing deviations from a rising trend, not from an unchanging average. In a growing economy, demand must grow in order

[15] Among recent contributions is Michael Darby, "Three-and-a-Half Million U.S. Employees Have Been Mislaid: Or, an Explanation of Unemployment, 1934–1941," *Journal of Political Economy,* February 1976. Darby argues that unemployment is mismeasured after 1933 because those on government work relief programs are counted as unemployed. Adjusted for those individuals, the unemployment rate falls rapidly from 20.6 percent in 1933 to below 10 percent in 1936. See also Thomas Mayer, "Money and the Great Depression: A Critique of Professor Temin's Thesis," *Explorations in Economic History,* April 1978, and Karl Brunner (ed.), *The Great Depression Revisited* (Boston: Martinus Nijhoff, 1981).

[16] See, too, the history of the New Economics in W. W. Heller, *New Dimensions of Political Economy* (New York: Norton, 1967). Walter Heller, now a professor at the University of Minnesota, was one of the chief architects of the economic policies of the Kennedy-Johnson administration. With him, as members of the Council of Economic Advisers or staff economists, were highly distinguished economists: James Tobin, Kenneth Arrow, Robert Solow, Otto Eckstein, Gardner Ackley, and the late Arthur Okun. Paul A. Samuelson served as an unofficial adviser.

to maintain full employment of labor and full utilization of capacity at stable prices. The economy is not performing satisfactorily unless it is almost continuously setting new records of production, income, and employment. Indeed, unless production grows as fast as its potential, unemployment and idle capacity will also grow. And when the economy starts from a position well below potential, output must for a time grow even faster than potential to achieve full utilization.

The contrast between economic policy in the thirties and economic policy in the sixties is marked. In the sixties, policy makers came into a not very difficult economic situation with well-thought-out theories and policies to apply. Those policies were based on the Keynesian analysis that developed in the thirties and out of the experience of the thirties. In the thirties, policy fumbled, and badly, for some way to get the economy moving again. The Roosevelt administration did run budget deficits, but most unwillingly, and it had no concept of the full-employment surplus; the Kennedy-Johnson administration, by contrast, planned a tax cut in 1963–1964 when the budget was in deficit, and sold the policy to a skeptical Congress.

The New Economics emphasized the goal of reattaining full employment after the high unemployment levels of the late 1950s. We briefly review the basic analytical concepts of the New Economics before concluding this section by discussing what was new in the New Economics.

Potential Output and the GNP Gap

To focus attention on the target of full employment and for use as an operating guide to policy, the *Council of Economic Advisers* (*CEA*), and particularly Arthur Okun, developed and stressed the concept of potential output. Potential output, or full-employment output, measures the level of real GNP the economy can produce with full employment. The full-employment rate of unemployment used in defining potential output in the sixties was about 4 percent.[17] Figure 16-2 shows potential output for the 1956–1971 period.

Along with the concept and measurement of potential output went the notion of the GNP gap. The gap is the difference between actual and potential real output. For the years 1961–1965, actual GNP was below its potential level, and the GNP gap was therefore positive. At the beginning of 1961, the GNP gap was more than 7 percent of GNP. A gap of that magnitude clearly called for expansionary monetary or fiscal policy to raise aggregate demand to a level closer to the economy's potential.

The notions of potential output and the GNP gap seem very simple, but they are important. They dramatize the costs of unemployment in easily understood terms of output lost due to unemployment—and make it easy to understand what alternative target levels of GNP, at which policy makers might aim, would mean for the level of unemployment.

[17] We introduced potential output in Chap. 1. Remember that we pointed out there that new measures of potential output (to be discussed in Chap. 17) take an unemployment rate of as much as 6 percent to represent full employment.

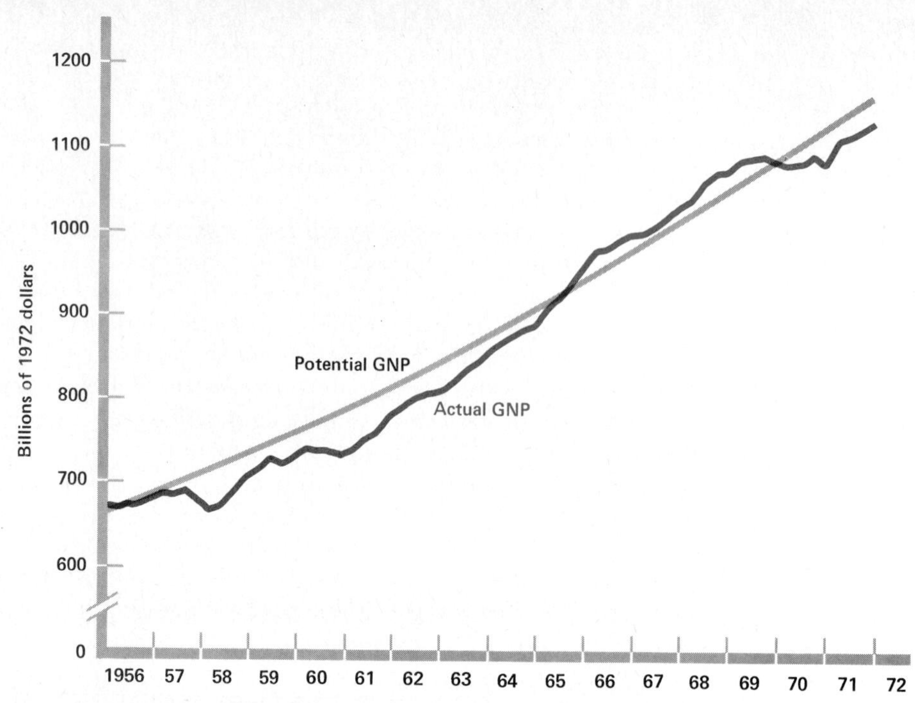

FIGURE 16-2 ACTUAL AND POTENTIAL GNP (BILLIONS OF 1972 DOLLARS)
(*Source: The Survey of Current Business*, April 1982 and 1983, and Data Resources, Inc.)

The Full-Employment Budget Surplus

The full-employment budget surplus was discussed in Chapter 3, and we will therefore be brief here. The concept had been introduced before the 1960s, most notably to study fiscal policy in the thirties. The concept is important and useful because it directs attention away from the actual budget, which is a misleading indicator of fiscal policy, toward the full-employment surplus—a more relevant, although still imperfect, indicator of policy.

The New Economists planned to use fiscal policy as the instrument with which to close the GNP gap. It was important to get across to Congress and the public the idea of the full-employment surplus because the federal budget was in an actual deficit. Any proposals to increase spending or cut taxes would certainly imply a larger deficit. Congress could be relied upon to look with great suspicion on any policy that might increase the budget deficit. By focusing attention on the full-employment budget, the New Economists appropriately succeeded in shifting attention away from the state of the actual budget to concern with how the budget would look at full employment—which had the side benefit of focusing attention on the full-employment issue itself.

Growth

The New Economics emphasized economic growth in two ways. First, there was the need for aggregate demand to grow in order to achieve full employment. In that respect, growth was a matter of achieving full employment and maintaining it. Second, there was an emphasis on achieving a high rate of growth of potential output itself. The emphasis was on investment spending to encourage growth in productive potential. To that end the administration introduced an investment tax credit (see Chapter 7) in 1962.

The Behavior of Money Wages

The New Economists emphasized the behavior of money wages relative to productivity in affecting the rate of inflation. This is in accord with the analysis of inflation in Chapters 12 and 13.

Early in the Kennedy-Johnson years, in 1962, the Council of Economic Advisers set up *guideposts*[18] for the behavior of money wages. The basic guidepost was that money wages should not grow faster than the average rate of productivity increase in the economy. In 1965 and 1966, the guideposts were made more explicit, and the rate of wage increase of 3.2 percent became the general criterion for noninflationary wage increases.

In setting up the criterion for noninflationary wage increases—that wages should not increase faster than labor productivity—the CEA also suggested that rapid investment could contribute to price stability. The notion was that rapid investment would increase the amount of capital employed in the production of output, and would thus increase the productivity of labor. For a given rate of wage increase, this greater productivity would mean less inflation. High investment spending was thus thought helpful in containing inflationary pressures. A similar argument was advanced in the early 1980s by supply-side economists.[19]

What Was New?

What was new about the New Economics? Was the approach to stabilization policy along the lines of fiscal activism, potential output objectives, and the emphasis on the full-employment budget surplus in fact new? The answer here is not simple. It is true that the activism the CEA displayed was unprece-

[18] For an interesting, and sometimes amusing, discussion of the guideposts, see George P. Shultz and Robert Z. Aliber (eds.), *Guidelines* (Chicago: The University of Chicago Press, 1966).

[19] The argument that more rapid productivity growth helps reduce the inflation rate is correct, but it is important to get the orders of magnitude right. Given the growth rate of money, an increase in the growth rate of output results in a lower rate of inflation—because the demand for real balances grows faster when output grows faster. (See the discussion in Chap. 13 of the relation between money growth and inflation.) It is unlikely that a 1 percent increase in the growth rate of output would on those grounds reduce the inflation rate by more than 1 percent. Thus increased productivity growth, while of great importance for long-run standards of living (see Chap. 17), would not have large effects on inflation.

dented. But it is true, too, that the tools and concepts the Council used were main-line professional macroeconomics. The idea of active fiscal policy as a countercyclical measure and the notion that there was nothing particularly desirable about a balanced budget were certainly not new.

Even so, the active use of fiscal policy met much resistance in the political process at the time. Herbert Stein, himself chairperson of the CEA under President Nixon, reviews the progress toward the major policy measure of the early sixties, the 1964 tax cut, in his book *The Fiscal Revolution*.[20] He shows how the Kennedy administration first had to get accustomed to the idea that, during recession, a move toward an increased budget deficit was not a step toward fiscal irresponsibility. By the same token, Congress had to find its way toward expansionary fiscal policies, away from balanced budgets or tax cuts accompanied by offsetting reductions in public spending. Eventually, many recognized that a measure to expand aggregate demand was necessary in order to cope with high unemployment.

Thus, what was new about the New Economics was not the analysis, which was standard macroeconomics, but rather the active and successful use of that analysis in the operation of fiscal policy.

The New Economics and the Economy

The most ambitious and successful policy action of the Kennedy-Johnson administration was the tax cut of 1964, which we analyzed in Chapter 5. The tax cut kept the economy growing rapidly through the mid-sixties, thus reducing the unemployment rate. At the same time, as Figure 16-3 shows, the inflation rate stayed below 2.5 percent per year.

Through the middle of the sixties, the economy was behaving as well as it ever has. Productivity growth was high, output was growing fast, unemployment was falling, and the inflation rate was low. It is little wonder that there was considerable optimism about the possibilities of the New Economics.

In the late sixties things began to go wrong. Part of the problem was political. Government spending for the Vietnam war was rising rapidly, but President Johnson was not willing to push for a tax increase to finance the war, fearing that a tax increase would make the war more unpopular. In 1966 and 1967, it was left to monetary policy to fight the increasing expansionary pressure of fiscal policy. Only in 1968 was the Johnson administration willing to ask Congress for a tax increase to try to contain the expansionary pressure of military spending.

The decision was made to go for a transitory tax increase. The contractionary effect of the tax increase was overestimated, so that by the end of the Johnson administration at the beginning of 1969, the inflation rate was up to more than 5 percent. To be sure, the unemployment rate was below 4 percent, and the economy was still in its longest expansion on record: there was no recession between 1961 and 1969.

The record of the 1960s is one of full employment, expansion, and rising

[20] Chicago: The University of Chicago Press, 1969.

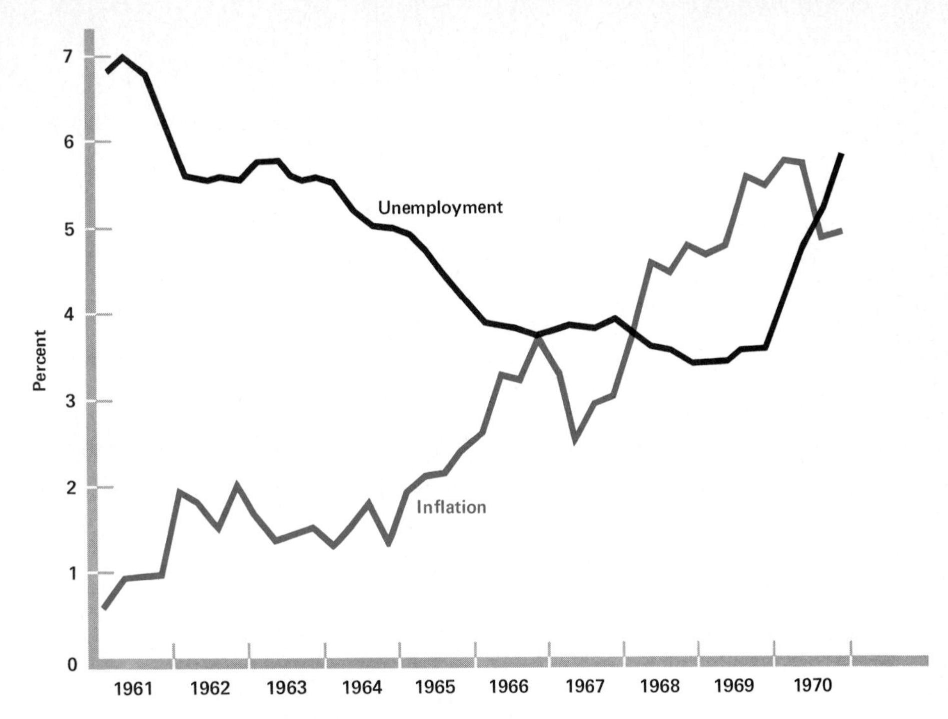

FIGURE 16-3 INFLATION AND UNEMPLOYMENT 1961–1970 (*Source:* Data Resources, Inc.)

inflation. Keynesian economics, or the New Economics, received the popular credit for the expansion of the mid-sixties following the tax cut. Similarly, it received the blame for the rising inflation, even though many of the economic advisers to the President were urging a tax increase as early as 1966.

The rising inflation of the sixties was accompanied by increasing money growth, as can be seen in Figure 16-4. By the beginning of the Nixon administration in 1969, concern over inflation and the constant emphasis by monetarists on the relationship between money growth and inflation had combined to reduce confidence in the New Economics and turn attention toward monetarism.

16-4 THE ECONOMY: 1969–1983

Before we turn to monetarism and subsequent developments in macroeconomics, we describe the behavior of the economy from 1969 to 1983. Table 16-3 summarizes the contrast between the average rates of growth, inflation, unemployment, and money growth for the 1961–1968 and 1969–1983 periods. Growth in the sixties was substantially higher, and inflation and unemployment were lower, than in the subsequent years.

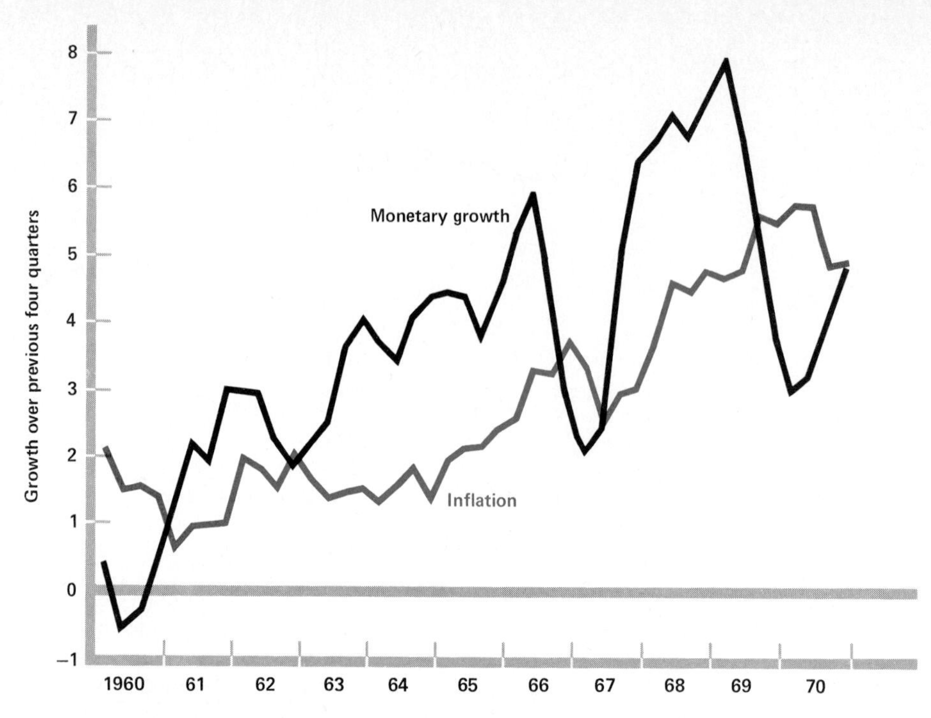

FIGURE 16-4 INFLATION AND MONETARY ($M1$) GROWTH, 1960–1970
(*Source:* Data Resources, Inc.)

Figure 16-5*a* shows the unemployment and inflation rates over the 1969–1983 period. In part (*b*) we show the growth rate of $M1$ and fiscal policy for the period. There were four recessions (shaded) during this period, by contrast with none during the previous 8 years. The 1973–1975 and 1981–1982 recessions were the deepest since World War II.

The period opened with restrictive monetary and fiscal policies designed to reduce the inflation rate below the 5 percent level it had reached at the end of 1968. The restrictive policies were kept in place for over 2 years. But when the inflation rate proved resistant to conventional aggregate demand policies, the Nixon administration turned in 1971 to wage and price controls, aiming to bring the inflation rate down rapidly through direct measures.

From 1971 to 1973 the economy boomed, with the encouragement of

TABLE 16-3 COMPARATIVE ECONOMIC PERFORMANCE, 1961–1968 AND 1969–1982, (%)

	Growth rate of real GNP	Unemployment rate	Inflation (CPI)	Money growth ($M1$)
1961–1968	4.9	4.8	2.2	4.3
1969–1982	2.3	6.4	7.5	6.4

Source: Data Resources, Inc.

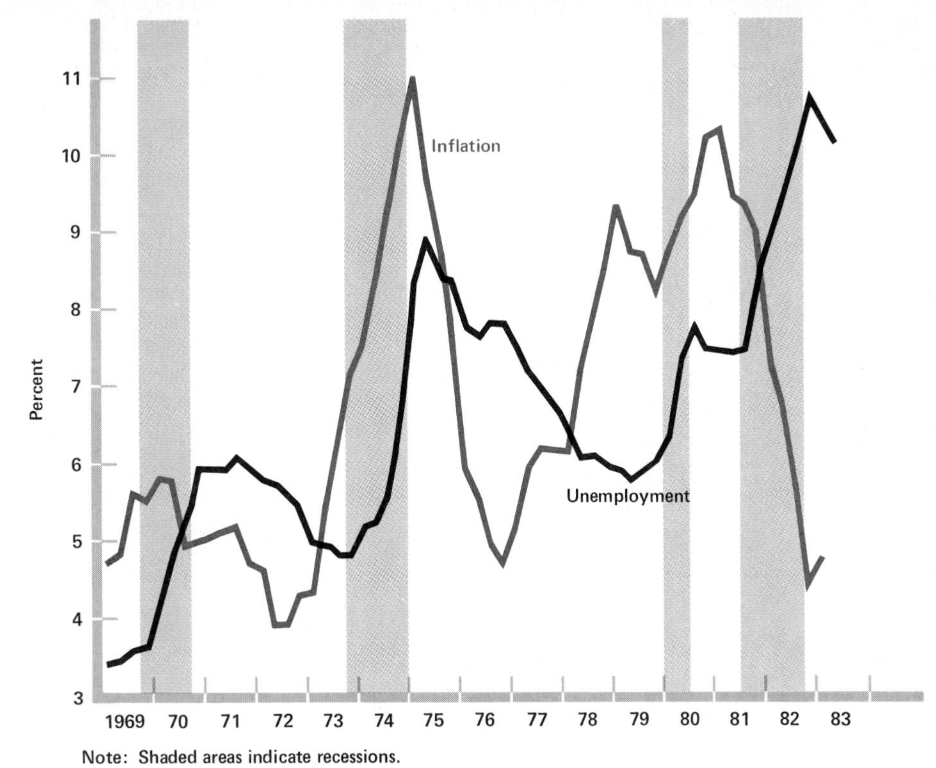

FIGURE 16-5a INFLATION AND UNEMPLOYMENT, 1969–1983 (*Source:* Data Resources, Inc.)

expansionary monetary and fiscal policies. During 1973 food and raw materials prices rose sharply, and then at the end of 1973, the first oil price shock hit the economy. The rapid rises in food and raw materials—particularly oil—prices constituted the first serious supply shock to hit the economy in the post-World War II period. Policy makers and economists were perplexed about how to respond to the shock. The high inflation rate seemed to call for restrictive monetary and fiscal policy, but the supply shock was reducing output; so perhaps policy should have been expansionary or at least accommodating of the shock. In any event, monetary policy became restrictive to fight the inflation. As late as the end of 1974, with the recession well under way, the administration was still considering a tax *increase* to fight the inflation. By early 1975, though, fiscal policy became expansionary; consumers were given a tax rebate on their 1974 taxes, and the investment tax credit was increased.

The 1973–1975 recession reduced the inflation rate. Consumer prices rose less than 5 percent during 1976. From the low-inflation/high-unemployment situation at the beginning of 1975, the economy grew rapidly. The growth rate of GNP was 5 percent per year or more in each year from 1976 to 1978. This was a strong recovery from the recession. The only fly in the ointment—and it was no small fly—was the rising inflation rate. In 1979 a

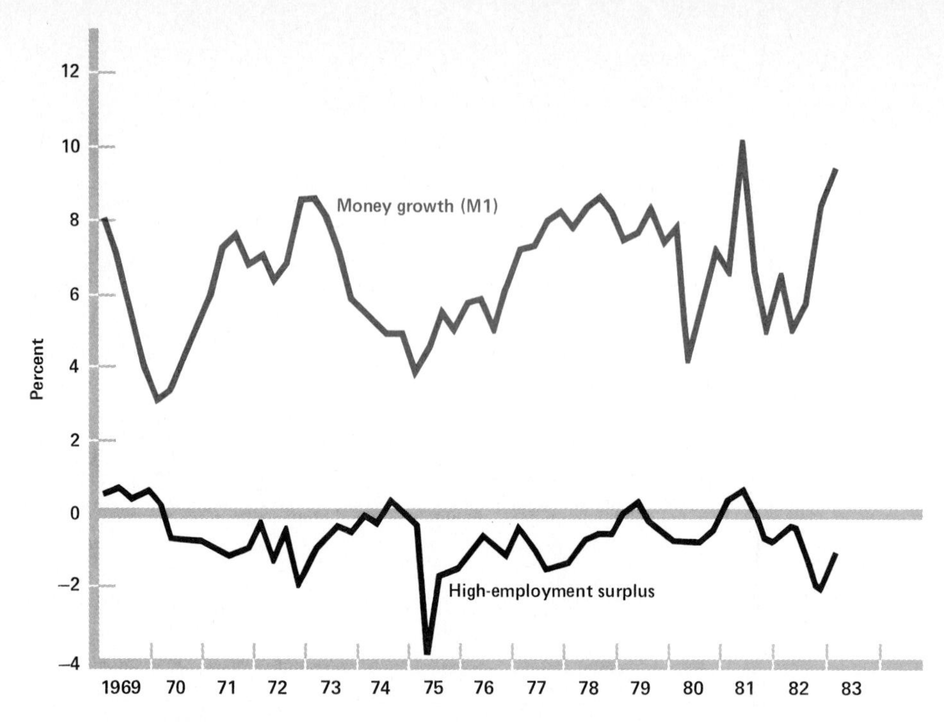

FIGURE 16-5*b* MONEY GROWTH AND THE HIGH-EMPLOYMENT SURPLUS (PERCENTAGE OF GNP) (*Source:* Data Resources, Inc.)

second oil price shock caused the inflation rate to rise sharply again. In response to the high inflation, the Fed in October 1979 adopted its new monetary policy, which was henceforth to concentrate on keeping the growth rate of money under control and on target. Over the next 4 years, there were two recessions. During this period, too, the Reagan administration introduced its fiscal policy, with a commitment to sharply reducing taxes and the size of the government.

By the middle of 1983, with the inflation rate down to less than 5 percent, it was reasonable to hope that the inflation of the past decade had been broken. Whether the economy was entering a new expansionary era, such as that of the sixties, or, alternatively, was at the beginning of a typical cyclical period of expansion such as that of 1975–1979 could not be predicted.

The poor economic performance of the 1969–1983 period raised interesting and important questions for economists and for the future of the economy. The problem of inflation received most attention. How could inflation be reduced? Was there a better way than through recessions? How could the inflation rate be kept low when the economy recovered? What is the right way to respond to supply shocks? The low real growth of the period also raised questions, all coming down to one essential issue: is there any way to get the economy moving again at the high growth rates of the sixties?

In searching for answers to these questions, macroeconomics developed and moved away from the New Economics of the sixties. The emphasis in 1969 was on monetarism, which promised control of inflation by controlling the money supply.

16-5 MONETARISM

Milton Friedman and monetarism are almost synonymous. Monetarism appears, however, in many shades and covers quite a spectrum from a hard monetarism, beyond the Friedman variety, to eclectic Keynesianism. In that spectrum one would include Karl Brunner of the University of Rochester, Allan Meltzer of Carnegie-Mellon, Thomas Mayer of the University of California at Davis, Phillip Cagan of Columbia University, David Laidler and Michael Parkin of the University of Western Ontario, and William Poole of Brown University, to name only some of the most prominent. Monetarism is not confined to academic economists. Indeed, the Federal Reserve Bank of St. Louis has long been a haven of a monetarist perspective on macroeconomics, and so have congressional committees. If monetarism admits of some diversity, it nevertheless comes down to the proposition that money is extremely important for macroeconomics, that money is more important than other things such as fiscal policy, and, in some variants, that money is virtually all that matters.

We define monetarism by describing Friedman's views, but we should warn you that in so doing we overemphasize Friedman's role in developing and sustaining monetarism. Friedman's views on macroeconomics have been laid out in a series of scholarly articles, books, and popular writings.[21] Outstanding among his publications is *A Monetary History of the United States, 1867–1960,* written jointly with Anna J. Schwartz of the National Bureau of Economic Research. We have already noted the influential monetary explanation of the great depression in the *Monetary History.* More generally, the *Monetary History* is an absorbing book that skillfully relates the behavior of the economy to the behavior of the stock of money.

What are the main features of monetarism?

Emphasis on the Stock of Money

Monetarism emphasizes the importance of the behavior of the money stock in determining (1) the rate of inflation in the long run and (2) the behavior of real GNP in the short run. Friedman has said[22]:

> I regard the description of our position as "money is all that matters for changes in *nominal* income and for *short-run* changes in real income" as an exaggeration but one that gives the right flavor of our conclusions.

[21] In addition to the books referred to earlier in the chapter, see *The Optimum Quantity of Money* (Chicago: Aldine, 1969) and *A Program for Monetary Stability* (New York: Fordham University Press, 1959).

[22] "A Theoretical Framework for Monetary Analysis," *Journal of Political Economy,* March/April 1970, p. 217.

The view that the behavior of the money stock is crucial for determining the rate of inflation in the long run is consistent with the analysis of Chapter 13, as we noted there. The view that the behavior of the money stock—by which Friedman usually means the *growth rate* of the money stock—is of primary importance in determining the behavior of nominal and real GNP in the short run is not one we have accepted. Our treatment so far has given emphasis to *both* monetary and fiscal variables in determining the short-run behavior of nominal and real GNP. But there is no doubt that monetary variables play an important role in determining nominal and real GNP in the short run.

An important part of monetarism is the insistence that changes in the growth rate of money—accelerations and decelerations—account for changes in real activity. Instability in monetary growth is mirrored in variability in economic activity. Thus Friedman argues[23]:

> Why should we be concerned about these gyrations in monetary growth? Because they exert an important influence on the future course of the economy. Erratic monetary growth almost always produces erratic economic growth.

Monetarists point to a number of economic expansions and recessions as being caused by monetary accelerations and decelerations. These would certainly include the 1966 slowdown of economic activity in response to the credit crunch, the failure of the 1968 tax surcharge because it was swamped by expansionary monetary policy, and the 1970, 1980, and 1981–1982 recessions.

Friedman's view of the primary importance of money is based in part on his careful historical studies, in which he was able to relate the booms and recessions of U.S. economic history to the behavior of the money stock. In general, it appeared that increases of the growth rate of money produced booms and inflations, and decreases in the money stock produced recessions and sometimes deflations.

Long and Variable Lags

Monetarism has emphasized that although the growth rate of money is of prime importance in determining the behavior of GNP, the effects of changes in the growth rate of money on the subsequent behavior of GNP occur with long and variable lags. On average, it takes a long time for a change in the growth rate of money to affect GNP, and so the lag is long. In addition, the time it takes for this change to affect GNP varies from one historical episode to another—the lags are variable. These arguments are based on empirical and not theoretical evidence. Friedman estimates the lags may be as short as 6 months and as long as 2 years.

[23] "Irresponsible Monetary Policy," *Newsweek*, Jan. 10, 1972. Reprinted in Friedman's collection of public policy essays, *There's No Such Thing as a Free Lunch* (La Salle, Ill.: Open Court Publishing, 1975), p. 73.

The Monetary Rule

Combining the preceding arguments, Friedman argues against the use of active monetary policy. He suggests that because the behavior of the money stock is of critical importance for the behavior of real and nominal GNP, and because money operates with a long and variable lag, monetary policy should not attempt to "fine-tune" the economy. The active use of monetary policy might actually destabilize the economy, because an action taken in 1984, say, might affect the economy at any of various future dates, such as in 1985 or 1986. By 1986, the action taken in 1984 might be inappropriate for the stabilization of GNP. Besides, there is no certainty that the policy will take effect in 1986 rather than 1985. For example, suppose that the economy is currently in a recession, and that the money supply is increased rapidly today to increase the growth rate of real GNP. Today's increase in the growth rate of money might affect GNP within 6 months, and achieve its purpose. However, it might work only in 2 years, by which time GNP might well already have increased without the aid of the monetary policy action. And if the expansionary monetary policy affects an economy by then close to full employment, inflation will result.

Thus monetarists argue that although monetary policy has powerful effects on GNP, it should not be actively used lest it destabilize the economy. Accordingly, their view is that the money supply should be kept growing at a constant rate, to minimize the potential damage that inappropriate policy can cause.[24]

The Unimportance of Interest Rates

In the *IS-LM* model changes in the money stock affect the economy primarily by affecting interest rates, which, in turn, affect aggregate demand and thus GNP. When interest rates are low, monetary policy seems to be expansionary, encouraging investment and thus producing a high level of aggregate demand. Similarly, high interest rates seem to indicate contractionary policy. Since the Fed can control the level of interest rates, and since interest rates provide a guide to the effects of monetary policy on the economy, it seems perfectly sensible for the Fed to carry out monetary policy by controlling interest rates. Through the 1950s and most of the 1960s, the Fed did carry out its monetary policy by attempting to set the level of interest rates.

Friedman and monetarism brought two serious criticisms of the Fed procedure of attempting to set interest rates as the basis for the conduct of monetary policy. The first is that the behavior of nominal interest rates is not a good guide to the direction—whether expansionary or contractionary—of monetary policy. The *real* interest rate, the nominal interest rate minus the expected rate of inflation, is the rate relevant to determining the level of

[24] For a concise statement, see Milton Friedman, "The Case for a Monetary Rule," *Newsweek*, Feb. 7, 1972. Reprinted in Milton Friedman, *Bright Promises, Dismal Performance* (New York: Harcourt, Brace, Jovanovich, 1983), pp. 225–227. See too his article "The Role of Monetary Policy," *American Economic Review*, March 1968.

investment. But a high nominal interest rate, together with a high expected rate of inflation, means a low real rate of interest. Thus monetary policy might be quite expansionary in its effects on investment spending even when nominal interest rates are high. Consequently, Friedman and other monetarists argue that the Fed should not concentrate on the behavior of nominal interest rates in the conduct of monetary policy.

The second criticism is that the Fed's attempts to control nominal interest rates might be destabilizing. Suppose the Fed decides that monetary policy should be expansionary and that the interest rate should be lowered. To achieve these goals the Fed buys bonds in the open market, increasing the money supply. The expansionary monetary policy itself tends to raise the inflation rate. It thus tends to raise the nominal interest rate as investors adjust their expectation of inflation in response to the behavior of the actual inflation rate. But then the Fed would have to engage in a further open market purchase in an attempt to keep the nominal interest rate low. And that would lead to further inflation, further increases in nominal interest rates, and further open market purchases. The end result is that an attempt to keep nominal interest rates low may lead to increasing inflation. Therefore, Friedman argues, the Fed should not pay attention to the behavior of nominal interest rates in the conduct of monetary policy, and should, rather, keep the money supply growing at a constant rate.[25]

Each of these arguments on the dangers of conducting monetary policy by reference to nominal interest rates is important. It is indeed correct that real, and not nominal, interest rates provide the appropriate measure of the effects of monetary policy on aggregate demand. It is also true that the Fed could, by attempting to keep nominal interest rates low forever, destabilize the economy. However, once the latter danger has been pointed out, the probability that the Fed will destabilize the economy by operating with reference to interest rates is reduced. The use of interest rates as a guide to the direction of monetary policy does not mean that the Fed has to attempt to keep the interest rate fixed forever at some level. Instead, it may aim each month or quarter for an interest rate target that it regards as appropriate for the current and predicted economic situation.

The monetarist case for concentrating on the behavior of the money stock in the conduct of monetary policy is a strong, but not conclusive, one. The major weakness in the argument is that the demand for real balances may shift over time, as it has done since 1973 (see Chapter 8). A simple numerical example should help make the point. Suppose that real income is constant, and that the nominal interest rate is constant. Suppose also that the demand for real balances is constant. Then if the money supply grows at, say, the rate of 5 percent, the price level, too, will grow at 5 percent, so that the stock of real balances remains constant. Now suppose, instead, that the demand for real balances is falling by 2 percent per year. Then if the nominal money supply increases at 5 percent per year, the price level has to increase at

[25] The details of the argument are spelled out in Friedman's "The Role of Monetary Policy," *American Economic Review*, March 1968.

7 percent per year to keep the supply of real balances equal to the demand. Thus, shifts in the demand for money affect the rate of inflation, given the growth rate of money. In this example, if the demand for real balances grew at 5 percent per year, 5 percent money growth would not be inflationary at all. These shifts in demand raise the possibility that concentration on the behavior of the nominal money stock may be seriously misleading and inappropriate for the conduct of monetary policy.

The problem of shifts in the demand-for-money function became particularly acute in the early eighties, following the change in Federal Reserve monetary policy in October 1979. The policy change was intended to place more emphasis on keeping the growth rate of money under control. But at the same time there were extensive reforms of the monetary system, which, as we discussed in Chapter 8, shifted the demand function for (and definitions of) money. With a shifting demand function it became unclear what the right rate of growth of money was to keep the economy on track. At the end of 1982 the Fed announced it was temporarily abandoning its $M1$ money growth rate targets, until the shifts in the demand function for money were completed.

Given the possibility, and the actual experience, of shifts in the demand for money, we see that the behavior of the money stock is not a perfect guide to the conduct of monetary policy. Neither is the behavior of nominal interest rates. However, the behavior of the nominal money stock and the behavior of nominal interest rates *both* provide some information about the direction in which monetary policy is pushing the economy, imperfect as each measure is. Accordingly, the Fed should pay attention to the behavior of both interest rates and the quantity of money in the conduct of its monetary policy.[26]

The Importance of Fiscal Policy

Friedman has frequently, if tongue in cheek, said that fiscal policy is very important. Although we noted earlier that he argues fiscal policy itself is not important for the behavior of GNP, he does contend that it is of vital importance in setting the size of government and the role of government in the economy. Friedman is an opponent of big government. He has made the interesting argument that government spending increases to match the revenues available. The government will spend the full tax collection—and some more. Accordingly, he is in favor of tax cuts as a way of reducing government spending. This argument was probably influential in the Reagan administration's 1981 decision to pass tax cuts well before it had figured out how to cut government spending.

Friedman stands out in arguing that fiscal policy does not have strong effects on the economy except to the extent that it affects the behavior of money. Thus he has remarked[27]:

[26] The argument is worked out in Benjamin M. Friedman, "Targets, Instruments, and Indicators of Monetary Policy," *Journal of Monetary Economics*, October 1975.

[27] Milton Friedman, "Higher Taxes? No," *Newsweek*, Jan. 23, 1967. Reprinted in *There's No Such Thing as A Free Lunch*, op. cit., p.89.

> To have a significant impact on the economy, a tax increase must somehow affect monetary policy—the quantity of money and its rate of growth. . . .
>
> The level of taxes is important—because it affects how much of our resources we use through the government and how much we use as individuals. It is not important as a sensitive and powerful device to control the short-run course of income and prices.

The Inherent Stability of the Private Sector

The final aspect of monetarism we consider here is the monetarist view that the economy, left to itself, is more stable than when the government manages it with discretionary policy, and that the major cause of economic fluctuations lies in inappropriate government actions. This view is quite fundamental in that it underlies many other monetarist positions, and it may be the litmus test for distinguishing monetarists from other macroeconomists. It is because this point is so fundamental that a major stage in the acceptance of monetarism occurred when Friedman and Schwartz published their *Monetary History of the United States.* In it they provided evidence for the view that the great depression was the result of bad monetary policy rather than private sector instability, arising, say, from autonomous shifts in consumption or investment demand.

Summary: We Are All Monetarists

From the viewpoint of the conduct of economic policy, the major monetarist themes are (1) an emphasis on the growth rate of the money stock, (2) arguments against fine tuning and in favor of a monetary rule, and (3) a greater weight that monetarists, as compared, for example, with Keynesians, place on the costs of inflation relative to those of unemployment.

Although we describe these as the major monetarist propositions relating to policy,[28] it is not true that macroeconomists can be neatly divided into two groups, some subscribing to the monetarist religion and the others to a less fundamentalist faith called neo-Keynesianism. Most of the arguments advanced by Friedman and his associates are technical and susceptible to economic analysis and the application of empirical evidence. Many of those propositions are now widely accepted and are no longer particularly associated with monetarism. As Franco Modigliani has remarked, "We are all monetarists now." He adds that we are monetarists in the sense that all (or most) macroeconomists believe in the importance of money.

Much of the analysis of this book would, a few years ago, have been considered monetarist. For example, we have assumed the long-run Phillips curve is vertical, a proposition that was originally associated with monetarism. We have laid considerable stress on the behavior of the money stock and have

[28] For a range of views on monetarism, see Franco Modigliani, "The Monetarist Controversy," *American Economic Review*, March 1977; Thomas Mayer, *The Structure of Monetarism* (New York: Norton, 1978); D. Batten and C. Stone, "Are Monetarists an Endangered Species?", Federal Reserve Bank of St. Louis, *Review*, May 1983; and J. H. McCulloch, *Money and Inflation* (New York: Academic Press, 1982).

emphasized that fiscal policy affects long-run inflation to the extent that it affects the long-run growth rate of money. Older readers will doubtless detect other places at which we appear monetarist to their eyes. That is all to the good. If economists did not modify their analyses in the light of new theories and evidence, the field would be barren.

Friedman and his associates have indeed changed macroeconomics. The forceful and persuasive way in which he has emphasized the role of money has changed the views of most economists on the importance of monetary policy. It is always possible that those views would have changed anyway, in the light of the increasing inflation of the sixties. The fact remains, however, that it was Friedman, and not someone else, who hammered away at the importance of money.

Monetarism and the Economy

Over the period since World War II there has been an increasing emphasis on limiting money growth as an essential ingredient in controlling inflation. In 1975 the United States adopted money growth targets for one or more monetary aggregates (*M*1, *M*2, high-powered money, etc.). All major nations now have such targets.[29] The adoption of money targets is a result of the monetarist emphasis on the importance of money. Thus monetarism has certainly had an impact on the way in which monetary policy is carried out.

Of course, having a target and hitting it are not the same thing. No central bank is so committed to its money target that it wants to hit it regardless of what else is happening in the economy. As we saw in the case of the United States in Chapter 9, when interest rates start rising rapidly, the central bank typically compromises on its money target, letting the money stock go above target to avoid interest rates rising too far. Despite such compromises, the central bank does try to adhere to its targets unless there is a compelling reason not to. By announcing the targets, the central bank also takes on the responsibility of explaining why it departs from those targets when it does.

Beyond the general monetarist influence visible in the adoption of money targets, there have been several policy episodes that are more narrowly monetarist. Among these are the period 1969–1971 in the United States, when policy aimed to reduce the inflation rate of 5 percent inherited from the Johnson administration, by gradually slowing the money growth rate; the policies of the Thatcher government in Britain from 1979, which attempted to reduce the inflation rate; and the Fed's adoption of a new monetary policy in 1979.

The lesson of these episodes is broadly in agreement with the predictions of monetarism. It is possible to reduce the inflation rate by controlling the growth rate of money. But the lags emphasized by Friedman are indeed long. Figure 16-6 shows the effects of tight money in the United States in the 1969–1971 period. Money growth is cut back sharply at the beginning of 1969. Inflation continues to rise into 1970 before beginning to come down slowly.

[29] Data are published in the OECD's *Economic Outlook*, which appears twice a year.

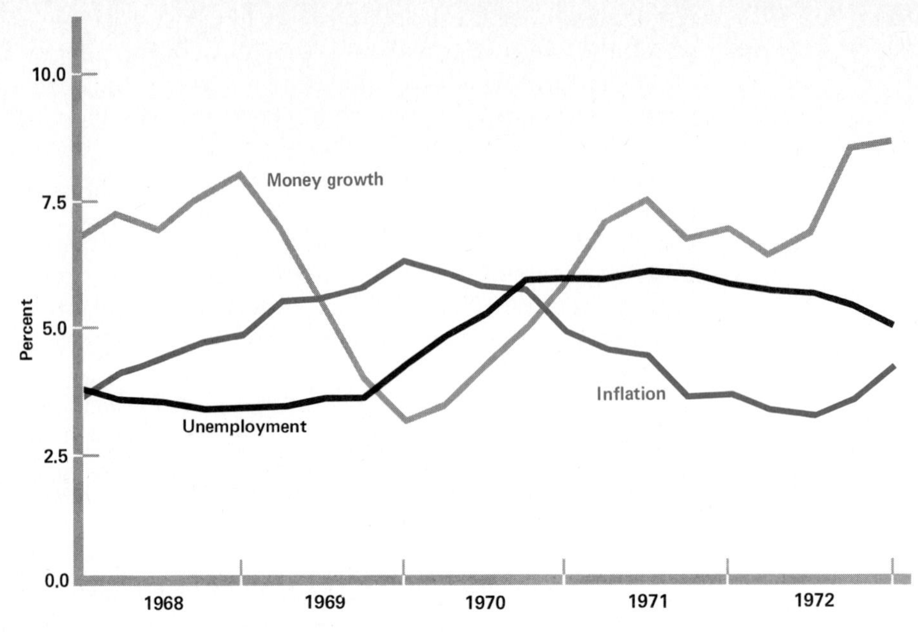

FIGURE 16-6 THE GROWTH RATE OF MONEY ($M1$) AND THE RATES OF INFLATION AND UNEMPLOYMENT, 1968–1972. (*Source:* Data Resources, Inc.)

Further, as the analysis of Chapter 13 shows, monetary policy reduces the inflation rate only by producing a recession. It is only after the sharp increase in unemployment starting at the end of 1969 that the inflation rate begins to come down. Similarly, the reductions in inflation in Britain between 1980 and 1983, and those in the United States between 1981 and 1983, were accompanied by deep recessions.

Monetarist economists often warn that getting rid of inflation is a long, slow business—as it turns out to be. Even so, monetarists have on occasion been too optimistic. Milton Friedman, writing in May 1969, said[30]:

> If the Fed continues its present policy of moderate growth in the money supply, we should start seeing results in the near future. By summer or early fall, the rise in income should start slackening. The effect will be first on output. However, by fall at the latest, the pace of price rise should be coming down.

The political process could put up with a 1-year delay in the effects of slower money growth on inflation. But looking at Figure 16-6, we see that the inflation rate at the end of 1970 was no lower than it had been at the beginning of 1969. The Nixon administration could easily see in the high rate of

[30] Reprinted in *An Economist's Protest* (New York: Horton, 1972), pp. 51–52.

unemployment the price that had to be paid to get rid of inflation. But it was not so clear that there was a payoff in terms of lower inflation. By August 1971, patience had worn off completely. The Nixon administration imposed a price and wage freeze as a quicker, surer way of getting the inflation rate down. It was no longer willing to wait for the slow monetarist medicine to work, because it was afraid the public was not willing to wait either. In the cases of Mrs. Thatcher in Britain and the Reagan administration, at the beginning of the eighties, the public appeared more patient. Probably this was because by 1980 there had been another decade of inflation at well above the 5 percent rate of 1969.

Nonetheless, the question remains why it takes so long to reduce the inflation rate through restrictive aggregate demand policy. Early in the 1970s, a radical new development in macroeconomics seemed to promise improved understanding of the effects of policy measures on the economy. This was the rational expectations approach.

16-6 THE RATIONAL EXPECTATIONS APPROACH

The failure to reduce inflation in the 1970s and the apparent inability of macro policy to achieve its goals led to a reconsideration of the premises of modern macroeconomics. The reconsideration places great emphasis on expectations, on the credibility of policies, and on the limited scope for discretionary stabilization policies. The general emphasis on expectations and the credibility of policies is widely shared. Indeed, we have explained much of the behavior of the inflation rate and wage increases by appealing to expectations of inflation and the belief that anti-inflationary policies would not be long-lived. But the emphasis and its implications have been taken further by a group of economists who have developed the *rational expectations approach* to macroeconomics. Among the leading members of the school are Robert Lucas of the University of Chicago and Thomas Sargent and Neil Wallace of the University of Minnesota.[31] Most other macroeconomists have by the 1980s accepted some parts of the rational expectations approach.

We distinguish between two aspects of the rational expectations approach.

1 *Rational expectations as a theory of expectations.* As a theory of expectations, the notion of rational expectations assumes that individuals use information efficiently and do not make *systematic* mistakes in expectations. This assumption is made on occasion by almost all macroeconomists, and its use does not automatically qualify the user as a member of the rational expectations school.

[31] For an introduction, see Thomas Sargent and Neil Wallace, "Rational Expectations and the Theory of Economic Policy," *Journal of Monetary Economics*, April 1976. See also the very useful paper by Bennett McCallum, "Macroeconomics after a Decade of Rational Expectations: Some Critical Issues," in Federal Reserve Bank of Richmond, *Economic Review*, November/December 1982; and R. Lucas and T. Sargent, "After Keynesian Macroeconomics," Federal Reserve Bank of Minneapolis, *Quarterly Review*, Spring 1979. (Also in Federal Reserve Bank of Boston, *After the Phillips Curve*, Conference Series No. 19, 1978.)

Rational expectations as a theory of expectations implies that policy cannot rely for its effectiveness on systematic misunderstandings by the public. For instance, if at first the public does not understand that countercyclical tax changes are transitory, those changes will have powerful effects on the economy. But as people begin to realize that tax changes are reversed as the economy reaches full employment, such a policy comes to have less powerful effects because the tax changes are understood to be transitory. The expectations part of rational expectations suggests that it is best, in formulating policy, to assume that the public will soon understand how a particular policy is working. It also implies that any policy which works for some time only because the public does not correctly anticipate its effects is doomed to eventual failure.

2 *The market clearing approach.* Economists belonging to the rational expectations school (as we define it here) assume that markets always are in equilibrium, or *clear*, and that economic agents set wages and prices, given the information they have, so as to achieve maximum profits and utility.

It is the market clearing assumption that distinguishes the rational expectations school. This strong assumption has three major implications. The first is that there is no involuntary unemployment. Why? Because anyone who expects to be unemployed, or who is currently unemployed and would prefer to work, can find work by asking for it at a wage below the existing wage. If, at the existing wage, the individual prefers not to work but rather to continue searching for a job, then the unemployment is voluntary. Of course, the theory recognizes that there is some normal level of unemployment corresponding to individuals who are between jobs or looking for their first job.

If there is no involuntary unemployment, why, then, does the level of output vary? Here the theory points to two factors. The first consists of changes in the level of potential output. The second, more important, involves mistakes in perceiving the current economic situation. Suppose that individuals do not know the aggregate price level in the current period. Of course, they do know the wage at which they can work. They have to form an estimate of the *real* wage on the basis of the price level they expect to hold during the period. Now, if the price level should turn out to be unexpectedly high, then individuals overestimate the real wage and work harder than they would if they knew the true situation. Thus, *unexpectedly* high prices lead to a higher level of output than at full employment. Individuals are working harder than they would at full employment.

This mechanism is very subtle,[32] and it is regarded by some as implausible. It clearly requires that individuals do not have complete information about the current state of the economy. Otherwise, with all markets clearing, the economy would be at the full-employment level of output. Indeed, one of the consequences of the development of the rational expectations school has been a growing emphasis on the information that individuals use and process in making their economic decisions.

[32] The mechanism is discussed in more detail in Robert E. Lucas, Jr., "Understanding Business Cycles," in Karl Bruner and Allan Meltzer (eds.), *Stabilization of the Domestic and International Economy*, Carnegie-Rochester Conference Series, vol. 5.

The second implication follows closely from the first. It is that the level of output cannot be affected by changes in monetary policy unless those changes are not perceived by individuals in the economy. Suppose that it is believed and known that the money supply has changed. Then individuals know the price level should be higher and adjust their prices and wages accordingly so as to produce full employment immediately. If there is a lag in the publication of data on the money stock, individuals will adjust prices to the level of the money stock they expect. If the money stock turns out to be higher than expected, aggregate demand will be higher, and output will rise because of the mechanism, described earlier, in which individuals mistakenly work harder, believing the real wage is above the level at which it currently is. We thus arrive at the most famous proposition advanced by the rational expectations school, that *with regard to monetary policy, only unexpected changes in the stock of money affect the level of output.*

The lack of policy effectiveness that the rational expectations school advances as a central proposition is well summarized in the following quote[33]:

> Whatever the government does, individuals will catch on, and if not immediately, then quickly. . . .
>
> That is what the rational expectations hypothesis says: individuals, anxious to do as well as they can, make the best possible forecasts. And it is an implication that the government cannot influence the unemployment rate, except maybe over a very short short run.
>
> It may be a bit hard for you to swallow, my contention that the public is always pretty much aware of what the government's stabilization policy is—what its objectives are and what it will be doing to achieve those objectives. Each of us has at least one rather dim relative, an uncle perhaps, maybe even an aunt, who does not have the faintest notion what the phrase "stabilization policy" means, let alone know what the actual policy of the moment is. It is, however, not required that everyone know, only some, those who are strategically located. For example, where trade unions represent workers, it is enough that the leadership know. And it would seem right that the typical present-day union leadership is pretty well informed.

If only unanticipated changes in the stock of money affect the level of output, then monetary policy cannot affect the level of output except by producing *surprises.* This leads to the third implication: Under these circumstances, there appears to be no role for monetary policy systematically to affect output or unemployment. Any systematic policy, such as increased monetary expansion in a recession (remember that recessions are possible as a result of surprises), would be predicted by market participants, and wages and prices would be set accordingly. Unless the Fed had better information or shorter reaction lags than the market, it could not, according to this theory, have a systematic *real* effect.

[33] J. Kareken, "Inflation: An Extreme View," Federal Reserve Bank of Minneapolis, *Quarterly Review*, Winter 1978.

The proposition that only monetary *surprises* affect output has been the subject of intense empirical research. Early work by Robert J. Barro[34] appeared to support the proposition. Later research by, among others, Frederic Mishkin and Robert Gordon cast substantial doubt on the early findings.[35] The later results suggest that both expected and unexpected changes in the money stock affect output. By this stage, the evidence does not support the strong implication of the market clearing approach that only unanticipated changes in the money stock affect output. Accordingly, the evidence also does not support the view that systematic monetary policy does not affect the behavior of output.

Relative Wages, Wage Contracts, and Rational Expectations

The strongest form of the rational expectations theory just outlined, which assumes market clearing in every period and attributes fluctuations to imperfect information, has not been supported by the evidence and is not widely accepted. There are, however, models that use rational expectations as a theory of expectations but also recognize economic institutions such as long-term contracts and the importance of the relative wages of various groups in the labor market[36]. Relatively simple amendments have gone far in removing some of the least plausible implications of the strong market clearing form of rational expectations theory.

Suppose we have 2-year labor contracts and that half the contracts in the economy come up for renewal every year. Suppose further that we start from price stability and that an unanticipated decline in the money stock occurs. If all wages and prices were instantaneously flexible, they would immediately decline in proportion to the fall in money, and no real effects would arise. This does not occur, however, if we have long-term contracts that fix nominal wages. With a lowering in the money stock, there is potentially a decline in employment. Unemployed workers whose wages come up for renewal now have the choice of reducing their wages enough to become employed. If they do so, the price level will fall because the average wage has fallen. But when the price level falls, the real wage being paid to workers on existing contracts rises (the nominal wage they receive is fixed, and the price level has fallen), and some of them lose their jobs.

In addition, workers may be concerned that their *relative* wages not fall. If those whose contracts come up for renewal now accept cuts in wages large

[34] Robert J. Barro, "Unanticipated Money, Output, and the Price Level in the United States," *Journal of Political Economy*, August 1978.

[35] Frederic Mishkin, "Does Anticipated Monetary Policy Matter? An Econometric Investigation," *Journal of Political Economy*, February 1982 (this is difficult reading); and Robert Gordon, "Price Inertia and Policy Ineffectiveness in the United States, 1890–1980," *Journal of Political Economy*, December 1982.

[36] The discussion here follows a paper by John Taylor, "Staggered Wage Setting in a Macro-Model," *American Economic Review*, May 1979. For a careful, advanced introduction see D. Begg, *The Rational Expectations Revolution in Macroeconomics* (Baltimore: Johns Hopkins University Press, 1983).

enough to keep them fully employed, their wages will have to fall relative to those whose wages were negotiated earlier. Workers may be willing to accept some unemployment if they can keep their wages in line with those of others. If so, current wages will be set somewhere in between the full-employment level and the level of wages on contracts still running. That means wages do *not* adjust immediately to money changes; that is, wages are less than fully flexible. It takes some time until the whole wage structure adjusts. The fact that we have long-term, nonsynchronized wage setting, and that relative wages matter, directly implies the possibility of extended periods of wage stickiness and unemployment.

The model is thus able to explain simultaneous wage inflation and unemployment. Suppose there is a contraction in demand, as we have just discussed, and that labor knows that policy will be expansionary in the future. Then those whose wages are currently up for renegotiation recognize that if they set too low a wage, they will be out of line with the wages that will be set next year by a group that will then be facing strong demand. Accordingly, even with the possibility of current unemployment, the prospect of expansionary aggregate demand policies in the future will make current economic slack less effective in dampening wage and price inflation. Rational expectations enter here in that the groups currently setting their wages look ahead and ask themselves what will be the macroeconomic environment in which other groups set their wages next period. If the policy setting next period is expected to be expansionary, this fact will already be anticipated in this year's wages.[37]

The relative wage model, combined with rational expectations, thus has two important features: first, wages are sticky downward in the face of unemployment; and second, wage inflation may persist in the face of unemployment. The extent of persistence is determined by, among other things, the degree to which the policy setting is accommodative or not.

Rational Expectations, Credibility, and Disinflation

At the end of Chapter 13 we discussed the choice between gradualist and cold turkey approaches to inflation reduction. That choice was widely considered in the United States at the end of the 1970s as the inflation rate increased to the double-digit range and the costs in terms of unemployment of policies to reduce inflation were weighed against the costs of continued inflation.

Members of the rational expectations school took a more optimistic view of the costs of reducing the inflation rate than did other economists. In its most extreme form, the rational expectations (market clearing) approach would argue that it takes only the announcement of a permanently lower growth rate of the money stock to get the inflation rate down immediately. But there were few who took such a suggestion seriously. Almost all economists recognized that some unemployment would be necessary to reduce the inflation rate.

[37] Similar implications follow if workers are concerned about the real wages they will be receiving in future years, rather than relative wages.

BOX 16-1

DISEQUILIBRIUM ECONOMICS AND POST-KEYNESIAN ECONOMICS

In the main text we have developed the history of ideas as running from Keynesian economics to monetarism and the rational expectations challenge, with supply-side economics as a flashy sideshow. However, two other strands of macroeconomics are sufficiently distinct and fruitful to deserve attention.

THE DISEQUILIBRIUM APPROACH

As early as the 1950s economists recognized the implications of disequilibrium in one market for supply or demand in other markets. If workers cannot sell all the labor they wish at the going wage, and cannot borrow, how will this affect their consumption decision? If they cannot buy all the goods they wish at the going prices, how does this affect their supply of labor or their demands for money and other assets. If firms cannot sell at the going price all the output they would like to produce, how does this affect their demand for labor?

The disequilibrium approach answers these questions by constructing a model of the economy that explicitly takes into account the ***quantity constraints*** on the decisions which households and firms face. Quantity constraints are present when households or firms cannot at the going wages or prices buy or sell all the quantities they wish. Central to the approach is the assumption that wages and prices do not move rapidly, leaving markets in disequilibrium, which gives rise to quantity adjustments. These quantity adjustments in different markets are interdependent through the quantity constraints under which households and firms make their optimal decisions.*

The most interesting contribution of the disequilibrium approach so far has been to influence empirical work. For example, studies of consumption pay close attention to the role of income and wealth, reflecting the possibility that individuals cannot borrow against future income so that ***liquidity constraints*** affect spending behavior. In studies of the labor market the approach suggests the important distinction between "high-wage" or classical unemployment on one side and Keynesian or "lack of demand" unemployment on the other. (See Box 14-1.)

POST-KEYNESIAN ECONOMICS

Post-Keynesians are a diverse group of economists who share the belief that modern macroeconomics leaves aside or explicitly assumes away many of the very central elements of Keynes' *General Theory*.†

Five elements of this approach stand out distinctly. First, adjustment, just as in the disequilibrium approach, takes place primarily through quantity adjustment, not price changes. Indeed, price changes where they occur are often seen as disequilibrating. Second, the

* The early reference is D. Patinkin, *Money, Interest and Prices* (New York: Harper & Row, 1956). The complete working out of these ideas can be found in R. Barro and H. Grossman, *Money, Employment and Inflation* (London: Cambridge University Press, 1976); and E. Malinvaud, *The Theory of Unemployment Reconsidered* (Oxford: Basil Blackwell, 1977), and *Profitability and Unemployment* (Oxford: Basil Blackwell, 1981).

† For an introduction see A. Eichner (ed.), *A Guide to Post-Keynesian Economics* (White Plains, N.Y.: M. E. Sharpe, 1979), and the essays on post-Keynesian economics in the *American Economic Review*, May 1980.

distribution of income between profits and wages plays a central role in affecting consumption and investment decision. Third, expectations (Keynes' animal spirits), together with profits, are the chief determinant of investment plans. Fourth, institutional features—credit constraints on households and self-finance by firms, as well as the financial structure involving credit creation in a pyramid—interact in shaping the business cycle and on occasion financial crises. Finally, unlike in classical macroeconomics, the focus of post-Keynesian economics is to explain why the economy does not work well.

Post-Keynesian economics remains an eclectic collection of ideas, not a systematic challenge, as, for example, the rational expectations hypothesis. It has influenced economists in their research program. But the deliberate downplaying, indeed rejection, of individual rationality and maximization as a basis of behavior by firms and households has kept the approach at odds with the mainstream of the profession that has been attempting to bring macroeconomics into closer touch with microeconomics.

Members of the rational expectations school were on the more optimistic side, though.

The more optimistic view of the rational expectations school was based on two factors. First, like others, the members emphasized the role of expectations of inflation in determining the response of wages and prices to changes in policy. Second, they argued that the effects of policy depend on the *credibility* (believability) of the policy. In particular, they argued that if the Fed implemented a new policy, and was understood to be serious about the change in policy (that is, if the policy was credible), expectations would adjust rapidly and the recession could be short-lived.

The disinflation of 1981–1983 was not as fast as the proponents of rational expectations predicted. But it was slightly faster than would have been predicted on the basis of Phillips curves estimated through the 1970s. Part of the speedup of the disinflation was probably based on the credibility of the inflation-fighting determination of the Fed under Chairman Volcker. The credibility factor emphasized by the rational expectations school is thus of practical significance. Of course, the rational expectations approach also warns us that policies are credible in the long run only if they do what they promise to do.[38]

Policy Making under Rational Expectations

The rational expectations approach has led to a more sophisticated view of policy making than prevailed earlier. The rational expectations approach emphasizes that economic agents do not react mechanically to every policy change. Rather, they try to figure out what the policy change means for the

[38] The importance of the credibility of policies has been particularly emphasized by William Fellner, *Towards a Reconstruction of Macroeconomics* (Washington, D.C.: American Enterprise Institute, 1976). See also the discussion in the *American Economic Review*, May 1982.

behavior of the economy, and for future changes in policy. And they behave accordingly. For instance, as we noted in Chapter 6, economic agents adjust their consumption more in response to a permanent income tax cut than to a transitory tax cut of the same size.

The approach leads also to an emphasis on institutional changes as ways of altering the behavior of the economy. Members of the rational expectations school are less interested in what policy should be *now* than they are in ways of making it possible for policy to operate better in general. The quote from Robert E. Lucas at the beginning of this chapter shows a general attitude toward attempts to predict the effects of a particular policy action. Members of the rational expectations school doubt that we know enough to predict how the public will respond in the short run to a particular policy change, because the response depends on how the policy measure affects expectations. But in the long run the public will catch on to the effects of any policy change, and it thus becomes possible to predict the long-run effects of long-run policy changes. A member of the rational expectations school might support a constitutional amendment to balance the budget, in part because a constitutional amendment should have a very strong predictable effect on expectations.

Similarly, a rational expectations economist confronted with the inflationary experience of the seventies would argue that the best way to change the behavior of the Fed is to change the institutional environment in which it works. Accordingly, such an economist is likely to support a monetary rule for the Fed, for example, requiring the money supply to grow at 4 percent per year.[39]

Monetarists, too, support a monetary rule. Indeed, there is considerable overlap between the policy views of monetarists and those of members of the rational expectations school. The similarity extends to the usually conservative views of policy held by members of both groups. But there are important differences between the monetarist and rational expectations approaches to macroeconomics. Monetarists are willing to assume that expectations may be systematically wrong and that markets are very slow to clear, whereas a member of the rational expectations school would not make such assumptions. Monetarism can be viewed as operating within the same framework and model as Keynesianism, while disagreeing over the relative importance of monetary and fiscal policy. The rational expectations school believes that the standard framework is fundamentally flawed and thus has developed the market clearing approach, which argues that imperfect information is responsible for the business cycle. It is thus a more radical attack on standard macroeconomics than is monetarism.

[39] You might wonder why members of the rational expectations school should care at all about monetary policy if they believe that (*a*) only unexpected changes in money affect real output, and (*b*) the public's expectations eventually catch up with reality. The two assumptions (*a*) and (*b*) seem to suggest that whatever the Fed is doing, it will eventually have no effect on real output. However, the strong form of rational expectations does not argue that monetary policy is irrelevant to the behavior of *prices*. Thus members of the rational expectations school concerned about keeping inflation low can logically be in favor of a monetary rule that will prevent the average rate of growth of money from becoming high.

Where will the rational expectations attack on conventional macroeconomics lead? It had already had a substantial influence on the way macroeconomists think. First, rational expectations is widely used as a theory of expectations. Second, the sophisticated view of policy, in which responses to policy depend on the public's analysis of what policy measures will do to current and future behavior of the economy, is widely adopted. The market clearing approach, however, is more controversial than other components of the rational expectations view, and seems to be inconsistent with the slow reaction of the economy to policy measures.[40] A modified approach, such as that described above involving wage contracts and other institutional features of the economy, may emerge as a synthesis of the rational expectations approach and more traditional macroeconomics. Such a synthesis is fully consistent with the approach to macroeconomics developed in this book.

16-7 SUPPLY-SIDE ECONOMICS

Supply-side economics was all the rage in the United States in 1981, the first year of the Reagan administration. It was the guiding principle behind the tax cuts voted in August of that year, and served as the justification for the optimistic scenario presented by the administration's first budget. The budget predicted that inflation could be reduced without creating a recession. It also predicted that the tax cuts would lead to a rapid increase in growth, and therefore would produce more rather than less tax revenue for the government.

Supply-side economists lay heavy stress on the incentive effects of taxation in determining the behavior of the economy. Beyond that broad agreement there are really two separate supply-side groups. The mainstream group includes economists such as Martin Feldstein of Harvard, once President of the National Bureau of Economic Research, and from 1982 Chairman of the Council of Economic Advisers, and Michael Boskin of Stanford University. This group stresses the importance of tax incentives in promoting growth, by affecting saving and investment. Similarly, it analyzes the effects of tax changes on labor supply, the effects of social security on saving and on retirement decisions, and a host of other important issues.

The mainstream group has been presenting the results of its research in scholarly journals for many years and is influential and active within the economics profession. There are few economists who believe incentives are unimportant. Indeed, as we noted earlier in the chapter, it was the New Economics that was sufficiently concerned about growth in 1962 to introduce investment incentives through the investment tax credit.

But it was the radical fringe of the supply-side group that received most of

[40] See the discussion, especially by A. Okun, "Rational Expectations with Misperceptions as a Theory of the Business Cycle," in the special issue of the *Journal of Money, Credit and Banking*, November 1980.

the publicity.[41] This group made exaggerated claims for the effects of tax cuts on savings, investment, and labor supply and for the effects of tax cuts on total government revenue from taxation. Among the leaders of the radical fringe are Arthur Laffer of the University of Southern California, whose curve was described in Chapter 15, and George Gilder, whose radical supply-side book *Wealth and Poverty*,[42] was on the best-seller list in 1981. Radical supply-siders were installed in the Treasury, and included Norman Ture who had the responsible position of Under Secretary. The radical fringe argued (*a*) that tax rate reductions would have such powerful effects on work effort that total tax revenues would rise, and (*b*) that the supply-side effects of the tax cuts would have a powerful effect in reducing inflation by increasing the growth rate of output.

Radical supply-side economics was an essential part of the rhetoric supporting *Reaganomics*. There is no precise definition of Reaganomics, other than that it is the economic policies pursued by President Reagan in 1981–1982. The most important factor in these policies was the President's determination to cut taxes. This was done in the belief that the government was too large and that government spending could be cut by denying tax revenue to the Congress to spend. Arguments by supply-siders that tax cuts would rapidly increase economic growth and reduce inflation were certainly welcome, but it is quite likely that President Reagan would have proceeded with his policies even had he known they would result in a 2-year-long deep recession, so long as they would reduce inflation and the size of government.

Supply-side predictions were criticized at the time by mainstream macroeconomists. The evidence is that tax reductions do affect incentives and that tax cuts would increase output.[43] But there is no evidence that the incentives would be so strong as to result in higher government revenue after a tax cut. Similarly, an increase in the growth rate of output will contribute to reducing the inflation rate—but the effects are unlikely to be powerful.

The events of the 2 years following the Reagan tax cuts do not support the views of the radical supply-siders. Inflation was indeed reduced, but the reduction was a result of tight monetary policy and not of expansionary fiscal policy. Output fell rapidly; it did not increase. These events led to the departure of the radical supply-siders from responsible policy-making positions, but did not slow down their claims that supply-side economics (of the radical branch) was the solution for the economy's problem.

[41] The distinction between mainstream and radical groups is drawn by Harold McClure and Thomas Willett in "Understanding the Supply Siders," in W. C. Stubblebine and T. D. Willett (eds.), *Reaganomics A Midterm Report (*Institute of Contemporary Studies, 1983). See this paper and a paper by Richard Rahn in the same volume for more details on supply-side economics and for lists of the players in the two groups.

[42] New York: Basic Books, 1981.

[43] Some of the evidence is examined in Chap. 17. The effects of cuts in tax rates on tax revenue were discussed in Chap. 15.

16-8 WHERE DOES IT ALL LEAD?

At the start of this chapter we asked why macroeconomics suffers from such rapidly changing opinions. The answer is that it doesn't. There has been an evolution from simple Keynesianism toward a more sophisticated approach, not a series of rapidly changing beliefs. Macroeconomics has evolved, and it now gives more weight to monetary factors and to aggregate supply, emphasizing the roles of both expectations and labor market institutions. However, the rational expectations approach does pose a more radical challenge to the standard way of viewing the economy, and has already had a major impact on mainstream macroeconomics. Whether it will lead to the replacement of current mainstream macroeconomics with a new standard model remains to be seen—and time and evidence will determine that.

If there haven't in fact been frequent changes of opinion in macroeconomics, why does it still seem that way? Because macroeconomic issues are important, macroeconomics is both news and politically useful. Politicians look for economists with the arguments to support their positions. Supply-side economists had an influential role in the Reagan administration because the President wanted to cut taxes and needed professional support. No matter that the radical supply-side arguments were accepted by only a very small part of the profession: they provided at least some intellectual support for a policy that was based more on the President's ideology than on a detailed analysis of the potential effects of the tax cuts.

It is hoped that careful study will cumulate over the years to improved knowledge. Opinions, of course, change as new evidence accumulates, but genuine revolutions in thinking are rare. There was a Keynesian revolution in the thirties, and a significant shift toward monetarism in the fifties and sixties—which was easily accommodated by expanding the Keynesian framework. There may be a rational expectations revolution in progress. Even if it succeeds, it will build in much of the existing structure of macroeconomics. And even if it does not radically reshape macroeconomics, it will, nonetheless, make for serious changes in understanding of the formation of expectations and the operation of economic policy.

There was never a radical supply-side revolution.

The hope is that study of existing macroeconomics combined with the right degree of scepticism and questioning will make it possible for you to reach your own conclusions when the next brand of economics hits the headlines.

16-9 SUMMARY

1 The great depression shaped both modern macroeconomics and many of the economy's institutions. The extremely high unemployment and the length of the depression led to the view that the private economy was

unstable and that government intervention was needed to maintain high employment levels.

2 Keynesian economics succeeded because it seemed to explain the causes of the great depression—a collapse of investment demand—and because it pointed to expansionary fiscal policy as a means of preventing future depressions.
3 Keynesian views did not much affect economic policy making in the United States until the New Economics of the Kennedy-Johnson administration. The greatest success of the New Economics was the tax cut of 1964. The New Economics is perceived by the public as having been responsible for increasing inflation during the sixties.
4 Economic performance in the United States (and other countries) was much worse from 1969 to the present than during the sixties. There were four recessions in the latter period and none in the 1961–1969 period. The poor economic performance led to a search for explanations and cures.
5 Monetarism lays heavy stress on the money stock as determining the level of output in the short run and the inflation rate in the long run. The essential step in the advance of monetarism was the Friedman-Schwartz analysis of the great depression as having been significantly worsened by extremely poor monetary policy.
6 Monetarists generally view the money supply as having powerful, but not easily predictable, effects on the economy. Money works with long and variable lags. For that reason monetarists favor a monetary rule. Monetarists argue that interest rates are a poor guide to the direction of monetary policy. They also believe that the private economy is inherently stable.
7 Monetarism's influence on economic policy can be seen in the adoption of money targeting in major countries. Monetarism has also been influential in several policy episodes in which tight money was used to bring down the inflation rate. This takes a long time, and works by creating a recession that puts pressure on wages and prices.
8 The rational expectations approach to macroeconomics has two components. The first is a theory of expectations, arguing that people form expectations using all available information, and do not make systematic mistakes. The second is the market clearing approach. This assumes that markets are in equilibrium each period, and attributes deviations of output from full employment to imperfect information.
9 The market clearing approach implies that monetary policy can affect real output only by creating surprises. Early empirical evidence supported this view, but later evidence is less favorable.
10 A synthesis of rational expectations with more standard macroeconomics combines rational expectations assumptions with institutional features of the economy, such as long-term labor contracts. This can explain the slow adjustment of the economy to changes in monetary policy.
11 The rational expectations approach emphasizes the credibility of policies

as an important factor determining their success or failure. The approach also views institutional reform as the main way to get better policy.

12 Supply-side economics focuses on the incentive effects of taxation. There are two supply-side groups — mainstream and radical. The radical group attracted most of the attention at the time the Reagan administration was formulating its tax cut and budget plans. They argued that incentive effects were powerful enough that cuts in tax rates would increase government revenue and have a powerful supply-side effect on inflation. Neither argument was supported by later events. Mainstream supply-siders continue to be influential in both policy making and economics.

KEY TERMS

New Deal
New Economics
Council of Economic Advisers (CEA)
Guideposts
Monetary rule
Rational expectations approach
Market clearing approach
Credibility
Supply-side economics
Reaganomics

PROBLEMS

1 It is sometimes said that the great depression would have been a severe recession if it had stopped in 1931, but would not have been the calamity it was.
   (*a*) From Table 16-1 calculate the rate at which GNP was falling from 1929 to 1931.
   (*b*) How does this compare with the rate at which real GNP fell during the 1981 – 1982 recession?
   (*c*) Do you agree with the first sentence in this question? Explain.

2 Using Table 16-2, explain why concentration on the actual budget deficit might have given a misleading impression of fiscal policy at some stages between 1929 and 1933.

3 Evaluate the argument that increased government spending or deficits would have crowded out private spending in 1933.

4 In Table 16-1 examine the behavior of the short-term (commercial paper) interest rate and the growth rate of money.
   (*a*) Explain why a Keynesian might have thought monetary policy was expansionary during the great depression, while a monetarist would argue that monetary policy was, on the contrary, contractionary.
   (*b*) What do you think happened to real interest rates during the depression?

5 From the data in Figure 16-4 and at the end of the book, compare the average rate of money growth from 1961 to 1964 with that from 1965 to 1969. Also compare the inflation rates over those periods. The increasing inflation and falling unemployment of the 1961 – 1969 period are usually attributed to fiscal policy. Could they equally well have been attributed to monetary policy?

6 What, if anything, was new about the New Economics?

7 The growth rate of money for the 1968 – 1972 period is shown in Figure 16-6. Is there evidence in the figure that monetary policy contributed to the rapid inflation that began in 1973?

8 Outline the main tenets of monetarism.

9 Distinguish the two components of the rational expectations approach to macroeconomics.
10 Supply-side economics points, appropriately, to the importance of incentives in determining economic behavior. Why, then, have mainstream macroeconomists generally been critical of radical supply-side economics?
11 Why is there so much disagreement among macroeconomists, and why do opinions change so frequently?
12 Evaluate the quote by Keynes with which this chapter begins.
13 In the introduction we note the contradictory advice of two unnamed economists. Martin Feldstein, Chairman of The Council of Economic Advisors, believes the budget deficit is the problem of the 1980s, while Paul Craig Roberts, formerly a Treasury official, recommends financing the government by borrowing (deficits), not taxes. What is your opinion of the issue in the light of Chapter 15 and the material of this chapter?

17

LONG-TERM GROWTH AND PRODUCTIVITY

From 1889 to 1983 per capita real GNP in the United States grew at an average annual rate of 1.8 percent. With a growth rate of 1.8 percent, per capita GNP doubles every 39 years. A 20-year-old student could anticipate per capita GNP doubling before he was 60, if the growth rate of GNP were at its long-run historical average.

Table 17-1 shows that growth in the United States in the period from 1973 to 1983 was below the historical average. During that decade per capita real GNP grew at only nine-tenths of one percent per year. At that rate per capita GNP would take 76 years to double, and a 20-year-old student could look forward to a level of per capita GNP that was only 44 percent higher by the time he turned 60.

In this chapter we turn our attention away from the short-run problems of the business cycle, and look at where the economy has been and may be heading in the long term. Figure 17-1 shows actual GNP and a trend line for GNP since 1889. Over long periods actual output fluctuates around the long-run trend, and unemployment fluctuates around the full-employment output level.

To analyze the long-run behavior of the economy we thus focus on *trend* or *potential output*. The major question we pose is, What determines the *growth rate* of potential output? Given today's level of potential output,

TABLE 17-1 AVERAGE ANNUAL GROWTH RATES, 1889–1983

	1889–1983		1953–1973		1973–1983	
	GNP, real	Per capita real GNP	GNP, real	Per capita real GNP	GNP, real	Per capita real GNP
GNP growth, % per year	3.2	1.8	3.6	2.1	1.9	0.9
Time for per capita GNP to double, years		39		33		76

Note: The difference between the growth rate of GNP and per capita GNP is the growth rate of population, for example, growth rate of population between 1889 and 1983 was 1.4% per year (= 3.2% − 1.8%).
Source: U.S. Department of Commerce. Long-Term Economic Growth, 1860–1970 (1973): Economic Report of the President, *1983; and estimate for 1983 by authors.*

and the growth rate of potential output, we then know also what determines the *level* of potential output in the future. In terms of Figure 17-1, we are asking what is behind the trend output line.

In discussing the growth rate of potential output, we are discussing the important question of what future levels of real GNP will be. Table 17-1 shows that small differences in the growth rate of output cumulate over time to large differences in levels of GNP. To see this, compare the number of years

FIGURE 17-1 REAL GNP IN THE UNITED STATES: 1889 to 1983. (*Sources:* Data Resources, Inc., and *Historical Statistics of the United States,* U.S. Bureau of the Census, 1976.)

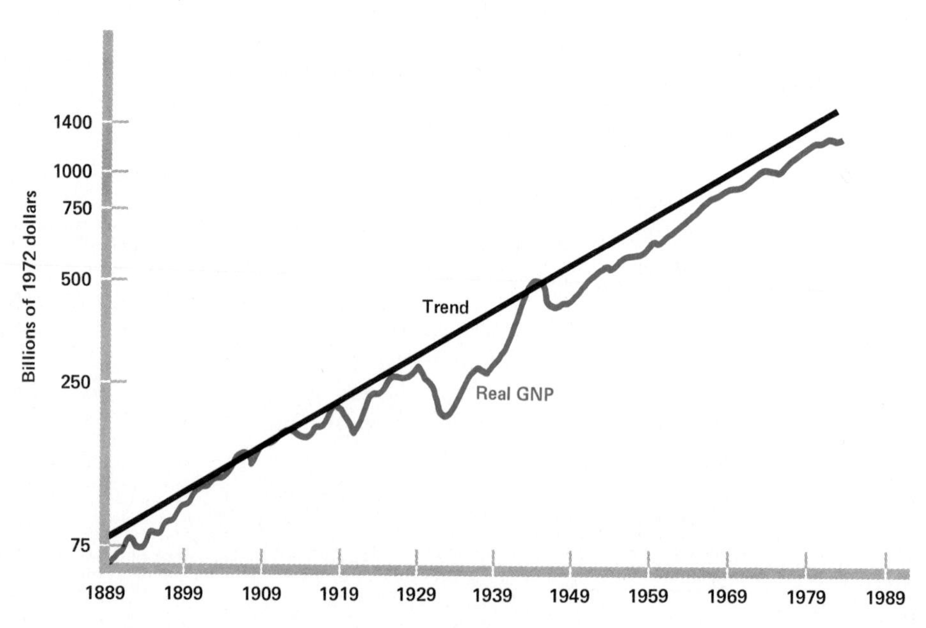

it takes for GNP per capita to double when the growth rate is 2.1 percent with the number of years it takes when the growth rate is 0.9 percent. Despite the difficulties of using GNP as a welfare measure, we can be quite sure that people with a 60 percent higher level of per capita GNP would be materially much better off.

Because future per capita GNP levels are so sensitive to the growth rate of potential output, it is worth worrying about changes of even 1/10 of 1 percent in the long-run growth rate of output. Certainly the large change between 1953–1973 and the following decade has been the cause of such concern. Is the change a lasting one, resulting from the beginning of an "age of limits," as many argued after the oil shock of 1973? Or is the sharp decline seen in Table 17-1 merely a temporary setback, soon to be reversed?

To answer questions about the growth rate of potential output, we go back to fundamentals. With output at the full-employment level, and hence the available factor supplies fully utilized, there are only two possible sources of growth. *Factor supplies may grow, or the productivity of factors of production may increase.* This, in turn, raises the questions of what determines the growth of factor supplies, including the role of supply-side fiscal policies, and what is the quantitative link between growth in factor supplies and output growth.

There are two complementary approaches to these questions. One is *growth theory*, which models the interactions among factor supplies, output growth, saving, and investment in the process of growth. The other is *growth accounting*, which attempts to quantify the contribution of different determinants of output growth. The two approaches draw on a common analytical framework which we now outline.

17-1 SOURCES OF GROWTH IN REAL INCOME

In this section we use the production function to study the *sources of growth*. We show that growth in labor, growth in capital, and improved technical efficiency are the three sources of growth.

The Production Function

In earlier chapters we introduced the concept of a production function. The *production function* links the amount of output produced in an economy to the inputs of factors of production and to the state of technical knowledge. Equation (1) represents the production function in symbols:

$$Y = AF(K,N) \tag{1}$$

where K and N denote the inputs of capital and labor and A denotes the state of technology. The production function $AF(K,N)$ in (1) states that the output produced depends on factor inputs K and N and on the state of technology. Increases in factor inputs and improved technology lead to an increase in output supply.

The next step is to make these links more precise by looking at an expression for the growth rate of output. In Equation (2) (which is derived in the Appendix) we show the determinants of output growth[1]:

$$\underset{\text{growth}}{\underset{\text{Output}}{\Delta Y/Y}} = \underset{\text{share}}{\underset{\text{labor}}{(1-\theta)}} \times \underset{\text{growth}}{\underset{\text{labor}}{\Delta N/N}} + \underset{\text{share}}{\underset{\text{capital}}{\theta}} \times \underset{\text{growth}}{\underset{\text{capital}}{\Delta K/K}} + \underset{\text{progress}}{\underset{\text{technical}}{\Delta A/A}} \qquad (2)$$

where $(1 - \theta)$ and θ are weights equal to the income shares of labor and of capital in production.

Equation (2) summarizes the contributions of growth of inputs and of improved productivity to growth of output:

1 The contribution of the growth of factor inputs is seen in the first two terms. Labor and capital each contribute an amount equal to their individual growth rate *multiplied by the share of that input in income.*
2 The rate of improvement of technology, called *technical progress* or the *growth of total factor productivity,* is the third term in Equation (2). The growth rate of total factor productivity is the amount by which output would be increasing as a result of improvements in methods of production, with all inputs unchanged. In other words, there is growth in total factor productivity when we get more output from the same factors of production.[2]

EXAMPLE

Suppose the income share of capital is 0.25 and that of labor is 0.75. These values correspond approximately to the actual values for the U.S. economy. Furthermore, let labor force growth be 1.2 percent and growth of the capital stock 3 percent, and suppose technical progress increases at the rate of 1.5 percent. What is the growth rate of full-employment output? Applying Equation (2) we obtain a growth rate of $\Delta Y/Y = 3.15$ percent ($= 0.75 \times 1.2$ percent $+ 0.25 \times 3$ percent $+ 1.5$ percent).

An important point to note in Equation (2) is that the growth rates of capital and labor are weighted by the respective income shares. The reason for these weights is that the importance of a 1 percent change in capital or labor to production differs, and that difference in importance is measured by their relative income shares. Specifically, if labor has a larger share than capital, output rises more when labor increases by, say, 10 percent than if capital increases by 10 percent.

Returning to our example, if labor alone grows by 1 percent, output will

[1] Equation (2) applies when there are *constant returns to scale* in production; that is, increases in both inputs, in the same proportion, increase output in that proportion.

[2] There is a distinction between *labor productivity* and total factor productivity. Labor productivity is just the ratio of output to labor input, Y/N. Labor productivity certainly grows as a result of technical progress, but it also grows because of the accumulation of capital per worker.

grow by 0.75 percent, using the 0.75 income share for labor. If capital alone grows by 1 percent, output will only grow by 0.25 percent, reflecting the smaller importance of capital in production. But if each grows by 1 percent, so does output.

This point—that growth in inputs is weighted by factor shares—turns out to be quite critical when we ask how much extra growth we get by raising the rate of growth of the capital stock, say by supply-side policies. Suppose in the example above, with everything else the same, capital growth had been twice as high, 6 percent instead of 3 percent. Doing the calculations with the help of Equation (2) we find that output growth would increase to 3.9 percent, rising by less than a percentage point even though capital growth rises by three percentage points.

17-2 EMPIRICAL ESTIMATES OF THE SOURCES OF GROWTH

The previous section prepared us for an analysis of empirical studies that deal with sources of growth. Equation (2) suggests that the growth in output can be explained by growth in factor inputs, weighted by their shares in income, and by technical progress. An early and famous study by Robert Solow of MIT dealt with the period 1909–1949 in the United States.[3] Solow's surprising conclusion was that over 80 percent of the growth in output per labor hour over that period was due to technical progress, that is, to factors other than growth in the input of capital per labor hour. Specifically, Solow estimated for the United States an equation similar to Equation (2) that identifies capital and labor growth along with technical progress as the sources of output growth. Of the average annual growth of total GNP of 2.9 percent per year over that period, he concluded that 0.32 percent was attributable to capital accumulation, 1.09 percent per annum was due to the increases in the input of labor, and the remaining 1.49 percent was due to technical progress. Per capita output grew at 1.81 percent, with 1.49 percent of that increase resulting from technical progress.

The very large part of the growth contribution that is taken up by "technical progress" makes that term really a catchall for omitted factors and poor measurement of the capital and labor inputs. Further work therefore turned quite naturally to explore this residual, that is, growth not explained by capital accumulation or increased labor input.

Perhaps the most comprehensive of the subsequent studies is that by Edward Denison.[4] Using data for the period 1929–1969, Denison attributed 1.8 percent of the 3.4 percent annual rate of increase in real output to increased factor inputs. Output per labor hour grew at the rate of 2.09

[3] "Technical Change and the Aggregate Production Function." *Review of Economics and Statistics*, August 1957.

[4] *Accounting for United States Economic Growth 1929–1969* (Washington, D.C.: The Brookings Institution, 1974). See also E. Denison's *Accounting for Slower Economic Growth: The United States in the 1970s* (ibid., 1980).

TABLE 17-2 SOURCES OF GROWTH OF TOTAL NATIONAL INCOME, 1929–1969

Source of growth	Growth rate, percent per annum
Total factor input	1.82
Labor: 1.32	
Capital: 0.50	
Output per unit of input	1.59
Knowledge: 0.92	
Resource allocation: 0.30	
Economies of scale: 0.36	
Other: 0.01	
National income	3.41

Source: E. Denison, Accounting for United States Economic Growth 1929–1969 *(Washington, D.C.: The Brookings Institution, 1974), p. 127.*

percent, of which 1.59 percent was due to technical progress. Denison's findings thus support Solow's estimate that most of the growth in output per labor hour is due to technical progress. Table 17-2 shows a breakdown of the increased factor inputs.

Technical progress explains almost half the growth in output, with growth in total factor inputs accounting for the other half of growth. Consider now the breakdown between the various components of increased factor use. Here increases in the labor force get a very large credit for their contribution to growth. Why? Because labor grows very fast? The answer is provided by Equation (2), which suggests that labor's growth rate has a relatively large weight mainly because labor's share of income is relatively large. The counterpart is obviously the relatively low share of capital. As noted above, even if capital and labor grew at the same rate, the fact that they have different shares in income—labor having a share of about 75 percent and capital having a share of about 25 percent—implies that labor would be credited with a larger contribution toward growth.

Next we look at the various sources of increased factor productivity or increased output per unit factor input. Here the striking fact is the importance of advances in knowledge that account for almost two-thirds of the contribution of technical progress toward growth. Two other sources of increased factor productivity are worth recording. One is the increase in productivity that stems from improved resource allocation. Here we can think of people leaving low-paying jobs or low-income areas and moving to better jobs or locations, thus contributing to increased output or income growth. An important element is relocation from farms to cities.

The remaining significant part of technical progress is *economies of scale.* This is a bit troublesome because we assumed away economies of scale in deriving Equation (2). In deriving that equation, we explicitly assumed constant returns to scale, but we find now that more than 10 percent of the average annual growth in income is due to an expanding scale of operation. As the scale of operation of the economy expands, fewer inputs are required per unit output presumably because we can avail ourselves of techniques that are economically inefficient at a small-scale level but yield factor savings at a larger scale of production.

The major significance of Denison's work, and the work in this area of others, including Simon Kuznets and J. W. Kendrick, is to point out that there is no single critical source of real income growth. The early finding by Solow that growth in the capital stock makes a minor, though not negligible, contribution to growth stands up well to the test of later research. Capital investment is certainly necessary—particularly because some technological improvements require the use of new types of machines—but it is clear that other sources of growth can make an important contribution. Furthermore, since for most purposes we are interested in output per head, we have to recognize that we are left with only technical progress and growth in capital to achieve increased output per head. Here we have to ask, What are the components of technical progress? *Advances in knowledge stand out as a major source and point to the roles of research, education, and training as important sources of growth.*[5]

The Decline in Growth

We saw in Table 17-1 the decline in U.S. output growth in the 1970s. The decline in growth was not limited to the United States. In the 1970s trend growth rates of output declined throughout the industrialized world. Pinpointing the exact source of the decline remains a controversial issue, but the growth accounting framework of Equation (2) provides some help. We can rewrite that equation, taking employment growth to the left-hand side, to obtain an equation that gives the determinants of the growth in output per head, $\Delta Y/Y - \Delta N/N$:

$$\Delta Y/Y - \Delta N/N = \theta\,(\Delta K/K - \Delta N/N) + \Delta A/A \qquad (2a)$$

The equation states that output per head grows either because capital per head increases or because total factor productivity rises.

Table 17-3 (see page 593) compares the sources of growth over the 1960–1973 period with those of the more recent 1973–1979 period of slowdown. The data are presented for the United States, Japan, and Germany.[6] In each case there is a large reduction in the growth of output per hour of labor. The growth reduction, in each case, is a reflection of reduced capital accumulation and of reduced total factor productivity growth. Moreover, the decline in advances in knowledge, which includes all items not otherwise classified, represents a very significant part of the reduction in growth. In the United States, part of this decline has been attributed to a decline in government spending for research and development.

[5] A collection of useful papers on the sources of growth are contained in Edmund Phelps (ed.), *The Goal of Economics Growth* (New York: Norton, 1969), and Dennis C. Mueller (ed.), *The Political Economy of Growth* (New Haven, Conn.: Yale University Press, 1983).

[6] Note the amazing growth rate of Japanese output from 1960 to 1973. By 1973 the output per labor hour was almost three times the 1960 level.

Government regulation appears in each case as a negative contribution to growth. In comparing the two periods, regulation is one of the items responsible for the reduced growth in the 1970s. Interestingly, increased regulation accounts for a much smaller cost in terms of reduced growth in the United States, where regulation is a big issue, than in Japan:

In principle, government regulation could be a source of increased efficiency and therefore of growth. But in none of the nine countries and two subperiods studied by Kendrick is this the case. Government regulation, from this account, appears harmful to growth. But in interpreting that finding we must bear in mind that the regulation, which reduced pollution, brought improvements in the quality of the environment. These improvements make us better off but do not show up in GNP.[7]

17-3 OUTPUT GROWTH AND SUPPLY-SIDE ECONOMICS

In the early 1980s, partly as a result of disappointment with slow growth and generally poor macroeconomic performance, *supply-side economics* attracted much attention. We have already discussed supply-side economics in Chapters 15 and 16. Here we concentrate on the solid part, which argues that the level and/or the growth rate of output could be significantly increased through policies designed to promote greater efficiency, reduced regulation, greater willingness to work, and greater willingness to save and invest.

In discussing full-employment output in earlier chapters we took the labor supply to be given and independent of the real wage, and similarly, we assumed a given stock of capital. But the basic premise of supply-side economics is that capital and labor supplies are not given, independent of incentives to work, save, and invest. On the contrary, it is argued that the labor-leisure choice is strongly affected by the *after-tax* real wage and that the willingness to save and invest is likewise affected by the *after-tax* rates of return on assets. This perspective directs attention to fiscal policy as influencing factor supplies and hence the level and rate of increase of output.

Labor Supply

Households have to choose how much labor to supply. In practice that means choosing how many members of the family work and for how many hours per week or month. At first sight there appears to be little choice since the typical job comes with a given number of working hours per week. But that is not quite the case once we take into account the possibility that more than one family member might work, or the possibilities of working overtime hours or holding part-time jobs. Households' labor supply can thus vary in response to incentives.

[7] For a further discussion of the slowdown in growth, see E. F. Denison, "Explanations of Declining Productivity, "*Survey of Current Business*, August 1979, part II.

The main determinant of labor supply is the after-tax real wage. Suppose the after-tax real wage increases. There are two effects on labor supply. First, a given number of working hours now gives a higher income than before. Thus the worker can maintain the same income as before, while working fewer hours and enjoying more leisure. This is the *income effect*, tending to reduce the quantity of labor supplied when the real wage rises. But, second, every hour spent in leisure is more expensive in terms of real income foregone, tending to make the worker substitute work for leisure. This is the *substitution effect* of the higher real wage. The net effect of these two forces is, in general, uncertain, and we must therefore turn to empirical studies of the labor supply to find which effect dominates and whether the labor supply response is large.

EMPIRICAL EVIDENCE

Jerry Hausman of MIT has shown in a number of studies that the household labor supply increases *significantly* in response to increased after-tax real wages.[8] This implies that changes in the tax structure that increase the after-tax real wage would increase labor supply and output. Hausman finds that the progressivity of income taxes reduces labor supply. The magnitude of the effect can be judged from the following experiment. Suppose the progressive income tax structure were eliminated and replaced by a flat 15 percent income tax which would lead to the same amount of revenue. What would happen to labor supply? Hausman estimates that total labor supply would rise by 5 percent. With an income share of 0.75, a 5 percent growth in labor supply would increase the level of full-employment output by 3.75 percent. This is certainly a nonnegligible gain, although the policy experiment—the move to a flat income tax—would be a major and controversial change in the structure of taxation.

Supply of Capital

The supply of capital represents the cumulation of past investment. The capital stock grows if additions to the stock more than offset the depreciation due to wear and tear and to obsolescence.

A supply-side point of view emphasizes the links between saving and investment. Recall that when the goods market clears and when net exports are zero, investment minus saving equals the budget surplus, or

$$I = S + (T - G) \tag{3}$$

Equation (3) shows that to raise investment and thus growth of the capital stock, we require increased saving or reduced government budget deficits.

[8] J. Hausman "Labor Supply and the Natural Unemployment Rate," in L. Meyer (ed.), *The Supply-Side Effects of Economic Policy* (St. Louis: Center for the Study of American Business, 1981), and "Labor Supply," in H. Aaron and J. Pechman (eds.), *How Taxes Affect Behavior* (Washington, D.C.: The Brookings Institution, 1981).

Supply-side economics has focused on the incentives to save and invest. Supply-side economists argue that regulation has reduced the productivity of investment and that corporate and personal income taxes further reduce the rate of return eventually received by the savers who provide the funds needed to finance investment. If savers receive a lower rate of return as a result of taxation, say the supply-siders, they reduce saving, and therefore capital accumulation is reduced.

For instance, consider an investment that yields 12 percent per year in real terms. That is, someone who undertakes the investment, costing $100 in year 1, earns $12 per year in real terms forever after (net of labor and material costs). If the income tax rate is 40 percent, the saver can at most earn, after tax, 60 percent of 12 percent, or 7.2 percent. As a result of taxation, the return to saving is substantially reduced. Accordingly, claim supply-siders, the higher the tax rate, the less saving there will be.[9]

What supply-side policies increase the yield on saving? There are a variety of means of exempting the return on saving from taxation. For instance, an individual can contribute up to $2,000 per year to an IRA (individual retirement account). The amount contributed is not counted as income for federal tax purposes, and the interest is not taxed either. There are other such tax-free means of saving. There is also considerable support for the use of a *consumption tax* rather than the income tax. A consumption tax levies taxes only on consumption spending, not on income. Since the difference between income and consumption is saving, a consumption tax effectively exempts any amount that is saved from being taxed in the year it is earned, and thereby encourages saving.

There is considerable disagreement on the issue of the response of saving to changes in its return. The contention that increased after-tax rates of return to saving will *strongly* raise saving does not have much support. Once again we have two opposing effects: With increased interest rates, less saving is needed to ensure a given future income, say, for retirement. This effect (actually an income effect) reduces saving. At the same time a dollar saved today yields increased future wealth and consumption and would therefore lead households to postpone consumption and increase saving (this is the substitution effect). The balance of effects is theoretically uncertain.

The empirical evidence does not settle the issue of whether changes in the after-tax rate of return affect the rate of saving.[10] Therefore policies that reduce taxes on saving as a means of generating more saving, capital formation, and growth have an uncertain effect on the economy.

Another line of argument questions the quantitative importance of policies to promote saving. We note from the growth Equation ($2a$) that growth in

[9] See M. Boskin "Economic Growth and Productivity," in M. Boskin (ed.), *The Economy in the 1980s: A Program for Growth and Stability* (San Francisco: Institute for Contemporary Studies, 1980); the *Economic Report of the President*, 1982 and 1983; and especially, Michael K. Evans, *The Truth about Supply-Side Economics* (New York: Basic Books, 1983).

[10] Gerald A. Carlino, in "Interest Rate Effects and Intertemporal Consumption," *Journal of Monetary Economics*, March 1982, reviews and extends the (ambiguous) evidence.

capital receives a very small weight in determining output growth. Even if policies led to a 10 percent rise in the capital-labor ratio, output per head would only increase by 2.5 percent. But to achieve a 10 percent rise in the capital-labor ratio, say, over 10 years, net investment as a share of GNP would have to double.[11]

Regulation

Government regulation involves a tradeoff. Government regulations serve some social purpose (the environment, safety, conservation), but they also involve costs to firms that have to abide by them. Regulation therefore reduces business profitability. Policy makers are keenly aware that the tradeoff exists and therefore, rightly, focus on inefficient regulation and particularly costly (nonmarket) regulation as requiring review. That process has been under way for some time, but it would be a mistake to expect major growth in output from reduced regulation.

Budget Deficits and Growth

In Equation (3) we showed that private investment and capital formation will be higher when saving is higher and the government budget deficit is smaller.[12] Government budget deficits thus imply, other things equal, a reduction in full-employment output growth. Government budget deficits absorb private saving—households buy government securities rather than the stocks or bonds that firms issue to finance their investment. Therefore funds are diverted from growth toward other purposes. It is clear that if the only objective is to promote growth, the government should balance the budget or even run a surplus to free resources for investment. However, there is a tradeoff between growth and the social objectives that may lie behind a budget deficit.

Evaluating Supply-Side Economics and Growth Incentives

The emphasis on increasing incentives to work, save, and invest is the valid core of supply-side economics. There are two questions here. The first is, will the proposed policies work, that is, increase future potential output? The second question is, If the policies do work, how far should we go in creating incentives to increase future potential output?

Policies to increase the labor supply by reducing taxes and policies to increase investment by reducing government budget deficits and through investment subsidies would be effective in increasing potential output today

[11] Suppose the capital stock is equal to 3 times output. Then a 10 percent increase in capital represents an amount equal to 30 percent of GNP, or over a 10-year period, an increase in net investment of 3 percent of GNP. *Net* investment is now between 2 and 5 percent of GNP. The increase therefore would imply doubling the share of net investment in GNP.

[12] We implicitly assume that all investment is undertaken by the private sector, not by the government. But in many countries government investment is a large part of total investment.

and in the future. Thus supply-side policies are available. But we can also go overboard on such policies. If we are reducing government budget deficits while reducing other taxes, we are also reducing government spending. We could reduce government spending by getting rid of the army. But most people would think it better to have higher taxes and some army than lower taxes and no army. And similarly, the government provides many useful services through its welfare programs—services that most people prefer to have—rather than aiming purely to maximize the level of investment.

Further, given government spending, and at full employment, increases in saving imply reductions in consumption. Thus in supply-side economics we are trading off current consumption for future consumption. We are trading off the consumption of those now alive for the consumption of their children and children who come later yet. This process also can go too far. In the extreme, we (society) would not want to force the current generation to consume at a bare survival level just so their grandchildren can sit around their pools doing very little work while automated factories made possible by a huge volume of past investment produce a high level of output. Somewhere between not saving now and saving almost all of output, there is an optimal amount of saving to be done.

It is no easy task for society to decide what that optimal amount of saving is. Those who will be consuming in the future are not here to vote, because they have not yet been born. And those who are around now will have different views. Some may ask, as reportedly has Joan Robinson, the famous English economist, "What did posterity ever do for us?" Others may feel it is the duty of the parents to sacrifice for their children's sake. Ultimately the policy decisions that affect growth are settled politically.

17-4 MEASURING POTENTIAL OUTPUT

When policy makers decide to use monetary or fiscal policy to bring the economy closer to full employment, they need to know where to aim. If the full-employment unemployment rate were 6 percent, it would not make much sense to use expansionary fiscal policies at a 5.5 percent unemployment rate. Thus we need measures of the full-employment unemployment rate and the corresponding level of *potential output* or *full-employment output*. The concept draws on the ideas of growth accounting to construct a GNP series that can serve as a benchmark for policy planning.

There are two approaches to constructing a series for potential output. Both approaches use the production function of Equation (1) as a conceptual framework, but they use it differently.

1 Data on capital, labor, and material inputs are used to estimate the production function. Then estimates of the high-employment factor supplies are inserted to calculate what potential output is. This point is expanded upon below.
2 The alternative approach does not attempt to identify the separate contri-

butions to output of capital, labor, and other factors, but rather focuses on employment and labor productivity.

We start by sketching the second approach.

The Traditional Approach to Estimating Potential Output

The basic equation of the traditional approach uses as a starting point an identity that relates output to employment and to labor productivity, or output per hour of labor:

$$\text{Output} = \text{output per hour of labor} \times \text{total labor hours} \tag{4}$$

or in fewer words, output = productivity × hours. To move from here to potential output we need estimates of (*a*) the *high-employment* level of labor productivity and (*b*) the *high-employment* total labor hours. Because both labor hours and productivity vary over time and cyclically, the problem is to determine the high-employment value of each and to guess their future course.[13]

HIGH-EMPLOYMENT LABOR HOURS

Consider first the calculation involved in finding the high-employment number of work hours. This is the product of hours worked per person employed and the number of persons employed. The number of persons employed is a function of the employment rate, the labor force, and the labor force participation rate in the population. Say the working age population is 200 million people, of whom 60 percent are in the labor force, of which, in turn, at full-employment 95 percent are employed, each of whom works for 2,000 hours per year. Then total high-employment work hours are 228,000 million hours. Equation (5) shows the formula:

$$\begin{matrix}\text{Total high-} \\ \text{employment} \\ \text{hours}\end{matrix} = \begin{matrix}\text{hours} \\ \text{per} \\ \text{worker}\end{matrix} \times \begin{matrix}\text{employment} \\ \text{ratio}\end{matrix} \times \begin{matrix}\text{labor force} \\ \text{participation} \\ \text{ratio}\end{matrix} \times \begin{matrix}\text{working} \\ \text{age} \\ \text{population}\end{matrix} \tag{5}$$

where each of the ratios on the right-hand side is evaluated at the high-employment level.

Equation (5) is interesting because it points to a number of different factors influencing labor hours. Among the factors, for example, is the sex and age composition of the labor force, which has a strong influence on the participation rate. But institutional factors, and tax incentives as we saw

[13] See A. M. Okun, "Potential GNP: Its Measurement and Significance," reprinted in his book *The Political Economy of Prosperity* (New York: Norton, 1970); and G. Perry, "Potential Output: Recent Issues and Present Trends," in *U.S. Productive Capacity* (St. Louis: Center for the Study of American Business, Washington University, 1977).

above, also influence the fraction of the population that is in the labor force. Shifts over time in the underlying determinants will change the labor force participation rate and hence, given the other determinants, total hours and potential output.

The employment ratio, or 1 minus the unemployment rate, is one of the determinants of high-employment hours. Here an estimate must be made of what is the high-employment rate of unemployment. The unemployment rate, as we saw in Chapter 14, is a weighted average of the unemployment rates of different groups — experienced workers and young people, men and women, each of which has different unemployment characteristics. The aggregate unemployment rate is therefore affected by shifts in the age-sex composition of the labor force. Young people, for example, have a higher full-employment unemployment rate. Therefore an increase in the proportion of young people in the labor force, as a consequence of the baby boom, would raise the aggregate full-employment unemployment rate.

The number of hours per workweek changes over time. The tendency has been toward a reduction. At the same time, because different sectors of the economy (manufacturing, services, construction) have slightly different work weeks, the economywide average is also influenced by the trend changes in the composition of output. Because the workweek is strongly influenced by cyclical factors, the trend and cyclical factors need to be disentangled here too.

PRODUCTIVITY

The second determinant of high-employment output in Equation (4) is labor productivity. In Table 17-3 we saw the determinants of labor productivity, or output per hour. These include not only increases in capital per work hour, but also changes in the quality of labor, in knowledge, and in the regulatory environment. As we have seen, productivity growth has not been constant in the past. It changes over time and very significantly over the business cycle. Once again it is necessary to disentangle the trend, change in trend, and cyclical factors to find out what the behavior of cyclically adjusted or high-employment productivity is.

THE HIGH-EMPLOYMENT BENCHMARK

The most difficult point in estimating potential output arises when we have to specify the benchmark unemployment rate that corresponds to full employment.

Estimates of potential output were published by the Council of Economic Advisers through 1981 and are still published by the Department of Commerce. The full-employment rate of unemployment was taken to be 4.0 percent in 1955, rising to 4.9 percent in 1973. The increase represents shifts in the composition of the labor force that we discussed above. Further shifts in the composition of the labor force raised official estimates of the high-employment level to above 5 percent by 1981.

TABLE 17-3 THE SLOWDOWN IN GROWTH

	United States		Japan		Germany	
	1960–1973	1973–1979	1960–1973	1973–1979	1960–1973	1973–1979
Output per labor hour	3.1	1.1	9.9	3.8	5.8	4.3
Contribution to growth						
Capital per labor hour	1.2	0.5	3.3	2.0	2.6	2.2
Total factor productivity; of which:	1.9	0.6	6.6	1.8	3.2	2.1
Labor quality	0.3	0.4	1.8	0.6	0.3	0.3
Scale and capacity utilization	0.5	0.1	1.1	0.1	0.5	0.1
Regulation	−0.1	−0.4	−0.2	−1.0	0	−0.4
Knowledge	1.2	0.5	3.9	2.1	2.4	2.1

Source: J. W. Kendrick, "International Comparisons of Recent Productivity Trends," in W. Fellner (ed.), Contemporary Economic Problems *(Washington, D.C.: American Enterprise Institute, 1981), pp. 140–141.*

Figure 17-2 shows actual and potential output as estimated by the Department of Commerce, using the 1955 and 1973 benchmark unemployment rates. Note that the gap between actual and potential output is, by construction, zero in the two high-employment years.

FIGURE 17-2 ACTUAL AND POTENTIAL OUTPUT: 1955–1983. (Billion 1972 $.) (*Sources: Survey of Current Business*, November 1980 and April 1983 and Data Resources, Inc.)

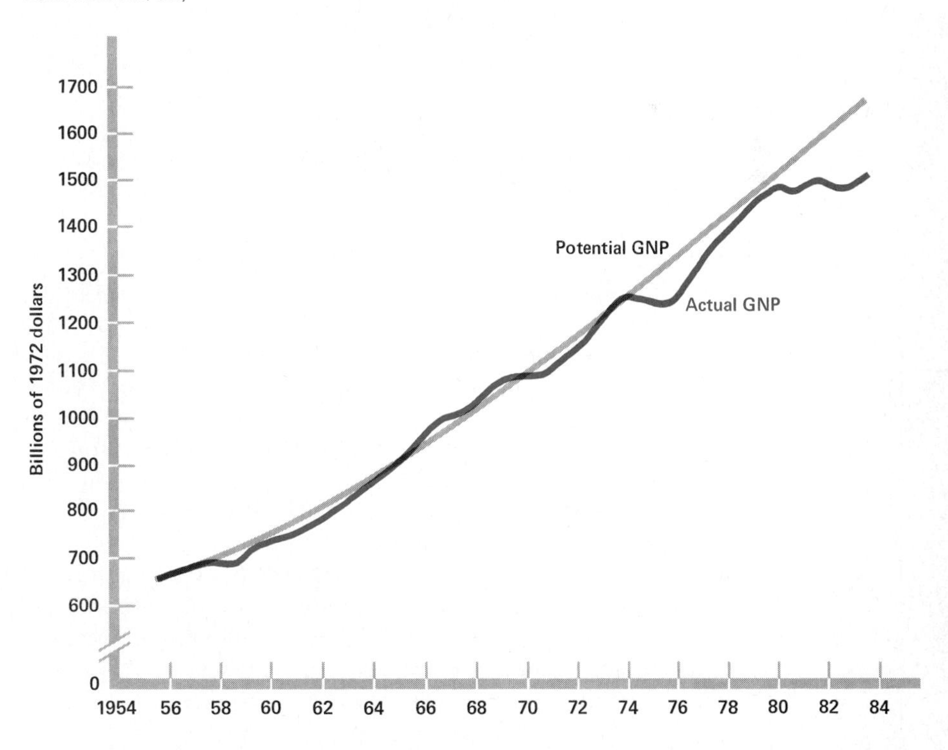

TABLE 17-4 ACTUAL PRODUCTIVITY GROWTH AND ESTIMATED GROWTH OF POTENTIAL OUTPUT *(Average annual rates).*

	1960–1973	1973–1979	1979–1982
Productivity growth	2.9	0.8	0.5
Potential output growth	3.6	3.3	2.6

Source: Economic Report of the President, *1983, and* Survey of Current Business, *April 1982 and April 1983.*

Note also that the growth rate of potential output declines over time. This decline reflects an estimate of reduced productivity growth and changes in the trend rate of increase of the labor supply. We discussed reasons for the decline in productivity growth in Section 17-2, with the contributions of the various causes listed in Table 17-3. Table 17-4 shows the growth rates of actual productivity (output per labor hour) and estimated growth rate of potential output. A slowdown occurs in 1973–1979, and a further reduction occurs in the post-1980 period.

UNCERTAINTY ABOUT POTENTIAL OUTPUT AND PRODUCTIVITY GROWTH

The low growth rate of output and the high-unemployment rates of the last decade have created considerable uncertainty about both the full-employment unemployment rate (and thus about potential output) and the growth rate of potential output. In response to the uncertainty, the Council of Economic Advisors stopped publishing calculations of potential output in 1982.

The reason for uncertainty is that since 1973, the unemployment rate has not been as low as 5 percent, the number used by the Department of Commerce in its *Survey of Current Business.* Since that time, the unemployment rate went below 6 percent only in 1978 and 1979. Even then the lowest civilian unemployment rate was 5.6 percent. It seems almost certain that full employment corresponds more realistically to a benchmark rate of about 6 percent, and many argue for an even higher rate. If the 6 percent rate is right, then potential output measures have to be reduced below the levels seen in Figure 17-2.

Estimates of the growth rate of potential output too are subject to unusual uncertainty at present. That is in part because it is difficult to separate the role of the energy crisis in the 1970s in reducing the growth rate of output from changes in long-term trends.

Table 17-5 presents alternative estimates of both the full-employment unemployment rate and the growth rate of potential output. The Budget Office in preparing actual and full-employment budget forecasts assumes an annual growth rate of potential output of 2.6 percent for the period

TABLE 17-5 POTENTIAL OUTPUT GROWTH AND FULL-EMPLOYMENT UNEMPLOYMENT RATE: PROVISIONAL ASSUMPTIONS

Potential output growth	Full-employment unemployment rate
2.6–2.9%	6.0%

Sources: Congressional Budget Office, Reducing the Deficit. *A Report to the Senate and House Committees on the Budget, Washington, D.C., February 1983; and Joseph Pechman (ed.),* Setting National Priorities *(Washington, D.C.: The Brookings Institution, 1983), app. A.*

1983–1988 and a benchmark unemployment rate of 6 percent. These are close to what would be a consensus of opinion in the early eighties.

Despite the uncertainties about both the benchmark unemployment rate and the growth rate of potential output, we should note that we are talking about a relatively narrow range of unemployment rates. There is no doubt that the full-employment rate of unemployment is far below the 10 percent ranges of 1982–1983, and estimates above 7 percent are rare indeed. Estimates of the growth rate of potential output are more uncertain—but those estimates are of less immediate relevance to stabilization policy. The concept of potential output is still a highly useful one in understanding both the current state of the economy and the budget—since estimates of the high-employment budget depend on the estimate of full-employment output.[14]

The Production Function Approach

An alternative to Equation (5) is to attempt directly to estimate the production function relation between output and the inputs of capital, labor, and materials. Once estimates of the relation between output and the inputs are obtained, the level of high-employment output can be calculated by using a high-employment series for capital and labor and a measure of the use of materials.

The production function approach attracted interest in part because it seemed a way of finding out just how important the energy shocks of the 1970s were in reducing the level or growth rate of potential output. The energy shocks were prime suspects in the search for an explanation of lower productivity growth because productivity growth fell most dramatically after the first oil shock in 1973. By using an explicit production function framework, an estimate can be obtained of the effect of increased energy prices on energy use and hence on output. This approach has turned out to be controversial. The reason is that the production function approach suggests a very

[14] William Fellner has sharply questioned the entire idea of potential output. He argues that the notion of potential output is not useful because it seems to imply that only demand variables (reflected in the unemployment rate) determine the economy's potential output. But, says Fellner, supply-side variables also matter. See William Fellner, *The High Employment Budget and Potential Output* (Washington, D.C.: American Enterprise Institute, 1982).

significant decline in real potential output in response to increased energy costs.[15]

One recent study finds that a 10 percent rise in the real price of energy reduces output in the short run by 0.89 percent and in the long run by 1.22 percent. In the period 1974–1982 the real price of energy increased by 68 percent, which implies a reduction of potential output of about 8 percent.[16] For many observers this estimate of the role of energy is far too high. There is no question that energy does matter, but the precise estimate remains a subject of further research.

Conclusion

We use measures of potential output to judge fiscal policies and to plan stabilization policies. The measures of potential output we have are far from perfect. They attempt to estimate from the actual behavior of output, productivity, and employment what would be the behavior of output along a full-employment path. But because of the difficulties discussed above, the measures of potential output are subject to a wide margin of error. In the recent past, potential output measures have been revised almost each year, and occasionally by large amounts, and in 1982–1983 were no longer made public by the Council of Economic Advisers.

The disappearance of a well-defined and easy-to-measure potential output series is very disturbing, given how central it is to many policy questions. But two points need to be made. The first is that the *theoretical concept* of full-employment output—even if that output is responsive to supply-side policies—remains entirely intact. The second is that controversies surrounding the *measurement* of potential output are in part a reflection of the puzzles about productivity growth in the 1970s. If and when these puzzles are better understood, potential output measures will again become more widely used.

*17-5 GROWTH THEORY

We turn now from empirical issues and the historical record to the theory of economic growth. The theory of economic growth asks what factors determine the full-employment growth rate of output over time. Growth theory is important because it both helps explain growth rates and helps explain why per capita income levels differ among countries. One of the central results of growth theory, for example, is the proposition that between two countries

[15] See R. Rasche and J. Tatom, "Energy Resources and Potential GNP," Federal Reserve Bank of St. Louis, *Review*, June 1977; J. Tatom, "Potential Output and the Recent Productivity Decline," ibid., January 1982. J. Tatom, "Investment and the New Energy Regime," in Board of Governors of the Federal Reserve, *Public Policy and Capital Formation*, Washington, D.C. 1981; and J. Perloff and M. Wachter, "A Production Function-Nonaccelerating Inflation Approach to Potential Output," in K. Brunner and A. Meltzer (eds.), *Carnegie-Rochester Conference Series*, vol. 10 (Amsterdam: North-Holland, Publishing Company 1979).

[16] This is the most recent estimate provided in Tatom, "Potential Output," op cit., p. 7. See, however, the discussion in Dension, "Explanations of Declining Productivity," op cit.

with the same technology and saving rates the one that has the higher rate of population growth will eventually have lower per capita income.

We have already examined the sources of growth in Equation (2), where we showed that full-employment output growth depends on the growth in factor inputs and on technical progress. In this section we pursue the issue further to ask what determines the growth of factor supplies and what is the link to long-run per capita incomes or standards of living.

We take a rather simple formulation here by assuming a given and constant rate of labor force growth, $\Delta N/N \equiv n$, and also that there is no technical progress, $\Delta A/A = 0$.[17] With these assumptions the only variable element left in Equation (2) is the growth rate of capital.

Capital growth is determined by saving, which, in turn, depends on income. Income or output, in turn, depends on capital. We are thus set with an interdependent system in which capital growth depends, via saving and income, on the capital stock. We now study the short-run behavior, the adjustment process, and the long-run equilibrium of that interdependent system.

Steady State

We start by discussing the steady state of the economy. Here we ask whether in an economy with population growth and saving, and therefore growth in the capital stock, we reach a point where output per head and capital per head become constant. In such a steady state, current saving and additions to the capital stock would be just enough to equip new entrants into the labor force with the same amount of capital as the average worker uses.

The idea of a steady state is simply this: If capital per head is unchanging, given technology, so is output per head. But for capital *per head* to remain unchanging even though population is growing, capital must grow at just the right rate, namely, at the same rate as population. More formally, if output per head is to remain constant, output and population must grow at the same rates, or $\Delta Y/Y = \Delta N/N = n$. Therefore, from Equation (2*a*), setting productivity growth and growth in output per capita equal to zero, we have $0 = (\Delta K/K - n)$, or

$$\Delta K/K = n \tag{6}$$

Equation (6) states that in the steady state the growth rate of the capital stock is equal to the growth rate of population. Equivalently, in the steady state the amount of capital per head is constant.

We now show the steady state graphically in Figure 17-3. We put output per head on the vertical axis and capital per head on the horizontal axis. The production function, which is central to understanding growth, exhibits diminishing returns. As capital per head increases, so that workers use increasing amounts of machinery, output per head increases, but at a diminishing

[17] For further simplicity we also assume that the entire population works, so that the labor force and the population are the same.

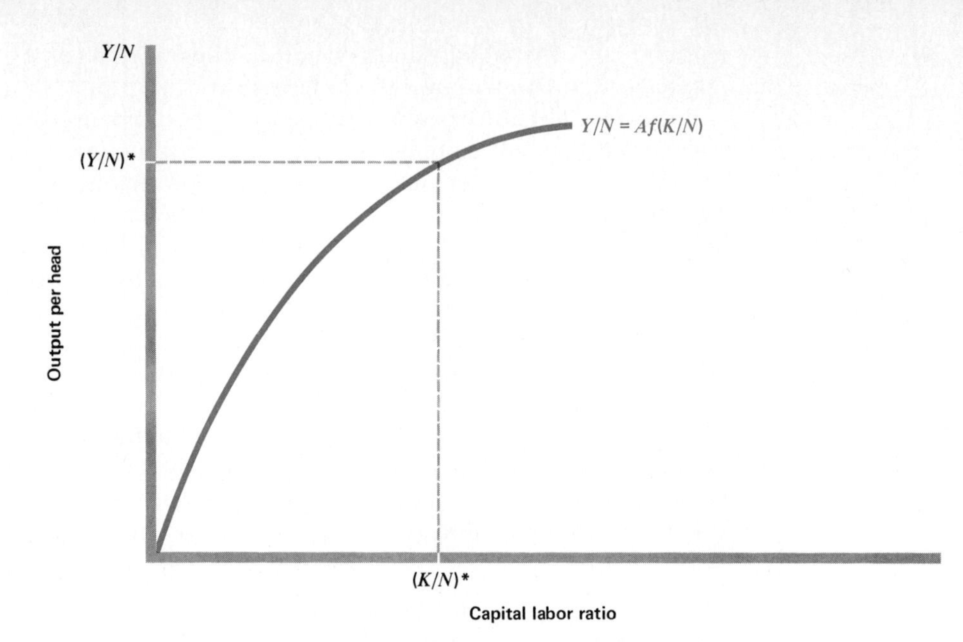

FIGURE 17-3 OUTPUT PER HEAD AND THE CAPITAL-LABOR RATIO. The production function shows output per head as a function of the amount of capital per head, or the capital-labor ratio. The higher the capital-labor ratio is, the higher output per head is. But the increment to output from raising the capital-labor ratio grows progressively smaller as the capital-labor ratio rises.

rate. Thus an increase in the capital-labor ratio is productive, but there are diminishing returns. In steady state, the economy settles down to a fixed capital-labor ratio, $(K/N)^*$. The production function shows the corresponding amount of output per head, $(Y/N)^*$.

SAVING AND GROWTH

We gain insight by examining the link between saving and the growth in capital. We are assuming there is no government. Accordingly, investment, or the gross increase in capital, is equal to saving. To obtain the increase in the capital stock, however, we have to deduct depreciation. Therefore the net addition to the capital stock is equal to saving less depreciation.

$$\Delta K = \text{saving} - \text{depreciation} \tag{7}$$

Two assumptions take us from (6) and (7) to a complete description of the steady state. In (7) we need to specify saving behavior and to make an assumption about depreciation. We assume first that saving is a constant fraction s of income (Y). Second, depreciation is at a constant rate of d percent of the capital stock. Concretely, we might assume that people save $s = 15$ percent of their income and that depreciation is at a rate of 10 percent per year so that every year 10 percent of the capital stock needs to be replaced to offset wear and tear.

Substituting these assumptions in Equation (7) yields

$$\Delta K = sY - dK \tag{7a}$$

or placing the right-hand side in Equation (6), we arrive at the following result that describes the steady state[18]:

$$sY = (n + d)K \tag{6a}$$

Equation (6*a*) states that in the steady state, saving (sY) is just sufficient to provide for enough investment to offset depreciation (dK) *and* to equip new members of the labor force with capital (nK). If saving were larger than this amount, net investment would be sufficiently large to make capital per head grow, leading to rising income per head. Conversely, if not enough were saved, capital per head would be falling and with it income per head.

The Growth Process

We next study the adjustment process that leads the economy from some initial capital-labor ratio over time to the steady state. The critical element in this transition process is the rate of saving and investment compared with the ratio of depreciation, and population growth.

NOTATION

The argument is made easier by a bit of new notation. We define the amount of output per head as $x = Y/N$ and the amount of capital per head, or the capital-labor ratio, as $k = K/N$. This is simply notation and in no way changes our model.

$$k = \text{capital-labor ratio} = \frac{K}{N} \qquad x = \text{output per head} = \frac{Y}{N} \tag{8}$$

Thus in terms of Figure 17-3 the vertical axis will be labeled x and the horizontal axis k.

CAPITAL ACCUMULATION

We now turn to the transition to the steady state. Note from Equation (2) that output her head will grow if capital per head grows and that capital per head will grow if saving is *more than sufficient* to cover depreciation of the capital

[18] Placing Eq. (7*a*) in Eq. (6) yields $(sY - dK)/K = n$. By multiplying both sides by K and collecting terms, we obtain $sY = (n + d)K$.

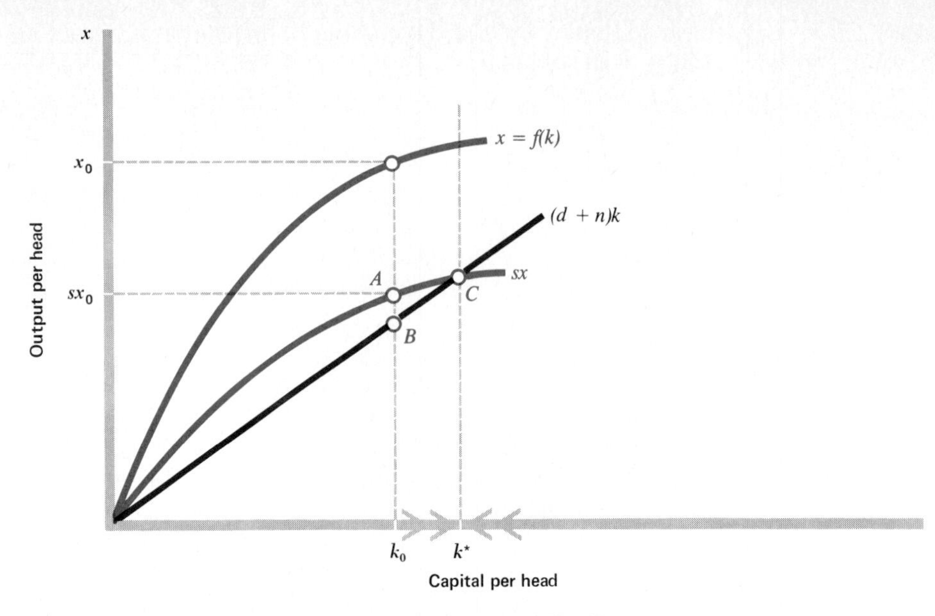

FIGURE 17-4 SAVING, INVESTMENT, AND CAPITAL ACCUMULATION. The saving function shows at each capital-labor ratio the part of income that is saved, sx. The straight line $(d + n)k$ shows the investment requirement. At low capital-labor ratios, saving exceeds the investment requirement, and hence output per head grows. Conversely at high capital-labor ratios, saving is less than the investment requirement, and capital per head is falling. The steady-state capital-labor ratio is k^*, where saving is just sufficient to maintain the capital-labor ratio constant.

stock and also to equip new members of the population with capital. This can be formalized by writing the change in the capital-labor ratio as follows[19]:

$$\Delta k = sx - (n + d)k \tag{9}$$

The growth process can now be studied with the help of Equation (6*a*) and Figure 17-4. Here we reproduce the production function from Figure 17-3, writing output per capita as a function of the capital-labor ratio.

We have added the savings function, which, for each capital-labor ratio, is simply the fraction s of output. Thus, for any capital-labor ratio, say, k_0, the corresponding point of the saving schedule tells us the amount of saving per head, $sx(k_0)$, that will be forthcoming at that capital-labor ratio.

We know that all saving is invested, so that gross investment or gross additions to the capital stock, in per capita terms, are equal to sx, given a

[19] The percentage growth rate of the capital-labor ratio is equal to the difference between the growth rate of capital and the growth rate of labor, or $\Delta k/k = \Delta K/K - n$. Now using Eq. (7*a*) to replace ΔK, we have $\Delta k/k = sY/K - d - n = \dfrac{s(Y/N)}{K/N} - (d + n) = \dfrac{sx}{k} - (d + n)$. Multiplying both sides by k yields Eq. (9) in the text.

capital-labor ratio of k_0. We know, too, from Equation (9) that the increase in the capital-labor ratio falls short of that gross addition for two reasons:

- Depreciation reduces the capital-labor ratio, and part of gross investment must be devoted to offsetting depreciation. In particular, if the depreciation rate is d, an amount dk is required as a depreciation allowance. For example, if the depreciation rate is 10 percent and the capital-labor ratio is 10 machines per person, each year the equivalent of 1 machine would depreciate and would have to be replaced; that is, 10 percent times 10 machines equals 1 machine that has to be replaced.
- Growth in the labor force implies that with a given stock of capital, the capital-labor ratio would be declining. To maintain the amount of capital per head constant, we have to add enough machines to the stock of capital to make up for the growth in population; that is, we need to invest at the rate nk.

It follows that we can write the investment required to maintain constant the capital-labor ratio in the face of depreciation and labor force growth as $(n + d)k$. When saving and hence gross investment are larger than $(n + d)k$, the stock of capital per head is increasing. If saving and gross investment are less, then we are not making up for depreciation and population growth, and, accordingly, capital per head is falling. We can therefore think of the term $(n + d)k$ as the investment requirement that will maintain constant capital per head and therefore, from Figure 17-3, output per head.

In Figure 17-4 we show this investment requirement as a positively sloped schedule. It tells us how much investment we would require at each capital-labor ratio just in order to keep that ratio constant. It is positively sloped because the higher the capital-labor ratio, the larger the amount of investment that is required to maintain that capital-labor ratio. Thus, with the depreciation rate of 10 percent and a growth rate of population of 1 percent, we would require an investment of 1.1 machines per head per year at a capital-labor ratio of 10 machines per head to maintain the capital-labor ratio constant. If the capital-labor ratio were 100 machines per head, the required investment would be 11 machines (=100 machines per head times 11 percent).

We have seen that the saving schedule tells us the amount of saving and gross investment associated with each capital-labor ratio. Thus, at a capital-labor ratio of k_0 in Figure 17-4, saving is sx_0 at point A. The investment requirement to maintain constant the capital-labor ratio at k_0 is equal to $(n + d)k_0$ at point B. Clearly, saving exceeds the investment requirement. More is added to the capital stock than is required to maintain constant the capital-labor ratio. Accordingly, the capital-labor ratio grows. Not surprisingly, the increase in the capital-labor ratio is equal to actual saving or investment less the investment requirement and is thus given by the vertical distance AB.

In the next period, capital per head will be higher. Thus on the horizontal axis we draw an arrow showing k increasing. You recognize the line of argument we are taking. From Figure 17-4 it is clear that with a somewhat higher capital-labor ratio, the discrepancy between saving and the investment requirement becomes smaller. Therefore the increase in the capital-labor ratio becomes smaller. However, the capital-labor ratio still increases, as indicated by the arrows.

The adjustment process comes to a halt at point C. Here we have reached a capital-labor ratio k^* for which saving and investment associated with that capital-labor ratio exactly match the investment requirement. Given the exact matching of actual and required investment, the capital-labor ratio neither rises nor falls. We have reached the steady state.

We can make the same argument by starting with an initial capital-labor ratio in excess of k^*. From Figure 17-4 we note that for high capital-labor ratios, the investment requirement is in excess of saving and investment. Accordingly, not enough is added to the capital stock to maintain the capital-labor ratio constant in the face of population growth and depreciation. Thus, the capital-labor ratio falls until we get to k^*, the steady-state capital-labor ratio.

To review our progress so far:

- To maintain the capital-labor ratio constant, saving and investment have to be sufficient to make up for the reduction in capital per head that arises from population growth and depreciation.
- With saving a constant fraction s of output, we established that the capital-labor ratio moves to a steady-state level k^* at which output and therefore saving (investment) are just sufficient to maintain constant the capital-labor ratio.
- The convergence to a steady-state capital-labor ratio k^* is ensured by the fact that at low levels of the capital-labor ratio, saving (investment) exceeds the investment required to maintain capital per head and therefore causes the capital-labor ratio to rise. Conversely, at high capital-labor ratios, saving (investment) falls short of the investment requirement, and thus the ratio declines.

Now we turn to a more detailed study of the steady-state equilibrium and the adjustment process. We note that the steady-state level of capital per head is constant, and thus the steady-state level of output per head is also constant. The steady state is reached when all variables, in per capita terms, are constant. This means that in the steady state, output, capital, and labor all grow at the same rate. They all grow at a rate equal to the rate of population growth. Note particularly that the steady-state growth rate is equal to the rate of population growth and therefore is *not* influenced by the saving rate. (Recall that we are assuming no technical progress.) To explore this property of the steady state in more detail, we investigate the effects of a change in the saving rate.

A Change in the Saving Rate

Why should the long-run growth rate be independent of the saving rate? If people save 10 percent of their income as opposed to 5 percent, should we not expect this to make a difference to the growth rate of output? Is it not true that an economy in which 10 percent of income is set aside for additions to the capital stock is one in which capital and therefore output grow faster than in an economy in which only 5 percent of income is saved?

We show here that an increase in the saving rate does the following: In the short run, it raises the growth rate of output. It does not affect the *long-run growth rate* of output, but it raises the long-run level of capital and output per head.

Consider Figure 17-5 with an initial steady-state equilibrium at point C, where saving precisely matches the investment requirement. At point C, exactly enough output is saved to maintain the stock of capital per head constant in the face of depreciation and labor force growth. Next consider an increase in the saving rate. For some reason, people want to save a larger fraction of income. The increased saving rate is reflected in an upward shift of the saving schedule. At each level of the capital-labor ratio, and hence at each level of output, saving is larger.

At point C, where we initially had a steady-state equilibrium, saving has

FIGURE 17-5 AN INCREASE IN THE SAVING RATE. An increase in the saving rate implies that at each capital-labor ratio a larger fraction of output is saved. The saving schedule shifts upward to $s'x$. At the initial steady state, saving now exceeds the investment requirement, and hence the capital-labor ratio rises until point C' is reached. An increase in the saving rate raises steady-state per capita income. The growth rate rises only in the transition from C to C'.

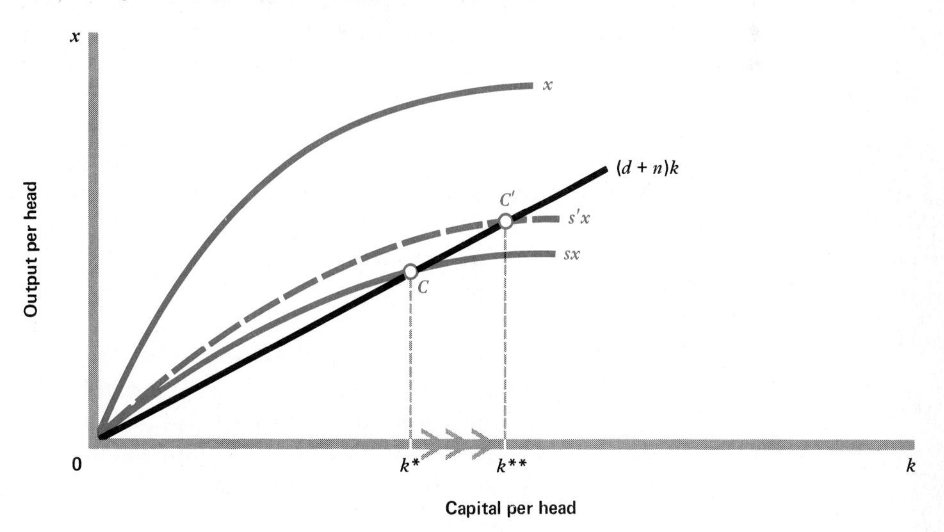

now risen relative to the investment requirement, and as a consequence, more is saved than is required to maintain capital per head constant. Enough is saved to allow the capital stock per head to increase.

It is apparent from Figure 17-5 that the capital stock per head will keep rising until we reach point C'. At C', the higher amount of saving is just enough to maintain the higher stock of capital. At point C', both capital per head and output per head have risen. Saving has increased as has the investment requirement. We have seen, therefore, that an increase in the saving rate will in the long run raise only the level of output and capital per head, but not the growth rate of output per head.

The transition process, however, involves an effect of the saving rate on the growth rate of output and the growth rate of output per head. In the transition from k^* to k^{**}, the increase in the saving rate raises the growth rate of output. This follows simply from the fact that the capital-labor ratio rises from k^* at the initial steady state to k^{**} in the new steady state. The only way to achieve an increase in the capital-labor ratio is for the capital stock to grow faster than the labor force (and depreciation). This is precisely what happens in the transition process where increased saving per head, due to the higher saving rate, raises investment and capital growth over and above the investment requirement and thus allows the capital-labor ratio to rise.

In summary, the long-run effect of an increase in the saving rate is to raise the level of output and capital per head but to leave the growth rate of output and capital unaffected. In the transition period, the rates of growth of output and capital increase relative to the steady state. In the short run, therefore, an increase in the saving rate means faster growth, as we would expect.

Figure 17-6 summarizes these two results. Figure 17-6*a* shows the level of per capita output. Starting from an initial long-run equilibrium at time t_0, the increase in the saving rate causes saving and investment to increase, the stock of capital per head grows, and so does output per head. The process will continue at a diminishing rate. In Figure 17-6*b* we focus on the growth rate of output and capital. The growth rate of output is equal to the growth rate of population in the initial steady state. The increase in the saving rate immediately raises the growth rate of output because it implies a faster growth in capital and therefore in output. As capital accumulates, the growth rate decreases, falling back toward the level of population growth.

Population Growth

The preceding discussion of saving and the influence of the saving rate on steady-state capital and output makes it easy to discuss the effects of increased population growth. The question we ask is, What happens when the population growth rate increases from n to n' and remains at that higher level indefinitely? We will show that such an increase in the rate of population growth will *raise* the growth rate of output and *lower* the level of output per head.

The argument can be conveniently followed in Figure 17-7. Here we show the initial steady-state equilibrium at point C. The increase in the

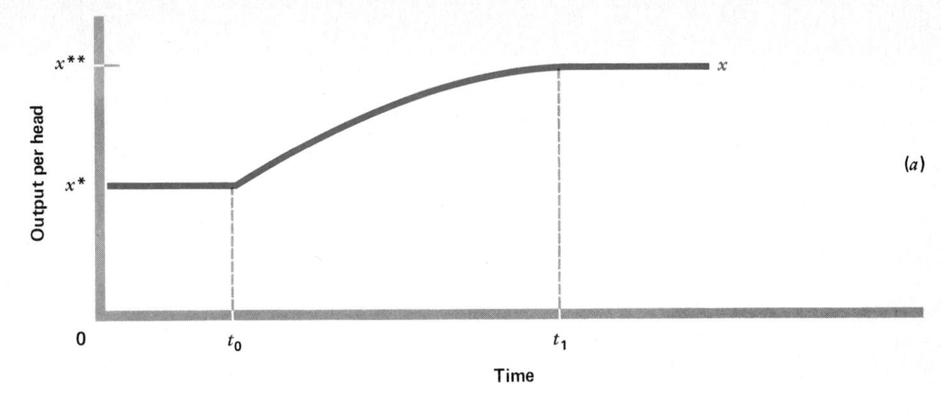

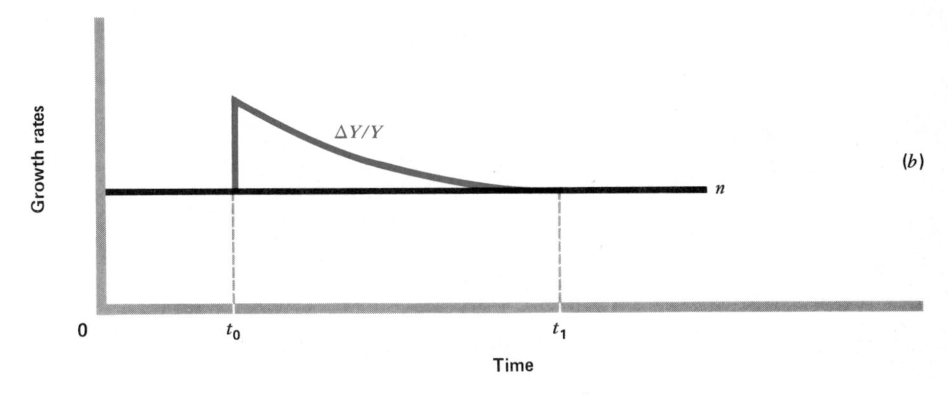

FIGURE 17-6*a* THE TIME PATH OF PER CAPITA INCOME. A rise in the saving rate leads to a rising capital-labor ratio and therefore to increasing output per head until a new steady state is reached.

FIGURE 17-6*b* THE TIME PATH OF THE GROWTH RATE OF OUTPUT. An increase in the saving rate raises investment above the investment requirement and thus leads to capital accumulation. Output growth transitorily rises and then falls back to the growth rate of population.

growth rate of population means that at each level of the capital-labor ratio, it takes a larger amount of investment just to maintain the capital-labor ratio constant. Suppose we had 10 machines per head. Initially, the growth rate of population is 1 percent and depreciation is 10 percent, so that we require per year 11 percent times 10 machines, or 1.1 machine, just to offset population growth and depreciation and thus maintain capital per head constant. To maintain the capital-labor ratio constant in the face of a higher growth rate of population, say, 2 percent, requires a higher level of investment, namely, 12 percent as opposed to 11 percent. This is reflected in Figure 17-7 by an upward rotation of the investment requirement schedule.

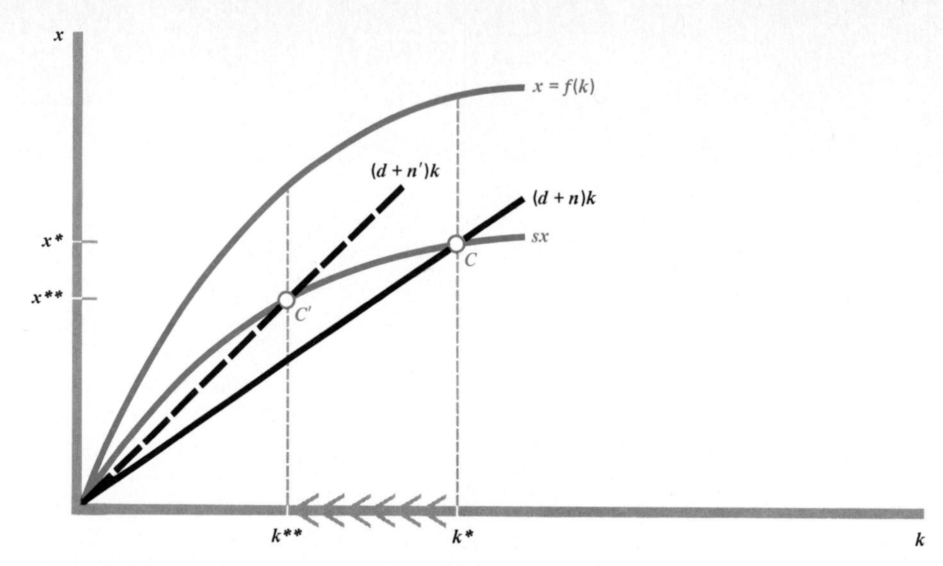

FIGURE 17-7 AN INCREASE IN THE POPULATION GROWTH RATE REDUCES PER CAPITA INCOME. Increased population growth raises the investment requirement, rotating the schedule upward to $(d + n')k$. At point C saving is insufficient to maintain capital per head constant in face of the more rapidly growing population. Capital and output per head decline until a new steady state at C' is reached.

It is clear from the preceding argument that we are no longer in steady-state equilibrium at point C. The investment that was initially just sufficient to keep the capital-labor ratio constant will no longer be sufficient in the face of higher population growth. At the initial equilibrium, the higher population growth with unchanged saving and investment means that capital does not grow fast enough to keep up with labor force growth and depreciation. Capital per head declines. In fact, capital per head will keep declining until we reach the new steady-state equilibrium at point C'. Here the capital-labor ratio has declined sufficiently for saving to match the investment requirement. It is true, too, that, corresponding to the lower capital-labor ratio, we have a decline in output per head. Output per head declines from x^* to x^{**}.

The decline in output per head as a consequence of increased population growth points to the problem faced by many developing countries. Fast growth in population, given the saving rate, means low levels of income per head. Indeed, in poor countries one can trace poverty, or low income per head, to the very high rate of population growth. With high population growth, saving will typically be too small to allow capital to rise relative to labor and thus to build up the capital-labor ratio to achieve a satisfactory level of income per head. In those circumstances, and barring other considerations, a reduction in the rate of population growth appears to be a way of achieving higher levels of steady-state per capita income and thus an escape from poverty.

BOX 17-1

THE LIMITS OF GROWTH

The record of growth since 1889 reviewed in Table 17-1 is impressive indeed. Per capita GNP in the United States has been doubling in less than 40 years over a period of nearly a century. And the growth certainly goes back further than that. The question of the limits to growth is whether limited resources and the pressure of population on scarce land and food will ultimately bring the growth process to a dramatic halt. Are growing economies headed toward stagnation or even disaster?

The disaster scenario is a simple one. First, only so much oil, coal, copper, and other raw materials are in the earth. One day they will all be used up. Then what do we do? The "one day" seemed to come very close in the early seventies when many experts were predicting we would run out of oil by the year 2020. Second, there is the problem of an ever-growing population. The world, being of finite size, cannot accommodate an ever-growing population. Unless we can colonize other planets, population growth has to decline. In particular, there is the problem of food. Can we grow enough food to feed the nearly 6 billion people (compared with a current 4.5 billion) expected to be alive at the turn of the century? If not, will world population be forced down through starvation, as Malthus long ago predicted?*

The standard retort of the growth-oriented economist is to point out that all the concerns we have today about the limits to growth were equally valid a century ago. Indeed, in 1865 the famous English economist W. S. Jevons wrote a book about the impending exhaustion of Britain's coal resources — coal that is still being mined today.† The experience after the oil price shock in 1973 was that price changes can cause massive conservation of resources, and thus there is reason to hope that most ***exhaustible*** resources — resources present on earth in limited quantities — will be around for a long time, albeit with rising relative prices.

A more important challenge to the limits set by exhaustible resources is technical progress. Much technical progress takes the form of inventions and processes that save on scarce resources used up in production. The expectation or hope is that the same technical progress that has proved an important source of real growth in the last century will help overcome the effects of the reduced availability of raw materials.

Of course there is no assurance that the right technical progress will come along to bail us out when coal or oil run short in supply. Perhaps one should not bank on technical progress, innovation, and ingenuity to help us out. At the same time, it would surely be irresponsible to dismiss entirely the extraordinary record of technical progress that has contributed around one-half the average growth in real income. Public policy directed at encouraging research and development could help ensure continued technical progress.

* Thomas Malthus, *The Principle of Population,* 1798 (Homewood, Ill.: reprint by Richard D. Irwin, 1963).
† W. S. Jevons, *The Coal Question,* 1865 (New York: reprint by Augustus M. Kelley, 1865).

17-6 SUMMARY

1 A production function links factor inputs and technology to the level of output. Growth of output, changes in technology aside, is a weighted average of input growth with the weights equal to income shares. The production function directs attention to factor inputs and technological change as sources of output growth.

2 Growth theory studies the determinants of intermediate-run and long-run growth in output.

3 In U.S. history over the 1929–1969 period, growth in factor inputs and technical progress each accounted for roughly one-half the average growth rate of 3.4 percent of output. Growth in the stock of knowledge along with growth in labor input, was the most important source of growth.

4 Per capita output grows faster, the more rapidly the capital stock increases and the faster is technical progress. In U.S. history since 1889, output per head has grown at an average rate of 1.8 percent.

5 Potential output grew at nearly 4 percent in the sixties, but its growth rate has fallen to less than 3 percent since then. The fall is in large part due to the decline in productivity growth. The prospects for a return to the high productivity growth rates of the 1948–1973 period are slim, but some improvement from the poor performance of the late seventies is likely.

6 Supply-side economics proposed to raise the level and growth rate of full-employment output by creating improved incentives for work, saving, and investment and through reduced regulation. Empirical research suggests that incentives would be successful on the labor supply side, and that reduced government deficits would stimulate investment.

7 Potential output or full-employment output is estimated as the product of the high-employment level of work hours and high-employment productivity. Important changes in the labor market and the puzzling reduction in productivity growth have led to questions about the appropriateness of the traditional potential output concept and measure.

8 Production function estimates of potential output show a very important role for energy. According to these estimates, a doubling of energy prices would lead to a fall in potential output of about 12 percent. These numbers are very large and remain the topic of research.

9 The concept of steady-state equilibrium points (in the absence of technical change) to the conditions required for output per head to be constant. With a growing population, saving must be just sufficient to provide new members of the population with the economywide amount of capital per head.

10 The steady-state level of income is determined by the saving rate and by population growth. In the absence of technical change, the steady-state growth rate of output is equal to the rate of population growth. An increase in the growth rate of population raises the steady-state growth rate of total output and lowers the level of steady-state output per head.

11 An increase in the saving rate transitorily raises the growth rate of

output. In the new steady state, the growth rate remains unchanged, but the level of output per head is increased.

12 With technical change, per capita output in the steady state grows at the rate of technical progress. Total output grows at the sum of the rates of technical progress and population growth.

13 Potential limits to growth pose a serious question about continued increases in real per capita income or even the maintenance of current consumption standards. The historical record is one of technological progress that offsets limitational factors and scarce resources. There is no certainty that this offset will continue, but so far it has done so. Public policy to encourage research and development can make a contribution in that direction.

KEY TERMS

Potential output
Production function
Growth accounting
Sources of growth
Labor productivity
Technical progress
Growth of total factor productivity
Supply-side economics
Steady state
Limits of growth

*APPENDIX: PROPERTIES OF THE PRODUCTION FUNCTION

In this Appendix we briefly show how the fundamental growth equation (2*a*) is obtained. The material is presented for completeness; it is not essential to an understanding of the text.

We start with a production function that exhibits constant returns: increasing *all* inputs in the same proportion raises output in that same proportion. Thus if we double all inputs, output will double. With that property the change in output due to technical progress and to changes in inputs can be written as

$$\Delta Y = F(K,N)\ \Delta A + MPK\ \Delta K + MPN\ \Delta N \tag{A1}$$

where MPK and MPN are the marginal products of capital and labor, respectively. We remember that the marginal product of a factor tells us the contribution to output made by employing one extra unit of the factor. Dividing both sides of the equation by $Y = AF(K,N)$ yields the expression

$$\Delta Y/Y = \Delta A/A + (MPK/Y)\ \Delta K + (MPN/Y)\ \Delta N \tag{A2}$$

Equation (A2) further simplifies by multiplying and dividing the second term on the right-hand side by K and the third term by N.

$$\Delta Y/Y = \Delta A/A + (K \cdot MPK/Y)\ \Delta K/K + (N \cdot MPN/Y)\ \Delta N/N \tag{A3}$$

We now argue that the terms in parentheses are the income shares of capital and labor. In a competitive market factors are paid their marginal product. Thus the term $N \cdot MPN/Y = wN/Y$, where w is the real wage. The right-hand side is recognized as the ratio of labor income to total income or the share of labor in income. Similarly, the term $K \cdot MPK/Y$ is the share of capital in income. With constant returns and competition, factor payments exhaust the total product. Therefore the shares of capital and labor sum to unity. Denoting the share of capital in income by θ and the labor share by $1 - \theta$, we arrive at Equation (2*a*) in the text.

We note a further property of the constant returns production function. When returns to scale are constant, we can write the production function as follows:

$$Y = AF(K,N) = NAf(K/N) \tag{A4}$$

or using the notation $x = Y/N$ and $k = K/N$,

$$x = Af(k) \tag{A5}$$

This is the form used in the growth theory section of the text, where output per head is a function of the capital-labor ratio.

PROBLEMS

1. Which of the following government activities have effects on the long-term growth rate? Explain how they can do so.
   (*a*) Monetary policy
   (*b*) Labor market policies
   (*c*) Educational and research programs
   (*d*) Fiscal policy
   (*e*) Population control programs
2. Discuss the role of government policy in raising (*a*) the supply of labor and (*b*) the supply of capital. How successful can such policies be?
3. Discuss why the 5.0 percent full-employment benchmark may no longer be a sensible basis for potential output calculations. What do you think should be done: abandon the potential output concept, or assume some new benchmark?
4. Since 1973, the growth rate of productivity has sharply declined in most industrialized countries. List several of the factors that are responsible for this decline and discuss why the decline in productivity growth is an important issue.
5. Suppose the share of capital in income is 0.4 and the share of labor is 0.6. Capital grows by 6 percent, and labor supply declines by 2 percent. What happens to output?
6. An earthquake destroys one-quarter of the capital stock. Discuss in the context of the growth model the adjustment process of the economy, and show, using Figure 17-4, what happens to growth.
7. (*a*) In the absence of technical progress, what happens to output per head and total output over time? Why?
   (*b*) What is the long-run effect of the saving rate on the *level* of output per capita? On *growth* of output per capita?
8. Evaluate this statement: "The saving rate cannot affect the growth of output in the economy. That is determined by the growth of labor input and by technical progress."

*9 Suppose we assume a production function of the form

$$Y = AF(K,N,Z)$$

where Z is a measure of the natural resources going into production. Assume this production function obeys constant returns to scale and diminishing returns to each factor [like Equation (1)].

(*a*) What will happen to output per head if capital and labor grow together but resources are fixed?

(*b*) What if Z is fixed but there is technical progress?

(*c*) Interpret these results in terms of the limits to growth.

*10 Use the model of long-run growth to incorporate the government. Assume that an income tax at the rate t is levied and that, accordingly, saving per head is equal to $s(1 - t)x$. The government spends the tax revenue on public consumption.

(*a*) Use Figure 17-4 to explore the impact of an increase in the tax rate on the steady-state output level and capital per head.

(*b*) Draw a chart of the time path of capital per head, output per head, and the growth rate of output.

*(*c*) Discuss the statement: ''To raise the growth rate of output, the public sector has to run a budget surplus to free resources for investment.''

11 Use Figure 17-4 to explore the impact of a *once-and-for-all* improvement in technology.

(*a*) How does technical progress affect the level of output per head as of a given capital-labor ratio?

(*b*) Show the new steady-state equilibrium. Has saving changed? Is income per head higher? Has the capital stock per head increased?

(*c*) Show the time path of the adjustment to the new steady state. Does technical progress transitorily raise the ratio of investment to capital?

12 Discuss the statement: ''The lower the level of income, the higher the growth rate of output.''

PART FOUR

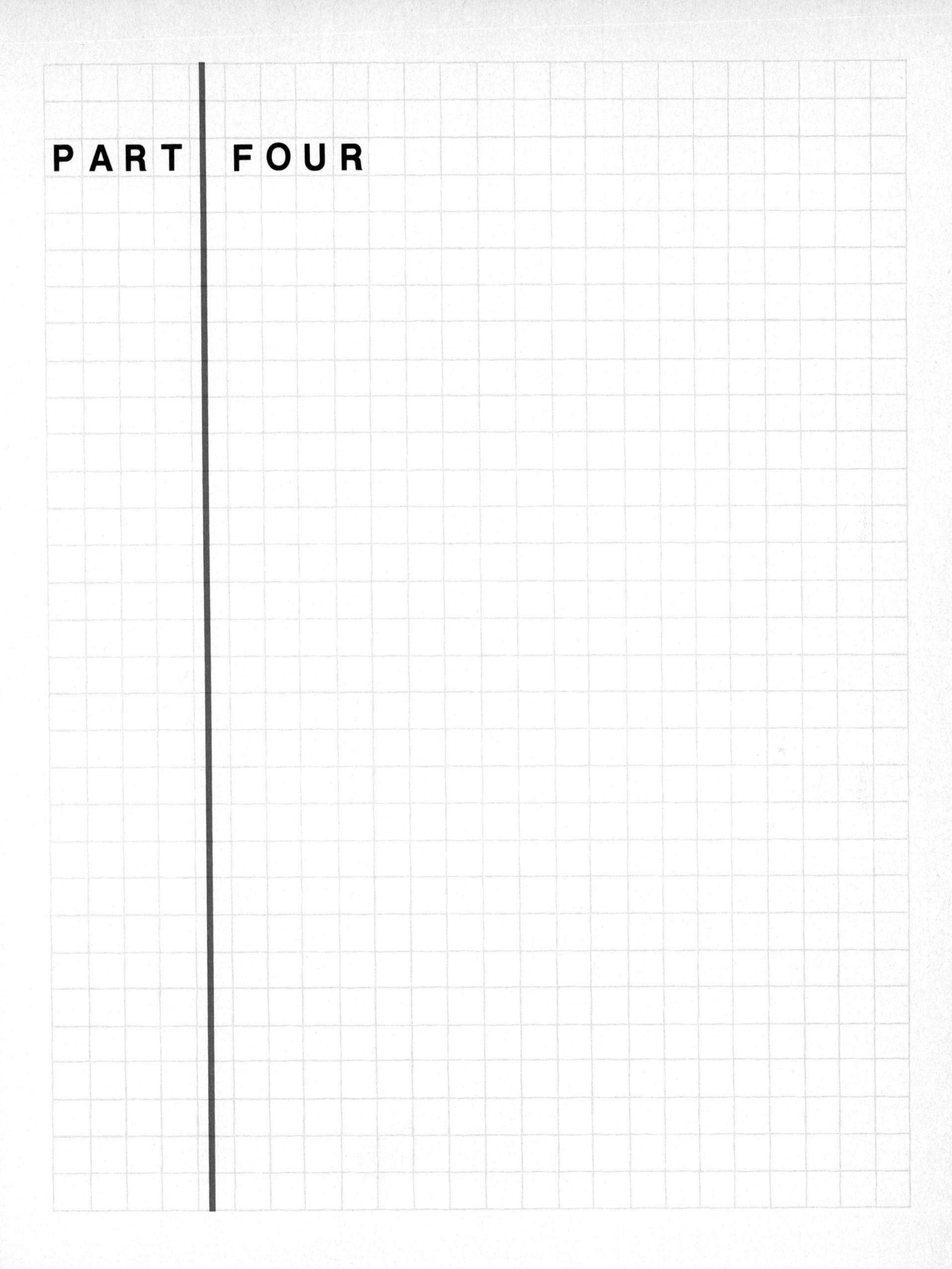

18

MACROECONOMICS IN THE OPEN ECONOMY: TRADE AND CAPITAL FLOWS WITH FIXED EXCHANGE RATES

This is the first of two chapters analyzing foreign trade and its effects on the economy. It extends the macroeconomics we have learned to open economies — economies that trade with others. Trade among economies takes place in both goods and services — Americans buy German cars, and Europeans buy American brokers' services — and in assets — Americans buy Japanese stocks, and Arabs buy American real estate. Since all economies engage in international trade, all economies are open.

The degree of *openness*, as measured by the ratio of imports to GNP or GDP, varies widely. In Table 18-1 we show this ratio for different countries. Note the large differences in openness as measured by the imports/GDP ratio. Mexico and the United States appear as relatively closed economies, whereas the Netherlands is very open with the value of imports being more than 50 percent of production.

This chapter begins with a brief description of the balance of payments accounts — the record of the country's transactions with other economies. Section 18-1 also describes the two basic exchange rate systems: the fixed and flexible rate systems. In a *fixed exchange rate system,* central banks fix the prices of foreign currencies and stand ready to buy and sell foreign currencies at those prices. The world was essentially on a fixed rate system from 1946 to 1973, though there were occasional adjustments of exchange

TABLE 18-1 MEASURES OF OPENNESS, 1981*

	Canada	Mexico	Netherlands	U.K.	U.S.
Imports/GDP, %	26.7	13.5	54.6	24.5	10.5

Source: International Financial Statistics, *April 1983.*
* For Mexico, figure is for 1980.

rates during that period. In the *flexible exchange rate system,* the exchange rate is determined in the foreign exchange market and can change from moment to moment. After 1973, exchange rates between the dollar and other currencies were allowed to float, to be determined by the supply and demand for foreign exchange.

The rest of this chapter analyzes trade in goods and assets in a fixed exchange rate system. Section 18-2 examines the way in which foreign trade affects goods market equilibrium and the determinants of the balance of trade in goods and services. Section 18-3 examines the effects of devaluation and looks at the financing of deficits. Trade in assets is studied in Section 18-4, as are the implications of such trade for the conduct of monetary and fiscal policy. Chapter 19 presents an analysis of international trade under flexible exchange rates.

18-1 THE BALANCE OF PAYMENTS AND EXCHANGE RATE REGIMES

The *balance of payments* is the record of the transactions of the residents of a country with the rest of the world. There are two main accounts in the balance of payments: the current account and the capital account.

The *current account* records trade in goods and services, as well as transfer payments. Services include freight, royalty payments, and interest payments. Transfer payments consist of remittances, gifts, and grants. We talk of a current account surplus if exports exceed imports plus net transfers to foreigners, that is, if receipts from trade in goods and services and transfers exceed payments on this account.

The *capital account* records purchases and sales of assets, such as stocks, bonds, and land. There is a capital account surplus, or a net capital inflow, when our receipts from the sale of stocks, bonds, land, bank deposits, and other assets exceed our payments for our own purchases of foreign assets.

Closely related to the current account are certain subaccounts that we mention here for completeness. The *trade balance* simply records trade in goods. Adding trade in services and net transfers, we arrive at the current account balance.

SURPLUSES AND DEFICITS

The simple rule for balance of payments accounting is that any transaction that gives rise to a payment by U.S. residents is a deficit item. Thus, imports of cars,

TABLE 18-2 U.S. BALANCE OF PAYMENTS ACCOUNTS (*In billions of dollars*)

	1960–1969, average	1970–1979, average	1980	1981	1982
Current account	3.33	−0.23	1.52	4.47	−8.09
Capital account	−4.59	−13.98	−8.81	−4.08	10.01
Official reserve transactions	1.26	−14.21	−7.29	0.39	1.92

Sources: Economic Report of the President, 1983 *and* Economic Indicators, *April 1983.*

use of foreign shipping, gifts to foreigners, purchase of land in Spain, or deposits in a bank in Switzerland are all deficit items. Surplus items, by contrast, would be U.S. sales of airplanes abroad, payments by foreigners for U.S. licenses to use American technology, pensions from abroad received by U.S. residents, and foreign purchases of GM stock.

The overall *balance of payments* is the sum of the current and capital accounts. If both the current account and the capital account are in deficit, then the overall balance of payments is in deficit. When one account is in surplus and the other is in deficit to precisely the same extent, the overall balance of payments is zero—neither in surplus nor in deficit. We record these relationships in Equation (1)[1]:

$$\text{Balance of payments surplus} = \text{current account surplus} + \text{capital account surplus} \quad (1)$$

Table 18-2 presents the U.S. balance of payments accounts. We show the averages for the 1960s and 1970s and several recent years. During the 1960s the current account was in surplus; in the 1970s it averaged to a deficit, although there were wide swings that we look at below. The U.S. capital account is in deficit most of the time. This means that there has been a net capital *outflow*, or U.S. residents have purchased more assets abroad than foreigners have acquired in the United States. We read often of foreigners buying U.S. assets, such as land or banks: such transactions cause a capital account surplus. But U.S. residents on balance typically buy even more assets from foreigners, thereby creating, in total, a capital account deficit.

Making International Payments

Any transaction which gives rise to a payment by U.S. residents to foreigners is a deficit item. An overall deficit in the balance of payments—the sum of the current and capital accounts—means, therefore, that U.S. residents make more payments to foreigners than they receive from foreigners. Since for-

[1] In using Eq. (1), recall that a deficit is a negative surplus.

eigners want to be paid in their own currencies,[2] the question arises of how these payments are to be made.

In Table 18-2, the "Official reserve transactions" entry measures the overall balance of payments deficit.[3] When the overall balance of payments is in deficit[4]—when the sum of the current and capital accounts is negative—Americans have to pay more foreign currency to foreigners than is received. The Fed and foreign central banks provide the foreign currency to make payments to foreigners, and the net amount supplied is "official reserve transactions." When the U.S. balance of payments is in surplus, foreigners have to get the dollars with which to pay for their excess of payments to the United States over their receipts from sales to the United States. The dollars are provided by the central banks.

Fixed Exchange Rates

We now examine in more detail the way in which central banks, through their official transactions, *finance,* or provide the means of paying for, balance of payments surpluses and deficits. At this point we distinguish between fixed and floating exchange rate systems, which we defined above.

In a fixed rate system, foreign central banks stand ready to buy and sell their currencies at a fixed price in terms of dollars. In Germany, for example, the central bank, the Bundesbank, would buy or sell any amount of dollars in the 1960s at 4 Deutsche marks (DM) per U.S. dollar. The French central bank, the Banque de France, stood ready to buy or sell any amount of dollars at 4.90 French francs (FF) per U.S. dollar. The fact that the central banks were prepared to buy or sell *any* amount of dollars at these fixed prices or exchange rates meant that market prices would indeed be equal to the fixed rates. Why? Because nobody who wanted to buy U.S. dollars would pay more than 4.90 FF per dollar when francs could be gotten at that price from the Banque de France. Conversely, nobody would part with dollars in exchange for francs for less than 4.90 francs per dollar if the Banque de France, through the commercial banking system, was prepared to buy dollars at that price.

In a fixed rate system, the central banks have to finance any balance of payments surplus or deficit that arises at the official exchange rate. They do that simply by buying or selling all the foreign currency that is not supplied in

[2] An exception occurs if foreigners want to be paid in dollars to add to their assets. In that case, we conceptually separate, first, our demand for imports, which gives rise to payments in foreign currency that appears in the current account, from, second, foreigners' demand for dollars, which appears in the capital account as an inflow.

[3] The official presentation of balance of payments statistics as in Table 18-2 was stopped in mid-1976 after a review committee suggested that official reserve transactions are not a full measure of foreign exchange intervention. Nonetheless everyone but the government presents the data as in the table.

[4] We include in Table 18-2 the statistical discrepancies that arise from incomplete recording of actual trade in goods and services and assets. The data are reconciled by an entry called "errors and omissions" which are believed to arise largely from unreported capital flows. The difference between the sum of the *current* and capital accounts in Table 18-2 and "official reserve transactions" is equal to errors and omissions.

private transactions. If the United States were running a deficit in the balance of payments vis-à-vis Germany, so that the demand for marks in exchange for dollars exceeded the supply of dollars in exchange for marks from Germans, the Bundesbank would buy the excess dollars, paying for them with marks.

Fixed exchange rates thus operate like any other price support scheme, such as in agricultural markets. Given market demand and supply, the price fixer has to make up the excess demand or take up the excess supply. In order to be able to ensure that the price (exchange rate) stays fixed, it is obviously necessary to hold an inventory of foreign exchange that can be provided in exchange for domestic currency.

RESERVES

Foreign central banks held *reserves*—inventories of dollars, and gold that could be sold for dollars—that they would sell in the market when there was an excess demand for dollars. Conversely, when there was an excess supply of dollars, they would buy up the dollars, as in our example of the U.S. balance of payments deficit vis-à-vis Germany.

INTERVENTION

Intervention is the buying or selling of foreign exchange by the central bank. What determines the amount of intervention that a central bank has to do in a fixed exchange rate system? We already have the answer to that question. The balance of payments measures the amount of foreign exchange intervention needed from the central banks. So long as the foreign central bank has the necessary reserves, it can continue to intervene in the foreign exchange markets to keep the exchange rate constant. However, if a country persistently runs deficits in the balance of payments, the central bank eventually will run out of reserves of foreign exchange and will be unable to continue its intervention.

Before that point is reached, the central bank is likely to decide that it can no longer maintain the exchange rate, and will devalue the currency. In 1967, for instance, the British devalued the pound from \$2.80 per pound to \$2.40 per pound. That meant it became cheaper for Americans and other foreigners to buy British pounds, and the devaluation thus affected the balance of payments. We shall study the way in which devaluation affects the balance of payments in Section 18-3.

We have so far avoided being specific on exactly which central banks did the intervening in the foreign exchange market in the fixed rate system. It is clear that if there were an excess supply of dollars and an excess demand for marks, either the Bundesbank could buy the dollars in exchange for marks, or the Fed could sell marks in exchange for dollars. In practice, during the fixed rate period, each foreign central bank undertook to *peg* (fix) its exchange rate vis-à-vis the dollar, and most foreign exchange intervention was undertaken by the foreign central banks. The Fed was nonetheless involved in the management of the exchange rate system, since it frequently made dollar loans to foreign central banks that were in danger of running out of dollars.

Flexible Exchange Rates

We have seen that the central banks have to provide whatever amounts of foreign currency are needed to finance payments imbalances under fixed exchange rates. In flexible rate systems, by contrast, the central banks allow the exchange rate to adjust to equate the supply and demand for foreign currency. If today's exchange rate against the mark were 50 cents per mark, and German exports to the United States increased, thus increasing the demand for marks by Americans, the Bundesbank could simply stand aside and let the exchange rate adjust. In this particular case, the exchange rate could move from 50 cents per mark to a level such as 52 cents per mark, making German goods more expensive in terms of dollars and thus reducing the demand for them by Americans. In Chapter 19 we shall examine the way in which exchange rate changes under floating rates affect the balance of payments. The terms *flexible rates* and *floating rates* are used interchangeably.

FLOATING, CLEAN AND DIRTY

In a system of *clean floating*, central banks stand aside completely and allow exchange rates to be freely determined in the foreign exchange markets. The central banks do not intervene in the foreign exchange markets in a system of clean floating, and official reserve transactions would, accordingly, be zero in such a situation. That means the balance of payments would be zero in a system of clean floating: The exchange rate would adjust to make the current and capital accounts sum to zero.

In practice, the flexible rate system, since 1973, has not been one of clean floating. Instead, the system has been one of *managed*, or *dirty*, *floating*. Under managed floating, central banks intervene to buy and sell foreign currencies, in attempts to influence exchange rates. Official reserve transactions are, accordingly, not equal to zero. The reasons for this central bank intervention under floating rates are discussed in Chapter 19.

Terminology

The use of language with respect to exchange rates can be very confusing. In particular, the terms *depreciation* and *appreciation* and *devaluation* and *revaluation* will recur throughout this chapter and the next.

Figure 18-1 shows the dollar-sterling exchange rate since 1960. We use the figure to clarify some points of terminology. The vertical axis shows the exchange rate measured as $U.S. per pound sterling. First note that we show two subperiods, the fixed rate period lasting through the 1960s until 1973 and then the flexible rate regime. During the fixed rate period the dollar price of sterling remained constant. It was constant, or pegged, at a given level by the Bank of England except for two adjustments. Until 1967 the exchange rate was $2.80 per pound sterling, but in that year sterling was devalued and the rate became $2.40 per pound. In 1971 sterling was revalued to $2.60 per

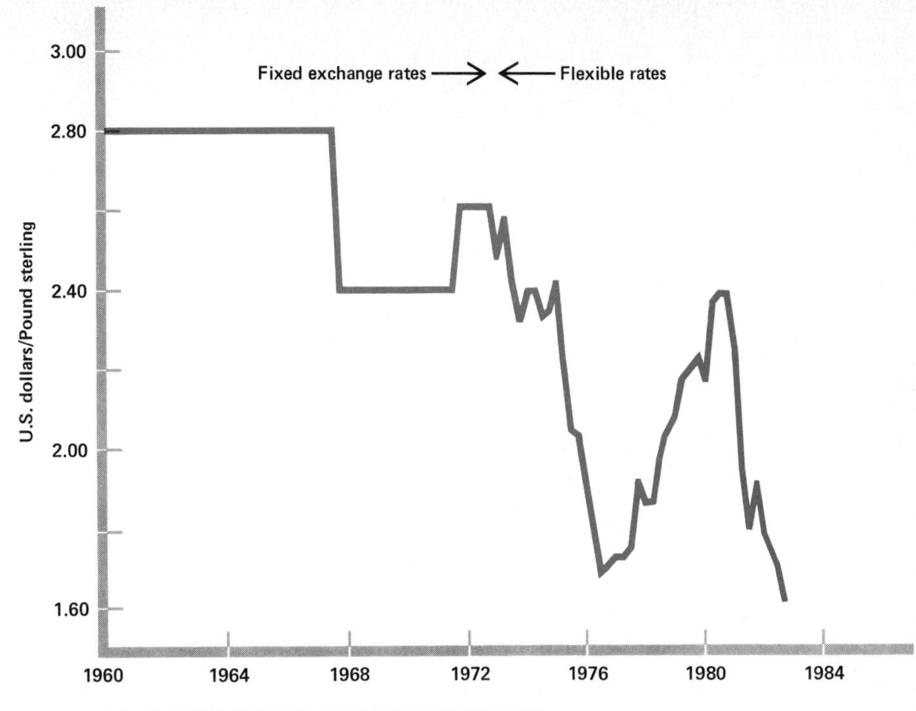

FIGURE 18-1 THE DOLLAR-POUND STERLING EXCHANGE RATE.

pound. A *devaluation* takes place when the price of foreign currencies under a fixed rate regime is increased by official action. A devaluation thus means that foreigners pay less for the devalued currency or that residents of the devaluing country pay more for foreign currencies. The opposite of a devaluation is a *revaluation*.

Changes in the price of foreign exchange under flexible exchange rates are referred to as *currency depreciation* or *appreciation*. A currency *depreciates* when, under floating rates, it becomes less expensive in terms of foreign currencies. For instance, if the exchange rate of the pound sterling changes from \$1.50 per pound to \$1.47 per pound, the pound is depreciating. By contrast, the currency *appreciates* when it becomes more expensive in terms of foreign money.

For example, in Figure 18-1 we see that in 1975–1976 and again in 1982–1983 sterling was depreciating, meaning that it took less and less dollars to buy a pound sterling. By contrast, in 1979–1980 sterling was appreciating. Although the terms devaluation/revaluation and depreciation/appreciation are used in fixed and flexible rate regimes, respectively, there is no economic difference. These terms describe the direction in which an exchange rate moves.

Summary

1 The balance of payments accounts are a record of the transactions of the economy with other economies. The capital account describes transactions in assets, while the current account covers transactions in goods and services and transfers.
2 Any payment to foreigners is a deficit item in the balance of payments. Any payment from foreigners is a surplus item. The balance of payments deficit (or surplus) is the sum of the deficits (or surpluses) on current and capital accounts.
3 Under fixed exchange rates, central banks stand ready to meet all demands for foreign currencies arising from balance of payments deficits or surpluses at a fixed price in terms of the domestic currency. They have to *finance* the excess demands for, or supplies of, foreign currency (that is, the balance of payments deficits or surpluses, respectively), at the pegged (fixed) exchange rate by running down, or adding to, their reserves of foreign currency.
4 Under flexible exchange rates, the demands for and supplies of foreign currency can be made equal through movements in exchange rates. Under clean floating, there is no central bank intervention and the balance of payments is zero. But central banks sometimes intervene in a floating rate system, engaging in so-called dirty floating.

18-2 TRADE IN GOODS, MARKET EQUILIBRIUM, AND THE BALANCE OF TRADE

We now study the effects of trade in goods on the level of income, and the effects of various disturbances on both income and the trade balance—which, from now on, we use as shorthand for the current account. We also examine policy problems which arise when the balance of trade and the level of income require different corrective actions. We do not at this stage include the capital account, so that for the present the current account and the balance of payments are the same.

In this section we fit foreign trade into *IS-LM* framework. As in Chapters 3 to 5, we assume that the price level is given, and that output that is demanded will be supplied. It is both conceptually and technically easy to relax the fixed price assumption, and we shall briefly do so later. But it is important to be clear on how the introduction of trade modifies the analysis of aggregate demand, and for that reason we start from a familiar and basic level.

A word of warning is in order before you start working through the following sections. The exposition here assumes you are thoroughly at home with the *IS-LM* analysis and therefore proceeds quite rapidly. However, the material is not more difficult than that of earlier chapters and should, with careful and active reading, be totally accessible.

Domestic Spending and Spending on Domestic Goods

In this subsection we want to establish how foreign trade fits into the *IS* schedule. In an open economy, part of domestic output is sold to foreigners (exports), and part of spending by domestic residents falls on foreign goods (imports). We accordingly have to modify our analysis of aggregate demand developed in Chapters 3 and 4.

The most important change is that it is no longer true that domestic spending determines domestic output. What is true now is that *spending on domestic goods* determines domestic output. Spending by domestic residents falls in part on domestic goods but also in part on imports. Part of the typical American's spending is for imported beer, for instance. Demand for domestic goods that determines output, by contrast, includes exports or foreign demand along with part of spending by domestic residents.

The way in which external transactions affect the demand for domestic output was examined in Chapter 2. Recall the definitions:

$$\text{Spending by domestic residents} \equiv A \equiv C + I + G \tag{2}$$

$$\begin{aligned}\text{Spending on domestic goods} \equiv A + NX &\equiv (C + I + G) + X - Q \\ &= (C + I + G) + NX\end{aligned} \tag{3}$$

where X is the level of exports, Q is imports, and NX is the trade balance (goods and services) surplus. The definition of spending by domestic residents $(C + I + G)$ remains that of the earlier chapters. Spending on domestic goods is total spending by domestic residents *less* their spending on imports *plus* foreign demand or exports. Since exports minus imports is the trade surplus, or net exports NX, spending on domestic goods is spending by domestic residents plus the trade surplus.

With this clarification we can return to our model of income determination. We will assume, as in Chapter 4, that domestic spending depends on the interest rate and income, so that we can write

$$A = A(Y, i) \tag{4}$$

Further, we assume for the present that foreign demand for our goods, or exports X, is given and equal to $\overline{X}$. Domestic demand for foreign goods, or imports Q, is assumed to depend only on the level of income, so that $Q = Q(Y)$. As income rises, part of the increase in income is spent on imports, while the rest is either spent on domestic goods or saved.

Now the trade balance is

$$NX \equiv X - Q = \overline{X} - Q(Y) \tag{5}$$

With our assumptions, the trade balance NX is a function only of the level of income. The trade balance is shown as a function of income in Figure 18-2. Imports are small at low levels of income, so that given the fixed level of exports, there is a trade surplus, $NX > 0$. As income rises, import spending increases until we reach income level Y_B, where imports match exports, so that trade is balanced. A further increase in income gives rise to a trade deficit. We can thus write

$$NX = NX(Y, \overline{X}, \ldots) \tag{5a}$$

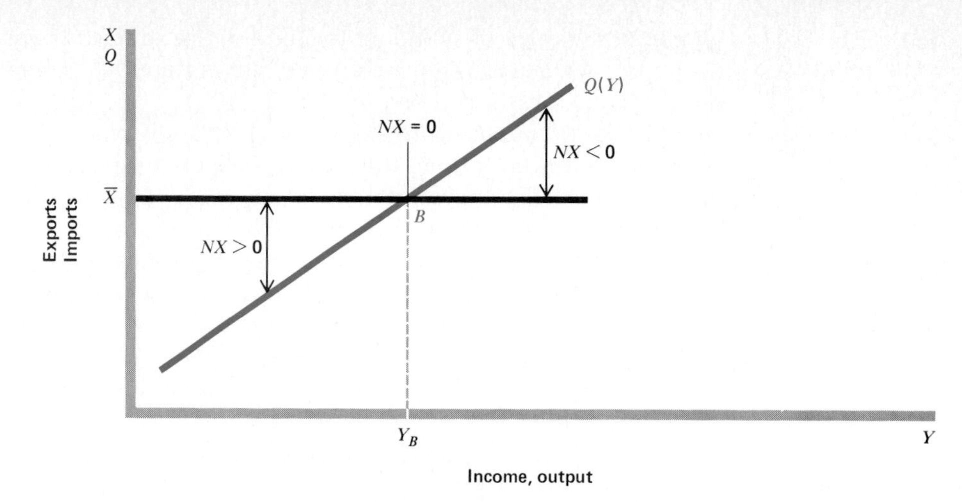

FIGURE 18-2 THE TRADE BALANCE AS A FUNCTION OF INCOME. The level of exports is given and equal to $\overline{X}$. Imports depend on the level of income. The schedule $Q(Y)$ shows that imports increase with the level of income. The slope of the schedule is the marginal propensity to import. For income levels less than Y_B, export earnings exceed import spending, and hence the trade surplus, equal to the vertical distance between the schedules, is positive. At Y_B there is trade balance equilibrium, and for higher income levels there are increasingly larger deficits.

where $\overline{X}$ denotes the given level of exports and the dots denote the other variables, such as exchange rates and prices, which we hold constant for now.

Goods Market Equilibrium

There is equilibrium in the domestic goods market when the amount of output produced is equal to the demand for that output. The value of output produced continues to be equal to income.[5] The equilibrium here is different from that in Chapter 3 in that the demand for domestically produced goods includes net exports:

$$Y = A(Y, i) + NX(Y, \overline{X}) \tag{6}$$

Figure 18-3 illustrates the goods market equilibrium condition (6). We still refer to it as a goods market equilibrium schedule, or *IS* curve, though it is important to recognize that now the trade surplus, or net exports *NX*, appears as a component of demand for output. The schedule is downward-sloping

[5] We assume that all factors of production are owned by domestic residents, who in turn own no factors of production abroad. If foreigners owned some of the factors of production located in our country, GNP would differ from GDP (see Chap. 2). If GDP exceeds GNP, then the value of production in the country exceeds the income earned by domestic residents.

because an increase in output causes an excess supply of goods: the increase in income is only partly spent on domestic goods, the rest being either saved or spent on imports. To compensate for the excess supply, interest rates have to decline to induce an increase in aggregate demand, and the *IS* curve therefore slopes down. The *IS* schedule is drawn for the given level of foreign demand $\overline{X}$.

We have also shown, in Figure 18-3, the trade balance equilibrium schedule $NX = 0$. Given exports, we see from Figure 18-2 and Equation (5) that there is some level of income, Y_B, at which import spending exactly matches export revenue, so that trade is balanced. Points to the left of the $NX = 0$ schedule are points of trade surplus. Here income and hence import spending are low relative to exports. Exports accordingly exceed imports. Points to the right of the $NX = 0$ schedule, by contrast, are deficit points. Here income and hence import spending are too high relative to exports for trade to be balanced. Finally, we have drawn, too, the *LM* schedule, which is precisely the same as in our study of the closed economy.

Equilibrium Income and the Balance of Trade

The next question to address, using Figure 18-3, is where the short-run equilibrium of the economy will be. It will be at point *E*, the intersection of the *IS* and *LM* curves. At point *E*, demand for domestic goods equals supply, and

FIGURE 18-3 GOODS AND MONEY MARKET EQUILIBRIUM. The *LM* schedule is familiar from the closed economy. The *IS* schedule represents goods market equilibrium but now includes net exports *NX* as a component of demand. Given exports, there is a unique level of income Y_B at which trade is balanced. This is shown by the vertical $NX = 0$ schedule. Equilibrium obtains at point *E*, where goods and money markets clear. At *E* there is a trade surplus associated with the goods and money market equilibrium.

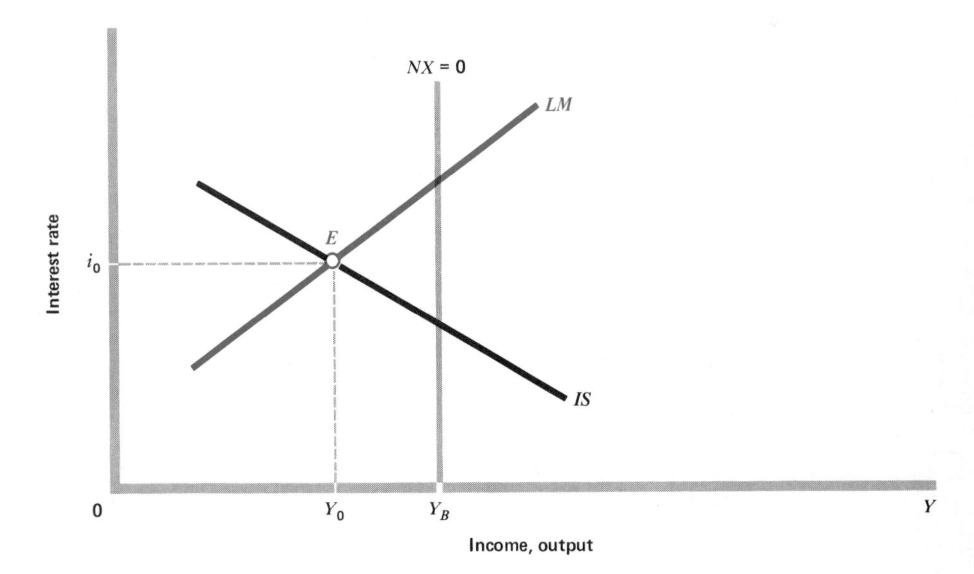

money demand equals money supply. Therefore, both the goods and money markets are in equilibrium.

The trade balance need not be in equilibrium. In the short run, a trade balance deficit can be financed by running down foreign exchange reserves, and a surplus can be financed by building up reserves. The assumption is that the central bank finances the trade deficit by selling foreign exchange and thus maintains the exchange rate at its pegged level in the face of a trade and balance of payments deficit, or that the bank purchases foreign exchange if there is a surplus.[6] We assume the goods and money markets clear sufficiently quickly so that equilibrium is determined at point E in Figure 18-3. As we have drawn the equilibrium, the trade balance is in surplus.

Disturbances

How do internal and external disturbances—shifts in the level or composition of spending, or changes in exports—affect equilibrium income and the balance of trade? To answer that question, it is important to remember that both the IS and the trade balance schedules are drawn for a given level of exports, $\overline{X}$.

We can think of three types of disturbances, the effects of which we will briefly analyze in turn: (1) an increase in autonomous domestic spending that falls on our own goods, (2) an increase in exports, and (3) a shift in demand from domestic goods to imports.

Before going through the exercises, we indicate the results we expect to find. First, any autonomous increase (decrease) in spending on our goods should result in an increase (decrease) in equilibrium output and income. But we would expect the trade balance to worsen if domestic income expands because the higher income leads to increased import spending. Second, it is not so clear how an increase in exports affects the trade balance. Say exports increase, and as a consequence, domestic income rises. This income increase, in turn, raises import spending, and we are not certain whether the net effect on the trade balance is an improvement or a worsening. In fact we can show that the net effect is actually an improvement—induced import spending dampens but does not offset the trade balance improvement resulting from an increase in exports. Table 18-3 summarizes those results.

The Effects of an Increase in Autonomous Spending

We now proceed to our analysis. First, consider an autonomous increase in our spending on domestic goods, perhaps because of expansionary fiscal

[6] We are abstracting here from a complication that is suggested by our study of the money supply process in Chap. 9. We saw there that foreign exchange transactions may have an effect on high-powered money and thus on the money supply. A trade deficit would cause the central bank to lose foreign exchange and, as a counterpart, would cause the monetary base and the money supply to fall. We are assuming here that the central bank automatically engages in offsetting open market operations that keep the money supply constant. In the case of a deficit, such a *sterilization* operation would require a purchase of debt in the open market to offset the reduction in the monetary base due to the trade deficit, as we saw in Chap. 9.

TABLE 18-3 THE EFFECT OF DISTURBANCES ON INCOME AND ON THE TRADE BALANCE

	Autonomous increase in spending on domestic goods	Autonomous increase in exports	Shift in demand from imports to domestic goods
Income	+	+	+
Trade Balance	−	+	+

policy. In Figure 18-4, we show the effect to be a shift in the *IS* curve. At the initial equilibrium *E* there is an excess demand for goods, and accordingly, the equilibrium income level increases. The new equilibrium is at point *E*′, where output and interest rates have risen and where we have a reduction in the trade surplus. The expansion in output increases import spending, and thus at *E*′ the trade surplus is less than at *E*. The first lesson is, therefore, that expansionary domestic policies or autonomous increases in spending raise income but cause a worsening of the trade balance.

A second point worth making concerns the size of the income expansion induced by an expansionary policy, that is, the size of the multiplier. By comparison with a closed economy, we have less of an expansion in an open economy. Multipliers are smaller because induced spending on domestic goods is less. Part of an increase in income is now spent on imports rather than

FIGURE 18-4 THE EFFECTS OF AN INCREASE IN DOMESTIC SPENDING. Starting from equilibrium at *E*, there is an increase in our spending that falls on domestic goods. Accordingly, the *IS* schedule shifts to the right to *IS*′, and the new equilibrium is at point *E*′, where goods and assets markets clear. The increase in demand raises income. It also worsens the trade balance because of increased import spending.

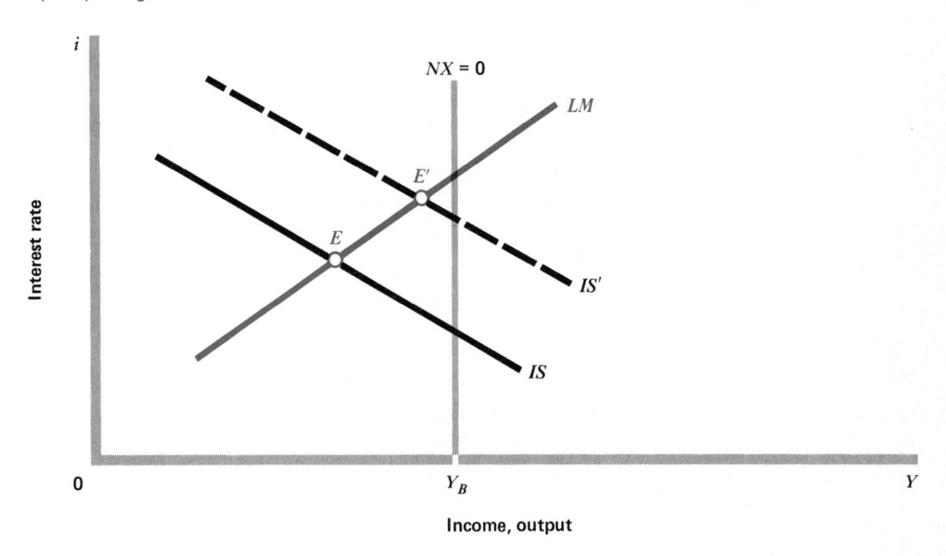

domestic goods. Imports are a *leakage* from the domestic multiplier process. Indeed, the larger the fraction of an increase in income that is spent on imports, the smaller the multiplier, because there is relatively little induced spending on domestic goods.[7]

The Effects of an Increase in Exports

The next disturbance we consider is an increase in exports. An increase in exports raises the demand for domestic goods and thus shifts the *IS* curve to the right (to *IS′*), as shown in Figure 18-5. At the same time, the increase in exports implies that at each level of income the trade balance is improved. Given the higher exports, trade will now be balanced at a higher level of income. Thus, the trade balance schedule shifts to $NX' = 0$.

Starting from a position of balanced trade at point *E*, we find that the increase in exports raises equilibrium income and improves the balance of trade at point *E′*. The first part is quite intuitive. Higher demand for our goods leads to an increase in equilibrium output. The trade balance improvement, though, is less intuitive. The increase in exports by itself improves the trade

[7] See the Appendix to this chapter.

FIGURE 18-5 THE EFFECT OF AN INCREASE IN EXPORTS. Starting from an equilibrium at *E*, there is an increase in exports. The trade balance improves at each income level. It now takes a higher level of income to induce enough import spending to match the higher level of exports. Accordingly, the trade balance equilibrium schedule shifts to the right to $NX' = 0$. Higher exports means increased demand for domestic goods. Therefore the *IS* schedule also shifts to the right. But it shifts by less than the trade balance schedule. The new equilibrium is at point *E′*. Interest rates and income rise. At the same time, the trade balance improves.

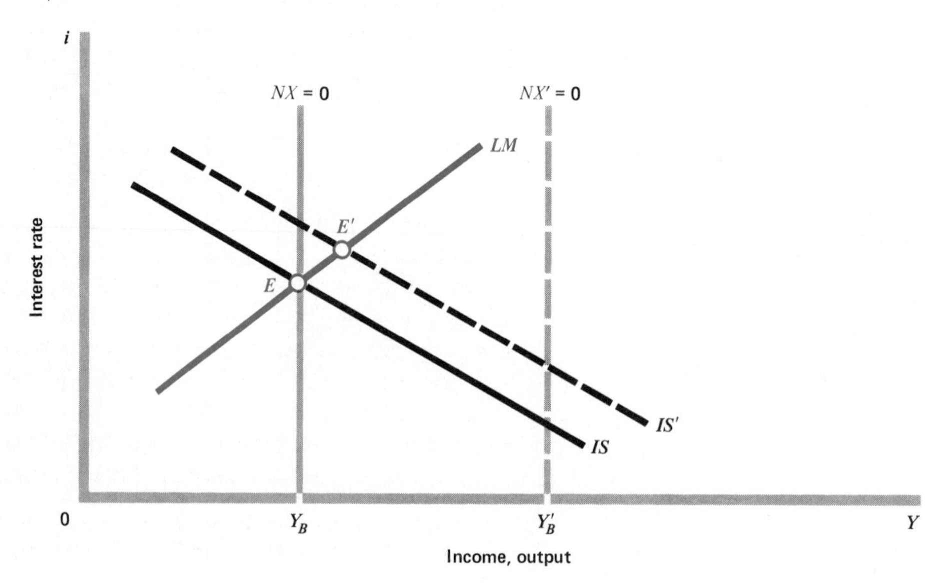

balance, but the increase in income leads to increased import spending, which, it seems, could perhaps offset the direct improvement from the export increase. This is, in fact, not the case, and we leave the demonstration of that result to the Appendix and Problem 1 at the end of this chapter.

A Shift in the Composition of Demand

The last disturbance we consider is a shift in demand from imports to domestic goods. You will recognize that this has the same effects as an increase in exports. It means increased demand for domestic goods and also an improvement in the trade balance.

Internal and External Balance

We have now constructed and used, in Figures 18-3 through 18-5, our basic diagrammatic apparatus for embodying trade in the *IS-LM* model. We draw on the analysis of income and trade balance determination to ask about economic policy making. From a policy perspective we would want to be able to achieve both *internal* and *external balance.* Internal balance means that output is at the full-employment level $\bar{Y}$. External balance occurs when the trade balance is zero.

It is clear enough why internal balance should be an aim of policy. But why is external balance desirable? In a fixed exchange rate world, a balance of payments deficits cannot be maintained indefinitely, as the financing of the deficits requires the country to use its reserves of foreign currency. Such reserves will run out in the face of continual deficits. Hence, a country on a fixed exchange rate cannot aim to run a balance of payments deficit[8] indefinitely. On the other side, a country on fixed rates wants to avoid running a permanent surplus, because that causes it to acquire foreign currencies to add to its reserves indefinitely. Since the foreign exchange could be used to buy and consume foreign goods, the country is permanently forgoing some consumption it could otherwise have had, when it chooses to run permanent balance of payments surpluses.

The policy problem is illustrated in Figure 18-6. The problem is that for a given level of exports we may not be able to achieve *both* internal and external balance. In Figure 18-6, we have drawn the trade balance schedule, $NX = 0$, for the given level of exports. We have drawn, too, the full-employment level of output $\bar{Y}$, and the two lines do not coincide.

We can break up Figure 18-6 into three regions. To the left of the trade balance schedule, we have a trade surplus, and to the right we have a deficit. To the left of the $\bar{Y}$ schedule, we have unemployment, and to the right we have overemployment, or a boom.

From a policy viewpoint, regions I and III present no problem. In region I we want to pursue an expansionary policy so as to raise employment *and*

[8] In the absence of capital movements, and grants, remittances, etc., the balance of payments is equal to the balance of trade.

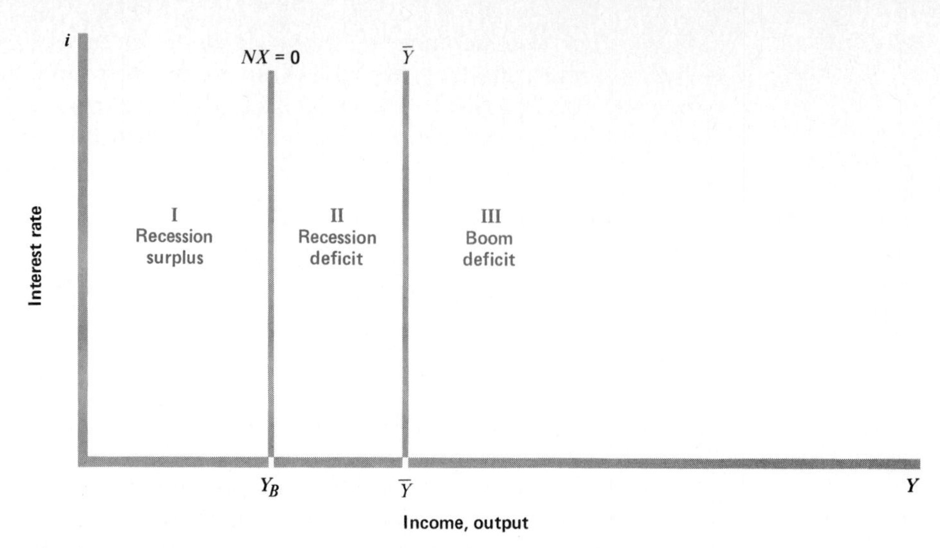

FIGURE 18-6 INTERNAL AND EXTERNAL BALANCE AND THE POLICY DILEMMA

reduce the trade surplus. Until we get to trade balance equilibrium, there is no issue, since both the internal and external targets call for expansionary policies. Similarly, in region III we want to pursue restrictive policies to reduce overemployment and the trade deficit. Until we get to full employment, there is no issue.

POLICY DILEMMAS

The dilemma area is region II. Here we have to choose whether we want to use tight policies to achieve trade balance equilibrium or expansionary policies to achieve full employment. Not only are we unable to reach both targets simultaneously by manipulating aggregate demand, but any attempt to reach one target gets us further away from the other. Such a situation is called a *policy dilemma,* and it can always arise when there are more targets of policy than instruments with which to move the economy toward its targets. In our case we have only one policy instrument—aggregate demand policies—but we have two independent targets—external and internal balance.

The policy dilemma can be solved by finding another policy instrument to cope with the multiple targets. What is needed is some policy that shifts the trade balance schedule to the right until it overlaps with the full-employment level of output line, $\overline{Y}$. An obvious policy would be to cut down on imports at each level of income. Such a policy would reduce import spending at each level of income and thus shift the trade balance schedule to the right.

How can we cut import spending? We can use any of a number of tools, among them tariffs and exchange rate changes. Tariffs are taxes on imported goods. A tariff raises the cost of imports to domestic residents and thereby diverts demand away from imports to domestic goods. A 10 percent tariff on imported shoes, for instance, makes imported shoes more expensive relative to domestically made shoes and shifts demand to locally made shoes. A devaluation, as we shall see, achieves the same effect by raising import prices relative to the prices of domestically made goods. In summary, if we have a trade deficit at full employment—as in Figure 18-6—we require a policy that directly affects the trade balance so as to give us trade balance equilibrium at full employment.

The Use of Expenditure Switching/Reducing Policies

The argument of the previous subsection needs to be spelled out in more detail to focus attention on a subtle and important point: Policies to shift spending from imports to domestic goods generally also affect aggregate demand in the goods market. Accordingly, policies to shift the $NX = 0$ line generally have to be accompanied by policies that adjust aggregate demand.

Figure 18-7 shows a situation in which the level of output in the economy is at $\bar{Y}$, but the balance of payments is in deficit, since the $NX = 0$ line is to the

FIGURE 18-7 THE POLICY DILEMMA WITH A TRADE DEFICIT. An initial equilibrium at *E* involves a trade deficit. To correct the external balance a tariff is imposed, and this policy move shifts demand from imports to domestic goods. The trade balance equilibrium schedule shifts to $NX' = 0$ because imports are reduced at each income level. The *IS* schedule shifts right to *IS′* because of increased demand for domestic goods. A further policy change is now required to avoid the overemployment equilibrium at the intersection of *IS′* and *LM*. A reduction in money, shifting the *LM* schedule up and to the left, could restore full-employment equilibrium.

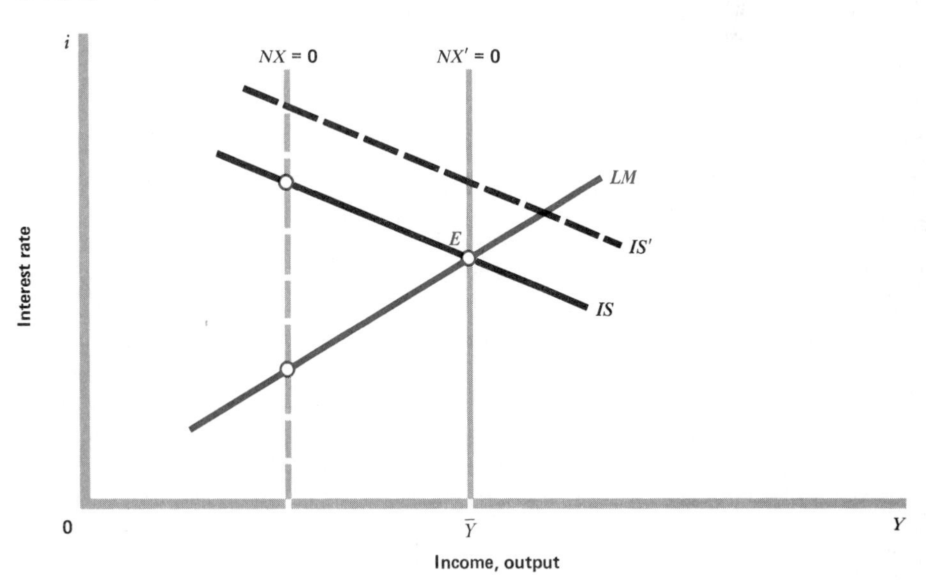

left of $\bar{Y}$. As we saw earlier in this chapter, aggregate demand policies cannot, in this case, both keep us at full employment and reduce the trade deficit. Consider using a tariff which shifts demand from imports to domestic goods. By using the tariff, we reduce import spending and shift the trade balance line to the right until it coincides with the full-employment line.

But the tariff will also affect the demand for domestic goods. The spending which at a given level of income no longer goes to imports goes to domestic goods instead. We are simply *switching* expenditures from imports to domestic goods. Accordingly, the tariff shifts the *IS* curve out to the right to *IS*′. We therefore have to use a further policy to offset the expansionary effect of the tariff in the domestic goods market. We could use either monetary or fiscal policy to shift the economy's equilibrium back to the full-employment level $\bar{Y}$.

The important point is: In general it is necessary to combine both *expenditure switching policies,* which shift demand between domestic and imported goods, and *expenditure reducing* (or *expenditure increasing*) *policies,* to cope with the targets of internal and external balance. This point is of general importance and continues to apply when we take account of capital flows and other phenomena omitted in this section.

Interdependence and Repercussion Effects

The next topic to be taken up in this section is the interdependence of income determination in the world economy. An increase in income in one country (country A), by increasing country A's imports, affects demand for output abroad and leads, in turn, to a foreign expansion in imports from country A.

These *spillover effects* in the income determination process have two implications: (1) Countries cannot, in general, decide on appropriate stabilization policies without knowing what policies or income levels will prevail abroad and hence what the world demand for their exports will be. This suggests that coordination of stabilization policy between countries may be necessary or desirable. (2) One country's income and import expansion spills over to increases in income abroad. But, in addition, the foreign income increase which the spillover induces leads to increased foreign import demand. There is thus a *repercussion effect* that we have so far ignored by assuming that export demand is autonomous. The repercussion effect is the additional effect on country A's income caused by the reaction of foreign countries' income to an initial increase in aggregate demand in country A.

We consider first the very important problem posed by spillover effects. For example, during the 1981–1982 recession some countries, such as Germany, were relying on the U.S. recovery to pull them out of their own recession. How? It was expected that U.S. monetary and fiscal policies would stimulate the level of income in the United States and therefore U.S. imports. With part of U.S. imports coming from Germany, this would lead to increased German exports. Increased exports, in turn, mean increased income and employment. Thus, a recovery in Germany could have been started off by an increase in exports. For obvious reasons, such a recovery is called an *export-led recovery*.

A critical question in the policy decision to wait for an increase in foreign demand rather than to undertake domestic action must be the size of the impacts of one country's income growth on another country's exports and thus on the latter's income. In the case of Germany, the question is by how much a 1 percent increase in U.S. income, say, increases German income. If the number were of the order of 0.5 percent, then U.S. growth could make an important contribution to German recovery, and disregard of U.S. policy could lead to serious policy errors.

ESTIMATED REPERCUSSION EFFECTS

Table 18-4 provides estimates of the size of repercussion effects and the importance of international linkages. The table, derived from an econometric model of the OECD, shows income multipliers associated with an expansion in one country on that country itself and on other countries.[9] Consider first the case of the United States. An increase of 1 percentage point in U.S. autonomous spending would raise U.S. income by 1.47 percent.

What is the impact on selected other countries? Looking at the top row, we find that German income growth rises by about ¼ percent, and the same is true for Japan. Thus, U.S. expansion does affect these countries, although the size of the effect is not overwhelming. The comparison with Canada is of interest here. A U.S. expansion by 1.47 percent raises Canadian income growth by nearly 0.7 percent. Thus Canada appears considerably affected by U.S. expenditure disturbances. The last entry in the top row of Table 18-4 shows the impact of a U.S. expansion on industrialized countries as a group.

[9] The OECD (Organization for Economic Cooperation and Development) is a grouping of 24 industrialized countries, based in Paris, which serves as a framework for international policy discussion. Among the members are the few listed in Table 18-4, plus Italy, the United Kingdom, France, and seventeen others.

TABLE 18-4 THE INTERNATIONAL TRANSMISSION OF AGGREGATE DEMAND DISTURBANCES

	AFFECTED COUNTRY OR GROUP (PERCENTAGE CHANGE IN INCOME)				
Initiating country or group (1 percent increase in autonomous spending)	United States	Germany	Japan	Canada	OECD
United States	1.47	0.23	0.25	0.68	0.74
Germany	0.05	1.25	0.60	0.60	0.23
Japan	0.04	0.05	1.26	0.06	0.21
Canada	0.06	0.03	0.03	1.27	0.10
OECD	1.81	2.38	1.84	2.32	2.04

Source: OECD Occasional Paper, "The OECD International Linkage Model," January 1979.

The impact here is to increase the group's combined income by three-quarters of a percentage point.[10]

Consider for comparison a Canadian expansion. The multiplier for Canadian income growth of a 1 percent increase in Canadian autonomous spending is 1.27, about the same as the 1.47 multiplier for the United States. The impact on the rest of the world is quite minor, though. The most substantial impact is on the United States (0.06 percent induced income growth) and only 0.03 percent increased growth for Germany or Japan.

What determines the size of the multipliers and spillover effects? Three chief factors should be taken into account in interpreting the multiplier patterns revealed in Table 18-4. First, the size of the country is important. A Canadian expansion, for example, induces only a small percentage increase in U.S. income because a given dollar change in Canadian income and imports will be only a small fraction of U.S. income. By contrast, a given increase in U.S. income and imports will be a relatively large fraction of Canadian income.

The second important determinant of multiplier patterns is openness to trade. The spillover effects of an expansion in any one country on the rest of the world will be more substantial the more open the expanding economy.[11]

The third point to note is the extent to which trade patterns are reflected in the multipliers. The United States, for example, benefits relatively more from a Canadian expansion than does Germany. This reflects the fact that Canada has a high marginal propensity to import from the United States in comparison with its propensity to import from Germany.

Table 18-4 allows us to study not only the effects of an individual country's expansion and the induced spillovers but also the effect of a simultaneous joint expansion in all industrialized countries. The last row of the table provides the multipliers for this experiment. Clearly, if all countries expand together—each raising autonomous expenditure by 1 percent—the multiplier effects are much more substantial. Each country benefits not only from its own expansion and its repercussion effects through induced expansion abroad, but also from the autonomous foreign expansion. Accordingly, the multipliers are around 2 in this case, while being in the range of 1.2 to 1.5 for the case of an isolated expansion.

We can now return to the question of export-led recoveries and ask what contribution U.S. real growth could have made to Germany. The answer from Table 18-4 is that the impact would not have been large. In the short run, U.S. autonomous spending would have to increase by more than 4 percent (1/0.23) to raise German income by only 1 percentage point. The transmission effect in

[10] Do you see why the relative effect on total OECD income (0.74 percent) of a 1 percent increase in U.S. autonomous spending is smaller than the relative effect on U.S. income (1.47 percent)? (*Hint:* Consider (*a*) on which OECD country the U.S. expansion has the largest effect and (*b*) the size of total OECD income relative to that of the United States.)

[11] There is, however, an offset to this, since a more open economy (as measured by the marginal propensity to import) will have a smaller multiplier, so that a given demand expansion will induce a smaller increase in imports. The net effect of more openness, though, is to increase the spillover effects.

this instance would have been quite small, although for a country like Canada, U.S. growth is a critically important determinant of short-run growth performance.

Interdependence, Relative Growth, and the Current Account

The effects of changes in the level of income in one country on income in another, studied in the preceding section, are transmitted through changes in the levels of imports and exports. The spillover and repercussion effects therefore also affect the current account.[12] A country that is growing rapidly tends to increase its imports relatively fast. The current account of the rapidly growing country therefore tends to go into deficit.

Such effects have been important for the United States in the past few years. Table 18-5 presents relevant facts on income growth and the current account. The "Big Six" are Japan, Germany, France, the United Kingdom, Canada, and Italy, the United States' major trading partners within the OECD. Consider first 1975, the trough of a worldwide recession. United States income fell absolutely by 1.2 percent, more of a decline than the 0.3 percent fall abroad. With the substantial fall in income at home relative to that abroad, our *net* imports fell very substantially, and consequently, the current account shows a record surplus for that year. The magnitude of the worldwide recession in 1975 reflects the fact that the decline in activity in each area spread, through multiplier effects, throughout the world, thus deepening the recession. In 1976, growth patterns were roughly the same in all countries, and the United States experienced a reduction in the current account, surplus. An interesting year is 1977. Here U.S. growth ran substantially ahead of growth abroad. The consequence was a massive turnaround in the U.S. current account, a deficit of $14 billion. With nearly matching growth rates, there remained a deficit in 1978.

A word of warning is needed here. The behavior of the current account reflects more than relative income growth. Factors such as changes in the exchange rate, exogenous shocks such as the oil price increase, and shifting

[12] Estimates of current account effects of expansion in different countries are provided in the OECD Occasional Paper, "The OECD International Linkage Model," January 1979.

TABLE 18-5 REAL INCOME AND THE U.S. CURRENT ACCOUNT

	1975	1976	1977	1978	1979
	REAL INCOME GROWTH, PERCENT PER YEAR				
United States	−1.2	5.4	5.5	5.0	2.8
Big Six	−0.3	5.4	3.3	4.3	4.3
	CURRENT ACCOUNT, BILLIONS OF DOLLARS				
United States	18.3	4.4	−14.1	−14.8	−0.5

Sources: Economic Report of the President *and* OECD Economic Outlook.

trade patterns due to the emergence of new competitors and the spread of technology abroad all affect the current account as well. Even so, Table 18-5 shows *relative* cyclical performance as one essential determinant of the current account.

External Balance, Money, and Prices

The analysis has been developed so far on the assumption that domestic prices do not respond at all to changes in demand. This is a convenient assumption for expository purposes, but we know it is not realistic. We therefore turn to a complete model, parallel to the aggregate demand and supply analysis of Chapters 11 and 12.

We start by reviewing the main points. Aggregate demand depends on the level of prices. A higher level of prices implies lower real balances, higher interest rates, and lower spending. In an open economy, the relation is slightly more complicated because now an increase in our prices reduces demand for our goods for two reasons. The first is the familiar higher interest rate channel summarized above. The second is that an increase in our prices makes our goods less competitive with foreign-produced goods. When the prices of goods produced at home rise, and given the exchange rate, our goods become more expensive for foreigners to buy, and their goods become *relatively* cheaper for us to buy. An increase in our prices is thus an increase in the *relative price* of the goods we produce, and shifts demand away from our goods toward imports, as well as reducing exports.

In summary, then, an increase in our price level reduces the demand for our goods both by increasing the interest rate (and reducing investment demand) and by reducing net exports—by making the goods we produce relatively more expensive than foreign-produced goods. In Figure 18-8 we show the downward-sloping demand schedule for our goods, AD. Demand is equal, as before, to aggregate spending by domestic residents, plus net exports, $AD \equiv A + NX$.

The demand for domestic goods, AD, is drawn for a given level of foreign prices, a given nominal money supply, and given fiscal policy. Remember, too, that the exchange rate is fixed. An increase in the nominal money stock shifts the schedule upward, as does expansionary fiscal policy. We show, too, the short-run aggregate supply schedule AS and the full-employment level of output $\bar{Y}$. Initial equilibrium is at point E, where we have unemployment.

Next we look at the trade balance equilibrium schedule, $NX = 0$. An increase in our income raises imports and worsens the trade balance. To restore trade balance equilibrium, domestic prices would have to be lower. This would make the home country more competitive, raise exports, and reduce imports. Thus, we show the trade balance equilibrium schedule as downward-sloping.[13] We assume that it is steeper than the demand schedule

[13] We assume that a decline in prices improves the trade balance. This requires that exports and imports are sufficiently responsive to prices. There is a possibility that a reduction in our price level (which reduces the prices of our exports) lowers our revenue from exports—because the increased sales are not sufficient to compensate for the lower prices. We shall assume that this possibility does not occur. We shall assume, too, that import spending does not depend on the interest rate.

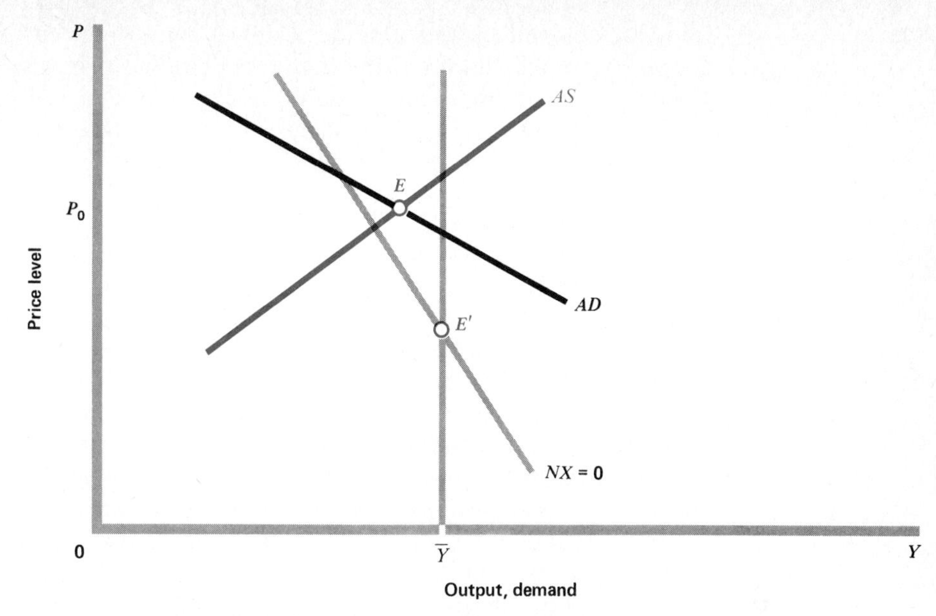

FIGURE 18-8 OPEN ECONOMY EQUILIBRIUM WITH PRICE ADJUSTMENT. Net exports and the demand for domestic goods depend on the relative price of our goods. Demand for domestic goods also depends on the price level because this affects the real money supply and hence interest rates. *AD* is the aggregate demand schedule. It is downward-sloping because a reduction in our prices raises the real money stock, lowering interest rates, and because lower prices for our goods increase our international competitiveness. The trade balance equilibrium schedule is also downward-sloping, reflecting the increased competitiveness that we derive from a lower relative price of our goods. Macroeconomic equilibrium obtains at *E*, where aggregate demand equals aggregate supply. This need not be a point of full employment and external balance, which obtain at *E′*.

for domestic goods. The schedule is drawn for a given level of prices abroad. The short-run equilibrium at point *E* is one where the home country has a trade deficit. Our prices are too high or our income is too high to have exports balance imports. To achieve trade balance equilibrium, we would have to become more competitive, thus exporting more and importing less. Alternatively, we could reduce our level of income in order to reduce import spending.

The Adjustment Process

Consider next the policy options in terms of external and internal balance. At point *E* there is unemployment and a deficit. To restore full employment, we could expand aggregate demand, or else wait for wages and prices to fall sufficiently to raise the demand for our goods through the interest rate and increased net exports channels. From an external point of view, we have to achieve a decline in income or in prices to restore balance.

At point *E′* we have both internal and external balance, that is, full employment and balanced trade. But we cannot get to that point except through a protracted recession that cuts domestic prices sufficiently to shift the aggregate supply schedule down. This adjustment process would indeed occur if the government did not pursue any stabilization policy and simply pegged the exchange rate. The process is sufficiently important to deserve more attention.

AUTOMATIC ADJUSTMENT

First we look at the aggregate demand side. We remember that there is a link between the central bank's holdings of foreign exchange and the domestic money supply, assuming now no sterilization, as defined in footnote 6. When the central bank pegs the exchange rate, selling foreign exchange, it reduces domestic high-powered money and therefore the money stock. This is exactly what happens in the case of a deficit. Thus the trade deficit at point E implies that the central bank is pegging the exchange rate, selling foreign exchange to keep the exchange rate from depreciating, and reducing the domestic money stock. It follows immediately that over time the aggregate demand schedule (which is drawn for a given money supply) will be shifting down and to the left.

On the aggregate supply side, we remember that unemployment leads to a decline in wages and costs, which is reflected in a downward-shifting aggregate supply schedule. Over time, therefore, the short-run equilibrium point E moves down as both demand and supply schedules shift. The points of short-run equilibrium move in the direction of point E', and the process will continue until that point is reached. (The approach may be cyclical, but that is not of major interest here.)

Once point E' is reached, we have achieved long-run equilibrium. Because the trade balance is in equilibrium, there is no pressure on the exchange rate and therefore no need for exchange market intervention. Accordingly, there is no influence from the trade balance on the money supply and thereby on aggregate demand. On the supply side, we have reached full employment. Therefore wages and costs are constant, so that the supply schedule is not shifting. At point E' we have a combination of relative prices, demand, and employment that gives both internal and external balance. The adjustment of the level of prices ensures that we can—in the long run—have both full employment and trade balance equilibrium.

The adjustment process we have just described is called the *classical adjustment process.* It relies on price adjustments and an adjustment in the money supply based on the trade balance. The adjustment process "works" in the sense that it moves the economy to a long-run equilibrium of internal and external balance. However, the mechanism is far from attractive. There is no good case for a protracted recession simply to achieve a cut in prices. A preferable policy is to resort to expenditure switching policies, or to exchange rate changes, as a means of achieving internal and external balance.[14]

[14] An exchange rate depreciation, or a policy that shifts demand from imports to domestic goods, would shift both the net export schedule and the aggregate demand schedule up and to the right.

The Monetary Approach to the Balance of Payments

How important are monetary considerations in explaining balance of payment problems? Is it true that balance of payments deficits are a reflection of an excessive money supply? These questions must be raised because it is frequently suggested that external balance problems are monetary in nature.

There is a simple first answer. It is obviously true that for any given balance of payments deficit, a sufficient contraction of the money stock will restore external balance. The reason is that a monetary contraction, by raising interest rates and reducing spending, generates a contraction in economic activity, a decline in income, and therefore a decline in imports. It is equally true that this result could be achieved by tight fiscal policy, and so there is nothing especially monetary about this interpretation of remedies for external imbalance.

A more sophisticated interpretation of the problem recognizes the link, examined in the previous sections, between the balance of payments deficit, foreign exchange market intervention, and the money supply. The automatic mechanism is for a sale of foreign exchange—as arises in the case of deficits—to be reflected in an equal reduction in the stock of high-powered money. The central bank merely sells one asset (foreign exchange) and buys another (high-powered money). This process will automatically lead to a decline in the stock of money in deficit countries and an increase in the money stock in surplus countries. Given that the money supply is thus linked to the external balance, it is obvious that this adjustment process must ultimately lead to the right money stock so that external payments are in balance. This is the adjustment process discussed above.

STERILIZATION

The only way the adjustment process can be suspended is through *sterilization operations.* We discussed this in Chapter 9 on the money supply. There we noted that central banks frequently offset, or sterilize, the impact of foreign exchange market intervention on the money supply through open market operations. Thus, a deficit country that is selling foreign exchange and correspondingly reducing its money supply may offset this reduction by open market purchases of bonds that restore the money supply.

Such a practice suspends the automatic adjustment mechanism. Persistent external deficits are possible because the link between the external imbalance and the equilibrating changes in the money stock is broken. It is in this sense that persistent external deficits are a monetary phenomenon: by sterilizing, the central bank actively maintains the stock of money too high for external balance.

THE MONETARY APPROACH AND THE IMF

The emphasis on monetary considerations in the interpretation of external balance problems is called the *monetary approach to the balance of pay-*

TABLE 18-6 BALANCE SHEET OF THE MONETARY AUTHORITIES

Assets	Liabilities
Net foreign assets (*NFA*)	High-powered money (*H*)
Domestic credit (*DC*)	

ments.[15] The monetary approach has been used extensively by the International Monetary Fund (IMF) in its analysis and design of economic policies for countries in balance of payments trouble. We give the flavor of the approach by describing typical IMF procedure in analyzing a balance of payments problem.

We start with the balance sheet of the monetary authority, typically the central bank, as in Table 18-6. The monetary authority's liabilities are high-powered money, as explained in Chapter 9. But we recognize on the asset side that it can hold both foreign assets—including foreign exchange reserves, gold, and claims on other central banks or governments—and domestic assets, or *domestic credit.* Domestic credit consists of the monetary authority's holdings of claims on the public sector—government debt—and claims on the private sector—usually loans to banks.

From the balance sheet identity, we have

$$\Delta NFA = \Delta H - \Delta DC \qquad (7)$$

where ΔNFA denotes the change in net foreign assets, ΔH the change in high-powered money, and ΔDC the change in domestic credit. In words, the change in the central bank's holdings of foreign assets is equal to the change in the stock of high-powered money minus the change in domestic credit.

The important point about Equation (7) is that ΔNFA is the balance of payments: recall from Section 18-1 that official reserve transactions, which is all that ΔNFA is, are equal to the balance of payments.

The first step in developing a stabilization policy package is to decide on a balance of payments target, ΔNFA^*. The IMF asks how much of a deficit the country can afford and then suggests policies to make the projected deficit no larger. The target is based largely on the availability of loans and credit from abroad and the possibility of drawing down existing reserves.

The next step is to ask how much the demand for money in the country will increase. The planned changes in the stock of high-powered money ΔH^* will have to be just sufficient to produce, via the money multiplier process, the right increases in the stock of money to meet the expected increase in demand. Then, given ΔNFA^* and ΔH^*, Equation (7) tells the monetary author-

[15] For a collection of essays on this topic, see Jacob Frenkel and Harry G. Johnson (eds.), *The Monetary Approach to the Balance of Payments* (London: Allen & Unwin, 1976). See also *The Monetary Approach to the Balance of Payments* (Washington, D.C.: International Monetary Fund, 1977).

ity how much domestic credit it can extend consistent with its balance of payments target and expected growth in money demand. Typically, a stabilization plan drawn up by the IMF will include a suggested limit on the expansion of domestic credit.

The limit provides a *ceiling on domestic credit expansion.* The adoption of such a ceiling helps the central bank avoid the temptation of expanding its loans to the government or private sector in the face of rising interest rates or government budget deficits.

HOW DOES IT WORK?

The simplicity of Equation (7) raises an obvious question. Since all it takes to improve the balance of payments is a reduction in the rate of domestic credit expansion, why not balance payments immediately and always? To answer this question, we need to understand the channels through which the curtailment of domestic credit improves the balance of payments.

Controlling domestic credit means operating a tight money policy. Consider an economy that is growing and has some inflation, so that the demand for nominal balances is rising. If domestic credit expansion is slowed, an excess demand for money develops. This, in turn, causes interest rates to rise and spending to decline. The increase in interest rates leads to a balance of payments improvement. That is, the monetary approach as used by the IMF relies on restrictive monetary policy to control the balance of payments. There is, though, a subtle difference between domestic credit ceilings and ordinary tight money. In an open economy with fixed exchange rates, the money stock is endogenous. The central bank cannot control the money stock, since it has to meet whatever demand arises for foreign currency. But it can make "money" tight by reducing the growth of domestic credit. That will imply that the only source of money growth becomes an increase in foreign exchange reserves or foreign borrowing. The economy has to go through enough of a recession or rise in interest rates to generate a balance of payments surplus.

The use of domestic credit ceilings is a crude policy to improve the balance of payments. But the simplicity of the conceptual framework, and the apparent definiteness of the policy recommendations to which it leads, frequently makes it the best policy tool available, particularly if dramatic action is needed and the credibility of the government's policies needs to be restored.

THE MONETARY APPROACH AND DEPRECIATION

Proponents of the monetary approach have also argued that depreciation of the exchange rate cannot improve the balance of payments except in the short run. The argument is that in the short run the depreciation does improve a country's competitive position and that this very fact gives rise to a trade surplus and therefore to an increase in the money stock. Over the course of time, the rising money supply raises aggregate demand and therefore prices

BOX 18-1

BRAZIL AND THE IMF: ADJUSTMENT UNDER CONDITIONALITY

Late in 1982 Brazil surprised the world capital markets when it suddenly became clear that the country could not pay its bills nor pay interest on its large foreign debt. The crisis was solved by short-term loans from the main industrialized countries and by borrowing from the IMF and accepting an adjustment program (also called *conditionality*) worked out with the IMF. Here we consider how Brazil got into trouble and what an adjustment program looks like.

Brazil's growth and balance of payments performance is shown in Table 1. Until 1978 real growth was very high. But the current account moved into *large* deficits when world oil prices increased in 1979. Spending on oil imports increased with the higher prices, and export earnings were not enough to pay for the oil and other imports.

The country started borrowing on a very large scale in world markets, year after year. Soon interest payments on the external debt came to be sizeable. By 1981 troubles were plainly acute: the second oil shock and the sharp increase in world interest rates meant that spending on just oil and interest payments more than absorbed the entire export revenues. The 1982 world recession further increased Brazil's difficulties by causing a decline in export earnings.

In late 1982 Brazil had to tell the bankers who had provided more than $80 billion in loans that there was a crisis: Brazil was unable to pay its bills. Indeed, it needed even more loans just to keep going while an adjustment program was put into effect.

Brazil went to the IMF and in early 1983 secured a loan of over $4 billion together with an agreement from the banks to renew credit lines and help the country through the crisis. But the adjustment was to be drastic. Inflation was to be brought under control, and the government budget deficit that had sustained the high growth rates had to be eliminated. The current account deficit had to be reduced sharply. These targets are set out in Table 2.

The adjustment program implies a dramatic restructuring of the Brazilian economy away from government and toward increased net exports. But what happens in an economy when the budget deficit is cut by an amount equal to 8 percent of GDP without an offsetting increase in demand? The answer is, of course, a quite enormous recession. The Brazilian government has therefore been reluctant to implement the program.

But can the adjustment be delayed for long? Yes, if bankers are reluctant to call their loans,

TABLE 1 BRAZIL: GROWTH AND EXTERNAL BALANCE (Annual Averages)

	1971–1973	1974–1978	1979–1980	1981	1982
Real GDP Growth (%)	12.5	7.0	7.3	−1.9	−1.2
Current account deficit (billion $US)	1.5	6.2	11.8	11.7	12.5
Exports (billion $US)	4.6	10.3	17.7	23.3	20.2
Interest payments (billion $US)	0.5	2.2	6.5	10.3	10.7
Oil payments (billion $US)	0.5	3.5	8.1	11.0	10.2

Source: Data Resources, Inc.

TABLE 2 THE ADJUSTMENT PROGRAM

	1981	1982	1983*	1984*	1985*
Inflation (%)	95.2	99.7	87.0	40.0	20.0
Public sector deficit (% of GNP)	12.7	16.9	8.8	5.5	4.0
Current account deficit (% of GDP)	3.6	4.5	2.2	1.5	1.1

Source: IMF Survey, *March 21, 1983, p. 93.*
* Planned.

preferring to put more money in rather than risking a Brazilian default. Rapid and sustained world recovery, lower oil prices, and lower real interest rates all could help turn matters around without dramatic adjustment. But should these not come in time, the adjustment will have to be huge.

until the economy returns to full employment and external balance. Devaluation thus exerts only a transitory effect on the economy which lasts as long as prices and the money supply have not yet increased to match fully the higher import prices.

The analysis of the monetary approach is entirely correct in its insistence on a longer-run perspective in which, under fixed exchange rates, prices and the money stock adjust and the economy achieves internal and external balance. It is also correct in arguing that monetary or domestic credit restraint will improve the balance of payments. But this mechanism is not painless, since the tight money policy produced by slow domestic credit growth typically produces a recession.

The approach is misdirected when it suggests that exchange rate policy cannot, even in the short run, affect a country's competitive position. More important, exchange rate changes frequently occur from a position of deficit and unemployment. In that case, a depreciation moves the economy toward equilibrium. It eases the adjustment mechanisms by achieving an increase in competitiveness through an increase in import prices rather than through a recession-induced decline in domestic prices.

Summary

1 The introduction of trade in goods means that spending by domestic residents is no longer equal to the demand for domestically produced goods. Some of our demand for goods goes for imports, and some of the demand for our goods comes from foreigners, to whom we export.

2 There is equilibrium in the goods market when the demand for our goods, consisting of spending by domestic residents, plus net exports, is equal to the output of domestic goods.
3 In short-run equilibrium, there is no guarantee that trade balances. In our simplest model, there is a unique level of income at which trade balances, and this is not necessarily the income level at which the economy comes into short-run equilibrium.
4 An increase in autonomous demand for domestic goods increases domestic output and worsens the trade balance. An increase in exports increases domestic income and reduces the trade deficit. A shift in demand toward domestically produced goods increases the level of income and reduces the trade deficit, or increases the trade surplus.
5 Because trade does not necessarily balance in short-run equilibrium, there may be a *policy dilemma* in attempting both to move income to the potential output level and to balance trade. Increasing the level of income to move it closer to potential may well worsen the trade balance.
6 The use of *expenditure switching* policies, which change the relative prices of domestic and imported goods, combined with *expenditure reducing* policies, can move the economy to full employment with balanced trade.
7 Foreigners' demand for our goods, their imports, depends on their level of income. Therefore demand for our goods depends also on the foreign level of income. An increase in foreign income increases our exports and increases our level of income, and therefore our imports.
8 There are *repercussion effects* by which a change in foreign income eventually induces an increase in the demand for foreigners' goods through exports. The size of these interdependence and repercussion effects depends on the relative size and openness of the economy. A small economy may be very dependent on a larger one, but a larger economy's level of income does not depend much on the income level in small foreign economies.
9 Once we allow for price flexibility with fixed exchange rates, we use the analytical apparatus of Chapter 12. Price flexibility ultimately leads an economy to full employment with balanced trade. The mechanism involves changes in the domestic money supply which occur as the central bank keeps selling foreign exchange to domestic residents in exchange for domestic currency (essentially an open market sale of foreign currency). The falling money stock reduces our prices and therefore improves the balance of trade. Policy can be used actively to bring about adjustments without relying on this automatic and slow-moving mechanism.
10 The monetary approach to the balance of payments emphasizes the central bank's balance sheet identity, Equation (7), which shows that sufficient contraction of domestic credit will improve the balance of payments. This improvement comes about through higher interest rates and lower domestic income. We should also note that the link between

the balance of payments and the domestic stock of money, which is central to the monetary approach, can easily be broken through sterilization operations by the central bank.

So much for where we have been. In the next section, we compare the alternatives of *financing* a trade deficit by the central bank's drawing down its reserves (or by borrowing) with adjustment through *devaluation*. Then in Section 18-4 we introduce trade in assets, so-called *capital mobility*, and analyze its implications for stabilization policy.

18-3 FINANCING OF DEFICITS AND DEVALUATION

In a fixed exchange rate system, it is possible for the central bank to use its reserves to finance temporary imbalances of payments—that is, to meet the excess demand for foreign currency at the existing exchange rate arising from balance of payments deficits. Other ways of financing temporary payments imbalances are also available. A country experiencing balance of payments difficulties can borrow foreign currencies abroad. The borrowing may be undertaken either by the government (usually the central bank) or by private individuals. Although borrowing may be undertaken to finance both current and capital account deficits, we concentrate in this section on the current account.

A current account deficit cannot be financed by borrowing from abroad without raising the question of how the borrowing will be repaid. If the counterpart of the current account deficit is productive domestic investment, there need be little concern about paying back the interest and capital borrowed. The investment will pay off in terms of increased output, some of which may be exported, or which may replace goods that previously were imported. The investment would thus yield the foreign exchange earnings with which to *service* (make payments on) the debt. However, problems may well arise in repaying the foreign debt if borrowing is used to finance consumption spending.

Maintaining and financing current account deficits indefinitely or for very long periods of time is impossible. The alternative to financing deficits is *adjustment of deficits* in the current account through policy measures to reduce the deficits. We examined in Section 18-2 one method of adjusting a current account deficit, through the imposition of tariffs. However, tariffs cannot be freely used to adjust the balance of trade, partly because there are international organizations and agreements such as GATT (General Agreement on Tariffs and Trade) and the IMF (International Monetary Fund) that outlaw, or at least frown on, the use of tariffs. Tariffs have generally fallen in the post-World War II period as the industrialized world has moved to desirably freer trade between countries.

Another way of adjusting a current account deficit is to use a restrictive domestic policy. In this regard, it is worth repeating that a trade deficit reflects an excess of expenditure by domestic residents and the government over income. In Chapter 2 we showed that

$$NX \equiv Y - (C + I + G) \quad (8)$$

where NX is the trade surplus and I is actual investment. Thus, a balance of trade deficit can be reduced by reducing spending $(C + I + G)$ relative to income (Y). The trade deficit can be eliminated by reducing aggregate demand, by reducing C, or G, or I. In terms of Figure 18-6, the trade deficit can be eliminated by using restrictive monetary and/or fiscal policy to shift the intersection of the *IS* and *LM* curves to the level of income at which trade balances. The costs of this policy, in terms of unemployment, are obvious.

DEVALUATION

The unemployment that typically accompanies adjustment through recession and the desirability of free trade, which argues against the use of tariffs, both suggest that an alternative policy for reconciling internal and external balance be considered. The major policy instrument for dealing with payments deficits in the dilemma situation is *devaluation*—which usually has to be combined with restrictive monetary and/or fiscal policy. A devaluation, as we noted in Section 18-1, is an increase in the domestic currency price of foreign exchange. Given the nominal prices in the two countries, devaluation increases the relative price of imported goods in the devaluing country and reduces the relative price of exports from the devaluing country.

Table 18-7 shows the effects of an exchange rate shift on relative prices. Recall that we are assuming that nominal prices in the home currency in each country are fixed. We assume that we (Americans) produce and export Chevrolets and they (Germans) produce and export Volkswagens (VWs). The Chevrolet is priced at $8,000 and a VW at DM16,000. These prices, in terms of the respective producer's currencies, are assumed to remain constant.

Now, at an exchange rate of $0.40 per mark, the relative price of a VW in terms of Chevrolets is $6,400/$8,000 = 0.8, meaning that a VW costs 80 percent as much as a Chevrolet. Next, consider a devaluation of the dollar by 50 percent. The table shows that the dollar price of a VW rises and that the

TABLE 18-7 THE EFFECTS OF EXCHANGE RATE CHANGES ON RELATIVE PRICES

	Volkswagen	Chevrolet
Dollar price		
(*a*) $0.40/DM	$6,400	$8,000
(*b*) $0.60/DM	$9,600	$8,000
DM price:		
(*a*) $0.40/DM	DM16,000	DM20,000
(*b*) $0.60/DM	DM16,000	DM13,333

mark price of a Chevrolet declines. Both in the United States and in Germany, Chevrolets become *relatively* cheaper, or VWs become relatively more expensive. The dollar devaluation lowers the mark price of U.S. goods and raises the dollar price of German goods. The exchange ratio for German and U.S. cars now becomes $9,600/$8,000 = 1.20, so that a VW now costs 20 percent more than a Chevrolet. Clearly, the increase in the relative price of German goods will affect the pattern of demand, increasing both U.S. and German demands for Chevrolets at the expense of the demand for VWs.

Internal and External Balance

How does a devaluation assist in achieving internal and external balance? Let us take first a special case of a country that has been in full employment with balance of trade equilibrium, as shown by point E in Figure 18-9. Now let there be an exogenous decline in export earnings, so that the $NX = 0$ schedule shifts to the left to $NX' = 0$. At the given exchange rate and relative prices—that is, prices of domestic goods relative to world prices—the foreign demand for domestic goods is assumed to decline. In the absence of domestic policy intervention, and with fixed rates, output would decline. The IS schedule moves to the left as a result of the fall in exports, and the resultant income decline to point E' lowers imports, but not enough to make up for the

FIGURE 18-9 THE EFFECTS OF A DECLINE IN EXPORTS ON INCOME AND THE TRADE BALANCE. The initial equilibrium at point E is disturbed by a decline in exports. To restore external balance, imports must decline, and that means income must fall. Hence the trade balance equilibrium schedule shifts to $NX' = 0$. Because the reduction in exports is a reduction in demand for domestic goods, the IS schedule shifts to IS'. The new equilibrium is at point E', where output has declined and the trade balance is in deficit.

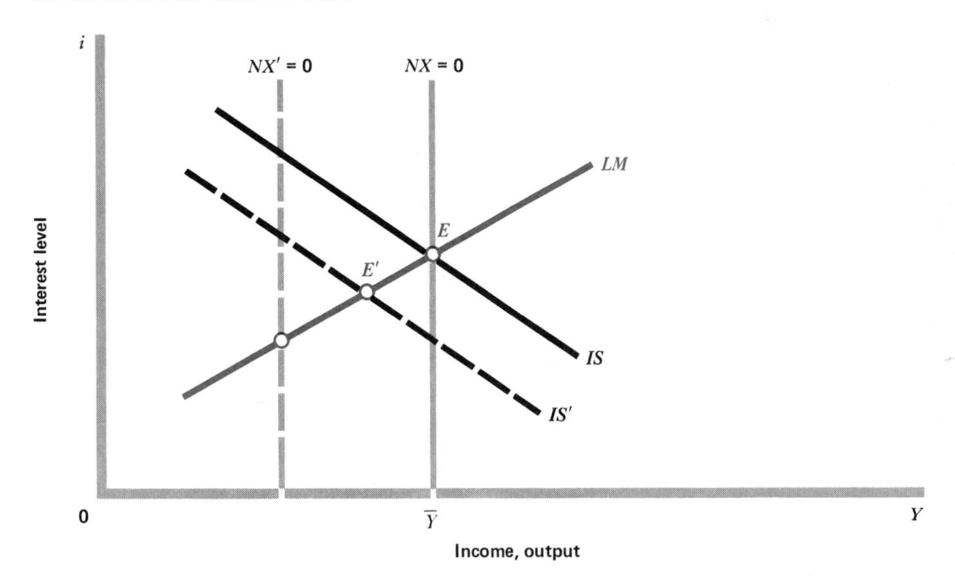

loss of export revenue. The net effects are therefore unemployment and a trade deficit.

Next, we ask how the home country can adjust to the loss of export markets. One possibility is to go through an adjustment process of declining domestic wages and prices as the high unemployment slowly reduces wages or slows down their rate of increase. This is the process described earlier. Such an adjustment would, over time, lower domestic costs and prices as compared with the prices of foreign goods. The home country would gain in competitiveness in world markets and thus restore export earnings and employment. This is a feasible adjustment process, and, indeed, is the process that would occur by itself, given enough time.

An alternative solution is to recognize that in order to restore full employment and export earnings, the home country must become more competitive in the prices charged for exports and imports. To restore competitiveness, domestic costs and prices have to decline *relative* to foreign prices. That adjustment can occur in two ways: (1) through a decline in domestic costs and prices at a given exchange rate and (2) through a depreciation of the exchange rate with unchanged domestic costs and prices.

The latter strategy has the obvious advantage that it does not require a protracted recession to reduce domestic costs. The adjustment is done by a stroke of the pen—a devaluation of the currency. Why would a devaluation achieve the adjustment? *Given* prices of foreign goods in terms of foreign currency (for example, the mark prices of German goods), a devaluation, as shown in Table 18-7, raises the relative price of foreign goods. The effect is to induce an increased demand for American goods and a reduction in demand for imports in the United States.

The case we have just considered is special, however, in one important respect. The economy was initially in balance of trade equilibrium at full employment. The disturbance to the economy took place in the trade account. Accordingly, if we could move the $NX = 0$ locus back to the full-employment level of income—as we could with a devaluation—both internal and external balance would be attained. Put differently, the reason there was an internal balance problem of unemployment in Figure 18-9 was the reduction in exports and consequent external balance problem. Both problems could thus be cured through devaluation.

TARGETS AND INSTRUMENTS OF POLICY

In general we cannot secure both external and internal balance following a disturbance by using just one instrument of policy. A general rule of policy making is that we need to use as many policy instruments as we have policy targets. Thus if the disturbance causes a trade deficit, it will, in general, not be enough just to have a devaluation.

To make that point we look at a reduction in saving or an autonomous increase in spending at home. The increased spending, by assumption, falls entirely on imports. Interest rates and income at home are unchanged because demand for domestic goods is unchanged, but there is now a trade deficit.

Since we are no longer in external balance, corrective action requires some measure to improve the trade balance. Suppose a devaluation is used and successfully shifts demand from imports to domestic goods. External balance now is secured, but we have done so by shifting demand to domestic goods. If initially there was full employment, the higher level of demand now means overemployment. Accordingly, we need a further policy, in addition to the devaluation, that ensures maintenance of full employment. A restrictive monetary or fiscal policy would do the job. Thus external balance adjustment involves an adjustment of the entire economy.

We should not fool ourselves into believing that just because full employment can be maintained, current account adjustment with a devaluation is costless. Current account adjustment involves not only a cut in spending to the level of income, but also, in many instances, a worsening of the *terms of trade*—the price of exports relative to imports. Foreign goods become more expensive, thus reducing the purchasing power of the goods we produce. Therefore our standard of living falls.

Finally, a comment on the role of the exchange rate in a fixed rate system: In the fixed rate system, the exchange rate is an *instrument of policy.* The central bank can change the exchange rate for policy purposes, devaluing when the current account looks as though it will be in for a prolonged deficit. In a system of clean floating, by contrast, the exchange rate moves freely to equilibrate the balance of payments. In a system of dirty floating, the central bank attempts to manipulate the exchange rate while not committing itself to any given rate. The dirty floating system is thus intermediate between a fixed rate system and a clean floating system.

18-4 CAPITAL MOBILITY AND THE POLICY MIX

So far, we have been assuming that trade is confined to goods and services and does not include assets. Now we allow for trade in assets and see the effects of such trade on the equilibrium of the economy and its desired policy mix.

One of the striking facts about the international economy is the high degree of integration or linkage among financial or capital markets—the markets in which bonds and stocks are traded. The capital markets are very fully integrated among the main industrial countries. Yields on assets in New York and yields on comparable assets in Canada, for example, move closely together. If rates in New York rose relative to those in Canada, investors would turn to lending in New York, while borrowers would turn to Toronto. With lending up in New York and borrowing up in Toronto, yields would quickly fall into line.

Figure 18-10 shows the yields on U.S. short-term securities and their Canadian counterparts.[16] The yield differential is consistently small. There is impressive evidence in Figure 18-10 of the linkage of international capital

[16] The yield on Canadian securities in Fig. 18-10 is "covered," which means that it is without exchange risk. Any yield differential in Fig. 18-10 is *not* a reflection of exchange risk.

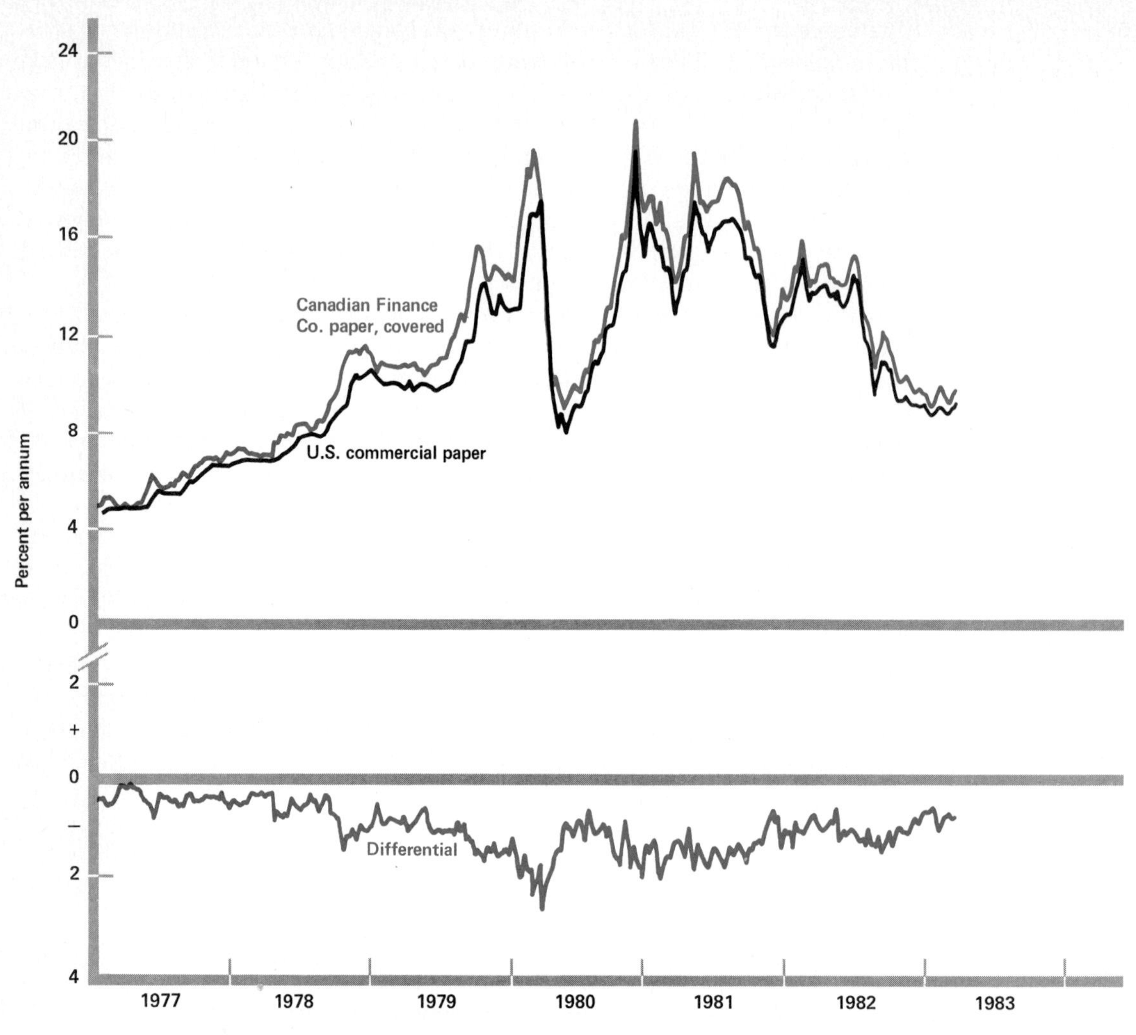

FIGURE 18-10 INTERNATIONAL INTEREST RATE LINKAGES. (*Source:* Board of Governors of the Federal Reserve, *Selected Interest Rates and Exchange Rates.*)

markets that ensures consistency among interest rates in different countries. That consistency arises because the flow of capital—lending to and by foreigners—to countries with higher interest rates soon equalizes such rates.

The high degree of capital market integration that is reflected in Figure 18-10 suggests that any one country's interest rates cannot get too far out of line from those in the rest of the world without bringing about capital flows that tend to restore yields to the world level. As we have noted, if Canadian yields fell relative to U.S. yields, there would be a capital outflow from Canada because lenders would take their funds out of Canada and borrowers would try to raise funds in Canada. From the point of view of the balance of payments, this implies that a relative decline in interest rates—a decline in our rates relative to those abroad—will worsen the balance of payments because of the capital outflow—lending abroad by U.S. residents.

The recognition that interest rates affect capital flows and the balance of payments has important implications for stabilization policy. First, because monetary and fiscal policies affect interest rates, they have an effect on the capital account and therefore on the balance of payments. The effects of monetary and fiscal policy on the balance of payments are *not* limited to the trade balance effects discussed in Section 18-2 but extend to the capital account. The second implication is that the way in which monetary and fiscal policies work in affecting the domestic economy and the balance of payments changes when there are international capital flows. We will examine the monetary-fiscal policy mix that can be used to achieve internal and external balance, and see that capital flows can be used to *finance* the trade balance and thus help in achieving overall balance of payments.

The Balance of Payments and Capital Flows

We introduce the role of capital flows in a framework in which we assume that the home country faces a given price of imports and a given export demand. In addition, we assume that the world rate of interest is given and that capital flows into the home country at a rate that is higher, the higher the home country's rate of interest. That is, foreign investors purchase more of our assets the higher the interest rate our assets pay relative to the world interest rate. The rate of capital inflow, CF, or the capital account surplus, is an increasing function of our rate of interest. At a level equal to the world rate, $i = i^*$, there are no capital flows. If the domestic interest rate is higher, there will be an inflow, and conversely, if the domestic interest rate is lower, there will be a capital outflow.

Next we look at the balance of payments. The balance of payments surplus BoP is equal to the trade surplus NX plus the capital account surplus CF:

$$BoP = NX(Y, \overline{X}, \ldots) + CF(i, i^*) \tag{9}$$

In Equation (9) we have shown the trade balance as a function of income and the capital account as a function of the domestic interest rate. An increase in income worsens the trade balance, and an increase in the interest rate raises capital inflows and thus improves the capital account. It follows that when income increases, an increase in interest rates could maintain overall balance of payments equilibrium. The trade deficit would be financed by a capital inflow. That idea is extremely important because it suggests that in the short run we can get out of the internal-external balance dilemma of Section 18-2.

The problem, we remember, was to achieve simultaneously internal and external balance from a position of deficit and unemployment or surplus and boom. The presence of interest-sensitive capital flows suggests that we can run an expansionary domestic policy without necessarily running into balance of payments problems. We can afford an increase in domestic income and import spending, provided we accompany it by an increase in interest rates so as to attract a capital inflow. But how can we achieve an expansion in domestic income at the same time that interest rates are increased? The answer is that we use fiscal policy to increase aggregate demand to the full-employment level and monetary policy to get the right amount of capital flows.[17]

Internal and External Balance

In Figure 18-11 we show the positively sloped schedule $BoP = 0$, derived from Equation (9), along which we have balance of payments equilibrium. To derive the slope of the $BoP = 0$ line, start with an income expansion, which raises imports and worsens the balance of payments. To restore balance of payments equilibrium, interest rates have to be higher to attract the capital

[17] The idea of the policy mix for internal and external balance was suggested by Robert Mundell in his important paper, "The Appropriate Use of Monetary and Fiscal Policy under Fixed Exchange Rates," *I.M.F. Staff Papers*, March 1962. Mundell's work on international macroeconomics has been extraordinarily important, and the adventurous student should certainly consult his two books: *International Economics* (New York: Macmillan, 1967) and *Monetary Theory* (Pacific Palisades, Calif.: Goodyear, 1971).

FIGURE 18-11 INTERNAL AND EXTERNAL BALANCE. Full employment obtains at an output level $\bar{Y}$. The internal balance schedule is therefore the vertical line at $\bar{Y}$. Along $BoP = 0$ the balance of payments is in equilibrium. A rise in income worsens the trade balance, and therefore higher interest rates are required to attract capital inflows that finance the trade deficit. Points above and to the left of the BoP schedule correspond to surpluses and points below and to the right to deficits in the balance of payments. The higher the degree of capital mobility, the flatter the BoP schedule, since then a small increase in our interest rates creates large capital flows.

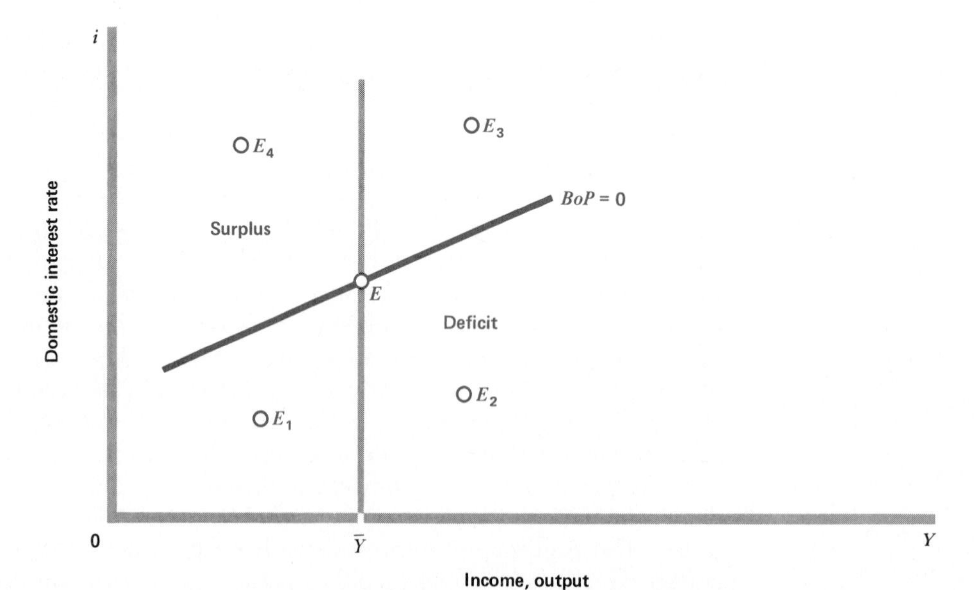

flows that finance the trade deficit. Thus to maintain payments balance, an income increase has to be matched by a higher interest rate, and the $BoP = 0$ line is therefore upward-sloping.

The schedule is drawn for given exports and a given foreign interest rate. The higher the degree of capital mobility, the flatter the schedule. If capital is very highly responsive to interest rates, then a small increase in the interest rate will bring about very large capital flows and thus allow the financing of large trade deficits. The larger the marginal propensity to import, the steeper the schedule. An increase in income worsens the trade balance by the increase in income times the marginal propensity to import. Thus, a high propensity to import means that a given increase in income produces a large deficit and thus requires a large increase in interest rates to bring about the right amount of capital flows to offset the trade deficit. Points above and to the left of the $BoP = 0$ schedule correspond to a surplus and points below and to the right to a deficit. We have also drawn, in Figure 18-11, full-employment output $\bar{Y}$. The full equilibrium with both internal and external balance is at point E.

We can talk about policy problems in terms of points in the four quadrants of Figure 18-11. Each such point would be an intersection of an *IS* and an *LM* curve, and the question is how to use monetary and fiscal policy—shifting the *IS* and *LM* curves—to get to full equilibrium. Thus, point E_1, for example, corresponds to a case of unemployment and deficit. Point E_2, by contrast, is a case of deficit and overemployment. What are points E_3 and E_4?

The Policy Mix

Suppose that the economy is at point E_1. The appropriate policy to produce internal and external balance requires a higher level of employment for internal balance and higher interest rates and/or a lower level of income for external balance.

In terms of the earlier analysis there is a policy dilemma at E_1 because employment considerations suggest income should be raised and balance of payments considerations suggest it should be reduced. However, now there is a way out of the dilemma. Suppose we reduce the money supply and thus raise interest rates. To offset the effects of the higher interest rates on income, we could use expansionary fiscal policy. Clearly, we would keep income constant and reach balance of payments equilibrium by getting interest rates high enough. However, we can do better. We can use fiscal policy to get us all the way to full employment and use tight money, in the form of higher interest rates, to achieve balance of payments equilibrium. Thus we can get to point E with both internal and external balance.

The lesson we have just derived is that under fixed exchange rates, we should expand income through fiscal policy whenever there is unemployment and use tight money whenever there is a balance of payments deficit. The combination of policies moves us to both internal and external balance. With a situation like point E_4, we want to use the same principle, but the economic conditions are different. Here we have a surplus and unemployment. Accordingly, we need expansionary fiscal policy to achieve full employment and expansionary monetary policy to reduce interest rates. Point E_4 is actually *not* a dilemma situation, since any form of expansionary policy moves us in the right direction with respect to both targets.

We leave it to you to work through the remaining cases and note here merely the principle: Under fixed exchange rates and with capital mobility, we use monetary policy to achieve external balance and fiscal policy to achieve full employment. What is the experience with such a rule? There is little doubt that tight money, for balance of payments reasons, is the oldest remedy in the policy maker's medicine chest. Since monetary policy is a flexible tool, attainment of external balance in the short run through tight money is relatively easy.

Limitations of the Policy Mix

The argument for a fiscal-monetary policy mix to handle both internal and external balance problems is persuasive, but it overlooks three important limitations. The first problem is that fiscal policy may not be sufficiently flexible to implement the needed policy mix. The discussion of lags in Chapter 10 made the point that the inside lag for fiscal policy is quite long. If fiscal policy cannot be modified readily, then all the policy maker can do is control the balance of payments, *or* employment, through monetary policy. We are back in a dilemma situation, because there are two targets—internal and external balance—but only one instrument—monetary policy.

The second point is that a country will typically not be indifferent to the level of domestic interest rates. Even if fiscal policy were sufficiently flexible to implement the policy mix, it would still be true that the composition of domestic output would depend on the mix. Thus, a country that attempts an expansion in aggregate demand, together with tight money, effectively restricts the construction sector and investment spending in general. The notion of a policy mix with monetary policy devoted to the balance of payments therefore overlooks the fact that the interest rate determines the composition as well as the level of aggregate spending.

The final consideration concerns the composition of the balance of payments. Countries are not indifferent about the makeup of their balance of payments between the current account deficit and the capital account surplus. Even if the overall balance is in equilibrium so that one target is satisfied, there is still the problem that a capital account surplus or capital inflow means net external borrowing: our country's debts to foreigners are increasing. Those debts will eventually have to be repaid.

Under a system of fixed exchange rates, there are circumstances under which a country—much like an individual—will find it useful to borrow in order to finance, say, a transitory shortfall of export earnings. But continued large-scale borrowing from abroad is not consistent with a fixed exchange rate over long periods. Large-scale borrowing eventually places the country in a position where the interest payments to foreigners become a major burden. Faced with the prospect of continued foreign borrowing on a large scale in order to maintain its exchange rate fixed, a country would be well advised to implement adjustment policies that improve the current account balance.

Such policies would typically be a devaluation accompanied by restrictive monetary and/or fiscal policy to reduce domestic demand.

18-5 SUMMARY

1 The balance of payments accounts are a record of the international transactions of the economy. The current account records trade in goods and services as well as transfer payments. The capital account records purchases and sales of assets. Any transaction that gives rise to a payment by U.S. residents is a deficit item for the United States.
2 The overall balance of payments is the sum of the current and capital accounts. If the overall balance is in deficit, we have to make more payments to foreigners than they make to us. The foreign currency for making these payments is supplied by central banks.
3 Under fixed exchange rates, the central bank maintains constant the price of foreign currencies in terms of the domestic currency. It does this by buying and selling foreign exchange at that fixed exchange rate. For that purpose, it has to keep reserves of foreign currency.
4 Under floating or flexible exchange rates, the exchange rate may change from moment to moment. In a system of clean floating, the exchange rate is determined by supply and demand without central bank intervention to affect the rate. Under dirty floating, the central bank intervenes by buying and selling foreign exchange in an attempt to influence the exchange rate.

The remainder of the chapter studies the role of international trade in goods and assets under fixed exchange rates:

5 The introduction of trade in goods means that some of the demand for our output comes from abroad and that some spending by our residents is on foreign goods. There is equilibrium in the goods market when the demand for domestically produced goods is equal to the output of those goods.
6 In short-run equilibrium, the balance of trade may be in deficit. If there is no trade in assets, there may be a policy dilemma in that balanced trade and full employment cannot be attained merely through the manipulation of aggregate demand by fiscal and monetary policy. Expenditure switching policies that change the allocation of spending between imports and domestic goods are needed to solve the problem.
7 Over long periods, an automatic adjustment mechanism in the economy eventually leads to full employment at balanced trade under fixed exchange rates. A balance of trade deficit leads to a reduction in the domestic money stock, which leads to falling domestic prices that, given the foreign price level, switch spending away from imports and increase foreign demand for our goods. In the long run, domestic wages will also adjust to ensure full employment.
8 However, there are alternative mechanisms for achieving balanced trade

without going through an adjustment process involving falling domestic prices. A devaluation, combined with restrictive aggregate demand policies, can lead to balance of payments equilibrium from a situation of trade deficit at more than full employment.

9 The introduction of capital flows points to the effects of monetary and fiscal policy on the balance of payments through interest rate effects on capital flows. An increase in the domestic interest rate, relative to the world interest rate, leads to a capital inflow that can finance a balance of trade deficit.

10 Policy dilemmas can then be handled by combining restrictive monetary policies to improve the balance of payments through higher interest rates and capital inflows, with expansionary fiscal policy to increase domestic employment.

11 However, such policies cannot be used in the long run to maintain balanced payments at the fixed exchange rate. The interest burden of the policies would, in the long run, be excessive, and the exchange rate could not be maintained. If balance of payments deficits are not temporary, then adjustment policies, such as devaluation with accompanying monetary and fiscal changes, have to be undertaken to correct the imbalance.

KEY TERMS

Openness
Fixed exchange rates
Flexible exchange rates
Balance of payments
Current account
Capital account
Trade balance
Intervention
Clean floating
Dirty (managed) floating
Devaluation
Revaluation
Currency depreciation
Currency appreciation
Sterilization
Internal and external balance
Expenditure switching policies
Expenditure reducing (or increasing) policies
Repercussion effect
Classical adjustment process
Monetary approach to the balance of payments
Financing of deficits
Adjustment of deficits
Targets and instruments of policy
Capital mobility
Policy mix

PROBLEMS

1 This problem formalizes some of the questions about income and trade balance determination in the open economy. (Before doing it, read the Appendix to this chapter.) We assume, as a simplification, that the interest rate is given and equal to $i = i_0$. In terms of Figures 18-3 and 18-4, the monetary authorities hold constant the interest rate so that the *LM* curve is flat at the level $i = i_0$.

We assume aggregate spending by domestic residents is

$$A = \overline{A} + cY - hi$$

Import spending is given by

$$Q = \overline{Q} + mY$$

where $\overline{Q}$ is autonomous import spending. Exports are given and equal to

$$X = \overline{X}$$

(a) What is the total demand for domestic goods? The balance of trade?
(b) What is the equilibrium level of income?
(c) What is the balance of trade at that equilibrium level of income?
(d) What is the effect of an increase in exports on the equilibrium level of income? What is the multiplier?
(e) What is the effect of increased exports on the trade balance?

2 Suppose that, in problem 1,

$\overline{A} = 400$ $\quad c = 0.8$ $\quad h = 30$ $\quad i_0 = 5$ (percent) $\quad \overline{Q} = 0$
$m = 0.2$ $\quad \overline{X} = 250$

(a) Calculate the equilibrium level of income.
(b) Calculate the balance of trade.
(c) Calculate the open economy multiplier, that is, the effect of an increase in $\overline{A}$ on equilibrium output.
(d) Assume there is a reduction in export demand of $\Delta\overline{X} = 1$ (billion). By how much does income change? By how much does the trade balance worsen?
(e) How much does a 1 percentage point increase in the interest rate (from 5 to 6 percent) improve the trade balance? Explain why the trade balance improves when the interest rate rises.
(f) What policies can the country pursue to offset the impact of reduced exports on domestic income and employment as well as the trade balance?

3 It has been suggested that the smaller the marginal propensity to import, the larger the cost of adjustment to external imbalance. What is the reason for this argument? Do you agree?

4 It is sometimes said that a central bank is a necessary condition for a balance of payments deficit. What is the explanation for this argument?

5 Consider a country that is in a position of full employment and balanced trade. Which of the following types of disturbance can be remedied with standard aggregate demand tools of stabilization? Indicate in each case the impact on external and internal balance as well as the appropriate policy response.
(a) A loss of export markets
(b) A reduction in saving and a corresponding increase in demand for domestic goods
(c) An increase in government spending
(d) A shift in demand from imports to domestic goods
(e) A reduction in imports with a corresponding increase in saving.

6 (a) Use the formula $1/(m + s)$ for the foreign trade multiplier (see the Appendix) to discuss the impact on the trade balance of an increase in autonomous domestic spending.
(b) Comment on the proposition that the more open the economy, the smaller the domestic income expansion.

7 Use the central bank balance sheet to show how a balance of payments deficit affects the stock of high-powered money under fixed exchange rates. Show, too, how sterilization operations work.

8 Discuss the manner in which income, price adjustments, and money supply adjustments interact in leading the economy ultimately to full employment and external balance. Choose as an example the case where a country experiences a permanent increase in exports.

9 In relation to external imbalance, a distinction is frequently made between imbalances that should be "financed" and those that should be "adjusted." Give examples of disturbances that give rise, respectively, to imbalances that require adjustment and those that should more appropriately be financed.

10 Consider a world with some capital mobility: The home country's capital account improves as domestic interest rates rise relative to the world rate of interest. Initially, the home country is in internal and external balance. (Draw the IS, LM, and $BoP = 0$ schedules.) Assume now an increase in the rate of interest abroad.
   (*a*) Show the effect of the foreign interest rate increase on the BoP schedule.
   (*b*) What policy response would immediately restore internal and external balance?
   (*c*) If the authorities took no action, what would be the adjustment process along the lines described by the "monetary approach to the balance of payments"? (You may refer here to your answer to problem 8.)

*11 Consider again the case of a country that faces some capital mobility. What monetary-fiscal policy mix should be pursued to offset the following disturbances?
   (*a*) A transitory gain in exports
   (*b*) A permanent gain in exports
   (*c*) A decline in autonomous spending
   (*d*) An increased rate of capital outflow (at each level of domestic interest rates)

*12 This question is concerned with the repercussion effects of a domestic expansion once we recognize that as a consequence output abroad will expand. Suppose that at home there is an increase in autonomous spending, $\Delta\bar{A}$, that falls entirely on domestic goods. (Assume constant interest rates throughout this problem.)
   (*a*) What is the resulting effect on income, disregarding repercussion effects? What is the impact on our imports, ΔQ?
   (*b*) Using the result for the increase in imports, we now ask what happens abroad. Our increase in imports appears to foreign countries as an increase in their exports and therefore as an increase in demand for their goods. In response, their output expands. Assuming the foreign marginal propensity to save is s^* and the foreign propensity to import is m^*, by how much will a foreign country's income expand as a result of an increase in its exports?
   (*c*) Now combine the pieces by writing the familiar equation for equilibrium in the domestic goods market: change in supply, ΔY, equals the total change in demand, $\Delta\bar{A} + \Delta X - m\,\Delta Y + (1 - s)\,\Delta Y$, or

$$\Delta Y = \frac{1}{s + m}(\Delta\bar{A} + \Delta X)$$

   Noting that foreign demand ΔX depends on our increased imports, we can replace ΔX with the answer to 12(*b*) to obtain a general expression for the multiplier with repercussions.
   (*d*) Substitute your answer for 12(*b*) in the formula for the change in foreign demand, $\Delta X = m^*\,\Delta Y^*$.
   (*e*) Calculate the complete change in our income, including repercussion effects. Now compare your result with the small-country case where repercussion effects are omitted. What difference do repercussion effects make? Is our income expansion larger or smaller with repercussion effects?
   (*f*) Consider the trade balance effect of a domestic expansion with and without reper-

cussion effects. Is the trade deficit larger or smaller once repercussion effects are taken into account?

APPENDIX

This Appendix briefly shows how to extend the simple Keynesian model to the open economy. We derive expressions for the equilibrium level of income, the foreign trade multiplier, and the trade balance.

Aggregate demand, in the simplest case, depends on autonomous spending and on income: $A = \overline{A} + cY$, where c is the marginal propensity to consume *all* goods, domestic plus imports. But there is also an equation describing spending on imports, Q. Import spending depends on some autonomous level and on income: $Q = \overline{Q} + mY$. Here m is the marginal propensity to spend on imports or the fraction of an extra dollar of income that is spent on imports. Finally, exports are taken as exogenous at the level $\overline{X}$. With these assumptions we can look at the equilibrium in the market for domestic goods. Equilibrium requires that output equals demand for domestic goods:

$$Y = A + X - Q = \overline{A} + cY + \overline{X} - \overline{Q} - mY \tag{A1}$$

Collecting terms and remembering that the sum of the propensity to consume (all goods) and to save is one, $1 = c + s$, we have

$$Y = \frac{\overline{A} + \overline{X} - \overline{Q}}{s + m} \tag{A2}$$

Thus equilibrium income depends positively on the autonomous levels of domestic demand and exports and negatively on autonomous import spending $\overline{Q}$. The multiplier now is given by

$$\text{Open economy multiplier} \equiv 1/(s + m) \tag{A3}$$

The smaller the marginal propensity to consume, the larger the multiplier. If a large part of an extra dollar income is spent on imports rather than domestic goods, then induced demand at home will be relatively small and so will be the cumulative income expansion brought about by, say, a fiscal expansion.

We can use the expression for equilibrium income to calculate the trade balance. Using the definition of the trade balance, $NX \equiv X - Q$, and substituting import demand, we have

$$NX = \overline{X} - \overline{Q} - mY = (\overline{X} - \overline{Q})\frac{s}{s + m} - \frac{m}{s + m}\overline{A} \tag{A4}$$

where we have substituted for Y from (A2) and collected terms.

You should now use (A2) and (A4) to check the results in Table 18-3.

19

TRADE AND CAPITAL FLOWS UNDER FLEXIBLE EXCHANGE RATES

From 1946 to 1973 most countries had exchange rates that were fixed in terms of the dollar. This was the *Bretton Woods system* that at the end of World War II replaced the unstable exchange rates and restrictive trade policies of the 1930s. Under the Bretton Woods system countries fixed the exchange rates among currencies. This was achieved by specifying the rate at which the central bank would buy and sell dollars in the foreign exchange market, for example, DM4/$. These exchange rates were to remain fixed over time, or at least change only infrequently.

A system of fixed exchange rates requires that countries pursue very similar policies so that prices of goods in different countries do not get out of line. Otherwise goods in one country become cheaper than in another country, and everyone wants to buy from the country where goods are cheaper. To avoid such a growing discrepancy, inflation rates in different countries have to stay closely in line.

But that was not the case in the late 1960s, when U.S. inflation increased significantly without a similar increase abroad, especially in Germany. The United States was losing competitiveness (its goods were becoming increasingly expensive for foreigners to buy), and Germany was gaining. The difference in inflation rates led to the belief that the Deutsche mark would be revalued (for example, from DM4/$ to DM3/$). That way

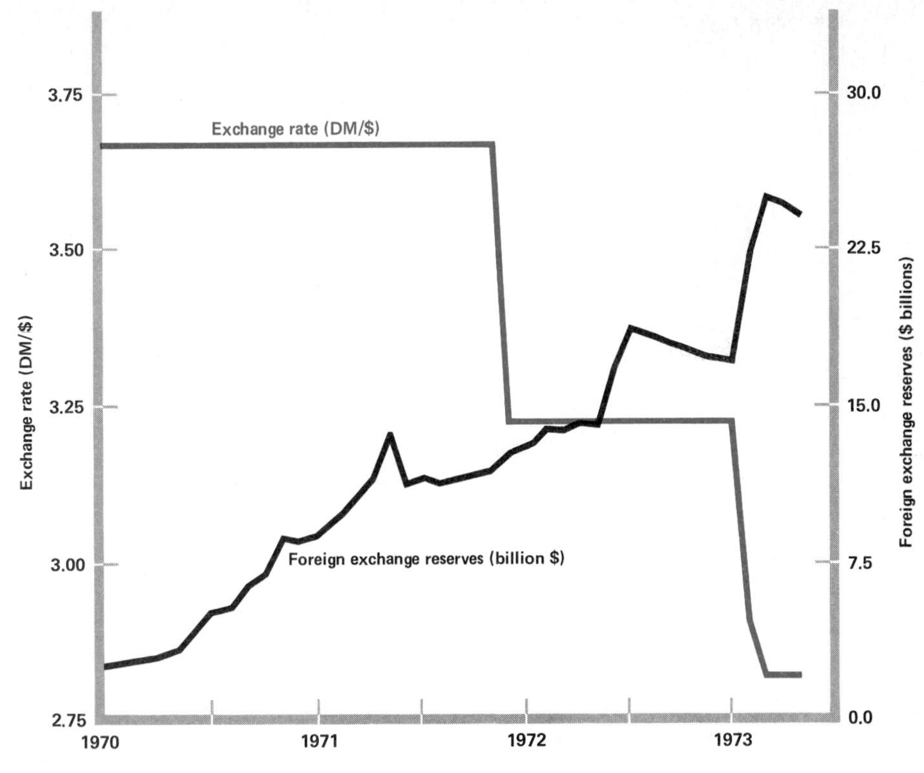

FIGURE 19-1 THE DEUTSCHE MARK/DOLLAR EXCHANGE RATE AND GERMAN FOREIGN EXCHANGE RESERVES, 1970–1973.

the prices of German goods would rise relative to the prices of American goods, and trade between the countries would come closer to being balanced.

Investors expecting a revaluation of the DM favored holding DM assets rather than dollar assets. That way they would benefit if there was a change in the exchange rate. For instance, anyone using $1 million to buy DM4 million worth of German bonds before the revaluation could sell them after a revaluation for $1.333 million — a nice profit. The speculation in favor of the mark and against the dollar meant that capital was flowing from the United States toward Germany. Germany's balance of payments showed a large surplus, and the central bank was forced to buy large amounts of dollars as it kept the exchange rate fixed. Germany's continued purchases of dollars grew into increasingly large holdings, as Figure 19-1 shows. At the same time the German inflation rate began to increase as aggregate demand in all countries shifted toward the relatively low-priced German goods. This was called "imported inflation."

To German policy makers, forced to buy dollars and facing imported inflation, the fixed rate system became more and more difficult to accept and, because of *speculation*, increasingly difficult to maintain. Speculation involves buying an asset cheaply in the expectation that it can be resold dearly. Speculators bear the risk that they will lose their money if their predictions turn out to be wrong.[1]

But there was little risk of loss in the case of the dollar-DM exchange rate. Speculators forced a one-way bet. The Deutsche mark could only be *revalued* against the dollar. There was no risk that it could be *devalued*. No one could be certain when revaluation would take place, but anybody who was willing to be patient could be almost certain to win if she placed her bets on a Deutsche mark revaluation. Capital therefore flowed into Germany, and in defending the overvalued dollar and the undervalued DM, the Bundesbank (German central bank) bought up huge amounts of dollars.

Figure 19-1 shows the stock of dollars accumulated by the Bundesbank. From less than $3 billion at the beginning of 1970 it grew to more than $25 billion in 1973. But the problems of the fixed rate system were not limited to rapid increases in foreign exchange reserves. In buying dollars in the foreign exchange market, countries increased their own money supplies—because they bought the dollars with their own currencies.

The monetary expansion increased aggregate demand and inflationary pressures in foreign countries. At the same time in the United States the outflow of dollars forced the Fed to pursue a tighter monetary policy than it would otherwise have chosen. The system could not last. On three occasions the dollar-DM rate was changed. A first revaluation of the DM or devaluation of the dollar occurred in 1969, a second occurred in 1971, and a third in 1973. Every time, the adjustment lasted only a short period before investors again saw an undervalued DM or an overvalued dollar and once again speculated against the dollar. In May 1973, after a last unsuccessful attempt to keep exchange rates fixed, the fixed rate system broke down, and the world economy moved to *flexible exchange rates* between the dollar and other important currencies such as the yen or the DM.[2]

Under flexible exchange rates, central banks do not undertake to buy and sell foreign exchange at a fixed price. They may, though, intervene (buy or sell foreign exchange) in the foreign exchange market to influence the exchange rate. We shall see in this chapter how a system of flexible exchange rates works. Once we have understood the macroeconomics of flexible rates, we turn to the reasons why a central bank may be tempted to try to make rates move less than they would in a market without any government intervention.

[1] In speculation, for every winner there must be a loser, either another speculator or the central bank. That means speculation is risky. Keynes is said to have lost two fortunes and made three, speculating on German currency during the hyperinflation of the 1920s. Irving Fisher is said to have speculated on the stock market in the 1930s, making two fortunes and losing three. For a good but technical text on finance, see K. Garbade, *Securities Markets* (New York: McGraw Hill, 1982).

[2] In Europe exchange rates have remained fixed (with occasional adjustments) among currencies such as the DM and the Dutch guilder, the Italian lira, and the French franc. The arrangement today is called the *European monetary system*, or EMS for short.

We start with a model of output and exchange rate determination. Our discussion extends the analysis of Chapter 18, where we looked at income determination in an open economy. In that chapter, we assumed capital mobility, sticky prices, demand-determined output, and fixed exchange rates. Here, we maintain all these assumptions except the last and now allow the exchange rate to be flexible. Our analysis proceeds as follows: First, we review the role of exchange rates in determining the relative prices of imports and domestically produced goods and thereby the demand for domestic output. Next, we develop the equilibrium conditions in the goods and money markets and in the external balance. Finally, we use our model to show the implications of monetary and real disturbances for the level of output and the exchange rate. These results are directly compared with those for the fixed exchange rate world. After making the comparison, we proceed in the following sections to alternative assumptions about capital mobility and to a discussion of longer-term adjustments of prices and output.

Exchange Rates and Competitiveness

A central piece of macroeconomics under flexible exchange rates is the role of the exchange rate in affecting a country's competitiveness in the world goods markets and therefore the world demand for the country's goods. We measure *competitiveness* by the price charged by a country's trading partners relative to its own prices. A country gains in competitiveness if the price of its goods falls relative to those of the competitors. Thus, as a country gains competitiveness, its goods become cheaper relative to those produced in other countries.

We now define the relative price or competitiveness more precisely. Let P be the price of goods we produce—say, our GNP deflator—and P^* the price of foreign goods. Our price is measured in dollars per unit of output; their price in, say, DM per unit of their good. The exchange rate e is the price in dollars of one Deutsche mark. With these definitions we measure our competitiveness by the ratio of their prices relative to our own, both expressed in the same currency:

$$\text{Competitiveness} = eP^*/P \tag{1}$$

From the definition we see that we become more competitive if their prices (measured in dollars) eP^* rise relative to our own prices P. It does not matter whether their prices in dollars rise because there is inflation abroad (P^* rises), or whether we pay more per unit of foreign exchange (e increases), or whether prices at home decline (P falls). Whichever happens, or any combination, a rise in eP^*/P means that we are more competitive.

A common measure of competitiveness is the *terms of trade.* Terms of trade is defined as the ratio of the prices of a country's imports relative to its exports, both measured in the same currency. We can interpret eP^*/P as the terms of trade, with eP^* our import price and P the price of the goods we export. The crucial point about competitiveness or the terms of trade is the following: When we become more competitive, world demand shifts away from foreign goods toward our goods. Our exports increase, and our imports decline, and therefore our trade balance, or net exports, improves.

COMPETITIVENESS AND NET EXPORTS

In Equation (2) we summarize the discussion by writing the trade balance, or net exports NX, as a function of domestic income and foreign income and of the relative price. We take foreign income as given.

$$NX = NX(Y, Y^*, eP^*/P) \tag{2}$$

We show the role of competitiveness in relation to trade flows in Figure 19-2. We measure competitiveness on the vertical axis and net exports on the horizontal axis. An increase in competitiveness leads to an increase in net exports. This is shown by the positively sloped NX schedule which is drawn for given domestic and foreign incomes. The reason for the positive slope is that we can export more when we become more competitive because world demand shifts away from foreign goods toward our goods. At the same time we buy less imports and more domestic goods instead. For both reasons net exports rise.[3] The diagram shows that there is a deficit when competitiveness

[3] We assume that elasticities are large enough so that an increase in import prices leads to a reduction in import spending. We return to this question below under the subheading "Relative Prices and the Trade Balance: The J Curve."

FIGURE 19-2 NET EXPORTS AND COMPETITIVENESS. Competitiveness is measured by trading partners' prices relative to our own. A rise in competitiveness, an increase in eP^*/P, shifts demand toward our goods and away from foreign goods. Exports rise, and spending on imports declines. Thus net exports increase as our competitiveness improves. At high levels of competitiveness, other things equal, there is a trade surplus; at low levels a deficit.

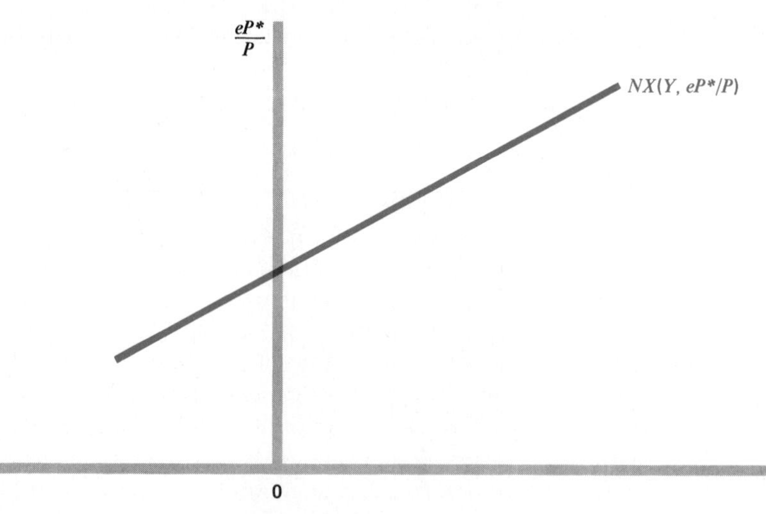

is low. At high levels of competitiveness, exports are higher and import spending is lower, and accordingly, other things equal, there is a surplus.

Changes in either prices or exchange rates can lead to changes in competitiveness. We concentrate now on the case where prices are given in each country, or P and P^* are given. That leaves the exchange rate as the only variable to influence competitiveness. The case is not altogether unrealistic because exchange rates do change frequently and sometimes rapidly, while prices are sticky in the short term.

Exchange rates therefore do have important effects on competitiveness, at least in the short run. With the assumption that prices are given, we have very simple relations between exchange rate movements and changes in competitiveness. An exchange rate depreciation leads to a gain in home country competitiveness, and an exchange appreciation leads to a loss in home competitiveness. To give an example, if we have to pay 20 percent more to buy a Deutsche mark, then for given prices in Germany we have to pay 20 percent more for German goods. German goods have become 20 percent less competitive, or our goods have become 20 percent more competitive.

We have now seen that exchange rates can affect competitiveness and thereby influence trade flows. The next question is how exchange rates themselves are determined and what role they play in the economy. To analyze that, we extend our simple *IS-LM* of model to include trade.

Relative Prices, Net Exports, and Demand for Domestic Output

The demand for domestic output comes from both domestic residents and the rest of the world. We showed in Chapter 18 that we can write demand for domestic goods as the sum of total spending by domestic residents (including spending on imports), A, plus net exports or the trade surplus, NX. Domestic aggregate spending depends on interest rates i and income Y. Net exports [Equation (2)] depend on foreign income, which we take as given, domestic income, and relative prices, eP^*/P.

Output is assumed to be determined by demand, and prices are given. Equilibrium requires that output equal the demand for domestic goods or, equivalently, aggregate spending plus the trade surplus:

$$Y = A(i, Y) + NX(Y, eP^*/P) \tag{3}$$

We show in Figure 19-3 the *IS* schedule that represents goods market equilibrium, given an exchange rate of, say, e_0. What happens to the *IS* schedule if the exchange rate depreciates?

Exchange depreciation will, under our assumptions, raise the relative price of imports or lower the relative price of our own goods. With our own goods more competitive, there is increased net demand arising from increased net exports. Thus, for a given interest rate and income level, exchange depreciation must lead to an excess demand for our goods. To restore equilibrium, output would have to rise or interest rates would have to increase. In Figure 19-3, we accordingly show that exchange depreciation shifts the *IS*

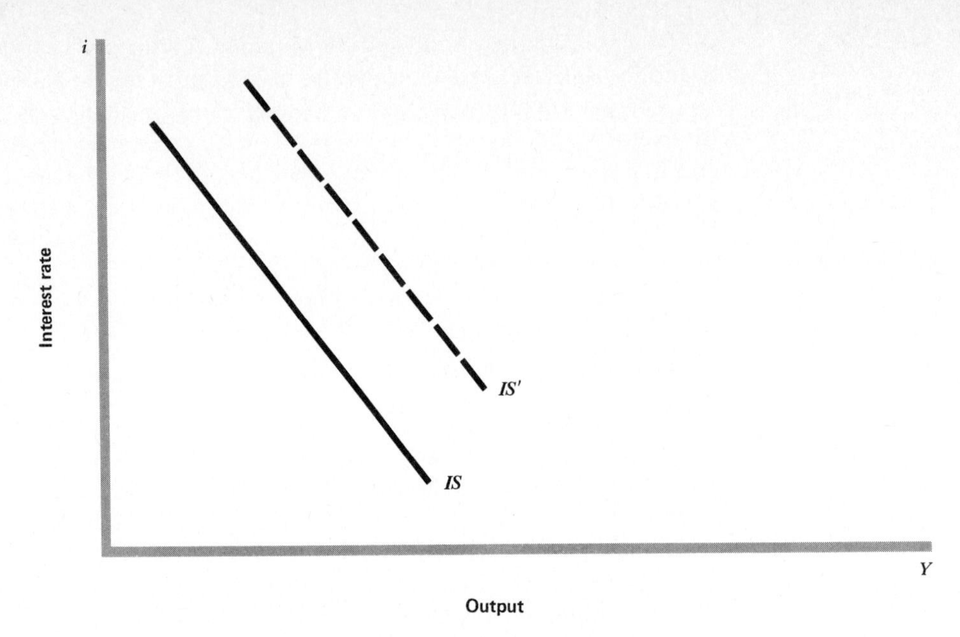

FIGURE 19-3 EFFECT OF EXCHANGE RATE DEPRECIATION ON THE IS CURVE. Each *IS* curve is drawn for a given relative price eP^*/P. A depreciation which makes us more competitive and thus increases aggregate demand shifts the *IS* curve to the right. The shift is larger the larger the response of the trade balance to a change in competitiveness and the larger the multiplier.

schedule up and to the right. The schedule *IS'* is drawn for a higher relative price of imports. Conversely, an appreciation and fall in import prices would, of course, lead to an excess supply of our goods and a downward shift of the *IS* schedule.

We now develop the remaining parts of our model of exchange rate and output determination, namely, the money market equilibrium condition and the balance of payments.

Monetary Equilibrium and Payments Balance

The condition of monetary equilibrium is the familiar *LM* schedule of earlier chapters. Given prices P and nominal money M, we have a given real money stock, M/P. Equilibrium in the money market requires that the demand for real money balances equals the existing real money stock:

$$\frac{M}{P} = L(i, Y) \tag{4}$$

Real money demand in (4) is a decreasing function of the interest rate and an increasing function of the level of income. The *LM* schedule is shown in Figure 19-4 for a given real money stock.

We draw on the discussion of capital mobility in Chapter 18 to develop our balance of payments equation. The balance of payments surplus *BP* is equal to net exports *NX* plus the net rate of capital inflow *CF*.

$$BP = NX(Y, eP^*/P) + CF(i - i^*) \tag{5}$$

We have already introduced the fact that the trade balance depends on income and relative prices. We now have added the rate of capital flow as a function of the difference between our interest rate, i, and the given interest rate abroad, i^*. If our interest rate increases relative to that in the rest of the world, then there will be a net capital inflow.

For the present, we make the simplifying assumption that capital mobility is very high, so that we can have payments balance only at the world interest rate. If our interest rate were lower, there would be large-scale capital outflows swamping any current account surplus. Conversely, with a higher interest rate than the rest of the world, the capital inflows would swamp any deficit in the current account. We represent this assumption of high capital mobility in Figure 19-4 by a flat *BB* schedule. Points above it correspond to a balance of payments surplus and points below it to a deficit.

FIGURE 19-4 EQUILIBRIUM OF THE GOODS AND MONEY MARKETS AND THE BALANCE OF PAYMENTS. The *LM* schedule is familiar from the closed economy. The *IS* schedule is drawn for a given exchange rate. The schedule *BB* shows equilibrium in the balance of payments with capital flows financing trade imbalances. The schedule is horizontal in the case of perfect capital mobility where any divergence of home interest rates from those abroad leads to unlimited capital flows. Only at an interest rate $i = i^*$ can the balance of payments then be in equilibrium.

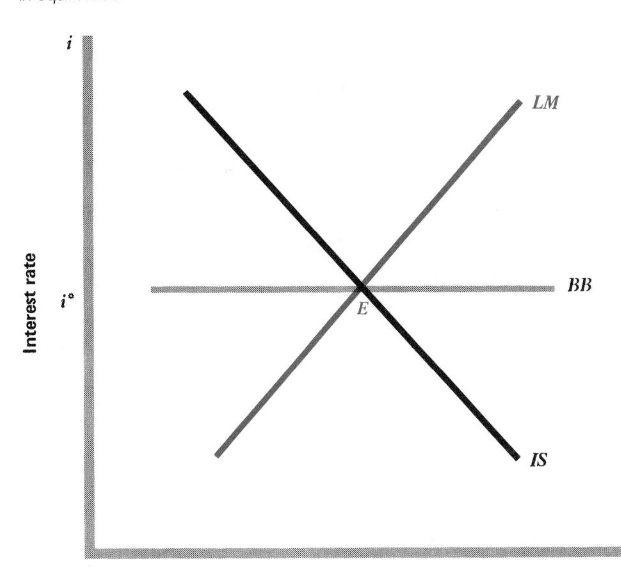

Adjustment to a Real Disturbance

We have now completed our model, represented by Equations (2) through (5) and Figure 19-4, and can ask how the economy will adjust to disturbances. In particular, we want to know how various changes affect our level of output, the interest rate, and the exchange rate. The first change we look at is an exogenous rise in the world demand for our goods, or an increase in exports. The change in export demand is a real disturbance to the economy, or a disturbance that originates in the goods market.

Starting from an initial equilibrium at point E in Figure 19-5, we see that the increase in foreign demand implies an excess demand for our goods. At the initial interest rate, exchange rate, and output level, demand for our goods now exceeds the available supply. For goods market equilibrium, at the initial interest rate and exchange rate, we require a higher level of output. Accordingly, the *IS* schedule shifts out and to the right.

FIGURE 19-5 EFFECTS OF AN INCREASE IN THE DEMAND FOR EXPORTS. A rise in foreign demand for our goods, at the initial exchange rate and interest rate at point E, creates an excess demand for goods. The *IS* schedule shifts out to *IS'*, and the new goods and money market equilibrium is at point E'. But at E' our interest rate exceeds that abroad. Capital will tend to flow into our country in response to the increased interest rate, and the resulting balance of payments surplus leads to currency appreciation. The appreciation means that we become less competitive. The *IS* schedule starts shifting back as a result of the appreciation, and the process continues until the initial equilibrium at E is reached again. In the end, increased exports (or a fiscal expansion) do not change output. They simply lead to currency appreciation and thereby to an offsetting change in net exports.

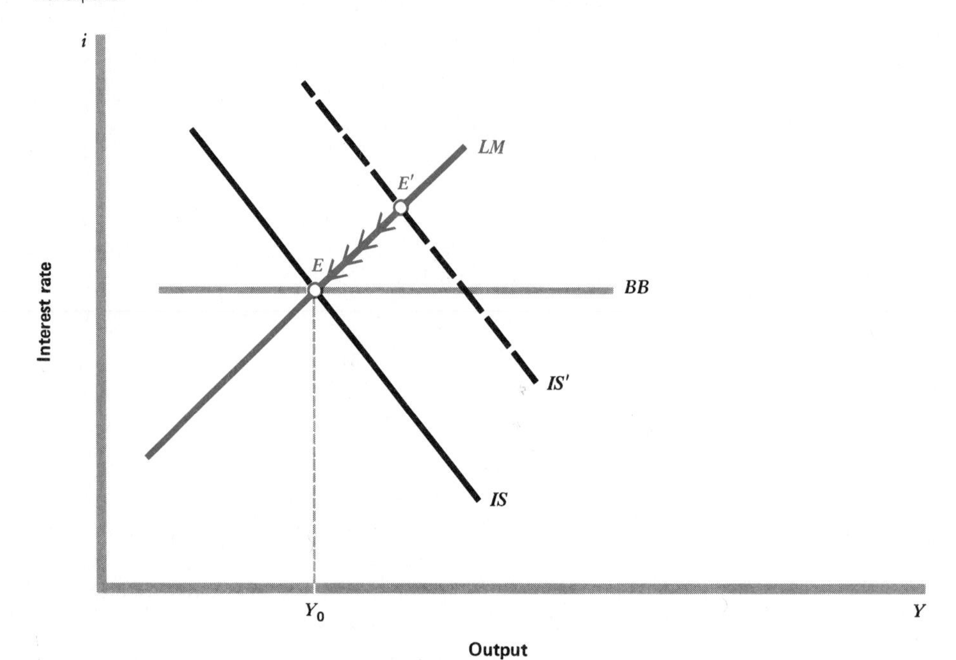

Now consider for a moment point E', where the goods and money markets clear. Here output has increased to meet the increased demand. The rise in income has increased money demand and thus raised equilibrium interest rates. But is point E' an equilibrium? It is not, because the balance of payments is not in equilibrium. In fact, we would not reach point E' at all. The tendency for the economy to move in that direction, as we show now, will bring about an exchange rate appreciation that will take us all the way back to the initial equilibrium at E.

THE ADJUSTMENT PROCESS

Suppose, then, that the increase in foreign demand takes place and that, in response, there is a tendency for output and income to increase. The induced increase in money demand will raise interest rates and thus will bring us out of line with interest rates internationally. The resulting capital inflows immediately put pressure on the exchange rate. The capital inflow causes our currency to appreciate.

The exchange appreciation means, of course, that import prices fall and that domestic goods become relatively more expensive. Demand shifts away from domestic goods, and net exports decline. In terms of Figure 19-5, the appreciation implies that the *IS* schedule shifts back from *IS'* to the left. Next, we have to ask how far the exchange appreciation will go and to what extent it will therefore dampen the expansionary effect of increased net exports.

The exchange rate will keep appreciating as long as our interest rate exceeds the world level. This implies that the exchange appreciation must continue until the *IS* schedule has shifted back all the way to its initial position. Thus adjustment is shown by the arrows along the *LM* schedule. Only when we return to point E will output and income have reached a level consistent with monetary equilibrium at the world rate of interest.

We have now shown that under conditions of perfect capital mobility, an expansion in exports has no lasting effect on equilibrium output. With perfect capital mobility the tendency for interest rates to rise, as a result of the increase in export demand, leads to currency appreciation and thus to a complete offset of the increase in exports. Once we return to point E, net exports are back to their initial level. The exchange rate has, of course, appreciated. Imports will increase as a consequence of the appreciation, and the initial expansion in exports is in part offset by the appreciation of our exchange rate.

FISCAL POLICY

We can extend the usefulness of this analysis by recognizing that it is valid not only for an increase in exports. The same analysis applies to a fiscal expansion. A tax cut or an increase in government spending would lead to an expansion in demand in just the same way as increased exports do. Again, the tendency for interest rates to rise leads to appreciation and therefore to a fall in exports and increased imports. There is, accordingly, complete crowding out here. The crowding out takes place not as in Chapter 5 because higher interest rates

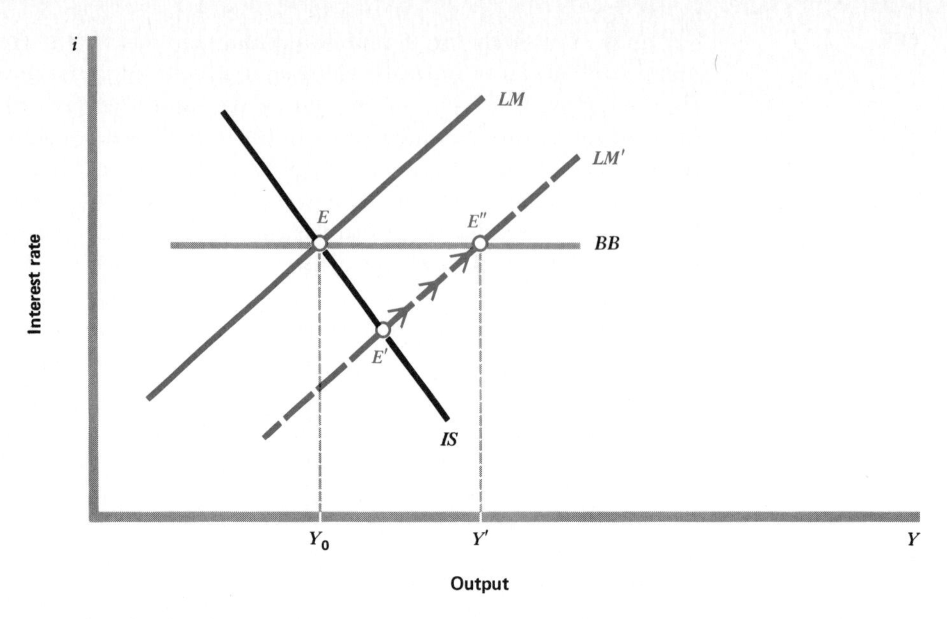

FIGURE 19-6 EFFECTS OF AN INCREASE IN THE MONEY STOCK. A monetary expansion shifts the LM schedule to LM'. At point E' the goods and money markets clear, but our interest rate is below the world level. Therefore capital will tend to flow out, the balance of payments goes into deficit, and the exchange rate depreciates. The depreciation means that we become more competitive. Net exports rise, and therefore the IS curve shifts out and to the right. The process continues until we reach point E''. Interest rates are again at the world level, and the depreciation has led to a higher level of income. Monetary policy thus works by increasing net exports.

reduce investment, but because the exchange appreciation reduces net exports.

The important lesson here is that real disturbances to demand do not affect equilibrium output under flexible rates with perfect capital mobility. We can drive the lesson home by comparing a fiscal expansion under flexible rates with the results we derived for the fixed rate case. In Chapter 18, we showed that with fixed rates, fiscal expansion under conditions of capital mobility is highly effective in raising equilibrium output. For flexible rates, by contrast, a fiscal expansion does not change equilibrium output. Instead, it produces an offsetting exchange rate appreciation and a shift in the composition of domestic demand toward domestic goods and away from net exports.

We turn next to the analysis of a monetary disturbance.

Adjustment to a Monetary Disturbance

We now show that under flexible exchange rates, an increase in the money stock leads to an increase in income and a depreciation of the exchange rate. The analysis uses Figure 19-6. We start from an initial position at point E and consider an increase in the nominal quantity of money, M. Since prices are given, we have an increase in the real money stock, M/P. At E there will be an excess supply of real balances. To restore equilibrium, interest rates would have to be lower or income would have to be larger. Accordingly, the LM schedule shifts down and to the right to LM'.

We ask once again whether point E' is the new equilibrium. At E', goods and money markets are in equilibrium (at the initial exchange rate), but it is clear that interest rates have fallen below the world level. Capital outflows will therefore put pressure on the exchange rate. The exchange depreciation caused by the low level of interest rates implies that import prices increase, domestic goods become more competitive, and, as a result, demand for our output expands. The exchange depreciation therefore shifts the IS curve out and to the right. As the arrows indicate, exchange depreciation continues until the relative price of domestic goods has fallen enough to raise demand and output to the level indicated by point E''. Only at E'' do we have goods and money market equilibrium compatible with the world rate of interest. Consequently, there is no further tendency for exchange rates and relative prices, and hence demand, to change.[4]

We have now shown that a monetary expansion leads to an increase in output and a depreciation of the exchange rate under flexible rates. One way of thinking about this result is that with P fixed, an increase in M increases M/P. The demand for real balances is, from Equation (4), equal to $L(i, Y)$. Since i cannot differ from the world rate of interest, Y has to rise to equate the demand for money to the supply. The exchange depreciation raises net exports, and that increase in net exports, in turn, sustains the higher level of output and employment. One interesting implication of our analysis, then, is the proposition that monetary expansion improves the current account through the induced depreciation.

How do our results compare with those of a fixed exchange rate world? We argued in Chapter 18 that under fixed rates, the monetary authorities cannot control the nominal money stock and that an attempt to expand money will merely lead to a reserve loss as the central bank attempts to prevent the tendency for the exchange rate to depreciate in response to declining interest rates. Under flexible rates, by contrast, the central bank does not intervene, and so the money stock increase is *not* reversed in the foreign exchange market. The depreciation and expansion in output actually do take place, given the assumed sticky prices. The fact that the central bank *can* control the money stock under flexible rates is one of the most important aspects of that exchange rate system.

Beggar-Thy-Neighbor Policy and Competitive Depreciation

We extend the analysis of the fixed price variable employment model with a brief discussion of the international implications of exchange depreciation

[4] In the problem set at the end of this chapter we ask you to show that the current account improves between E and E'', even though the increased level of income increases imports.

and changes in net exports. We showed that a monetary expansion in the home country leads to exchange depreciation, an increase in net exports, and therefore an increase in output and employment. But our increased net exports correspond to a deterioration in the trade balance abroad. The domestic depreciation shifts demand from foreign goods toward domestic goods. Abroad, output and employment therefore decline. It is for this reason that the depreciation-induced change in the trade balance has been called a *beggar-thy-neighbor policy*—it is a way of exporting unemployment or of creating domestic employment at the expense of the rest of the world.

The recognition that exchange depreciation is mainly a way of shifting demand from one country to another, rather than changing the level of world demand, is important. It implies that exchange rate adjustment can be a useful policy when countries find themselves in different stages of a business cycle—for example, one in a boom (with overemployment) and the other in a recession. In that event, a depreciation by the country experiencing a recession would shift world demand in that direction and thus work to reduce divergences from full employment in each country.

By contrast, when countries' business cycles are highly synchronized, such as in the 1930s or in the aftermath of the oil shock in 1973, exchange rate movements will not contribute much toward world full employment. The problem is then one of the level of total world spending being deficient or excessive while exchange rate movements affect only the allocation of a *given* world demand between countries. Nevertheless, from the point of view of an individual country, exchange depreciation works to attract world demand and raise domestic output. If every country tried to depreciate to attract world demand, we would have *competitive depreciation* and a shifting around of world demand rather than an increase in the world level of spending. Coordinated monetary and/or fiscal policies are needed to increase demand and output in each country.

* Imperfect Capital Mobility

The case of perfect capital mobility is extreme, and it probably overstates the speed with which capital moves internationally in response to interest rate differentials. It is therefore important to consider the effects of more moderate capital mobility, or *imperfect capital mobility*. In this case, the rate of capital flows increases as the international interest differential increases, but it remains finite. In equilibrium, interest rate differentials are possible. The larger the equilibrium differential, the larger the associated capital flow and therefore the current account imbalance.

How would monetary and fiscal policy work in a world of imperfect capital mobility? We leave as an exercise at the end of the chapter the demonstration of the following results: First, a fiscal expansion at home raises our interest rate and increases our income. With the higher interest rate, there will be an increased inflow of capital. This implies a deterioration in the current account, since the sum of the current and capital accounts is zero.

However, the current account deteriorates by less than the fiscal expansion. There is less than full crowding out, and hence, income rises.

In the case of a monetary expansion, our interest rate falls, income rises, and the current account must improve. We know that the current account must improve since the lower interest rate implies increased capital outflows which, for payments to balance, must be offset by an improvement in the current account.

The case of imperfect capital mobility clearly qualifies our earlier results. Now both monetary and fiscal policies are effective and the extent to which fiscal policy can affect income depends on the extent to which changes in interest differentials affect capital flows.

Summary

So far, we have studied the role of exchange rates in a world of fixed prices. In this setting, movements in exchange rates change the relative prices of foreign versus domestic goods. An exchange depreciation both raises foreign demand for our goods and moves our own demand away from imports toward domestic goods. The exchange rate thus plays a central role in the determination of macroeconomic equilibrium.

An examination of real and monetary disturbances under flexible exchange rates, fixed prices, and perfect capital mobility gave us the following results, summarized in Table 19-1.

1 A fiscal expansion leaves output unchanged. The fiscal expansion tends to increase income and raise interest rates. The tendency for interest rates to rise leads to appreciation of the exchange rate as capital is attracted from abroad. The appreciation, by lowering import prices, shifts demand away from our goods and thus offsets the expansionary effect of fiscal policy.
2 This result is the opposite of that derived under fixed exchange rates. The difference results from the fact that under flexible rates, the money stock is exogenous and is kept fixed when fiscal policy changes, while under fixed rates, exchange rate stabilization makes money endogenous and thus accommodates the fiscal expansion.

TABLE 19-1 THE EFFECTS OF MONETARY AND FISCAL POLICY UNDER PERFECT CAPITAL MOBILITY

	Fixed rates	Flexible rates
Monetary expansion	No output change; reserve losses equal to money increase	Output expansion; trade balance improves; exchange depreciation
Fiscal expansion	Output expansion; trade balance worsens	No output change; reduced net exports; exchange appreciation

3 For a monetary expansion, conclusions were also opposite to those for fixed rates. A monetary expansion leads to an increase in income and to exchange depreciation. The tendency for interest rates to fall as a consequence of monetary expansion leads to a capital outflow that causes the exchange rate to depreciate and thereby to raise demand for domestic output.
4 In the case of a fiscal expansion, the induced appreciation of the exchange rate leads to a reduction in net exports, offsetting the increased domestic spending. With a monetary expansion, the depreciation that ensues leads to an improvement in net exports. The trade balance effects of the two policies are thus quite different.
5 With imperfect capital mobility, interest rates can differ internationally, and both monetary and fiscal policies can affect the level of output.

The fixed price assumption of this section cannot be expected to hold over long periods. We would not expect wages and prices to stay fixed if there was substantial unemployment or if demand increased when the economy was already at full employment. Therefore we have to expand the model of this section to incorporate the flexibility of prices as well as exchange rates. Still, as in earlier chapters, the analysis of the fixed price case will be needed in understanding the flexible price situation, to which we now turn.

19-2 EXCHANGE RATES, MONEY, AND PRICES

In this section we take the implications of price flexibility into account. In particular, we study the effects of price level and exchange rate adjustments on the level of output and the interest rate. To do so, we will have to ask what factors cause the exchange rate and the price level to change.

The Adjustment Process

We make two strategic assumptions to describe the adjustment process: First, whenever output exceeds full employment, prices are rising. Conversely, when output is below potential, prices are falling. Second, we assume that capital mobility is perfect. That implies we are always on the *BB* schedule because our interest rate cannot diverge from that in the rest of the world. An incipient decline in interest rates, say, because of a monetary expansion, leads to *immediate* depreciation and an increase in net exports, income, money demand, and interest rates, putting us back on *BB*. Conversely, a tightening in money or a fiscal expansion leads to a tendency for interest rates to rise. In response, capital flows in, and the currency appreciates. There is a loss in competitiveness and a fall in net exports, income, and money demand, and therefore the pressure on interest rates to rise is offset. Conversely, a monetary expansion leads to depreciation and income expansion, which counteract the tendency for interest rates to fall below the world level.

With these assumptions we can study the adjustment process in terms of

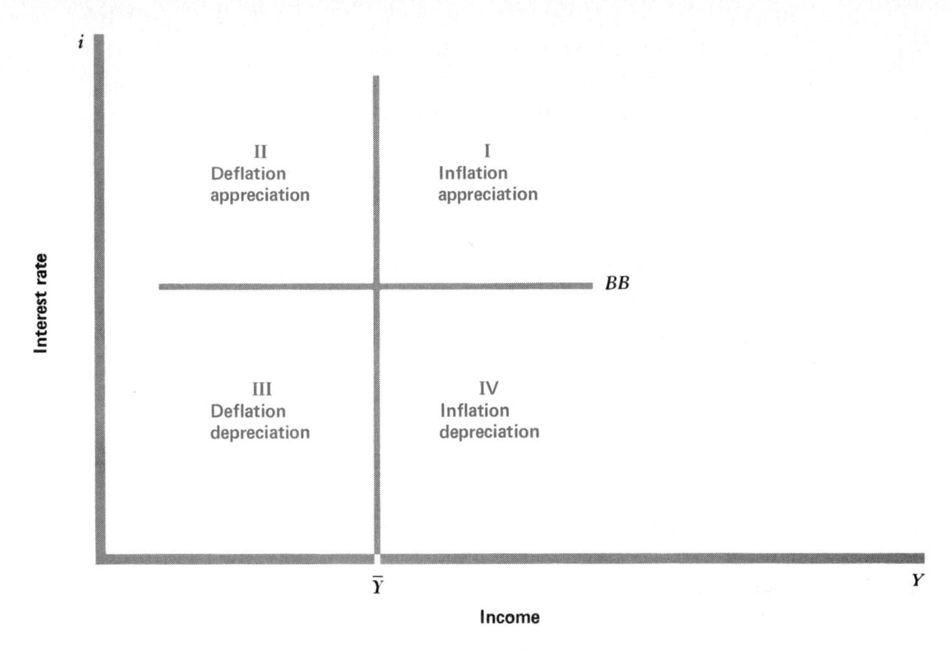

FIGURE 19-7 ADJUSTMENT OF EXCHANGE RATES AND PRICES. Prices move in response to the deviation of the economy from full employment. When output is above potential, prices are rising (regions I and IV), and they are falling at output levels below potential (regions II and III). With perfect capital mobility the balance of payments is highly sensitive to interest rates. If our interest rate falls below the world level, capital tends to flow out, and that leads to a deficit and depreciation of the exchange rate (regions III and IV). Conversely, a rise in interest rates leads to capital inflows, a surplus, and appreciation (regions I and II).

Figure 19-7. Anywhere to the right of $\bar{Y}$, prices are rising and to the left prices are falling. Points above *BB* lead to capital inflows and appreciation; points below to capital outflows and depreciation. Moreover, with capital mobility that is extremely high, the exchange rate will adjust very rapidly so that we are practically always on the *BB* schedule.

A Monetary Expansion: Short- and Long-Run Effects

We saw earlier that with given prices a monetary expansion, under flexible rates and perfect capital mobility, leads to depreciation and increased income. We ask how that result is modified once we take adjustments in prices into account. We will show that the output adjustment is now only transitory. In the long run a monetary expansion leads to exchange depreciation and to higher prices with no change in competitiveness. Figure 19-8 helps make these points.

In Figure 19-8 we start at an initial equilibrium with full employment, payments balance, monetary equilibrium, and equilibrium in the domestic goods market. All this occurs at point *E*. Now a monetary expansion takes place and shifts the *LM* schedule to *LM'*. The new goods and money market

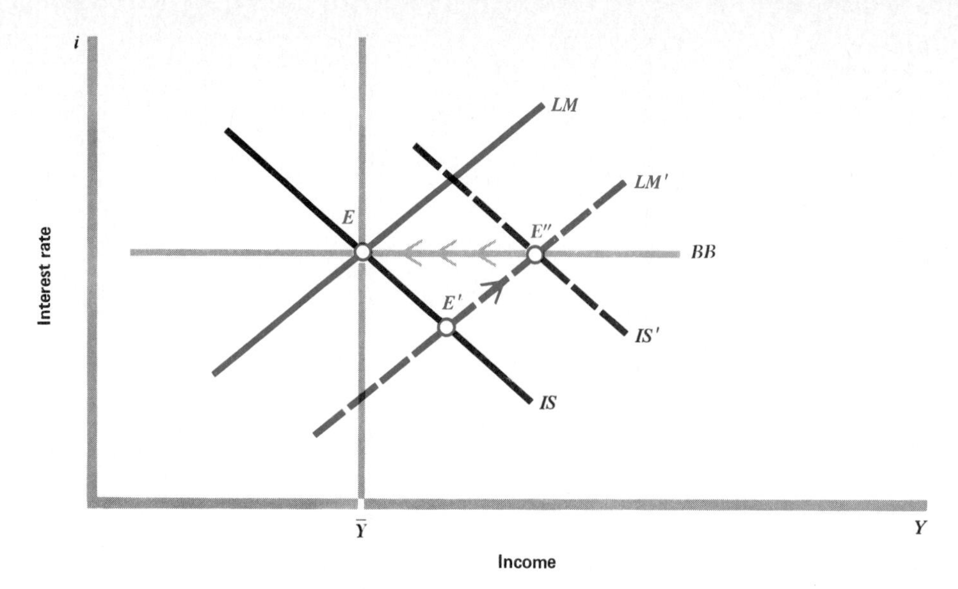

FIGURE 19-8 THE SHORT- AND LONG-RUN EFFECTS OF A MONETARY EXPANSION. The economy is in initial equilibrium at E when a monetary expansion shifts the LM schedule to LM'. The goods and money market equilibrium at E' involves an interest rate below the world level. Capital outflows now lead to immediate exchange depreciation, and therefore the IS schedule shifts to IS'. The economy thus moves rapidly from E to E''. But at E'' there is overemployment, and hence prices are rising. Rising prices reduce real balances and shift the LM schedule back toward E. As real balances decline, interest rates tend to rise, drawing in capital and leading to appreciation, which shifts the IS' schedule back toward E. In the long run, output returns to normal, and money, prices, and the exchange rate all rise in the same proportion.

equilibrium at E' involves an interest rate below the world level, and therefore the exchange rate immediately depreciates, raising home competitiveness and thus shifting the IS schedule to IS'. The economy moves rapidly from E via E' to E''. Output has risen, the exchange rate has depreciated, and the economy has thereby gained in external competitiveness. But that is not the end of the story.

At E'' output is above the full-employment level. Prices are therefore rising, and that implies real balances are falling. As the real money stock M/P declines because of rising prices, the LM schedule starts shifting to the left. Interest rates tend to rise, capital tends to flow in, and the resulting appreciation leads now to a decline in competitiveness that also shifts the IS schedule back toward the initial equilibrium. Both the IS and LM schedules thus move back toward point E. The process continues until point E is reached again.

What adjustments have taken place once the economy is back to point E? At point E interest rates have returned to their initial level and so have relative prices eP^*/P. In moving from E to E' the exchange rate depreciated immediately, ahead of the rise in prices. But when prices increased and real balances fell, some of that depreciation was reversed. Over the whole adjustment

TABLE 19-2 THE SHORT- AND LONG-RUN EFFECTS OF A MONETARY EXPANSION

	M/P	e	P	eP^*/P	Y
Short run	+	+	0	+	+
Long run	0	+	+	0	0

process, prices and exchange rates rose in the same proportion, leaving relative prices eP^*/P and therefore aggregate demand unchanged. In the long run money was therefore *entirely neutral.* Table 19-2 summarizes these results. Neutrality of money means, in terms of the second row of the table, that nominal money, prices, and the exchange rate all increase in the same proportion so that real money and relative prices are unchanged.

Exchange Rate Overshooting

The analysis of monetary policy under flexible exchange rates given above leads to an important insight about the adjustment process. The important feature of the adjustment process is that *exchange rates and prices do not move at the same rate.* When a monetary expansion pushes down interest rates, the exchange rate adjusts immediately, but prices adjust only gradually. Monetary expansion therefore leads in the short run to an immediate and abrupt change in relative prices and competitiveness.

Figure 19-9 shows time paths of nominal money, the exchange rate, and the price level implied by the analysis of Figure 19-8. For each of these variables we show an index that is initially equal to 100. The economy starts at long-run equilibrium. Then, at time T_0, the money stock is increased by 50 percent. Thus the money stock rises from 100 to 150 and stays at that higher level as shown by the solid schedule. The exchange rate immediately depreciates. In fact the exchange rate index rises by more than money, say, from the initial level of 100 at point A to a new level of 170 at point A'. Prices do not move rapidly.

Following the impact effect at time T_0, further adjustments take place. Because the gain in competitiveness at time T_0 has raised output above potential, there is now inflation. Prices are rising, and at the same time the exchange rate is appreciating, thus undoing part of the initial, sharp depreciation. Over time, prices rise to match the increase in money, and the exchange rate will also match the higher level of money and prices. In the long run, real variables are unchanged. The adjustment pattern for the exchange rate seen in Figure 19-9 involves *overshooting.* The exchange rate overshoots its new equilibrium level when, in response to a disturbance, at first it moves *beyond* the equilibrium it ultimately will reach and then gradually returns to the long-run equilibrium. Overshooting means that changes in monetary policy produce large changes in exchange rates.

Figure 19-10 shows an index of the DM/$ exchange rate for the period since 1979. We notice the sharp depreciation of the DM or appreciation of the dollar. We also show an index of the relative price, eP^*/P, using consumer prices in Germany and the United States. The diagram shows clearly that along with an appreciating dollar there occurs a loss in U.S. competitiveness as eP^*/P declines. The dollar appreciation is to be explained by the shift toward tight money in the United States, starting in late 1979. Our model predicts that in the case of tight money there would be an immediate appreciation of the dollar. Moreover, in the short run, prices would respond relatively little, and therefore competitiveness would immediately decline, almost one for one with the appreciation. The episode supports strongly the notion that under flexible exchange rates monetary policy has powerful effects on the exchange rate, competitiveness, and net exports.

These effects are so strong that they have become a source of major concern. Those who believe that exchange rate overshooting introduces an

FIGURE 19-9 THE ADJUSTMENT TO AN INCREASE IN MONEY. The diagram shows an index for prices, money, and the exchange rate. Initially the economy is in full equilibrium, and the value of each index is chosen as 100. A permanent increase in the money stock of 50 percent takes place at time T_0, as shown by the solid schedule. The exchange rate immediately depreciates from A to A', more than the increase in money. Prices adjust only gradually. In the short run, the relative price of imports, eP^*/P, thus increases sharply. That gain in competitiveness causes a transitory income expansion. But over time prices rise and the exchange rate appreciates somewhat, undoing the initial overshooting. In the long run, nominal money, the exchange rate, and prices all rise in the same proportion (50 percent, from 100 to 150), and real balances and the relative price of imports are therefore unchanged.

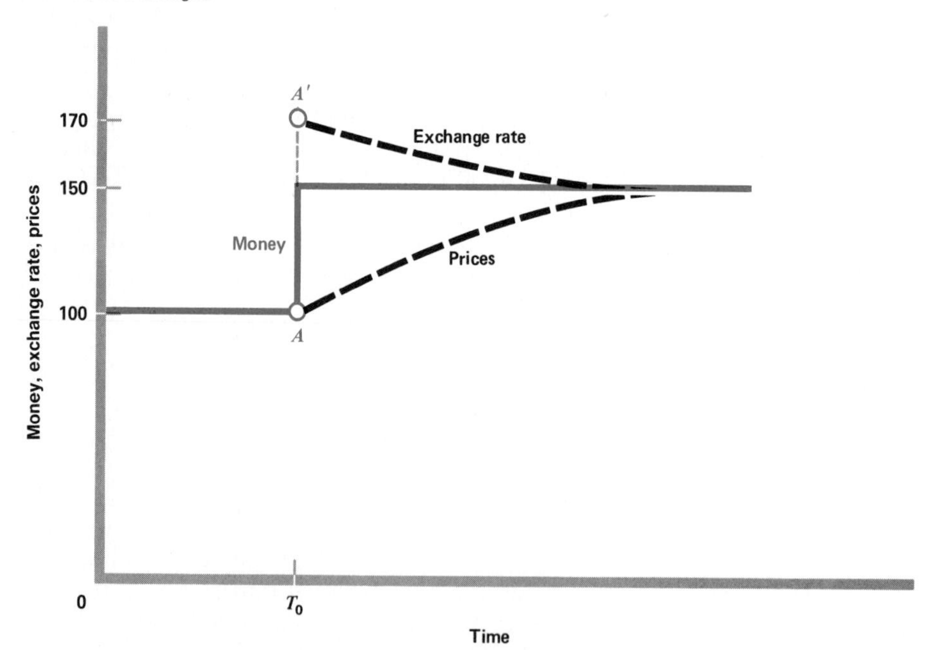

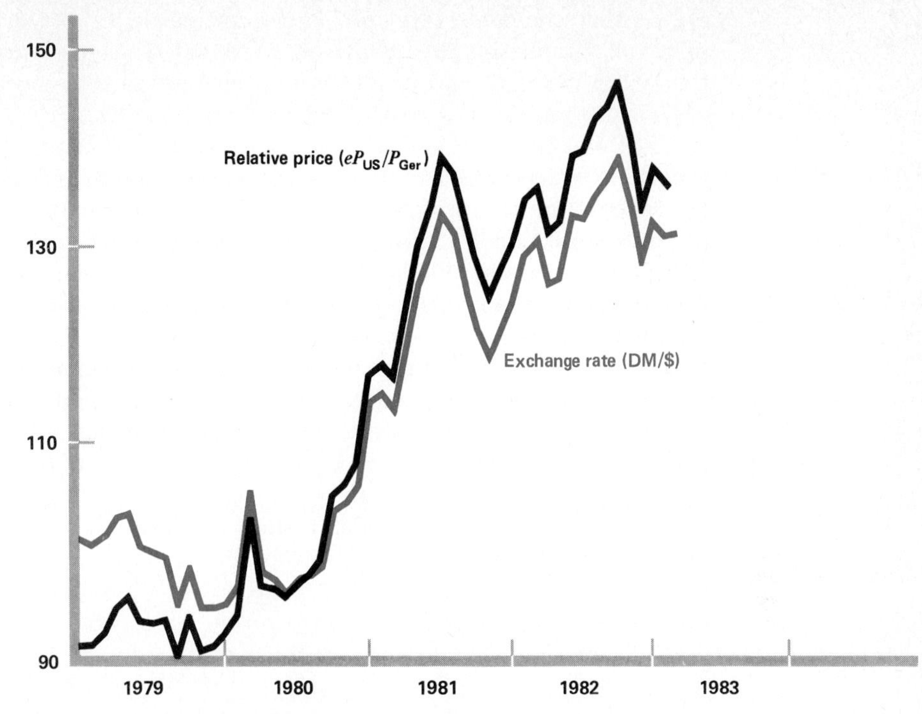

FIGURE 19-10 THE EXCHANGE RATE AND RELATIVE PRICES: GERMANY–UNITED STATES (index: 1980 = 100).

undesirable instability into the economy argue that governments should intervene in foreign exchange markets to avoid large, excessive exchange rate fluctuations. The sharp dollar appreciation of 1980–1981 strongly reinforced the call for such intervention.

Purchasing Power Parity

The long-run neutrality of money discussed above illustrates the potential role of exchange rates in offsetting the effects of changes in the price level at home and abroad on the terms of trade. In the preceding analysis, the exchange rate rose by precisely the right amount to offset the effects of domestic inflation on the terms of trade. That is, the exchange depreciation maintained the *purchasing power* of our goods in terms of foreign goods between the initial and the final equilibrium positions.

An important view of the determinants of the exchange rate is the theory that exchange rates move primarily as a result of differences in price level behavior between the two countries in such a way as to maintain the terms of trade constant. This is the *purchasing power parity* (PPP) theory. The theory argues that exchange rate movements primarily reflect divergent rates of inflation. Examining the terms of trade, eP^*/P, the theory maintains the following: When P^* and/or P change, e changes in such a way as to maintain eP^*/P constant.

PPP is a plausible description of the trend behavior of exchange rates, especially when inflation differentials between countries are large. In particular, we have seen that the PPP relationship does hold in the face of an increase in the money stock. If price level movements are caused by monetary changes—as they are likely to be if the inflation rate is high—then we should expect PPP relationships to hold in the long term.

But qualifications are necessary. First, even a monetary disturbance affects the terms of trade in the short run. Exchange rates tend to move quite rapidly relative to prices, and thus in the short term of a quarter or a year, we should not be at all surprised to see substantial deviations of exchange rates from the rates implied by PPP. And indeed, the terms of trade do move in the short run, as we already saw above.

The second important qualification concerns the role of nonmonetary disturbances in affecting exchange rates. For example, we saw that an increase in exports improves our terms of trade or leads to currency appreciation at unchanged domestic prices. Or if we look at an increase in potential output as another example, we will find that the equilibrium terms of trade worsen. To absorb the increased output, demand must rise, implying a decline in the relative price of our goods. Thus, it is apparent that, over time, adjustments to *real* disturbances will affect the *equilibrium* terms of trade. In the longer run, exchange rates and prices do *not* necessarily move together, as they do in a world where all disturbances are monetary. On the contrary, we may have important changes in relative prices. Such changes run counter to the purchasing power parity view of exchange rates.

Figure 19-11 shows the level of prices in the United Kingdom compared with the United States. The index $P_{U.K.}/P_{U.S.}$ measures the relative prices. It rises when inflation in the United Kingdom exceeds that in the United States. It remains flat when inflation rates are the same. We also show an index of the exchange rate, measuring the price in dollars of a pound sterling.

Strict PPP theory would argue that the exchange rate index and the relative price level should move in line. But that clearly is *not* the case. For example, in 1976, the exchange rate depreciated more than relative prices changed. Conversely, in 1980–1981, relatively high inflation in the United Kingdom was not at all matched by depreciation. Thus in the short run, and over longer periods, exchange rates can diverge from the evolution of relative prices. "Real" factors, such as a change in fiscal policy, discovery of North Sea oil, or supertight money, have short-run effects on the exchange rate, and some can even change long-run relative prices.

As an empirical matter, PPP views of exchange rates work well when, as frequently happens, inflation differences predominate. Thus PPP is an important explanation of some large exchange rate movements, particularly in hyperinflations. But not all exchange rate changes are caused by monetary disturbances, and PPP does not provide a good explanation for the short-run behavior of exchange rates.

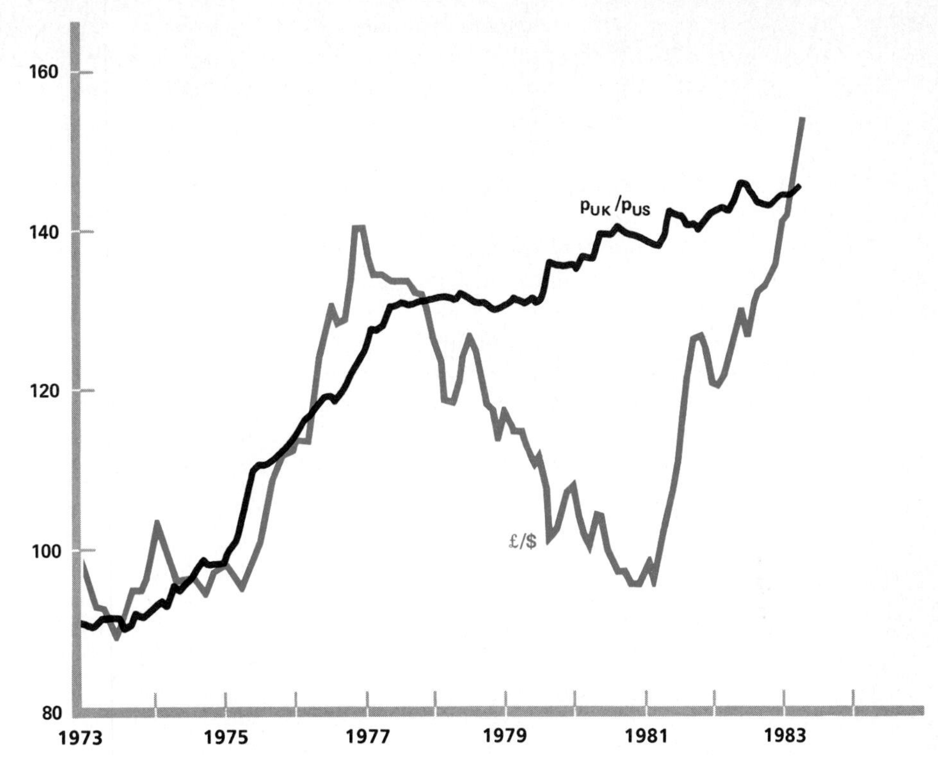

FIGURE 19-11 PURCHASING POWER PARITY? RELATIVE PRICES AND THE EXCHANGE RATE, U.K./U.S. 1973–1983 (indices: 1973–1975 = 100).

Summary

In this section we allowed for price flexibility as well as exchange rate flexibility. We assumed that the price level increases when output is above the full-employment level and that the exchange rate appreciates when the interest rate is above the world level, and there is therefore a capital inflow. The examination of monetary disturbances under flexible prices and exchange rates gave us the following results:

1 Price level and exchange rate adjustments affect the level of income and the interest rate. An increasing price level reduces real balances, tending to increase the interest rate. Changes in the price level and the exchange rate also affect the terms of trade and thus influence the demand for our goods.
2 A monetary expansion in the long run increases the price level and the exchange rate, keeping real balances and the terms of trade constant. In the short run, though, the monetary expansion increases the level of output and reduces the interest rate, depreciating the exchange rate. The exchange rate overshoots its new equilibrium level.
3 Purchasing power parity theory argues that exchange rate changes are, in

practice, caused by divergences in inflation rates between countries, with the exchange rate changing in a way that maintains the terms of trade constant. This theory is a good predictor of the behavior of the exchange rate over long periods when disturbances are caused mainly by monetary factors, such as in hyperinflations. But in the short run, monetary disturbances are not neutral, and even in the long run the exchange rate can change as a result of real disturbances. Examples include changes in technology in different countries, shifts in export demand, and shifts in potential output.

We have now completed the core of this chapter. The remaining sections take up a number of issues that extend the basic analysis.

19-3 INTEREST DIFFERENTIALS AND EXCHANGE RATE EXPECTATIONS

A cornerstone of our theoretical model of exchange rate determination in Sections 19-1 and 19-2 was international capital mobility. In particular, we argued that with capital markets sufficiently integrated, we would expect

FIGURE 19-12 THE INTEREST RATE ON U.S. CERTIFICATES OF DEPOSIT AND FOREIGN INTEREST RATES. (*Source:* Board of Governors of the Federal Reserve, *Selected Interest Rates and Exchange Rates.*)

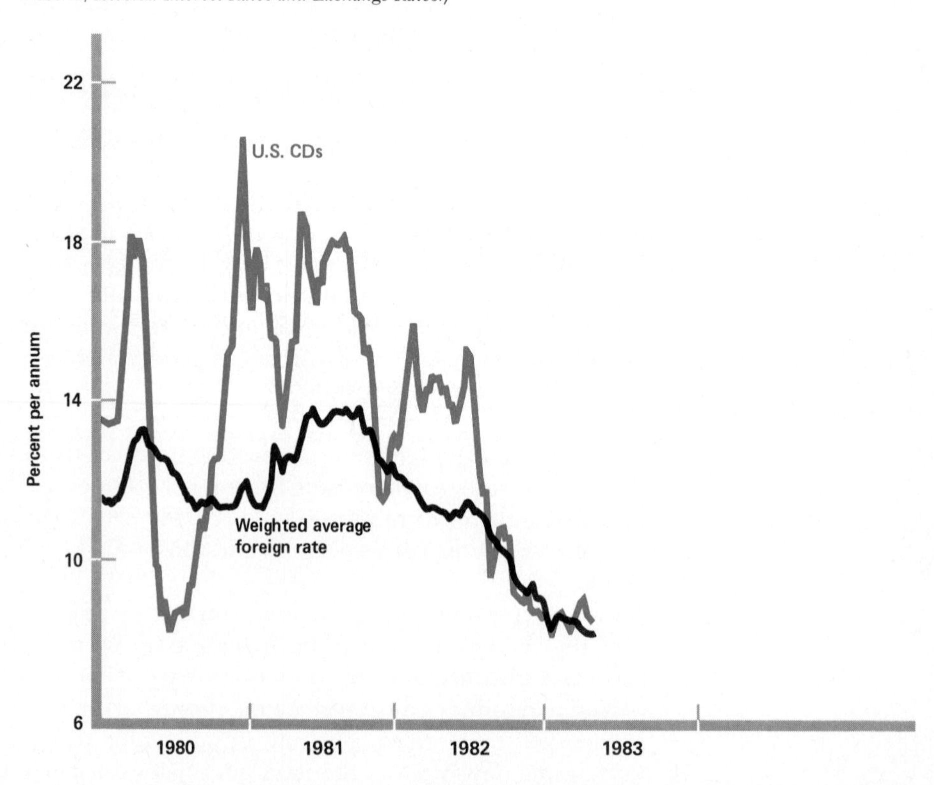

interest rates to be equated across countries. How does this assumption stand up to the facts? In Figure 19-12 we show the U.S. interest rates on certificates of deposit (CDs) and an average of interest rates in major industrialized countries. It is quite apparent from the chart that these rates are certainly not equalized. Thus, in late 1980 and in 1981, the interest differential ranged upward of four percentage points. How do we square these facts with our theory?

Exchange Rate Expectations

Our theoretical analysis in Sections 19-1 and 19-2 was based on the assumption that capital flows internationally in response to nominal interest differentials. For example, if domestic interest rates were 10 percent and foreign rates 6 percent, we would, according to the earlier sections, expect a capital inflow.

However, such a theory is incomplete in a world where exchange rates can, do, and are expected to change. For example, consider a situation where the Deutsche mark is expected to appreciate by 5 percent over the next year relative to the dollar. Suppose the interest rate in Germany is 6 percent. Anyone buying German bonds will earn a return in Deutsche marks of 6 percent. Suppose now that the U.S. interest rate is 10 percent. A German investing in the United States for a year will, at the beginning of the year, exchange his Deutsche marks for dollars and then earn 10 percent on his dollars. At the end of the year, he will want to change his dollars back into Deutsche marks to spend in Germany. But he expects that by the end of the year, each dollar will be worth 5 percent less in terms of Deutsche marks, as a result of the expected depreciation. Therefore, in terms of marks, he will expect to earn only 5 percent (10 percent minus 5 percent) by investing in American bonds, whereas he earns 6 percent by investing in German bonds. He will naturally prefer to invest in German bonds.[5]

It is clear, therefore, that we must extend our discussion of interest rate equalization to incorporate expectations of exchange rate changes. Table 19-3 gives some combinations of the domestic interest rate i, the foreign

[5] You should confirm that an American who expects the dollar to depreciate by 5 percent would, given the 6 percent and 10 percent interest rates, also prefer to buy German bonds.

TABLE 19-3 INTEREST RATES AND EXCHANGE DEPRECIATION (*In percentages*)

Case	Domestic interest rate i	Foreign interest rate i^*	Depreciation $\Delta e/e$	Adjusted interest differential, $i - i^* - \Delta e/e$
1	10	5	0	5
2	10	15	−5	0
3	10	15	−2	−3
4	10	15	−10	5

interest rate i^*, and exchange rate changes $\Delta e/e$. Suppose we want to know the return, in terms of domestic currency, of investments here compared with those abroad. For domestic investments we just look at the interest rate i. For foreign investments, we look at the interest rate i^* *and* at the exchange depreciation. Suppose foreign interest rates were 5 percent and exchange rates did not change. This occurs in case 1, and the *adjusted* interest differential $(i - i^* - \Delta e/e)$ is 5 percent in favor of the home country. Case 2 considers the case where interest rates abroad are high (15 percent), but where our currency appreciates at the rate of 5 percent or the foreign currency depreciates by that amount. Here the depreciation exactly offsets the higher foreign interest rates, and the adjusted differential is zero—what would be gained in interest is lost through the foreign depreciation. Cases 3 and 4 show circumstances where the foreign depreciation falls short of, and exceeds, the interest differential, respectively. In cases 1 and 4, we would want to invest in the home country; in case 2 we are indifferent; and case 3 favors the foreign country.

The trouble, of course, is that we do not know ahead of time how the exchange rate will move. We know the interest rates on, say, 3-month Treasury bills in the United States and the United Kingdom, so that we can compute the interest differential, but we do not know whether the pound will appreciate or depreciate over the next 3 months. Even if we somehow knew the direction, we would certainly not know the precise amount.

Investors then have to form *expectations* about the behavior of the exchange rate; that is, in deciding whether to invest at home or abroad, they have to make forecasts of the future behavior of the exchange rate. Given these forecasts, we would expect that in a world of high capital mobility, the interest differentials, adjusted for *expected depreciation*, should be negligible. That means that a country that is certain to depreciate will have interest rates above the world level, and conversely, a country that is expected to appreciate will have interest rates below the world level.

The introduction of exchange rate expectations modifies our equation for the balance of payments. Now capital flows are governed by the difference between our interest rate and the foreign rate adjusted for depreciation, $i - i^* - \Delta e/e$. An increase in foreign interest rates or an expectation of depreciation, given our interest rates, would lead to a capital outflow. Conversely, a rise in our rates or an expectation of appreciation would bring about a capital outflow. We thus write the balance of payments as

$$BP = NX(Y, eP^*/P) + CF(i - i^* - \Delta e/e) \qquad (5a)$$

The adjustment for exchange rate expectations thus accounts for international differences in interest rates. These differences are by and large due to differences in inflation rates and are reflected in trend movements of the exchange rate. High-inflation countries have high interest rates and depreciating currencies. We thus have an international extension of the Fisher equation discussed in Chapter 13. The international extension relies on PPP

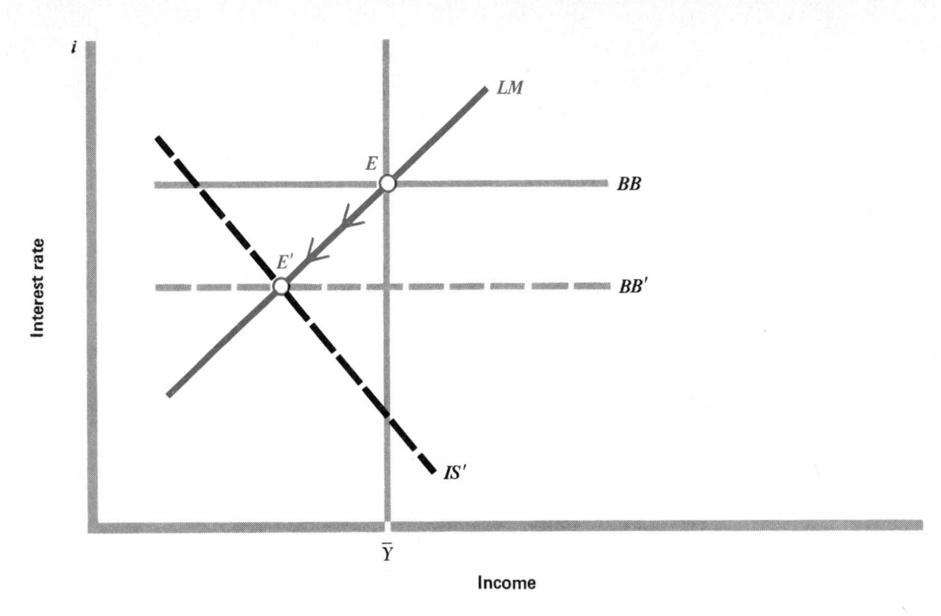

FIGURE 19-13 RESPONSE TO AN EXPECTED APPRECIATION OF THE CURRENCY. The initial equilibrium at E is disturbed by the expectation that the home currency will appreciate. The BB schedule shifts down to BB', reflecting the fact that people are willing to hold domestic assets at a reduced interest rate since they are compensated for the differential by anticipated appreciation. At E there is now a capital inflow that leads to exchange appreciation. The IS schedule (not drawn) shifts to IS', and the economy moves into a recession. The capital inflow has brought about a loss of trade competitiveness and thus unemployment at point E'.

to argue that inflation differentials internationally are matched by depreciation. Our long-term relation then is

$$\text{Inflation differential} \simeq \text{interest differential} \simeq \text{depreciation rate}$$

(The $\simeq$ sign means "approximately equal to.") The relation is only approximate because, as we have seen, exchange rates can move independently of prices and also because obstacles to capital flows may create long-term interest differentials.

There is another respect in which the introduction of exchange rate expectations is important and that concerns speculative capital flows and their impact on macroeconomic equilibrium. The point is made with the help of Figure 19-13. Here the *BB* schedule is drawn for a given foreign interest rate and a given expected rate of change for the exchange rate, say, zero. Suppose that we start in full equilibrium at point *E* and that the market develops the expectation that the home currency will appreciate. This implies that even with a lower home interest rate, domestic assets are attractive, and so the *BB* schedule shifts down by the amount of expected appreciation.

Point *E* is no longer an equlibrium, given the shift of the *BB* schedule to *BB*′, but rather a position of surplus with large-scale capital inflows motivated by the anticipation of appreciation. (This might well describe the case of the United Kingdom after awareness of British oil discoveries spread in the market.) The surplus causes the exchange rate to start appreciating, and we move in a southwesterly direction, as indicated by the arrow. The speculative attack causes appreciation, a loss in competitiveness, and, consequently, falling output and employment.

This analysis confirms that exchange rate expectations, through their impact on capital flows and thus on actual exchange rates, are a potential source of disturbance to macroeconomic equilibrium.

19-4 EXCHANGE RATE CHANGES AND TRADE ADJUSTMENT: TWO EMPIRICAL ISSUES

In this section we take up two important empirical issues related to the possibilities for adjusting current account imbalances by changes in the exchange rate. In our theoretical model of Section 19-1, we assumed that prices here and abroad were fixed, so that exchange rate changes affected relative prices one for one. In Section 19-2, by contrast, we explored a world where prices (and wages) are flexible and full employment is maintained in the long run. In this section, we consider the alternative possibility, that wages and prices are flexible, but that they may respond to movements in the exchange rate in a way that makes it impossible or at least difficult to change relative prices through changes in the exchange rate. This issue is particularly important if formal wage indexation arrangements link wage behavior to import prices and thus to the exchange rate.

The second issue we consider is whether changes in relative prices, assuming that they are possible, will affect the current account in the direction we have so far assumed. The assumption, so far, has been that a decline in the relative price of our goods improves the current account. But the possibility arises that at least in the short run there might be a perverse reaction. With import prices rising, for example, import demand may not decline sufficiently to compensate for higher prices, and thus total import spending (price times quantity) may actually increase. We turn now to these two issues.

Exchange Rates and Relative Price Adjustment

In studying the flexible wage-price model of Section 19-2, we assumed that wages and prices adjust to achieve full employment. Now we consider as an alternative the possibility that prices are based on labor cost or wages and that wages are inflexible in real terms. Suppose that labor wants to maintain the purchasing power of wages or to keep real wages constant. In such a world, changes in the cost of living would lead to changes in money wages, in labor cost, and therefore in prices, which in turn feed back into wages. Two points emerge from this description. The first is that in such a world, we may not be able to get to full employment. Labor may set the real wage too high, and at least in the intermediate run, the full-employment level of output cannot be sustained. The second point is that a process in which changes in prices feed back into wages and from there into prices is one of a *wage-price spiral* that may produce considerable volatility in the price level. Small disturbances can set off quite large changes in the price level.

Suppose, first, that the real wage is fixed in terms of the consumer price index that includes both domestic goods and imports. Let us assume, second, that changes in the consumer price index are fully passed on into wages, and third, that changes in wages are fully passed on into increased domestic prices. Now assume that starting from an initial equilibrium, there is an exchange depreciation brought about by some short-term, reversible disturbance. The depreciation raises import prices and thereby has a direct effect on consumer prices and wages. To maintain the purchasing power of their wages, workers increase money wages and firms pass on the wage increase into higher prices. Where are we after the process ends? Real wages are constant, which means wages and the price level (a weighted average of the prices of domestic and imported goods) have risen in the same proportion; wage increases have been fully passed on, which means that real wages *in terms of domestic output* are also unchanged. The two results imply that relative prices are unchanged, or that the exchange depreciation is fully matched by domestic inflation.

Of course, this is not really the end because we have to ask how the higher price level affects the macroeconomic equilibrium. To the extent that lower real balances lower aggregate demand, we would have a reduction in employment. To round out our story, we can imagine that the central bank steps in to prevent unemployment by raising the money stock. If nominal money rises in proportion to the price increase, then the full-employment equilibrium, at the same terms of trade, is reestablished but, of course, at a higher level of wages and prices. This is an economy where there is very little stability in the price level because the slightest change in exchange rate expectations leads to actual exchange rate movements that are fully *validated* by domestic wage, price, and monetary developments.

A second context in which the idea of *sticky real wages* is important is that of real disturbances. Suppose our export demand declines permanently because of, say, the introduction of superior technology abroad. To return to full employment, we saw in Section 19-2 that the relative price of our goods must fall so as to encourage foreign demand. But how can the relative price fall? In Section 19-2, we argued that the exchange rate will depreciate, thereby raising import prices relative to domestic prices and restoring our competitiveness. In the present context we have to recognize that import price increases would be immediately matched by wage increases and that these wage increases would be fully passed on into price increases. Relative prices cannot change. The consequence would, of course, be protracted unemployment. Unemployment would continue until the *real* wage declines.

The empirical question, then, is, How flexible are real wages? That is, to an important extent, a question of institutional arrangements. In small open economies with substantial cost-of-living indexation in wage agreements, it may indeed be very difficult to change real wages and relative prices through exchange rate changes.

Relative Prices and the Trade Balance: The J Curve

We come now to the second issue, the effect of changes in relative prices on the trade balance and the possibility that a depreciation *worsens* the trade balance. To make this point, we write out the trade balance, measured in terms of domestic goods, as

$$NX = X - \frac{eP^*}{P} \cdot Q \qquad (6)$$

where X denotes the foreign demand for our goods or exports and Q denotes our own import quantity. The term $(eP^*/P)Q$ thus measures the *value* of our imports in terms of domestic goods.

Suppose that we now have an exchange depreciation and that in the first instance, domestic and foreign prices, P and P^*, are unchanged. Then the relative price of imports, eP^*/P, rises. This leads to two effects. First, if the physical *volume* of imports does not change, their *value* measured in domestic currency unambiguously increases because of the higher price. With unchanged physical import volume, Q, higher prices mean increased import spending and thus a worsening of the trade balance. This is the source for the potentially perverse response of the trade balance to exchange depreciation. However, there is an adjustment that runs in the opposite direction. The increased relative price of imports makes us more competitive and shifts demand in volume terms toward domestic goods. This *volume effect* of substitution in response to changed relative prices shows up in Equation (6) in the form of increased export volume, X, and reduced import volume, Q. The volume effects thus unambiguously improve the trade balance.

The question, then, is whether the volume effects on imports and exports are sufficiently strong to outweigh the price effect, that is, whether depreciation raises or lowers net exports. The empirical evidence on this question is quite strong and shows the following result: *The short-term volume effects, say, within a year, are quite small and thus do not outweigh the price effect.*[6] *The long-term volume effects, by contrast, are quite substantial, and certainly enough to make the trade balance respond in the normal fashion to a relative price change.*

Where does this asymmetry come from, and what does it imply about trade adjustment to relative prices? First, the low short-term and high longer-term volume effects result from the time consumers and producers take to adjust to changes in relative prices. Some of these adjustments may be

[6] See Michael C. Deppler and Duncan M. Ripley, "The World Trade Model: Merchandise Trade," *IMF Staff Papers*, March 1978; and Duncan M. Ripley, "The World Model of Merchandise Trade: Simulation Applications," *IMF Staff Papers*, June 1980.

instantaneous, but it is clear that tourism patterns, for example, may take 6 months to a year to adjust and that relocation of production internationally, in response to changes in relative costs and prices, may take years. A case in point is increased foreign direct investment in the United States—say, Toyota moving from Japan to California. In the long term, such direct investment leads to reduced imports by the United States, and thus to an improved trade balance, but such an adjustment takes years, not weeks or months.

The lag in the adjustment of trade flows to changes in relative prices is thus quite plausible. The next question is, What do these lags imply about the impact of relative price changes on the trade balance? Suppose that at a particular time, starting with a deficit, we have a depreciation that raises the relative price of imports. The short-term effects result primarily from increased import prices with very little offsetting volume effects. Therefore, the trade balance initially worsens. Over time, as trade volume adjusts to the changed relative prices, exports rise and import volume progressively declines. The volume effects come to dominate, and in the long run, the trade balance shows an improvement. This pattern of adjustment is referred to as the *J-curve effect,* because diagrammatically the response of the trade balance looks like a *J*.

The medium-term problem of sticky real wages and the J-curve effect are important qualifications to the macroeconomics of flexible rates as spelled out in Sections 19-1 and 19-2. They imply that flexible exchange rates do not provide for instant, costless flexibility of relative prices and trade flows. At the same time, these considerations provide important clues for the interpretation of macroeconomic experiences across countries, particularly in showing why depreciations typically do not lead to improvements in the current account in the short term.

19-5 EXCHANGE RATE FLUCTUATIONS AND INTERDEPENDENCE

In the 1960s there was growing dissatisfaction with fixed exchange rates. The Bretton Woods system was called a crisis system because from time to time exchange rates would get out of line and expectations of exchange rate changes would mobilize massive capital flows that often precipitated the exchange rate changes that speculators expected. Is the flexible rate system of the 1970s and early 1980s better? Is it less crisis-prone, and does it provide a better framework for macroeconomic stability? Before providing an answer, we look briefly at how flexibly the system has, in fact, operated.

Dirty Floating and Intervention

Under *fully* flexible exchange rates the government takes no action in the foreign exchange market. Far from buying or selling foreign exchange at a fixed price, the government does not conduct *any* foreign exchange transactions. It stays out of the foreign exchange market, whatever happens to the exchange rate. Such a system is almost unheard of, although the United States did behave that way in 1981–1982. More commonly, governments intervene in the foreign exchange market to a lesser or greater extent. Foreign exchange market *intervention* occurs when a government buys or sells foreign exchange in an attempt to influence the exchange rate. The extent to which governments intervene varies substantially. They may only try to offset short-term fluctuations and buy or sell foreign exchange to maintain "orderly markets." But they also may try to keep an overvalued exchange rate from depreciating or an undervalued exchange rate from appreciating. *Dirty floating* (as opposed to clean) is the practice of using substantial intervention to try to maintain an exchange rate against the pressure of market forces.

During the 1973–1983 period, exchange market intervention has been of the decidedly dirty variety. Governments have intervened on a very large scale. This leads naturally to the question of why a government should try to resist market forces, to prevent an appreciation or a depreciation of the currency.

Why Governments Intervene

Central banks intervene to affect exchange rates for several reasons. Probably the main reason is the belief that many capital flows merely represent unstable expectations, and that the induced movements in exchange rates move production in the economy in an unnecessarily erratic fashion. The second reason for the intervention is a central bank's attempt to move the real exchange rate in order to affect trade flows. The third reason arises from the effects of the exchange rate on domestic inflation. Central banks sometimes intervene in the exchange market to prevent the exchange rate from depreciating, with the aim of preventing a depreciation-induced increase in the inflation rate.

Should central banks intervene in the exchange market? The basic argument for such intervention is that it is possible for intervention to smooth out fluctuations in exchange rates. At one extreme, the argument would assert that any movements in exchange rates produce unnecessary fluctuations in the domestic economy and that exchange rates therefore ought to be fixed. This is the basic argument for dirty floating. The only—and overwhelming—objection to the argument that the central bank should smooth out fluctuations is that there is no simple way of telling an erratic movement from a trend movement. How can we tell whether a current appreciation in the exchange rate is merely the result of a disturbance which will soon reverse itself, rather than the beginning of a trend movement in the exchange rate? There is no way of telling at the time a change occurs, although with the benefit of hindsight, one can see which exchange rate movements were later reversed.

There is one circumstance under which central bank intervention might be desirable. It is clear from our earlier analysis that one of the key determinants of exchange rate behavior consists of expectations of economic policy. It may sometimes be possible to make it clear that there has been a change in policy only by intervening in the foreign exchange market. This is a case of putting your money where your mouth is.

SHOULD GOVERNMENTS INTERVENE?

There is disagreement on whether governments should intervene in the foreign exchange market. The United States, for example, in 1981–1982 strongly refused consideration of any kind of intervention. The reason was that policy makers in the United States, unlike those in Europe, felt the market knows better than policy makers what level the exchange rate should be. But there is another and more interesting disagreement: it concerns the effectiveness of intervention. Does it make any difference to the exchange rate if the Bundesbank sells $1 billion from its reserves?

To judge the effectiveness of intervention we must make a distinction between *sterilized* and *nonsterilized intervention.* In the case of sterilized intervention a central bank, say, buys foreign exchange, issuing domestic money. But then the increase in home money is reversed by an open market sale of securities. In the sterilized intervention case, therefore, the home money supply is kept unchanged. By contrast in the case of nonsterilization, there is a change in the money stock equal to the amount of intervention.

Thus nonsterilized intervention results in a change in the money stock. It is widely agreed that nonsterilized intervention, because it changes the money supply, will affect exchange rates. There is widespread skepticism, however, about the effectiveness of sterilized intervention. In 1978–1979 the U.S. dollar was depreciating in currency markets even though there was intervention on a massive scale. But that intervention was carefully sterilized. Only in late 1979, when the dollar depreciation had come to alarm the Fed, did a change in policy take place. Monetary policy was tightened, and immediately the dollar depreciation was stopped and soon massively reversed.

The episode strongly suggests the effectiveness of nonsterilized intervention and of intervention that is backed by credible policies. It also suggests that without such policies intervention accomplishes little.[7]

Interdependence

It used to be argued that under flexible exchange rates countries can pursue their own national economic policies — monetary and fiscal policy and the inflation rate — without having to worry about the balance of payments. That is certainly correct, but it is also misleading. There are important linkages between countries *whatever the exchange rate regime.*

These *spillover*, or *interdependence*, effects have been at the center of the discussion about flexible exchange rates. The effects of the tight U.S. monetary policies in 1980–1982 created problems for all industrialized countries. The reason is clear from our models: As the United States tightens monetary policy, our interest rates rise, and that attracts capital flows from abroad. The

[7] In 1982–1983 the main industrialized countries conducted a study of intervention to try to reconcile their different views. The result is contained in the *Report of the Working Party on Foreign Exchange Market Intervention,* U.S. Treasury, Washington, D.C., 1983.

TABLE 19-4 THE INTERNATIONAL EFFECTS OF U.S. TIGHT MONEY

	U.S.	Abroad
Output and employment	−	+
Inflation	−	+

dollar appreciates, and foreign currencies depreciate. Table 19-4 shows the effects on other countries.

The U.S. appreciation implies a loss in competitiveness. World demand shifts from U.S. goods to those produced by our competitors. Therefore, at home, output and employment decline. Abroad, our competitors benefit from the depreciation of their currency. They become more competitive, and therefore output and employment abroad expand. Our monetary tightening thus tends to promote employment gains abroad, which come, of course, at the expense of our own employment.

There are also spillover effects through prices. When our currency appreciates, import prices in dollars fall. Therefore our inflation tends to decline quite rapidly when there is a sharp dollar appreciation. But abroad the opposite occurs. Their currency depreciates, and therefore prices in foreign currency tend to increase. Inflation abroad thus rises. Foreigners might welcome an increase in employment as a side effect of our monetary policy, but they certainly can do without the inflation that comes from currency depreciation.

Policy makers abroad therefore must decide whether to accept the higher employment–higher inflation effects of our policies or whether they should change their own policies. If inflation is already a problem abroad, or if the rest of the world is highly averse to inflation, then the policy response abroad to this *imported inflation* may well be to tighten money. A monetary contraction abroad, matching our own, ensures that exchange rates will not move or at least will move less. But it also means that our own tight money and recession become the world's tight money and a world recession. This was substantially what happened in the worldwide recession of 1981–1982.

POLICY SYNCHRONIZATION

The large changes in exchange rates that arise when policies are not fully synchronized between countries pose a major threat to a world of free trade. When import prices fall by 20 or 30 percent because of a currency appreciation, large shifts in demand will occur. Domestic workers become unemployed, and they have no trouble seeing that it is foreigners who gain the jobs they just lost. Accordingly, there will be pressure for protection — tariffs or quotas — to keep out imports that are "artificially cheap" due to the currency appreciation. In the United States repeated calls for protection in the automobile industry, in steel, and in many other industries reflect in large part the side effects of a dollar that appreciated sharply in response to tight money.

On the question of independence or interdependence under flexible exchange rates, the experience of the last 10 years offers a quite unambiguous answer. Under flexible exchange rates there is as much or more interdependence as there is under fixed rates. Moreover, because exchange rates are so flexible and so ready to respond to (bad) policies, macroeconomic management does not become easier. Further, to the extent that exchange rate overshooting causes sharp changes in competitiveness, it leads to protectionist sentiment.

On all counts then, flexible rates are far from being a perfect system. But there is no better system. Therefore we can ask only whether through international coordination of interests and policies, we can make the system work better than it has in the recent past.

19-6 SUMMARY

1. Under flexible exchange rates, without government intervention, the exchange rate adjusts to ensure equilibrium in the overall balance of payments. The sum of the current and capital account deficits is zero with floating rates and no intervention.
2. The demand for our goods depends on the exchange rate which, given foreign and domestic prices, affects the relative price of imports versus exports. An increase in the exchange rate—a depreciation—increases the demand for domestically produced goods by reducing imports and increasing exports.
3. When capital is very mobile, so that the interest rate essentially cannot differ from the world rate, fiscal policy becomes totally ineffective in changing the level of income. An increase in government spending merely reduces net exports, with the trade deficit being financed by a capital inflow.
4. Monetary policy—given prices—retains its effectiveness when capital is very mobile. An increase in the money stock leads to a depreciation of the exchange rate and an improved foreign balance, which increases demand for domestic output.
5. If an economy finds itself with unemployment, the central bank can intervene to depreciate the exchange rate and increase net exports and thus aggregate demand. Such policies are known as beggar-thy-neighbor policies, because the increase in demand for domestic output comes at the expense of demand for foreign output.
6. In the long run, exchange rate movements in the absence of real disturbances reflect changes in the price levels in the two countries concerned. A country with a more rapid rate of inflation will find its exchange rate depreciating against the currency of a country which is inflating less rapidly. The exchange rate movements induced by the price level changes merely keep the relative prices of goods produced in the two countries constant.

7 In the short run monetary disturbances lead to exchange rate overshooting.
8 Exchange rate expectations introduce divergences among nominal interest rates internationally. The international interest differential equals the anticipated rate of depreciation when capital is highly mobile. A country that is expected to have a depreciating currency will have higher nominal interest rates than the rest of the world.
9 A currency depreciation can, in the short run, lead to a worsening of the trade balance. This occurs when the effect of changes in relative prices on the volume of trade is small because adjustments take time. Over time, trade adjusts and the depreciation improves the trade balance. This is called the J-curve effect.
10 Because it raises import prices, depreciation of the exchange rate raises the cost of living and may spill over into increased wage demands. If such spillovers are substantial, then a flexible rate system will have large movements in nominal prices, and exchange rate movements may perform poorly in bringing about relative price changes.
11 Since the beginning of the flexible rate system in 1973, there have been substantial fluctuations in exchange rates. These movements are hard to explain. They affect the allocation of resources. A central bank which wants to intervene to smooth out the fluctuations has to know when an exchange rate change is going to be reversed and when it is permanent. For this reason, foreign exchange intervention to smooth out exchange rate fluctuations is extremely difficult.
12 Under flexible exchange rates, there are significant spillover effects from one country's prices to another country's employment and inflation. These spillover effects make it important to coordinate policies internationally, even under flexible exchange rates.

KEY TERMS

Competitiveness
Terms of trade
Real wage rigidity
Beggar-thy-neighbor policy
Exchange rate overshooting
Purchasing power parity
Expected depreciation
J curve
Intervention
Sterilized and nonsterilized intervention
Imported inflation
Policy synchronization

PROBLEMS

1 Explain why the belief that a devaluation is imminent makes a devaluation more likely in a fixed exchange rate system.
2 Why do you think countries were reluctant to move away from the system of fixed exchange rates during the late sixties and early seventies, even though it was by then not operating very well? Also explain what "not operating very well" means.

3 Explain why an expansionary fiscal policy "beggars our neighbors" less than direct intervention by the central bank in the foreign exchange markets to depreciate the exchange rate.

4 Assuming there are no capital flows, explain how an increase in the domestic interest rate (which we have assumed fixed, so far) affects the level of income and the exchange rate. How could the domestic interest rate be changed?

5 (*a*) What are the terms of trade?
(*b*) Why does expansionary policy affect the terms of trade in a floating exchange rate system?

6 Assume that capital is perfectly mobile, the price level is fixed, and the exchange rate is flexible. Now let the government increase purchases. Explain first why the equilibrium levels of output and the interest rate are unaffected. Then show whether the current account improves or worsens as a result of the increased government purchases of goods and services.

7 Assume that there is perfect mobility of capital. How does the imposition of a tariff affect the exchange rate, output, and the current account? (***Hint:*** Given the exchange rate, the tariff reduces our demand for imports.)

8 Explain how and why monetary policy retains its effectiveness when there is perfect mobility of capital.

9 Consult the *Wall Street Journal* or some other newspaper which has foreign exchange rates listed on its financial pages. For some countries, such as Britain and Germany, you should find future prices listed. This is the price to be paid today to receive one unit of the foreign currency in the future. A 30-day future price for the pound sterling, say, is the price paid today to receive 1 pound 30 days from now. Explain why the future prices are not generally equal to the spot prices—the price paid today to receive the foreign currency today. See whether you can explain the difference between the relationship of spot and future prices for the pound and Deutsche mark, respectively.

10 Assume you expect the pound to depreciate by 6 percent over the next year. Assume that the U.S. interest rate is 4 percent. What interest rate would be needed on pound securities—such as government bonds—for you to be willing to buy those securities with your dollars today, and then sell them in a year in exchange for dollars? Can you relate your answer to this question to your answer to problem 9?

11 What considerations are relevant for a country deciding whether to borrow abroad to finance a balance of trade deficit, or to adjust?

12 Explain the purchasing power parity theory of the long-run behavior of the exchange rate. Indicate whether there are any circumstances under which you would not expect the PPP relationship to hold.

13 This problem deals with the current account effect of an expansion in the money stock, given prices, perfect capital mobility, and flexible exchange rates.
(*a*) Given the interest rate i^*, the real money stock M/P, and the money market equilibrium condition

$$\frac{M}{P} = kY - hi$$

solve for the equilibrium level of income Y_0 that is compatible with monetary equilibrium.
(*b*) Consider next the goods market equilibrium condition:

$$Y = A(Y, i) + NX$$

Let $A = \overline{A} + cY - bi$. Substitute for $i = i^*$ and the equilibrium level of income from 13(*a*). What is the equilibrium value of the trade balance NX?

14 Assume capital is imperfectly mobile, so that the higher the interest rate at home, the higher the rate of capital inflow, but that the flows remain finite. Then we can write the balance of payments as

$$BP = NX\left(\frac{eP^*}{P}, Y\right) + CF(i - i^*)$$

where CF denotes the net rate of capital inflow and i^* is the given foreign interest rate.

(*a*) Suppose the exchange rate adjusts to maintain payments equilibrium. Then $BP = 0$, and the current account surplus equals the capital account deficit:

$$NX\left(\frac{eP^*}{P}, Y\right) = -CF(i - i^*)$$

Suppose the goods market is *also* in equilibrium, so that

$$Y = A(i, Y) + NX\left(Y, \frac{eP^*}{P}\right)$$

Substituting for the current account in the goods market equilibrium condition yields

$$Y = A(i, Y) - CF(i - i^*)$$

Show this equation graphically in i, Y space and interpret it.

(*b*) Also draw an LM schedule in the same space and interpret the intersection point.

(*c*) Show now the effect of a fiscal expansion in the home country on interest rates, income, and the current account.

(*d*) Show the effect of a monetary expansion on income, interest rates, and the current account.

15 Suppose in year 1 we have price levels $P = 100$ and $P^* = 100$. Suppose next that in year 2 the respective price levels are $P_2 = 180$ and $P_2^* = 130$. Let the exchange rate initially be \$2/£.

(*a*) If there were no real disturbances between year 1 and year 2, what would be the equilibrium exchange rate in year 2?

(*b*) If the terms of trade eP^*/P had deteriorated between year 1 and 2 by 50 percent, what would the exchange rate be in year 2?

16 This problem draws on the discussion of stabilization policy and beggar-thy-neighbor policy in Section 19-1. Suppose we have two countries with full-employment output levels of $\overline{Y}$ and $\overline{Y}^*$ at home and abroad, respectively.

(*a*) Draw a diagram with actual output levels, Y and Y^*, on the axes. Draw also lines corresponding to potential output levels. Label the resulting four quadrants I, II, III, and IV.

(*b*) Identify for each of the quadrants the state of demand in each country as boom or recession.

(*c*) Which policies can be pursued when output exceeds potential in each country? When output exceeds potential in one but falls short of potential in another?

(*d*) In which quadrants are beggar-thy-neighbor policies particularly dangerous? Where is coordination of policies essential?

INDEX

  compared to policy in the 1930s, 549